Legal Issues In School Health Services

A Resource For
School Administrators
School Attorneys
School Nurses

Foreword by
Gerald N. Tirozzi
Executive Director, National Association of Secondary School Principals
Former Assistant Secretary of Elementary and Secondary Education
U.S. Dept. of Education

Editors
Nadine C. Schwab and Mary H. B. Gelfman

Authors Choice Press
New York Lincoln Shanghai

Legal Issues In School Health Services
A Resource for School Administrators, School Attorneys, School Nurses

Authors Choice Press
an imprint of iUniverse, Inc.

iUniverse books may be ordered through booksellers or by contacting:

iUniverse
2021 Pine Lake Road, Suite 100
Lincoln, NE 68512
www.iuniverse.com
1-800-Authors (1-800-288-4677)

Originally published by Sunrise River Press

Edited by Nadine C. Schwab and Mary H. B. Gelfman

This publication is designed to provide accurate and authoritative information in regard to the subject matter covered. It is sold with the understanding that the publisher is not engaged in rendering legal, clinical, or other professional services. If legal advice or other expert assistance is required, the services of a competent professional person should be sought.

ISBN-13: 978-0-595-35813-7
ISBN-10: 0-595-35813-6

Printed in the United States of America

To our husbands

Jack & Nels

And our children and their significant others,
John, Michael, Celia and Tom, Kay, and David and Eleanor

NCS & MHBG

and in memory of friends,

Janet and Claire
NCS

Contributors

NADINE C. SCHWAB, RN, MPH, PNP, FNASN

Nadine Schwab is the nursing supervisor for Westport Public Schools, Connecticut and a school health consultant/principal with Schwab & Associates. She is an Associate Clinical Professor at Yale University School of Nursing and the University of Hartford, Division of Nursing, a co-editor of the Section on Legal and Ethical Issues, *Journal of School Nursing*, and nurse consultant to the Section on School Health of the American Academy of Pediatrics. She worked ten years (1989–1999) as Consultant for School Health Services at the Connecticut State Department of Education and seven years as Director of School Health Services, Hamden, Connecticut. Ms. Schwab's prior professional experience included clinical practice as a pediatric nurse practitioner, administration of community health programs, and public health nursing.

Ms. Schwab served as an elected officer of the National Association of State School Nurse Consultants 1992-97, including two years as president. She is a recipient of the Distinguished Service Award of the National Association of School Nurses and the Outstanding Service Award, Committee on School Health, Connecticut Chapter of the American Academy of Pediatrics. She is a Fellow of the National Association of School Nurses, a Sigma Theta Tau community leader, and a nationally certified school nurse. Ms. Schwab has authored several professional publications and journal articles, and delivered numerous national and regional presentations on topics related to legal and clinical issues in school health. A graduate of Boston College (BSN), Columbia University (MPH), and the University of Connecticut Pediatric Nurse Practitioner Program, Ms. Schwab has served on a number of national task forces and is a member of several professional organizations concerned with child, adolescent, and school health.

MARY HUGHES BOYCE GELFMAN, MA, JD

Attorney Mary H.B. Gelfman practices in the area of school law, and writes and presents professional development programs in that area. She is admitted to practice in the State and Federal Courts of Connecticut. She is currently a Hearing Officer for state-level special education appeals, and student expulsion hearings in the state-run vocational-technical high schools for the Connecticut State Department of Education.

Ms. Gelfman has spoken on school law and special education issues, at local school districts, statewide special education meetings in Utah, Wisconsin, New Jersey, West Virginia, South Dakota, New Hampshire, and Vermont as well as Connecticut; regional meetings, and national meetings, including the National Association of School Nurses, the American Academy of Pediatrics, and the Education Law Association. In addition to her published articles about legal issues in school health, student discipline, and confidentiality of student records, she co-authored with Jim Rosenfeld and Linda Bluth *Education Records: A Manual* in 1997. In 1993, the School Health Committee of the Connecticut Chapter of the American Academy of Pediatrics presented Ms. Gelfman with a citation for assistance with research and policy development concerning school health.

A graduate of Swarthmore College, Ms. Gelfman also has an MA from Teachers College, Columbia University, and a JD from the University of Connecticut School of Law. Previously a high school teacher and an eleven-year member of a local board of education, she worked for the Due Process Unit, Bureau of Special Education and Student Services, Connecticut State Department of Education 1979-84. She is a member of the Board of Contributing Editors for EDLAW Briefing Papers.

MILA ANN AROSKAR, RN, EDD, FAAN

Mila Aroskar is an Associate Professor, School of Public Health and Faculty Associate, Center for Bioethics, University of Minnesota, Minneapolis, Minnesota. She is a Fellow of the American Academy of Nursing, a member of Sigma Theta Tau, and a Fellow of The Hastings Center, a national organization for the study of ethics in health care and society. She is an author of the book, *Ethical Dilemmas in Nursing Practice*, now in its 4th Edition, and has authored numerous professional publications and journal articles. She has served on several institutional ethics committees and made numerous presentations nationally and internationally. She serves as Chair of the ANA Advisory Board, Center for Ethics and Human Rights. Her awards include Distinguished Alumni Award, Columbia University-Presbyterian Hospital, School of Nursing Alumni Association; Distinguished Alumni Achievement Award for Nursing Practice, Nursing Education Alumni Association, Teachers College, Columbia University; and has been inducted into the Teachers College Nursing Hall of Fame, Columbia University.

Dr. Aroskar received undergraduate degrees from the College of Wooster and Columbia University Department of Nursing; an MEd from Teachers College, Columbia University; and her EdD from the State University of New York at Buffalo. Dr. Aroskar's previous professional experiences include ambulatory care, public health nursing, and faculty member in undergraduate and graduate nursing education programs.

MARTHA DEWEY BERGREN, RN, MS, DNSC

Martha Dewey Bergren is a faculty member of the School of Nursing at the University of Minnesota teaching both undergraduate child health and graduate school nursing curriculum. She is also a consultant and national speaker on nursing informatics and telecommunications. Ms. Bergren has been the Section Editor for the Information Technology column for the *Journal of School Nursing* since 1993. She founded and has managed SCHLRN-L, a 1600 subscriber international Internet discussion list for school nurses since 1994. She is also the co-chair of the Information Technology Committee and webmaster for the School Nurses of Minnesota. She was formerly the Information Technology Consultant for the National Association of School Nurses.

Ms. Bergren received the 1997 National Association of School Nurses Recognition Award for contributions to school health in information technology and telecommunications. She was also the recipient of the 1995 Excellence in Teaching Award from the University at Buffalo Graduate School, 1992 Ruth McGrory Leadership Award from the University at Buffalo School of Nursing, and the 1992 National Association of School Nurses Lillian Wald Research Award. She received the 1994 First Doctoral Award at the IMIA

International Conference on Nursing Use of Computers and Information Science for her research poster, "Diffusion of Information: The Adoption of Information Technology by School Nurses". She is a graduate of the Pennsylvania State University (BS) and the University at Buffalo (MS) and is presently a doctoral candidate at the University at Buffalo. Ms. Bergren has practiced in child health in the acute, community, and school settings for more than 20 years.

SARAH D. COHN, RN, JD, FACNM

Sarah Cohn is a registered nurse, certified nurse midwife, and attorney in the state of Connecticut. She has been Director of Medicolegal Affairs for the Yale New Haven Hospital and Yale University School of Medicine since 1998 and was Associate Counsel for Medicolegal Affairs for 14 years prior to becoming Director. She is a lecturer at the Yale University Schools of Nursing and Medicine, a Fellow of the American College of Nurse Midwives, and the author of numerous professional book chapters and journal articles on legal and clinical issues in nursing, nurse midwifery, and medicine. Among her contributions to school health, Ms. Cohn has published and contributed to state agency deliberations and guidelines related to legal issues in school health services, provided legal consultation to school nurse managers, and delivered key presentations on legal issues in school nursing. Ms. Cohn's prior professional experience includes clinical practice as a nurse midwife and newborn special care nurse, and lecturer in the advanced practice nurse midwifery program at Yale University School of Nursing.

A graduate of Georgetown University School of Nursing (BSN), Yale University School of Nursing (MSN), and Yale Law School, Ms. Cohn was admitted to the Connecticut Bar in 1983. Ms. Cohn is a member of numerous professional organizations, including the Connecticut Bar Association, National Health Lawyers Association, and American Society of Law & Medicine. She is a long-standing member of the Board of Directors and Executive Committee of the Planned Parenthood League of Connecticut, Inc., and has served as Chair of the Division of Competency Assessment of the American College of Nurse Midwives (ACNM), and Chair of the Connecticut Chapter of ACNM.

CAROL C. COSTANTE, RN, MA, NCSN, FNASN

Carol Costante is supervisor of school health nursing for the Baltimore County Public Schools, Maryland, the 25th largest school system in the U.S. She has 21 years of experience in school health, 15 of which have been in administration. In addition, she is Courtesy Faculty at both the Johns Hopkins University and the University of Maryland Schools of Nursing, and the Johns Hopkins University, graduate School of Public Health. With the National Association of School Nurses (NASN), Ms. Costante served on the Board (1991-98), as Education Committee chair (1992-95), on the Executive Committee (1993-98), and as an elected officer (1995-98), including president (1996-97). She has continued to work extensively in the national arena of school health in diverse ways. Lecturing widely to state, national, and international health and education audiences, Ms. Costante has also authored many professional publications and journal articles on issues related to school health, including DNR and future issues in school nursing. She is a Fellow of the NASN, a nationally certified school nurse, and a Sigma Theta Tau community leader.

In her home state of Maryland, Ms. Costante has been honored by the Governor for service and distinguished leadership in promoting and developing services to students, by the Maryland House of Delegates for dedication and support to school children and school nurses, and by the Baltimore County Executive for distinguished service for developing health services for school children. She is a graduate, cum laude, of the Washington Hospital Center School of Nursing (nursing diploma), Johns Hopkins University (BS), and Towson University (MA).

WENDY J. FIBISON, PHD, MHSC, PNP

Wendy J. Fibison is Associate Director, Division of Intramural Research, National Institute of Allergy and Infectious Diseases, National Institutes of Health, in Bethesda, Maryland. She is also a Special Volunteer in the National Human Genome Research Institute, conducting research in the Clinical Gene Therapy Branch. The focus of her research is nonviral approaches to gene therapy and single cell analysis of gene therapy, which is an extension of her postdoctoral work conducted in the laboratory of R. Michael Blaese. Prior to this, she was a consultant for ethical, legal, social, and educational issues related to advances in genetics and biotechnology and she has published in these areas. She has held faculty positions at Yale University, the University of Connecticut, and McMaster University, and has served as a World Health Organization consultant. As a Pediatric Nurse Practitioner, she served underserved populations in rural and urban settings.

Dr. Fibison received the annual prize from the American Society of Human Genetics for outstanding work in predoctoral clinical research, which defined the critical region for the Digeorge Syndrome.

ELIZABETH "NANCY" GAFFREY, MSN, RN

Nancy Gaffrey is a Master's prepared Clinical Nurse Specialist in Family Health. She has recently retired from her position as the Medi-Cal Coordinator for the San Diego Unified School District. Now working as an independent contractor, she is currently the Nurse Consultant to the San Diego County Office of Education, which provides services to 43 school districts. A published author and a presenter at national conferences, Gaffrey's research includes issues dealing with School Health, Managed Care, Quality Assurance, and Health Care for the Homeless.

ELIZABETH KENNEDY GREGORY, PHD, RN, NCSN, FNASN

Betty Gregory, a school health consultant, is a former school nurse and nurse consultant for health services and health education. Dr. Gregory is a graduate of Bellevue School of Nursing, Johns Hopkins University, Loyola College, and Texas Woman's University, and a member of Sigma Theta Tau. She is a Fellow, National Association of School Nurses. Dr. Gregory has authored several professional journal articles and manuals and has delivered many presentations on school health topics. In addition she was an officer in local, state, and national school nursing and school health associations and a member of the National Board for Certified School Nurses for six years, two as president.

JANIS HOOTMAN, RN, PHD, MST, BSN, NCSN

Janis Hootman has 19 years of school nursing experience and is currently in the position of Supervisor for the Department Of School Health Services, Multnomah Education Service District, Portland, Oregon. She is an adjunct professor at Oregon Health Sciences University. Dr. Hootman served 4 years as a Director for the National Association of School Nurses (NASN), 2 years as NASN Research Chair, and currently serves as the NASN Vice President. Her awards include the Distinguished Service Award of NASN. She is a member of Sigma Theta Tau and a nationally certified school nurse. Dr. Hootman has authored several professional publications and journal articles. She has presented at state and national conferences on a variety of school nursing issues. Dr. Hootman has degrees in nursing, health education, and health administration. Her prior professional experience includes community health, pediatric hospital administration, and clinical pediatric practice.

ANN B. MECH, RN, MS, JD

Ann B. Mech, an attorney, is Assistant Professor and Coordinator, Legal Services, University of Maryland School of Nursing. The School of Nursing operates several school-based health centers in Baltimore and surrounding Maryland counties. She also chairs the Board of Health of Howard County, Maryland, and is a member of the Board of Trustees of Howard County General Hospital.

WANDA R. MILLER, RN, MA, FNASN

Wanda R. Miller is the administrator for the Saint Paul Public Schools, Student Wellness Department, St. Paul, Minnesota. Ms. Miller was the winner of the 1998 NASN School Nurse Administrator of the Year Award. She has published and presented nationally on school health issues and is a Fellow of the National Association of School Nurses.

KATHERINE J. POHLMAN, RN, JD

Katherine J. Pohlman is a nurse attorney in private practice in Minneapolis, Minnesota. She focuses her practice on health-related matters and is also General Counsel to the National Association of School Nurses. She is also the owner of kjp kommunications, a firm that provides writing and editing services to health care and health law clients.

SUSAN E. PROCTOR, BSN, MPH, DNS

Susan Proctor is a Professor of Nursing and Coordinator, School Nurse Program, California State University, Sacramento. In these roles, she has been involved in the education of several hundred Northern California school nurses over nearly three decades. In the late 1980s, she served as chair of a statewide task force which identified educational standards and competencies for school nursing practice in California. This work in turn provided a template for *School Nursing Practice: Roles and Standards* (1993) published by the National Association of School Nurses and for which she was primary author. From 1996-1999, Dr. Proctor served as Executive Editor of the *Journal of School Nursing*, an official publication of the National Association of School Nurses. She is a fellow in NASN's Academy of Fellows and was the 1998 recipient of the NASN Distinguished Service Award. She has also been a long-time member of the California School Nurses Organization. Dr. Proctor has authored several publications in the areas of school nursing and adolescent childbearing. A graduate of the College of St. Teresa, Winona, Minnesota (BSN), the University of California, Berkeley (MPH), and the University of California, San Francisco (DNS), she was also a Peace Corps volunteer nurse in East Africa. She is credentialed by the state of California as a school nurse.

SUSAN J. WOLD, BSN, MPH, PHD, RN

Susan Wold is an Associate Professor in the College of Nursing at Valdosta State University in Georgia. In all, she has more than 25 years' experience as a nursing educator, including 15 years at Metropolitan State University (ultimately as Professor and Director of Graduate Studies) and six years at the University of Minnesota. In addition, she is self-employed as a writer and consultant in the areas of community and school health. Dr. Wold has numerous publications to her credit including journal articles, book chapters, and two books, *School Nursing: A Framework for Practice* and *Community Health Nursing: Issues and Trends*. She has received awards for teaching excellence and public service from the University of Minnesota and in 1982 received an American Journal of Nursing Book of the Year Award for her school nursing textbook. Dr. Wold is a member of Sigma Theta Tau and is a past president of Zeta chapter and president-elect of Epsilon Pi chapter. She is also a member of such professional organizations as the American Public Health Association, the American School Health Association, and the National Association of School Nurses. Dr. Wold holds three degrees from the University of Minnesota: Bachelor of Science in Nursing (BSN, awarded with distinction), Master of Public Health (MPH), and Doctor of Philosophy (PhD) in Higher Education.

Acknowledgments

It is impossible to thank all of the individuals and groups of individuals who inspired, supported, or contributed in some way to the creation, content, production, and achievement of this book.

Above all, we thank our family loved ones, whose sacrifices, support, patience, prodding, and laughter made this book possible.

We are very grateful to the following:

- **Contributing authors** whose expertise, excellent manuscripts and dedication to the fields of school nursing, education, law, ethics, technology, and genetics made this book a reality.

- **Students**—of all ages, personalities, sizes, and needs —for they are the most fundamental reason for school personnel to support quality practices and diminish safety and liability risks related to the delivery of health services in our nation's schools.

- **Families** who advocate for their children, raise issues, and spur us to better understand their priorities for education, health care, and community collaboration.

- **School nurses, school nurse managers, and state school nurse consultants** across the country, so many of whom contributed the energy, questions, expertise, leadership, information, and cases that inspired and enhanced our ability to produce a resource book on legal issues—especially one relevant to practice in today's schools.

- **Former colleagues in education, special education, and health** in Connecticut—at the Bureau of Special Education and Pupil Services, State Department of Education, as well as administrators in local school districts and regional education service centers, and at the State Department of Public Health and local health departments, so many of whom have supported quality school health services programs and broadened our horizons.

- **Attorney colleagues in education (representing both districts, families, and state agencies) and in health (representing nurses and state boards of nursing)** who consistently place top priority on the health, safety, and confidentiality of students and patients, some of whom have also been our mentors and sounding boards.

Thank you to the following individuals who, over time, have significantly influenced our approach to legal issues in school health or provided special support:

Charlotte Burt	Judy Maire
Ellen Campbell	Carol Passarelli
Theresa DeFrancis	Jim Rosenfeld
Roger Frant	Mary Schulze
Tom Gillung	Anne Sheetz
Lynne Gustafson	Martin Sklaire
James Hadler	Marie Snyder
Marie Hilliard	Joseph Sullivan
Susan Kennedy	Elizabeth Thomas
Patricia Krin	Elizabeth Truly

Thank you also to the individuals who contributed materials for the book—ideas, stories, queries, cases, resources, or critiques that, whether or not explicitly used, improved our understanding of specific issues and consideration of risk management strategies. These individuals are either cited directly in the text or are listed below:

Vivian Ashworth	Carol Iverson
Nela Beetem	Mary Jackson
Nancy Birchmeyer	Jan Ozias
Shirley Carstens	Veronica Puleo
Deborah Culligan	Vincent Sacco
Colette Gardner	Jan Sanderson
Luanne Grennan	Claire Taylor
Judy Harrigan	Gail Terry
Kathleen Hunthausen	Elizabeth Thomas

Without the ongoing support and patience of Dave and Martha Arnold, publishers, this project would not have come to fruition. Although the years we spent working on it were far beyond our wildest predictions (and expectations), and the final product may be a strange cousin to the initial proposal, they nevertheless continued to support our efforts and, for that, we are grateful.

Special recognition and appreciation are extended to the following individuals for their professional expertise, technical skills, and collaboration in producing this book:

- Sarah Zaino, who was always there to help put initial drafts on chapters and reference lists into proper style and format;

- Martha Arnold, who meticulously produced an incredibly comprehensive index for this book— its most important tool; and

- Monica Dwyer Abress, Managing Editor, who transformed a rough and uncoordinated manuscript into a polished, accessible, organized and pleasing final product—despite many ordinary and extraordinary challenges along the way.

Finally, we acknowledge those who haven't been specifically named above or cited in the book, but who influenced our thinking, supported our efforts, or otherwise contributed wittingly (or unwittingly) to the production of this book.

Nadine C. Schwab and Mary H. B. Gelfman, Editors

Contents

SPECIAL TOPICS

Foreword

The need for such social and health services is often inseparable from the support that students require for successful academic achievement.

—The National Association of Secondary School Principals, 1996, p. 91.

Health and education are two major determinants of whether a child will grow up to be a self-sufficient and productive member of society.

—Council of Chief State School Officers, 1991, p. iii.

Effective team leaders realize they neither know all the answers, nor can they succeed without the other members of the team.

—J. R. Katzenback & D. K. Smith, 1993, p. 86.

Over the past four decades, this country has witnessed fundamental changes in its public schools and, today, continues to grapple with serious challenges to the educational system. The population of children attending school has changed dramatically. As American society has become increasingly complex, its communities more diverse in culture and language, and the gap between poor and well-to-do families ever wider, public and private initiatives have supported experimentation with new roles for schools and new strategies for improving educational outcomes for all students.

Some school reform efforts, including new models for the delivery of school health programs, have been quite successful in individual schools. As recently reported by Straub (2000), however, these successes are often short term and, for children living in poverty, they significantly diminish in effect as students grow older. Based on his research into school reform successes and failures, Straub concludes that schools alone cannot solve the problems of urban poverty that result in educational inequality and vast discrepancies in student achievement. What he does embrace, along with the more radical concept of moving families to new environments, is the notion that ensuring the success of all students requires the collaboration of many institutions and the support and coordination of effort among all segments of our society.

This book offers an opportunity to improve the collaboration of educators and health services providers in promoting student learning and success. While this collaboration is only one piece to the larger, unresolved challenges discussed above, it is, nevertheless, a critical one. As pointed out by McKenzie and Richmond (1998, p. 11), "Education reform initiatives will succeed only if they also address students' health and well-being." This book addresses the spirit and letter of the laws and related standards that affect the delivery of health services within educational settings and conflicts between them. Some of these laws address educational standards that health professionals need to be knowledgeable about in order to be effective members of school teams. Others address health standards that educators, administrators, and school attorneys need to understand in order to foster school practices that are effective in promoting and maintaining student health and well being.

While the book's focus is on legal issues that educators, school nurses, and other school health and mental health professionals wrestle with in day-to-day practice, the emphasis is on the spirit of the laws and how they are intended to support successful outcomes for students. According to Justice William J. Brennan, Jr., "The law is not an end in itself, nor does it provide ends. It is preeminently a means to serve what we think is right" (in Peter, 1977, p. 290). Thus, school leaders, staff, and expert advisors need to understand the thinking behind various legal standards that apply to health services in schools, including where and why there are conflicts between standards. Better understanding of the rationale for the standards, as well as practice issues related to them, will improve communication across disciplines and enhance collaborative efforts on behalf of students and families. Better understanding should also promote coordinated strategies to improve or eliminate the laws and regulations that no longer serve what the broad community "thinks is right" about school health services.

As a resource on the legal aspects of school health services, this book addresses practice issues and dilemmas that face school administrators, school nurses, other school health professionals, and policy makers on a regular basis. It is not so much about "how to" answers, but rather, about concepts and standards that underlie quality school health services and nursing practice today. Specific laws and cases are discussed to illuminate risk management principles and pitfalls, as well as trends and differences in state and school district approaches to practice; sample policies, laws, and other materials that support effective risk-management strategies are referenced in the text or included in the appendices.

More than a resource, this book constitutes a challenge to the status quo. It is a call to interdisciplinary dialogue and collaborative action towards improving the quality of, and reducing unnecessary risks in, the delivery of health services in schools. The chapter authors provide unique perspectives on the legal implications of current practices and directions in school health, and emphasize cross-disciplinary approaches to resolving difficult issues. It is an important contribution to the fields of education, school nursing and school law, particularly for the administrators, policy makers, practitioners, and legal and medical advisors of school health services programs, and the higher education faculty members who prepare them.

Gerald N. Tirozzi, PhD
Executive Director, National Association of
Secondary School Principals
Former Assistant Secretary of Elementary and
Secondary Education, U.S. Dept. of Education

REFERENCES

Council of Chief State School Officers. (1991). *Beyond the health room.* Washington, DC: Author.

Katzenback J. R. & Smith, D. K. (1993). *The wisdom of teams: Creating the high performance organization.* New York: HarperBusiness.

McKenzie, F.D. & Richmond, J.B. (1998). Linking health and learning: An overview of coordinated school health programs. In Marx, E. & Wooley, S.F. (with Northrop, D.), Eds., *Health is academic: A guide to coordinated school health programs.* New York: Teachers College Press.

Peter, L.J. (1977). *Peter's quotations: Ideas for our time.* New York: William Morrow and Company, Inc.

The National Association of Secondary School Principals. (1996). *Breaking Ranks: Changing an American Institution.* Reston, Virginia: Author.

Traub, J. (January 16, 2000). Schools are not the answer. *The New York Times Magazine,* 52-57, 68, 81, 90 & 91.

Introduction

The primary purpose of this book is to provide a legal resource for education and health professionals who are involved in the development, implementation, and evaluation of school health services and for attorneys who advise school districts and families about those services. It is published at the turn of the 21st century, a time when the demands for, and complexity of, health services delivered to students age 3 (or younger) to 21 years is unprecedented in the history of U.S. public schools. These demands and complexities present school districts with challenges across the spectrum of regular and special education that are financial, clinical, operational, legal, and ethical in nature. While the focus of this book is on the legal challenges inherent in providing health services in education settings today, one theme of the book is the crucial link among these challenges. Furthermore, while the book addresses those health services provided primarily by school nurses, many of the issues, standards, and risk management principles explored are applicable to the services of other school health and mental health professionals.

McKenzie and Richmond (1998, p. 4) define school health services, one of eight components of coordinated school health programs, as

- preventive services, education, emergency care, referral, and management of acute and chronic health conditions;

- designed to promote the health of students, identify and prevent health problems and injuries, and ensure care for students.

Duncan and Igoe (1998, pp. 172–176) further describe the essential functions of school health services as follows:

- screening, diagnostic, treatment, and health counseling services (including urgent and emergency care, timely identification of and appropriate intervention for health problems, mandated and necessary screenings for all students, assistance with medication during the school day, and health services for children with special needs and health counseling);

- health promotion, prevention education, and preventive services; and

- referrals to and linkages with other community providers.

Teamed with other school health and mental health professionals and paraprofessionals, teachers, administrators, medical advisors, and families, school nurses play a prominent role in the delivery, coordination, and supervision of these school-based services. (See also the opening of chapter 6 for the National Association of School Nurses' definition of school nursing practice.)

In 1992, the National School Boards Association (NSBA) issued the first of a series of *Issue Briefs* on the relationship between health and learning in children and the need for communities to design and implement school health programs tailored to the needs of their individual student populations. The Executive Director's introduction to the series of briefs began with this paragraph (Shannon, 1992):

> Education in the 1990s and beyond must focus on the needs of the whole child. The task of balancing the physical, mental, emotional and social needs of children against the public school district's responsibility to provide excellent and equitable education requires a comprehensive approach, especially in light of fiscal realities. The healthy child of today ensures the development of a life long learner who is the productive citizen and parent of tomorrow.

While national and international experts in the fields of education, health, and child development would not argue with Shannon's premise, the actual task of achieving that balance is often fraught with barriers that appear to be, and have sometimes become, insurmountable. These barriers cover a range of factors—from resource limitations, divergent political priorities, and bureaucracy, to ineffective communication, an absence of collaboration, and educators and nurses who are ill prepared to understand the legal framework of each other's professions.

In promoting the effectiveness of coordinated school health programs, McKenzie and Richmond (1998, p. 2) suggest that what is new about these programs is "not their individual components—many schools already have most in place—but their quality, sophistication, and coordination of effort." A major theme throughout this book is that, regardless of program model, quality services—provided by competent education and health practitioners who communicate and collaborate with each other, families, and community experts—protect against liability risks. Stated conversely, inadequate knowledge, competence, communication, and collaboration can become the substructures of poor quality programs and the causes of legal challenges in the arena of school health services.

The *Issue Brief* cited above (NSBA, 1992, p. 2) described two major trends in the United States over the prior two decades that altered the public school's responsibility for student health:

- the emergence of behavior-related chronic diseases, rather than infectious diseases, as the leading causes of morbidity and mortality in the United States; and

- dramatic changes in the structure of the family and demographics of the school-age population.

These trends have had a wide range of effects on school health programs. For example, mothers who used to be home and available to schools when their children became ill or injured are now in the work force, and parents are difficult to reach or unable to take time away from their jobs. Other new demands on the responsibility of public schools include those fostered by students who come to school today with complex medical and psychiatric needs, including life-sustaining technology, medical treatments, and behavioral interventions.

Two additional trends over these decades are relevant to legal issues in school health services:

- significant restructuring of the health care delivery system; and

- increasing challenges to, and liability of, public school districts and school health professionals related to the provision of health services in schools.

Despite national and state efforts to increase health care insurance for children, access to health care and limitations to that care remain significant factors in the daily lives of many children who are poor and have physical and mental health problems. As a result, school nurses are often used by families as the first line of medical care and advice for their children, not unlike the country doctor or family physician in eras past. Additionally, it is not unusual for a student with a major mental health crisis—for example, a suicide attempt related to severe depression—to be hospital-ized one day and back in school the next, without any coordinated plan for the student's care. Students with complex physical problems also experience hospitalizations for a number of reasons, from immediate crises to scheduled surgical procedures, and find themselves rapidly returned to school without sufficient communication and advanced planning between the school, family, and health care providers.

The trend in legal challenges and liability associated with school health services—in both regular and special education venues—is related, in part, to each of the other trends discussed above. It also underscores the need for school nurses, administrators, and attorneys to be knowledgeable regarding applicable law, quality practices, and risk management strategies. It is interesting to note, for example, that in a 1987 book on legal issues in nursing, Northrop (p. 223) reported that no case law existed regarding school nurses' responsibilities related to medication administration. That statement is no longer true, as cases highlighted in this book demonstrate.

In a presentation to school nurses in the early 1990s, Madelon Baranoski, a pediatric nurse practitioner and clinical psychologist at Yale University, addressed the issue of communication and collaboration through the "sandbox" analogy. She suggested that school nurses are "playing in someone else's sandbox." If they want to succeed in that sandbox, she said, school nurses must learn the culture, foundation, process, and language of education. Similarly, in terms of risk management, nurses must not only have a thorough understanding of law related to nursing practice, but they must also acquire a working knowledge of relevant legal standards in the field of education.

To carry Dr. Baranoski's analogy one step farther, the owner of the sandbox (i.e., the school district) needs to learn about the culture, foundation, process, and language of its "guest playmates." In other words, if school districts want to be successful in providing school health services, their administrators and attorneys need to acquire a working knowledge of legal and clinical practice standards relevant to the health professionals working in their schools. In particular, they need to become knowledgeable about those standards that promote student safety, support quality health services programs, and minimize liability risks. Both groups need some of this knowledge before communication and collaboration can become truly effective.

Admittedly a difficult experiment in addressing a "culturally diverse" audience, this book attempts to bridge some of the knowledge gaps related to legal standards between professional groups. Hopefully, it will foster more effective communication and collaboration among players in the sandbox of school health services—students, nurses, administrators, attorneys, medical advisors, families, other educators, other school health and mental health professionals, and school board members. Many of the issues addressed and case examples cited are based on a collection of questions, concerns, and anecdotes gathered over several years, mostly from school nurses, school administrators, and parents. In raising the issues, we tried to provide content that supports safe practice, critical thinking, collaborative problem solving, a balanced view of realities across the country, and reasonable risk management strategies. We also sought contributors with expertise in a variety of areas, including education, special education and health law, school nursing practice, school health services management, higher education, ethics, and genetics.

Another important theme in this book is that state and federal law in the area of school health services is fluid and varied. The period of 1994–1999 demonstrated that fluidity and variety in many ways:

- After many court decisions that drew the line for school health services at individual nursing care for medically complex children, the U.S. Supreme Court decided the issue in *Cedar Rapids Community School District v. Garret F.* (1999): If a child requires a service in order to benefit from special education, and if the service does not require a physician, it is a related service and the school must provide it.

- The 1997 amendments to the Individuals with Disabilities Education Act were followed by the 1999 revised regulations, which, among other changes, included a provision encouraging states to set standards for paraprofessionals who participate in the delivery of special education and related services.

- After a period of confusion about sexual harassment, the U.S. Supreme Court spoke clearly in *Davis v. Monroe County School District* (1999), holding school districts responsible for damages if the school district had notice of harassment that was severe, persistent, or pervasive and did not investigate and, if necessary, take steps to stop it.

- Although confidentiality of medical records had been primarily a state law issue, the 1998 enactment of the Kennedy-Kassenbaum bill included a provision that encouraged states to review their confidentiality requirements, recognizing the widespread use of computerized records and electronic transmission of medical records. This activity revived concerns

that school health records, while serving as education records, are also medical records and should be protected appropriately.

One of the results of this legal activity is increased recognition of the significant role of the school nurse as an integral member of the school staff, as well as a health care provider in school. Another theme of the book is the critical importance of school nurse participation on IEP and § 504 teams that consider and make decisions about school health-related services for students with special needs. In some cases, the school nurse's role includes recommending that the team include a consulting physician or other health care provider.

Finally, we hope this book will assist school leaders and practitioners alike in understanding the complexity of demands being made on schools in general and on school health services programs in particular. A careful reader will detect both differences of opinion and differences in priorities among the contributors to this book. That too reflects the current state of school health services: There are gaps, for example, between the nursing services now expected in school and full recognition of the education and licensing required in each state for the professional delivery of these services. While observing the trend toward making schools a base for the delivery of many types of services to children, like others we recognize the incredible challenges that school staff face when, already overburdened with academic demands, they must also prepare to function as an efficient health care team.

We hope this book helps school districts, school personnel, and families understand and address these challenges together, for together we have the best opportunity to improve the learning and health of our nation's children and youth.

CAUTIONS AND NOTES

The general recommendations made in this book should never be substituted for legal counsel in a particular situation, nor for the collective wisdom of a team representing families, students, and health, education, and legal professionals collaborating in their own community. Families, school districts, communities, regions, and states differ—in their customs, laws, policies, resources, and priorities. While the book identifies many legal issues in school health services today, we caution readers that not all issues are addressed, nor will potential solutions work in all situations. Furthermore, not only the answers (where there are answers), but also the issues themselves will continue to change and will continue to vary from district to district and state to state.

A few sample materials—policies, protocols, guidelines, and forms—are included in individual chapters and appendices. We share these materials with readers not because they are either perfect or adaptable to all situations, but because they represent a collaborative effort to identify a reasonable approach to solving a problem. School districts are encouraged to use them as a point of discussion and for adaptation, if applicable, to their own needs.

As a final word of caution, it is important for readers to know that there are far more health-related cases brought against school districts, administrators, and nurses than are ever adjudicated in court. In other words, a majority of cases are settled out of court, before a jury verdict, and sometimes for very substantial amounts of money. These cases are difficult, if not impossible, to research unless involved individuals provide information. There are several "settled" cases that influenced policy and practice recommendations in this book but, because of confidential settlements, could not be cited.

An important note needs to be made regarding gender pronouns. To enhance readability of the text, singular pronouns that refer to a nonspecific person (e.g., a student) have often been randomly assigned either the male gender (e.g., "he") or the female gender (e.g., "she"), rather than using both (e.g., "he or she"). No other intent should be inferred from any assignment of a gender pronoun to a nonspecific person.

NOTE ON LEGAL REFERENCES AND LEGAL RESEARCH

Many of the references in this book are court decisions, laws and regulations, and rulings or advice from an administrative agency, the U.S. Department of Education. Court decisions can be published in an "official" report designated by the court and also appear in other legal publications. Some of the court decisions cited here have been published in the official legal report of the court; many others are not officially published and have been provided to the biweekly service *Individuals with Disabilities Education Law Report (IDELR)*, published by LRP. A few agency communications have not been published anywhere and are identified as "unpublished": These communications are available from the agency under the Freedom of Information Act. The following examples should explain the form of these references:

1. Court decision:
   Patricia P. v. Board of Education of Oak Park & River Forest High School District No. 200, 7 Fed. Supp.2d 801, 28 IDELR (LRP) 298 (N.D. Ill. 1998).

   Meaning of reference: Name of Plaintiff versus Name of Defendant; Volume 7 of the Federal Supplement Second, page 801 [Court Reporter Reference]; Individuals with Disabilities Education Law Report, volume 28, page 298; (Court, Year). This case was heard in the Federal District Court of the Northern District of Illinois.

2. Administrative ruling:
   Fairfield (CT) Public Schools, 29 IDELR (LRP) 42 (OCR 1997).

   Meaning of reference: School district against which complaint was filed; Individuals with Disabilities Education Law Report, volume 29, page 42; (Office for Civil Rights, U.S. Department of Education, Year). This administrative ruling was made by the Office for Civil Rights, U.S. Department of Education.

3. Law and regulation:
   20 U.S.C. § 1415.

   Full reference: Title 20, United States Code, Section 1400. This cites the beginning of the federal special education law.

   34 C.F.R. § 300.562.

   Full reference: Title 34, Code of Federal Regulations, Section 300.1. This cites the beginning of the federal special education regulations.

Reference information on court cases and Office for Civil Rights decisions is provided separately from other reference material at the end of each chapter. Reference information on all federal statutes and regulations that are cited in the book is provided in a **Table of Federal Statutes and Regulations** on page 623 of the book. Reference information on state statutes is provided in the chapter content.

Legal research can be conducted in a law library or on the Internet, although most electronic legal research services are available only on a paid basis. Some may require subscriptions, while others may provide access on a fee-for-service basis. Law libraries can be found in most courthouses and law schools and in some cities are provided by a local bar association. Large school districts, law firms that represent school districts, state and regional education agencies, and special education resource centers may also subscribe to IDELR and the Education Law Reporter. The Education Law Reporter publishes advance sheets of court decisions involving schools and colleges and commentary concerning related legal issues. Court decisions related to health care and nursing practice in general are most easily accessed through an on-line service.

REFERENCES

Baranoski, M. (1997, June 25). *Only a school nurse: The vision, the challenge, the partnership.* Keynote presentation at the 29th Annual Conference of the National Association of School Nurses, Dallas, TX.

Duncan, P., & Igoe, J. B. (1998). School health services. In E. Marx & S. F. Wooley (Eds.), *Health is academic.* New York: Teachers College Press.

McKenzie, F. D., & Richmond, J. B. (1998). School health services. In E. Marx & S. F. Wooley (Eds.), *Health is academic.* New York: Teachers College Press.

National School Boards Association. (1992). *Issue brief number 1—School health: Helping children learn.* News Service. Alexandria, VA: author.

Northrop, C. (1987). School nursing. In C. Northrop & M. Kelly (Eds.), *Legal issues in nursing.* St. Louis: C. V. Mosby.

Shannon, T. A. (1992). Letter to Federation member executive director. In *Issue brief number 1—School health: Helping children learn.* News Service. Alexandria, VA: National School Boards Association.

Chapter One
School Health Services: History and Trends

Susan J. Wold

INTRODUCTION

The purpose of this first chapter is to set the stage and provide a context for the discussion (in subsequent chapters) of legal issues in school health. Accordingly, this chapter will do the following:

1. Provide a historical overview of school health services;

2. Justify continuation of school health programs, documenting their contribution to the achievement of national and local public health agendas;

3. Review the essential and recommended components of school health programs and their intended outcomes;

4. Clarify the contribution of school nurses within school health programs and identify educational preparation and credentials needed for effective role performance;

5. Identify emerging school health/school nursing issues and trends.

THE EMERGENCE AND DEVELOPMENT OF SCHOOL HEALTH SERVICES

European Origins of School Health Services

School health services originated in Europe during the 19th century with medical inspection of schools and children. According to Struthers (1917), inauguration of inspections and other health services in the schools was prompted by the realization that the efforts of social workers and others to improve the health and living conditions of poor adults had produced only temporary relief. As Struthers (1917, pp. 13-14) further explains:

> The futility of the methods applied to adults and the practical failure to save men and women from the abyss of drink, crime, and immorality forced the attention of the thoughtful upon the child problem…. It was quickly observed that the maximum result could be best obtained through the medium of the school.

The first country to mandate medical inspections was France, which in 1837 passed a royal ordinance requiring school authorities to "supervise" the health of schoolchildren and to ensure that schools were maintained in a "sanitary condition" (Gardner, 1916, p. 263). However, it was nearly 40 years until the next note-worthy development: the appointment of school physicians in Brussels in 1874. Brussels thus became the first city to implement a *system* of school inspections (Gardner, 1916). Other countries in Europe (Germany, England, Sweden, Russia, Austria, and Hungary) and elsewhere (e.g., Argentina, Chile, and Egypt) soon followed, requiring school medical inspections (Gardner, 1926).

European Origins of School Nursing

In 1892, 55 years after the inception of school medical inspections in France, school nursing began in England. The first school nurse was Miss Amy Hughes, the Superintendent of Queen's Nurses in London's Bloomsbury Square. Having been consulted about proper nutrition and feeding for children attending a Drury Lane elementary school, Miss Hughes began making weekly visits to the school. Miss Hughes soon discovered that many children suffered needlessly from untreated minor ailments and were consequently too often absent from school. As a result of Miss Hughes's efforts, Queen's Nurses were placed in a number of London schools (Gardner, 1916).

In 1898 the London School Nurses' Society was formed "as a forerunner and example of what might be done" (Gardner, 1916, p. 265). However, because they believed that school nursing should be publicly financed, members of this voluntary society did not attempt to provide large-scale services. Instead, the Society sought funding from the London School Board, which grudgingly approved a salary for one school nurse in 1900 to deal with a ringworm epidemic. In 1904 the London School Nurses' Society successfully lobbied the London County Council to hire a staff of school nurses and a superintendent, all to be paid with public funds (Gardner, 1916).

Origins of School Health Services and School Nursing in America

By this time, school health services had also spread to the United States, beginning with medical inspections in the Boston schools in 1894 (Gardner, 1916; Struthers, 1917). Other cities soon followed (Struthers, 1917), including Chicago (1895), New York (1897), and Philadelphia (1898). In New York City, the mandatory medical inspections were conducted by 150 physicians, who were employed by the health department to work one hour per day inspecting schoolchildren and excluding those with contagious conditions (Pollitt, 1994). In 1900, the secretary of the London School Nurses' Society visited New York, returning home with ideas for improving London's medical inspections. A year later, Lillian Wald, the American nurse who had established New York's Henry Street Settlement in 1893, traveled to London, where she was "equally impressed with the possibilities of school nursing" (Gardner, 1916, p. 266).

Meanwhile, life on New York City's lower East Side at the turn of the century was, in a word, "appalling," as Christy (1970, p. 51) explains:

> Sweat shops still flourished and housing reform was only beginning…. Immigrants were pouring in, many finding life in New York a place of cruel hardship rather than the "promised land." Persons who were ill were afraid to go to the public hospitals which had high mortality rates and reputations for poor treatment. The sick often lay without medical or nursing care, and, if the illness were of a contagious nature, infected others in the desperately overcrowded homes. The streets were filthy, there were few parks, and the slum children played dangerously in the stifling traffic.

Because Miss Wald and her Henry Street Settlement nurses lived and worked in this neighborhood, they were painfully aware of the overwhelming public health needs that surrounded them. While the original purpose of the Henry Street Settlement was to provide

visiting nurses to care for the sick poor in their homes (Pollitt, 1994; Woodfill & Beyrer, 1991), the health and well-being of school-age children was also of concern.

By 1900 compulsory school attendance was the law in New York City, exacerbating the existing problems of overcrowding and inadequate sanitation (Pollitt, 1994; Thurber, Berry, & Cameron, 1991). Consequently, the public schools too often became "veritable hot beds of major and minor contagion" (Gardner, 1916, p. 267), contributing to the spread of both major (e.g., diphtheria, pertussis, scarlet fever, measles, and mumps) and minor (e.g., ringworm, scabies, head lice, and conjunctivitis) communicable diseases (Gardner, 1916; Pollitt, 1994). Thus, the mandatory daily medical inspections of school children and exclusion of those deemed "physically unfit to associate with the others" seemed to be the "easy way out" of the overcrowding/contagion problem (Gardner, 1916, p. 266).

However, the many school-age children observed roaming the neighborhood near the Henry Street settlement soon led Miss Wald to conclude that medical inspection and exclusion were ineffective (Dock, 1902; Gardner, 1916). Indeed, not only were excluded children *not* receiving needed treatment and other follow-up; they also were *not* prevented from associating with healthy children who remained in school! In fact, Gardner (1916) notes that children sent home because of minor communicable conditions like scabies or ringworm often waited for their playmates outside the school at the end of the day, thereby defeating the purpose of the exclusion (i.e., the protection of non-infected children).

Bringing these concerns to the attention of New York City's health commissioner and the chairman of the school board, Miss Wald noted that illness-related absentee rates in the public schools averaged 10–20% (Struthers, 1917). Because children of the poor typically left school at age 14 seeking paid employment to help their families, *any* disruption of their too-brief educational opportunities due to preventable illnesses or problems might limit their marketable job skills and reduce their lifelong wage-earning potential (Dock, 1902; Struthers, 1917). Thus, the students who could afford it least had the most to lose by missing school (Gardner, 1916).

Therefore, in an effort to reduce health-related absenteeism, Miss Wald offered to place one of her nurses in the four schools with the highest absentee rates as an experiment for one month. That first school nurse was Lina Rogers Struthers, who began work on October 1, 1902. By the end of one month, the results were so promising that the New York City Board of

Health offered her a continuing school nurse appointment, to begin November 7, 1902 (Struthers, 1917). In December 1902, the then Miss Rogers was named Superintendent of School Nurses and a staff of 12 nurses was appointed; in February 1903, 15 additional school nurses were hired, for a total staff of 27 (Struthers, 1917, pp. 26–27).

New York thus became the first city in the world to publicly fund and oversee school nursing services (Struthers, 1917). After only one year of school nursing, the results were astounding. Although 10,567 children had been excluded from New York City public schools during September 1902 (prior to Miss Rogers' appointment), only 1,101 students—a reduction of nearly 90%—were excluded during September 1903 (Gardner, 1916, p. 268). This "experiment" was clearly a success. Impressed with these results, other large American cities also began hiring school nurses (Struthers, 1917, pp. 30–34), including Los Angeles (1904), Boston (1905), Philadelphia (1908), and Chicago (1910).

Evolution of American School Health and School Nursing Services

From its promising beginnings in New York City in 1902, U.S. school nursing evolved unevenly during the 20th century, following a rather rocky course. However, because lengthy discussion of the history of school nursing is beyond the scope or intent of this chapter, readers seeking a more detailed account may wish to consult other sources (Wold & Dagg, 1981b; Woodfill & Beyrer, 1991; Hawkins, Hayes, & Corliss, 1994). Instead, the remainder of this section will briefly highlight major developments and trends.

School Health and School Nursing: The First Four Decades

As previously noted, the early years of school health and school nursing services focused almost exclusively on *medical inspection* of schools to ensure safe and sanitary conditions and medical inspection of schoolchildren to detect and prevent the spread of communicable disease (Gardner, 1926). However, the need for a more holistic view of children's health was soon apparent. Thus, the next emphasis in school health was on *medical examination* to detect and correct other kinds of health problems and "physical defects" that might interfere with a child's ability to learn (Gardner, 1926). Conducted in the school by a physician (assisted by the school nurse), these medical examinations assessed the health of students' eyes, ears, nose, throat, mouth (including teeth), heart and lungs,

"nervous system," spine and extremities, and general nutrition (Struthers, 1917, pp. 85–88).

However, officials soon recognized that this emphasis on casefinding and disability limitation was shortsighted in that it did not address disease prevention or health promotion (Gardner, 1926). This realization led to the incorporation of *health education* into the school curriculum, for the purpose of helping children "learn for themselves the principles and acquire the habits of health" as individuals and members of a community (Gardner, 1926, pp. 324–325). Initially, the school nurse provided health education via three- to five-minute talks in the classroom on such topics as hygiene, toothbrushing, and so on. Later, efforts were made to incorporate these health talks into teachers' lesson plans. Eventually, health education evolved into a curriculum that was mutually planned by the school nurse and classroom teacher (Gardner, 1926; Wold & Dagg, 1981b).

As detailed elsewhere (Wold & Dagg, 1981b), the increased workload associated with expansion of the school nurse's role to include health teaching and home visiting (in addition to assisting with medical inspection and examination of children) eventually resulted in problems of overextension. As a result of their overextension and role overload, school nurses were doing nothing well—a fact verified by a 1934 survey that showed that the poorest quality of public health nursing was that being done in the schools (Wales, 1941, p. 112).

Added to the problem of role overload was concern about school nurses' role confusion, which has been variously attributed to both inadequate educational preparation and employers' divergent role expectations. That is, some experts (Cromwell, 1946; Troop, 1963) suggested that school nurses' role confusion was at least partly due to their inadequate, hospital-based education, which taught nurses *how* to perform tasks without teaching them *why* they should perform them. Among the identified gaps in school nurses' preparation were principles of public health nursing, educational psychology, educational philosophy and teaching methods, pediatrics, and sociology (Troop, 1963; Hawkins, Hayes, & Corliss, 1994). Consequently, experts (e.g., Freeman, 1945) voiced the need for broader, college-based education for school nurses, including preparation for leadership roles within the school health program.

Compounding these concerns about the inadequacy of school nurses' educational preparation were the often divergent role expectations of school nurses' two most frequent employers: public health departments or agencies and educational systems. Thus, some school nurses were employed by public health departments or other health agencies (e.g., visiting nurse services) to provide either full-time or part-time school nursing services. These nurses, like the agencies that employed them, operated out of the public health model, with its underlying community-based philosophy. Consequently, these school nurses were primarily identified—by themselves and others—as public health nurses (Hawkins, Hayes, & Corliss, 1994). In contrast, school nurses who were employed directly by school systems or boards of education identified more readily with educators than with public health nurses. Reflecting their perceived alliance with educators, then, many school nurses employed by educational systems began to identify themselves as "school nurse teachers" or "teacher nurses" (Troop, 1963; Hawkins, Hayes, & Corliss, 1994).

The role divergence and confusion that resulted from school nurses' aligning themselves either with public health nurses or teachers also fueled debate about educational preparation for school nursing. According to Troop (1963), the debate centered on both the nature of the credential needed for school nursing (e.g., a hospital school nursing diploma versus a college degree) and the content of the preparatory curriculum for school nurses. As noted previously, experts (Freeman, 1945; Cromwell, 1946) called for curricula to include more public health nursing, pediatrics, leadership, counseling, and educational theory and teaching methods. Although standards for minimal versus ideal educational preparation for school nursing continue to be debated today, the discussion of these issues during the 1920s–1940s helped raise expectations regarding school nursing role preparation and practice (Dilworth, 1949). Thus, as will be discussed later in this chapter, fundamental agreement has been reached regarding national educational and practice standards for school nursing.

Another factor contributing to school nurses' overextension during the 1940s was the advent of World War II, which resulted in the recruitment of many nurses—including school nurses—into military service. Indeed, whereas only 1,600 nurses were on duty in the Army and Navy in September 1940, by September 1943 the number of nurses in the military had swelled to more than 24,345 (Dilworth, 1944, p. 443). With fewer civilian nurses available during World War II, dramatic cutbacks in school nursing would have been logically expected. However, the rejection of 25% of the 18- and 19-year-old males drafted for military service in 1943 for health reasons (Palmer, 1944, p. 221)

reinforced the need to maintain school health and school nursing services.

At the same time, however, the shortage of available school nurses, along with the previously described problems of overextension, led to the realization that school nurses needed to relinquish some of their existing duties and delegate to others so that they could concentrate their time and energy on the "wartime essentials" (Randle, 1943; Palmer, 1944; Dilworth, 1944), including the following:

- ongoing consultation to administrators regarding the school health program and incorporation of community resources;

- inservice education for teachers regarding health services (e.g., vision screening, daily inspections) they were to conduct;

- interpretation of health examination data to parents, teachers, and children with referral to community resources for follow-up as needed;

- home visiting to promote continuity of care for children and their families.

Thus, during this era, school nurses relied on classroom teachers to conduct routine physical inspection of children, vision screening, and height/weight measurement; when teachers noted health problems or defects, these were brought to the school nurse's attention. In addition, classroom teachers assumed major responsibility for teaching health in the classroom, with nurses functioning as health advisors, curricular consultants, and occasional guest speakers (Wales, 1941; Freeman, 1945).

In keeping with the public health model widely used in school health programs, school-home coordination and use of community resources were emphasized. Consequently, parents were now expected to be involved with and responsible for their children's health. Thus, instead of providing routine physical examinations at the school, schools now required parents to arrange for these on their own and to follow up with recommended treatments (Dilworth, 1944). Further evidence of this shared responsibility for children's health was the formation of "school health councils," composed of students, teachers, parents, administrators, health professionals, and community members. These advisory health councils participated in planning and implementing school health programs (Freeman, 1945).

Perhaps the most far-reaching development in school health during the 1940s, however, was the introduction of lay assistants into the school health program. As previously noted, classroom teachers were among the first of these lay assistants to whom the school nurse delegated such activities as daily inspection of students, periodic height/weight measurement, and (most significantly) teaching health classes. While delegation to teachers did relieve the school nurse of some duties, the shortage of civilian nurses during World War II raised concerns about the feasibility of achieving school nursing's wartime essential activities. Therefore, to enable school nurses to carry out the essential tasks, the National Organization for Public Health Nursing (NOPHN) recommended that "those tasks frequently performed by public health [school] nurses which do not require nursing skills be allocated to others, . . . [including] available volunteers, auxiliary aides, . . . teachers and community welfare workers" (Palmer, 1944, p. 222). The school nurse was still expected to train these assistants and coordinate their activities. Although it was not controversial at the time, in retrospect the decision to incorporate lay assistants into the school health program was tantamount to opening Pandora's box. Indeed, the issue of delegation to and use of unlicensed personnel in the school health program continues to be a two-edged sword for today's school nurses, as will be further discussed later in this chapter.

School Health and School Nursing: The 1950s–1990s

By the 1950s, it was generally accepted that "health is the first objective of education" (Brown, 1952, p. 219), and that the school health program should aim "to help every child to achieve the highest degree of physical, mental, social, and spiritual health" possible (Sellery, 1952, p. 121). It is therefore not surprising that the school nurse's most important role during the 1950s was that of health educator (Wold & Dagg, 1981b; Brown, 1952; Dierkes, 1951). Furthermore, the "teamwork" philosophy that had been established of necessity during the 1940s continued to grow in the next decade. The classroom teacher shouldered the ongoing responsibility for day-to-day observation of children's health and well-being, collaborating with the school nurse as needed to address identified health needs and problems (Wold & Dagg, 1981b).

Other significant developments during the 1950s included establishment of the family life curriculum (with the school nurse as a consultant) and an increased emphasis on students' nutrition and mental health (Wold & Dagg, 1981b). To encourage students to develop healthy eating habits, the school lunch

program was born; this program aimed to provide nutritionally complete, low-cost meals. Likewise, in recognition of the stresses associated with such developmental milestones as beginning school or reaching adolescence, the school health program increased its attention to mental health by providing a supportive classroom learning environment and promoting students' self-esteem (Wallace, 1959; Wold & Dagg, 1981b).

Politically, the 1960s were a more liberal and unsettled decade, defined by massive government programs like the "Great Society" and by polarizing issues like the Vietnam War (Wold & Dagg, 1981b). Likewise, civil rights and the quest for world peace were among the thorny issues occupying center stage on the American political agenda as the nation grappled with its social conscience. Fueled by national concern for equal educational opportunity and optimal health for all children, school health programs began to address the special needs of disabled and disadvantaged children, an emphasis previously suggested by Wallace (1959). However (as will be discussed later in this chapter), it was not until the 1970s that caring for and educating children with disabilities became a major influence in school health and school nursing.

During the 1960s, school nurses continued to struggle to define and communicate their roles and establish boundaries for their practice. In part, their persistent role confusion resulted from the varying educational levels and perspectives of school nurses as well as the nature of their employer. For example, Fricke (1967) found that school nurses with a baccalaureate or higher degree were substantially more likely than diploma graduates to regard leadership as an important role element. Lacking the leadership and assertiveness skills to clearly define and delimit their roles, many school nurses found themselves carrying out visible yet nonessential tasks (e.g., giving minor first aid, filling out health records, arranging bus schedules, or delivering faculty paychecks) at the expense of health counseling and health education (McAleer, 1965).

At the same time, an important shift in employers was occurring. That is, whereas originally school nurses were public health nurses employed primarily by agencies or health departments, there was a definite trend toward employment of school nurses by boards of education instead (McAleer, 1965). Although this change in employers meant that school nurses were now part of the school organization, their role and position were by no means certain. During this decade, other professionals, including counselors, social workers, health teachers, and psychologists, were also being added to the school's health team (Wold & Dagg, 1981b). Consequently, school nurses found that the roles and functions of these added personnel overlapped their own. For example, while school nurses busied themselves with routine first aid and record-keeping, social workers "took over" the home visiting function that had been a mainstay of the public health-oriented school nurse since the very beginning (Wold & Dagg, 1981b).

Further compounding school nurses' role-definition woes was the expanded use—and misuse—of unlicensed assistants, primarily school health aides (Tipple, 1964). The documented problems associated with the use of these aides ranged from school nurses' inability or unwillingness to "give up" nonessential tasks to the aides, to inappropriate delegation of nursing responsibilities that required professional judgment. Even more disturbing was the realization that in some settings, unlicensed personnel were not assisting school nurses but were instead replacing them (Tipple, 1964). Thus, although delegation to unlicensed assistants was intended to free nurses to carry out essential professional responsibilities requiring expert skill and judgment, the inclusion of unlicensed assistants in the school health program raised legal and professional practice issues that persist even today.

By the end of the 1960s, even as school nurses struggled to define their roles and manage their workloads, school districts across the country were facing fiscal problems requiring budgetary cutbacks. As they sought to cut programs and services deemed most expendable, the unthinkable happened: school districts proposed trimming or eliminating school health programs and services. Suddenly, school health and school nursing were scrutinized as luxuries, rather than essential services, taking a backseat to what had become, for many school districts, more important (and more costly) budget items, like competitive sports (Fredlund, 1967).

Unprepared to defend their worth with facts and figures, school nurses entered the 1970s caught between opposing trends. On the one hand, the literature urged role expansion (e.g., the school nurse practitioner [SNP] option), better credentialing (master's degrees), and greater community involvement. On the other hand, however, school nurses confronted role confusion, role reduction, and possible job loss (Wold & Dagg, 1981b). Indeed, in answer to his own probing question, "Is there a school nurse role?" sociologist Norman Hawkins (1971, p. 744) offered a shocking conclusion: "Probably not."

Ironically, even as school nurses' fortunes declined, the health needs of children and adolescents changed and expanded during the 1970s. Drug use and chemical dependency increased dramatically, as did sexual experimentation and its accompanying problems: sexually transmitted diseases (STDs) and unwanted pregnancy. In addition, the women's movement led to changing gender roles, and the family unit began to waver under a rising divorce rate and the decision of many couples to cohabit without marrying. Because children and youth were too often caught in the middle of this social upheaval, their need for health counseling and education was greater than ever before.

To better prepare school nurses to meet students' increasingly complex health needs, the University of Colorado developed the nation's first school nurse practitioner (SNP) program in 1970. As envisioned by Loretta Ford (1970, p. 22), the SNP would be "a first rate wellness clinician" skilled in physical and psychosocial assessment and able to manage common problems of school-aged children, youth, and their families in collaboration with physicians and other health care providers. Because these advanced practice nurses would have clearly defined roles, be able to manage minor illnesses, and thus be more judicious about referrals to outside providers, SNPs were expected to improve students' health while also demonstrating the cost-effectiveness of school nursing services.

Described in detail by Igoe (1981), the University of Colorado's SNP program required 16 months to complete and included both on-site study in Denver over two summers and a supervised clinical preceptorship in students' home states. The program prepared its graduates to "perform competent health evaluations, identify and manage various health problems in consultation with a physician, develop and implement directly health maintenance plans, and appropriately refer children requiring the services of other health and educational specialists" (Igoe, 1981, p. 470). Following Colorado's lead, SNP programs subsequently emerged in such states as California, Connecticut, Texas (American Association of Colleges of Nursing, 1994), Pennsylvania, and New Jersey, and are typically associated with master's degree programs in nursing.

The second major development in school health during the 1970s (along with emergence of the SNP role) was renewed interest in the needs of children with disabilities. An outgrowth of the 1960s' civil rights movement, concern for equal educational access for disabled children dominated the school health agenda, culminating in the 1975 passage of PL 94-142: The Education for All Handicapped Children Act. Described in greater detail elsewhere (Wold, 1981; Hertel et al., 1982; American Nurses' Association Divisions on Nursing Practice, American School Health Association, & National Association of School Nurses, 1980), this landmark legislation required that a "free appropriate education" be provided for all children with disabilities, ages 3–21, in the "least restrictive environment" based on development of an "individualized educational program (IEP)" (Wold, 1981, p. 66). In 1986, PL 94-142 was amended (via PL 99-457) to include early intervention services for preschoolers (infants and toddlers) with special needs (Oberg, Bryant, & Bach, 1994). In 1990, PL 94-142 was updated and renamed the Individuals with Disabilities Education Act (IDEA) (Bonaiuto, 1995).

As will be further discussed in this and subsequent chapters, PL 94-142 profoundly affected the role and workload priorities of school nurses, raising a number of thorny legal and ethical issues along the way, many of which remain unresolved more than 20 years after its enactment. Indeed, devising a school health program to meet the needs of both mainstreamed children with disabilities and the school community at large in an era of fiscal restraint and health care reform requires an artful balance of ethics and economics—and more than a little political and moral courage.

By the early 1980s, the numbers of students with disabilities and special needs in the schools had increased dramatically as a consequence of PL 94-142. In rural New Hampshire alone, Desrosiers (1989) reported that 18,000 special education students were accommodated *each year*. As the numbers of disabled and technology-dependent children increased, however, a frightening reality became apparent: many school nurses lacked the skills and/or experience to competently care for them (Desrosiers, 1989).

Fortunately, the University of Colorado anticipated school nurses' need for additional preparation to care for children with chronic and disabling conditions and began offering the School Nurse Achievement Program (SNAP) in 1981 as a nationwide continuing education program (Goodwin, Igoe, & Smith, 1984). The goals of SNAP included the following: (a) improving school nurses' knowledge and skills in assessing and caring for students with chronic illnesses, physical disabilities, emotional and mental disorders, and learning disabilities; (b) educating school nurses about PL 94-142 and other federal and state laws concerning students with handicaps; (c) increasing school nurses' participation in development of appropriate IEPs; and (d) promoting collaboration with other school personnel and community agencies (Goodwin, Igoe, & Smith, 1984). Between 1981 and 1984, approximately 2,000 school nurses in 18 states successfully completed SNAP. Preliminary evalua-

tion data from a sample (N = 124) of the first SNAP graduates revealed that more than 70% of respondents found the program helpful in increasing their knowledge and, to a somewhat lesser extent, skills (Goodwin, Igoe, & Smith, 1984). Buoyed by this early success, the University of Colorado marketed the program throughout the country.

With the economy in a recession and the school-age population declining, the budgetary cutbacks that had threatened school health and school nursing a decade earlier were once again a problem during the early 1980s (Green, 1981). As a result, many districts cut back their school nursing staff and/or replaced them with unlicensed assistants (Whited & Starke, 1989), thereby fulfilling Tipple's grim predictions (1964). The "rewards" for those school nurses who "survived" the cutbacks included larger student populations to serve and "hectic to impossible" job demands (Custer, 1984, p. 259).

A further consequence of the nation's worsening economy was the fact that, in about two thirds of the families with school-age children, both parents needed to be employed outside the home. As a result, neither parent was likely to be at home during the school day to seek medical care if a child became ill at school. In addition, as the costs of health care became prohibitive, nearly one third of school-age children had *no* ongoing source of health care (Igoe, 1980a, 1980b). Thus, some experts (Igoe, 1980b; DeAngelis, 1981) began calling for expansion of the existing school health services—which consisted primarily of screening activities—to include ambulatory care and expanded preventive services (e.g., immunizations).

To that end, the Robert Wood Johnson Foundation launched its pioneering National School Health Program in 1978, using four states (Colorado, Utah, New York, and North Dakota) as 5-year demonstration sites (DeAngelis, 1981). Established in schools whose students lacked access to adequate medical and dental care, the school-based clinics (SBCs) formed under this program were each staffed with an SNP (who also served as the "team's" coordinator), a school health aide, and a part-time physician (DeAngelis, 1981). The clinics were intended to provide school-based primary care for two populations: (a) students lacking other health care resources, and (b) physically or developmentally disabled students attending school under the provisions of PL 94-142 (Igoe, 1980a). These SBCs proved to be very successful, particularly for medically underserved (and underinsured) populations, since physicians did not object to "competition" from SNPs (Igoe, 1980a, 1980b). SBCs were also successful for adolescents, who are far more likely to seek care and comply with treatments on-site (at school) than if they are referred to health care providers in the community (Green, 1981; Igoe & Giordano, 1992).

Although expansion of school-based health services was an important achievement of the 1980s, unquestionably the most remarkable milestone of the decade was the development of national practice standards for school nursing. In summarizing unmet needs and problems facing school nursing, Wold (1981, pp. 478–493) concluded that "inadequate quality assurance due to lack of mandated standards for school nursing practice" (1981, p. 492) was a major roadblock to the survival and growth of this nursing practice specialty. Her proposed solution (Wold, 1981, p. 491) was creation of a national task force, including representatives from "pertinent" professional organizations, such as the American Nurses' Association (ANA), the American School Health Association (ASHA), and the National Association of School Nurses (NASN), to develop and unanimously endorse "acceptable, meaningful, and appropriate school nursing standards."

Despite the seeming complexity of the charge and the number of organizations whose cooperation would be needed, this task was completed in 1983 with ANA's publication of *Standards of School Nursing Practice.* Furthermore, three other organizations (the Public Health Nursing Section of the American Public Health Association [APHA], the National Association of State School Nurse Consultants, and the National Association of Pediatric Nurse Associates and Practitioners [NAPNAP]) collaborated in drafting and endorsing the standards. By definition, these standards "represent agreed-upon levels of quality in practice . . . [and] have been developed to characterize, measure, and provide guidance in achieving excellence in care" (American Nurses' Association, Task Force on Standards of School Nursing Practice, 1983, p. 1).

To facilitate implementation and evaluation of the standards, several additional publications have since appeared. The first was *An Evaluation Guide for School Nursing Practice Designed for Self and Peer Review* (National Association of School Nurses, 1985). This document presents ANA's *Standards of School Nursing Practice* (1983) in the format of an evaluation tool that individual nurses can use to rate their own or a peer's performance. A more detailed set of interpretive guidelines, the *Implementation Guide for the Standards of School Nursing Practice,* was subsequently published (1991) by the American School Health Association. Like other professional practice guidelines, however, the standards for school nursing practice must be regarded

as a living, "in progress" document, subject to ongoing review and updating based on changes in the profession and the practice environment. Accordingly, the National Association of School Nurses adapted the ANA standards (1983, 1991), publishing the following two explanatory documents: *Guidelines for a Model School Nursing Services Program* (Proctor, 1990) and *School Nursing Practice: Roles and Standards* (Proctor, 1993).

During the 1990s, the needs of students with physical and developmental disabilities continued to dominate the school health agenda for several reasons. First, the passage of PL 94-142 in 1975 guaranteed access to education in the least restrictive environment, resulting in an increase in the number of children with special needs in public schools. In addition, due to technological advances in health care, children who would not previously have survived major congenital anomalies or chronic illnesses were now attending school (Iverson & Hays, 1994). In fact, Passarelli (1993, 1994a, 1994b) reports that approximately 10–15% of American children have a chronic health condition and that 10% of those are "severe." Furthermore, Palfrey et al. (1992) estimate that 20,000 to 100,000 children, including 1 in 1,000 children in Massachusetts alone, are "technology dependent," requiring daily nursing assistance for respiratory care (oxygen, ventilators), ostomy care, urethral catheterization, intravenous feeding, and dialysis, to name a few nursing needs.

Due to the 1990s' theme of "inclusion," then, the number of disabled and chronically ill students in regular classroom settings increased, as did the acuity of their health needs. So school nurses now were expected to care for "medically fragile" and "technology dependent" children in addition to meeting the health needs of the rest of the school population, prompting some experts (Bonaiuto, 1995) to question school nurses' competence to take on these expanded responsibilities. Moreover, the time required to meet the needs of these special students also became an issue, as school districts continued their struggle to stretch scarce dollars.

As a result, ethical dilemmas arose concerning the distribution and use of resources. For example, some taxpayers and health care providers objected to school nurses spending so much time meeting the needs of (comparatively) few students with disabilities, while health promotion and health education initiatives for well children received less time and attention. For school nurses, other ethical dilemmas were even more troubling, such as the issue of DNR (do not resuscitate) orders in the schools. As Rushton, Will, and Murray (1994, p. 582) point out, the presence in school of a child with a DNR order "forces everyone to face the reality that a child is going to die." In addition, the legal and ethical issues inherent in responding to DNR orders may result in conflict between the child's family and school personnel, setting the stage for legal challenges.

Amid the ongoing debate over school health priorities, including the needs of medically fragile versus able-bodied students, national concern over rising health care costs and suggestions that some health services be rationed or restricted sparked the health care reform movement. The notion of "managed care" as a means of expanding health care access, improving quality, and controlling costs was widely debated. Although the Health Security Act proposed in 1993 by President Clinton did not become law, it did incorporate comprehensive school health education plus mechanisms for developing school-based health services (Salmon, 1994).

Despite being derailed by partisan politics in Washington, the health care reform movement refused to die. Proponents have continued to advocate improved health care access and controlled costs both nationally and on a state-by-state basis. For example, Salmon (1994) and other experts (Igoe & Giordano, 1992) have ardently promoted expansion of the "school-based and school-linked health services" (Salmon, 1994, p. 137) that had been proposed in Clinton's Health Security Act. And, while politicians continue to debate the feasibility and advisability of funding school-based health services, there is evidence that some school districts are forging creative collaborations to provide essential services. For example, a community hospital, a school district, and a private pediatrician in Phoenix, Arizona, collaborated to sponsor a school-based clinic to ensure that all children attending five inner-city elementary schools had access to adequate health care (Wenzel, 1996). Similarly, responding to an inner city elementary school's daily absentee rate of 10–12% and asthma rate of nearly 17% (one in six children), four competing health plans have cooperatively planned and funded a school-based clinic in Minneapolis (Lerner, 1996).

As these creative models suggest, an unresolved and pressing issue for the 1990s and beyond is funding of school health and school nursing services. In the absence of federal legislation supporting school health programs and services, school districts struggle fiscally and philosophically to determine which services are essential and affordable. At the heart of all the debate, of course, is money. Because low-income children and their families are the least likely to have health insurance, the quest for equal access to health care resources has intensified efforts to obtain Medicaid reimburse-

ment for school nursing services. Indeed, the National Association of State School Nurse Consultants (1996b) has explicitly stated that Medicaid reimbursement should be provided for school nursing services delivered to Medicaid-eligible students. This would allow school districts to use their limited budgets and tax revenues to underwrite needed programs and services for which no other funding or reimbursement is available.

Although improving health care access, controlling costs, and creating new funding mechanisms are laudable goals of the 1990s' health care reform movement, perhaps the most serendipitous outcome for school health has been the suggestion (Salmon, 1994; Uphold & Graham, 1993) that school health programs broaden their focus to include integrated, multidisciplinary services for families and communities, with an emphasis on health promotion and illness prevention. For example, Salmon (1994) calls for a return to "school *health* nursing" in which nurses are broadly concerned with the wellness of school populations and communities, rather than focusing solely on individuals' needs. As she explains (Salmon, 1994, p. 138):

Clearly, the fundamental underpinnings of health care reform call for a nurse . . . who can be part of creating new paradigms for school health. . . . The issues of quality, access, and cost fundamental to health care reform are best addressed through a service paradigm in which health promotion and disease prevention represent central components. . . . The role of schools is deliberately being broadened and changed. Schools no longer are being viewed solely as society's mechanism for educating children . . . [but instead] as a highly desirable vehicle through which significant gains in the health status of children and families can be made.

Endorsing this proposed paradigm shift, other experts (Uphold & Graham, 1993; Igoe & Giordano, 1992) suggest that school-based clinics (SBCs) be reconfigured as "family services centers" or "family health centers" that provide universal access to a broad array of well-coordinated educational, health, social, and economic services for families in the community. Such centers are expected to improve clients' health status and outcomes, while empowering individuals and families, through education and counseling, to assume responsibility for their own health. Ultimately, such expanded school health programs may prove to be an innovative strategy for "using the nation's schools to improve the nation's health care system" (Uphold &

Graham, 1993, p. 204). Time and history alone will judge.

TO BE OR NOT TO BE: A RATIONALE FOR CONTINUATION OF SCHOOL HEALTH PROGRAMS

As the preceding pages illustrate, school health has historically followed a rather rocky course over the past 100+ years, beset by such problems as ambiguous mission, role confusion and overlap, inadequate educational preparation of school nurses and other personnel, and inadequate funding to meet documented health needs. Given these persistent issues as well as the trend toward ever leaner school budgets, an obvious question comes to mind: Do the outcomes of school health programs justify their continuation, given their associated economic and other costs—or are school health programs expensive anachronisms that should be eliminated? The following pages will address that fundamental question.

Schools and Health

Because of compulsory attendance laws, schools are the only public institutions that can reach most of the nation's children and youth (Satcher, 1995). In fact, 95% of the United States's 48 million children ages 5–18 are enrolled in school, with an average daily attendance of 90% nationally (Kann, Collins, et al., 1995; Walker-Shaw, 1993). Because these children are typically in class 6 hours per day, 180 days per year, "schools have more influence on the lives of youth than any other social institution except the family" (Kann, Collins, et al., 1995, p. 291). The schools are thus widely regarded (Baker, 1994; Kann, Collins, et al., 1995; Lavin, Shapiro, & Weill, 1992; Walker-Shaw, 1993; Wold, 1982) as a primary site and vehicle for influencing students' health status, attitudes, and behaviors. Furthermore, experts (Fryer & Igoe, 1995; Igoe, 1995; Walker-Shaw, 1993; McGinnis & DeGraw, 1991; Healthy People 2000, 1991; U.S. Department of Health and Human Services, 1991) agree that the schools play a pivotal role in promoting achievement of those *Healthy People 2010* objectives (U.S. Department of Health and Human Services, 2000a, 2000b) that pertain to school-age populations.

Thus, one rationale for implementing school health programs is the fact that U.S. students represent a "captive well population" for whom meaningful health protection and health promotion can be provided (Wold, 1982). A second, frequently cited rationale is that, by promoting students' wellness, school health programs enable students to benefit optimally from their classroom learning opportunities; in short,

healthy kids are better learners (Kann, Collins, et al., 1995; Killip, Lovick, Goldman, & Allensworth, 1987; Allensworth & Kolbe, 1987; Fryer & Igoe, 1995; Lavin, Shapiro, & Weill, 1992; Wold, 1982). Furthermore, research (Fryer & Igoe, 1995) suggests that some indices of child well-being (e.g., death rate of children ages 1–14, percent of births to unwed teens, and on-time high school graduation) are associated (at statistically significant levels) with the availability of school nurses and nursing services (as measured by pupil–school nurse ratios).

Despite the documented contribution of school health programs to students' health status and ability to learn effectively, it can also be argued that children's health is the responsibility of their parents, not of the schools. However, because children are under the protection and supervision of the schools for up to six hours each day, parents must delegate some responsibility for children's health to schools. A third rationale for implementing school health programs, then, is to assist parents in carrying out their responsibilities (American School Health Association, 1974; Wold, 1982).

For example, schools may offer comprehensive health education and counseling to empower students to (ultimately) assume responsibility for their own health. In addition, schools may facilitate students' and parents' compliance with legally mandated requirements, such as immunization schedules, by offering immunization clinics on-site. Likewise, when school-based clinics (SBCs) are available to provide routine pediatric care on-site, parents (especially those with low incomes) may be less likely to postpone treatment of such common health problems as ear and throat infections. If the school can provide prompt, low-cost treatment (e.g., using pharmaceutical samples), unnecessary complications and/or hospitalizations can be avoided (Igoe, 1995). Thus, school health programs can indeed assist, but not supplant, parents' efforts to assume responsibility for children's health.

A final justification for continuing school health programs is related to the overarching purpose of schools in society: namely, to educate and develop young people into productive adults. In turn, for young people to become productive, contributing members of society, they need to be "healthy," however defined. As Kann, Collins, et al. (1995, p. 291) explain:

The goals of schools are consistent with the goals of health promotion. Because healthy children learn better than children with health problems, to achieve their education mission, schools must help address the health needs of students. Furthermore, the underlying responsibility of schools to prepare youth to lead productive lives makes health promotion a central facet of the education mission.

Indeed, analyzing data from the 1991 edition of *Kids Count* (Center for the Study of Social Policy, 1994) and from *School Health in America* (Lovato, Allensworth, & Chan, 1989), Baker (1994, p. 182) concludes that, despite considerable state-to-state variation in spending for education and school health, there appears to be "a positive relationship between economic investment in children, children's well-being, and SAT performance." As she further explains (Baker, 1994, p. 182):

> The states that care about their children as reflected in higher educational expenditures, health insurance coverage, and mandated school health programs tend to rank higher in the well-being of their children. This means that these states have a lower percent of low-birth-weight babies, a lower infant mortality rate, lower child death rate, lower teen violent death rate, lower percent of teen out-of-wedlock births, lower juvenile incarceration rate, fewer children in poverty, and a higher percentage of high school graduates and pupils sitting for the SAT.

In short, for all of the reasons cited in the preceding pages, there is a place for health programs in the schools. At the same time, however, escalating costs and eroding budgets are also realities confronting today's schools and health programs. Consequently, producing significant outcomes, such as the improved child well-being described by Baker (1994), is no longer enough. Instead, schools are expected to produce positive outcomes *cost-effectively.* As will be discussed next, an important way to accomplish this is to regard the school health program as part of the community's public health agenda.

Integrating School Health into the Community's Overall Health Agenda

In an editorial on "Bridging the Gap Between Community Health and School Health," Green (1988, p. 1149) acknowledges the tendency of "public health people" to make schools the scapegoat for such community health problems as drug abuse, teen pregnancies, increased teen suicides, "couch-potato television viewing," and the consequent "decline of physical

fitness in youth." However, citing a personal communication from Marshall Kreuter, Iverson (1981, p. 7) points out that *schools* do not have these health problems: "rather the community in general and families specifically have these problems. The problems are brought to the school but their existence there is a direct reflection of the problems as they exist in families and the total community."

The solution to these problems, then, requires the cooperation and involvement of all three constituencies: families, schools, and the community at large (Iverson, 1981; Nader, 1990). Endorsing this notion of schools partnering with the community to address shared health concerns, Elders (1993, p. 312) predicts that in the 21st century schools will become the "centerpieces" of communities and will serve as the "hub" for integrating a broad range of health and social services for children and communities. Other experts (Green, 1988; DeGraw, 1994; Killip et al., 1987) agree. Green (1988) believes that ending the finger-pointing and "buck-passing" concerning health problems of school-age children and youth will require shared responsibility by schools, health agencies, and parents. In turn, such "intersectoral and multidisciplinary collaborations" will depend on coalition building at the community level (Green, 1988, p. 1149). Furthermore, efforts must be made to help students develop the requisite knowledge and skills to assume responsibility for their own health (Green, 1988).

Noting the renewed interest in schools as community institutions, DeGraw (1994, p. 192) underscores the *complexity* of children's health and educational problems and calls for "multiple, broad-based approaches" to solve them. DeGraw further believes that new models of school health will be required that are "flexible, adaptable, and specific to the needs of students they serve" (p. 192). Echoing the importance of a collaborative approach to integrating school health and community health programs, Killip et al. (1987, p. 437) offer additional rationales. First, because they rely on public tax dollars for their very existence, schools do not (and cannot) exist in isolation from the community. Second, students are more likely to adopt "health enhancing behaviors" if they receive "consistent messages…through multiple channels (home, school, community, media)… [from] multiple sources (parents, peers, health and educational professionals, and media)."

Despite such widespread agreement about the need to integrate and coordinate school health and community health programs and initiatives, there are potential barriers to such cooperative efforts, including conflicting agency goals or policies and inadequate resources. However, as Iverson (1981, p. 9) observes, "the greatest barrier to cooperative efforts . . . is the prejudices and inflexibilities of persons working within the affected systems." Therefore, education and health professionals must curb their tendencies toward territoriality, recognizing that "synergism is more helpful . . . than antagonism" (Iverson, 1981, p. 10).

To meet the mandate of providing cost-effective school health programs, then, schools must collaborate with families and other community agencies and groups to offer health programs that meet the needs *of their particular community* (Doering, 1996). A critical first step, therefore, is conducting a needs assessment to clarify community characteristics (including age, race, income levels, cultural diversity, etc.) and identify health risk factors (Elders, 1993; Nader, 1990). Consistent with this first step of identifying the community's needs is the goal for the collaboration: development of a school health "system" that incorporates the following principles (DeGraw, 1994, pp. 192–194):

1. Although the school may be the "hub" or focal point, the school health program must be part of a larger *community-based* system, recognizing that families and communities strongly influence students' health attitudes and behaviors.

2. The system should be *"student-focused and needs-driven,"* with its success measured in terms of student outcomes developed in response to the community needs assessment.

3. The school health system must also be *culturally sensitive* to the diversity of the school and community populations, ensuring that the system is indeed accessible and responsive to all.

4. The school health system must *comprehensively address students' health needs,* offering a broad array of health and support services and incorporating innovative delivery options (e.g., new technologies).

5. Furthermore, school health system *components must be coordinated and integrated* to ensure efficient and effective use of limited resources.

6. To ensure optimal student health outcomes, the system must be *prevention-oriented,* beginning its health promotion efforts early in life (e.g., during the preschool years).

7. The system must also be readily *accessible* to those it serves, which requires communication about availability of services and expectations, and development of multiple entry points.

8. To remain responsive to students' changing needs as well as to changes in health care, community dynamics, and resources, the school health system must be *flexible.*

9. Finally, to ensure long-term viability, the system must demonstrate its *accountability* to taxpayers, other funding sources, administrators, school boards, parents, the students it serves, and the community at large.

To meet the goal of developing a school health system with the foregoing characteristics requires coalition-building at the community level (Iverson, 1981; Killip et al., 1987; DeFriese, Crossland, MacPhail-Wilcox, & Sowers, 1990). As Iverson (1981, p. 9) explains, community-based coalitions are needed to "build an active constituency for school health programs" that will enlist community support and funding for school health. These coalitions should represent broad segments of the community, such as health and education agencies (public and private), funding agencies (e.g., United Way), health service agencies, professional organizations, churches, neighborhood associations, the PTA, and so on (Iverson, 1981).

In summary, building coalitions to develop an integrated, coordinated school health system is a "win-win" situation with benefits for all involved (Killip et al., 1987). For example, students benefit because their health program becomes a higher priority in the community for funding and ongoing support. In turn, the schools gain increased funding and other resources to implement health programs, including controversial (e.g., innovative, experimental) programs that could not otherwise be launched. For their part, the other community agencies and groups benefit from increased visibility, cost savings associated with avoiding duplication of services and more effective deployment of resources, heightened public awareness of their contributions and services, and a consequently enhanced ability to mobilize additional resources (Killip et al., 1987).

SCHOOL HEALTH PROGRAMS: SCOPE AND FOCUS

Now that the necessity for health programs in the schools and for a coordinated approach to planning and implementing them has been established, the logical questions that arise include the following: What is the scope of school health programs? What are their intended outcomes? What are the school health program components used to achieve these goals? These questions are addressed next.

The Scope of School Health Programs: Traditional vs. Comprehensive

For most of the 20th century, school health programs were structured according to the traditional "three-pronged" approach, focusing on (a) providing necessary health services (such as screening and emergency care) for students; (b) implementing K–12 health education programs and curricula; and (c) maintaining a safe and healthy school environment (Allensworth & Kolbe, 1987; Davis & Allensworth, 1994; Kann, Collins, et al., 1995; Resnicow & Allensworth, 1996). However, as the complexity of students' health concerns and problems increased, the limited ability of traditional school health programs to address them became more apparent.

Therefore, in an effort to make school health programs more effective, Allensworth and Kolbe (1987) proposed a configuration that expanded the traditional three-pronged school health program into an eight-pronged "comprehensive" school health program. To broaden the so-called "classic triad" of health services, health education, and healthy environment (Resnicow & Allensworth, 1996), then, Allensworth and Kolbe (1987) added five components: (a) physical education; (b) nutrition and food services; (c) school counseling, psychology, and social services; (d) school-based wellness programs for faculty and staff; and (e) collaborative school-community health promotion efforts. These eight components interact to "influence not only the health but the cognitive performance of school students, faculty, and staff" (Davis & Allensworth, 1994, p. 400). Indeed, not only is the interaction of these components complementary, it may even prove to be synergistic (Allensworth & Kolbe, 1987).

The Comprehensive School Health Program

Definition and Purpose

But what precisely is a "comprehensive school health program"? The literature includes a number of definitions (DeFriese, Crossland, MacPhail-Wilcox, & Sowers, 1990; Comprehensive School Health Education Workshop, 1993; American School Health Association, 1994; Kann, Collins, et al., 1995). For example, DeFriese et al. (1990, p. 183) suggest that a comprehensive school health program includes "a broad spectrum" of intersecting activities and services intended to provide students and their families "with exposure to a range of cognitive, affective, and skill development opportunities that contribute to overall competence with respect

to health." Such knowledge and skills, they further contend, are necessary "for personal growth and development throughout the life cycle" and help ensure "long-term life satisfaction and personal competence" (DeFriese et al., 1990, p. 183).

Endorsing that view, the American School Health Association (1994) indicates that the broad spectrum of activities and services included in the comprehensive school health program occurs both in the school and surrounding community to "enable children and youth to enhance their health, develop to their fullest potential and establish productive and satisfying relationships in their present and future lives" (1994, p. 1). Accordingly, a *comprehensive school health program* may be defined (American School Health Association, 1994, p. 21) as "an organized set of policies, procedures and activities designed to protect and promote the health and well-being of students and staff" incorporating these eight components: (a) health services; (b) health education; (c) healthy environment; (d) physical education; (e) food and nutrition services; (f) counseling, psychological, and social services; (g) worksite health promotion for faculty and staff; and (h) integration of school-community health programs and initiatives.

Although each school health program must determine its own goals, based on a needs assessment and community-wide collaborative planning effort (discussed previously), comprehensive school health programs, by definition, share some fundamental purposes and need to address some common goals. For example, according to the American School Health Association (1994, p. 1), inherent in a "comprehensive" approach to school health programming are the following goals:

- to promote health and wellness;

- to prevent specific diseases, disorders, and injury;

- to prevent high-risk social behaviors;

- to intervene to assist children and youth who are in need or at risk;

- to help support those who are already exhibiting special health care needs;

- to promote positive health and safety behaviors.

As stated, these are not true "goals" because they do not specify measurable *outcomes*. Instead, these represent broad program *strategies,* or actions intended to produce desired results. Fortunately, specific, measurable intended outcomes (goals) concerning the health of children and youth are included in publications regarding *Healthy People 2010* (U.S. Department of Health and Human Services, 2000a, 2000b). Thus, individual school health programs can incorporate and/or adapt goals concerning physical fitness, nutrition, immunization levels, environmental safety, and so on from these publications for their own use. Strategies and resources for implementing the 2000 goals as suggested by Allensworth, Symons, & Olds (1994) may be helpful in adapting 2010 goals.

School Health Program Components: A Closer Look

Having defined the nature of a comprehensive school health program, identified its components, and summarized its broad purposes and goals, this chapter next will briefly consider each of the eight program components identified previously—as well as a ninth component (program management) proposed by experts (Davis & Allensworth, 1994; Resnicow & Allensworth, 1996). Table 1-1 summarizes the discussion, describing each component's overall emphasis, identifying possible outcomes and strategies, and citing recommended references. Note that the outcomes and strategies listed are intended to be *descriptive*, not *prescriptive*, and that they are only examples: the list provided is not exhaustive.

As noted earlier, the school health program must "fit" or match the needs, values, and resources of the particular community and school/district that implements the program. The first step in planning a school health program is therefore to complete a needs assessment (Elders, 1993; Nader, 1990). In addition to needs assessment data, however, school health program planners must also incorporate legally mandated services and expectations. Examples of these include (but are not limited to) (a) screening specific age groups or populations for particular problems (e.g., vision and hearing); (b) ensuring compliance with immunization laws; (c) obtaining/reviewing the findings of periodic physical examinations; (d) compliance with specified maintenance standards for the school's physical plant and playground equipment; (e) educating students about particular health topics at designated age or grade levels; and (f) compliance with nutritional guidelines and food service safety regulations. Thus, the relative emphasis of any school health program on and within particular program components is determined by review of needs assessment data and legal mandates. For that reason, school health programs are like snowflakes: no two are exactly alike.

Health Services. Mistakenly regarded (on occasion) as the essence of the school health program, health services are intended to ensure that students are as healthy as possible so that they can benefit maximally from their school-based learning opportunities. Depending, again, on results of the needs assessment and applicable laws and regulations, the health services included in a school's health program may include such activities as (a) screening; (b) immunization surveillance and enforcement; (c) periodic health histories and physical examinations; (d) emergency nursing care (i.e., professional assessment and intervention) or, in the absence of a school nurse, first aid by trained lay personnel in response to on-site illnesses or accidents; and (e) case management, health supervision, administration of treatments, medications, and other services for students with chronic and/or disabling conditions. Furthermore, depending on geographic and financial accessibility to health care resources in the community, some health services may be offered on-site via a school-based health center (SBHC) or by referral to private providers in the community. Thus, continuity of care issues are determined by community need and resource availability.

Health Education. The purpose of health education in a comprehensive school health program is to provide students (and, by extension, their families) with the requisite knowledge, attitudes, and skills to grow and develop into self-actualized persons who are physically, mentally/emotionally, spiritually, and socially healthy. To accomplish that, schools typically offer an outcomes-oriented, sequential curriculum that considers the particular learning needs, interests, and developmental stage of students at each grade level.

Community needs assessment data and legal mandates also influence development of the curriculum. For that reason, even mandated topics like safety and environmental health may be addressed differently by particular schools. For example, in rural areas prevention of farm accidents may be an important safety emphasis, whereas in urban areas gang violence may be a more relevant topic. Likewise, rural students and their families may be more immediately concerned about pesticides and herbicides as threats to environmental health, whereas urban students may regard air pollution and toxic waste dumps as urgent environmental health issues.

For all students, however, use of multiple teaching-learning strategies is advised (Seffrin, 1990; Allensworth, 1994), along with ample opportunities for students to practice and assimilate their newly acquired health knowledge, attitudes, and behaviors. Furthermore, students need ongoing access to qualified, authoritative health education resources, including

Table 1-1. Comprehensive School Health Program Components: A Summary

School Health Program Component	Emphasis	Sample Outcomes	Sample Strategies	References
HEALTH SERVICES	Plan, deliver, and evaluate the effectiveness of needed and legally mandated health services to assess, promote, maintain, and/or restore students' health.	Evaluation of students' health status to ensure normal growth and development and to detect problems that may interfere with learning and/or self-actualization.	Periodic completion/review of health histories, physical examinations, dental examinations, and other health observations as needed or mandated.	Allensworth et al., 1994 Allensworth & Kolbe, 1987 ASHA, 1994 DeFriese et al., 1990 Elders, 1993 Healthy People 2000, 1991 Igoe & Giordano, 1992 Kolbe et al., 1995 Lovick, 1988 Nader, 1990 Small et al., 1995 Uphold & Graham, 1993 Wold, 1982 Zanga & Oda, 1987 Zimmerman & Reif, 1995
		Achievement/maintenance of mandated immunization levels.	Ongoing surveillance of immunization levels via maintenance and review of students' immunization records, and referral/follow-up as needed. Sponsoring and/or conducting periodic immunization clinics to facilitate compliance.	
		Early identification and prompt treatment for vision and hearing problems, scoliosis, and other defects or abnormalities.	Periodic screening and follow-up for vision and hearing, scoliosis, and other remediable diseases and defects (e.g., hypertension, tuberculosis, etc.).	
		Prompt, accurate triage, first aid, and referral as needed for illness and injuries at school.	Development and implementation of policies and procedures that ensure provision of prompt, safe, and legal emergency and urgent care for illness and injuries at school.	

School Health Program Component	Emphasis	Sample Outcomes	Sample Strategies	References
HEALTH SERVICES *continued*		Continuity of care for students with chronic and/or disabling conditions. Access to primary care for all students and families.	Provision of case management services, development and implementation of individualized health plans (IHPs), administration of prescribed treatments and medications as needed (per policies). Provision of school-based clinics (SBCs) staffed by SNPs/PNPs and other qualified providers or negotiation of contracts for school-linked services.	
HEALTH EDUCATION	Develop, implement, and evaluate a comprehensive, outcomes-oriented health education program emphasizing knowledge, attitudes, skills, and behaviors that promote physical, mental/emotional, spiritual, and social health.	Implementation of a formal, planned, sequential, comprehensive (preschool–grade 12) health curriculum that includes age-appropriate objectives and topics, varied teaching-learning strategies, and multiple opportunities to practice newly acquired skills (such as CPR or conflict resolution).	Topics and teaching methods varied by age and developmental level that may include personal health habits, health decision-making, disease and injury prevention, safety, first aid, nutrition, exercise/fitness, stress management, growth and development, sexuality and reproduction, human/family life/relationships, consumer health, conflict resolution and violence prevention, substance (alcohol, drugs, and tobacco) use/abuse, community health, and environmental health.	Allensworth, 1994 Allensworth et al., 1994 Allensworth & Kolbe, 1987 ASHA, 1994 Bartlett, 1981 Collins, et al., 1995 Comprehensive School Health Education Workshop, 1993 DeFriese et al., 1990 Healthy People 2000, 1991 Jackson, 1994 Lohrmann, Gold, & Jubb, 1987 Nader, 1990 Seffrin, 1990 Wold, 1982

School Health Program Component	Emphasis	Sample Outcomes	Sample Strategies	References
HEALTH EDUCATION *continued*		Availability of health education and related preventive services to students' families and the community. Appropriateness of staffing levels and material resources (including films, models, pamphlets, and other teaching aids) to meet identified needs.	Annual health fairs for the school community. / Adequate staffing (school nurse, SNP, health educator, etc.) to capitalize on "teachable moments" (unplanned, spontaneous, one-to-one teaching/learning opportunities). Accessibility of pamphlets and other teaching aids to students and faculty.	
HEALTHY ENVIRONMENT	Maintain the school's physical plant (including buildings, campus, playground, equipment, etc.) according to statutory and other standards, and promote a positive (nurturing, supportive, safe, and respectful) psycho-social climate for students, faculty, and staff.	Compliance of physical plant with accepted construction specifications and safety and maintenance standards. / Maintenance of an on-site accident and injury rate less than or equal to the school's targeted goal.	Periodic inspection of physical plant, assessing structural integrity, lighting, temperature, humidity, noise, ventilation, water supply, sanitation, and so on. / Periodic safety inspection of playground equipment and athletic facilities (including swimming pool); removal/repair/replacement of hazardous items. Follow-up of accident reports; correction of hazards. / Supervision of playgrounds, athletic facilities, and other recreational areas.	Adams et al., 1991; Allensworth et al., 1994; Allensworth & Kolbe, 1987; ASHA, 1994; DeFriese et al., 1990; Healthy People 2000, 1991; Nader, 1990; Rowe, 1987; Schultz, Glass, & Kamholtz, 1987; Wilson, 1990; Wold, 1982

School Health Program Component	Emphasis	Sample Outcomes	Sample Strategies	References
HEALTHY ENVIRONMENT *continued*		Maintenance of a clean and orderly school plant.	Sponsorship of an annual "School Clean-Up Day" as part of a science unit on ecology.	
		Reports by students, faculty, and staff of feeling "safe" from crime at school.	Locked school doors and/or employment of security guards during school and school events. Continuous patrolling of the school plant by security guards and/or school staff. Required sign-in and display of "Visitor" badges for non-school personnel or students on-site.	
		Creation of a classroom climate conducive to learning and personal growth.	Use of cooperative learning strategies (groups of 3–5 students). Teachers' acknowledgment and affirmation of each student's strengths and oral contributions to class discussions.	
		Respect and value for cultural and other differences.	Implementation of an annual "Diversity Fair" featuring food, clothing, music, etc., from cultural and ethnic groups represented in the student body, school faculty and staff, and surrounding community.	
		Valuation of studying, learning, and academic achievement.	Awards for effort, improvement, and scholastic achievement.	

School Health Program Component	Emphasis	Sample Outcomes	Sample Strategies	References
PHYSICAL EDUCATION	Promote optimal cardiovascular and respiratory function, development of motor skills and lifelong physical fitness, sports, and recreational activities, and encourage use of physical activity to relieve stress.	Participation at School X by 90% of the students in physical education classes for at least 1 hour/week. Implementation of a physical education curriculum that promotes development of skill in sports, movement, and other physical activities in which students can engage throughout their lives. Emphasis in the physical education curriculum on physical activity and fitness as integral to overall health. Achievement of national fitness standards by at least 70% of the students (during annual testing).	Completion of physical education classes stressing moderate to strenuous physical activity that promotes muscular strength, endurance, and flexibility required for all students, according to their health and ability. Classes to be offered at least three times/week. Emphasis in physical education classes on aerobics, walking, running, tennis, swimming, bicycling, dance, and other activities that can be used (with modification) throughout life. Emphasis on lifelong physical activity as part of a healthy lifestyle (including as a means of stress management) and on meeting the Healthy People 2000 objectives. Curricular focus on teaching skills included in national fitness standards; testing of all students (at least annually).	Allensworth et al., 1994 Allensworth & Kolbe, 1987 ASHA, 1994 Healthy People 2000, 1991 Kolbe et al., 1995 Nader, 1990 National Association for Sport and Physical Education, 1995

School Health Program Component	Emphasis	Sample Outcomes	Sample Strategies	References
FOOD & NUTRITION SERVICES	Provide on-site food service that is nutritious and affordable in a setting that encourages students to make appropriate food choices.	Compliance of all school meals served with USDA (U.S. Department of Agriculture) standards for nutritional content and food safety. Selection by students at least 70% of the time of nutritious foods (e.g., high fiber, low fat, low refined sugar, etc.) that meet national dietary intake guidelines. Participation by all eligible students in the subsidized school breakfast and lunch program.	Emphasis in school breakfasts and lunches on fruits, vegetables, and grain products, while minimizing intake of salt, refined sugar, and cholesterol. Administration of the school cafeteria/food service by a qualified food service manager or dietitian to ensure that all foods are prepared, served, and stored according to accepted health regulations and guidelines. Use of interactive computer programs (including games) to teach students to choose nutritious foods. Inclusion in on-site vending machines of healthy foods (fruits, yogurt, popcorn, soups, whole-grain cereal, etc.) instead of high-fat, sugar-laden products (potato chips, candy, cookies, sodas, etc.). Assessment by school personnel of students' financial and health needs, identification of those eligible for free/reduced cost breakfasts and/or lunches, and completion of arrangements to ensure their participation.	Allensworth et al., 1994 Allensworth & Kolbe, 1987 ASHA, 1994 Healthy People 2000, 1991 Kolbe et al., 1995 U.S. Dept. of Health and Human Services, 1991

School Health Program Component	Emphasis	Sample Outcomes	Sample Strategies	References
COUNSELING, PSYCHOLOGICAL, AND SOCIAL SERVICES	Promote students' mental, emotional, and social health through availability of counseling, guidance, and social services, along with psychological testing and assessment, consultation, intervention, and referral.	Full-time availability of school counselors to assist students with problem solving, crisis intervention, and other guidance needs, and to provide emotional support in small groups (e.g., re: coping with parents' divorce) or one-to-one.	Availability of certified/licensed counselors, psychologists, & social workers before, during, and after school hours by appointment and on a walk-in basis for one-to-one counseling, consultation and referral, and support groups re: coping with grief and loss, family issues, etc.	Allensworth et al., 1994 Allensworth & Kolbe, 1987 ASHA, 1994
		Curriculum emphasis on development of problem-solving and life skills, self-esteem and self-control, coping with change and loss, withstanding peer pressure, violence prevention, and conflict resolution.	Consultation from school counselors, psychologists, and social workers for curriculum development and implementation re: these issues and concerns.	
		Establishment of individualized multidisciplinary health/education plans (IHPs/IEPs) for all students with behavioral or emotional problems and/or who have handicaps that may interfere with learning.	Interdisciplinary teams of school nurses, psychologists, counselors, social workers, and others to develop and review IHPs and IEPs.	
		Availability of trained students to assist peers with problem solving, conflict mediation, peer and family communication, drug and alcohol use questions, sexuality issues, etc.	Availability of trained peer mediators to assist students as needed.	

School Health Program Component	Emphasis	Sample Outcomes	Sample Strategies	References
WORKSITE HEALTH PROMOTION	Decrease direct and indirect health care costs for school employees and provide positive role models re: a healthy life-style by educating, motivating, and assisting faculty and staff to protect and promote their own health.	Congruence of the school's worksite health promotion program with the known health needs/risks of its employees.	Annual surveys of employees re: their interest in/need for on-site programs re: weight management, stress management, physical fitness, smoking cessation, etc. Review of health care utilization aggregate data to identify patterns and risks. Offering periodic (annual?) on-site screening for common adult health problems, e.g., hypertension, diabetes, obesity, etc., to identify at-risk individuals.	Allensworth et al., 1994 Allensworth & Kolbe, 1987 ASHA, 1994 Blair et al., 1987 Hoffman et al., 1993 McKenzie, 1988 U. S. Dept. of Health and Human Services, 1991
		Availability of group and/or individualized interventions for employees at risk for specific health problems or needs (e.g., hypertension, overweight, etc.) and those with unhealthy lifestyles (e.g., sedentary persons, tobacco smokers, etc.).	Offering programs (support groups, classes, etc.), services (discounted health club memberships, groomed outdoor walking trails, etc.), and/or individualized interventions (counseling, exercise and diet regimens, etc.) to help employees lower their health risks.	
		A ≥10% decrease in employee health care costs and absenteeism within two years.	Provision of incentives (release time, rewards, prizes, etc.) to encourage participation in the worksite health promotion program by ≥75% of employees, including those known to be at risk.	

School Health Program Component	Emphasis	Sample Outcomes	Sample Strategies	References
INTEGRATION OF SCHOOL-COMMUNITY HEALTH PROGRAMS	Ensure that school health is integrated into the community's overall health program by forming partnerships or coalitions among schools, families/ students, and citizens/organizations within the community at large to plan, deliver, and evaluate comprehensive school health programs.	Coordination of school health program planning efforts with community health program planning efforts. Development of a school-based clinic (SBC) to offer primary care to students, their families, and community members.	Creation of a school health program planning commission whose appointed members include representatives of school administrators, school health personnel (e.g., a school nurse, health educator, social worker, psychologist, nutritionist, etc.), community agencies/health care providers, families of students, and other interested community members. Creation of a committee of local health care providers, school administrators, SNPs and/or school nurses, community residents, and students/families to plan (based on assessed community needs and preferences) the scope and focus of clinic services and clinic operations (including budget and funding sources, administrative structure, and policies and procedures).	Allensworth et al., 1994 Allensworth & Kolbe, 1987 ASHA, 1994 DeFriese et al., 1990 Doering, 1996 Elders, 1993 Iverson, 1981 Killip et al., 1987

School Health Program Component	Emphasis	Sample Outcomes	Sample Strategies	References
PROGRAM MANAGEMENT	Create and implement an administrative model that addresses assessed community needs, promotes collaboration, and ensures efficient and effective use of resources to meet school health program objectives.	Designation of a "lead" person to oversee coordination of school health program planning, implementation, and evaluation. Ongoing thorough, systematic evaluation of all school health program components, accompanied by corrective action as indicated.	Development of a task force of school administrators, health personnel, community members, and families of school children to develop a position description, identify qualifications, and oversee the hiring of the school health program coordinator. Oversight (by the coordinator) of development, implementation, and evaluation of a written school health program plan to ensure that students' documented health needs are met, *Healthy People 2010* objectives are attained, and both outcomes and processes (program implementation strategies) are carefully reviewed and refined as needed.	Belzer & McIntyre, 1994 Davis & Allensworth, 1994 Doering, 1996 Resnicow & Allensworth, 1996

credentialed school nurses and health educators/ teachers, as well as appropriate multimedia resources (pamphlets, models, films, and the like).

Healthy Environment. According to experts (ASHA, 1994; Allensworth & Kolbe, 1987; Schultz et al., 1987; Wold, 1982), schools are obligated to maintain a safe and healthy physical environment and should promote a positive psychosocial climate. Ensuring a safe physical environment requires that the school's physical plant (including playgrounds, athletic facilities, equipment, and parking lots) be constructed and maintained according to accepted standards, to minimize the risk of accidents and injuries. Furthermore, the physical plant should be monitored to prevent and control hazards and to ensure compliance with accepted/legally mandated standards for use and disposal of wastes (e.g., biological, chemical, or solid). Potential sources of environmental health hazards include temperature (excessive heat or cold), humidity, lighting, ventilation, noise, radiation, mechanical vibration, chemical agents (such as asbestos, lead, pesticides, cleaning agents, and wastes from science labs), biological agents (including microorganisms, live and dead animals used in science labs, and blood and other bodily fluids), and food, water, and air contaminants.

A positive psychosocial environment is a social-emotional climate that is "productive, nurturing . . . and supportive" (Schultz et al., 1987, p. 432) as well as "friendly . . . [and] respectful of differences" (ASHA, 1994, p. 3) for both students and school staff. In such a climate, students and staff should feel and be "safe" from crime, violence, and intimidation, even if on-site security guards are needed to achieve that (Nader, 1990). Consequently, a positive school climate fosters learning, development of self-esteem, effective communication, social networking and cooperation, resolution of conflicts, and development of problem-solving and decision-making skills (ASHA, 1994; Schultz et al., 1987). Sample goals and strategies to promote and maintain the school's physical and psychosocial environment are provided in Table 1-1.

Physical Education. The fourth component of a comprehensive school health program is physical education. Because less than 10% of Americans exercise vigorously three or more times per week, while nearly 25% of adults report that they engage in *no* leisure physical activities (U.S. Department of Health and Human Services, 1991), the federal government is rightly concerned about the fitness levels of Americans, including children and youth. Since school-age children and youth are a "captive population" whose lifestyle choices (including physical activity level) are still being formed, the school's physical education curriculum is regarded as an important means of achieving national health and fitness goals (Allensworth, Symons, & Olds, 1994; ASHA, 1994; Healthy People 2000, 1991; National Association for Sport and Physical Education, 1995; U.S. Department of Health and Human Services, 1991).

As with other school health program components, the specific fitness goals/standards used to structure a school's physical education curriculum vary according to state and district mandates, assessed community needs, and the age, grade, and developmental level of students. In general, however, the physical education curriculum emphasizes (a) improving physical activity and fitness levels; (b) developing physical, emotional, social, and cognitive skills related to sports and physical activity; (c) promoting safety and preventing injuries; and (d) developing skill in sports and physical activities, such as walking, running, swimming, and tennis, that can be enjoyed throughout the life span as part of a healthy lifestyle. Although curricular details are available elsewhere (Allensworth, Symons, & Olds, 1994; ASHA, 1994; Healthy People 2000, 1991; National Association for Sport and Physical Education, 1995), Table 1-1 provides sample physical education outcomes and strategies for achieving them.

Food and Nutrition Services. The school food and nutrition service exists to ensure that students (and faculty/staff) have access to nutritious meals and snacks at an affordable cost. Indeed, for children whose families live at or below the poverty line, school breakfasts and lunches may be the only meals they have on some days. For all children, of course, sound nutrition is essential for normal growth and development. In addition, dietary intake is a known factor in the prevention and/or management of a number of chronic illnesses, including diabetes, cardiovascular disease, obesity, and some cancers. Therefore, the school health program should not only provide access to nutritional meals, but should also teach students to choose foods based on sound nutritional principles.

Standards for food storage and preparation, menu selection, health surveillance of food handlers, and so on are provided by federal and local government agencies (e.g., the U.S. Department of Agriculture and state and local health departments). Additional standards and strategies are available elsewhere (Allensworth et al., 1994; ASHA, 1994; Healthy People 2000, 1991; U.S. Dept. of Health and Human Services, 1991), while sample goals and strategies are included in Table 1-1.

Counseling, Psychological, and Social Services. This fifth component of a comprehensive school health program relies on the knowledge and skills of three professions—counseling, psychology, and social work—to promote and maintain students' mental, emotional, and social health. The specific services offered depend on the school's assessed needs, priorities, and available resources, but school counselors, psychologists, and social workers generally collaborate with school nurses and others, particularly when an individual student is referred for evaluation of an emotional, mental, or behavioral problem. In such instances, the "team's" purpose is to develop an individualized health care plan (IHP) and/or an individualized educational plan (IEP), in accordance with PL 101-476, the Individuals with Disabilities Education Act (IDEA) (Allensworth & Kolbe, 1987; Haas, 1993; Yates, 1994a).

Counselors, psychologists, and social workers also assist students in managing both the expected changes and transitions in their lives (e.g., moving from elementary school to junior high) and the unexpected events, crises, and losses (e.g., parental divorce or the death of a fellow student). While students may receive one-to-one or small group counseling for these issues, another important purpose of school-based counseling, psychological, and social services is to ensure that the school's curriculum promotes development of (a) "life skills," problem solving, and coping abilities; (b) positive self-esteem, self-control and discipline; (c) nonviolent conflict resolution skills; and (d) healthy peer and family relationships.

Worksite Health Promotion. Employee health promotion programs in the schools represent an extension of the types of worksite health programs that have long been available in the corporate sector. The primary purpose of school-based employee health programs is to ensure that the school's faculty, administrators, and staff are physically, mentally, and emotionally healthy enough to perform their jobs without compromising their own or others' (including students') safety or well-being. A related benefit of having healthy employees, of course, is that they (in turn) can serve as positive role models for students regarding health and a healthy lifestyle (Allensworth & Kolbe, 1987; Blair, Tritsch, & Kutsch, 1987; Allensworth, Symons, & Olds, 1994). At the same time, healthy employees have fewer illnesses and injuries and therefore miss fewer workdays and incur fewer health care expenses. Consequently, worksite health promotion programs in schools can lower both direct (health insurance) and indirect (absenteeism, disability, and staff substitutes/replacements) employer costs (Blair, Tritsch, & Kutsch, 1987; McKenzie, 1988).

Along with the "captive well population" notion, another advantage of offering worksite health promotion programs in the schools is the availability of personnel (such as school nurses, psychologists, counselors, and food service staff) and facilities (gymnasium and exercise equipment, health office/equipment, classrooms, etc.) needed to plan and implement the program (Allensworth & Kolbe, 1987). Consequently, such programs are generally convenient and have minimal start-up costs.

Although the specific emphases, outcomes, and strategies used to promote employee health must be based on the needs of the school's employee population and must conform to school district guidelines and policies (ASHA, 1994), it is important to package health promotion services and initiatives as a program, rather than as ad hoc activities. That is, health promotion services should be planned using a population-based versus individual-employee focus to achieve lasting behavior change in the employee population (Blair, Tritsch, & Kutsch, 1987). To facilitate this, McKenzie (1988) proposes a 12-step process for developing, implementing, and evaluating a school-based employee health promotion program. Examples of goals and strategies that might be used in such programs are included in Table 1-1. (See also the report by Hoffman et al. [1993] concerning their use of health risk appraisals and other screening methods to assess school employees' health promotion needs.)

Integration of School-Community Health Programs. The eighth and final comprehensive school health program component proposed by Allensworth and Kolbe (1987) is integration of the school's health program into the community's overall health program. As discussed previously, such collaboration between schools and communities offers numerous benefits, including (a) increased community support (and funding) for school health; (b) cost savings associated with avoiding service gaps or duplication of efforts; (c) more effective use of limited resources; and (d) (ultimately) improved health outcomes for students and the community.

As indicated in Table 1-1, efforts to integrate school and community health programs emphasize formation of partnerships or coalitions among schools, students and their families, and citizens and other organizations in the community at large to plan, deliver, and evaluate comprehensive school health programs that complement overall community/public health goals. Thus, school health program planning requires formation of a committee or commission with representation by all interested parties. This interdisciplinary commission begins by assessing the community's health needs and proposes services (e.g., development of a school-based health center) that efficiently and effectively address those needs.

Program Management. In their discussion of integrating school and community health programs, Killip et al. (1987) explore a number of models. They state that there is no one "ideal" model and that selection of a particular approach to integrating school and community health programming is the prerogative of individual school districts. Indeed, other experts (Elders, 1993; Belzer & McIntyre, 1994; DeGraw, 1994) describe a variety of models that have been successfully used in a number of communities and school districts in the United States and Canada to implement comprehensive school health programs. After carefully studying existing statewide school health programs in Nebraska ("Healthy Kids, Healthier Nebraska") and Iowa ("Iowa...A Place to Grow Healthy"), however, Davis and Allensworth (1994) concluded that formal leadership and coordination of the eight-pronged comprehensive school health program is critical to successful implementation. Thus, Davis and Allensworth (1994) proposed the addition of a "program management" function to integrate and coordinate the other eight school health program components.

Although they might be either advisory boards or designated individuals, Davis and Allensworth (1994) observed that effective program managers/leaders needed certain competencies and characteristics, including a programmatic vision as well as skill in leadership/management, program planning, evaluation, and communication. By 1996, however, Resnicow and Allensworth (1996) formally recommended that program management be added as a recognized component of a comprehensive school health program and that the program manager or coordinator be a specific person (a "lead" individual).

Going a step further, Belzer and McIntyre (1994) recommend use of a model studied in Dartmouth, Nova Scotia. In this model, which resembles nursing process, program management is the responsibility of the Coordinator of Planning and Implementation (CPI). The role of the CPI includes such functions as (a) assembling a committee to plan and implement the comprehensive school health program; (b) generating and selecting ideas for the health program; (c) pilot-testing program activities; (d) empowering committee members and overseeing implementation of program activities; and (e) evaluating results (Belzer & McIntyre, 1994).

Although the CPIs in this study were health educators, this author believes that well-educated school nurses (i.e., with master's preparation in school nursing that includes coursework in leadership, management, and program development) would be readily able to serve as school health program managers. As Table 1-1 indicates, then, the program management component emphasizes the designation of a qualified person to oversee collaborative planning, implementation, and evaluation of the school health program, addressing the efficiency and effectiveness of both program outcomes and processes (strategies).

CONTRIBUTIONS OF SCHOOL NURSES WITHIN SCHOOL HEALTH PROGRAMS

As this chapter's discussion of the historical evolution of school health revealed, the role of school nurses within school health programs has been debated in the literature over time. Despite such widespread attention, however, there is still no consensus regarding the role of the school nurse or the credentials and skills needed to effectively implement it. Indeed, as the discussion of legal cases later in this book demonstrates, confusion over the school nurse's role, necessary educational credentials and skills, and expected professional practice standards may have serious consequences for school districts and individual nurses. Accordingly, this section will begin by addressing role clarity and confusion, followed by discussion of school nursing roles and goals, practice standards, and educational preparation and credentials.

School Nursing: Role Clarity and Confusion

Despite ongoing evolution and expansion of American school nursing from 1902 to the present, role clarity has been elusive. Consequently, school nurses continue "to confront a poorly articulated set of role expectations" (Parsons & Felton, 1992, p. 498). Indeed, following their survey of state education departments (N = 50), Thurber, Berry, and Cameron (1991, p. 139) concluded that nearly half of the states (N = 23) "do not seem to be able to define what they expect of their school nurses."

In turn, such role ambiguity and confusion make it difficult to meet role obligations and expectations, especially when exacerbated by role conflict and overload (Parsons & Felton, 1992; Kozlak, 1992). McCarty-Marple (1994, p. 20) speculates that school nurses' role ambiguity is due, in part, to their status as "boundary dwellers"—that is, health care professionals (nurses) employed in a non–health care setting (the school), which is dominated by other professionals (educators). Thus, school nurses provide services that may be regarded as having a lower value and priority than those provided by teachers and other school employees.

In addition to role conflict with teachers and other personnel, school nurses also may experience role overlap and conflict with other members of the school health team. In particular, where school-based clinics are available, Salmon (1994) observes that school nurses may have difficulty distinguishing the boundaries of their role from that of the school nurse practitioner (SNP). Furthermore, in locales where public health nurses employed by outside agencies provide part-time school nursing services to a number of public and/or parochial schools, establishing clear role boundaries and expectations is essential; to that end, a close and cooperative relationship between administrators of the school(s) and the public health agency is critical (Conrad & Wehrwein, 1992). In addition, open discussion by the public health/school nurse with school officials helps ensure that the school health program will meet legal requirements while addressing the school's priorities and values (Conrad & Wehrwein, 1992).

Most troubling, however—and a potential source of legal liability—is the confusion of roles between the school nurse and unlicensed assistants, who are generally called school health aides (Fryer & Igoe, 1996). As noted earlier, when school budgets shrink, school nurses are too often replaced by school health aides, whose salaries are lower than those of nurses. In such cases, the school health program may be coordinated and staffed by a nonprofessional person, which raises questions of program quality and effectiveness.

Of equal concern to this writer, however, are registered nurses who accept employment as unlicensed assistants (school health aides). Are these individuals legally accountable only as health aides—or are they expected to perform proficiently as registered nurses? Although that issue will be explored further later in this book, the scenario (e.g., Brown, 1995) is troubling. Even more alarming is the scenario in which an unlicensed assistant takes charge of the school health office and program. Indeed, what school administrator has not shuddered upon hearing an unlicensed assistant identify herself/himself as "the nurse" or "the school nurse" when answering the telephone in the school's health office?

In short, school nurses' role confusion and ambiguity is associated with a variety of factors, including (a) their status as boundary dwellers in the school setting; (b) lack of clear, appropriate, and agreed-to role expectations; and (c) role conflict within the school and

school health team. However, some experts (Thurber, Berry, & Cameron, 1991, p. 140) believe that school nurses themselves must accept some responsibility for role confusion, since "many of the inconsistencies [in role expectations and performance] may result from the [nurses'] own inability to adequately perceive [their] role within the schools or to articulate that role to others." Mindful of this lingering role confusion and ambiguity, then, what *are* the expected roles and goals for school nurses? That question is addressed next.

School Nursing Roles and Goals

A number of organizations and individuals (American School Health Association, 1974; American Nurses' Association, Task Force on Standards of School Nursing Practice, 1983; Wold & Dagg, 1981a; Proctor, 1993) have devised lists of roles and/or goals for school nurses. While some roles are mentioned on virtually all of these lists (for example, manager/administrator, health service deliverer/provider, and health educator), each list includes some unique role, such as client advocate (Wold & Dagg, 1981a) or nurse investigator (Proctor, 1993). Since no one list has been universally adopted, this chapter will focus on the five role/goal dyads proposed by Wold and Dagg (1981a): manager, deliverer of health services, health educator, counselor, and advocate.

The School Nurse as Manager of Health Care

As manager of health care, the school nurse's goal is to participate in the planning, implementation, and evaluation of the school health program (Wold & Dagg, 1981a). Because school health program planning is a collaborative process that addresses the assessed needs of the community, the school nurse should not be expected to independently plan, implement, and evaluate the school health program (Wold & Dagg, 1981a). Instead, as a leader and administrator, the school nurse cooperates with other stakeholders within the school and surrounding community (e.g., school administrators, teachers, other school and community-based health professionals, students and families, and community residents) to determine school health programming needs, goals, and priorities. Underscoring the importance of the school nurse's ability and willingness to work with other stakeholders, Oda (1992) notes that collaboration enhances the school nurse's visibility—and visibility can be equated with viability.

Thus, collaborative planning and coordination of program activities and personnel are key elements of the school nurse's role as manager of health care (Oda, 1992; Kozlak, 1992). As Conrad and Wehrwein (1992) point out, for public health nurses employed by agencies that contract with school systems to provide health services and programs, collaborative planning and coordination are especially important. Indeed, unless school administrators and public health nurses/agency administrators communicate openly and reach agreement about the school health program's intended scope and focus, goals and priorities, staffing needs (e.g., hours per week and schedule of nursing services), and other details, the program's effectiveness may be stymied by conflicting goals and expectations.

Although experts (Wold & Dagg, 1981a; American School Health Association, 1991; Proctor, 1993; Oda, 1992; Salmon, 1994) agree about the importance of the school nurse's role as a leader, manager, and administrator within the school health program, school nurses may need help to embrace and effectively perform these roles. For example, Kozlak (1992) suggests that school nurses need to first acknowledge their role as managers and understand how to implement the managerial functions described elsewhere (Wold, 1981), including planning, organizing, directing and heading (leading), and controlling (evaluating). Endorsing that view, Salmon (1994, p. 139) encourages school nurses to "become expert and credible as administrators" and to regard school health program management as part of their "professional domain." Moreover, school nurses need to recognize that "their presence and effectiveness in administrative processes is requisite to realizing their potential in school health programs of the future" (Salmon, 1994, p. 139).

To demonstrate their "presence" in the school health program, school nurses must also assert themselves as leaders, by virtue of their expertise in nursing and community health. Accordingly, school nurses "can take a leadership role in formulating goals, policies, and procedures relating to school health" (American School Health Association, 1991, p. 11). However, as Kozlak (1992, p. 476) cautions, school nurses "must be willing to do the hard work required to be leaders," including (a) developing a "vision" for their comprehensive school health program; (b) upgrading their education as needed to develop skills in leadership, management, administration, and political activism; and (c) assuming and accepting their leadership role.

In sum, by whatever labels it may be known (manager, leader, administrator, collaborator, planner, and coordinator), the school nurse's role as a manager and leader within the school health program is vitally important and serves as the linchpin for the remaining roles and goals. As school health programs become more comprehensive and complex, so too will the nurse's role as leader and manager. Consequently, as will be discussed later in this chapter, master's-level educational preparation may soon be a necessity for the majority of school nurses.

The School Nurse as Deliverer of Health Services

The second school nursing role identified by Wold and Dagg (1981a) is that of deliverer of health services to the client system, which includes the aggregate student population, individual students and their families, school staff, and other community members. Comparable to the "provider of client care" role described by Proctor (1993), the goal of the nurse as deliverer of health services is to identify and address clients' health needs using clinical skills (helping relationship/communication skills, screening/casefinding, and health assessment) and systematic processes, such as nursing process, health education, and epidemiology.

Because school nursing is a subspecialty of community health nursing, health promotion and disease/injury prevention should be the "backbone" of the services offered (Oda, 1992). Likewise, program planning should address the needs of the school population as a whole (aggregate), even though many services are provided to individuals. Furthermore, services provided should be based on state and local mandates, assessed needs of the school community, the goals and priorities of the particular school health program, and available human and material resources.

The nature of the health services to be offered is also influenced by local and national trends in morbidity and health care delivery/reform. For example, today's school nurses must address what Miller (1990, p. 29) calls the "new morbidities," including teen pregnancy, depression and suicide, substance abuse, and nutritional "deficits." To that list, one might add HIV/AIDS and gangs and violence. Services that the school nurse might provide to these students include physical and psychosocial assessments, individual and/or group health education and counseling, and referral to other resources. Too, given the increased numbers of children with chronic illnesses and disabilities attending school (from birth to age 21, in some cases) and their often complex daily health needs, school nurses may spend much of their time delivering services to this population. For example, school nurses may be expected to (a) oversee (and/or directly administer) treatments and medications for these students; (b) counsel students, families, teachers, and others regarding the illness or disability and its impact on the student's education; and

(c) facilitate access to and use of community resources (Yates, 1994a).

In some instances, the school nurse may become the case manager for a child with a chronic illness or disability, working to coordinate the efforts of all concerned parties, including the child, parents, health care provider(s), and school personnel (such as teachers, social workers, and administrators). Indeed, some experts (e.g., Joachim, 1989) believe that the school nurse is ideally qualified to serve as case manager for such children, given the nurse's knowledge and skills and commitment to health promotion.

Although (as previously noted) the types of school health services offered should be based on assessed needs and legal mandates, other factors may also influence the nature and relative priority of services provided. One such factor is the expectations and perceptions of school administrators (e.g., principals). For example, in their study of school health services provided by public health nurses (via agency contract), Conrad and Wehrwein (1992) found that although school administrators selected "health education" as the most important category of the school nursing role, the specific school nurse *activities* they rated as most important were communicable disease control and monitoring compliance with immunization requirements. These authors (Conrad & Wehrwein, 1992) suggest that if nurses can develop clear policies and procedures to address administrators' concerns regarding communicable disease control, immunizations, and other "health supervision" needs, they may then be able to devote more time to health education.

Another factor affecting the nature and relative priority of school health services is demand, as measured by the "foot traffic" into the nurse's office and the types and frequency of assistance requested. For example, in their study of office visits to the school nurse, Jones and Clark (1993) found that the most common nursing diagnoses (identified for 43% of students visiting the nursing office) involved pain and its causes (such as headache, menstrual cramps, and injuries). Furthermore, of the 2,300 student office visits made during the one-week study period, 1,379 (60%) were for medication administration. Reflecting differences in developmental levels, Jones and Clark (1993) also noted that administration of medication was the most frequent nursing intervention for elementary school students (38% of visits), whereas counseling with students (22%) and parents (32%) was used most frequently in high schools.

In short, the nurse's role as deliverer of health services may include both aggregate activities, such as screening programs and immunization clinics, and individual activities, such as medication administration and staff blood pressure checks. The nature and focus of service delivery is determined through careful planning and should reflect assessed community and school needs as well as legal mandates.

The School Nurse as Health Educator

The third school nursing role identified by Wold and Dagg (1981a) is that of health educator. Because it is an integral part of health promotion, health education is a core function of the school nurse. Indeed, as noted previously, Conrad and Wehrwein (1992, p. 14) found that health education is perceived by school administrators as *the* priority focus for school nurses. However, a survey (Thurber, Berry, & Cameron, 1991) of the education departments in all 50 states found that while 70% (N = 35) of all states mandate health education in the schools, the expected role of the school nurse regarding health education is not clear. In 34% (N = 17) of the states, school nurses are expected to be "involved" in health education, either as "primary disseminators" or resource persons (re: health education materials or information); in the remaining 66% (N = 33) of states, teachers may address health education goals without school nurses' input or assistance (Thurber, Berry, & Cameron, 1991).

Interestingly, a descriptive study of the school nurse's role as health educator found that, when asked to rank eight common tasks based on their importance (#1 = high and #8 = low), school nurses ranked classroom teaching about health as #6 and consulting with classroom teachers about health topics as #7; ironically, even record keeping (ranked #3) was regarded as more important than health education (Van Cleaf, Young, & Hamilton, 1990). Furthermore, teachers who requested classroom presentations by school nurses rated the nurses' performance substantially higher than did the nurses themselves (Van Cleaf, Young, & Hamilton, 1990). Thus, although teachers value the school nurse's role as health education consultant and classroom teacher, school nurses may need encouragement to raise the priority they assign to health education and may need further preparation to improve their performance of and comfort with the health educator role.

In short, the school nurse's role as health educator is an important one. In particular, education of school staff regarding the health and educational needs of students with chronic and/or disabling conditions is an area of growing concern, as mainstreaming and "inclusion" initiatives increase the number of such children in regular classrooms (Yates, 1994a). School nurses in all settings thus need to improve their teaching skills and participate actively in planning and developing the health curriculum (Kozlak, 1992).

The School Nurse as Health Counselor

Closely related to the health educator role is the school nurse's role as health counselor. This role involves providing advice or guidance to students, families, and school staff regarding health concerns and resources (Wold & Dagg, 1981a). For example, the school nurse might help students newly diagnosed with chronic illnesses such as diabetes or asthma express such feelings as anger, frustration, or loss and identify positive coping strategies; the nurse might also provide referrals to other resources (for example, a diabetes education center or the local chapter of the American Lung Association) or might begin a support group. Likewise, the school nurse may counsel and offer support to family members and to school personnel regarding their own or students' health concerns.

Because providing support for clients has long been an integral part of nursing, the relatively high proportion of time school nurses spend on counseling should come as no surprise. To illustrate, in their study of office visits to the school nurse, Jones and Clark (1993, p. 14) found that nearly 29% of school nurses' interventions involved counseling of students (14%), parents (14%), or teachers (0.8%). Furthermore, as previously noted, counseling was the most frequently used intervention for high school students and their parents (Jones & Clark, 1993). In addition, these authors noted that high school students' visits to the school nurse were longer than those of younger students; 47% of high school students stayed in the nurse's office for 30–60 minutes, compared to 7% of grade school students and 9% of middle school students. Therefore, Jones and Clark (1993) concluded that the school nurse's counseling role is influenced by the amount of time the nurse is available in the school, plus "the age and stage of development of the student as well as the presenting problem, and the counseling skill level of the nurse" (p. 16).

The School Nurse as Advocate

The fifth and last school nurse role envisioned by Wold and Dagg (1981a) is that of advocate for children's health rights, which entails speaking on behalf of school-age children and youth to ensure that their health needs and rights are respected and addressed. Accordingly, the school nurse may advocate for specific children and their families or on behalf of a larger community or aggregate. For example, the school nurse may function as the case manager for a student with a chronic illness or disability; as such, the nurse might help the family obtain needed resources (e.g., a personal care attendant) while educating school staff about necessary classroom accommodations to promote the child's health, safety, and learning (Joachim, 1989).

In contrast to the individualized approach just described, the school nurse may also advocate for the health rights and concerns of communities or aggregates (populations with shared needs or characteristics). Examples of these at-risk populations are students with HIV/AIDS (Brainerd, 1989) and homeless students and their families (Chauvin, Duncan, & Marcontel, 1990). Advocacy for such populations exemplifies what Salmon (1994) calls school *health* nursing, which requires school nurses "to move well beyond simply talking about the health of children to actually developing proactive, cross-sectoral programs that work" (p. 138).

That is, such advocacy demands that school nurses become politically visible and proactive (rather than merely reactive) in seeking passage of federal and state legislation that promotes the health, safety, and well-being of children. Thus, school nurses, acting alone or through their professional associations, might lobby for passage of bills that provide funding for school health programs and services, or on behalf of laws that require up-to-date immunizations for school enrollment. Oda (1992) agrees that "activism" is an important element of school nursing, urging school nurses to continue developing their "political acumen" (p. 113).

Yates (1994a, p. 18) observes that being proactive is essential in today's "new paradigm" of school health; she goes on to suggest that nurses interact with legislators, school officials, and relevant others to ensure that children's health needs are understood and that programs to address them are available. Likewise, Bradley (1997) reminds school nurses that, as citizens, taxpayers, and voters, they have an obligation to be politically informed and involved. She therefore urges school nurses to serve on policy-making committees and to pressure politicians to articulate their positions concerning school health and to be accountable for their campaign promises (Bradley, 1997). However, as school nurses become more comfortable with aggregate-level advocacy, perhaps more of them will seek the ultimate advocacy challenge: serving as elected officials themselves.

Practice Standards

In carrying out their roles and goals, school nurses (like all other professionals) are held legally accountable for their decisions and actions. That is, school nurses are expected to meet existing practice standards. In this context, a standard is "a norm that expresses an agreed-upon level of practice that has been developed to characterize, to measure, and to provide guidance for achieving excellence" (ANA, 1983, p. 17). In other words, a standard of nursing care means that "an ordinary [sic] prudent nurse would have performed in the same or similar manner" (Schwab, 1988, p. 14). But for which standards are school nurses accountable? As will be discussed in detail in chapter 4, standards may be determined nationally (e.g., by professional organizations), at the state level (e.g., via the Nurse Practice Act), and locally (e.g., via school district policies and school nurses' position descriptions) (Schwab, 1988).

Thus, school nurses must determine which standards are applicable to their practice and familiarize themselves with those standards. What makes that especially challenging, however, is the fact that there is no *one* set of universally accepted national standards for school nursing practice. Although (as noted earlier) the American Nurses' Association (ANA) publication of *Standards of School Nursing Practice* in 1983 was the culmination of a collaborative effort by several professional organizations to produce agreed-on national standards for school nursing, less than 10 years later, the National Association of School Nurses (NASN) identified a need for revisions. Accordingly, Proctor (1993) wrote *School Nursing Practice: Roles and Standards*, which is a substantially revised set of standards that incorporates the ANA's *Standards of Clinical Nursing Practice* (1991). This document was formally adopted by the NASN Board of Directors in 1992 (Proctor, 1993).

Despite the endorsement of the NASN Board of Directors, however, this writer believes that discussion of national school nursing standards needs to be ongoing, with input from a broad cross-section of school health/school nursing professionals and constituencies. Accordingly, this writer concurred with the recommendation of the National Nursing Coalition for School Health (NNCSH) that a national committee be appointed to "improve, review, and update existing standards . . . and generate consensus about the standards among relevant national organizations" (1995, p. 372). Fortunately, NASN provided leadership for that initiative by appointing a task force to revise the standards. The NASN Standards of Practice Task Force included representatives of NNCSH's constituent organizations, which are the American Nurses' Association (ANA), American Public Health Association (APHA) School Health Section, American School

Health Association (ASHA) School Nurse Section, National Association of School Nurses (NASN), and the National Association of State School Nurse Consultants (NASSNC) (National Nursing Coalition for School Health, 1995). As a result of this initiative, NASN (1998) published new national standards for school nursing, reflecting the format and language of ANA's generic nursing standards (1998). This collaborative initiative provided the clarity and genuine endorsement needed to successfully implement national standards. Once these national standards have been widely adopted and disseminated, school nurses will then need to attend to states' nurse practice acts, local ordinances and policies, job descriptions, and other sources to ensure their compatibility with national norms. See Appendix A for these Standards.

Educational Preparation and Credentials

By now it should be apparent that carrying out the complex roles and goals previously described, while also meeting national, state, and local practice standards, is not a job for the faint of heart or the undereducated. Indeed, school nursing is a highly complex subspecialty of community health nursing—and, therefore, requires specialized educational preparation (Wold, 1981; Bachman, 1995).

As will be discussed later in this chapter, an issue of persistent concern is the wide variability in educational preparation (from associate degree to doctorate) and school nurse licensure requirements across the United States (Miller, 1990; Oda, 1993; Passarelli, 1994a, 1994b; Bradley, 1997). Increasingly, though, a baccalaureate degree in nursing is being recognized and endorsed as *minimal* preparation for entry into school nursing (Kornguth, 1990; Passarelli, 1994a, 1994b; National Nursing Coalition for School Health, 1995).

Furthermore, a number of experts have proposed the content of the baccalaureate education needed by school nurses, beginning with Salmon's assertion that school nurses "must possess a broad and deep, interdisciplinary knowledge base that allows them to serve as a bridge, translator, link, and *health* expert . . . [and that is] of a caliber equal to that of their colleagues in the school context" (1994, p. 138). At the very least, experts (Wold, 1981; Oda, 1993; National Nursing Coalition for School Health, 1995) agree that baccalaureate education for school nurses should emphasize public/community health nursing concepts and principles, including school nursing and community assessment. Supervised clinical experience in community health nursing and school nursing is also recommended.

Normal growth and development, expanded health assessment skills, and screening methods and principles are also key content areas to be included. Too, given the complex health needs of many students, especially those with chronic and/or handicapping conditions who are mainstreamed into regular schools and classrooms, school nurses need preparation in case management and relevant laws (e.g., IDEA and Section [§] 504 of the Rehabilitation Act) (Oda, 1993). In addition, to work effectively with other school and community health team members, school nurses need to develop skill in collaboration and team building and must be computer literate (National Nursing Coalition for School Health, 1995). Likewise, given the expansion of the school health program from three to eight components and changing staffing patterns, school nurses need strong preparation in leadership, school health program development and management, and delegation to and supervision of unlicensed personnel (Wold, 1981).

As if this list of expected content were not already long enough, research (Van Cleaf, Young, & Hamilton, 1990) has documented the importance of the school nurse's role as health educator and curriculum consultant—and school nurses' perceived inadequacies in meeting these expectations. Therefore, preparation in educational theories, methods, and resources, including classroom teaching experience, should be part of the preservice education for school nurses. Finally, given the dynamic nature of education, health care, and population trends, school nurses must be "educated to deal with change" (Collis & Dukes, 1989, p. 110). That is, school nurses need to know how to anticipate and *plan for* change; this will enable them (individually and collectively) to be proactive, rather than merely reactive.

Perusal of the foregoing list of knowledge and skills needed by school nurses will no doubt be troubling to nursing educators. Speaking from more than 20 years' experience teaching in baccalaureate and higher degree programs in nursing, this writer and others (Bachman, 1995; Oda, 1993) understand all too well that baccalaureate programs in nursing are intended to prepare *generalists,* not specialists. And school nursing is clearly a *specialty* practice, one that requires sophisticated knowledge of program planning and administration and staffing and legal issues (including education and civil rights law), in addition to population-based health care and interdisciplinary collaboration. Furthermore, given the trends toward inclusion of students with moderate to severe disabilities in regular classrooms, and expansion of primary care services via school-

based health centers (SBHCs) and third-party reimbursement in the schools, school nursing leaders polled by Oda (1993, p. 230) expect that nurse practitioner preparation will be "critically important in the future."

Therefore, despite the present dearth of graduate nursing programs in some regions of the country, this writer believes that school nursing *must* be acknowledged as the complex, advanced practice nursing specialty that it is. As such, school nursing *requires* advanced academic and clinical preparation as part of a master's degree program in nursing that addresses the unique knowledge and skills needed by school nurses. Such programs need to be affordable and accessible, taking advantage of distance learning strategies and accommodating the calendar and schedules of most school nurses. For example, programs that can be completed during the summer, through evening classes, and via the Internet or interactive television should be developed and marketed.

Finally, in addition to post-baccalaureate or master's education for school nurses, there is also the issue of credentials. While a baccalaureate or higher degree from an accredited program/institution is regarded as a measure of educational quality, obtaining certificates from other organizations is a further endorsement of a professional's knowledge and skill. School nurses may achieve national certification by passing standardized tests offered by the American Nurses' Credentialing Center (ANCC) or the National Board for Certification of School Nurses (Bradley, 1997). School nurses who complete nurse practitioner programs may also seek national certification as school nurse practitioners (SNP), pediatric nurse practitioners (PNP), or family nurse practitioners (FNP) via ANCC testing. Obtaining nurse practitioner certification is especially important for nurses working in primary care (i.e., SBHCs) and/or seeking prescriptive authority and third-party reimbursement. Because some states also require school nurses to be certified as teachers or administrators, Proctor (1993) urges faculty in master's programs to carefully consider the school nurse licensure and certification requirements in their respective states when developing curricula.

SCHOOL HEALTH/SCHOOL NURSING: ISSUES AND TRENDS

The preceding sections of this chapter have (a) documented the emergence and development of school health services, (b) provided a rationale for continuation of school health programs, (c) described the scope and focus of school health programs, and

(d) clarified the role and contributions of the school nurse in such programs. The remaining task, then, is to identify salient issues and trends expected to shape the future of school health and school nursing services in the 21st century. Although in "real life" school health and school nursing issues and trends defy tidy compartmentalization, the following pages will briefly discuss issues and trends associated with (a) administration and leadership of school health programs, (b) students' health concerns and conditions, (c) health services access and delivery, and (d) the school nurse role: clarity, preparation, and performance.

Administration and Leadership of the School Health Program

By definition, administration and leadership issues are associated with planning, implementation, and evaluation of the school health program; that is, such issues pertain to the structure and day-to-day operations of the program. Because efficient, effective administration and leadership are essential for achievement of the school health program's overall objectives, the following related issues and trends merit some attention here: (a) program funding and resource adequacy; (b) effective school health program administration/management: what and by whom; (c) staffing; and (d) ethical priority-setting and resource distribution within the school health program.

Program Funding and Resource Adequacy

From the very beginning, schools have struggled to obtain the fiscal and human resources needed to deliver quality school health programs and services. Sadly, nearly 100 years later, economics remains "a major consideration" in providing school health and school nursing services (National Nursing Coalition for School Health, 1995, p. 375) because most school health funding typically comes out of state and local (not federal) education funds (National Nursing Coalition for School Health, 1995; Baker, 1994; DeFriese et al., 1990). Thus, the amount of school health funds allocated (and, hence, the number and level of school nursing positions available) is more likely to depend on the amount of money available than on the assessed health needs of students and the community (National Nursing Coalition for School Health, 1995).

Because school systems' budgets vary cyclically between prosperity and austerity, school health budgets may also fluctuate (National Nursing Coalition for School Health, 1995). Consequently, achieving stable funding and planned growth in school health programs

may prove elusive at best. Therefore, in an effort to achieve more stable, predictable funding for school health, some states are exploring other funding sources, including federal programs like Title V (Maternal and Child Health block grants) and Medicaid (Title XIX) as well as private foundations such as the Robert Wood Johnson Foundation (Igoe, 1995; Lear, Montgomery, Schlitt, & Rickett, 1996).

The challenge for school districts, then, according to the National Nursing Coalition for School Health (1995, p. 375), is to accomplish a "creative blending of funding streams" to support achievement of school health program goals. In turn, this will require school nurses and school nursing leaders to be more visible and proactive in the school health program budgeting process. It will also require that school nurses, particularly those serving as school health program administrators or coordinators, develop grant-writing skills and an awareness of potential private funding sources. Likewise, as advocated by the National Association of State School Nurse Consultants (1996b), a concerted effort should be made to obtain Medicaid reimbursement for such eligible school nursing services as case finding (e.g., screening), direct nursing care (e.g., administration of medications and treatments), care coordination (e.g., referrals and case management), health counseling and education of students, and emergency care.

In short, allowing school health programs, the mission of which is to promote and safeguard children's health, to be held hostage by the vagaries of local politics and unstable school system budgets is unconscionable. If school health programs are ever to achieve funding levels approaching those of intermural athletics or other equally costly but nonessential activities, school nurses must become politically involved while creatively exploring private funding sources as well.

Effective School Health Program Administration/ Management: What And By Whom

As noted earlier in this chapter's discussion of school health program components, "program management" is a necessary function to integrate and coordinate the other (eight) components of a comprehensive school health program (Davis & Allensworth, 1994). Given the breadth of school health programs today and the inherent complexities of integrating the school's health program into the community's overall health program, experts (Resnicow & Allensworth, 1996; Belzer & McIntyre, 1994) recommend that a specific "lead" individual or "point person" be designated as the school health program manager or coordinator.

While the notion of a designated school health program coordinator/manager is not controversial per se, there *is* continuing debate about who is eligible for this role and what qualifications and preparation are needed to successfully implement it. The laundry list of competencies that experts (Resnicow & Allensworth, 1996, p. 62) believe are needed by the school health program coordinator includes "organizational management, school administration, group facilitation, social marketing, health education counseling, teacher training, program evaluation, accounting, financial planning, health care financing, fund raising, and grant writing."

Although Resnicow and Allensworth (1996) acknowledge that "this diverse set of skills may seem beyond the capacity of any one individual" (p. 62), they propose creation of master's-level programs to prepare a new breed of health professional: the School Health Coordinator (SHC) whose "multidisciplinary role" would be to oversee program administration, including quality control (Resnicow & Allensworth, 1996, p. 62). Because creation of graduate programs to prepare SHCs is at best a long-term strategy, Resnicow and Allensworth (1996) suggest that, as a short-term measure, "training programs" be developed to "retrofit" school health personnel for the role. In particular, these authors recommend that health educators be groomed for the role.

This author contends, however, that knowledge and skill concerning (a) assessment and management of student and staff health needs, (b) relevant health laws and regulations, and (c) community resources are also important, thereby placing the role of school health program coordinator within the scope of the school nurse's practice. Moreover, this author believes that merely "training" or "retrofitting" existing personnel is not a viable solution. Instead, master's degree programs in nursing need to be provided to prepare advanced practice school nurses who also have expertise in school health program management. Such individuals would be ideally suited to serve as school health program managers or coordinators. The time is now for qualified school nurses and their national organizations and leaders to step forward and claim this role.

Staffing

Another key element associated with leadership and management of the school health program is staffing. Although school health program staffing issues have been of concern for most of this century, discussion and debate have intensified over the past decade as school budgets and resources have dwindled. In partic-

ular, two related topics continue to be debated today: (a) staffing levels and ratios, and (b) use of unlicensed assistive personnel (UAPs), including delegation and supervision issues.

School Health Program Staffing Levels and Ratios. Administratively, there is always tension between the desire to provide optimal staffing in order to achieve program outcomes and the need to control costs. And, because personnel costs (salaries and fringe benefits) tend to be the largest line item in any budget, many school districts tend to employ as few school nurses as they legally can. Further complicating the issue of staffing adequacy is the fact that only 16 states require school health services to be provided by a registered nurse (RN), and only 2 states mandate minimal nurse-student ratios (National Nursing Coalition for School Health, 1995).

Because school health program staffing levels are thus left (for the most part) to the discretion of local authorities, the fact that staffing levels vary widely across the country should come as no surprise. Indeed, citing data from a 1994 NASN study, Igoe (1995, p. 13) reports that school nurse-student ratios range from the sublime (1 nurse to 486 students in New Hampshire) to the ridiculous (1 nurse to 10,814 students in Tennessee). However, adopting a national perspective, the National Nursing Coalition for School Health (1995) notes that there are approximately 30,000 school nurses in the United States to address the health needs of 42 million students, resulting in an overall school nurse-student ratio of 1:1,400—nearly double the recommended ratio (1:750) and up from the 1:1,280 ratio reported by NASN members (NASN Membership Survey, 1993).

So, what are the recommended staffing levels and how should they be determined? Experts (ANA, 1983; ASHA, 1991; Proctor, 1993; N. Schwab, personal communication, April 28, 1998) recommend that staffing levels be based on consideration of a number of factors, including (a) the numbers of students to be served; (b) the number of school sites to be served, their relative geographic proximity (and proximity to emergency health care facilities), and the amount of time allocated to each; (c) federal, state, and local mandates, regulations, and funding; (d) program goals and priorities; (e) student characteristics such as socioeconomic status, mobility, age, and developmental level; (f) the complexity of students' health needs (for example, the number of students with chronic and/or disabling conditions, and/or who are technology-dependent or require treatments such as suctioning or tube feeding); (g) the number of students with complex social backgrounds (e.g., students whose families live in poverty, are disrupted or violent, or are migrant workers); and (h) the availability of other pupil services professionals (such as health educators, school psychologists and counselors) and health assistive personnel (such as school health aides) within the school and health and social agencies within the community.

Cautioning that staffing levels must be determined locally after considering the above list, the American Nurses' Association (1983, p. 18) and the American School Health Association (1991, p. 12; 1994, p. 7) propose the following minimum standard ratios of school nurses to students:

1. 1:750 for the general student population,

2. 1:225 for special-needs students mainstreamed into the general student population,

3. 1:125 for severely/profoundly disabled students.

ASHA (1994, p. 7) goes on to state that students with "complex medical needs" may require even lower ratios. Such staffing decisions must be made on a case-by-case basis. Application of such staffing ratios, however, is further complicated by the reality that many school populations include students in all three of these categories (i.e., the "general" or "well" population, students with special needs, and students with severe and profound disabilities). Therefore, the "ideal" ratio of school nurses to students may lie somewhere between 1:125 and 1:750, depending on the acuity and "mix" of students' health needs.

In addition to the total number of students to be served, a related issue to consider is the number of school buildings that one school nurse can safely and realistically be assigned. Nurses who must "cover" more than one school during the day or week may have more difficulty becoming accepted, trusted members of the school staff and integral members of the § 504, IDEA, and student assistance teams because they cannot invest as much time in any one school as full-time staff members do. Likewise, the presence of a different principal in each school also means that nurses will have multiple bosses—each of whom might have conflicting demands and expectations. Furthermore, if a complex emergency or other situation requiring the nurse's professional judgment arises when the nurse is not in the building, the nurse and the school may face legal consequences if the situation is not handled properly.

The fundamental problem associated with assigning nurses to multiple schools, however, is one of access for students. For example, in their study of school nurses in the southwestern United States, Jones and Clark (1993) found an inverse relationship between the number of schools for which a nurse is responsible and the number of students seen by the nurse in each school. They speculate that trying to "cover" more schools by assigning nurses to multiple sites actually *decreases* the accessibility of nurses, resulting in fewer student contacts and less time available per student.

In short, based on the previously cited fact (National Nursing Coalition for School Health, 1995) that the United States has only 30,000 school nurses to meet the needs of 42 million students (a 1:1,400 ratio), another 26,000 school nurses (for a total of 56,000) would be needed to reach the recommended minimum ratio of 1:750. If there were also a commitment to minimize the number of school buildings to which individual nurses are assigned, then the number of additional school nurses needed would exceed 26,000. Clearly, like funding and resource adequacy, staffing is another priority that school nurses need to address.

Use of Unlicensed Assistive Personnel. Numbers and ratios aside, another staffing issue to be addressed is the use (and sometimes misuse) of unlicensed assistive personnel (UAPs), who may be school health aides, school secretaries or clerks, teachers, volunteers, or others. As previously discussed, the relative merits of UAPs have been vigorously debated for the past 40 years. At this juncture, the dilemma of whether or not to continue using UAPs is moot: because they serve as low-cost "school nurse extenders," UAPs are here to stay. Indeed, this author believes that UAPs are a necessary adjunct to the school health program, who, if properly trained and supervised, can increase the cost-effectiveness of the school health program. Fryer and Igoe (1996) would no doubt agree. In their study of 482 randomly selected U.S. school districts, Fryer and Igoe (1996) found that nearly 31% of the districts employed UAPs and 63% had been "satisfied" or "very satisfied" with their job performance. Furthermore, litigation concerning care provided by UAPs had occurred in only 8 (1.7%) of the 482 districts (Fryer & Igoe, 1996).

Key factors for effective use of UAPs include role definition, adequacy of training, and appropriate delegation and supervision. Because these are addressed at length elsewhere (Wold, 1981; National Council of State Boards of Nursing, 1990, 1991; Hootman, 1994; National Association of State School Nurse Consultants, 1995, 1996a; Schwab & Haas, 1995; Panettieri & Schwab, 1996) and later in this book, only a few observations will be made here. First, school nurses need to be familiar with their state nursing practice acts so that they know what the scope of their own practice is and so that they understand what can and cannot be delegated to non-nurses. Armed with that understanding, school nurses (in consultation with school and district administrators) should develop a clear, limited, written position description for the UAPs with whom they work, including any unpaid assistants (volunteers).

Once the UAP's role and position description are clearly articulated, the school nurse must ensure that the UAP has been adequately trained and is competent to perform the identified tasks. When delegating tasks and functions to the UAP, then, the school nurse needs to verify that the UAP has the knowledge and skill to carry them out safely and effectively. Because *the school nurse remains legally accountable* for nursing tasks delegated to UAPs, the nurse must carefully supervise the UAP. Supervision involves monitoring the UAP's performance, coaching and counseling to help improve it, taking corrective action when needed—and documenting (in writing) the entire process to prove that it was done.

If school nurses adhere to accepted principles of delegation and supervision (National Council of State Boards of Nursing, 1990; Schwab & Haas, 1995; Panettieri & Schwab, 1996), misuse/overuse of UAPs will be minimized. However, there are potential pitfalls. For example, in their survey of Minnesota school nurses (N = 161), Josten, Smoot, and Beckley (1995) found that 25% of school nurses had received *no* education about delegation, and only 28% reported that their schools had delegation policies. Furthermore, 74% stated that they were uncomfortable and concerned about the competency of the UAP, while 13% admitted delegating to UAPs without verifying their knowledge or ability to carry out the task. In all, 35% of the nurses admitted delegating "against their better judgment" and 26% said they delegated to UAPs because someone else (such as a school administrator or parent) told them to do so (Josten, Smoot, & Beckley, 1995, p. 12). These frightening findings illustrate that before school nurses can be expected to delegate safely and appropriately, they will need inservice training, including a review of their state's nursing practice act and discussion of what can be delegated, to whom, by whom, by what method, and how supervision should be provided.

Ethical Priority Setting and Resource Distribution within the School Health Program

The last, but assuredly not least, aspect of administration and leadership to be addressed here is priority setting and resource distribution within the school health program. Paralleling the managed care/managed cost initiatives now sweeping the U.S. health care system are ongoing efforts to control and reduce federal, state, and local public spending on everything from welfare to education. Border states like California, Texas, and Florida have considered a number of extreme solutions to their budget woes, such as refusing to educate children of illegal immigrants or to provide health care or welfare for undocumented residents.

Although other citizens may decry the ethics of denying health and education benefits to low-income children and families, school health programs across the country confront a Solomon-like dilemma every day. That is, how can admittedly too few resources be expended on students' health in the most cost-effective way? And who should decide on whom those scarce dollars will be spent?

To some extent, legal mandates and regulations already make some of the decisions. For example, federal laws requiring mainstreaming of students with disabilities into regular classrooms (the least restrictive environment) consequently shift some of the school health program's emphasis and resources away from more generalized student services and toward accommodating special needs students. Accordingly, the nursing and school health literature has discussed approaches to assessing and managing the nursing needs of students with chronic illness, disability, and technology dependence (Schwab, 1991; Yates, 1992; Palfrey et al., 1992; Bonaiuto, 1995) while considering the impact of legislation and health care reform (Oberg, Bryant, & Bach, 1994; Palfrey, Samuels, Haynie, & Cammisa, 1994) on the ability of students with chronic and/or disabling conditions to obtain mandated services.

However, there is another, less politically correct question imbedded in all the rhetoric about meeting the needs of these vulnerable children: namely, if a large portion of school health's shrinking pot of resources is expended to meet the needs of the estimated 10–15% of students with chronic illnesses (Hootman, 1994), will there be enough dollars left to meet the health promotion/disease prevention needs of the 85–90% of students in the generalized population? At least one study (Cowell, 1988) suggests that the answer is "Probably not." In her study of how a sample of urban, suburban, and rural school nurses in northern Illinois spent their time, Cowell (1988) found that nurses spent 48.2% of their time addressing the needs of special education students, who constituted 9.6% of the total enrollment. Thus, nearly half of the school nurses' time was concentrated on only a small percentage of the total student population.

So, how can increasingly scarce school health resources be equitably distributed? This question has no easy answers. On the one hand, society is obligated to provide services for vulnerable children to help them grow into adults who are as independent and productive as possible. On the other hand, comprehensive health promotion and disease prevention strategies applied to the 85–90% of schoolchildren who are a "captive well population" could go a long way toward deferring or decreasing chronic illnesses later in their lives that otherwise will cost our health care system millions of dollars to treat. For now, school districts will likely continue to juggle these competing demands, achieving an uneasy year-to-year truce. Eventually, however, as resources further erode, hard choices will have to be made and school nurses will likely find themselves in the uncomfortable and unfamiliar position of being at the center of the debate.

Students' Health Concerns and Conditions

Along with administrative/leadership issues, school health programs are also confronted with changes in the health concerns and conditions of students. That is, while school-age children and youth are generally regarded as a "captive well population," increasing numbers of students today are neither "captive" nor "well." Consequently, school health programs need to extend beyond vision and hearing screening and other "routine" activities to address students' lifestyle issues and the "new morbidities" that are evident among school populations.

Factors Influencing School Attendance

In order to benefit maximally from their educational opportunities, students must attend school consistently and be well enough to learn and participate. However, American students miss an average of five days of school each year; girls miss slightly more days than boys, while low-income children miss nearly twice as many days as upper-income students (Klerman, 1988; Pigg, 1989). Indeed, poverty is a significant predictor of poor health and school absence (Kornguth, 1990; Igoe, 1995; Newacheck, Jameson, & Halfon, 1994). Given estimates (Passarelli, 1993, 1994a, 1994b) that 60% of children in urban schools live in poverty, the potential impact on school health resources is sobering. Low-income families, as well as migrant workers, may move frequently, thus disrupting school attendance for their children. Likewise, the increasing incidence of homelessness profoundly affects children, resulting in both physical and emotional health problems; consequently,

meeting the health needs of homeless children poses a special challenge for today's school nurses (Chauvin, Duncan, & Marcontel, 1990).

Students with chronic illness and disabilities also tend to have higher absentee rates and more prolonged absences than the general student population (Hootman, 1994). Thus, these children, like those whose families are poor, mobile, and/or homeless, are not consistently "captive" as full-time students. Unfortunately, unless their school attendance patterns can be improved, these students are at risk for scholastic underachievement and eventual school failure (Hootman, 1994; Igoe, 1995).

Immunization Levels and the Incidence of Preventable Diseases

In addition to being less often "captive" and available to learn, increasing numbers of today's students are not "well," either. In fact, as documented in the literature (Pigg, 1989; Igoe & Giordano, 1992; Passarelli, 1993, 1994a, 1994b; Baker, 1994; Hootman, 1994; Igoe, 1995), the range of physical, social, and emotional health issues confronting today's children and youth—and hence school health programs—is staggering. For example, due to falling immunization levels nationally, preventable childhood diseases are on the rise. In fact, only 50% of U.S. children are fully immunized by age 2; consequently, more than 30,000 cases of measles, mumps, and pertussis were reported in 1990 (Igoe & Giordano, 1992, p. 35). Efforts to improve and verify students' compliance with immunization laws and guidelines therefore continue to be a school health program priority.

Indeed, the incidence of a number of communicable diseases, including tuberculosis (TB), HIV/AIDS, and other sexually transmitted diseases (STDs) has risen in recent years. Because TB, AIDS, and other STDs can be prevented or controlled by lifestyle changes and detected early through screening, school health program planners should determine (based on the assessed needs of their school's population) which educational and/or screening strategies to include in their programs.

Asthma and Other Chronic Conditions

Another health problem on the rise is asthma, which affects 1 in 12 American children and is "the most common cause of school absence" (Passarelli, 1994b, p. 143). Because they may need medication (via inhaler or nebulizer) and respiratory assessment/monitoring during the school day, as well as ongoing health teaching and counseling, students with asthma may consume substantial amounts of school nursing time. Similarly, students with other chronic conditions such as diabetes may also require significant school nursing time and attention.

Students with Disabilities, Medically Fragile Conditions, and Technology Dependence

As noted earlier, laws mandating inclusion of all students with disabilities in regular schools and classroom settings (as appropriate) have prompted school health programs to redirect substantial portions of their resources to care for these children. In recent years, the severity of students' impairments has increased, no doubt reflecting medical breakthroughs that have improved the survival rates for children with profound disabilities. Consequently, increased numbers of children who are medically fragile and technology dependent (i.e., on ventilators) are now attending public schools (Bonaiuto, 1995). Meeting the needs of these children will require schools to (a) review their school health programming priorities and resources; (b) implement procedures to ensure student safety; (c) ensure collaboration by involved physicians, school nurses, classroom teachers, and paraprofessionals on behalf of affected students; and (d) provide inservice education to attain and maintain school nurses' competency to care for such students.

Emotional/Mental and Behavioral Health Concerns

Within the realm of emotional/mental and behavioral health, a number of concerns and conditions affect school health program planning. One such concern is depression and suicide among children and adolescents. Pigg (1989) reports that 20% of school-age children have symptoms of depression. Igoe (1995) notes that children living in poverty are twice as likely to experience mental health problems but are less likely to have access to effective treatment. Suicide is also a significant problem, especially among adolescents, although very young children have also committed suicide. Because untreated mental health problems can be debilitating and may persist into adulthood, mental health promotion needs to be a strong component of school health programs.

Teen Pregnancy. Another behavioral concern is the rising rate of pregnancy among teens. Because more than half of adolescents age 15–19 are sexually active (Igoe & Giordano, 1992, p. 35), it is not surprising that teen pregnancy rates have more than doubled in the past 20 years (Passarelli, 1993, 1994a, 1994b). According to Pigg (1989), more than 1 million teens get pregnant each year, of whom half give birth. To ensure that teen

parents complete their formal education while learning to be effective parents to their infants, some cities have created special schools and health programs, offering classes for the teens plus on-site day care for their babies; St. Paul's AGAPE program is a good example (Passarelli, 1993, 1994a, 1994b). Since adolescent sexual activity and pregnancy are not likely to go away, schools will need to intensify their health promotion and health education efforts to ensure responsible sexual behavior and to reduce the incidence of STDs and unplanned pregnancy.

Attention Deficit Hyperactivity Disorder (ADHD). Another behavioral health issue is the increasing number of children diagnosed with ADHD, Attention Deficit Hyperactivity Disorder. Although the causes of this disorder are not well understood, medication is commonly prescribed to control the symptoms. Children with ADHD can be disruptive in class and may have difficulty concentrating and learning; they may also experience side effects from their medications. Therefore, school nurses and school health programs need to plan how they will address the needs of this population.

Substance Use and Abuse. Use and abuse of such substances as tobacco, alcohol, and street drugs continue to rise, even among elementary school children (Igoe, 1995; Pigg, 1989). Such behavior is of concern not only because of the risk of injury or death from the substances themselves, but also because of the behaviors students may engage in while they are "high." For example, students who are intoxicated with alcohol or drugs may engage in unsafe sex or be vulnerable to injury from sexual assault, driving while intoxicated, or getting into fights.

Violence. Substance abuse may also be a contributing factor in violence, which is another problem on the rise. Increasingly, adolescents are both victims and perpetrators of violent crime. In fact, Pigg (1989) notes that 34% of teens report being threatened or hurt by someone; 13% report being attacked either at school or on a school bus, and nearly 25% of teen boys admit carrying a weapon to school at least once within the past year. Hootman (1994) reveals that young people are becoming increasingly violent and have greater access to weapons. Even more shocking is the fact that homicide is now the second leading cause of death for teens age 15 to 19 (Hootman, 1994).

Family violence, including child abuse, also persists. Igoe and Giordano (1992, p. 35) indicate that 2.2 million children were reported abused or neglected in 1989, an increase of 147% over the previous 10 years.

Compounding the violence issue is the growth of gangs in the United States. Although gang membership may meet the socialization and esteem needs of some children and youth, it may also lead to criminal activity and imprisonment, as well as increasing the risk of violent injury or death. The school health program can and should teach students to settle conflicts without violence and to meet their esteem and belonging needs without gangs.

Eating Disorders. Likewise, efforts to promote self-esteem in children and youth will continue to be important mental health goals for the school health program. The persistence of eating disorders, including bulimia and anorexia, particularly among young girls, is cause for concern. Bulimia affects an estimated 5–25% of teenage girls (Pigg, 1989); in contrast, the incidence of anorexia is much lower, but the consequences are potentially far more deadly. Pigg (1989, p. 27) estimates that 1 in 250 girls (0.4%) between ages 12 and 18 will become anorexic; two thirds of them will fully recover; about one third will remain chronically ill—and 5% of them will die.

Summary

In short, the health needs of today's school-age children and youth are becoming increasingly complex and acute. Therefore, school health program planners will need to carefully weigh the needs of their particular student populations against the limited "pot" of resources available for planning and implementing a school health program and set thoughtfully derived priorities.

Health Services Access and Delivery

In addition to program administration issues and the changing health needs and concerns of students, a third set of issues shaping the future of school health and school nursing is health services access and delivery. Indeed, as previously noted, lack of access to primary health care is a major problem today, especially for low-income students and their families, who are disproportionately burdened by illness and health defects (Igoe & Giordano, 1992; Igoe, 1995; Newacheck, Jameson, & Halfon, 1994). Contributing to these health care access problems are a number of barriers, including (a) lack of transportation; (b) inconvenient clinic/facility hours; (c) financial pressures, such as low income and inadequate insurance coverage; and (d) perceived socioeconomic and/or cultural insensitivity (Igoe & Giordano, 1992).

School-based Health Centers

As discussed earlier, school-based health centers (SBHCs) emerged in the early 1980s as a means of overcoming these health care access barriers and providing on-site primary care for students who lacked other resources and those with physical or developmental disabilities (Igoe, 1980a). Buoyed by the success of the early demonstration clinics, Yates (1994b) reports that between 1985 and 1993 the number of school-based clinics increased tenfold, from 50 to 500; by the end of 1995 there were 700 school-based health centers in the United States (Lear, Montgomery, Schlitt, & Rickett, 1996). Because the school nurse practitioners who head SBHCs are able to diagnose and treat routine illnesses on-site, SBHCs can effectively reduce absenteeism (Kornguth, 1990). By thus preventing disruptions in students' attendance, SBHCs ideally enable students to benefit more fully from their educational opportunities.

Despite the documented success of school-based health centers in improving both health care access and outcomes, their future is clouded by a number of issues that will affect school health programming in the 21st century. A major issue, in fact, is long-term funding for SBHCs. That is, communities must determine whether to finance their SBHCs with federal block grants (e.g., Title V), state and local public funds, third-party reimbursement (e.g., Medicaid, HMOs, or other private insurance), and/or private monies (Lear, Montgomery, Schlitt, & Rickett, 1996). However, both private foundation and local school system sponsorship of SBHCs have declined, resulting in an unstable financial status for SBHCs (Yates, 1994a). Lear et al. (1996, p. 83) explain the problem as follows:

> Public support for establishing school-based health centers has outstripped understanding of how to pay for them in the long term. As a result, a large number of school-based health centers have been started without a clear notion of how they will be sustained. . . . A substantial portion of these centers face staffing and service cuts if stable funding mechanisms . . . are not put into place.

Another issue that the presence of school-based health centers raises is liability. That is, are schools accountable for the quality of care provided in their on-site SBHCs? And who is liable if a student or other client of the SBHC sues after receiving treatment or other services? The answers to these questions depend on the health center model being used and how the center is sponsored or funded. In any event, however, these questions need to be addressed up front.

Communication with other school personnel and the corollary issue of maintaining confidentiality also must be addressed when on-site health care is provided via a school-based center. Too, when there is a "regular" school nurse in the building along with the school nurse practitioner in the SBHC, role overlap and confusion may be an issue. Therefore, to the extent possible, the roles (position descriptions) for the school nurse and school nurse practitioner should be clarified before the SBHC is launched.

Finally, in those communities in which school-based health centers are expected to grow and thrive, the nature of the SBHC's mission and long-range development needs to be thoughtfully considered. That is, should the SBHC focus exclusively on providing primary care to under-insured and under-served children and their families? Or should the SBHC evolve more broadly into the kind of family health resource center envisioned by Igoe and Giordano (1992)? The answers to these questions will also help shape the future of school health.

Emergency Care

Another issue that will shape the future of school health and school nursing concerns the response to "routine" student complaints and the provision of emergency care at school. As noted earlier, the expectation of some administrators and others that school nurses will personally handle *all* minor illnesses and injuries is unrealistic, costly, and inappropriate because (a) in many areas, school nurses must "cover" more than one school and so are not available full-time in any one building, and (b) preoccupation with minor illnesses or injuries may prevent nurses from handling other, more weighty issues that demand their education and expertise. However, it *is* appropriate for school nurses to oversee development and implementation of a comprehensive emergency care plan for the school, including designation and training of "first responders." This is particularly important in schools that enroll medically fragile students. In addition, school nurses should monitor compliance with the emergency plan over time to ensure that it is followed when school nurses are not in the building.

Caring for Chronically Ill, Disabled, and Medically Fragile Students

The continued and increasing presence in school of students with chronic illnesses and disabilities, as well as those who are medically fragile or technology dependent, also stimulates questions that will affect the future of school health and school nursing. One such

question concerns *who* will deliver the complex, often time-consuming services (such as assessments and treatments) during the school day. How can disruption in the classroom be minimized while such services are being provided? Who will pay for such services? Who will supervise the person(s) delivering care to these vulnerable students? What is the role of the school and school nurse in all this? That is, schools must ensure competent provision of care while seeking funding and reimbursement. (See chapters 11 and 12 for further discussion.)

Medication Administration. A related issue concerns administration of medications at school. A key issue is *who* should be authorized to dispense medications to students in school. Because there are (typically) too few registered nurses employed in schools, medications are too often dispensed by secretaries, teachers, or paraprofessionals (Francis, Hemmat, Treloar, & Yarandi, 1996). Given that reality, it is especially important for school districts to have clear, written policies about medication administration to minimize liability risks. Detailed recommendations about this are available elsewhere (Office of School Health Programs, 1990).

DNR Orders. An even more thorny concern prompted by the increasing number of seriously ill children attending regular schools and classrooms is the issuance of "Do Not Resuscitate" (DNR) orders. Although their purpose is to ensure that dying children receive supportive, compassionate care without prolonging the process or discomforts of dying, DNR orders raise troubling ethical, moral, and legal issues (Rushton, Will, & Murray, 1994). The fact is, however, that children *are* dying and that some of them (or their families) may obtain DNR orders—which they expect the school to obey. Therefore, to avoid facing this dilemma without prior preparation, school districts are advised to develop written policies to guide schools' (and school nurses') responses to DNR orders. Failure to do so could be costly—to the student and the school. (See also chapter 14.)

The School Nurse Role: Clarity, Preparation, and Performance

The final group of issues and trends expected to shape the future of school health and school nursing concerns the role of the school nurse, who is (and has been from the beginning) the mainstay of the school health program. Because discussion of many of these issues and trends is a thread woven throughout this chapter, the following pages need only serve as a postscript.

Role Clarity

Just as they have for nearly 100 years, today's school nurses must confront the realities of a role that is too broad, ill defined, and ever changing (Thurber, Berry, & Cameron, 1991; Zimmerman, Wagoner, & Kelly, 1996). Compounding those challenges is the too-frequent expectation of school administrators and others that school nurses should be able to (a) effectively promote students' health through health education and counseling; (b) safely meet the needs of students with disabilities, medically fragile conditions, and technology dependence; (c) conduct periodic screenings to detect vision, hearing, and musculoskeletal problems; (d) monitor compliance with immunization laws and other statutes and regulations; (e) recruit, train, and effectively supervise volunteers and other unlicensed assistive personnel; and (f) accomplish it all on an already inadequate, ever-shrinking budget.

As this list of expectations reveals, the role of the school nurse has expanded almost continually since its formal beginning (in the United States) in 1902, spurred (in part) by such societafl changes as increased poverty and homelessness, violence, and family disruption. At the same time, advances in health care and medical technology have increased the survival rates and life expectancies of children with profound disabilities and illnesses, many of whom are now mainstreamed (by law) into regular classrooms across the United States. Because all these changes have increased the number and complexity of students' needs, they have increased the complexity of the school nurse's role as well.

Consequently, the boundaries between the school nurse's role and the roles of social workers, educators, psychologists, and others have blurred. Likewise, the addition of school-based health centers (SBHCs) in underserved areas, headed (generally) by school nurse practitioners (SNPs) with the knowledge and skill to diagnose and manage a variety of illnesses, has blurred (once again) the role boundaries between nursing and medicine, raising questions about scope of practice and legal liability along the way.

Furthermore, the trend toward greatly expanded reliance on unlicensed assistive personnel (UAPs) has proved to be a two-edged sword. On the one hand, judicious use of UAPs is now recognized as a cost-effective way to deliver school health programs. On the other hand, however, UAPs are too often mistaken for school nurses and sometimes have misrepresented themselves as school nurses, thereby exposing themselves, school nurses, and school districts to potentially disastrous legal consequences. Unfortunately, when registered nurses accept employment as UAPs or school health aides, as illustrated (for example) by Brown (1995), the legal, ethical, and professional issues become even murkier. (See also chapters 4 and 5.)

Role Preparation

Given the increasing complexity of the school nurse role and the broad array of constituencies to be served, including students, families, school personnel, and the community at large, it should be apparent that tomorrow's school nurses will need expanded preparation in order to effectively perform this specialized community health nursing role. Although national groups, such as the National Nursing Coalition for School Health (1995), have gone on record favoring the Bachelor of Science in Nursing (BSN) degree as the minimal entry credential for school nursing, this writer disagrees with the BSN as the minimal standard.

Instead, this writer strongly advocates movement toward the Master of Science in Nursing (MSN) degree as the minimal standard, including advanced preparation in community health nursing and role preparation as a pediatric nurse practitioner (PNP) or school nurse practitioner (SNP). Such preparation should help school nurses to adopt the aggregate-level view needed to plan, implement, and evaluate school health programs tailored to meet the needs of their particular communities. At the same time, role preparation as a PNP or SNP would enhance school nurses' assessment skills and confidence in their ability to develop individualized health plans and to serve as case managers for chronically ill or disabled students and for those who lack other health care resources or supervision (Urbinati, Steele, Harter, & Harrell, 1996).

Furthermore, master's-prepared school nurses with advanced practice nursing skills will be better equipped to define their role and test/document its effectiveness through outcomes research. Likewise, master's-prepared school nurses should also have substantial knowledge and skill in planned change and management (including delegation to and supervision of unlicensed assistants). Such preparation is clearly beyond the focus of baccalaureate nursing programs, which are designed to prepare generalists, not specialists (like school nurses). So, while others may protest that adopting the MSN as the minimal credential for entry into school nursing practice is unrealistic, unless the bar is raised, school nursing will never clear the hurdle of effective role preparation. The standard may be high, but its attainment is essential.

Role Performance

Assuming that school nurses will be able to clarify their role and identify appropriate role preparation and educational credentials, school nurses' ability to effectively perform their role requires completion of another task: clarification/revision of national standards. That is, although the adoption of school nursing standards in the 1980s (American Nurses' Association, 1983) was a landmark event, the need for revisions was recognized less than a decade later (Proctor, 1993). Because school health and school nursing have continued to evolve and change, the standards are once again being revisited.

Indeed, as recommended by the National Nursing Coalition for School Health (1995), a national committee has been formed to review and update the standards and to seek consensus among all relevant organizations. In this writer's opinion, the standards need to be enlarged and revised in at least two areas: staffing levels and role preparation. Regarding staffing levels, school nurse—student ratios need to be mandated for general school populations (1:750), mainstreamed special needs students (1:225), and severely/profoundly disabled students (1:125) (American Nurses' Association, 1983; American School Health Association, 1991, 1994). Furthermore, ratios of unlicensed assistants to school nurses should be specified, to prevent school nurses from having too large a span of control (i.e., too many UAPs to safely supervise).

Regarding role preparation standards, this writer believes (as previously noted) that the educational standard should be raised to the MSN level, particularly for those school nurses who manage school health programs and/or serve in urban or rural areas in which the school nurse is a primary health care resource for families. Requiring master's preparation would be an acknowledgment that school nursing is a highly complex, independent practice that requires education and credentials comparable to those of master teachers in the schools (Salmon, 1994).

Conclusion

To paraphrase Dickens, "It is the best of times, it is the worst of times." At the beginning of a new century, school nursing is once again at a crossroads. As Salmon (1994, p. 140) explains:

> For school health nurses, this is a particularly opportune moment. Policymakers and administrators alike are looking to expand the roles of schools and professionals who work in them as

[a] means for enhancing the health of children. However, school health nurses are also being challenged to develop clarity and a concerted sense of direction regarding their real abilities to contribute to school health services of the future.

Clearly, the time is now for school nurses to chart their course into the future. The health of America's children may well hinge on their success.

REFERENCES

Adams, R. M., Cole, H., Price, A. L., Lewis, R. C., Jr., & Cotton, W. H. (1991). Environmental health and safety in schools: An overview. *School Nurse, 7*(1), 14–18.

Allensworth, D. D. (1994). The research base for innovative practices in school health education at the secondary level. *Journal of School Health, 64*(5), 180–187.

Allensworth, D. D., & Kolbe, L. J. (1987). The comprehensive school health program: Exploring an expanded concept. *Journal of School Health, 57*(10), 409–412.

Allensworth, D. D., Symons, C. W., & Olds, R. S. (1994). *Healthy students 2000: An agenda for continuous improvement in America's schools.* Kent, OH: American School Health Association.

American Association of Colleges of Nursing. (1994, June). School nursing: Extending primary care's reach. *AACN Issue Bulletin,* 4 pp.

American Nurses' Association. (1998). *Standards of clinical nursing practice* (2nd ed.). Washington, DC: American Nurses' Publishing.

American Nurses' Association Divisions on Nursing Practice, American School Health Association, & National Association of School Nurses. (1980). *School nurses working with handicapped children* (ANA Publication No. NP-60). Kansas City, MO: American Nurses' Association.

American Nurses' Association, Task Force on Standards of School Nursing Practice. (1983). *Standards of school nursing practice* (Publication No. NP-66). Kansas City, MO: American Nurses' Association.

American School Health Association. (1974). *Guidelines for the school nurse in the school health program.* Kent, OH: Author.

American School Health Association. (1991). *Implementation guide for the standards of school nursing practice.* Kent, OH: Author.

American School Health Association. (1994). *Guidelines for comprehensive school health programs* (2nd ed.). Kent, OH: Author.

Bachman, J. (1995). A university's response to a need for school nurse education. *Journal of School Nursing, 11*(3), 20–22, 24.

Baker, C. M. (1994). School health: Policy issues. *Nursing & Health Care, 15*(4), 178–184.

Bartlett, E. E. (1981). The contribution of school health education to community health promotion: What can we reasonably expect? *American Journal of Public Health, 71*(12), 1384–1391.

Belzer, E. G., Jr., & McIntyre, L. (1994). A model for coordinating school health promotion programs. *Journal of School Health, 64*(5), 196–200.

Blair, S. N., Tritsch, L., & Kutsch, S. (1987). Worksite health promotion for school faculty and staff. *Journal of School Health, 57*(10), 469–473.

Bonaiuto, M. M. (1995). School nurses' competence in caring for students who depend on medical technology. *Journal of School Nursing, 11*(4), 21–22, 24–28.

Bradley, B. J. (1997). The school nurse as health educator. *Journal of School Health, 67*(1), 3–8.

Brainerd, E. F. (1989). HIV in the school setting: The school nurse's role. *Journal of School Health, 59*(7), 316–317.

Brown, C. (1995, November 9). Nurse! School health aides see themselves as educators as well as dispensers of TLC, bandages, ice packs. *Hastings Star Gazette*, p. 2A.

Brown, E. S. (1952). The role of the nurse in the school health program. *Journal of School Health, 22*(8), 219–224.

Center for the Study of Social Policy. (1994). *Kids count data book*. Washington, DC: Annie E. Casey Foundation.

Chauvin, V., Duncan, J. A., & Marcontel, M. (1990). Homeless students of the 1990s: A new school population. *School Nurse, 6*(3), 10–13.

Christy, T. E. (1970). Portrait of a leader: Lillian D. Wald. *Nursing Outlook, 18*(3), 50–54.

Collins, J. L., Small, M. L., Kann, L., Pateman, B. C., Gold, R. S., & Kolbe, L. J. (1995). School health education. *Journal of School Health, 65*(8), 302–311.

Collis, J. L., & Dukes, C. A. (1989). Toward some principles of school nursing. *Journal of School Health, 59*(3), 109–111.

The comprehensive school health education workshop: Background and future prospects. (1993). *Journal of School Health, 63*(1), 7–8.

Conrad, M., & Wehrwein, T. (1992). Public health nursing in schools: Perceptions of public school administrators. *Journal of School Nursing, 8*(4), 11–14.

Cowell, J. M. (1988). Health services utilization and special education: Development of a school nurse activity tool. *Journal of School Health, 58*(9), 355–359.

Cromwell, G. E. (1946). *The health of the school child*. Philadelphia: W. B. Saunders Company.

Custer, M. (1984). School nursing: A case of the forest and the trees. *Journal of School Health, 54*(7), 259–260.

Davis, T. M., & Allensworth, D. D. (1994). Program management: A necessary component for the comprehensive school health program. *Journal of School Health, 64*(10), 400–404.

DeAngelis, C. (1981). The Robert Wood Johnson Foundation National School Health Program: A presentation and progress report. *Clinical Pediatrics, 20*(5), 344–348.

DeFriese, G. H., Crossland, C. L., MacPhail-Wilcox, B., & Sowers, J. G. (1990). Implementing comprehensive school health programs: Prospects for change in American schools. *Journal of School Health, 60*(4), 182–187.

DeGraw, C. (1994). A community-based school health system: Parameters for developing a comprehensive student health promotion program. *Journal of School Health, 64*(5), 192–195.

Desrosiers, M. C. (1989). The School Nurse Achievement Program in New Hampshire. *Journal of School Health, 59*(8), 364–366.

Dierkes, K. (1951). The nurse in a generalized program. *Journal of School Health, 21*(4), 131–135.

Dilworth, L. P. (1944). Essential school nursing in wartime. *Public Health Nursing, 36*(9), 443–447.

Dilworth, L. P. (1949). The nurse in the school health program. *Public Health Nursing, 41*(8), 438–441.

Dock, L. L. (1902). School-nurse experiment in New York. *American Journal of Nursing, 3*(2), 108–110.

Doering, R. G. (1996, January 23). *School boards must address needs of the whole child: Healthy children are better learners* (3 pp.). Press release from the NSBA News Service. Alexandria, VA: National School Boards Association.

Elders, M. J. (1993). Schools and health: A natural partnership. *Journal of School Health, 63*(7), 312–315.

Ford, L. C. (1970). The school nurse role—A changing concept in preparation and practice. *Journal of School Health, 40*(1), 21–23.

Francis, E. E., Hemmat, J. P., Treloar, D. M., & Yarandi, H. (1996). Who dispenses pharmaceuticals to children at school? *Journal of School Health, 66*(10), 355–358.

Fredlund, D. J. (1967). The route to effective school nursing. *Nursing Outlook, 15*(8), 24–28.

Freeman, R. (1945). Developments in education of public health nurses for school health work. *Public Health Nursing, 37*(9), 454–455.

Fricke, I. B. (1967). The Illinois study of school nursing practice. *Journal of School Health, 37*(1), 24–28.

Fryer, G. E., & Igoe, J. B. (1995). A relationship between availability of school nurses and child well-being. *Journal of School Nursing, 11*(3), 12–14, 16, 18.

Fryer, G. E., & Igoe, J. B. (1996). Functions of school nurses and health assistants in U.S. school health programs. *Journal of School Health, 66*(2), 55–58.

Gardner, M. S. (1916). *Public health nursing.* New York: Macmillan.

Gardner, M. S. (1926). *Public health nursing* (2nd ed.). New York: Macmillan.

Goodwin, L. D., Igoe, J. B., & Smith, A. N. (1984). Evaluation of the School Nurse Achievement Program: A follow-up survey of school nurses. *Journal of School Health, 54*(9), 335–338.

Green, L. W. (1981). Lessons from the past, plans for the future. *Health Education Quarterly, 8*(1), 105–117.

Green, L. W. (1988). Bridging the gap between community health and school health. *American Journal of Public Health, 78*(9), 1149.

Haas, M. B. (Ed.). (1993). *The school nurse's source book of individualized healthcare plans* (Vol. 1). North Branch, MN: Sunrise River Press.

Hawkins, N. G. (1971). Is there a school nurse role? *American Journal of Nursing, 71*(4), 744–751.

Hawkins, J. W., Hayes, E. R., & Corliss, C. P. (1994). School nursing in America—1902–1994: A return to public health nursing. *Public Health Nursing, 11*(6), 416–425.

Healthy People 2000: National Health Promotion and Disease Prevention Objectives and Healthy Schools. (1991). *Journal of School Health, 61*(7), 298–328.

Hertel, V. , Brainerd, E., Desrosiers, M., Fisher, C., Hatfield, M. E., Lewis, P., Markendorf, J., & Quinnell, N. (1982). National Association of State School Nurse Consultants define role of school nurse in "PL 94-142—Education for All Handicapped Children Act of 1975." *Journal of School Health, 52*(8), 475–478.

Hoffman, M. A., Freeman, V. S., Kaplan, T. M., Behmer, C. L., & Kangas-Packett, S. (1993). Assessment of health and stress levels in school personnel. *Journal of School Nursing, 9*(4), 6–11.

Hootman, J. (1994). Nursing our most valuable natural resource: School age children. *Nursing Forum, 29*(3), 5–17.

Igoe, J. B. (1980a). Changing patterns in school health and school nursing. *Nursing Outlook, 28*(8), 486–492.

Igoe, J. B. (1980b). What is school nursing? A plea for more standardized roles. *MCN, 5*(5), 307–311.

Igoe, J. B. (1981). The educational preparation and role of the school nurse practitioner. In S. J. Wold, *School nursing: A framework for practice* (pp. 468–475). North Branch, MN: Sunrise River Press.

Igoe, J. B. (1995). School health: Designing the policy environment through understanding. *Nursing Policy Forum, 1*(3), 12–16, 18–19, 30–36.

Igoe, J. B., & Giordano, B. P. (1992). *Expanding school health services to serve families in the 21st century* (ANA Publication Code CH-21). Washington, D. C.: American Nurses Publishing.

Iverson, C. J., & Hays, B. J. (1994). School nursing in the 21st century: Prediction and readiness. *Journal of School Nursing, 10*(4), 19–24.

Iverson, D. C. (1981). Promoting health through the schools: A challenge for the eighties. *Health Education Quarterly, 8*(1), 11–14.

Jackson, S. A. (1994). Comprehensive school health education programs: Innovative practices and issues in standard setting. *Journal of School Health, 64*(5), 177–179.

Joachim, G. (1989). The school nurse as case manager for chronically ill children. *Journal of School Health, 59*(9), 406–407.

Jones, M. E., & Clark, D. (1993). What school nurses really do: A study of school nurse utilization. *Journal of School Nursing, 9*(2), 10–17.

Josten, L., Smoot, C., & Beckley, S. (1995). Delegation to assistive personnel by school nurses—One state's experience. *Journal of School Nursing, 11*(2), 8–10, 12, 14, 16.

Kann, L., Collins, J. L., Pateman, B. C., Small, M. L., Ross, J. G., & Kolbe, L. J. (1995). The School Health Policies and Programs Study (SHPPS): Rationale for a nationwide status report on school health programs. *Journal of School Health, 65*(8), 291–294.

Killip, D. C., Lovick, S. R., Goldman, L., & Allensworth, D. D. (1987). Integrated school and community programs. *Journal of School Health, 57*(10), 437–444.

Klerman, L. V. (1988). School absence—A health perspective. *Pediatric Clinics of North America, 35*(6), 1253–1269.

Kolbe, L. J., Kann, L., Collins, J. L., Small, M. L., Pateman, B. C., & Warren, C. W. (1995). The School Health Policies and Programs Study (SHPPS): Context, methods, general findings, and future efforts. *Journal of School Health, 65*(8), 339–343.

Kornguth, M. L. (1990). School illnesses: Who's absent and why? *Pediatric Nursing, 16*(1), 95–99.

Kozlak, L. A. (1992). Comprehensive school health programs: The challenge for school nurses. *Journal of School Health, 62*(10), 475–477.

Lavin, A. T., Shapiro, G. R., & Weill, K. S. (1992). Creating an agenda for school-based health promotion: A review of 25 selected reports. *Journal of School Health, 62*(6), 212–228.

Lear, J. G., Montgomery, L. L., Schlitt, J. J., & Rickett, K. D. (1996). Key issues affecting school-based health centers and Medicaid. *Journal of School Health, 66*(3), 83–88.

Lerner, M. (1996, May 15). Minneapolis school to set up clinic: Officials hope to counter absentee, asthma rates. *Minneapolis Star Tribune, 15*(41), p. B3.

Lohrmann, D. K., Gold, R. S., & Jubb, W. H. (1987). School health education: A foundation for school health programs. *Journal of School Health, 57*(10), 420–425.

Lovato, C. Y., Allensworth, D. D., & Chan, F. A. (1989). *School health in America: An assessment of state policies to protect and improve the health of students* (5th ed.). Kent, OH: American School Health Association.

Lovick, S. R. (1988). School-based clinics: Meeting teens' health care needs. *Journal of School Health, 58*(9), 379–381.

McAleer, H. S. (1965). What's new in school nursing. *Journal of School Health, 35*(2), 49–52.

McCarty-Marple, M. (1994). Stressors and coping in the school setting. *Journal of School Nursing, 10*(1), 20–25.

McGinnis, J. M., & DeGraw, C. (1991). Healthy schools 2000: Creating partnerships for the decade. *Journal of School Health, 61*(7), 292–297.

McKenzie, J. F. (1988). Twelve steps in developing a schoolsite health education/promotion program for faculty and staff. *Journal of School Health, 58*(4), 149–153.

Miller, J. S. A. (1990). Implications of role expansion for school nurse managers. *Journal of School Health, 60*(1), 29–30.

Nader, P. R. (1990). The concept of "comprehensiveness" in the design and implementation of school health programs. *Journal of School Health, 60*(4), 133–138.

NASN membership survey. (1993). *Journal of School Nursing, 9*(4), 28–35.

National Association for Sport and Physical Education. (1995). *Moving into the future: National physical education standards: A guide to content and assessment.* St. Louis: Mosby-Year Book.

National Association of School Nurses. (1985). *An evaluation guide for school nursing practice designed for self and peer review.* Scarborough, ME: Author.

National Association of School Nurses. (1998). *Standards of professional school nursing practice.* Scarborough, ME: Author.

National Association of State School Nurse Consultants. (1995). Position paper: Delegation of school health services to unlicensed assistive personnel. *Journal of School Nursing, 11*(4), 13–14, 16.

National Association of State School Nurse Consultants. (1996a). Delegation of school health services to unlicensed assistive personnel: A position paper of the National Association of State School Nurse Consultants. *Journal of School Health, 66*(2), 72–74.

National Association of State School Nurse Consultants. (1996b). Medicaid reimbursement for school nursing services: A position paper of the National Association of State School Nurse Consultants. *Journal of School Health, 66*(3), 95–96.

National Council of State Boards of Nursing. (1990). *Concept paper on delegation,* 4 pp. (mimeo).

National Council of State Boards of Nursing. (1991). *Nursing care in the school setting: Regulatory implications.* Chicago: Author (mimeo).

National Nursing Coalition for School Health. (1995). School health nursing services: Exploring national issues and priorities. *Journal of School Health, 65*(9), 369–389.

Newacheck, P., Jameson, W. J., & Halfon, N. (1994). Health status and income: The impact of poverty on child health. *Journal of School Health, 64*(6), 229–233.

Oberg, C. N., Bryant, N. A., & Bach, M. L. (1994). Ethics, values, and policy decisions for children with disabilities: What are the costs of political correctness? *Journal of School Health, 64*(6), 223–228.

Oda, D. S. (1992). Is school nursing really the "invisible practice"? *Journal of School Health, 62*(3), 112–113.

Oda, D. S. (1993). Nurse administrators' views of professional preparation in school nursing. *Journal of School Health, 63*(5), 229–231.

Office of School Health Programs, University of Colorado Health Sciences Center. (1990, January). *National guidelines for the administration of medications in schools.* Denver, CO: Author.

Palfrey, J. S., Haynie, M., Porter, S., Bierle, T., Cooperman, P., & Lowcock, J. (1992). Project school care: Integrating children assisted by medical technology into educational settings. *Journal of School Health, 62*(2), 50–54.

Palfrey, J. S., Samuels, R. C., Haynie, M., & Cammisa, M. L. (1994). Health care reform: What's in it for children with chronic disease and disability. *Journal of School Health, 64*(6), 234–237.

Palmer, M. F. (1944). Essentiality of school nursing. *Public Health Nursing, 36*(5), 221–222.

Panettieri, M. J., & Schwab, N. (1996). Delegation and supervision in school settings: Standards, issues and guidelines for practice (Part 2). *Journal of School Nursing, 12*(2), 19–27.

Parsons, M. A., & Felton, G. M. (1992). Role performance and job satisfaction of school nurses. *Western Journal of Nursing Research, 14*(4), 498–511.

Passarelli, C. (1993, November). *School nursing: Trends for the future* (National Health/Education Consortium Occasional Paper #9), 24 pp.

Passarelli, C. (1994a). School nursing: Trends for the future. *Journal of School Nursing, 10*(2), 10, 12, 14, 16–21.

Passarelli, C. (1994b). School nursing: Trends for the future. *Journal of School Health, 64*(4), 141–145.

Pigg, R. M., Jr. (1989). The contribution of school health programs to the broader goals of public health: The American experience. *Journal of School Health, 59*(1), 25–30.

Pollitt, P. (1994). Lina Rogers Struthers: The first school nurse. *Journal of School Nursing, 10*(1), 34–36.

Proctor, S. T. (1990). *Guidelines for a model school nursing services program.* Scarborough, ME: National Association of School Nurses, Inc.

Proctor, S. T. (with Lordi, S. L., & Zaiger, D. S.). (1993). *School nursing practice: Roles and standards.* Scarborough, ME: National Association of School Nurses, Inc.

Randle, B. B. (1943). Wartime essentials in school nursing. *Public Health Nursing, 35*(9), 482–483.

Resnicow, K., & Allensworth, D. (1996). Conducting a comprehensive school health program. *Journal of School Health, 66*(2), 59–63.

Rowe, D. E. (1987). Healthful school living: Environmental health in the school. *Journal of School Health, 57*(10), 426–431.

Rushton, C. H., Will, J. C., & Murray, M. G. (1994). To honor and obey—DNR orders and the school. *Pediatric Nursing, 20*(6), 581–585.

Salmon, M. S. (1994). School (health) nursing in the era of health care reform: What is the outlook? *Journal of School Health, 64*(4), 137–140.

Satcher, D. (1995). Foreword. *Journal of School Health, 65*(8), 289.

School health nursing services: Exploring national issues and priorities. (1995). *Journal of School Health, 65*(9), 370–389.

Schultz, E. W., Glass, R. M., & Kamholtz, J. D. (1987). School climate: Psychological health and well-being in school. *Journal of School Health, 57*(10), 432–436.

Schwab, N. (1988). Liability issues in school nursing. *School Nurse, 4*(1), 13–21, 24–25.

Schwab, N. (1991). Students with complex health care needs: Role of the school nurse. *School Healthwatch, 3*(1), 3–5.

Schwab, N., & Haas, M. (1995). Delegation and supervision in school settings: Standards, issues and guidelines for practice (Part 1). *Journal of School Nursing, 11*(1), 26–35.

Seffrin, J. R. (1990). The comprehensive school health curriculum: Closing the gap between state-of-the-art and state-of-the-practice. *Journal of School Health, 60*(4), 151–156.

Sellery, C. M. (1951). The nurse in the school health program—The administrator's point of view. *Journal of School Health, 21*(4), 119–124.

Small, M. L., Majer, L. S., Allensworth, D. D., Farquhar, B. K., Kann, L., & Pateman, B. C. (1995). School health services. *Journal of School Health, 65*(8), 319–326.

Struthers, L. R. (1917). *The school nurse: A survey of the duties and responsibilities of the nurse in the maintenance of health and physical perfection and the prevention of disease among school children.* New York: G. P. Putnam's Sons.

Thurber, F., Berry, B., & Cameron, M. E. (1991). The role of school nursing in the United States. *Journal of Pediatric Health Care, 5*(3), 135–140.

Tipple, D. C. (1964). Misuse of assistants in school health. *American Journal of Nursing, 64*(9), 99–101.

Troop, E. H. (1963). Sixty years of school nurse preparation. *Nursing Outlook, 11*(3), 364–366.

Uphold, C. R., & Graham, M. V. (1993). Schools as collaborative services for families: A vision for change. *Nursing Outlook, 41*(5), 204–211.

Urbinati, D., Steele, P., Harter, J. E., & Harrell, D. (1996). The evolution of the school nurse practitioner: Past, present, and future. *Journal of School Nursing, 12*(2), 6–9.

U.S. Department of Health and Human Services. (2000a, January). *Healthy People 2010* (Conference edition, Vols. I-II). Washington, DC: Author.

U.S. Department of Health and Human Services. (2000b). *Healthy People 2010: Understanding and improving health.* Washington, DC: U.S. Government Printing Office.

U.S. Department of Health and Human Services/Public Health Service. (1991). *Healthy people 2000: National health promotion and disease prevention objectives*

(DHHS Publication No. [PHS] 91-50212). Washington, DC: U.S. Government Printing Office.

Van Cleaf, D., Young, A. A., & Hamilton, P. A. (1990). The educational role of the school nurse: Perceptions of school nurses and teachers. *School Nurse, 6*(4), 8–10.

Wales, M. (1941). *The public health nurse in action.* New York: Macmillan.

Walker-Shaw, M. (1993). Applying community organization to developing health promotion programs in the school community. *Journal of School Health, 63*(2), 109–111.

Wallace, H. M. (1959). School health services. *Journal of School Health, 29*(8), 283–295.

Wenzel, M. (1996). A school-based clinic for elementary schools in Phoenix, Arizona. *Journal of School Health, 66*(4), 125–127.

Whited, F., & Starke, T. (1989). School nurses: Saving an endangered species. *Journal of School Health, 59*(10), 446–447.

Wilson, C. J. (1990). Playground safety. *School Nurse, 6*(3), 36, 38–39.

Wold, S. J. (1981). *School nursing: A framework for practice.* North Branch, MN: Sunrise River Press.

Wold, S. J. (1982). Levels of school nursing service: Impact on the scope and quality of the school health program. In G. D. Miller (Ed.), *Differentiated levels of student support services: Crisis, remedial and developmental/preventive approaches* (monograph). St. Paul: Minnesota Department of Education.

Wold, S. J., & Dagg, N. V. (1981a). Philosophy, roles, and goals of school nursing. In S. J. Wold, *School nursing: A framework for practice* (pp. 20–29). North Branch, MN: Sunrise River Press.

Wold, S. J., & Dagg, N. V. (1981b). School nursing: A passing experiment. In S. J. Wold, *School nursing: A framework for practice* (pp. 3–19). North Branch, MN: Sunrise River Press.

Woodfill, M. M., & Beyrer, M. K. (1991). *The role of the nurse in the school setting: A historical perspective.* Kent, OH: American School Health Association.

Yates, S. R. (1992). The school nurse's role: Early intervention with preschool children. *Journal of School Nursing, 8*(4), 30–37.

Yates, S. (1994a). The practice of school nursing: Integration with new models of health service delivery. *Journal of School Nursing, 10*(1), 10–14, 16–19.

Yates, S. (1994b). School health delivery programs throughout the United States. *Journal of School Nursing, 10*(2), 31–36.

Zanga, J. R., & Oda, D. S. (1987). School health services. *Journal of School Health, 57*(10), 413–416.

Zimmerman, B. J., Wagoner, E. F., & Kelly, L. E. (1996). A study of role ambiguity and role strain among school nurses. *Journal of School Nursing, 12*(4), 12–18.

Zimmerman, D. J., & Reif, C. J. (1995). School-based health care centers and managed care health plans: Partners in primary care. *Journal of Public Health Management and Practice, 1*(1), 33–39.

See page 625 for Table of Federal Statutes and Regulations.

Chapter Two
Fundamentals of U.S. Law

Nadine C. Schwab
Mary H. B. Gelfman
Sarah D. Cohn

INTRODUCTION

This chapter reviews general concepts concerning the sources of law in the United States, as well as the different classifications of law as they pertain to school health. It also includes a brief summary of the major laws that impact the provision of health care services in schools. While several areas of education and health law will be addressed in depth in later chapters, this overview should help the reader understand the breadth of laws that apply to school health services, potential conflicts among them, and the difficulty of addressing one area of law in isolation from others. It

should also enable the reader to better understand the topics and issues covered in other chapters of the book. The last section of the chapter examines, in general terms, the legal concepts of liability, negligence, and standards of care, as well as defenses against negligence, liability risks in school health practice, and implications for school districts. Later chapters, especially chapters 4, 5, and 6, deal with specific liability issues in school nursing.

For information on how to read and access legal citations, see the Introduction to this book, pages 1–5.

SOURCES OF LAW

There are three major sources of law in the United States: federal and state constitutions (known as constitutional law), federal and state statutes (known as statutory law), and the decisions of judges (known as case law, common law, or decisional law). Although administrative law, or "the law of administrative agencies," is a subset of statutory law, it is sometimes viewed as a fourth category or source of law. School health professionals need to have a general understanding of each of these sources of law and their relevance to school health practice.

Although not often addressed as such, the underlying source of all law is ethics, which is a system of values and beliefs that governs conduct in order to protect individual rights. According to Hall, law is minimum ethics written down and enforced; it addresses behavior that is mandated, not just desirable (Hall, 1996, p. 49). The principles of ethics, which are addressed in chapter 3, must also be understood by school health professionals, not only because they form the basis for law, but because the law does not address the multiple situations and practice dilemmas that health professionals regularly deal with in schools and other practice settings. While the law sets minimum

standards for acceptable behavior in order to protect society from significant harm, ethics guides behavior and decision making based on desirable standards of right and wrong (morality) that are adhered to by an individual or group, such as a profession. Most health and education professional organizations publish codes of ethics that set the moral code for decision making within that profession. (See chapter 3 for further information regarding ethical values and principles.)

Federal and State Constitutions

The primary source of law in this country is the United States (U.S.) Constitution, which establishes the authority and functions of each branch of the federal government. The three branches of the U.S. government are

- the legislative branch, which makes the laws (U.S. Const. Art. I, Sec. 1);

- the executive branch, which administers the law (U.S. Const. Art. II, Sec. 1); and

- the judicial branch, which interprets the law (U.S. Const. Art. III, Sec. 1 and 2).

The U.S. Constitution includes nothing about education or health care. The 10th amendment reserves to the states or to the people those powers not delegated to the federal government, and the 14th amendment provides for equal protection of all citizens and due process of law prior to a citizen's deprivation of life, liberty, or property (U.S. Const. amend. XIV, Sec. 1). The 14th amendment has been used to bring cases challenging state public education systems that did not provide reasonably equal educational opportunity for all children. In the case of *Brown v. Board of Education* (1954), the U.S. Supreme Court ruled that separate schools for black children were not equal educational opportunity. Using *Brown,* the cases of *Mills v. District of Columbia Board of Education* (1972) and *North v. District of Columbia Board of Education* (1979) established that children with disabilities were entitled to appropriate educational opportunities. These cases relied on the legal principle that if a state offers public education to children under the 14th amendment, it must provide public education to all children, regardless of race or disability.

Similar to the U.S. Constitution, each state's constitution is the primary basis for law within that specific state. Although all state constitutions require the same branches of state government as the U.S. Constitution mandates in the federal government, there are many variations in how the executive, legislative, and judicial branches of state governments are constructed to conduct their business. The laws in one state apply only within that state, but the "full faith and credit" clause of the U.S. Constitution (U.S. Const. Art. IV) extends recognition of state law matters, such as marriage and divorce, to other states (e.g., a marriage in one state is recognized in all other states).

Legislation (Statutory Law)

In addition to the federal and state constitutions, which are rather general in language, there are other important sources of law. The first is legislation—that is, laws that are enacted by the U.S. Congress and state legislative bodies. Laws, which are also referred to as statutes, are second only to the federal and state constitutions in their authority to compel behavior. An example of a law passed by the federal government is the Family Educational Rights and Privacy Act, which protects the privacy of student records in schools, and an example of a state law or statute is the nursing practice act for each state, which defines the scope of nursing practice therein. State child abuse reporting laws, another example of state statutes, were generally passed in response to a federal law that offers some financial

assistance to states that participate in certain activities concerning child abuse. Federal law applies to all states and U.S. citizens, while state laws pertain only to those who reside or work in that particular state.

Health and social service laws deal with funding for various types of health and welfare services, including Medicaid funding, the legal scope of practice of health and social services professionals, the maintenance and confidentiality of medical records, the extent to which minors may seek medical treatment without parental involvement, the regulation of health care facilities, and the authority of state and local public health agencies to act when, for example, a communicable disease threatens the health of the general public. Public education is established and regulated by state law with a few specific federal laws setting national standards. School health issues are addressed in federal and state law and in health and education statutes.

Administrative Law or the Law of Government Agencies

For the purposes of this book, administrative law, an important subset of statutory law, is discussed in relation to the following entities:

- state boards of nursing, which regulate the practice and licensing of nurses;

- state and federal departments of education, which regulate public education and related funding;

- federal agencies for labor, health, and social services, which regulate or fund activities that affect schools, such as occupational health and safety standards, child abuse reporting, and drug and alcohol treatment records; and

- state departments of health, which are responsible for a variety of disease prevention and health promotion activities that are directed at school-age children.

In general, government agencies are created by laws that define their missions, and these agencies develop regulations that elaborate their responsibilities. These regulations are subject to public notice and hearing requirements. The regulations interpret, but may not expand beyond, the original statutory authority of the law. For example, a state legislature, when enacting a nursing practice act, delegates to the state's nursing board its authority to regulate nursing practice, but only within the constraints of the authorizing statute. The statute may also require the nursing board to promulgate regulations to provide specific details of how it will exercise its authority.

Government agencies also issue advisory or declaratory rulings in response to inquiries and hold contested case hearings in areas specified by law. The state boards of nursing define the practice of nursing for the state; they may issue, deny, or revoke professional licenses, and they sometimes invoke other types of sanctions upon proof of professional misconduct. The state and federal education departments have authority to enforce statutory requirements for schools, including mandatory health education and health services in schools, and may provide or deny various types of financial assistance to local districts. Depending on the state, the state department of education may also do the following:

- certify teachers and hold hearings to revoke teaching credentials (every state);

- mediate and arbitrate in school labor disputes (Connecticut);

- approve text books for use in schools (Texas); and

- develop curriculum (New York).

State health departments may define the immunizations required for school attendance, the content and frequency of school physical exams, requirements for medication administration in schools, and the nature of school health screening programs. They regulate health care agencies in the state and the practice of various health professions through licensure or certification. For example, a state department of health may license health care institutions, medical laboratories, day care and preschool programs, as well as license or certify various health professionals and paraprofessionals. State health departments also set health standards for communicable disease reporting and follow-up, quarantine and closing of public facilities, and regulate the authority and responsibilities of local and regional health departments. Through the use of incentive grant funds, a state health department may support the development of specific programs to address identified needs, such as injury prevention programs, school-based health centers for the delivery of primary care services to children and youth in underserved communities, and local screening programs to identify individuals with such health conditions as tuberculosis and lead poisoning.

The Federal government and most states have adopted Uniform Administrative Procedures Acts (UAPA), laws that apply to all governmental agencies.

These laws include rules for agency procedures like adoption of regulations with timelines, agency rules of practice, and mechanisms for appealing an agency decision to court. Almost all federal laws concerning education and health care have regulations, many state laws concerning education and health care have regulations, and most of the laws that are the subject of this book have interpreting regulations. It is important to know how these administrative regulations apply to schools and the practice of health professionals in school settings.

These government agency regulations are generally considered under the executive branch of the government (state or federal) because the executive branch directs the agencies to whom the legislature delegates authority (Aiken, 1994, p. 5). Administrative agencies are sometimes referred to as the "fourth branch of government." In his 1994 book, *The Death of Common Sense: How Law Is Suffocating America*, Howard observes that administrative law in this country has become so focused on "process" that state and federal agencies are profoundly bogged down in rules and procedures that "do away with individual responsibility" and preclude the exercise of expert judgment and compassion. While that may be true, practitioners in education and health nevertheless do need to have some knowledge of the myriad administrative rules and procedures, including due process procedures, relating to the delivery of health services in school settings.

Case Law or The Law of Judicial Decision (Also Called Common Law)

Another important source of law evolves from the judicial branch of government or the federal and state judicial (court) systems. Judicial law—the law of judicial decision—is also referred to as case law, judge-made law, or common law. When a law suit is filed by a plaintiff (the party bringing the action), the defendant (the party against whom the complaint is brought) is notified, and both parties prepare for trial before a judge, sometimes with a jury. Courts are regularly required to determine whether a statute, regulation, or interpretation of either is constitutional (that is, compatible with either state or federal constitutional principles) or at odds with those principles and, thus, illegal.

An example of the interpretive function of the courts can be found in a number of landmark cases through which the U.S. Supreme Court established that the right to privacy, although not explicitly stated in the U.S. Constitution, is nevertheless constitutionally guaranteed through the 14th amendment. These cases established the right of every person "to withhold his or her person, personality, and property from unwarranted public scrutiny" (Bernzweig, 1996, p. 394). This includes a corollary that certain personal information belongs to the individual, who has the right to decide whether that information should be disclosed to others. (See chapter 8 for specific information on privacy and confidentiality.)

In addition to the function of interpretation, the courts are asked to settle controversies or conflicts in situations where statutes do not exist to resolve the issues. Most of negligence law, under which professional liability actions are brought, is found in case law, not in statute.

An example of an important legal concept in education that evolved from common law or court decisions is known as *in loco parentis.* This concept means "standing in place of the parent" and refers to the authority of school personnel, in the absence of the parent, to exercise judgment regarding, and to act toward, a student in the same way that the parent would judge and act in similar circumstances. *In loco parentis* served as a critical legal standard underlying the right of teachers to use corporal punishment, since parents legally have the right to use physical means, within reason, to discipline their own children. Of course, what is considered "within reason" has also changed as society and the decisions of judges have embraced other legal concepts, such as those related to the abuse of children by parents and other care givers, and certain rights of minor children and youth. Although the concept of *in loco parentis* has served as a major legal principle in public and private education and has been an especially strong concept where students reside in the school, its scope and applicability is gradually being narrowed by the courts owing to changing societal values and the increase of opposing legal principles. In the case of *New Jersey v. T.L.O.* (1985), the U.S. Supreme Court recognized that the authority of a public school to search a student in a disciplinary situation is not based entirely upon the principle of *in loco parentis,* but also springs from the specific relationship between the public school and its minor students.

In addition to the principal's general authority to make staffing decisions, the notion of *in loco parentis* may sometimes be the basis for a school administrator's belief that he or she can, at the request of the parent, "stand in" for the parent by performing (or assigning another staff person to perform) specialized health services for a student that the parents perform at home. If the administrators do not know the licensure laws for health professionals and their applica-

bility in schools, they may assume that the traditional legal concept of *in loco parentis* supports them if they take on such responsibilities. Furthermore, *in loco parentis* does *not* extend the traditional legal immunity from suit that applies to family members caring for each other. A principal in an Oregon public school, at the request of a student's parent, assigned a health aide, Carol Mitts, the task of performing clean intermittent catheterization for that student. When the health aide, who had been trained by the parent, sued the district and the principal, the Oregon State Board of Nursing (1989) was consulted by the court and ruled that the principal was practicing nursing without a license. Following the Declaratory Ruling, the case was settled out of court (Gary Smith, Court Clerk, Washington County Courthouse, written communication to Nadine Schwab, May 30, 1997). (See also the discussions of licensure and delegation in chapter 4 and "Staffing for Individualized School Health Services" in chapter 12.)

Precedent and Jurisdiction

Specific court decisions may become precedent for later cases that address the same legal issue. Earlier decisions of the court usually cannot be contraindicated in later decisions; this legal principle is referred to as *stare decisis,* meaning "to stand by things decided" or "let the decision stand" (Bernzweig, 1996, p. 309). Thus, using the written precedent provided by decisions in other cases, the courts also have the power to make law. For example, the court decisions establishing the right to privacy as a guaranteed right under the 14th amendment of the U.S. Constitution became the basis for further rulings on privacy and related issues. In 1985, a New Jersey court decided the controversy in the Karen Quinlan case regarding the right to refuse or discontinue treatment. The court held that the right to privacy found in the 14th amendment protects an individual's right to forego or terminate life-prolonging treatment and permitted the guardian to consent to the removal of Ms. Quinlan's respirator (*In re Quinlan,* 1976). Thus, the first case decisions regarding the right to privacy became the basis for further legal actions and interpretations.

Just as state statutes are binding only in the state that enacts them, case law is binding in the court jurisdiction that made the ruling, whether it is a state court, a federal district court, or the U.S. Supreme Court. Jurisdictional authority is based on federal and state constitutions and statutes. The federal courts have jurisdiction over federal issues and conflicts between citizens from different states. State courts hear cases involving state issues and disputes, and when both federal and state laws are involved in a particular case, the choice between federal or state court becomes another issue to be determined in litigation. Some courts, such as state juvenile courts, are specialized and only have jurisdiction in the specialty area.

Although one court's decision may not strictly apply to a similar issue in another jurisdiction, it is typical for attorneys who are arguing a difficult issue for the first time to cite decisions from other states or federal courts addressing the same problem. While decisions from one state are not binding on neighboring states, state court judges do consider relevant decisions from other jurisdictions.

Despite such considerations, differences in decisions do occur and conflicts in the case law surrounding school health services issues do exist, as later chapters will illustrate. Conflicts among courts in a single state must be resolved by the highest court in that state (usually, but not always, called the "State Supreme Court"); conflicts among federal districts are resolved by the appropriate federal circuit Court of Appeals, and, if the appeals courts are in conflict, the issue remains to be resolved by the U.S. Supreme Court. If the U.S. Supreme Court has ruled on an issue, that decision is binding on all state and federal courts at all levels. For example, when the U.S. Supreme Court ruled on the issue of whether or not "private duty" nursing services are related services under IDEA (March, 1999), its ruling became binding on all federal district courts, including those that had previously ruled differently (*Cedar Rapids Community School District v. Garret F.,* 1999). (See chapter 13 for further discussion.)

In terms of hierarchy, courts will give deference to the Constitutions, federal and state in that order, then to statutes, then to regulations, and then to other sources in deciding a conflict. With rare exceptions, courts will not decide theoretical questions; they are limited to considerations of current cases or controversies. (See Appendix C for information regarding the federal court system).

Precedent by Standard Setting

Unlike most laws, the federal Individuals with Disabilities Education Act, or IDEA (formerly called the Education of All Handicapped Children Act, or EHA) focuses on individual needs by specifically requiring that public schools evaluate children with disabilities and, if necessary, develop individualized education programs for each such child according to his or her

disability. Thus, an appropriate educational program for one child with a disability (and court decisions regarding it) will have no relevance for another child, with or without disabilities. When the educational program for a child with a disability is appealed to court, new law may be created by the court in developing the standards to be applied or procedures to be followed in the decision-making process. These standards or procedures are considered precedent in future cases; however, whether the specific program is found acceptable or not will usually have no impact on other children's educational rights—that is, will not constitute precedent for future cases.

The following cases are examples of court-provided standards, which are discussed in greater detail in chapters 12 and 13. In *Rowley* (*Board of Education of the Hendrick Hudson Central School District v. Rowley,* 1982), the U.S. Supreme Court established the standard for court review of special education appeals. *Tatro* (*Irving Independent School District v. Tatro,* 1984) and *Detsel* (*Detsel v. Auburn Enlarged City School District Board of Education,* 1987), among others, concern whether specific health care services required by individual children must be provided, free of charge, by the public schools in which they are enrolled, as services related to special education. *Honig* (*Honig v. Doe,* 1988) established some basic procedural requirements for discipline of students with disabilities. The standards established by these cases are frequently cited in later cases that address similar issues.

Other Legal Standards

In addition to constitutional, statutory, and case law, there are additional legal standards that may apply to schools and school health practices.

Opinions of Attorneys General

The Attorney General in a state is the official charged with giving legal advice to state agencies and officials. The Attorney General may respond to a request for an opinion on a particular legal question; the opinion of the Office of the Attorney General provides information to the public about the position the state would take if the issue were to be challenged in court. The agency that the opinion affects generally will follow the opinion or, if the agency disagrees, will seek to change the relevant statute or regulations on which the opinion is based. Attorneys General have issued opinions directly and indirectly relevant to school health services—for example, on a public school's responsibility to accept DNR orders (Maryland) and the limits of practice of certified emergency medical technicians (Connecticut).

Opinions of state Attorneys General are usually available in two ways: through the state agency to which a specific opinion applies and through law libraries that include published state material. However, since opinions are not always indexed and publication schedules may be slow, an inquiry to the state agency may yield more prompt answers.

Declaratory Rulings

A declaratory ruling is a determination by a court or an administrative agency of the rights of an individual, a class of people, or the parties in a dispute; it can also be an opinion on a matter of law. Administrative agencies can issue declaratory rulings that interpret a law or regulation within their authority. In some states, boards overseeing the practice of health professionals do not have the power to issue regulations directly, but must do so through a more complicated process of review by the state health department. Where this is true, professional boards have sometimes chosen to issue "declaratory rulings." These documents, which are not issued through the formal regulation making, are primarily used by the professional board to guide administrative proceedings, including those related to discipline issues. While not binding *per se,* such rulings may be considered "standards of practice" within the state and may be cited as such in a civil suit. For example, the Connecticut Board of Examiners for Nursing issued a declaratory ruling on the Scope of Practice of Licensed Practical Nurses (LPNs) in 1989 and another on Delegation by Licensed Nurses to Unlicensed Assistive Personnel in 1995. These rulings, once issued, became a practice standard for nurses working in Connecticut. Declaratory rulings are usually not indexed and may be difficult to locate. A letter to the professional board or pertinent governmental agency, requesting a copy of any rulings related to a specific topic, may be the best way to determine whether any rulings pertaining to the issue exist in the state. Access to such state agency documents is assured by the Freedom of Information Act in most states.

Municipal Enactments

Within counties, cities, or other governmental subdivisions, there may also be municipal enactments, often called ordinances. These rules will rarely directly affect the educational environment, but depending upon the subject, they may be important. For example, some cities now limit, by zoning ordinance, the minimum distance that certain businesses must be from school

grounds. Municipal requirements for public employees may affect school staff members or public health nurses assigned to work in public schools. Examples of such requirements are hiring, supervision, and discipline and termination procedures; residence requirements; and pension plans.

Public Agency Interpretations: Policy Statements and Guidelines

Federal and state agencies may issue guidelines and policy statements. Although these guidelines do not have the same force as law and regulation, they usually function as interpretations or "standards of practice" that, if applicable, do have implications for school districts and their personnel. (See the section below on "Negligence and Liability" for further discussion.)

CLASSIFICATION OF LAWS

There are two major classifications of law for consideration within this book: criminal law and civil law. While this book primarily addresses civil law, it is important to understand the differences and implications of each.

Criminal Law

Criminal law addresses violations of specific criminal statutes. Criminal actions are statutory in nature and are brought by a governmental authority, such as a state or federal law enforcement agency, not an individual. At one time, criminal law had little application to schools or school nursing services. Today, however, with the escalation of violence, drug problems, weapons possession, and crimes on school grounds, it is important to know one's obligations under the state's criminal statutes to report observations of criminal behavior of students. Criminal law also applies to school nurses and other school professionals should they be involved in illegal behavior, such as stealing controlled drugs or falsifying student medication records. Failure to report suspicion of the abuse or neglect of a student, depending on the state's law and regulations, or violation of the state's nurse practice act (e.g., practicing nursing without a license) may also precipitate criminal charges. In criminal actions, the standard for finding the defendant guilty is "beyond a reasonable doubt."

Civil Law

Civil actions may include lawsuits such as those alleging negligence, breach of contract, discrimination (under state or federal law), product liability, and many others. These cases may be brought by governmental authorities or by individuals; remedies sought can include monetary relief or injunctive relief, which is designed to prevent further episodes of the same conduct. Most civil actions involving public schools or school personnel fall into the categories of administrative proceedings and tort actions, as explained below.

Civil actions are brought in state or federal court, depending upon whether the conflict relates to underlying state or federal law. Issues raising purely state questions may not be filed in federal court, although some federal actions may be heard in state court. Where the issue is a purely state one, a decision by the highest state court is final and binding on the citizens of that state, but not on those of other states. An appeal of these state issues may be brought into the federal court system only where there is an issue of federal law. Thus, not all state issues may be appealed to the U. S. Supreme Court. Issues of federal law are generally filed in the federal courts. Similar to the state system, when a federal case is appealed to the U.S. Supreme Court, and the court rules on the topic at issue in the case, its decision is binding on the entire country.

Administrative Proceedings

Congress and the state legislatures provide administrative procedures within many governmental agencies to address civil issues that fall within the technical expertise of the specific agencies. Complainants are required to exhaust these designated administrative remedies in an attempt to resolve the conflicts prior to going to court. Three examples of administrative relief or remedy that are important in this book are special education hearings under the Individuals with Disabilities Education Act (IDEA); discrimination complaints under Section (§) 504; and proceedings before state licensing boards.

Special education hearings may be requested by the parent of a child with a disability or by the school district responsible for providing the child's education to address complaints based on state or federal special education regulations. Such complaints may concern the following:

- access to public school records about the child's identification, evaluation, and educational placement, and provision of a free appropriate public education;

- notice by the school district concerning a proposal or refusal to initiate or change the identification, evaluation, or placement, or provision of a free appropriate public education; and

- an opportunity to present complaints concerning the identification, evaluation, or educational placement of a child, or the provision of a free, appropriate public education.

Federal IDEA regulations provide some states with the option of having a two-level system of hearings (New York, Pennsylvania, and Michigan) or a one-level system (Connecticut, Iowa, and Utah). In either case, the hearing officer or hearing panel acts independently. After receiving the final written decision from a hearing, parties to a special education dispute may appeal that decision in federal district court or in a state court under state law, as applicable.

Under § 504 of the 1973 Rehabilitation Act, the Office for Civil Rights (OCR) at the U.S. Department of Education investigates complaints of discrimination on the basis of disability in public schools that receive federal funds. OCR provides administrative remedies including a form of mediation, investigation, and letter rulings. Under limited circumstances, either party (family or school district) may appeal the OCR ruling to the federal court system.

Another type of administrative procedure occurs when a licensed health professional is reported to his or her state licensing board for unsafe or poor practice. Under state statute, such boards have the authority to investigate complaints and take disciplinary action, including suspension or revocation of the professional's license to practice in the state. The professional must be given notice of the complaints and an opportunity to respond. For example, in the *Mitts* case, cited in the section on "Case Law" above, the Oregon Board of Nursing suspended the license of the school nurse. After the licensing board has taken action, the action or decision may be appealed to a state court.

Tort Actions

Tort law, one branch of civil law, addresses wrongful acts that are committed by individuals against other individuals or entities. These actions are considered private wrongs, rather than wrongs against society, as in criminal actions. A tort results from the breach of a legal duty that "exists by virtue of society's expectations regarding interpersonal conduct as opposed to a legal duty that exists by virtue of a contractual relationship" (Springhouse Corporation, 1996, p. 202). Most court actions involving personal injuries, including negligence and malpractice cases, are tort actions. Tort law provides injured individuals the opportunity to seek compensation, usually financial, for the damages suffered. Torts are generally classified as intentional, if the defendant intended the harm, or unintentional, if the defendant only intended the act (or omission of an act), not the harm. The tort of negligence does not require any intent on the part of the defendant, but intention is required in the torts of assault, battery, invasion of privacy, libel, false imprisonment, and intentional infliction of emotional distress (Bernzweig, 1996, p. 21; Brent, 1997, p. 108).

CONFLICTS BETWEEN LAWS

A major point of discussion in the chapters that follow is the extent to which laws within states conflict with one another and, as a result, appear to place conflicting responsibilities over the same issues upon educators and school health professionals. In addition to conflicts within state law (that is, among the education code and the health code), there are also inconsistencies between federal and state laws, and even among federal laws.

It is a general principle of federal Constitutional law that, where there is a conflict between federal and state law, the federal law will prevail. However, there are many areas in which the federal government may not directly legislate or does not have jurisdiction. For example, the legal regulation and licensure of health care providers is generally accomplished within the states. This accounts for the variation among states in the scope and regulation of nursing practice and the variation among states in the identification of health care professionals who must be licensed. With the major exception of health care funding, in fact, most aspects of health care are regulated within states, while education law, some of which addresses the same subject matter, is both state and federal (for example, education records and confidentiality of student information).

Beyond conflicts among laws, there are also conflicts between ethical principles that guide professional decision making. Conflicts in the law and in ethical principles give rise to the "legal and ethical dilemmas" regularly faced by school health professionals. In a discussion of the fundamental elements of ethics, Purtilo points out that "[a]lmost all ethical conflicts in health care arise from clashes among two or more duties, two or more competing rights, or duties competing with rights" (Purtilo, 1996, p. 29).

It is no wonder, then, that school health professionals are sometimes confused or uncertain about their legal and ethical obligations to students, staff, and employers. These conflicts, which will be further explained in later chapters, create philosophic, practice, and legal dilemmas both for educators and health care providers, as they seek to comply with all of the rele-

vant, and sometimes inconsistent, law and with ethical standards of practice.

RELEVANT FEDERAL LAWS

The focus of this book is on the laws that impact the provision of health services within or linked to schools. Chapters 12 and 13 will offer limited discussion of private special education programs into which students with disabilities are placed by school districts and school health services provided at public expense in private schools. In order to provide a background for the more detailed material discussed in later chapters, the following sections will address, in very general terms, the most important laws governing health services in school settings.

Many federal laws directly and indirectly affect public education in the United States; private education is less extensively regulated, and except for anti-discrimination laws and federal funding requirements, regulation of private schools is left to the states. In general, the important federal laws can be categorized as related to education, civil rights, or health.

Federal Education Laws

Federal education laws, usually referred to as "funding statutes," have been enacted by Congress to provide grant incentives to state and local education agencies to develop or improve specific programs, such as special education, or to stipulate practices that state and local agencies must follow in order to receive federal funds. States can choose not to apply for a specific grant, and some grants are only available to a limited number of states or local districts. When the Education of All Handicapped Children Act (now IDEA) was enacted in 1975, all states were eligible to apply for grants; for many years, however, New Mexico chose not to request federal assistance to support educational programs for children who required special education. Similarly, although all states were eligible for funding to establish an early intervention system for infants and toddlers with disabilities, under Part C (previously Part H) of the Individuals with Disabilities Education Act (IDEA), some states chose not to apply for the grant monies available.

When states choose not to apply for federal grants, it is usually because they consider the stipulations that come with the funds too costly or too difficult to implement—or, on occasion, that the state can do a better job without the grant. There are, however, a few federal education laws that state education agencies and local school districts are generally careful to comply with because violations can result in the loss of all federal education revenue. An example is the federal law establishing standards for confidentiality of student information, called the Family Educational Rights and Privacy Act (FERPA). Only those federal education laws that are universally applicable across states and most directly related to the provision of health services in schools will be addressed below. Many other federal laws that provide incentive grants to states—for example, in the areas of school lunch, nutrition education, and assistive technology—while important to understand for practice purposes, generally have fewer legal stipulations directly relevant to school health services programs and are not addressed in this book.

Individuals with Disabilities Education Act

This section provides an introduction to this significant federal education law and its basic provisions, while chapter 12 examines it in much greater depth, especially in regard to health services. Chapter 13 addresses current controversial issues and case law related to special education.

The Individuals with Disabilities Education Act (IDEA) was a 1990 update and renaming of the 1975 Education of All Handicapped Children Act (EHA). Several amendments were enacted in 1997, and the U.S. Department of Education published final revised IDEA regulations in 1999. Under the Act, free and appropriate education means "special education and related services provided at public expense, under public supervision and direction, without charge, which meet the standards of the state educational agency, and are in conformity with the Individualized Education Program (IEP)" as defined in the Act. Important amendments to EHA included provisions, among others, that

- required states to provide special education services to eligible preschool children;

- enabled parents who prevail over school districts in special education due process proceedings to recover their legal fees;

- changed the law's name to the "Individuals with Disabilities Education Act" (IDEA); and

- stipulated that parents must be members of the IEP team.

IDEA provides the standards for distribution of federal funds to states that provide a free, appropriate education in the least restrictive environment to students who qualify as disabled under the law. Each

state must submit a State Plan to the U.S. Department of Education for approval; the State Plans describe in detail how each state complies with the requirements of IDEA. In addition, the regulations that accompany this federal law provide that students must be evaluated for eligibility and, if eligible, shall receive special education and, if appropriate, related services such as the following:

- assistive technology services and devices;

- audiology;

- counseling services;

- early identification;

- medical services for evaluation purposes;

- occupational therapy;

- orientation and mobility (services);

- parent counseling and training;

- physical therapy;

- psychological services;

- recreation;

- rehabilitation services;

- planning for transition from programs for infants and toddlers to those for preschoolers; programs for preschoolers to those in primary and secondary public schools; and secondary school programs to post-secondary education and job training, or adaptive and life-skills training;

- school health services;

- social work services;

- speech language pathology;

- communication development services;

- therapeutic recreation; and

- transportation.

Special education and related services must be documented in an individualized education program (IEP) and/or individualized family service plan (IFSP) (Rosenfeld, 1994; updated for IDEA 1997 and 1999 regulations).

Procedural Requirements. IDEA requires school districts to follow certain procedures. Districts must do the following:

- seek out children with disabilities (a procedure referred to as "Child Find");

- secure parental consent prior to evaluation;

- evaluate to identify the child's strengths and weaknesses;

- develop, in a multidisciplinary team meeting including the child's parents, an individualized education program (IEP) to meet the child's individual educational needs;

- obtain parental consent prior to a special education placement;

- make an educational placement for the child in the least restrictive environment for that child;

- review the child's progress at least annually; and

- re-evaluate the student, with parental consent, at least every three years.

Eligibility under IDEA. Students who may be eligible for special education must have a disability that significantly interferes with learning—that is, that adversely affects their educational performance. IDEA defines a "child with a disability" as a child with

mental retardation, hearing impairment (including deafness), speech or language impairments, visual impairments (including blindness), serious emotional disturbance, orthopedic impairments, autism, traumatic brain injury, other health impairments, or specific learning disabilities and who, by reason thereof, needs special education and related services.

For students in elementary and secondary public schools, eligibility for special education requires the presence of a disability or disabilities as defined above. The disability must be identified by professional evaluation techniques AND must be shown to interfere with the student's educational progress. Children with a disability or disabilities that do not interfere with learning may be eligible for support under § 504, which is a civil rights law. Children with learning problems (e.g., poor reading skills), but no identifiable disability, may be eligible for remedial services under regular education but are not eligible for special education. The diagnosis of a disability that interferes with learning requires specific procedures identified in the IDEA regulations. While states must serve students who qualify according to the 10 federally defined categories of disabilities cited above, states may choose to provide special education services to students who qualify under additional categories of disabilities defined within the state's education statutes. It is important to

note that all students who qualify for services under IDEA are also qualified for protection under federal civil rights legislation as described later in this chapter.

Eligibility for 3- to 5-year-olds. IDEA, Part B, addresses special education eligibility for students between 3 and 21 years of age. Between the ages of 3 and 5 years, children who demonstrate a disability or developmental delay that is likely to significantly interfere with future educational performance are eligible for special education services. The federal law does not require that such students be identified within one of the disability categories listed above for school-age children, only that they be at risk for such a disability. Therefore, children with chronic illness or other chronic health conditions may be eligible for preschool special education services if it can be demonstrated that they are already developmentally delayed or their condition puts them at significant risk for educational disability in the future. (See chapter 12 for "Determination of Eligibility for Special Education.")

Individualized Education Program. Under Part B, a child who is determined eligible for special education and related services is entitled to an Individualized Education Program (IEP), which specifies (1) the child's current strengths and weaknesses; (2) individual student objectives for learning; (3) appropriate program modifications, curriculum adaptations, and related services that are necessary in order for the student to make appropriate educational progress; (4) related services to be provided; 5) participation in the regular education program; and (6) timelines and methods of evaluation to determine if the student-specific objectives are being met.

Eligibility under IDEA, Part C. IDEA, Part C, addresses early intervention services for infants and toddlers. Criteria for identification and eligibility vary from state to state. In some states, the infant or toddler must have a diagnosed condition that is known to lead to significant developmental delay or learning disability (e.g., Down Syndrome) or must demonstrate significant developmental delay in one or more areas of development. In other states, infants and toddlers who are at significant risk for such delays or disabilities, but do not yet have a diagnosed condition, are also served under these birth-to-three early intervention services. The purpose of Part C legislation is to provide incentive funding to states to assist them in creating a system of early intervention services for infants, toddlers, and their families in order to maximize the children's potential for development and learning. The lead state agency for birth-to-three services under Part C varies;

in many states it is the state department of health, while in others it may be a state department of education or social services, or another state agency.

Individualized Family Service Plan. Under Part C, an infant or toddler who is determined eligible for services is entitled to an Individualized Family Service Plan (IFSP) that specifies the following:

- individualized child objectives for development and learning;

- an appropriate program, to the extent possible in "natural settings" with the modifications, adaptations, related services, and parent supports that are necessary in order for the child to make appropriate developmental progress; and

- timelines and methods of evaluation to determine if the child- and family-specific objectives are being met.

Appeal Process. IDEA specifies an appeal process for parents and school districts when the two do not agree on the eligibility of, or IEP for, a student. It also specifies an appeal process on the eligibility of, or IFSP for, an infant or toddler. The legal option of parents to challenge an eligibility, placement, or program decision is most often referred to as the child's or family's "due process right." Due process complaints beyond the local or regional level are processed through the state department of education and, if not settled satisfactorily at that level, may become civil actions in the regular court system.

See "Administrative Proceedings" earlier in this chapter for a simple introduction to the due process provisions of IDEA and chapter 12 for detailed information regarding IDEA, its provisions, and procedural requirements. Chapters 12 and 13 contain significant case law decisions about students with health-related disabilities under IDEA and associated issues for school and health professionals.

Family Educational Rights and Privacy Act

The Family Educational Rights and Privacy Act (FERPA) is a federal education law that was enacted in 1974 in response to reported abuses of confidentiality, denial of parental access to student records, poor or inconsistent record-keeping practices in school districts across the country, and other records issues. Also known as the Buckley Amendment, FERPA is the primary federal legislation that affects record keeping in public schools, including the records of school health

and related services personnel (Gelfman & Schwab, 1991). Indeed, school health records—that is, records kept by school nurses, physicians, psychologists, and social workers under the auspices of a school district or by contract to a district—and records sent to a school district for educational planning by outside health care agencies, are all considered education records under FERPA. In many states, medical records released to schools with consent are subject to protections under both FERPA and the state medical records laws. These protections are not always consistent. (See chapter 9 for further discussion.) Among other requirements, FERPA requires education agencies to protect the confidentiality of all student records and to provide parents with access to all of the school records of their children. (See chapters 8, 9, and 10 for additional information on confidentiality and student records.)

Elementary and Secondary Education Act

The Elementary and Secondary Education Act (ESEA) of 1974 and subsequent amendments, including the Improving America's Schools Act of 1994, are best explained by quoting the Congressional statement of policy that introduces the law:

> The Congress declares it to be the policy of the United States that a high-quality education for all individuals and a fair and equal opportunity to obtain that education are a societal good, are a moral imperative, and improve the life of every individual, because the quality of our individual lives ultimately depends on the quality of the lives of others (20 U.S.C. 6301).

Congress's Statement of Purpose for the ESEA is also instructive:

> The purpose of this subchapter is to enable schools to provide opportunities for children served to acquire the knowledge and skills contained in the challenging State content standards and to meet the challenging State performance standards developed for all children. This purpose shall be accomplished by
>
> (1) ensuring high standards for all children and aligning the efforts of States, local education agencies, and schools to help children served under this subchapter to reach such standards;

(2) providing children an enriched and accelerated educational program, including, when appropriate, the use of the arts, through school wide programs or through additional services that increase the amount and quality of instructional time so that children served under this subchapter receive at least the classroom instruction that other children receive;

(3) promoting school-wide reform and ensuring access of children (from the earliest grades) to effective instructional strategies and challenging academic content that includes intensive complex thinking and problem-solving experiences;

(4) significantly upgrading the quality of instruction by providing staff in participating schools with substantial opportunities for professional development;

(5) coordinating services under all parts of this subchapter with each other, with other educational services, and, to the extent feasible, with health and social service programs funded from other sources;

(6) affording parents meaningful opportunities to participate in the education of their children at home and at school;

(7) distributing resources, in amounts sufficient to make a difference, to areas and schools where needs are greatest;

(8) improving accountability, as well as teaching and learning, by using State assessment systems designed to measure how well children served under this subchapter are achieving challenging State student performance standards expected of all children; and

(9) providing greater decision making authority and flexibility to schools and teachers in exchange for greater responsibility for student performance (20 U.S.C. 6301).

Over time, a variety of specialized federal programs have been incorporated into ESEA, with the requirement that states and local school districts meet all ESEA standards if they expect to receive any ESEA federal funding. While the amounts of such funding may be relatively small for each separate program, the total amounts are significant enough that states are reluctant to challenge federal requirements that may differ from earlier state mandates.

A recent example is the Gun Free Schools Act of 1994, which requires expulsion for at least one year for public school students found in possession of a firearm in school. The Act provides for discretion by the school superintendent to modify expulsion requirements on a case-by-case basis. Many states already had student discipline statutes, which included weapons offenses and penalties, and there has been a long history of court decisions in the area of students' rights in suspensions and expulsions. The new federal requirement, while a popular response to reports of increasing violence in schools, could be seen as intruding into an area where state legislatures and courts have been providing sufficient direction.

General Education Provisions Act (GEPA) and Education Department General Administrative Requirements (EDGAR)

The general purpose of this law and its regulations is to provide the rules under which the U.S. Department of Education operates in dealing with state and local education agencies. Matters such as requirements for grant applications, federal monitoring and auditing, and due process protections for fund recipients are found here. In addition, there is a requirement that children who have been enrolled in private schools by their parents be provided with a "genuine opportunity" to participate in federally funded educational programs. (See chapter 12 for further details.)

Hatch Amendment

In reaction to questions raised about curriculum and testing practices, Congress passed the Hatch Amendment to GEPA in 1978, amending it in 1994. After a general requirement that all instructional materials be available for parental inspection, there is a specific requirement for parental consent prior to any "survey, analysis, or evaluation" in a federally funded program concerning

political affiliations; mental and psychological problems potentially embarrassing to the student or his family; sex behavior and attitudes; illegal, anti-social, self-incriminating and demeaning behavior; critical appraisals of other individuals with whom respondents have close family relationships; legally recognized privileged or analogous relationships; or income.

While the intent to protect family privacy is reasonable, it is difficult to measure compliance with this law. Additionally, strict compliance with the parental consent requirements could jeopardize timely assessment and referral of students seeking professional advice concerning health and mental health issues or for suspected child abuse and may be in conflict with specific federal and state confidentiality requirements.

Federal Civil Rights Legislation

The Rehabilitation Act of 1973, in particular § 504, and the American with Disabilities Act of 1990 are the major federal laws that address the civil rights of individuals with disabilities. Because students with disabilities, including many who have chronic health conditions, may be "eligible" for protection under these laws, it is important for school- and community-health professionals to know their eligibility requirements and protected rights. In particular, education and health professionals should understand how these laws apply to school settings, school health services, and student rights, and how to explain these provisions to families of students who may be eligible. As an important distinction from the IDEA, these civil rights laws are not funding provisions and, while they mandate that state and local education agencies comply with the law's requirements, no funding is provided. A third civil rights mandate, 42 U.S.C. § 1983 (originally the Ku Klux Klan Act of 1871), enables individuals injured by public officials who abuse their authority to sue and recover damages from those individuals.

Section 504

Section 504 of the Rehabilitation Act of 1973 is a civil rights provision that prohibits discrimination, on the basis of handicap, by recipients of federal funds. Therefore, state and municipal agencies, most schools and hospitals, many employers, and other agencies that receive any federal funding have been prohibited since 1973 from discriminating against individuals who qualify under the law's definition of "handicapped." In simple terms, § 504 requires all public schools, and those private schools that also receive federal funding, to provide individuals with disabilities "access" to their buildings, programs, and services, and prohibits them from excluding a child solely because of a "physical or mental handicap."

Eligibility. A child (or individual) with a disability is broadly defined under the law (see chapter 11 for the specific § 504 definitions of a "handicapped individual") and includes children with a physical or mental health impairment that "substantially interferes with a major life function." Examples of such major life functions, as cited in the Act, include "caring for oneself, performing manual tasks, walking, seeing, hearing, speaking, breathing, learning and working." Because the law does not provide an exhaustive list of all such major life functions, it is incumbent on health professionals to identify when a condition does interfere with a major life function, interpret how it does so, and communicate that information to parents and educators. For example, a 5-year-old boy with diabetes has a condition that substantially interferes with normal metabolism (certainly a "major life function"). This student cannot be discriminated against—that is, the school district cannot bar him from attending school or refuse to provide appropriate "aids and services" related to his health condition that are necessary for him to access an "appropriate" education. Furthermore, the district cannot keep the student from participating in field trips and other non-academic and extracurricular activities on the sole basis of his disability; nor can it require the parent to provide the necessary health services or monitoring required by the student. Thus, if the student is a young, brittle diabetic who requires glucose monitoring, the administration of insulin on a regular or as-needed basis, modifications for snacks and meals, daily monitoring of health status, and education regarding self-care in order to maintain his health and to access the regular school program, the school district may be required to provide those services, even if they require the part-time services of a qualified registered nurse, and even if such a nurse is not usually available in the school. An alternative plan for the young student with brittle diabetes might be to transport him to a school within the district that has better nursing coverage and more rapid access to 9-1-1 services.

Among all students who qualify as disabled under § 504, only those whose disabilities significantly interfere with the major life function of *learning,* and fit within one of the 10 eligibility categories, also qualify under IDEA as eligible for special education and related services (see "Individuals with Disabilities Education Act" above). All students eligible under IDEA qualify as disabled under § 504; special education students are a smaller subset of § 504-eligible students. The student who is a brittle diabetic but is progressing normally in school would be eligible for services under § 504, but not under IDEA, because his condition is not interfering with learning. On the other hand, if his health status is sufficiently unstable that he is frequently absent from school and his classroom performance is significantly affected by fluctuating blood sugar levels, his health condition might be interfering with learning and he should be evaluated for eligibility under IDEA as "other health impaired."

Identification. Parents, health care providers, and school nurses are likely individuals to refer children with health-related disabilities to the school for identification and educational planning under § 504. However, § 504 also mandates that state and local education agencies identify unserved children with disabilities. Parents usually require assistance in obtaining information, education, and resources related to the provisions of these laws, their children's rights under the laws, and procedures for referral and participation in the decision-making process.

Procedural Safeguards. Section 504 is a civil rights statute, not a funding statute like IDEA, and its requirements are stated in general terms. The regulations for § 504 identify areas in which school districts must not discriminate on the basis of disability, but these regulations do not spell out procedures for school districts the way IDEA and its regulations do. In fact, because of the lack of specific requirements and the lack of funding, many school districts have been slow to recognize their responsibilities under § 504.

Nevertheless, each school district that receives *any* federal financial assistance must establish procedural safeguards to insure compliance with § 504. At a minimum, the safeguards must include annual notice of rights, including designation of a coordinator, right of parental access to student records (as required under FERPA; see chapter 9), and an opportunity for a hearing. The § 504 regulations cite special education procedural safeguards as an acceptable way of meeting the hearing requirement, but some states have not given § 504 jurisdiction to state special education hearing officers for complaints with no IDEA claims. Once again, there is variation from state to state and from school district to school district.

Appeal Process. Complaints under § 504 can be filed with the Office for Civil Rights (OCR) of the U.S. Department of Education. OCR has 10 regional offices that handle most complaint investigations. (See Appendix D.) In some states, § 504 complaints must be submitted to the Complaint Officer at the State Department of Education prior to filing with OCR. (A detailed discussion regarding § 504, including the rights of students under this legislation, eligibility requirements, due process rights, OCR decisions, case law examples, and specific issues for school health professionals, is provided in chapter 11.)

The Americans with Disabilities Act

The Americans with Disabilities Act (ADA) of 1990 reaffirms the civil rights of individuals with disabilities and extends their right of access to the "full range of services provided by both the public and private sectors, excluding religious entities and private clubs." In effect, the ADA expanded the scope of the civil rights mandates under § 504, such that the prior obligations of public agencies are now extended to private businesses and organizations, including private day care programs, nursery schools, elementary and secondary schools, and colleges and universities, regardless of whether or not they receive any federal funding. Therefore, preschoolers and students with health conditions that significantly interfere with a major life function cannot be discriminated against by the private sector.

Without additional cost to the family, private school or day-care programs, exclusive of those owned and operated by a religious entity, must provide certain accommodations, aids, and services to enable children with disabilities to access those programs so long as the students are otherwise eligible to attend. There are limitations to the extent of accommodations that might be required in an individual circumstance. For example, a private home day-care program with space for six infants and toddlers would probably not be required by the ADA to provide a full-time nurse for a ventilator-dependent toddler so that the toddler could safely attend the day-care program; the cost would be prohibitive and might force the day-care program out of business. Should the same toddler apply for attendance in a much larger day-care center where the cost of the nurse might not be so prohibitive and other children could profit from the presence of the nurse, the day-care program might, indeed, be required to provide that service, at no extra cost to the family. Because such services must be at no extra cost to the child with the disability (since that would constitute discrimination), the increased costs must be equally distributed across the tuition of all participants in the program. Litigation continues in this area.

Complaint Process. Parallel to the requirements of § 504, the ADA requires school districts to adopt policies and procedures to insure compliance with the Act. Complaints related to public schools may be filed with the local school district or with OCR at the U.S. Department of Education. Complaints related to private entities, such as private day care and nursery school programs, are filed with the Department of Justice.

(For further information about the ADA and its relevance for school health professionals, see chapter 11.)

Section 1983

Section 1983 is a federal civil rights law that provides a right of action for persons injured by public officials who abuse their authority. Accordingly, the U.S. Code provides that

> [e]very person who, under color of any statute, ordinance, regulation, custom or usage, of any State or Territory or the District of Columbia, subjects or causes to be subjected, any citizen of the United States or other person within the jurisdiction thereof to the deprivation of any rights, privileges, or immunities secured by the Constitution and laws, shall be liable to the party injured in an action at law, suit in equity, or other proper proceeding for redress.

Some claims against schools have been made under § 1983, which may be useful if no other law applies (e.g., § 504 or IDEA). For example, a parent might use § 1983 to challenge the use of excessive force by a school administrator in a discipline situation.

Federal Health Laws

Like federal education laws, there are federal laws related to health services far too numerous to mention in this book. Therefore, only those with the most direct applicability to the provision of health services within or linked to schools are mentioned below, and only those with the most significance related to legal issues in school health will be discussed in detail in other chapters.

Occupational Health and Safety Administration

Congress created by statute the Occupational Safety and Health Administration (OSHA), the federal agency responsible for issuing and enforcing regulations and investigating complaints related to the safety and health of employees in the workplace. OSHA requirements are applicable to private employers and are usually, but not universally, adopted by states making them applicable to public employers, as well. The various Occupational Safety and Health Administration (OSHA) mandates obligate employers to create and maintain a safe working environment for employees. While these requirements do not directly benefit students who are present in the school environment, they may indirectly influence safety conditions, such as the safe sterilization of medical equipment and other infection control measures that are necessary to protect students, as well as staff. In states where schools are required to meet OSHA standards, school districts can be (and have been) fined when they are investigated and found out of compliance with the OSHA regulations. Complaints or questions related to unsafe or unhealthy working conditions for employees in school settings should generally be reported to the OSHA section of the state's department of labor; the state's department of health may also be of assistance.

Regulations Related to Bloodborne Pathogens. Under the Occupational Safety and Health Act and its regulations related to occupational exposure to bloodborne pathogens, school districts are generally required, among other things to

- educate their personnel;

- document the training;

- offer, at no charge to the employees, hepatitis B vaccine to employees who have potential risk of contact with bloodborne pathogens within their regular job responsibilities, for example, special education teachers who work with young, developmentally delayed students or students with significant behavior problems, school nurses, coaches, others who provide direct health care (e.g., school physicians), first aid providers (e.g., health aides), and janitors; and

- provide employees with protective equipment and clothing (e.g., goggles, gloves, laboratory coats) when they are providing care that carries risk of contact with bloodborne pathogens.
(See chapter 6 for additional information.)

Tuberculosis. At the time that this chapter is being written, OSHA has reviewed public comments on its draft of the Compliance Directive for Occupational Exposure to Tuberculosis but has not implemented it. The Directive provides guidance and parameters to regional investigators for examining the compliance of facilities to the guidelines (American Nurses Association, 1995). It is not yet clear how, if implemented, this Directive will impact schools across the country. It should be noted that some states and some school districts are already testing students for tuberculosis and have adopted policies and procedures to prevent the spread of this disease.

Medical Records and Confidentiality

There are also federal laws protecting the confidentiality of medical records that deal with the evaluation and treatment of individuals for mental health and drug and alcohol abuse problems. Under the Alcohol and Drug Abuse Prevention and Treatment Act, these protections extend to minors when they seek treatment for drug and alcohol abuse. It is noteworthy that the federal requirements that protect the confidentiality of individuals receiving drug and alcohol services, including minors who seek help from student assistance teams in schools, are in conflict with the provisions of the Family Educational Rights and Privacy Act (FERPA), which requires that schools give parents access to all the school records of their minor children. (Further discussion of this issue, and other conflicts in the law related to minor's rights, can be found in chapters 8 and 9, and issues specifically related to the security of electronic data and computerized health records are addressed in chapter 10. Minors rights, *per se,* are discussed in chapter 7.) At the time this book is going to press, the U.S. Congress is considering establishing national standards of confidentiality for all medical records as part of a proposed "Patient's Bill of Rights" and a variety of other bills related to protecting the privacy of individuals' health care information.

Clinical Laboratory Improvement Amendments of 1988

The Clinical Laboratory Improvement Amendments of 1988 (CLIA) require that medical laboratories, hospitals, physician offices, and other entities that provide any on-site laboratory services, including such tests as hematocrits or throat cultures, meet federal standards as defined in the regulations. Therefore, school districts and school-based health centers providing any type of laboratory services, including those in the categories of "waived" tests, moderate-complexity tests, and high-complexity tests, are subject to these requirements. High-complexity tests are unlikely to be provided in any laboratory facility located in schools.

Home-style glucose monitoring kits and other tests "simple in complexity," such as dipstick urinalysis, are considered "waived tests." In a 1996 update of the regulations, a rapid strep test was also granted waived status with the provision that the user follow the manufacturer's instructions. School districts providing only waived tests must be registered with the Health Care Financing Administration (HCFA) of the U.S. Department of Health and Human Services under a "Certificate of Waiver." Districts that provide only waived tests are not required to conduct proficiency testing and are not subject to other quality control requirements of the law, although HCFA can inspect any site to investigate complaints or ensure that only waived tests are being performed. When students self-administer glucose

monitoring tests with their own kits, the requirements of CLIA do not apply.

According to CLIA requirements, the federal program for registering, monitoring, and inspecting laboratories must be self-supporting and must pay a yearly registration fee commensurate with the level of laboratory testing provided. Registration with a "Certificate of Waiver" requires payment of an annual user fee. School health services programs and school-based health centers will be monitored and inspected regularly if they are providing tests in the moderate-complexity category (e.g., standard throat culture). School districts need to pay one fee only (as an "umbrella agency" rather than on a per-building basis), and may not need to register at all if the samples are collected in school, but testing actually takes place in a community medical laboratory, physician's office, or other registered facility.

School districts and school-based health centers that provide nursing and primary care services to students (or any other clients) should stay apprised of changes in the CLIA regulations that may be pertinent to school settings.

RELEVANT STATE LAWS

State laws are generally organized by topical sections, such that one section contains the state's education statutes, another the state's health-related statutes, and so on. Statutes in a different section of the law from education can still directly impact schools and school personnel. There are requirements in the health sections of state statutes, for example, that can apply to schools. Many, but not all, state laws are accompanied by regulations that are written after the law is passed to further define the requirements and intent of the law. (See "Administrative Law or the Law of Government Agencies" under "Legislation [Statutory Law]" above).

Public education and the practice of medicine, nursing, and other health care professions are extensively regulated by state governments. Therefore, there can be considerable difference between the laws and practices in one state and those in another. Ellen Johnson, a school nurse in Tulsa, Oklahoma, lost her position in a local school district for refusing to administer medications under unsafe conditions and for trying to change what she considered to be dangerous medication practices: no physician orders were required; pills were delivered in plastic bags; and sometimes parent medications were brought in for school personnel to give to their child (*Ellen F. Johnson v. Independent School District No. 3* of Tulsa County, Oklahoma, 1989). In her previous position as a school nurse in New Jersey, state law had prohibited her from administering medications *except* with a physician's order, parental authorization, and delivery to the school in a properly labeled, original pharmacy container. In Oklahoma, medication administration in schools was not specifically regulated except by the nursing practice act (which was not enforced at that time), while in New Jersey it was highly regulated. Therefore, it is critical for school health professionals to know the state laws, regulations, and local customs that govern and influence education and health care practices.

State Education Laws

These statutes cover a diverse range of topics and issues related to education. Examples of such mandates, depending on the state, may include the following:

- the age range for mandatory school attendance,
- eligibility requirements for teacher certification,
- curriculum standards,
- continuing education requirements for teachers,
- mandated school health screenings,
- student immunization requirements,
- medication administration in schools,
- qualifications of coaches,
- student rights in suspensions and expulsions, and
- graduation requirements.

Depending on the state, pupil services professionals (e.g., school counselors, nurses, psychologists, social workers, and speech/language pathologists) may be eligible for, or required to hold, teacher certification in order to practice in schools. Other education statutes may define the qualifications for health professionals who work in schools but are not required to be teacher certified, such as school physicians, occupational and physical therapists, and sometimes school nurses. Certain communications between students and school personnel may also be the subject of a state mandate—for example, a Connecticut statute concerning private communications regarding assistance for a drug or alcohol problem (Sec. 10-154a, C.G.S.).

Also found within the education section of state laws are the state versions of, or companion versions to, federal education legislation. For example, each state legislates its own version of the federal special education mandates (IDEA); it may expand upon the federal

requirements according to the individual needs of the state, so long as the state's version meets the minimum requirements of the federal law. State mandates related to student records and confidentiality of student information largely follow the requirements of the federal Family Educational Rights and Privacy Act, as discussed above, but variations at the state level do exist. Therefore, it is important for school health professionals to become familiar with their state education laws, in addition to the federal education mandates.

State Health Laws

Like education laws, each state code has a section of law primarily related to health. These state health laws are even more diverse and numerous than those in the education section because

- they address topics and issues related to a more variable range of services, service providers, and sites of service;
- substandard services may lead to significant harm or even death; and
- health has been a more litigated area of the law.

Health laws that may be relevant to schools include those related to licensure of health professionals, paraprofessional certification, minors' rights to seek treatment for certain health conditions, and public health requirements. Public health laws may affect schools in relation to requirements for immunizations, reporting communicable diseases and excluding students with acute communicable infections, such as measles or Hepatitis A, and the health and safety requirements for, and inspections of, school facilities and grounds. In addition, state health mandates include companion requirements to federal health laws that impact schools, such as those related to the requirements of the Occupational Safety and Health Administration.

Not only should health professionals be familiar with state health mandates relevant to schools, but so should education administrators who have responsibility for the supervision of health professionals and sometimes even for carrying out delegated nursing activities. In addition, attorneys who advise districts on educational matters today need a working knowledge of these laws and their applicability to schools.

Licensure of Health Professionals

All states mandate the licensure of registered nurses, clinical psychologists, and physicians. Most states also license or certify social workers, occupational and physical therapists, speech-language pathologists, respiratory therapists, and others, including chiropractors and naturopaths. While schools are not considered by educators to be health care settings, professional practice acts are state laws that define the scope of practice of the profession within the state, regardless of the practice setting. Thus, the practice of these professions remains a licensed function whether it occurs in a private practice, hospital, home, or school. Furthermore, if unlicensed personnel are used in school settings to carry out nursing tasks, a professional nurse who delegates to such a person may be regulated by the state board of nursing as to how and under what circumstances such delegation takes place. (See chapter 4 for additional information.) It is also true, however, that certain states (e.g., Texas, Kansas, and West Virginia) include provisions in the regulations or declaratory rulings of the state board of nursing that distinguish, in general terms, between practice requirements in health care institutions, such as acute care hospitals and rehabilitation centers, and those in community settings, such as homes, schools, and group homes (Schwab & Haas, 1995).

In general, state licensure requirements set only minimal qualifications for the practice of health professionals within a state. While these licensure laws are found in the health section of state statutes, education law may provide further regulation for practice in schools. For example, education regulations in several states (e.g., California, Massachusetts, Illinois, Pennsylvania, and Connecticut) require credentials beyond registered nurse (RN) licensure for qualified school nurses and nurse practitioners. Beyond state laws, agency credentialing requirements, professional standards, and institutional policies may further dictate personnel qualifications: a school physician may be required to be a pediatrician and a school nurse may be required to hold a bachelor's or master's degree in nursing, even though these qualifications are beyond the minimum standards necessary for state licensure. Related to the licensure and education requirements for health professionals, but stemming instead from special education law, the IDEA regulations require professionals serving special education students to meet the highest entry-level requirements for practice of the profession in that state (34 Code of Federal Regulations [C.F.R.] 300.136).

Conflicts may arise in a state when the licensure requirements for health professionals, such as nurses or therapists, set legal practice standards that are not recognized in schools or are even countermanded by education law, regulations, or state education agency

guidelines. Such conflicts most frequently arise from questions of who can perform a health care activity (e.g., medication administration, activities of daily living, or range of motion exercises), who makes the decision about who will perform such activities for a specific student, and who is responsible for supervising the assigned individual. (See chapters 4 and 5 for further discussion.)

Certification of Health Care Paraprofessionals

Many states have mandates regarding the functions, training, and qualifications of health care paraprofessionals, such as occupational therapy assistants, physical therapy assistants, nursing assistants, and home health aides. Regulation most often relates to the content of their training courses and the requirement that they function under the supervision of the licensed professional. In health care settings, health professionals usually assign or delegate client care to certified and legally recognized assistants. In some states, these laws may provide that particular health care professionals (e.g., occupational therapists) can only delegate tasks that are within their scope of practice to individuals with certain credentials (e.g., certified occupational assistants). When this is true, conflicts may arise when the health professional is expected to teach certain health care activities to other members of the education team who do not hold those credentials. Since the 1997 IDEA amendments allow states to use paraprofessionals to assist in providing special education and related services, so long as they are "appropriately trained and supervised," relevant state health laws may establish standards in this regard (34 C.F.R. 300.136(f)). (Further discussion of paraprofessionals can be found in chapters 4 and 5 and, in relation to IDEA, chapters 12 and 13.)

Minors Rights

Each state regulates the age at which persons are considered to have reached the age of majority, at which time they are considered capable of marrying, voting, and contracting legally, among other obligations. This age is set at 18 years in all but three states: the age of majority is 19 in Alabama and 21 in Mississippi and Pennsylvania, except that Mississippi law specifies that anyone 18 or older is considered an adult for purposes of consenting to medical care (Donovan, 1997). However, the law realizes that persons under the age of majority are not necessarily incapable of all decision making. Thus, states generally permit minors (at various ages, depending on the statute) to seek and receive certain types of health care, such as treatment for venereal disease, drug abuse, or pregnancy, without parental involvement. This creates conflicts between state health law and federal education law (see discussion of FERPA earlier in the chapter) if the records of that treatment or referral for treatment are transmitted to the schools, and it creates confidentiality dilemmas for school nurses, social workers, psychologists and other pupil services specialists who work with minors seeking confidential health and counseling services or referral for such services. (These state health laws and other federal and state mandates that may pertain to the rights of minors in school settings are discussed in detail in chapter 7. See also chapter 8 regarding confidentiality, chapter 9 for further details on FERPA provisions, and chapter 12 for related IDEA provisions.)

Other Relevant State Mandates

Many other state laws impact the responsibilities of school staff members, including school health professionals. One example is reporting suspected child abuse. Under a federal requirement that each state address the issue of child abuse (Child Abuse Prevention and Treatment Act), states must establish procedures for the reporting, investigating, and prosecuting of child abuse. With some variation among states, these laws designate professionals and paraprofessionals who work with children as "mandatory reporters" and provide the reporters with immunity from prosecution for good faith reports. These state statutes are usually the responsibility of the state child care agency, but reporting and documentation requirements do impact school systems; reporting, where required, is not optional, and the failure to report a reasonable suspicion of abuse and neglect is often punishable by a fine or other court action. (Further discussion of school responsibilities in reporting suspected child abuse is found in chapters 6 and 7; related confidentiality concerns are addressed in chapter 8.)

NEGLIGENCE AND LIABILITY

For background to this section on negligence law and liability, it may be helpful to refer back to the earlier section on "Sources of Law," as well as previous discussions of "Case Law," "Civil Law," "Administrative Proceedings," and "Tort Actions." *Negligence* means the failure to act as an ordinary prudent person would have acted in the same or similar circumstances; the term *malpractice* refers to negligence by a professional. Malpractice, then, means the failure of a professional to act as a reasonably prudent member of the same profession would have acted in the given circumstances. Nursing negligence is conduct that is unreasonable

under the circumstances and fails to meet the nursing standard of care (Aiken, 1994, p. 285).

Negligence law, which encompasses malpractice law, is that section of tort law that addresses unintentional conduct or unintentional legal wrongs. Law suits relating to negligence are brought by one or more private persons against another private person or legal entity who caused the wrong (Bernzweig, 1996, pp. 22–23). Negligence law is applicable to school systems and school personnel, although it may be subject to certain constraints if a public school system or its personnel are considered part of the state (see "Defenses in Negligence Actions" below). Liability in a negligence action does not require intent on the part of the defendant. Rather, it requires proof that the defendant's conduct did not conform with a standard of care (Brent, 1997, p. 107). An 18-year-old Louisiana student died of an asthma attack at Lawless Senior High School, New Orleans Parish, after school officials delayed calling 9-1-1 as the student had requested, while trying to contact the student's mother to see if she would pay for the ambulance. In a negligence action brought by the family, a state district judge found the school principal, a guidance counselor, and the school board negligent in the student's death for the following reasons:

- the principal had "shirked his duty to protect the child from harm";

- the counselor "had abandoned common sense and placed rigid rules before a dying child's request"; and

- the school board had failed to provide adequate training for its employees or to have a clear policy on medical emergencies.

The family was awarded $1.6 million; $1.4 million was to be paid by the insurance companies of the principal and counselor, and $200,000 was to be paid by the school board (*Declovet v. Orleans Parish School Board*, 1998).

While negligence actions are usually brought by individuals, they may also be brought by an insurance company or the state on behalf of a class of victims. This type of civil action always claims monetary damages; an individual who is found negligent is called "liable," rather than "guilty," as in a criminal action. Liability, then, refers to a finding in civil cases that the defendant was responsible for the plaintiff's injuries, as in the Louisiana case cited above.

The Four Elements of Negligence

In order to prevail in a negligence action, the plaintiff must prove that all four elements of negligence are present and are more probably true than not true. In other words, the four elements of negligence must be proven by a "preponderance of the evidence," not "beyond a reasonable doubt," which is the standard prevailing in criminal actions. A preponderance of the evidence means that more than 50% of the evidence must indicate that the defendant was responsible for the plaintiff's injuries. The four elements of negligence are described below.

Duty

The plaintiff must prove that the provider had a duty of care to the person injured. In a standard negligence action, this would require that the school have a duty to keep its premises safe from hazards that caused a particular fall, for example. In the context of a professional liability action, proof of duty would require that the school nurse have a duty to care for the students in the school according to the relevant standards of care, which are discussed briefly below and in greater depth in chapter 4. The element of duty may be argued when the person injured is a trespasser to the premises or when a student is harmed after leaving the premises; but otherwise, duty of care is not generally disputed. In general, school nurses owe a duty, in varying degrees, to every student in the school or schools to which they are assigned and, as needed, to all students in the school or school district for which their services have been engaged. They specifically owe a duty to every student who comes to the health room seeking nursing assessment or advice regarding a health concern. It would be difficult for a school nurse, for example, to claim that he or she did not need to assess or provide care for a student's complaint (that is, did not owe a duty to the student) because the student's injury or illness occurred over the weekend or began at home; it would also be difficult to refuse to travel to another school in the district to care for an injured student even if that school is not regularly assigned to the nurse. The extent of the nurse's duty, however, may be proportional to her or his job responsibilities, assignments, and availability at the time the student was injured, among other variables.

Breach of Duty

Once a duty of care has been established, the plaintiff must prove that the defendant breached the duty owed. In proving that the defendant failed to execute his or her duty, the plaintiff must demonstrate that the defendant did not act in the same manner as another reasonable person would have acted in order to avoid causing harm to others. In a malpractice action, it must be proved that what the defendant did (or refrained

from doing) did not meet the applicable professional standard of care. This portion of a malpractice case must be proven by expert testimony. The expert testifies as to the action required, for example, of a reasonable nurse, with similar training and experience and under the same circumstances, and compares the required action with the care provided by the defendant. It is critical to note that the standard of care varies according to circumstances, as discussed under "Standards of Care" below.

Proximate Cause

Once a breach of duty has been established, the plaintiff must prove that the defendant's breach of duty actually caused the damages claimed by the plaintiff. In other words, it must be demonstrated that what the defendant did (or failed to do) was causally and reasonably related to the harm suffered by the plaintiff.

Damages

The plaintiff must demonstrate damages—that is, demonstrate that harm or injury was sustained by the plaintiff. Usually physical damages are required before emotional distress may be claimed, but certain types of allegations may merit emotional distress damages only. A civil action in negligence cannot be successful if damages cannot be proved, even if the defendant did breach his or her duty to the plaintiff.

Case Examples

The four elements of negligence are illustrated by the following case, decided in 1970 by a court in Louisiana. It involves a 16-year-old boy, Robert Mogabgab, who on August 16, 1966, at 5:20 p.m., became ill during football practice. His mother was not notified until 6:45 p.m., and it was she who called for medical assistance. Robert arrived at the hospital at 7:30 p.m.; he died at 2:30 a.m. the next morning of complications of heat stroke.

Following these events, his parents sued the coaches involved, the principal, the superintendent of the school board, the supervisor of physical education in the school system, and the school board itself. There was no dispute that the school personnel had a duty to respond to symptoms of illness experienced by a boy participating in football practice. There was, however, considerable dispute about what the coaches should have done—that is, the standard of care in that situation. For example, at 5:50 p.m., a blanket was placed over the boy who was, by that time, lying on the cafeteria floor. Expert testimony demonstrated that such an action was medically incorrect and could have contributed to a worsening of Robert's condition. In addition, the standard required that Robert be provided with immediate medical attention; instead, apparently a first aid book was brought into the cafeteria and the coaches discussed what should be done.

There was a vigorous dispute about causation in this case, since it was not certain that Robert would have survived even had he been transported to the hospital more expeditiously. The court held that certainty is not required and found that the plaintiff had proven that it was "more likely than not" that Robert would have survived had he received prompt medical attention.

Finally, monetary damages were awarded by the trial court, and affirmed on appeal. Judgment was entered against the coaches only (*Mogabgab v. Orleans Parish School Board*, 1970).

A second case illustrates the same issues. In a New York case (*Griffin v. New York*, 1986), an asthmatic student complained to the school nurse that she was ill. She was sent back to class without treatment and then left the school premises and walked home. Her mother was at home and went to the kitchen to call an ambulance. The child, unable to breathe, opened a window, leaned out, apparently lost consciousness, and fell to the ground. The mother sued the New York Board of Education for damages suffered by her daughter.

The court dismissed this action for two reasons. First, it held that the school owed no further duty to the student after her mother had assumed control over her. Second, the court held that even if the school had violated a duty owed to the student, that violation of duty was not a proximate cause of the injuries in this case. It held that the student's fall from the window at home was not reasonably foreseeable (*Griffin v. New York*, 1986). It should be noted that, had the student fallen from a window at school after having been sent back to class, the court may have determined that the school had a duty to protect the student from harm, that the duty was violated, and, finally, that this violation was the proximate cause of the student's fall.

Standards of Care

The standards of care to be used in negligence actions are those that were in effect at the time of the incident, not those that might be in place at the time the claim is brought or at the time the case is tried, which may be several years later. The applicable standard of care in a civil suit against a health care professional can be based on the following standards, as they existed at the time of the incident:

- legal standards, for example, licensure laws and regulations;

- the professional's education, qualifications, and experience;

- professional standards of practice;

- agency policies and procedures, especially the individual's job description;

- current practice in the community; and

- other relevant information from that point in time, such as guidelines, professional journal articles, and textbooks.

- some or all of the above.

The expected standard of care varies according to specific circumstances in the situation. Some examples that apply to schools are as follows:

1. The standard of care for students who have known special health and safety needs should be higher than the standard of care for students who have no identified special needs.

2. The standard of care for triage and treatment in an acute care hospital emergency department differs (at least in part) from that provided in a school nurse's office. Critical thinking and actions should be alike; resources, equipment, and intervention options are not alike. It should be noted, however, that in the case of a Minnesota school nurse who was sued in the asthma-related death of a student (*Schluessler v. Independent School District No. 200*, et. al., 1989), an expert witness from a major hospital emergency room in the community testified that the school nurse should have responded as an emergency room nurse would have responded to meet the standard of care, and the school nurse was found liable, in part.

3. The school nurse who functions primarily as a consultant to a large county school district with 40,000 students would not be held to the same standard for developing and implementing individualized health care plans as would a school nurse who works full time in one building with 500 students.

(Standards of care for school nursing are discussed in more detail in chapters 4, 5, and 6.)

Defenses In Negligence Actions

In addition to proving that the defendant "acted reasonably under the circumstances" and arguing, for example, that the plaintiff has not proven that the defendant's conduct breached a standard of care or that evidence of proximate cause was lacking (i.e., all elements of negligence were not proved), there are other defenses to a professional liability action. Some of these are statutory, and some are found in case law.

The most widely known defense is the statute of limitations. This statute, which exists in all states but has varying provisions, sets forth the time within which a suit must be brought. Beyond that time limit, the suit will be barred from going forward in the courts. Generally, the statutes require that suit be brought within a specified number of years from the date of the negligent conduct, or in some states, the date on which that conduct reasonably could have been discovered. In the Mogabgab case above, the date of the negligent conduct was clear—August 16, 1966—and suit was brought within the required time. However, for cases like exposures to asbestos in a stage curtain, for example, one may not be aware of a problem until much later, so some statutes permit suit to be brought after "discovery" of the problem. In keeping with the same principle and of importance in schools, the statute of limitations does not begin to count time when a minor is injured until such time as the minor becomes "aware of the injury," which legally means at the age of majority, or 18 years.

Another common defense is to allege "contributory" or "comparative" negligence. This defense is used when the conduct of the plaintiff is said to have contributed to or caused all or part of the damages in the case. For example, if a nurse instructs an 18-year-old not to walk on a wet floor, and the student does so and falls, contributory or comparative negligence may be used by the defense. These defenses are most commonly used to allocate responsibility between the plaintiff and defendants—for example, a court might find a plaintiff 20% responsible for his injuries and deduct that percentage from the jury verdict.

In a school setting, however, this defense has limited applicability to the students. The younger or the more mentally impaired the student, the less likely that a court will find that the student was capable of making a decision to disregard instructions. This defense still can be used to allocate responsibility to a parent, however. For example, if a student is sent home with a parent, who is instructed to have the child promptly examined at a hospital but does not do so, subsequent harm may be the sole or partial responsibility of the parent.

Another defense that is applicable in varying degrees in many states is the principle of sovereign immunity, based on state statute, which protects public employees from liability for acts committed within the scope of

their employment. Thus, in a 1987 case in Texas in which a student with cerebral palsy was pushed into a stack of chairs, sustaining a head injury followed by a convulsion, cold sweats, and incoherence, the student was then brought to the school nurse, who kept the student in school and did not contact the parent or student's physician. The district, bus supervisor, principal, school nurse, and teacher were found not liable for negligent acts due to such immunity under Texas law. There were, however, dissenting opinions in the case (*Spring Independent School District v. C. A. Hopkins*, 1987). It is important to note that sovereign immunity does not usually protect public employees from liability if their actions constitute gross negligence or are construed as willful or wanton.

A similar defense that applies to public employees in some jurisdictions is called discretionary function immunity, which provides public employees immunity from liability for good-faith mistakes in judgment (i.e., for exercising discretion) in the course of their employment. Again, where such immunity exists, it is not without exception. In 1986, the Appellate Court of Illinois upheld the decision of the Circuit Court in which the plaintiff was awarded $2.5 million for damages suffered in 1978 when, as a sixth-grade student, he did not receive prompt medical treatment after receiving a blow to the head on the school playground. The Court found that both the school staff and the Emergency Medical System (EMS) staff acted willfully and wantonly causing unwarranted delays in emergency medical care for the student. Therefore, they were not protected by the state's rule of immunity for discretionary acts of public employees (*Barth by Barth v. Board of Education*, 1986).

Principles related to discretionary function immunity, which can help a defendant in responding to a law suit, include qualified immunity from liability and the concept of "foreseeability of harm." An example of these two principles is found in a 1993 Alabama case in which a student with spina bifida brought a $2 million suit against a school principal, school nurse, special education director, and special education aide, claiming that 1) the aide had negligently failed to catheterize her, resulting in physical injuries and mental trauma; and 2) the principal, nurse, and special education director had "negligently or wantonly failed to supervise and train the aide." The trial court dismissed the suits against all but the aide, because the three were protected by discretionary function immunity, and

- such delegation was within the scope of the supervisors' responsibilities and no one could have predicted (foreseen) that the aide would neglect to carry out the catheterization on that day; and

- they were protected by qualified immunity from liability for wanton misconduct, absent a showing of bad faith (*Nance v. Matthews*, 1993).

In a Minnesota case ruling in 1996, both a school counselor and school district were found entitled to "discretionary function immunity" and "common law official immunity" in a student's death from suicide, despite the fact that the counselor had been notified and counseled the student about details of the student's plan to commit suicide, but had not contacted the family. A dissenting opinion in the case agreed that it was within the discretionary function of the school to adopt or not adopt a written suicide prevention policy, but that the counselor and district "owed a duty" to the student to inform the parents (*School Health Professional*, May, 1996, p. 4). (See also the discussion of statutorily-limited liability in chapter 4.) Of course, the best defense to a potential negligence action is documented evidence that the standard of care was met, which can be provided by the written nursing record in conjunction with expert testimony.

Negligence Cases in School Health

In the *School Health Professional* article cited above (1996, p. 4), it was reported that, while the courts have generally "accorded schools and educators immunity from charges of negligence or malpractice," deferring instead to the "professional expertise of educators," parents and students do sue schools. The article cites negligence cases against school districts as frequently related to the following:

- injuries, especially related to participation in physical education and sports;

- actions taken or not taken by guidance counselors (e.g., failure to report suicidal intent of student);

- rights of schools to provide sex education and reproductive health counseling;

- failure to prevent sexual assault by personnel and student-to-student sexual abuse; and

- failure to meet the needs of students with disabilities.

Parents also sue school districts and school personnel, including school nurses, in cases related to student deaths from acute episodes of asthma and anaphylactic (allergic) reactions and, in 1999, for not obtaining informed consent for in-school, mandated physical exams. Most often, more than one party is named as defendant and, when a staff person is sued, usually the district, the person's supervisor, and one or more school administrators will be named in the suit. School physicians acting on behalf of school districts may also be named as defendants, as in the 1999 case mentioned above. (See chapter 6, "Parental Permission for School Nursing and Health Services," for additional information.)

As with guidance counselors, negligence cases against school nurses are generally based on allegations that actions taken or not taken do not meet the standard of care. Recurring themes in successful suits against school nurses include the following:

- failure to keep abreast of nursing knowledge;

- failure to document adequately;

- failure to recognize urgent and emergency situations;

- failure to follow school district policy; and

- failure to challenge administrative decisions that put students at risk.

As in all areas of civil suits, out-of-court settlements between the plaintiff and defendant are not infrequent. Because the details of such settlements are frequently kept private or are hard to obtain, it is difficult to know how many cases are actually brought and what the outcomes of those settlements are.

(Refer to chapter 4 for further discussion of nursing negligence and liability insurance and to chapter 6 for other civil actions related to school nursing services within general education.)

ISSUES AND IMPLICATIONS

High Risk Aspects of School Health Nursing Practice

As reported by Schwab (1988), certain aspects of school health practice put school nurses at higher risk for liability than their colleagues in other settings (p. 17), including the following:

- professional isolation,

- a wide range of responsibilities,

- conflicts between policies of boards of education and professional standards of care, and

- conflicts between education law and health law.

Not only are school nurses practicing in settings outside the mainstream of health care, but, in addition, their roles and competencies vary enormously based on state- and locally-mandated qualifications for school nurses, available funding streams, availability of qualified nurses, state and district interpretation of federal law (e.g., special education and civil rights laws), as well as state law (e.g., licensure statutes), and district staffing patterns. Another area of risk—for all school professionals—is the difficulty in today's society of establishing and maintaining effective working relationships with families. High mobility of families, language and cultural differences, the high percentage of parents in the workplace, and the rapid pace of society make ongoing communications with parents far more challenging than in the past. It is important for both district administrators and school nurses to keep these areas of high risk in mind when planning risk-management strategies for school health services programs.

Lack of Knowledge

While practitioners in education or in health may know the area of law that relates to their own area of expertise—that is, educators generally know the laws that are contained within the education sections of state and federal law and health practitioners generally know state and federal mandates relating to health—few practitioners or school administrators understand both sets of laws. Nor do they understand how the laws overlap, where they conflict, or how to determine their impact on the current responsibilities of school districts, school employees who provide school health services, or employees of other agencies who deliver health services within the education agency (e.g., the public health nurse employed by a visiting nurse association or the social worker employed by a hospital-operated, school-based health center). Often, lawyers hired by boards of education to provide legal counsel do not fully understand—or even know of—certain federal and state health mandates or the potential impact of those mandates on the responsibilities of school districts and their personnel. Similarly, lawyers with expertise in the health arena typically lack expertise in education law and how those mandates may affect the provision of health services in schools.

Even at the state agency level and attorney general's office, legal consultants may not know both areas of the law, although, in an attorney general's office, lawyers representing many areas of expertise consult and collaborate with one another when they are aware of conflicts or crossover implications. As a result, it is not unusual that on a particular issue, such as Do-Not-Resuscitate orders in schools, the opinions or interpretations of education lawyers may differ significantly from those of health lawyers.

Implication for School Districts

It is extremely important for school districts and state education agencies to obtain the counsel of legal experts from both fields when health problems or practices are at issue in education settings. In all such situations, collaboration among health and education administrators and, when necessary, consideration of legal advice from experts in both fields are critical to sound decision making. Furthermore, consideration of both health and education laws that may apply in a given situation better protects education agencies and the personnel who work within them from potential liability.

When the Law Is Not Enough

In many situations in schools, laws, regulations, and even case law precedent do not provide answers or solutions to the numerous ethico-legal dilemmas facing education and health professionals on a daily basis. In some cases, they even create further conflicts and, in general, the law lags far behind cutting-edge practice. As a result, sound risk-management strategies require school professionals to

- know the various laws and standards that apply to their practice;
- understand the principles of ethics and how to apply them to decision-making and student-care dilemmas;
- learn how to access expert information about federal and state laws and regulations;
- learn how to access expert consultation regarding ethical issues;
- collaborate with colleagues (across disciplines) to find joint solutions to difficult problems;
- focus on the needs of students, including the needs of their families, as appropriate, when making judgments regarding student care and work responsibilities; and
- promote and maintain good communications and working relationships with families.

School districts should consider establishing school health advisory councils (or healthy-school teams) and quality assurance and ethics committees representative of families, students, all professional disciplines within schools, and community experts. Such advisory councils and committees promote the ability of school districts to

- develop policy, procedures, and guidelines in the school health arena that best meet the needs of the school and wider community;

- explore and resolve ethical and legal issues and dilemmas;

- promote up-to-date professional practice;

- employ effective risk-management strategies; and

- maintain quality programs.

REFERENCES

Aiken, T. D. (with Catalano, J. T.). (1994). *Legal, ethical and political issues in nursing.* Philadelphia: F. A. Davis Company.

American Nurses Association. (1995). *Capitol update, 13*(19), 5.

Bernzweig, Eli P. (1996). *The nurse's liability for malpractice: a programmed course* (6th ed.). St. Louis: Mosby.

Brent, N. J. (1997). *Nurses and the law: A guide to principles and practice.* Philadelphia: W. B. Saunders & Co.

Donovan, P. (1997). Teenagers' right to consent to reproductive health care. Guttmacher Institute [Online]. Available: http://www.agi-usa/pubs/ib21.html

Gelfman, M., & Schwab, N. (1991). School health services and educational records: Conflicts in the law. *Education Law Reporter, 64,* 319–338.

Hall, J. K. (1996). *Nursing ethics and law.* Philadelphia: W. B. Saunders Company.

Howard, P. K. (1994). *The death of common sense: How law is suffocating America.* New York: Random House.

Oregon State Board of Nursing. (1989). *Declaratory Ruling: In the Matter of the Petitions for Declaratory Ruling by Hillsboro Union High School No. 3, et al., and by Carol Mitts.* Beaverton, OR: Author.

Purtilo, Ruth. (1996). *Ethical dimensions in the health professions* (2nd ed.). Philadelphia: W. B. Saunders Company.

Rosenfeld, L. R. (1994). *Your child and health care: A "dollars and sense" guide for families with special needs.* Baltimore: Paul H. Brookes Publishing Company.

School Health Professional. (1996, May 22). Why schools get sued, and for what. *School Health Professional,* pp. 4–5.

Schwab, N., & Haas, M. (1995). Delegation and supervision in school settings: Standards, issues and guidelines for practice (Part 1 of 2). *Journal of School Nursing, 11*(1), 19–27.

Schwab, N. (1988). Liability issues in school nursing. *School Nurse, 4*(1), 13–25.

Springhouse Corporation. (1996). *Nurse's legal handbook* (3rd ed.). Springhouse, PA: Author.

TABLE OF CASES

Barth by Barth v. Board of Education, 490 N.E.2d 77 (Ill. App. 1 Dist. 1986).

Board of Education of the Hendrick Hudson Central School District v. Rowley, 102 S. Ct. 3034, EHLR 553:656 (U.S. 1982).

Brown v. Board of Education, 347 U.S. 483 (U.S. 1954).

Cedar Rapids Community School District v. Garret F., 29 IDELR 966 (U.S. 1999).

Declouet v. Orleans Parish School Board, 715 So.2d 69 (La. App. 4 Cir. 1998).

Detsel v. Auburn Enlarged City School District Board of Education, 820 F.2d 587, EHLR 558:395 (2nd Cir. 1989).

Ellen F. Johnson v. Independent School District No. 3 of Tulsa County, Oklahoma, 891 F.2d 1485 (10th Cir. 1989).

Griffin v. New York, 507 NYS 2d 445 (AD 2 Dept. 1986).

Honig v. Doe, 484 U.S. 305, 108 S. Ct. 592, EHLR 559:231 (U.S. 1988).

In re Quinlan, 355 A.2d 647 (N.J. 1976).

Irving Independent School District v. Tatro, 104 S. Ct. 3371, EHLR 555:511 (U.S. 1984).

Mills v. District of Columbia Board of Education, 348 F.Supp. 866 (D DC 1972).

Mitts, Carol v. Hillsboro Union High School District No. 3, et al., Washington County Circuit Court, Case No. 87-1142C. (1990).

Mogabgab v. Orleans Parish School Board, 239 So. 2d 456 (La. App. 1970).

Nance v. Matthews, 622 So.2d 297, 20 IDELR 3 (Ala. 1993).

New Jersey v. TLO, 469 U.S. 325 (U.S. 1985).

North v. District of Columbia Board of Education, EHLR 551:157 (D DC 1979).

Schluessler v. Independent School District No. 200, et al, August, 1989 Minnesota Case Reports 652, Dakota County District Court.

Spring Independent School District v. C. A. Hopkins, 736 S.W.2d 617 (Texas 1987).

See page 625 for Table of Federal Statutes and Regulations.

Chapter Three
Exploring Ethical Challenges in School Health

Mila Ann Aroskar

INTRODUCTION

Health and education professionals who provide school health services frequently have to make decisions that require attention to ethics and values. While this book focuses on the legal aspects of school health, several chapters deal with ethical matters that are often components of situations requiring legal information and interpretation. Although legal and ethical factors are often both part of the problems confronting school health professionals such as school nurses, educators, and others, it is not always possible to reach conclusions that resolve both facets of the question. Ethical quandaries may persist even when legal requirements are clear. One example is a legal obligation to report a specific communicable disease as required in state statute when a student has demanded that this information not be shared with anyone else.

Situations that call for making decisions about difficult issues often create ethical conflict. Such situations include establishing health goals and priorities, protecting the privacy of student health information, determining rights and responsibilities of students and parents, identifying the ethical obligations of school health nurses and educators, meeting health needs of individual students versus health needs of a school population, preventing HIV infection and AIDS, educating students for prevention of pregnancy, and delegating duties to unlicensed assistive personnel. Ready-made answers for such conflicts often do not exist, and decision makers must struggle to develop responses that are ethically, legally, and practically supportable.

It is important to recognize from the beginning that school health nurses in public schools work in environments in which the primary goal is education. Schools consider health a means to acquiring an education for the purpose of becoming an effective and productive citizen in society. Maintaining health, promoting health, and alleviating the physical or emotional suffering of students support the primary goal of education in schools. In healthcare institutions, these goals and means are reversed. Health and health-related goals are primary, and education is one of the means to achieving those goals. The role of the school health nurse is fraught with ethical tensions similar to those of the nurse who is employed in an occupational or other public health setting. Also, school health nurses cannot focus solely on individual students but must include the well-being of the student population in their decision-making as they respond to ethical conflicts that arise in treating students. These and other factors such as the multicultural composition of many school populations make ethical decisions particularly challenging for nurses who have learned to be advocates for individual patients in a society that emphasizes individual freedom and rights.

The purpose of this chapter is to discuss three areas related to decision making in situations that require explicit attention to ethical principles, values, and concepts in order to develop reasoned and justifiable responses. The first section presents criteria for identifying situations in school health that create ethical conflict and presents a framework for decision-making and problem solving that incorporates ethical principles and concepts. The second section presents ethical theories, values, principles, and other ethical concepts such as rights and responsibilities that underlie the decision-making framework. The third section uses the framework to respond to two school health situations that present ethical conflicts for school health nurses and others involved in or affected by the potential consequences of each situation.

From this discussion, it will become evident that even the explicit consideration of ethical aspects does not automatically lead to one "right" response or set of responses with which everyone agrees. There may be more than one response that can be supported ethically, a quick initial response that will be ruled out, or a choice that will be required among seemingly equal and unattractive choices. Consider a situation in which the parents of a pregnant teen are contacted about needed health care solely because the parent will receive a bill for services, even though the teen has told the nurse that she does not want her parents contacted. Clearly,

there is more at stake here than simply assuring payment for needed services. Respecting individuals and preventing harm are significant ethical principles underlying this and similar troubling situations.

PROBLEM SOLVING: AN ETHICAL FRAMEWORK

Working through a troublesome situation for which the right response is not apparent requires the decision maker to resolve whether it is primarily an ethical problem or whether it simply contains some ethical elements that require attention. Other situations might require information about current law or more effective communication among the affected parties.

Identifying an Ethical Quandary

An ethical problem in school health has one or more of the following six characteristics:

- it is a situation with conflicts in values, obligations, loyalties, interests, or needs among an identified individual student and other students or conflicts among students, health professionals, and other involved parties such as parents or school administrators.

- it requires a decision about the morally right action that should be made reflectively and thoughtfully;

- it requires that the choice be influenced by ethical principles and values;

- the identified choices for action seem to be equally problematic from an ethical perspective for those affected directly and indirectly;

- the choices are affected by the feelings and values of the involved individuals and by the demands or context of the situation;

- the conflict requires an interdisciplinary approach for an ethically justifiable response.

It is important to clarify the existence of some or all of these characteristics in a given situation to assure that the situation is not primarily an issue of inadequate communication or clearly a legal issue that requires a first response informed by legal counsel .

Ethical Framework for Decision Making

Once a troubling situation has been identified as primarily an ethical problem or set of problems, a

framework is useful for analysis and the development of ethically reasoned responses. This process may be initiated by an individual or a group of involved colleagues or affected parties. The following elements constitute such a framework:

- ask yourself what is going on in the situation and identify all relevant information to the degree that this is possible;

- identify the affected parties or stakeholders such as the individual student(s), other students involved or at risk, faculty, administration, parents, community organizations, and others;

- identify the specific ethical issues or conflicts, such as respect for an individual's privacy versus the safety of others whose welfare may be in jeopardy, or respect for individual freedom versus fairness for all;

- identify choices for action and the ethical justification for each option, such as avoiding or preventing harm to a student or group of students or identifying a threat to the health of others;

- identify the foreseeable consequences of the different options for action, including the practical (legal, economic, social, and political) constraints;

- select a course of action and evaluate the actual consequences of such a course; and

- identify what has been learned for use in similar problem-solving or decision-making situations.

Using this process to make decisions requires attention to the ethical values and principles at stake and to the unique characteristics of the situation that demand an individualized response. The goal of the process is to develop a response that is reasoned, reflective of attention to morally relevant features of the situation, and sensitive to the humanity of those involved. Protecting relationships, supporting those making difficult decisions, and promoting effective communication are often additional goals in responding to ethically troublesome situations.

ETHICAL THEORIES, PRINCIPLES, VALUES, AND CONCEPTS

This section discusses the ethical theories, principles, values, and concepts that inform use of the ethical framework. Selected theories that support different ethical principles and values are discussed briefly as background. The discussion of principles and concepts is drawn primarily from the American Nurses Association (ANA) Code of Ethics (1985), the bioethics literature, and the nursing ethics literature. (See Appendix B for the ANA Code of Ethics.)

Ethical Theories

Ethical theories from various traditions of moral philosophy show how philosophers have struggled over time to determine what is "right" or "good" character, conduct, and action. While there is no single ethical theory that assists decision makers in determining responses to specific ethical quandaries, it is important to be familiar with different theoretical approaches that have been developed and debated over time. Awareness of these different approaches helps us understand the views that individuals or groups express as they confront ethical dilemmas. Decision makers may use one or more of these approaches implicitly without being aware of them. Their approaches may be based primarily on consideration of virtue or character, consideration of principles, considerations of caring, or considerations that begin with a focus on community.

For the past two decades, bioethical decisions have been founded on principle-based theories. More recently, there is a resurgence of attention to other approaches to ethical concerns and questions of right and good. These approaches, some old, some new, include concern for the moral virtues of individuals and organizations, attention to caring as an ethic, and a focus on the good of the community.

Virtue or Character Theory

The place of the moral character or virtue of decision makers has a long tradition in ethics and moral philosophy. Issues of character are significant in professional practice generally and specifically in school health nursing. It can be argued that the character and integrity of school health nurses acting as moral agents will influence whether they identify ethical concerns and how they develop their responses to these concerns.

Virtues refer to character traits such as trustworthiness, respectfulness, honesty, and kindness as they are demonstrated by a person's behavior. Character traits also reveal ethical principles such as truthfulness and respect for other people. Attention to character as a way of being rather than a way of acting based on abstract ethical principles is viewed as enriching to professional ethics (Drane, 1994). Both dimensions are important to the integrity of individual nurses, to their practice, and to practice environments. A nurse's character and behavior influence the practice environment and the behavior of others as well. Conversely, school and other practice environments influence individual attitudes and behavior. An example is the school health nurse who influences students' respect for each other by his or her own behavior and attitudes of respect for students, parents, and colleagues. Conversely, a school environment where students and faculty are not respected can contribute to negative behavior. Employees may become frustrated with their attempts to demonstrate respectful behavior to students and others.

Principle-based Theories

Two principle-based families of ethical theory have received the most emphasis in bioethics over the past three decades. One is Kantian or duty-based theory. The second is Utilitarianism, or consequence-based theory. Both theories are based on acts or rules to determine what is right or good.

Kantian (Duty-based) Theory. The Kantian ethical approach focuses on principles that express duties and obligations (Davis, Aroskar, Liaschenko, & Drought, 1997, pp. 49-50). An act such as showing respect for a person is right by virtue of its inherent moral significance. According to Kant's "categorical imperative," decision makers, as moral agents, must be willing to universalize a decision made in one set of circumstances to any similar set of circumstances or people. A school nurse, considering this theory, must be willing to treat students in similar circumstances of health or illness similarly independent of a student's socioeconomic class, race, religion, or gender.

A second element of Kant's categorical imperative is that human beings should never be treated solely as means to ends, including research or advancing special interests. This ethical approach, which considers the moral significance of both acts and rules, does not consider the consequences of proposed actions or the consequences of following particular moral rules such as "Always tell the truth."

Decision makers using this approach need to prioritize principles and duties when they conflict in real-life situations. There is often no clearly correct answer on which everyone will agree because principles do not automatically fall into a hierarchical order and they are often too abstract for dealing with a specific situation. However, a theoretical approach does assist the decision maker to identify what counts from an ethical perspective when there is disagreement. And principles still serve as guides for action. From an ethical perspective, we must consider principles such as respect for people and avoiding or preventing harm when making decisions that have consequences for others.

Utilitarian (Consequence-based) Theory. Utilitarianism is a form of consequentialist theory that relies on the single principle of utility as happiness or pleasure to be pursued. It emphasizes the consequences of rules and actions. The right action or rule results in the greatest good and least amount of harm for the greatest number of persons, assuming that one can weigh and measure harms and benefits and arrive at an accurate measure of good over evil for the most people (Davis, et al., 1997, pg. 56). From this perspective, school health nurses should calculate the potential benefits and harms of a given decision or action for the student population rather than just for the student who is most directly affected by the decision. Even though each student is considered in decision making, the one(s) most directly affected, such as the student who brings a lethal weapon to school, may end up in a minority position when the consequences have been considered for all. Administrators and public health professionals find this approach to be more congenial for the types of difficult decisions they are required to make than the clinician who prefers to advocate for an individual patient.

One of the limitations of a utilitarian perspective is its potential conflict with more traditional nursing goals of advocacy for patients based on need and traditional medical goals of doing everything possible for an individual patient. A further limitation is the inability of this approach to deal adequately with claims of individual rights and justice, such as fairness. In everyday life, decision makers must consider a variety of values other than the single value of utility when they develop a response that shows respect for individual needs.

In summary, Kantian and utilitarian theories offer different perspectives to be considered in ethical decision making. Both are examples of "principled" approaches for developing responses to ethical dilemmas in school health settings. While both have strengths and limitations, they are helpful in considering what is morally and ethically significant in a situation and may lead to rejecting some possible responses. Many "real-life" situations require the consideration of both approaches by decision makers.

Theory of Care

An ethical theory based on caring has more recently been developed within the broader field of feminist philosophical theory. This provides another perspective from which to respond to ethical concerns in a more comprehensive way than an appeal solely to abstract principles such as respect for autonomy (Davis et al., 1997, pp. 57-59). This theory is particularly relevant for nurses, because the ANA Code for Nurses (1985) emphasizes respectful care of individuals as its major principle.

In an ethic of care, decision making focuses on responsibility for developing decisions and actions that promote and maintain human relationships. People are viewed as unique individuals within networks of relationships rather than as isolated bodies claiming individual autonomy or simply as members of a population at risk. This concept of caring supports school nurses who involve all persons significant to student well-being in discussions and decision making at some level. This may include individuals who are affected directly or indirectly by the decision to be made. An ethic of care is fundamental to the nursing profession, which is responsible for caring for individuals, for families, for communities, for the environment, and for the profession itself.

Caring focused on individuals and their relationships is only one element of the broader field of feminist ethics. A second element is attention to oppression and dominance where they occur in relationships or organizations. This is an important dimension to nurses, including school nurses, who often work in organizations in which power differentials and inequalities affect their ability to influence decision making and policy development. This element of feminist ethics reflects the need to balance caring for and meeting the needs of others with efforts to develop non-oppressive relationships and work environments that enhance respect for all persons and their contributions to the mission of the organization.

An ethical benchmark in any organization, including schools, measures relationships and structures as they affect the humanity of all—teachers, students, health care personnel, other employees, administration, and parents or guardians. This aspect of caring connects respectful care for individuals with the broader public health perspective of promoting the common good.

While the concept of an ethic of care needs more development in order to provide a structure for a professional ethic, it still provides a different starting point for deciding what is "right" in an ethically problematic situation than a sole focus on individualism and individual rights.

Communitarian (Community-based) Theory

School health nurses may find it helpful to become acquainted with the communitarian ethic (Beauchamp & Childress, 1994, pp. 77-78) that is a community-based rather than an individual-based ethic. This is a more controversial ethic, in light of our societal focus on individual rights, with its claim that fundamentals in ethics derive from communal values, social goals, and cooperative virtues. Yet it is important to consider in the decision making required of school health nurses who have obligations to a school population as well as to individual students. Communitarianism, in common with an ethic of care, calls attention to the importance of responsibilities as well as rights, the importance of creating communal ties, and the importance of promoting the common good. Explicit attention to more community-oriented values could be helpful in school health decision making and policy development even if total agreement on ethical values is an improbable goal in our pluralistic society.

In summary, familiarity with ethical theories or approaches does not provide a formula for resolving ethical concerns and problems in real-life. The theories are, however, examples of ethical elements that should be considered in more holistic decision making, even though they do not provide an easy answer in a specific situation. Though they may not be made explicit in discussions of complex ethically troubling situations, ethical theories or approaches may be used implicitly as school health nurses seek to resolve conflicts individually or in concert with others. These are often situations in which no ready-made answers exist or accurate legal information does not adequately address a decision maker's ethical worries.

ETHICAL VALUES AND PRINCIPLES

Ethical values and principles such as respect for persons and prevention of harm are considered here as general guides to decision making and action. Like ethical theories, values and principles do not provide an automatic answer when considered in specific situations. This is often a source of frustration for decision makers who must respond when there is limited information, time constraints, or a troubling situation with many involved parties to consider. Still, considering ethical principles and values can guide nurses in developing responses to difficult situations. One example is the challenge of developing a plan of care for an elementary school student who has epilepsy that is not well controlled with medication. The parents have notified the school nurse but demand that no one be told. A second

example is the demand by parents for a terminally ill child who has a DNR order to attend school. The school has been dragging its feet on developing policy even though there are legal requirements to do so.

These examples represent situations where there are many people to be considered, time is an element to be considered, and limited information may be available. As a member of the school team, a school health nurse has an obligation to point out that ignoring ethical values and principles may lead to decisions or actions that are harmful to students or the school and that could possibly be prevented. Explicit attention to ethical values and principles can promote a humane approach to troubling situations where there are no ready-made answers and existing law can only be helpful to a limited degree.

Values

The philosophical study of values in philosophy is known as the field of axiology, the study of the general theory of value deriving from the Greek work *axios*, meaning "worthy" (Davis et al., 1997, p. 36). There are many definitions of value. One view is that the term refers to strongly held ideals, attitudes, beliefs, or commitments that are fundamental to the way we live. Decision makers encounter both ethical or moral values and non-moral values. Non-moral values include social, religious, economic, aesthetic, and political values. Ethical/moral values reflect strongly held beliefs about the inherent dignity of human beings, attitudes about honesty, ideals about the "good" person, and obligations to one's self, family, or profession. Agreement about the importance of specific values is elusive, and the emphasis placed on different values varies in our pluralistic society. For example, public schools focus on the values of education and citizenship.

Values such as respect, fairness, and avoiding harm have many roles in our daily lives even though we do not often think about them or articulate them to someone else. Values provide direction to both our individual and our common life. They influence our perceptions and views of the world. They also guide and, in some instances, determine our everyday decisions and actions. Values also provide benchmarks for appraising our own decisions and actions and the decisions and actions of other individuals, groups, or communities. Values may also conflict. School health nurses and educators may find that one's dedication to promoting and maintaining health conflicts with the other's education values when it comes to setting priorities for the allocation of limited financial resources. Or an individual's religious values may conflict with the health and social values of childhood immunization or birth control.

Ethical Principles

In this chapter, ethical principles are viewed as reflective of ethical values, and the two terms are used interchangeably. Both serve as standards for evaluating attitudes and behavior. Principles are more often formally stated or articulated guides to action, whereas values may or may not be identified or stated to others. Yet values and personal and professional principles influence and direct our actions in powerful ways.

Principle of Respect for Persons

According to the ANA Code for Nurses (1985), the fundamental ethical principle that should guide nursing practice is respect for persons. Other principles such as beneficence stem from this principle. Respect for persons is a broader principle than respect for autonomy or self-determination, a major value for patients and clients in nursing, health care, and in society. Respect for persons has two major elements. One is respect for individual autonomy. This element of respect for persons mandates that each individual be treated as unique and as equal to every other individual. Interfering with or intervening in an individual's own purposes, privacy, or behavior requires special justification (Jonsen & Butler, 1975). The second element is respect for persons as interrelated members of the human community. This element reflects the reality that decisions we make as individuals often have consequences for others as well as ourselves.

The principle of respecting persons as individuals and as interconnected members of the community requires attention to one's duties and obligations to others as well as to one's self. A teenage student's selling of illegal drugs to other students or lying about such activities to school authorities has repercussions beyond that individual student. In addition to the legal aspects of this situation, claims of individual autonomy or rights do not inevitably trump other ethical principles and values such as avoiding or preventing harm to other people.

Commitment to the principle of respect for persons influences whether and how troubling ethical situations are dealt with in a school, including health clinics. It also influences relationships in the school and beyond. In addition to thinking about teenage students as autonomous individuals with rights, school health nurses in their advocacy role also need to think about students as members of families, school groups, and the wider community. Using this principle, a specific decision for action or non-action is justified on the moral basis of whether the proposed action protects or enhances individual autonomy and takes into account the potential consequences of individual choices for the well-being of others. It also requires a student to consider not only their rights but also their responsibilities and obligations to others. This is a different rationale than solely using a legalistic, bureaucratic justification based on school administrative rules and regulations. Decision-making that incorporates ethical considerations does take time and not all will agree with the choices made. However, attention to ethical principles and values will make decisions more comprehensive and thoughtful.

Principle of Beneficence/Non-Maleficence

The ethical principle of beneficence may be viewed on a spectrum ranging from not inflicting/preventing harm to providing benefits (Davis et al., 1997, pp. 52-53). The two ends of the spectrum may be divided into two separate principles of non-maleficence and beneficence. The principle of beneficence is usually considered as a positive duty or obligation. The duty not to inflict or to prevent harm generally takes precedence over providing benefits in a conflict situation in which everything else is equal. One could also argue that avoiding or preventing harm to an individual is a benefit, even though the recipient of the benefit is not aware that this benefit has occurred. For example, basic public health benefits that avoid or prevent harm, such as a safe drinking water supply in school buildings or safety during school lunches, are usually taken for granted until they become identified hazards to health.

Preventing harm and providing benefits are both obligations that school health nurses should take into account in decision making. When there is conflict in a situation, the principle of beneficence tells us to promote good while preventing or minimizing harm for individuals. This principle does not tell us how we should balance burdens and benefits when all cannot benefit from a decision in a particular situation. The allocation of finite economic resources in schools for health and education programs or the allocation of professional time and expertise are examples of situations in which there are competing needs and goals. Additional considerations that may take precedence in a particular situation include state legal requirements or economic constraints that may dictate a response that is not ethically ideal. Allocation decisions and other questions of fairness require attention to the principle of justice.

Principle of Justice

The principle of justice is fundamental to how we live together in groups and communities and to social institutions including schools. This is not to say that there is much explicit public discussion about concepts of justice. But issues and concepts of justice are implicit in many of the dilemmas confronting us as individuals and members of society.

There are many ideas and no consensus about what constitutes justice in our pluralistic society. Most individuals have some sense of justice and most of us could probably agree on instances of injustice, such as lack of access to needed health care for the uninsured or situations in which the heaviest burdens of poverty fall on vulnerable children. Still, there is no agreement on an operational definition of justice to guide public and institutional policy development or to resolve discussions about individual claims of rights when there are conflicts. This reality presents a profound challenge to policy makers and others who must make decisions about allocating finite resources such as health and education money.

Distributive justice is only one of the many different kinds of justice found in the literature of moral philosophy and political theory. School health nurses may encounter discussions of distributive, individual, social, retributive, and compensatory justice even though they are not explicitly identified as such. Ideas about distributive justice are frequently invoked implicitly in health care decision making and policy development. Distributive justice is concerned with the distribution of goods and evils or burdens and benefits in any society in which resources are limited. Ideally, in a just society, the goal would be to treat people in similar situations similarly, for example all pre-school children in need of immunizations. Treating people in similar situations differently requires special justification.

Considerations of justice are often about comparative treatment of individuals. In order to justify variances in the distribution of burdens and benefits, one must be able to point to morally relevant differences between individuals or groups. There are several ideas about how people differ that might justify different distributions of benefits and costs of health care and education to individuals or groups. These criteria include individual effort, need, ability to pay, societal contribution, contract, and equal shares. Different bases for distribution of burdens and benefits are used in different societal contexts. The welfare system, for example, has usually distributed payments on the basis of need, while individual achievement and merit are the usual considerations in the distribution of jobs and promotions (Beauchamp & Childress, 1994, p 331). Using age as a criterion for allocating resources is very controversial, especially for technologically sophisticated and expensive health care services at the end of life.

According to the ANA Code for Nurses (1985), individual need should be the basis for distributing the benefits of nursing and health care. *Medical necessity* is a frequently used concept to justify health plan benefits in managed care arrangements even though this language merits caution because it does not carry the same meaning for everyone. While need seems to be the most easily justified basis for distribution of nursing and health care, there are challenges to this concept of distributive justice. One important issue is defining need as opposed to demands, wishes, and desires. Fundamental needs are defined as those needs that, if not met, will result in irreparable harm. One example is a student who is bleeding profusely after receiving a serious injury while playing in a school sports program and requires emergency treatment. Other examples, such as continuing needs for all children to have adequate nutrition and psychological/emotional support in order to learn, are less dramatic but have significant short- and long-term implications.

Philosopher John Rawls (1971) provides another way to look at justice as fairness and as the foundation of social structures. He makes the case for a fair distribution of what he calls primary social goods such as wealth, income, liberty, opportunity, and the bases of self-respect. Rawls draws on economics, moral philosophy, and political theory for his concept of justice as fairness. His concept is significant to discussions of policy on resource allocation and other decision making required in health care and other settings. The heart of his theory is the idea of an "original position" from which people negotiate the principles of justice by which all are then bound to live. The negotiators are rational, intelligent people who wish to pursue their life plans in a more just society. One condition of the negotiations is that these negotiators do not know what their position will be in society. They will not know their socioeconomic circumstances or class, race, or sex. The negotiators are placed in this situation in order to consider both their own interests and the interests of others because any one of the negotiators might be one of the least fortunate or less advantaged individuals in a given situation or community. According to Rawls, if one thinks of schools as communities and uses this negotiating model in discussions of justice and fairness, principles of fairness that take everyone's interests into account would be developed.

Rawls' theory postulates that inequalities are permissible to improve the condition of the least fortunate or most vulnerable such as children in poverty or children with serious disabilities. The least advantaged or most vulnerable then become the benchmark for decision making and policy development in school communities under this notion of fairness. While the most advantaged may still benefit, consequences to the least advantaged must always be considered. This is a way to think about the allocation of resources that mandates that the most vulnerable populations always be considered in the development of institutional and public policy. Rights and responsibilities also proceed from this perspective of justice as fairness, taking the most vulnerable and least advantaged groups into consideration.

RIGHTS AND RESPONSIBILITIES

In our society, the past two centuries have seen a dramatic change from an emphasis on obligations and responsibilities of citizens to a society that now focuses more on rights of citizens and protection of those rights, including a right to health care. Claims of rights to health care often conflict with current goals and policies that influence health care financing and delivery. Cost containment goals and ever-expanding technological capabilities also affect school health and health-related services.

Like other social institutions, schools must deal with issues of rights and responsibilities, and school nurses find these to be factors in many of the decisions they make. Claims of individual rights arise from our society's emphasis on individualism and individual freedom. Examples include a right to make choices, rights to privacy and protection of confidentiality, and a right to freedom from bodily harm. The fact that most students in public schools have not reached the age of legal majority only adds to the complexity of discussions about rights and responsibilities. One example is mothers in a student population who have attained legal majority simply by becoming mothers. Yet they may not even be close to the chronological age of majority in a particular state.

A narrow focus on rights for one group and responsibilities for another is an inadequate perspective for considering the principle of respect for persons, a principle that includes both respect for individual autonomy and respect for persons as interconnected members of the human community. School nurses are confronted with situations in which claims of rights by individuals are only the beginning point for discussion—not the end of the discussion. Claims of individual rights alone do not trump all other considerations, such as avoiding harm to a group of students when a single student's behavior endangers others.

ANA Code for Nurses and Rights

The ANA Code for Nurses (1985) uses the language of "rights" in its major provisions and interpretive statements, which include nurses' obligations to safeguard client rights to privacy as an inalienable and basic human right in health care. Claims of client rights in the Code incorporate nurses' obligations to provide care based on respect for human dignity and the uniqueness of the client and to protect confidentiality. This perspective often creates conflict for school nurses and educators who have more goals to consider than simply honoring the rights that individual students claim.

The Code also recognizes implicitly that individuals have moral and legal rights to determine what is to be done to their bodies, to be given information that is necessary for informed decision making, and to be told the possible effects of care. School nurses need to take these aspects of informed decision making and consent into consideration when counseling students and making recommendations about their health problems and health-related behaviors.

In determining the extent of a student's involvement in making decisions, school nurses will have to consider a variety of factors besides autonomy, including chronological age and the student's capacity to understand the consequences for himself or herself and for others. One option is to include students in the decision making process in a position of limited power. In this capacity, students may not legally provide sole consent, but they may provide (or withhold) assent to a decision about participation. This concept has limits based on the nature of the consequences for an individual and others who may be affected by a decision. An example is students claiming a "right" to smoke wherever they wish. Students then need to be part of discussions about responsibilities as well as rights. They are not only individual persons but also citizens of the school community.

Different Types of Rights

Part of the challenge of using the language of rights is that there are many different types of rights and views of what constitutes a right. Rights also need to be distinguished from privileges. Privileges are benefits or advantages provided by someone else, such as the privilege of driving a car. The state provides this privilege to people who meet certain requirements. The underlying notion of rights is grounded in respect for human beings in their social context, that is, as individuals embedded in a network of interconnecting relationships (Davis et al., 1997, p. 84). Paying attention to this reality reaffirms that students are usually not isolated from others but rather interconnected with others in their school and community.

Two major types of rights are moral, or human, rights and legal rights. Human rights have been described as moral rights of fundamental importance. They are more important from a societal perspective than other rights, even legal rights, and are shared equally by all persons. If an individual is deprived of a human right, there is a grave affront to justice (Bandman, 1978). Many human rights are stated as negative rights, such as the right not to be tortured or the right of non-interference, rather than as positive rights, such as a right to an education or to health care. Negative rights are generally considered by the liberal individualist tradition to be stronger than claims of positive rights (Beauchamp & Childress, 1994, p. 73). This is similar to the strength of the ethical principle of preventing or avoiding harm in relationship to the principle of beneficence or providing benefits. It can be argued from this perspective that school health nurses have a stronger obligation to avoid harm to individuals and to other students than to provide an individual with the benefit of protecting confidentiality when others are in jeopardy. An example is a student who is known to be using drugs and tells the nurse that another student supplied them.

A narrower view of rights falls under the category of legal rights created by law. Rights exist by virtue of having been enacted by courts or legislatures. Simply claiming a right does not mean that it exists in the legal sense or that anyone legally has an obligation or responsibility to honor that claim. This is a key issue when it comes to claims about rights to health and access to health care. Constitutional amendments provide citizens with a broad sweep of rights but there is no constitutional amendment that is specific to health or health care as a legal right for all.

Many concepts of rights, such as a right to privacy or to health care, are associated with a specific social system and its legal institutions (Davis et al., 1997, p. 85). Some groups in our society, prisoners in correctional facilities and Native Americans, for example, have legal rights to health care. Many more in our society have no legal right to health care. In claiming a legal right, one must demonstrate that an individual's person or property is endangered. Once that has been

demonstrated, a second question arises: Who, if anyone, has a legally enforceable duty to honor an individual's claim of a right? The second part of a legitimate claim is that an individual, such as a school nurse, or entity, such as a school, has a corresponding duty or obligation. School nurses, for example, have professional duties to provide competent care and ethical duties to avoid or prevent harm not only to individual students but also to the school population for which they are responsible.

Framing an issue solely in terms of rights, without clarifying what kinds of rights are being claimed, often leads to an adversarial confrontation rather than a resolution of conflict. While rights that have legal standing frequently identify individuals or institutions that have corresponding duties, moral or human rights do not automatically have this feature. When rights fall into the category of human or moral rights rather than legal rights, it is difficult—but necessary—to identify who has the corresponding duties to honor the rights that are claimed.

The Patient's Bill of Rights, which has legal standing in some states, creates institutional responsibilities to patients as holders of these rights. Health care institutions can be held legally accountable for respecting and upholding patients' rights in these states. Many existing patient's bills of rights are not exclusively about rights but also define patients' responsibilities, such as showing respect for other patients. Patient's bills of rights and responsibilities in health care services can serve as guides for schools wishing to develop similar documents, with students and staff working collaboratively to prevent identified or potential ethical problems.

Considering both rights and responsibilities will create a more useful framework for a discussion than solely focusing on rights, particularly when the claimed rights have no legal standing.

Nurses and educators will find it useful to understand the different kinds of rights that students or parents might claim and to make these differences clear to them. If the rights are not legally mandated, they can still be discussed and the conflict resolved, but they can be put in a broader ethical framework for discussion and problem solving. Regardless of their legal or philosophical basis, the claims should be discussed in an atmosphere of mutual respect and with an assurance that everyone's voice will be heard.

In summary, claims of individual rights are only the beginning, not the end, of responding to situations in which ethical concerns predominate. An attempt to respond to a claim of rights as the sole issue in a conflict is limited and generally unsatisfactory unless the rights have legal standing. There is much more to be considered, such as clarifying that situation, determining what kind of right is being claimed, and identifying the responsibilities of the parties involved.

SITUATIONS FOR DECISION MAKING AND PROBLEM SOLVING

The ethical framework for decision making and problem solving presented earlier in this chapter will be used in this section to illustrate how it can help participants discuss and develop responses to ethical quandaries. Developing resolutions to ethical disagreements and conflicts is a fundamental component of the school health nurse's role as identified in chapter 1 by Wold. School nurses can also be advocates for inclusion of ethical considerations in decision making and policy development in their schools.

Two situations with ethical conflicts for decision makers in school settings are presented below. The brief discussion does not exhaust all the possibilities for consideration; rather, it indicates directions in which the school nurse's reasoning and reflection might go before a decision is made or action taken when ethical issues are part of the situation.

Situation One: Jim

Jim, a 17-year-old senior, is a popular athlete in a large, urban high school. He lives with his parents and his two younger siblings. He comes to the school health clinic and tells the nurse that he has experienced night sweats and intermittent diarrhea for the past three months.

The nurse does a brief physical examination and discovers swollen lymph nodes and oral thrush. Jim refuses to answer inquiries about his use of intravenous drugs or his sexual behavior, saying that he has a "right" not to answer questions. He mutters something about AIDS but does not respond when asked for clarification of what he said. He has never had a blood transfusion as far as he knows.

The nurse recommends that Jim make an appointment for a complete physical examination and possible further testing. He tells her that he is covered under his dad's health insurance plan. He does not want his parents to know anything about his health concerns or the recommendations for further testing and observation. He also claims that he has "rights" to complete privacy and demands that the nurse not tell anyone about this visit or his symptoms.

The nurse is concerned about how she should respond to Jim's claims about his rights. She wants to take the "right" actions and to fulfill her obligations to Jim, to other students, to his parents, and to school administration. Upon reflection, she recognizes that this situation may be characterized as an ethical problem because of the conflicting needs and interests of all the parties involved or affected and because ethical principles and values are at stake. She also knows that students and health professionals may experience different feelings and emphasize different values in determining the right action to take in this and similar troubling situations.

The nurse's ethical concerns include balancing or reconciling issues of privacy and confidentiality, claims of rights, how to respect Jim as an individual, and how to avoid actual or potential harm to him as well as potential harm to other students who are in contact with him.

Turning to the framework presented in this chapter, the nurse decides that she must systematically think through the ethical aspects of the situation, determine the options that stand the test of ethical reflection, and discuss these options and her rationale with a colleague if she feels that this is necessary. Her initial steps are to identify what is going on in the situation, including all relevant information and key stakeholders, to the degree that this is possible. For example, she knows that Jim has had good grades all through school and that his grades have been dropping. She also knows that Jim has sometimes missed team practices and even recently missed a game. These behaviors are quite unlike his past scholastic performance and sports involvement. She also knows Jim's parents and appreciates the concern that they have always shown for their children. She realizes that they have high expectations for Jim as the oldest son.

The nurse ponders the fact that Jim would not discuss his sexual history. Since she does not have access to a sexual history for Jim, she can only assume that he may be sexually active. Therefore, she is very concerned about the welfare of other students who may be Jim's sexual partners. The nurse also recognizes that school administrators and faculty have a stake in this situation. They, too, are responsible for protecting students from harm and promoting health as a means of achieving an education. The nurse realizes that Jim must trust her because he came to her about his health concerns even if he was not forthcoming with any details. He also may be terribly worried and embarrassed to find himself in this situation.

Considering the parties involved and the available information, the nurse identifies the ethical issues or conflicts in the situation and the ethical principles and values at stake. She knows that protection of privacy and confidentiality is clearly an issue given Jim's request and the potential sensitivity of the situation. Such protection, if treated in an absolute way, will conflict, however, with the principle of non-maleficence—that is, avoiding or preventing further harm to Jim and to others in jeopardy from his past behavior or currently unknown health status. She also considers respect for persons, which includes respect for self-determination, but also respect for individuals as interconnected and interdependent members of the school community and the wider society. Jim does not exist in isolation from his family and other students. They are affected by his health-related behavior and decisions and are possibly endangered by his behavior.

Protection of privacy and confidentiality and respect for individual claims of rights do not automatically or always trump other important ethical considerations such as avoiding identifiable or potential harm to others. Harm to identifiable persons should usually receive more weight in decision making than potential harm to unidentified persons. Such a determination is often a matter of judgment on which reasonable people may disagree even after much ethical reflection.

The school nurse considers options that can be justified from an ethical perspective. This clearly rules out the option of doing nothing or simply taking Jim's claim about his rights of confidentiality and withholding information as the last word on the subject. One option is to call Jim in to her office for further discussion of her concerns about his health and to ask him what he thinks is a reasonable next step or set of steps for follow-up. This is an opportunity to demonstrate her respect for Jim as an individual and to help him clarify his responsibilities to himself and to others. They can talk about how he might respond if one of his friends were in a similar situation and how important it is to care for one's friends and family when the decisions that one makes potentially affect their well-being. Her assumption, if she does this, is that Jim is a reasonable person who may choose to take responsible action after this preliminary discussion, action that assures attention to his own health and the well-being of others. The nurse may also offer to accompany Jim to talk with his parents if he is reluctant to face them alone. Jim is covered under their health plan and she knows that parents are ultimately responsible for the medical bills of minors. The nurse may consider talking with a trusted colleague whose perspective she values in order to identify any further options before taking action. An outline of the situation can be presented as hypothetical without any personal identifiers as one

way to protect Jim's privacy and confidentiality as requested. As a last resort, if Jim refuses to follow recommendations for further assessment and the nurse's offers of assistance, the nurse can consider going beyond the nurse-student relationship in order to meet her professional obligations to Jim and other students in the school.

One of the difficulties for school nurses, administrators, and parents of students in situations like this is that students may take action not in their best interests, such as leaving home or school in order to avoid confronting a health crisis. For the nurse, however, the potential for negative consequences does not justify doing nothing or simply allowing student demands to be her only consideration.

An argument can be made for using communitarian ethical theory to inform a response to troubling student situations like Jim's. Communitarian theory would be helpful to the school nurse because Jim's decisions potentially affect others in the school with whom he is interconnected. It justifies actions that are more community-oriented instead of leaving the nurse to make a decision based solely on a claim of individual rights. Using communitarian theory, she can give attention to communal values, social goals, virtues of cooperation, and the importance of individual responsibility, as well as to the student's claim of rights.

Consideration of communitarian ethical theory also affirms Jim's role as a citizen in the school and community. Two parts of the concept of citizenship are important for school nurses and other decision makers in education (Danis & Churchill, 1991). One part requires deliberation about a person's legal rights and duties and protects the private self. The second part emphasizes the communitarian, social, and moral aspects of citizenship with a focus on our common purposes and shared vulnerabilities. Thinking about Jim's situation from both sides of the citizenship coin puts a different perspective on his claims about rights and does not automatically require the nurse to make a decision based solely on his demands. Claims of individual rights, even if they are legal rights, usually require a broader context of discussion before anyone can take action.

Considering more than one ethical approach or theory does not often result in easier decision making or make it easier to identify a single right action. But broad ethical reflection does help decision makers take a more comprehensive approach to the issue and to rule out some options. For example, accepting Jim's claim of a right to refuse to answer questions as meaning she need take no further action is not an option to the nurse after she has taken a broader ethical perspective. The school nurse's recognition that systematic ethical reasoning is required rules out any simplistic response to Jim's situation.

Situation Two: Carol

This case study involves Carol, a terminally ill 9-year-old student who has developed fatal complications of a kidney disease and still wants to attend school. Carol does not want any of her classmates or other students to know that she is terminally ill. She has a do-not-resuscitate (DNR) order that has just been written, and the school nurse is developing a plan for her care while in school.

Carol attends a public school where she is in a third-grade, rather than fourth-grade, class because she has frequent absences due to her illness. She has had two kidney transplants that have failed. She is now on kidney dialysis three times a week and is not a candidate for a third transplant owing to other medical complications. She has participated in the decision about the DNR order. Carol has had periodic tutoring at home but has difficulty keeping up with her classmates academically because of her medical treatments and lack of energy. She has a strong will and wants to be "one of the kids." She becomes upset when treated differently because of her illness even though her classmates know that she is very ill. Carol's parents are determined that she attend school whenever possible so that she can be with her friends and kids near her age. Two younger siblings attend the same school.

This situation is worrisome to the school nurse who is developing Carol's plan of care because the school has never had a student with a DNR order. The nurse is concerned about Carol's well-being while in school and the well-being of other students. Even though in the past she has urged the school to be proactive in developing a plan for such students, the school has been reluctant to do so.

Key school administrators and some members of the school board are ambivalent about children with DNR orders attending school. They have been informed about the Americans with Disabilities Act of 1990 and the Individuals with Disabilities Education Act of 1990 that mandate the same level of education for children like Carol as for all other students. This situation raises many ethical and legal issues that schools have not encountered in the past when students who were ill generally remained at home for their care and received home tutoring. School administrators and school health professionals struggle with new obligations to respond to student situations covered by these mandates.

The nurse determines that she must make both short- and long-term plans in order to respond most effectively to this situation. She knows that her immediate plan must be comprehensive regarding: Carol's medical status; sensitivity to the many ethical and legal issues; and the feelings and values of those affected by this situation. For example, when parents choose to refuse specific life-prolonging treatments for a child, many school employees struggle with their obligation to honor this decision when the child is in school. Honoring this parental right may conflict with rights and obligations to other students and with strongly held moral beliefs of school personnel who will be in contact with Carol. While she has not been in school recently, Carol will return to school as soon as she is stronger, probably within the next week or two. So planning for her return has a time factor as well.

The nurse arranges a meeting with Carol's parents and school administrators to share information and to provide them with an opportunity to voice their concerns, and to provide input for the plan of care. After this meeting, she plans to meet with Carol's teachers and their assistants to provide information about Carol's situation, to hear the teachers' concerns, and to discuss their responsibilities to Carol and her parents and to their other students.

Determining the level of responsibility that is appropriate in medical crises for teachers and other school employees who are not medical personnel raises many concerns that must be addressed (Rushton, Will, & Murray, 1994). Legal opinions have not been unanimous about the duty of schools to comply with duly authorized DNR orders for students, and, in any event, it is unclear whether physicians can give a medical order to individuals who are not licensed health care professionals (i.e., laypersons). (See chapter 14 for further discussion of this issue.) School nurses, other educators, and administrators must have accurate information about their own state laws on this matter. Regardless of the existence or lack of specific state law, schools may still consider that they have an ethical obligation to proactively educate school employees and their students about the issues involved in these situations. Still, reasonable people disagree about what constitutes an appropriate response even when it involves health education and discussion that is couched in terms of prevention.

The school nurse realizes that Carol's situation requires a response that goes beyond just this one case, as does the allocation of resources for dealing with these situations. Therefore, she puts them on her agenda for future attention, realizing that fairness and justice are issues here and that a plan for Carol cannot wait for future-oriented education plans and allocation of resources in the next fiscal budget. She recalls that there is no consensus on what constitutes justice in our society. She also knows that the allocation of financial and human resources in a school district and within individual schools has no single or easy formula and that several stakeholders are involved.

In 1994, the National Education Association (NEA) published guidelines that serve as a resource for school nurses and administrators to use in developing a response to DNR order in schools (Rushton et al., 1994). The guidelines suggest minimum conditions for school boards to consider if they choose to develop policy in this area:

- there should be a written request accompanied by a written order from the student's physician;

- the school should establish a team to consider the written request and the available alternatives;

- if no other alternatives are available, a medical emergency plan should be developed; and

- staff and students should receive training and counseling as part of an overall response or policy.

Elements of a medical emergency plan are also identified, including the following:

- briefing other school employees who supervise the student;

- requiring an ID bracelet indicating that the student has a DNR order;

- establishing parental responsibility for executing a contract with the local emergency medical service, with a copy to the school superintendent; and

- conducting an annual team review of the plan.

The initial plan that the school nurse has developed, using the NEA guidelines, shows that she has considered the ethical principles and values of respect for the student and parents as individuals and as members of the school community. It also shows her concern for avoiding or preventing harm to key stakeholders such as the student's classmates and those who teach or supervise a student with a DNR order. Expressing concern for all the key stakeholders in this situation also demonstrates her attention to the school's responsibilities to individuals and the wider school population. Justice and fairness are important ethical values and principles at stake in this and similar situations.

Thus the nurse has been able to develop a plan that includes short- and long-term aspects supported by ethical reasoning and reflection.

CONCLUDING COMMENTS

School nurses have professional and ethical obligations to individual students, to their parents, to school administration, to the school community composed of students and employees, and to the school board. Ethical obligations may sometimes conflict with existing law and with personal and professional values and interests. Nevertheless, school nurses and administrators should have policies and procedures in place to respond to these conflicts in ethically responsible ways. School nurses and other decision makers should not be abandoned in their search for ways to respond to tough ethical issues. The leadership in schools and school districts and related professional organizations should provide assistance and guidance in this search as interdependent members of school and wider communities. School nurses are in a key position to initiate thoughtful ethical responses to the many challenges confronting them in their promotion and protection of healthy students and schools.

REFERENCES

American Nurses Association. (1985). *Code for nurses with interpretive statements.* Kansas City, MO: American Nurses Association.

Bandman, B. (1978). The human rights of patients, nurses, and other health professionals. In E. L. Bandman & B. Bandman (Eds.), *Bioethics and human rights* (pp. 321–322). Boston: Little, Brown.

Beauchamp, T. L., & Childress, J. F. (1994). *Principles of biomedical ethics* (4th ed.). New York: Oxford University Press.

Danis, M., & Churchill, L. R. (1991). Autonomy and the common weal. *Hastings Center Report, 21* (1), 25–31.

Davis, A. J., Aroskar, M. A., Liaschenko, J., & Drought, T. S. (1997). *Ethical dilemmas and nursing practice* (4th ed.). Stamford, CT: Appleton & Lange.

Drane, J. F. (1994). Character and the moral life. In E. R. DuBose, R. Hamel, & L. J. O'Connell (Eds.), *A matter of principles? Ferment in U.S. bioethics* (pp. 284–309). Valley Forge, PA: Trinity Press International.

Jonsen, A., & Butler, L. (1975). Public ethics and policy making. *Hastings Center Report, 5* (4), 19–31.

Macklin, R. (1976). Moral concerns and appeals to rights and duties. *Hastings Center Report, 6* (5), 31–38.

Rawls, J. (1971). *A theory of justice.* Cambridge, MA:
    Harvard University Press.

Rushton, C. H., Will, J. C., & Murray, M. G. (1994). To
    honor and obey—DNR orders and the school. *Pedi-
    atric Nursing, 20* (6), 581–585.

**See Page 625 for Table of Federal Statutes and
Regulations.**

Chapter Four

Legal Framework and Financial Accountability for School Nursing Practice

Katherine J. Pohlman

INTRODUCTION

Like other nursing subspecialties, school nursing rests upon a foundation of general nursing practice. Similarly, an understanding of the licensure and certification requirements for school nursing requires an understanding of basic concepts and general principles related to nursing licensure and practice.

This chapter outlines the legal framework for nursing practice. It discusses nursing licensure generally and describes the role of the board of nursing as it relates to nursing education, nursing licensure, and disciplinary action. It provides a historical perspective on the debate over entry-into-practice requirements and practice in the expanded role. Additional sections discuss standards of practice, the standard of care, negligence, and issues related to delegation, training, and supervision by school nurses. The chapter briefly reviews selected issues related to relationships between school nurses and other professionals, including health care providers and school personnel. The final section reviews the financial accountability for practice, including professional liability insurance, statutorily limited liability, indemnification, and hold harmless agreements.

LICENSURE

Licensure is the process by which an agency of a state government grants permission to an individual to practice a particular profession or engage in a certain occupation. Although the reader may first think of licensure only in terms of the professions—such as medicine, nursing, education, or law—most states license a large number of occupations as well, such as morticians, beauty operators, and plumbers. To ensure protection of the public's health, safety, and welfare, prior to granting a license, the state requires that an applicant demonstrate a minimal degree of competency. A state licensing scheme may adopt one of two approaches to licensure, either mandatory or permissive. A mandatory statute regulates the practice of the profession and requires compliance if an individual performs activities that fall within the scope of practice as defined by the statute. A permissive statute regulates the use of a title and requires compliance only if an individual intends to use the title regulated by that statute.

Prior to the first nursing licensure law, anyone could care for the sick. Because early licensure laws regulated use of the title "nurse," an individual could still care for the sick, provided that individual did not use the title *nurse*. Although North Carolina was the first state to adopt a mandatory nursing licensure law (Hadley, 1989), eventually the remainder of the states followed suit and passed statutes that are now frequently referred to as nurse practice acts. A nurse practice act defines the scope of nursing practice, establishes the requirements for entry into practice, and also sets forth the penalties for violations of the statute. Additional provisions also address related issues, such as the board of nursing (BON). Those issues are discussed later in this chapter.

A brief summary of the relationship between the federal and state governments facilitates an understanding of the source of the state's authority to license the professions. The United States government is based upon the principle of federalism, with power divided between the federal and state governments (Black, 1979). As discussed in chapter 2, the United States (U.S.) Constitution reserves for the states those powers not specifically delegated to the federal government. The Supremacy Clause (Article VI, Section 2) of the U.S. Constitution declares that federal laws and treaties are superior to any conflicting state law or state constitution.

Because the U.S. Constitution does not specifically control licensure, the power to regulate licensure is reserved for the states. Each state possesses what is known as "parens patriae" power under which it can create laws to protect the public's health, safety, and welfare. The state's police power permits it to limit certain individual rights when creating laws necessary to protect the public (Kelly, 1991). If the federal government passed legislation concerning licensure, to the extent that the federal law conflicted with a state law, the federal law would prevail.

One example of a federal law related to licensure is the Health Care Quality Improvement Act (HCQIA) of 1986. Congress passed that Act in an attempt to protect the public from what it perceived as the dangers associated with ineffective peer review. Without any national peer review system, incompetent health care providers could conceivably face disciplinary action and loss of professional licensure in one state, but later obtain a license in another state. HCQIA created the National Practitioner Data Bank, which is discussed in greater detail later in this chapter.

When Congress first passed HCQIA, each state had the opportunity to "opt out" and create its own statutory scheme to accomplish the goals of HCQIA (Horner, 1990). Because of the Supremacy Clause discussed above, those states could not create provisions more lenient than HCQIA, but they were free to adopt more stringent provisions. Similarly, nothing in those state laws could override or conflict with the provisions of the HCQIA (Horner, 1990).

PRACTICE ACTS

Although state statutes may differ, most nurse practice acts define the scopes of practice for the various levels of licensed nurses, such as registered nurse (RN) and licensed practical nurse (LPN), outline the requirements for licensure and entry into practice, create and empower a board of nursing, and set forth grounds for disciplinary action against licensees.

Board of Nursing

Most state legislatures pass laws that create and empower a board of nursing (BON) to enforce the nurse practice act. Most BONs exercise only the powers granted by the nurse practice act or those reasonably implied as necessary to carry out the responsibilities assigned by the practice act. In that respect, boards of nursing are typical of most governmental or administrative bodies (Northrop, 1987). Although most BONs exercise rule-making power over regulatory and disci-

plinary matters involving licensees, the authority of boards differs from state to state and can vary from fully autonomous to advisory only (Northrop, 1987). Rule-making power enables a BON to promulgate the rules and regulations necessary to carry out the provisions of the nurse practice act.

The composition and organization of BONs varies across the states. Some are composed of only registered nurses, while others include licensed practical nurses and/or public representatives. Most BONs rely on committees to carry out the discretionary responsibilities, with the disciplinary committee often one of the most active. Ministerial responsibilities are often performed by BON administrative staff rather than board members.

Declaratory Rulings

As part of their rule-making power, many BONs are also empowered to issue declaratory rulings or opinions. Such opinions clarify the scope of nursing practice as defined in the nurse practice acts. Examples of questions for which the Iowa Board of Nursing has issued declaratory rulings include the following:

1. May a teacher instructed and supervised by an RN insert and remove a catheter into a continent gastrostomy for the purpose of administering liquids? (1989)

2. May non-nursing staff discontinue a nasogastric tube in a school setting after the school nurse has inserted the tube and started the feeding and medication? (1988)

3. Does state law allow registered nurses to administer over-the-counter medications to children enrolled in the public school system upon parental request? (1985)

The ruling in a case decided by the Supreme Court of Alabama underscores the importance of the BON's power to issue declaratory rulings (*Stamps v. Jefferson County Board of Education*, 1994). Several special education teachers sought a declaratory judgment from the circuit court, claiming that certain functions (including suctioning of tracheotomies, medication administration, gastrostomy feedings, etc.) assigned to them as a routine part of their jobs constituted the practice of nursing without a license. The circuit court entered a judgment for the Board of Education, finding that the teachers were not unlawfully practicing nursing. The Alabama Supreme Court dismissed the subsequent appeal, opining that the circuit court did not have jurisdiction to enter any judgment because the BON, a necessary party, was not named in the lawsuit.

Legal Counsel for the Board of Nursing

The type of legal counsel available to a BON varies according to the state's governmental structure. A BON in a heavily populated state with several large urban areas is likely to have jurisdiction over a significant number of nurse licensees. That type of board may have an attorney whose sole client is that BON, or it may share an attorney with other health-care related boards. A board in a sparsely populated state may be represented by an attorney responsible for serving multiple unrelated administrative agencies. Obviously, an attorney responsible for representing many diverse administrative agencies is not likely to acquire the same level of expertise in the various substantive areas regulated by those agencies as an attorney responsible for representing only boards that regulate health care professionals.

School nurses often face a similar phenomenon when employed by a school district or other educational or administrative agency. The employer is responsible for providing counsel to the school nurse when necessary, often through the services of an attorney who represents the employing school district, board, or administrative agency. Because school health and nursing services represent a very small percentage of the attorney's responsibilities, such an attorney may have had relatively little opportunity to become familiar with nursing licensure and practice issues.

Although the challenges associated with such a situation are discussed in greater detail later in this chapter, a short example illustrates the phenomenon described above. A recent publication featured an article critical of the result in *DeBord v. Board of Education of the Ferguson Florissant School District* (a 1996 case discussed in greater detail later in this chapter in the section entitled "The Role of Organizational Policies in Establishing the Standard of Care"). In his critique, the author, an education attorney, alleged that the Board of Education was practicing medicine without a license because it had supported a school nurse's compliance with school policy, which required her to refuse to administer excessive doses of Ritalin to a student. After inviting a state school nurse consultant and this author to submit a rebuttal for publication, he rejected the submission because he believed it was non-responsive to his article. He apparently based his belief upon the fact that the rebuttal focused on the school nurse's legal duty, under the nurse practice act, to consider student safety and independently evaluate physician orders

before administering medication. Commenting that his article had not even discussed the school nurse's role at any length, he explained that he saw her actions as irrelevant to any analysis of the situation. An attorney familiar with nursing licensure and practice issues would have understood clearly not only the relevance but the pivotal nature of the nurse's legal duty in that case.

Regulation of Nursing Education

In addition to responsibilities related directly to licensees, many BONs also regulate nursing education programs. Most require that programs obtain accreditation, often from the National League for Nursing (NLN). Prior to granting accreditation, most accrediting bodies conduct a thorough evaluation to ensure that an applicant organization or program meets established standards. Some nursing education programs may be subject to additional accreditation beyond the BON, such as requirements contained in the state statutes related to the general regulation of educational institutions.

Regulation of Nursing Practice

The BON is usually responsible for defining the requirements for entry into practice. Most BONs also administer license renewal requirements, including continuing education in those states where the nurse practice act mandates a certain number of credits per licensure period.

Among other things (such as payment of a fee and submission of the requisite application), the requirements for entry into practice include either successful completion of an examination or satisfaction of requirements other than examination, such as reciprocity based upon valid licensure in another state. The BON also defines the eligibility criteria for licensure by examination. That one responsibility, seemingly minor among the board's many other duties, may be the single most historically controversial issue boards face. Known throughout the profession as the entry-into-practice debate, it rages on and is discussed in greater detail later in this chapter.

Disciplinary Proceedings

Most nurse practice acts empower the BON to take action against a nurse's license for grounds defined in the state statute or related regulations. Traditionally, the BON can deny, limit, suspend, revoke, rescind, or otherwise act upon a license for grounds that frequently include substance abuse, incompetence, negligence, criminal activity, or violation of the Nurse Practice Act (NPA) (Northrop, 1987). Examples of disciplinary action against nursing licenses are discussed in various sections throughout this chapter.

The Health Care Quality Improvement Act (HCQIA) currently requires health care entities to report to the board of medicine (BOM) any disciplinary actions against physicians that affect clinical privileges for more than thirty days. The health care entities report such actions to the board of medicine and it, in turn, reports them to the National Practitioner Data Bank (NPDB), a data bank created by HCQIA. Some think HCQIA should be amended to require reporting of disciplinary action against nurses as well. (For more information on the NPDB, see the discussion of medical malpractice payment reporting in the Negligence Section of this chapter.)

Issues Related to Nurse Practice Acts

Telenursing

Even though the nurse practice act defines the scope of nursing practice, questions often arise concerning the application of that definition to real-life circumstances. (See earlier discussion in the section on Declaratory Rulings.) Telenursing, case management, and utilization management are three sets of circumstances where the BON may be called upon to decide whether certain activities constitute the practice of nursing.

As in other health care disciplines, such as medicine, the advancement of telecommunications has introduced into the professions an important debate. Does the provision of services over electronic media constitute the practice of the profession? At least one nursing organization has answered that question in the affirmative. The National Council of State Boards of Nursing (NCSBN) defines telenursing as "the practice of nursing over distance using telecommunications technology" (1997b).

Although the telephone may be the most frequently used technology, the issues are similar when information is transmitted through facsimile, video phones, teleconference, computer, video conference, or interactive television. The telephone has long been an important part of nursing practice, with nurses taking orders from a doctor located elsewhere, whether in the same building or off-site. The rapid development of sophisticated telecommunication technologies has made possible many communication methods never before imagined. The push to save health care dollars has ignited interest in such methods.

Telenursing can encompass a number of different scenarios. Perhaps the communication occurs between a nurse and patient over the telephone where physical assessment of the patient's symptoms is not possible. Perhaps it occurs through the use of interactive television located in a patient's home, where visual communication accompanies the verbal. Perhaps the communication is between a nurse assisting with surgery, where the surgeon giving orders is consulting from another state via video-conferencing. These are but a few examples of the current arrangements that fall within the definition of telenursing.

In telenursing, the legal issue is not so much use of the telephone, but rather the practice of nursing across state lines. Because each state regulates the practice of nursing in that state, regulatory issues surface when a nurse physically present in one state performs tasks or functions in another state. The issues exist regardless of whether the nurse is assessing and diagnosing a patient in another state or accepting and carrying out orders from a physician present in another state. The question arise then whether the nurse practice act in each state permits practice across state lines and whether both nurse practice acts define the task or function as within the scope of nursing practice.

Some state laws may address practice across state lines, but in a fashion that fails to fully clarify the issue. For example, the Connecticut nurse practice act's general definition of nursing is silent on the issue of practice across state lines, but a later section of the same law specifically states that an RN or LPN employed by a home health care agency may execute a medical regimen under the direction of a physician licensed in a state that borders Connecticut (Connecticut General Statutes 20–87[a]) Additionally, the same Connecticut practice act states that an advanced practice nurse may prescribe, dispense, and administer medical treatments under the direction of a physician licensed in Connecticut. Because the practice act contains only very specific references to telenursing, it remains unclear what the BON might conclude in a factual situation not directly addressed by the law.

In Connecticut, school nurses face further confusion. While the practice act does not contain any general permissive language about practicing across state lines, the education law in that state specifically permits school nurses to administer medication prescribed by physicians licensed in a state other than Connecticut (C.G.S. 10-212a). The fact that the education law permits that practice does not prevent the BON from deciding that such actions are not consistent with the scope of practice as defined in the Connecticut nurse practice act. As discussed in several sections throughout this and other chapters, school nurses find themselves facing such situations frequently. There are numerous instances of overt conflict between the nurse practice act and education laws, as well as other instances of more subtle or potential conflicts like the Connecticut example described above.

A 1995 NCSBN survey assessed the nurse practice acts in 41 jurisdictions. The results revealed that

- 31% permitted taking orders only from a provider licensed in that state;

- 14% prohibited taking orders from a provider licensed in another state; and

- 58% were silent on the issue (NCSBN, 1997c).

The survey of nurse practice acts and the Connecticut example discussed show that the current status of the law leaves unanswered many of the complex regulatory issues raised by telenursing. It should come as no surprise that nursing organizations have begun to propose strategies to answer some of those questions and provide clarity for the practicing nurse. A later section of this chapter discusses in greater detail one of those strategies—the mutual recognition model or regulation.

It may seem that telenursing is of great concern only in certain nursing subspecialties or within certain delivery systems. Those thinking only of the school nurse who practices in the traditional role within a public school district (usually, by definition, within a single state's boundaries), may mistakenly assume it to be of little concern in school health. Those more familiar with the broad boundaries of the school health subspecialty rapidly realize the many situations in which cross-state practice issues may arise. A nurse accompanying students on a field trip in another state, a child whose family chooses a primary health care provider in a neighboring state, an educational system with multiple state sites, a child who pays to attend a public school in an adjoining state, a rural setting where the closest acute care facility is within another state's boundaries—all present issues similar to those regularly discussed as part of the telenursing debate.

Managed Health Care: Case Management and Utilization Management

Nurses are involved in managed care in a variety of roles, including that of care provider, case manager, and utilization management nurse. Some of those roles, such as case manager and utilization manager, involve

activities that use telecommunications technologies across state boundaries.

Case management is the process of managing chronic or serious conditions likely to require multiple providers and involve costly health resources. Case managers handle each patient individually, working with providers to identify and make available the most cost-effective treatments within the bounds of the patient's health care coverage. Utilization management involves review of the appropriateness, necessity, and quality of health care services or supplies. That review may occur before the delivery of services or after, as part of the claims payment process.

Both case management and utilization management responsibilities are frequently performed by nurses in conjunction with health plan medical directors. Because health plans are often not administered from the same state in which a patient resides or receives care, the nurse involved may be evaluating aspects of client health care provided in another state. Although health plans usually insist that case and utilization management decisions be based on the availability of benefits rather than the actual health care services required or provided, courts have increasingly rejected that distinction as artificial. Patients rarely have resources to obtain health care not covered by some type of reimbursement plan, whether private or governmental, and courts have relied on that fact to find health plans liable for the denial of benefits in certain circumstances (*Wickline v. State of California*, 1986).

Some health plans take the position that case and utilization management nurses are not practicing nursing when performing their responsibilities. Although this author has not identified any BON declaratory rulings that have held otherwise, boards of nursing may well disagree with the health plan view. A 1992 memorandum from the Wisconsin Department of Regulation and Licensing held that a medical director engaged in retrospective utilization review activities was not practicing medicine, although the opinion indicated that prospective or current utilization review might constitute the practice of medicine in certain circumstances. A 1998 Arizona appeals court ruling clearly established that a medical director who denied benefits because gall bladder surgery was not medically necessary was practicing medicine and, therefore, under the jurisdiction of the board of medicine (*Murphy v. Arizona Board of Medical Examiners*). While different jurisdictions may continue to reach conflicting conclusions, it is more likely that the most recent case represents a trend, based upon an increased understanding of managed care.

Some health plans have attempted to distinguish between the roles of physicians and nurses involved in case and utilization management activities. Proponents of that distinction claim nurses face minimal liability because they do not deny benefits, but rather rely on protocols to approve benefits and refer all potential denials to a physician for review and final determination. In reality, courts have considered the nurse's activities and judgment as a significant factor when finding health plans liable for damages based upon utilization management decisions (*Jass v. Prudential Health Care, Inc.*, 1996).

While health plans may attempt to make a distinction between physicians and nurses regarding whether either is practicing a profession when performing case and utilization management responsibilities, many health care management nurses would reject any attempt at that distinction. Most accept that BOMNs will likely ultimately agree with the Arizona court that found the BOM had jurisdiction over a managed care medical director engaged in utilization management activities.

Reciprocity and Mutual Recognition Licensure

Because nursing licensure is regulated individually by each state, a nurse interested in relocating to a new state must deal with the administrative issues related to obtaining licensure in that new state. Assuming the original requirements for licensure are similar in the two states, usually a nurse must simply complete an application for licensure based upon reciprocity, pay a fee and demonstrate that the license in the first state is in good standing.

If the National Council of State Boards of Nursing (NCSBN) has its way, license by reciprocity may become a thing of the past. The NCSBN's mission is to lead in nursing regulation by assisting Member Boards, collectively and individually, to promote safe and effective nursing practice in the interest of protecting public health and welfare (August 29, 1997). It is the organization through which boards of nursing act and counsel together on matters of common interest. (August 29, 1997).

In August of 1997, the NCSBN's Delegate Assembly met and unanimously adopted the following resolution: "That the NCSBN endorses a 'mutual recognition' model of nursing regulation and authorizes the Board of Directors to develop strategies for implementation to be adopted by the Delegate Assembly" (August 25, 1997). Reasons cited by the NCSBN for the resolution include the following:

- New practice modalities and technology are raising questions regarding issues of current compliance with state licensure laws.

- Nursing practice is increasingly occurring across state lines.

- Nurses are practicing in a variety of settings and using new technologies that may occur across state lines.

- Expedient access to qualified nurses is needed and expected by consumers without regard to state lines.

- Expedient authorization to practice is expected by employers and nurses.

- Having a nurse demonstrate the same licensure qualifications to multiple states for comparable authority to practice is cumbersome and is neither cost-effective nor efficient (NCSBN, August 25, 1997).

In a special session held in December 1997, the NCSBN approved proposed language for an interstate compact in support of a standard approach to mutual recognition licensure. Under the mutual recognition model of regulation, nurses will hold a license in their state of residency, but will be able to practice in any state that has signed onto the interstate compact, provided the nurses follow the laws and regulations of the state in which they practice (NCSBN, December 16, 1997). Before implementation could occur, the states would need to take the compact back to their legislatures for enactment. Delegates attending the special session agreed to recommend that state legislatures adopt laws codifying the compact no earlier than January 1, 2000. As of 1999, Arkansas, Maryland, Texas, and Utah had adopted the interstate compact. Iowa, Nebraska, North Carolina, and Wisconsin were considering legislation introduced to adopt the compact (NCSBN, 1999).

The progress of these efforts will prove interesting to follow. As discussed later in this chapter, the nursing profession historically has encountered many obstacles when attempting to lobby for changes in its entry-into-practice requirements. On of these obstacles was divisiveness within the nursing profession as its members debated whether to define a two-, three-, or four-year nursing degree as the minimum educational requirement for entry into practice as a registered nurse. (See discussion later in this chapter.)

Mutual recognition may, on the surface, appear to be a less controversial issue than entry-into-practice; or perhaps the controversies have not yet emerged. For example, If North Dakota, as the only state that requires a BSN for entry into professional nursing practice, signs on to an interstate compact, will RNs in all other participating states be permitted to practice as professional nurses in North Dakota? Or will only RNs with a BSN be allowed? How the two issues will interface remains to be seen.

Boards of Registration for Other Professions

Most states license a number of other health care professionals in addition to nurses, including physicians, chiropractors, dentists, physician assistants, occupational therapists, social workers, and psychologists, to name a few. Some states choose not to regulate certain types of providers, despite the fact that other states require licensure for such professionals. Examples of providers that may need licensure in one state but not another are naturopaths and lay midwives. In situations where the activities of those unlicensed individuals closely resemble or overlap those of licensed health care professionals, it is not uncommon to see a licensing board (such as the BON) take legal action against an unlicensed individual (such as a lay midwife) for practicing the profession without a license.

Boards of registration for other licensed professionals (such as physicians, social workers, and psychologists) function in much the same manner as the BON. Each is charged with regulating a particular profession. Most enjoy rule-making power and are responsible for interpreting the scope of that particular profession's practice. In some states, particularly those less populated, the total number of practitioners in a given profession may not be very high, and a single administrative agency, such as the health department, may be charged with regulatory responsibility for various professions, such as occupational therapy, physical therapy, or acupuncture.

EDUCATIONAL REQUIREMENTS FOR ENTRY INTO NURSING PRACTICE

Practice as a Registered Nurse

No issue has been as divisive within the nursing profession as educational requirements for entry-into-practice. Although each state is free to regulate nursing licensure, and thus the educational requirements for entry into practice, all states historically adopted two categories of nursing licensure—licensed practical or licensed vocational nurses (LPNs or LVNs) and registered nurses (RNs).

Despite many efforts to change history, as of 2000, all but one state retained the traditional two nursing licensure categories. In March 1986, North Dakota changed its administrative regulations and became the first state to require a Bachelor of Science in nursing (BSN) degree for entry into professional nursing practice. Although Maine also adopted 1986 legislation that required a BSN for entry into professional nursing practice and an associate degree (AD) for entry into associate nursing practice, the implementation originally scheduled for 1995 met obstacles, and the law was not enforced.

The history of the debate over entry into practice dates back as far as 1964, when the American Nurses Association (ANA) resolved that by 1985, all states should require the BSN for entry into professional practice. When that proved unrealistic, ANA revised the timetable, calling for all states to do so by 1995. According to Wertz (1995), that timetable also proved unrealistic because ANA diverted resources throughout the 1980s and early 1990s to another compelling professional issue—health care reform. When 1995 arrived and only North Dakota had achieved the goal, that state led the charge to pass a new resolution, again in support of the original proposal to require the BSN for entry into practice.

Many factors contribute to what, at times, seems to be the unattainable goal of the BSN degree as the requirement for entry into professional nursing practice. Some are issues within the nursing profession itself, such as the inability to agree upon title and the scope of practice for each of the two proposed levels of nursing.

Other factors with a more indirect effect relate to the predominance of women within the profession and the difficulty women's professions have traditionally had lobbying successfully when those in power, still men for the most part, see the issues differently.

Although nursing as a labor force has always been far larger than medicine, the physician lobby has met with greater success when championing its positions to the legislature. While that may be related to gender, it is also most likely a result of the proportionately higher esteem granted to physicians. Although the percentage of women entering the medical profession has increased significantly over the last two decades, men continue to occupy many of the more powerful leadership positions within that profession, particularly within certain high-profile and high-dollar subspecialties, such as surgery, cardiology, and neurology.

Regardless of the reasons, 2000 finds nursing in much the same position as in 1965 with respect to licensure, with a few exceptions. Other than North Dakota, each state still permits all RN applicants to sit for the same licensure examination, regardless of educational preparation. Upon successful completion of the examination, each applicant still receives the same RN license. Nothing about that RN license informs the public whether the nurse graduated from a four-year college or university with a BSN degree, a two-year community college with an AD degree, a two- or three-year hospital school with a diploma, or a graduate-level nursing program with a masters or doctoral degree obtained after earning a bachelors degree in a non-nursing field.

Perhaps more than in the acute-care setting, the continued variability of various states' entry-into-practice requirements presents persistent problems for school nursing practice. Hospitals seem to have more readily acknowledged that different levels of competencies exist based upon the variable educational backgrounds of nurses. Often such facilities create career ladders, both clinical and administrative, that permit advancement according to increasing educational preparation.

Unfortunately, school districts and boards have been more resistant to such concepts. Many continue to disregard basic distinctions among the different types of nurses, including the difference between an RN and LPN or an RN and an advanced practice nurse. In the interest of budgetary concerns, some even attempt to inappropriately use LPNs rather than RNs as independently functioning school nurses. Because school districts are reluctant to acknowledge the existence of professional clinical standards for RN school nurses and the reality that LPNs cannot meet such standards, the competencies of school nurses often vary widely from school district to school district.

Additional Credentials—Certification

Beyond entry-into-practice requirements, nurses with baccalaureate or master's degrees (depending on the type and level of practice and certification prerequisites) who have specific experience can apply for certification in a particular area of practice from a national nursing organization. Generally, the applicant must present the requisite qualifications and pass an examination that demonstrates expert knowledge and judgment in the practice area. (Certification options for school nurses are discussed in chapter 5, as is teacher certification, a different type of credential altogether.)

Practice in the "Expanded Role"

Until 1971, all nurse practice acts included language that prohibited nurses from engaging in diagnosis or treatment—activities viewed as exclusively within the scope of medical practice (Hadley, 1989). Idaho changed that pattern and became the first state to recognize practice in the "expanded role" when it amended its practice act in 1971 (Hadley, 1989). Rather than delete the prohibition against diagnosis and treatment, Idaho added a phrase that permitted nurses to do so pursuant to rules and regulations created jointly by the Idaho BON and Board of Medicine (Hadley, 1989).

Between 1971 and 2000 all states, except Tennessee, revised their practice acts to formally recognize practice in the expanded role (Pearson, 2000). Although many of the statutes use different terminology to describe practice in the expanded role, the most commonly used term for a nurse practicing in that role is an Advanced Practice Nurse (APN) or Advanced Practice Registered Nurse (APRN). Each state statute is slightly different, but most fit one of four categories described by Pearson and set forth in Table 4-1 (2000).

The categories of APN licensure identified in Table 4-1 fall along a continuum, ranging from those that preserve the maximum amount of autonomy for the nursing profession to those that permit control by other disciplines. States where the nursing profession has the least amount of autonomy vest the regulatory power in the BON and the board of medicine (BOM) and require physician supervision of each APN as well. Those where nursing has the greatest degree of control vest the regulatory power solely in the BON and have no supervision requirement. For a detailed discussion, see "The Annual Legislative Update: How Each State Stands on Legislative Issues Affecting Advanced Nursing Practice" in the January 2000 issue of *Nurse Practitioner* (Pearson, 2000).

Certification for APNs

Although they vary somewhat, most states require APNs to obtain some type of certification for specialty practice by a recognized professional association, the most popular being the American Nurses Association (ANA). Certification programs for nurse practitioners today require completion of a specific course of study at the master's degree level and successful performance on an examination, which may include clinical as well as written components. For example, specialty certification is available for pediatric nurse practitioners, school nurse practitioners, and family nurse practitioners.

Prescriptive Authority

The nursing profession's battle to obtain prescriptive authority bears a striking resemblance to its earlier

Table 4-1. Comparison of State Practice Acts Affecting APN Licensure

States with Nurse Practitioner* Title Protection and the Board of Nursing as Sole Authority in Scope of Practice with No Requirements for Physician Collaboration or Supervision	Alaska, Arizona, Arkansas, Colorado, District of Columbia, Hawaii, Iowa, Maine, Michigan, Montana, New Hampshire, New Jersey, New Mexico, North Dakota, Oklahoma, Oregon, Rhode Island, Texas, Utah, Washington, West Virginia, Wyoming
States with Nurse Practitioner* Title Protection and the Board of Nursing as Sole Authority in Scope of Practice, but Scope of Practice Has a Requirement for Physician Collaboration or Supervision	California, Connecticut, Delaware, Florida, Georgia, Illinois, Indiana, Kansas, Kentucky, Louisiana, Massachusetts, Maryland, Minnesota, Missouri, Nebraska+, Nevada, New York, Ohio, South Carolina, Vermont, Wisconsin
States with Nurse Practitioner* Title Protection But Scope of Practice Is Authorized by the Board of Nursing and the Board of Medicine	Alabama, Mississippi, North Carolina, Pennsylvania, South Dakota, Virginia
States without Nurse Practitioner* Title Protection Where APNs Function under a broad Nurse Practice Act	Tennessee

* may include other Advanced Practice Nurses (APNs), such as clinical nurse specialists, nurse midwives, and nurse anesthetists
+states with an ARNP board

Modified with permission from: *The Nurse Practitioner, 25*(1): 18. Copyright Springhouse Corporation, 2000.

battle to obtain the legal right to diagnose and treat patients independent of physician supervision. The first victory came when North Carolina amended its nurse practice act and granted limited prescriptive authority to APNs—in 1975 for APNs and in 1977 for Certified Nurse Midwives (CNMs) (Hadley, 1989). The victory was bittersweet in many respects. A number of other states quickly followed suit and adopted statutes with similarly limited authority, most of which have proved difficult to amend to incorporate broader authority. As of 2000, nurse practice acts in every state include some type of prescriptive authority for APNs, although many retain restrictions adopted when the statutes were first amended to incorporate that authority (Pearson, 2000).

Many of the early statutes limited APN prescriptive authority to specific practice settings, facilities, or drug formularies. A number of practice acts still contain such restrictions. In states where APN practice requires physician supervision or approval by the BOM, prescriptive authority is usually subject to those same requirements. Hadley discusses the various statutory approaches, labeling them either substitutive (those that authorize nurses to function independently of a physician) or complementary (those that require nurses who prescribe to function as complements to physi-

cians) (1989). *The Nurse Practitioner*'s annual update adopts a different classification, organizing the various statutes into the four models set forth in Table 4-2 (Pearson, 2000).

STANDARDS OF PRACTICE AND STANDARD OF CARE

Because each phrase contains the word "standard," people tend to use "standard of care" and "standard of practice" interchangeably. In fact, the phrases have different but related meanings.

Webster's (1986) defines standard as something that is established by authority, custom, or general consent as a model or example to be followed. That definition offers the key to understanding the distinction between standards of practice and standard of care. While each is a model or example, the court establishes the standard of care and a profession usually establishes standards of practice.

Another aid to understanding the distinction requires careful attention to use of the singular versus plural with each term. Although defined by information from multiple sources, a singular standard of care is used to judge a defendant's actions. A singular standard of practice may apply to a particular clinical situa-

Table 4-2. Comparison of State Practice Acts Affecting APN Prescriptive Authority

States Where NPs* Can Prescribe (Including Controlled Substances) Independent of Any Required Physician Involvement in the Actual Prescription Writing	Alaska, Arizona, District of Columbia, Iowa, Maine, Montana, New Hampshire, New Mexico, Oregon, Utah**, Washington**, Wisconsin, Wyoming
States Where NPs* Can Prescribe (Including Controlled Substances) with Some Degree of Physician Involvement of Delegation of Prescription Writing	Arkansas, California, Colorado, Connecticut, Delaware, Florida^^, Georgia, Hawaii, Idaho, Illinois^^, Indiana, Kansas, Massachusetts, Maryland, Michigan, Minnesota, Nebraska, North Carolina, North Dakota, New Jersey, New York, Oklahoma, Pennsylvania^^, Rhode Island, South Carolina, South Dakota, Tennessee, Vermont, West Virginia
States Where NPs* Can Prescribe (Excluding Controlled Substances) with Some Degree of Physician Involvement or Delegation of Prescription Writing	Alabama, Kentucky, Louisiana, Mississippi, Missouri, Nevada, Ohio^, Texas, Virginia
States Where NPs* Have No Statutory Prescribing Authority	None

* may include other APNs (i.e., clinical nurse specialists, nurse midwives, and nurse anesthetists)
** Schedule V Only
^^ pending approval of rules and regulations
^ in narrowly specified situations
Modified with permission from: *The Nurse Practitioner, 25*(1): 21. Copyright Springhouse Corporation, 2000.

tion or question, but the phrase is more often used in its plural sense to refer to the standards of practice for a profession, discipline, or subspecialty.

Standards of Nursing Practice

Professions establish standards of practice primarily to communicate within the profession uniform expectations with respect to the care delivered. Despite standards of practice, each practitioner must also continually exercise professional clinical judgment, taking into account all facts relevant to each particular patient. Standards of practice are but one factor considered by a professional when caring for a patient. Other factors include the patient's condition and wishes, the setting, available resources, and applicable law, to name a few.

Actively involved in standards development since the 1960s, the American Nurses Association (ANA) published the first standards of nursing practice in 1973. Those standards applied generally to nursing practice. Since that time, numerous other professional organizations have developed standards for specialty nursing practice, some acting independently and others in collaboration with the ANA. For example, in 1983 the ANA published the first standards of school nursing

practice written by a task force with representatives of organizations including the ANA, the National Association of School Nurses (NASN), the National Association of State School Nurse Consultants (NASSNC), the American Public Health Association (APHA), and American School Health Association (ASHA).

In 1991, after collaborating with the specialty organizations, the ANA revised its general clinical standards and published the *Standards of Clinical Nursing Practice.* The ANA published the second edition of those standards in 1998. (In 1995, a process was established to facilitate revisions of the ANA *Standards* every 5 years.)

As the voice for school nurses nationwide, NASN participated in the collaboration that led to publication of the 1991 ANA standards, as well as the efforts that culminated in 1995 with adoption of the revision process. In 1993, NASN published guidelines for school nurses entitled *School Nursing Practice: Roles and Standards* (Proctor, 1993). In addition to applying ANA's *Standards of Clinical Nursing Practice* to the specialty practice of school nursing, that publication focused on school nurse role synthesis and role actualization (Proctor, 1993). In 1998, NASN published the *Standards of Professional School Nursing Practice,* which are reprinted with permission in Appendix A of this book. (See chapter 1 for additional discussion.)

Standard of Care

Standards of practice are but one factor considered by a court when determining the applicable standard of care in professional liability cases (also called medical malpractice cases). For a more detailed discussion of medical malpractice, see the section on "Negligence" later in this chapter. Other factors considered include expert testimony, applicable laws (including the relevant practice act), organizational policies and procedures (including job descriptions), and any other sources considered authoritative with respect to the professional's actions.

Black's Law Dictionary (1979) relates the definition of the standard of care to the law of negligence, identifying it as the degree of care that a reasonably prudent person should exercise under the same or similar circumstances. Black continues and clarifies that in medical malpractice cases, a standard of care is applied to measure the competence of the professional. Therein lies the confusion. When attempting to define the standard of care in a professional liability case, the court must look to a number of sources, one of which is the applicable standard of practice.

The Role of Expert Testimony in Establishing the Standard of Care

One of the ways in which a party in a lawsuit often introduces evidence regarding the applicable standard of care, including information about the professional standards of practice, is through the use of an expert witness. Expert witnesses also help the judge and/or jury understand the damages alleged in a malpractice lawsuit. Although the practice is changing, historically it has not been uncommon for attorneys to use physician experts to testify to the standard of care by which a nurse's actions should be judged. Reasons include the small number of malpractice suits against nurses as compared to physicians and the refusal of the court system to recognize nursing as a profession with an independent body of knowledge (Northrop & Mech, 1981). Until the courts adopt a requirement that nurse expert witnesses testify where nursing malpractice is at issue, the practice of using physician experts is likely to continue in the few remaining states in which it is still permitted. The following case is an example of that practice.

The defense attorney in a Rhode Island case chose a board-certified emergency-room physician to testify that a school nurse met the standard for emergency care by attempting to clear the airway in order to perform CPR on a teenager who suffered a severe allergic reaction to nuts. (*Federico v. Order of St. Benedict in Rhode Island*, 1995). Other experts, including a school nurse supervisor and an associate clinical professor at a well-known university, testified that the applicable standard of care included the immediate administration of epinephrine, alleging it would have saved the boy's life (Carole Passarelli, personal communication, April 2, 1999). The court ruled in favor of the boarding school involved, and the plaintiffs appealed, claiming that the lower court improperly interpreted the school's legal duty. The appellate court upheld the lower court's decision.

The Role of Organizational Policies in Establishing the Standard of Care

A case involving a Minnesota school nurse illustrates the role organizational policies can play in establishing the applicable standard of care in a malpractice lawsuit. (*Schluessler v. Independent School District*, 1989) After a high school student died during an asthma attack at school, the family sued, claiming the school nurse's negligence had caused the student's death. In addition to claims that the nurse had failed to properly assess the severity of the attack and summon emergency care, the plaintiffs claimed that the nurse violated school policy by failing to report to school authorities the student's use of another student's inhaler and by failing to call the parents. The presence of a school policy was clearly a factor in determining the applicable standard of care and, ultimately, the outcome of the case. The jury agreed with the plaintiffs and awarded the family $142, 289.00.

In addition to the civil lawsuit discussed above, the school nurse involved faced disciplinary charges before the BON (Minnesota Board of Nursing, 1989). Rather than face revocation of her license, the school nurse voluntarily entered an agreement with the BON. The BON placed her license on conditional status, based upon the school nurse's commitment to an agreement that included additional education, training, monitoring, and reporting to the BON.

Organizational policies and procedures also played a role in determining the outcome of a 1996 Missouri case that involved medication administration (*DeBord v. Board of Education of the Ferguson Florissant School District et al.*). The court ruled in favor of a school district in that case, which involved the administration of high doses of Ritalin, the level of which had been confirmed by the prescribing physician. Consistent with the school district's policy against knowingly administering medication in an amount that exceeds the recommended daily dosage, a school nurse refused to give a student her afternoon dose of Ritalin. The school offered several accommodations to permit the student to receive the afternoon dosage, including early dismissal from school and administration by the parent or designee.

A different judge in the same court dismissed a similar case brought shortly after *DeBord* was decided. The Davis family sued the Francis Howell School District when the school nurse refused to administer a dosage of Ritalin in excess of the amount recommended by the manufacturer's insert and the *Physician's Desk Reference,* a standard drug resource widely used by health care professionals. The school nurse refused only after consultation with the assistant superintendent, the district's nurse coordinator, the district's consulting pediatrician, the student's treating physician, and a consulting physician chosen by the family. The court concluded that the school district's refusal to administer the prescribed dose did not violate the Americans with Disabilities Act or § 504 since the refusal was not based upon the student's disability, but rather on the defendants' concern about potential future harm to the student and the district's potential liability (*Davis v. Francis Howell School District,* 1997).

Conflicting Laws and Standards of Practice

An example involving abortion illustrates the distinction between standards of practice and the standard of care as applied in a medical malpractice action. Federal regulations first introduced in 1988 prohibit certain federally funded projects from engaging in abortion-related counseling, referrals, and advocacy. When the regulations were first introduced, clinicians protested loudly. Most believed that the standards of practice required the disclosure of all treatment options, regardless of whether available resources would support those options. A review of the standards of practice for maternal child nurse practitioners and obstetricians and gynecologists supported that belief.

Many clinicians were afraid that they would face liability if they omitted abortion from a discussion with a patient about her pregnancy treatment options. They perceived the decision to be at odds with the applicable professional standards of practice. On the other hand, they also feared civil and criminal penalties if they disregarded the federal law that prohibited the same discussion compelled by those standards of practice.

A court determining the standard of care in a malpractice lawsuit filed for failure to advise a patient about abortion would look not only at the standards of practice, but at the federal regulations that prohibited discussion of abortion as a treatment option, as well as

any other relevant laws or cases. Thus, in establishing the standard of care, the court would look at both the standards of practice and the applicable law, as well as the apparent conflict between the two.

In the abortion situation discussed above, the court would likely consider other court opinions that addressed the federal regulations. *Rust v. Sullivan* (1991) is one such case. That case alleged that the regulations violated First Amendment freedom of speech rights of family planning clinics, as well as the Fifth Amendment right of a woman to terminate her pregnancy. The court found that the regulations did not violate such Constitutional rights, nor did they limit a physician's ability to provide abortion counseling to a pregnant woman. Clearly, that ruling provided no reassurance to clinicians concerned about liability exposure for failure to fully advise a woman of her options regarding pregnancy. Most were left with a dilemma similar to that faced by school nurses when an employer mandates an action at odds with professional standards of practice—a choice between the risks associated with loss of employment for failure to follow policies and procedures and the risks associated with violating applicable standards of practice or, in many instances, the nurse practice act.

The school health setting is replete with professional dilemmas such as the one described above, where two sources of authority appear to dictate different courses of behavior. Those related to delegation are perhaps the most troubling and are discussed in a later section of this chapter. Others include dilemmas related to the conflicting rights of parents and children regarding the confidentiality of school health and medical records. Other chapters in this book discuss in detail the dilemmas school nurses face when the standards of practice conflict not only with a single law, but with multiple inconsistent laws.

In lawsuits involving conflicting laws and laws that clearly conflict with professional standards, the court must consider not only the standards of practice in defining the applicable standard of care, but the conflicting laws as well. For school nurses, the challenge seems to be to substitute their judgment for the court's—second-guessing the court before the fact—if they hope to avoid liability. Such defensive practice is often uncomfortable for health care professionals. It also represents the antithesis of what most feel should be the proper paradigm for professional decision-making, where the patient's welfare and priorities—rather than economics, liability, or criminal penalties—should be the single most important determinant.

The Role of Other Laws and Standards in Establishing the Standard of Care

The court must consider many factors when establishing the standard of care. In addition to those already discussed, depending on the facts involved, other laws and standards may prove relevant. Examples include the medical practice act, the pharmacy practice act, education laws, informed consent laws, and laws that cover reporting of communicable disease or child and vulnerable adult abuse.

NEGLIGENCE

Ordinary Negligence

According to Black (1979), ordinary negligence is the failure to use such care as a reasonably prudent and careful person would use under similar circumstances. To succeed in a lawsuit based upon a claim of negligence, a plaintiff must show that the defendant had a legal duty to exercise a certain level of care, that the defendant breached that duty, and that the breach actually caused the damages that the plaintiff suffered. The plaintiff must prove each of those four elements—duty, breach, causation, and damages—by what is known as a preponderance of the evidence. Preponderance of the evidence is a level of proof that means it is more likely than not that the defendant was negligent. If a quantitative value could be placed upon that level, it would be 51%.

The standard of care applied to a defendant's actions in an ordinary negligence case is that of the reasonably prudent person. Essentially, that means the plaintiff must establish through various types of evidence, including testimony and any relevant documents, what another ordinary citizen acting reasonably would have done in a similar situation under similar circumstances.

Professional Negligence and Malpractice

Professional negligence is the term used to describe negligence of a licensed professional, such as a physician, attorney, accountant, or school nurse. Malpractice is simply an alternative term for professional negligence, one used more often by lay people than by those who are part of the legal system. Cases based upon professional negligence claims related to health care services are usually broadly referred to as medical malpractice actions, whether against a physician, nurse, dentist, podiatrist, chiropractor, or other health care provider. (See chapter 2 for a more detailed discussion of nursing negligence in the school health setting.)

One significant difference between ordinary negligence and professional negligence is the standard of care applied to the defendant's conduct. Malpractice cases apply the professional standard and require expert testimony. The defendant's conduct is evaluated against the testimony of a similarly educated and experienced expert, almost always of the same profession. Although historically some states permitted physicians to testify to the standard of care in nursing negligence cases, most now require that an expert nurse witness provide such testimony.

Reporting Medical Malpractice Payments to the National Practitioner Data Bank

As mentioned earlier in this chapter, in 1986 Congress passed the Health Care Quality Improvement Act (HCQIA) for public protection purposes. That Act created a data bank, the National Practitioner Data Bank (NPDB), that contains primarily two kinds of information. The first—that concerning disciplinary actions against certain health care providers—is discussed in greater detail earlier in this chapter in the "Disciplinary Proceedings" section.

The second kind of information concerns medical malpractice settlements. HCQIA requires any entity that makes a payment to settle or satisfy a written claim for malpractice to report that payment to the NPDB. Insurance companies that sell a large volume of medical malpractice policies are quite familiar with these reporting requirements. Self-insured school districts may be unaware of, or at least less familiar with, such requirements because medical malpractice claims against school nurses may arise very infrequently as compared to the other types of lawsuits handled by such districts.

Statutes of Limitations

An example of procedural rather than substantive law, a statute of limitations defines the period of time within which a lawsuit must be filed. The periods of time differ depending on the type of lawsuit and, because each state defines its own statutes, they differ from state to state. Federal law also has statutes of limitations for various federal actions. Statutes of limitations for professional negligence actions usually range from one to three years, whereas statutes of limitations for ordinary negligence are typically longer. Many indicate that the time begins to run from the occurrence or discovery of the negligent act or omission. Most also include a provision that prevents the time from beginning to run for children until they reach the age of majority, defined as 18 in many states. Of particular importance to school nurses who work closely with children, that means the period during which an injured child can sue may be very long. The impact of that prolonged period on insurance coverage is discussed later in this chapter in the "Insurance" section under "Types of Policies."

Because it has the potential to block recovery of what may otherwise be a viable lawsuit, the statute of limitations is a very important consideration in malpractice. In 1996, the Oklahoma Supreme Court reversed an appellate court decision affirming the lower court, which had found that the parents of a student who had died of a severe asthma attack at school could not proceed with their lawsuit because of the statute of limitations *(Calvert v. Tulsa Public Schools)*. The parents in that case filed the original lawsuit within the defined time but were not appointed as the child's personal representatives until after the statute of limitations ran out. The Oklahoma Supreme Court's decision was based upon its interpretation of the term "personal representative" in the 1997 Governmental Tort Claims Act in Oklahoma and made it possible for the parents to proceed with their original lawsuit.

DELEGATION, TRAINING, AND SUPERVISION

Long a difficult issue in the school health setting, delegation continues to plague school nurses. Given the reality of school nurse-to-student ratios and the increasing complexity of student health needs, delegation is unavoidable. Therefore, a school nurse must understand the related legal issues. This section reviews the legal basis for nursing delegation and outlines the decision-making process that should be used when determining whether or not to delegate nursing activities. It also compares and contrasts the issues involved in (1) delegation to unlicensed assistive personnel (UAP), who have no legal scope of practice encompassing the delegated activity; and (2) the assignment of certain functions or tasks to other licensed nurses whose legal scope of practice encompasses the same functions or activities (i.e., assignment by an RN to another RN or, in some instances, to an LPN).

Definitions of Terms Related to Delegation

A clear understanding of several terms is essential to any discussion of the related issues. Unfortunately, state laws, regulations, and related documents often use the terms interchangeably—contributing to rather than clarifying the confusion (Schwab & Haas, 1995). As you might expect, the nursing literature—particularly standards and guidelines—use the terms more precisely. This section discusses the issues generally, in a manner

that corresponds to the conceptual principles espoused in the nursing literature. It does not provide an exhaustive or detailed analysis of the many nurse practice acts or regulations but cites examples to illustrate the principles reviewed.

Delegation is defined as "transferring to a competent individual the authority to perform a selected nursing task in a selected situation" (NCSBN, 1996). It is important to understand that the nurse remains accountable for the delegation and the actions of the individual to whom a task or function is delegated (the delegatee). Although the jurisdictions differ in their approaches, RNs may delegate to LPNs or unlicensed assistive personnel (UAP) certain tasks or functions within the scope of RN practice. In some jurisdictions, LPNs may also delegate to UAP certain tasks within the LPN scope of practice.

The NCSBN defines accountability as "being responsible and answerable for actions or inactions of self or others in the context of delegation" (1996). The NCSBN model curriculum defines supervision as "the provision of guidance or direction, evaluation and follow-up by the licensed nurse for accomplishment of a nursing task delegated to unlicensed assistive personnel" (1996). Although the definitions of supervision may vary from state to state, most require that the supervisor be available to the delegatee to provide direction, either in person or through the use of some alternative method of communication that permits immediate accessibility, such as the telephone. Because of such supervision requirements, school nurses responsible for students located in multiple buildings may find the opportunities for delegation somewhat limited, or at least replete with logistical and pragmatic challenges.

The NCSBN model curriculum contrasts delegation to assignment. It defines assignment as "giving someone a task within the person's own scope of practice." Assignment does not involve the transfer of the legal authority to complete a nursing task because the actor already has the legal authority to perform the task or activity.

Although the NCSBN refers only to unlicensed assistive personnel (UAP) in its definition of supervision, an RN may also supervise an LPN in the performance of a delegated task if that task is not within the scope of the LPN's practice. ANA's definition reflects that broader use of the term supervision: "The active process of directing, guiding and influencing the outcome of an individual's performance of an activity" (ANA, 1994). Supervision is generally categorized as on-site (the nurse being physically present or immediately available while the activity is being performed) or off-site (the nurse has the ability to provide direction through various means of written and verbal communication). Because of the nurse-to-student ratios in most school districts, off-site supervision is common in school nursing.

Since it is the source of much of the controversy associated with delegation, perhaps the most important term to understand is "unlicensed assistive personnel" (UAP). According to NCSBN (1996), UAP refers to any unlicensed individual, regardless of title, to whom nursing tasks are delegated. UAP can include other licensed professionals, such as social workers, psychologists, or occupational therapists whose licensed scopes of practice do not include the nursing function or activity in question.

The distinction between delegation and assignment depends on the actor's (delegatee's) source of authority for the function or task delegated. In an assignment, a nurse requests that another nurse complete a task or activity that is within the scope of practice of both nurses. The assignment may be by an RN to another RN, or by an RN to an LPN. In the latter situation, the LPN's scope of practice (and thus scope of authority for the particular task involved) may require supervision by the RN. In such situations, (for example, in a state where the practice act allows an LPN to function only under the direction or supervision of an RN, physician, podiatrist, or dentist), it would be inaccurate to say an RN "assigns" a nursing task to an LPN. In those circumstances, the RN delegates to an LPN and when doing so, must follow the same process used when determining whether to delegate to UAP. When delegating to UAP, the licensed nurse actually transfers to the UAP the authority to complete the task or function, since the UAP has no license or individual scope of practice. In either case, the nurse remains accountable for the appropriateness of the assignment or delegation.

The term delegation may often be used improperly to refer to the assignment of tasks within the scope of both the delegating nurse and delegatee's scope of practice. Likewise, what should properly be called assignment has long been viewed as simply an effective management technique rather than a source of controversy. While there may be questions regarding the appropriate level of supervision necessary by the assignor, the intensity of the debate has never reached the fever-pitch of the debates associated with delegation to UAP. While some accept delegation to UAP as a necessary and effective management technique, many believe that it results in poor quality of care and moves nurses further away from where they belong—doing direct patient care (Schwab & Haas, 1995).

Sources of Authority for Delegation

Federal and State Laws and Regulations

The process used to analyze the legal basis for delegation does not differ substantially from the process used to analyze the legality of any other nursing function. The analysis itself may prove more complex in certain practice settings, such as school health, because of the number of conflicting laws and regulations. The process requires analysis of federal law and regulations, state law and regulations, local laws, regulations, and ordinances, professional standards of practice and guidelines, and applicable organizational policies and procedures, as well as job descriptions.

Several federal laws indirectly affect delegation and contribute to the complexity of the delegation dilemmas in the school health setting (§ 504 of the Rehabilitation Act of 1973, the Americans with Disabilities Act of 1990, and the Individuals with Disabilities Education Act [IDEA] of 1990. These are discussed in detail in Chapters 11, 12, and 13 and in the section of this chapter entitled "Delegation of Nursing Tasks in the School Setting." Although each law addresses slightly different issues, all essentially require that school health services be provided as a related service for eligible students. Few school districts are staffed to easily meet such requirements without delegation by school nurses. Interpretations of those laws vary, and thus, not all school districts fulfill their obligations in the same manner (Schwab & Haas, 1995). One school district may interpret the federal law to require it to provide certain services in the school setting, regardless of the legality of delegating the nursing tasks necessary to accomplish that end. Another school district may not interpret the law to obligate it to provide services in the school setting at all, the result being that the child is educated in isolation at home or in a facility other than the local school.

A review of state nurse practice acts reveals wide variation in how each addresses delegation. The continuum ranges from practice acts silent on the issue to those that have adopted specific standards for delegation across practice settings, including school health. Some enumerate tasks and functions that may not be delegated, while others instead address the decision-making process. A few states have issued declaratory rulings to interpret a current provision of the nurse practice act or related regulations rather than amend the law to specifically address delegation (Schwab & Haas, 1995).

In some jurisdictions, state agencies other than the BON have addressed delegation in the school setting in sections of the state law separate and distinct from the nurse practice act (Schwab & Haas, 1995). Some state agencies, such as the departments of health or education, publish guidelines based upon their own laws (Keen, 1996, and Ahearn, Gloeckler, & Walton, 1993). In a state where laws and/or guidelines conflict, it is difficult for the school nurse to know which law controls unless an advisory opinion has been issued interpreting the applicable nurse practice act.

Professional Standards of Practice on Delegation

Because controlling laws and regulations are often unclear or nonexistent, professional standards of practice are useful not just to guide clinical judgment and behavior, but to evaluate that judgment and behavior in a subsequent lawsuit. A number of professional groups have issued position statements and developed standards and guidelines for delegation in the school health setting.

In 1992, the ANA released a position statement, *Registered Nurse Utilization of Unlicensed Assistive Personnel.* Published in 1994, ANA's standards, *Registered Professional Nurses & Unlicensed Assistive Personnel,* summarize current trends, provide specific guidelines, and discuss relevant legal risks associated with delegation to a UAP. Both are available through ANA's website (www.nursingworld.org).

In 1996, the National Council of State Boards of Nursing (NCSBN) published *Delegation: Concepts and Decision-making Process,* a document intended as a guide to the process of delegation in clinical and administrative settings. The NCSBN is also in the process of developing a model curriculum based upon the information in its delegation document. Designed to assist those who teach nurses how to delegate, the learning objectives for that curriculum address the nurse-UAP relationship, the process for making decisions about delegation, and the principles and practical issues underlying effective delegation (Massachusetts Board of Registration in Nursing, 1997). Both NCSBN documents, as well as other valuable resources on delegation, can be obtained from the section of NCSBN'S website (http://www.ncsbn.org/files/delegation.asp) that focuses specifically on delegation to UAP issues.

The National Association of School Nurses (NASN) has published several documents that address delegation, including guidelines and a compendium (Luckenbill, 1996), a position statement (1995), and standards (Proctor, 1993). Many can be accessed online (www.nasn.org). In 1997, NASN surveyed its Board of Directors to assess the need for a curriculum for school nurses to use in training UAPs. (See chapter 5 under

"Accountability for Health Assistants (UAP)" for information on a curriculum for training assistants and preparing school nurses for their teaching and supervisory role with UAPs.)

In 1995, the National Association of State School Nurse Consultants issued a position statement entitled *Delegation of School Health Services to Unlicensed Assistive Personnel: A Position Paper of the National Association of State School Nurse Consultants.* That position statement identifies as critical two questions pertaining to delegating and supervising a nursing care activity:

- Is the activity a nursing task under the state's definition of nursing?

- Can the activity be performed by unlicensed assistive personnel under the supervisions of a registered nurse?

The position statement also lists 11 determinations that a registered nurse makes when delegating and supervising a nursing care activity for a particular student. It is under revision in 2000.

Despite differences in the approaches of state legislatures, the underlying principles embodied in state laws and regulations are quite similar to those supported by the professional standards of practice available on delegation (Schwab & Haas, 1995). Most define delegation, identify what tasks or functions can be safely delegated, the circumstances under which delegation can occur, and to whom care can be delegated (Brent, 1993).

Organizational policies on delegation

Education law may empower an administrator in a certain school setting to delegate or assign tasks (Luckenbill, 1996). In that role, the administrator may create policies on delegation or make decisions about delegation that conflict with the laws that regulate nursing practice. School nurses faced with such dilemmas face difficult decisions.

Decision-Making Process for Delegation

In its 1997 *Curriculum on Delegation,* the NCSBN outlines the five rights of delegation and suggests using them as a mental checklist to determine when delegation is safe and appropriate in the practice setting. Those rights are (1) the right task, (2) the right circumstances, (3) the right person, (4) the right direction/communication, and (5) the right supervision.

The NCSBN also published a decision-making model, useful for helping the nurse ensure appropriate assessment, planning, implementation, and evaluation. That model guides the nurse through the delegation decision-making process by breaking it down into the following five steps and explaining each in greater detail:

1. Assess the situation.

2. Plan for the activity.

3. Assure appropriate accountability.

4. Supervise the performance of the activity.

5. Evaluate the entire delegation process.

At least one state's BON advocates relying on a similar model to promote regulatory compliance, since that state's regulations are incorporated into the five questions that logically flow from the five rights of delegation discussed above (Massachusetts Board of Registration in Nursing, 1997). Set up as a decision tree, the following series of questions allow the nurse to proceed to the next question only after answering the prior one in a manner indicating that delegation may be appropriate:

1. Is the activity within the nurse's (RN/LPN) scope of practice to perform?

2. Are the activities to be performed ones that require nursing assessment and judgment during implementation?

3. Is there UAP available who can perform the activity safely?

4. Is the nurse able to provide appropriate supervision of the UAP during the implementation and performance of the activity?

5. Are there any other considerations that would prohibit delegation by a reasonable and prudent nurse?

Delegation of Nursing Tasks in the School Setting

While delegation has long been a part of nursing practice (ANA, 1994), the cost containment movement and the push to do more with less has resulted in a renewed focus on delegation and related issues. That renewed focus has been felt acutely by school nurses forced to grapple with the increased number of students with complex health needs, many of whom require specialized services during the school day (Beister, 1993). Often, school nurses struggle to do so with staffing based upon nurse-to-student ratios set long before the days when federal and state laws began

requiring that students with complex health needs be taught in the least restrictive environment and included in the regular school setting.

Federal and state laws also grant to many disabled students the rights to certain specialized services that must be provided in the school setting. Ideally, nurse-to-student ratios would permit school nurses to provide many of those services. While some health services may be provided only by nurses, many can be delegated to UAP who are trained by nurses to perform them. To complicate matters, school nurses are often the only licensed health care professionals in an educational setting where their legal, professional, and ethical responsibilities are different from those of the educators who dominate and control such settings. Surrounded by competing pressures, administrators may instruct school nurses to conduct themselves counter to the dictates of the nurse practice act.

Given the reality described above, it is no surprise that litigation involving school nurses often involves delegation issues. In Oregon, a school health assistant turned to the court to obtain an order preventing the school district from compelling her to perform clean, intermittent catheterization (CIC) on a new student with spina bifida (*Mitts v. Hillsboro Union High School District*, 1987). The student's mother taught the technique to the assistant, with the school nurse present during the training session to answer questions. Although the school nurse did not provide any written instructions to the assistant, at the insistence of the school district she provided periodic observation and monthly supervision.

The court asked the Oregon State Board of Nursing (the Oregon Board) for a declaratory ruling on whether CIC could be lawfully delegated to an unlicensed person trained on the technique. The Oregon Board opined that the school principal was practicing nursing without a license when he assumed responsibility for the assessment, diagnosis, and planning of the student's health needs. Because she followed the principal's directive, the school health assistant was also unlawfully practicing nursing. The Oregon Board further found that the nurse failed to conform to the applicable nursing standards when she accepted the principal's assignment. The Board subsequently disciplined the school nurse for failing to make her own assessment regarding the appropriateness of the delegation decision and failing to comply with the applicable regulations regarding delegation (Oregon State Board of Nursing, 1989).

The Oregon case makes it clear that a school nurse must refuse to comply with an educator's or administrator's directive if it runs afoul of the nurse practice act. Unfortunately, as many school nurses know, that refusal may cost a school nurse her job. Although the facts of the case involve medication policies rather than delegation policies, *Johnson v. Independent School District* (1989) provides an example of what can happen when a school nurse challenges administrative policies that place her in danger of disciplinary action from the Board of Nursing if she follows such policies.

In that case, the school nurse challenged a medication policy that required nurses to administer prescription and over-the-counter medication with merely a note from the parent and without any requirement that the medication come in its original labeled container. She initially worked with a group of colleagues to develop a new policy that required a physician's order, consistent with a communication from the Oklahoma BON that interpreted the nurse practice act to include such a requirement. Eventually, most of those colleagues withdrew their support, fearful they would lose their jobs when it became clear that the administration was unsympathetic to the proposed changes. When the school board refused to adopt the proposed policy, the school nurse retained an attorney to advise her regarding the risks of working under the questionable policy. The school board eventually voted not to renew her contract, claiming that the school nurse had been disruptive and caused divisiveness when she spoke out against the administrative policies. Although the jury found for the school nurse in a ruling based upon first amendment grounds, the court set aside the jury's verdict. Upon appeal, the Court of Appeals upheld the lower court decision.

Many school nurses face dilemmas such as those discussed in the two preceding cases. On one hand, if they fail to challenge unclear or conflicting policies such as those that exist when a departmental guideline runs counter to the apparent dictates of the nurse practice act, they face liability for any harm that may befall a student. On the other hand, if they challenge such policies they run the risk of losing their jobs. School nurses in such situations are well advised to gather as much information as possible, including information from authoritative sources, such as the BON, and a state nurse consultant, if there is one in the state's department of health or education. A school nurse armed with a declaratory ruling from the BON and guidelines from a state agency may find administrators less resistant to her position or at least less likely to fire her for advocating her position.

Often, school nurses who face dilemmas such as those discussed above fear repercussions if they document their concerns and actions. While school nurses should follow applicable district policy when raising such issues, at some point documentation is likely to be necessary whether required by policy or not. When such situations eventually result in disciplinary inquiries or actions by the BON for alleged violations of the nurse practice act, school nurses armed with documentation will find themselves better equipped to respond to the BON's questions and avoid action against their licenses.

Despite the importance of the issue and the number of lawsuits related to delegation, very little data exist regarding delegation by nurses to UAP. Josten, Smoot, & Beckley (1995) conducted a survey of Midwestern school nurses. They found that some nurses have not received training regarding delegation, nor did school policies and procedures exist to guide them. The survey revealed that the most frequently cited concerns about delegation were the competency of the UAP, the child's condition, and the nature of the procedures. Some of the respondents admitted delegating against their nursing judgment, most because they had been instructed to do so by administrators.

Delegation by Physicians

The legal analysis for delegation by physicians is very similar to that used for delegation by nurses. Because only licensed physicians can practice medicine, in most states physicians cannot delegate tasks involving medical judgment. In many states, physicians routinely delegate specific tasks to other licensed practitioners, such as physician assistants or nurses. They often do so through various formal mechanisms, including physician orders, standing orders, or protocols. Like the nurse who delegates specific nursing tasks to other licensed practitioners or unlicensed personnel, the physician remains responsible for training and supervising the individual to whom medical tasks are delegated.

Most medical practice acts (and the accompanying regulations) do not specifically address delegation to anyone other than another licensed practitioner. However, like nursing delegation, this does not imply that physicians may delegate to unlicensed personnel. Connecticut is one example of a medical practice act that clearly prohibits delegation to UAP; that state's act specifies that physicians can "delegate certain licensed functions to other licensed health care providers under his/her supervision, but not to unlicensed persons" (Connecticut State Dept. of Education, 1992).

At least one state has addressed the issue of physician delegation in its administrative code. The Texas regulations related to the state medical practice act (22 Texas Administrative Code 193.4) state the following:

Providing the authorizing physician is satisfied as to the ability and competence of those for whom the physician is assuming responsibility, and with due regard for the safety of the patient and in keeping with sound medical practice, standing delegation orders may be authorized for the performance of acts and duties which do not require the exercise of independent medical judgment.

Another section of the same regulation clearly indicates that the limitations in that section do not apply to care delivered by physician assistants or advance practice nurses, as authorized under the Texas Medical Practice Act. It also includes examples of the various tasks that standing delegation orders may address, including taking histories, ordering tests, and administering vaccines (22 TAC 193.4).

SCHOOL NURSES' RELATIONSHIPS WITH OTHER HEALTH CARE PROVIDERS

Licensed Practical Nurses (LPNs)

Because some nurse practice acts permit LPNs to practice only under the direct supervision of an RN, school districts in such states cannot legally hire an LPN to function independently as a school nurse. LPNs that accept such positions expose themselves to disciplinary action for practicing outside the legal scope of nursing practice.

In some school districts, LPNs may function under the direction of an RN, with the RN responsible for assessing and determining what nursing tasks are appropriate for delegation to the LPN. In those settings, the RN must develop an individualized plan of care and procedures to assure that the tasks are performed safely. The latter includes an assessment by the RN of the LPN's ability to perform the delegated tasks and, if necessary, additional training for the LPN. Once the tasks are delegated, the RN remains responsible for supervising the LPN. The RN may not delegate to an LPN decisions that involve professional nursing judgment.

Often outside agencies assign LPNs to provide private duty nursing care for students with medically complex health care needs. The cost of such services may be covered by Medicaid or the family's insurance program. Because all applicable state laws still apply, the school nurse and private duty LPN must clearly establish the boundaries of such a relationship, including details related to their respective responsibilities, supervision and direction, and the applicability of school policies and procedures. Many school districts memori-

alize the details in a written contract, which should clearly differentiate between routine and emergency events.

Although most state laws do not specifically require that an agency RN provide supervision and direction for a private duty LPN, outside agency and school district policies and procedures should clearly dictate such an arrangement. (See Appendix J.) Because of the limited nature of the relationship between the school nurse and the LPN, a school nurse who takes the responsibility for supervising and directing a private duty LPN also invites an increased risk of liability. In addition to the private duty LPN's direct responsibility to the student, the LPN is also responsible for complying with school policies and procedures, including those applicable to any emergency involving that student, as well as for functioning within their scope of practice. Despite the absence of a formal supervisory relationship with a private duty LPN, a professional school nurse is responsible for reporting any deficiency or incompetency observed as the LPN provides services to the student. While school district policy usually dictates to whom the school nurse must report such observations (such as administrator, principal, or parent), the school nurse must also evaluate whether the state nurse practice act requires a report to the BON.

Emergency Medical Technicians (EMTs)

If educators are unfamiliar with the laws that apply to nursing practice, they may make decisions that jeopardize student safety, as well as expose the school nurse to liability risks. One such example is a district that hires emergency medical technicians (EMTs) to accompany students with complex health needs when the students are being transported in school vans or assigns a teacher who is also an EMT to administer medication to students. A memorandum from the Connecticut Attorney General makes it clear that, in Connecticut, EMTs may not function other than in relationship to an emergency medical services provider or facility and, if they do so, they may be found to be practicing medicine without a license (Comerford, J. D., Assistant Attorney General of Connecticut, memorandum, May 13, 1994).

A school nurse responsible for student health needs in a district that decides to hire such personnel faces a dilemma similar to those discussed throughout this chapter. If she challenges an administrator determined to use EMTs, she faces a politically difficult employment situation. If she fails to do so, based upon her legal duty to the student she may face liability for any injuries sustained by the student and disciplinary action by the BON.

Physicians

In addition to their independent scope of practice, nurses have a dependent scope of practice under which they carry out medical orders from physicians. These include orders for various medications and treatments that students need in school. None of those orders is as troubling to school nurses as Do Not Resuscitate (DNR) orders. Such orders raise not only legal but ethical issues for all involved.

DNR orders are commonplace, although less so for children than adults, in many health care settings today—particularly in acute-care settings such as intensive care and in chronic-care settings such as hospices and nursing homes. DNR orders are not commonplace in schools, and as a result, they generate considerable controversy. As is often the reality with cutting-edge medico-legal issues, the practice dilemmas are steps ahead of the law, leaving school nurses with little specific guidance. As more and more children with medically complex needs are educated in the regular school setting, perhaps school nurses will see more DNR orders, or at least see more clarity in the policies regarding such orders. (For further detailed discussion of DNR orders in schools, see chapter 14.)

School-Based Health Centers

In addition to school health programs that offer routine health services, some schools may operate school-based health centers, either independently or through partnerships with other entities (such as a health department, university, or health care provider group). Unlike the routine services offered in school health programs, school-based health centers offer primary care services such as diagnosis and treatment of acute and chronic conditions, preventive health and dental services, and mental health counseling. In most instances, nurse practitioners serve as the primary care providers in school-based health centers, with physician involvement at the oversight level. (See chapter 15 for a more detailed discussion of school-based health centers.)

Although many school-based health centers provide similar core primary health services, all differ slightly because of their organizational models and their funding arrangements. It is important to define clearly the relationships between school-based health center staff, the individuals involved in providing routine school health services, and the community or emergency providers to whom both groups of school-based professionals often refer students for follow-up services or services not provided in the school setting. In some situations, community providers may treat clients whom they then refer to the school-based setting. To insure coordination of health care from providers at multiple sites, each group of providers must be familiar with the services provided by the others, as well as the medical records kept by each.

Managed Health Care

Providers of routine school health services and providers in school-based health centers are increasingly confronting issues related to the large numbers of students covered through managed health care plans. Although there may be many related issues, particularly troublesome ones include reimbursement for services provided in the school setting and coordination of care and medical records.

Although Medicaid reimbursement for services rendered in the school setting is available, it is relatively recent and many schools are not yet well versed in the bureaucratic requirements for processing such claims. Historically, private insurance companies and managed care plans did not provide reimbursement for services provided by school health personnel, often because school districts did not seek such reimbursement. Because state and local laws vary—as do benefits provided by various insurance programs and managed care plans—it is impossible to make any generalizations about what services may be reimbursable. Schools are increasingly seeking such reimbursement with at least modest success. (See chapter 15 for a more detailed discussion of reimbursement for school-based health services.)

Since many managed care plans limit benefits to services delivered by providers included in a specific network, services offered in the school setting may not be reimbursable. School-based centers are increasingly seeking recognition as "primary-care providers" eligible for membership in such provider networks. Despite network membership, school-based providers may not be allowed to serve as "gatekeepers"—in managed care, the focal point for the coordination of care. Because school-based health care is usually not available 24 hours a day or in the summer, managed care has been resistant to designating such providers as gatekeepers.

FINANCIAL ACCOUNTABILITY FOR PRACTICE

Professional Liability Insurance

Nurses often express uncertainty about the need for professional liability insurance. Many frequently ask,

"Should I buy my own policy?" Unfortunately, the answer—"It depends"—likely contributes further to confusion and uncertainty about the decision.

In its pamphlet on this subject, The American Association of Nurse Attorneys (1989) states:

1. All professional nurses engaged in the practice of nursing should be insured against liabilities to third parties arising out of their professional practice.

2. The means by which a nursing professional elects to insure professional practice should be based on an informed decision.

While all professionals, nurses included, should make certain they have insurance to cover their practices and liabilities, there are many factors to consider in determining how best to accomplish that end.

Types of Policies

A professional liability policy is a written agreement between the professional and the insurance company. Many types of professionals may seek liability insurance, including attorneys, architects, accountants, and health care providers, such as nurses, physicians, and dentists, to name a few. Under the terms of a professional liability agreement, the insurance company agrees to compensate a person for injuries caused by the insured professional. Injuries may be caused by an act or omission by the insured.

Professional liability policies are increasingly being written to include additional coverage for disciplinary actions against the insured professional. Usually, such policies provide reimbursement for legal fees incurred by an insured who faces disciplinary action by the licensure board. Typically, reimbursement is limited to a specific dollar amount, usually between two and five thousand dollars.

A professional liability insurance policy may be either an occurrence-based policy or a claims-made policy. An occurrence-based policy covers injuries that occur while the policy is in effect, a time referred to as the policy period. A claims-made policy covers only those injuries that (1) occur during the policy period and (2) are reported to the insurance company during the policy period or during the uninterrupted extension of that policy period, known as a tail.

Once a claims-made policy is no longer in force, without a tail, a nurse remains exposed to liabilities for injuries that were caused, but not reported, during the policy period. The tail can provide continuous protection during whatever future time period a viable claim

may be filed. The length of that period depends on the applicable statute of limitations in the jurisdiction where the plaintiff files the claim. In subspecialties involving the care of children (such as school nursing, pediatrics, labor and delivery, and neonatology), nurses may need occurrence-based coverage or a very long tail for a claims-made policy. Many states suspend the statute of limitations for minors until the age of majority (usually 18 or 21), permitting minors, once they reach majority, to sue during the period defined by the statute of limitations. (See the discussion of statutes of limitation earlier in this chapter.)

Self-Insurance Programs

Some school districts may elect to self-insure rather than cover risk through a commercial insurance program. School nurses evaluating their own risk based upon coverage available through a self-employed employer should review the terms of that self-insurance program much the same way they would review a commercial policy. Issues to explore include the scope of the program (that is , does it cover professional liability risks?), the limits available, the point at which the program provides coverage (i.e., is there some level of personal responsibility similar to a deductible on a commercial policy?), the reporting obligations, the nature of any exclusions, and details related to legal counsel available through the plan. School nurses should assess the solvency of the self-insurance program, just as they would assess the security and solvency of a commercial insurance company before purchasing insurance from that company. Self-insurance programs should have adequate funds segregated from general assets (usually in a trust account) to cover anticipated losses. The self-insurance program should also have in place written claims-processing guidelines and procedures.

Selection of counsel is an issue of particular importance to self-insurance programs. Some self-insured districts may hire outside attorneys to handle lawsuits; others may use district or school board attorneys for all lawsuits or those under a certain dollar amount. Because education attorneys often are not familiar with the legal issues raised in a medical malpractice action against a school nurse, they may not be in a position to provide the best defense. School nurses employed by a self-insured district that uses its own education attorneys to handle all the lawsuits may wish to explore with the district the possibility of involving an experienced medical malpractice attorney when facing a lawsuit that includes allegations of professional negligence. If the district refuses, the school nurse should evaluate the representation available and consider a consultation with a medical malpractice attorney, at her or his own expense if feasible or necessary.

If a school district self-insures only the risks associated with its educational activities, prior to accepting a position with that district the school nurse should explore obtaining an individual professional liability policy at the district's expense. If the school district is reluctant to cover the cost of such a policy because it believes the school nurse is adequately protected by some type of sovereign immunity available, rather than rely on the district's opinion, the school nurse should seek legal advice and reach an independent conclusion on that issue. The next section of this chapter discusses sovereign immunity in greater detail. If the school nurse remains uncomfortable with the risks after considering all the factors, an individual professional liability policy may be the solution.

Ownership of a Policy

The insured may be covered by a policy issued to one of three types of owners—institutional, group, or individual. Frequently, nurses are covered as employees of a health care organization on an institutional liability policy, which usually covers employees and volunteers and may even cover consultants with whom the organization has a contractual relationship. A group policy covers a group of licensed professionals engaged in practice through some type of corporation or partnership. A medical group composed of physicians and nurse practitioners would likely be covered through a group policy. Finally, a nurse may be covered through an individual policy purchased to cover only the nurse-owner of the policy, or the nurse and her employees or agents as well.

Because health care organizations usually purchase claims-made policies, nurse-employees relying solely on that coverage may face a dilemma upon terminating employment. If the organization cancels its policy without purchasing a tail, the nurses remain exposed to liabilities related to injuries that occurred during their employment for which claims are filed after cancellation of the claims-made policy. A nurse involved in that type of situation might face payment of significant defense costs or a judgment if the organization is unable or unwilling to cover such costs. To avoid this situation, individuals and groups usually purchase occurrence-based policies.

In addition to the dilemma associated with termination of employment, a nurse relying on coverage through an employer's institutional policy may face liability risks related to nursing practice outside the scope of employment. Coverage for such activities is typically excluded from institutional policies. (See discussion of Exclusions later in this section.) A nurse engaged in volunteer work, consulting, or any other nursing activity beyond the scope of work defined by the employer may wish to consider purchasing an individual professional liability policy.

Nurses frequently ask whether an employer that has unsuccessfully defended a case against a nurse based upon an obligation to do so under the employer's institutional liability policy will bring an action seeking indemnification from the nurse for any judgment the employer had to pay. While an employer may have a legal right to do so, in reality few exercise that right. Given the average salary of nurses, most do not have sufficient personal assets to make it cost-effective for the employer to attempt to recover the judgment through an indemnity claim against the nurse.

Scope of Coverage

Policy Forms. A nurse considering the question of professional liability coverage should also evaluate the scope of the coverage. Depending on the policy form chosen, the policy may define the insurance company's obligation differently and perhaps offer coverage more limited than appropriate for a particular professional. One form limits the company's obligation to damages for injuries to a patient or client caused by a medical incident, while another more broadly applies that obligation to damages for injuries arising out of the rendering or failure to render professional services.

The difference in the policy forms may be particularly meaningful in subspecialties such as occupational health or school nursing, where the nurse is often involved in educational or policy-making activities with the potential to impact a broad group of patients. Even when no nurse-patient relationship has been established, an individual may still claim to have been injured as a result of the nurse's educational or policy-making responsibilities and decisions. An insurance policy issued on the more limiting "medical-incident" form described above might not cover such injuries.

Exclusions. All professional liability policies include what are known as exclusions. While some exclusions are specific, such as claims arising out of sexual abuse or criminal activity, others exist as a result of the type of policy issued and should be evaluated carefully.

For example, institutional policies typically cover only claims falling within the nurse's scope of employment. A nurse may possess certain skills that fall clearly within the definition of nursing practice, but outside the scope of her job description. While individual policies are typically broader and cover claims related to the rendering of professional services, it is conceivable that a dispute may arise over whether a particular act actually falls within the definition of nursing practice. In such situations, an insurance company may send what is known as a reservation of rights letter. Under a reservation of rights, the insurance company undertakes the cost of defense, subject to a later factual determination that the claim was actually covered by the policy (i.e., in the example above, that the act fell within the scope of nursing practice). If the facts reveal that the claim was not covered, the nurse is responsible for any judgment or settlement, as well as for reimbursement for defense costs.

Deductibles and Policy Limits. Several issues related to deductibles and policy limits bear discussion. The policy defines the amount that the insurance company agrees to pay on behalf of an insured as the limit of liability. References to that number are usually expressed as "limits" because there are two components to the number. The per-incident or per-occurrence limit is the amount paid for any single incident. The aggregate limit is the amount paid in any single policy year. Although they can vary considerably by subspecialty, limits ranging from $1 million–$3 million to $1 million–$5 million are fairly common for nurses.

Although all cover the costs of defense, policies vary according to how they consider defense costs. A policy that covers defense costs outside, or in addition to, the limits of liability provides more money for the insured. If defense costs fall within the limits of liability, fewer dollars remain to satisfy any judgment or pay any settlement.

Most policies also have a deductible, which may vary from as little as one hundred dollars to several thousand dollars. The deductible is that portion of the loss (including defense costs) that the nurse must bear before the insurer begins to pay.

The Insured's Rights

Selection of Counsel. Although a few insurance companies may permit the insured to select counsel, most do not. Insurance companies usually develop relationships with a panel of attorneys experienced in defending health care professional liability matters (medical malpractice) and choose from that panel for each new claim. Although the attorney technically represents the individual nurse as the insured, it is not uncommon for the insurance company—usually

through a claims adjuster or representative—to play an active role in managing the claim. At times, this practice can cause concerns for the insured, who may feel that the attorney is treating the claims adjuster, rather than the insured, like the client. Any nurse involved in a claim where such concerns arise should voice those concerns directly to the attorney and the company's claim representative.

Attorney-Client Relationship and Attorney-Client Privilege. Despite the claims adjuster's legitimate interest in a lawsuit, the attorney-client relationship is between the insured (the client) and the attorney assigned to represent that client. The implications of that relationship are significant, and a nurse involved as a defendant in any lawsuit should understand them at the start of the lawsuit.

In addition to the attorney's other ethical obligations to the client, the attorney must honor the attorney-client privilege. The attorney-client privilege allows the client to refuse to disclose certain communications between the client and his or her attorney. It also permits the client to prevent anyone else, including the attorney, from disclosing such communications. To be covered by the privilege, communications must have been made confidentially between the client and attorney for the purpose of obtaining legal advice or representation. If another person, such as the claims adjuster, is present during the communication the privilege does not apply.

Multiple Defendants and Conflicts of Interest. Nurses often inquire whether an attorney provided through an employer's institutional policy (as opposed to an individual policy owned by the nurse) can adequately represent the nurse's interests, particularly if the employer is also a defendant in the lawsuit and represents both defendants. In many cases where the plaintiff names multiple defendants, such as an institution, an administrator, and a school nurse, the defense strategy for each is similar enough to permit representation by a single attorney. If conflicts of interest exist between the defendants, the defense strategies will not be compatible and defendants with conflicting interests need separate representation. An attorney undertaking representation of multiple defendants is obligated ethically to evaluate such issues initially and throughout the case. If facts emerge at any point in the case that create a conflict among defendants, separate representation should be arranged.

Settlement Issues. In cases involving multiple defendants, each may approach settlement decisions with differing interests and concerns. Many licensed health care professionals, such as school nurses, weigh the merits of a case more heavily than do institutional defendants when the settlement question arises. To professionals, settlement often seems like an admission of wrongdoing rather than a mutually negotiated resolution based upon other factors, such as the projected cost of trial. Individual practitioners may also have strong feelings about issues that are of less concern to institutions, such as the reporting of a settlement to the National Practitioner Data Bank. (See the earlier discussion in the "Negligence" section of this chapter.) When faced with a settlement situation involving multiple defendants, a school nurse should raise any and all concerns with counsel before agreeing to settle.

Policies differ about whether an insurance company must obtain the insured's consent to settle a claim. If the policy requires that the insurance company obtain the insured's consent and the insured unreasonably refuses, the insured may be liable for the portion of any judgment that exceeds the settlement offer. On the other hand, if the insurance company refuses to accept a reasonable settlement offer and the ultimate judgment exceeds policy limits, the company may be liable for the entire judgment. If the insurance company fails to extend to the insured an opportunity to accept or refuse settlement when required by the policy to do so, the insurance company is in breach of the policy agreement and is liable for any damages, even those that exceed the policy limits.

Statutorily Limited Liability

Sovereign Immunity

Under the historic doctrine of sovereign immunity, no one could sue a sovereign (governmental entity) without its consent. While most governments have abolished sovereign immunity, many states have placed limits on the amount a plaintiff can recover in a tort claim against a governmental entity or employee. Although amounts vary, most states have a limit on such liability, either by common law or statute. Often called Tort Claims Acts, many of the state statutes are modeled after the federal act of the same name. The laws also vary regarding whether the limits apply to the amount of liability or the ability even to file a lawsuit for injuries or damages. A school nurse employed by a governmental agency, such as a school board or department of education, may be protected by these laws.

If a governmental entity (such as a state, municipality, or township) has some form of sovereign immunity, it usually also distinguishes between absolute and qualified immunity. Often the entity itself is entitled to absolute immunity, while governmental employees may be entitled to qualified immunity, depending on the type of activities that gave rise to the lawsuit.

Although the distinction is often quite difficult to make, laws regarding sovereign immunity usually further distinguish between discretionary functions (for which employees are entitled to qualified immunity) and ministerial functions (for which employees are not entitled to immunity). *Black's Law Dictionary* (1979) defines a discretionary act as one that requires the exercise of judgment and choice. It defines a ministerial act as one performed by a person in a prescribed manner in obedience to authority without regard to the exercise of judgment. Activities that involve some element of professional judgment—such as clinical assessment—are often viewed as discretionary, whereas those that involve merely the implementation of orders or policies—such as tabulating attendance records—are usually viewed as ministerial.

Two cases illustrate the importance of these concepts. In one, the Alabama Supreme Court upheld a lower court decision dismissing a lawsuit against a principal, school nurse, and special education director based upon discretionary function immunity *(Nance v. Matthews,* 1993). In that case, a female student had allegedly been injured by a special education aide's failure to catheterize her. The plaintiff claimed that the defendants negligently retained and supervised the aide. Because the court held that the supervision and training responsibilities of the defendants were discretionary functions entitled to immunity under the applicable law, the court did not even consider whether the defendants had carried out those responsibilities in a negligent fashion.

In another case that settled for a large amount before going to trial, a 10-year-old twin suffered severe brain damage, allegedly from a hypoxic episode that occurred when her tracheotomy became plugged during school *(Vinci v. Ames Community School District,* 1997). Although a school secretary attempted to clear the tracheotomy, there was no suction machine available at the school. In response to the school district's motion for summary judgment, the court determined that the decision whether to have a suction machine available was a discretionary function and dismissed claims against the school that were based upon its failure to provide the machine. As in the Nance case, the court held that the defendants' actions were discretionary functions entitled to immunity and did not even consider the issue of whether the absence of a suction machine was negligent.

The school district's motion for summary judgment also sought dismissal of other claims that would have remained for trial had the case not settled, including whether the school nurse was negligent for failing to update the health plan and delegating tracheotomy care to non-nursing personnel, and whether the school district was negligent for failing to assure that a nurse was available on-site when the child suffered her injuries (Terence Sibbernsen, personal communication, March 11, 1998). Despite its dismissal of the claim related to the suction machine based upon discretionary function immunity, the court refused to dismiss the plaintiff's claim that the school was negligent for failing to provide a full-time educational assistant "with a nursing background" for the child. In its ruling, the court found that once the school had made the decision to provide the assistant and documented it in a memorandum, it could not shield itself from the question of negligence by claiming that the decision was a discretionary function. Had the case not settled, the court would have heard evidence on that issue and reached a determination as to whether the district had been negligent in its failure to hire the assistant.

The court also refused to conclude that discretionary immunity protected the district from liability for the school nurse's failure to train "qualified designated personnel to deliver and perform special health services"—specifically, care of the new tracheotomy tube. Because the health plan explicitly required training of qualified personnel, the district was not entitled to discretionary immunity for its failure to do so. As with hiring the assistant, had the case not settled, the court would have considered the question of whether the district was negligent when it failed to provide training on care of the new tracheotomy tube.

While the findings in these types of cases may be favorable to the school employees involved, the results generate considerable controversy within the community. Many feel that outcomes based on procedural issues like discretionary immunity leave families, hurt already by the injuries inflicted and pain suffered, further distraught because they are without recourse for what might otherwise be a very legitimate claim for negligence.

Indemnification and Hold Harmless Agreements

A nurse should understand several issues related to indemnification and hold harmless agreements. *Black's Law Dictionary* (1979) defines indemnification as reimbursing one for a loss already incurred. It defines a hold harmless agreement as a contract where one party assumes the liability inherent in a situation and relieves the other party of responsibility. Practically speaking, the concepts operate similarly.

Nurses often ask whether an organization will seek indemnification from a nurse when it is forced to pay a loss on behalf of that nurse-employee, either because the loss falls within the deductible or exceeds the policy limits. As mentioned earlier in this chapter in the "Professional Liability Insurance" section, while permitted to do so in most states, an organization typically does not pursue such recovery. Political considerations and concern for its reputation may be primary factors, but pragmatic considerations often come into play as well. In many situations, the organization will forgo indemnification because of the financial cost of recovery and the fact that many nurse-employees have limited assets available to satisfy such debts.

Nurses may also encounter indemnification when providing services for an organization that does not provide professional liability insurance but promises in a written agreement to indemnify the nurse for any losses suffered as a result of performing those services. In those circumstances, nurses should evaluate issues similar to those considered when purchasing insurance. For example, they should consider the financial stability of the organization making the promise, the scope of the indemnification, and the terms under which the organization will handle lawsuits. They should inquire in detail about such terms, including how much control the nurse will have over defense of the action, whether the organization will pay defense costs up front, whether it will permit the nurse to select counsel, and whether the organization can settle the lawsuit without the nurse's consent.

CONCLUSION

In summary, nurses must be prepared to accept legal and financial accountability for their practices. That includes understanding the legal framework for practice, including the nurse practice act, applicable regulations and standards, and the principles related to professional negligence and professional liability insurance. Keeping up-to-date on the laws, regulations, standards, and principles that control nursing practice requires considerable effort and energy, just as keeping current on clinical issues requires continuing education.

Because the laws regulating education and the health care professions are not always consistent, school nurses face difficult dilemmas and may be exposed to unique legal and financial risks. They are well advised to seek counsel as necessary when attempting to resolve such dilemmas.

REFERENCES

Ahearn, K. A., Gloeckler, L. J., & Walton, A. L. (1993). *Guidelines for school districts regarding the rights of students under § 504 of the rehabilitation act of 1973.* Albany: The State Education Department/The University of the State of New York.

The American Association of Nurse Attorneys. (1989). *Demonstrating financial responsibility for nursing practice.* Baltimore: Author.

American Nurses Association. (December 11, 1992). *Registered nurse utilization of unlicensed assistive personnel* (Position statement) [On-line]. Available: http://www.nursingworld.org/readroom position / /uap/uapuse.htm

American Nurses Association. (1994). *Registered professional nurses & unlicensed assistive Personnel* (Position statement). Washington, DC: Author.

American Nurses Association. (1991). *Standards of clinical nursing practice* (1st ed.). Washington, DC: Author.

American Nurses Association. (1998). *Standards of clinical nursing practice* (2nd ed.). Washington, DC: Author.

American Nurses Association Task Force on Standards of School Nursing Practice. (1983). *Standards of school nursing practice.* Washington, DC: The American Nurses Association.

American Nurses Association. Website at http://www.nursingworld.org

Beister, D. J. (1993). Delegation: Professional judgment or economic necessity? *Journal of Pediatric Nursing, 8*(1), 50–1.

Black, H. C. (1979). *Black's Law Dictionary* (5th ed.). St. Paul, MN: West Publishing Company.

Brent, N. J. (1993). Delegation and supervision of patient care. *Home Healthcare Nurse, 11*(4), 7–8.

Connecticut State Department of Education. (1992). *Serving students with special health care needs.* Hartford: Author.

Hadley, E. H. (1989). Nurses and prescriptive authority: A legal and economic analysis. *American Journal of Law & Medicine, 15*(2–3), 245–299.

Horner, S. (1990). The health care quality improvement act of 1986: Its history, provisions, applications and implications. *American Journal of Law & Medicine, 16*(4), 455–498.

Iowa Board of Nursing. (July 25, 1985). *Declaratory ruling No. 3. Administration of o-t-c medications by school nurses.*

Iowa Board of Nursing (January 27, 1988). *Declaratory ruling no. 19. Removal of ng tube.*

Iowa Board of Nursing (December 7, 1989). *Declaratory ruling no. 47. Teacher inserting gastrostomy tube in a continent gastrostomy.*

Josten, L., Smoot, C., & Beckley, S. (April 1995). Delegation to assistive personnel by school nurses—one state's experience. *Journal of School Nursing, 11*(2). 29–45.

Keen, T. P. (March 1996). *Guidelines for specialized health care procedures.* Virginia Department of Health.

Kelly, M. E. (1991). Introduction to federal and state systems of government. In C. E. Northrop & M. E. Kelly (Eds.), *Legal issues in nursing.* (pp. 3–12). St. Louis, MO: C. V. Mosby Co.

Luckenbill, D. H. (1996). *The school nurses' role in delegation of care: Guidelines and compendium.* Scarborough, ME: National Association of School Nurses.

Massachusetts Board of Registration in Nursing. (1997, Summer). Delegation decision-making. (Special Issue). *Nursing Board News, 3*(2) 1–8.

Minnesota Board of Nursing. (December 7, 1989). *Stipulation and order of the board of nursing in the matter of Gretchen M. McMahon, R.N.*

National Association of School Nurses. (1995). *Position statement on delegation.* Scarborough, ME: Author.

National Association of School Nurses. (1998). *Standards of professional school nursing practice.* Scarborough, ME: Author.

National Association of State School Nurse Consultants. (1996). Delegation of school health services to unlicensed assistive personnel: A position paper of the National Association of state school nurse consultants. *Journal of School Health, 66*(2), 72–74.

National Council of State Boards of Nursing. (August 25, 1997). *Boards of nursing adopt revolutionary change for nursing: Mutual recognition model of nursing regulation* (Press release) [On-line]. Available: http://www.ncsbn.org/files/newsreleases/970825dial.html

National Council of State Boards of Nursing. (December 16, 1997). *Boards of nursing approve proposed language for an interstate compact for a mutual recognition model of nursing regulation* (Press release) [On-line]. Available: http://www.ncsbn.org/files/newsreleases/971216dial.html

National Council of State Boards of Nursing. (1996). *Delegation: Concepts and decision-making process.* Chicago: Author.

National Council of State Boards of Nursing. (1997a). *Draft curriculum on delegation.* Unpublished manuscript.

National Council of State Boards of Nursing. (1999). Mutual recognition: From concept to reality in Arkansas. *Issues, 20*(2) [On-line]. Available: www.ncsbn.org/files/publications/issues/vol202/mrarkansas202.asp

National Council of State Boards of Nursing. (August 29, 1997). *National council concludes 1997 annual meeting: Mutual recognition model for nursing regulation adopted* (Press release) [On-line]. Available: http://www.ncsbn.org/files/newsreleases/970825dial.html

National Council of State Boards of Nursing. (1997b). *National Council of State Boards of nursing position paper on telenursing (1997): A challenge to regulation.* (Position statement) [On-line]. Available: http://www.ncsbn.org/files/positions/telenrsg.html

National Council of State Boards of Nursing. (1997c). Telenursing: The regulatory implications for multi-state regulation. *Issues, 17*(3) [On-line]. Available: http://www.ncsbn.org/files/positions/telenrsg.html.

Northrop, C. E. (1987). Licensure revocation. In C. E. Northrop & M. E. Kelly (Eds.), *Legal issues in nursing* (pp. 405–422). St. Louis: C. V. Mosby Company.

Northrop, C. E., & Mech, A. (1981). The nurse as expert witness. *Nursing Law & Ethics, 2*(3), 1–8.

Oregon State Board of Nursing. (1989). *Declaratory Ruling: In the Matter of the Petitions for Declaratory Ruling by Hillsboro Union High School No. 3, et al., and by Carol Mitts.* Beaverton, OR: Author.

Pearson, L. (2000). Annual legislative update: How each state stands on legislative issues affecting advanced nursing practice. *Nurse Practitioner, 25*(1), 16–68.

Proctor, S. T. (with Lordi, S. L., & Zaiger, D. S.). (1993). *School nursing practice: Roles and standards.* Scarborough, ME: National Association of School Nurses, Inc.

Schwab, N., & Haas, M. K. (1995). Delegation and supervision in school settings: Standards, issues and guidelines for practice. Part 1. *Journal of School Nursing, 11*(1), 19–28.

Webster's third new international dictionary of the English language: unabridged. (1986). Springfield, MA: Merriam-Webster, Inc.

Wertz, E. (1995). And a little state shall lead them . . . educational requirements for nurses. *Prairie Rose, 64*(3), 1, 4.

TABLE OF CASES

See page 625 for Table of Federal Statutes and Regulations.

Chapter Five

School Nursing Practice: Professional Performance Issues

Nadine C. Schwab
Janis Hootman
Mary H. B. Gelfman
with Elizabeth K. Gregory and Katherine J. Pohlman

INTRODUCTION

This chapter focuses on program foundation and contemporary *professional* performance issues that have implications for school district and school nurse liability. Professional performance issues include those responsibilities and practice parameters in school health nursing, other than direct care, that enhance the quality of programs and services, such as compliance with legal and ethical standards of practice and maintaining one's professional competence. The emphasis in this chapter is on those professional performance issues that impact day-to-day practice in and beyond the school nurse's office, also known as the "school health room," "health center," "health clinic," or "wellness center." Rather than addressing every issue, this chapter discusses those that are fundamental to quality health-services programs serving the general school population, pre-k through 12th grade, with emphasis on high-priority risk-management concerns. Chapter 6, a companion chapter, explores *clinical* performance issues in school nursing practice. Other chapters in this book address many of these issues from different perspectives; these are cross-referenced for the reader's benefit.

In all aspects of American life, including public education, today's culture expects a "fast-food" approach to service delivery and problem resolution. Yet, as chapter 1 describes, students' health issues are increasing in complexity and variety and presenting schools with unique ethical, legal, administrative, and financial challenges. School nurses must provide services according to scientifically validated nursing principles, local, state, and national standards for general nursing practice, and specialty school nursing practice, as well as legal mandates and professional ethics. Professional standards describe competent nursing

service delivery and benchmarks for quality client care and professional performance. (See also chapter 4.)

Quality care in schools implies delivering nursing services that enhance student learning by maintaining or improving student health and well being. As such, nursing standards for the school setting are critical to an effective school health program. Legal standards must also be considered in establishing effective school nursing programs, although it is important to remember that laws and regulations tend to describe minimal standards and frequently lag well behind current professional standards and general practice in the field. Working toward legislative change can be an effective way to update the standards set by law.

Practicing within both legal and professional parameters should decrease the potential for civil and criminal liability in the event of legal action against a nurse or school district. Nevertheless, determining the best course of action in individual situations remains a challenge. At times, education law, health law, school policy, and nursing standards of practice may conflict with each other. Such conflicts increase the potential for civil liability of both school districts and school nurses and the potential for disciplinary action by the state's board of nursing against school nurses (See chapters 2 and 4 for additional information). Therefore, communication and collaboration among school nurses and school administrators with input from parents, students, school staff members, medical advisors, community providers, and other interested parties are essential for the development of policies, procedures, and strategies that enhance student learning, protect students from harm, and minimize the exposure of school districts to unwarranted liability in the school health arena. Regular communication with parents, consultation with other school health experts, such as school medical advisors and state school nurse consultants, and the effective use of school health advisory councils are critical components to effective risk-management programs in today's public schools. Duncan & Igoe (1998, p. 189) recommend the use of "Healthy School Teams," rather than school health advisory councils, and list critical team members in their description of "Action Steps for Implementing School Health Services."

It is important to remember that the authority of a court decision may be limited to the court's own jurisdiction. (See chapter 2 for further explanation of case law and precedent.) Furthermore, because the Individuals with Disabilities Education Act (IDEA) is based on the individual needs of each student, a decision regarding one child, even in the same federal district, may not be applicable to another (see chapters 2, 12, and 13). However, because national and state professional standards of practice are increasingly recognized by courts as applicable to determining the "standard of care" in cases of negligence (see chapters 2 and 4), state agencies and regional and local school districts should consider these standards in developing state and district policy.

PROGRAM FOUNDATION

The foundation for school nursing and school health services programs is addressed in this chapter from a legal perspective. For an in-depth description of the essential functions of school health services programs today from a systems and practice perspective, the reader is referred to chapter 1 and to Duncan and Igoe's chapter "School Health Services" in the book *Health Is Academic: A Guide to Coordinated School Health Programs* (1998).

State Mandates, Policies, and Guidelines

State Mandates

States vary in their mandates related to nursing and other health services in public schools. These variances are not surprising considering the lack of a universal definition of "school nursing services" or "school health services," changing concepts of what constitutes the components of these services, lack of clarity and understanding in communications between education and health professionals at local, state, and national levels, and the laws and resources of different states and communities. Most of the specific mandates for school health services (e.g., what kind and how much) derive from state law rather than federal law, as discussed in chapter 2. Relevant state legislation may include, but is not limited to, mandates for school nurses and school medical advisors, education and certification of school nurses, student immunizations, student health assessments and health screenings, medication administration, and health content of curricula for students and staff in-service programs.

Federal civil rights and special education laws require all schools to assume greater accountability for student health services. *Macomb County Intermediate School District v. Joshua S.* articulates this responsibility: "The reason for mandating the provision of supportive services . . . is to guarantee handicapped students an opportunity to gain an education" (1989, p. 602). According to Palfrey (1995), "Probably more than any other aspect of the law [Public Law 94-142; IDEA], the related services provision transformed the educational environment and changed schools from solely scholastic institutions into therapeutic agencies" (p. 265). State laws usually mirror these federal laws. See chapter 11 for in-depth information regarding federal civil rights laws (§ 504 of the Rehabilitation Act and the Americans with Disabilities Act) and chapters 12 and 13 regarding federal special education law and current issues.

State mandates related to health services may not always reflect federal requirements and may be at odds with other state mandates, as well. For example, in Connecticut, state education law and regulations provide that "medication administration is not required in schools" and permit local and regional school districts to choose whether or not to have a policy allowing it (Regulations of Connecticut State Agencies, §§ 10-212a-2(a) and 10-212a-2(a)(1)). Under federal law, however, refusal to administer a medication that a student requires during the school day in order to attend school, and that meets safety standards, would be considered discriminatory. Thus, in reality, Connecticut school districts do not have a choice as to whether or not they will have a policy regarding the administration of medication.

Legislation can support the establishment and retention of health services when there is temptation to eliminate such programs. For example, in *Liebowitz v. Dinkins* (1991), an injunction preventing elimination of school health services in New York City public schools was upheld because state law required these services. In another case, *Kelly v. Parents United for the District of Columbia Public Schools* (1994), parents in the school district sued when budgetary constraints impeded implementation of District of Columbia law. The law required that registered nurses be assigned to all schools for specified hours each week and also required nurses or certified athletic trainers at "every school-sponsored athletic event." The lower court granted a permanent injunction to require that services be provided as required by law, and the injunction was upheld on appeal.

Legislation also supports quality health services, including safe environmental conditions in schools. Quality health services programs are affected by laws and regulations related to nursing practice, medical advisors, student immunization requirements, medication administration, health education, communicable disease control, training of first-aid assistants employed in schools, and health inspections of school buildings and grounds, among others. They are also affected by legislation that stipulates financial support for school health services programs, including criteria for obtaining funding and determining how the dollars can be spent. For example, in Massachusetts, the state and local shares of public school budgets, including those for school health services, are specified in the Massachusetts Education Reform Act of 1993 and its foundation budget. This foundation budget, identified as "Foundation Health Care Staff," called for one nurse for every 500 elementary students and one nurse for every 667 middle and high school students, and provided a basic level of state support for school health service programs (Massachusetts Department of Public Health [MDPH], 1998, p. 15). MDPH reported that the foundation budget "is currently providing an estimated $49M annually for health services in public schools. . . . [Additionally,] the Health Protection fund provides $5M annually for partial support of the School Nurse Institute, 31 school-based health centers (SBHCs), 10 planning grants for SBHCs, and 26 enhanced school health programs [and] almost $25M . . . for school-based health education that links with school health services" (1998, p.5). Of additional interest, in 1996 the Massachusetts legislature called for the formation of a Commission on School Nursing to address "issues pertaining to the provision of nursing services in the public and non-public primary and secondary schools of the Commonwealth." The Commission was designated responsibility for identifying the current health needs of students and staffing patterns of nurses across the state and for making recommendations to the legislature regarding standards, models, and funding for school nursing services. Among several recommendations made by the Commission was one calling for one registered nurse in every school building, with extra

staffing for schools with more than 500 students (extra registered nurses [RNs] at the rate of one tenth of a full-time RN for every 50 students). As required by the 1996 legislation, MDPH subsequently submitted to the legislature a plan for implementing the Commission's recommendations (April 1, 1998). The report outlines a

projection of costs and funding sources associated with said implementation, the identification of mechanisms to promote the development of collaborative partnerships between school districts, health care providers, and health care insurers, and the identification of criteria necessary to insure that school health services are targeted to high priority sites.

The MDPH report describes three different models for school health services: Standard School Health Services (with nursing staff levels as described above), Standard School Health Services with Enhanced Coordination, and Standard School Health Services with School-Based Health Center.

It is not uncommon for state mandates to become outdated as society (including families) and education and health care systems change. Laws that once supported quality school health services when they were enacted may, in the future, be insufficient to ensure minimum safety standards or may even become barriers to creative, positive change. In order to effect statewide change, therefore, state mandates may need to be revised or eliminated and new mandates may be indicated. This can be a tedious, long process, but a crucial one for which educators and school health professionals should provide leadership within their communities and states. Such leadership requires, first and foremost, informing and educating the public and their legislative representatives of the issues and implications of old and newly proposed legislation. Excellent communication skills, collaboration, and compromise are required for success—to say nothing of patience, timing, and vigilance throughout the political process. It took the New Jersey State School Nurse Association, in collaboration with the New Jersey Education Association and other interested parties, approximately 18 years to change their mandate from one certified school nurse per district to the requirement that all school nurses must be certified (Carol McGotty, personal communication, July 10, 1999). (See the section on "Accountability for Non-certified Registered Nurses [RNs]" later in this chapter for additional information.)

State Agency Policies and Guidelines

State agencies may issue policies and guidelines that directly affect the provision of school nursing services in the state. Until 1995, state policy in Tennessee assigned responsibility for providing health care services to students, including procedures such as catheterization and suctioning, to classroom personnel, that is, teachers and teacher aides (National Education Association, 1995). This policy did not reflect the requirements of special education law restricting the provision of related services to qualified individuals (see chapter 12), nor did it reflect the requirements of state licensure laws that define who in the state is qualified to provide health care services (i.e., licensed health professionals). In response to pressures brought by the Tennessee Education Association (TEA), however, state policy was changed in 1995 when Tennessee's Special Education Director issued a new directive, warning that unlicensed school employees who perform health care procedures risked liability for practicing medicine without a license (National Education Association, 1995; Hatfield, 1997, p. 7). The pressures brought by TEA further resulted in legislation in 1996, mandating Tennessee school districts to employ or contract with certified health professionals to provide health services in schools. This legislation resulted in a significant change to school nurse staffing patterns in Tennessee, increasing the number of nurses in some districts by as many as 60 (Robinson, 1997a, p. 6). Many state health and education agencies have published guidelines for school districts to follow in developing local policies. Some address school nursing and health services programs in their entirety, and others address certain practice issues, such as health services for special needs students or child abuse prevention and reporting. For example, the Wisconsin Department of Public Instruction published *School Nursing and Health Services: A Resource and Planning Guide* (Ericksen, 1998) in order to

> Assist school districts, health personnel serving schools, and community partners to design and provide safe, effective school health systems that promote health, development, and well-being and remove health-related barriers to learning for all children in Wisconsin schools.

Similarly, the Massachusetts Department of Public Health published *The Comprehensive School Health Manual* (Goodman and Sheetz, 1995) as a resource "providing guidelines for acceptable practice and policy development, and orienting new school nurses." In 1992, the Connecticut Department of Education

published guidelines, entitled *Serving Students with Special Health Care Needs,* to assist districts "to develop, enhance and promote safe and appropriate educational opportunities for students with special health care needs." State agencies in many other states have published such guidelines and, while they are not policy directives or legal mandates per se, they are consistent with or founded on legal requirements and establish state standards for local and regional school districts to follow.

State agencies may also define performance measures for school health services programs and require school districts to report aggregate data for monitoring and evaluation purposes. In 1999, for example, the New York State Department of Education, in collaboration with other partners, drafted a "Report Card for School Health Services." This draft assessment tool is intended to "provide consistency with educational strategies already utilized in New York State and also to provide schools with a tool for self-assessment and monitoring their own health services" (University of the State of New York, New York State Department of Education, Comprehensive Health and Pupil Services Team, & Statewide Advocacy for School Health Services Center, June 21, 1999). The tool establishes a set of standards in eight areas of school health services practice. The standards in each area are defined according to the following descriptors:

- Below Standard

- Standard

- Proficient

- Distinguished

The eight areas of practice are Immunization Policy and Practice; Infectious/Communicable Disease Control; Special Health Care Needs; Emergency Procedures; Administration of Medications; Screening Procedures; Health Office; and Health Services Personnel. Each area of practice has several categories of standards. For example, the first category of standards under "Immunization Policy and Practice" is "Immunization Status." Standards for "Immunization Status" are defined as follows:

- **1.1. Below Standard:** Verbal statements (e.g., by parents, physician offices, etc.) are accepted as proof of immunizations.

- **2.1. Standard:** All student cumulative health records contain the required written certificate of proof or legitimate exception.

- **3.1. Proficient:** In addition to meeting the requirements given in 2.1, a list that identifies students who have not been vaccinated according to national recommendations is readily accessible in the event of an outbreak.

- **4.1. Distinguished:** In addition to meeting the requirements given in 3.1, immunization records are computerized on a secure system that is used to monitor the immunization status of each student.

Once the pilot project phase of this initiative is complete, these standards will be used for monitoring compliance with established standards, as well as evaluating different outcomes and attributes of school health services programs in the state (University of the State of New York, et al., 1999). These standards, then, define expected levels of care for school districts and their personnel.

Risk Management Issues

Because the level of school nursing services mandated by state and federal law has significantly increased, in terms of both the number of students requiring services and the complexity of nursing care required, there is enhanced risk for litigation. Thus, district administrators and school boards need to work collaboratively with qualified nurses and physicians to develop sound policy and procedural guidelines, identify health and safety risks, promote a safe environment, and ensure the maintenance or improvement of student and employee health in the school community. Qualified school nurses who adhere to professional and legal practice standards can provide districts with considerable protection against litigation. Those who practice outside these standards put a district and themselves at considerable risk of liability. (See also chapter 17.)

Whether school nurses are employed by an educational or health agency, they must know and comply with both educational and health care laws, regulations, policies, and standards. School administrators and medical advisors should be familiar with these laws, as well. While mandates can positively impact the outcome of school nursing programs—for example, by requiring qualified personnel through teacher certification and establishing systems for student health surveillance—laws and regulations that become outdated can be more problematic than supportive to the provision of quality services. When state mandates do not reflect current practices in schools, it is essential, from a risk management point of view, that school district policies and procedures do reflect the current practice of its

personnel and that the practices are in keeping with current professional standards.

In terms of state agency policy directives and guidelines, it is important to remember that the content in these documents can sometimes be used by the plaintiff in a negligence action against a school district to help establish the duty or "standard of care" that was owed to the student. New school nurses, medical advisors, and administrators should always contact both their state education and health agencies to determine if relevant guidelines exist and request a copy of such guidelines for their own use.

School Medical Advisors

Many states require the appointment of a school medical advisor to assist school districts in addressing health issues. The role of the medical advisor includes administration and planning in collaboration with the school nursing staff and school administrators, implementing state and district school health requirements, health education, consulting with school staff on a variety of topics, identifying and minimizing hazards in the school environment, and sports medicine (Sklaire, 1990). More specifically, the school medical advisor may be involved in diverse activities such as the following:

- developing and revising standing orders for emergencies and routine medical intervention;

- consultation regarding medication administration issues;

- athletic physical exams and supervision (team physician);

- medical advice to the school district regarding individualized school health services for students pursuant to § 504 and/or IDEA, including participation in team meetings, as needed;

- consultation on school absenteeism issues, including review of requests for home instruction, as requested;

- employee health;

- safety and environmental assessment;

- formulating school district policy regarding immunizations and consulting concerning individual requests for exemption or partial exemption from immunization requirements; and

- consultation concerning suspected child abuse. (American Academy of Pediatrics, Committee on

School Health, 1993; Connecticut Advisory School Health Council, 1997).

In addition, the school medical advisor serves as a connection between the local medical community and the schools. At various places in this book, references are made to consultation with the school medical advisor. Given the variation in requirements and role definitions for school medical advisors across the country, it would be difficult to propose one standard. Many states provide a standard in statute, however simplified or outdated. School districts need to define the school medical advisor's role from state statute and from the needs of the district. That role definition then becomes school district policy and the basis for a contract between the district and the medical advisor. A critical element of any role description comprises the qualifications of persons who can fill the position. From a risk-management perspective, school districts are wise to seek medical advisors whose qualifications and competencies include demonstrated, up-to-date expertise in the medical care of children and adolescents.

Even if state law does not require that school boards appoint a medical advisor, school districts need competent medical advice on a regular basis. Also from a risk-prevention perspective, school administrators must remember that medical decisions should be made by health care professionals; others risk charges of practicing medicine without a license. From an administrative point of view, medical consultation may provide answers to significant questions (e.g., is the request medically reasonable?) and additional options for consideration in many school-related contexts, including health services, safety management, health education, special education, mental health issues, and environmental concerns.

District Policies and Procedures

In cases of nursing malpractice, courts take into consideration many standards that might apply to the expected standard of care. One critical standard is the health care facility's (or school district's) "rules and policies" (American Nurses Association, 1998a, p. 11). School districts detail their understanding and application of state mandates, as well as their beliefs and preferences regarding nursing services, through the on-going development, review, and revision of district policies and procedures.

Without adequate policy and procedural guidelines, school districts and their employees are at greater risk for performance errors, including discrimination, safety violations, and other actions that are not compliant with federal and state mandates. Furthermore, poor risk management may result in harm to students and litigation against employees and school districts that might otherwise be avoided.

Without policy and procedures, school personnel have no reliable source of direction from the district regarding their service parameters or protection regarding alleged violations of their responsibilities. In a 1991 Louisiana case (*Declouet v. Orleans Parish School Board*, 1998), officials of a school failed to respond to an 18-year-old girl's pleas for an ambulance during an asthma attack, resulting in the student's death. The family of the student won a $1.6 million settlement, which was confirmed on appeal. The school district was found liable for

- failure to have a clear policy on medical emergencies,

- failure to adequately train its employees, and

- failure to protect the student from harm.

In this case, the assistant principal had instructed a counselor to contact the student's mother regarding authorization to call an ambulance before calling the emergency medical system (EMS). No policy required personnel to call EMS immediately (and first) in an emergency or consult with the school nurse if unsure when a health complaint might constitute an urgent health problem. The school nurse was actually present on the campus at the time, but was not contacted by the principal or counselor (personal communication with Yvonne LaGasse, June 1997).

Examples of significant practice issues that require clear policies and procedures include those related to medication administration, communicable disease control, health screenings, "do not resuscitate" (DNR) orders, crisis intervention, and transportation of students experiencing illness or injury at school.

Well-developed policies and procedures can prove critical to school districts' defense strategies when they are sued. In *Hickingbottom v. Orleans Parish School Board* (1993), the Louisiana Court of Appeals reversed a lower court's finding that a school board was liable for negligence when a fourth-grade student, following dismissal, permanently injured the little finger on his dominant hand. The injury occurred when the child's father sent him back on school property to find his sister. Another student allegedly assaulted him in the school, throwing him on the ground and injuring his finger. The Appellate Court cited, among other findings, the existence of a standard dismissal policy, which was properly followed by the teacher. For this and additional reasons, the school was not liable for the student's injury.

In a potentially far-reaching case against a Missouri school district, parents cited violation of their daughter's rights under the Americans with Disabilities Act (Title II), § 504 of the Rehabilitation Act of 1973, and 20 U.S.C. 1983; see chapter 2 for introductory information regarding these federal laws and regulations.) The district's school nurse refused to administer to their daughter Ritalin prescribed in a dosage far in excess of that recommended by the manufacturer and the *Physician's Desk Reference*, a standard resource for appropriate dosages and other information critical to safe administration of medication (*DeBord, Allen, et al. v. The Board of Education of the Ferguson Florissant School District, et. al.*, 1996). The federal district court found for the defendants (the district and its personnel, including the school nurse) for several reasons. One reason was the existence of a school district policy that supported the school nurse's professional judgment regarding medication administration safety (*DeBord*, 1996, Memorandum of Decision, footnote 3, p. 2). The school nurse may determine, based on her professional judgment, whether a prescribed medication should be administered at school. The policy states that physician prescribed medications must be "cleared with the school nurse before being taken while in school." This decision was upheld on appeal to the 8th Circuit Court of Appeals (1997).

A similar case (*Davis v. Francis Howell School District*, 1997), brought by a family in another Missouri school district but heard in the same federal district court, involved similar megadoses of Ritalin ordered for a student by the same physician. In this case, the district's medication procedures were one of several important defenses against a finding of discrimination under § 504 or the Americans with Disabilities Act of 1990. The procedures specifically state that the nurse has a "right and obligation to verify the validity of any medication order" and to "refuse to give any medication that he or she feels does not meet the criteria established in the Board Policy for giving medication" (Robinson, 1997b). Because of the similarity to findings in the *DeBord* case, the Court ruled for the school district in the *Davis Case* (1997), and the ruling was upheld on appeal to the 8th Circuit Court (1998). (These cases are also discussed in chapters 4, 6, and 11.)

In order to avoid liability in civil cases, it is critical for school nurses both to know the policies and procedures of the school district they are working in and to follow them. Agency policies hold employees to a specified standard of behavior. School nurses should

encourage districts that lack sufficient policy and procedures for nursing services to develop them. School nurses can facilitate policy formation by reviewing established policies from other school nursing (health services) programs and constructing a draft for their district's review and endorsement.

In a Minnesota case (*Schluessler v. Independent School District No. 200, et al.*, 1989), a school nurse and school district were found liable in the death of an 18-year-old student who had an asthma attack in school. The court determined that the school nurse failed to make a proper asthma assessment and violated school district policy by her failure to notify school administration and the parent of the student's use of another student's medication. Despite several mitigating circumstances in favor of the nurse (Cynthia K. Silkworth, personal communication, April 1999), failure to follow district policy (i.e., to notify an administrator of a student's unauthorized use of another's medication—in this case, a friend's inhaler) contributed to the finding of negligence.

Policies and procedures need to reflect current standards of practice and should be periodically reviewed and revised. Considering professional practice standards and the rapid changes in scientific and professional information and technology, a review should be done at least every 5 years; some policies or procedures may require annual review. Policy changes must be memorialized in writing, not merely communicated verbally. Policies should be specific and avoid any recommendation that would extend a nurse's responsibility beyond the scope of professional practice defined in the state's nurse practice act or require a nurse to perform beyond his or her professional preparation and experience.

District policies are generally approved by school boards, and procedures are developed and reviewed with school administration. School districts should include the school nurse and other appropriate health care specialists in the ongoing process of developing, reviewing, and revising relevant policies and procedures. Relevant policies and procedures include those that directly address the delivery of professional services (e.g., nursing, counseling, social work, physical therapy) and those that address health-related student concerns (e.g., absenteeism, homebound services, school entry requirements, behavior management plans, and "do not resuscitate" [DNR] orders).

Current policies should be available to staff for their reference at all times, and staff should be not only informed about policy changes, but also provided with timely written updates. Supervisors should ask staff to "sign off" on policies to verify that they have read and understood them to establish that the supervisor (and district) acted responsibly in making the policies accessible to staff. Administrators and supervisors responsible for school nursing services also need to ensure that outdated policies are removed from each school's health policy book and that new ones are inserted in the proper order.

Subsequent to the student's death from asthma in the case cited above (*Declouet),* the school system did review and revise emergency procedures in the district. However, due to inadequate dissemination of the improved policy and procedures, many staff members were never notified or instructed regarding them. As a result, another student with asthma was endangered the following year, at the same site, when a staff member told a student in respiratory distress to "go outside for air," instead of calling for emergency medical assistance. Recognizing that inadequate dissemination of policy and procedures, especially addenda to policies and procedures, was problematic in their large school district, the Medical and Health Department of the district began issuing to all personnel an annually reprinted policy directive. The directive states that 9-1-1 must be called in an emergency and specifies what constitutes an emergency—for example, breathing problems, uncontrolled bleeding, and head, neck, or back injury (Iris Haydel, telephone communication, July 1998). Although calling the school nurse, after 9-1-1, is not included in the emergency protocol of the district, it would be an appropriate addition. In the Declouet case, immediate respiratory assessment by—or even telephone consultation with—the school nurse might have saved the student's life.

It is wise for school districts to publish significant school health services policies in documents such as student handbooks or newsletters that are disseminated to parents. Publication facilitates annual parent notification and family communication. Examples of significant policies are as follows:

- Management of medical emergencies. (Policy example: Call 9-1-1 in all medical emergencies with notice to parents as soon as possible.)

- Transportation of students. (Policy example: Transportation to the hospital emergency room will be provided only by the Emergency Response System [or EMS]. The parent is responsible for the cost of such transportation.)

- Medication administration. (Policy example: Medication administration at school requires a prescription written by an authorized prescriber as well as written parental authorization. The medication must be delivered to the health office in a properly labeled, original-pharmacy container.)

- Early dismissal for illness or injury conditions. (Policy example: Students may not be dismissed early without parental authorization.)

- Communicable disease management—prevention of Hepatitis A outbreaks. (Policy example: No home-prepared foods may be distributed to students at school or school-sponsored activities.)

- Communications between school health professionals and community health care providers. (Policy example: When in-school medical treatments are ordered for students, including the administration of medication, the school nurse will communicate with the prescriber, when necessary, to confirm and clarify treatment orders and to ensure safe care. Such communications will be limited to discussion of the treatment orders and their implementation in the school setting or to a health or safety emergency.)

- Animals in school buildings. (Policy example: For health and safety reasons, animals will be allowed in school only with prior approval of building principals and in accordance with established procedures of the Board of Education).

Heightened Risk: Cases Involving Student Deaths

In developing state and school district policies and procedures, it is important to consider relevant court cases and their implications for the development of effective risk-management strategies in school settings. Cases involving student deaths generally have heightened liability risks for school districts and school employees. Some are explored in this section, therefore, as a tool for gleaning lessons that can be applied to policies and practice standards in schools.

When a student dies at school or after sustaining an injury at school, the question of liability is often raised by grieving parents. The following cases illustrate issues of standards of care for school nurses as well as broader issues of supervision, hazardous conditions, and staff responsibilities. These cases could be considered extensions of the more numerous cases involving injuries of students. Discussing liability cases involving special education students who were injured at school, Pitasky (1995) concludes:

> Viewing the body of significant special education student injury lawsuits as a whole, a

> common theme is obvious. . . . Time after
> time, that theme has been one of no liability
> in absence of gross negligence.

This conclusion also appears to apply as consistently to cases of student death.

Two cases concerning students who died of acute asthma after requesting help at school, *Declouet* and *Schluessler*, have already been discussed above. In a third case, *Calvert v. Tulsa Public Schools*, 1996, a 10-year-old Oklahoma student died at school during an asthma attack, and her parents sued the school, alleging that her requests for help were ignored. The suit was dismissed on the technical ground that it could only be filed by an appointed personal representative. Later, the parents were appointed as personal representatives, and they moved to amend their original petition. This request was denied on the technical ground that the time limit for filing the suit had passed prior to the motion to amend. The appellate court affirmed this decision, commenting that the state Government Tort Claims Act barred granting the motion to amend. The state supreme court vacated the appellate decision, reversed the lower court decision, and remanded the case for trial, finding that the parents had standing to file the suit either as parents or as personal representatives, under state law, and that the specific requirements of the Government Tort Claims Act had been met. Although most of the discussion in the decision concerns the application—and misapplication—of procedural requirements to the situation, this decision is also an example of the application of equitable principles. The technical outcomes seem completely unfair in the specific circumstances: equity means that courts may, in some circumstances, consider basic justice and fairness.

The most important message from these three cases of deaths related to asthma is the importance of emergency planning, including instructions for the entire school staff on the dangers of asthma and the need for rapid assessment of the student's status by knowledgeable health professionals. To expedite calls to 9-1-1, there should be an agreement between the school district and the local emergency services concerning arrangements when payment is required.

In two cases where students died as the result of violence at school, the lower courts had found for the school districts based on governmental immunity without examining the negligence claims (*Brum v. Town of Dartmouth*, 1998 and *Etheredge v. Richland School District*, 1998). In both cases, the appellate court

reversed and remanded for a fuller analysis of the negligence claims, and the outcomes were pending when this book went to press.

In *Brum*, there was an altercation among students and at least one outsider on school grounds before school started. The school administration intervened and one of the students warned the principal that some of the combatants had threatened to return to the school to retaliate. The Massachusetts court decision indicates that school administrators observed the return of three young people carrying knives and other weapons, and did not intervene. The three youths entered a classroom and stabbed a student, who died. The appellate court found that the failure of the school district to adopt security policies and procedures for the school, as required by state law, and the failure of the principal to respond to a warning of further violence could have been found to be negligent. The lower court's dismissal had denied the plaintiff parent an opportunity for a trial on the issue of negligence, and the appellate court reversed and remanded for trial.

In *Etheredge*, one student shot another to death in a South Carolina school. The lower court granted summary judgment for the school district, based on governmental immunity under state law. The appellate court relied on the affidavit of a school security guard, who reported numerous examples of students out of control at the school, as well as the rejection of his requests for equipment and authority. The school did provide this and another guard with radios, but they lacked uniforms, badges, or any form of weapon to assist them in maintaining order. After reviewing a series of prior hair-raising cases in which student injuries at the hands of other students led to law suits, and analyzing the school district's largely procedural objections, the appellate court reversed and remanded for trial the issue of whether the district had been grossly negligent, which would constitute an exception to the state immunity law.

In a 1997 Texas case, the issue was whether a student's death from heat exhaustion during an August football practice session was the result of school district negligence (*Roventini v. Pasadena Independent School District*). In response to a motion to dismiss, the federal court found that negligence claims could not be dismissed without trial, citing intensive first day practice without appropriate conditioning, rest periods, or sufficient water to prevent dehydration. The student in question complained to the coaches and was told to continue with the drills. After the student collapsed, coaches failed to provide immediate assistance, and he died a few hours later. The court dismissed from the case school officials who were not directly involved but had been cited in the claim for relief, and ordered the matter to go forward against the coaches.

An 8-year-old Mississippi special education student ran away from school after being disciplined and was found dead in a nearby creek the next day. The parent's suit included claims under the IDEA concerning the appropriateness of the student's school placement, under state law for wrongful death and emotional distress, and under § 1983 for violation of the student's civil rights (*Brown v. Houston School District*, 1997). The lower court dismissed the case in a summary judgment, citing sovereign immunity or qualified immunity. The state supreme court upheld this decision, confirming that the district had immunity from suit and that the IDEA and § 1983 claims were without factual basis.

An Ohio student who had a seizure disorder and a heart condition, of which the school district was aware, collapsed on the school bus on the way home after school (*Sargi v. Kent City Board of Education*, 1995). The bus driver's attempt to radio the bus garage for assistance failed, and she continued on her route. Using a phone provided by a parent, the driver later called the bus garage and asked the secretary to call the student's home. The student had stopped breathing by the time the bus reached her home, and she died three days later. The parent sued under § 1983 and state law, claiming that lack of school district policies concerning emergencies and lack of training of school staff, including bus drivers, had deprived her daughter of life and liberty. The federal district court found that the school district did not cause the student's death and that the district was immune from liability under state law, and granted the school district's motion for summary judgment. On appeal, the Sixth Circuit Court of Appeals affirmed, stating in part:

> Therefore, we hold that there is no special relationship between decedent and the school district that gave rise to a constitutional duty on the part of the Board to protect her from the consequences of a seizure while she was on the school bus. We do not hold that school districts have no duty of protection of students in other situations not before us. The nature and extent of such duties will have to be decided case by case.

Finding further that the school district itself had not made a deliberate choice to take the student home without medical intervention, and that lack of training

of bus drivers for medical emergencies did not constitute "deliberate indifference," the appellate court rejected the parent's claims concerning policies and training. Addressing the claim that the lack of policies and training caused the danger that resulted in the student's death, the court found no affirmative act by the school district that created a danger for the student. The Sixth Circuit upheld the district court's summary judgment on both constitutional and state immunity law grounds.

After a Georgia student collapsed on a school staircase and later died, her parents sued the school district claiming violations of § 504 (*Crisp County School District v. Pheil*, 1998). The lower court denied the school district's motion for summary judgment, and the district appealed. The appellate court found that although the required handrail was missing from the stairs, the parents did not show that the missing rail caused the injury that resulted in her death. The parents relied on § 504 claims in attempting to defeat the school district's immunity under state law, but failed to establish that the district's failure to make specific accommodations for their daughter's allergies and headaches caused her fall. Although the student had complained to her parent about the difficulties of changing classes, the school had never been notified of this problem. The court reversed the lower court's denial of summary judgment for the school. This case stresses the importance of making causal connections between the defendant's actions and omissions and the resulting injury and death. In most states, the governmental immunity that supports dismissal or summary judgment in this type of case can be defeated by a showing of gross negligence. Given the specific facts of this case, the court implies that a missing staircase railing was not gross negligence.

An Arizona school district had a "closed campus" policy at the high school, requiring that students remain on campus all day. After a group of students left campus during the day and were involved in an automobile accident that killed some of them, parents sued the school district for failure to supervise and enforce the policy (*Tollenaar v. Chino Valley School District*, 1997). The trial court granted summary judgment for the school district, citing an earlier case in which the court found that an "open campus" policy did not create an unreasonable risk of automobile accidents involving students. While recognizing that failure to enforce the closed campus policy is somewhat different from adopting an open campus policy, the appellate court found only "the ordinary risks" of automobile use. The court also rejected a claim that the closed campus policy represented an assumption of additional responsibility for the protection of students.

A private residential school in Rhode Island had been informed by the parents that a student with asthma had a severe allergy to peanuts (*Federico v. Order of Saint Benedict in Rhode Island,* 1995). During an evening dorm party, the student unknowingly ate food containing peanuts, which presumably triggered an anaphylactic (life-threatening allergic) response complicated by asthma. The dorm parents had not been informed of the student's severe allergic condition and there was no individualized health care plan in place. The school nurse was notified, asked someone else to call emergency services, and went to the student's aid. However, the nurse did not bring to the scene the epinephrine (injectable medication) that was on hand in the health office and, if administered in a timely fashion, would likely have saved his life, and did not notify the school's physician. School staff members, other students, and the nurse made a variety of efforts to assist the student but did not administer the epinephrine. The student was not breathing when he was taken to the hospital, and he died soon afterwards. Although the trial court heard from medical experts concerning standards of care, it barred testimony on a technicality concerning nursing standards of care and the development of individualized emergency care plans by schools. (See also chapter 4 for discussion of this case under "The Role Of Expert Testimony In Establishing the Standard Of Care.") The jury found for the school. The parents requested a new trial, which was denied, and then appealed to the First Circuit Court of Appeals. This court upheld the district court's instructions to the jury concerning standard of care:

A school is required to do whatever a reasonably prudent school would do in safeguarding the health of its students, providing emergency assistance to them when required and arranging for appropriate medical care if necessary. That does not mean that a school is responsible for guaranteeing the health of its students. Obviously no one can guarantee anyone's health. Nor does it mean that a school is expected to have the knowledge of a physician or to assume the role of a physician in diagnosing or treating its students. What it means is that a school must act as a reasonable school in responding to medical needs of the students.

The appellate court upheld these jury instructions and upheld the decision to deny a new trial. This case might have come out quite differently if the school

involved had been a public school and the student had had a § 504 accommodation plan, if the school had had a standing order concerning acute allergic reactions, or if it had been tried in another court. If the nursing standard of care had been admitted into evidence, it is also likely that the outcome would have been different.

While each of the above cases involves unique facts and most of them involve individual state immunity laws, the general rule proposed by Pitasky (above) appears to apply. In other words, without proof of gross negligence, the school defendants usually prevail. However, as attorneys become more familiar with nursing standards of care in schools, the finding of gross negligence may become slightly easier. It is useful to consider these issues when developing risk management strategies and policies and procedures for school health.

PROFESSIONAL PERFORMANCE

Professionalism implies expert knowledge, credibility, critical thinking, sound decision making, innovation, continuous learning, and respect for legal and ethical frameworks. The performance of school nurses can be measured by comparing their practice to professional standards, applicable laws and regulations, job descriptions, agency policies and procedures, guidelines of state agencies and professional organizations, nursing curricula, and professional literature. Some of the primary indicators of professional performance are discussed in the remainder of this chapter.

Standards of Practice

Standards of practice are important from a risk-management point of view because, as explained in chapter 4, they are increasingly cited in civil court cases to demonstrate the applicable standard of care. It is important to note that professional nurses today are held to the legal standard of what a reasonably prudent *nurse* would have done in the same circumstance, not just what a reasonably prudent *person* would have done. The American Nurses Association states in its publication *Legal Aspects of Standards and Guidelines for Clinical Practice* (1998a, p. 10) that in addition to holding nurses "to standards of the nursing profession," some states recognize an even higher standard of care for specialty and advanced practice nurses.

The *Standards of Professional School Nursing Practice,* published by the National Association of School Nurses (NASN) in 1998, and the American Nurses Association's (ANA) *Standards of Clinical Nursing Practice,* also published most recently in 1998 (1998b), are the primary professional practice standards for school nurses. ANA (1998b, p. 1) defines standards as "authoritative statements by which the nursing profession describes the responsibilities for which its practitioners are accountable." It further clarifies that the *Standards of Clinical Nursing Practice* "delineate the professional responsibilities of all registered nurses engaged in clinical practice, regardless of setting" (1998b, p.5). NASN's standards, based on the ANA standards, further define school nurses' professional responsibilities. The importance of these standards and the history of their development are addressed from different perspectives in chapters 1, 4, and 17. See Appendix A for the National Association of School Nurses *Standards of Professional School Nursing Practice*, including the standards of care and standards of performance.

The NASN Standards of Care, like ANA's standards, specifically address each step of the nursing process and provide measurement criteria for determining how each step of the process is achieved in actual practice. In the 1950s, nursing adopted a scientific method for problem solving, usually referred to as the *nursing process:* "The process is an orderly, prudent method of planning, providing, and evaluating nursing care" (Hootman & Carpenito, 2000, p. 2). School nurses are accountable under the standards of care for applying this scientific, problem-solving approach to client care. Elaboration on the value of the nursing process and the techniques for its application may be found in numerous texts, including NASN's *Nursing Assessment of the School Age Youth: Using the Nursing Process* (Hootman & Carpenito, 2000) and Atkinson and Murray's *Understanding the Nursing Process: Fundamentals of Care Planning* (1990).

Several cases against school nurses highlight the importance of practicing according to legal and professional nursing standards. In a Connecticut case settled out of court several years ago, a school nurse was sued for failing to intervene in order to prevent the progression of anaphylaxis in and eventual death of an elementary school student. The student had a known history of peanut allergy and asthma, and medical orders for emergency medication were on file in her school health record. The student complained that she thought she had eaten something with peanuts. The school nurse, however, relied on the telephone consultation of a doctor who was taking calls for the student's regular physician. The doctor recommended that the nurse should monitor the student for a period of time and, if there were no problems, send her back to class. No medications were given. The student was sent back to

class, later complained again, and vomited; eventually she turned cyanotic, stopped breathing, and died on the way to the hospital.

The student's record did not include any documentation of a professional nursing assessment of the student's respiratory status or vital signs. Had the case gone to trial, the school nurse could not have demonstrated application of the nursing process, and her actions, based on the written record, would not have met the standard of care of a reasonable nurse in the same or similar situation. This case was settled out of court.

In another case, *Mitts, Carol v. Hillsboro Union High School District No. 3, et al.* (1990), it was determined that the school nurse violated the nursing process by accepting and acting on the improper "assessment" of unlicensed school personnel. In this case, a health aide sought to obtain declaratory relief and money damages and to prevent the school district, assistant superintendent, school nurse, parent, and student's physician from "compelling and/or conspiring to compel" her to unlawfully practice medicine or nursing. The part-time school nurse had acquiesced to the school principal's directives when he assigned the school's health aide to perform daily clean intermittent catheterization (CIC) for a new student with myelodysplasia (spina bifida), after training by the parent, and assigned the nurse to supervise the health aide in performing this procedure. The court asked the Oregon State Board of Nursing to issue a declaratory ruling on the question of whether CIC could be lawfully delegated to a trained unlicensed person. The Board of Nursing determined that the principal, other school authorities, and the health aide were practicing nursing without a license. The Board also found that the school nurse's actions in accepting the principal's assessment of the student's health care needs in school, despite the parent's agreement, were below the applicable standards of nursing practice; that is, she failed to use the nursing process and did not complete her own assessment of the student's needs:

The Board expects the licensed nurse to take an active role in applying the nursing process. [The school nurse's] role was passive in that she accepted the assessment by school authorities regarding [the student's] health care needs and acted on the assessment by supervising [the health assistant].

(For further details regarding this case, see the section on "Delegation of Nursing Tasks in the School Setting" in chapter 4.)

In the *Schluessler* case, cited previously in the section on "District Policies and Procedures," the court not only found that the school nurse had failed to follow district policy, but that she had violated the applicable standards of school nursing practice. It determined that the school nurse did not meet practice standards because she failed to provide sufficient nursing assessment of the student's respiratory status and to intervene accordingly. Her failure to report the student's use of another student's medication also violated legal and professional standards of practice for medication administration, not only district policy, since such standards provide that a medication may only be used for the client for whom it is prescribed. (Medication administration issues are discussed in detail in chapter 6.)

Nursing standards are periodically reviewed by the respective national organizations to assure that they promote quality services based on current nursing, medical, and other biopsychosocial sciences. Position papers and publications from these professional organizations can assist school nurses and administrators in preparing and implementing policies and procedures that support these standards. (Appendix E lists authoritative organizations and agencies that school nurses and school administrators can access for information and assistance.)

State nursing organizations may also publish standards that are state specific. For example, in 1997, the Minnesota Nurses Organization published a position paper on *Delegation and Supervision of Nursing Activities*. This publication specifies the responsibilities of Minnesotan registered professional nurses in delegating nursing activities and supervising those to whom they delegate, as well as the person receiving delegation and the agency or employer. It also provides guidelines for RNs to follow in making delegation decisions. State nursing standards related to specialty practice are usually based on national standards.

As addressed in the section above, state education or health agencies may publish guidelines or policy directives that set certain expectations for professional performance standards in school nursing. See Appendix F for an example of guidelines, published by the State of Connecticut State Department of Education, for school district use in evaluating school nursing programs. These guidelines are excerpted from a larger publication, titled *Guidelines for Pupil Services Programs: A Self-Evaluation Guide* (1999), which includes generic standards for an entire pupil services department, as well as individual standards for discipline-specific pupil services programs.

Nurse Practice Acts

School nurses *should not* violate nursing practice laws and regulations or other health care legislation to follow school policy, especially if such violation increases the risk of harm for students or school personnel. If they violate such mandates, they are subject to discipline by their state's board of nursing. Nurse practice acts specify the parameters of the profession's practice regardless of the practice setting (e.g., hospital, home, or school), and are intended to protect the public from harm at the hands of unqualified persons. Because they are "the law," according to Guido (1997), "state boards of nursing cannot grant exception or waive [their] provisions" (p. 192). While a school nurse's job description may be one of the most important local standards against which his or her performance will be measured in a civil case, the nurse practice act is the most important state standard. (See chapter 4 for information on nurse practice acts and their significance to nursing practice in any setting.)

In a case related to the reporting of child abuse (claim brought by Lavery against the Capital Region Board of Cooperative Educational Services in 1995), a school nurse was directed by her school administrator not to report to protective services her suspicion that a student was suffering medical neglect. As a mandated reporter under New York State's statute, and having an obligation to safeguard the client, the school nurse informed the administrator of her responsibility and proceeded to report her suspicion to protective services. Thereafter, the school nurse was interrogated and disciplined by her immediate supervisor and the school administrator. Stating that their administrative directions were causing her to violate state nurse practice requirements, the school nurse advised the school of the need to terminate her employment as soon as a replacement could be found. After leaving her employment in the summer program in August 1995, the school nurse took legal action to recover the loss of her pay and, in 1996, a settlement was made in the school nurse's favor (Joyce Lavery, RN, personal memorandum with attachments to Nadine Schwab, February 11, 1997).

In preparing her legal case, Ms. Lavery had inquired of the Office of the State Board for Nursing in New York what her responsibility under the Nurse Practice Act was in this situation, given her suspicion of medical neglect. The Board responded to the inquiry with the following opinion (Milene A. Sower, Executive Secretary, letter, November 15, 1995):

The failure to report a case of child abuse which came before a registered nurse in her professional capacity would be considered unprofessional conduct ... subject to the penalties ... which range from censure and reprimand to suspension or revocation of the license to practice. Your actions ... appear to be completely in accord with your obligations under the Nurse Practice Act.

Clearly, if the school nurse had followed the principal's directive , she could have been both liable for not following New York state child abuse reporting laws and in jeopardy of disciplinary action for not meeting the requirements of the state's nurse practice act. (This case is also discussed in the section on "Child Abuse and Neglect—Reporting of Suspicion," chapter 6.)

The state's nurse practice act also provided the basis for the Connecticut Board of Examiners for Nursing's decision, in 1997, to open investigations in two Connecticut school districts after receiving complaints that licensed practical nurses (LPNs) were functioning outside their scope of practice and receiving inadequate direction from registered nurses (RNs). School nurses in Connecticut are required to be RNs with additional qualifications as specified in the Connecticut General Statutes (C.G.S.), Section 10-212. A query from the supervising school nurse in one district, a complaint from a concerned parent in the other, and testimony by representatives of the Association of School Nurses of Connecticut led to the Connecticut Board of Examiners for Nursing's (CBEN) decision to investigate. Both the query and the complaint alleged that the districts' staffing policies did not allow the school nurse adequate time to direct the licensed practical nurses (LPNs), as required by the Connecticut Nurse Practice Act (C.G.S., Section 20-87). Both districts' policies permitted LPNs to function without a school nurse on-site and, allegedly, with insufficient direction and supervision. Connecticut education law requires a district to have "one qualified school nurse or nurse practitioner," whose qualifications must include registered nurse (RN) licensure, but is silent on the issue of assistants to school nurses, such as LPNs or nursing aides.

In these cases, a collaborative effort between the CBEN, Departments of Public Health and Education, Association of School Nurses of Connecticut, Association of Licensed Practical Nurses of Connecticut, and school district superintendents resulted in changes to school staffing patterns, including increased school nurse supervision and direction of the LPNs. As a

result, CBEN action against individual nurses was avoided and a cautionary statement reminding the nursing community and employers that LPNs must have "RN supervision that is immediately available, if not continuously on-site, in the community setting" was published in CBEN's *Newsletter* (Connecticut Board of Examiners for Nursing, 1998). The same edition of the *Newsletter* reviewed the scope of practice of LPNs who, in Connecticut, must always practice under the direction of an RN or advanced practice registered nurse (APRN). Had the investigations proceeded without this collaborative intervention, both the LPNs and school nurses might have been at risk of disciplinary action by the Board. The LPNs were at risk if it was determined that they were functioning outside their scope of practice, that is, without RN direction.

The district's school nurses who were aware of this situation, but did not take action to promote change, might also have been at risk of disciplinary action by CBEN if it had been determined that they neglected to report or try to change an unsafe client-care situation. The school nurse supervisor in one of the districts, who queried CBEN about her liability in this situation, was not likely to be at risk for discipline because she had taken actions to try to clarify and change the situation. However, this supervisor subsequently resigned from the position, believing that an unsafe situation still existed due to inadequate school nurse (RN) staffing (Donna Hemmann, personal communication, May 16, 1999). (See chapter 4 for further discussion of nurses' obligations to put their clients [students] first and to practice according to the state's nurse practice act, even in situations that may put the nurse's job in jeopardy.)

The National Association of State School Nurse Consultant's position paper, *Delegation of School Health Services to Unlicensed Assistive Personnel* (1995), includes a section, "If Care Cannot Be Safely Provided in School." While guidance under this section of the position paper targets unsafe situations related to delegation, the steps outlined are appropriate for other situations where school policy and procedures are in conflict with the requirements of a state's nurse practice act and regulations. This position paper is included in Appendix G.

Nursing Protocols and Clinical Practice Guidelines

Increasingly, nursing standards in health care settings include the use of clinical protocols or practice guidelines that specify the desired outcomes in patients with specific medical conditions, as well as the nursing care necessary to achieve those outcomes. These clinical protocols define expected nursing care parameters for given conditions and include applicable nursing diagnoses, care planning, and interventions, as well as criteria for evaluating actual patient outcomes.

Within an agency or institution, these nursing protocols or guidelines direct the nursing process, set local standards of care, and permit documentation by exception, a time-saving form of recording patient care (see the section "Documentation" later in this chapter and chapter 9). The National Association of School Nurses (NASN) publishes a reference book, *Quality Nursing Intervention in the School Setting: Procedures, Models and Guidelines* (Hootman, 1996a), that provides school nursing protocols for a myriad of student health complaints, from head lice to acute asthma to child abuse. Such protocols, if refined and adopted by a school district, guide nursing practice in the district and decrease the potential for wide variations in health problem assessment and management. Appendix H contains two examples of different protocols: one from NASN's publication referenced above (Hootman, 1996a) and the other developed by a committee of the Ridgefield Public Schools in Connecticut. *The School Nurse's Source Book of Individualized Healthcare Plans*, Volume 1, edited by Haas (1993), and Volume 2, edited by Arnold & Silkworth (1999), do not provide nursing protocols, but they set a framework and parameters for developing individualized health care plans for students with specific medical conditions.

Through a training grant from the Maternal Child Health Bureau of the U.S. Department of Health and Human Services, entitled *Nursing Graduate Program for Leadership Development: Children & Adolescents with Special Health Care Needs, Families and Communities*, the University of Washington School of Nursing developed "clinical paths" for nutrition, asthma, and attention deficit-hyperactivity disorder (ADHD). A product of this grant, the 1999 manual, *Children with ADHD: A Manual with Decision Tree and Clinical Path for Health Care Professionals*, identifies four specific goals:

- to promote a systematic and comprehensive approach to the assessment process;

- to enhance a comprehensive and multimodal intervention plan;

- to enhance collaboration among the various providers of care, child, and family; and

- to enhance cultural sensitivity of care (Magyary, Brandt, & Kovalesky, 1999).

At the core of the manual is a "decision tree," or diagram with decision steps, and a Clinical Path to guide clinicians along two timelines: the assessment and diagnostic decision-making phase and the management and follow-up phase. Both parts are based on current research, professional literature, and best-practice standards. The Clinical Path includes outcome statements oriented toward the child and family (Magyary, Brandt, & Kovalesky, 1999). An excellent resource, this manual provides a clinical protocol (path, guideline) for collaborative use between primary health care providers (e.g., advanced practice nurses, pediatricians, and mental health clinicians), and school nurses, other pupil services professionals, and educators in assessing and managing children and adolescents with ADHD-like symptoms.

The legal implications of nursing protocols and clinical guidelines are unclear. They are widely used and endorsed in nursing care today, so a lack of nursing protocols in a district that employs nurses to deliver services to students could potentially be cited by a state board of nursing as a sign of substandard practice by school nurses in the district. The lack of nursing protocols could also be cited by an expert witness in a civil case as evidence of poor management practices by school administration. Whether or not deviations from standard nursing protocols would constitute evidence of negligence in a civil case or in a disciplinary action against a school nurse is a different and unresolved question. In medicine, for example, the use of "Clinical Practice Guidelines" has been embraced by the American Medical Association, health care policy makers, and many state legislatures as a way to minimize unnecessary and ineffective medical care, thereby improving both the quality and cost-effectiveness of medical interventions (Oetgen & Wiley, 1998). The Institute of Medicine (1990) defines Clinical Practice Guidelines as "systematically developed statements of recommendations for patient management to assist practitioner and patient decisions about appropriate health care for specific clinical circumstances." According to Oetgen & Wiley (1998), no jurisdiction has permitted a deviation from a practice guideline to be equated with conclusive evidence of medical malpractice, although some jurisdictions (not all) may allow the admission of a practice guideline as one piece of evidence, among others, to demonstrate conformity with or variation from the expected standard of care.

In school nursing, the use of clinical protocols is an important way for school districts and supervisors to demonstrate their efforts to support and promote quality nursing care of students. This can be an especially useful risk-management strategy in school settings because school nurses practice in significant isolation from each other and from mainstream health care. When they are kept up-to-date, nursing protocols assist a district in directing their school nurses to address student health needs in a standardized and safe fashion and according to policy within the district. Nursing policies and protocols must, however, allow for nursing judgment in individual situations. Curtin (1999, p. 2) cautions that, while practice guidelines ought to be respected and applied appropriately, they should not become "substituted judgments." Rather, intuition, common sense, and professional judgment ("for which there is no substitute") must continue to play a "vigorous role in professional life." While deviations from usual nursing protocols should be acceptable based on individual student needs and situation variables, written documentation of reasons for any deviation is essential for defense of the nurse's judgment in a given situation.

Research in the Clinical Setting

Research is essential to maintain quality in nursing services. Research moves nursing forward, validates the principles and skill techniques of school nursing practice, and leads to improved services for students. For example, a research study verified that the implementation of a hand washing program had positive outcomes—25% fewer student visits to their physicians and 86% fewer medications were needed, and absences decreased by 22% (Monsma, Day, & Arnaud, 1992). According to the *Standards of Clinical Practice*, published by the American Nurses Association (1998b), the *Standards of Professional School Nursing Practice*, published by the National Association of School Nurses (1998), and Proctor's *School Nursing Practice: Roles and Standards* (1993), school nurses are professionally accountable for implementing the findings of, and participating in, relevant research.

The school nurse, medical advisor, and school administrator must know district policy as well as ethical codes of conduct regarding research before beginning any investigation. There are a variety of ethical conduct codes to reference, including the following:

- the Nuremberg Code, developed in 1947, which addresses the protection of human subjects, especially in terms of their informed consent;

- the Declaration of Helsinki, developed in 1964 by the World Medical Association, which reinforces the Nuremberg Code and enhances the protection of subjects' rights by stressing minimal risk to subjects;

- the Patient's Bill of Rights, promulgated first by the Joint Commission on the Accreditation of Hospitals (JCAH) in 1970, formally adopted by the American Hospital Association (AHA) in 1973, and revised in 1992, which emphasizes the right to choose or decline participation in human experimentation (Rothman, 1991, p. 145); and

- Nursing Codes, including the 1893 Nightingale Pledge (McBurney & Filoromo, 1994), *The Code for Nurses with Interpretive Statements* (American Nurses Association, 1985a), *Guidelines for the Investigative Functions of Nurses* (American Nurses Association, 1981), and *Human Rights Guidelines for Nurses in Clinical and Other Research* (American Nurses Association, 1985b).

The school district may also have guidelines regarding research studies, including confidentiality requirements. (See chapters 8 and 9 for information regarding confidentiality, the requirements of the Family Education Rights and Privacy Act, and student records.) If a district does not have policies related to research activities, it should develop, document, and publish such policies for staff and community reference. A widely representative advisory committee from the school and community, including families, as well as health, education, and ethico-legal professionals, may be the best strategy for developing, implementing, evaluating, and revising such policies.

Qualifications and Certification of School Nurses

The board of nursing in each state specifies the minimum qualifications for licensure—that is, for practicing as an entry-level professional (registered) nurse, within its geographical boundaries. State and local boards of education may stipulate additional credentials and competencies that professional nurses must have in order to be hired as school nurses. Several states require school nurses to be certified as teachers and stipulate specific course work and competencies required for eligibility (e.g., California, Illinois, Massachusetts, Ohio, and Washington). Those requirements are usually set forth in the educational section of a state's laws and are administered or enforced through state and local school boards rather than a nursing organization or state health agency.

Where teacher certification is not required for employment as a school nurse, other guidelines may be available to help districts determine the level of preparation and qualifications appropriate for nursing personnel functioning independently in schools. For example, professional nursing organizations support national nursing certification to enable nurses to demonstrate, through examination, competency and expertise in specialty areas of nursing practice. According to Guido (1997, p. 209), "certification indicates a level of competence above minimum criteria for licensure and verifies that an individual has met certain standards of preparation and performance." For the specialty practice of school nursing, the certifying body is the National Board for Certification of School Nurses, Inc. (NBCSN), which is affiliated with the National Association of School Nurses. The American Nurses Credentialing Center (ANCC), which is affiliated with the American Nurses Association, also provided certification for school nurses but withdrew from this activity as of 2000.

Other than certification examinations, there are no nationally established knowledge, content, and skill competencies that all school nurses must be able to demonstrate for safe or optimal practice. Several states have established standards through teacher certification requirements, other state laws, or state agency guidelines; in some states, state school nursing organizations have developed recommended competencies for practice within that state (e.g., Minnesota, Kansas). Consequently, there are considerable variations across states and, in states where teacher certification is not required, across districts. Districts interested in hiring qualified school nurses and establishing appropriate role descriptions should reference the following sources:

- state law and regulations, if applicable;

- the standards of practice published by the National Association of School Nurses (1998) and American Nurses Association (1998b);

- the minimum requirements set by the above organizations for eligibility to sit for their respective certification exams;

- state guidelines; and

- faculty expertise regarding content provided in and professional competencies expected from successful completion of undergraduate and graduate university nursing preparation programs.

Professional publications may be useful for reference. For example, the ANA published *Nursing's Social Policy Statement* (1995), which explains nursing's knowledge base and scope of practice at the basic and advanced levels of practice. It also addresses professional regulation of nursing practice.

In states that do not legislate school nurse qualifications, school districts should take special care to obtain consultation from appropriate nursing educators and expert clinicians when determining essential qualifications for nursing personnel and staffing patterns. Claiming ignorance of nursing licensure requirements, scope of practice issues, levels of educational preparation, professional standards, or the health needs of their student population is unlikely today to be an adequate defense against a negligence action against the district and district's nursing personnel. Furthermore, because licensure laws and regulations generally set minimal requirements for entry into practice and lag well behind practice standards, districts should seek qualifications beyond those mandated by law. The latter recommendation is critical in states that do not mandate qualifications of school nurses beyond basic licensure to practice nursing.

(For additional information and recommendations regarding school nurse qualifications, see also the following chapters: chapter 1, which addresses the academic preparation of school nurses in relation to the specialty nature of school nursing; chapter 4, which discusses educational requirements for entry into nursing practice; and chapter 17, which explores the implications of different levels of nursing preparation in relation to independent practice in community settings, such as schools, contemporary needs of students, schools and communities, and school district liability.)

Continuing Education

States vary in their expectations for nurses' continuing education. Considering the vast, ongoing expansion of scientific knowledge and medical technology, school nurses should regularly pursue professional education. Continuing education—a professional performance expectation in all clinical settings—facilitates practitioner growth and ability to stay current in clinical knowledge and skills. This expectation is affirmed for school nurses by the National Association of School Nurses' Position Statement on "Continuing Education" (1997):

> It is the position of the NASN that the professional school nurse should participate in continuing education to expand and update knowledge and practice to meet the increasing demands and expectations of the school and health community.

(Chapter 17 presents continuing education options for school nurses that are based in universities and community colleges.)

A standard of nursing practice in any setting is that nurses cannot accept assignments that are beyond their skill level because to do so may put patients at risk of receiving poor or inadequate care The fact that a nurse has not performed a particular medical treatment or nursing intervention for many years, or has never done so in a school setting, is not by itself a reason to refuse a student access to the nursing intervention or to school. Rather, the school nurse needs to inform the district of the continuing education and clinical experiences that she needs in order to update her competencies and of how these experiences can be obtained. Sheehan (1999, p. 72) warns nurses that, although they put both their license and patients in jeopardy when they take on a responsibility for which they are not adequately prepared, simply refusing an assignment can leave the nurse "open to charges of abandonment." In addition to requesting continuing education, Sheehan recommends asking for supervision and, if the request goes unanswered, "going up the chain of command and documenting the request in a memo."

On the other hand, if the responsibility is beyond the scope of practice of the nurse (e.g., *dispensing* of medication), continuing education alone will not suffice to permit the nurse to carry out that function. State medical and pharmacy practice acts prohibit the dispensing of medication by individuals other than those licensed as physicians, pharmacists, and, in many states, advanced practice registered nurses and physician assistants. Licensure, subsequent to required education, and satisfaction of licensure requirements, is legally necessary for practice. (See chapter 4 for further explanation of licensure issues.)

Lack of awareness and lack of district funding for continuing nursing education do not excuse incompetent, unsafe performance. It is the nurse's responsibility as a licensed health professional, not the employer's obligation, to seek out learning opportunities and to stay up-to-date. On the other hand, prudent employers should facilitate ongoing education to promote competency of their nursing staff and avoid potential harm to clients. This is especially true if a district directs a nurse to obtain knowledge or skills not previously required in the position or if a district hires a nurse who does not have the requisite competencies of a school nurse in the first place. District responsibility to provide a certain amount of support for continuing education of personnel may also be the subject of union or other employer-employee contracts. Resources for continued learning include targeted programs developed collaboratively with community organizations (e.g., universities, teaching hospitals, and public health nursing

agencies), professional journals and texts, formal academic programs, in-service training, study and discussion groups, independent learner activities, such as mentoring experiences, and participation in national, state, and local professional organizations.

Case Loads and Staffing

Concern frequently arises regarding district expectations of school nurses and student safety issues in relation to the number of students and school buildings in a school nurse's assigned case load. As discussed in chapter 1, in 1972 the National Association of School Nurses published recommended guidelines for school nurse-to-student ratios. These guidelines recommend 1 school nurse to 750 regular education students, 1 to 250 students with disabilities, and 1 to 75 students with severe and profound disabilities; these recommendations also reflect the wide variations in staffing that existed across the country at the time of their publication. These guidelines, however, do not take into account the many factors that operate in schools today—in particular, the "inclusion" of most students with disabilities into regular classrooms and neighborhood schools, including those with complex behavioral, psychiatric, and medical needs; the increasing racial and ethnic diversity, as well as income disparity among children (Federal Interagency Forum on Child and Family Statistics, 1999); problems in accessing medical care; and increased numbers of students requiring medication administration and related supervision in school settings (Davis, Fryer, White, & Igoe, 1995). NASN is aware that its recommendations regarding case loads were made before these and other societal changes impacted schools; therefore, school nurses and administrators should be cautious about using them as sole criteria for staffing decisions. Some states have much better staffing ratios than the NASN recommendations; others are not yet close to approaching them. According to Davis, Fryer, White, & Igoe (1995), staffing for school health services is generally improving across the country.

Individual states, for example, Pennsylvania, have mandated the maximum numbers of students that school nurses can have in their caseloads (1:1500). Other states, such as Connecticut (Krin, 1997) and New Hampshire (Harvey, 1997), have not mandated the school nurse-to-student ratio but maintain average ratios of 1:500. School nurse-to-student ratios may also vary depending on the qualifications mandated for school nurses.

In 1995, the State of Washington, Office of the Superintendent of Instruction (OSPI) published recommended staffing guidelines for school health services based on supervisory ratios, as well as certified school nurse-to-student ratios (Maire, 1995). No specific mandate existed. These guidelines recommended minimum school nurse staffing standards in Washington, including one model for individual school districts (see Figure 5-1) and another model for professionals hired by regional Educational Service Districts (see Figure 5-2).

The development of these guidelines required critical collaboration between the state's board of nursing (now titled "Nursing Care Quality Assurance Commission") and the state's education agency (OSPI), with the input of local school district administrators and the School Nurse Organization of Washington (SNOW). This collaboration was facilitated by the state school nurse consultant whose position is supported equally by Washington's state education and health agencies. Accordingly, the collaborators addressed and incorpo-

rated the following standards and issues:
- school nurse certification requirements under state education statutes and regulation;
- licensure, delegation, and supervisory responsibilities of registered nurses in relation to licensed practical nurses, certified or registered nursing assistants, and unlicensed assistants) under Washington state statute and regulations related to nursing care;
- NASN staffing ratio guidelines; and
- poor school nurse-to-student staffing ratios and limited district resources at the time of publication.

Despite the 1995 guidelines, however, staffing and service levels for nursing care in Washington's public schools continued to be determined by local districts, staffing remained uneven across the state, and the health care needs of students continued to increase. In

Figure 5-1. Recommended Health Care Staffing: District Models I & II

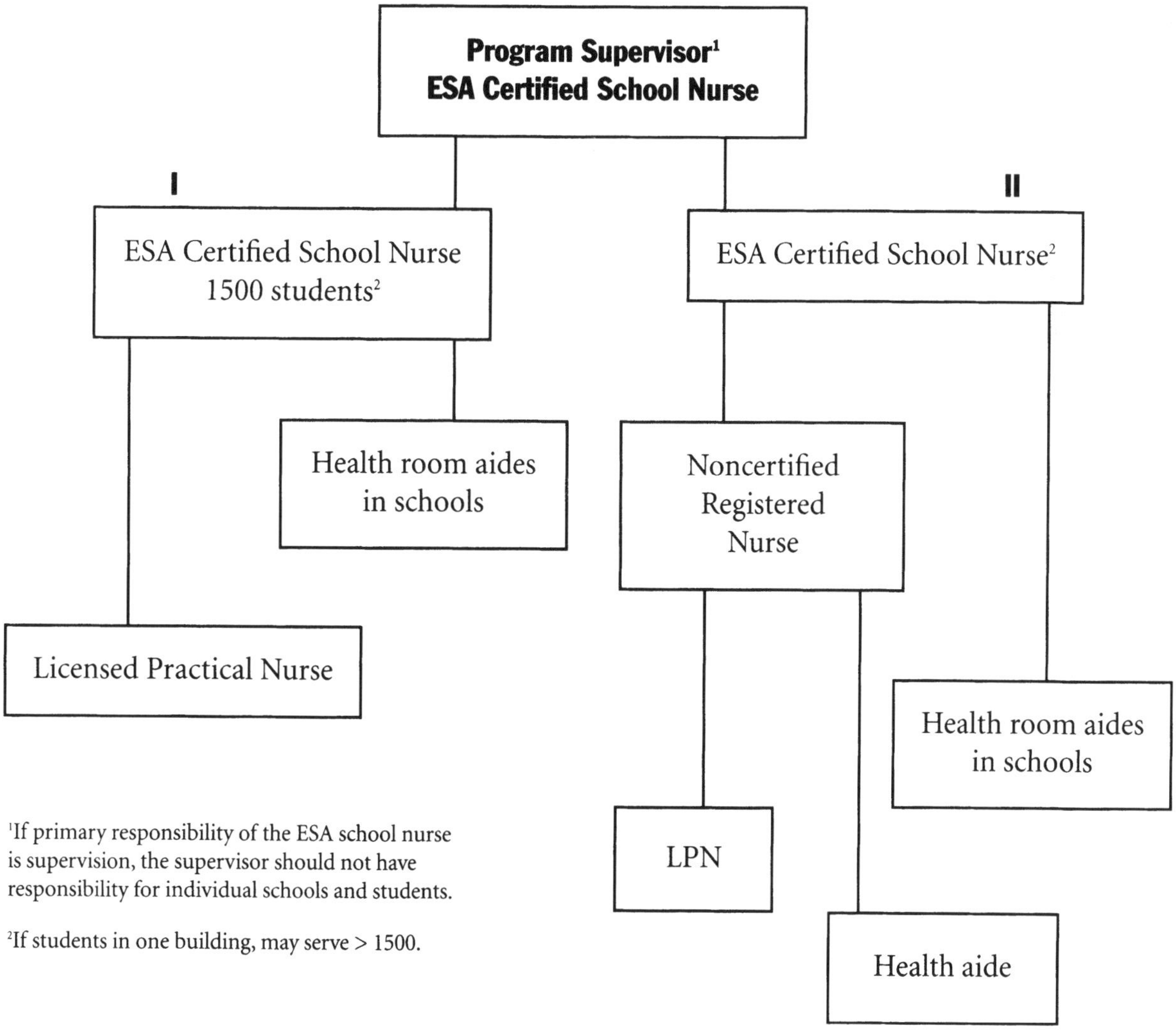

¹If primary responsibility of the ESA school nurse is supervision, the supervisor should not have responsibility for individual schools and students.

²If students in one building, may serve > 1500.

Used with permission: Maire, J. (1995). *Recommended Staffing for School Health Services.* Olympia, WA: Superintendent of Public Instruction.

Figure 5-2. Recommended Health Care Staffing: Educational Service District Models I & II

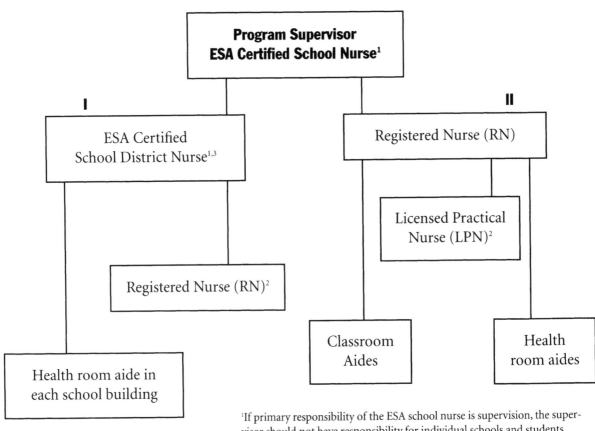

[1]If primary responsibility of the ESA school nurse is supervision, the supervisor should not have responsibility for individual schools and students.

[2]Provides care to those students requiring health care by licensed individuals.

[3]Additional detail on Diagram 1.

Used with permission: Maire, J. (1995). *Recommended Staffing for School Health Services.* Olympia, WA: Superintendent of Public Instruction.

1997, the State of Washington Joint Legislative Audit and Review Committee, in collaboration with the state's school nurse consultant and SNOW, conducted a survey of school districts to "provide the legislature with information on the number of school nurses and other health workers in the K–12 system, the nature and frequency of services provided and to identify current student health conditions." Based on this report (Washington State Joint Legislative Audit and Review Committee, 1997), OSPI submitted within its budget proposal in January 1999 an initiative for "Comprehensive Health Services" (Office of Washington State Superintendent of Public Instruction, 1999) and in June the state legislature appropriated $5.2 million to fund 9 regional nursing consultants and 37 school nurses.

The regional consultants, in addition to providing consultation and supervisory services in their regions, collaborated with the state school nurse consultant to assign these state-funded nurses to schools with the highest student health care needs and least school nursing coverage. Of interest, the proposal stated that the alternative of requiring a ratio of one professional nurse to every 750 students "would be expensive and inefficient since it would not target resources to those districts and buildings with students enrolled that need nursing care" (Office of the Superintendent of Public Instruction, 1999, p.4). The legislative proposal further stated:

OSPI staff will . . . identify or develop the reporting system used to collect data on student health, to supervise the pilot software program, and to institute the system statewide. The data gathered will form a basis for appropriate staff assignments and for the monitoring of health care needs of students. Additionally, a statewide health database will give nurse supervisors and OSPI the tools needed to identify the greatest need for nursing staff. It will establish the level of care required by students and provide the basis to efficiently assign appropriately trained or licensed staff.

In order to determine which schools have the highest need, the Washington State Nursing Care Quality Assurance Commission and OSPI convened a committee of school nurse managers (supervisors) to develop a model for determining the level of nursing care required by students in a school building and for the district, based on the severity of their diseases and conditions, and for assigning nursing and paraprofessional resources accordingly. This model is intended to supersede the 1995 model. See Figure 5-3 for definitions of each level of severity of student health condition and the level of nursing care required, as described in the model. Although not included in the Figure, it is important to note that the model includes consideration of additional factors that may increase students' health care risks, such as co-morbidity, English as a second language, homelessness, poverty, and others (Washington State Nursing Care Quality Assurance Commission and Washington State Office of the Superintendent of Public Instruction, 1999).

Although the Healthy People 2010 objectives for the nation (U.S. Department of Health and Human Services, 2000) include increasing the number of schools having a ratio of one nurse to every 750 children, staffing ratios alone, as implied by the Washington draft model, are not necessarily sufficient as the sole criterion in determining safe and appropriate staffing for individual schools, especially since the student mix and school climate can change significantly from one year to the next. A *School Health Intensity Rating Scale*, based on a well-established community health nursing model (Community Health Intensity Rating Scale), may become an important tool in addressing staffing for nursing services and related resource allocation in school districts and individual buildings (Burt, Beetem, Iverson, Hertel, & Peters, 1996). Developed, piloted, and studied for inter-rater reliability in the Midwest, this promising tool requires further studies for application beyond elementary schools and in other geographical areas before it is refined and validated for use with students of all ages across the country (Klahn, Hays, & Iverson, 1998). It is intended to assist districts in determining appropriate nursing coverage for individual school buildings and modifying that coverage as student populations change each year. It may be that data regarding the intensity of services

required to meet the health needs of each student within a building, compiled in aggregate for each school's student population, better describes what school nurses can safely manage for caseloads and what districts need to provide for staffing. A current limitation of the tool results from its lack of attention to school nurse responsibilities that are not student specific, such as mass screenings, participation on crisis intervention teams, and contributions to the development and implementation of health education curricula (G. E. Fryer, Health Sciences, University of Colorado, personal communication, February 24, 1999).

Since each student is unique, assessment for service intensity will remain a challenge. Other factors that warrant consideration in determining safe staffing patterns include school climate, staffing patterns of teachers and other pupil services specialists, school and community environmental and socioeconomic factors, and student access to primary health care. Student use of the school health room (i.e., traffic to the nurse's office) may be a factor, but is not necessarily a reliable source of information since students' use of services may simply reflect the services currently available to them—specifically, the level of provider and that provider's competencies. If the current quality of services is poor or the level of provider is inadequate to meet student needs (e.g., no nurse is available and first aid is provided by an unlicensed person), students may be able to access first aid, but not professional nursing services such as respiratory or mental status assessment, counseling to promote healthy behaviors, and health teaching to enhance self-care capabilities. Since students will not use the health room for professional services if they are not available, data documenting student visits will not be a reliable indicator of the need for those services.

Caseload requirements frequently require school nurses to prioritize student needs and nursing interventions according to those issues impacting student safety and learning at school. Health services resources available to the district must also be considered in determining appropriate nursing roles and assignments. From a risk management perspective, the following considerations are important in addressing concerns related to unsafe staffing conditions:

- When the current staffing pattern appears unsafe for students, school nurses should always report the identified problem to and ask for assistance from their supervisor. Notification of unsafe staffing conditions should be made in writing.

Figure 5-3. Required Nursing Services by Level of Student Health Condition

Level	Definition	Requirements
A: Nursing Dependent	These students require 24 hours/day, frequently one-to-one, skilled nursing care for survival . . . most are dependent on technological devices . . . and, without effective use of this technology, the student will experience irreversible damage or death.	• Assessment by professional registered nurse (RN) prior to entry. • Immediate availability of the nurse (RN or LPN)—on the premises and within audible and visual range of the student . . . and the student has been assessed by the RN prior to delegation of duties to any caregiver.
B: Medically Fragile	These students face daily the possibility of a life-threatening emergency requiring the skill and judgement of a professional nurse.	• A completed and current Individual Health Plan developed by a professional RN. • Full time nurse in the building — on the premises, quickly and easily available and the student has been assessed by the RN prior to delegation of duties to any care giver. • Professional RN determines who will be trained to provide care during transportation.
C: Medically Complex	These students have a complex and/or unstable physical and/or social-emotional condition that requires daily treatments and close monitoring by a professional RN. Life threatening events are unpredictable.	• Professional RN in the building a full day a week and available on a daily basis; the RN may not be on the premises but has previously given written instructions for the care and treatment of the student and the student has been assessed by the professional RN before delegation of duties to any care giver. • If any alteration of the written plan is required, it must be made by the professional nurse.
D: Health Concerns	These students have physical and/or social-emotional conditions that are currently uncomplicated and predictable. Occasional monitoring is required, from biweekly to annually (e.g., migraines, orthopedic conditions requiring accommodations).	• Assessment by the professional RN at least once a school year. • Reassessment occurs as the condition requires and the nurse's judgment determines.

Excerpted with permission from: Nursing Care Quality Assurance Commission and Office of the Superintendent of Public Instruction. (1999). *Staff Model for the Delivery of School Health Services.* Olympia, WA: Authors.

- When, over time, efforts to improve unsafe conditions are not successful, the school nurse must determine if continued employment in the school district is consistent with ethical and legal standards of nursing practice.

Despite a staffing shortage, school nurses must be careful not to devise restrictions that limit services to students for arbitrary reasons—for example, because a student's injury or complaint originated off school property (e.g., a twisted ankle that occurred over the weekend or illness that started at home the night before). Turning a student away from the health room before assessing the complaint and determining the level of care or referral required could be viewed as client abandonment.

As a method of notifying school administrators of staffing and related safety issues, the Federation of Nurses/United Federation of Teachers (UFT) has developed several forms for use by school nurses working for the New York City Board of Education. The first is an "Additional Staffing Request," asking for supervisory evaluation of the need for another nurse at the school and increased coverage until the evaluation is complete. The second form, "Unsafe Staffing Notification," is used when the evaluation results in denial of additional staff and the school nurse still believes that "the health and safety of the students is being compromised." When this system of notifying administrators of unsafe staffing conditions in writing has been used, it has been effective (B. J. Darby, UFT, personal communication, August 24, 1999). A third form notifies supervisors that the health records of one or more students currently attending school in a given building have not been received by the school nurse. These forms are published by the American Federation of Teachers (1997, pp. 89–91). (See also the section "Accountability for Health Assistants (UAP)" later in this chapter.)

Job Descriptions

There is no universal job description for the role of a school nurse. School districts' role descriptions for school nurses and expectations of their job responsibilities and performance differ across communities, regions, and states. These variations depend on multiple factors such as socioeconomic, demographic, and political variables. Job descriptions that are current and reflect the actual, specific role and responsibilities of the school nurse best ensure mutual understanding between the nurse and the district. Job descriptions serve as the most important local stan-

dard of care against which a school nurse's performance will be measured in a civil action to determine if the nurse met the standard of a reasonable, prudent school nurse.

Job descriptions provide objective data for comparisons of knowledge, skills, education, experience, and certification required for job performance (DeCenzo, 1994). The NASN document *Guidelines for School Nursing Documentation: Standards, Issues and Models* addresses the issue of differences in school nurse responsibilities, depending on their caseload and assignments, in relation to standards and systems of documentation (Schwab, Panettieri, & Bergren, 1998, p. 2). Similarly, the job description for school nurses assigned full time to buildings with 350 to 550 students, for example, will detail responsibilities for direct student care, membership on special education, crisis intervention, § 504, and staff wellness teams, leadership of a school health advisory council, and other building-level responsibilities. In contrast, the job description for school nurses covering 1,500 to 5,000 students in several different buildings across significant distances must necessarily describe less responsibility for direct care and building level services and significantly more responsibility for services as a consultant to the district. Examples of those types of responsibilities include the following:

- providing consultation to district-wide administrators;
- ensuring district compliance with state mandates;
- delegation to and training and supervision of assistive personnel, when appropriate (e.g., for administering first aid and carrying out screening programs);
- identifying, prioritizing, and assisting the administrators in addressing the most critical health and safety issues in the district; and
- making recommendations to improve the quality of the School Health Services program, including budgetary recommendations for staffing and other essential resources.

School nurses who function primarily as consultants should have job descriptions that support the consultant role; school nurses who function primarily as direct service providers should have job descriptions that support the clinician role.

When applicable, job descriptions should clearly articulate the supervisory role of school nurses in directing and evaluating the performance of assistive personnel. Job descriptions are also essential for any assistive personnel (both aides and LPNs) for whom the school nurse is directly accountable, including any volunteers assisting the nurse (e.g., nurses, parents, and physicians). Job descriptions should be regularly reviewed to assure accuracy in the specified job expectations and employee qualifications.

Conflicts Between Job Descriptions and Licensure Requirements

From a risk management point of view, it is inadvisable for licensed nurses to work in positions with job descriptions that do not require and support their licensed responsibilities to clients. For example, the licensed nurse may be in some legal jeopardy when he or she takes a position as a health aide in a school district. In an emergency (e.g., status epilepticus, respiratory distress, or anaphylaxis) where the student comes to harm and the family sues, the nurse has two disparate standards of care by which her performance may be measured. The first standard is that of the RN license, which would require her to call 9-1-1 *and* intervene at the level of a professional RN, with immediate nursing assessment, medication administration, oxygen administration, CPR, and other appropriate measures. The second standard is that of her job description. As a health aide, her job description would support calling 9-1-1 and, if trained, administering CPR, but would not support administration of PRN medication and oxygen, at least not without RN delegation as permitted by the state's nurse practice act. Regardless of the nurse's actions, as she meets one applicable standard, she violates the other.

This same problem exists when RNs take paid positions as LPNs, since RNs are expected by their license to function at the professional level of practice, not the assistive, technical level. Good Samaritan provisions (see chapter 6) are unlikely to apply, since the nurse would be acting in the capacity of a salaried position and, in a legal action, there would be no question of whether a duty was owed the student. The question would be what level of care was owed, professional or nonprofessional. School nurses are advised to consult with the board of nursing in their state regarding this issue. If a ruling does not exist, putting the question in writing to the board may be useful. For example, responding to the query of a "School Health Advisor" in the Massachusetts Department of Health, the Nursing Practice Coordinator of the Massachusetts Board of Registration in Nursing (Bette Lindberg, letter to Constance Brown, April 1, 1993) wrote that

It is the Board's determination that licensed nurses who are employed in non-nursing positions may not perform the activities of a licensed nurse in that position. The nurse employed as a health aide is restricted to the activities described in the job description of the health aide.

Nurses who are no longer licensed have no such conflict. Also, it may be feasible for a district to develop a job description that accommodates a combined role, for example an "LPN/teacher aide." This job title allows a role description for a one-to-one paraprofessional, serving a student who requires continual, individualized nursing *and* educational services in the classroom. If the role description details and supports both the LPN's licensed scope of practice, including assistive responsibilities to (and direction from) the school nurse/RN, *and* assistive responsibilities to the classroom teacher, the LPN will not be in a legal bind if faced with a medical emergency or a civil action against her. Although this may require the district to pay the LPN/aide a higher salary, the increased amount is negligible compared to the potential cost of liability in a civil suit.

Of significance, the 1997 amendments to the Individuals with Disabilities Education Act (IDEA) include a section recognizing the possibility of state standards for paraprofessionals employed to assist in providing special education and related services. In establishing state standards for paraprofessionals, states have an opportunity to explore and, perhaps, resolve these types of conflicts.

Performance Appraisals

Evaluation of performance is a professional responsibility intended to enhance one's professional growth and competencies. Since only nurses can accurately evaluate the clinical, technical, and judgment aspects of nursing practice, it is important to have nurse supervisors evaluate those aspects of a school nurse's performance. In California, the Board of Registered Nursing has ruled that non-medical personnel cannot evaluate nurses. Otherwise, non-nurse evaluators determining the appropriateness of a nurse's clinical decisions and actions might be considered practicing nursing without a license (Bourne, 1997). Very small districts can facilitate appropriate nursing supervision and evaluation by contracting with a school nurse supervisor from a neighboring locality or joining other small districts jointly to contract with one clinical supervisor (Connecticut State Department of Education, 1993).

School administrators can certainly judge non-clinical aspects of a school nurse's performance, such as interpersonal and communication skills, team functioning, organization, and self-direction. NASN's *Job Performance Evaluation Guidelines for School Nurses* (Ackerman, 1995) is a good reference source when establishing evaluation criteria.

Licensed and unlicensed assistive personnel (e.g., LPNs and health aides) require supervision, not just for delegation purposes, but also for performance evaluation, and are entitled to periodic feedback about their performance. School nurses should know and follow their district's evaluation policy and practices and participate in review and revision of the policy and practices. Performance evaluation, like delegation responsibilities, requires on-site supervision (at least some of the time), including direct observation of performance and skills, thorough record review, and discussion of student care and assigned responsibilities.

Unsafe Practice by Others

Regardless of whether a school nurse is a supervisor or a provider of direct health services, all nurses are responsible for functioning according to the state's nursing practice act and rulings of the board of nursing. These mandates stipulate the scope of practice of nursing and conditions of unprofessional conduct that must be reported to the board of nursing. Many nurse practice acts have whistle-blowing provisions that both require nurses to report unsafe case practices and protect them when they do. Nurses can jeopardize their own licenses by failing to report violations of the nurse practice act by others, including unlicensed individuals who are practicing nursing without a license.

Likewise, professional nurses who have concerns about the competence of or substandard care provided by another health care provider (e.g., another nurse, emergency response staff, or a physician), must speak up on behalf of the client's (student's) safety. For example, if a school nurse observes that an ambulance attendant fails to describe clearly to a parent the potential risks to the student for whom the parent is refusing ambulance transport, the school nurse should report the observation to an appropriate authority (e.g., the ambulance company or, for an egregious error, the state agency that certifies the attendant, usually the state department of health). If a school nurse, other school employee, or parent believes that a nurse is using alcohol or drugs while working or otherwise exhibits repeated impaired functioning that places students at risk of receiving inadequate care, the nurse or other individual should report this information to the state's board of nursing, as well as to the school principal or school district superintendent.

Accountability for Health Assistants (UAP)

A systematic random sample of 482 school districts within 45 states completed by the University of Colorado (Fryer & Igoe, 1996) identified 148 districts that employed school health assistants (also referred to in nursing literature as "unlicensed assistive personnel" or "UAP"). Unless otherwise defined, the terms "health assistant" and "nursing assistant" may also include licensed assistants, i.e., practical (vocational) nurses (LPN or LVN). Since this section of the chapter is specifically targeted to unlicensed assistants, the term "UAP" will be used instead. It is important to keep in mind, however, that under most state nurse practice acts, registered nurses are responsible for directing, delegating to, and supervising UAPs *and* LPNs; therefore, many of the principles discussed below apply to school nurse responsibilities for LPNs as well as UAP.

Unlicensed assistive personnel (UAP) assist the school nurse in managing the health office, performing clerical functions, and carrying out simple, delegated nursing activities on behalf of students. State nurse practice acts and regulations or delegation procedures require school nurses to ensure that UAP are appropriately trained and receive sufficient and ongoing supervision. The definition of what constitutes "appropriate training" may be found in state statutes (e.g., certification requirements similar to those for credentialed "certified nursing assistants") or guidelines, or left entirely to the discretion of local school districts. Minimum requirements usually include a high school diploma, current certification in CPR and first aid, and on-the-job training in such things as infection control, universal precautions, confidentiality, and body mechanics for injury prevention. In some states, such as Minnesota, preparation of school health assistants occurs in community colleges; and a standard curriculum is used and usually taught by qualified school nurses (Minnesota Department of Health and Hutchinson-Willmer Regional Technical College & St. Cloud Technical College, 1995). The University of Colorado, Office of School Health, with funding from the U.S. Department of Education, developed a national model for teaching school nurses how to train, delegate to, and supervise UAP who plan to or already work in school health programs (Uris, 1996); Minnesota's curriculum for the UAP-training component was adapted for use in the Project Assist model.

Necessary training and continuing education for UAP must include and emphasize the limitations of their role and responsibilities. Training and written protocols should include direction for specific events and circumstances that must be reported to the school nurse. In addition, to safeguard students and avoid putting the UAP at risk of practicing nursing or medicine without a license, written policies, procedures, and job descriptions should specify the limitations of the UAP's job activities. Assistive personnel name badges should specify the assistant's job title (e.g. "nurse assistant" or "health aide,"), and telephone, written, and electronic communications between UAP and others—parents, students, and school personnel—should clearly identify the UAP and the limitations of his or her responsibilities. School nurses should always document direction given to UAP regarding student care and provide them with *written* directions. (See, for example, Appendix I: Mitts Declaratory Ruling.) Written protocols and directions provided to UAP must be specific and ensure that they are not required to make a clinical assessment or nursing judgment. For example, caregivers should never be asked to determine whether a child is having an "asthmatic reaction." Rather, caregivers must be given information regarding specific symptoms to observe for, what those symptoms will look like in a particular student, and directions to follow when the symptoms are observed. This specificity to the *functional* health needs of individual students supports the use of nursing diagnoses rather than medical diagnoses in communicating with other school personnel (Schwab, Panettieri, & Bergren, 1998; Hootman, 1996b). Directions to the caregiver should also stress the importance of immediate contact with the school nurse or emergency services when the student's symptoms are unusual.

School nurses have a responsibility to monitor students for expected outcomes of care provided by UAP, such as blood pressure or height and weight measurements. The professional nurse must "ensure that the tasks delegated to UAP are within the nurse's scope of practice and that tasks requiring licensure (nursing judgment or skill) are not delegated to UAP. Once a task is delegated, the nurse must ensure that the action was performed and performed correctly" (Guido, 1997, p. 286).

Supervision of UAP

The school nurse should be immediately accessible, if not directly on-site, to provide necessary direction to unlicensed assistive personnel (UAP). If hired as part-time employees, school nurses cannot be responsible for delegating to, or supervising, full-time UAP. When school nurses delegate responsibilities to UAP, they must be available to provide direction, supervision, and immediate intervention in a situation, as needed, whenever the UAP are functioning in a UAP or nursing assistant role. If UAP provide nursing services as delegated by the nurse without the immediate availability of the registered nurse in the district, they may be practicing nursing or medicine without a license. When a supervising or delegating school nurse is absent from the district, substitute school nurse coverage must be provided to ensure appropriate direction and supervision of UAP.

State law, regulations, standards, and rules set by the state board of nursing may determine whether off-site supervision of UAP is an option in school settings within a particular state. If it is an option, the school nurse, based on nursing assessment of the health status of the student population (or an individual student, depending on the situation), and related factors such as the school/classroom environment, must determine when off-site supervision is safe, and how frequently on-site supervision is indicated. (See chapter 4 for additional discussion of nursing licensure and delegation, and related cases.)

There is little data to identify safe ratios of nurse-to-UAP or nurse-to-students when school nurses supervise unlicensed assistants in school settings. From a legal point of view, the nurse must make the decision about the use of assistants on a case-by-case basis because each student's health needs are unique and student populations vary from building to building and year to year. Depending on the needs of the student population, the school nurse must determine whether it is safe to delegate nursing activities to UAP. Furthermore, staffing ratios of school nurses to assistants and the amount of on-site supervision required in each situation are not constants. School nurses must make recommendations for change when the health service needs of an individual student or the student population as a whole warrant it, and they need the support and collaboration of school administrators in addressing these ever-changing student health needs.

School boards and school administrators may not be able to respond immediately to staffing recommendations, but they should be kept informed about the changing health needs of their student population and work with school health professionals to ensure safe educational programs for all students. When school health professionals and administrators or school boards cannot agree, or when districts are unsure that staffing recommendations made by their personnel are correct, districts may be wise to obtain a second opinion from an outside expert. Such experts include school nurse supervisors or school nurse consultants with recognized clinical and administrative expertise.

Student safety is the primary concern for determining whether or how unlicensed assistants can be used to enhance health services. Fryer & Igoe (1996) report that litigation is more frequently filed in cases when care is provided by UAP than in cases when care is provided by school nurses or classroom personnel. Appropriate nurse-to-UAP ratios and on-site supervision are essential to ensuring the safe delivery of nursing services to students. (For further discussion of nurses' legal responsibilities in delegating health care responsibilities to UAP, see chapter 4.)

School nurses who are responsible for supervising other personnel, whether UAP, LPNs or other RNs, should understand their potential liability and legal protections as supervisors. For example, in *Nance v. Matthews* (1993) the school nurse, principal, and supervisor of special education were found to have immunity from liability in a suit concerning injuries to a student with spina bifida when a paraprofessional failed to catheterize the student. In this case, the trial court dismissed the suits against all but the aide, finding that the others were protected by "discretionary function immunity." In other words, supervisors have within their responsibilities *the discretion* (authority) to make certain decisions, including assignment of other personnel to certain tasks. If the nurse fulfills her responsibilities as a supervisor (e.g., makes an appropriate assignment or delegation, trains and supervises the UAP, and evaluates student outcomes and UAP performance on a periodic basis), the supervising nurse should not be liable for the unpredictable errors of the UAP. (See chapter 2, under "Defenses in Negligence Actions" for further information on sovereign immunity and discretionary function immunity.)

Accountability for LPNs (LVNs)

Although there are variations in specific requirements among states, licensed practical nurses (in several states referred to as "licensed vocational nurses") are trained to assist registered nurses (RNs) in the care of patients in acute and long-term health care facilities. Pre-service preparation of licensed practical nurses (LPNs) typically consists of a 12-month, post-high school program offered, for example, in a vocational-technical high school or community college. For licensure, LPNs must pass an examination and demonstrate successful completion of a program approved by the state board of nursing or other agency authorized to define LPN scope of practice and requirements for LPN preparation programs in the state.

School nurses and school administrators should clearly understand the scope of practice of LPNs and their legal relationship to RNs before LPNs are hired to work in a school setting. See Figure 5-4 for Krin's model of the clinical-legal relationship of LPNs to RNs. This model was approved by the Connecticut Board of Examiners for Nursing and is likely applicable in most other states. Depending on state laws, LPNs can carry out more nursing tasks than health assistants because of their technical training, but they are neither prepared nor licensed to function at the professional level of nursing. LPNs can contribute to each step of the nursing process, but cannot "*independently* assess the health status of any student or student's care environment, make nursing diagnoses or determine when delegation of care to UAP is appropriate" (Panettieri & Schwab, 1996).

Staffing decisions, therefore, must be based on careful scrutiny of the assistive services that are needed, the LPN scope of practice, the individual LPN's competencies, the school nurse's legal relationship to an LPN, and the amount of time that the school nurse (RN) will be required both on-site and off-site to provide necessary direction and supervision to the LPN. Depending on state licensure laws and other mandates, school nurses usually must determine that delegation or assignment of school nursing and health service activities to LPNs is appropriate in a situation before an LPN can take on such responsibilities. In Iowa, for example, LPNs may be prohibited from working in a school unless a school nurse is on-site at all times; or, as in Maryland, they may be prohibited from working in schools at all (Collins, 1996). (See chapter 4 for further discussion of school nurse [RN] delegation to LPNs.)

In a few states, education statutes and guidelines permit school principals to assign health care tasks to UAP and LPNs, probably based on the waning principle of "*in loco parentis*." With the increased acuity of health care needs of students in schools today, and federal civil rights and special education laws, it is unlikely that a "standard of health care" for students that is established by a school administrator (non-health professional) acting alone would be considered reasonable or acceptable. (See chapter 2 for further discussion of "*in loco parentis*" and chapter 4 for discussion of delegation of health care procedures by unlicensed school officials.)

Figure 5-4. Conceptual Framework for RN Delegation of Nursing Functions to the LPN in School Health Services

In the school setting, as in any setting, the LPN must perform his or her nursing functions and **shared nursing responsibilities under the direction of a registered nurse.** As stated in the 1989 Connecticut Board of Examiners for Nursing Declaratory Ruling, the LPN is properly allowed to participate in all phases of the nursing process. The extent of this participation is portrayed in the model below.

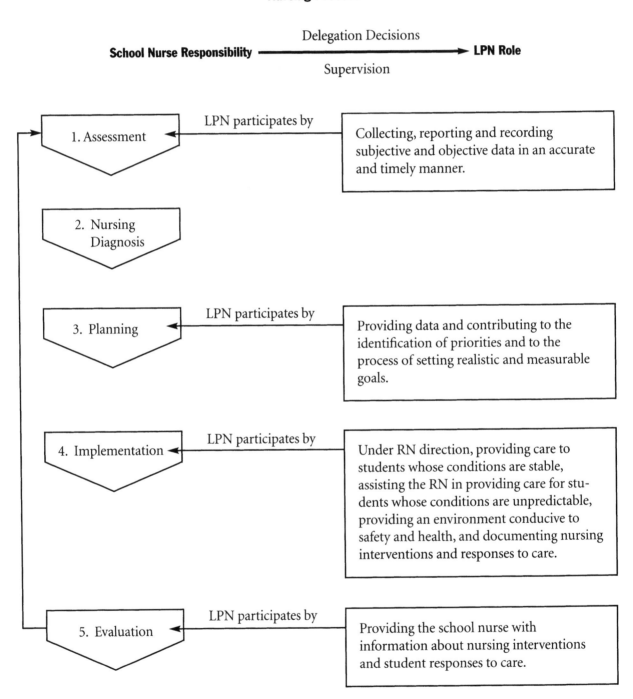

© Patricia Krin, RN, BSN, C.S.N., 1997

In terms of risk management, school nurses who are responsible for supervising LPNs must ensure that they have adequate time to direct and supervise them. Many of the risk management principles discussed in the section above on "Accountability for Health Assistants," including the use of written protocols, relate to school nurse relationships with LPNs as well as health assistants and, therefore, need not be repeated here. When school nurses make sound decisions about assignments and delegation to LPNs, ensure training (when indicated), provide supervision, including on-site supervision, are immediately available to provide direction (as required by state law and student-specific needs), and regularly evaluate student outcomes, they should not liable for errors of judgment made by LPNs whom they supervise.

Figures 5-5 and 5-6 provide sample written protocols for LPNs who work under the direction of a school nurse. These protocols are written specifically for LPN assistants and are not intended as protocols that would be appropriate for UAP. School nurses also have a responsibility to report unsafe and illegal practice of others, including LPNs, if they observe it. (Chapter 4 provides additional information on the legal aspects of school nurse-LPN relationships.)

Accountability for Non-Certified Registered Nurses (RNs)

In some states, only RNs who meet the additional education and experience qualifications stipulated by the state's department of education may work as school nurses. (See the section above, "Qualifications and Certification of School Nurses," regarding types of certification for school nurses.) For example, in June 1999, the New Jersey legislature passed P.L. (Public Law) 1999, C. 153, requiring public school nursing services to be provided by "certified school nurses." Certified school nurses are RNs who must meet additional qualifications specified by New Jersey Administrative Code 6:11-11.7 (i.e., a bachelor's degree with specified credits in both general education and the specialty area, such as school nursing, public health, foundations of education, and mental health). Accordingly, an RN who meets the specified academic requirements may obtain an educational services certificate with an endorsement as a "school nurse." Prior to this legislation, a "school nurse" had to be certified, but districts were only mandated to hire one school nurse.

Historically, most districts in New Jersey had hired certified school nurses for all of their schools, but recent changes in the health care system and tight school budgets resulted in a few local school district experiments with privatization of school nursing services. These districts contracted with local hospitals or other health agencies, newly in competition for community-based business, to take over their school health services programs. In so doing, the health agencies sometimes used non-certified nurses in the same capacity as certified school nurses—that is, the agencies assigned them as "school nurses" (Carol McGotty, personal communication, July 9, 1999).

The 1999 legislation stipulated that school districts may supplement the services of a certified school nurse provided that the non-certified nurse is assigned to the same building or complex as the school nurse. Thus, all nurses who are hired to work as school nurses in New Jersey public schools must now be certified by New Jersey's State Department of Education. It appears from the language of the Act that any other nurse must work as an assistant to, and under the immediate direction of, a certified school nurse. However, actual definitions and interpretations must be established and the State Board of Education must adopt administrative rules and regulations that will clarify the intent of the law (Marilyn Kent, personal communication, July 15, 1999, and April 6, 2000).

If this legislation intends to ensure that the certified school nurse has the responsibility for the outcomes of nursing care for all of the students in the building or complex, it also means that the school nurse may assign certain nursing responsibilities to a non-certified RN who is hired by the district or placed there under contract by an outside agency. In terms of liability in this situation, the school nurse is responsible for

- making appropriate assignments to the RN (as with other assistants);

- providing supervision appropriate to the situation; and

- evaluating student outcomes of care.

Given that the school nurse carries out those responsibilities in a manner consistent with that of other reasonable school nurses, the school nurse should not be responsible for errors in judgment made by a non-certified RN, who is independently licensed to practice nursing according to his or her own qualifications and experience.

Figure 5-5. Protocol for School Nurse Delegation to LPN Management of Abdominal Pain

PROTOCOL FOR SCHOOL NURSE DELEGATION TO LPN MANAGEMENT OF ABDOMINAL PAIN

Student Name: _____   **Date:** _____

Subjective:

Objective:

Temp _____		If >100, call RN
Abdominal injury?	❑ Yes ❑ No	If yes, call RN
Food allergies?	❑ Yes ❑ No	If yes, call RN
Location and type of pain		
Duration of pain		
Frequency of pain		
Intensity of pain (scale of 1-10) _____		
Relief with change of position?	❑ Yes ❑ No	
Does pain increase with movement?	❑ Yes ❑ No	
Pain with "heel jar"	❑ Yes ❑ No	If yes, call RN
When did the student last eat?		
What did the student last eat?		
Constipation?	❑ Yes ❑ No	
Diarrhea?	❑ Yes ❑ No	
Last BM?		
Frequency and/or burning on urination?	❑ Yes ❑ No	If yes, call RN
Nausea?	❑ Yes ❑ No	
Vomiting? X _____	❑ Yes ❑ No	If yes, call RN

Plan:

In absence of abdominal injury, fever, vomiting, or frequency and/or burning on urination have student rest for 10-20 minutes. If pain subsides and student feels better return to class. Instruct student to return to health office if pain increases or localizes, if vomiting occurs, or if the student feels worse in any way.

If abdominal injury, fever, vomiting or urinary tract symptoms, or student does not feel better within 10-20 minutes, call RN.

Other pertinent information:

RN called _____   **Time** _____   **Date** _____

Signed _____ **, LPN**

Used with permission: P. Krin, RN, C.S.N., 1998

Accountability for School Nurse Assistants: Volunteers, Students, and Student Nurses

Volunteers

Volunteers are sometimes recruited to function as assistants to school nurses in health services programs. District policy should specify, at a minimum, the procedures related to recruitment, safety, confidentiality, job qualifications, job descriptions and limitations, and necessary on-the-job training. Additionally, nursing protocols that stipulate to whom the volunteer should direct student health concerns are essential. A protocol should help the volunteer to decide whether to call 9-1-1, the nurse, the principal, or the parent and, if more than one is indicated, in what order. If volunteers are first-aid trained (a recommended minimum standard for an individual assigned to work in a health center), they can be expected to provide minor first aid under nursing protocols and supervision (including on-site supervision). (Refer to chapter 8 for further detail on confidentiality and volunteers.)

There are legitimate legal concerns regarding the use of volunteers to "cover" the school nurse's office. Both districts and potential volunteers should carefully analyze the risks and benefits and seek legal advice regarding the implications of volunteer status under education and health law. School nurses and administrators with supervisory responsibility for volunteers who assist in providing nursing services should also seek administrative and legal advice.

Questions to consider include these:

- How will the volunteer's competency in the performance of assigned tasks be assured?

- Will the volunteer's service time and capabilities be worth the nurse's time to (1) complete sufficient training, (2) provide the volunteer with on-site direction and consultation by telecommunications, and (3) conduct regular on-site performance monitoring of the volunteer? All of this must be done while the nurse continues to provide follow-up of students requiring nursing services and maintains up-to-date knowledge of changing student health needs in the building.

- Is the nurse available to step in whenever a situation requires nursing judgment?

- Does the district have responsibility for protective measures for the volunteers, for example, hepatitis immunization, compensation for injury occurring while volunteering, and liability insurance?

- Can the volunteer document on and have access to school records?

- Who will be responsible for medication administration and meeting other special health care needs of students with chronic conditions?

- What are the legal issues related to using volunteers to tend to ill and injured students (e.g., what training and supervision should volunteers receive)?

- If the volunteer is an RN, what is an appropriate role description to cover the RN's status as both volunteer and as a licensed health professional? If the volunteer RN is a parent?

- What is the state board of nursing's position on licensed nurses as volunteers?

- What liability insurance, if any, covers the RN volunteer in this situation?

- How does the district's insurance company view this situation?

- Can the school nurse delegate nursing tasks to volunteer nurses (RNs; LPNs)?

- If so, for what is the delegating school nurse accountable?

Guido (1997) shares some considerations for nurses and school districts regarding many of the above questions:

- The legal status of volunteers may not be well defined because donated services do not fall within the auspices of state nurse practice acts. Most nurse practice acts apply only to compensated services.

- The location of services does not exempt nurses from a possible lawsuit or from the standard of the reasonably prudent nurse. The state's nurse practice act still guides one's professional responsibilities.

- The nurse-patient relationship is initiated when care is first given. Once established, the same duty of care owed a hospital or paying patient is owed this [non-paying] patient (Lunsford v. Board of Nurse Examiners, 1983).

In any event, the standard of care for licensed nurses remains the same under most circumstances; the minimum standard of care owed by licensed nurses to their clients is unlikely to change due to their status as volunteers. Good Samaritan laws may provide some protection in emergency circumstances, but their provi-

Figure 5-6. Protocol for LPN Management of Head Injury in the School Setting (Front)

PROTOCOL FOR LPN MANAGEMENT OF HEAD INJURY IN THE SCHOOL SETTING

Student Name: _____   **Date:** _____

Subjective:

Objective:

			Initial	5 Min	10 Min	30 Min	Pupillary Size mm (approx)
1. **Best** Eye Opening	Spontaneous To voice To pain None Swollen shut	4 3 2 1 0					1. • 2. • 3. ●
2. **Best** Verbal Response	Oriented Confused Inappropriate words Incomprehensible sounds None	5 4 3 2 1					4. ● 5. ●
3. **Best** Motor Response	Obeys commands Localizes pain Withdraws to pain Flexes to pain Extends to pain None	6 5 4 3 2 1					6. ● 7. ●
Glascow Coma Scale **Total**							8. ● 9. ●

Pupils			Initial	5 Min	10 Min	30 Min	
Right		Size					
		Response					
Left		Size					
		Response					

Pupillary Response
C = Constricted	D = Dilated
E = Equal	F = Fixed
NR = Nonreactive	R = Reactive
S = Sluggish	U = Unequal

If GCS <15 at any time, call RN
Pupillary response other than equal and responsive to light and accommodation at any time, call RN.

Continue to collect data on other side:

Figure 5-6. Protocol for LPN Management of Head Injury in the School Setting (Back)

Data Collection continued:

> **Questions answered Yes in this box require immediate activation of Emergency Medical Services.**
>
> A person with significant head injury is always at high risk for a spinal injury. **Always take spinal precautions if a person is down with a head injury.**
>
> **Observe for:**
>
> | | | |
> |---|---|---|
> | Obstructed airway? | ❑ Yes ❑ No | *If yes have someone call 9-1-1 first, then call RN. Stay with student. Reposition head to remove obstruction while waiting, initiate CPR if indicated.* |
> | GCS < 9? | ❑ Yes ❑ No | *If yes at any time call 9-1-1 first, then RN* |
> | Pupils fixed and/or nonreactive? | ❑ Yes ❑ No | *If pupils are fixed and/or nonreactive at any time, call 9-1-1 first, then call RN* |

BP _____   P _____   R _____   Notify RN for parameters outside of NL for age of student.

If the answers to any questions below are yes, call RN

Dizziness?	❑ Yes ❑ No	
Altered or unusual behavior?	❑ Yes ❑ No	
Distorted memory of incident?	❑ Yes ❑ No	
Vision blurred?	❑ Yes ❑ No	
Eyes fail to move together?	❑ Yes ❑ No	
Fluid leakage/bleeding from eyes and ears?	❑ Yes ❑ No	
Very severe headache?	❑ Yes ❑ No	
Seizure?	❑ Yes ❑ No	
Mobility or strength of arms or legs altered or unequal?	❑ Yes ❑ No	
Vomited?	❑ Yes ❑ No	
Bleeding from injured area?	❑ Yes ❑ No	
Scratch or abrasion?	❑ Yes ❑ No	**Cleanse, apply dressing if indicated.**
Laceration?	❑ Yes ❑ No	**Apply pressure to control bleeding.**
Swelling?	❑ Yes ❑ No	**Apply ice.**

Plan:
In the absence of any of the above, observe student for 10 minutes and reevaluate. If condition remains unchanged, return to class, send head injury letter home with student. Direct student to report back if he/she doesn't feel well, has nausea, vomiting, blurred vision, increased pain, etc.

Other pertinent information:

RN called _____ **Time** _____ **Date** _____

Signed _____ **, LPN**

sions are generally limited to the "unexpected" emergency when the health professional is not working in a professional capacity, for example, stopping to assist at a roadside accident. Specific provisions related to schools may not cover the nurse volunteer.

Students as School Nurse Assistants

Caution is recommended when considering the use of students as assistants in the health center. For confidentiality, safety, and legal reasons, it is never appropriate to assign students to perform triage or assessment functions. Students certified in first aid can legally carry out first aid techniques, but should do so after initial assessment by the nurse to rule out other needs and confidentiality concerns. Important risk management strategies include clear role descriptions and role limitations through orientation, and direct on-site supervision by the school nurse. Furthermore, students who do assist school nurses in any first aid tasks must be properly informed, trained, immunized, and protected from risk of exposure to blood-borne pathogens, and a parent's informed consent is appropriate.

For confidentiality reasons, students who wish to "shadow" the school nurse as a means of career sampling are best assigned to settings other than their home school. This protects the privacy of peers in the home school and avoids conflicts and barriers that might be perceived by students seeking assistance from the school nurse.

University Student Nurses

Student nurses are not volunteers. Typically, as part of required academic coursework and clinical rotations, university students are seeking a real-world learning experience in providing nursing services to children and youth in community settings. Indeed, student nurses who are enrolled in bachelor and master degree programs in nursing may even be a source of supplemental nursing services for a district. While they do require an investment of school nurse time (i.e., for direction, consultation, and supervision), clinical experiences in school settings prepare professionals to be competent recruits for future school nurse positions. Just as schools assist in the preparation of teachers by participating in practice teaching programs, they should participate in the preparation of school nurses.

Arranging for student nurses to have clinical experiences in a school district includes the development of a contractual agreement between the district and the university or college. A contract clarifies the responsi-

bilities of both parties and is necessary to ensure the quality of nursing services provided to the district's students and the quality of clinical experience provided for the student nurse. For example, the agreement should require that the university permit only competent students to practice in the district, and that the school district maintain safe and adequately staffed clinical sites. The contract should also address malpractice insurance coverage (for the student and faculty member), immunization requirements for the student nurse, and issues regarding confidentiality of student information and records.

A student nurse should always be under the direct supervision of a clinical instructor from the university's faculty, and the relationship of the student nurse to the school nurse should be well delineated. Objectives for the student nurse's clinical experience should be compatible with the district's and school nurse's program goals and priorities. Generally, the school nurse or school nurse supervisor is responsible for protecting the district's interests by

- orienting the student nurse to district policies and procedures;

- helping to define appropriate assignments for the student nurse;

- consulting with the faculty preceptor and student nurse, as needed;

- providing appropriate oversight and follow-up of nursing services provided to district students;

- identifying concerns regarding student nurse or faculty actions, if any; and

- participating in evaluation of the student nurse's performance and the district's provision of an appropriate clinical experience for the student.

While nursing students retain accountability for their own actions (Guido, 1997), nursing faculty and school personnel may become responsible for student nurse incompetence or lack of adequate preparation if they neglect their responsibilities to inform, teach, and supervise the student nurse. Nursing students and faculty, like district staff, must follow district policy and procedures. Because mentoring a student nurse takes time, school nurses require administrative support for this activity.

Documentation

Documentation challenges many nurses, regardless of their clinical setting. This challenge reflects the underlying conflict between time available to provide direct care to clients (never enough) and time consumed by indirect services, especially writing. Studies consistently report that documentation takes 15–25% of a nurse's time (Burkle, Kuch, Passian, Prokosch, & Dudeck, 1995; Pierpont, & Thilgen, 1995). Practical concerns aside, documentation is an essential tool in risk management programs in medicine and nursing. A physician-attorney expert, in a discussion of ethical and legal duties of clinicians to diagnose and treat patients according to acceptable standards of practice (Bianco, 1998, p. 19), states that

clinicians who closely adhere to all ethical duties imposed by their professions will almost assuredly overcome any allegations of malpractice. This is especially true when pertinent medical records reflect, directly or indirectly, that standard procedures were used.

Addressing pediatricians regarding medical record practices, Karp (1996, p.18) states:

Documentation made at the time care was rendered is a defendant's most convincing evidence that care standards were met. Unclear, ambiguous and incomplete records are a leading reason medically defensible medical liability claims are filed and ultimately decided in the plaintiff's favor.

Although nursing standards of documentation do not change across practice settings, the content of the client's record may vary. It is appropriate to use time-saving mechanisms such as charting by exception (following predetermined protocols of care so that documentation consists mainly of content related to any exceptions made to the general protocol), flow records, and care plan templates to decrease time spent in documentation. It is not acceptable to compromise the quality or confidentiality of documentation in these time-saving efforts.

Documentation is critical to the development and maintenance of school health services programs. It is essential to the practice of professional nursing and a fundamental component of the nursing process (Schwab, Panettieri, & Bergren, 1998.) Among other things, documentation:

- validates that the nursing process was followed;

- provides a basis for evaluating the accuracy of identified nursing diagnoses, as well as the effectiveness of school health programs;

- demonstrates that the school nurse met the standard of care of a reasonable, prudent school nurse;

- facilitates communication with other nurses, school physicians, and community health care providers regarding care already provided to or planned for students; and

- provides necessary data for research and funding initiatives. (Hootman & Carpenito, 1997; Iyer & Camp, 1995; Kozier, Erb, Berman, & Burke, 2000)

In the Connecticut case discussed under "Standards of Practice" above, even if the school nurse had used the nursing process in her approach to caring for the student, there was no documentation of an appropriate nursing assessment. This left the school nurse open to the presumption by others, including an expert witness and potential jury, that a clinically competent nursing assessment had not been performed. The National Association of School Nurses (NASN) *Guidelines for School Nursing Documentation: Standards, Issues, and Models* (Schwab, Panettieri, & Bergren, 1998, p. 4) includes the following statements regarding documentation as legal evidence:

In legal actions against school nurses (as well as nurses in general), inadequate documentation of care is generally considered synonymous with inadequate or poor-quality care. According to Springhouse Corporation, 1996, documentation of care has become synonymous with care itself, and failure to document implies failure to provide care.

Hence the well-known adage, "if it wasn't documented, it wasn't done." Furthermore, failure to record essential information [in a medical record] can occasionally have catastrophic consequences (Bernzweig, 1996) and, in a malpractice suit, nursing documentation may actually determine the outcome of the case (Baldwin-Mech, 1987). Documentation, then, can be critical to the protection of school nurses, school districts and other employers against threats of malpractice claims.

The nursing record is evidence of the nursing assessments, treatments, and evaluations performed for a student and the nursing diagnoses, care plans, and student goals determined or developed on his or her behalf. The nursing record ensures that a break in nursing services will not occur because a student is transferred to another building within the district or a new nurse is assigned to the student's school. It also provides complete, historical information regarding a student's health status and needs in school and on transfer to a new district.

Documentation and Risk Management

Three examples from the experiences of school nurses further highlight the central importance of documentation to risk management strategies in school nursing practice. The first two examples demonstrate the potential importance of nursing documentation to school districts; the third example demonstrates its importance to the school nurse.

Situation One: South Carolina

In the first situation, a student on crutches in a South Carolina school, following major surgery on his leg from a hockey injury, slipped and fell on a wet floor at school. The leg was reinjured, requiring an "extensive procedure to reset his leg." When the mother confronted the school nurse, indicating her belief that the school was responsible, the school nurse reminded the parent that, when the student had returned to school, a meeting was held with the student and mother to discuss special needs and safety issues. The school nurse had strongly recommended the use of a wheel chair, rather than crutches, and had written the recommendation into the student's IHP. Both the recommendation itself and the written evidence that it was made averted potential litigation against the school district (Hatfield, 1997).

Situation Two: Connecticut

In the second situation, a Connecticut school district has been notified of a parent's intent to sue the school for damages in excess of $1 million for respiratory problems incurred by his daughter "because of fungus growth present in the building" (Szabo, 1998). According to the news report, air problems were caused by the growth of a fungus stemming from water leak problems in a part of the school that had been recently renovated. The attorney for the family claimed that the student suffered the following:

- respiratory and breathing problems causing illness and absence from school;

- a surgical procedure for treatment;

- the opinion of school officials that her problems were not medical in nature but, rather, related to adjustment problems from her recent transfer to the school;

- delays in getting homebound instruction; and

- a loss of credit for the school year.

As this case goes forward, the school nurse's documentation of the student's visits to the health center for complaints of illness may provide critical information to support the school district's position that the student's symptoms may have been caused by factors other than the fungus. When the student had visited the health center with complaints, the school nurse completed and documented thorough nursing assessments, with nursing diagnoses and interventions, that linked the student's "present complaints" (when visiting the school nurse) to prior medical conditions (district's school nurse [not named due to ongoing legal proceedings], personal communication, July 20, 1999, and April 7, 2000). These records may be especially powerful because they reflect what happened *before* the problem with the fungus was discovered and because evaluation of the student's health-related complaints was completed and documented by a well-qualified school nurse.

Situation Three: New York

The third case, which demonstrates the importance of documentation for the school nurse's own protection against liability for malpractice, is important for many reasons, not only documentation. It is also profoundly sad. This lengthy story is based on the report of the Office of the Special Commissioner of Investigation for the New York City School District (Stancik, 1995) and interviews in June of 1998 with B. J. Darby, Chapter Leader, Federation of Nurses, United Federation of Teachers (UFT), and two other individuals who were involved, directly or indirectly, in these events. The latter two individuals asked that their names be withheld from print.

In a New York City public school in 1995, an 8-year-old male student with multiple disabilities, transported by a special education van that was staffed with a monitor, arrived at school "unable to be awakened." One of two school nurses in the building was summoned to the cafeteria, where students were served breakfast before going to home room, and immediately observed that the child, Q. M., had fully-dilated pupils, no vital signs, and was so rigid that his tightly closed jaws made CPR impossible. While directing someone to call 9-1-1, the school nurse observed additional signs indicating that rigor mortis (stiffening of the body from death) may have already set in. Following the student's death on January 20, 1995, the parent communicated her intent to sue the district and an investigation was conducted by the Office of the Special Commissioner of Investigation for the New York City School District into "the role played by school personnel during the final days and hours of Q. M.'s life" (Stancik, 1995).

This nonverbal, severely disabled student with cerebral palsy, weighing 27 pounds at death (down from 34 pounds in August of 1994), had attended the special education program at a school in Brooklyn for a total of 4 days prior to the day on which he was apparently dead on arrival at school; those days were January 4, 5, 18, and 19, 1995. Between October 28, 1994, and January 3, 1995, Q. M. had been absent from school for 37 consecutive days due to illness, according to the mother. During that time, his family had moved and Q. M. had been reassigned from a school in Queens to one in Brooklyn, nearer to where the family had moved, although the Queens school continued to have him on its attendance roll. According to the report of the investigation, hereafter referred to as "Stancik's report," Q. M. had been enrolled in and on the bus route of two schools during November and December, but attended neither. No investigation of the student's absences ensued, as would have been required by district policy. Q. M.'s return to school in January coincided exactly with the date of a decrease in hours of a home-care attendant provided for Q. M. by Medicaid. Although he had been transferred to the new school by the end of November 1994, no school records, not even the student's medical and school health records, had been forwarded to the new school, despite district policy requiring the timely transfer of such records. They were finally delivered to the school on January 23, 1995, three days after the student's death.

The special education nurse had not been notified of the new student's enrollment in the school and had had no opportunity to obtain information from the parent or child's physician or develop an individualized health care plan prior to his arrival at school. It was the policy of the district that the Committee on Special Education determined where students would be placed and, although the committee did not include a nurse or physician, whether or not the student had any medical problems that the school needed to address. If so, a "Medical Alert" form was supposed to be filled out and sent with the student to the school. No such form preceded or arrived with this student. School nurses in the district generally had no opportunity to do advanced assessment and planning (prior to school entry) to ensure a safe environment and appropriate health services for students with medical needs. Furthermore, when new students appeared without notice, nurses had no authority to refuse the students entry until medical records, medical orders, supplies, equipment, and parent

permissions for treatment were obtained and individualized health and emergency care plans were developed. It is significant to note that, for several years prior to this incident, the UFT Chapter of the Board of Education's School Nurses and Therapists had recommended that a nurse participate as a member of the Committee on Special Education when students with special health care needs were being considered or, at the least, be consulted regarding interpretation of student's medical records and needs.

On January 4, Q. M.'s mother visited the school along with Q. M. This gave the nurse the opportunity to obtain brief information about Q. M.'s diet, medications, and general health. The mother stated that he would get his medication at home, not in school. He was observed to be extremely thin, but alert and responsive. No prior data was available to determine whether he had recently lost weight or what his baseline weight and nutritional status were, although his mother reported that he was under the regular care of a physician, whom she named.

Q. M. came to school on January 5, the first real day of school for him, and was then absent from January 6 through January 17. According to Board of Education policy, the school nurse had called the mother to determine why Q. M. was absent and to inform the mother that a physician's note was required for his return after an absence of 3 or more days. Q. M.'s home-care attendant said that it was the mother who had been ill, but that Q. M. already had an appointment scheduled with his physician the next day. Q. M. returned to school on January 18 with a note from his physician, who reported that he had examined Q. M. the day before (January 17) and that he was fine to return to school. School personnel described him as even thinner than before.

Alarmed by the further deterioration of Q. M.'s general condition and the finding of a decubitis ulcer (breakdown of the skin, usually from pressure and poor circulation), the special education nurse asked the other (regular education) nurse in the building to assess Q. M. with her. Both agreed that he was emaciated and generally in poor condition, although his vital signs were normal. They estimated a weight at 31 pounds. Q. M. had also been observed to be a very poor and slow eater. The school nurses called the physician's office to share their concerns and ask for information regarding Q. M.'s baseline weight, whether Q. M. might benefit from supplemental feedings, and whether any medical assessment related to the efficacy of a gastrostomy tube had been completed. The physician's office staff said that the physician would be away until January 20 but affirmed that the doctor had examined Q. M. the day before and that Q. M. was all right to be in school. The staff also declined to share any medical information relevant to the school nurses' concerns.

The school nurses both tried unsuccessfully to reach the mother to share their concerns regarding Q. M.'s weight, fragile condition, and skin ulcer. After several attempts, according to the nurses' testimony, one call got through to the mother's work office but was interrupted by an operator for emergency reasons. (Stancik's report alleges that they made only one attempt to call the mother.) Finally, the special education nurse went to find the teacher, hoping at least to communicate with the mother through the student's back-and-forth notebook, but Q. M. had already left on the bus and the teacher was gone as well.

On the following day, January 19, a substitute nurse was scheduled to work for the special education nurse and accompany Q. M.'s class on a field trip to the supermarket. Therefore, in addition to documenting her assessment and interventions on Q. M.'s health record, the school nurse reported that she had left a long note for the substitute nurse, not only about Q. M.'s fragile condition, but about all of the students. Included in the note were directions for the care of other students in the class, including the administration of medications. Although the students apparently received their medications that day and the substitute nurse's report had been that "all of the students were fine," Stancik's report states that the substitute nurse denied seeing any note from the school nurse. That afternoon, the school bus delivered Q. M. into the care of his after-school, home-care attendant, who later told investigators that the mother had instructed her by phone not to feed Q. M. supper, which the attendant usually did. She also reported that the food that Q. M.'s mother usually left for him was "inappropriate and lacking in nutritional value." The next day, January 20, is the day that Q. M. died—when, exactly, is not clear since the mother had made an unusual request to the bus monitor to "let him sleep" and the bus monitor had not interacted with or observed him except from behind the wheelchair. Transportation on the bus took 1 1/2 hours, from 7:15 to 8:45 a.m. The monitor reported after Q. M.'s death that, although he had "wept" on the bus to and from school on January 19 (the day before), she did not think it was her place to tell anyone. The monitor's description of her job responsibilities, which included never touching a student, and her lack of CPR, first aid, or other medical training were verified by another monitor, but were "in sharp contrast" to the written job description of the district.

The Office of the Special Commissioner of Investigation's report is lengthy, exploring in detail the many errors that occurred in providing an appropriate education program for this student, as well as apparent errors at home and by the student's physician. Many of the school-based errors, whether or not they contributed to the tragic outcome, might have been avoided if district policies had been followed and if policies had required nursing participation in the advanced assessment and planning necessary for the safe care of students with complex medical problems. The parent withdrew her threat to sue the district when, on autopsy, it was determined that Q. M. died between 4:00 and 8:45 a.m. from a "dangerously toxic level" of Phenobarbital, which was administered only at home. The autopsy report also stated that contributing to his death were his seizure disorder, severe dehydration, and pneumonia. No food was found in his stomach. The mother declined to testify during the investigation, citing Fifth Amendment rights, but had given three different accounts of Q. M.'s condition when she put him on the bus that morning. Also, despite a subpoena, she failed to produce Q. M.'s back-and-forth notebook, which she had taken from the school on the day he died.

Despite the autopsy findings and all other factors in this case, Stancik's report on the role of school personnel places more "blame" on the special education school nurse than on anyone else. It recommended that she receive "severe disciplinary action which could appropriately include her termination of employment from the Board" for failing "to carry out her responsibility to Q. M." The report suggests that if Emergency Medical Services had been called on January 18, perhaps a different outcome might have been possible.

Stancik's report also intimated that the regular education nurse, the first one to assess Q. M. the morning of his death, should have performed CPR and that better communications with the 9-1-1 operator about the seriousness of the emergency might have influenced the outcome. Investigators strongly challenged her decision not to administer CPR and her ability to assess his condition—that is, that his tightly clamped jaws made CPR ineffective and that his body temperature, color, lack of vital signs and rigid muscle tone, among other assessment findings, were indicative of rigor mortis. The report notes that the emergency medical technician (EMT), also noting that Q. M.'s jaw was "clamped closed," did attempt to administer CPR and continued this effort until they reached the hospital, where Q. M. was then pronounced dead. The report supported the EMT's actions without mentioning that EMTs are required by EMS protocol to administer CPR, regardless of the patient's condition. Although the regular education nurse was criticized, rather than acknowledged for her nursing assessment skills and efforts to maintain calm in front of the other students and staff, no recommendations for disciplinary actions were made against her.

Stancik's report also recommended that a letter of reprimand be placed in the personnel file of the school nurse supervisor, one of two Board administrators admonished in the report. The rationale was that her report was too favorable to the school nurses involved, that her omissions in the report (e.g., the nurse's failure to initiate CPR) might have been "calculated," and that she had failed to provide supervision and take actions to "prevent similar errors in the future." In other words, the supervisor's assessment that the nurses had performed adequately in the circumstances was discounted and investigators felt she deserved to be disciplined for not taking action against one or both of them.

On the other hand, classroom personnel were all commended for their concern and caring toward this child. The district was not taken to task for not requiring sufficient medical information to be available to the school nurses who were responsible to provide health services for Q. M. and other special-needs students. The supervisor of the bus monitor was not admonished for not training the bus monitors, as required by district policy. No one mentioned how it was decided that this medically fragile student should ride on a bus to school for 1 1/2 hours each way. Only one other administrator – one who no longer worked for the district – was criticized for not reporting accurately why district policy on following up absent students was not followed in this case. The physician was referred to the state medical board for investigation by that body.

It was the strong belief of the school nurses that they would have been disciplined or fired had it not been for the following factors:

- they had good documentation of their assessments and interventions, including physical assessment data and efforts to obtain baseline and past medical history information; and

- they had proof of excellent nursing knowledge and skills. Both nurses had strong nursing backgrounds in emergency and intensive care nursing, both were CPR certified (even though the Board did not provide such training for school nurses at that time), and they had demonstrated appropriate assessment and effective CPR and emergency skills in prior emergencies with other students.

Whether the Office of the Special Commissioner of Investigation felt that the district might need to find blame, given the possibility of a law suit, or simply had insufficient knowledge and understanding of nursing practice requirements and how to determine the appropriate standard of care, or perhaps both, is unclear. Certainly a nurse should be held to a higher standard of assessment and observation regarding health status than educators. On the other hand, these nurses were dealing with several factors out of their control, especially the lack of health records and baseline data of any kind, but also the lack of authority to send Q. M. home, the brief time that he had been in school, and the physician's report that he was well enough to be there. However, given the multiple, significant issues and errors inside and outside the school system, it is notable that the only school personnel who were recommended for discipline were nurses, with the one exception of the special education administrator who no longer worked for the district when the report was written.

Without their documentation, one or both of the school nurses may well have been fired or even criminally investigated in this student's death. It was bad enough that the report was summarized in the local newspapers, including the name of the nurse recommended for dismissal. It was worse that the initial result of the autopsy was "death by natural causes" and the toxicology report was not made known for some time, a very long time for those apparently being blamed, at least in part, for this tragedy.

As of April 11, 2000, no disciplinary action had been taken against the special education nurse, nor had the recommendation for disciplinary action been rescinded. Furthermore, the union's long-standing recommendation that a school nurse participate as a member of, or consultant to, the Committee on Special Education had still not been implemented. Students who were medically fragile and had complex health needs were still arriving at New York City schools without prior notice, medical records, medical orders, or advanced assessment, planning, and preparation by appropriately licensed health professionals (B. J. Darby, personal communication, April 11, 2000).

The NASN guidelines cited above provide school nurses and administrators with a resource for the rationale, standards, and principles of school nursing documentation, current models, and related legal issues. (Many of those issues are explored in depth throughout this book. Chapter 7 addresses a minor's right to treatment statutes; chapter 8 discusses confidentiality; and chapters 9 and 10 explore legal aspects of paper and electronic records and principles of nursing documentation.)

CONCLUSION

Clinicians and administrators responsible for developing, delivering, evaluating, or advising school districts about school health services programs should be knowledgeable about the standards that apply to school health services programs and professional performance. These standards include the laws, regulations, and state guidelines from both health and education agencies that apply to practices in their state, as well as methods for managing risks and resolving potential conflicts inherent in delivering a wide variety of health and mental health services in school settings. The development and regular updating of policies, procedures, and clinical protocols are critical for establishing local standards that support safe practice, improve student health and learning, and avoid potential charges of harassment, discrimination, or negligence.

Quality professional performance by school nurses is best assured when compliance with professional standards of practice, the state's nurse practice act, and up-to-date job descriptions is supported by school administrators and school district policy, and when decisions related to fundamental program issues, such as staffing and program policies, are collaboratively made. Quality professional performance also requires continuous learning, ongoing performance appraisal, open communications, and critical thinking skills that include the perspectives of individual students, the student body, the school district, families, colleagues, and the community at large. The next chapter, "School Nursing Practice: Clinical Performance," builds on the risk management principles discussed in this chapter. It addresses specific clinical responsibilities and concerns of schools that regularly challenge school nurses, administrators, and medical advisors.

REFERENCES

Ackerman, P. (1995). *Job performance evaluation: A guide for school nurses.* Scarborough, ME: National Association of School Nurses.

American Academy of Pediatrics, Committee on School Health. (1993). *School health: Policy and practice* (5th ed.). Elk Grove, IL: American Academy of Pediatrics.

American Federation of Teachers. (1997). *The medically fragile child in the school setting* (2nd ed.). Washington, DC: Author.

American Nurses Association. (1985a). *The code for nurses with interpretive statements.* Washington, DC: American Nurses Publishing.

American Nurses Association. (1985b). *Human rights guidelines for nurses in clinical and other research.* Washington, DC: American Nurses Publishing.

American Nurses Association. (1981). *Guidelines for the Investigative Functions of Nurses.* Washington, DC: American Nurses Publishing.

American Nurses Association (1995). *Nursing's social policy statement.* Washington, DC: American Nurses Publishing.

American Nurses Association. (1998a). *Legal aspects of standards and guidelines for clinical practice.* Washington, DC: American Nurses Publishing.

American Nurses Association. (1998b). *Standards of clinical nursing practice* (2nd ed.). Washington, DC: American Nurses Publishing.

Arnold, M., & Silkworth, C. (Eds.). (1999). *The school nurse's source book of individualized healthcare plans* (Vol. 2). North Branch, MN: Sunrise River Press.

Atkinson, L. D., & Murray, M. E. (1990). *Understanding the nursing process, fundamentals of care planning* (4th ed.). New York: Pergamon Press.

Baldwin-Mech, A. (1987). Quality assurance and documentation. In C. E. Northrop & M. E. Kelly (Eds.), *Legal issues in nursing* (pp. 453-465). St. Louis: C. V. Mosby Company.

Bernzweig, E. P. (1996). *The nurse's liability for malpractice* (6th ed.). St. Louis: Mosby.

Bianco, E. A. (1998). Iatrogenic drug related diseases. *The Journal of Nursing Risk Management 1998.* Department of Legal Medicine, The Armed Forces Institute of Pathology [Continuing Education On-Line: 19–21]. Available: www.afip.org/legalmed/jnrm.html or www.afip.org/legalmed/lmof.html

Bourne, L. (1997). Evaluations [On-line]. Available E-mail: lcbourned@pa. mother.com

Burkle, T., Kuch, R., Passian, A. Prokosch, U., & Dudeck, J. (1995). The impact of computer implementation on nursing work patterns: Study design and preliminary results. *Medical Informatics (8 Pt.) 2*, 1322–5.

Burt, C. J., Beetem, N., Iverson, C., Hertel, V., & Peters, D. A. (1996). Preliminary development of the School Health Intensity Rating Scale. *Journal of School Health, 66*(8), 286–290.

Collins, M. (1996). *A summary of school health staffing patterns concentrating on the utilization of LPNs.* Kent, OH: National Association of State School Nurse Consultants.

Connecticut Advisory School Health Council. (1997). *Qualifications and Roles of School Health Personnel.* Middletown, CT: Connecticut State Department of Education.

Connecticut Board of Examiners for Nursing. (1998). School nurse. LPN scope of practice. *Newsletter, X*(1), 6.

Connecticut State Department of Education. (1992). *Serving students with special health care needs.* Hartford: Author.

Connecticut State Department of Education. (1993). *Evaluating pupil services specialists.* Hartford: Author.

Connecticut State Department of Education. (1999). *Guidelines for pupil services programs: A self-evaluation guide.* Hartford: Author.

Curtin, L. (1999). Editorial opinion: Going from the gut . . . *CurtinCalls, 1*(5): 1–2.

Davis, N., Fryer, G., White, S., & Igoe, J. (1995). *A closer look: A report of select findings from the National School Health Survey 1993–1994.* Denver: Office of School Health, University of Colorado Health Services.

DeCenzo, D., & Robbins, S. (1994). *Human resource management: Concepts and practices* (4th ed.). New York: John Wiley & Sons, Inc.

Duncan, P., & Igoe, J. B. (1998). School health services. In E. Marx & S. F. Wooley with D. Northrop (Eds.), *Health is academic: A guide to coordinated school health programs* (pp. 169–194). New York: Teachers College Press.

Ericksen, C. (1998). *School nursing and health services: A resource and planning guide.* Madison, WI: Wisconsin Department of Public Instruction.

Federal Interagency on Child and Family Statistics. (1999). *America's Children: Key National Indicators of Well-being, 1999.* Washington, DC: Author. Available On-line: http//childstats.gov/ac1999/ac99.asp

Fryer, G., & Igoe, J. (1996). Functions of school nurses and health assistants in U.S. school health programs. *Journal of School Health, 66*(2), 55–58.

Goodman, I. F., & Sheetz, A. H. (1995). *The comprehensive school health manual.* Boston: Massachusetts Department of Public Health.

Guido, G. W. (1997). *Legal issues in nursing* (2nd ed.). Stamford, CT: Appleton & Lange.

Haas, M. (Ed.) (1993). *The school nurse's source book of individualized healthcare plans* (Vol. 1). North Branch, MN: Sunrise River Press.

Harvey, G. (1997). Reply, school districts with many nurses, October 6, 1997 [On-line]. Available E-mail: gmh@cyberportal.net

Hatfield, M. E. (Ed.). (1997). School nurse expansion in Tennessee. *School Nursing News, 17*(1): 7.

Hatfield, M. E. (Ed.). (1997). Caution by School Nurse prevents lawsuit over hallway accident. *School Nursing News, 17*(1): 7.

Hootman, J. (1996a). *Quality nursing intervention in the school setting: Procedures, models, and guidelines.* Scarborough, ME: National Association of School Nurses.

Hootman, J. (with Carpenito, L. J.). (1996b). *Nursing diagnosis: Application in the school setting.* Scarborough, ME: National Association of School Nurses.

Hootman, J., & Carpenito, L. J. (2000). *Nursing assessment of school-age youth: Nursing process.* Scarborough, ME: National Association of School Nurses.

Institute of Medicine. (1990). *Clinical practice guidelines: Directions for a new program.* Washington, D.C.: National Academy Press.

Iyer, P., & Camp, N. (1995). *Nursing documentation, a nursing process approach* (2nd ed.). St. Louis: Mosby.

Karp, D. (1996). Accurate medical records provide strong defense. *AAP News,* April edition.

Klahn, J. K., Hays, B. J., & Iverson, C. J. (1998). The school health intensity rating scale: Establishing reliability for practice. *Journal of School Nursing, 14*(4), 23–28.

Kozier, B., Erb, G., Berman, A. J., and Burke, K. (2000). *Fundamentals of nursing: Concepts, process and practice* (6th ed.). Upper Saddle River, NJ:. Prentice Hall Health.

Krin, P. (1997). Reply, school districts with many nurses, October 1997 [On-line]. Available E-mail: patricia.krin@snet.net

Magyary, D., Brandt, P. & Kovalesky, A. (1999). *Children with ADHD: A manual with decision tree and clinical path for health care professionals.* Seattle: University of Washington, School of Nursing.

Maire, J. (1995). *Recommended staffing for school health services.* Olympia, WA: Office of the Superintendent of Public Instruction.

Massachusetts Department of Public Health. (April 1, 1998). *Options for developing school health services in the Commonwealth of Massachusetts: A report to the Committees on Ways and Means of the Massachusetts Senate and House of Representatives.* Boston: Author.

McBurney, B. H., & Filoromo, T. (1994). The Nightengale Pledge: 100 years later. *Nursing Management, 25*(2), 72–74.

Minnesota Department of Health and Hutchinson-Willmer Regional Technical College & St. Cloud Technical College. (1995). *Assisting the licensed school nurse: School health paraprofessional curriculum.* Minneapolis: Minnesota Department of Health and St. Cloud Technical College.

Minnesota Nurses Association. (1997). *Position paper: Delegation and supervision of nursing activities.* Minnesota: Author.

Monsma, M., Day, R., & Arnaud, S. (1992). Handwashing makes a difference. *Journal of School Health, 62*(3), 109–111.

National Association of School Nurses. (1972). *Caseload assignments resolution.* Scarborough, ME: Author.

National Association of School Nurses. (1997). *Position statement: Continuing education.* Scarborough, ME: Author.

National Association of School Nurses. (1998). *Standards of Professional School Nursing Practice.* Scarborough, ME: Author.

National Association of State School Nurse Consultants. (July 1995). *Position paper: Delegation of school health services to unlicensed assistive personnel, revised.* Kent, OH: Author.

National Education Association. (1995). *NEA TODAY.* November issue.

Oetgen, W. J., & Wiley, M. J. (1998). Clinical practice guidelines: Is cookbook health care here? *The Journal of Nursing Risk Management 1998.* Department of Legal Medicine, The Armed Forces Institute of Pathology [Continuing Education On-Line: 2–6]. Available: www.afip.org/legalmed/jnrm.html or www.afip.org/legalmed/lmof.html

Palfrey, J. (1995). Amber, Katie, and Ryan: Lessons from children with complex medical conditions. *Journal of School Health, 65*(7), 265–267.

Panettieri, M. J., & Schwab, N. (1996). Delegation and supervision in school settings: Standards, issues and guidelines for practice (Part II). *Journal of School Nursing, 12*(2), 11–18.

Pierpont, G., & Thilgen, D. (1995). Effect of computerized charting on nursing activity in intensive care. *Critical Care Medicine, 23*(6), 1067–73.

Pitasky, V. M. (1995). *Liability for injury to special education students.* Horsham, PA: LRP Publications.

Proctor, S., (with Lordi, S., & Zaiger, D.). (1993). *School nursing practice: Roles and standards.* Scarborough, ME: National Association of School Nurses, Inc.

Robinson, V. (Ed.). (1997a). Tennessee's upsurge in school nurses. *School Health Professional, 4*(6), 6.

Robinson, V. (Ed.). (1997b). Courts uphold nurse's judgment on Ritalin. *School Health Professional, May 7: 2 & 4.*

Rothman, D. J. (1991). *Strangers at the bedside. A history of how law and bioethics transformed medical decision making.* New York: Basic Books, Harper Collins Publishers.

Schwab, N., Panettieri, M. J., & Bergren, M. (1998). *Guidelines for school nursing documentation: Standards, issues and models* (2nd ed.). Scarborough, ME: National Association of School Nurses.

Sheehan, J. (1999). Advice of Counsel: When you're given an assignment you're not trained to do. *AJN 62*(4): 72.

Sklaire, M. W. (1990). Role of the pediatrician in school health. *Pediatrics in Review, 12*(3).

Springhouse Corporation. 1996. *Nurse's legal handbook* (3rd ed.). Springhouse, PA: Author.

Stancik, E. F. (with Lupuloff, K., Keith, L., & Fernbacker, J.). (1995, September). *An investigation into the death of eight-year old Quentin Magee.* New York City: Office of the Special Commissioner of Investigation for the New York City School District.

Szabo. (1998, August 20). Amity High sued by parent. *The Bulletin, 14*(32), 1.

University of the State of New York, New York State Department of Education, Comprehensive Health and Pupil Services Team, & Statewide Advocacy for School Health Services Center. (1999, June 21). *Report card for school health services,* draft edition. Albany: Authors.

Uris, P. F. (1996). *Supervisory leadership: A training manual for school nurses working with school health paraprofessionals.* Denver: Office of School Health, University of Colorado.

U.S. Department of Health and Human Services, Office of Disease Prevention and Health Promotion. (2000). *Healthy People 2010,* Conference Edition. [On-line]. Available: http://www.health.govhealthypeople/Document/Table of contents.htm

Washington State Joint Legislative Audit and Review Committee. (1997). *Survey of school nurses: Report 97-5.* Olympia: author.

Washington State Nursing Care Quality Assurance Commission and Washington State Office of the Superintendent of Public Instruction. (2000). *Staff Model for the Delivery of School Health Services.* Olympia, WA: Authors.

Washington State Office of the Superintendent of Public Instruction. (January 1999). *Comprehensive health services, EB.* Olympia, Washington: Author.

TABLE OF CASES

Brown v. Houston School District, 704 So.2d 1325 (Miss. 1997)

Brum v. Town of Dartmouth, 690 N.E.2d 844 (Mass. Ct. App. 1998)

Calvert v. Tulsa Public Schools, 932 P.2d 1087 (Okl. 1996).

Crisp County School District v. Pheil, 27 IDELR 1033 (Ga. Ct. App. 1998).

Davis v. Francis Howell School District, (104 F.3d 204, 25 IDELR 212 (8th Cir. 1997); 138 F.3d 754, 27 IDELR 811 (8th Cir. 1998)).

DeBord, Allen, et al. v. The Board of Education of the Ferguson Florissant School District, et. al., Case No. 4:96-CV634 (CEJ) (E.D. Mo. 1996); 126 F.3d. 1002., 26 IDELR 1133 (8th Cir. 1997).

Declouet v. Orleans Parish School Board, 715 So. 2d 69 (La. Ct. App. 4 Cir. 1998).

Etheredge v. Richland School District, 499 S.E.2d 238 (S.C.App.1998).

Federico v. Order of Saint Benedict in Rhode Island, 64 F.3d 1, 23 IDELR 215 (1st Cir. 1995).

Hickingbottom v. Orleans Parish School Board, 623 So. 2d 1363 (La. Ct. App., 1993).

Kelly v. Parents United for the District of Columbia Public Schools, 641 A.2d 159 (D.C. Ct. App., 1994).

Liebowitz v. Dinkins, 575 N.Y.S. 2d 827 18 IDELR, 506, 1ECLPR 185, 575 N. Y.S.2d 827 (N.Y. App. Div., 1991).

Lunsford v. Board of Nursing Examiners, 648 S.W. 2d 391 (Tex: App. 3 Dist., 1983).

Macomb County Intermediate School District v. Joshua S., EHLR 441:600 (ED Mich. 1989).

Mitts, Carol v. Hillsboro Union High School District No. 3-8Jt, et al., Washington County Circuit Court, Case No. 87-1142C (1990).

Nance v. Matthews, 622 So.2d 297, 20 IDELR (LRP) 3 (Ala. 1993).

Roventini v. Pasadena Independent School District, 981 F.Supp. 1013 (S.D. Tex. 1997).

Sargi v. Kent City Board of Education, 70 F.3d 907, 23 IDELR 431 (6th Cir. 1995).

Schluessler v. Independent School District No. 200, et al., 1989 Minnesota Case Reports 652 (Dakota County District Court, 1989).

Tollenaar v. Chino Valley School District, 945 P.2d 1310 (Ariz.App.Div. 1, 1997).

See page 625 for Table of Federal Statutes and Regulations.

Chapter Six
School Nursing Practice: Clinical Performance Issues

Janis Hootman
Nadine C. Schwab
Mary H. B. Gelfman
with Elizabeth K. Gregory and Katherine J. Pohlman

School nursing is a specialized practice of professional nursing that advances the well being, academic success, and life-long achievement of students. To that end, school nurses facilitate positive student responses to normal development; promote health and safety; intervene with actual and potential health problems; provide case management services; and actively collaborate with others to build student and family capacity for adaptation, self management, self advocacy, and learning.

National Association of School Nurses
May 1999

INTRODUCTION

This chapter focuses on *clinical* performance issues that have implications for school district and school nurse liability. Clinical performance issues are those directly related to the delivery of health services to students and staff, such as communicable disease control and medication administration services. The reader is directed first to chapter 5, a companion chapter that addresses the *professional* performance issues and standards critical to the foundation of a quality health services program. This chapter builds on that foundation by exploring legal issues related to the clinical, or direct-care responsibilities of schools and school nurses in providing a wide range of health services to students and staff. Emphasis is on those clinical performance issues that impact day-to-day practice in and beyond the school's health and wellness center. Rather than addressing every issue, the chapter discusses those that confront school nurses and administrators in serving the general school population, pre-k through 12th grade, with emphasis on high-priority risk management concerns. Other chapters in the book address many of these issues from different perspectives; these are cross-referenced for the reader's benefit.

Like it or not, schools are in the business of delivering health services today. While these are typically not the "primary health care services" that individuals iden-

tify with going to their regular physicians and nurse practitioners for health assessments, and the diagnosis and medical management of health problems, they are, at a minimum, health promotion, health maintenance, and early identification and intervention services. *Health maintenance services* refers to the nursing and other related services necessary to ensure that students with chronic health conditions such as asthma, diabetes, and clinical depression, and those with complex medical problems and medical-technology dependence can maintain or improve their health status in school, rather than experience health deterioration from inadequate or poor care during the school day. In addition to implementing health promotion, early intervention, and accommodation strategies to enhance learning, school nurses frequently carry out or direct others to carry out a therapeutic medical regimen for students, under medical orders from authorized prescribers (i.e., physicians, advanced practice nurses, and physician assistants, depending on the state).

Whether school districts want to take on these health care responsibilities does not matter; their obligation to provide services when students require them to access an appropriate education and to provide them safely is clearly supported in federal and state statute and court decisions. Some schools provide ongoing primary health care services, as well; these services are the main focus of school-based health centers. (See chapters 15 and 16, respectively, for information on school-based health centers and school-based managed care initiatives and contracts.)

As addressed in the introduction in chapter 5, effective communication with parents, consultation with other school health experts, such as school medical advisors and state school nurse consultants, and the effective use of school health advisory councils are critical components of effective risk-management programs in today's public schools. Caution is again recommended in applying the authority of court decisions to other situations, as the decisions may be limited to the court's own jurisdiction.

SAFETY MANAGEMENT

As chapter 1 describes, today's students come to school with a multitude of acute and chronic health conditions, both physical and psychological. Many of these conditions, which vary from mild to severe, directly and indirectly impact student safety and learning. In response, schools provide a wider range and more intense level of nursing services than ever before. Health promotion and safety programs, consultation with community physicians and other community experts, and school team-family collaboration are not only critical strategies for enhancing student health and learning, but also for eliminating potential causes of legal action. This section addresses legal considerations related to specific safety issues in schools, including environmental conditions and individual student health needs.

School districts have a duty to address health and safety issues that impact student learning and threaten student and staff well being. Safety concerns in the school environment, for example, should always be investigated. "Asking me to overlook a simple safety violation would be asking me to compromise my entire attitude towards the value of your life" (Sheldrake, 1997). Many federal and state mandates address and promote student and employee safety, and district policies interpret these regulations for local application.

Prevention is the first priority in safety management. Historically, schools focused on environmental safety precautions, for example, fire and earthquake drills, playground equipment maintenance, and removal of lead or asbestos in buildings. Schools today are responsible for safety in the school community beyond the physical environment, including violence prevention, behavior management, and promotion of a healthy school climate.

Emergency, First Aid, and Crisis Preparedness

School districts are accountable for developing programs that prevent, when feasible, and ensure an effective response to urgent and emergency health problems of students, staff, and even visitors to school buildings. The exact level of accountability of the school nurse in a specific urgent or emergency situation will depend on multiple factors, such as the nurse practice act, relevant national and state standards, the school nurse's job description and assignments, and district policies and procedures.

Assessing Emergency Situations

Due to their professional preparation and license, school nurses ordinarily have the primary responsibility for assessing and managing urgent health problems of students and staff. The standard of care applicable to school nurses' responses to such problems is well above that of teachers, principals, health aides, and licensed vocational or practical nurses. The nursing standard requires clinical assessment, diagnosis, and intervention at the professional level of knowledge and skill; in most instances, the nursing standard of care is well beyond that of simple first aid. The nursing standard also includes directing others in a health-related crisis.

Guido (1997, p. 332) cites the case of *Schluessler v. Independent School District No. 200 et al.* (1989), in a comment on the standard of care expected of school nurses in health-related emergencies. "School nurses have a higher duty of care than hospital nurses to make an assessment of the need for emergency services." Because schools do not have immediate access to emergency room personnel and equipment, as in a hospital, school nurses must be prepared to rapidly:

- *recognize* impending and actual emergencies;
- *summon* appropriate emergency medical services; and
- *stabilize* affected individuals.

School nurses cannot and should not be the sole responders to urgent health situations in schools. Even when school nurses are assigned full time to a building, they may not always be on-site or readily available at the location of an emergency. Building administrators and school nurses should ensure that schools have reasonable plans for recognizing and responding to urgent and emergency health problems that can be reasonably anticipated in the student population. The school nurse should assist not only in the development of student-specific plans for children with special health care needs (described below under "chronic health conditions"), but also in the development of generic school-emergency plans (e.g. responses to chemical exposure, respiratory distress, seizure or head injury management, and violence in the environment).

The Office for Civil Rights, U.S. Department of Education, recognized the need for both generic and student specific emergency plans in the case of *Conejo Valley Unified School District* (1993). (See chapter 11 for further discussion of this case of a student with diabetes.) The responsibility of school personnel to prevent and be responsive to student injuries and illnesses is, in part, related to the legal principle of *in loco parentis* (care for a child in "the place of the parent"). For example, the family of a student with Down Syndrome brought a case of negligent supervision against the New York City Board of Education following injuries sustained when an "unsecured wooden platform" that was resting on the back wall of the gym fell on him (*Farrukh v. Board of Education of the City of New York*, 1996). The family sued the board for both inadequate supervision and negligence, but the trial court dismissed the action related to inadequate supervision and the jury found for the board on the action related to negligence. The family appealed and the appellate court reversed, holding that

- the jury's finding that the board was not negligent went against the weight of the evidence; and

- the trial court had "erred in dismissing the action for inadequate supervision as a matter of law, since the record showed that the student had established a prima facie case [a very strong and undisputed case of the facts] that the board had failed to exercise the degree of reasonable care that a parent of ordinary prudence would have exercised under comparable circumstances" ("Injured student established case of negligent supervision," 1996).

Thus, a district's standard of care for preventing accidents will frequently be considered that *degree of reasonable care that a parent of ordinary prudence would exercise under comparable circumstances.*

In the New Orleans case discussed in chapter 5 under "District Policies and Procedures" (*Declouet v. Orleans Parish School Board*, 1998), the student with asthma died when school officials failed to respond to her pleas for an ambulance. Not only did school officials fail to recognize the student's life-threatening condition and summon an ambulance, but they compounded that failure by not seeking direction from the school nurse who was present on the campus (personal communications with Yvonne LaGasse, June, 1997 and Iris Haydel, July, 1998). The school district's liability was based, in part, on its failure to adequately train school personnel in emergency procedures; it also failed to act with the same degree of care with which a reasonable parent would have acted in the same circumstance.

School district policies and procedures and staff job descriptions should reflect staff responsibilities and district expectations for staff actions in an emergency situation. School nurses and principals should collaboratively identify designated first aid providers. It is important for these persons to be willing, consistently available, physically and emotionally competent, and appropriately trained. Collaboration is important because, while administrators generally determine employee assignments, the clinical expertise and professional judgment of the school nurse may be critical in identifying individuals who will be both willing and capable in the role of first-aid provider. Northrop (1987, p. 224), in discussing school nurse responsibilities for arranging in-service programs to train school personnel in first aid and emergency response, asserts that school nurses must also "assess the level of proficiency" of personnel at the end of the program.

First Aid and CPR

Individuals relied on by the district to provide first aid and CPR in an emergency should have regularly updated formal training. Formal training programs for generic first aid and CPR should meet the standards of prescribed courses, such as those developed by the American Heart Association, American Red Cross, Medic First Aid from EMP International, Inc., and the National Safety Council. These standard courses allow for the retrieval of content should there be a question about what was covered in the training. They also reflect standardized criteria for quality training and certification of competent course participants. In addition to training courses for personnel, it is necessary to purchase appropriate first aid and CPR equipment and supplies, properly maintain them, and ensure that they are accessible to emergency responders.

Crisis Intervention

Schools districts should establish and update mechanisms for preparing rapid, coordinated responses by qualified school personnel and community experts to crises that may occur at the school building, school district and wider community levels. While such crises may affect students, staff, and families directly or indirectly, they nevertheless require knowledge-based, collaborative, planned, and immediate approaches, as well as sustained efforts, that ensure effective interventions to minimize trauma and promote healing in those affected. Crises can vary from acts of violence with intended injury to natural disasters, outbreaks of communicable disease, and accidental death.

Lichtenstein, Schonfeld, Kline, and Speese-Lineham (1995, pp. 4–5) describe four key concepts essential to an effective approach to crisis response:

- preparation is absolutely essential to ensure effective response to a school crisis;

- there is no ideal crisis preparation and response plan that will work best in all schools and school districts;

- to whatever extent feasible, every school should develop the capacity to deal with crisis situations; and

- crisis response is just one component in the overall constellation of mental health and social development efforts within the school community.

As these authors wisely observe in supporting a team approach to crisis response (p. 8), "The greatest beneficiary of a team approach…is the school administrator, who bears a weighty responsibility for major decisions affecting the school." In any event, in advance of any crisis, school administrators, teachers, and school health and mental health professionals, working through school health advisory councils or "healthy school teams" (Marx & Wooley, 1998), should collaborate with parents and community experts, including emergency medical services (EMS) staff, to establish a workable, planned, and organized framework for crisis response. In addition, this collaborative group must develop a mechanism for later evaluation of the actual handling of any crisis situation, including revision of the framework. Cashin (1999) points out to school nurses that, by analyzing a multi-student event, they can help to identify areas requiring improvement in a school's response plan, such as triage, space management, traffic control, communications, and readiness of supplies and equipment.

A principle of risk management—that it is always better to be prepared—is certainly true with regard to crisis response. No school or school district in the United States today can claim that there is no potential for a major crisis in their school or community, or that they have no responsibility for planning an adequate response. Another principle, that prevention is the best remedy, requires school districts, communities, individual citizens, and the nation to examine the causes of violence and other potentially preventable crises, and to make changes that will prevent their occurrence in the first place.

Emergency Procedures for Students with Special Health Care Needs

In order to meet the ordinary standard of care for safeguarding the health and safety of students, districts must act on the information and knowledge available to them. In the past, school systems' accountability for responding to emergencies and urgent health problems focused primarily on first-aid measures related to in-school injuries and minor, acute illness. Today, school district responsibilities include planning for and addressing complex medical and nursing needs of students with physical and mental health disabilities. This may include emergency conditions, such as anaphylaxis, hypoglycemia, airway obstruction, and suicide attempt.

Federal law clearly specifies school district responsibility for addressing the health needs of students. Section (§) 504 of the Rehabilitation Act of 1973 (see chapter 11 for detailed information) prohibits discrimination against individuals with disabilities. This law requires schools to provide the accommodations and related services, including school health services, necessary for students with disabilities to safely access school programs to which they would otherwise be eligible. For example, a district should act on the knowledge that an enrolled student is at high risk for an emergency situation that requires professional nursing assessment and intervention in order to prevent significant harm or death. In some circumstances, the nurse may be able to delegate to, and train, unlicensed personnel in providing specialized care and emergency interventions for individual students (as permitted by state laws and regulations). In other situations, the district may need to ensure that a school nurse is available on-site to provide professional level services when a student's condition is unstable, or when urgent or complex health needs can be anticipated on a frequent basis.

In making recommendations and decisions regarding emergency plans for students with special health care needs, school nurses must know, and interpret for districts, the following:

- State licensure laws and regulations that address delegation by registered professional nurses (RNs) to LPNs and unlicensed assistive personnel;

- relevant declaratory rulings from the state board of nursing, if any;

- education laws and regulations that address delegation by registered professional nurses (RNs) to LPNs and unlicensed personnel, if any; and

- related standards of practice for professional nurses.

These laws and their interpretations vary significantly from one state to another. (See chapter 4 for a thorough discussion of *nursing delegation*. For further discussion, see chapter 11 regarding § 504, and chapters 12 and 13 regarding the Individuals with Disabilities Education Act, relative to emergency planning and health services for students with special health care needs. See also the subsections on "Students with Chronic Conditions: Planning and Implementing Care" and "Individualized Health Care Plans" later in this chapter for additional standards of care related to students with special health care needs.)

Good Samaritan Laws

Frequently, queries are posed regarding protection granted by state *Good Samaritan Laws*. The initial intent of this legislation was to encourage medical personnel to stop at accident scenes to provide emergency medical interventions. The laws are meant to protect volunteers from criminal and civil liability for good faith efforts to help at the scene of an accident. In an emergency, the volunteer is expected to provide the kind of care any reasonable person with similar training would provide in similar circumstances. Good Samaritan laws vary from state to state.

School personnel who may be first-aid responders in the absence of a school nurse or physician need to know the following:

- relevant state laws and regulations;

- if these laws and regulations apply to their "on the job" responsibilities; and

- where and under what circumstances they apply.

In addition to verifying who is covered, it is important to clarify in what locations Good Samaritan coverage applies. Some states limit covered occurrences to roadside events. Washington state law (RCW § 4.24.300) defines the scene of an emergency as "an

accident…which calls for immediate action other than in a hospital, doctor's office or other place where qualified medical personnel practice or are employed" (Matsen, 1998). Other states allow for emergency care wherever the need, including hospitals, physicians' offices, and schools. Michigan law (MCLA § 691.1501), for example, provides that a physician, registered professional nurse, or licensed practical nurse who in good faith renders care at the scene of an emergency is generally immune from civil liability. Immunity is not provided, however, if the provider is grossly negligent or engages in willful or wanton misconduct, acts beyond the scope of his or her license, or had a pre-existing relationship with the patient. Several states specify that Good Samaritan coverage applies only to settings *outside the workplace* (i.e., when the responder is not employed). Most states require the care to be voluntary and unpaid.

If a state's Good Samaritan law addresses procedures that are also addressed in other states' laws, districts should seek legal advice regarding which law takes precedence in a given situation. For example, the Good Samaritan law may cover properly trained school personnel who administer medication by injection in the event of anaphylaxis. However, if the state's education or health code contains a mandate specific to medication administration in schools, including the administration of epinephrine for anaphylaxis, the requirements of the medication administration law may take precedence over Good Samaritan, especially when students are known reactors.

In Connecticut, protected responders under the state Good Samaritan law can be any school personnel who have had a course in first aid and a course in injection technique taught by a physician (C.G.S. § 52-557b(e)). However, the medication administration law for public schools limits who can administer medication in schools (only nurses, teachers, and principals), requires all medication administration to be under the general supervision of the school nurse, and calls for training of non-nurses to be provided by the school nurse or physician (C.G.S. § 10-212a and Connecticut Regulations § 10-212a-3). The education law takes precedence when students have a medical order for emergency medication and authorization from the parent, as required by the statute; Good Samaritan applies to Connecticut school personnel who may need to administer medication by injection under "standing orders" to first time (unknown) reactors.

Of interest, a more recent trend is for states to mandate emergency assistance in certain circumstances. Guido (1997, p. 103) cites Vermont (Vermont Statutes Annotated, Title 12, Sec. 519 (1968)) as the first state to enact a law "requiring persons to assist others when exposed to grave physical harm as long as the assistance can be given without endangering themselves. Reasonable assistance should be given and violation of the statute is punishable by fines." In any event, when Good Samaritan provisions are applicable under state law, one can further limit risk of liability by refusing compensation and not forcing services.

Preparation of School Personnel to Respond to Student Health Care Needs

Beyond first aid and CPR, school personnel may require additional preparation for responding to student health needs, both individual and population-based. This preparation may be the responsibility of the school nurse, a nursing supervisor, or a nursing educator in collaboration with a team of school professionals. Planning for school and individual emergencies includes the following:

- the development and testing of a general emergency disaster plan;

- the development of crisis intervention procedures;

- the development and communication of individualized emergency health care procedures for students with special needs; and

- ongoing staff training and supervision of performance, as applicable.

The services required by students with special health needs vary, depending on their individualized responses to and the acuity of their medical conditions. For example, two students diagnosed with asthma may have considerable variation in their symptoms, precipitating factors, acuity level, risk for emergency, and need for education and monitoring related to self-care. During an acute episode of asthma, the first student might consistently respond well to medication self-administered through an inhaler. The second student might always require nebulizer treatments during asthma attacks and have a history of several episodes requiring cardiopulmonary resuscitation (CPR) and emergency transportation from home or school to the local hospital.

The individualized health care plans and immediate interventions for these students must be different. In the first instance, it may be reasonable to delegate medication administration to a trained, unlicensed staff member, for example a teacher, with periodic reassessment by the school nurse. In the second instance, the

emergency plan may require the immediate availability of a professional nurse in the same building or on the same campus. Under § 504, such nursing services, if necessary for the student to access an appropriate education, would be required. (See chapter 11 for additional information.)

Emergency protocols developed for classroom teachers or other emergency responders should stipulate when to call Emergency Medical Services (EMS; 9-1-1), the school nurse, and the parents, and in what order. In the asthmatic death of the New Orleans student (*Declouet v. Orleans Parish School Board*, 1998), the nurse was present on the campus, but not summoned or consulted by the school administrator or guidance counselor. In this case, 9-1-1 should certainly have been called first, then the school nurse (who may have been able to intervene until EMS arrived), and finally the parents. In this case, had the nurse been called, even immediate consultation by phone may have precipitated a 9-1-1 call early enough to save the student's life.

The extent of responsibility of other school personnel for responding to students' health conditions depends, in part, on the

- needs and health status of the students;

- professional nursing coverage in the school;

- availability of school nurses to provide training and supervision when nursing activities are delegated;

- competencies, willingness and training of the unlicensed personnel (e.g., teachers, teacher aides); and

- state laws and regulations.

School nurses and physicians who participate in developing emergency plans for individual students need to distinguish between what can be safely carried out by trained personnel and what requires professional nursing assessment and judgment. (See also chapter 4 on delegation, and chapters 11, 12, and 13 on students' rights under § 504 and IDEA.)

Transportation Issues

Advanced planning and special accommodations for transportation and field trips are necessary for students with health conditions that may require immediate intervention. The school nurse should identify these students, collaboratively develop a plan of action for each student, and review the plan with individuals responsible for the student's care. This planning should be part of the IEP process for students requiring special education.

Student Care During Transportation

Individualized health care plans need to identify responsible caregiver(s), when needed, during transportation. Drivers cannot safely drive and simultaneously respond to a student's health problems. While the driver should be prepared "to handle a true emergency, he must never be utilized to provide routine or intermittent care to an individual student during actual transport" (Connecticut State Department of Education, 1992, p. 55). In its guidelines, *Serving Students with Special Health Care Needs* (1992, p. 56), the Connecticut Department of Education advises that the level of care that a student requires in school is generally the same level of care that the student requires during transportation and field trips. This standard is also found in *Macomb County Intermediate School District v. Joshua* (1989), which is discussed in detail in chapter 12. In order to be safe during transportation to and from school, some students with special health care needs require a professional nurse or delegated caregiver (LPN or unlicensed assistant) to accompany them. The student's individualized health care plan should identify the appropriate caregiver(s) and equipment necessary to maintain the student's health status during travel.

Aides and monitors on buses must be adequately trained to provide care to students. In a New York City school district, a student arrived at school dead and an investigation ensued. Among numerous school district errors cited in the investigator's report was the fact that, although district policy required bus monitors to be trained, the monitor riding the bus that morning and the day prior when the student cried continuously, had not received training (Stancik, 1995). (See chapter 5 under "Documentation" for details of this incident.)

As a related matter, the District of Columbia was cited as not providing adequate transportation when a bus driver was not aware that an adolescent with a disability was having a seizure. The court found that the district's failure to provide adequate transportation constituted a violation of federal laws and regulations, specifically, the Individuals with Disabilities Education Act (Schwaderer, 1996, p. 1).

School Bus Accidents

School districts need to plan in advance how they are going to handle bus accidents, whether on or off school property. In the event of an accident, the driver or a school official available by beeper should have information about students with high-risk health conditions, such as bleeding disorders. Consultation with the school nurse should occur as rapidly as possible. Students may be too traumatized or embarrassed to

self-identify significant health histories, but may require special attention in injury assessment.

At times, school nurses have been directed to leave their assigned school(s) to provide urgent care to students off-campus (e.g., at the site of a bus accident en route to school). Rarely is this advisable since EMS is better prepared to handle a true emergency, with necessary equipment and an ambulance, and the school nurse may be needed to care for other students in the school building. Once the students arrive at school, however, the school nurse should triage, assess, and intervene, as appropriate, to address student health needs. When districts or principals do expect school nurses to travel off campus to the site of accidents or to attend ill persons on adjacent property, it is wise to first obtain consultation about this expectation from the school nurse supervisor, the school district's attorney, and the state board of nursing. School district or campus planning should address who will do what and when. Crisis drills help to eliminate spontaneous but ill-conceived reactions.

Transporting or Accompanying Injured and Ill Students to a Medical Facility

Transporting students in private vehicles can leave the school nurse and school district vulnerable to liability should the passenger(s) sustain injury. An injury can be sustained by the student due to an automobile accident or by development of complications related to his or her own health condition. The school nurse cannot attend the student and drive a car at the same time, nor do private vehicles have emergency equipment (including telecommunications) should a student require emergency care during travel. Furthermore, school personnel who transport students may not be covered by school insurance should an accident occur, or they may be covered by the school's insurance only after the staff's personal insurance is expended. Transporting students may also be considered under state law or insurance provisions as using a private automobile as a business vehicle.

Transportation of students for health reasons should not be an expectation placed in the job description of school nurses, other pupil services' professionals, or assistants. Depending on the student's health status, transportation should be provided by the parent, the district in its own vehicles, a contracted transportation company, an ambulance or, when appropriate, by public transportation, such as a taxi. Guidelines for when it is appropriate to use public transportation and how it is paid for should be included in district policy and procedure.

If the job description of school nurses in a district includes transportation of students in their own vehicles, the school nurses should obtain written evidence of the district's policy and insurance coverage. Additionally, they should review their personal auto coverage and should request from an administrator an opportunity to consult with the district's attorney. They should also consider consultation with a personal attorney regarding the implications of this responsibility with respect to personal liability and auto insurance.

District Policy on Emergency Transportation. School districts should have a policy that clearly specifies how school personnel should proceed when parents are not available to or cannot provide transportation to an appropriate health care facility for their ill or injured child. Policies and procedures should clearly state that EMS (9-1-1) will be called in **all** emergencies and that parents will be responsible for the expenses incurred. School district policy should never allow parental "choice" on whether or not the school should call an ambulance in a true emergency and the meaning of "emergency" should be clearly defined in district policy. The only exception to this policy, if allowed by law, should be for a student with a DNR (Do Not Resuscitate) order that has been legally executed, authorized by the parent, and incorporated into an individualized emergency plan for the student. (For more information on DNR orders, see especially chapter 14, but also chapters 3, 4 and 11).

Accompanying Students on an Ambulance. If a parent is not immediately available in an emergency, it is reasonable, prudent, and compassionate for a school official to accompany a student being transported by ambulance to the hospital and remain with the student until a parent arrives. A school official can provide support to a frightened student, give general information, and demonstrate to parents that the school did not abandon their child. Since ambulance attendants are fully trained to handle emergencies and become legally responsible for a student's care as soon as they arrive at the scene and during transportation, it is rarely appropriate for a school nurse to leave her school-wide responsibilities to accompany one student on an ambulance. This is true, as well, for a health aide who is responsible for first aid for the other students in the building.

It is sound policy for school nurses and school principals to collaborate in identifying the most appropriate person in each situation to accompany a student to the hospital in an ambulance (or to meet the ambulance

there). No school staff member, including a school nurse, who accompanies a student in an ambulance or waits at the hospital for arrival of the parents is authorized to provide care and rarely, if ever, would he or she have legal authority to consent to care in place of the parent. Since sending the school nurse leaves the rest of the school, or in some cases the entire district, without a nurse to respond to the health and safety needs of other students, it is usually more appropriate to send another professional to support the student until a parent arrives.

Although school nurses are rarely the best choice among school officials to accompany a student to the hospital, it is important to understand the concept of "abandonment" in relation to this issue. Abandonment is the "unilateral termination of the health care provider-patient relationship before further health care providers have arrived to continue the care" (Brainerd, 1997). It is not considered abandonment for the school nurse to leave her school building for a good reason unless he or she knowingly leaves behind a student in need of urgent or constant nursing services. It is abandonment if the school nurse observes an emergency, or initiates care in an emergency, and leaves the scene or refuses to provide care before other qualified individuals (e.g., EMS personnel) arrive to take over.

The difference is highlighted by the following example. A school nurse is attending two students in the school health center: one student whose respiratory status is compromised due to an acute episode of asthma, and a second student whose seizures have continued beyond 20 minutes (i.e., status epilepticus, a medical emergency). For the student with seizures, the nurse calls 9-1-1 and summons an ambulance. If the school nurse should then decide (or follow an administrative directive) to accompany the student with seizures on the ambulance, leaving behind the asthmatic student (whose respiratory function is compromised but responding to medication), that nurse may be liable for using poor judgment—and for abandoning the asthmatic student—should the student's airway stop responding to the medication, leading to deterioration of respiratory function, and eventual harm to the student.

On the other hand, there are rare occasions when it may be appropriate for the school nurse to accompany a student during transportation to an emergency room. For example, a student who has a history of being abused and is consequently extremely fearful of strangers, especially males, requires emergency transportation due to a head injury sustained from falling off a swing. If the ambulance crew is all male, the school nurse is the only female readily available, and another nurse in the district can take call (provide back-up) for the school, it may be appropriate for the nurse and principal to decide that the nurse should accompany the fearful student until the parent or guardian arrives at the hospital. However, a back-up plan for covering urgent or emergent health needs of other students must be reasonable (under the circumstances) and activated.

The Final Decision to Transport in an Emergency. When students or parents decline emergency transportation, EMS should still be called (as required by district policy) and EMS personnel should make the final decision regarding the situation. Police can be summoned for assistance in life-threatening circumstances. The police have authority to restrain an individual when he or she is at high risk of personal injury or of harming others. The school nurse or other school official should make every attempt to talk through a student's (or parent's) anxiety and resistance before resorting to authoritarian coercion. Sometimes, direction from an authority figure will help calm a combative student.

Concern regarding the family's financial expense for an ambulance should never cause a delay in calling for an ambulance in a true emergency. School districts and their personnel are first responsible for student safety. When there is disagreement between an administrator and a school nurse, and the school nurse's clinical assessment and judgment indicate the need for emergency transportation to a hospital, the nurse's professional judgment must prevail, regardless of any directive to the contrary. In a civil action, it is likely that the court would hold the nurse to a higher standard of care than the administrator, based on the nurse's preparation and license as a health care professional. From a risk management perspective, an administrator is wise to follow the medical advice of the health professionals hired by the district to make such medical decisions, rather than assume responsibility for decisions that he or she is neither educationally prepared, nor legally qualified to make.

General Disaster Planning

Since school districts are required to take reasonable steps to protect the safety of their student population, they must prepare not only for individual emergencies, but also for crises that produce multiple casualties. Examples of multiple casualty events include mace sprayed into the environment, multiple injuries occurring from violence at school, and trauma experienced during bad weather, such as earthquakes and torna-

does. Preparation should be targeted to those disasters that can reasonably be expected to occur in the community or region in which the school is located.

Disaster planning requires collaborative efforts between the school district and other community organizations, including the local Emergency Medical System (EMS), and police and fire departments. Planning should include the determination of necessary supplies, including first-aid materials, water, food, emergency medications, utensils such as shovels, and protective mechanisms from inclement weather, such as plastic bags for ponchos. Periodic testing of the disaster plan demonstrates a good faith effort on the part of the school district to appropriately prepare school personnel to handle such events.

Parental Permission for School Health and Nursing Services (Parental Notice and Consent)

State laws and regulations, common law, and professional practice standards in education and health govern requirements related to parental notice and consent for student participation in specific school nursing and health services programs. With or without mandates, schools should minimally provide parental notice regarding general health services provided in the district, for example, in the student handbook or annual calendar. Such notice should include information regarding the credentials of personnel providing health services and the amount of time they are available in the school, as well as relevant policies and procedures (e.g., medication administration and emergency procedures). Notice should be given to parents prior to all routine health screenings. Notice allows parents to question the screening (e.g., rationale, methodology) and to refuse their child's participation. When screenings for communicable disease or infestation are indicated, parents should be notified, although notice may occur at the end of the first day of screenings and should include appropriate educational information for additional screening and management at home.

Parental notice may also be required by law or district policy prior to health education programs. Regardless of whether required, it may be prudent practice, especially when the health education content is controversial in the community. From a practice point of view, parent participation and collaboration in developing, implementing, and evaluating health education and health services are critical to the long-term success of such programs.

When health services for a student requires nursing assessment or intervention beyond those provided to all students, written informed parental consent is essential. For example, schools must obtain specific, written parental authorization for any medical treatment to be provided for their child at school, including medication administration, and for any in-depth assessment which is significantly different from routine nursing services. They must also obtain written informed consent for physical examinations that schools offer students to help them meet requirements for sports participation and state- or school-mandated health assessments. (See the 1999 Pennsylvania case discussed two paragraphs below. Parental notification and consent issues are also discussed in chapter 7 related to minor's rights, chapter 12 in relation to special education and early intervention and later in this chapter under "Immunizations" and "Child Abuse").

"The right of consent involves the right of refusal" (Guido, p. 128). In our pluralistic society, schools can anticipate that some parents will determine that certain health services or programs are not in their child's best interests. This determination may be based on religious or philosophic beliefs, social or cultural mores, preferences for alternative health practices or other reasons. The law generally allows parents wide discretionary authority in child rearing, but there are variations in state law regarding parental consent requirements and permitted exemptions to student health requirements for attendance in public schools.

In a 1999 Pennsylvania case (*Doe v. Vahanvaty, MD et al. & Tucker v. Vahanvaty, MD et al.*) a federal jury awarded $7,500, payable by the East Stroudsburg School District, to each of eight girls whose Fourth Amendment rights protecting them against "unreasonable searches" were violated, according to a federal court judge's ruling, when external genital exams were performed by a school physician to meet the requirements of state-mandated physical exams. Prior to the judge's ruling, the jury had returned a verdict that neither the girls nor their families had given informed consent for the genital exams. The physical exams were provided by the middle school following seven written notifications that the physicals were required for school attendance and that, if not obtained from students' own physicians, would be provided in school by a school physician, as required by law. When the cutoff date came, those students who did not have the required physical exam report on file and whose families had not responded to the notification of the scheduled in-school exam were examined. While families were notified of the exams, details of the exams were not provided and written informed consent was not obtained. The school district may also be liable for approximately one half million dollars in attorneys' fees incurred by the families

who brought the case. Originally, the district, school nurses and school physician were named in the suit; the cases against the school nurses were dismissed, and the physician settled separately out of court following the jury's verdict. Reportedly, the physician's insurance company agreed to pay $25,000 to each family. The case will not be appealed by the school district or physician (McDonald, 1999; Grossman, 1999; Groff, 1999; "Federal case will have impact on community," 1999).

Permission for Emergency Treatment

It is not wise for districts to "ask permission" of parents to allow them to intervene in a true emergency to save the life or limb of a student or to transport the student by ambulance to a hospital when necessary. School districts should have policy and procedures that clearly delineate actions that school personnel will take in all cases of actual and potential emergencies, and they should annually notify parents of such policies and procedures. The only exception to this policy should be for students who have an individualized emergency care plan under § 504 or IDEA that directs personnel to take specified actions for that student. For example, it is appropriate to collaboratively develop an individualized emergency care plan when a minor student has a legally executed—and accepted—DNR (Do Not Resuscitate) order from the student's physician and documented authorization from the parent. (See chapter 14, in particular, as well as chapters 4, 6 and 11.)

Information about a district's policies and procedures on handling accidents, illnesses and emergencies, including when 9-1-1 will be called, should be clearly explained in appropriate language(s) and written materials sent to all parents. An important opportunity for providing emergency policy and procedure information is when the "emergency information card" is sent home for parents to fill out and sign. This card should request information on how to contact the parent or other responsible adult in an emergency. Since a doctor can legally provide immediate treatment without parental consent to save a minor patient's life or prevent the loss of an organ, limb or function (Springhouse Corporation, 1996), asking the parent to sign consent for such emergency treatment is not necessary and, when consent is refused, is legally and clinically problematic. Furthermore, since a signed authorization card gives only general consent to treatment, it is unlikely to meet the standard of "informed consent" in a given situation, and a physician is unlikely to treat a minor's non-emergency condition with only the parent's *general* consent in hand. "The doctrine of informed consent reminds us to respect persons by fully and accurately providing information relevant to exercising their decision-making rights" (Committee on Bioethics, p. 2). (See chapters 7 and 8 for additional information regarding informed consent, and chapter 3 for additional information on ethical principles.)

This is true regardless of whether parents have written the school specifying that no medical treatments should ever be administered to their child. Except when a legally valid DNR order is in effect, school officials must take action to preserve the life or limb of a student in a life-threatening emergency. District policies and procedures should include explicit directions regarding actions school personnel must take when confronted with true emergency circumstances. Parents of students with complex medical conditions and repetitive medical emergencies (e.g., seizures for more than 20 or 30 minutes) sometimes refuse to give the local hospital permission for emergency interventions or ask the school not to transport their child by ambulance, even if school personnel judge the student's condition to constitute an emergency. In these situations, districts need to inform the parents, in writing, that the district's policy in an emergency is to call EMS (9-1-1) and let the EMS personnel make the decision regarding transportation to the hospital by ambulance.

Schools should adequately prepare their personnel to recognize actual and potential emergency situations and to take actions accordingly. Personnel responsible for determining that an emergency exists should be qualified and trained to make that determination, especially for students with known risks of health emergencies. The inability of school personnel to recognize impending emergencies may be a cause of later findings of liability for school districts, and inadequately prepared nurses are not immune from making poor judgments in this regard.

Parental Authorization for Communications Between Authorized Prescribers and School Nurses Executing Medical Orders

Neither health professionals nor educators may release specific information about students without parental authorization. Therefore, under most circumstances, school personnel must request parental permission to share student health information with a child's physician or other health care provider, and the health care provider must have parental permission to share information with appropriate school personnel. However, a different legal relationship exists between a health care provider (e.g., physician, advanced practice registered nurse, dentist) and the school when the provider "orders" a medical treatment to be given to a

student at school by a health professional (e.g., medication administration or clean intermittent catheterization) and the parent gives informed consent for the school to implement the medical order. This legal relationship is based on licensure laws. These laws both limit who can carry out such orders and, in the case of orders to nurses, require nurses to work under the direction of a physician (or other authorized prescriber) when carrying out prescribed medical therapies and treatments. This relationship also exists between authorized prescribers and other health professionals who implement medical orders, for example, physical therapists, occupational therapists, and speech and language pathologists. Both the mandated "direction," usually given in the form of "medical orders," and standards for ensuring safety in implementing such orders, require communication between the prescriber and the professional carrying out the order.

When a parent gives informed consent for a medical therapy or treatment to be provided in school, consent (permission) is given with the expectation that the care will be provided safely and according to professional standards of practice. In order to give "informed" consent, parents need information that explains the rationale for and limitations of appropriate communications between an authorized medical prescriber and school nurse (or other school health professional responsible for implementing the order of a medical prescriber). This information should be clearly written on every parent authorization form, including authorization for medication administration and physical therapy. The form should state that, when parents authorize a medical treatment for their child in school, such authorization includes permission for appropriate communications between the school health professional and the medical prescriber related to the specific treatment in question. Legally appropriate school nurse-medical prescriber communications, based on the medical orders, generally include the following areas:

- the prescription or treatment itself (e.g., questions regarding dosage, method of administration, potential drug interactions, size of catheter for emergency insertion into the track of a dislodged gastrostomy tube);

- implementation of the treatment in school (e.g., questions regarding safety concerns, infection control issues, or modifications in the treatment order related to the school setting or student's academic schedule); and

- student outcomes from the treatment (e.g., questions regarding observed side effects, possible untoward reactions, observations of behavior changes in the classroom).

In addition to including this information on the parent authorization form, districts should establish and publish school policy that requires parents who request specialized health care services in school, including medication administration, to permit necessary communications between the prescriber and the school health professional (e.g., school nurse) responsible for implementing the specialized care. "Necessary communications" should be limited, as described above, and defined. The policy should also clarify that parents will be (1) notified of, and informed about, the purpose of such communications, preferably in advance of the communications, and (2) included in all decisions related to changes regarding an order or plan of care.

If a health professional is required to provide a medical therapy or treatment without the ability to confer with the authorized prescriber, it creates clinically unsafe situations for students and legally untenable situations for both the school district and school health professional. Parents rarely refuse to permit prescriber-school health professional communications, but occasionally some do. The best management for this possibility is prevention. As indicated above, the best preventive strategies are as follows:

1. implementing school policy that requires professional-prescriber communications and

2. developing consent forms that include parental authorization for such communications, as a necessary prerequisite to school-provided medical treatment.

If a district does not have such a policy in place, and informed consent is not requested on the district's parent-authorization forms, both the district and school health professional are wise to refuse to carry out medical orders for a student whose parent refuses to consent to reasonable and appropriately limited prescriber-school health professional communications.

Promoting Informed Consent

In addition to issues regarding communications, school nurses should share with parents all pertinent information necessary to assist them to

1. understand their options in the school environment, including pros and cons of alternate strategies for implementing the care requested;

2. make informed choices about those options; and

3. give informed consent.

Examples of the types of information that may be essential to informed consent include the following:

- modifications necessary in the school setting;

- impact on the student's academic schedule;

- differences between administration at home and in school (e.g., increased distractions);

- safety and privacy issues;

- plans for administration or monitoring, including credentials of assigned personnel;

- back-up plans; and

- appraisal of the student's self-care abilities.

Student Authorization for Specialized Nursing Services

As children mature, families, pediatricians, and nurses strive to involve them, as appropriate, in decision making about their own health care, including treatment procedures. Accordingly, school nurses should include students in the process of obtaining informed consent for treatments needed routinely at school. As with families, school nurses should share all pertinent information necessary to assist students in understanding their options in the school environment, making choices when feasible, and giving informed consent. Involvement of students in the decision-making process acknowledges their right to increasing autonomy in and responsibility for managing their own health care and promoting their own wellness. The pace at which students are involved in their own self-care, however, should generally be consistent with family preferences. Involving minor students in giving informed consent for themselves, therefore, requires family collaboration.

Employee Protections Under OSHA

Depending on state requirements and school district personnel assignments, job descriptions of school nurses may include some responsibility for employee health and safety programs. For example, school nurses and physicians may be responsible for carrying out the school district's obligations to protect its employees from known work hazards, including toxic and hazardous substances. Regulations of the Occupational Safety and Health Administration (OSHA) of the U.S. Department of Labor require such protection for employees in the private sector. It is easy to reference information about OSHA's various standards and requirements, including applicability to schools, at the department's website (www.osha.gov).

The intent of OSHA standards and regulations is to provide protection to workers. While OSHA regulations do not address client safety issues, or obligations of institutions or agencies in maintaining client safety, clients (e.g., students) benefit indirectly from these regulations. Federal authority extends to all private sector employers with one or more employees and to federal civilian employees. In addition, states may extend these protections to public employees under their own occupational safety and health programs, by submitting state plans for approval under § 18(b) of the Occupational Safety and Health Act. These plans must adopt standards and enforce requirements that are "at least as effective as federal requirements." In 1993, OSHA reported that of 25 state plans submitted by states and territories, 23 cover the private and public sectors and two cover the public sector only (U.S. Department of Labor, OSHA, 1993).

As with all OSHA regulations, penalties can be levied for lack of compliance with OSHA standards. In those states in which governmental agencies are required to meet OSHA standards, school districts have been inspected and fined by the responsible state agency for failure to comply with applicable regulations. School administrators and school nurses can benefit from consultation regarding the application of federal and state OSHA regulations in school settings in their state. Questions can be addressed to the state agency responsible for administering and interpreting OSHA requirements (e.g., state department of labor or occupational health) or, for federal requirements, to the regional offices of OSHA. (See the OSHA web site [above] for additional information.)

Two significant federal regulations of OSHA are the *Occupational Exposure to Bloodborne Pathogens*, December 6, 1991, with 1992 and 1996 amendments, and the *Hazard Communication Rule*.

Bloodborne Pathogen Standard

The intent of OSHA's Bloodborne Pathogen Standard, also referred to as "Universal Precautions," is to provide protection for employees against bloodborne diseases that are transmitted through exposure to infectious blood and other body fluids. The OSHA regulations, 29 CFR 1910.1030, can be accessed on the Web

(http://www.osha-slc.gov/OshStd_data/1910_1030.html). The Bloodborne Pathogen Standard was effective as of March 1992.

OSHA's term "Universal Precautions" is sometimes confused with "Standard Precautions." Distinct from OSHA, the Hospital Infection Control Practices Advisory Committee of the Centers for Disease Control (CDC), issued "new isolation guidelines for the care of hospitalized patients" in 1996. These guidelines rely on "an expanded set of universal practices, designated Standard Precautions, designed for the care of all patients regardless of their diagnosis or presumed infectious status." The expanded Standard Precautions apply to blood, all body fluids, secretions and excretions, nonintact skin, and mucous membranes, and are intended to "reduce the risk of the transmission of microorganisms from both recognized and unrecognized sources of infection in hospitals" (Committee on Infectious Diseases, American Academy of Pediatrics, 1997, pp. 100–101). Although OSHA only requires "Universal Precautions," prudent school employees should practice "Standard Precautions" to reduce the risk of communicable disease transmission.

In those states in which public schools are not mandated to follow OSHA regulations, school districts should consider the intent of the requirements, since their implementation can significantly benefit both school personnel and students. Regardless of state mandates, school districts should seek expert consultation regarding the costs and benefits of following the OSHA standard and the potential risks of not following it. When a school district makes reasonable efforts to implement Standard or Universal Precautions and related infection control practices, they demonstrate good faith efforts to protect the health and safety of staff and students, a risk-management strategy.

School nurses and administrators must collaborate in designating jobs and assigning school staff to jobs that may expose employees to bloodborne pathogens. Under OSHA, these job assignments can signal additional financial and legal commitments for public schools. The OSHA regulations obligate employers to provide training promptly after employment and yearly thereafter for personnel whose regular job responsibilities put them at risk for bloodborne pathogens exposure. The training must be offered during the employee's scheduled work hours and at no cost to the employee. Additionally, employers are responsible for providing the following, at no cost to employees at risk:

- accessible hand-washing facilities;
- personal protective supplies and equipment;

- approved disposal equipment (e.g. sharps containers and waste bags);

- hepatitis B immunizations;

- engineering controls (as ventilation devices and self-sheathing needles);

- policies and procedures (e.g. policies about not recapping needles and using protective devices); and

- immediate post-exposure medical evaluation and counseling.

Under Standard Precautions, several techniques of infection prevention and control are addressed, including hand washing, handling of appropriate equipment and supplies (e.g., gloves, masks, eye protections and shields, non-sterile gowns, mouth pieces, resuscitation bags, and other ventilation devices), and managing contaminated clothing and other materials. As the AAP *Red Book* (Committee on Infectious Diseases, 1997) states, in bold, "Hand washing before and after each patient contact remains the single most important routine practice in the control of nosocomial [hospital-spread] infections." Hand washing is also the first line of defense against the spread of infections in schools, both in the classroom and in the health center.

Use of Protective Devices by School Nurses

Whether a state requires public schools to comply with OSHA's Bloodborne Pathogen Standard, school nurses should always be prepared to respond to emergency situations with personal protective equipment. This is a standard of nursing practice to which nurses are accountable, no matter the clinical setting in which they practice. Furthermore, it could be considered abandonment if a nurse refuses to give CPR to a client due to the unavailability or inadequacy of protective devices. In Oregon, the State Board of Nursing clarified that the minimum protective equipment nurses should employ are a mask, gloves, and goggles (personal communication with M. A. Thompson, Oregon State Board of Nursing, November 1998). Equipment should be routinely checked to identify and remedy deterioration in the quality of barrier devices. School nurses can use situations requiring protective devices, including gloves, gowns and masks, as teaching opportunities to provide information and modeling for students, families, and school personnel regarding disease prevention and transmission.

OSHA's Hazard Communication Rule

The language of OSHA's Hazard Communication Rule, 29 CFR 1910.1200, requires that all employees be made aware of potentially hazardous chemicals used in a building. This regulation was first published August 24, 1987, and has been subsequently amended. All potentially hazardous chemicals now come with Material Supply Data Sheets (MSDS). The school nurse may be assigned to keep the source document current. Personnel must be advised about the location and contents of the MSDS information. The advisement should explain the "warning" symbols and information to which employees must pay heed. For example, chemical containers will have a warning diamond or statement to indicate flammability, reactivity, health warnings, and the personal protective equipment required during handling. The regulation can be found online (www.osha-slc.gov/OshStd_data/1910_1200.html).

School policies and procedures should require that employees check with the school's safety officer before bringing chemical products into the work environment. Employees are entitled to information on the chemicals that they might use in their job performance and the potential risks from exposure to those chemicals. For example, school personnel may routinely come in contact with toner fluid for copy machines. The MSDS information for the fluid should be in the work area where the product is used. Such products, if inhaled in quantity, can be potential hallucinogens or may ignite if exposed to heat. Pediculocides (products for the treatment of head lice) are an example of potentially hazardous chemicals. If school nurses apply such products, they should have access to the corresponding data sheets.

Environmental Safety Issues

The school environment can have a significant impact on the safety and well being of students and staff. Many environmental factors can pose potential risks, including temperature, air quality, allergens, water quality, food safety, and hazardous chemicals, waste, and equipment. Sometimes they can be as simple as wet floors, as in the South Carolina situation discussed under "Documentation" in chapter 5. Unfortunately, environmental issues can also be very complex, such as those related to air quality and "Sick Building Syndrome." Air quality issues are not uncommon in school buildings, both old and new. In the 1994 nationwide survey of 10,000 schools by the U.S. General Accounting Office, 60% of all schools surveyed reported at least one inadequate building feature (e.g., poor ventilation equipment, leaky roof) and 50% reported at least one unsatisfactory environmental factor (e.g., poor indoor air quality, inadequate heating) (Spindel, 1997).

Schools need to respond to concerns from students and families about the negative impact of the school environment on performance or attendance. In the cases of *Punxsutawney Area School District v. Kanouff* and *Punxsutawney Area School District v. Dean,* 1995), the district was found to be in violation of the Individuals with Disabilities Act (IDEA) because it failed to implement evaluation when the families of two students brought concerns to the district regarding the negative impact of the environment on their children's health. The students' symptoms caused extended absenteeism that resulted in deficient academic performance. One parent requested a transfer to a neighboring school, but the district offered home tutoring as the only option. The two students were awarded compensatory education.

Based on several federal and state laws and regulations, and case law decisions, employers, including school boards, have a "general duty" to provide a safe and healthy work environment. To do so, employers should conduct regular environmental assessments and undertake environmental maintenance and improvement activities, as indicated. Environmental assessments and recommendations for ongoing maintenance and improvement require knowledge of applicable laws and regulations, and collaboration with consultants in other systems, such as the state departments of environmental quality and protection, public health, sanitation, and labor. In some states, for example Connecticut, state law gives the school medical advisor responsibility for general oversight of environmental safety in public schools (C.G.S. § 10-20). The medical advisors delegate much of this responsibility to school nurses and public health sanitarians who, ideally, collaborate to inspect school buildings annually and submit written reports of such inspections to the medical advisor and school district authorities.

Prevention Strategies

School districts can best manage their obligations to address employee and student concerns regarding environmental conditions through a preventive health and safety program. Prevention of environmental problems, rather than more costly treatment and crisis intervention, should be the primary goal of health and safety programs. School nurses, in collaboration with school officials and other health professionals, can take a leadership role in the identification and implementation of

preventive measures in school settings. Such measures might include the following:

- assigning a subcommittee to the school district's school health advisory council or healthy school team to establish and oversee environmental prevention and intervention strategies for the district;
- implementing disease prevention and control methods (e.g., general hand washing and standard precautions education and practices);
- training on the identification of, and immediate response to, allergic reactions of students and staff;
- using incident and accident reporting data, as well as health room visit/nursing diagnosis data, to identify potential hazards in the school environment;
- routine inspection of playground equipment for structural and developmental safety;
- parking and idling buses in locations that eliminate the potential for intake of exhaust fumes in the school;
- developing guidelines regarding the appropriateness of and measures for handling animals safely in the classroom;
- scheduling activities, such as mowing grass and cleaning, to diminish student and employee exposure;
- implementing safe insecticide spraying programs, including notifying employees, students, and families, and coordinating alternative methods for pest control;
- providing guidelines for lifting and back safety awareness programs;
- ensuring adequate fresh air intake and humidity control; and
- instituting policies and procedures for handling the concerns of staff and students about environmental issues, including documentation.

In the March 24, 1997, edition of *MTA Today*, the Official Publication of the Massachusetts Teachers Association (MTA), one of several stories related to air quality problems in Massachusetts schools reported that significant illnesses and respiratory complaints of several teachers in a school in Haverhill had pointed to air quality as "at least one source of the problem." The local teacher's union had asked the MTA to have the building tested for air quality and several problems were identified. Because the school and district's administrators took the complaints, study findings, and ongoing problems seriously, however, "the [local union] did not have to file a single grievance over health and safety issues in the building." This was true despite the fact that not all existing problems with the building could be fixed, the state refused funding for renovations (not cost-effective), and the town defeated an alternative proposal to build a new school (Spindel, 1997).

This same edition of *MTA Today* contains legal advice for school personnel and local teacher unions regarding how to proceed when indoor air quality is problematic. A 1998 article, "The Indoor Air We Breathe," (Oliver & Shackleton) in the publication *Public Health Reports*, provides information about health problems related to poor indoor air quality today in buildings, including schools, prevention strategies, and the importance of taking complaints seriously.

One resource that may be helpful to school administrators, school nurses, teachers, parents, and other members of a school's or district's environmental committee, both for prevention purposes and for addressing specific problems or complaints, is a kit called "Indoor Air Quality: Tools for Schools." This kit was first made available in 1995 through a program of the U.S. Environmental Protection Agency (EPA) in collaboration with several co-sponsoring national organizations, such as the American Lung Association (ALA) and National Education Association. It may be available

through a state or local teacher union, state ALA office, or state parent-teacher association. Alternatively, contact the EPA in Washington, D.C. (202-233-9030).

Animals in schools. Schools should develop specific policies and procedures for animals and pets on school grounds and in the classroom. Exposing students and staff to some animals may be inappropriate for safety reasons (e.g. iguanas, ferrets, and raccoons, due to bites) or for communicable disease reasons (e.g. turtles, due to salmonella). Exposure to animals may be potentially unhealthy for individual students and staff (e.g., allergies, asthma, fears). Potential hazards for even a few students may conflict with anticipated benefits for others. Some school districts have barred all animals from the classroom, for these reasons.

Consultation with a local, regional, or state department of health regarding what animals to exclude from schools is essential when developing and reviewing related school policies. If animals are not barred entirely, school administrators responsible for making case-by-case decisions will want to confer with the school nurse regarding known health conditions of students in the classroom and building. See Figure 6-1 for a sample policy and Figure 6-2 for sample procedures from the Chisago Lakes Independent School District #2144. Figure 6-3 shows the District's teacher request form and Figure 6-4 shows its parent permission form.

Figure 6-1.

CHISAGO LAKES ISD #2144

Adopted: *8/13/98*
Revised: *2/11/99*

540   ANIMALS IN SCHOOL BUILDINGS

To insure the safety of students and community, animals will be allowed in school buildings *only with prior approval* of building principals or the Community Education Director and in accordance with the Guidelines & Procedures on Animals established by the Board of Education.

Figure 6-2.

540   Guidelines & Procedures on Animals in School Buildings

Chisago Lakes Area Schools is concerned about the health and safety of every individual that enters a school building in the district. Therefore, the following guidelines have been established by the school district with regard to animals.

1.   Animals, either live or dead, will be allowed in school district buildings <u>only</u> if they meet the following criteria:

   a.   air quality needs
   b.   health needs
   c.   curriculum goals
   d.   animal care & sanitation concerns

2.   The processing of large animals domestic or wild will be partnered with local businesses at their facilities.

3.   The teacher is responsible for:

   a.   notifying the building principal in writing that an animal will be in their classroom;
   b.   the cleanliness, containment, transportation and humane treatment of the animal;
   c.   maintaining a healthy classroom environment that responds to the sensitivity of students & staff with health concerns;
   d.   student hygiene after handling animals;
   e.   notifying parents of the instructional use of animals in the classrooms;
   f.   notifying the animal's owner of the responsibilities and the liabilities of bringing an animal to school.

4.   Parents must secure permission from the classroom teacher prior to bringing any animal to school and the classroom teacher must secure permission from the principal.

5.   Final authority regarding animals in school buildings rests with the individual building principal.

Used with permission, Chisago Lakes Area Schools ISD #2144, Lindstrom, Minnesota.

Figure 6-3.

CHISAGO LAKES ISD #2144
PERMISSION TO INCLUDE ANIMALS IN THE CLASSROOM

(To be completed by the TEACHER)

Teacher: _____

Class: _____

Name of Animal / Classification: _____

Brief description of how you will involve the animal(s) during instructional activities:

_____

_____

_____

Length of time the animal(s) will be housed in the classroom or on school grounds:

_____

History / origin of animal: _____

Plans for the release or disposition of animal(s) after instructional time: _____

_____

Animal handler / owner: _____

I have read and agree to abide by the guidelines for use of animals in the classroom.

Teacher's Signature: _____ Date: _____

(To be completed by the ANIMAL OWNER)

I understand that I am liable for my animal's actions while on school property.

Animal Owner: _____ *Date:* _____

Phone: _____

Homeowner's Insurance Company: _____ _____ *Policy #* _____

Attach copy of current rabies vaccination certificate if applicable.

Approved: ❏ Disapproved: ❏ _____	
Principal's Signature	*Date*

Original: Principal   *Canary: HS Health Office*   *Pink: Teacher*

Used with permission, Chisago Lakes Area Schools ISD #2144, Lindstrom, Minnesota.

Figure 6-4.

**CHISAGO LAKES ISD #2144
PARENT PERMISSION FOR STUDENTS
TO PARTICIPATE IN THE CARE AND HANDLING OF
ANIMALS IN THE CLASSROOM**

Dear Parents:

In the course of the year, your child may be exposed to the handling and care of animals in the classroom. More specifically, the animal(s) to be included in the instructional are:

_____

District procedures for the care and safety of your child and the animal have been developed. It is my intent to abide by these guidelines and insure the safety of the children in the classroom, to teach them the proper care and handling of such animals, and to provide hygienic conditions in the classroom. I would like your permission to allow your child to participate in this instructional activity. Please note any health concerns on the permission form, sign the form below and return it to me.

Sincerely,

_____
(Teacher)

Child's name: _____

As a parent of a child in _____ School, in _____
(teacher's name)

classroom, I give my permission for my child to be exposed to the animals included in that

classroom for instructional purposes. I understand that my child will be given proper instructions

in the handling and care of the animals.

Health Concerns: _____

_____

Parent/Guardian's **Signature:** _____ Date: _____

Please **print** parent/guardian's name: _____ Phone: _____

Used with permission, Chisago Lakes Area Schools ISD #2144, Lindstrom, Minnesota.

Incident and Accident Reports

A major function of school risk-management departments, administrators, or consultants is to assist districts in identifying risks that might precipitate illness or injury and eliminating them from the school environment. School nurses should be involved in risk management assessment in their building(s), both because of their knowledge base and the relevant information they collect through systematic documentation of student and staff visits to the health room for illness and injury care.

Excellent sources of data for risk management analysis are accident and incident reports. Generally, the purposes of accident and incident reports (also known as variance, situation, occurrence, or unusual reports) include the following:

- preventing student safety or care problems;

- providing timely notice to administration of incidents and accidents, as well as situations that could result in accidents;

- tracking potentially hazardous conditions for risk assessment and elimination;

- documenting facts for insurance claims; and

- preparing for the possibility of a suit.

From a legal perspective, accident and incident forms serve the same purpose—to bring attention to "an event that is inconsistent with the...ordinary routine, regardless of whether injury occurs" (Springhouse Corporation, 1996). In schools, accident forms are generally used when an injury to a student occurs and an incident form is used for an unusual event in which injury is not necessarily involved. In reality, an incident form can be used for both purposes and this chapter will refer to both as incident forms.

The risk management authority of a school district should provide guidelines for documenting incidents and accidents that occur on school grounds and in all school activities. The staff member witnessing or first arriving at the event should complete the portion of the form describing what happened and what was done at the scene. According to Springhouse Corporation (1996), nurses, aides, and managers have a duty to report any incident of which they have first-hand knowledge. If school nurses need to include second-hand information in a report, they should use quotation marks to designate material provided by others (e.g., Mrs. Daly reports that "Jessy tripped on the sidewalk curb after exiting the bus"). Other witnesses

should cosign the form, agreeing with or adding additional observations to the description of what occurred. Such documentation, using district-approved forms, should be completed factually, promptly (the same day), and thoroughly.

While legal advice to school districts will vary depending on the attorney advisor, the characteristics of the school district, local and state variations in legal precedence and practices, and school district policy should specify the content of incident reports, the number of copies made, and their circulation. In general, circulation of an incident form should be limited to those who need it to fulfill the purpose of the form (for instance, risk management administrator, business manager, school nurse supervisor). Copies should be limited to the number required to provide those individuals with the information they need, or fewer if the copies can be shared, and should be filed according to district policy and procedures.

Only factual information limited to observations of what happened, preferably first-hand, should be recorded. No notation of potential liability or liability concerns should ever be recorded on an incident form. Furthermore, suggestions for correcting an underlying potential cause should not be included except when the form specifically requests information related to possible causes and recommendations for corrective actions. If a district's form does request such information, it should also require the appropriate supervisor and risk manager to document any corrective actions taken and plans for follow-up. If such outcome information is not asked for on the incident form itself, it should nevertheless be documented in order to demonstrate the district's good faith efforts to identify and eliminate potential risks to students and staff.

Confidentiality of health information on incident forms can be enhanced by using students' initials in place of their full names, as is the practice in many health care settings. Furthermore, only information specific to the incident, that is, factual data about what happened, should be recorded on the form. Confidential information from the student's health record, for example, medical diagnoses or medications (e.g., "student has a past history of drug use"), and speculation regarding possible etiology should never be documented on an incident report.

An incident report does not replace the need for nursing documentation if the nurse evaluates and intervenes with a student or employee. As with any student visit, the school nurse should document the nursing assessment, nursing diagnoses, and actions taken, including notification of the family. Incident reports are filled out in addition to the nursing record, for the reasons cited above, but should not be referred to in the nurse's progress notes.

Incident reports are considered internal, administrative communications, rather than part of the student's health record. If left in a student's health record that is subpoenaed during the discovery phase of a civil action against the school district, an incident form may alert the opposing attorneys to additional situations or information that was not the original intent of the record review. Nevertheless, under FERPA, parents have access to all student records, including incident reports, about their child. Similarly, Aiken and Catalano (1994) advise that incident reports "should not be used for disciplinary action against staff" and "must not be made a part of the employee's personnel file because the file may be subpoenaed" (p.231).

The district's risk management administrator should develop and disseminate clear procedures for directing inquiries of staff, students, and parents regarding incidents at school, incident reports, and potential compensation regarding incidents.

Students with Chronic Health Conditions: Planning and Implementing Services

It is evident that advances in medical technology and changes in the structure of American families and society in general have increased the numbers of students attending school who require direct and indirect professional nursing services. Terms such as *medically fragile, medically complex,* and *technology dependent* are used to refer to 2-4% of U.S. children with high technology or complex medical care needs, while the term "special health care needs" generally refers to a wider spectrum of children and youth with chronic health conditions. The National Center for Health Statistics (1997) reports that

16 to 18% of U.S. children under age 18 currently have a chronic physical, developmental, behavioral, or emotional condition and also require health or related services beyond those required by children generally. This does not include children at elevated risk for chronic physical, developmental, behavioral, or emotional conditions.

Examples of students whose chronic health conditions may require nursing assessment and consultation, as well as ongoing nursing monitoring or management, include those with ADHD, asthma, cere-

bral palsy, cystic fibrosis, depression, diabetes, suppression of the immune system, seizure disorder, and traumatic head injury. It is impossible to make a comprehensive list of conditions that may require ongoing nursing management or monitoring at school. This is due, in part, to the unique response of each child to his or her disease or disabling condition, and individual life circumstances.

Professional nursing services, as they relate to the education of students with special health care needs, include the following:

- assessing student health and developmental status;

- diagnosing individual student responses to their health conditions;

- joint planning for necessary modifications, aids, and services in school, including identification of desired student outcomes;

- implementing or supervising nursing interventions required to promote student wellness, independence, and learning, and prevent complications of disease or disability; and

- evaluating student health outcomes in relation to educational progress.

Figure 6-5 lists responsibilities of school nurses for students with special health care needs. It is important to keep in mind that these responsibilities require collaboration and team decision making. However, the role of the school nurse is critical in assessing the implications of a student's health status and special needs in the school setting, and in making recommendations to the team regarding a safe environment, classroom accommodations, and health services necessary for the student to maintain his or her health and to progress in the educational program.

Once schools become aware of potential health and safety needs of students with chronic conditions, they have an obligation pursuant to § 504 of the 1973 Rehabilitation Act to provide appropriate school health support. While schools and hospitals are very different types of institutions, ensuring client safety (i.e., "doing no harm") is a basic responsibility of both. Failure of school staff to develop adequate emergency plans or provide appropriate assessment of student health status and needs, for example, for an asthmatic student, may have the same legal effect as failure of hospital staff to lower the bed and raise the bedside railings of a disoriented patient.

Figure 6-5.

SCHOOL NURSE RESPONSIBILITIES:
Students with Special Health Care Needs

Assessment

Student   health and development status, medical diagnoses, strengths, coping style, sense of different-
                ness, view of health condition, level of self-help skills, health needs in school, home care
                routine.
Family   vision, strengths, resources, priorities and preferences, coping styles of members, support
                liaison needs, sibling considerations.
Environment   access, personnel, safety, equipment, electricity, privacy, peers.
Medical Care   providers, communications, orders, procedural guidelines, emergency interventions.

Nursing Diagnoses/Collaborative Educational and Medical Problems

Planning/Management before Entry
    Obtain consultation and update knowledge and skills, as needed
    Initiate Individualized Health Care Plan (IHCP)*
    Recommend level of nursing care & program modifications to §504/IEP team
    Collaborate with team in finalizing IHCP
    Incorporate relevant health goal(s) & measurable short-term objectives into ß504 plan/IEP
    Provide personnel training; prepare staff and students, as needed
    Obtain equipment/resources, M.D. orders and parent authorization
    Develop back-up plans

Management after Entry
    Promote student independence, positive coping, least restrictive environment
    Provide expert nursing services - direct care
    Educate/train others to give care, when appropriate
    Supervise delegated care
    Provide consultation regarding student health needs
    Advocate for student/family
    Collaborate with family, team members, community providers & authorized prescribers
    Monitor progress

Evaluation
    Reassess student's health status
    Assess student outcomes with family and team
    Evaluate delegation/supervision plan
    Notify supervisor/administrator
    Alter IHCP accordingly

*IHCP Components
    Nursing diagnoses/collaborative educational and medical problems
    Expected student outcomes: educational/behavioral/physiological goals and objectives (in measurable
        terms)
    Interventions/level of care
    Responsible individuals
    Training/supervision
    Evaluation of student outcomes with timelines

Adapted with permission from the New England Regional Genetics Group (NERGG). Schwab, N. (Ed.). (1992). *Guidelines for the Management of Students with Genetic Disorders: A Manual for School Nurses* (1st ed.). Mount Desert, ME: NERGG.

Both as health professionals and school officials, school nurses should provide leadership in identifying, assessing, and planning for the special needs of students with chronic health conditions. This includes referring students for evaluation of eligibility under § 504 and the Individuals with Disabilities Education Act (IDEA). In *Grafton (ND) Public School* (1993), the school was found in violation of the American Disabilities Act (ADA) and § 504 regulations. The district failed to assign a tutor or accommodate, in any way, the student's numerous absences due to medical disabilities (severe asthma). A school nurse's assessment and referral for team evaluation and planning could have prevented this unfortunate circumstance. (Chapter 2 provides an introduction to these civil rights and special education federal laws. For more in-depth information, refer to chapter 11 regarding student rights and eligibility under § 504 and the Americans with Disabilities Act, and chapter 12 regarding student rights and eligibility under IDEA.)

A conservative estimate of school nurse time allocation indicates that up to 50% of school nurse hours are spent meeting the diverse needs of students with special health care needs (Harrison, Fairchild, & Yaryan, 1995, p. 58). Meeting the special health care needs of students with chronic health conditions presents clinical, ethical and legal challenges for school nurses, especially where staffing and resource allocation is not adequate for the increased health needs of student populations. According to Hootman (1996a), the first priority for care planning is life-threatening conditions, the second is basic needs, and the third is issues of greatest significance to students, parents, and school personnel. A system of prioritization, well-defined in district procedures, can provide a rationale for resource allocation, including staffing, and for decision making in day-to-day practice. The School Nurse Intensity Rating Scale (Klahn, Hays, & Iverson, 1998), Washington State's *Staff Model for the Delivery of School Health Services* (Nursing Care Quality Assurance Commission and Office of the Superintendent of Public Instruction, 2000), or another objective process for prioritizing student needs should assist districts and school nurses in making such decisions. (See chapter 5 under "Case Loads and Staffing" for further discussion.)

It is essential to remember that students who are eligible under § 504 and IDEA have certain rights, and districts have certain responsibilities to identify and provide necessary aids and related services. A district's regular staffing pattern is not an acceptable reason to deny students related services, including nursing services, when eligible students require them in order to access an appropriate education in the least restrictive environment. (See also discussion in chapters 11 and 12).

Policies and procedures of school districts should address the safety needs and specialized health services for students with chronic health conditions. Depending on the acuity and stability of the student's condition and the medical supports necessary to maintain the student's health status in school, these issues, some with legal implications, may include (but are not limited to) the following:

- advance assessment, planning, and preparation before student entry into school;

- collaboration and communication with health care providers and related services in the community, such as the fire department and Emergency Medical Services;

- education of appropriate personnel regarding the student's specialized needs, both routine and emergency;

- delegation and supervision requirements when nursing services are delegated to other personnel;

- back-up plans and equipment to implement them in the event of staff absences or equipment failure;

- development of a contract with an outside nursing agency to delineate the relationship between and responsibilities of both the school district and nursing agency if the latter is providing a private duty nurse for an individual student (see Appendix J for a sample contract between a school district and a private-duty nursing agency, provided by Baltimore County Public Schools); and

- accepting and implementing, or rejecting, Do-Not-Resuscitate (DNR) orders. (See chapter 14.)

Students with Life-Threatening Allergies

Issues regarding the rights of students with special health care needs to access an appropriate education under § 504 and the Americans with Disabilities Act (ADA) are covered in chapter 11. The particular question of accommodating students with life-threatening food allergies is not specifically discussed in that chapter, in part because, as Rosenfeld (1998, p. 3) points out, "no court has specifically…held [whether] a person with food allergies is 'disabled' within the meaning of § 504 or ADA." This appears true of students with latex allergies, as well, although these students often qualify for other reasons, such as the condition of myelodysplasia (spina bifida). Rosenfeld further describes the current dilemma related to students with severe allergies, which is not so much whether they should be accommodated, but rather, "exactly how far should a school go?"

A 1992 article in the *New England Journal of Medicine* (Sampson, Medelson, & Rosen), reports on a medical study of 13 children with food allergies—six who suffered fatal and seven who suffered near-fatal reactions from unwittingly eating food to which they were allergic. This study at Johns Hopkins University School of Medicine indicated that the deaths and near deaths "resulted largely from a failure on the part of adults to recognize how serious the situation was and to take proper action."

Clearly the results of this study point to the importance of planning and educating school personnel to recognize early symptoms of an anaphylactic reaction and to rapidly intervene. This is especially critical in schools, during transportation on school buses, and at other locations away from home where control over what students eat is significantly decreased. On the other hand, parental requests to ban a food, for example peanut butter, from entire school buildings is problematic for other students for whom this popular food is a lunch staple and sometimes for school lunch programs trying to provide nutritious menus on tight budgets.

There appears to be consensus in the health and education literature that accommodations must reasonably ensure students' safety, but not to the extent of total protection and isolation from the real world—neither is total protection achievable, nor is it in the best interests of a child's normal development. For example, Burke and Wheeler (1999) discuss the physician's role in prescribing a child's treatment protocol for school use, emphasizing that schools, health care providers and families can find ways to enable students to avoid allergic reactions yet "participate fully" in school activities. Rosenfeld (1998) provides useful suggestions addressed both to parents and schools for preventing anaphylactic events and accommodating students with severe food allergies.

The Food Allergy Network has published an excellent resource to assist school districts in planning appropriately for students with severe food allergies and high risk for anaphylaxis; this resource, including an educational video and written materials for various school personnel, is useful in planning accommodations, educating staff, and developing emergency

procedures (Munoz-Furlong, 1995). The American Academy of Allergy, Asthma and Immunology, another resource on this topic, can be reached at (414) 272-6071. For up-to-date information regarding latex allergy, contact the Spina Bifida Association of America, (202) 944-3285.

Each student is different from another, as is each family, school, and situation. Therefore, judicious assessment of the clinical risk of a particular child, individualized, collaborative planning, excellent school-family-health care provider communications, staff education, and creative problem-solving are essential for effective student services and risk management.

Field Trips and Summer Programs

The principles for planning field trips and summer programs for students who require specialized nursing services during the school day are the same as those outlined for medication administration starting on page 222. (See also chapters 11, 12, and 13 regarding § 504 and IDEA, and chapter 4 regarding delegation of nursing activities and functions.)

Individualized Health Care Plans

Students who have mild to severe special health care needs that require nursing services or supervision at school should have an individualized health care plan (IHP) on file. IHPs are also referred to as individualized health care plans (IHCPs), school health management plans (SHMPs) and nursing care plans. IHPs are specifically required by the American Nurses Association's *Standards of Clinical Practice* (1998) and the National Association of School Nurses' *Standards of Professional School Nursing Practice* (1998). The importance of IHPs is also cited in numerous state agency guidelines and professional publications (e.g., Haas, 1993; Hootman, 1996a; Schwab, Panettieri, & Bergren, 1998; Arnold & Silkworth, 1999). Therefore, judicious use of the IHP as a vehicle to ensure safe nursing services and continuity of care for students with special needs is a standard of care against which a school nurse's conduct can be judged in a legal proceeding. In addition, the IHP provides a mechanism for evaluating the quality of services provided by school health personnel and a basis for hiring and assigning staff.

Although developed primarily by and for nursing staff rather than for other school personnel, IHPs should provide the foundation for the health component of § 504 plans and individualized education programs (IEPs), when applicable. Sec. 504 plans and

IEPs are collaboratively developed with school team members, based on students' educational and related services needs, including needs for health services. Students' health-related IEP goals and objectives should be framed in terms of expected outcomes for student learning. (See Appendix K for a list of potential learning objectives by nursing diagnosis and a sample care plan demonstrating their use.) These educational objectives are appropriate for § 504 plans, as well.

All student assessments and IHPs must be individualized. The case of *Conejo Valley (CA) Unified School District* (1993) affirms the value of individualized evaluation in creating emergency response procedures for students. The parent of a six-year-old student with Down syndrome and diabetes filed a complaint with the Office for Civil Rights (OCR), U.S. Department of Education, when the school district failed to provide appropriate support and emergency planning. (For a detailed discussion of this case and district violations of § 504 as cited by OCR, see chapter 11.)

The IHP is based on nursing assessment of the student and the identified nursing diagnoses (Hootman, 1996b, p. 19). It describes the nursing interventions to be implemented and specifies student outcomes expected as a result of the nursing services provided. A plan may contain modifications in a student's school program, nursing interventions (e.g., instruction in self-care), medical treatments, and "designated caregivers." The term caregivers usually refers to school nurses, other nurses working under the direction of a school nurse, and unlicensed assistive personnel (UAP) to whom a school nurse has delegated certain nursing care activities or procedures in order to meet a student's health needs. (See chapter 4 and, in chapter 5, "Accountability for Nursing Assistants" (UAP) and "Accountability for Licensed Practical (Vocational) Nurses" and for further information on delegation.)

Developing and documenting an IHP is not enough; the written plan must be implemented and revised when additional data is available. In an Iowa case, the school district moved to have the case dismissed (i.e., moved for summary judgment) on the basis that, under Iowa law, the district could not be liable due to discretionary function immunity (*Jennifer Vinci, et al. v. Ames Community School District, et al.,* 1997). (See chapter two for a discussion of discretionary function immunity.) In this case, the school nurse had developed an IHP for a student with a new tracheostomy that did not provide for one-on-one nursing care. Rather, it called for several designated employees (school nurse, principal, and secretaries) to help Jennifer with any problems from the tracheal tube. Shortly thereafter, Jennifer required additional surgery to first insert a new type of tracheal tube, and then a stent (plug) to separate her vocal chords and promote healing. As a result of the surgery, air could no longer be exchanged around the outside of the tracheal tube. This carried a much higher risk to the student in the event of blockage of the tube from mucous secretions than had the prior tube and its placement.

Aware of this risk, the district's special education director documented a planned change in staffing for Jennifer on her return from the surgery. A full time one-on-one educational assistant with "nursing background" was to be with the student. However, the plan was not immediately implemented. Jennifer returned from the surgery, suffered acute airway obstruction from a mucous plug when only a secretary was available to respond to the emergency, and sustained severe oxygen deprivation and brain damage. The court refused to grant summary judgment for the defendants on two of the four charges of negligence because (1) "once the School District made its discretionary decision about Jennifer's supervision…[as written in the IHP], it had no choice but to implement that decision"; and (2) the school nurse who, according to the IHP, was to "update knowledge and skills to meet the student's special health service needs," failed to "keep abreast of Jennifer's health needs." Therefore, the court found that the district could be found liable for those two charges of negligence. Furthermore, an expert school nurse witness involved in the case, after a review of the records and the school nurse's deposition, concluded that the nurse functioned below the standards of school nursing practice with respect to nine different issues. One issue was that she "did not update the individual health care plan as Jennifer's physical condition changed" (Homola-Portuondo, 1995). The district subsequently settled out of court for a very significant sum of money.

In developing IHPs, the school nurse must determine what, if any, care can be delegated to UAP, and what training and school nurse supervision is required. (See chapter 4 for information regarding delegation.) Furthermore, some procedures cannot be safely or legally delegated. For example, in the *Vinci* case cited above (Homola-Portuondo, 1995), the expert witness found that the school nurse had

...used poor judgment in delegating nursing functions to unlicensed assistive personnel; as these functions went beyond meeting the basic human needs such as feeding, drinking, ambulating, grooming, toileting, dressing; into an area requiring professional knowledge, judgment, and skill.

Each IHP should include a review date, based on the individual health status and needs of the student. Students with more complex health care needs and those with health conditions that are unstable require more frequent nursing evaluation. In any event, no more than one year should ever lapse between review cycles.

The IHP must anticipate events such as field trips, off-campus work experiences, bus transportation, and classroom parties. In *Macomb County Intermediate School District v. Joshua S.* (1989), the court affirmed that students are entitled to the same level of service on the bus (during transportation) as in the classroom. This student required constant attention to his respiratory function and tracheostomy tube and positioning in his wheelchair. (Further discussion of field trips and summer programs can be found later in this chapter and further discussion of these plus transportation and special activities [e.g., swimming programs] can be found in chapters 12 and 13.)

Parents, students, physicians, and other health care providers should participate in planning, authorizing, and implementing individualized health care plans and their associated components (e.g., health teaching, self-care promotion and special procedures). For example, parents should always authorize (in writing) medical care and invasive procedures for their minor children, and physicians or other authorized prescribers must write orders for medical treatments that require implementation at school. Another finding of the expert witness in the Jennifer Vinci case was that the school nurse "did not actively seek physician orders to promote safe/quality care and a safe environment."

The quality standards against which a care plan and other nursing services will be evaluated include the following:

• consistency with minimum standards;

• accuracy with safety criteria; and

• quality control through periodic review (Hootman, 1996a, pp. I-2,3).

These standards assist the professional nurse in preventing omissions in care and increasing efficiency

in service delivery. (For resources regarding IHPs, see such sources as Haas [1993], Hootman [1996a & 1996b], Hootman & Carpenito [1997], and Arnold and Silkworth [1999]).

District policies and procedures should clearly specify what medical supplies, equipment, and services must be provided to students under § 504 and IDEA. School policy related to who must finance and supply personnel and equipment, as well as medical evaluations, should be based on the requirements of IDEA and § 504 (see chapters 11 and 12) and state guidelines to ensure consistent minimum standards across and within districts. While school districts can always provide more than the law allows, and each child's needs must be individually addressed, a claim of discrimination might be valid if random or arbitrary decisions are made in this regard. For example, in *Huntsville City (AL) School District*, 1996), an individual alleged that the school district discriminated against students with diabetes by requiring students to come to the office to use a glucometer. The district's medication policy required students to come to the office, and the district had determined that this included glucometers. The district had made an exception for the student to carry the glucometer but required testing in the office. It was determined that no violation of § 504 occurred. This reinforces the importance of policy and its consistent application within a district. On the other hand, exceptions to policies may be acceptable in individual situations and should be considered when indicated by the § 504 or individualized education program (IEP) team, and explicitly documented in the student's 504 plan or IEP.

Policy and state guidelines notwithstanding, school personnel, and especially school nurses, should have expert knowledge regarding and facilitate referrals to resources within the school, community and state where families can obtain additional support and assistance in accessing necessary medical and social services, including medical supplies and equipment. School nurses may also need to advocate for their students with other local and state agencies. (See chapters 11 through 13 for in-depth information on the requirements of § 504 and IDEA as they apply to students with chronic health conditions. Those chapters review many additional Office for Civil Rights [OCR] decisions and court cases, including cases related to least restrictive environment, inclusion of students with disabilities in regular classrooms, funding responsibilities for health and medical services and equipment, and appropriate locations for administering student health treatments.)

SPECIAL HEALTH AND BEHAVIOR ISSUES

Communicable and Chronic Infectious Diseases

Historically, statutes and case law have designated authority to state and local public health agencies to protect the public from unwarranted exposure to communicable disease. Some authority may also be extended by law and regulation to other public institutions, such as schools and physicians. For example, school districts may be required to report the in-school incidence of communicable diseases on an immediate, 24 hour, weekly, or monthly basis, depending on the specific disease and state requirement. School districts are also usually delegated responsibility by statute for routine communicable disease control strategies in schools. Accordingly, states may mandate districts to require physical examination of students prior to school entry and at other intervals during elementary, middle, and high school years, and to deny attendance to those with acute contagious disease and inadequate immunization protection.

School boards and administrators generally assign the responsibility for communicable disease management to school nurses and, where applicable, school medical advisors (e.g., C.G.S. § 10-20). Screenings of students may be necessary at school to control the spread of communicable disease or infestations, for example, head lice or scabies. While professional nurses at the baccalaureate level are educated to perform physical assessment, recognize variations from the normal, and make nursing diagnoses, only certified and licensed advanced practice registered nurses can make medical diagnoses and treat medical conditions. Therefore, based on their assessment findings of variation from the normal, school nurses frequently must exclude students from school for definitive medical diagnosis and initiation of treatment.

State and local health agencies may provide guidelines to schools regarding mandated reporting by schools, exclusion requirements, including the length of exclusion, and treatment for communicable diseases. For authoritative information on infectious diseases—specifically, their prevention, identification, control, expected course, potential complications, and treatment, including specific information for school settings, school nurses and medical advisors should refer to the latest edition of the *Red Book* of the American Academy of Pediatrics (Committee on Infectious Diseases, 2000). The American Public Health Association's book, *Control of Communicable Diseases Manual* (Chin, 2000) is another important reference and is also regularly updated.

School districts must be consistent in their application of exclusion and readmittance criteria to avoid claims of discrimination or harassment. For example, determining on a case-by-case basis whether or not to apply a "no nit" policy risks charges of discrimination. Conversely, it is not harassment to screen students who are repeatedly infested with head lice as a measure to prevent (to the degree possible) infestation of others, so long as all infested students are treated consistently.

Districts should have written policies and procedures on communicable disease management for reference in every school building's health office. Such direction helps to avoid unnecessary exclusions, and promotes fair application of the rules district-wide. These policies and procedures must address confidentiality requirements related to student screenings, school and community notification, reporting to state and local health departments and related issues. The Committee on Infectious Diseases (2000, p. 120) states that "in all circumstances requiring intervention to prevent the spread of infection within the school setting, the privacy of children who are infected should be protected." (See chapter 8 regarding confidentiality and privacy issues.) It is critical that parents receive in writing, at least yearly, the district's policy and procedures for communicable disease management, including screening, exclusion and readmittance criteria, and confidentiality provisions.

In outbreaks of communicable disease, and in any related crisis, collaboration with local and state health officials is essential since they hold legal authority and responsibility within a state to manage such occurrences. Preferably, schools should avoid crisis management by engaging in programs to prevent communicable disease outbreaks. School districts should seek direction and advice from local and state health agencies and should implement policies that will minimize outbreaks of disease and infestations in school communities. For example, district policies and procedures may specify hand-washing, food-handling, and food-sharing practices for staff and students to minimize the spread of hepatitis A and other diseases that are spread through the fecal-oral route.

In relation to the case *School Board v. Arline* (1987), McNary-Keith (1995, p. 74) writes:

Although the court acknowledges that few handicaps give rise to as much apprehension as does a contagious disease, the court concluded that although contagious diseases might adversely affect others, automatic exclusion under § 504 is not warranted unless there is a significant risk that others will be infected.

While this quotation is in reference to tuberculosis, it applies to all communicable diseases. District policy not only gives direction to school personnel, but also serves as the reference document for inquiries from concerned citizens about screening and exclusion procedures.

Tuberculosis

Tuberculosis (TB) testing requirements vary from state to state. The primary objective of school testing is to identify infected children before their infection progresses to an infectious (communicable) stage. The incidence of TB is increasing for all ages, not only in developing countries, but also in the industrialized world. The true prevalence of TB in children is unknown because reporting of positive test results is not mandated in the United States and there have been no national surveys since. "The rise for infection by Mycobacterium tuberculosis among children depends primarily on the level of risk of developing infectious TB from adults in their immediate environment, especially their household." (Kahn, 1995, p. 1)

Gravatt (1999, p. 29) states that the incidence of TB has been associated with three factors:

- The connection between TB and HIV infection;

- Immigration of people from countries with high incidence of TB;

- Diminished effectiveness of public health care in many areas of the U.S.

The changing epidemiology of TB suggests that consultation with local health departments is prudent for districts to assist in targeting defined high-risk populations needing screening and treatment.

Appropriate health information provided by school nurses can assist students, families, and school personnel in understanding the disease, its transmission, the meaning of "exposure" versus active disease, and current prevention and treatment regimens. Appropriate information decreases anxiety and facilitates the development of health-promoting life skills and well-being.

Most children needing treatment for TB are not communicable to other students. If a communicable situation occurs, the school nurse should work with appropriate medical providers and public health officials to determine whether mass testing at school is indicated. Compliance with consistent and complete medication treatment is essential for effective TB treatment but often problematic. To improve patient compliance, public institutions are increasingly taking

on the role of "direct observation therapy" (DOT) in a concerted effort to assist public health officials in managing at-risk clients. School districts are among those institutions. In some states, such as Texas (telephone communication with Mary Jackson, Texas Department of Health, October, 1997), DOT means having the patient observed when taking their medication—to ensure that the medication is taken as prescribed. When student compliance with a treatment regimen for TB is poor, DOT at school may be an appropriate public health and treatment strategy. As with all medications, TB medication needs to be administered safely and students taking TB medications should be monitored for side effects.

Human Immunodeficiency Virus (HIV)

HIV is a virus that affects the body's ability to resist infections caused by other agents, referred to as opportunistic or secondary infections. Historically, these repeated and rampant secondary infections were lethal for most HIV infected persons. Considerable progress in HIV treatment has been made in recent years, however, and infected individuals are now surviving long-term with rigorous and difficult treatment regimens. In addition to dealing with very demanding treatment regimens and multiple medications, students with HIV disease continue to be susceptible to secondary infections and related health complications that may require nursing support and supervision at school.

Students with HIV may not be discriminated against or denied enrollment. "The primary enforcement mechanisms are…§ 504 of the 1973 Rehabilitation Act, and IDEA. Other enforcement mechanisms may also exist under state law, other federal statutes, and the equal protection clause of the Fourteenth Amendment" (McNary-Keith, 1995, p. 71). (For a discussion of court cases concerning the rights of students with HIV, see chapter 11.)

Courts have also ruled that teachers infected with HIV should be able to preserve their classroom status. In *Chalk v. United States District Court* (1988), for example, the court granted an injunction and reinstated Mr. Chalk to classroom duties. On the basis of his status of HIV infection, he had been reassigned to an administrative position (McNary-Keith, p. 76). In these cases, court decisions were based on the prevailing scientific evidence regarding the modes of HIV transmission and the risk of transmission in school.

There are no reported cases of transmission of the AIDS virus in a school setting. The Committee on Infectious Diseases, (AAP, 2000, p. 345) reaffirms scientific research, advising that "in the absence of blood exposure, HIV infection is not acquired through the types of contact that usually occur in school settings, including contact with saliva or tears." The AAP also provides specific recommendations for schools including housekeeping procedures for handling spills of blood and other body fluids (pp. 298-301). District-wide implementation of Standard Precautions should be required by school policy and procedures. Standard precautions should be taught to all staff through in-service training programs, and students' education should be an integral part of the school curriculum. These measures provide appropriate protection against the transmission of HIV in schools.

In the event of a possible body fluid exchange, such as may occur in student fights or biting incidents, parents of the involved students should be advised of the incident. Although state laws concerning confidentiality of HIV information vary and are frequently amended, neither party can be forced to divulge communicable disease status or compelled to take a blood test. Sometimes parents may give permission to let their child's physician talk directly to the physician of the other child. This option can be suggested to parents and, if both sets of parents agree, the names of the physicians can be shared. The name of the other child does not need to be shared with each consenting parent and only the physicians need to have both students' names. Parents would need to give to their child's physician informed, written consent to share relevant information from their child's medical history with the other student's doctor. State law provisions for significant exposures and other strategies for managing individual situations should be explored with an HIV expert at the state department of health. (See also chapter 8 regarding confidentiality and HIV.)

Hepatitis

Hepatitis is an infection of the liver, caused by different viruses—e.g. A, B, C, D, E. The infection can be acute to chronic and can be fatal.

Hepatitis A is more commonly spread by the fecal-oral route and through contaminated food or water. Thus, schools may place restrictions on food sharing and food preparation in the school environment as a preventive measure against spreading the virus within the school community. Policies should be in place to facilitate safe food handling within the school.

Hepatitis B and C are caused by bloodborne viruses that are spread through body fluid exposure. Although somewhat more communicable than HIV, hepatitis B and C are still not easily transmitted if Standard

Precautions are routinely practiced. While hepatitis A may require exclusion during the period of acute illness due to communicability, chronic infection with hepatitis B and C do not justify the exclusion of a child or school staff from school, except in unusual and temporary circumstances. As with HIV, multiple court cases have determined that hepatitis B infected students are entitled to an education in the least restrictive environment. In the case of *Jeffrey S. v. State Board of Education State of Georgia, et al.*, (1989), a school district suspended and then denied homebound instruction for a student with disabilities who was a carrier of hepatitis B. Finding discrimination under § 504, the court ordered the child back into school. In *Robert H. v. Fort Worth Independent School District* (1988), the student was mentally retarded and a carrier of hepatitis B and had displayed increasingly aggressive behavior. The school district had changed the student's placement from the local school to a state facility for mentally retarded people. The parties reached a settlement to return the student to the local district and procedures were established for student carriers of hepatitis B.

Other Infectious Diseases

When questions arise regarding chronic and acute infectious diseases of staff or students or the development of related policies and procedures, it is important to refer to the two books mentioned earlier in this section (Committee on Infectious Diseases, 2000; Chin, 2000) and to consult with local and state public health officials. Collaboration with the latter experts helps to ensure that appropriate steps are taken in evaluating a situation, determining appropriate actions and precautions, educating personnel and the community, and establishing sound policy. This collaboration is especially critical when dealing with a new issue, for example, frequently hospitalized students who are colonized with Methicillin-resistant Staphylococcus Aureus (MRSA) or other multi-drug resistant bacteria.

Immunizations and Vaccine Preventable Diseases

Every state has immunization laws to prevent the spread of traditional childhood illnesses (Gordon, Zook, Averhoff, & Williams, 1997). Although the requirements vary from state to state, failure to be properly immunized generally means that a student will be denied enrollment or attendance in school. It is important that districts comply with enrollment regulations to avoid claims of discrimination or harassment, as well as liability risk for negligently carrying out their responsibility to maintain a safe school environment for all students.

Exemptions from immunization requirements have traditionally been made for two very different reasons—medical contraindications and religious beliefs. More recently, exemptions have been allowed for philosophical reasons. Some states allow personal exemptions—for example, California, where "personal exemption" refers to both religious and philosophical exemption. While most states allow religious exemptions (all but Mississippi and West Virginia), 15 states allow philosophical exemptions. The criteria for religious, philosophical, medical and personal exemptions vary among the states. (National Vaccine Advisory Committee, Working Group on Philosophical Exemptions, 1998).

Students may have temporary or permanent medical exemptions. Temporary exemptions should be renewed at least annually. Examples of reasons for temporary medical exemptions include pregnancy and chemotherapy. An example of a permanent medical exemption is history of a significant adverse reaction, for example, to pertussis vaccine. Permanent exemption signifies that a medical provider determines it is not safe for the student to ever receive the specified vaccination in question. Generally, a medical exemption is for a specific immunization. State laws dictate how medical exemptions are reviewed and accepted or rejected. Courts have affirmed that exemptions must be granted for valid medical conditions. In the case of *Lynch v. Clarkstown Central School District* (1992), however, the child's physician requested an exemption based on the diagnosis of Rett's Syndrome. The school district's denial of this request was upheld by the Court, citing a lack of credible medical evidence.

Historically, state laws have allowed religious exemptions based either on religious affiliation (e.g. membership in a Christian Science congregation) or "sincere religious belief." The latter can be a statement about the religious belief of the child. New York cases in which religious exemption has been upheld include *Berg v. Glen Cove City School District* (1994), *Sherr v. Northport-East Northport Union Free School District* (1987), and *Levy v. Northport-East Northport Union Free School District* (1987). On the other hand, exemptions to state immunization requirements for school attendance have been denied in some cases. Examples include *Hansel v. Arter* (1985)— denial of exemptions on the basis of "chiropractic ethics," and *Mason v. General Brown Central School District* (1988)—denial of exemption from immunization as "contrary to the genetic blueprint of the child." When parents objected to a required tetanus shot for student participation in interscholastic baseball, the court found immunization not unreason-

ably burdensome, since participation in interscholastic sports is "not an important government benefit" (*Calandre v. State College Area School District*, 1986).

The process for accepting religious exemptions varies from state to state. Proof of religious affiliation cannot be required according to guidelines from the Centers for Disease Control and Prevention (CDC) and, as cited above, case law. While some states or localities may still require a parent's statement to be notarized and annually renewed, general practice based on case law precedent is that a written statement of the child's or family's religious belief is sufficient to warrant exemption from state immunization requirements.

Regardless of whether an exemption is for religious or philosophical reasons, it is wise for district personnel (school nurses) to inform parents and older students, in writing, of the possible complications and sequelae of the disease, if contracted. Such written notice should also inform families of the district's procedures for exclusion of unimmunized students during an outbreak of communicable disease in the school or community. Parents and eligible students should be asked to sign the notice form to indicate that they have read the information. The district should keep the original signed form in the student's record with other documentation of the exemption.

Exclusion of students during a disease outbreak, regardless of exemption status, has been upheld in Nebraska and Arizona cases, *Maack v. School District of Lincoln* (1992), and *Maricopa County Health Department v. Harmon, et al.* (1987). The length of exclusion will vary according to the incubation period of the particular disease. State requirements and school district policies may also vary regarding specific exclusion requirements. For example, in Harris County public schools (Texas), a student must produce a positive antibody blood titer for the organism or remain out of school for two communicable disease cycles.

School health records are generally considered legal records of immunizations. Such records, as part of the school record, are confidential and cannot be released without parental permission, even to physician offices, unless the immunization was given in school under a medical order from the physician requesting information. A student may be able to use a copy of a school health record as official proof of immunization status, for example, for college entrance.

It is not ethical to withhold the immunization records as leverage to compel families to pay fees owed to schools or medical providers. In both California and Oregon, spokespersons for the state medical societies have supported this ethical concept for physicians' local medical practice. In Connecticut, state law specifies that the true copy of the state-required school health record and state required health assessment forms, including immunization data, must be forwarded to the next district in which a student enrolls (C.G.S. § 10-206). Thus, Connecticut districts are prohibited from holding on to a student's health record, even temporarily, when a student transfers. As a result, students are rarely denied entry into another Connecticut school district due to lack of immunization data.

Families should be taught the importance of maintaining personal records of their child's immunizations and provided, as needed, a copy of school immunization records. School personnel can use enrollment activities and health room encounters, to reinforce with parents and students the necessity of maintaining immunization records at home.

Many districts provide immunizations on-site at school. In order to provide immunizations, there must be access to vaccine, supportive district policy, parental informed consent (or student informed consent if 18 years or older), and medical orders authorizing nurses to give the immunizations according to medical protocols. Even when students are younger than 18 years, they should be informed of the risks and benefits commensurate with their age and competence. The National Childhood Vaccine Injury Act (NCVIA) of 1986, as amended, requires notification of patients and parents about vaccine benefits and risks. When administering any vaccine containing diphtheria, tetanus, pertussis, measles, mumps, rubella, polio, hepatitis B, haemophilus influenzae type B (Hib), or varicella, a Vaccine Information Statement (VIS), developed and distributed by the CDC, must be shared and discussed with patients and parents prior to immunizing the patient. In 1994, an amendment to the NCVIA disallowed providers flexibility in creating their own materials. Copies of the VISs are available from CDC and state and local health departments; and on the National Immunization Program's Internet website (http://www.cdc.gov/nip). VISs no longer require a patient/parent signature. However, documenting that the information was given and discussed is essential.

It is the intent of the law that clients have certain information. If clients are unable to read, the provider must read, paraphrase, or facilitate translation of the VIS. There are presently no official CDC translations of the VISs. Several states have translated the VISs into other languages, however, and CDC does not require approval of the translated documents. Refer to state law for specific "informed consent" requirements regarding immunization. The specifications should include

procedural (for example, oral vs. written consent) and content (type of information) regulations. (Refer to the American Academy of Pediatrics *Red Book* [Committee on Infectious Diseases, 1997, p. 681] or to the state health department for detailed information regarding specific immunizations covered by the Program. Information on providers' responsibilities under the NCVIA can be found at CDC's website (www.cdc.gov/nip/vacsafe/vaccinesafety/providers/ncvia.htm) and at the website about the National Vaccine Injury Compensation Program (VICP) (www.hrsa.dhhs.gov/bhpr/vicp/).

Parent or guardian consent is necessary prior to administering immunizations, just as it is for any other medical treatment. Failure to obtain informed consent is reasonable grounds for a legal action against a school district, as well as disciplinary action against a school nurse. For example, in an Illinois case (*Board of Education of the City of Chicago v. Illinois State Board of Education*, 1987), a tenured school nurse was fired for failure to secure parental consent prior to immunization. Although there was no question that her failure to obtain consent deserved disciplinary action, she was able to obtain reinstatement to her position on the basis of tenure and technical employment law.

District policies and procedures should clearly state whether telephone authorization by a parent is an option to provide informed consent. From a legal point of view, phone authorizations from parents should be discouraged for any type of treatment or medication, including immunizations. There is greater assurance that communication accomplished in person or in writing allows for mutual understanding of the pros and cons of immunization, thereby enhancing informed consent. While phone authorization is never wise, if absolutely necessary, two persons can listen to and document a parent's verbal permission or refusal.

The risk of liability regarding vaccine administration can never be eradicated, but is relatively minimal for districts when standards of practice for immunization administration are followed. For example, in the Texas Torts Claims Acts there is protection for school districts from all liability for negligence unless it involves the use or operation of a motor vehicle (Texas Civil Practice and Remedies Code § 101.051). Thus, negligence actions in Texas would likely be dismissed even if a district allows an outside organization to host the immunization program on school premises. While many states do not have immunity provisions as strong as those in the Texas Torts Claims Act, there is generally some immunity for public employees whose conduct is not willful and does not constitute gross negligence. Additionally, the Vaccine Injury Compensation Program (VICP) discussed above provides no-fault insurance to persons unavoidably injured by vaccines. It requires injured persons to pursue their tort claims exceeding $1000.00 through the VICP before going to state courts. It will not, however, protect nurses or physicians who negligently administer immunizations. For more information on VICP and liability risks related to immunizing children, see the references, VICP (1999) and Texas Department of Health (1994), respectively.

Health Screenings

With the escalation of health care costs and managed care dominating health care delivery in the United States, there is once again greater impetus for preventive health services. Although school health services were initially organized to address communicable disease control and severe problems with school attendance, school health services today have expanded to include other aspects of direct care and health promotion. Schools have long been identified as excellent environments for delivering cost-effective, population-based health screenings. Schools provide almost all our youth access to these preventive and early identification health programs. "Every school day, more than 95% of the nation's 5- to 17-year-olds attend one of almost 110,000 elementary and secondary schools" (Vernon, Bryan, Hunt, Allensworth, & Bradley, 1997, p. 252). In addition to health services, schools generally provide health instruction.

Health screenings at school, including periodic health assessments, provide opportunities for early identification of emerging health problems and reinforcement of preventive health management strategies. Remediation of problems identified in these screenings can positively impact student learning, defray financial costs incurred by families, schools, and health care systems when such problems are not identified early, and enhance affected students' emotional well being and readiness to learn. For example, "Abnormal visual acuity is the most common chronic medical condition in children of industrialized nations" (Yawn, Lydick, Epstein, & Jacobsen, 1996, p. 171). Vision and hearing impairments, if uncorrected, can significantly affect reading and writing abilities and language acquisition and comprehension, all essential for academic success. Early detection and treatment of scoliosis can save significant health care dollars in surgical and hospital expenses and diminish school absence and the physical and emotional trauma of surgery for affected students. However, with the demands for expanding school health services, some districts are having to make hard

choices about the efficacy and level of services that can be offered.

Cost-effective screening programs are ones that can identify all individuals at risk for the specified problem while minimizing over-identification, that is, without producing too many false positive results. The most common state-mandated screenings in schools include vision, hearing, and spinal (postural) screening. Other screenings, for example, for TB, lead poisoning, blood pressure, and anemia, may be required by law or district policy as part of mandated physical exams, or as mass screenings in school.

Schools, like health care providers, cannot force minor students to participate in screenings against their will or that of their parents. To do so can result in a charge of assault and battery against the screener and the school. (See chapter 7 for additional discussion of consent issues.) When a student refuses to participate, the refusal should be documented in the student's health record to protect the school against a future civil action. If a minor student refuses a screening when the parent has not refused it, the parent should be notified and parental notification should be documented.

Documentation should include details of the screening and the specific findings, both normal and abnormal. District procedures for all screening programs should be kept on file to demonstrate the standards for training screeners, and conducting, reporting, following up, and documenting all screenings.

The maintenance of student privacy during screenings is essential. All students are entitled to preservation of their dignity and confidentiality regarding screening results. During in-school physical examinations, including screening examinations for curvature of the spine, the need for a witness in the examination room, or on the other side of a curtain or partially opened door should be considered. When any doubt exists, providing a witness to the examination is wise. The individual who acts as a witness must be trained regarding confidentiality and his or her name should be included in documentation of the exam. Physical examinations, including sports physicals, are usually best provided by the child's own health care provider, including a school-based health center provider, so that ongoing primary health care services and follow-up care are better ensured.

School district policies and procedures should require that parents be provided with advance written notice of screenings and a timely written report of any results requiring further medical assessment. States vary in their mandates regarding scoliosis screening and notification. In two New York cases that examined whether scoliosis screening procedures were adequate and results were properly communicated to parents, the courts found no liability on the part of school districts. In *Bello v. Board of Education of Frankfort-Schuyler Central School District* (1988), a parent sued based upon the school's alleged failure to report results of the child's scoliosis test until 14 months later, and claimed that, as a result, the condition was aggravated. The court ruled that the district was not liable because it was not required to report the results of the tests. In *Grindle v. Port Jervis Central School District* (1986), the parents sued for damages, alleging that the school failed to examine the child for scoliosis. The court found no private right of action in the state statute requiring scoliosis screening. This decision was upheld on appeal. In a different state, in a different circumstance, or in the future, the outcomes of such cases may be different. Many state statutes and regulations do specifically require the following:

1. parental notice of questionable or abnormal screening results;

2. referral of the student to an appropriate provider for further assessment; and

3. follow up to determine the outcome of the referral.

When the law and school policy do not require notification, referral or follow up, nursing standards of practice and ethical principles do require such action. Determining the outcome of the referral and its potential impact on the student's learning is an essential component of quality screening services. Common sense dictates that there is little reason to subject students to screening examinations if nothing is done with abnormal findings.

Violence and Abusive Behaviors

According to Furst (1995, p. 13),

The United States is awash in a sea of violence. Estimates are that more than 3 million assorted crimes occur each year in the 85,000 public schools in the United States, representing about 11% of all crimes committed in the country.

District policies must be in place to manage violence. These policies should give a message that children (and adults) must be safe at school, and violence will not be tolerated. District policies and procedures should also highlight training of students and staff, in order to prevent, predict when possible, and intervene during acts of violence.

Furst (1995, p. 27), feels that school districts are obliged to provide supervision among those in their care who do not possess the maturity or self-discipline to police themselves:

Among the duties that a school district and its employees assume in their care for children is adequate supervision. Because of their lack of maturity, children are not able to foresee situations that might be hazardous to their well-being, and adults have a responsibility to care for them and to protect them from physical harm.

In *Mirand v. City of New York* (1994), one student threatened another because the first child bumped into her in a school building. The victim student told the teacher, who consequently directed her to the security office. The victim went to the office twice and found no one present. At the end of the school day, she and a sibling were accosted and seriously injured by several students. No security personnel were present. The school was subsequently found liable for negligent supervision.

The case of *Hickingbottom v. Orleans Parish School Board* (1993) reinforces the importance of school district policy. The school had followed standard after-dismissal procedure and was not found liable for the student's injury when he returned to school and became involved in a fight with another student. (This case is discussed also in chapter 5 in the section on "Policies and Procedures.")

(See also the section on "Crisis Intervention" earlier in this chapter.)

Sexual Harassment

The issue of sexual harassment in the workplace has received significant attention since the early 1990s. Less attention has been directed toward student-to-student sexual harassment, at least until the 1999 case decided by the U.S. Supreme Court (*Davis v. Monroe County Board of Education*, 1999). Title IX of the Education Amendments of 1972 prohibits discrimination against students on the basis of gender. This prohibition includes sexual harassment of students by employees of a school district and by other students, whether or not they are in a position of authority over the student.

Sexual harassment refers to any unwelcome sexual advance or request for sexual favors, including both actual harassment ("quid quo pro harassment") and harassment that creates a "hostile learning environment." Guidelines from the Office for Civil Rights (OCR), U.S. Department of Education (1997), define these terms with respect to schools. A district violates Title IX when it fails to investigate a student's complaint or the suspicion of a third party regarding harassment of another student. For example, if a student confides in the school nurse that her friend is being harassed by a clique of boys, the nurse must report the information to the Title IX coordinator or an appropriate administrator, and the district must investigate. Absent a complaint, if the school district should have known about the harassment anyhow, the district may be in violation of Title IX, and investigation alone does not suffice to meet Title IX requirements. Following investigation, the district must take appropriate actions to prevent further harassment. (See chapter 11 for additional information on Title IX requirements, relevant court decisions, and school policy issues.)

Child Abuse and Neglect—Reporting of Suspicion

Every state has laws that require individuals with professional responsibilities for children to report suspected abuse (Schwab, 1989, p. 18). In fact, there can be penalties for not reporting suspicions to either police or child protective agencies. Nurses and physicians are mandated reporters of suspected child abuse or neglect. School staff members became mandated reporters of suspected child abuse or neglect under the 1974 Federal Child Abuse Prevention and Treatment Act. This act, amended in 1992, offers a small amount of federal funding to states that enact legislation requiring the reporting of suspected child abuse or neglect and provision of services to affected children and their families.

School district policies and procedures should clearly define roles and responsibilities of school personnel, including requirements of the state reporting laws, necessary staff training, reporting criteria, reporting procedures, assessment of student health status, emergency procedures, parental notification and documentation requirements. To the extent feasible, policies and procedures should define terminology, for example, the meaning of "reasonable cause to suspect" or "reasonable suspicion." It is especially important to clarify that mandated reporters are required to report suspicion of neglect and abuse, not to investigate that suspicion. School policy should clearly identify the state agency responsible for determining whether or not abuse and neglect have actually occurred, and should define the relationship between that agency and the school district when reports are filed by school district personnel.

Lack of awareness is not an adequate defense in cases of negligence by school personnel. In the case of *Morris*

v. State of Texas (1992), a teacher appealed her conviction for failure to report abuse of a pre-school child with severe and profound disabilities by two classroom aides. The conviction was upheld, with all technical points of the appeal rejected by the Court. In the case of the *State of Minnesota v. Grover* (1989), a school principal charged with failure to report suspected child abuse was acquitted on the argument that the state statute was unconstitutionally vague and over-broad. The state appealed the dismissal, and ultimately the Minnesota Supreme Court reversed and remanded the case for trial.

Health care providers are accountable for complying with professional standards of practice for assessing and reporting potentially abused and neglected children. Failure to practice competently or to follow legal mandates can result in the loss of one's professional license. In the case of *Landeros v. Flood* (1976), a physician failed to perform a complete examination of a child and to report suspected child abuse. The court determined that the physician had, therefore, failed to meet California's professional standard of care for physicians.

In a New York case that was settled in 1996, a school nurse was working in a summer program for medically involved students run by the Capital Region Board of Cooperative Educational Services (BOCES). The school nurse assessed the right hand and thumb of an 8-year-old student whose hand had been closed in a car door over the weekend. The school nurse's examination revealed swelling, discoloration, limited range of motion, and pain. Both the school nurse and social worker tried to get the mother to take the student for a medical examination, and the nurse facilitated an appointment at the local medical center. When the parent refused to take the student for medical care and the student was subsequently absent from school, the nurse informed the principal of the school and later the BOCES supervisor of her concerns for the student, suspicion of medical neglect, and intent to make a report to Child Protective Services (CPS). Not only did the school nurse meet considerable resistance from these two administrators, but she was also informed that the BOCES principals and supervisors make such decisions, not nurses. Unable to find district support for her decision to make a report, the school nurse called CPS for direction. The CPS legal liaison and supervisor agreed that the school nurse had reasonable suspicion of abuse or neglect, and advised her that, as a mandated reporter, she must report her suspicion, regardless of administrative direction to the contrary. The school nurse filed the report with CPS and notified the principal and supervisor of her actions.

The following day the school nurse was reprimanded and directed to go through the agency's social workers for any future communications with parents. Finding this directive contrary to professional practice standards, the nurse decided to terminate her employment as soon as the BOCES could find a replacement, and advised the district accordingly. Two days later, she was replaced (Lavery, 1997). With assistance from the New York School Nurse Association and National Association of School Nurses, the school nurse obtained legal counsel and pursued legal action against Capitol Region BOCES. Her actions were supported, not only by the state and national school nurse organizations, but also by the New York State Board of Nursing and Child Protection Agency. A settlement was reached, and the BOCES agreed to pay the school nurse monetary damages to compensate her for the loss of salary and legal expenses.

It is critical for school health and education professionals to know state law and regulations regarding the reporting of child abuse and neglect. For example, Texas law requires the "outcry witness" (the individual who first recognizes signs of suspected abuse or to whom the child first discloses) to do the reporting; others may allow the report to be submitted by the employee's supervisor, or by a team of employees. Some states require school personnel to provide a written report to the child protective agency within a certain number of days, in addition to an oral report. In states that permit or require a supervisor or administrator to file a report of suspected abuse, the administrator is legally required to make the report. In other words, if a staff person has a reasonable suspicion that a student is being abused or neglected and reports it to the administrator, as required or permitted by state statute, the administrator has *no option* but to file a report with the child protection agency on the staff member's behalf. His or her opinion about the staff member, report, family, student, circumstances, or any other issue is not relevant to the obligation of filing the report. Support services professionals, including school nurses, are legally and ethically bound to ensure that reports regarding suspicions of other staff members, for example, a teacher afraid to file the report herself, are filed on behalf of students.

School staff must know the warning signs of child abuse and neglect and be prepared to perform and document an appropriate assessment. It is critical when obtaining assessment data that questions are posed in a fashion that are not "leading" the student. Generally, open-ended questions facilitate the collection of information without directing student responses. For example, the nurse might say, "Tell me about the bruise on your face," rather than, "Who hit you?" Furthermore, only that information which is necessary to formulate suspicion and make a report should be sought. Other agencies, not schools, are legally responsible for investigating and determining whether abuse and neglect actually is occurring or occurred (usually CPS, police, and designated hospitals, when a child is assessed by or admitted to the latter).

Documentation is crucial for accurate recall of specific incidents of suspicion, assessment findings, and prior reports of suspected abuse or neglect. District policy should specify how to document and where to store child abuse reports. Often courts are dependent on documentation from such incidents and reports for evidence needed to intervene with a family when a pattern of neglect or abuse exists but the family refuses to cooperate with child protective services. It is critical for reports of suspected abuse and neglect to be stored in a well-protected file in the building in which the student is located. That allows staff making a current report to child protective services to consult the file for incidents of prior suspicion. In instances where the CPS agency has not found grounds to conclude that abuse occurred, repeated reports (especially when citing a history of prior incidents) can lead to CPS intervention. Connecticut State Department of Education guidelines (1994) recommend that copies of any reports of suspected abuse be filed in the student's state-mandated health record and transferred as part of the record when the student moves to another district.

Objective, detailed documentation of what the student and caretaker (if appropriate) say, and what the professional nurse or physician observes on examination is essential. Reports of physical findings by individuals other than those licensed (i.e., recognized as having sufficient expertise) to perform such assessments are usually not admissible in court proceedings. School district policy should limit who can perform physical assessment of students to nurses and physicians. Any pertinent assessments and observations made by other staff members should be added to the report, either on the form itself, or as attachments, and signed by the responsible staff member.

Taking photographs of physical findings is generally not the responsibility of school personnel unless the police or a protective service agent requests otherwise, or state law specifically allows it. State laws may or may not address the issue of who is permitted to photograph physical findings of suspected abuse. In states where the law is silent on this issue, it is best to obtain consultation from the state board of nursing, the child protective agency, and a state school nurse consultant prior to developing district policy or using photography to document suspicious signs of physical abuse. This extent of assessment and documentation may be considered outside the realm of determining "suspicion" and more akin to investigation, a CPS responsibility.

Occasionally, school nurses may suspect that a student's health and well being are imminently or chronically threatened by lack of medical treatment. These circumstances may require referral to CPS or police under state child abuse and neglect statutes. As agents of the state, these authorities may limit parental refusal of medical treatment for their children based on legal interests of the state regarding the following:

- Preservation of life;

- Protection of minor dependents;

- Prevention of irrational self-destruction;

- Maintenance of the ethical integrity of health professionals; and

- Protection of the public's health (Guido, p. 129).

In some circumstances, a hospital will seek a court order to override parental denial of consent to treat a child in a life-threatening situation.

Issues of confidentiality, privacy, and consent related to child abuse and neglect reporting are addressed in chapter 8. This content is essential to developing or revising district policies and procedures, providing staff training, and professional decision making in clinical dilemmas related to child abuse reporting.

Child Abuse and Neglect—Assessment of Physical and Emotional Status

State laws related to child abuse and neglect reporting generally do not address other concerns of a school district when suspicion of abuse or neglect occurs. Because the suspicion is often based on the observation of physical signs of injury or a complaint of abuse disclosed by the student, school districts have an additional obligation to the student beyond reporting, that is, to ensure that the student is not in danger related to the abuse and stress of disclosing it to others, while waiting for CPS personnel to arrive at school or otherwise intervene. It is essential to assess the student for signs of urgent or emergency medical or psychiatric conditions that require immediate referral for evaluation. For example, if the student sustained a

blow to the head, further physical assessment is critical to identify potential signs of concussion or skull fracture. If warranted for emergency medical or psychiatric reasons, 9-1-1 should be called and the student should be transported to the hospital for further evaluation and treatment.

In situations in which CPS personnel are unable to reach school before bus time and school personnel believe that returning home will further endanger the student, either arranging emergency transportation to the hospital or calling the police for assistance is appropriate. School personnel themselves should never assume the responsibility for taking a student off school grounds; such actions might be construed as kidnapping. Parents should also be notified if a student is being detained. School district policy should provide that parents are notified if a student is being detained at school, regardless of the reason.

Some situations warrant police presence at school after filing a report of suspected abuse with CPS, for example, if a family member is threatening or has a history of violence. The school administrator should take responsibility for contacting the police and making suitable arrangements.

Restraints in the School Environment

Students with aggressive and self-injurious behaviors are increasingly placed in school classrooms and may sometimes require restraint. "Physical restraint is a final option for dealing with aggressive behaviors. In general, the use of physical restraint is discouraged except in an emergency situation" (Ruhl, 1985, p. 33). Emergency situations are those in which a student may injure himself or others. Similarly, current standards of the Joint Commission on the Accreditation of Healthcare Organizations (JACHO) require that "physical restraint be applied only when there is adequate clinical justification and encourage the use of alternate interventions…[with] the implied intent that the use of physical restraint be eliminated" (American Nurses Association, 1997).

The use of restraints signals an aggressive and intrusive management of behavior problems, and frequently precipitates a struggle. Restraints are not only dehumanizing, they also pose risk of injury to students who are restrained and to staff who do the restraining regardless of setting. In a 1997 Connecticut incident, an adolescent patient at a psychiatric hospital died from suffocation while being restrained by staff during an emergency. According to news reports, the patient was positioned face-down on the floor, with arms crossed under his chest, as additional force was applied to restrain him. The parent filed suit against the hospital and the case is pending at press.

School personnel have been sued as early as 1944 for not applying restraint procedures in a "judicious manner" (*Calway v. Williamson*, 1944). School policies and procedures should specify under what circumstances restraints may be used, the methods that are allowed and prohibited, and necessary training of staff who may need to use restraint techniques. If an injury occurs to a student or staff member during any physical intervention, an assessment should occur and an accident or incident form should be completed (Wood, 1982). The need to use physical restraint should always precipitate a team review of the changes in the student's educational, health, and behavior status, and of the appropriateness of the student's educational program.

It is critical for school personnel to follow school district policy (assuming that the policy and procedures are reasonably expected to protect student and staff safety). In a Louisiana case (*Juneau v. Louisiana Board of Elementary and Secondary Education*, 1987), a school nurse was fired when she used aversive stimuli (a cold shower) on a student without first notifying her supervisor. The nurse sued her district for loss of employment, but her dismissal by the district was upheld in court since school policy required staff to notify a supervisor before using aversive stimuli on a student.

In a West Virginia case (*Ronnie Lee S. v. Mingo County Bd. of Education*, 1997), the parents of an elementary student with autism filed a complaint in state court against a school district and a number of its employees, claiming that the defendants, against the parents' wishes, frequently used a restraining device on the student, causing physical and psychological injuries. At the request of the defendants, the trial court granted summary judgment for the district, finding that parents had entered into a written settlement agreement with the district and that the parents had to exhaust IDEA administrative remedies prior to filing suit. The appeals court reversed, concluding that the trial court had erred, since

1. the parents had exhausted their administrative remedies when they requested due process;

2. the remedies sought (money and injunctive relief) were not IDEA claims anyhow; and

3. although a settlement was reached, it specifically did not release any claim related to the restraining device.

(See chapter 11 for further discussion of restraints, student rights and school district responsibilities.)

In testimony before the Restraint Task Force of the JACHO, the American Nurses Association (ANA) (1997) testified that

...except in those areas such as critical care units where the problem of treatment interference is intensified, it sees no role for the use of physical restraint. Rather, emphasis must remain on the availability of professional presence and adequate staffing...to make the necessary assessments in order to individualize patient care and take the necessary actions to resolve the patient's' problem(s). There is no empirical support for the implementation of clinical protocols to guide the use of restraint in the absence of a licensed independent practitioner's order.

ANA further testified that, in order to accomplish a restraint-free environment, there must be a consistent agency philosophy and administrative support to

- enable implementation of an individualized care plan;

- provide for sufficient continuing education for staff;

- engender the support of medical colleagues;

- ensure adequate professional staffing;

- provide appropriate environmental adaptation; and

- make available necessary equipment.

These recommendations are applicable in educational settings where student behavior raises the potential need for restraint strategies. Because decisions about the use of any type of restraint involves complex ethical, clinical, and legal considerations, a team approach to assessment of a student's behavior, and to planning, implementing, and evaluating the effectiveness of interventions is essential, including the advice and consultation of experts. Families and students must be involved in the decision making and, except in a true emergency, restraints should not be used without informed parental consent.

MEDICATION ADMINISTRATION

Liability Issues

According to Springhouse Corporation (1996), "Administering drugs to patients continues to be one of the most important—and, legally, one of the most risky—

tasks [nurses] perform." Not only is medication administration an increasing source of civil and administrative liability for school nurses, but it also tops the list of activities "most likely to lead to legal problems" for counselors, psychologists, and social workers: "If they make mistakes in the dosage or if, through some confusion or error, one student's medicine is given to another, the counselor is likely to be found liable for injuries suffered by students" (Fischer & Sorenson, 1996, p. 51).

Liability for non-nurse school employees (i.e., UAP) is likely to be highest in states where a state law permits medication administration by UAP, but does not require it to be

1. under the direction of a professional school nurse, with adequate training and ongoing supervision by the nurse; and

2. according to current health care standards for safe medication administration.

Districts that do not follow the requirements of such laws, even in states where they exist, or do not provide sufficient staffing for safe medication practices will also be at higher risk of liability for medication errors. Applicable health care standards include legal, professional, and ethical principles for medication administration in nursing, medicine, and pharmacy practice. These standards, with reasonable modifications, can be implemented in schools to enhance safe care of students and protection against district and staff liability.

Attention to safety in medication administration is more important today than ever before. There are many reasons why districts should carefully analyze their current practices and update them as needed. Those reasons are listed below:

• It is well documented by school health services programs across the country that significantly more students in 2000 require medication during the school day than did students even 10 years ago. Most of this increase is in the use of controlled drugs.

• Preventable medication errors and adverse reactions to drugs are on the rise in this country, in general, due to the growing number of medicines and prescriptions

• Errors in the administration of drugs, including over-the-counter (non-prescription) drugs, can cause significant harm and even death.

• Nursing errors in the administration of drugs causing significant harm or death can result not only in civil liability, but potentially criminal liability (see, for example, Kowalski and Horner, 1998, regarding the Denver case in which three hospital nurses were indicted for criminally negligent homicide in the death of a healthy newborn due to medication error).

• Most of the medications in schools are administered in a two-hour time frame (11 a.m. to 1 p.m.), which is also the busiest time of day for visits to the nurse for illness and injury complaints.

• Unlicensed personnel, even when sufficiently trained, are often required to administer multiple drugs to multiple students, in a short time frame, with competing job responsibilities and, generally, without sufficient ongoing supervision by a professional school nurse.

• There are increased reports to state school nurse consultants of theft of controlled drugs from school health offices and sales of personal prescription drugs from one student to another.

• Because of errors and court cases against nurses and physicians in other health care settings, standards of practice related to medication administration change; these changes are not always known by school nurses, physicians, and administrators.

• As the legal principles of "*in loco parentis*" and sovereign immunity continue to wane as defenses in liability cases (see chapter 2), and meeting the special needs of students becomes routine in all school settings, districts and their personnel will increasingly be held accountable for actions or inaction regarding safe medication administration practices.

Applicable Federal Laws

Both federal and state laws apply to medication administration in public schools.

Under federal civil rights legislation (§ 504 of the 1973 Rehabilitation Act), administration of medication in school is a related service that must be provided when students require the medication during the school day in order to access an appropriate public education. Medication administration, including monitoring students for the therapeutic, untoward, and side effects of medication, may also be required under IDEA if the IEP team includes it as a related health service in the IEP.

Many § 504 decisions issued by the Office for Civil Rights, U.S. Department of Education (OCR) and court cases brought under IDEA that relate to medication administration are discussed in chapters 11 and 13.

Brief examples of such OCR decisions and court cases are included here. In *Berlin Brothers Valley (PA) School District* (1988), the district's administrative requirements (i.e. discretion to administer medication, requiring a waiver of liability from parents) were found to violate § 504. OCR also ruled that the school district could not limit this service by requiring parents to sign waivers of liability. In *Pearl (MS) Public School District* (1991), a school policy denying administration of Ritalin to students with Attention Deficit Disorder during the school day was found discriminatory and in violation of § 504.

In *Ian E. and T.L.C. v. Board of Education, Unified School District, No. 501, Shawnee County, Kansas* (1994), the plaintiff was awarded reimbursement for expenses in connection with action against the school district. Initially, the district had refused to administer Clonidine at school, citing safety concerns. The district had agreed to transfer the student closer to the parent's work site in order for the parent to administer the medication. While the district later reconsidered and agreed to administer the medication, it was still found liable for the expenses incurred by the family in filing for due process and having legal counsel present at meetings.

District policy should clearly state the purpose of medication administration in the district (e.g., to provide essential medications necessary during the school day in order for the student to attend school or benefit from the educational program) and conditions under which the district will provide the service. Medications considered essential for students to receive in school include those requiring dosage during school hours for the management of seizures, disruptive or inattentive behavior, asthmatic or allergic reactions, diabetes, and other chronic health and mental health conditions. Rarely do antibiotics have to be administered in schools today since two or three times-per-day dosage can usually be managed at home, outside of school hours. At times, exceptions to this policy may be appropriate. For example, a student may not be receiving essential medications at home, as prescribed, due to home circumstances or developmental issues, such as asserting "independence and autonomy" (Scott, Love, & Owen, 1992, p. 479). These students may benefit from a school's willingness to provide in-school medication administration, even though the medication can technically be administered outside of school hours. Such situations, however, should be treated as exceptions to a district's general policy, and should be individualized in a § 504 plan or IEP.

Applicable State Laws

State laws vary regarding medication administration at school. Medication administration is usually the licensed function of physicians and nurses and is not delegated to unlicensed persons except when administrative mandates of state agencies specifically permit others to carry out this function. These state agency mandates act as exceptions to the licensure laws. Some state education or health codes, for example, have provisions allowing school nurses to delegate medication administration to unlicensed assistive personnel (UAP) in schools. Other state agencies, for example, departments of mental retardation and child protective services, often have similar provisions, allowing nursing personnel to delegate medication administration to trained assistants in their settings (e.g., group homes, residential centers for youth in state custody). These administrative regulations usually apply only to public entities unless specifically stipulated otherwise in the law.

In most states where education or health code provisions allow UAP to administer medication in schools, they can do so only with delegation, training, and direction by a professional school nurse. As exceptions to the licensure laws, these provisions attempt to achieve a balance between safety standards for medication administration, and reasonableness in schools, given limited resources, rights of students to access an appropriate education, and the assumption that students constitute a "well" client population. (See Appendix L for the Massachusetts medication administration regulations. These regulations provide an excellent example of state mandates that represent both an exception to the licensure laws and sufficient health care standards to reasonably ensure safe medication practices in Massachusetts schools.)

In a few states, for example, Texas, state law (Tex. Stat. 21-914) allows superintendents to assign medication administration to school personnel in their buildings—without delegation and direction by a professional school nurse. These school personnel may be unlicensed (e.g., teacher, health aide, secretary) or licensed, that is, registered nurse (RN) or licensed practical or vocational nurses (LPN/LVN). Wisconsin state law allows school district administrators and principals to authorize unlicensed school personnel to administer oral medications without delegation and direction from a professional nurse or physician, but does recommend that the district "seek the assistance of a registered nurse and a physician, both of whom are licensed to practice in Wisconsin and are in good professional standing, in developing a written district policy" (Wis. Stat. 118.29).

Conflicts between state laws and rulings of state boards of nursing regarding medication administration are not unusual. However, they are best managed when the relevant state agencies work together with interested parties, including the state's school nurse, school administrator, and teacher and parent organizations, to develop regulations that are consistent with applicable laws and safe practices for students.

For example, in Connecticut, the Board of Examiners for Nursing issued a 1995 declaratory ruling on delegation that permits professional nurses (RNs) to decide when and what is appropriate to delegate in a given instance, except that "no task may be delegated which requires an understanding of nursing process and principles necessary to recognize and/or manage complications…and medication administration by any route remains a licensed activity" that can never be delegated "unless a specific statutory exemption exists" (p. 10). This ruling reflects the Connecticut Nurse Practice Act (Connecticut General Statutes (C.G.S.) § 20-87, et seq.) but conflicts, in intent, with C.G.S., § 10-212a, which permits medication administration in schools by teachers and principals under the direction of a school nurse. In other words, C.G.S. § 10-212a, a law in Connecticut's Education Code, is a statutory exemption to the nurse practice act, a law in Connecticut's Health Code. In order to manage these opposing interests, regulations to the education statute are developed jointly by the state Departments of Education and Public Health, with input from the Board of Examiners for Nursing and many other interested parties in the fields of health, education, and consumer protection. Collaboration is essential in order to ensure the incorporation of sufficient professional practice standards to safeguard students. As described by Sheetz and Blum (1998, p. 95), the current regulations for minimum standards of medication administration in Massachusetts schools (see Appendix L) were developed through "discussion and compromise by a widely representative Advisory Committee" over a two-year period.

When principals and other administrators are responsible for directing school personnel in medication administration, there may be fewer safety nets incorporated into the actual procedures for medication administration, such as appropriate training and supervision of personnel. This can lead to situations that are more precarious for students (clinically), but less precarious for school nurses (legally), since they are not involved in the decision-making process. Regardless of a state's legal provisions regarding medication administration in schools, however, professional and ethical standards of practice require nurses and physicians who observe unsafe client conditions to either change those conditions or, after good faith efforts to effect change, remove themselves from employment in a position that directly or indirectly supports the unsafe conditions.

A state's laws and regulations generally grant immunity to school personnel who, according to legal requirements, administer medications in schools, for example, Texas law (*Administering of Medications by School District Employees: Immunity from Liability,* Texas Code 21.914 (1979)). Wisconsin's statute, cited above, provides immunity from civil liability for any person administering medication and any administrator or principal who authorizes such administration, according to the provisions of the statute, except when the act or omission, or the authorization, constitute a "high degree of negligence." Immunity notwithstanding, schools are accountable to provide safe, legal, and appropriate care for students in their schools.

School District Policy

Applicable state education and health laws and regulations related to medication administration and related professional standards of practice should form the basis of school district policies and procedures. School policies and procedures should never conflict with state law, regulations, and standards related to medication administration in schools, the practices of dentistry, medicine, nursing, pharmacology, and other health fields similarly governed, or legal requirements related to controlled drugs. If a conflict between laws exists, it is still necessary to implement relevant standards of safety in medication administration. In terms of potential liability, districts are best protected when they require medication administration to be under the direction of a professional school nurse, and when policies and procedures are collaboratively developed and revised with a school nurse supervisor and school medical advisor, as well as other interested parties. In 1990, the Office of School Health programs at the University of Colorado Health Sciences Center published national recommendations for medication administration in schools, including the suggestion that public deliberation and local policy development were essential to sound policy development (Igoe, 1990).

In addition to parent representation in policy and procedure development and revision efforts, all parents should be advised in writing, at least yearly, of the district's medication policies and procedures and district procedures for handling an unexpected emergency. It is best if the policies and procedures are contained in a student/parent handbook or comparable document that will not be easily lost at home. District medication forms should be included for family reference and use, when needed.

Two cases (*DeBord, Allen, et al. v. The Board of Education of the Ferguson Florissant School District, et. al.*,1996, and *Davis v. Francis Howell School District,* 1997) emphasize the respect the Missouri Federal District Court and the Eighth Circuit Court of Appeals hold for district policy regarding medication safety. In *Davis vs. Howell* (1997), the parents' contention that they had been irreparably harmed as a result of having to rearrange schedules and the resulting family stress from ensuring someone went to the student's school to give him medication was rejected by the court. In both cases, the school nurse and district were supported in their refusal to administer medication prescribed in unusually high doses. The school district was willing to administer the maximum dose recommended in the PDR, as provided in district policy. (See chapter 5, under "District Policy and Procedures" for additional information about these cases.)

Medication Procedures

Significant items to address in district policy and procedures may vary according to, and should reflect, state law and regulations, but include the following:

- All medications should be delivered to school by the student's parent or another responsible adult in the original pharmacy-labeled or manufacturer's container. Medications must be left in and dispensed from the properly labeled container.

- All medications require written orders from legally authorized prescribers and signed parental permission before they can be administered in school. (In some states, the prescription label may be used as the provider's written directions.)

- All medications, upon receipt, should be counted or measured, and the initial quantity delivered to school should be documented. Preferably, the medication is counted with and signed off by the parent. Alternatively, parents may be asked to document the quantity of medication they send to school, and the medication delivered can be counted, upon receipt, with another staff person.

- Controlled drugs should be counted on arrival at school, daily by the individual administering the medication *and* at least weekly with a witness (e.g., school nurse and trained teacher or principal). All counts should be documented and signed by the

individual administering and counting the medications and the witness, as applicable.

- Prior to administering any medication in school, the school nurse should review each medication order, as well as the delivered medication, for the correct drug, safe dosage, correct amount, administration directions, and compatibility with other medical treatments and academic scheduling and, based on the review, should develop an individualized medication plan for the student.

- Standard safety mechanisms should be followed in school by all responsible staff, including checking the "five rights" of medication administration:
  1. the right student,
  2. the right medication,
  3. in the right dose,
  4. at the right time, and
  5. by the right route.

  Springhouse Corporation (1996) suggests adding a sixth "right" to the original five: "by the right technique."

- Medications that exceed established medical safety parameters should not be administered in school.

- All medications must be stored according to both state and federal regulations. Since locked and secured cabinets or containers are required, a plan for quick retrieval of medications used in emergent situations, such as glucagon, epinephrine, and seizure-controlling agents, must be developed. Controlled drugs should be stored in double-locked containers or cabinets that are securely bolted to a closet wall or comparable surface. Massachusetts regulations require a locked cabinet that is "substantially constructed and anchored securely to a solid surface…used exclusively for medications" (Sheetz and Blum, 1998, p. 96). Safe storage includes directions regarding refrigeration, security of refrigerated drugs, and limited access to the refrigerator by school personnel. Refer to the state agency responsible for the oversight of controlled drugs, such as health or consumer protection. For additional information on federal regulations, review Registration of Manufacturers, Distributors, and Dispensers of controlled substances (21 CFR 1301.72).

- Access to medications must be strictly limited to the school nurse and selected, trained personnel who are currently designated to be responsible for medication administration.

- Keys to the medication cabinet must be secured

from general access; ideally, only the school nurse and one other school official should have a key to the medication cabinet. School officials who do have responsibility for the key, including the school nurse, must secure the key and maintain responsibility for its whereabouts at all times (see the cases discussed below).

- Medication must never be left out on counters, pre-poured in anticipation of student arrival, or pre-poured for another person to administer.

- Appropriate initial and refresher training should be required and documented for unlicensed staff assigned to administer medications to students. Training should include all standards of safe medication administration (i.e., general principles), as well as direction regarding student-specific medications and needs. General training should cover all legal and nursing practice standards including, for example, the "rights" of medication administration, when to call the school nurse, the need to be entirely free of distraction in all phases of the medication administration process, and the need to observe students placing the medication into their mouths and swallowing it.

- Ongoing direction and supervision of UAP and LPNs assigned to administer medications to students should always be provided by professional school nurses. Adequate staffing is essential to support this supervisory—and safety—function. (Refer also to the Massachusetts regulations, Appendix L.)

- When school nurses are expected to provide supervision and direction to UAP or LPNs who can administer medication in schools, district policy must support their option to delegate—or not to delegate—the administration of medication for a particular student, in a particular circumstance, to a particular UAP. This policy provision is essential regardless of state law provisions that may permit the principal or an administrator to "assign" the task. Furthermore, a school nurse's delegatory decisions must be defensible based on professional-clinical criteria related to student health and safety, and should be clearly communicated to the family, health care provider, and school team.

- Documentation should be completed promptly for all medications administered, including any errors occurring in the administration process.

- All errors in medication administration, including errors of timing (longer than 30 minutes before or

after the prescribed time) and missed doses should be recorded on incident forms and always reported to the parents, school nurse (if not the provider), building administrator, and risk management department.

- All medications not picked up by or returned to parents at the end of a course of treatment or the school year should be destroyed according to requirements of the state health, environmental safety, or consumer protection agency (controlled drug division). It is prudent to have a witness observe the disposal of drugs, especially controlled drugs.

- All information regarding medication and health status is confidential and, without parental permission, cannot usually be discussed by unlicensed personnel administering medication with anyone except the delegating school nurse and, when appropriate, the school principal. Students are entitled to privacy during the administration of their medication. (See "Parental Permission for Medication Administration" below for a discussion of nurse-prescriber communications.)

It is necessary for school personnel to consistently follow established policies and procedures in all aspects of medication administration, including administration at all school-sponsored, off-campus events. Otherwise, schools can be vulnerable to charges of negligence and discrimination. For example, *Pueblo (CO) School District* (1993) was found by OCR to discriminate. The district had refused to administer the student's eye drops for lack of directives from both the prescriber and parent, but OCR found that selective enforcement of district policy was retaliatory against the parent and, therefore, the parent's complaint was justified. This determination was based on evidence that the school district did not, in the preceding two years, always require both physician orders and written parental permission to administer medication at school. Rather, the district was randomly enforcing its policy. This arbitrary application of the policy was considered discrimination, even though the policy's requirements were both prudent and mandated under the law.

Delegation of Medication Administration

School nurses must know the provisions of their state's laws and regulations regarding medication administration and nursing delegation. Delegation of medication administration, other than topical and oral medications, may not be permissible by state law. For example, delegation of injectable, intravenous (IV) or rectal medications may not be permissible, or delegation of injectable medications may be limited to life-saving emergencies only. Where state law does permit professional school nurses to delegate medication administration to unlicensed school personnel, nurses should do so only when it is safe for students. In other words, school nurses should not delegate medication administration when there is an unreasonable risk of harm to the student; to do so puts the student in harm's way and the nurse at risk for disciplinary action, even if the law provides immunity from civil liability. Making decisions about delegation requires collaboration with the student, family, health care providers, school physician, and other school team members.

The potential benefits and risks for students must be weighed and balanced in each situation. For example, the desired outcomes of student attendance at his or her neighborhood school, increased student independence in self care, and improved self image may be positive benefits of nursing delegation of medication administration. Undesirable outcomes might be harmful to the student from improper dosing or administration, or failure of the staff member (delegatee) to recognize untoward effects of the medication. The school nurse and school physician should assist the school team and family in recognizing and weighing these potential risks and benefits before the school nurse makes a final decision regarding delegation. District resources (or lack of resources) and administrative preferences are important factors to consider in the decision-making process, but these must never take precedence over student safety and learning needs.

If assessment of a student's health status (e.g., cardiac or respiratory status) is necessary before a medication can be administered, school nurses cannot delegate administration of the medication to unlicensed personnel (UAP). To do so would be asking the UAP to make professional nursing judgments. In some instances, however, school nurses may be able to use the physician's written orders and nursing assessment data to construct a step-by-step protocol with specific directions that would permit administration of medication by unlicensed personnel. In other words, the protocol would not require professional nursing judgment to carry it out, but may require telephone contact with the school nurse for decision-making and direction. The professional decision regarding delegation will depend on multiple factors, including these:

- stability of the student's medical condition;
- complexity of the medication administration process;

- potential for risks to the student from medication side effects or error;
- competency of the caregiver; and
- availability of the school nurse for direction and supervision.

Insulin is an injectable medication that usually involves assessment prior to administration and requires a professional nurse to be on site for its administration. In many states, medication by injection, with the exception of epinephrine for anaphylaxis, cannot be delegated to UAP under any circumstances. However, if compatible with state regulations, delegation of insulin administration may be possible for certain students. In other words, the school nurse must determine that administration of insulin for the student does not require nursing assessment or judgment in order to ensure reasonable student safety. Should delegation of insulin administration be legal, as well as reasonable according to nursing delegation standards, it is imperative that adherence to all components of the delegation process occur. (See chapter 4.)

If unlicensed personnel are involved in medication administration, they must consistently follow all aspects of the district's medication policies and procedures and individual student medication plans or protocols.

Over-the-Counter Medications

Medications administered in school environments fall into two general categories-prescription and over-the-counter (OTC) medications. The same guidelines for administering prescription medications should be used for OTC medications. In many states, OTC medications are treated exactly the same as prescription drugs and cannot be administered in school without the order of an authorized prescriber and the written permission of the parent. All drugs, whether prescribed or OTC, have potential side and untoward effects; if used in excess, they can cause harm and even death.

There are both pros and cons to using OTC medications in school. On the positive side, appropriate use of OTC medication can assist students to stay in school and facilitate a level of well-being that may enhance student participation in the classroom. On the negative side, the kinds of complaints for which students may seek OTC medications are often best managed by other means. In other words, it is better care for students to learn to use healthier self-care strategies for managing headaches, mild cramps, stress, stomachaches, the common cold, and similar complaints—before resorting to management by drugs. Good nutritional habits, regular exercise, adequate sleep, relaxation techniques, and seeking assistance with problem solving, for example, should be encouraged in place of OTC drugs, as appropriate. If fever onset occurs during the school day, antipyretic medications (e.g., Tylenol, Ibuprofen) may mask symptoms of a significant underlying condition. Furthermore, antipyretics are not necessarily the treatment of choice. The fever most often indicates an infectious (and communicable) illness and the student generally needs sleep and care at home.

School nurses and school physicians should establish safety mechanisms for OTC drug use at school, especially if OTC medications are not covered in state law and regulations governing prescription of medication. The wisest policy from a legal perspective is to apply the same requirements to OTC medications as are applied to prescription medications. Sometimes, community groups or media reports scoff at nurses "who can't even give out aspirin." From a health promotion perspective, responses to these misconceptions can (and should) generate community discussion about the wisdom of drug use by children and youth. School nurses and physicians should educate their communities about the risks, negative health messages, and contraindications inherent in administering these types of medications to children and youth and why precautions are especially appropriate in schools.

In states where the law and regulations do not address OTC medications, or where practice allows schools to administer such medications solely on the basis of parental request, licensed nurses must determine whether their nurse practice act allows them to administer OTC medications to clients without the order of an authorized prescriber. Most nurse practice acts, if not all, prohibit nurses from administering to a client any medical therapeutic, including OTC medications, except under the direction of a physician or other authorized prescriber. To do so may be construed as practicing medicine without a license. Wisconsin guidelines (Erickson, 1998), for example, clarify that

> The Wisconsin Board of Nursing governs administration of OTC medications by nurses. School nurses may administer OTC medications to students based on standing orders developed in collaboration with the district's medical advisor, provided that the school board allows the use of such standing orders.

Other issues to be considered include who pays for OTC medications as they could conceivably become a significant budgetary item for school districts, and whether administering a medication from a stock bottle is considered administration or dispensing of medication. Generally, only physicians, pharmacists, and advanced practice registered nurses can dispense.

PRN (as Needed) Medications

Some medications are not ordered on an everyday basis, but rather, on an "as needed" basis (medically referred to as "PRN"). All medications, whether OTC or prescription, ordered on a PRN basis, generally require an assessment to determine the underlying cause of the student's symptoms and rule out improper use of the drug. Close monitoring may also be needed to prevent overuse and observe for untoward interactions with other drugs. For example, when a student has a PRN order for Ibuprofen for menstrual cramps, it may be appropriate to rule out abdominal pain from other causes, such as gastroenteritis and appendicitis, before administering the medication.

If it is legal in the state to do so and school nurses are considering delegation of the administration of an individual student's PRN medication, they must be able to provide to the unlicensed assistant (UAP) written directions that eliminate the need for nursing assessment of such factors. A nursing protocol must be developed that outlines a step-by-step process for proceeding according to the protocol or calling the school nurse for direction. Information that should be incorporated into a medication administration protocol for a PRN drug ordered for an individual student include the following:

- expected signs and symptoms in the student that indicate the need for PRN medication;

- medication frequency and dosage;

- action(s) to take prior to medication administration (e.g. take temperature and call nurse if fever);

- action(s) to take when data collected by the protocol indicate that the administration of this medication is not appropriate;

- action(s) to take if medication is administered and symptoms are not relieved;

- when to consult with the school nurse;

- when and how to notify the parent that a medication has been administered or requested and not administered, and why; and

- when the school nurse will consult with the medical prescriber or school medical advisor.

See Figures 6-6 and 6-7 for sample written protocols for use by the UAP to whom a school nurse delegates responsibility for administering an individual student's PRN medication. The PRN medication in these examples are ordered for menstrual cramps in student "A" and headache in student "B."

Standing Orders for PRN Medications

A PRN medication order from an authorized prescriber for an individual student is entirely different from a standing PRN medication order written by one physician for a whole population of students from both clinical and legal perspectives. Standing orders that cover a group of patients (in this case, students) are risky, as discussed below, and are generally not acceptable today in health care institutions.

These constraints notwithstanding, it is important to acknowledge that standing orders for emergency medication in schools, specifically epinephrine, can (and do) save the lives of children and adult members of the school community who experience their first anaphylactic reaction to food or a bee sting while in school. Therefore, standing orders are intended to cover those individuals who are not yet identified as known reactors and, for that reason, do not have their own emergency medication and individualized medical order in place. From an ethical perspective, it is appropriate for schools to undertake some risk in providing a service that has proven to be life saving in school districts across the country. Standing orders for epinephrine need to be written as part of an entire emergency protocol, including the order in which 9-1-1 is called, epinephrine is administered, a second dose is given, and other emergency interventions are employed, such as CPR. The order also needs to distinguish between the dosage required for younger/smaller students and the dosage appropriate for older/larger students and adults. Some state Good Samaritan laws provide protection for school employees who administer medication by injection in an emergency if they have had appropriate training. (See the Food Allergy Network's manual [Munoz-Furlong, 1995], discussed under the subsection "Students with Life-Threatening Allergies" earlier in the chapter, for additional information regarding emergency protocols.)

Standing orders for non-emergency medications, particularly OTC drugs, such as Tylenol, Ibuprofen, and antacids, are currently used in some districts and states, but are legally risky for several reasons. From a policy perspective, districts are wisest to require that students have an individual medical order from their own health care provider for all medications, including OTC drugs.

Reasons for such a policy position include the following:

1. Standing orders increase the risk of medication errors and, therefore, harm to students.

2. Standards of nursing and medical practice in other health care settings no longer include the routine (non-emergency) use of standing orders for medication administration for groups of patients.

3. Wellness promotion techniques include teaching children and youth to become independent in assessing their own health complaints and in making healthy choices to manage them. There are numerous strategies for managing the majority of routine, temporary health complaints of students (e.g., headache, stomachache, malaise) that, in the long run, are more effective and healthy than using drugs.

4. Medications can mask the early symptoms of significant medical conditions (e.g., fever, pain), and interfere with the body's normal immune responses to infection.

5. The use of OTC drugs in schools enable students to stay in school during the most contagious stages of common communicable illnesses, such as viral upper respiratory infections and streptococcal pharyngitis.

6. Refusal to use standing orders for non-emergency PRN medications does not prohibit students from obtaining medical orders for OTC drugs, when appropriate. Their own primary health care providers, who know the details of students' individual medical histories, including other medications they may be on at home, can write an order tailored to the needs of the individual student. A written medical order for Ibuprofen for menstrual cramps, for example, along with written authorization from the parent, can enable a student to manage the discomfort and stay in school.

Additional questions related to use of standing orders for non-emergency drugs that should be addressed if a district is using or considering using them include these:

- Who, other than physicians and professional nurses, can (legally) and should (clinically) assess students to determine if using a standing order in a given situation is appropriate?

- Should schools be ordering, using, and storing stock containers of OTC drugs?

Figure 6-6.

PROTOCOL FOR SCHOOL NURSE DELEGATION TO LPN OR UNLICENSED STAFF
ADMINISTRATION OF PRN
MEDICATION FOR MENSTRUAL CRAMPS

Student Name: _____   Date: _____

To be used only in the event that a student specifically requests medication for menstrual cramps, not to be given for complaints of abdominal pain or stomachache.

Subjective:

        Date of last menstrual period _____

        Is student actively menstruating?   [ ] Yes [ ] No   **If no, call RN**

        Pain other than menstrual cramps?   [ ] Yes [ ] No   **If yes, call RN**

Objective:

        Student's age _____

Plan:
Determine that the student has written physician's order and written parental permission for this medication on file. If student is actively menstruating, give medication according to physician's order. Have the student check back with you in one half-hour if pain is no better or becomes worse. Call RN if student returns. **Administer medication only one time during the school day unless directed otherwise by RN.** Document administration of medication on student's medication record.

Other pertinent information:

RN called _____ Time _____ Date _____

Signed _____ Title _____

STUDENTS WHO REQUEST PAIN MEDICATION FOR MENSTRUAL CRAMPS MORE FREQUENTLY THAN TWO TIMES PER MONTH MUST BE REFERRED TO THE SCHOOL NURSE FOR FURTHER ASSESSMENT.

Figure 6-7.

PROTOCOL FOR SCHOOL NURSE DELEGATION TO LPN OR UNLICENSED STAFF
ADMINISTRATION OF PRN MEDICATION FOR HEADACHE

Student Name: _____   Date: _____

To be used only in the event that a student specifically requests medication for headache, medication should not be offered to a student who complains of a headache.

Subjective:

Vomiting?	[ ] Yes [ ] No	**If yes, call RN**
Head Injury?	[ ] Yes [ ] No	**If yes, call RN**
Location and type of pain		**If describes that type of pain has changed from onset, call RN**
Duration of pain		**Call RN if pain has been present more than one day.***
Intensity of pain (scale of 1-10)		_____: **Call RN if student unable to function due to pain.**
When did the student last eat?		**If missed last scheduled meal, offer crackers & milk; rest 30 mins; if not improved and no other indicators to call RN, give RX**
Pain other than headache?	[ ] Yes [ ] No	**If yes, call RN**

Objective:

Temperature	_____	**If > 100, call RN**
Visual changes, severe stiff neck, incoordination/one-sided weakness	[ ] Yes [ ] No	**IF yes, call RN**

***If pain not yet present for one hour, offer water and rest for 30minutes and then if pain does not subside follow medication protocol.**

Plan: Determine that the student has a written physician's order and written parental permission for medication on file. In the absence of fever, vomiting or head injury, if the student has eaten his or her last regularly scheduled meal, and pain has been present for at least one hour, give medication according to physician's order. Have the student check back with you in one half-hour if the headache is no better or becomes worse. Call RN if student returns. **Administer medication only one time during the school day unless directed otherwise by RN.** Document administration of medication on student's medication record.

Other pertinent information:

RN called _____ Time _____ Date _____

Signed _____ Title _____

STUDENTS WHO REQUEST PAIN MEDICATION FOR HEADACHE MORE FREQUENTLY THAN TWO TIMES PER MONTH MUST BE REFERRED TO THE SCHOOL NURSE FOR FURTHER ASSESSMENT.

©Patricia Krin, RN, CSN. Used with permission.

- Should school personnel pour individual doses from a stock bottle?

- What state laws, regulations, and standards of care govern these practices?

- Does the state's board of nursing have a relevant ruling or guideline?

- Is the school's insurance agent aware of the district's practices in this regard?

- Are licensed nurses, physicians, and other school personnel adequately covered by the insurance policy to administer OTC drugs by standing order?

- Does the medical advisor's malpractice insurance cover this activity?

- What ethical issues should be discussed and weighed in deciding whether standing orders for non-emergency OTC drugs are in the best interests of students?

- What are potential short and long term benefits and harms for students? Parents? Staff? Other students?

- Do the potential benefits outweigh the potential harms?

Standing orders for emergency medications and others, if applicable, should be regularly reviewed and updated at least annually. The responsible physician must annually sign these medication orders, including those for emergency medications, before they can be implemented. School nurses who administer a medication without the updated order of the physician risk the consequences of practicing medicine without a license. Each school health office in a district should have a copy of the original order as it was executed for the district's central office.

Physician's Orders for Medication

Nursing and medical practice acts *never* authorize registered nurses, unless they are otherwise licensed as advanced practice registered nurses (APRNs), to make medical diagnoses, prescribe medication or administer medication without physician (or other authorized prescriber) direction and authorization. This may include the administration to clients of OTC medications, such as topical ointments, lotions, and pediculocides. Nurses (and others) who, for remuneration, diagnose or treat others (including administering medication of any kind) risk disciplinary action for practicing medicine without a license and penalties under state law (e.g. fines, jail sentence). A nurse prac-

tices nursing independently, but carries out medical treatments (or "the medical regimen") under the direction of a physician, including medication administration, unless he or she is legally practicing as an APRN. Because medical direction is required for dosage, timing, and route of administration, nurses cannot accept from a parent, without written physician confirmation, a request for change in the dosage, timing, or route of administration of a prescribed medication.

As suggested above, school districts should have "standing orders" from their school medical advisors for handling potential emergencies at school. These orders are appropriate due to the relative isolation of schools from medical treatment centers and the need for rapid interventions in emergencies. Appropriate medications for standing orders may be those critical for life-threatening, previously unknown conditions, e.g., epinephrine in a student or staff member who first experiences an anaphylactic reaction to food or a bee sting. A students who is a known reactor should already have on record a physician's order and parent's permission for administration of epinephrine specific to that student's individual needs.

Physician orders provide directions for safe medication use and ensure compliance with state licensure laws. Therefore, requiring individual physician orders for students is the most prudent route for schools to take. See Figure 8 for a sample medication authorization form used in a California school district.

Verbal and Faxed Orders

Medication and treatment orders should be written with the authorized prescriber's original signature. There are times when a change in dose or a new order needs to be implemented immediately and a written, signed order cannot be obtained the same day. School districts should have policies and procedures, based on federal and state laws and regulations and health care standards, that provide school nurses with guidance regarding the legality of verbal, fax and electronic-mail medical orders.

States vary regarding the legal standing of these temporary measures to expedite care. Faxed orders may be more desirable than verbal orders because they provide a copy of the order, if not an original, and are becoming more widely accepted as an alternative to written orders in those situations "when the original record or mail-delivered copies will not meet the needs of immediate patient care" (American Health Information Management Association, 1996). Unless otherwise directed by law, regulation, an attorney general's opinion, or a state board of nursing guideline, however,

Figure 6-8.   [front]

MEDICATION AUTHORIZATION AND PLAN   ____ IHP   ____ 504 (office use only)

*All students receiving medication at school require a Medication Authorization and Plan. This Authorization serves as an Individual Health Plan (IHP) for Special Education students or a Section 504 Accommodation Plan for other students. Prescription and non-prescription medications are permitted at school only when a completed Medication Authorization and Plan is on file. If any of the conditions of this Authorization change, a new form must be completed and signed by the parent and health provider. A fax copy may be accepted until the original can be mailed or brought to the health office. **This form is valid for school year 20____ to 20____ .**

****

PARENT SECTION:

I, the undersigned as legal parent/guardian of _____ (student's name) _____ (birth date) attending _____ School, Grade _____, request a designated member of the school staff make available the following listed medication(s) to my child as prescribed on this Authorization and in accordance with California law as referenced below. I also authorize, as needed, the sharing of information related to my child's health between the school nurse (or designee) and the health care provider listed below. I will comply with the procedure listed on the back of this form related to dispensing medication at school.

_____   _____   _____

Date   Parent/Guardian Signature   Student Signature (self-medication)

_____   _____   _____

Home Address   Work Phone   Home Phone

****

HEALTH PROVIDER SECTION:

I hereby instruct a designated school staff member to assist the above student in taking:

Medication	**Dose**	**Route**	**Time**	**Diagnosis/condition:**

Side effects that may be experienced even if given as prescribed: _____

Other medications taken by this student _____

EMERGENCY PLAN: _____

I have instructed this student in the proper use of the above listed medication(s). In my professional opinion _____ MAY / MAY NOT carry and use this medication him/herself.

(CIRCLE ONE)

_____ MD/DO/DDS/DPM/NP/PA _____

Printed name of provider   **Telephone #**

_____   _____ _____

Signature of provider   **CA license #**   **Date**

Approved by: _____ (school nurse) Date _____

REFERENCES: *California Education Code Section: :* 49423 Medication at school; 49480 Continuing Medication. *Business and Professional Code :* 2725 Verbal Orders; 4033 Definition of a Physician; 4036 Definition of a lawful prescription; 4051 Restrictions on furnishing medications without prescription. (CUSD 12/98)

The procedure covering prescription and non-prescription medication listed on this form will be executed under the following conditions:

Figure 6-8.   [back]

1. Only medication prescribed by the student's health provider as being necessary to be taken by the student in the manner listed on this form may be brought to school. Written parent permission is also required. Self-medication requires student signature.

2. Such medication shall be taken directly by the student in accordance with instructions from the provider as listed on this Authorization.

3. Medication brought to school will be given to the student according to the provisions listed on this form. The prescription or manufacturer's container must be clearly labeled with :
    - the name of the student;
    - the name of the prescribing provider;
    - the pharmacy who dispensed the medication or the manufacturer;
    - the strength of the medication and the amount to be given (dose);
    - the method of administration (oral, inhaled, topical, etc);
    - the specific time and or specific situations the medication is given.
(Parents may want to ask the pharmacist for "school packaging"—a separate container labeled just for the school time dose).

4. All medication will be kept in a secure place. Any special instructions for storage or security measures must be written by the health care provider and given to school personnel.

5. Students carrying and administering their own medication must have the provider circle consent on the front of this form. The student will comply with the order as written and maintain the safety of the medication at all times. Students who need medication while at school may carry medication (such as, asthma inhalers, insulin, severe allergic reaction injections - Epi-Pen and migraine medicines) and self-administer such medication under the supervision of school personnel, provided the following conditions are met: (1) the student is physically, mentally, and behaviorally capable, in the written opinion of the parent, physician, and the credentialed school nurse, to assume that responsibility and has been adequately instructed at home; (2) the medication is necessary to the student's health and must be taken during school hours; (3) the student has successfully demonstrated self-administration of the medication to the school nurse; and (4) supervision is provided by the credentialed school nurse, when available, or by designated school personnel.

6. Parent or responsible student (generally 6th grade or above) shall deliver the medication and the completed form to the school health office for review by the school nurse. Fax copies of this form are permitted until the original signed copy can be forwarded to the health office (within 5 days). CHS/CMS Fax - _____.

7. A new Medication Authorization form must be completed for any change in dose, time or method of administration. It will be valid for the current school year or until discontinued.

8. Medications must be picked up by the parent or guardian within one day of the end of the school year or they will be discarded.

9. For students with a current IEP from Special Education, this Authorization serves as an Individual Health Plan (IHP) added to the Special Education file. For other students, this Authorization serves as a Section 504 Plan to accommodate the health needs of the student while at school.

10. Additional copies of this form are available at each school's office or on line at: www.coronado@K12.ca.us. Look under CHS, Administration, Nurse, Forms.

11. Direct questions concerning medications at school to your school nurse: _____
    _____.

Used with permission, Ann F. Holler, 9/1998.

a written order should be obtained within 48 hours of accepting the phone, fax or E-mail order. (See chapter 10 for additional information.)

For liability reasons, it is wise for the school nurse accepting verbal orders to ask a second party to listen on the phone and to verify in writing the verbal order given by the physician or other authorized prescriber. District policy should specify who may accept verbal orders and under what circumstances. The American Society of Hospital Pharmacists' guidelines recommend that only an RN or pharmacist accept verbal orders (Gobis, 1997). State licensing laws may prohibit individuals other than nurses and pharmacists from accepting such orders; in other words, a teacher, social worker, or special education director who accepts a medical order related to medication administration may be practicing nursing or pharmacy without a license. Whether licensed practical (vocational) nurses can accept and implement verbal orders in a school setting, without direction from an RN, is a matter of state law, regulation or board of nursing and state agency interpretation. School nurses (and other school personnel, if applicable) should never accept an order, or change in order, that comes through a third party (e.g., parent or other staff member who is not licensed to receive or give such orders).

Parent Authorization for Medication Administration

In emergencies, school personnel administering medication may assume that parent permission is granted, even when written authorization is not available. Except in cases of gross negligence, the doctrine of "*in loco parentis,*" the state's Good Samaritan Law or immunity provisions for public employees will generally apply in emergency situations. In any event, if there is any question whatsoever, it is better in an emergency to err on the side of acting to save a life (or limb) than on the side of failing to act. See discussions earlier in this chapter, under "Emergency, First Aid, and Crisis Preparedness," regarding the death of a New Orleans student when school officials failed to respond to her request for an ambulance during an acute episode of asthma (*Declouet v. Orleans Parish School Board*, 1998). In this case, immediate action to obtain medical intervention may have saved the student's life and avoided a large monetary award against the school personnel and district.

Districts are best protected from liability in emergencies—and from legal disputes with families—if they annually notify families of their policies and procedures for handling health and safety emergencies. Such notifi-

cation should clarify that emergency procedures are applicable to *all* students. The only exceptions to implementing such procedures should be for students with individualized emergency care plans, particularly those with DNR orders. (See also chapters 11 and 14.) See Figure 8 for a sample medication authorization form that includes key requirements of the district's medication policy and procedures.

Districts should always have written parental permission to administer medication to students—for all non-emergency situations, including routine OTC drugs, such as acetaminophen for headache or temperature. Parent permission should also be obtained for emergency medication when students have individual medical orders and are known to be at risk for a medical emergency. Without parent permission, administering a medication to a minor, except in an emergency, may be construed as assault and battery.

State laws, regulations, and practices vary regarding the use of standing orders for OTC drugs and procedures for obtaining parental permission to administer these drugs to their children. Some districts rely on permission slips that list medications offered under the standing orders of a school physician. Parents are asked to authorize administration of such OTC medications by checking off which medications, including dosages, their children may receive in school, when indicated.

Some districts require telephone authorization by the parent before each dose is given. While sufficient manpower to make the necessary phone calls may present a challenge, this requirement is a reasonable precaution for both safety and risk management, if standing orders are allowed at all. Indeed, speaking with a parent may yield additional information, for example, another medication given by the parent that morning or symptoms the parent observed at home the night before. Since it is better in all cases to have both the individualized order of a physician and written authorization of a parent prior to administering any medication to a minor, it is safest when standing orders, except to save life or limb, are eliminated. However, until a district's policy can be changed to eliminate the use of such orders, requiring telephone permission for each dose is a practical strategy to limit the use of such orders and minimize certain types of medication errors. (See also the section concerning "Standing Orders for PRN Medications.")

Self-Administration of Medications by Students

Self-administration of medication in schools refers to situations in which students carry their own medication *on their person* and administer that medication to themselves during the school day, as ordered by their physician and authorized by their parent and the school district. This medication is not handled by school personnel, nor is it stored in the school's medication cabinet or in a teacher's locked file. State laws and regulations may permit self-administration of medication by students when districts support it through policy and procedure. (See, for example, Massachusetts regulations in Appendix L.)

Self-administration of medication by students with chronic health conditions, such as asthma and severe food allergy, is strongly advocated by health care experts. The major short-term goal of self-administration of medication is immediate treatment of symptoms in order to minimize effects of the disease and prevent unnecessary progression of an acute episode. For students with the potential for anaphylaxis, having the medication immediately available may be a life-saving strategy. The major long-term goals of medication self-administration, in addition to optimal treatment outcomes, are student independence, competence in self-care, and enhanced self-image. The sample authorization form in Figure 6-8, including authorization and requirements for self-administration, is designed for inclusion in a § 504 plan or IEP; alternatively, it constitutes the § 504 plan if no other accommodations or services are required (personal communication with Ann Holler, September, 1998). (See chapter 11 for additional information regarding § 504 and student rights related to medication administration in schools.)

School policy and procedures must clearly define when and under what circumstances self-administration of medication is permitted and the decision making process. Policies that limit who may self-administer medication strictly by grade level may be unwise, since developmental stages may have as much to do with a student's compliance and competence at a given time as age. Policies and procedures should also be in keeping with state mandates, as applicable, and with health and education standards for student safety related to medication administration. Safety issues for both the student in question and other students in the school should be considered. Where specific regulations or guidelines do not exist, the Massachusetts regulations in Appendix L provide a useful template. Some state's health or education agencies have guidelines that address self-administration of medication, for example, Virginia (Virginia Department of Health, 1996, p. III-5).

Many districts have policies that do not permit students to carry medications on their persons on school property or at school events. When families request permission for students to carry their own medication at school, it is necessary to assess safety issues, therapeutic issues, student development and competence, and related management issues and options. The desired outcome of all health interventions for students with chronic health conditions is independence in self-care, including student management of their own medication regimens, when reasonable, in the school setting. The school nurse should be involved in determining when a student has the proficiency to be independent in management techniques needed during the school day or, alternatively, can benefit from supervised self-administration. In some cases, such as students with Type 1 insulin-dependent diabetes, the medical team may be aggressively teaching and promoting self-management, including self-glucose monitoring and self-injection of insulin for students as young as five or 6 years old. This may work well at home, but may be more challenging to implement in school for a variety of reasons. The school nurse can serve as a mediator between the health care team, school, family, and student to plan an effective self-management program at school, recognizing family, school, and health care priorities. See Appendix H for an example of a school district's protocol for making decisions regarding diabetic self-care, including location of care. This protocol was developed by a representative committee that included the school nurse supervisor, special education director, school medical advisor, and parents of students with diabetes in a Connecticut school district.

Students and parents need clear direction as to what defines "medication" and "drug." Products such as multiple vitamins and cough drops are examples where variable interpretations may be made regarding whether they constitute a medication. In Iowa and New York, for example, districts may require students to have parental and physician authorization in order to carry and use cough drops at school.

Students who need immediate access to their emergency medications for life-threatening conditions should receive periodic nursing assessment, including evaluation of their self-management skills. Huang (1998) reported that of 98 patients surveyed, 93 of whom were patients under the age of 18 years, at least 75% reported that neither the physician or his or her staff had demonstrated correct use of the device. Furthermore, many children over age 12 and many parents of children 12 years or younger failed to operate the EpiPen correctly. For these students, the IHP should include plans both for enhancing their self-administration skills, and for ensuring assistance in the event a student becomes unable to independently manage his or her urgent care.

For students who are too young to carry their own emergency medication, the medication can be taped up high on the inside of a closet door in the classroom or otherwise made readily accessible to the teacher or other staff member who is likely to be the first responder to an emergency situation. While accessibility to the responsible adult is important, the medication cannot be accessible to other students. When students carry emergency medication on their own persons, a back-up supply of medication should be available in the school health office.

In *Culver City (CA) Unified School District* (1990), the parents had sought permission for their severely asthmatic child to carry his inhaler with him, rather than having it available in the school office, where it was frequently inaccessible when needed. In addition to finding that the district's original plan was an inadequate accommodation for the student, OCR determined that the district should have trained school staff members to assist in emergency use of the inhaler. (See chapter 11 for further discussion of § 504 decisions, including this one.)

Another example of medication that is appropriate for self-administration is enzyme therapy for students with cystic fibrosis. Because the enzymes are essential for proper absorption of nutrients, they must be taken with each meal. Because they would not usually be harmful to other students who ingested them, and there is an immense therapeutic effect from ingestion of the enzymes with a meal, students with cystic fibrosis should never be denied the opportunity to include these medications in their lunch boxes. Indeed, in some school districts where "self-administration of medications" is not permitted, these relatively benign enzyme medications have been treated as necessary food supplements.

Experimental Medication

Sometimes medications that are approved for use in treating one type of medical problem are ordered for a different health condition. Medications known to be safe for adults, but without long term studies in children, such as mood altering drugs, may be ordered for students, especially in the psychopharmacology area. An experimental drug that is not in the PDR may be used for a student with cancer. Policies and procedures should be in place to address these situations. The school nurse should have resources for information sufficient to support administering the drug in school. Such resources include current medical texts, such as

Child and Adolescent Clinical Psychopharmacology (Green, 1995), current medical and nursing journal articles, or a drug information center within a medical center.

Naturopathic and Homeopathic Remedies: Dietary Supplements and Drugs

An increasing interest in alternative or complementary therapies for management of health problems is evident in the number of requests received by schools for treatments from providers other than those practicing traditional American medicine. As a result, parental requests for the administration of naturopathic and homeopathic preparations and herbal remedies is a current issue in many states. State laws generally determine whether school nurses in the state can accept and carry out orders from naturopathic and homeopathic practitioners. It is critical for school nurses to know the state's law regarding medication administration in schools, the scope of practice of licensed providers, and the categories of licensed providers from whom the school nurse may implement treatment orders. This can help the nurse to determine whether the licensed provider has authority to write the prescriptive directions being requested for implementation at school and whether the nurse can act on it.

In states where school nurses cannot accept a medication order from a naturopathic or homeopathic practitioner, parents can be advised to ask the practitioner to work in collaboration with a medical physician who might provide the order, or to order doses that do not have to be given during school hours. It is important to support parents in their preferences for health care and help them find safe solutions to such dilemmas. It is also important to share why, should school personnel administer substances without sufficient scientific data regarding safety, it can be risky for both the student and the school.

Some states, such as Washington and Oregon, allow nurses to carry out orders from naturopathic doctors, although Oregon does not address the administration of dietary supplements in schools, and school districts must develop appropriate policy. Others, such as Connecticut, do not allow school nurses to carry out such orders. Section 10-212a of the Connecticut General Statues allows school nurses and, under the supervision of a school nurse, other nurses, teachers, and principals to administer medications. There must be a written order specifically from a physician, physician's assistant, advanced practice registered nurse, or dentist, and the written authorization of the parent. Because naturopathic and homeopathic practitioners are not physicians, as defined under § 10-212a-1 of the Connecticut Administrative Regulations, school nurses cannot accept medication orders from them. (See chapter 4 for further discussion of health professional practice acts and licensure.)

In Nebraska, the board of nursing clarified the responsibility of Nebraska nurses vis-à-vis prescriptive authority and administration of over-the-counter medications (Burbach, 1997, p. 3):

Prescriptive authority is required for legend [prescription] drugs and controlled substances making RN administration of such dependent upon a lawful medication order. Prescriptive authority is not required for over-the-counter (OTC) drugs; therefore, a registered nurse may legally administer such without a lawful medication order unless restricted by the facility/employer [and] may recommend to a consumer the use of an OTC drug/medication. If the RN elects to recommend and/or administer an OTC drug/medication, the nurse is directly accountable and responsible to the consumer for the quality of nursing care rendered...including knowledge of the indications, contraindications, and potential side effects from the medication/drug [and] such knowledge should be used in concert with nursing assessment of the consumer needs and health status...[and] consumer education.

In the same newsletter, Burbach, a Nursing Practice Consultant at the Nebraska Department of Health and Human Services, goes on to address the question of "School Nurses and Natural Remedies and Supplements" (p. 3). Since Nebraska nurses can recommend and administer OTC drugs according to the above stipulations, Burbach states that "the legal question of authority to administer medications without a lawful order is not the issue. The issue becomes nursing judgment," with consideration being given to the lack of usual standards and research data, as well as the potentially negative effect (on the consumer and consumer-nurse relationship of a school nurse's refusal to administer the substance. Burbach suggests that, if a school nurse is simply "providing" the medication (i.e., holding it and making it available to the student as like a paraprofessional does), as opposed to "administering" it (which requires professional judgment about the appropriateness of the medication, review of contraindications, observing for therapeutic effect or side effects and evaluating the "medication profile in relation to consumer assess-

ment"), that it might be acceptable for the school nurse to do. Burbach further suggests that it is a matter of the nurse's contract with the consumer, which, "if necessary, should be in writing."

School nurses are strongly cautioned about this interpretation, which should be used as a basis for practice only in Nebraska. Even in Nebraska, applying the regulatory language used to define medication practices by aides and other unlicensed persons to the practice of licensed professional nurses poses ethical, clinical, and legal questions and risk management concerns. Nebraska Administrative Regulations, chapter 95, "Regulations Governing the Provision of Medications by Medication Aides and Other Unlicensed Persons," do distinguish between the terms "provision of medication" and "administering medication":

[The provision of medication consists of] giving or applying a dose of a medication to an individual and includes helping an individual in giving or applying such medication...according to the five rights and recording medication provision. [It] does not include observing, monitoring, reporting, and otherwise taking appropriate actions regarding desired effects, side effects, interactions, and contraindications associated with the medication (Nebraska Regulations (NR), Title 172, chapter 95, 002.17).

The regulations go on to require (at NR, Title 172, chapter 95, 006) that "medications may be provided by medication aides and other unlicensed persons only when direction and monitoring are provided and documented" by a medication-capable recipient (patient) who is 19 years or older, a caretaker (parent, foster parent, family member, friend, or legal guardian), or a licensed health professional acting "within the prevailing standards of the profession." The latter phrase appears inconsistent with Burbach's suggestion that school nurses can operate under standards for paraprofessionals, rather than standards for nurses. For example, medication administration defined within the Nursing Intervention Classification system (NIC) is defined as "preparing, giving, and evaluating the effectiveness of prescription and nonprescription drugs" (Anderson, 1998). As it would be difficult to distinguish between the terms "provide" and "give," the NIC definition indicates that if a nurse gives (or provides) a medication, he or she must also ensure its safe preparation and evaluate its effects on the student.

Whether the nurse is administering a medication directly or monitoring an aide who is doing so, the prevailing standards of the profession require nurses to be knowledgeable about care they provide and to safeguard clients from harm. *Agreeing to "provide" a medication instead of "administering" the medication is not likely to relieve a school nurse from his or her obligation to follow standards of practice for the safe administration of medication, whether over-the-counter or prescription. This is especially true when clients are minors.* Furthermore, licensed professional nurses owe a higher standard of care to clients than do paraprofessionals.

Most states do not distinguish between providing and administering, and in states where school nurses can implement orders from naturopathic or homeopathic practitioners, a dilemma still exists. For all medications administered to clients, nurses are accountable for knowing therapeutic effects, safe dosage, contraindications, and potential side effects. For traditional drugs that are researched and reviewed by the FDA prior to sale in the U.S., nurses and physicians can use the *Physician's Desk Reference* (PDR) and other standard nursing and medical drug reference books to review such information. For homeopathic preparations and herbal remedies, however, references are not yet available with the same scientific, research-based information with which to verify the appropriate use, safe range of dosage in children, and potential therapeutic and untoward effects (short and long term). Homeopathic products, according to *The Medical Letter* (Homeopathic products, 1999), have not been proven effective for any clinical condition. Even if classified as food supplements, natural substances and herbs are not without potential harm, including life-threatening conditions (Mitchell, 1998).

Herbal products and dietary supplements have not been subject to the scrutiny of the Food and Drug Administration (FDA) and in the United States, as in most countries, dosage and purity have not been regulated for these products. Since the FDA's Commission on Dietary Supplement Labels proposed that labels should be made more uniform and reliable, however, the U.S. Pharmacopeia (USP) is establishing "authoritative standards for botanical and non-botanical dietary supplements" (U.S. Pharmacopeia, 1999a). Information provided by the USP is helpful in establishing what information is and is not known about the efficacy and safety of these supplements. Furthermore, while not yet required, products labeled with USP and NF (National Formulary) will indicate compliance with new USP quality and purity standards for these dietary supplements. Currently, the American Medical Association is calling upon Congress to modify the Dietary Supple-

ment Health and Education Act to require that dietary supplements and herbal remedies, including the products already in the marketplace, meet USP standards for identity, strength, quality, purity, packaging, and labeling (U.S. Pharmacopeia, 1999b).

If school nurses are expected to administer such preparations, they should ask the responsible practitioner to provide written, factual information about the medication or dietary supplement, desired results, appropriate dosage range for the age or weight of the student, necessary precautions, contraindications, and possible side effects, as well as a resource for checking on standards and research data about the substance. Another option is to let parents come to school to administer the desired product. Medication administration is basically an access issue—an accommodation made to allow students, who might otherwise have to remain home or forego treatment, to come to school. Therefore, requesting research evidence supporting the need for a product *to be given in school* is appropriate. Even where permitted by state law, not all medications—or alternative products—need be accommodated at school.

While states vary on this issue, and "prevailing practice" and regulation may change as standardization occurs and more information is known about these products, school nurses and administrators are cautioned, from a risk management perspective, to consider the following:

- School nurses should know and practice within the laws of their state.

- If the law does not sufficiently address this issue, or ethical issues remain, obtain a written opinion from the Board of Nursing and encourage collaboration between the Boards of Nursing, Medicine and Pharmacy and the state departments of health and education.

- Consider convening a committee on ethics, with appropriate representation and expertise from the school and community, to explore and advise on the issues.

- School district policies and procedures should meet professional standards of practice for safe medication administration and should be followed consistently.

- School policy should prohibit students from carrying and personnel from administering any substance that could be construed as a drug or medication, including natural remedies, herbs, and nutritional supplements, without the explicit order of an authorized prescriber in the state, parent authorization, verification that a product is safe to administer to children in the prescribed dosage, and reasonable information regarding therapeutic and untoward effects.

- Not administering a product in school does not prevent parents from administering it at home or coming to school to administer it themselves.

If school policy is focused on student safety and founded on scientific knowledge, if parents receive adequate information and explanations, and if the policy is enforced without exception, school districts should not be liable if parents charge them with discrimination. In a case in Montana, OCR found no discrimination in the school's refusal to administer medication prescribed by naturopathic physician (East Helena, MT, Elementary School District #9, 29 IDELR 796 (OCR1998)). On the other hand, when scientific evidence and safety parameters are available, efforts to accommodate parental preferences are exceedingly important. School nurses need to keep up to date with current research and standards in these fields and with the culture and health interests of their community's members. Again, a school health advisory council or healthy school team and ethics committee can be invaluable in helping a school district to research the issues and develop appropriate policies and procedures in this challenging area of school health practice.

Emergency Medications, Including Oxygen

Several, if not all, states have legislation allowing unlicensed individuals to receive training in recognizing students with anaphylactic shock reactions and responding, by injection of epinephrine (e.g., Oregon Statute 433.800 and Florida Statute 232.465). In these states, schools that do not train personnel or stock emergency medication for response in a crisis can be vulnerable to findings of negligence for being unprepared to respond to such emergencies. While permissive in language, these laws set a standard for districts with respect to schools' emergency responses to student emergencies.

The American Academy of Pediatrics (AAP) has taken a position in favor of anaphylaxis protocols in the school setting (AAP, 1990). Nurses who do not have prescriptive authority require an order from an authorized prescriber in order to administer any medication, including epinephrine in the event of anaphylaxis, regardless of the clinical setting (hospital, school, day

care, for example). Unlicensed personnel can only respond to this type of emergency if they have completed a training program required by enabling legislation or through a delegation from the school nurse. Some state nurse practice acts may prohibit such delegation since injection of medication is an invasive procedure and errors can cause significant harm. (See chapter 4 for further discussion of delegation.)

There are an increasing number of issues regarding the advisability of oxygen at school. Schools should obtain guidance from their medical advisor and EMS system regarding the need for oxygen as a standing order for students with unexpected medical problems and whether it is advisable to make it available in the district, or in a particular school setting. Oxygen for an individual student with an order from the physician and related to an underlying medical condition is a different issue. (See chapters 11 and 12 regarding the rights of students with special health care needs under § 504 and the IDEA.)

Schools are not required by civil rights legislation to provide emergency medication for individual students with special needs. Even in an emergency, medication supplied for one student, including siblings, should *never* be used for another student. Such a course of action leaves the second student without medication in the event that he or she requires it. Furthermore, the nurse is at risk of practicing medicine without a license in using a medication not specifically ordered for that child, and would likely be in violation of school policy which should prohibit the use of one student's medication by another student. (See the case of *Schluessler v. Independent School District No. 200, et al.* [1989], as discussed in chapters 4 and 5.)

When parents fail to provide necessary medication and supplies, the school nurse should involve the school administrator. Only the school administrator has authority for determining whether the student's attendance at school should be temporarily denied on the basis of the school's inability to provide for the student's safety during an emergency until essential supplies are delivered. Schools should be cautious about providing medication for indigent families, or funding medical services that are not part of a student's IEP, as they may be found in violation of discrimination laws if they are not providing similar products and services to all families. It is better to work with other community agencies and health care providers to find assistance for the family.

Field Trips and Summer Programs

Standards for safe medication administration,

including delegation procedures and school nurse supervision, do not change when students are on field trips or in summer programs sponsored by their school district. The related service of medication administration must be provided for students who are otherwise eligible to participate in field trips and summer school programs and eligible under § 504. (See chapter 11.) In other words, all members of a class are eligible for a class outing, and all baseball team members are eligible for a baseball team outing. Regardless of setting or time of the year, legal and clinical standards of safe medication administration still apply, as do standards for other health care that students require. Given the significant increase in students with special health care needs, including medication administration, school district policy should require that planning for field trips and summer programs is (1) initiated before school starts or early in the year, and (2) the product of collaboration between school administrators, teachers and nurses, as well as families, school medical advisors, and community health care providers, as appropriate.

Legal considerations in planning for field trips, summer programs and other district-supported student activities include the following:

- Students cannot be denied access to school programs and activities on the basis of their disability. (See chapter 11 on § 504 requirements and chapter 13 on current issues under IDEA.)

- Parents can be asked to accompany their child on a field trip, but cannot be required to do so.

- The level of nursing or health care services required for a student in the classroom is, at a minimum, the same level of care that the student requires during school programs outside the classroom. Therefore, if a student requires medication by injection to be administered in school only by a nurse, then sending a nurse on the field trip with the student is likely the appropriate plan of care.

- If delegation of a nursing function to assistive personnel (LPNs or UAP) is either illegal or judged by the school nurse to be unsafe when the student is in the classroom, it is likely to be illegal or unsafe during a field trip or summer program.

- If delegation of medication administration by a school nurse to an LPN or UAP is based on the premise that the nurse will be *immediately available* in a crisis (i.e., one that can be reasonably anticipated), then delegation of the administration of medication on an excursion away from the school—in particular, away from the availability of the school nurse to intercede in a crisis—will not be appropriate.

- Since delegation of medication administration, or any other nursing function, requires the delegating nurse to direct and supervise the delegate and evaluate the outcomes of client care, the school nurse must remain reasonably available to the delegate through telecommunications or other means. Summer school programs, for example, cannot have a trained, unlicensed person administering medications to students, even if they have done so during the school year, unless the professional nurse who is delegating that responsibility is reasonably available to provide direction, consultation, and supervision as indicated. Reasonably available means that a qualified nurse is hired (on staff) and within reasonable proximity to provide the necessary direction and supervision—which will vary depending on the needs of the students and competencies of the delegate. If the nurse is on vacation and not available to provide these functions, the situation is likely to be illegal, unsafe for students, and highly risky for the district in terms of potential liability.

- Administration of medication does NOT include dispensing of medication. Under the licensure laws in most states, only physicians, pharmacists, and advanced practice registered nurses (APRNs) may *dispense* drugs. Nurses, unless otherwise licensed as APRNs, may only administer medication and, therefore, may only delegate the administration of medication.

- Procedures for medication administration must be consistent with licensure, state law and regulations specific to medication administration in schools, and controlled drug and pharmacy mandates in the states. During field trips, individual student medications should be individually packaged by a pharmacy in "travel packs" (one dose per package) or sent in their original containers. Original containers can include small, properly labeled containers from a pharmacy filled only with the number of doses needed on the field trip.

- Transferring a drug from its original container into another (including an envelope) for administration to a student at a later time is generally considered dispensing medication and, therefore, not a nursing function. Placing a pill into an envelope, even with descriptive information, also increases the potential for dosage errors, access by unauthorized individuals and loss of medication. See below, however, for additional considerations regarding original containers versus one-dose containers.

- Medications taken on field trips must be appropriately secured (e.g., in a double-locked, sturdy box) and well-supervised throughout the trip. Given the numbers of medications that need to be taken on field trips today, and the increasing number of thefts of controlled drugs in and around schools, adequate security may be problematic. Therefore, sending full bottles of Ritalin and other controlled substances may not be any more desirable than sending one pill in a properly labeled envelope for each student medication. Guidance from the state agencies responsible for controlled drugs and pharmacy practice, as well as the state board of nursing, may best assist in solving this dilemma. In Connecticut, for example, the State Department of Public Health, in collaboration with the Departments of Education and Consumer Protection (Controlled Drug Division), provided school districts with written guidance regarding field trips. The guideline stated that, while sending *one* dose of a medication in a properly labeled envelope "falls within the scope of administration vs. dispensing medication," sending multiple doses in this fashion does not (Christoffers, 1990, p. 2). *Since this is a matter of guidance in one state, and since state employees who give such guidance change, school nurses must keep current on acceptable practice in their states.*

- Students who require ready access to medication during the trip, for example, asthma inhalers, should never be significantly separated from the person designated to carry or administer the medication. Where reasonable, self-administration plans, allowing competent students to carry and administer their own medication, is desirable. However, a back-up plan for adult assistance is essential.

- Arrangements for overnight and out-of-state field trips should be made on a case-by-case basis, depending on the needs, ages, and competence of the students, the destination, and the responsible adults on the trip. While safety must be the foremost consideration, creativity in achieving reasonably safe conditions for students is important as well. Advance information about EMS and availability of specialty medical services at the destination for some students may be necessary.

- If school personnel will need to administer or students will need to self-administer medications ordi-

narily not required during the school day, the same policies and procedures should be followed as are required for medications given during school (i.e., parent permission, physician order, properly labeled container, etc.).

- When it is decided that a school nurse will travel with a group of students on a field trip, a substitute nurse should be provided to address the health care needs of students remaining at school. Alternatively, it may be more appropriate to send the substitute nurse on the field trip.

Many issues related to medication administration at off-school-grounds programs, including work-site experiences, field trips, and outdoor camping experiences, are not well addressed through existing law or regulation. Perhaps more appropriate than mandates, in any event, are professional judgment, creativity, and collaboration with students, families, and other members of the education and health care teams. These are essential elements to finding the right balance between requirements for safety in a given situation and the personal risk-taking that is reasonable in order for the student to participate, learn and progress toward independence. The ethical concept of "dignity of risk" is addressed by the Committee on School Health of the American Academy of Pediatrics both in its guidelines for day and residential camps (1991, p. 117) and in its book, *School Health: Policy and Practice* (1993, p. 203). The former "maintains that children must be safeguarded but not overly protected" and the latter states that children with severe disabilities deserve the "same dignity for risk taking that is part of everyone's daily life."

The administration of controlled drugs during overnight field trips can be especially problematic, since even mature students should not be permitted to carry or self-administer these medications—on or off school property. Since self-administration means that the student carries or keeps the drug on his or her person, or is otherwise in charge of it at all times, this is not appropriate with controlled drugs for several reasons:

- students who require controlled drugs in school often require them for disabilities that affect their learning, memory, and organizational skills;

- these medications have a street value related to their use as "recreational" drugs, making them high risk for misuse, sale to others, and theft;

- controlled drugs have serious side effects, both physical and psychiatric, including death from overdose; and

- school policies and procedures must, to the extent possible, work to prevent the sale and theft of controlled drugs between students at school and during all school events, including field trips. This safety requirement should override any individual student's or family's preference regarding self-administration of medication, regardless of the student's competence.

Careful review of state law, regulations, and standards for the administration of controlled drugs, judicious planning, and flexible problem solving are required to manage medications on trips away from school.

Students Who Fail to Come for, or Refuse, Medication

To promote the intended benefits of medication therapy, doses of medication should always be administered in a timely fashion—that is, within 30 minutes before or after the prescribed time. When students do not appear at the scheduled time for their medications, school personnel remain responsible for timely administration of the dose, and should have a plan for handling "no-show" students. In essence, a medical order remains an order and, once the school has agreed to accept the order, it is obligated to do so within standard parameters for medication administration.

School districts should have policies and procedures that ensure safe medication administration, including how to handle "no-shows" and refusals by students. The best way to do that is to have a medication plan for each student requiring medication in school (and for each drug), with a section that addresses no-shows and refusals on an individual basis. For example, if a student frequently forgets to come for medication, or when it can be reasonably anticipated that a student will forget, the plan could include prompts from a wrist-watch alarm or from the classroom teacher to remind the student to go to the health room. If a student is rarely forgetful, the plan may simply require the school nurse or other person responsible for medication administration to follow up to determine if the student is absent from school or failed to come to the health room for another reason. If medication is not administered or is delayed beyond 30 minutes, parents should be advised and an incident report should be filed. Omissions and late doses of medication should always be treated as medication errors.

When medication plans are not achieving the desired result (i.e., timely administration and therapeutic effects), the student's needs should be reassessed and the plan revised accordingly. Individualized medication plans should be also be considered § 504 accommodation plans (most students requiring medication have a physical or mental disability that significantly interferes with a major life function) and, for IDEA-eligible students, should be incorporated into their IEP. (See chapters 11 and 12.) "Punishing" a student for forgetting to go to the health room, especially when the need for medication or "forgetfulness" itself is related to the student's disability, might be construed as discrimination against the student. (See also chapter 11.)

Student refusal to take medication is a different issue. While school personnel should make all reasonable attempts to give a student medication that is ordered, physical force and restraining devices should not be used to achieve this purpose. District policy should address the extent to which school personnel will attempt to administer medication and parent notification procedures when students refuse to take authorized medication (Murdock, 1990). Using force to administer medication may be construed as assault and battery against the child. However, when students are resistant to taking medication, schools must work with parents, other school personnel (e.g. administrator, counselor), and the student's physician to develop alternative approaches. Furthermore, since psychoactive medications work best when the individual being medicated is cooperative, they may be less effective if forced ("Medication for Behavioral Control," 1994, p. 6.).

Students cannot be denied attendance at school while awaiting control through medical management. In *Valerie J. v. Derry Cooperative School District* (1991), it was determined that the school district could not require a student with ADHD to be medicated as a condition of school attendance. The decision supported the position that, if a parent refuses to medicate his child, the school must devise a program to appropriately address the child's disability. Should the student's behavior present an imminent risk of harm to self or others, referral for medical or psychiatric evaluation, including exclusion until emergency assessment and treatment are provided, may be legitimate. Parents should be provided necessary information on available community resources and school support services to which students are entitled.

CONCLUSION

Quality school nursing services should result in healthy outcomes and improved learning for students; they are based on professional standards of practice and legal and ethical parameters for health services in school settings. Quality services mean that the right services are delivered at the right time and in the right way. In schools, quality nursing services require constant collaboration among school administrators, other educators, parents, students, community health care providers, school medical advisors, and school nurses and the exercise of their collective wisdom.

Qualified school nurses can assist school districts in providing quality health services. Legal mandates, district policy, and professional standards of practice provide the cornerstones for developing, implementing, and evaluating the quality of nursing services and competence of individual nurses. "No longer can nurses rely on a working ignorance of the law and legal doctrine. Today's professional practitioners must know, understand, and apply legal decisions and doctrines to their every day nursing practices" (Guido, p. 3). They must also be prepared to problem solve and identify strategies for addressing ethical and legal dilemmas in collaboration with their colleagues, and to maintain their qualifications through ongoing study and adherence to legal and professional standards.

To promote quality school nursing services, school nurses must be more than expert clinicians; they must also be expert communicators. Communication skills are essential in order for school nurses to clarify to others how and why legal mandates, ethical principles, and professional standards in the health field can or should do the following:

- be creatively adapted in schools;

- improve student performance;

- assist with problem solving;

- improve school climate and programs; and

- reduce district and staff liability.

Furthermore, effective communication is essential to collaboration and cooperation. "The law requires it" and "it's on my license" are never sufficient explanations of why something should be done in a certain way. Why the required action will make a difference for students and the school, what the bottom-line safety issues are, where flexibility is possible and risk-taking is reasonable in order to promote student independence and support family preferences—these are key areas of professional judgment that school nurses must be able to address and communicate in effecting change and promoting quality services for students.

REFERENCES

Aiken, T., & Catalano, J. (1994). *Legal, ethical, and political issues in nursing.* Philadelphia: F. A. Davis.

American Academy of Pediatrics. (1990). Policy Statement: Guidelines for Urgent Care in School (Re9193). *Pediatrics, 86*(6), 999–1000 [On-line]. Available: http://www.aap.org/policy/03376.html

American Health Information Management Association (AHIMA). (1996). Issues: Facsimile transmission of health information. *Practice Brief* (July/August). Chicago: Author.

American Nurses Association. (1997). Testimony of the American Nurses Association before the Restraint Task Force, Joint Commission of the Accreditation of Healthcare Organizations. *ANA Policy Series.* Washington, DC: Author.

American Nurses Association. (1998). *Standards of clinical nursing practice* (2nd ed.). Washington, DC: American Nurses Publishing.

Anderson, K. (Ed.). (1998). *Mosby's medical, nursing & allied health dictionary* (5th ed.). St. Louis: Mosby.

Arnold, M., & Silkworth, C. (Eds.). (1999). *The school nurse's source book of individualized healthcare plans* (Vol. 2). North Branch, MN: Sunrise River Press.

Brainerd, E. F. (1997). *School nurse emergency medical services for children program.* Farmington, CT: University of Connecticut Department of Pediatrics.

Burbach, V. (1997). School nurses and natural remedies and supplements. *The Lamplighter.* Lincoln, NE: State Department of Health and Human Services, School Health Program.

Burke, W., & Wheeler, L. (1999). Peanut-free or peanut-smart? Allergy education vital in schools. *AAP News,* February 20.

Cashin, D. (1999). Crisis preparedness. *Journal of School Nursing, 15*(2), 26–27.

Chin, J. (Ed.). (2000). *Control of communicable diseases* (17th ed.). Washington, DC: American Public Health Association.

Christoffers, C. (1990, April 16). Memorandum to school nurse supervisors: Revised regulations on administration of medications by school personnel. Hartford: State of Connecticut Department of Health Services, Community Nursing and Home Health Division.

Committee on Bioethics. (1995). Informed consent, parental permission, and assent in pediatric practice. *Pediatrics, 95*(2), 1–8.

Committee on Infectious Diseases, American Academy of Pediatrics. (2000). *Red Book 2000: Report of the Committee on Infectious Diseases* (25th ed.). Evanston, IL: American Academy of Pediatrics.

Committee on School Health of the American Academy of Pediatrics. Medical guidelines for day camps and residential camps (1991). *Pediatrics, 87*(1), 117–118.

Committee on School Health of the American Academy of Pediatrics. (1993). *School health: Policy and practice.* Elk Grove, IL: American Academy of Pediatrics.

Connecticut Board of Examiners for Nursing. (1995). *Memorandum of decision in re: Declaratory ruling—delegation by licensed nurses to unlicensed assistive personnel.* Hartford: Author.

Connecticut State Department of Education. (1992). *Serving students with special health care needs.* Hartford: Author.

Connecticut State Department of Education. (1994). *Guidelines for the development of school district policy and procedures: Reporting of child abuse and neglect; Youth suicide prevention and youth suicide attempts.* Hartford, CT: Author.

Ericksen, C. (1998). *School nursing and health services: A resource and planning guide.* Madison, WI: Wisconsin Department of Public Instruction.

Federal case will have impact on community. (Editorial, August 1, 1999). *Pocono Record* [On-line]. Available: http://www.winternet.com/radama/exams/t3.html or http://poconorecord.com/1999

Fischer, L., & Sorenson, G. P. (1996). *School law for counselors, psychologists, and social workers.* White Plains, NY: Longman Publishers USA.

Furst, L. (1995). When children assault children: Legal and moral implications for school administrators. 102 *Education Law Reporter* (13), 13–33.

Gobis. (1997). Can unlicensed staff relay verbal orders? *American Journal of Nursing, 97*(4), 72.

Gordon, T., Zook, E., Averhoff, F., & Williams, W. (1997). Consent for adolescent vaccination: Issues and current practices. *Journal of School Health, 67*(7), 259–264.

Gravatt, B. (1997). Current concepts in the pharmacologic treatment and management of tuberculosis. *Journal of School Nursing, 13*(4), 28–38.

Green, W. H. (1995). *The child and adolescent clinical psychopharmacology* (2nd ed.). Baltimore: Williams and Wilkins.

Groff, B. (1999). Upset father discloses tentative settlement with physician (August 11). *Pocono Record* [On-line]. Available: http//www.poconorecord.com/1999/groff/bg081199.htm

Grossman, E. (1999). Court: Genital exams violated rights. *Pocono Record* (Morning Call) [On-line].

Available: http://www.winternet.com/radama/exams/t3.html or http://poconorecord.com/1999

Guido, G. W. (1997). *Legal issues in nursing* (2nd ed.). Stamford, CT: Appleton & Lange.

Haas, M. K. (Ed.). (1993). *The school nurse's sourcebook of individualized healthcare plans* (Vol. I). North Branch, MN: Sunrise River Press.

Harrison, B., Fairchild, J., & Yaryan, L. (1995). The impact of legislation and litigation on the role of the school nurse. *Nursing Outlook, 43*, 57–61.

Homeopathic products. (1999). *The Medical Letter, 41*, 20–21.

Homola-Portuondo, P. (1995). Letter to Attorneys Kavit, Gass & Weber, S.C., in re Jennifer Vinci (summary and findings concerning the care received at school between 8/30/93 and 11/3/93). Expert testimony for *Jennifer Vinci, et al. v. Ames Community School District, et al.*

Hootman, J. (1996a). *Quality nursing interventions in the school setting: Procedures, models and guidelines.* Scarborough, ME: National Association of School Nurses.

Hootman, J. (with Carpenito, L. J.). (1996b). *Nursing diagnosis: Application in the school setting.* Scarborough, ME: National Association of School Nurses.

Hootman, J., & Carpenito, L. J. (1997). *Nursing Assessment of School Age Youth, Using the Nursing Process.* Scarborough, ME: National Association of School Nurses.

Huang, S.-W. (1998). Incorrect use of Epi-PENS. *J Allergy Clin Immunology, 102*, 525–536.

Igoe, J. (1990). *National guidelines for the administration of medications in schools.* Denver: University of Colorado Health Sciences Center.

Injured student established case of negligent supervision. (1996). *The Special Educator, 12*(3), 11.

Khan, E. A., & Starke, J. R. (1995). *Diagnosis of tuberculosis in children: Increased need for better methods. Emerging Infectious Diseases, 1*(4), 115–123.

Klahn, J. K., Hays, B. J., & Iverson, C. J. (1998). The school health intensity rating scale: Establishing reliability for practice. *Journal of School Nursing, 14*(4), 23–28.

Kowalski, K. & Horner, M. (1998). A legal nightmare: Denver nurses indicted. *MCN, 23*(3), 125–129.

Lavery, J. (1997). Memorandum and attachments from Joyce Lavery to Nadine Schwab, February 11, 1997.

Lichtenstein, R., Schonfeld, D. J., Kline, M., & Speese-Lineham, D. (1995). *How to prepare for and respond to a crisis.* Alexandria, VA: Association for Supervision and Curriculum Development.

Marx, E., & Wooley, S. F. (with Northrup, D.). (1998). *Health is academic.* New York: Teachers College Press.

Matsen, J. (1998). *Washington's good samaritan statute* (act) [On-line]. Available: http://www.wsffa.org.goodsam.html

McDonald, J. (1999). Exam violated girl's civil rights (July 28); Doctor denies forcing exams on schoolgirls (July 15); Jury gives $7,500 each to girls in genital exam case (July 30). *Pocono Record* [On-line]. Available: http://www.winternet.com/radama/exams/t3.html or http://poconorecord.com/1999

McNary-Keith. (1995). AIDS in public schools: Resolved issues and continuing controversy. *Journal of Law and Education, 24*(1), 69–80.

Medication for behavioral control. (1994, May). *School Health Alert,* p. 6.

Mitchell, A. (1998). Herbal therapies take some heat. *Pediatric Alert, 23*(18), 105–107.

Munoz-Furlong (Ed.). (1995). *The school food allergy program.* Fairfax, VA: The Food Allergy Network.

Murdock, K. (1990, February). Giving medication in the school. *EDU-GRAM.*

National Association of School Nurses. (1998). *Standards of professional school nursing practice.* Scarborough, ME: Author.

National Center for Health Statistics. (1997) [On-line]. Available: http://cdc.gov/nchswww/data

National Vaccine Advisory Committee, Working Group on Philosophical Exemptions. (1998, January 13). Report of the NVAC Working Group on Philosophical Exemptions. Atlanta, GA: CDC.

Northrop, C. E. (1987). School nursing. In C. E. Northrop & M. E. Kelly, *Legal issues in nursing.* St. Louis: C. V. Mosby.

Nursing Care Quality Assurance Commission and Office of the Superintendent of Public Instruction. (2000). *Staff model for the delivery of school health services.* Olympia, WA: Office of the Superintendent of Public Instruction.

Office of Civil Rights. (1997). Sexual harassment guidance: Harassment of students by school employees, other students, or third parties. *62 Fed. Reg. 12034 (March 13).* Washington, DC: U.S. Department of Education.

Oliver, L. C., Shackleton, B. W. (1998). The indoor air we breathe. *Public Health Report, 113*(5), 398–409.

Rosenfeld, J. (1998). Why and how to accommodate food allergies. *EDLAW Briefing Paper, 8*(5), 1–8.

Ruhl, K. (1985). Handling aggression: Fourteen methods teachers use. *The Pointer, 29*(2), 30–33.

Sampson, H. A., Medelson, L., Rosen, J. P. (1992). Fatal and near-fatal anaphylactic reactions to food in children and adolescents. *New England Journal of Medicine, 327*(6), 350–354.

Schwab, N. (1989). Child abuse and neglect: Legal and clinical implications for school nursing practice. *School Nurse, 5*(4), 17–28.

Schwab, N. (Ed.). (1992). *Guidelines for the Management of Students with Genetic Disorders: A Manual for School Nurses* (1st ed.). Mount Desert, ME: NERGG.

Schwab, N., Panettieri, M. J., & Bergren, M. (1998). *Guidelines for school nursing documentation: Standards, issues and models* (2nd ed.). Scarborough, ME: National Association of School Nurses.

Schwaderer, R. (Ed.). (1996). DC school bus driver does nothing when child has seizure on bus. *Transporting Students with Disabilities, 7*(19): 1–4.

Scott, C. S., Love, C., & Owen, R. G. (1992). Increasing medication compliance and peer support among psychiatrically diagnosed students. *Journal of School Health 2*(10), 478–480.

Sheetz, A. H., & Blum, M. S. (1998). Medication administration in schools: The Massachusetts experience. *Journal of School Health, 68*(3), 94–98.

Sheldrake, A. (1997, August). Presentation at Multnomah Education Service District, Portland, OR.

Spindel, J. (1997). Sick building syndrome: Grim, hopeful local actions. *MTA Today, 27*(6), 1.

Springhouse Corporation. (1996). *Nurse's legal handbook* (3rd ed.). Springhouse, PA: Author.

Stancik, E. F. (with Lupuloff, K., Keith, L., & Fernbacker, J.). (1995, September). *An investigation into the death of eight-year old Quentin Magee.* New York: Office of the Special Commissioner of Investigation for the New York City School District.

Texas Department of Health. (1994). *The liability risks associated with immunizing children.* Austin: Author.

U.S. Department of Labor, OSHA. (1993). *Occupational exposure to bloodborne pathogens* (reprinted). Washington, DC: U.S. Government Printing Office.

U.S. Pharmacopeia. (1999a). *Dietary supplements* [On-line]. Available: http://www.usp.org/

U.S. Pharmacopeia. (1999b, July/Aug). AMA recognizes USP's role in off-label uses and dietary supplement standards. *The Standard* [On-line]. Available: http://www.usp.org/cgi-bin/catalog/SoftCart.exe/catalog/frameset.htm?E+us pstore1999

Vernon, M., Bryan, G., Hunt, P., Allensworth, D., & Bradley, B. (1997). Immunization services for adolescents within comprehensive school health programs. *Journal of School Health, 67*(7), 252–253.

VICP (Vaccine Injury Compensation Program). (1999) [On-line]. Available: http://www.hrsa.dhhs.gov/bhpr/vicp/

Virginia Department of Health. (1996). *Guidelines for specialized health care procedures.* Richmond, VA: Author.

Wood, F. (1982). *Developing guidelines for the use of nontraditional educational interventions.* Lincoln, NE: Support System Project for Behaviorally Impaired, 1-46.

Yawn, P., Lydick, E., Epstein, R. & Jacobsen, S. (1996). Is school vision screening effective? *Journal of School Health, 66*(5), 171–176.

TABLE OF CASES

Bello v. Board of Education of Frankfort-Schuyler Central School District, 527 N.Y. S. 2d 924 (A.D. 4 Dept. 1988).

Berg v. Glen Cove City School District, 853 F.Supp.651 (E.D.N.Y. 1994).

Board of Education of the City of Chicago v. Illinois State Board of Education, 112 Ill.Dec.236, 513 N.E.2d 845 (Ill. App. 1 Dist. 1987).

Calandre v. State College Area School District, 512 A.2d. 809 (Pa. Cmwlth. 1986).

Calway v. Williamson, 36 A.2d. 377 (Conn. 1944).

Chalk v. United States District Court Central District of California, and Orange County Superintendent of Schools, 840 F. 2d 701 (9th Cir. 1988).

Davis v. Francis Howell School District, (104 F.3d 204, 25 IDELR 212 (8th Cir. 1997); 138 F.3d 754, 27 IDELR 811 (8th Cir. 1998)).

Davis v. Monroe County Board of Education, 119 S.Ct. 1661 (U.S. 1999).

DeBord, Allen, et al. v. The Board of Education of the Ferguson Florissant School District, et. al., Case No. 4:96-CV634 (CEJ) (E.D. Mo. 1996); 126 F.3d. 1002., 26 IDELR 1133 (8th Cir. 1997).

Declouet v. Orleans Parish School Board, 715 So.2d 69 (La. Ct. App. 4 Cir. 1998).

Doe v. Vahanvaty, MD et al., No 3:CV-96-852, No 3:CV-98-464 (M.D. Pa. 1999).

Farrukh v. Board of Education of the City of New York, 24 IDELR 407 (N.Y. Ct. App. 1996).

Grindle v. Port Jervis Central School District. 500 N.Y.S. 2d 314 (App. 2 Dept. 1986).

Hansel v. Arter (1985) 625 F. Supp. 1259 (S.D. Ohio 1985).

Hickingbottom v. Orleans Parish School Board, 623 So. 2d 1363 (La. Ct. App., 1993).

Ian E. and T. L.C. v. Board of Education, Unified School District No. 501, Shawnee County, Kansas, 21 IDELR, 980 (D. Ka. 1994).

Jeffrey S. by Ernest S. v. State Board of Education State of Georgia, et al., EHLR Dec. 441:576 (S.E. Ga. 1989).

Jennifer Vinci, et al. v. Ames Community School District, et al., CV 36870, Iowa District Court for Story County, 1997.

Juneau v. Louisiana Board of Elementary and Secondary Education, 506 So. 2d 756 (La. Ct. App. 1 Cir. 1987).

Landeros v. Flood, 551 P.2d 389 (Cal. 1976).

Levy etc., et al., v. Northport-East Union Free School District, et al., 672 F. Supp. 81 (E.D.N.Y. 1987).

Lynch v. Clarkstown Central School District, 590 N.Y.S.2d 687, 19 IDELR (LRP) 659 (N.Y. Sup.Ct. 1992).

Maack v. School District of Lincoln, 241 NEB.847, 491 N.W. 2d 341 (Neb. 1992).

Macomb County Intermediate School District v. Joshua S., EHLR 441:600 (E.D. Mich. 1989).

Maricopa County Health Department v. Harmon, et al., 750 P.2d 1264 (Ariz.Ct. App. 987)

Mason v. General Brown School District, 851 F.2d 47 (2nd Cir. 1988).

Mirand v. City of New York, 84 N.Y. 2d 44, 614 N.Y.S. 2d 372, 637 N.E. 2d 263 [92 Ed. Law Rep.[957] (N.Y. 1994).

Morris v. State of Texas, 19 IDELR 96 (Tex. Ct. App. 1992).

Punxsutawney Area School District v. Kanouff and Dean, (1995) 23 IDELR (2), 73–77.

Robert H. v. Fort Worth Independent School District, EHLR 559:509 (N.D. Tex. 1988).

Ronnie Lee S. v. Mingo County Board of Education, 27 IDELR 202 (W. Va. 1997).

Schluessler v. Independent School District No. 200, et al., 1989 Minnesota Case Reports 652 (Dakota County District Court. 1989).

School Board v. Arline, 480 U.S. 273 (1987).

Sherr v. Northport-East Northport Union Free School District (1987), 672 F.Supp.81 (E.D.N.Y. 1987).

State of Minnesota v. Grover, 437 N.W. 2d 60 (Minn. 1989).

Tucker v. Vahanvaty, MD et al., No 3:CV-96-1714 (M.D. Pa., 1999).

Valerie J. v. Derry Cooperative School District, 17 EHLR Dec. 1095 (D.N.H. 1991).

OFFICE FOR CIVIL RIGHTS (OCR) DECISIONS

Berlin Brothers Valley (PA) School District, EHLR 353:124 (OCR 1988).

Conejo Valley (CA) Unified School District (1993), 20 IDELR 1276 (17) (OCR 1993), 1276–1281.

Culver City (CA) Unified School District, 16 EHLR 673 (OCR 1990).

East Helena (MT) Elementary School District #9, 29
    IDELR (OCR 1998).
Grafton (ND) Public School, 20 IDELR 82 (OCR
    1993).
Hunstville City (AL) School District, 25 IDELR 70
    (OCR 1996).
Pearl (MS) Public School District, 17 EHLR 1004 (OCR
    1991).
Pueblo (CO) School District #60, 20 IDELR 1066 (OCR
    1993).

**See page 625 for Table of Federal Statutes and
Regulations.**

Chapter Seven

Adolescent Issues and Rights of Minors

Sarah D. Cohn
with Mary H. B. Gelfman
and Nadine C. Schwab

INTRODUCTION

Since school systems and their personnel must deal with students whose ages range from at least 3 to over 20, it is important to understand how the law treats minors and their parents. This chapter discusses the law regarding minors and informed consent generally and, using that background, addresses specific clinical areas, including reproductive services, mental health, child abuse, and Do-Not-Resuscitate orders. The law that governs minors' rights is state law and can vary considerably among the states. While the discussion contained in this chapter illustrates some of the variations, school nurses and school administrators must know the important aspects of this law in the state in which they have responsibility for minor students.

CONSENT TO TREATMENT

A competent adult may consent to, or refuse, what is to be done to his or her body, including any medical or surgical treatment. In the Cruzan case (*Cruzan v. Director, Missouri Dept. of Health*, 1990), the U.S. Supreme Court recognized that a competent adult has a constitutionally protected right to refuse unwanted medical treatment, even when it is life-saving. It further clarified that even an incompetent adult, in this case one who is comatose, can exercise his or her right to refuse treatment so long as there is "clear and convincing" evidence of what the individual, if competent, would want. Such autonomy to consent to or refuse treatment is not absolute, although adults are presumed to be legally competent unless declared otherwise by the courts. In addition, relevant laws vary from state to state, and certain situations, such as those involving drug abuse, are particularly problematic for health care providers.

Usually the age of majority is 18 years in the United States. The implications are discussed below, but, in general, the law presumes that one becomes a competent adult upon reaching that age. If a person is not competent at age 18, a guardian (who may also be called a conservator) may be appointed by a court for personal decision-making, financial decision-making, or both. Usually, parents are guardians of their minor children; when one parent dies, the remaining parent is the guardian. When the last parent dies or becomes incompetent, or where the child is abused or neglected, guardianship may be transferred away from the parent. The guardian, who may be appointed temporarily or permanently by a court may be a relative, stepparent, foster or adoptive parent, or state welfare agency. Where a guardian has been appointed for a minor under the age of 18, and it is considered necessary to continue the guardianship as an adult, most states require a new competency hearing and guardianship appointment once the adolescent is 18.

It is quite common for children to be living with family members who have not been formally appointed as guardian. A child whose mother has died or disappeared, and whose father is not involved, may be living with a grandparent, for example. Since a court proceeding to appoint a guardian has financial costs associated with it and takes time, many families simply do not seek formal guardianship, although the child may have been living in the household for years. If a guardian has not been legally appointed, it is customary to accept substituted consent from family members for most, but not all, types of medical treatment. Consent of family members can also be accepted to enroll a child in school. This custom has developed because it is not possible to force the appointment of a legal guardian if the family does not wish to apply to the court for this appointment, unless school personnel or others who may be concerned, like hospital or health care providers, intervene and file the application themselves. If schools or health care providers take the position that consent can only be given by a formally appointed guardian, as a practical matter many children will not receive the services that they should receive.

The traditional law held that persons under the age of majority were not capable, as a matter of law, of exercising sufficient judgment to make an adequate decision about health care and other serious matters. For example, in recognition of this principle, by statute or case law very young children are found legally incapable of forming the necessary intent to commit a crime. This legal principle still underlies the requirement that parental consent be sought prior to the medical evaluation and treatment of minors under the age of 12–14, depending upon the state.

The only exception to this parental consent requirement involves medical emergencies. An emergency is a condition that is life threatening—that is, one that poses an immediate, serious health threat. Holder (1987) defines an "emergency" as any condition that requires prompt treatment and is not restricted to a condition that may cause death or disability.

This definition is somewhat broader for a minor than for an adult because, while a competent adult may be permitted to refuse, for example, treatment for a broken leg, few health care providers would permit a parent to refuse such treatment on behalf of the minor child. Faced with this situation, which carries with it the chance of life-long disability for the patient, most health care providers would contact child welfare authorities or seek a court order for treatment. Similarly, a Massachusetts court authorized a hospital to provide all reasonable medical care, including blood transfusions, to an 8-year-old child, thereby overruling the parents' refusal, on the basis of religious beliefs, to consent to such treatment (*Matter of McCauley*, 1991). Despite the fact that the parent may not be permitted to refuse, and while evaluation and treatment may begin in an emergency, the health care provider, whether school or hospital, must make—and should document—all reasonable efforts to find and locate at least one parent.

Informed Consent

When issues of consent, by adults and minors alike, are encountered in practice, the underlying principle of "informed consent" is critical to understand and apply to the decision-making process. Informed consent in the medical context, according to Bernzweig (1996, p. 467), is a legal doctrine that holds that a patient's consent to treatment is not valid unless the patient fully understands the following:

- the nature of his or her condition;

- the nature of the proposed treatment or procedure;

- the alternatives to such course of action;

- the risks involved in both the proposed and the alternative procedures; and

- the relative chances of success or failure of the proposed and alternative procedures.

Underlying informed consent is the assumption, as discussed above, that the patient has the capacity to understand and make judgments regarding the information provided. As a rule, the more invasive a treatment and the more serious the potential outcomes of accepting or rejecting treatment, the more critical informed consent becomes as a legal requirement in the health care field.

Critical to the notion of informed consent is the process of the patient's "gaining information, deciding, and consenting [to treatment], not [just putting] . . . a signature on paper" (Hall, 1996, p. 222). This legal principle requires full disclosure of the relevant facts so a client can make an intelligent decision to accept or reject treatment. If all the facts are not clearly explained, then the signature of a patient on a consent form may not be legally valid; the client's full understanding of a treatment is far more critical than the signed consent itself. While the client's signature demonstrates a certain level of consent, it may not prove *informed* consent should a client bring suit for battery against the provider. Furthermore, a proper written consent from a patient does not make the health care professional immune from liability if substandard care is rendered (Bernzweig, 1996, p. 217).

Consent is usually given to the health care provider who is to carry out the treatment or surgery. Even when that person is a doctor, advanced practice registered nurse, or physician's assistant, staff nurses working with the client are still held accountable for ensuring that the client has provided informed consent to treatment. Accordingly, Hall (1996, pp. 224–225) states,

> Nurses are held responsible for patient advocacy, including advocacy in the consent process. Nurse responsibility for consent includes communication between doctor and patient, reporting to management (and perhaps even regulatory agencies, if consent is not obtained) and ultimately (if necessary) quitting the job.

While school nurses are not usually in the situation of mediating informed consent for medical treatment or surgery by other providers, as they are in health care institutions, they are accountable, and therefore liable, for ensuring that proper consent is provided by the parent, student, or both, as applicable for executing a medical treatment in the school setting; they are also responsible for fully informing both the parent and the student's health care provider(s) of environmental and clinical issues in the school setting that may affect potential outcome(s) of care or alter the risk/benefit ratio of providing treatment in that setting. A case regarding informed consent for the performance of state-mandated, in-school physical exams is discussed in chapter 6.

In the educational context, the notion of informed consent refers to the full disclosure of relevant facts related to, for example, the release of confidential student information to third parties or parental permission to evaluate a student for special education eligibility. (See also the discussion of the release of student records in chapter 9 and requirements for evaluating students for special education in chapter 12.)

Parental Consent or Substitute Consent

Where parental consent is required, the consent of one parent is normally adequate. Under some circumstances, the consent of both parents is required, but this is unusual. Notification or consent of both parents is required in certain states for abortion services. (Parental consent and notification requirements related to abortion services for minors is discussed later in the chapter.) In addition, if a minor is to participate as a research subject in a medical study that carries more than minimal risk and where the study will not provide direct benefit to the minor, consent of both parents may be required. (See federal regulations at 45 CFR 46.408 regarding Protection of Human Subjects; see also English, 1995, for a summary of research requirements when adolescents participate in research.)

These days, children may reside with one parent, who may not have legal custody pursuant to a divorce decree. For example, a child or adolescent may be visiting a non-custodial parent over a school vacation or may be living there permanently, although the divorce decree has never been modified. Nevertheless, if the child requires medical treatment, the consent of that parent may be presumed adequate; school personnel and health care providers may presume that the consent of only one parent is needed even if the parents have joint legal custody. Generally, school personnel have no obligation to examine legal documents in order to determine the right of a parent to consent.

If the documents do contain a requirement that only one parent may consent, it is likely that the parent holding that power will bring the matter to the attention of the school. Under unusual circumstances, however, a related or unrelated adult may have court-granted limited guardianship over a child. When this occurs, it may be necessary to examine the court documents to determine the limits of the powers that the court has given the guardian. These documents may be obtained from the guardian or from the court that appointed the guardian. It is preferable to obtain them from the guardian since, as a practical matter, guardians are appointed in the town, city, or county of residence, and most states do not maintain a central listing of guardianship appointments; therefore, school personnel would have to know where the appointment was made in order to determine which court to contact.

When school personnel permit someone other than a parent to enroll the child in school, consent to medical treatment, or provide other consent, it is advisable to document the social history and the whereabouts of the parents, whether known or unknown, in order to prove a good faith effort to determine who might act for the child.

Where a child has been abused, neglected, or abandoned, guardianship may be held by a state welfare or other state agency; in these cases, a representative of the agency has the authority to consent. When a child is in a foster home, the situation can be quite complicated legally. Most often in these cases, however, guardianship is held, either temporarily or permanently, by the welfare agency that placed the child in the foster home. In these situations, the foster parent may be permitted to consent for routine care and treatment, like a pediatric visit with routine immunizations, but the consent of the agency should be sought for more serious treatment, like surgery, or the disclosure of sensitive information, like HIV status. If the foster parent and the representative of the agency do not agree in situations like health care, confidentiality, participation in school activities, or other matters, and the issues cannot be resolved by meeting with all of the parties, the view of the court-appointed guardian will prevail. If the school nurse or school administration strongly disagree with the views of the state agency, the only alternative may be a court action to replace the guardian with another; this will usually not be possible if the state agency is appointed in a child abuse situation.

Mature Minors

Over time, it has proven impractical to require parental consent for every aspect of medical care. A well known Tennessee case documents the general legal principles related to "mature minors." In that case, a 17-year-old young woman sought care from an osteopathic physician for her back problems. The physician was one her father had seen; he performed certain manipulations in the office for a subluxation of the spine and a bilateral sacroiliac slip. Later that day, she developed urinary retention and had problems walking. Testing revealed a slipped (herniated) disc in her back, and she underwent a laminectomy to remove it. A malpractice case was filed against the physician. At the time the case was tried, the patient still had residual neurological deficit that resulted in difficulty walking.

Among other claims in this case was one of battery, in which the physician was viewed as having treated the patient without valid consent (since she was a minor and had consented to the physician's treatment, and her parents were not involved). In this case (*Cardwell v. Bechtol*, 1987), the Tennessee Supreme Court formally adopted the "Rule of Seven." It noted that minors have varying degrees of maturity and that

- under the age of 7, there is no capacity to consent;

- between the ages of 7 and 14 there is a rebuttable presumption of no capacity; and

- over 14, there is a rebuttable presumption of capacity.

Those states that have adopted the so-called "mature minor" rule have not abandoned the usual requirement of parental consent. Instead, where the health care provider has considered the age of the minor and the ability, experience, education, demeanor, and perceived maturity of the minor, the minor may be treated without parental consent. The burden is on the health care provider to document the ability of the minor to appreciate the risks, benefits, and alternatives of treatment.

Based on this case and subsequent ones, the mature minor rule confirms that treatment can generally be provided under this rule when the following conditions are met (Holder, 1985, p. 134):

- the minor is 15 years old or older, even if residing at home;

- the proposed treatment is for the benefit of the minor, and not for the benefit of someone else;

- the proposed treatment is necessary, based on the professional judgment of the health care provider;

- the minor is able to give informed consent—that is, the minor appears to have sufficient intellect and maturity to be able to understand the risks and

benefits of the treatment and make a reasoned decision based on the information provided; and

- the treatment does not involve complex, high-risk medical or surgical treatment or procedures.

As a practical matter, many health care providers render only "routine" evaluation and treatment under the auspices of the "mature minor" rule. However, that might include a throat culture and antibiotic treatment, which is not entirely without risk. It also seems certain that the osteopath in the Tennessee case believed that the manipulations being applied were not likely to cause serious harm, but they did.

A recurring question when minors are permitted to consent to medical treatment is how the school nurse or other health care provider is to evaluate, as a practical matter, whether the minor understands enough to consent. A recent article from the *Annals of Emergency Medicine* provides a useful framework. The article (Tsai, et al., 1993) suggests that the following criteria be assessed:

- *Understanding*: Can the minor accurately paraphrase the information given?

- *Reasoning*: Can the minor think abstractly, consider multiple factors, hypothesize, and predict future consequences?

- *Voluntariness*: Is the minor coerced or unduly influenced by others?

- *Nature of decision*: What is the gravity of the situation? Is an immediate decision necessary? Can choices later be reversed? What is the risk/benefit ratio?

Documentation that the minor appeared to understand the decisions being made should be entered in the health record.

In order to achieve some certainty for providers and patients alike, some states have adopted a form of the "mature minor" rule through statute. Some statutes are fairly restrictive, while others are more liberal. For example, Rhode Island law states that a minor age 16 or older, or married, "may consent to routine emergency medical or surgical care" (R.I. Gen. Laws § 23-4.6-1, 1995). South Carolina law provides the following:

Any minor who has reached the age of sixteen years may consent to any health services from a person authorized by law to render the particular health service for himself and the consent of no other person shall be necessary unless such involves an operation which shall be performed only if such is essential to the health or life of such child in the opinion of the performing physician and a consultant physician if one is available (S.C. Code Ann. § 20-7-280,1993).

In a few states, such as Arkansas and Mississippi, the law authorizes any minor who is sufficiently mature to understand the nature of the treatment to give consent to surgical or medical care (no age is specified); and in Alabama, minors 14 and older may consent to general medical care (Donovan, 1997). The majority of states do not have these statutes, but where they exist, the school health provider should understand their terms and restrictions, if any. Unfortunately, states rarely have a publication that summarizes these matters. However, information can be obtained from the state department of health or education, from a local hospital legal or risk management office, or, if the provisions are in statute, from statute books in a local library.

In summary, health care providers should know the provisions of state laws, if any, that govern the provision of routine treatment for minors. In states that do not have these laws, it is generally permissible, but not required, for a health care provider to render routine evaluation and treatment to a minor who meets the criteria discussed above. Special laws governing consent for drug and alcohol abuse, sexually transmitted diseases (STDs), abortion, and other specific situations are discussed below.

Emancipation

The concept of emancipation is somewhat different from the "mature minor" rule, although where emancipation is found, the effect is the same: that is, no parental consent is required for treatment.

Either by statute or by case law, a minor may be found to be emancipated from his or her parents if the minor meets certain criteria. These criteria vary among the states. In some states, statutes list the requirements. Wyoming law (Wyo. Stat. § 14-1-101(b)) states the following:

(b) A minor may consent to health care treatment to the same extent as if he were an adult when:

  (i)   The minor is or was legally married; or

  (ii) The minor is in the active military service of the United States; or

  (iii) The parents or guardian of the minor cannot

with reasonable diligence be located and the minor's need for health care treatment is sufficiently urgent to require immediate attention; or

  (iv) The minor is living apart from his parents or guardian and is managing his own affairs regardless of his source of income; or

  (v)   The minor is emancipated under W.S. 14-1-201 through 14-1-206.

The last section of this statute refers to a court proceeding in which a minor can petition the court for an order of emancipation. If granted, such an order recognizes the minor as an adult for the purposes of entering into a binding contract, suing and being sued, buying and selling real property, establishing a residence, and being subject to the criminal law in the state. The order of emancipation also terminates parental rights and responsibility (Wyo. Stat. § 14-1-202 (a), 1996).

Minnesota law has fewer requirements:

Notwithstanding any other provision of law, any minor who is living separate and apart from parents or legal guardian, whether with or without the consent of a parent or guardian and regardless of the duration of such separate residence, and who is managing personal financial affairs, regardless of the source or extent of the minor's income, may give effective consent to personal medical, dental, mental or other health services, and the consent of no other person is required (Minn. Stat. § 144.341, 1995).

Some states require, as one of the criteria for emancipation, that the minor has lived apart from a parent for a period of time (Nevada requires a period of four months [Nev. Rev. Stat. Ann. § 129.030 (1)(a), 1995]), or that the minor be either pregnant or a parent (410 ILCS 210/1,1996). Some emancipation statutes deny even emancipated minors the right to consent to sterilization (Nev. Rev. Stat. Ann § 129.030, 1995) or to sterilization and abortion (Mass. Ann. Laws ch. 112, § 12F, 1996). In most states where the emancipation requirements are met, emancipation exists without further action.

As is the case with the mature minor rule, school health providers and school administrators must become familiar with the relevant state emancipation requirements. In all cases, if a minor is emancipated, he or she has the right to enroll in school, contract, and consent to all medical treatment. In essence, if a minor is truly emancipated, the rights and responsibilities of parents are virtually eliminated. Therefore, if a school or school health provider is accepting a minor's consent to treatment or anything else under emancipation provisions, it is wise to document that decision and the factors on which it is based.

Emancipation provisions also have an impact on the services offered in a school-based health clinic; an emancipated minor does not need parental consent to obtain health care in the clinic. However, for reasons based on the agreement between the Board of Education and the clinic, it may be necessary to obtain consent from the adult with whom the minor is living. If the minor is homeless or not living with an adult, it may be necessary to waive the signature of any adult.

Age of Majority

In most states, the age of majority is 18. At that time, a minor becomes an adult and may legally undertake adult decision-making (other than the decision to consume alcoholic beverages in many states). A person who has reached the age of majority is presumed to be legally competent to enter into contracts, execute a testamentary or living will, and make all health care decisions, no matter how serious. For example, Wyoming statutes provide that

> …upon becoming eighteen (18) years of age, an individual reaches the age of majority and as an adult acquires all rights and responsibilities granted or imposed by statute or common law, except as otherwise provided by law (Wyo. Stat. § 14-1-101(a) (1996)).

Parents are no longer authorized to access medical records of their now-adult children, even if the care was rendered when the adult was a minor.

School records also become accessible to students when they become 18. However, the parent may also retain access if the student is reported as a dependent on the parent's income tax form. Under the Family Educational Rights and Privacy Act (FERPA) (1974), all records contained in a student's school files are accessible to the parents and to the student when he or she is 18. A possible result is that records concerning mental health, drug or alcohol evaluation and treatment, or treatment for a sexually transmitted infection, which might not be accessible to the parent in the original setting, become more accessible to the parent if copies are sent to the school to assist in planning school services. This conflict suggests that the school should be quite precise about the records it requests for school

purposes, and it should retain only those records it actually needs to justify the decisions made about placement and services. Appendix M contains a copy of FERPA. (For more information on school health records, see chapter 9; see chapter 8 regarding confidentiality.)

If an 18-year-old is not competent, the standard laws for the appointment of a guardian may be used to appoint an adult to act for the student. However, as is the case with many minors, many persons 18 or older who would not be considered competent due to mental retardation, or in rarer cases mental illness (mental illness by itself does not necessarily render a person incompetent as a matter of law), do not have a guardian appointed. These situations can be very complicated. For example, if a severely retarded 19-year-old has abdominal pain but is not permitting anyone to touch her, it would be unwise to permit that student to refuse evaluation. However, if the student is moderately retarded and taking illegal drugs, as a practical matter the appointment of a guardian will not stop her from obtaining the drugs, since the student is ambulatory and not constantly supervised.

There is additional confusion regarding the age of majority for special education students. The Individuals with Disabilities Education Act (IDEA) requires that special education continue until a student either graduates from high school or reaches the age of 21. Interpretations of age 21 vary from state to state, with some providing services through the school year in which the student turns 21 and others stopping at the student's birthday. Initially, IDEA provided all rights (such as notice of meetings, consent, and appeal) to the parents of students eligible for special education. In the case of *Mrs. C. v. Wheaton* (1990), the court found that notice of a team meeting to discuss an adult special education student's decision to withdraw from school should have been sent to the student's parent as well as to the student. The 1997 IDEA amendments include a provision that transfers special education procedural rights from the parent to the student when the student reaches the age of 18, unless a guardian has been appointed. IDEA also notes that state procedures should be developed to provide assistance for students over age 18 who do not have guardians but may need assistance in IEP team meetings. Students 18 years of age and older may request that notices be sent to their parents and may bring their parents with them to IEP meetings. For additional information, see chapter 12.

In FERPA, the parental right of access to a student's school records transfers to the student at age 18. Schools are not required to allow access by an adult student to medical "treatment records" and may permit access by a physician designated by the adult student instead. Parents whose adult students are listed as dependents on the parental federal income tax return continue to have access to their adult student's education records.

SPECIFIC CLINICAL ISSUES

The following sections discuss specific health care issues that frequently raise questions and challenges regarding the rights and responsibilities of minors. Several of the sections address minor consent-to-treatment statutes; the remaining sections address others minors' rights issues, particularly from the health care perspective.

The state minor consent-to-treatment statutes in this section are specific to particular conditions and, therefore, differ from the statutes discussed under "Mature Minors" that provide a more global right to consent to medical care. According to Donovan (1997), the trend for the last three decades has been to expand teenagers' authority to make health care decisions for themselves for two main reasons: (1) the increasing recognition that many minors are capable of making informed decisions about medical care and that confidentiality can be essential to encouraging young people to address sensitive health concerns in a timely fashion; and (2) the U.S. Supreme Court rulings that extend the constitutional right to privacy to a minor's decision to obtain contraceptives and the decision to terminate an unwanted pregnancy.

Recently, however, there have been numerous challenges to minors' rights to consent to the termination of pregnancy and a few efforts to curtail minors' rights to give consent for contraceptive services. Education personnel, in particular school administrators and school health and mental health professionals, must be knowledgeable about the relevant minor consent-to-treatment laws in their state and must keep up-to-date with statute changes and relevant court decisions. These laws have implications for practice in schools; they may have an impact on such issues as referrals for health care services, documentation, confidentiality, and release of health care information, as well as liability concerns.

Sexually Transmitted Infections

Almost all states have made provisions for minors who seek care for the evaluation and treatment of a sexually transmitted infection (STI) or sexually transmitted disease (STD) (which is still usually referred to as a venereal disease in the statutes). While the specific provisions do vary, the laws state that the minor may consent to the

medical evaluation of and treatment for STIs; a few state that it is not necessary to obtain parental consent or prohibit contacting the parent without the minor's consent. For example, Arizona law states,

> Notwithstanding any other provision of the law, a minor who may have contracted a venereal disease may give consent to the furnishing of hospital or medical care related to the diagnosis or treatment of such disease.... The consent of the parent, parents, or legal guardian of such a person shall not be necessary in order to authorize hospital or medical care (A. R. S. § 44-132.01 (1995)).

As a corollary to these requirements, it is often true that the minor is responsible for the costs associated with the evaluation and treatment (Minn. Stat. § 144.347 (1995)); sending a bill for these services to a parent may be prohibited by the statute in order to preserve confidentiality (Ct. Gen. Stat. § 19a-216 (1996)). Even without a statutory prohibition on billing a parent or guardian, billing anyone other than the minor, including an insurance carrier, for a service that can be sought confidentially should be done carefully, and in some cases, should not be done at all. Inadvertent breaches of confidentiality during the billing and reimbursement process have occurred; for example, explanations of benefits are often sent to the holder of the insurance, who may be the parent, not the patient. Private insurers, public and private providers of gynecology services, including school-based health centers, and managed care organizations have struggled with these issues. Many providers use general gynecology codes rather than those that are specific for STIs, while others use STI or STD codes but make sure that the bill does not state the diagnosis. Whatever system is designed, confidentiality of the services provided should be considered in advance and discussed with the patient.

The application of the general rule that minors can consent to STI treatment without parental involvement is often complicated by the facts of the case presented to the school nurse. For example, if a minor who seeks STI evaluation and treatment is sick enough to require in-patient treatment, it is likely that no health care provider would permit the minor to refuse the treatment since the consequences can threaten fertility and life, and after warning the minor, would contact a parent. In addition and for practical reasons, the admitting hospital is likely to contact a parent, in order to at least let the parent know where the minor will be living for the next few days.

What the staff then shares with the parents regarding

the medical reasons for hospitalization or the specifics of the diagnosis becomes a matter of professional judgment, especially when the parents believe that their daughter has never been sexually active. The preferred method of communication in these situations is to inform the minor that parents have inquired about the cause of the pelvic infection and to assist the patient in participating in the disclosure of the necessary facts.

As part of a few state STI treatment statutes, and not very well known, are provisions that if the minor with a venereal disease is under a certain age, which is 12 in Connecticut (Ct. Gen. Statutes, § 19a-216 (a)), the health care provider must report the matter as suspected sexual abuse to the child welfare authorities. Whether or not the statute contains such a requirement, sexual abuse is reportable as child abuse; if the school health provider believes that an STI may have occurred as the result of sexual abuse, the matter is reportable to child welfare authorities despite what may seem contradictory statutory confidentiality provisions.

Contraception

Donovan (1997) reported that 27 states have no laws addressing these services and 24 states have statutes authorizing minors to consent to contraceptive services. Where there are no statutes addressing contraceptive services for minors, health care providers do provide contraceptives to minors without parental notification or consent. Some state laws restrict, or some would say clarify, consent for contraceptive services for minors. For example, in Maine, family planning services

> …*may* [emphasis added] be furnished to any minor who is a parent or married or has the consent of his or her legal guardian or who may suffer in the professional judgment of a physician probable health hazards if such services are not provided (22 M.R.S. § 1908 (1995)).

In Tennessee, the law provides that "contraceptive supplies and information" may be furnished "by physicians" to any

> … minor who is pregnant, or a parent, or married, or who has the consent of such minor's parent or legal guardian, or who has been referred for such service by another physician, a clergyman, a family planning clinic, a school or institution of higher learning, or any agency or instrumentality of this state or any subdivision thereof, or who requests and is in need of birth control procedures, supplies or information (Tenn. Code Ann § 68-34-107 (1995)).

Table 7-1 demonstrates the considerable differences in state requirements regarding a minor's right to consent to reproductive health care. Note, however, that this Table is based on 1997 data. The Alan Guttmacher Institute's update of this Table (Boonstra, H. & Nash, E. 2000) demonstrates how much change is occurring in this area of state law.

If contraceptives are provided, the provider is responsible for making the determination that the minor has the intelligence and maturity necessary to understand the risks and benefits of the contraceptive method under discussion. It is also important to be practical—a minor may be competent to consent to the use of Norplant but it is unlikely, given Norplant's placement under the skin of the arm, that the parent will not notice the implanted contraceptive.

The privacy of records involving contraceptive care provided to minors is often uncertain. It is for this reason that minors might prefer to seek contraceptive advice from a source other than their usual pediatric or family health care providers. This decision must be made depending upon the providers involved and the trust and preferences of the adolescent. However, most reproductive health care providers will use every effort to resist providing information to a parent against the wishes of the minor patient and will notify the adolescent if the law would appear to compel the release of the records.

Condom Distribution

With growing awareness that the use of condoms could substantially limit the spread of the HIV epidemic, school health services and school-based health centers began considering ways to reach sexually active students with this vital information. In time, some school districts and health centers began to make condoms available to students. In response came lawsuits and federal legislation.

When the New York City schools made condoms available to high school students on request as a part of an HIV/AIDS prevention program, parents sued to stop condom distribution to minor students without parental consent. The initial claim was dismissed. On appeal, the condom distribution plan was rejected by the court because it interfered with parental rights. When this decision was appealed, the appellate court found that condom distribution in schools was a health service, and that there must be either parental consent or an "opt out" provision for minor students (*Alfonso v. Fernandez,* 1993). Parents could "opt out" for their children by notifying the school. If no "opt out" was received from parents, students could participate in the program.

It should be noted that parental consent require-

Table 7-1. Teenagers' Right to Consent to Reproductive Health Care: State Requirements as of 1997, page 1 of 3

MC=Minor authorized to consent or decide. PC=Parental consent explicitly required. PN=Parental notice explicitly required. NL=No law found.

State	Contraceptive Services	Prenatal Care	STD-HIV/AIDS Services	Treatment for Alcohol and/or Drug Abuse	Outpatient Mental Health	General Medical Care	Abortion Services
Alabama	NL	MC	MC2,3,4	MC	MC	MC5	PC
Alaska	MC	MC	MC	NL	NL	MC6	NL
Arizona	NL	NL	MC	MC2	NL	NL	NL
Arkansas	MC	MC7	MC	NL	NL	MC8	PN9
California	MC	MC7	MC2,10	MC2,4	MC2	NL	NL
Colorado	MC	NL	MC10	MC	MC4,11	NL	NL
Connecticut	NL	NL	MC10	MC	MC	NL	MC
Delaware	MC2,4	MC2,4,7,8	MC2,4,10	MC2	NL	NL	PN12
Dist. Columbia	MC	MC	MC	MC	MC	NL	MC
Florida	MC13	MC8	MC3	MC	MC14	NL	NL
Georgia	MC	MC7	MC3,4	MC4	NL	NL	PN
Hawaii	MC4,15	MC4,7,15	MC4,15	MC4	NL	NL	NL
Idaho	MC	NL	MC3,15	MC	NL	MC	PN9,16
Illinois	MC13	MC8	MC2,3	MC2	MC2,4	MC6,8,17	NL
Indiana	NL	NL	MC	MC	NL	NL	PC
Iowa	NL	NL	MC10,18	MC	NL	NL	PN12
Kansas	NL	MC8,19	MC4	MC	NL	MC8,19,20	PN
Kentucky	MC4	MC4,7	MC3,4	MC4	MC4,20	MC4,6,8	PC
Louisiana	NL	NL	MC4	MC4	NL	MC4,8	PC
Maine	MC13	NL	MC4	MC4	MC4	NL	MC21
Maryland	MC4	MC4	MC4	MC4	MC4,20	MC4,6	PN22
Massachusetts	NL	MC7	MC	MC2	MC20	MC6,8,17	PC
Michigan	NL	MC4	MC4,10	MC4	MC15	NL	PC
Minnesota	NL	MC4	MC4	MC4	NL	MC6	PN9
Mississippi	MC	MC8	MC3	MC4,11	NL23	MC23	PC9

* See note on page 241 regarding updated information

Table 7-1. Teenagers' Right to Consent to Reproductive Health Care: State Requirements as of 1997, page 2 of 3

MC=Minor authorized to consent or decide. PC=Parental consent explicitly required. PN=Parental notice explicitly required. NL=No law found.

State	Contraceptive Services	Prenatal Care	STD-HIV/AIDS Services	Treatment for Alcohol and/or Drug Abuse	Outpatient Mental Health	General Medical Care	Abortion Services
Missouri	NL	MC4,7,8	MC4,8	MC4,8	NL	MC6,8	PC
Montana	MC4	MC4,8	MC4,8,10	MC4,8	MC20	MC4,6,8	PN
Nebraska	NL	NL	MC	MC	NL	NL	PN
Nevada	NL	NL	MC3	MC	NL	MC	NL
New Hampshire	NL	NL	MC15	MC2	NL	MC	NL
New Jersey	NL	MC4,8	MC4,8	MC4	NL	MC4,6,8,17	NL
New Mexico	MC	NL	MC10	MC	MC	NL	NL
New York	MC	MC	MC10	MC	MC	MC6	NL
North Carolina	MC	MC7	MC3	MC	MC	NL	PC12
North Dakota	NL	NL	MC15	MC15	NL	NL	PC9
Ohio	NL	NL	MC10	MC	MC15	NL	PN24
Oklahoma	MC4,25	MC4,7	MC3,4	MC4	NL	MC4,6,8	NL
Oregon	MC4	NL	MC3,8	MC4,15	MC15	MC4,8,11	NL
Pennsylvania	NL	MC	MC3	MC4	NL	MC25,26	PC
Rhode Island	NL	NL	MC10	MC	NL	NL	PC
South Carolina	NL27	NL27	NL27	NL27	NL27	MC27	PC12
South Dakota	NL	NL	MC	MC	NL	NL	PN
Tennessee	MC	MC	MC3	MC	MC20	NL	NL
Texas	NL	MC4,7,8	MC3,4,8	MC4	MC	NL	NL
Utah	NL	MC	MC	NL	NL	NL	PN9,16
Vermont	NL	NL	MC2,3	MC2	NL	NL	NL
Virginia	MC	MC	MC3	MC	MC	NL	PN
Washington	NL	NL	MC3,15	MC15	MC14	NL	NL
West Virginia	NL	NL	MC	MC	NL	NL	PN28
Wisconsin	NL	NL	MC	MC2	NL	NL	PC12
Wyoming	MC	NL	MC3	NL	NL	NL	PC

Table 7-1. Teenagers' Right to Consent to Reproductive Health Care: State Requirements as of 1997, page 3 of 3

MC=Minor authorized to consent or decide. PC=Parental consent explicitly required. PN=Parental notice explicitly required. NL=No law found.

State	Contraceptive Services	Prenatal Care	STD-HIV/AIDS Services	Treatment for Alcohol and/or Drug Abuse	Outpatient Mental Health	General Medical Care	Abortion Services
Total MC	24	28	50	46	22	22	3
Total PC/PN	0	0	0	0	0	0	30
Total NL	27	23	1	5	29	29	18

Table Notes

1. Includes only laws that are currently enforced. These laws include a judicial bypass except where indicated. Eight states (AK, AZ, CA, CO, IL, NV, NM and TN) have parental consent or notice laws that have been enjoined and therefore are not in effect.
2. Minor must be 12 or older.
3. State officially classifies HIV/AIDS as an STD or infectious disease, for which minors may consent to testing and treatment.
4. Doctor may notify parents.
5. Minor must be 14 or older, a high school graduate, married, pregnant or a parent.
6. Minor may consent if has a child.
7. Excludes abortion.
8. Includes surgery.
9. Involvement of both parents required in most cases.
10. Law explicitly authorizes minors to consent to HIV testing and/or treatment.
11. Minor must be 15 or older.
12. Notice or consent may be given to or by grandparent or, alternatively, in DE to a licensed mental health professional, or in WI by another adult relative over age 25.
13. Minor may consent if has a child or doctor believes minor would suffer "probable" health hazard if services not provided; in FL and IL, also if minor is pregnant; in IL, also if referred by doctor, clergyman or Planned Parenthood clinic.
14. Minor must be at least 13.
15. Minor must be at least 14.
16. Does not include judicial bypass.
17. Minor may consent if pregnant.
18. Parent must be notified if HIV test is positive.
19. Minor may consent if parent is not "available," or in the case of general medical care, "immediately available."
20. Minor must be 16 or older.
21. Minor may be counseled by physician or a counselor in lieu of obtaining parental consent or court authorization.
22. Law has no judicial bypass; however, a physician may waive notification if the minor does not live with a parent; or if doctor determines that the minor is mature enough to give informed consent or that notification may lead to physical or emotional abuse of the minor or otherwise to be contrary to her best interests; or if reasonable effort to give notice was unsuccessful.
23. Any minor who is mature enough to understand the nature and consequences of the proposed medical or surgical treatment may consent.
24. Stepparent, grandparent or sibling over age 21 may be notified if minor files affidavit stating she fears physical, sexual or severe emotional abuse from parent.
25. Minor may consent if she has ever been pregnant.
26. Minor may consent if has graduated from high school.
27. Any minor 16 and older may consent to any health service other than operations. Health services may be rendered to minors of any age without parental consent when the provider believes services are necessary.
28. Notice or judicial bypass can be waived if second physician determines that minor is mature enough to give consent or that notice would not be in her best interest.

ments make student participation dependent on an affirmative act by the parent and assume that lack of consent means that parents do not support their child's participation. "Opt out," on the other hand, requires an affirmative act by the parent to bar participation and assumes that no response from a parent is implied consent to participation. This decision required the school health services to provide for parental notice of the program and either require consent from parents of minor students or allow individual parents to "opt out," preventing their children from participation.

Philadelphia parents objected to a condom distribution plan that included parental consent or "opt out," and the parents filed suit in federal district court. Organizations that supported the plan intervened, and the federal court granted summary judgment for the school district, upholding the plan. Upon appeal to the Third Circuit, the decision was upheld. The appellate court stressed the voluntary nature of the program:

> We recognize the strong parental interest in deciding what is proper for the preservation of their children's health. But we do not believe the Board's policy intrudes on this right. Participation in the program is voluntary. The program specifically reserves to parents the option of refusing their child's participation. Once the parents have returned the opt out form, their child will not be able to receive either counseling or condoms (*Parents United for Better Schools, Inc., v. School District of Philadelphia Board of Education*, 1998).

After a court upheld a condom distribution program for junior and senior high schools in Falmouth, Massachusetts, the Massachusetts Supreme Judicial Court upheld the decision (*Curtis v. School Committee of Falmouth*, 1995). Under this program, condoms were available at the junior high school through the school nurse, who would also provide counseling and written materials on HIV/AIDS and sexually transmitted diseases. At the high school, free condoms would be available from the school nurse and condom machines would be installed in specified girls' and boys' bathrooms. The high school would also designate staff members to be available for counseling on HIV/AIDS and make written materials available to students. No notice to parents was required, and parental consent was not required. In response to parents' claims of liberty and privacy in matters concerning the raising of their children, the court said:

> We discern no coercive burden on the plaintiffs' parental liberties in this case. No classroom participation is required of students. Condoms are available to students who request them and, in the high school, may be obtained from vending machines. The students are not required to seek out and accept the condoms, read the literature accompanying them, or participate in counseling regarding their use. . . . For their part, the plaintiff parents are free to instruct their children not to participate. The program does not supplant the parents' role as adviser in the moral and religious development of their children.

In response to an argument that the program interfered with the religious freedom of some students and parents, the court found that:

> Although the program may offend the religious sensibilities of the plaintiffs, mere exposure at public schools to offensive programs does not amount to a violation of free exercise [of religion]. Parents have no right to tailor public school programs to meet their individual religious or moral preferences.

Included among the general prohibitions concerning use of federal financial assistance to schools under the Elementary and Secondary Education Act, 20 U.S.C. § 8901 specifically prohibits the use of federal funds "to operate a program of condom distribution in schools." The same section of the federal law recognizes in general terms the autonomy of states and local school districts to control curriculum and other services provided in schools and the discretion to spend state and local funds.

In weighing the institution of condom distribution programs, local boards of education are influenced by community attitudes as well as the recommendations of school and health professionals. While Curtis upheld a voluntary program that did not require parental consent, it is likely that many communities would be more comfortable with the Philadelphia program, which required parental consent or provided for parental opt-out. Based on a review of the issues raised concerning condom distribution programs, Bjorklun (1994) recommends parental consent requirements.

Pregnancy

A minor who becomes pregnant is legally permitted to determine whether she wishes to continue the pregnancy (see the section on "Abortion" below) and may, in most states, consent to the prenatal and delivery care required. Typical of these laws is a Minnesota statute:

> Any minor may give effective consent for medical, mental and other health services to determine the presence of or to treatment of pregnancy and conditions associated therewith,…and the consent of no other person is required (Minn. Stat. § 144.343 (1995)).

One exception is Kansas, where the statute provides the following:

> Notwithstanding any other provision of the law, an unmarried pregnant minor where no parent or guardian is available may give consent to the furnishing of hospital, medical and surgical care related to her pregnancy. …The consent of a parent or guardian of an unmarried pregnant minor shall not be necessary in order to authorize hospital, medical and surgical care related to her pregnancy, where no parent or guardian is available (K. S. A. § 38-123 (1995)).

Even in states where pregnancy does not automatically emancipate a minor, the minor should be able to consent to all aspects of prenatal care, fetal testing, and delivery, even if it is by caesarean section. Further, no matter what the age of the mother, she may consent for health care delivered to her child. Although it is not absolutely necessary, many states have made this explicit, as has Rhode Island. There the statute provides that a "minor parent may consent to treatment of his or her child" (R.I. Gen. Laws § 23-4.6.1 (1995)). In a few states, this creates unusual situations: a 15-year-old, who is not emancipated despite having delivered a child, may consent for treatment of that child's brain tumor but may not consent to treatment of a tumor of her own.

The law is often silent about the circumstances under which a school nurse or any other health care provider may or must notify a parent when a minor says she is or may be pregnant or the nurse believes her to be. However, the American Academy of Pediatrics, among other professional organizations, has stated that information about the diagnosis and treatment of pregnancy "should not be offered to anyone, including the patient's parents, without the patient's permission" (American Medical Association, Chicago, 1993). The current standard of practice seems to confirm that pregnancy-related information will be kept confidential and not disclosed against the wishes of the minor, even to a parent, unless there is a life-threatening emergency.

For example, if a pregnant minor begins to experience heavy vaginal bleeding and must be taken to the hospital, the nurse must inform the parent—not necessarily that the minor is pregnant, but that there is vaginal bleeding and that the minor is on her way to a hospital emergency department.

Despite the general rule that pregnancy-related information will be confidential, the nurse may share that information with selected others in the school health system, like a substitute nurse or a social worker, so that if the student has health difficulties during school hours, those caring for her know the relevant history. It also remains good professional practice for the school nurse, who knows the student and sees her intermittently, to encourage that student to communicate with her parents about the pregnancy.

There are non-life-threatening situations where a nurse may feel it critical that a parent be notified. The issue becomes particularly difficult when the pregnant student chooses to continue the pregnancy but not seek prenatal care. The nurse must finally make an assessment to determine if the student is putting herself at risk of excessive harm. For example, instances in which a minor is developing pregnancy-related hypertension or approaching term and has no plans for delivery and care of the baby should raise justifiable concerns.

At the point where the minor refuses to address these concerns, for example, by refusing to permit the nurse to make an appointment for care, refusing care, or rejecting any other mutually agreeable solution, then the nurse must consider the possibility of notifying parents. Consultation with other school colleagues may be useful as the decision is made. If the school nurse or other provider intends to notify parents, it is important and often useful to tell the minor in advance; this may force the minor to undertake the discussion with her parents in advance of the call or visit from the nurse or other school personnel. (See also chapter 8 regarding making contracts with students.) It may also be appropriate to assist the student in discussing her pregnancy with her parents; this can be done by inviting the parent(s) to school for a conference in which the student participates. A home visit can also accomplish the same goal if the provider feels that the student and the provider will be safe in that environment. One advantage of disclosure in the school environment is that help is more readily available if the student is correct in predicting that her parent will react explosively to the news of her pregnancy. Whether the decision is to notify parents or not, the nurse should document the decision making in the student's confidential health (nursing) records.

If the student has reached the age of majority, the

school nurse and other school personnel may not notify parents, even if the student still lives at home. If, however, the student is an adult but has a mental handicap, an assessment must be made of the competence of the student to make the decision to decline prenatal and other health care. The practical standard for making this assessment can be the same as the one used to determine if a minor is presumptively competent to consent to the use of a particular contraceptive method: that is, does the student seem to have sufficient intellect to understand the risks and benefits and come to a reasoned decision? If this standard is met, the decision reached need not be reasonable, since a competent adult may make an unreasonable and unwise decision as long as he or she understands the potential consequences of making that decision. Therefore, the question to be addressed in these situations is whether the student does possess a reasonable understanding and ability to recall and discuss the risks, benefits, and potential consequences, not whether the decision she makes is reasonable.

Where the provider or other school official has serious doubt that the student does have this understanding and the situation is potentially serious, then the school may consider notification of the parent or guardian. Whether or not to notify the parent or guardian can bring legal risk no matter what action is taken; therefore, it is important that the school nurse or administrator make a real effort to balance the needs and rights of the student with the potential harm to be caused; documentation of the thought process in the school or school health record is important. (See also chapter 3 regarding ethical dilemmas and chapter 8 regarding confidentiality.)

Abortion

Since 1973, when the U.S. Supreme Court decided *Roe v. Wade*, there has been considerable federal and state legislative and court activity; for some, the goal is to limit the availability of abortion services, and for others, the goal is to make abortion generally available on demand.

Case law has confirmed that the minor herself may decide whether to continue the pregnancy. All courts that have considered the issue have held that neither the father of the baby (who may be liable for child support payments) nor a parent may compel a minor to undergo an abortion if she does not want the procedure done. Two cases are illustrative of this point.

Even before *Roe v. Wade* came down, Maryland courts had decided a case involving Cindy Lou Smith. Cindy was 16 and pregnant; the father of the baby was

also 16. Cindy and her mother had discussed an abortion, but Cindy did not wish to abort the pregnancy. Therefore, Cindy's mother sought a court order in Juvenile Court, which, among other things, would keep her in the custody of the Sheriff of Kent County, and as a "Special Condition" declare that Cindy "shall obey her Mother in submitting to the medical procedures at (the)…[h]ospital to terminate the pregnancy." The Court further declared "that the request and instructions from her Mother shall be sufficient authority for any medical doctor or hospital to provide this treatment." The lower court granted this request on September 26, 1972, and the decision was immediately appealed to the Maryland Court of Special Appeals. Interpreting Maryland statutes, the Court found that the "Juvenile Court did not have the power to compel Cindy to resort to medical procedures relative to a termination of her pregnancy on the ground that her mother wanted her to have an abortion" (*Matter of Cindy Lou Smith*, 1972).

A subsequent case in New York held that a 15-year-old could refuse an abortion that her mother wanted her to have; it went further and noted the following:

> The petitioner mother is ordered not to interfere with Mary's determination to deliver her child nor to attempt to force Mary to have an abortion. Among the permissible penalties for failure to comply with the order of protection is a jail term not to exceed six months (*In the Matter of Mary P.*, 1981).

Therefore, while a provider can and should perform an indicated appendectomy with parental consent over the refusal of a minor, it is legally unwise to perform an abortion under the same circumstances. On occasion, however, the provider will care for a patient who, due to mental retardation or psychosis, does not understand that she is pregnant or the consequences of that pregnancy. Under these circumstances, parental consent for abortion may be possible; since these procedures are usually done in a hospital or surgical center, facility policy will govern whether a parent or guardian may consent to the abortion.

Other major abortion-related issues for minors have involved both parental consent and notification requirements.

Parental Consent

There are no federal requirements that are currently applicable to the states other than U.S. Supreme Court cases that define the limits on a state's ability to restrict a minor's access to abortion. The Supreme Court has held that a state may not under all circumstances require parental consent for abortion (*Planned Parenthood of Central Missouri v. Danforth*, 1976). However, subsequent cases have clarified that if a state wishes to require the consent of one or both parents, it must offer an alternative for a minor who does not wish to involve her parents.

This alternative has generally required the minor to go to court, in an expedited fashion, to authorize the minor to give consent herself or to request authorization from a judge. This is known as the "judicial bypass procedure" because it allows the minor an avenue for bypassing the parental consent requirement contained in the statute. If the state requires the consent of both parents, and one parent is unavailable or refuses consent, the minor and the other parent may need to use the judicial bypass procedure. Most parental-involvement statutes requiring either consent or prior notification of parents for a minor to obtain abortion services currently include the judicial bypass procedure because it permits a minor to obtain authorization from a judge for an abortion without informing her parents, a condition the U.S. Supreme Court has said is necessary to protect a minor's constitutional right to privacy (Donovan, 1997).

Parental Notification

There has been considerable state legislative activity involving parental notification prior to abortion. The U.S. Supreme Court standard for this legislation is lower than the standard for parental consent, since the court does not view parental notification to be as great a barrier to access to abortion services as parental consent requirements are. The Supreme Court has explained its position in this matter by noting that a notification provision does not permit anyone to "veto" the abortion decision (*H. L. v. Matheson*, 1981). Several state statutes containing parental notification requirements have been tested in federal court.

In *Hodgson v. Minnesota et al.* (1990), the court considered a two-parent notification requirement contained in Minnesota statute (Minn. Stat. § 144.343 (1995)). That statute requires that an abortion cannot be performed on a minor until at least 48 hours after written notice of the abortion has been *delivered* to a parent. *Parent*, for these purposes, is defined as "*both* [emphasis added] parents of the pregnant woman if they are both living, one parent of the pregnant woman if only one is living or if the second one cannot be located through reasonably diligent effort, or the guardian or conservator if the pregnant woman has

one" (Minn. Stat. § 144.343 (3) (1995)). If the pregnant minor does not allow notification of one or both parents, then she may petition a court to authorize the performance of the abortion. A hearing is required, after which the judge must find that the minor is "mature and capable of giving informed consent to the proposed abortion" (Minn. Stat. § 144.343 (6) (c)(i) (1995)). This judicial bypass procedure is required to be expeditious and no court fees are permitted, so that the minor can access the court without cost. The procedure must be used even in circumstances where the minor agrees to notification of one parent and not the other; the judge still must be involved to authorize the procedure.

The U.S. Supreme Court found the two-parent notification requirement unconstitutional, but despite this, found the overall statute, including that requirement, constitutional because the consequences of two-parent notification could be avoided by using the judicial bypass.

In *Ohio v. Akron Center for Reproductive Health* (1990), the court considered an Ohio statute that required that the physician who intends to abort an unmarried, unemancipated minor give one of her parents at least 24 hours telephone or written notification. Alternative notice can be given to other relatives if the minor filed a sworn affidavit with a court expressing fear of abuse from the parent or guardian who otherwise would have been notified. In the event that the minor does not wish to notify a parent or guardian, a judicial bypass procedure is available, by which the minor can seek permission to consent to the abortion herself. Judicial bypass requires the minor to file a legal action claiming that she

- is pregnant;

- is unmarried, under 18 years of age and unemancipated; and

- wishes to have an abortion without notification of her parents, guardian, or custodian.

In addition, the minor must file a statement that either or both of the following is true:

- that she is sufficiently mature and well enough informed to intelligently decide whether to have an abortion without the notification of her parents, guardian, or custodian;

- that one of her parents, her guardian, or her custodian was engaged in a pattern of physical, sexual, or emotional abuse against her, or that the notification of her parents, guardian, or custodian otherwise is not in her best interest (ORC Ann. § 2151.85 (1995)).

While Ohio passed a revised law requiring parental consent, that law has been challenged and is under a court injunction (Alan Guttmacher Institute, 1999).

Like Ohio, other states have experienced recent and sometimes multiple changes and challenges to parental consent and notification provisions. In August 1997, for example, the California Supreme Court struck down the state's never-enforced 1987 parental consent law—just a little more than a year after the same court upheld the law. In its new decision, the court held that mandatory parental consent violated minors' right to privacy under the California constitution.

Similarly, state constitutional provisions are the basis for challenges to these laws in other states. For example, despite a U.S. Supreme Court ruling that the Montana Parental Notice of Abortion Act (Title 50, Chapter 20, part 2, MCA) was constitutional under the U.S. Constitution (*Lambert v. Wicklund*, 1997), a Montana court issued an injunction on February 13, 1998, prohibiting enforcement of the Act. The injunction was issued on the basis that the state's constitution, "being more strict than the right offered by the U.S. Constitution," guarantees minors the fundamental right to privacy (which includes the right to choose to have an abortion) and the "plaintiffs made a prima facie showing that the Act infringes a minor's fundamental right to obtain an abortion" (*Wicklund et al. v. State of Montana*, 1998).

Parental Consent and Notification: A Summary

As of July 2000, the majority of states have adopted a statute that requires either parental consent or notification for abortion services; most, but not all, include a judicial by-pass procedure and a number require either the consent or notification of both parents. In several states, parental involvement requirements have been enjoined until current court challenges are resolved. Nine states do not require parental involvement (Alan Guttmacher Institute, 2000). The school health professional must be aware of state requirements in order to counsel students about the law and what can be expected if they seek abortion services. See Table 7-2 for 2000 information on state-specific parental consent and notification requirements. Readers are cautioned, however, that these provisions may have changed and may continue to change on a regular basis.

In dealing with the question of a pregnancy termination, school nurses and others must remember that, regardless of their own personal beliefs and the law,

abortion remains a topic that arouses strong emotions. In counseling a student, it is wise to document that the student was told of options in addition to abortion and that the importance of notifying a parent was at least discussed. The following case is illustrative.

In 1986, suit was brought against a Board of Education, a guidance counselor, and the school principal by a male and female student and their parents. The complaint alleged that the Board employees coerced the female student into having an abortion and forbade the students from notifying their parents about the pregnancy; the conduct was said to be racially motivated, since the students were black. The court found for the Board of Education, based on evidence that the defendants had counseled the students about notifying their parents and had discussed options for the pregnancy. The court noted what is still true: "No federal or state statute or other rule or regulation requires parental notification by school officials of pregnancy or abortion plans of minors reporting pregnancy or abortion plans to public school officials" (*Arnold et al. v. Board of Education*, 1990).

HIV Testing

The majority of states now have laws addressing the requirements for HIV testing, and many of these laws include provisions for the testing of minors. Minors may be tested with parental consent, but questions have arisen where the minor is requesting testing without parental involvement. Where any statute is silent on this question, health care providers may test under the mature minor or emancipation provisions of the individual state's law.

Where statutes do exist, some have created more problems than they have solved. For example, the Connecticut HIV testing statute was amended in 1993 explicitly to permit HIV testing *and treatment* for minors with HIV without parental consent. The statute prohibits the health care provider from notifying a parent of a minor without the minor's consent, even if the test result is positive or if the minor refuses adequate disease follow-up. Practically, this means that a health care provider who agrees to accept the minor's consent for testing may not notify a parent of the positive result, as long as the minor refuses to consent. However, the statute merely permits, but does not require, testing at the request of a minor. Therefore, a health care provider may choose to require parental involvement prior to testing. If testing or treatment without parental consent occurs, the parent is not financially responsible for the charges incurred (Ct. Gen. Statute, § 19a-581-585).

Table 7-2. The Status of Major Abortion-Related Laws and Policies in the United States

Parental Involvement

Compiled by The Alan Guttmacher Institute and reflecting the status of state provisions as of May 2000

(Except where indicated, laws require the involvement of one parent and include a judicial bypass procedure. Laws in bolded states include some alternative to parental involvement or judicial bypass. In South Carolina, for instance, consent may be given by a grandparent; in Virginia, notice may be waived by a physician if the minor declares she is a victim of abuse or neglect and the physician has reason to suspect that is the case.)

Sixteen states require parental consent before a minor may obtain an abortion:

Alabama	Louisiana	**North Carolina**	Tennessee
(Arizona)[1]	Massachusetts	North Dakota[3]	**Wisconsin**
(Idaho)	Michigan	Pennsylvania	Wyoming
Indiana	Mississippi[3]	Rhode Island	
Kentucky	Missouri	**South Carolina**	

In three states, parental consent requirements are enjoined:

Alaska	California	New Mexico[4]

Fifteen states require parental notification before a minor may obtain an abortion:

Arkansas[3]	Kansas	South Dakota
Delaware	**Maryland**	Texas
Georgia	Minnesota[3]	Utah[4]
Idaho[3,4]	Nebraska	**Virginia**
Iowa	**Ohio**[5]	**West Virginia**

In six states, parental notice requirements are enjoined:

Colorado[3,4]	**Illinois**	Nevada
Florida	Montana	New Jersey

Nine states do not require parental involvement:

Connecticut[6]	New Hampshire	Oregon
Hawaii	New York	Vermont
Maine[7]	Oklahoma	Washington

[1] A new parental consent law is slated to be enforced in July 2000, barring any legal challenges. State is not included in total tally.

[2] A new parental consent law is slated to be enforced in July 2000, replacing the current parental notification law. State is not included in total tally.

[3] Involvement of both parents is required.

[4] Does not include a judicial bypass procedure.

[5] A revised law that requires parental consent is currently enjoined; meanwhile, the parental notification requirements remain in effect.

[6] Minor is required to receive counseling that includes a discussion of involving her parents.

[7] Minor may receive counseling in lieu of obtaining parental consent or court authorization.

Reproduced with permission of The Alan Guttmacher Institute from "The Alan Guttmacher Institute, The Status of Major Abortion-Related Laws in the United States," *Parental Involvement,* July 2000. Available on-line: http://www.agi-usa.org/pubs/abort_law_status.html#2.

Colorado takes a somewhat different approach. The statutes state that an institution or health care provider may examine and treat a minor with HIV if qualified to do so. The consent of the parent is not a "prerequisite" to that examination and treatment. If the minor is _ years of age or older, the "fact of the consultation, examination and treatment" of the minor is absolutely confidential (except that HIV is a reportable disease to the health department in Colorado, as in many states, and child abuse and neglect reports are still required, if indicated). If the minor is under 16 or not emancipated, the minor's parents or legal guardian *may* be informed. The law specifically requires that the minor be counseled on the importance of "bringing his parents or guardian into the minor's confidence about the consultation, examination, or treatment" (Colorado Rev. Stat. § 25-4-1405(6) (1995)).

While state laws may authorize testing a minor for HIV without parental involvement, no state *requires* that the health care provider order the test if a minor requests or demands it. The provision of testing, like all other health care to a minor without parental involvement, remains a matter of professional judgment. If a minor is to be offered HIV testing or treatment without parental knowledge (even if consent is not required), it is advisable that the health care provider clearly document the discussions with the minor. Documentation should include indication that the minor appeared to understand the potential risks and benefits to testing. Written, rather than oral, consent is often required by statute, as is pre- and post-test counseling.

Schools do not offer HIV testing; school-based health centers may have the ability to order the test and may draw the blood for testing. The provider who orders the test is responsible for complying with the relevant consent and counseling requirements. Anonymous testing is available in some communities, and a minor may be referred there for testing if it seems appropriate.

The ability of school personnel to have access to positive HIV results has caused some conflict between school personnel and school-based health centers and other providers. The release of HIV-related information is usually strictly regulated by state law; the school is not authorized to obtain that information without the permission of the patient or parent (Crocker et al., January 1994). While a general release signed by a parent, for example, will authorize the school to receive most medical information, in many states such a release will be insufficient to authorize the release of HIV-related information. In these states, the release must specify that HIV-related information is sought, in a manner that is similar to requirements for the release of drug, alcohol, and psychiatric information.

Drug and Alcohol Screening/Toxicology Screening

There are situations where a minor requests drug screening or, more likely, a parent requests that toxicology screening be done on the minor without the minor's knowledge. In many schools, there is no way to honor such a request. However, some school-based health centers may offer drug and alcohol screening tests. Although it may be legally permissible under some circumstances to do urine or blood testing for toxicology purposes without the knowledge of the minor and with the consent of the parent, many practitioners will refuse to do this (English & Tereszkiewicz, 1988, p. 19).

There are several reasons for this view. First, the American Academy of Pediatrics has stated the following:

Involuntary testing in a minor who lacks the capacity to make informed judgments may be done with parental permission. Parental permission is not sufficient for involuntary testing of the adolescent with decisional capacity, and the AAP opposes such involuntary testing. Suspicion that an adolescent may be using a psychoactive drug does not justify involuntary testing and it is not sufficient justification to rely solely on parental agreement to test the patient. Testing adolescents requires their consent unless: (1) a patient lacks decision-making capacity; or (2) there are strong medical indications or legal requirements to do so (American Academy of Pediatrics, Committee on Substance Abuse, August 1996).

In part, the reason for refusal is that the trust between the school nurse or nurse practitioner and the student body will be damaged, probably permanently. As a result, the nurse will not be able to convince a minor to be evaluated for anything, since every minor thereafter will believe that drug testing is being done in order to report to his or her parents. Therefore, most would suggest that the nurse inform the minor that the parent has made such a request and discuss with the student in advance how the results will be handled, regardless of what they show.

School-based health center staff who offer drug and alcohol testing must know the state-specific legal ramifications of a positive test result and provide information accordingly. For example, if testing is done pursuant to a student's request for drug evaluation and treatment (see below), the information is protected by federal law from disclosure to others, even to parents. However, if testing is to be done as part of a medical evaluation with a different purpose (such as participation in interscholastic sports), then the confidentiality of the results is subject to some question. In some states, a positive screen for an illegal drug like cocaine in a pregnant woman can have consequences for the placement of the child after birth. Therefore, health care providers who wish to test should obtain permission from the patient.

If there may be legal consequences to the results, then obtaining written consent from the student for testing is advisable. Otherwise, in many states, it is permissible to order toxicology screening without any explicit consent, just as is the case with most other laboratory work.

At least one case, in New Jersey, has addressed the right of a school district to adopt a policy requiring drug and alcohol screening on all students as part of the physical examination required prior to enrollment in school and yearly for continuing enrollment. A New Jersey court found the policy violated the New Jersey Constitution; specifically, the policy was found to be an unreasonable search and seizure, without due process, and also violated privacy rights (*Odenheim v. Carlstadt-East Rutherford Regional School District*, 1985).

This decision is to be contrasted with policies that require drug screening, not of all students, but of those who wish to participate in school sports.

Toxicology Screening for Participation in Sports

Many school districts and schools have adopted policies requiring routine or random screening of students who may participate in school athletic programs. There have been a number of legal challenges to these policies, and the law that has resulted varies among the states.

In 1995, the U.S. Supreme Court decided a case interpreting a policy from the Veronia School District in Oregon. The Veronia School District adopted a policy in 1989 authorizing random drug screening for students who wished to participate in the district's school athletic programs. In 1991, the plaintiff, James Acton, who was then in the seventh grade, refused to agree to sign the testing consent forms and was refused participation on the football team. He and his family sued, claiming that the Oregon and U.S. Constitutions were violated by the school district's policy. The U.S. Supreme Court held that the random drug screening for athletes did not violate the U.S. Constitution and was a permissible exercise of the District's authority. The Court, however, went on to caution that this

opinion should not be used to assume that "suspicion-less drug testing" would be constitutional in other contexts (*Veronia School District 47J v. Acton*, 1995).

Although the U.S. Constitution might find random or routine drug screening of athletes constitutionally acceptable, states may adopt a more, but not less, stringent standard. In the *Acton* case above, a subsequent court held, without discussion, that the Oregon Constitution would not offer greater protections than the U.S. Constitution did (*Acton v. Veronia School District 47J*, 1995). This result left the school policy intact.

In Arizona, a lower federal court decided that a policy similar to Oregon's violated the U.S. Constitution; however, it relied on an earlier *Acton* decision (decided prior to the U.S. Supreme Court decision and which had found the Oregon policy violative of the U.S. Constitution). The court did not conduct an independent examination of Arizona Constitutional protections (*Moule v. Paradise Valley Unified School District No. 69*, 1994).

Drug and Alcohol Abuse Evaluation and Treatment

There is both federal and state law dealing with drug and alcohol abuse evaluation and treatment. Federal law, which generally preempts less restrictive state laws, provides nearly absolute confidentiality protection to persons, including minors, who seek this kind of evaluation and treatment. In general, the law prohibits the disclosure of records or other information about *any* patient or student who seeks assistance from or is enrolled for treatment in a federally assisted drug or alcohol program. (See 42 U.S.C. § 290dd-2 and federal regulations at 42 C.F.R. Part 2.) Information can be disclosed in narrowly defined circumstances, including situations involving a medical emergency or where child abuse must be reported. There are both civil and criminal penalties for improper disclosure of this information.

Because of some confusion about what constitutes drug evaluation and treatment, there has been legal clarification by federal regulation. In general, if an individual goes to a hospital emergency department, for example, for detoxification only, these records may not be protected under the federal law, since only medical care was provided; in this situation, no real drug treatment was sought or provided. However, if a student even seeks information from a drug treatment program, including a drug counselor, student assistance team member, or school health professional, this information and the records that result are protected by federal law.

In trying to determine whether the drug- and alcohol-related information about a student is likely to be confidential and protected, even from parents, the school professional must consider the context in which the information was received. If the school nurse, for example, observes drug use in the school, then the matter may be treated as a criminal offense or a violation of school policy that should be reported to school administration and may subject the student(s) to discipline. If a student shares drug or alcohol abuse information in a health care context, it is protected under general rules involving patient confidences, which may be disclosed under FERPA (because under this law, school health records are part of the educational record) or, under certain other circumstances, under state law, which may permit the release of this information to a parent. However, if the information was received in a context in which the student was requesting drug or alcohol abuse referral for evaluation or treatment, that information is absolutely confidential under federal law.

Student assistance programs (SAPs) are often set up in schools to provide drug and alcohol assessment and intervention for students. These programs are covered by the federal confidentiality provisions—they may consist of activities like group and individual counseling for students and treatment referrals (Legal Action Center, 1996 p. 5). By contrast, however, classroom education programs do not constitute protected drug and alcohol evaluation and treatment, even though a student may disclose drug abuse during the class session.

If the SAP is under the direct administrative control of the school, then relevant information about students in the program may be disclosed to school personnel who are members of the SAP. However, disclosure may be made only to provide effective drug and alcohol services. If the SAP is run by another group, such as a school-based health center, then information may not be transmitted to school personnel without the student's permission (Legal Action Center, p. 13).

Many states now provide the same types of protection to minors who seek drug and alcohol evaluation as are found in the laws about sexually transmitted infections. As in all the consent statutes, however, statutory provisions vary. For example, Arizona law states,

Notwithstanding any other provision of law, any minor twelve years of age or older who is found, upon diagnosis of a licensed physician, to be under the influence of a dangerous drug or narcotic, which includes withdrawal symptoms, may be

considered an emergency case and such minor is to be regarded as having consented to hospital or medical care needed for treatment for such.... The consent of the parent, parents or legal guardian of such minor is not necessary to authorize hospital or medical care, except that such consent shall be equally valid if obtained (A.R.S. § 44-133.01 (1995)).

Minnesota law provides that "any" minor may give effective consent to "determine the presence of or to treat" alcohol and other drug abuse, and the consent of no one else is required (Minn. Stat. § 144.343(1) (1995)).

Some state laws permit parental notification. For example, Louisiana statutes permit a minor to consent to care for drug addiction. However, the law goes on to state that

...upon the advice and direction of a treating physician, or, in the case of a medical staff, any one of them, a physician or a member of a medical staff may, but shall not be obligated to, inform the spouse, parent or guardian of any such minor as to the treatment given or needed, and such information may be given to, or withheld from the spouse, parent or guardian without the consent and over the express objection of the minor (La. R. S. § 40-1096 (C) (1996)).

Under this sort of law, school nurses, social workers, and others could make such a notification only after consultation with the student's treating physician. These notification laws may be in conflict with federal law, if the facility or provider receives federal funds. In addition, as a practical matter, if the minor resides with a parent and needs in-patient treatment, notification of the parent(s) regarding the whereabouts of the student is required in order to inform them that their child has not run away, been in an accident, or been abducted.

Generally, if a person may consent to treatment, he or she may also refuse the same treatment. In Maryland, however, the law provides that a minor may consent to treatment or advice about drug abuse and alcoholism, but the capacity of the minor to consent to treatment for drug and alcohol abuse "does not include the capacity to refuse treatment for drug abuse or alcoholism in an inpatient alcohol or drug abuse treatment program...for which a parent or guardian has given consent" (Md. Health—General Code Ann. § 20-102 (c-1) (1995)).

Mental Health Treatment and Suicide

While the age of majority for most other medical purposes is 18 years, many states permit minors to consent to mental health treatment at an earlier age. For example, in Connecticut, the age of majority for mental health purposes is 16 (Ct. Gen. Stat, § 17a-75). However, the statute is silent on the extent to which the medical records of a 16-year-old are protected from parental discovery; under other circumstances they would be available to a parent.

Standards for involuntary commitment for mental health reasons do vary, but they include suicidal and homicidal intent. Involuntary commitment provisions also vary from state to state, as do the rights of the committed minor and his or her parents to request a hearing if they disagree with the commitment.

When a student threatens suicide (or homicide), the threat should be taken seriously, particularly since the rates of attempted and completed suicides have been rising among young people (Bjorklun, 1996). The National Center for Injury Prevention and Control (2000) reports that between 1980 and 1997 the incidence of suicide among adolescents aged 15–19 increased by 11%, and among children aged 10–14 by 109%. Furthermore, between 1980 and 1996, the rate of suicide for African-American males aged 15–19 increased by 105%. A real suicide threat should be reported to a parent or a known therapist or, if imminent, the student should be transported to an emergency department for evaluation. If the school nurse is unable to determine if the threat is a real or imminent one, then a mental health evaluation must be arranged, through a parent or otherwise. Regardless of the decision, the nurse should document what she or he was told by the student or others who may have knowledge of a suicide threat and what actions were taken.

Most of the law suits against schools are grounded in negligence theory, alleging inadequate supervision, duty to warn parents of symptomatic behavior observed in school, or failure to train staff to identify students at risk of suicide and to intervene appropriately. In many cases, the courts have held that the general supervisory duty of the school does not include one-to-one, full-day monitoring of individual students: in some states, a sovereign immunity defense has been successful. However, these results do not relieve schools of all responsibility for awareness of depression in students, behaviors suggestive of suicidal intent, and general suicide prevention programs.

While some students with suicidal tendencies may be found among the population identified as seriously emotionally disturbed for special education eligibility,

anecdotal experience suggests that others remain unidentified and may present no obvious warning signs to their friends, family, or school staff members. The school nurse is in a unique position to detect, from careful scrutiny of the record of visits to the health office or from analysis of candid remarks from students, some of the students at risk. Whether working as part of a planned intervention team or independently, school nurses should follow up all possible evidence of suicidal risk and inform parents and others needed to reduce the risk and assist in addressing student needs.

The following sampling of court decisions concerning possible school liability in student suicide cases is intended to assist school nurses and school districts in identifying policies and procedures that will assist students at risk and limit school district liability. These cases also illustrate the interplay of state and federal court jurisdiction when claims are made under state and federal law. The issues of liability and immunity are usually matters of state law, while special education and other civil rights claims may be matters of both state and federal law.

An Idaho high school student was assigned to write in a daily journal in his English class. After a few months, he told his teacher that her reading of the entries inhibited his writing, and she agreed to review only the dates and length of entries to ensure that assignments had been done. Thereafter, she did not read the content of his daily entries. The journal entries were from September 1990 through December 1990. In January 1991, the student committed suicide. After the student's death, his English teacher read through the journal and gave it to a school counselor, who in turn gave it to the student's parents. The parents sued the teacher and the school district for failing to intervene and prevent the suicide (*Brooks v. Logan*, 1997). The suit alleged "a duty to take affirmative action to detect and assist students who suffer from depression or suicidal ideation." There was a dispute as to whether the English teacher had read specific journal entries.

The first trial court found the district immune from liability to institute a suicide prevention program or to train staff in suicide prevention, but found that the teacher's failure to warn the student's parent after reading journal entries suggestive of suicidal ideation was negligent. On appeal, the state supreme court pointed out that the trial court should have determined whether or not the teacher had read the entries in question prior to the student's death as there was conflicting evidence on the record. On remand, the trial court found that the teacher had "no actual knowledge of [the student's] disturbed emotional state, nor actual knowledge of his suicidal ideation" prior to his suicide. The state supreme court upheld summary judgment for the defendant school district based on immunity. Idaho state law provides the following:

> A governmental entity and its employees while acting within the course and scope of their employment and without malice or criminal intent and without reckless, willful and wanton conduct…shall not be liable for any claim which…arises out of injury to a person or property by a person under supervision, custody or care of a governmental entity (Idaho Code § 6-904A(2)).

On remand, the trial court again granted summary judgment for the school district and the teacher, citing another case for the standard: "simply a duty to exercise reasonable care in supervising students while they are attending school" and finding that they were immune under state law. The Idaho Supreme Court upheld the decision. This case leaves a troubling awareness concerning the assignment of personal journal writing and the role of teachers. Should assignments be limited to "safe" areas, and should teachers be scrutinizing student writing and oral comments for non-academic content? A prudent teacher who has read troubling writing by a student should certainly consult the student's guidance counselor or the school nurse if there is no school procedure in place.

A 16-year-old New Mexico student identified as learning disabled with "other psychological and emotional problems, including impulsivity and depression," was suspended after harassing a younger student in school and sent home, where he shot himself. When the student met with the school principal at the time of the incident, he threatened the teacher and the teacher's son. While a school staff member was driving him home, the student appeared to be "very angry." The school policy regarding suspensions included a provision that when parents were not at home, the student would be held in in-school suspension. The student's parents were not notified of the suspension and were not at home. The student had made statements suggestive of suicidal ideation to a school paraprofessional, and the school staff knew that there were firearms available in student's home. When the parents sued the school district on a variety of grounds, the District Court denied the school's defense of immunity, rejected parents' claims under IDEA, and found a triable issue under a state-law "danger creation" theory of liability.

The school district appealed the denial of immunity

and the parents cross-appealed the rejection of IDEA claims. The Tenth Circuit Court of Appeals upheld the rejection of IDEA claims, reversed summary judgment for some school staff members because of facts in dispute related to the danger creation theory, and remanded the case to the District Court (*Armijo v. Wagon Mound Public Schools*, 1998). This decision does not finally resolve all claims, but it does illustrate the role of a school policy in establishing a standard of care. When school staff members failed to follow the policy that parents be notified immediately of a suspension and failed to follow procedures provided for a student whose parents are not at home, they risked a finding of negligence.

A Florida student who had attempted suicide twice at school tried and succeeded a third time, at home (*Wyke v. Polk County School Board*, 1997). After each of the student's suicide attempts at school, although the school was "somewhat aware" of the attempts, the school did not inform the parent or grandparent with whom the student was living. Based on a telephoned report from a parent of the student's classmate, who had reported an attempt by the student to hang himself in a school bathroom, the school's Dean of Students met with the student but did not notify anyone else. The student also discussed his problems with a school custodian and she reported her concerns to the school's vice principal without identifying the student. The custodian was reprimanded and there was no follow-up inquiry.

The next day the student did kill himself at home. The parent's suit under 42 U.S.C. 1983 alleged that the school's failure to train employees in suicide intervention/prevention "constituted deliberate indifference to [the parent's] constitutional rights to the care, custody, management, companionship, and society of her son." The parent's suit also included a state wrongful death claim. The Federal Judge Magistrate dismissed the first claim because the school had no responsibility for supervision of the student in his own home and tried the state wrongful death issue. The jury found the school guilty of failure to supervise the student and divided a monetary award among the school, the parent, and grandparent, based on a theory of shared responsibility. On appeal to the Eleventh Circuit, the verdict on wrongful death was upheld but the issue of the parent's and grandparent's liability under state law was remanded to the Florida State Supreme Court.

In upholding the lower court's rejection of the parent's constitutional claim, the Circuit Court reiterated the position that mandatory school attendance does not impose a duty of care, citing many cases from many courts. The court found the school district negligent in its failure to notify the parent of suicide attempts at school. Citing a state School Health Services Manual in use at the time of the student's suicide attempts, which recommends parental notification of student injuries at school, the court referred to the definition of an "acute emotional state" as an emergency. Noting that ordinarily one cannot be found liable for the suicide of another, which is "an independent act," the Eleventh Circuit found that in this case the suicide was foreseeable after the two attempts at school. Once again, a school procedure concerning notice to parents might have prevented the ultimate suicide of this student.

After an Illinois student told other students he was going to kill himself and wrote suicide notes, a school counselor questioned him and called his mother, suggesting that she take him for drug overdose treatment but failing to mention the suicide threats. The student killed himself later that day by jumping off a highway overpass. When the parent sued the school district, the school offered a defense of immunity (*Grant v. Board of Trustees of Valley View School District*, 1997). Summary judgment for the school was based on the state's immunity provisions, including a specific finding that the counselor's conduct was not willful or wanton. This ruling was upheld on appeal. With a different school policy concerning notice to parents or a different state immunity law, this case might have gone the other way.

A Montana high school student who had been diagnosed as depressed attempted suicide. The school responded by holding a § 504 meeting and planning for a "support person of the student's choice" to accompany her at all school activities, on and off campus, at which "stress becomes a problem." The student's parents transferred her to another school and filed a complaint with the Office for Civil Rights (OCR), U.S. Department of Education. After an investigation, the OCR found the school district's plan was not a substantial change in the student's program and was not discriminatory (Harlowton (MT) Public Schools, 1997).

Notwithstanding the possibility of the immunity defense, school districts should have policies and procedures in place for addressing student suicide attempts and evidence of suicidal ideation by students. Parental notice is an essential component of such procedures. The school nurse plays an important role both as a potential reporter and as a member of the school emergency intervention team.

Sexual Assault/Acquaintance Rape

Data suggest that the rate of sexual assault and acquaintance rape is increasing among students. This increase may be due in part to attitudes of the students themselves. In a study published in 1993, 237 students, ninth to twelfth grades, responded. Analysis of that study's data showed that 20% of the students had experienced what they considered forced sex; only half of those had told anyone about the experience. Sixty percent of the boys found it acceptable under some circumstances to force sex on a girl; attitudes among the girls were often troublesome as well (Davis et al., 1993).

In their criminal statutes, all states define the age at which the law presumes that a minor, generally a female (although some laws also include males), is capable of giving consent to sexual intercourse. Below that age (16 in some states, but as low as 12 in others), sexual activity constitutes statutory rape on the part of the partner, whether or not the conduct seemed consensual at the time. Some statutes prohibit the prosecution of the male unless he is of a certain age or a certain number of years older than the female.

The U.S. Supreme Court has addressed the constitutionality of statutory rape laws. In *Michael M. v. Superior Court*, the court considered a California statute that defined statutory rape for a female and not a male. In this case, a 17 1/2-year-old male was charged under a law that defined unlawful sexual intercourse as "an act of sexual intercourse accomplished with a female not the wife of the perpetrator, where the female is under the age of 18 years." The court found the California law constitutional, although it punished only males and not females of the same age and for the same behavior (*Michael M. v. Superior Court of Sonoma County*, 1981).

The magnitude of statutory rape is not known. However, the existing data are troublesome. A 1995 Alan Guttmacher Institute Study found that 65% of mothers 15–19 years of age had children by men who were 20 years old or older. Half of the teens in the 15–17-year age group had children by older men, and 20% of the men were six or more years older (Darroch, Landry, & Oslak, 1999). Despite this, statutory rape is rarely prosecuted, but it may be if the minor or a parent makes a complaint to police.

Sexual assault, which is sexual activity, from touching of sexual body parts to sexual intercourse and sodomy, without consent of one of the parties, is also treated as a criminal offense. Most states do not address the circumstances under which a minor may be evaluated for rape or lesser sexual assault; minors are evaluated under the mature minor and other exceptions to parental consent requirements. Under the general rules protecting the confidentiality of patient information, a health care provider may not notify police of a sexual assault, even of a minor, without the minor's consent.

Whether a parent may or must be notified is less certain. Health care providers and school authorities who wish to override a minor's refusal to allow parental notification should clearly document their reasons, including the fears that the minor will have expressed.

Under certain circumstances, the health care provider or the school will know the name of the alleged perpetrator, especially if the rape was an acquaintance rape. Whether the nurse who is told this information then has a duty to inform school officials depends upon the capacity in which the health care is delivered. If the nurse is a school employee or contracted employee, the school may require such disclosure. If the nurse is part of a school-based health center or other provider that is not part of the school system, disclosure without the permission of the minor is not permitted.

An intermediate position may be taken when, for example, health care providers, whether school employees or contracted personnel, become aware of sexual activity occurring in particular locations on school premises, such as a bathroom. At that point, school officials should be notified that there may be a safety problem in a particular bathroom, without specifying the names of the participants.

In general, it is unwise for school or other authorities to release information about the alleged perpetrator directly to the parent of the minor victim; the school will have gotten the information from the minor, it remains an allegation, and the parents have other methods to obtain unconfirmed information of this type.

Child Abuse/Sexual Abuse/Incest

Where a school health care provider becomes aware of known or suspected child abuse, the definition of which includes physical and sexual abuse, incest, psychological abuse, and physical and emotional neglect, the provider must report to the state child welfare authorities. There is no obligation on the part of the provider to investigate to determine if the suspicions are true prior to reporting, and in fact, a delay may subject the child to further harm and the provider to legal liability. As discussed in chapter 6, a reporter of known or suspected child abuse is immune from liability. This is true even if the report turns out to be incorrect, as long as the reporter made the report in good faith, and did not knowingly provide incorrect information in order to create problems for the accused.

As a rule, this system works well. But there are many situations in which the application is not clear. For example, the school nurse may be told by a 15-year-old student that she is having unprotected sexual intercourse with her 15-year-old first cousin and is actively trying to become pregnant. This situation does not explicitly involve sexual abuse, may not be statutory rape, and would not seem to require a report to the child welfare authorities. In addition, depending upon the circumstances in which the nurse learned of the facts, it also may not be possible to report the problem to the parents because the information was obtained during the provision of health care. Counseling and referral of the student, if the student will accept those services, may be the only option.

Another situation that can be difficult involves students who are moderately or severely cognitively impaired. If the students are 18 years or older and not declared legally incompetent (which would be accompanied by the appointment of a guardian, who could be a representative of a state agency), the law presumes competence. Therefore, the health care provider or school professional may be legally limited to counseling the student about her rights with regard to participation in or refusal of sexual activity and the potential for pregnancy.

If one or more students involved in sexual activities are under 18 years, a clinical assessment must be made about the ability of the student to understand the consequences of his or her activity. If that ability is so limited as to seriously impair the ability to give consent, consideration must be given to informing a parent or guardian of sexual activity. However, the purpose of the notification should be considered: if the notification is to try to prevent the sexual activity, this is likely to be ineffective if the student is ambulatory and not under constant supervision. If the notification is for the purpose of trying to provide effective contraception for the student, then a parent might be helpful to the situation.

Gay and Lesbian Rights

Some states protect gay and lesbian citizens from harassment and discrimination, either by protections in the State Constitution or by statutes making it a crime to harass someone based on sexual orientation. For example, Massachusetts has established a Commission on Discrimination that investigates complaints of, among other things, discrimination based on sexual orientation (not including those persons whose sexual orientation involves minor children as the sex object). Sexual orientation is defined as "having an orientation for or being identified as having an orientation for heterosexuality, bisexuality or homosexuality" (Mass. Ann. Laws ch. 151B, § 3 (6) (1996)). The school system should also have adopted statements or policies setting forth the handling of sexual and other harassment complaints. (See also the discussion below of sexual harassment of students by school employees and by student peers.)

If a student reports harassment based on sexual orientation, he or she should be told of the possible remedies, through the school or elsewhere. As in a case of sexual assault, a school health care provider may assist a student in making a report to the police but should not make the report without the permission of the student.

School health personnel should take care not to permit their personal beliefs about sexual orientation to affect the care of a student who may be gay or lesbian. Concerns about sexual orientation should not be reported to parents unless the student gives permission. If the school practitioner notes serious educational or mental health consequences, possibly related to sexual orientation, the student should be referred for evaluation of the depression, for example, and not specifically for sexual orientation.

Sexual Harassment

Title IX of the 1972 Education Amendments requires schools to adopt and publish grievance procedures to investigate and promptly resolve sexual harassment complaints; schools also must disseminate a policy prohibiting sex discrimination. Schools will be liable for failure to do these things, regardless of whether sexual harassment occurred in the setting. (For detailed discussion of court cases and recent Office of Civil Rights [OCR] guidance, see chapter 11.)

In determining whether sexual harassment occurred between a school employee and student, the OCR will consider whether the conduct was welcomed by the student. The OCR will never consider a sexual relationship welcome or consensual if it occurs between a school employee and an elementary student. If the student is in secondary school, the OCR will have a "strong presumption" that the relationship was not consensual; in considering whether the relationship was welcome, the OCR will consider the following:

- the nature of the conduct and the relationship of the school employee to the student, including the degree of influence (which could, at least in part, be affected by the student's age), authority, or control the employee has over the student; and

- whether the student was legally or practically unable to consent to the sexual conduct in question; for example, a student's age could affect his or her ability to do so; similarly, certain types of disabilities could affect a student's ability to do so.

In cases where "welcomeness" of behavior is in dispute, the OCR identifies the following information that may be helpful in resolving the dispute (Office of Civil Rights, U.S. Department of Education, 1997, pp. 12040–12041):

- statements by any witnesses to the alleged incident;

- evidence about the relative credibility of the allegedly harassed student and the alleged harasser;

- evidence that the alleged harasser has been found to have harassed others that may support the credibility of the student claiming harassment (conversely, the student's claim will be weakened if he or she has been found to have made false allegations against other individuals);

- evidence of the allegedly harassed student's reaction or behavior after the alleged harassment;

- evidence about whether the student claiming harassment filed a complaint or took other action to protest the conduct soon after the alleged incident occurred; and

- other contemporaneous evidence.

The OCR stresses that hostile environment sexual harassment is usually severe, persistent, or pervasive.

A school is liable for quid pro quo harassment by a school employee in a position of authority, such as a teacher or administrator, whether or not the conduct was known. It is also liable under most circumstances for hostile environment harassment.

Similarly, peer harassment in schools is prohibited. The school will be liable when the conduct was known or should have been known and the school failed to remedy the harassment in its education programs or activities (OCR, p. 12039). The OCR makes it clear that the school is not liable for the conduct of the student per se, but for its "own discrimination in permitting the harassment to continue once the school has notice of it" (OCR, p. 12039). In the same way, the school may be liable for the sexually harassing conduct of third parties who are not students at the school, such as visiting members of an athletic team (OCR, p. 12040).

The school nurse, and therefore constructively the school, may become aware of sexual harassment problems in a variety of ways. The nurse may see the conduct or it may be reported by the student-victim, another student, faculty, parents, a bus driver, or any other person. The nurse must be familiar with school policy to determine the proper—and prompt—action to take. There is no doubt that the nurse should ordinarily report to the school administration any circumstances that would appear to be sexual or gender harassment in the school, on the school bus, during athletics, or during any other school-sponsored activity.

The potential conflict between the roles of a nurse and a school employee becomes particularly evident, however, when the student confides the harassment or sexual activity as part of a health care contact, which would ordinarily be kept confidential. For example, a nurse may learn of sexual activity between a teacher and student when the student seeks evaluation for a possible pregnancy or sexually transmitted disease. Usually, the student, who "loves" the teacher or fears retribution, will plead or demand that no one be told of the sexual activity and may state that she will deny it if anyone asks.

Nevertheless, the school nurse, school psychologist, or any other school official who acquires this information must make a professional judgment about reporting. If there is sexual activity between an employee and an elementary student, between an employee and a student where the employee has authority over the student, or between an employee and a student who has disabilities that raise questions about the ability to consent, the school nurse should report the conduct according to school policy. If these are not the case and the nurse chooses not to report, the records should document the reasons that the information was kept confidential (the student claimed the conduct was welcome and she was 17, for example). These situations are legally and professionally troubling; consultation with peers and experts may be helpful.

Refusal of Treatment in Life-Threatening Situations

While the traditional law held that minors become capable of mature decision-making at age 18, courts have individually addressed cases in which minors with chronic diseases have sought to refuse treatment that either their parents or health care providers believed they needed. These cases have not involved cases of acute traumatic injury, which are treated as emergencies; it would be exceedingly unlikely that a hospital, for example, would accept refusal of treatment from a previously healthy and now traumatically injured minor.

In 1989, the Supreme Court of Illinois considered the following matter. A 17-year-old female, identified in the case as E. G. to protect her confidentiality, developed leukemia and required transfusion as part of the treatment. Both the patient and her mother refused transfusion on religious grounds. The child welfare authorities then petitioned and had E. G. declared a neglected child and appointed a guardian to consent to transfusion. An intermediate appeal court ruled that E. G. could refuse treatment as a mature minor but left intact the neglect ruling against the mother. The Supreme Court of Illinois reviewed the case. It agreed that E. G. could refuse blood transfusion as a mature minor and ordered the neglect finding against the mother removed from the records (In *Re E.G.*, 1990).

Two things are worth noting in this case. First, both parent and child refused the offered therapy. The court did not decide what it would have done had the minor refused life-saving treatment that the parent wanted the minor to receive. While the minor might have a legal right to refuse, the minor still would have to prove sufficient maturity to be permitted to make a decision such as this one. Second, there were several health care providers who testified that E. G. had the maturity of an adult and seemed quite competent to understand the consequences of her refusal, including death.

Cases like this are quite rare, and it is not possible to draw many generalizations from them. However, they do demonstrate that a minor *may* be permitted to refuse life-saving treatment, but courts will consider these cases individually based on the facts of the matter and the maturity of the minor. The impact of such a case on school health care will generally be indirect, in that a school nurse is unlikely to be involved in the family-physician decisions concerning medical treatment for life-threatening illness. Medical treatments and deviations from the usual emergency procedures in school depend upon orders from a physician and development of a plan requiring parental consent.

Do Not Resuscitate Decisions

Do Not Resuscitate (DNR) orders in schools are defined and explored in depth in chapter 14. This section briefly touches on DNR issues from a health perspective.

Schools have two types of students for whom "do not resuscitate" or DNR decisions may be involved. The first group includes students with a chronic, progressive, and eventually fatal disease like AIDS or certain types of cancer. The second involves students with severe disabilities who may develop life-threatening conditions, like status epilepticus, or go into cardiac arrest as a consequence of their underlying disorder. The law in many states now contemplates DNR orders for the terminally ill, for individuals who are permanently comatose, and for patients with certain other conditions. In New York, for example, a surrogate, like a family member, may consent to a DNR order on behalf of an individual if it has been determined to a reasonable degree of medical certainty that

- the patient has a terminal condition; or
- the patient is permanently comatose; or
- resuscitation would be medically futile; or
- resuscitation would impose an extraordinary burden on the patient in light of the patient's medical condition and the expected outcome of the resuscitation for the patient (N.Y. CLS Pub Health § 2965 (3)(c) (1996)).

Given that the case law involving adult patients and termination of ventilator and then food and fluid support began to develop in only 1976, it is not surprising that schools are just beginning to address these issues. The impetus compelling schools to address them has generally come from parents and concerned staff. A parent might, for example, be accustomed to authorizing a DNR order whenever their child is hospitalized and then be frustrated that the school, where the child spends a considerable period of time, refuses to consider their wishes for their child. The school, on the other hand, feels that it provides education and does not easily contemplate children dying on the premises. Since feelings on this subject tend to be very strong, whether they support a DNR order or do not, it is not surprising to find literature arguing that a school should honor the orders and other literature arguing that a policy can be drafted to limit the applicability of these orders in school.

Those who wish to support the use of DNR orders in schools cite a Maryland Attorney General's opinion that found that pursuant to Maryland law, a public school must accept a DNR order and refrain from interventions that are inconsistent with it (*79 Opinions of the Attorney General*, 1994). By contrast, the Washington State Board of Nursing has ruled that "the judgment of whether or not to resuscitate a student in the school setting is not within the purview of school nurse practice, and the nurse should resuscitate" (Brown, Patricia, letter to Judith Maire, 8-23-94). The Board went on to comment that it was not appropriate for a nurse to make the decision "whether a specific event is in fact an irreversible, terminal event or instead a correctable, reversible emergency, like choking." The nurse was instructed to treat all emergencies and transport the student to an emergency room. The Board decision explicitly did not address residential school settings and did not mention the fact that hospital-based nurses make exactly those assessments on a routine basis.

The one thing that all commentators seem to agree on is that the school system should develop its policy and procedures in advance of a request to implement a DNR order. This permits the school district and interested persons to determine a reasonable policy without the pressure and the politics involved with a particular child and unique set of facts.

School policies that address DNR orders will have to address some difficult issues that may not be obvious when discussions about the policy first begin. For example, a school nurse (unless prohibited by an interpretation of nursing licensure law, as in Washington), physician assistant, nurse practitioner, or physician should be on the premises to make an assessment of the student to determine whether a cardiac or respiratory arrest is occurring, rather than choking. Additionally, one should not contemplate honoring a DNR order if the respiratory arrest is precipitated by a reaction to a bee sting rather than as a consequence of the student's underlying disease. It is not reasonable or legally appropriate to require that a school principal, teacher, or other non-health care personnel take the responsibility for making what is a life or death assessment regarding the type of deterioration and the potential cause of it.

There must also be a mechanism for suspending a DNR order if the student decides he or she wishes all possible treatment to be given; such a circumstance must precipitate an immediate suspension of the order and a prompt discussion that includes the parent, the student, and school personnel to resolve any conflict and establish a new plan of care.

In some states, ambulance personnel, whether paramedic or other, will not honor a DNR order. In these areas, simply calling the 9-1-1 emergency response system will cause resuscitation to occur. Some states have enacted legislation to validate a DNR order that is worn by a patient in the form of a brightly colored orange bracelet (e.g., Ct. Gen. Stat. § 19a-580d, 1995). While the bracelet system acts as a universal method of communication regarding who has a valid DNR order within a state, it can also precipitate crisis. For example, a new student to the school may simply arrive with a DNR bracelet, but without the written authorization of the parent and physician and without an individual health plan in place for the student. In this situation, homebound tutoring may be appropriate for a few days until the necessary planning and written orders and agreements are in place.

(See chapter 14 for an in-depth discussion of DNR orders in schools and of the Massachusetts case in which it was determined that the parents had a constitutional right to refuse medical treatment for their minor child (*ABC School and DEF School v. Mr. and Mrs. M.*, 1997).)

School Violence

Recognizing that trends in society are often reflected in schools and student activity, both public and private schools have developed policies that address violence problems, including weapons in schools, the searching of lockers, and other safety-related issues.

With the adoption of the federal Gun Free Schools Act of 1994 (20 U.S.C. § 8921), the states are now required to have laws that mandate expulsion "for at least one year" of students who have brought a gun to school. This law provides that the superintendent may "modify such expulsion requirement for a student on a case-by-case basis." This qualifier was intended to provide for an appropriate determination of whether a student's disability played a role in the misbehavior. (See chapters 11, 12, and 13.) It is now also a federal requirement (20 U.S.C. § 8922) that any student who brings a weapon to school *must* be referred to the criminal justice or juvenile delinquency system. While these federal laws are quite narrow, most states have statutory "public school discipline" codes that provide more detail, and each school district's discipline code usually lists examples of offenses and punishments. (See also chapter 11 regarding discipline under § 504 of the Rehabilitation Act and chapters 12 and 13 regarding discipline under the Individuals with Disabilities Education Act [IDEA].)

In 1985, the U.S. Supreme Court held that the U.S. Constitution's 4th Amendment prohibition on unreasonable searches and seizures applies to searches carried out by public school officials, just as it does to searches undertaken by law enforcement officers. However, because the school has a legitimate interest in maintaining an environment in which learning can occur, school officials need not obtain a warrant to search a student. Therefore, the search of a student or a locker may be justified if there are reasonable grounds to suspect that the search will show that the student has violated or is violating either the laws or the rules of the school. This case validated the search of a purse of a student caught smoking in violation of school policy. The search revealed items suggesting the student was

dealing drugs; criminal delinquency charges were filed against the student (*New Jersey v. TLO*, 469 U.S. 325 (1985)).

Cases subsequent to this Supreme Court case have had varied outcomes. To the extent that there seems to be a unifying principle, it may be the balance between the perceived threat and the degree of intrusiveness involved in the proposed search. Therefore, a court may be more likely to approve a search when there was concern about a gun (In *Re Alexander*, 1990), than it would be to approve a strip search that seemed excessive and intrusive (*Cales v. Howell Public Schools*, 1985).

In general in most states, if lockers and other storage areas will be searched, there should be a school policy describing indications and procedures for search. Further, it is prudent and may be required that students and parents be notified at the beginning of the academic year that those areas are subject to search, either on a random basis (if legal in that state) or pursuant to a complaint or reasonable suspicion that a weapon, for example, is stored there. If a school proposes to search a student for a weapon that has been reported to school personnel, the school may choose to summon the police. If school personnel choose to search a student, a witness should be present to protect against allegations that the school employee behaved improperly during the search.

CONCLUSION

These days, minors have more rights than they once did. They certainly have more rights than in mid-seventh-century England, when a minor, who was anyone under 21 years, was a chattel of his or her father. Under this system, the father could sue a physician for damages for treating the child without his permission, since that treatment interfered with the father's right to control the child (Holder, 1987, p. 3400). It is not uncommon now for students to protest dress codes and other behavioral constraints as an infringement of their "rights." When health care is concerned, the rights of minors *have* been expanding to reflect both the more modern belief that one does not magically become a mature adult at age 18 and the needs of the diverse families that schools deal with today.

The law is always slow to respond to these realities; that is partly because a prudent legislature does not codify a fad in statutes but waits for the development to become more permanent. As a result, there are and will continue to be ambiguities and uncertainties in the background law on which the school and the school health professional must rely to make immediate decisions.

The nurse must have reasonable familiarity with the law in the state in which the practice is occurring; as the above discussions have demonstrated, the law of minors is uniquely state law, and there are considerable variations among the several states in addressing many of the issues that are relevant to school practice. In addition to familiarity, the nurse must also have a knowledge source within the school system, state department of education, or health or community agency to whom she or he may turn when questions with some immediacy must be answered.

REFERENCES

Alan Guttmacher Institute. (2000). *The Status of Major Abortion-Related Laws in the United States, Parental Involvement* [On-line]. Available: www.agi-usa.org/pubs/abort law status.html#2

American Academy of Pediatrics, Committee on Substance Abuse. (1996). Testing for drugs of abuse in children and adolescents. *Pediatrics, 98,* 305–307.

American Medical Association. (1993). *Policy compendium on confidential health services for adolescents* (J. Gans, Ed.). Chicago, p. 8.

Bernzweig, E. P. (1996). *The nurse's liability for malpractice: A programmed course* (6th ed.). St. Louis: Mosby.

Bjorklun, E. (1996). School liability for student suicides. *West's Education Law Reporter, 106,* 21.

Bjorklun, E. C. (1994). Condom distribution in the public schools: Is parental consent required? *West's Education Law Reporter, 91,* 11.

Boonstra, H. and Nash, E. (2000). Minors and the right to consent to health care. *The Guttmacher Report on Policy, 3* (4). Available online (www.agi-usa.org/pubs/journals/gr030404).

Crocker, A. C., et al. (1994). Supports for children with HIV infection in school: Best practice guidelines. *Journal of School Health, 64,* 33.

Darroch, J. E., Landry, D. J., & Oslak, S. (1999). Age differences between sexual partners in the United States. *Family Planning Perspectives, 31*(4), 160–167.

Davis, T. C., Peck, G. O., & Storment, J. M. (1993). Acquaintance rape and the high school student. *Journal of Adolescent Health, 14,* 220.

Donovan, P. (1997). Teen's ability to consent to reproductive health care commonly recognized at state level. *State Reproductive Health Monitor 893,* 4. As reprinted by The Alan Guttmacher Institute. (1998). Issues in Brief: Teenagers' Right to Consent To Reproductive Health Care [On-line]. Available at http://www.agi-usa.org.pubs/ib21.html

English, A. (1995). Guidelines for adolescent health research: Legal perspectives. *Journal of Adolescent Health, 17,* 277.

English, A., & Tereszkiewicz, L. (1988). *School-based health clinics: Legal issues.* Adolescent Health Care Project: National Center for Youth Law.

Hall, J. (1996). *Nursing ethics and the law.* Philadelphia: W. B. Saunders Company.

Holder, A. (1985). *Legal issues in pediatric and adolescent medicine* (2nd ed.). New Haven: Yale University Press.

Holder, A. (1987). Minors' rights to consent to medical care. *Journal of the American Medical Association, 257*(24), 3400.

Legal Action Center. (1996). *Legal Issues for School-Based Programs* (2nd ed.). New York: Author.

National Center for Injury Prevention and Control, Centers for Disease Control, U.S. Department of Health and Human Services. (2000). *Suicide in the United States: The problem.* [On-line]. Available at http://222.cdc.gov/ncipc/factsheets/suifacts.htm

Office of Civil Rights, U.S. Department of Education. (1997). Sexual harassment by school employees, other students or third parties. *Federal Register, 62*(49), 12034–12051

79 Opinions of the Maryland Attorney General. (1994). (Opinion No. 94-028 (May 13, 1994)).

Tsai, A. K., Schaefermeyer, R. W., Kalifon, D., Barkin, R. M., Lumpkin, J. R., & Smith, E. E. (1993). Evaluation and treatment of minors: Reference on consent. *Annals of Emergency Medicine, 22*(7), 1211–1217.

TABLE OF CASES

ABC School and DEF School v. Mr. and Mrs. M., 26 IDELR 1103 (Mass. Super. Ct. 1997).

Acton v. Veronia School District, 47J, 66 F.3d 217 (1995) (remand decision).

Alfonso v. Fernandez, 606 N.Y.S.2d 259 (A.D.2 Dept. 1993).

Armijo by and through Chavez v. Wagon Mound Public Schools, 159 F.3d 1235 (10th Cir. 1998).

Arnold et al. v. Board of Education, 754 F. Supp. 853 (S.D. Ala. 1990).

Brooks v. Logan, 944 P.2d 709, 710, 711 (Idaho 1997).

Cales v. Howell Public Schools, 635 F. Supp. 454 (E.D. Mich. 1985).

Cardwell v. Bechtol, 724 S.W.2d 739 (Tenn. 1987).

Cruzan v. Director, Missouri Dept. of Health, 110 S.Ct. 2841,111 L.Ed.2d 224 (1990).

Curtis v. School Committee of Falmouth, 652 N.E.2d 580 (Mass. 1995).

Grant v. Board of Trustees of Valley View School District No. 365-U, 221 Ill.Dec. 902, 676 N.E.2d 705 (Ill.App. 3 Dist. 1997).

H. L. v. Matheson, 450 U.S. 398, 411 (1981).

Hodgson v. Minnesota et al., (497 U.S. 417, 110 S. CT. 2926, 111 L.Ed. 2d 344 1990).

In Re Alexander, 220 Cal. App. 3d 1572, 270 Cal. Rptr. 342 (Cal. Ct. App. 1990).

In Re E.G., 549 NE 2d 322 (Ill. 1990).

In the Matter of Mary P., 111 Misc. 2d 532, 444 NYS 2d 545 (Fam. Ct., 1981).

Lambert v. Wicklund, 117 SCt. 1169 (1997).

Matter of Cindy Lou Smith, 16 Md. App. 209, 295 A.2d 238 (Md. Spec. App. 1972).

Matter of McCauley, 409 Mass. 134, 565 N.E.2d 411 (1991).

Michael M. v. Superior Court of Sonoma County, 450 U.S. 464, 101 S.Ct. 1200, 67 L.Ed.2d 437 (1981).

Moule v. Paradise Valley Unified School District No. 69, 863 F. Supp. 1098 (D. Ariz. 1994).

Mrs. C. v. Wheaton, 916 F. 2d 69, 16 EHLR (LRP) 1394 (2nd Cir. 1990).

New Jersey v. T.L.O., 469 U.S. 325 (985).

Odenheim v. Carlstadt-East Rutherford Regional School District, 510 A.2d 709 (Superior Ct. N.J. 1985).

Ohio v. Akron Center for Reproductive Health (497 U.S. 502, 110 S. Ct. 2972, 111 L.Ed 2d 405 (1990)).

Parents United for Better Schools, Inc., v. School District of Philadelphia Board of Education, 148 F.3d 260 (3rd Cir. 1998).

Planned Parenthood of Central Missouri v. Danforth, 428 U.S. 52 (1976).

Roe v. Wade, 410 U.S. 113 (1973).

Veronia School District 47J v. Acton, 115 S. Ct. 2386 (1995).

Wicklund, et al. v. State of Montana, Cause No. ADV 97-671, Order on Preliminary Injunction, Mont. 1st JD Ct, February 13, 1998 [On-line]. Available at: http://www.mt.net/~johnoitz/1stjd98/WICK-LUND_2_13.htm

Wyke v. Polk County School Board, 129 F.3d 560 (11th Cir. 1997).

OFFICE FOR CIVIL RIGHTS (OCR) DECISIONS

Harlowton (MT) Public Schools, 26 IDELR 1156 (OCR 1997).

See page 625 for Table of Federal Statutes and Regulations.

Chapter Eight
Confidentiality: Principles and Practice Issues

Nadine C. Schwab
Mary H. B. Gelfman

INTRODUCTION

The purpose of this chapter is to explain the legal and ethical bases and standards underlying confidentiality, as well as the limitations of confidentiality, particularly as they apply to student health information, nursing practice, and pupil-services issues in schools. Despite the promise of new federal and state laws to ensure the privacy of an individual's health information, the complexity of decision making about confidentiality issues in school health is unlikely to be significantly diminished in the near future. Indeed, new legislation may raise new questions and cause different practice dilemmas.

It is hoped that this chapter, together with chapters 9 (records and documentation) and 10 (electronic records and technology) will help education and health professionals to understand these complex issues and to collaborate in resolving dilemmas related to confidentiality of student health information. While the focus of this book is "health services," many of the same principles, issues, and guidelines described in this chapter are applicable to other pupil-services professionals and, with variations depending on their employers, school-based health center personnel as well.

This chapter's content is based on the works of experts in fields too numerous to mention here. However, the authors wish to acknowledge the Connecticut Committee on Confidentiality of Student Health Information (1996) for its contributions to their understanding of, and practical approaches to, problem solving in this complex area of school-based practice. (A full copy of the Committee's 1996 draft guidelines is included in Appendix N.) A diverse committee of approximately 42 members represented school principals, superintendents, special education directors, teachers, pupil-services professionals, parents, school and community health professionals, health and education lawyers, and a university-based ethicist, among others.

Confidentiality is an abstract concept that is inextricably intertwined with the individual's "right to privacy" and with communication and record-keeping practices in health care settings and schools. While the concepts of confidentiality and privacy are deeply rooted in long-standing ethical principles of most civilized cultures and in the legal tenets of our democracy, confidentiality issues pose complex challenges for health, education, and social service professionals in all practice arenas. With respect to minors in school settings, these challenges can be confounding.

Federal and state mandates and the common law addressing these concepts and practice issues are inexact and sometimes even in conflict with one another. As such, decisions related to the maintenance and disclosure of confidential student health information often require (1) the weighing and balancing of opposing ethical principles, (2) expert analysis of conflicting laws, and (3) highly sophisticated professional judgment.

In schools, confidentiality issues related to student health information usually revolve around the following questions:

- What is student health information?

- What student health information should be documented and where?

- What student health information may be shared?

- When may it be shared?

- With whom may it be shared?

- Who should consent to such sharing?

- Do special conditions apply to such sharing?

- On what bases should such decisions be made?

There are no simple answers to these questions and no answers that apply to all situations. Therefore, school professionals must understand the complex ethical and legal issues that underlie confidentiality concerns and rights of families and students, as well as the limits to those rights. Furthermore, they must learn to apply critical thinking and problem-solving strategies to individual situations. To assist school nurses and other school health professionals in understanding the legal and ethical issues inherent in maintaining and disclosing confidential health information of minor students, this chapter examines relevant principles of confidentiality found in ethics and law, general exceptions to the usual rule of maintaining confidentiality, the factors underlying special challenges faced in school settings, and general recommendations for approaching confidentiality issues.

Because the focus of this book is legal and ethical issues related to *school health*, the discussion on confidentiality targets *student health information*. It is important to note, however, that the same principles may apply to other student and family information that is private in nature. Furthermore, "health information," as defined by health professionals, encompasses a broad spectrum of health and mental health information related to an individual, including medical, social, psychological, lifestyle, family, and economic data. When the Connecticut Committee on Confidentiality of Student Health Information drafted policy guidelines for recommendation to the State Department of Education in 1996, the Committee defined "health information" as follows:

> Health information includes, but is not limited to, printed, oral and electronic communications regarding: details of a health and developmental history; current health status, illness or developmental concern; examination or assessment findings; medication requirements; treatment or intervention history and on-going progress notes; records of HIV testing and treatment; drug and alcohol abuse and psychiatric evaluation and treatment; health care facility and provider office records, including evaluation or testing summaries, discharge instructions, prescriptions, psychological evaluation and testing, and neuropsychiatric testing results; nursing, social work, and other pupil-services specialists histories, evaluations and progress notes relating to student or family health; and health-related planning and placement [special education] team records and communications.

It is of interest to note that the members of the Connecticut Committee, while charged with developing guidelines for student health information, determined over time that the same principles applied to all private student information and, therefore, the draft document was titled *[draft] Guidelines for Policy And Practice: Confidentiality of Student Information* (Connecticut Committee on Confidentiality of Student Health Information, 1996).

(Confidentiality and privacy issues are also addressed in other chapters of the book. See chapter 3 for ethical decision making in schools, chapter 7 for specific adolescent issues, including minor rights and informed consent, chapter 9 regarding the law related to education records and documentation systems for school health services programs, and chapter 10 for information related to technology and electronic records. Related discussion of confidentiality and informed consent may also be found in chapters 2 and 6.)

GENERAL PRINCIPLES AND SOURCES OF CONFIDENTIALITY

While "privacy" is a concept that usually refers to an individual, the notion of "confidentiality" refers to a relationship between two or more people where communication is protected. Purtilo defines confidentiality, in the context of the health professions, as "the practice of keeping harmful, shameful or embarrassing patient information within proper bounds" (1993, p. 97). The underlying principles of privacy and confidentiality are derived from both ethics and the law. Legal sources of privacy and confidentiality protections in this country include the U. S. and state Constitutions, federal and state laws, and case law. These ethical and legal standards that underlie the general principle of non-disclosure of personal health information are described below.

Ethical Principles

The importance of the confidentiality afforded patients in their relationships with health care providers is evidenced through an ancient tradition, the Hippocratic Oath. By this Oath, named for a Greek a physician who lived more than 2,000 years ago, physicians have, for centuries, sworn to protect the privacy of patient information. Maintaining patient confidentiality is considered a necessary prerequisite to establishing a trusting relationship and, thereby, encouraging patients to speak fully and candidly when seeking health care. Since factual and complete health and lifestyle information is critical to accurate diagnosis and effective treatment, patients must be confident that the information they share with health and social service providers will not be further disclosed. Similar concepts, including respect for individual autonomy and intimacy in relationships among human beings, form the basis of confidentiality in other special relationships, such as husbands and wives, clergy and confessors, and lawyers or counselors and their clients.

The ethical principles that underlie the concepts of confidentiality and privacy, according to Rushton and Infante (1995), include fidelity, respect for persons, and non-maleficence. Fidelity addresses the issue of keeping promises, that is, being faithful to the professional-client relationship that is based on mutual respect and trust. Fidelity requires health professionals to protect patient information from disclosure to others, except to members of the health care team working within the same agency who need to know the information in order to care for the patient. Since confidentiality is never absolute, however, fidelity also requires professionals working with both adult and minor clients to inform them, at the beginning of a professional-client relationship, what limitations exist to the usual rule of maintaining client confidentiality. Promises that cannot be kept should never be made.

Respect for persons, another ethical value, affords protection for the individual's preferences, self-determination, and need for privacy. Respect for persons includes the principles of autonomy (the right of individuals to determine their own actions—and to have sufficient information to make reasoned choices), veracity (truth-telling) and beneficence (promoting good). Promoting good for the client includes protecting the privacy of the client. The principle of autonomy requires that confidential information disclosed by an adult client in the course of diagnosis and treatment remain within the client's control. In other words, the client, not the professional, determines whether or not the information will be further disclosed. In health care, adolescents are generally, but not always, afforded similar control over their own health information. (See chapter 7, "Adolescent Issues and Rights of Minors.")

Non-maleficence refers to the ethical value of causing no harm. In health care, this principle obligates professionals to seek a course of action that minimizes harm to a client. It is related to beneficence, which

requires professionals to make choices that promote client well being and maintain client dignity. Inappropriate disclosure of confidential information, whether purposeful or inadvertent, can cause significant damage to individuals, including minor students and their families. At other times, failure to disclose confidential information may result in considerable harm to one or more persons.

Ethical values assist professionals in analyzing dilemmas, balancing potential good versus potential harm for the individual and others, making decisions, and choosing actions related to the protection and disclosure of confidential information. (See also chapter 3, "Exploring Ethical Challenges in School Health.") In keeping with these values, professional organizations of physicians, nurses, social workers, psychologists, and lawyers, among others, establish and promulgate ethical codes and standards of practice to guide the profession's members in applying the "values, ideals and norms of the profession, and in discharging their obligations to clients, the public, other members of the team, and the profession" (American Nurses Association, 1995).

Codes of ethics are especially important as guides for conduct when professionals are confronted with difficult dilemmas and changing practice realities. While not legally enforceable per se, a professional code of ethics can be used as a "standard of care" against which the performance of a professional can be judged in a civil action of negligence brought by a dissatisfied client, or in an administrative (disciplinary) action brought by the state agency or board that has oversight authority, including the power to grant and revoke professional licenses for the practice of that profession in a state. (See also chapters 2 and 4.) Professional codes of ethics are also cited in state agency guidelines as standards for pupil-services professionals (e.g., Connecticut Committee on Confidentiality of Student Health Information, 1996; Goodman & Sheetz, 1995).

The *Code for Nurses with Interpretive Statements* of the American Nurses Association (ANA, 1985) states that

The nurse safeguards the client's right to privacy by judiciously protecting information of a confidential nature.

In addition to the *Code for Nurses with Interpretive Statements*, Standard Five (V) of ANA's *Standards of Professional Performance* addresses ethics, saying that

The nurse's decisions and actions on behalf of clients are determined in an ethical manner.

The second measurement criterion for this standard (ANA, 1998) is, "The nurse maintains client confidentiality within legal and regulatory parameters. Like the ANA measurement criteria quoted immediately above, language recognizing legal constraints to the ethical value of confidentiality is more commonly found in contemporary professional codes of ethics than in past ones." (See appendix B.)

Similar performance standards and measurement criteria are found in the National Association of School Nurses' (NASN) *Standards of School Nursing Practice* (1998), and its Code of Ethics (1990). (See appendix A.) Furthermore, the ethical standard of maintaining student confidentiality is expressly cited as an ethical basis for school nursing practice in the 1993 NASN guidelines (Proctor, 1993). The National Association of State School Nurse Consultants issued a position paper on confidentiality of student health information in 1993, and is in the process of updating it for 2000.

State agency guidelines also set standards for practice. For example, in Washington, the state education agency has issued a publication, *Guidelines for Handling Health Care Information in School Records* (Billings, Pearson, Carthum, & Maire, 1995). Ethical considerations are addressed in the introduction (p. 1):

> In discussion, the Committee recognized the important concept of self-determination and dignity which are key confidentiality provisions. The legitimate purposes of information sharing must respect the person about whom the information is kept but it must not become the cloak behind which vital information is hidden.

Based on both legal and ethical principles, the guidelines specifically state that "Health care providers cannot disclose health care information to non-health care providers (teachers, etc.) until parent permission is obtained unless someone's health and safety is at risk" (p. 8).

State policies and guidelines vary considerably for this area of practice. The American Medical Association's *Policy Compendium on Confidential Health Services for Adolescents* (Gans, 1993), provides an overview of the ethical standards of practice, consensus, and policy recommendations of several national organizations of health professionals, including the American Academy of Pediatrics, the American Psychological Association, and the American Nurses Association, regarding confidential health services for adolescents. While not specifically targeted to

school settings, the publication is a useful source of general information related to confidentiality and adolescent health care. It includes model policy recommendations that are relevant to school health services and school-based health centers. (Additional discussion of the rights of adolescents to consent to health care is provided in chapter 7.)

The National Education Association's (NEA) *Code of Ethics for Teachers* in the *NEA Handbook 1991–1992* (1991) includes a standard for protecting the confidentiality of students. This ethical standard for educators is supported by the constitutional right to privacy, the Family Educational Rights and Privacy Act (the federal law passed in 1974 to allow parents access to their children's school records and to prohibit schools from disclosing confidential student information), the Individual's with Disabilities Education Act (IDEA), and other federal laws pertaining to education. However, the application of this standard in schools has been problematic, at best. Reasons that explain the discrepancy between standard and practice are discussed later in this chapter under "Variable Standards of Confidentiality," page 286. (See chapter 3 for further discussion of ethics in relation to school health services.)

Legal Principles

The main legal principle on which confidentiality of client information is based is the "right to privacy" which stems from but is not specifically mentioned in the U.S. Constitution. This personal right to privacy is also recognized in many state constitutions, and in federal, state, and case law. A second legal principle, referred to as "privilege," formalizes the common law tradition of confidentiality into state law, and is also well recognized in case law. Both are discussed below.

The right to privacy, described as "the right to be left alone" in a groundbreaking law review article by Brandeis and Warren in 1890, has been recognized by American courts as guaranteed in the U.S. Constitution. It not only reinforces the traditional confidential relationship between physician and patient established in ancient times, but is fundamental to the belief in individual freedom that American forefathers fought so hard to guarantee and protect. Alderman and Kennedy attempt to explain in the introduction to their book, *The Right to Privacy* (1997, p. xiii), why Americans "cherish" their privacy:

- It protects the solitude necessary for creative thought.

- It allows us the independence that is part of raising a family.

- It protects our right to be secure in our own home and possessions.

- It encompasses our right to self-determination and to define who we are.

- It allows us to keep certain facts to ourselves if we so choose.

- The right to privacy, it seems, is what makes us civilized.

Specific court decisions have helped to determine what the "right to privacy" actually means under the law. In a 1965 case, which challenged Connecticut's ban on family planning services (*Griswold v. Connecticut*, 1965), the U.S. Supreme Court defined a "zone of privacy" that included a woman's right to receive medical advice on reproductive matters. When the legality of a state's computerized registry of patients receiving prescribed narcotic drugs was challenged in 1977, the U.S. Supreme Court identified two types of individual privacy interests. These were interests in

- avoiding disclosure of personal matters, and

- independence in making certain kinds of important decisions (*Whalen v. Roe*, 1977).

These Supreme Court decisions both affirm that the U.S. Constitution guarantees U.S. citizens the right to privacy and help to define its legal parameters, especially in federal cases. Many state constitutions also recognize the right to privacy and it has been affirmed in many state and federal judicial decisions addressing a variety of different challenges to the right to personal privacy, including rights of the press, employer, and law enforcement to access certain kinds of information. These court decisions, or legal principles as they may become, vary depending on the specific issue involved.

Alderman and Kennedy's book (1997) addresses the major areas of conflict: privacy versus law enforcement, privacy and yourself (which include many health care issues), privacy versus the press, privacy versus the voyeur, privacy in the workplace, and privacy and information. The 1997 edition of this 1994 book includes an afterword that speaks to the alarming "erosion of medical confidentiality as a national concern" (p. 336).

Court decisions have further delineated two corollaries to the right to be left alone that are fundamental to the concept of confidentiality. They are that

- The individual has the right to decide whether, and to whom, personal information should be disclosed; and

- The individual has the right to expect that, when such information is disclosed, it will not be further disclosed without the individual's consent (Feldsman et al., 1992).

These corollaries support the concept that the individual is the "owner" of his or her own personal information, not the agency or professional with whom he or she shares it. Additionally, the right to privacy in health care refers to the right of a patient to accept or reject any recommendations regarding treatment or non-treatment (Rushton & Infante, 1996), and the right to keep private information about his or her health status. (Minors' rights regarding health care decisions are more variable and are discussed both below and in chapter 7.)

A related legal principle in the human service and health care realm, "privileged communications," is addressed in state law. Privileged communications under the law are protected from forced disclosure in judicial proceedings. Such protection is afforded under state laws because of the nature of the special relationship between two individuals, for example, the professional relationship between a physician and her patient or an attorney and his client. Privileged communication means that the individual (client) who discloses the confidential information within this special relationship also determines whether or not the information that was so disclosed can be revealed in a court proceeding. A professional receiving such communications cannot voluntarily disclose it or be legally compelled to disclose it as a witness without the permission of the client who made the disclosure (American Academy of Pediatrics, 1995, p.167).

It is important to understand that the "privilege" belongs to the individual, or client, not to the health care provider, social worker, or counselor. State laws usually define such privileges by specific professions. Generally, states have expanded the traditional protection of communications with members of the clergy, physicians, and lawyers to include licensed or certified health and mental health professionals, such as nurses, social workers, psychologists, and a variety of "counselors." Many states are experiencing pressure from professional organizations to expand the list of professionals provided with privilege and, as a result, the list varies from state to state and year to year.

There are additional principles of privacy and confidentiality embedded in international, federal, state, and judicial law, depending on the topic at hand and area of law. For the purposes of this chapter, however, only those principles and laws most relevant to school health are discussed. (See Alderman & Kennedy [1997] for a broad overview of the right to privacy.)

EXCEPTIONS TO THE GENERAL RULES PROHIBITING DISCLOSURE OF CONFIDENTIAL HEALTH INFORMATION

An individual's right to privacy is not absolute as there are competing interests that must be balanced against it. In the health care field, for example, practitioners, legislators, and the courts have recognized over time the necessity for exceptions to the general prohibitions against the disclosure of personal health information without the consent of the client or patient to whom the information belongs. These exceptions are few, but generally well defined in clinical health care settings, such as hospitals, community health care centers, nursing facilities, and private practitioner offices. Federal laws that address privacy issues, or include confidentiality requirements, generally include certain exceptions to those requirements, as does the Family Educational Rights and Privacy Act (FERPA), which is discussed in detail in chapter 9, and the federal drug and alcohol treatment requirements, which are discussed in this chapter. While certain exceptions to the confidentiality rules are contained in federal laws and, therefore, apply as a minimum standard across all states, individual states may have additional mandates and case law precedent that address both privacy rights and exceptions to those rights.

This section of the chapter addresses general exceptions to the confidentiality rule of non-disclosure of health information, rather than provisions specific to any law, except where noted. Because these limitations to confidentiality exist, it is critical that personnel understand them and that students who seek confidential services from school health professionals are informed that, even when they have a general right to confidentiality, the right is never absolute.

Written Informed Consent

When a client or, in the case of a minor, the parent or legal guardian of the client, gives written, informed consent for personal health information to be shared with others, it is permissible to share the specified information with the individuals or agencies indicated, and for the purpose(s) delineated in the permission. Written consents should be clear, sufficiently detailed, concise, and time-limited. See Table

8-1 for the items required in a "proper consent form" as specified in § 2.31 of the federal regulations governing the confidentiality of persons receiving services for drug and alcohol abuse, including students (42 C.F.R., Part II). Such written consent should meet the standard of "informed consent," that is, the client must fully understand what information will be shared, by and with whom it will be shared, and the expected outcomes and potential ramifications. Furthermore, when consent to share information is provided for one purpose, the information may not be used for another purpose. Under certain circumstances, minors may give their own consent to such information sharing, for example, when they consent to treatment for drug and alcohol abuse by a student assistance team or a health care provider in the community. (See also chapter 7 for discussion of informed consent and circumstances under which minors may consent to health care and to the release of confidential health information.)

Consent for Internal Sharing of Sensitive Health Information

In a majority of states at this time, there are no special provisions beyond FERPA regarding written consent for sharing confidential student health information among professional personnel working in a school district (i.e., employed or contracted by the district to provide services to students). Where legal guidance is lacking, good practice suggests that written consent should be obtained from the parent or guardian, and, in the case of an older student, the student as well to share sensitive confidential health information (e.g., a student's HIV or Hepatitis B diagnosis) even with school personnel who provide direct services to the student. The written consent should include the specific names of those individuals to whom the parent or legal guardian consents to disclose such information, how it will be used, and when the consent expires. Just putting "school nurse" on the consent form is not enough; the consent should specify "Mr. Smith, school nurse," or "Ms. Jones, school social worker."

In certain states like Washington, as referenced above, the school nurse must obtain written consent from the parent or guardian to share with other school personnel any specific medical information regarding a student (Billings et al., 1995), not just highly sensitive diagnoses. It is necessary to keep in mind that this personal information belongs to the student and family, not the school. Therefore, it is generally the student's (or parent's) right to control who has access to that

Table 8-1.

CONTENTS OF A PROPER CONSENT FORM

As Defined in Federal Regulations Regarding
Confidentiality of Individuals Receiving Services for Drug and Alcohol Abuse
(C.F.R. 42, Part II, § 2.31)

---

1. The name of the program(s) making the disclosure.
2. The name or title of the individual or organization that will receive the disclosed information.
3. The name of the patient [or student].
4. The purpose or need for the disclosure.
5. How much and what kind of information will be disclosed.
6. Statement that the patient [student] may revoke the consent at any time, except to the extent that the [student assistance] program has already acted in reliance on it.
7. The date, event, or condition upon which the consent expires if not already revoked.
8. The signature of the patient [student] and, in some cases, his or her parent.
9. The date that the consent is signed.

---

information, especially when disclosure might cause harm.

Interagency Sharing

Written informed consent is almost always required for sharing any type of identifiable student health information between two agencies, or between two professionals who work in different agencies. In other words, informed written consent of a parent, or student when applicable, is required in order for a school employee to share confidential information about the student (or family) with anyone outside the school district. This requirement is true for communications between school district personnel and school-based health center (SBHC) personnel unless the SBHC is owned and operated by the school district. Possible exceptions to the written consent rule for interagency communications are discussed under "Non-Identifying Information" and "Contracted Services" below.

Internal Communications

In general, written consent of a client is not required in order for personnel working within the same agency to share necessary client information for the purpose of treating or providing services to that client. For example, an individual who is admitted into a hospital signs a consent-to-treatment form, which generally authorizes disclosure of information for treatment and billing purposes (e.g., to third-party payors). Beyond

what is authorized, the hospital is expected to protect the patient's privacy by prohibiting the disclosure of medical status, health history, course of treatment, and any other confidential information to anyone inside the agency who doesn't need to know it in order to provide appropriate services, and to anyone outside the agency. However, it is implicit in the patient's general consent for treatment by the hospital that information the patient shares with one member of the hospital team can be shared with other hospital personnel *who need to know the information in order to benefit the patient*. In other words, the emergency room nurse does not need written consent from the patient to share his initial assessment with the attending physician, nor must the physician obtain written consent from the patient each time she needs to share patient information with other hospital staff for diagnostic and treatment purposes, for example, an x-ray technician or physical therapist.

Similarly, it is expected that staff members of a school district will—and they should—share with other district personnel confidential student information, including health information, *when necessary* in order to *benefit the student*, that is, to provide the students with appropriate educational services. The Family Educational Rights and Privacy Act (FERPA, 20 U.S.C. § 1232g) addresses this need by allowing internal communications regarding confidential student information when such sharing is for "legitimate educational purposes." Legitimate educational purposes includes, for example, school nurse-to-classroom teacher communications identifying a student who is at high risk for seizures, how to recognize the seizure, and what to do should one occur. The teacher does not need to know, however, the medical etiology of the seizures in order to provide a safe environment for the student, nor is it appropriate to post the student's name on a "Health Alert List" that is circulated among all teachers in a building. In the latter situation, not all teachers provide services to the student and, therefore, not all teachers need to know the information.

Sometimes the question of supervision of students at recess or the fact that older students have multiple teachers is raised as a reason for circulating a general list of students with health problems to all teachers. From both clinical and liability perspectives, it is more effective to provide all teachers with in-service programs to prepare them for handling potential emergencies than it is to circulate a list of all students' medical diagnoses. Such in-service programs should address how to recognize and provide first aid interventions for urgent and emergency health situations that can be reasonably anticipated to occur in school, such as head and neck injury, respiratory distress, seizure, hemorrhage, and anaphylaxis. The content of an in-service program will depend to some extent on the availability of health professionals in the school building and the needs of the student population. Written guidelines for simple first aid procedures that teachers can keep with them, both in the classroom and on the playground, are particularly useful. Both of these strategies demonstrate a school's efforts to protect the health and safety of its students, but do not require the disclosure of individual students' confidential health information.

In any event, a list of students and their medical diagnoses does not prepare a teacher to recognize or effectively intervene in an emergency (which may be related or unrelated to the condition). This list is also unlikely to be in the teacher's pocket at recess three months into the school year. In regard to older students with multiple teachers, older students are generally more independent in managing their health conditions and are able to communicate urgent problems directly with their teachers.

Informing teachers *individually* of students in their classroom who require accommodations or have the potential for an emergency situation is both necessary and appropriate. Variations in the extent of information sharing that is necessary depend on several factors, including the health and educational needs and competence of the student, safety risks involved, availability in

the building of a school nurse or other appropriately trained person, preferences of the family and student, and administrative issues. Falia, for example, defines categories of direction to include for caregivers (1992, p. 108):

1. Information (about the health condition, e.g., signs and symptoms for which to monitor and food items to avoid in the classroom);

2. Skills (to do necessary procedures, e.g., action to take during an asthmatic or hypoglycemic reaction); and

3. Educational implications, including physical education (impact on functioning and adaptations needed, e.g., decreased stamina and need to allow pacing of class work or sports participation or need for special classroom seating due to hearing or visual impairments).

The information that must be shared for the safety and health maintenance of a student rarely includes the medical diagnosis of a student. In fact, for educational purposes, medical diagnoses are non-specific, non-prescriptive, and lacking connections to student learning. The diagnosis of asthma, for example, applies both to Student A (who has very mild symptoms that occur only with strenuous exercise, are easily managed, and do not interfere with the student's academic performance) and to Student B (who has severe symptoms of disease, including respiratory distress, that are medically difficult to manage and interfere with the student's energy in the classroom and attendance in school). The use of medical diagnoses as communication vehicles between health and education professionals can also lead to discrimination, inappropriate performance expectations for students, and ineffective education programs.

Rather than the medical diagnosis per se, a classroom teacher needs to understand the *functional health problem* of the student, how to recognize the problem, and what to do if it happens. Nursing diagnoses, as standardized in classification languages already established (e.g., the classification of nursing diagnoses, as developed and regularly updated by the North American Nursing Diagnosis Association (1999), provide a universal language for describing the *functional health problems* of students. If used appropriately in schools, these functional diagnoses, coupled with individualized care plans for how to recognize and intervene in the classroom, can provide educators with excellent operational information about students' health needs. For example, the nursing diagnoses of "impaired mobility" or "ineffective airway clearance" can be used to describe a student's special health needs that require educational planning. They also eliminate the need for divulging the underlying medical diagnosis and help to protect confidentiality.

Whether the mobility limitation is caused by an underlying disease process, a birth defect, or traumatic injury is less important than whether it is mild, moderate, or severe, how it interferes with the student's development, learning, and independence, and what accommodations and services may be indicated. Similarly, whether the student's ineffective airway clearance problem is the result of a secondary infection from HIV, cystic fibrosis, or asthma is less important for the teacher to know than the severity of the problem, how it will be manifested, and what the student and teacher need to do about it (Schwab, Panettieri, & Bergren, 1998, p. 29). (For additional information on the use and implementation of nursing diagnoses in schools, see Leuhr, 1993; Hootman, 1996a, 1996b, and 1996c; and Poulton & Denehy, 1999. See Appendix K for a list of sample nursing diagnoses with related student objectives for § 504 and IEP [individualized education program] planning.)

School nurses also need to address necessary information sharing with school administrators. In a crisis, such as a case of hepatitis A in a pre-K class or several cases of scabies or ringworm in the seventh grade, school administrators need to be immediately advised of the situation. It is inappropriate for a school staff member to be informed without the principal being informed. Successful crisis management requires the principal to be aware before the crisis occurs (Majer, 1992, p. 24). On the other hand, the principal may not always need to know which students are infected in order to provide general administrative direction and respond to parental inquiries (e.g. in an outbreak of head lice).

Even outside of crisis situations, school administrators need sufficient information about the health and safety needs of students to plan appropriate programs, ensure a safe environment, and provide adequate staff training programs. They also need access to emergency care plans for student in their buildings. The use of nursing diagnoses, rather than medical diagnoses, can be helpful in protecting confidentiality when appropriate. An administrator's need to have sufficient information may include information regarding whether or not a student came to the health center at a particular time on a particular day, but does not translate to a right to access the content of the student's discussion with the nurse.

When to share student health information internally (within a school building and district) is, perhaps, one of the most challenging issues for school nurses. The definition of "legitimate educational interests" under FERPA is open to wide interpretation. Its interpretation by school administrators will often differ significantly from its interpretation by school nurses and other health professionals. Based on state nurse practice acts, and medical records and health care information laws, some states have provided school nurses with specific direction regarding limits to the internal disclosure of student health information in schools, for example, Washington (Billings et al, 1995) and Massachusetts (1995). However, to date, these states remain few in number. Further discussion of the complexities and dilemmas faced by school nurses in deciding what student health information to release internally and what to protect from release is found below under "Unique Challenges for School Health Professionals." (School health records and documentation are addressed in chapter 9.)

Non-Identifying Information

Communications that do not disclose the identity of the student or client, in other words, contain no personal identifying information, are generally permissible without the individual's written consent. Such communications include aggregate reports of data, for example, the total number of female students in a high school who, during a given school year, requested information from the school nurse about reproductive health. A second type of communications that fits into this category are consultations with supervisors, colleagues, faculty advisors (in the case of university students) and outside experts that are necessary for obtaining advice regarding services for the student. A "what if" scenario, omitting real names and other potentially identifying details, can be used to obtain the advice needed to manage a particular situation. Extreme care must be taken not to use a detail or descriptor that might identify the subject of the communication.

A third type of communications that fits within the general category of "non-identifying information" is general information shared internally, for example, with a teacher, that does not divulge the student's specific health problem or medical diagnosis so that, while the student is identified, the student's confidential health information is not. For example, it may be appropriate to share with a teacher that a student is experiencing stress and, as a result, requires temporary extensions on homework assignments. It is not necessary—or therefore appropriate—for the school nurse to share that the stress is caused by a change in medication, an exacerbation of chronic disease, or an impending divorce of the student's parents. Similarly, the federal confidentiality law and regulations governing drug and alcohol treatment records (42 U.S.C. § 290dd-2; 42 C.F.R. Part 2) allow communication of information without written consent if the information communicated does not disclose the student's status as someone with an alcohol or drug abuse problem (§ 2.12(a)(i); Legal Action Center, 1996, p.15). Accordingly, a school nurse can verify for an administrator that a student was in the health office for a consultation at 12 noon on Wednesday afternoon, but cannot disclose the student's reason for coming to the health office, which was to seek assistance with an alcohol problem.

Two important principles that support the limited sharing described in the two examples above are that (1) student health information should be shared internally only with those who need to know *for the benefit of the student* (not for the benefit of the provider); and (2) *only information necessary* to provide appropriate services to a student should be shared (Connecticut Committee on Confidentiality of Student Health Information, 1996, p. 3).

Contracted Services

Confidential information of a client, or student in the case of schools, can usually be shared between personnel in two agencies, without written consent, when a contractual arrangement exists between the two agencies for the provision of services to clients. In other words, if the personnel of the second agency are contracted by the first agency to provide services for clients of the first, or if the agency or individual is acting for, or in the place of, the first agency, sharing client information *with those who need to know the information in order to benefit the client* is generally acceptable. As with communications within the same agency, only that information necessary for the proper care and treatment of a patient (or student) should be shared, and contracted personnel must, as a minimum, abide by the confidentiality policies and procedures of the primary agency.

In school settings, such contractual arrangements are not unusual. For example, many city health departments and local or regional visiting nurse agencies provide nurses to staff local and regional health services programs in public schools through formal (and sometimes informal) contracts. In these situations, school nurses are *acting for the school district* and, therefore, may be considered contractual employees of the district for the purposes of team functioning and information sharing. They are strictly prohibited under FERPA from further disclosing student information to others, either those within their nursing or public health agency who do not have a need to know (to benefit the student), or to a third agency. To the extent that such contractual arrangements are in writing and reflected in school district and agency policy and procedures, personnel can be clear about permitted practices and their professional obligations regarding sharing of confidential student information with contracted personnel and agencies.

Under the federal law and regulations that protect the privacy of medical records of individuals who seek treatment for drug and alcohol problems, an agency that is under contract to a school district to provide drug and alcohol services is referred to as a "qualified service organization." The same exception to the usual non-disclosure rule, described above for contracted services, applies to qualified service organizations. It is important to note, however, that in cases where students seek assistance from a drug and alcohol student assistance program (SAP) in a school, the general exception for "internal communications" applies only to those staff who are members of the SAP team and to "an entity that has administrative control over the SAP" (Legal Action Center, 1996, p. 13). The SAP team within a school, if it "specializes, in whole or in part, in providing treatment, counseling, or assessment and referral services for students with alcohol or drug abuse problems" (42 C.F.R. § 2.12(e)) must comply with the federal confidentiality law and regulations for drug and alcohol treatment programs (42 U.S.C. § 290dd-2 and 42 C.F.R. Part 2). Staff who are members of the program team may share confidential student information "internally," that is, with other members of the SAP team or someone in administrative control of the program, but not with school personnel who are external to (i.e., not members of) the team or do not have direct administrative responsibility for the program (Legal Action Center, 1996). When internal disclosures of confidential drug and alcohol information are made, it should only be for the purpose of providing appropriate services to the student. This is no different than any other confidential health information.

Health or Safety Emergency

A widely recognized exception to the general prohibitions against sharing confidential client information is the health or safety emergency. FERPA addresses this exception, as do other federal and state laws, such as the federal drug and alcohol confidentiality requirements discussed above. Under the latter provisions, disclosure of information about a patient's (or student's) drug or alcohol condition, health status, or treatment is limited to those situations that pose an immediate threat to the health of the individual (§ 2.51). Furthermore, disclosures made for health emergencies may be made only to medical personnel. According to guidelines from the Legal Action Center of the City of New York (1996), an SAP that provides treatment, counseling, or assessment and referral services for students with drug and alcohol problems (p.18) can

> . .. notify a school nurse or physician about a suicidal student so that medical intervention can be arranged, and the school nurse or physician [can], in turn, notify the student's parents, so long as no mention is made of the student's drug or alcohol problem.

This exception generally refers to true emergency situations, that is, situations in which there is significant threat to the life or limb of an individual. For example, when a student has severe abdominal pain consistent with acute appendicitis, or is suspected to have overdosed on drugs or to be in labor, it is appropriate for the school nurse to share all pertinent information and assessment data with the emergency medical personnel who respond to the 9-1-1 call, and with hospital emergency room personnel where the student is being transported. The information is necessary for emergency personnel to assess and treat the student in the most expeditious manner possible. It is also appropriate to share sufficient information with parents and school administrators to convey the seriousness of the situation and enable them to respond accordingly. Details of the nursing assessment or initial impressions of the school nurse may not be appropriate to share, however, depending on the circumstances and age of the student. The medical diagnosis is not yet confirmed, the student's privacy should not be unnecessarily invaded, and the parent/guardian can obtain more detailed information directly from hospital personnel and the student.

A true health or safety emergency does not refer to a non-emergent situation, for example, when a student bites a teacher, or another student, and draws blood. While this situation needs immediate attention, it is not a health or safety emergency and is not, therefore, a situation in which the privacy of a student or family needs to be breached. Rather, there is time to obtain

consent for release of information or to obtain the assistance of local and state experts. Health professionals in health care facilities, including school-based health centers, while obliged to protect the right of minors to privacy in seeking treatment for certain medical conditions, as specified in state and federal law, must also notify a parent or guardian when a minor is in imminent danger of harm due to a health or safety emergency. Of note, the level of acuity and danger that is required to constitute a "health or safety emergency" in the health care field (i.e., imminent threat to life or limb) is generally higher than that construed under interpretations of a similar FERPA exception. The Connecticut Committee on Confidentiality of Student Health Information, in its draft guidelines (1996), recommended use of the health care standard for divulging confidential health information without written consent—that is, the health or safety emergency should constitute an imminent threat of serious harm to the student or others. (The health or safety exception to the general rule of non-disclosure, as it relates to adolescent health services, is discussed in chapter 7.)

Protection of the Public Health

As soon as medical science determined that certain diseases were contagious, it became possible to control or prevent their spread. This can be done by ensuring that infected individuals receive a full course of treatment and that their high-risk contacts also be tested and, if indicated, treated. In order to encourage individuals to agree to be tested and, even more difficult, to disclose their contacts (e.g., sexual partners), the assurance of absolute confidentiality beyond use of the information for medical and public health purposes, has been (and still is) critically important.

Beyond infectious diseases, the Supreme Court has identified other public health interests that warrant the release or partial release of patient information. For example, in *Whalen v. Roe* (1977), concerning the state registry of patients treated with narcotics, the Court ruled that the state's interest in protecting public health overrode the plaintiff's interest in preventing the potential disclosure of highly personal information. This case is also discussed above under "General Principles and Sources of Confidentiality."

An example of limited disclosure of public health information is that, when an individual third grader is absent because he has chicken pox, parents of other members of the third grade who had contact with that student are notified, although the name of the ill student is not given out. In practice, then, for public health reasons, potentially exposed students should be notified of an outbreak of communicable disease in the school, but disclosure of the identity of one or more infected students is not appropriate or necessary in order for classmates to benefit from the information.

The most frequent use of the public health exception is the state requirement that health care providers and, when applicable, medical laboratories, report to the local and/or state department of health the names and other relevant information regarding patients who are diagnosed with those communicable diseases that, if left untreated, pose considerable risk to the public's health. Such reportable diseases are determined by state law and include, among others, sexually transmitted infections (STIs), tuberculosis, salmonella, measles, hepatitis A, and bacterial meningitis. When patients who test positive for STIs or tuberculosis, for example, do not return to the health care provider for treatment, a state or local health department investigator will attempt to locate and require the individual to return for treatment. The individual's intimate contacts may also be located and informed of the need to be tested for the disease.

There may be times when a state department of health investigator attempts through the school to reach a student who has tested positive for an STI. While this may protect the confidentiality of the student in relation to home, contacting the student at school may be problematic unless it is handled through the school nurse or a school principal who allows the investigator access to talk to the student privately. The potential need for a health department official to contact a student at school is best addressed by the health department and the school district in advance of an incident. When based on both health and education laws, procedures can be established to meet the needs of the student and both institutions. Issues such as verification of the identity of the public health official, whether or not a witness should be present and, if so, who, should be addressed.

Reporting other communicable diseases solely by number may be required in order to track disease outbreaks within states and communities. For example, schools may be required to report monthly to the local board of health the number of known cases of diagnosed communicable diseases and infestations among students, such as streptococcal and staphylococcal infections, fifth disease, chickenpox, ring worm, scabies, and head lice. The names and addresses of individual students are not included, since follow-up by the health department is not required. Some states collect data from medical laboratories on the numbers of individuals who test positive to HIV, without personally identifying data, which allows tracking of the disease without compromising the privacy of those who seek testing. Others require medical practitioners and laboratories to report HIV positive information, including patient identification, again for public health and treatment purposes.

Child Abuse and Neglect

An important exception to the general rule of non-disclosure is the reporting of suspected child abuse and neglect. Statutes and regulations regarding reporting suspected abuse or neglect of a child by a caretaker or by school personnel differ among states. The purpose of these statutes is to require certain individuals who have caretaking responsibilities for children (e.g., day care providers, teachers, health professionals, social service providers) to report suspicions of abuse or neglect for the purpose of preventing harm or further harm to children and youth by parents or other caretakers who have been entrusted with their care. As a result, even when privacy rights of children and families might otherwise apply, confidential information can be shared with appropriate authorities when it is reasonably suspected that a child has been harmed or is at risk of harm due to abuse or neglect. Under this exception, the safety needs of the child override the privacy rights of the suspected parent (or other caretaker-abuser) to the extent necessary for school personnel to

- determine reasonable suspicion;
- make a report of suspected abuse or neglect to appropriate authorities;
- provide for emergency or immediate health needs of the child;
- address educational needs of the child; and
- monitor the child for further signs or symptoms of abuse or neglect.

This exception allows school personnel to share confidential information and concerns regarding suspected abuse with other members of the school team, provided that the information is shared only with those who have a need to know in order to provide appropriate services to the student and that only necessary information is shared. For example, after a school nurse reports an incident of suspected physical abuse by a caretaker to the appropriate child protection agency, the school nurse should tell the principal, if the principal has not already been notified, that such a report has been made, including the substantive basis for the suspicion. The principal will need substantive information, as she or he may need to allow the child-protection worker into the school, respond to an angry caretaker or parent, and ensure ongoing safety for the child. The nurse may also want to alert the classroom teacher who can observe the child for changing behaviors and future signs of abuse, but the classroom teacher may not need to know the details of the nurse's historical and physical findings that led to the report. For monitoring and support reasons, it may also be appropriate to share certain information regarding the suspected abuse or neglect with the school social worker who sees the student for counseling, or with other members of the school team who provide direct services to the student. Each situation and each disclosure requires individual judgment.

Of particular interest to staff members of student assistance programs (SAPs), federal law and regulations (42 U.S.C. § 290dd-2 and 42 C.F.R. Part 2) allow SAPs to disclose confidential student information or records related to assessment, counseling, treatment or referral services for drug or alcohol problems in order to comply with state child abuse reporting laws, but this exception applies only to the initial reporting of an incident of suspected abuse, not to "follow-up requests or even subpoenas for additional information . . . unless the student consents or the appropriate court issues an order under subpart E of the regulations" (Legal Action Center, 1996).

In most cases school staff members who are mandated reporters of suspected child abuse under state law are also provided with immunity from legal action by parents or other caregivers suspected of abuse. In the case of *Dunajewski v. Bellmore Merrick Central High School District* (1988), a school social worker reported her suspicion that a student was being abused by the child's grandfather. Subsequently, she shared that information with the school's Committee on the Handicapped (COH) (New York's previous term for the IEP Team). After the child protection agency found no support for allegations of suspected abuse, the child's grandfather filed a libel action against the social worker and school. The court found no absolute privilege for the report of suspected abuse: the grandfather had no right to confidentiality and the social worker had the right to share information within the COH team *for the student's welfare*. This case is important because it supports school personnel in sharing information with those staff members working directly with the student when sharing the information is deemed necessary for the monitoring and safety of the student.

In a few cases, parents have tried to use "privacy rights" against claims of child abuse. In the case of *Doe v. Bagan and Adams County School District* (1994), the Court held that the investigation of the report of suspected child abuse did not violate family privacy rights and that the child did not have the "right of assistance" (the right to have the parent present) in the interview with the caseworker. In the case of *Tenebaum v. Williams* (1994), parents filed a Section 1983 (civil rights) action against the school and the social service agency after their child was taken from school, without parental consent, and given an "invasive physical examination" following a report of suspected sexual abuse by the parent. The Court held that such an examination required probable cause and a warrant, but did not require parental consent.

The reporting of suspected child abuse usually overrides professional privilege or statutory confidential relationships. In the case of *Pesce v. J. Sterling Morton High School District #201* (1987), a school psychologist did not immediately report information received from a student because he felt that "counseling confidentiality" applied. When he was disciplined for a late referral, he appealed to the court. The court dismissed his appeal, citing a state law in Illinois, which specifically voided confidentiality when suspicion of abuse or neglect existed.

For further information regarding child abuse reporting, see chapter 9 regarding FERPA requirements, and chapter 6, under "Violence and Abusive Behaviors," for school nurse reporting and assessment responsibilities.

Court Orders

Confidential information can be released under a court order. A school's SAP, for example, can pursue obtaining a court order to release information without student consent to a parent when a student is refusing to comply with an agreed-to treatment plan. However, when school nurses or other school employees are the recipients of such orders, they should turn it over to an appropriate district administrator who, in turn, should consult with the school district's attorney prior to releasing any confidential information or records.

Privileged information, on the other hand, cannot be released without the express consent of the student, or the parent/guardian for a minor student, depending on state law, unless the court determines that the information is actually not privileged and orders it released. Court orders and subpoenas are not the same. The federal drug and alcohol confidentiality law, for example, prohibits SAPs from "disclosing information regarding current or former patients in response to subpoenas" (Legal Action Center, 1996, p. 47). (The responsibilities of school districts to respond to subpoenas and court orders under the Family Educational Rights and Privacy Act (FERPA), and the differences between subpoenas and court orders, are discussed in chapter 9.) In any event, school districts should obtain legal advice regarding any court order or subpoena received by any staff member.

Commission of a Crime

When a school district employee observes a student committing a crime, the employee (e.g., teacher, school nurse, social worker, school psychologist, health aide) must report the crime to school administrators and, when applicable, to the police. There is no special relationship, "privilege," or "right to privacy" in this situation. Minors may have the right to privacy in seeking help or treatment for specific health problems, but they do not have a right to privacy in committing illegal acts or violating school rules. Therefore, if a student seeks help from the school nurse because he has succumbed to drug use, and wants to overcome the problem, he has the right to confidentiality for assessment, treatment, counseling, and referral services, including the details that he shares with the school nurse regarding his actions and current or previous drug use. However, if the school nurse or another school employee witnesses a student in the stairwell smoking marijuana, or an intoxicated student comes to the health office to lie down or use the bathroom (i.e., is not seeking health care or counseling), or is brought in by an administrator for assessment, the school nurse is obligated to assess and then report the student. If the student is committing a crime, the nurse may be obligated to report to the police, as well. School health professionals must know and follow the state laws and school district policies that specify their obligations in this regard.

If, for example, a student tells the school nurse of another student who is selling drugs on school property, the nurse has an obligation to report the information to the school administration. The student who shares the information should be told that school administrators must be informed, both for the sake of the student who is selling and for those to whom she is selling. While students need to know that they can talk confidentially with school health professionals about their personal health and developmental concerns without fear of unwarranted disclosure to others, they also need to know that all school faculty and staff will take proper steps to protect students. If a student fears that disclosure of this information to the administration will result in retribution, one solution may be to

share the information with the administrator, while protecting the identity of the student who brought it to the nurse's attention. Sometimes only general information needs to be shared, for example, "I have second-hand information that drugs are being sold on school property, usually after school behind the auditorium." Another potential solution is to encourage the student to share the information directly with the administrator. It is important to be honest with students about the actions that must be taken. Furthermore, students should be given as much choice as is reasonable, and as much protection as is indicated, in a given situation. Whether or not students verbalize fear regarding their safety following such a disclosure, their protection should be an essential consideration of school authorities in deciding what to share and with whom. While school district policies and procedures should be developed to guide school nurses and other pupil-services professionals in handling information regarding behavior that may be criminal, not all scenarios will be specifically addressed, and the professional may need expert guidance.

Research

In general, personally identifiable information can be released for valid research purposes, without consent of the individual, so long as certain safeguards and limitations are met, as required by law. Federal confidentiality mandates (e.g., FERPA and the regulations on drug and alcohol treatment records), as well as state confidentiality mandates (e.g., medical records laws), support this exception to the general rule of privacy. Client or student privacy is maintained to the extent that the information must only be used for the approved purpose of the research and only by the researchers. Only aggregate data, that is, grouped data minus all personal identifiers, may be further released by the researchers. To the extent possible, researchers work with coded rather than real identifiers, and records of individual clients are returned or destroyed as soon as they are no longer needed for the purposes of the research.

Audit and Evaluation

Federal and state laws related to medical and education records do permit release of records without prior written consent of the individuals who are the subjects of the records for the purposes of audit or evaluation by local, state, and federal officials, including accrediting organizations. Again, certain safeguards and limits to protect individual privacy are defined in the laws or regulations and must be adhered to by those who are permitted access to medical or education records for these purposes.

ADDITIONAL CONCEPTS AND CONSIDERATIONS

HIV Confidentiality

Despite the existence in our society of deep-rooted legal and ethical principles protecting the confidentiality of individual health information, challenges to these principles occur because of actual and perceived conflicting obligations. Rushton and Infante (1995) describe a typical conflict between two duties: the duty to protect confidentiality and the duty to disclose information, such as suspected child abuse (see "Child Abuse" under "Exceptions" above). With the advent of a new infectious disease—especially a deadly one such as HIV—the obligations of protecting the infected individual from personal harm (such as loss of job, home, friends, or medical insurance) due to the unwarranted disclosure of private health information on one hand, and of protecting the general public from unwarranted spread of the deadly disease on the other hand, cause society to weigh the underlying principles. That is, indeed, what happened with the HIV epidemic.

Based on fear and lack of information, concerns regarding protection of the public health were initially misconstrued by many as weightier than concerns regarding the privacy rights of affected individuals. Eventually, however, scientific evidence demonstrated how the disease is (and is not) spread. This evidence provided a legitimate basis for decision making among experts and the courts on questions related to these conflicting interests. As a result of the scientific evidence, privacy rights of the individual prevailed, with the stringent exception of public health monitoring and, in some states, follow-up for persons testing positive for HIV and AIDS (see "Public Health Purposes" under Exceptions above). Because of the significant harm that can result from disclosing an individual's HIV status, the safeguards required to protect privacy have had to be even more stringent than those already in place in state statutes addressing medical information in general. As a result, many states passed laws specifically addressing HIV confidentiality.

Much of the initial controversy over school attendance of children who tested HIV positive, and those with AIDS, centered on a popular theory that a child in school with a "contagious disease" creates a "health and safety emergency." Only after medical authorities, such as the U.S. Surgeon General (*Understanding AIDS*, 1988; Koop, 1991), and the Centers for Disease Control,

U.S. Department of Health and Human Services (1985), produced evidence that the types of contacts that occur in school were not likely to result in transmission of HIV, were courts able to rule that children with AIDS, and those who had tested positive to the HIV virus but had no symptoms of disease, *must* be admitted to school (*Martinez v. School Board of Hillsborough County*, 1987; *Doe v. Dolton*, 1988; *Phipps v. Saddleback Valley Unified School District*, 1988; *Ray v. School District of DeSoto County*, 1987; *Robertson v. Granite City Community School District*, 1988; *Thomas v. Atascadero Unified School District*, 1987). Courts have also upheld school district and state policies concerning confidentiality of HIV status for all affected and infected individuals, including students (*Board of Education of the City of Plainfield v. Cooperman*, 1986; *Child v. Spillane*, 1989; *District 27 Community School Board v. Board of Education of the City of New York*, 1986). (For a discussion of the impact of AIDS on public schools, see McNary-Keith [1995] and Bogden, Fraser, Vega-Matos, & Ascroft [1996].)

While some state laws and many state and local school district policies require very strict confidentiality protections concerning a child's HIV status, school nurses who work with families of children with AIDS report a wide variety of family responses and needs. In many cases, when a child's health status requires school program modifications and health support services, parents have consented to share the child's HIV status with the school staff members responsible for daily educational services. In some cases, when a child's health status is deteriorating, parents have consented to share HIV information with the school community. The extent to which a family should be counseled to share their student's HIV status, however, is directly proportional to the extent to which school staff members can be trusted to maintain the confidence of an HIV-infected student and his family. Furthermore, even with written parental consent to share the HIV status of a student or family member, such information should be shared only with those who *need to know* in order *to benefit the student.*

An example of legislation which includes strong protection and a remedy for harm suffered from release of a patient's HIV status is the Connecticut AIDS statute (§19a-583(a)(7) through (10), C.G.S., 1995). This law provides confidentiality for any person's "HIV status," including a right to sue for damages if confidentiality is breached. Any disclosure requires the written consent of the individual, expressly designating the names of persons to whom the information can be disclosed. The law also includes a procedure for obtaining a court order for HIV testing when there has been a "significant exposure." Such state laws, although technically a reaffirmation of the general laws and ethical standards regarding confidentiality of health information, have been enacted as additional protections against the extreme prejudice and harm experienced by HIV-infected individuals and their families. For a more detailed discussion of these issues, see Harvey (1994). Despite such protections, in schools it is ironic—and problematic—that the diagnosis of HIV is frequently the only medical diagnosis not shared at IEP or other school intervention team meetings. As a result, the rare refusal to share a student's medical diagnosis with the team may actually communicate an HIV diagnosis, regardless of the parent and student's decision not to disclose that information to the entire team.

Hepatitis B and Other Chronic Infectious Diseases

Despite several court decisions and scientific evidence that chronic infectious hepatitis should not be a reason to exclude students from attendance in school (see chapters 6 and 11), Hepatitis B and, more recently, Hepatitis C continue to elicit reactions of fear among school personnel. Because these reactions frequently result in discriminatory treatment and stigmatization of affected students and their families, both in school and the community, the medical diagnosis of Hepatitis B or C and similar types of chronic infectious diseases should be treated with heightened confidentiality, similar to that of HIV. Students with other chronic infections, such as those colonized with antibiotic-resistant bacteria (e.g., multi-drug resistant strains of streptococcal and staphylococcal bacteria) also require heightened protections due to the significant harm that unwarranted disclosure can bring.

It is critically important to counter balance strict confidentiality protections for these students with the provision of pre-service and in-service education for teachers and school administrators, and on-the-job training, supervision, protective equipment, and other infection-control resources for all school personnel. These educational efforts are necessary to ensure that all staff understand and apply Standard Precautions and infection-control strategies in everyday interactions with students and other staff—and that they apply them at all times, not just with the one student who they believe to be infected. Furthermore, when disclosure to another member of the school team such as an administrator or teacher is indicated, further disclosure by that individual must be strictly prohibited. (See chapter 6 for additional information on infec-

tion-control standards and the requirements of the Occupational Safety and Health Administration.)

When school nurses and school medical advisors are unsure whether special precautions are indicated and whether other school personnel should be notified of a student's medical diagnosis, they should consult with their school nurse consultant at the state department of health or education and chief epidemiologist at the state department of health. The state school nurse consultant can provide school health professionals with information regarding applicable laws, regulations, guidelines, and related standards of practice for school settings. The chief epidemiologist, or a designee, can advise school health professionals of the latest scientific knowledge and public health practice standards in the control of these chronic infectious diseases. The expertise of these state-level health professionals is essential in developing statewide guidelines and problem solving in difficult situations. Consultation with ethical and legal experts may also be indicated.

Duty to Warn

In many respects, the "duty to warn" is closely linked to the duty to disclose information, a principle that underlies certain exceptions to the general rule of confidentiality in professional-client relationships, such as suspected abuse or medical emergencies. The "duty to warn" is a legal principle that provides an exception to "provider-client privilege," that is, to the special relationships of privilege recognized in state law (see "General Principles and Sources of Confidentiality" above), particularly with respect to psychiatrists and counselors who provide mental health counseling and therapy. While the "duty to warn" is often cited in discussions related to confidentiality, it is not well understood.

As laws concerning privileged relationships developed, legislatures began to consider the difficult issue of when, if ever, the recipient of such confidential, "privileged" information should be compelled to disclose it. Because most examples of this dilemma include an element of danger to another person, this issue is often called "a duty to warn." In the case of *Tarasoff v. Regents of the University of California* (1976), the parents of a murder victim sued the University because a university staff therapist, who learned of his student-patient's intention to commit murder, failed to warn the victim. The court analyzed the nature of the information disclosed to the therapist and the actions taken. After the therapist consulted his supervisors about his concerns, campus police were requested to assist in committing the patient to a mental hospital for observation. After meeting with the patient, the campus police determined that he was rational and warned him to stay away from the victim. The patient was not committed for observation, and in time he committed the planned murder. Finding that a duty to warn the intended victim overrode the confidentiality of therapist-patient communication in this situation, the California Supreme Court commented:

We conclude that the public policy favoring protection of the confidential character of patient-psychotherapist communications must yield to the extent to which disclosure is essential to avert danger to others. The [individual's] protective privilege ends where the public peril begins.

In a Louisiana case, the parents of children who had been sexually molested by another student in the district sued for damages and argued that the school district had a "duty to warn" the parents of other students about the presence of the molester. A lower court's ruling, citing evidence that the behavior of concern occurred off school grounds during a school vacation, and denying that the school district had such a duty, was upheld on appeal (*Morris et al. v. Canipe*, 1988). In other words, the plaintiff was unable to demonstrate that the school district had a duty to the student for events that occurred outside of school.

Not school-specific, but related in general, recent legal actions have resulted in a variety of state laws requiring the police to notify local residents when a person convicted of sexual abuse of children is released from prison. In each of these situations, the "right of potential victims" or "good of the community" is balanced against the "individual's right to privacy."

The question of whether there is or should be a "duty to warn" others in public schools about the HIV status of a student or staff member continues to be raised, despite long-standing scientific evidence regarding the modes of transmission of HIV, the extremely low risk factors in school settings, and case law decisions. For example, as recently as 1996, an Idaho school district revised two HIV-related policies that were first adopted in 1985, one for staff and one for students. These policies, still on record in 1999, required both employees and students who are HIV positive to disclose that information to the superintendent, who would share it with the school nurse, the district's consulting physician, the building principal, classroom teacher(s) (in the case of a student), other appropriate individuals as determined by the superintendent, and members of the Board of Trustees (www.sd331.k12.id.us/District/Policy Book).

While the policies also clearly stated that "further communication of such information is not permitted and violation of such provision of this policy may be grounds for discharge from employment," the disclosure requirement to the superintendent and other officials of the district, according to an Idaho American Civil Liberties Union consulting attorney, was probably unlawful under two federal laws, the Americans with Disabilities Act and Rehabilitation Act of 1973 (written communication from John C. Hummel to the Legal Committee of the Idaho ACLU, April 1996). In August 1999, the policies were referred to the district's attorney for legal review after coming to the superintendent's attention (personal communication with Dr. N. Hallett, August 18, 1999). These policies, and others like them, discriminate against individuals with HIV infection by requiring the unlawful and unethical disclosure of medical information, which is neither necessary for the benefit of the HIV infected person, nor for the protection of others in the school district. The potential harm from discrimination for the student or staff member (who is already dealing with a devastating medical condition) far outweighs the extremely remote potential of HIV transmission in school. Therefore, even if school health professionals believe that it is better to know about a student's HIV status, for example, in order to warn the family about communicable disease outbreaks, observe for symptoms of acute illness and support the student, it remains the family's and student's right to determine whether those services are more important to them than maintaining personal privacy. Respect for persons and autonomy are the ethical principles underlying that right. In this context, there is no "duty to warn," as there is no scientific reason or compelling public health need to do so.

The fact is, the risk of transmission of HIV in schools is very small, indeed. If Standard Precautions are used by all, and students and staff do not engage in risky sexual behaviors or needle sharing, the chance of an exposure to the virus in school is extremely remote. In other settings where significant exposures to blood and other infected body secretions are more likely, such as hospitals and medical laboratories, the risk of transmission is higher. To address these high-risk situations, some state legislatures have enacted public health laws or amended regulations permitting limited disclosure by designated institutions, public health officials, or physicians, depending on the state and the issue. For example, Connecticut General Statutes, § 19a-583(a)(7), allows a health facility, correctional institution, or other institution to disclose a patient's or person's HIV status to an individual who, in the course of his occupational duties, has sustained a "significant exposure" to HIV infection, as determined by an "exposure evaluation group." The group's determination must be made according to specific criteria provided in the law, including documentation of efforts to obtain voluntary release of the information from the patient or person. An example of a significant exposure might be when a tube of blood bursts in the hand of a laboratory technician, spraying a copious amount of blood on the technician's forearms, neck and face. Disclosure is limited to the patient's HIV status and does not include other confidential information, including patient-identifying information.

As with public health procedures for other sexually transmitted diseases, many states have laws that enable a medical provider or public health official to privately notify the sexual partner(s) of an HIV-infected person, who otherwise may be unaware of their exposure. This decision is made by the physician, public health authority, or other licensed heath care providers (such as a nurse practitioner) as determined by state law and regulation. Melroe, in an article addressing nurse clinicians' ethical and legal responsibilities when faced with the HIV-related "duty to warn"-versus-patient privacy dilemma (1990), discusses legal precedent for disclosure of communicable diseases by health authorities and potential guidelines for resolving ethical issues in individual cases. See also Swartz (1990) for further discussion of "duty to warn" in relation to persons infected with HIV, and Berger (1999) for a general discussion of physician liability in relation to the legal "duty to warn" third parties.

An exceedingly difficult ethico-legal dilemma regarding HIV and "duty to warn" does arise in school when a school professional knows or suspects that an HIV-infected student is engaging in behaviors that put other students at risk, usually through unprotected sex. Addressing the issue directly with the infected student is necessary and appropriate, but decisions regarding the disclosure of any information and "duty to warn" are not ones that should be made by school personnel alone, including school nurses and physicians. When faced with this type of dilemma, a school professional who holds the information and has the suspicion should obtain expert advice about (1) any state laws and regulations that might pertain to the dilemma; (2) ethical principles that should be considered; and (3) strategies for resolving the dilemma. Advice can (and should) be sought without divulging personally identifiable information, as discussed above under the subsection "Non-Identifying Information," and the resources suggested above under "Hepatitis B and

Other Infectious Diseases" are appropriate places to start, as is the HIV section of one's state department of health. University-based ethics experts, especially those with a background in public health, medical ethics or religious studies, are also excellent resources for help in processing and weighing the opposing ethical principles and potential outcomes of alternative actions. (See chapter 3 for a framework for approaching ethical dilemmas in schools.)

Right to Know

School personnel, and members of the public at large, often refer to the "right to know" in terms of a counter balance to another person's right to privacy. While there is no such guaranteed right in the U. S. Constitution, the notion is related to the common law precepts of "duty to warn" and "protection of the public health." It is often misconstrued, however, since a therapist's "*duty* to warn" a potential victim does not convert exactly to another's "*right* to know." In the context of providing health and education services to the public, there is no defined *right* of school personnel to know certain student information. There may be a demonstrable *need* for school personnel to have certain information in order for those staff members to provide appropriate services to the student, or in order for the school district to provide a student with an appropriate education, but that need does not usually extend to a legal "right."

An area of confusion between "need" and "right" in school nursing occurs when the school district is asked by a parent to deliver specialized health care services to his child and, to do so legally and safely, the school nurse needs medical direction and information. For example, if the school nurse is administering medication or oxygen to a student, according to parental request and under the order of a physician (as required by law), the nurse has a legal (and clinical) need to communicate with the physician, for example, to determine if the physician's order is accurate or has been changed or discontinued. The basis for this need is twofold: (1) the legal relationship between physician and nurses, as defined in state nurse practice acts, which requires most nurses to work under the direction of a physician when "carrying out the medical regimen" and (2) an ethical responsibility to the student to "do no harm." (This issue is also discussed in chapter 6, page 177 under "Parental Authorization for Communications Between Authorized Prescribers and School Nurses Executing Medical Orders.")

Some "privacy" versus "good practice" dilemmas that

school nurses face stem from poor relationships with families, including situations when a parent prohibits nurse-physician communications. Although not specific to school nursing, the following case of "parental negligence" may be instructive regarding underlying concepts of "right to know" versus "need to know" in school settings. In *Nieuwendorp v. American Insurance Company* (1993), a Wisconsin trial court awarded damages to a special education teacher as a result of a neck injury caused by the unruly behavior of a fourth grade student. The teacher claimed that the parents were negligent because they had failed to control their son's behavior and to exercise reasonable care with respect to him.

The case history indicates that the parents had discontinued their son's medication for ADHD, even though it had resulted in improvement in the symptoms of his condition, without consulting with his psychologist or physician, or informing the school. Symptoms of the student's condition included disruptive and aggressive physical behaviors, which were first manifested in the first grade. The insurance company appealed, arguing that there was insufficient evidence that the family's action was the proximate cause of the injury and, further, that public policy considerations did not require the family to "forcibly medicate their son." The teacher argued that the parents' legal duty to control their son required them to either continue the medication, while informing themselves of the consequences of discontinuing the medication and of alternative treatments, or to inform the school of their action so that other treatment and educational interventions could have been collaboratively planned and implemented.

The appeals court reversed the lower court's decision on the basis that it was only speculation that a consultation with a physician or notice to the school would have prevented the teacher's injury. The teacher appealed the reversal to the Wisconsin Supreme Court, which held for the teacher, citing another case (*Seibert v. Morris*, 1948). The latter provided that:

A parent is under a duty to exercise reasonable care so to control his minor child as to prevent it from intentionally harming others or from conducting itself as to create an unreasonable risk of bodily harm to them, if the parent (a) knows or has reason to know that he has the ability to control his child, and (b) knows or should know of the necessity and opportunity for exercising such control.

The court held that, while the parents' decision to take their son off of medication did not constitute negligence, nevertheless they were under an obligation to take reasonable steps to control his behavior. The court was "sympathetic" to the public policy considerations that were cited by the insurance company:

- Parents should not be required to control their children's behavior by involuntary medication;

- Patients should be allowed to make medical decisions without fear of being sued; and

- Patients should not be required to divulge their medical treatment decisions to third parties.

However, the court did not think that these concerns were applicable to the case, since the injury was not too remote from the negligence, and imposing liability in this case would not "place too unreasonable a burden on persons such as this student and his parents. . . ." This very fact-specific case does not stand for the proposition that parents must forcibly medicate their hyperactive children in order for their children to attend public school. Rather, it is a natural extension of the principle that recognizes parents' responsibility to exercise reasonable control over their children so as to prevent harm to others." Thus, the emphasis is on the parents' responsibility to control their child, rather than a specific legal "right" of the teacher to know the information.

The concept of "right to know" is most often discussed in schools in the context of a staff member's ability to protect against harm. For example, a classroom teacher may claim a "right to know" the HIV, Hepatitis B, or head-lice status of his students, in order to protect himself against disease and infestation. There is, however, no such guaranteed right. First, the teacher does not *need to know* who is infected in order to employ Standard Precautions and other infection-control strategies that will protect him from contact with bloodborne pathogens or infestation with head lice. From the public health point of view, it is best for the teacher to treat all students as if they are infected, and to employ Standard Precautions in every circumstance. Furthermore, when a teacher believes that he knows which students are infected, he also presumes that other students are not infected. This presumption is likely to put the teacher at far greater occupational risk, since he will not use proper or comparable precautions with those he presumes are not infected, but who may be.

School personnel may have certain rights under federal law to reasonable protection from known occupational hazards under federal and state Occupational Safety and Health Administration requirements, although there is variation in states' interpretation of the application of federal law and regulations to governmental agencies, including public school settings. These rights, when they do apply to schools, include the rights of personnel to:

- receive appropriate training, for example, in the use of Standard Precautions;

- have protective supplies and equipment available for use, for example, latex or non-latex protective gloves; and

- receive Hepatitis B vaccine if, as a regular part of their responsibilities, they are exposed to blood and other body fluids.

These protections do not include a "right to know" confidential student health information, but presume sufficient training that personnel will use appropriate infection-control techniques at all times. (See "Freedom of Information Acts" in chapter 9 for related information.)

UNIQUE CHALLENGES FOR SCHOOL HEALTH PROFESSIONALS

Issues of confidentiality and disclosure of client health information are challenging in any setting and with any client population. In school settings, these issues become even more complex and pose unique challenges for school health professionals and school administrators. These challenges emanate from multiple factors, including the following:

- characteristics of the client population;

- characteristics of the setting;

- conflicting laws;

- limited expertise;

- variable standards for confidentiality; and

- student records and documentation issues.

Characteristics of the Client Population

Elementary, middle, and high school students are primarily minors under the law and, if no longer minors, are usually still dependent on their parent(s). The legal principles and ethical issues related to the privacy rights of minors differ in significant ways from those of adults. According to English (1996), the Supreme Court has repeatedly held that minors, like adults, have constitutional rights, although there has

been considerable controversy over the scope of those rights, and state law provisions address specific rights of adolescents to access health care. Nevertheless, when minor children are the clients of health professionals, their parents are clients, too, albeit in varying degrees, depending on the child's age, competence, and the parent-child relationship. Indeed, parents generally have the legal right, authority, and responsibility to make health care decisions for their minor children, including decisions about disclosure of information and consent to, or refusal of, medical treatment.

From a clinical perspective, it is well known that effective services for minors require collaboration and communication between providers and parents. Even when minor youth have certain legal rights to confidentiality, for example, when seeking treatment for drug and alcohol abuse, sustained therapeutic success is most likely to occur when family members are included in the treatment process. Helping minors to understand the importance of working through real and perceived problems with their parents or seeking other appropriate adult assistance is a major responsibility of and intervention challenge for all professionals working with adolescents. In schools, this responsibility is of foremost importance.

While parents and guardians are integral members of a school health professional's client population, there are sometimes divergent interests between minors and their parents, as indicated in chapter 7. These can occur in life-threatening situations, such as when parents refuse life-saving measures (e.g., a blood transfusion) for their minor child. According to Kaar & Mawn (1998), "a parent may not intentionally endanger a child by failing to allow life and limb saving measures" (*People ex. Rel. Wallace v. Labrrez,* 1952; *Muhlenberg Hospital v. Patterson,* 1974). They can also occur when minors have the right to seek treatment for medical conditions without parental authorization or notification, usually for conditions that, when not treated, pose significant public health consequences.

These divergent interests can cause unique dilemmas for school nurses and other school professionals. For example, when a school nurse believes that other members of the education team need information about a student's health status in order to serve the student appropriately, and the parent refuses to give the nurse permission to share that information, the nurse is faced with an ethical dilemma. In this situation, the rights and needs of the student—as client—may need to be weighed separately from the rights and needs of the parent, although the interests of both must be considered from legal and ethical points of view. While parents' preferences usually carry more legal weight than those of their minor children, a parent's preference must sometimes be weighed against risk of harm to the minor. Solutions are possible, ranging from convincing parents to share limited information, to sharing only general, non-specific information with other team members, to reporting a parent for neglect, depending on the severity of the student's needs and risk of harm to the student if the information is not shared.

The challenge of providing health services to minor students is compounded by the fact that, under education law and culture, the legal right of parents to make decisions for their minor children is upheld almost without qualification. This right does not diminish with the age of the student, except when the student reaches the age of majority and, even then, parents may continue to have certain rights, for example, access to their dependent student's education records. In health care, however, the legal rights of parents to make decisions for their minor children give way, in part, to the rights of competent minors to seek, and make their own decisions regarding, certain types of health care (Holder, 1985 and English, 1996). This difference is well described by Siegler (1996, p. 259):

> The "education" of a minor is seen as an issue between the child, the school and the parents. On the other hand, the "medical" condition of the same minor is viewed as a matter to which only the patient and his/her health care providers need in all cases be privy.

This essential difference in parental rights adds confusion to confidentiality questions that health professionals who provide services to student populations, especially in middle and high schools, must address. It also leads to related dilemmas in documentation of those services on education records, and in providing safe services when parents refuse to allow a school nurse to communicate with their student's physician who has "ordered" medical care at school. (See the discussion above under "Right to Know.")

The right of minors to seek health care independent of their parents varies from state to state, depending on a state's "minor consent statutes," as discussed in chapter 7. These rights, where existent, are generally in proportion to the age and maturity or competence of the minor, type and invasiveness of the treatment, and potential consequences to both the minor and the public if the minor refuses to seek treatment due to fear of disclosure to parents or others. However, as English & Tereszkiewicz (1988) point out, it can be difficult to

determine, even with specific mandates, when a minor is mature or competent enough to seek and control privacy regarding health care and counseling. As they do in other health care settings, practice dilemmas arise when adolescents see school health professionals for information, assessment, or referral regarding sensitive health and mental health issues. Related confidentiality issues can be more problematic to resolve than in regular health care settings.

Other characteristics of student populations today are important to address. Major changes have occurred over the past two to three decades, especially in relation to the number, complexity, and acuity of students' medical and psychiatric problems. Students today come to school with every actual and potential physical and mental health condition, disability, and treatment modality possible. The only children who do not attend school today are those receiving acute, in-patient treatment in hospitals and a rare few who are still maintained in long-term rehabilitation settings. In the managed-care environment of today, hospitalization is infrequent and exceedingly brief. The children who in the past would have been in the hospital for medical or psychiatric care are now often sent back to school.

In many communities, student populations are also highly mobile and have inadequate access to continuous primary health care services. Access to care remains problematic despite federal and state initiatives to provide coverage for most of the nation's low-income uninsured and underinsured children. As a result, students and families bring primary health care issues to school nurses for assessment, diagnosis, intervention, and referral. Frequently, student information related to such primary health care issues is not relevant to learning or appropriate in education records (Siegler, 1996; Gelfman & Schwab, 1991; and Cohn, 1984). High mobility not only decreases continuity and quality of health and educational services, but also results in a multitude of school records on individual students with varying degrees of sensitive health information and even more variable protections.

Characteristics of the Setting

Unlike health care institutions and agencies, the primary mission of schools is education, not health care. Education laws, policies, and procedures derive from the core mission of schools, which is successful student learning. Health services programs in schools are organized to support, not supplant that mission. Therefore, the delivery of comprehensive primary health care services to students is neither the primary focus nor function of schools and the practice of school nursing is generally defined according to the institutional goals and culture of education. Nevertheless, students require health services during the school day for a variety of health and mental health conditions. Even when those conditions—and their treatments—directly relate to students' progress and performance in the classroom (e.g., the administration of controlled drugs for attention deficit [hyperactivity] disorder or seizures), decision making regarding how much information to share and with whom, and how much to document, can be very complex.

Furthermore, students frequently seek health information and services that are legitimately within the scope of nursing practice, but not directly related to student learning. In these situations, special challenges arise regarding both confidentiality and documentation, since sensitive health information and related nursing interventions may not always be appropriate in educational records (Gelfman & Schwab, 1991, Siegler, 1996). Where to document, then, becomes a challenge, and few school districts address this issue in policy or procedures. Quandaries related to consent for services (e.g., drug abuse counseling or referral to a clinic for HIV or family planning counseling) and consent to disclosure of confidential student health information are especially problematic.

Additional problems occur because the large majority of school nurses either do not have sufficient pre-service preparation to knowledgeably address these issues or do not function under the supervision and direction of a school nurse administrator-expert. According to Siegler (1996, p.260), even highly experienced nurses may be "unaware that the records they create in a school health office will not receive the same strict privacy as they would in [health] settings outside the school." See the subsection below on "Limited Expertise and Supervision" for additional discussion.

These same dilemmas are generally less problematic when nurses or nurse practitioners are hired by community health agencies (e.g., hospital, health department, university) to provide *primary health care services* (not "school health services") within a school-based health center (SBHC) on school property. There is general agreement that the health records of students that are generated in SBHC programs *operated by health institutions* (not schools) are considered medical records, not education records (Cheung, Clements, & Pechman, 1997; Siegler, 1996; English & Tereszkiewicz, 1988). Accordingly, medical records generated in a SBHC are governed strictly by medical records laws and sharing of confidential student information is generally prohibited between SBHC personnel and school

district personnel, including the school nurse, without the express written permission of the parent or guardian, and student when appropriate. Nevertheless, because SBHC providers are serving youth on school property, they are much more likely than traditional primary health care providers to interact with and witness their clients in everyday school life beyond the examination and consultation rooms. Whether they witness a student breaking school rules or learn about unsafe situations or crimes that are being committed in the building (e.g., drug or alcohol use or sale), their ethical and legal responsibilities to adequately communicate with school authorities are arguably different—and more challenging—than those of health care providers in other settings.

Conflicting Laws and Standards

Numerous conflicts have been identified between the laws that govern health and education records (see, for example, Cohn, 1984; Gelfman & Schwab, 1991; Schwab & Gelfman, 1991; Siegler, 1996; and Legal Action Center, 1996). These conflicts occur between federal laws, between federal and state laws, and between state laws. English (1996, p. 152) acknowledges conflicts, or at least lack of clarity in their application to minors, among confidentiality provisions of law and policy in the health field alone. In addition, conflicts concerning confidentiality issues exist between education laws and standards, and professional standards of practice for school health and mental health professionals.

Conflicts between Laws

An example of conflicting obligations under two federal laws arises from the issue of parental right of access to the records of their minor children. On one hand, the Family Educational Rights and Privacy Act (FERPA), which addresses record protections in public schools, gives parents complete access to their minor child's school records, including health records. On the other hand, the federal confidentiality requirements that address drug and alcohol treatment records (42 C.F.R. Part 2) require student assistance programs (SAPs) to protect the confidentiality of minor students who seek assistance for drug or alcohol problems; this means that minor students can refuse to release their drug treatment records, including to their parents. In recognition of this conflict, the U.S. Department of Education and the Alcohol, Drug Abuse and Mental Health Administration issued a joint opinion offering potential solutions (Sullivan and Rooker, 1990). This joint opinion suggests that local school districts resolve the conflict between these two laws by choosing one of the following options:

(1) Require that students consent to parental access to their records as a condition of receiving SAP services; or

(2) Require a court order to permit disclosure of SAP information to a parent who seeks it under FERPA; or

(3) Minimize documentation.

While the opinion is silent on the ethical and legal principles underlying these conflicting federal laws, it is helpful to consider them. According to Rushton (1997), FERPA recognizes the "rights of parents as decision makers, responsible for the health and well-being of their children." Because of these parental rights and responsibilities, it is important for health professionals to "acknowledge their need for information and try to give it." On the other hand, health professionals also recognize "the rights of the child, a right to privacy and confidentiality." These rights, such as the right to keep confidential drug and alcohol assessment and treatment information, are based in part on the ethical principle of non-maleficence or "doing no harm." In other words, if a troubled or ill minor refuses treatment for fear that his or her treatment records will not be kept confidential, further harm to the youth—and the public health—is likely. They are also based, in part, on the principles of respect for persons and autonomy, important values for maturing children and youth. Both laws involve the ethical concept of beneficence, since "doing good" underlies actions to make drug intervention services accessible to troubled adolescents, as well as actions to support parents in raising and helping their children.

While the Sullivan and Rooker opinion does not address the underlying conflict of duties and values, it does offer three potential courses of action, as indicated above. The first option is fundamentally problematic. On one hand, if students are required, as a condition of receiving any services, to give a blanket permission for parental access to their SAP (treatment) records, many adolescents will refuse to give that permission—thus refusing school intervention services altogether. The potential for refusal of health services on this basis is a major reason why minor consent-to-treatment laws emerged in the first place. On the other hand, school districts are placed in a difficult position with families if they refuse, even temporarily, a parent's request for full

disclosure of their child's school records.

Given the first two options, the second, providing intervention services to students, and later requesting a court order for release of the SAP records should parents request them, is probably a wiser course of action, both clinically and legally, than refusing needed services to students who seek help from qualified school personnel. The school nurse who chooses this option must inform the student at the beginning of the limitations to confidentiality inherent in obtaining services from school district SAPs when he or she first sees the student for drug and alcohol problems.

The third option, limiting documentation, is unclear in terms of practical application and is appropriate to the extent that only necessary information for assessment, interventions, and follow-up is included in the nursing or SAP record. No documentation of care is not an option because it increases the risks of both clinical errors and professional and school district liability. On the other hand, documentation should always be kept to the minimum necessary for safe care.

Conflicts also exist between federal laws and some state laws, for example, between FERPA and state laws that give minors the right to consent to medical treatment for certain health problems, such as tuberculosis, sexually transmitted diseases (STDs), and mental health concerns. School districts and their personnel may also have different obligations under state education and state health laws. The nature of these conflicts is the same as those between federal laws, as discussed above, and as those discussed in the following section.

Healthcare Information Privacy Acts: Recent Federal and State Initiatives

Since passage of the Health Insurance Portability and Accountability Act of 1996 (HIPAA), Congress has considered numerous versions of a federal law to protect the privacy of health care information in the age of electronic data. On September 11, 1997, the Secretary of Health and Human Services provided Congress with recommendations for federal legislation. They stated that federal legislation should do the following:

- allow for the smooth flow of identifiable health information for treatment, payment, and related operations, and for specified additional purposes related to health care that are in the public interest;

- prohibit the flow of identifiable information for any additional purposes, unless specifically and voluntarily authorized by the subject of the information;

- put in place a set of fair information practices that allow individuals to know who is using their health information, and how it is being used;

- establish fair information practices that allow individuals to obtain their records and request amendment of inaccurate information;

- require persons who hold identifiable health information to safeguard that information from inappropriate use or disclosure; and

- hold those who use individually identifiable health information accountable for their handling of this information, and to provide legal recourse to persons harmed by misuse (U.S. Department of Health and Human Services, 1999a & 1999b).

By the statutory deadline to meet the requirements of HIPAA, however, no law had been enacted by Congress. As a result, the Secretary of Health and Human Services was required to issue regulations containing standards for the privacy of healthcare information based on the authority of HIPAA. The Secretary's proposed regulations were published in the Federal Register, November 3, 1999 and commentary was permitted until February 17, 2000. While the proposed regulations implement many of the above principles, they do not support all of them. One limitation of the proposed Health and Human Services (HHS) regulations is that they address health care information that is maintained or transmitted electronically, but not records that are maintained solely in paper form. While the final Rules for Electronic Transactions was published on August 17, 2000 in the Federal Register, publication of the Standards for Privacy was delayed indefinitely. (For further discussion of HIPAA and related federal legislation, see chapter 10.)

School health professionals are clearly included as "health care providers" under the proposed rules, and certain principles clearly support the ethical standards of nurses and other school health professionals. For example, the amount of protected health information used or disclosed must be limited to the information necessary to meet the purpose of the use or disclosure. This rule supports limiting access to a client's healthcare information to a subset of an agency's employees who need to use the information in the course of their work, and limiting the amount of information disclosed from a record to the information needed by the recipient to fulfill the purpose of the disclosure. This principle may be either in conflict or compatible with the FERPA standard that student information can be shared internally in a school district for "legitimate education purposes,"

depending on how well the FERPA standard is defined and limited in individual school districts. Districts can define in policy, for example, which staff members have access to school health information, how much information, and who makes the decision.

Should federal legislation be passed in the future, it is unclear whether it will include competent minors among those who have a right to access and control certain information in their own health care records. Control of one's own heath care records implies the right to give or deny consent to the release of personal health information to others, including other health care providers, third-party payors, educators, and parents. Past proposed bills have included significant consequences for the failure of health professionals (and possibly others) to maintain the privacy of patients' health care information, whether they work in schools, universities, or other settings. Depending on its provisions, one or more requirements of a federal health care information privacy act may well be in conflict with one or more provisions of FERPA.

In the meantime, many states have moved forward to enact, or at least propose, their own legislation to better protect the privacy of patients' medical records in the electronic age. (See Health Privacy Project [1999] for additional information regarding state privacy mandates.) Most of these legislative initiatives have implications for the protection of confidential health information in any setting, including schools and universities, and in any form, including oral, written, and electronic. Like the federal proposals, state legislative initiatives generally have provisions that guarantee individuals access to and control of the health care information of which they are the subject. The provisions may extend to minors when, under state law, minors have the right to obtain health care services without parental permission or notification, such as for STDs, tuberculosis, reproductive health concerns, drug and alcohol problems and mental health.

State legislation that provides minors with the right to control the privacy of certain health care information will likely be in direct conflict with the provisions of both FERPA and state education records laws that give parents the right of access to all of their minor child's school records. Under education laws, parents' right to access their child's school records includes accessing documentation of a student's visit to a school nurse requesting treatment for a health concern that, under state law, a competent minor has the right to keep private. Whether visits to a school nurse for such issues are actually covered under state minor consent-to-treatment provisions is discussed in the subsection below, "School Nursing Services and Minor Consent-to-Treatment Laws."

Interim School District Options

Although the opinion of Sullivan and Rooker (see p. 282) is specific to the conflict that exists between FERPA and the federal drug and alcohol treatment confidentiality law, the options suggested can also be applied to other school health and mental health service records. For example, it may be appropriate to use the court order option if a school district receives a parent's request for access to all of his or her child's school health records when that record contains documentation of student services for a legally protected health condition and the student refuses release. In other words, when under state minor consent laws the student has a right to privacy in seeking treatment for an STI, and the student sees the school nurse to ask for assistance in obtaining confidential medical treatment, the school nurse's notes of the student's visit, including nursing assessment, counseling and referral to appropriate medical services in the community, should receive protection under the state law.

State statutes related to health care are not only potentially in conflict with federal and state education law. They are also frequently at odds with expectations of school administrators and other school personnel. To minimize misunderstandings and errors in judgment, it is important for school health professionals, school administrators, and attorneys to understand and collaboratively explore these issues. A school health advisory council, healthy school team (Fetro, 1998, p. 22), or an interdisciplinary school health services team (Duncan & Igoe, 1998, p. 183) are appropriate groups to explore the issues and make recommendations to the school district's administration. Experts in applicable areas of both health and education law should contribute to team and school district deliberations. Based on the recommendations of these groups and decisions of the administration, school districts should provide guidance to school health professionals and administrators regarding the following:

1. Information that should be shared with students regarding protections and limitations to protections provided for their school health records by law and school district policy; and

2. Procedures to follow when a parent requests a student's school health record that contains medical information to which the student has privacy protection under federal or state law.

School Nursing Services and Minor Consent-to-Treatment Laws

Whether visits to a school nurse for medical conditions are covered under state minor consent-to-treatment provisions for STIs, HIV, pregnancy, and drug addiction is often not clear in the laws themselves or through case law decisions (Siegler, 1996; Gelfman & Schwab, 1991). However, most school nurses have assumed that their assessment, counseling, and referral of students to community medical providers is covered by these laws, as they would be in health care settings (school nurse and school nurse supervisor communications with the authors at multiple presentation sessions across the country, 1990–2000). Legal interpretations in some states (e.g., Massachusetts and Washington), however, do clearly support extension of state confidentiality protections to minors who seek services from the school nurse. For example, Massachusetts guidelines on HIV issues direct school health providers to keep information of a strictly medical nature "in a locked file separate from the school health record ... [which is] only accessible to staff who have been given consent to view [them]" (Goodman & Sheetz, 1995, pp. 8–61).

Massachusetts also recommends that sensitive medical information not "relevant to the student's educational progress" be "placed in a nurse's personal files" (Goodman & Sheetz, 1995, pp. 2–28). Washington state guidelines (Billings et al., 1995) support keeping student health information, including student health records, protected from (not accessible to) any school personnel who are not licensed health care providers without a parent's express permission.

The assumption that minor consent-to-treatment laws apply to school nursing services is also consistent with the federal confidentiality protections for minors seeking treatment for drug and alcohol problems through school health professionals. The Institute of Medicine (IOM), Committee on Comprehensive School Health Programs, in its 1997 report on *Schools & Health* (p. 206) recommends that

... when state law eliminates the parental consent requirement for making specified counseling and treatment available to students, access to related medical records at school needs to be held to the same standards of confidentiality observed in other health care settings in communities in that state. In other words, confidentiality of school health records should be given high priority. Confidential health records of students should be handled and shared in a manner consistent with the handling of health care records in non-school health care settings.

For a copy of applicable minor consent laws in a particular state, contact the state school nurse consultant in the state health or education agency, or a state health agency attorney or consultant with expertise in the legal and ethical aspects of providing health care to adolescents in that state. As state laws change regularly, it is important to obtain updated information every year. (FERPA requirements are detailed in chapter 9 and the FERPA regulations, as of 1999, are included in Appendix M. For in-depth information on school-based student assistance programs and the federal confidentiality provisions that protect treatment records of drug and alcohol abuse patients, including minors, see the reference, Legal Action Center, 1996.)

Variable Standards of Confidentiality

As discussed at the beginning of the chapter, maintaining the confidentiality of patients and clients, including students and their families, is an ethical standard for health professionals, including nurses, physicians, social workers, therapists, and others. Health professionals have varying amounts of pre-service course work related to the confidentiality of patient health information and records. Even with considerable pre-service and ongoing education related to confidentiality, however, implementing legal and ethical principles in everyday practice and resolving related service dilemmas remain challenging to health professionals in all settings. They are, perhaps, most challenging to those who serve minors, especially those who provide health services to minors in non-health care settings.

The National Education Association's confidentiality standard in its code of ethics (1991) and the obligation of teachers to maintain student and family confidentiality has been present as an ethical standard in education for many years. Some states have encoded this obligation into state regulations for teacher certification (e.g., Connecticut State Agency Regulations, § 10-145d-400a). Nevertheless, the underlying principles of confidentiality, their application in schools, and special considerations regarding health care issues are rarely taught in pre-service preparation courses for teachers, or even in school administrator and teacher preparation at the graduate level. Teachers rarely receive preparation in public health practices, infection-control, epidemiology, and other related health topics.

These differences in preparation pose additional challenges in practice, since one staff person's understanding of his or her obligations regarding confidentiality may be significantly different from another's, despite use of the same terminology. A school administrator may understand the basic requirements of FERPA, but have no knowledge of state minor consent laws, the federal confidentiality requirements for SAP records, or ethical issues inherent in resolving dilemmas related to the protection and release of confidential health information. Special education directors, although knowledgeable about the confidentiality of special education records, may also lack knowledge of laws and professional standards related specifically to a student's health information and records. While it may be appropriate to share with a student's classroom teacher certain information related to the student's special health care needs, it may not be appropriate to share the information if it is not likely to be used appropriately and kept strictly confidential. Therefore, the school nurse needs to know that the information, if shared, will be used to benefit the student and will not be shared with other colleagues, posted in the teacher's lounge or on a classroom wall, or otherwise further disclosed.

The difference in preparation and obligations of these different professionals is addressed in varying ways in the current literature. Several states, for example, have addressed different aspects of confidentiality, documentation, and handling student health information through guidelines (e.g., Connecticut, Delaware, Maryland, Massachusetts, Virginia, Washington), and have made or proposed legislative changes (e.g., Massachusetts, Oregon). As discussed earlier, the Washington state guidelines, recognizing the differences in preparation and expertise of health and education professionals, provide that "health care providers cannot disclose health care information until parent permission is obtained unless someone's health and safety is at risk" (Billings et al., 1995, p. 8).

The Massachusetts guidelines (Goodman & Sheetz, 1995) also recognize these differences. After much deliberation, the Connecticut Committee on the Confidentiality of Student Health Information determined that, rather than make recommendations based on the differences in current preparation of school personnel, it would recommend that all school personnel be prepared at the same level of expertise as health professionals regarding privacy and confidentiality of student information. Thus, one recommendation of the Committee was that training of school personnel, including volunteers and contract employees, take place annually and during the orientation of new personnel (Connecticut Committee on the Confidentiality of Student Health Information, 1996).

In recognition of the need for better pre-service and in-service preparation of professional school personnel, several national organizations used a portion of their funding for cooperative agreements with the Centers for Disease Control (CDC), Division of Adolescent and School Health, to address student health confidentiality issues, especially those related to HIV. For example, the National School Boards Association addressed confidentiality in its publication *Someone at School Has AIDS* (Bogden et al., 1996), and the American Association of Colleges of Teacher Education published *InfoGuides* to be used in teacher preparation programs, including "Telling Tales Out of School: What Teachers Need to Know About Confidentiality and Student Health Information" (Schwab & Gelfman, 1998).

In 1997, the American School Health Association (ASHA) initiated a CDC-funded project to develop national guidelines on the confidentiality of student health information. In collaboration with the National Association of School Nurses and the National Association of State School Nurse Consultants, ASHA established a committee of representatives from national organizations to develop the document *Guidelines for Protecting Confidential Student Health Information* (National Task Force on Confidential Student Health Information, 2000). Reflecting the complexities and competing principles of law and ethics related to confidentiality, especially related to minors and health care services in school settings, there were multiple differences in constituent perspectives. Reaching consensus, even to identify basic underlying principles, was a major challenge for the committee and its leadership. Nevertheless, the need for better pre-service and in-service education programs for school personnel related to confidentiality and records keeping issues is a priority recommendation of the Committee, and is contained in several of the documents mentioned above as well.

Limited Expertise and Supervision

An additional complexity in managing student health information in a systematic, consistent fashion is that school nurses and other school health professionals (e.g., school medical advisors) often lack knowledge about education law and records, and education administrators generally lack knowledge about health (medical) law and records. As a result, neither school nurses nor school administrators are experts in the management of student *health* information within *education* records. This lack of expertise across systems and disciplines, in addition to the legal complexities discussed above, makes it extremely challenging for local and state leaders to develop and implement policies and procedures that will facilitate appropriate

sharing of student health information and ensure sufficient protections at the same time.

Lack of expertise among school nurses and school nurse managers regarding education law and standards, especially in this crucial area affecting everyday practice, supports Wold's view (see chapter 1) that school nurses should have specialty practice preparation at the Master's level, and Costante's view (see chapter 19) that school nurses entering practice at the baccalaureate level require direction from a Master's-prepared nurse administrator who is knowledgeable about the requirements of both health and education laws. Without specialty practice preparation of their own in a program that offers this content, or at least supervision by an expert school nurse administrator, nurses have little knowledge, direction or support for recommending workable policies and procedures, or for resolving conflicts inherent in delivering and documenting health services for minors in schools. Proctor (chapter 18) points out the potential connection between levels of school nurse education and liability protection for school districts; certainly confidentiality and minor consent to treatment issues can be considered high-risk areas of school nursing practice.

Many school nurses who work in small districts or alone in a school district have non-nursing supervisors, often the school principal. (The subject of school nurses working in "solo practice" is covered in more detail in chapter 18.) Even when nurse managers administer a school district's health services program, they are generally responsible for large numbers of school buildings within a district and are infrequently present in individual school buildings to provide personnel with individual direction and support. This adds to the challenges that school nurses face in recommending, implementing, and evaluating sound policy and procedures related to information sharing and documentation of communications with students, families, educators, and students' health care providers.

Similarly, school administrators lack adequate information and direction related to appropriate handling of student health information (oral, written, or electronic) and student health records. In general, health information in special education records receives better protections, although practices vary in this regard, as well. School administrators have little, if any, understanding of minor consent laws or their applicability in schools. School nurses have reported instances where school administrators believe they should have unrestricted access to all student health records, or require school nurses to publish and distribute to all faculty a complete list of students with health conditions, including students' medical diagnoses. While school nurses may understand that such practices do not meet standards for nursing and medical records, they sometimes lack sufficient expertise to convince their administrators that the practice(s) are inappropriate, possibly illegal and, in any event, not necessary to achieve the desired outcomes. Where knowledgeable school nurse managers are available, they should serve as first-line consultants both to school nurses and school administrators for policy development and assistance with exploring potential approaches to practice dilemmas.

Parents and other stakeholders also lack expertise regarding health and education standards for protection of student privacy, documentation, and record keeping. Parents rarely receive adequate information to make astute judgments regarding the release of—or refusal to release—their child's personal health information, either within or beyond the school district. Sometimes parents are advised by professionals in the community not to share significant or sensitive medical information with the school district when, in fact, confidentiality protections are adequate and the information might be essential to planning an appropriate education program and making accommodations that are advantageous to the student.

Not infrequently, community health care providers make recommendations to their patients regarding health-related, home-school communications without sufficient knowledge of a student's school system, its policies and procedures for health records and confidentiality, its personnel, or student and family rights to privacy under education law. Thus, education programs and strategies are also needed to help parents and community health care providers become more knowledgeable about laws and policies related to student health information, school health records, pros and cons of decisions they may make, and actual practices in their community's schools. The importance of sharing information with appropriate school personnel, given adequate protections, needs to be underscored in these educational efforts.

Student Records and Documentation Issues

The same unique challenges to managing student health information apply to student health records and nursing documentation. Sometimes on a daily basis, school nurses face dilemmas in deciding what and where to document confidential student and family health information. While school nurses handle oral, written, and electronic data governed by multiple health and education laws, school district record-keeping systems often provide limited security for such

sensitive data, and school nurses may have little control over the access of other school personnel to students' health records.

On one hand, school nurses whose districts have inadequate policies and records systems often face the dilemma of whether to document sensitive health information. On the other hand, the professional practice standards of the ANA (1998) and NASN (1998) require school nurses, like all nurses, to document each phase of the nursing process: assessment, diagnosis, outcome identification, planning, implementation, and evaluation. Indeed, good care is equated with good documentation (Springhouse, 1996), and, from a liability perspective, nurses who decline to document (even for ethical reasons) put themselves at increased risk. In negligence cases against nurses, including school nurses, the courts generally equate lack of documentation with lack of care. In other words, "if it wasn't documented, it wasn't done." (Records and documentation issues are discussed in greater detail in chapter 9 and issues related to electronic records and technology are addressed in chapter 10.)

ADDITIONAL PRACTICE CONSIDERATIONS

It is not the within the scope and purpose of this chapter to make recommendations for national, state, and local education and health agencies regarding these complex issues, and some work is already underway or accomplished at the state and national levels. For resources that may be helpful, readers are referred to the content and references in this chapter (e.g., state guidelines, the ASHA initiative, cited publications), as well as those in chapters 9 and 10, and to their state education and health agencies, and state and national professional organizations. Whether at the national, state, or local levels, health and education professionals, families, and other key members of the community, such as legal and ethical experts, need to collaborate to explore the issues and develop workable guidelines and policies for their schools.

Even making recommendations for professional practice at the practitioner level is daunting for the following reasons:

- there is no single prescription for managing confidential student health information across states and school districts;

- no two states have the same laws;

- no two communities have exactly the same values and resources;

- no two students (or staff, or families) are identical;

- no two ethical or legal dilemmas are precisely alike; and

- no formula can replace the need for expert knowledge, analytical skills, and judgment in resolving difficult confidentiality dilemmas.

Faced with a confidentiality dilemma regarding a particular student, school nurses (and other school personnel) should gather information related to the situation, analyze it, identify alternative options and, finally, choose a course of action. Aroskar (chapter 3) outlines a framework for addressing ethical dilemmas in schools. In addition, the following questions can be used to assist practitioners to obtain and consider information needed to make decisions in situations with opposing obligations:

1. What is the student's age and level of competency?

2. What is the relative sensitivity of the information or issue?

3. What are the preferences of the family and student?

4. What laws are applicable to the situation?

5. What school district policies and procedures apply to the situation?

6. What ethical considerations apply to the situation?

7. What would my colleagues do in the same situation?

8. What direction, if any, have I been given by my supervisor?

9. What advice have I sought and obtained from legal and ethical experts? Health experts? Education experts?

10. Are there additional considerations?

The following discussion breaks down each of these questions in further detail.

Question 1: What is the student's age and level of competency?

The student's age and competence to give consent or to follow through on a contract with the school nurse is one important criterion in the decision-making process. A 15-, 16-, or 17-year-old student requesting confidential referral to a health care provider or agency for pregnancy testing and counseling is very different

from a 12-year-old requesting the same referral. In the first situation, assuming a minor can legally give consent for reproductive health care in the state, the school nurse may contract with the student, agreeing to maintain the student's confidentiality if the student agrees to keep her appointment with the health care provider and to discuss the possibility of sharing the information with her family.

Follow-up is necessary to determine that the student is acting competently (e.g., has obtained family or other adult support, is keeping appointments with the health care provider, and making reasonable plans). If, for example, the student finds out that she is pregnant, refuses to tell anyone, doesn't keep appointments for prenatal care, and won't talk any further with the school nurse, the contract has been broken by the student. It is appropriate to get expert legal and clinical advice at that point about informing a parent, school administrator, or both. In the second instance, the nurse may help the 12-year-old student to share her concerns with her family or a school administrator, or both, and may need to consider referral to child protective services. Keeping this student's confidence strictly private is unlikely to be either legal, appropriate, reasonable, or in the student's best interests.

In risk-of-harm situations in which a school nurse agrees to maintain the confidentiality of a minor student, a student-nurse contract that requires the student to demonstrate his or her competence is useful. In these instances the nurse agrees to keep confidential the sensitive information so long as the student takes certain steps that they agree on and put in writing. Developing a contract together is also an effective strategy for clarifying when the risks of harm resulting from secrecy may begin to outweigh the risks of harm from disclosure. See Figure 8-1 for further discussion of contracts in relation to the case of a pregnant 16-year-old student who was indicted for manslaughter in the death of her newborn child.

Question 2: What is the relative sensitivity of the information or issue?

Generally, the more sensitive the information, the more likely that harm (e.g., discrimination) may result from disclosure or improper use of the information. When there are options, the potential risks of harm from disclosure should be balanced against potential positive outcomes of sharing the information. With whom and how much information will be shared is part of the equation. In other words, the sensitivity of the information must be weighed according to the situation, individuals involved and culture of the setting. The medical diagnoses of HIV and Hepatitis B

Figure 8-1.

Limits to Confidentiality: A Case in Point

In 1995, the body of a full-term newborn baby was found in double wrapped trash bags at a dump. The newborn was traced to a 16-year-old high school student who had delivered the baby at home into the toilet in her bathroom, unknown to anyone else. The following afternoon she had attended a football game at school and initially denied to the police that the baby was hers.

Subsequent to the discovery and the initial media report that no one had known of the girl's pregnancy, including the student's parents, a local newspaper reported, in an article titled "Nurse advised teen on pregnancy," that the school nurse had "advised her to seek family planning." A second article claimed medical confidentiality as the reason the nurse had not disclosed the information. The cause of death was consistent with drowning, and the teen was charged with first degree manslaughter, punishable by up to 20 years in prison. While the student's mother, a pediatric nurse, said she was unaware of the pregnancy, as were other school officials, the teen was a member of her school's swim team, and at least a few swimmers from other high schools' teams, observing her in a bathing suit, assumed she was pregnant. Almost two years later, the teen pleaded guilty to second-degree manslaughter and was sentenced to 18 months in jail. (This story is based on articles in the *New Haven Register,* November 1995–August 1997.)

The facts of any interactions between the school nurse and student are unknown to the authors. The story is relayed because it is a clear example of a teenager with a right under state law to have confidentiality in seeking counseling and care for pregnancy and family planning who, in fact, was not exercising that right because she wasn't seeking counseling or prenatal care. Indeed, it does not appear that she was acting in a competent way to safeguard herself or the baby she was carrying. While one might question whether she had a right *not* to seek prenatal care, her status as a minor does not ensure her such a right. Her choice not to seek care or tell her parent is a strong indicator that she may not understand the short- and long-term consequences of her actions.

In this type of situation, a nurse-student contract might require the student to keep an initial appointment with a health care provider and to come back to the school nurse with a plan for informing her parents or, minimally, another supportive adult in her life. Such a contract can be updated regularly, as circumstances change, for example, requiring the student to demonstrate that she is continuing to keep prenatal care appointments. If the student doesn't keep her part of the contract, the nurse should then engage the teen by giving her some choices of who will be told and how (e.g., parent, principal, social worker) and offering support in making the disclosure. Such contracts respect students' wishes to the extent that they can demonstrate competence in handling the difficult situation they are in, but also define for minor students the reasonable limits of confidentiality when they are at significant risk of harm.

---

are generally considered very sensitive because of public fear associated with them and the potential for discrimination. However, identification in school of a student with head lice, not a diagnosis generally considered sensitive by health professionals, may also result in embarrassment to and even discrimination against the student and family. Faced with a sensitive issue or dilemma, it is helpful when the nurse has worked in the school for enough time to have established trusting relationships with administrators, and to be familiar with the knowledge levels of individual personnel as well as the general culture of the school regarding confidentiality and health issues. However, individual parents may have different understandings

of the sensitivity of information from that of the general community.

Question 3: What are the preferences of the family and student?

It is critical to ascertain the preferences of the student, family, or both to give them as much information as possible to make informed decisions about information sharing, and to support their preferences to the extent allowed by law, policy, ethics, and safety standards. When the preferences of a student and his or her family differ, assisting them to resolve those differences may be appropriate, including referral to another school or community professional. When balancing student preferences in a dilemma, the nurse should give more weight to the preferences of mature students, who understand the consequences of the choices they make and take responsible steps to address their problem than to those of younger or less competent students. Also, in some instances, more than preference is involved and parents will have a clear legal right to make the decision to disclose or not disclose information, as will competent students who have reached the age of majority. (See Question 4 below).

Question 4: What laws are applicable to the situation?

State and federal laws (both health and education) may be directive about what can and cannot be released in a given situation, particularly when there are no conflicts between laws. It is critical to know the laws that may apply to a given situation, as well as any relevant attorneys general or state agency interpretations of the intent of the law(s). For example, if state law prohibits the release of a person's HIV status without the express, written consent of the person (or minor's person's parent), options to otherwise share the information internally (within the school) are eliminated. One exception to the prohibition of sharing the information without written consent might be in the case of a medical emergency where sharing the information with emergency medical personnel might be life saving for the student. Any case law decisions applicable to a particular situation might also be instructive.

Question 5: What school district policies and procedures apply to the situation?

The school nurse (or other school professional) must be cognizant of school district policies and procedures that might apply to a given situation. School policy should be followed unless compelling legal or ethical principles dictate otherwise. For example, it may be policy that the school nurse will inform the school principal of any student who is (or thinks she is) pregnant. However, it may be ethically and legally appropriate *not* to share this personal information with the principal when state law permits the student to independently and confidentially seek medical care and counseling, and the student is proceeding responsibly to obtain it. Even if the law requires parental consent for minor's access to reproductive health care services, it is still questionable whether the principal needs to be informed if there are no school-related issues or concerns about the student's safety, and the student agrees to inform her parents. Policies that do not sufficiently protect the confidentiality rights of students and families or do not conform with the law should be changed.

Question 6: What ethical considerations apply to the situation?

Ethical considerations are always important in decisions regarding the delivery of health services; they are especially critical when there are conflicting obligations and no one course of action appears or feels "right." As indicated earlier in this chapter and in chapter 3, laws, policies and professional standards of practice do not always provide clear answers to practice dilemmas. Sometimes there are conflicts or lack of clarity between laws, between laws and policies, or between laws or policies and professional standards of practice. Weighing and balancing opposing ethical values is important to deliberation about the appropriate course of action in a given situation. For example, the ethical principle of maintaining a client's confidentiality may be at odds with the principle of veracity, or telling the truth, an issue when a professional colleague asks for information about a student in order to better serve the student. In any situation, both legal and ethical principles, along with the specifics of the individual situation, must be weighed and balanced; achieving the least harm (or better good) for the client (student) must be a primary goal in reaching a decision. Considerations of least harm (and better good) for the family and school community must also be balanced in the decision-making process, as discussed by Aroskar in chapter 3.

Question 7: What would my colleagues do in the same situation?

It is helpful to consult with nursing colleagues, especially those with expertise and experience with similar challenges. This should be done without divulging information that might identify the student(s) in question. Colleagues may raise questions or issues that haven't been thought of or challenge a potential bias. They will also provide a perspective on "what another reasonable nurse would do in the same or similar circumstance." Non-nurse colleagues, for example a school social worker, can also be consulted for their knowledge and perspective.

Question 8: What direction, if any, have I been given by my supervisor?

Consulting with a supervisor is important, and protecting the identity of the student during the consultation is generally appropriate. Advice regarding school policy, the law, general practice in the district, and clinical considerations (if the supervisor is a nurse) can be gained. Supervisors may also help direct staff to outside experts for further consultation. There may be occasions when it is not appropriate to consult with one's supervisor. For example, if the school nurse's direct supervisor is the school principal, and the dilemma involves protecting the student's confidentiality about a medical issue, then consulting with the principal might not be appropriate since the principal is likely to surmise a student's identity from the situational facts, even without the student's name. In that case, it might be more appropriate for the school nurse to consult with a central office administrator, such as the special education director. There may also be a situation in which it would be wisest to seek outside expert consultation without going through a supervisor.

Question 9: What advice have I sought and obtained from experts: legal and ethical, health and education?

While colleagues and supervisors may provide sufficient assistance for many of the confidentiality dilemmas that school nurses face, there are times when additional expertise is indicated. Legal experts may be available through a state agency (e.g., department of education or health, or board of examiners for nursing), university (e.g., law school) or a legal aid center. Ethicists may be available through universities or professional organizations. If an issue has to do with adolescent health care, a pediatrician or advanced practice registered nurse with adolescent expertise from the community, a nearby hospital, or a university may be willing to consult. It may also be important to obtain input from both health and education experts, since legal and practical perspectives may differ significantly and both should be considered.

Question 10: Do I need to gather any additional information?

If, after obtaining assistance from the above sources and weighing and balancing the options that seem most appropriate, there is still a question about the best course of action, one should determine whether there are additional considerations. An examination of one's own competencies, attitudes, and biases may be appropriate in circumstances when one's personal beliefs or preferences and professional responsibilities seem in conflict. Also, it may be instructive to review the general rule for maintaining confidentiality, as well as the exceptions to those rules. There may also be a situation that should be turned over to a knowledgeable supervisor to handle.

SUMMARY

In summary, there are no easy answers to conflicts raised by confidentiality issues. School nurses and other school professionals must respect the right of parents and students to control their own information to the

extent possible. They must also share *necessary* information with other school team members to ensure student safety and promote student learning. In sharing information, they must consider that team members may lack preparation in the legal and ethical principles of confidentiality and privacy. Finding the right balance can be difficult; determining how much to document and what information in student health records to share with other members of the school team can be challenging. Ideally, all school personnel should receive training to enhance standards for both protecting the confidentiality of student health information and for enhancing positive communications among educators, health professionals, students, and families.

REFERENCES

Alderman, E., & Kennedy, C. (1997). *The right to privacy.* New York: Vintage Books.

American Academy of Pediatrics Committee on Medical Liability with Robertson, W., & Lockhart, J. (Eds.). (1995). *Medical liability for pediatricians.* Elk Grove Village, IL: American Academy of Pediatrics.

American Nurses Association. (1985). *Code for nurses with interpretive statements.* Washington, DC: American Nurses' Publishing.

American Nurses Association. (1998). *Standards of Clinical Nursing Practice* (2nd ed.). Washington, DC: American Nurses Publishing.

American Nurses Association, Center for Ethics and Human Rights. (1995). Nurses and unlicensed assistive personnel: Ethical perspectives. *Communique, 4*(2), 2–4.

Bergen, J. (1999). Legal "duty to warn" third parties not always clear: Seven guiding principles to minimize liability lawsuits. *AAP News, 15*(4).

Billings, J., Pearson, J., Carthum, H., & Maire, J. (1995). *Guidelines for handling health care information in school records.* Olympia, WA: Superintendent of Public Instruction.

Bogden, J. F., Fraser, K., Vega-Matos, C., & Ascroft, J. (1996). *Someone at school has AIDS.* Alexandria, VA: National Association of State Boards of Education.

Brandeis & Warren. (1890). The right to privacy. *4 Harvard Law Review, 193.*

Centers for Disease Control, U.S. Department of Health and Human Services. (1985). Education and foster care of children infected with human t-lymphotropic virus type III/Lymphadenopathy-associated virus, *Morbidity and Mortality Weekly Report, 34*(34).

Cheung, O., Clements, B., & Pechman, E. (1997). *Protecting the privacy of student records. Guidelines for education agencies.* Washington, DC: Council of Chief State School Officers and Policy Studies Associates.

Cohn, S. (1984). Legal issues in school nursing practice. *Journal of Law, Medicine and Health Care, 12*(5), 220–221.

Connecticut Committee on the Confidentiality of Student Health Information. (1996). *Draft Guidelines for policy and procedures: Confidentiality of student information.* Middletown, CT: Connecticut State Department of Education.

Duncan, P. & Igoe, J. B. (1998). School health services. In E. Marx & S. F. Wooley (Eds.). *Health is academic.* New York: Teachers College Press.

English, A. (1996). *Understanding legal aspects of care.* In L. S. Neinstein (Ed.), *Adolescent health care: A practical guide* (3rd ed.). Baltimore: Williams & Wilkins.

English, A., & Tereszkiewicz, L. (1988). *School-based health clinics: Legal issues.* San Francisco: National Center for Youth Law and Houston: The Center for Population Options.

Falia, S., & Todaro, A. (1992). Planning for a child with hydrocephalus: A guide for the school nurse. *Journal of School Health, 62* (3), 107–111.

Feldsman, Tucker, Leifer, Fidell, & Bank. (1992). *Legal issues in pediatric HIV practice: A handbook for health care providers.* Newark: National Pediatric HIV Resource Center.

Fetro, J. V. (1998). School health services. In E. Marx & S. F. Wooley (Eds.), *Health is academic.* New York: Teachers College Press.

Gans, J. (Ed.). (1993). *A policy compendium on confidential health services for adolescents.* Chicago: American Medical Association.

Gelfman, M., & Schwab, N. (1991). School health services and educational records: Conflicts in the law. *Education Law Reporter 64,* 319–338.

Goodman, I. F., & Sheetz, A. H. (Eds.). (1995). *The comprehensive school health manual.* Boston: Massachusetts State Department of Education.

Health Privacy Project. (1999). *The state of health privacy: An uneven terrain,* Executive summary. Washington, DC: Georgetown University Institute for Health Care Research and Policy. Available online: http://www.healthprivacy.org/resources/statereports/exsum.html

Holder, A. (1985). *Legal issues in pediatric and adolescent medicine* (2nd ed.). New Haven: Yale University Press.

Hootman, J. (1996a). *Quality nursing interventions in the school setting: Procedures, models and guidelines.*

Scarborough, ME: National Association of School Nurses.

Hootman, J. (1996b). Nursing diagnosis—A language of nursing; A language for powerful communication. *Journal of School Nursing, 12* (4), 19–23.

Hootman, J. (with Carpenito, L. J.). (1996c). *Nursing diagnosis: Application in the school setting.* Scarborough, ME: National Association of School Nurses.

Institute of Medicine, Committee on Comprehensive School Health Programs in Grades K–12. (1997). *School health: Our nation's investment.* Edited by D. Allensworth, E. Lawson, L. Nicholson, and J. Wyche. Washington, DC: National Academy Press.

Kaar, J. K., & Mawn, S. V. (1998). Health care decisions and third parties. *Journal of Nursing Risk Management 1998,* 22–26. [On-line] Available: www.afip.org/legalmed/jnrm.html

Koop, C. E. (1991). *Surgeon General's Report on Acquired Immune Deficiency Syndrome.* Washington, DC: U. S. Department of Health and Human Services.

Legal Action Center. (1996). *Legal issues for school-based programs* (2nd ed.). New York: Legal Action Center of the City of New York, Inc.

Luehr, R. E. (1993). Using nursing diagnosis in the school setting. In M. K. Haas (Ed.), *The school nurse's sourcebook of individualized healthcare plans.* North Branch, MN: Sunrise River Press.

Majer, L. (1992). HIV-infected students in school: Who really 'needs to know'? *Journal of Health, 62* (6), 243–244.

McNary-Keith, S. E. (1995). AIDS in public schools: Resolved issues and continuing controversies. *Journal of Law and Education, 24*(1), 6980.

Melroe, N. H. (1990). "Duty to warn" vs. "patient confidentiality": The ethical dilemmas in caring for HIV-infected clients. *Nurse Practitioner, 15* (2), 58–69.

National Association of School Nurses. (1998). *Standards of professional school nursing practice* (2nd ed.). Scarborough, ME: Author.

National Association of School Nurses. (1990). *Code of ethics with interpretive statements for the school nurse.* Scarborough, ME: Author.

National Association of State School Nurse Consultants. (1993). *Resolution on confidentiality of health information in schools* (rev). Kent, OH: Author.

National Education Association. (1991). *NEA handbook 1991–1992.* Washington, DC: Author.

National Task Force on Confidential Student Health Information. (2000). *Guidelines for Protecting Confidential Student Health Information.* Kent, OH: American School Health Association.

North American Nursing Diagnosis Association. (1999). *1999-2000 Nursing diagnoses: Definitions and classification, 3rd ed.* St. Louis: Author.

Poulton, S., & Denehy, J. (1999). Standardized languages in nursing: Integrating NANDA, NIC, and NOC into IHPs. In M. Arnold & C. Silkworth (Eds.), *The school nurse's source book of individualized healthcare plans: Vol. II. Issues and applications in school nursing practice.* North Branch, MN: Sunrise River Press.

Proctor, S. (with Lordi, S., & Zaiger, D.). (1993). *School nursing practice: Roles and standards.* Scarborough, ME: National Association of School Nurses, Inc.

Purtilo. R. (1993). *Ethical dimensions in the health professions.* Philadelphia: W. B. Saunders Company.

Rushton, C. (1997). Presentation to the National Task Force To Develop Guidelines For Handling Confidential Student Information in Alexandria, VA. In *Minutes of the First Meeting, May 27, 1997.* Kent, Ohio: American School Health Association.

Rushton, C., & Infante, M. (1995). Keeping secrets: The ethical and legal challenges. *Pediatric Nursing, 21* (5), 479–482.

Rushton, C., & Infante, M. (1996). Keeping secrets: The ethical and legal challenges: Confidentiality and Privacy. *Communique, 5* (1), 7–9. American Nurses Association Center for Ethics and Human Rights.

Schwab, N., & Gelfman, M. (1991). School health records: Nursing practice and the law. *School Nurse, 7* (2), 17–21.

Schwab, N. & Gelfman, M. (1998). Telling tales out of school. What teachers need to know about confidentiality and student health information—Ethical and legal dilemmas *(InfoGuide 4).* In *HIV/AIDS prevention in teacher education: InfoGuides.* Washington, DC: American Association of Colleges for Teacher Education.

Schwab, N., Panettieri, M. J. & Bergren, M. (1998). *Guidelines for school nursing documentation: Standards, Issues and Models* (2nd ed.). Scarborough, ME: National Association of School Nurses.

Siegler, G. E. (1996). What should be the scope of privacy protections of student health records? A look at Massachusetts and federal law. *Journal of Law and Medicine 25* (2), 237–269.

Springhouse Corporation. (1996). *Nurse's legal handbook* (3rd ed.). Springhouse, PA: Author.

State of Connecticut Department of Education. (1998). Developing quality programs for pupil services: A self-evaluative guide. Middletown, CT: Author.

Sullivan, F., & Rooker, L. (1990). *School-based Student Assistance Programs: Reconciling Federal Regulations under the Family Educational Rights and Privacy Act and the Alcohol and Drug Abuse Confidentiality Statutes,* Sept. 26, United States Department of Education and the Alcohol, Drug Abuse, and Mental Health Administration of the U.S. Department of Health and Human Services.

Surgeon General's Report on Acquired Immune Deficiency Syndrome, 1991, U.S. Department of Health and Human Services.

Swartz, M. (1990). Is there a duty to warn? *Human Rights, 17*(1).

Understanding AIDS. (1988). Washington, DC: Surgeon General and the Centers for Disease Control, U.S. Public Health Service, U.S. Department of Health and Human Services.

U.S. Department of Health and Human Services. (1999a). Proposed Standards for Privacy of Individually Identifiable Health Information. *Federal Register, 64*(212), 59918–59966. Available on-line: http://aspe.os.dhhs.gov/admnsimp/nprm/pvcnprm1 .pdf

U.S. Department of Health and Human Services. (1999b). Summary of Proposed Standards for Privacy of Individually Identifiable Health Information. Available on-line: http://aspe.os.dhhs.gov/admnsimp/pvcsumm.htm

TABLE OF CASES

Board of Education of the City of Plainfield v. Cooperman, 523 A.2d 655, 105 N.J. 587 (N.J. 1987).

District 27 Community School Board v. Board of Education of the City of New York, 502 N.Y.S.2d 326, EHLR 557:241 (Sup.Ct.N.Y.1986).

Doe v. Bagan and Adams County School District, 41 F.3d 571 (10th Cir. 1994).

Doe v. Dolton Elementary School District, EHLR Dec. 441:247 (N.D. Ill 1988).

Dunajewski v. Bellmore-Merrick Central High School District, 526 N.Y.S.2d 139 (A.D.2 Dept. 1988).

Griswold v. Connecticut, 381 U.S. 479, 14 L.Ed.2d 510, 85 S.Ct. 1678 (1965).

Martinez by Martinez v. School Board of Hillsborough County, Florida, 675 F.Supp. 1574, EHLR Dec. 559:281 (M.D.Fla. 1987) aff'd EHLR Dec. 441:257 (11th Cir. 1988).

Morris et al. v. Canipe et al., 528 So.2d 659 (La.App.2 Cir. 1988).

Muhlenberg Hospital v. Patterson, 320 A. 2d 518 (N.J. App. 1974)

Nieuwendorp v. American Family Insurance Company, 510 N.W.2d 779 (Wis. App. 1993; Wis.Sup. Ct., as reviewed at 21 IDELR 836).

*People ex. Rel. Wallace v. Labrrez,*104 N.E. 2d 769 (ILL 1952).

Pesce v. J. Sterling Morton H.S. District 201, 830 F.2d 789 (7th Cir. 1987).

Phipps v. Saddleback Valley Unified School District, 251 Cal. Rptr. 720 (Cal.App.4 Dist. 1988).

Ray v. School District of DeSoto County, 666 F.Supp. 1524 (M.D.Fla. 1987).

Robertson by Robertson v. Granite City Community School District, 685 F.Supp. 1002, EHLR Dec. 559:476 (S.D.Ill. 1988).

Seibert v. Morris, 252 Wis. 460, 463, 32 N.W.2d 239 (1948).

Tarasoff v. Regents of the University of California, 551 P.2d 334 (Cal. 1976).

Tenebaum v. Williams, 862 F.Supp. 962, 22 IDELR 209 (E.D.N.Y. 1994).

Thomas v. Atascadero Unified School District, 622 F.Supp. 376, EHLR Dec. 559:113 (C.D.Cal. 1987).

Whalen v. Roe, 429 U.S. 598 (1977).

See page 625 for Table of Federal Statutes and Regulations.

Chapter Nine
School Health Records and Documentation

Mary H. B. Gelfman with Nadine C. Schwab

INTRODUCTION

The purpose of this chapter is to discuss laws and professional standards that apply to student health records and documentation systems. Where federal and state health and education laws applicable to student health records are inconsistent or contradictory, conflicts of laws and related legal and practice issues are addressed. Additionally, practice standards and liability issues for school nurses, and policy concerns for local boards of education and school administrators are considered. Differences between school-based health centers and school health services records systems are highlighted where applicable.

This chapter is intended as a partner to chapter 8, "Confidentiality: Principles and Practice," since record keeping cannot be separated from matters of privacy and confidentiality. The emphasis in this chapter, however, is on systems issues. Principles of sound documentation from a legal perspective are discussed here and in chapters 5 and 8. It is also intended as a companion to chapter 10, "Electronic Records and Technology." Electronic systems are modeled on the paper systems they replace, but there are several areas of special concern. Security issues, both internal and during electronic transmission, are more complex. A well-designed electronic system can do more and do it faster than a paper system. It is likely that very soon virtually all school records, including student health information, will be handled electronically.

SCHOOL HEALTH RECORDS—MEDICAL OR EDUCATIONAL?

School health records exist because a student has enrolled in a school: does that make them education records? School nurses generate school health records: does that make them health care records? Since 1974, when the Family Educational Rights and Privacy Act (FERPA) established federal standards for confidentiality of and parent access to all personally identifiable student records, school nurses have been troubled by the classification of "education records." Nurses worry that as education records, school health records may be accessible to members of the school staff who may not understand medical terminology or the special needs for confidentiality concerning medical information. School staff members who are not health care professionals may resent any limits on access to student health information for staff members who share responsibility for the student.

Some, and perhaps all, student health information in school files is *both* an education record and a health care record. The confusion arises because health care records have traditionally been regulated by state law, while FERPA, a federal law, sets standards for education records. In some states, student health information or those parts of the record that are nursing progress notes and information released from health care providers to schools are classified as health care records, and access is limited to health care professionals unless specific consent has been provided by the parent. For detailed discussion of legal conflicts concerning school health records, see Gelfman & Schwab (1991), Schwab & Gelfman (1991), and Siegler (1996). Additional confusion concerning school health records is the result of current activity in the U.S. Congress addressing patients' rights to confidentiality and parallel activities in many state legislatures.

EDUCATION RECORDS: APPLICABLE LAWS

Until 1974, there was little regulation of school record keeping. As education was considered a state function, some states had laws concerning retention schedules for records of attendance, graduation, and the minimal content of school health records. Some school districts had policies or administrative procedures concerning record-making and record retention. Access within the school staff and by parents varied greatly.

There are many federal and state laws concerning student and employee records that impact on school documentation and record-keeping practices. The most important federal laws for school nurses are cited below; for more comprehensive lists, see Rosenfeld, Gelfman, & Bluth (1997) and Cheung, Clements, & Pechman (1997). For state requirements, consult state statutes and regulations.

FEDERAL LAWS

Family Educational Rights and Privacy Act (FERPA)

There was such disparity in school record keeping, parental access to a student's school records, and standards for record keeping and confidentiality (or lack of it) that in 1974 the U.S. Congress established nation-wide standards for student records. In every school, college, and university receiving federal financial assistance, the Family Education Rights and Privacy Act of 1974 imposes standards of confidentiality for information about individual students. For more detailed discussions of the legislative history of FERPA and subsequent court cases, see Johnson (1993), Mawdsley (1996), and Rosenfeld, et al. (1997). The regulations issued by the U.S. Department of Education to implement FERPA are found at Title 34, Code of Federal Regulations Part 99. The Family Policy Compliance Office (FPCO) of the U.S. Department of Education is responsible for investigating complaints of FERPA violations and answering questions of interpretation of the Act.

Definition of Records Under FERPA

In FERPA, "Education Records" includes any record containing personally identifiable information about a student and maintained by the school, by school staff members, or contracted employees. The FERPA regulations also define "records" to mean

> …any information recorded in any way, including but not limited to, handwriting, print, computer media, audio or video tape, microfilm, and micro-fiche.

To paraphrase this definition (Boomer, Hartshorne, & Robertshaw, 1995):

> An education record is any form of information directly related to a child which is collected, maintained or used by the school.

These records are about individual students, and they are maintained because the student is enrolled in school. In general, school health records are considered education records, whether the school nurse is employed by the school system or by another agency providing school health services by contract. The reason is that the records are maintained about individual students because they are enrolled in school.

Exceptions (or improvements) to this rule are found in the states of Massachusetts (Goodman & Sheetz, 1995) and Washington (Billings, Pearson, Carthum, & Maire, 1995), and in some individual school districts, in particular, the Multnomah Education Service District, Portland, Oregon. In these models, the traditional school health record with routine data (including documentation of immunizations, screenings, etc.) is considered an education record, but the nursing record, which is maintained separately from the school health record, is specifically identified as a medical, rather than education record. This standard is supported by the National Association of School Nurses in its publications: *Quality Nursing Interventions in the School Setting: Procedures, Models and Guidelines* (Hootman, 1996a) and *Guidelines for School Nursing Documentation: Standards, Issues and Models* (Schwab, Panettieri, & Bergren, 1998). The nursing record usually consists of health history information, documentation of student contacts with the nurse (nursing process notes), and third party medical records. In cases where a student requires specific medication, treatment, or nursing support in school, an individualized school health care plan and notes concerning daily implementation of that plan are included in the nursing record.

The records of a school-based health center (SBHC) which is operated by an independent agency, such as a hospital or community health service, are *not* education records. Students have the option of consulting with SBHC staff, and usually parental consent is required (see chapter 15). In some states and for specific locations, the parental permission form allowing a child to use the SBHC also includes permission for necessary health information to be shared between the SBHC and school personnel designated by title (i.e., school nurse, school social worker, guidance counselor). In Massachusetts, the permission form requires parents to allow the SBHC to share necessary medical information with the school nurse, and vice versa.

Internal Access to Education Records

Each education record must have an access log, which is used to record the name and title of the person accessing the record, and the reason for access, which must be for "a legitimate educational interest." In defining "school officials," the school district may include regular staff members and consultants. One example of a consultant to a school district is the attorney who represents the district.

Case example:

An Illinois court has found that release of student records to the attorney representing the school district, in order to prepare for litigation involving that student, is permissible under FERPA (*Aufox v. Board of Education*, 1992).

In defining "legitimate educational interest," the school district will usually include the titles of staff members who provide direct services to enrolled students (i.e., education, discipline, counseling, or health care) pursuant to an employment relationship. In a model school district policy provided by the U.S. Department of Education, a school official with a legitimate educational interest

- performs a task that is specified in his or her position description or by a contract agreement;

- performs a task related to a student's education;

- performs a task related to the discipline of a student; or

- provides a service or benefit relating to the student or student's family, such as health care, counseling, or job placement (*Student records policies and procedures for the Alpha School District* [1976]).

Regarding access to school health records, "legitimate educational interest" should be defined in terms of those who both "need to know to benefit the student" and who have the expertise to understand and interpret the health information in relation to school and education needs. In general, the school health professional (e.g., school nurse, nurse supervisor, or school physician) should maintain and interpret student health records, while incorporating the "need to know" information into individualized health and emergency plans and other summary information for sharing with school administrators, classroom teachers, and §504 and IEP teams who are also serving the individual students in question. Thus, information is shared when necessary for the student, but access to all of the students' medical and nursing records remains restricted to the school health professional(s) who are the makers, custodians, and interpreters of the record.

FERPA permits school districts to define in school district policy who has "legitimate educational interests"

for each type of school record. Therefore, a school district's records policy can distinguish among the different health and nursing records kept in school. For example, the classroom teacher of a student has a "legitimate education interest" in an individualized emergency care plan for that student and in information regarding the whereabouts of a student missing from class, but does not need access to the routine school health record (for immunization and screening information) or to nursing process records; the school principal has a "legitimate educational interest" in emergency plans for all students in his or her building, in the whereabouts of any student cutting class and in the routine school health records that demonstrate if students have complied with a variety of state laws related to school attendance, but does not require direct access to nursing records of student visits to the health room or to third party medical records.

When information in the protected records does become of "legitimate educational interest" to the principal or other school official, appropriate information should be released by the school health professional. As a simple example, it is appropriate information to verify that a "missing" student was at the wellness center (nurse's office) from 10:00–11:00 a.m. that day. In a second example, while the teacher and administrator do not have automatic access to nursing records, when a student's frequent visits to the health room for non-specific complaints are potentially indicative of a school-related concern, then the information should become part of the regular education records (including the traditional school health record)—and the nurse can (and should) share the information with the classroom teacher and principal. Information that is not relevant or necessary to indicating the need for school team action, however (e.g., the student's Hepatitis B carrier state), should not be shared. As a third example, the school district's attorney may have a "legitimate educational interest" in reviewing the student's health and nursing records in preparing a defense for an impending legal action, but would not otherwise have such access.

FERPA also provides for access to education records by state and federal officials (Ingram, 1995):

> While FERPA provides specifically for access by state and federal officials for audit and program monitoring purposes, such access must be recorded on the access record.

Additional FERPA Requirements

The confidentiality standards that FERPA imposes on all schools receiving federal financial assistance include the following:

1. The school is responsible for protecting personally identifiable student information, and may not release it beyond the school without written parental consent;
2. parents have access to all information about their children; and
3. the school district must issue annual notice of rights to parents and to students over age 18, providing information concerning the following:

   - rights to "inspect and review" education records;

   - right to request amendment of records believed to be inaccurate, misleading, or in violation of the student's right to privacy;

   - the requirement of consent for the release of education records, except for specific situations when consent is not required;

   - how to make complaints concerning alleged violations of FERPA to the U.S. Department of Education;

   - procedures for inspection and review and for requesting amendment; and

   - criteria for determining which school staff members have been designated as "school officials" and what is "legitimate educational interest" for staff access to education records.

For further discussion of FERPA requirements and sample forms for use by local school districts, see Cheung, et al., 1997.

Exceptions to FERPA Requirements

FERPA provides a few exceptions to what it defines as "education records." These exceptions remove categories of records from the protection of FERPA; however, state law or local school district policy may define protections—or lack of protections—for records not covered by FERPA.

Personal or "sole possession" notes that are made by a school staff member and are not accessible or revealed to any other person except for the staff member's temporary substitute, are not education records under FERPA. An example of a personal note is the note a school health office staff member might write as a reminder to follow up a concern with a student; the initial contact and the result of the follow-up should be recorded in the student's health record, but the reminder is a personal note. Interpretations of the "personal notes" exception by a court and by the

Office for Civil Rights (OCR) of the U.S. Department of Education illustrate recognition of the basic intent of FERPA that parents have a broad right of access to their children's education records.

Case examples:

In a Pennsylvania case, a school psychologist tried to use the personal notes exception to protect notes made in interviews of students who had been abused by a teacher. Parents of the children interviewed argued that their consent to interviews was conditioned on access to reports of the interviews. The lower court ruling, granting access to the parents of the children interviewed, was upheld on appeal, and the interview notes were found accessible to the parents (*Parents Against Abuse in Schools v. Williamsport Area School District*, 1991).

A teacher's record book (grade book) was found to be a personal note by the Office for Civil Rights (OCR) (Oklahoma Department of Education, 1984).

While the log of a student's behavior and performance, kept by a paraprofessional, might normally be considered a personal note, OCR found such a log to be accessible to parents when information from the log was entered on the record of a special education hearing (Oroville, 1980).

The above comments about a log of a student's behavior and performance, made by a paraprofessional, may be too narrow: the purpose of creating such a log is usually to have data to present to the IEP team or others considering the effectiveness of a student's school program or placement. Such sharing automatically makes the document accessible to the student's parent.

Treatment records for students who are over 18 years of age or attending college are not education records under FERPA. This provision protects college health service records from access by parents of adult students and college staff members in other departments, unless the student has consented to release. This requirement has only limited impact on secondary schools, where a few adult students may be receiving nursing services. This exception for adult and college students may also imply that such treatment records are considered medical or health care records, protected under state law and not subject to education law. For a discussion of confidentiality and record-keeping requirements applied to school counselors, psychologists, and social workers, see Fischer & Sorenson (1996), pp. 17–31 and 87–108.

Other exceptions of possible relevance to the school nurse include the following:

- records of a separate law enforcement unit within the school, which does not have access to other student records;

- employment records of students who are also employees, maintained only for employment purposes; and

- records about former students' activities after they leave school.

Protecting and Disclosing Education Records

Under FERPA, disclosure of confidential information in education records beyond the school is generally forbidden (see exceptions below) without written parental consent. The FERPA definition of disclosure is (34 C.F.R. § 99.3):

> To permit access to or the release, transfer, or other communication of personally identifiable information contained in education records to any party, by any means, including oral, written, or electronic means.

This regulation bars disclosure of information from education records without consent, except to those within the school who have been defined in district policy as school officials having a legitimate educational interest in access. Information released with consent under FERPA may not be re-released without an additional specific consent from the parent or adult student.

When a parent asks to see a student's education records, the school district policy usually requires that the request be in writing. Both parents have the right of access, unless the school has received a copy of a court order or other legally binding document that revokes parental rights.

FERPA allows access to education records by separated and divorced parents unless parental rights have been revoked by a court.

Case example:
A divorced, non-custodial New York parent was awarded access to education records and all notices of school activities, and attorneys' fees, by the court in a case where the school had denied access (*Fay v. South Colonie Central School District*, 1986).

The school must provide access within "a reasonable period of time, but in no case more than 45 days." (Note: IDEA provides that access must be provided prior to "any meeting regarding an IEP" or a special education due process hearing; see below.)

A recent amendment to the FERPA regulations provides: If circumstances effectively prevent the parent or eligible student from exercising the right to inspect and review the student's education records, the local school may provide copies or make other arrangements.

This language suggests the use of transmission by telecopier (FAX). The amendment may appear to vest school districts with the discretion to refuse copies of records to parents; however, IDEA contains a reference to providing copies to parents (see below) and OCR and several courts have ruled that parents have rights to copies of their children's records. The school district may charge a reasonable fee for copies, but it cannot charge for search for, or retrieval of, education records. The courts have addressed limitations on access and copying fees.

Case examples:
In a Florida class action which addressed many allegations of due process violations, the settlement agreement included a stipulation that the Board of Education would: 1) stop charging a fee for parental access to records; 2) make copy fees for special education student records and for regular education student records the same; and 3) provide parental access to education records "at reasonable hours on reasonable notice" (*S-1 v. Turlington*, 1986).

A Michigan challenge to copying fees for education records was remanded for findings about fees chargeable under the state Freedom of Information Act (*Tallman v. Cheboygan Area Schools*, 1990).

Explanations and interpretations of education records must be provided upon request from parents. Education records may not be destroyed when there is a request for inspection pending from a parent or an adult student.

There has been continuing discussion and disagreement concerning parental access to the actual questions and answers from psychological tests such as the Wecshler Intelligence Scale for Children (WISC). Schools have denied access for several reasons:

- concern that use of questions and answers to "prepare" students will undermine the validity of standardized test scores;

- copyright protection of standardized tests; and

- possible parental challenges to scoring and interpretation of tests by school psychologists and other school evaluators, including re-interpretation by parents' consultants.

Case example:
In a 1987 Illinois case, parents had requested access to their child's responses to a psychological exam. The lower court called the responses "personal notes," exempt from release under FERPA. On appeal, the responses were classified as "temporary education records" under state law, and found to be accessible to parents (*John K. and Mary K. v. Board of Education of School District #65, Cook County,* 1987).

The U.S. Department of Education has issued a variety of advisory letters concerning this issue:

- Rejecting an argument that the examiner's notes of a student's responses to questions were protected from parental access as "personal notes," the Department wrote that this material had been created by the student and the evaluator working together (Kelley, 1980).

- The Department wrote that test protocols that were "maintained in student files" were accessible to parents (Hill, 1981).

- In another letter, the Department wrote that parents had a right under FERPA to see their student's test answer sheet and a copy of the questions, and to have an explanation of the test (Letter, 1988).

- The Department's Family Policy Compliance Office, which is responsible for interpreting FERPA, and Office of Special Education Programs collaborated on a response to an inquiry which cited copyright protection of test questions as possibly precluding release. This response reaffirmed parental access, and cited the "Fair use" provision of the Copyright Act to permit limited copying of test questions (Thomas, 1986).

- The Office for Civil Rights has also found test protocols accessible for a special education hearing (Tri-County [IL] Special Education Cooperative, 1984).

In order to limit parental access to answer sheets, many school districts retain the sheets for a limited period of time, such as the school year in which the test was administered or 90 days after the test results have been provided to parents and discussed in an IEP meeting. OCR frowns on this approach.

OCR has ruled that protocols were accessible to parents and could not be destroyed (*In re St. Charles (IL) Community School District #303,* 1990).

Other interpretations have further muddied the waters—

- In 1993, the U.S. Department of Education wrote that test protocol sheets that did not contain any personally identifiable information [student name or identifying number] were not accessible to parents (MacDonald, 1993).

- In a New York case, the court found that state law restrictions on "psychiatric and psychological examination and evaluation records" prevented their release from health care providers in response to a school district subpoena (*In the Matter of a Handicapped Child,* 1983).

While requests to inspect or receive copies of the questions and a student's responses on standardized tests have been relatively few, psychologists and others who develop and administer these evaluative measures continue to argue that access beyond test scores and written professional interpretations should not be required, suggesting that answer sheets and the evaluator's rough notes be regarded as raw data or personal notes. FPCO has not been persuaded by this approach. For a detailed discussion of access to standardized tests under FERPA, see Rosenfeld, 1994.

Releasing Information from Education Records

With the exception of directory information, specific written consent from the parent or the adult student is required prior to the external release of any personally identifiable information from education records, and information so released may not be re-released without a new consent. School districts may define "Directory Information," and a district may elect to have *no* directory information available. FERPA defines "Directory Information" as

…information contained in an education record of a student which would not generally be considered harmful or an invasion of privacy if disclosed. It includes, but is not limited to the student's name, address, telephone listing, date and place of birth, major field of study, participation in officially recognized activities and sports, weight and height of members of athletic teams, dates of attendance, degrees and awards received, and the most recent previous educational agency or institution attended.

School districts must notify parents that they may request that information about an individual student be deleted from Directory Information. Increasing concerns about student safety have led many school districts to restrict the amount of information available as "directory information" and the individuals and groups to whom directory information may be released.

Consent for release of education records, and release of information from education records, must be obtained from the child's parent or guardian, or from a student who is 18 years old or older. A parent may request that copies of education records be released to his or her minor child. If a student over 18 is listed as a dependent on his or her parent's federal income tax return, that parent may have access to the student's records without consent from the adult student.

Exceptions to Consent Requirements

In the FERPA regulations, there are a few specific exceptions to the general requirement for parental consent prior to the release of a student's education records. For example, one exception to the parental consent-for-release requirement provides for disclosures to "state or local officials or authorities" as specified in state laws enacted prior to the passage of FERPA (November 19, 1974). Other exceptions in FERPA are discussed individually below. Consideration should also be given to specific state laws that preclude parental consent requirements for record release, such as suspected child abuse and neglect reporting laws, and others that may conflict with the FERPA parental consent requirement for the release of a student's education record. The latter include state minor consent to treatment provisions for mental health, drug and alcohol use, sexually transmitted infections, and reproductive health issues.

Except in life-threatening emergencies, school staff members should consult their supervisors and the attorney who represents the school district when they receive a request, without parental consent, for release of information from education records, including school health records. For a comprehensive summary of exceptions to the consent requirement with citations, see Zirkel (1997a).

Health and Safety Emergencies. FERPA provides for disclosure of confidential information about individual students in "health and safety emergencies." In general, "health and safety emergencies" refers to situations of immediate and serious danger, such as critical illness,

serious accident, or threatened homicide or suicide. For example, if the situation is serious enough to telephone for emergency services (call 9-1-1), release of sufficient student information to assist in emergency treatment is appropriate. Such release may be made only to "appropriate parties," and may be made only if knowledge of the specific information is "necessary to protect the health or safety of the student or other individuals."

The following two instances refer to cases where consent was deemed unnecessary because of the emergency that occasioned the medical care:

- The Family Policy Compliance Office (FPCO) of the U.S. Department of Education responded to a complaint concerning release of school information to a California child's physician without parental consent by finding that such a release could only occur in an emergency, in which the school staff member believed that the information being released was necessary for the health or safety of the student (Irvine Unified School District, 1996).

- In responding to an inquiry concerning identification to public health authorities of students who are suspected of having a reportable disease, FPCO found that these facts could be a health emergency. Release of information without parental consent was appropriate, with such release to be noted on the record access log (Barnett [personal communication], 1990).

Reporting Suspicion of Child Abuse and Neglect. FERPA allows school personnel to release information necessary to make reports of suspected abuse or neglect, as required by state law. (Child abuse reporting is discussed further under state laws below and in chapters 6 and 8.)

Student Transfers: District to District. FERPA provides for orderly transfer of records when a student moves from one school district to another. Parents must be given reasonable notice and an opportunity to review the records prior to transfer. However, the "sending" school does not need parental consent under FERPA, and parental requests to delete items from records to be transferred need not be honored, unless the challenged item is inaccurate, misleading, or in violation of the student's right of privacy (see below for amendments to records). The following two cases address problems concerning transfer of education records when students transfer to another school district:

- The Office of Special Education Programs of the U.S. Department of Education responded to an inquiry as to whether a school district is required to transfer a student's records when that student moves to another school district. The answer confirms that FERPA does not require such transfer (Kincaid, 1989).

- Maryland parents sued their former school district for release of education records including psychological reports to the school district to which they had moved. The court held that such release was not an invasion of privacy (*Klipa v. Board of Education of Anne Arundel County*, 1983).

School health records, and laws concerning their transfer, vary enormously from state to state. Since the student's health record from a prior district may be the best or only evidence of immunizations required for enrollment in a new school district, sending a copy to the new district can expedite enrollment.

The Washington State Department of Education Guidelines (Billings, Pearson, Carthum, & Maire, 1995) recommend that all information and copies of records received by the school from health care providers be kept separate from other education records, and be treated as health care records under state law. In this scheme, a specific parental consent would be required for transfer of health records to another school district. Another way to provide this level of protection is for the local school district to identify such records as requiring specific additional protections, including limiting internal access by school staff members.

The transfer of educational records for students who are incarcerated has often been problematic. In a class action concerning the rights of school-age prisoners in South Carolina, the court held that lack of access to student records, due to "reluctance" of school districts to send records to Corrections Department schools, interfered with the prisoners' right to educational services (*Bowers v. Boyd*, 1995).

Release to Law Enforcement Agencies. A 1994 amendment to FERPA and related amendments of the FERPA regulations in 1996 permit school districts to release student information to law enforcement agencies and to juvenile courts as provided by state law. If a student is involved in illegal activity or commits a crime at school, prompt referral to local police is encouraged and parental consent is not required.

Subpoenas and Court Orders. Education records may be released in response to a properly executed subpoena, provided that the school makes a reasonable effort to notify the parent of receipt of the subpoena. A subpoena is a written order to appear for a specific judicial proceeding, usually issued by an attorney for a party to the proceeding, or by a judge. It can be challenged by an appeal to the court, which may "quash" or void the subpoena, either if it was improperly written or served, or if the person upon whom it was served is protected by privilege (see below, and chapters 2 and 8). This notice provides time prior to release of the records for the parent to

- challenge the subpoena, including efforts to limit the scope of access; and

- exercise rights under FERPA to challenge material included in the education records to be released.

Case examples:
In a case addressing students' procedural rights, the court upheld the FERPA requirement that the school district notify parents of receipt of subpoenas for student records (*Mattie T. v. Johnson*, 1976).

In a class action concerning the effects of budget cuts at a New York State School for the Blind on services for individual children, the court upheld subpoenas issued to obtain student records, needed to show actual service reductions (*Gebhardt v. Ambach*, 1982).

The Connecticut Supreme Court has held that special education records and psychiatric records of two witnesses to a murder had been correctly barred from use to impeach the witnesses' testimony. In this case, the attorney for the defendant was unsuccessful in laying a foundation for the importance of admitting these documents. The director of special education was called as a witness, and she characterized the disabilities of the two witnesses in general terms. In this case, the witnesses' rights to privacy outweighed the defendant's argument for access (*State of Connecticut v. Martyn D. Bruno*, 1996).

In a similar New York case, the defendant in a sexual abuse trial attempted to use the victim's special education records: access to these records was denied by the court (*People of the State of New York v. Martin Manzanillo*, 1989).

FERPA also recognizes that student records must be released in response to an order from a judge or a grand jury. School staff members, including school nurses, should consult with their supervisors and the attorney who represents the school district prior to responding to a subpoena or a court order for education records.

Administration, Auditing, and Compliance. The FERPA regulations provide broad exceptions to the consent requirement for disclosure of education records to state and federal government officials responsible for supervising educational programs and auditing school funds. However, these exceptions apply only to officials within the education chain of command.

Case example:

In a case where the state comptroller requested access to student records for audit purposes, the court found no access under FERPA (*Board of Education of the City of New York v. Regan*, 1986).

It must be noted that the U.S. Department of Education requires retention of records concerning expenditures of federal funds for a period of at least three years after the completion of the funded program.

Educational Research. FERPA exempts from the consent requirement release of student information for specific educational research. The research must be within a narrow range, and the information must be used only for that research and must be destroyed after use. Best practice for school districts is the incorporation of approval by an institutional research committee for any research project, prior to consideration of release of data without consent. Such committees should be established by school district policy (if there is no state law addressing the issue) and should include representatives of the school system and the community. In some school districts, approval of staff research projects is available from the superintendent of schools. While this may prove an efficient method, it does not provide for an independent review.

Contractors' Records

It has been assumed that when a school district elects to provide education or support services by contract, contractors are bound by FERPA, for example, when a visiting nurse association or health department contract with a school district to operate and provide staffing for the school health services program. IDEA extends FERPA-type protections to special education contractors (see below).

School-based health centers (SBHCs), on the other hand, are operated by hospitals or community health clinics and provide services in school settings on a voluntary basis, but are NOT providing education or support services. Therefore, a school based health center that is operated independently in a school setting is not subject to FERPA. If the school based health center is operated directly by the school district, it is subject to FERPA. In that case, the district records policy should include the location of SBHC records and, access to such records should be limited to parents, adult students, school health staff, and counselors and social workers who are providing primary health and mental health services in the health center.

As mentioned above, when the school health services office is operated by contract, school health records are covered by FERPA, because they are: 1) related to students enrolled in the school; and 2) maintained because the children are enrolled in school.

Case example:

In a case where a mother attempted to secure access to juvenile court records that had been provided to the school board's attorney, the court ordered the board to release the records to the parent. Although the records were actually in the custody of an attorney, they were found to fall under FERPA because they had been released to the Board of Education, in the person of its attorney (*Belanger v. Nashua, New Hampshire, School District*, 1994).

Parental Requests to Amend Education Records

Under FERPA, parents may challenge information that is "inaccurate, misleading, or in violation of the student's rights of privacy" (34 C.F.R. § 99.20 (1996)). If a parent's request to amend the record is refused, the parent may request a hearing. A hearing officer for FERPA matters may be anyone who does not have an interest in the outcome of the case; school districts frequently designate an administrator without prior contact with the student or parent. If the parent's request is denied by the hearing officer, the parent may submit a written statement of his or her position on the challenged material, which must be filed with the challenged record and must be released with that record whenever it is released. For a discussion of the legislative history of this provision of FERPA and a few court cases concerning attempts to use FERPA to "correct" grades and related academic sanctions in higher education, see Baker (1997).

Case example:

In a case which reached the Fifth Circuit Court of Appeals, parents had challenged the special education classification of their children as "Mentally Retarded." The court upheld the school district's refusal to amend this record, because the classification was not inaccurate (*Carter v. Orleans Parish Public Schools*, 1984). This case supports a school nurse's position that specific diagnoses, symptoms, and other medical information in school health records, accurate at the time recorded, should not be altered in response to parental requests.

FERPA Complaints and Court Actions

Complaints concerning compliance with FERPA may be filed with the Family Policy Compliance Office (FPCO) in the U.S. Department of Education. FERPA does not provide access to the courts, although a few FERPA cases have succeeded under 42 U.S.C. §1983, a broad civil rights statute offering relief for violation of federal law by a public official. The penalty for proven violations of FERPA is the possible loss of federal funding. Enforcement procedures include investigation and an opportunity for a hearing.

Case example:
A family attempted to gain relief for publication of information about their child after personally identifiable information about reimbursement for travel expenses related to an out-of-district special education placement was recorded in public board of education minutes, as required by state law. An initial complaint to the Family Policy Compliance Office led to a finding that the Board had violated FERPA (Greater Hoyt School Board, 1993). Unsatisfied, the parent sued the school district. This lawsuit failed for a variety of technical reasons, but the court did find that §1983 provides legal access to the courts for FERPA violations (*Maynard v. Greater Hoyt School District*, 1995).

For a discussion of this case and related issues, see Zirkel (1997b).

Individuals with Disabilities Education Act (IDEA)

The basic elements of the FERPA scheme are also incorporated into the Individuals with Disabilities Education Act (IDEA), although regulations for these sections of IDEA include a few differences from FERPA. While FERPA applies only to education agencies receiving federal funds, the IDEA confidentiality provisions apply to all agencies involved in the special education process. This process includes identifying children with disabilities who may be in need of special education, evaluating them, and providing a free appropriate public education to those who are found eligible. Thus the records of a student with disabilities who is evaluated for a school district by a medical team in a hospital setting, and the records of a student with disabilities who has been placed in a private school by a school district would both be under IDEA and FERPA protection. The state education agency is also required, under IDEA, to give prior notice to parents concerning data collection necessary for monitoring of IDEA Child Find requirements. (See chapter 12 for more details concerning special education.)

The confidentiality requirements of IDEA exceed FERPA by requiring that the following occur:

- parents be informed that data about a student is being collected;

- parents be provided access to their student's education records prior to any meeting regarding an IEP [Individualized Education Program] or any hearing related to the identification, evaluation, or educational placement of the child;

- school personnel be trained regarding these requirements;

- names and positions of school staff members with access to student records be identified in school district policy; and

- a copy of procedures concerning destruction of education records be provided to parents, including the rights of a parent to request destruction when notified that information is no longer needed by the school for educational purposes.

The IDEA confidentiality and records provisions are significant "procedural rights" for parents of children with disabilities. Special education hearing officers and courts reviewing special education appeals consider compliance with the procedural requirements of IDEA to be one of two important tests which the school district must meet in providing a free appropriate public education to a child with disabilities. (See chapters 12 and 13.)

When considering providing notice to parents that special education records are no longer needed, school district staff must also meet federal auditing requirements that records of programs which have received federal funds must be retained for at least three years after completion of the program. (See chapters 2 and 12.)

Information Concerning Substance Abuse Treatment

A federal law encourages schools to provide assistance to students with drug and alcohol abuse problems. Student

Assistance Programs (SAPs) in public schools, developed to offer counseling and referrals for treatment for students with substance abuse problems, stress confidentiality for the student seeking assistance. Because maintaining absolute student confidentiality is a direct conflict with parental rights to access all education records under FERPA, in 1990 the U.S. Department of Education and the Alcohol, Drug Abuse and Mental Health Administration issued a joint memorandum to clarify students' confidentiality rights in federally funded Student Assistance Programs. Three options to resolve this conflict were suggested (Sullivan & Rooker, 1990):

1. Students could be asked or required to consent to their parents' access to SAP records upon entry into the program;
2. Student SAP records could be released only with written consent from the student or in response to court orders; or
3. SAPs should minimize record keeping.

None of these options is ideal. State laws regarding the confidentiality of drug and alcohol treatment records vary but reflect the federal requirements. (See chapter 8 for further discussion.)

STATE LAWS

"State FERPA"

Most states have some legal provisions concerning student records. While federal law (i.e., FERPA) has pre-empted this area, states may establish higher standards, and they may address areas not covered by FERPA. Examples include an Illinois definition for "temporary records" that will be destroyed at the end of the school year or sooner, and a Connecticut law requiring that education records which have been subpoenaed be kept confidential within court records. This Connecticut provision extends FERPA protections into the courthouse.

Reporting of Suspected Child Abuse

In compliance with the federal Child Abuse Prevention and Treatment Act of 1974, states now have laws concerning reporting of suspected child abuse and neglect, which make health care providers, teachers, and other school employees "mandated reporters." Reports of suspected child abuse, made to a child care agency or the police, are given confidentiality protection. Several cases have raised issues of parental access under FERPA versus the confidentiality of mandated reports of suspected child abuse. In response to a question

concerning parental access to the school's copy of a state form used to report suspected child abuse, the Family Policy Compliance Office (FPCO) advised in 1994 that while parents do have a right of access, the school may remove the name of the reporter from the copy of the form provided for parental inspection. (Sibner, 1994).

Case examples:

In one case related to the reporting of suspected abuse, the court upheld the immunity from suit of school staff and child welfare workers who care investigating suspected child sexual abuse, but found some violations of state procedures (*Tenenbaum v. Williams*, 1994).

In another case in which a family member was accused of sexual abuse of an emotionally disturbed 12 year old, a lower court quashed the subpoena for the victim's school records. On appeal, the victim's school records were found "evidentially relevant" and the subpoena was upheld (*Zaal v. State*, 1992).

Another growing group of cases addresses the question of whether a school staff member who has been accused of child abuse may have the record expunged when investigation showed insufficient evidence to sustain a finding of abuse. The circumstances of these cases, usually tried under state law, are too varied to draw conclusions at this time (*S. M. v. State of Florida Department of Health and Rehabilitative Services, 1995*, and *Korunda v. Department of Children and Family Services*, 1994).

Reports of suspected abuse by a teacher aside, as a general principle, reports of suspected abuse and neglect should be maintained in the student's file, as should documentation of the results of the child protection agency (CPA) investigation that tell whether a case is opened. Documentation of repeated reports of suspicion may be important information for the CPA or court in determining whether abuse or neglect is occurring and whether intervention is required (Connecticut State Department of Education, 1994; Schwab, 1989). (For additional information concerning reporting of suspected child abuse, see Chapters 6, 7, and 8.)

Retention and Destruction of Records of Public Agencies

Education records are also records of a public agency (local board of education) and are subject to state laws concerning maintenance of records (retention) and destruction of records no longer required by the public agency. Some states have statewide record destruction schedules; others simply require that local school district schedules meet state standards. A general example of state requirements is as follows:

- A minimal amount of information (attendance and graduation) about students must be retained forever;

- Significant items such as high school transcripts must be retained for 50 years; and

- All other records may be destroyed within five years of graduation or, for a student who transferred to another school district, within five years of the date of graduation had he or she remained in the district.

State public records administrators interpret state records laws, and make rulings under those laws.

In an appeal of a ruling by the Florida state pubic records authority by parents wishing to prevent destruction of a complaint they had brought concerning their child's special education program, the court found the case "not ripe" for adjudication, since the particular record was not yet due for destruction (*L. R. v. Department of State*, 1986).

Another concern here is the state statute of limitations for legal actions concerning health care provided by licensed health care professionals, such as school nurses and occupational, physical, and speech/language therapists. When a local school district develops policy concerning retention and destruction of education records, it is best practice to include a category of school health records that will be retained for at least the period of this statute of limitations.

Because school records of a child's disabilities may be valuable to former students and their families in establishing the history and extent of disability, school districts should provide an opportunity for records to be claimed by former students at the point of destruction. This is usually arranged by using legal notices in the local newspaper, such as the following:

Class of 1950 Records will be destroyed on or about June 30, 2000, unless claimed by individual former students. Persons wishing to claim their school records may make written application to [name and address of school administrator].

Federal Issues Can Complicate State Law Interpretation

When a school district has received federal funding for a program, records of that program must be maintained for at least three years after completion of the program for audit and compliance purposes.

FERPA includes no requirements concerning destruction of education records. IDEA includes a section that gives parents the right to request destruction of records when notified that such records are "no longer needed to provide educational services to the child" (34 C.F.R. § 300.573 (1999)). Although this regulation has a note which discusses reasons for permanent retention of special education records, there is no clear indication whether the audit and compliance retention periods are considered a part of "providing educational services," or whether data with personal identifiers deleted are acceptable for audit and compliance purposes.

The few published interpretations are too narrow to provide general guidance concerning the discretion of school staff members to retain or destroy records in response to parental requests. FERPA provides that a school district may, through an appointed hearing officer, refuse to agree to a parental request to amend an education record. Education records may also be important for unrelated purposes, including auditing and litigation.

In response to an inquiry from a Wyoming school district, the Office of Special Education Programs of the U.S. Department of Education advised that when parents have been notified that records are no longer needed to serve a student with disabilities pursuant to IDEA, the information must be destroyed at the request of the parent (Purcell, 1987).

A special education hearing officer may also interpret the IDEA provisions which incorporate, and in some cases expand, FERPA:

A Texas state special education hearing officer ordered destruction of records retained longer than the five year audit period. [The retention period was subsequently shortened to three years.] (Klein Independent School District, 1990).

Freedom of Information Acts (FOIA)

Many states now have Freedom of Information laws intended to ease public access to meetings and records of public agencies. While public school districts are public agencies, student records are usually among the categories of records excluded from public access under state law. If not specifically excluded, student records are protected under FERPA, which pre-empts state law by imposing stricter standards.

FOIA laws are often referred to as "Sunshine Laws" or "Right to Know Laws;" however, there is no state or federal right to know a student's education information. When a school maintains Directory Information (see above, FERPA disclosures), members of the public may request access under a state's FOIA. Some school districts have local policies that restrict release of Directory Information to individuals and organizations with valid interests, such as boy and girl scout groups, public recreation programs for children, etc. Other districts will accept for distribution to students material about these types of organizations, providing students' access to information without release of student information.

When student information is recorded in Board of Education minutes or other documents which are properly accessible under FOIA, problems will result. In the case of *Maynard v. Greater Hoyt School District* (1995), discussed above, details about the placement of a student with disabilities were included in Board minutes because the parents had requested reimbursement for transportation of the child. Most school districts have adopted the use of confidential student numbers when necessary, and make a practice of not recording individual student identification in minutes of Board meetings or records of payment for services.

HEALTH CARE INFORMATION LAWS

While the traditional general confidentiality of all communications between doctor and patient remains an ethical model, there are several areas in which this confidential relationship has changed. The most significant change is the powerful role played by insurers and other third-party payors of health care costs. Whenever a patient makes a claim for payment, the patient must also consent to the release of confidential information related to that claim. For a discussion of access to medical records see Shapiro & Annas (1994).

Concerns about whether patients approving release of information for an insurance claim should have separate notice of and an opportunity to deny access for other unrelated use or sale of their individual medical data have led to the introduction of a variety of bills in the U.S. Congress, most recently included within "Patients' Bill of Rights" proposals. As this book goes to press, Congress has not acted on this matter, and many state legislatures are discussing increased confidentiality protection for health care records. If federal law is enacted in this area, state laws may be at least partially pre-empted. (See also chapter 10.)

Federal law does protect confidentiality of information concerning the following: students participating in Student Assistance Programs for drug and alcohol abuse problems (see above); identity of students receiving free and low-cost school lunches; and a few other

categories of students receiving federal aid (see Rosenfeld, et al. 1997). The only other federal requirements with impact on student health care records are Medicaid provisions concerning confidentiality and consent for release. These Medicaid provisions must be addressed by states and school districts establishing systems for making claims for Medicaid reimbursement for related school health services provided to students with disabilities.

Until recently, both education and health care were considered to be areas reserved for state regulation under Article 10 of the U.S. Constitution. FERPA technically supplanted conflicting state laws concerning confidentiality and record-keeping practices for public schools.

All states, to varying degrees, regulate the confidentiality of health care records. (See chapter 8 for a detailed discussion of the reasons for providing confidentiality for health care records, and see also Siegler, 1996).

Traditionally, states did not require a physician to reveal treatment records to the patient; many states today, however, have passed laws to provide for patient access. Some states allow a physician or mental health care provider to limit access to material thought to be prejudicial to the patient's health or mental stability; in this case, the patient may be able to designate another physician to review the record. For additional discussion, see chapters 7 and 8, and also English, Matthews, Extavour, Palamountain, & Yang (1995).

The states of Massachusetts and Washington have classified health care records that have been released to schools and nursing or treatment records of care provided in schools as continuing to fall under the state health care record confidentiality requirements (Goodman & Sheetz [1995]; and Billings, Pearson, Carthum, & Maire [1995]). Local school districts may adopt policies that provide for the same level of confidentiality protection, including limiting internal access.

School districts provide for internal access to student records by defining in policy and procedures, by title, those staff members with a "legitimate educational interest." In school districts without nursing supervisors, in school buildings without full-time school nurses, and as a matter of general school supervision, building principals may have traditionally had access to school health records and, indeed, to all records within their buildings. While this may be considered a practical necessity to insure service delivery and communication of vital information in emergencies, records released from outside health care providers should be filed separately and not be accessible to other school staff members unless specific parental consent has been obtained.

In part because of increasing concerns about the security of electronically transmitted health information and in part because of the delay in Congressional action to protect the confidentiality of patients' health care information, many state legislatures are considering health care information acts which may incorporate a 1985 Model Act developed by the National Conference of Commissioners on Uniform State Laws. For the health care professionals' views of these issues, see Woodward, 1995; Council on Scientific Affairs, 1993; and Cassidy & Sepulveda, 1995. Current bills under consideration in several states include confidentiality protection by any and all "custodians" of health care information, which includes public schools. School nurses and administrators should keep current on their state's progress in strengthening state laws protecting health care information. (See chapter 10 for further information on electronic records, legislation and legal issues.)

RECORD KEEPING IN SCHOOL HEALTH OFFICES

Professional Medical and Nursing Documentation Standards

School nurses learn systems of documentation primarily required in health care settings. These requirements have evolved with the practice of medicine and nursing (Gelfman & Schwab, 1991). Currently, confidential health records are defined and regulated by 1) the individual hospital, clinic, medical practice, health maintenance organization, or home health nursing agency; 2) state law and regulations; 3) federal requirements for Medicare and Medicaid; and 4) the rules of accrediting organizations, such as the Joint Commission on the Accreditation of Healthcare Organizations, and of related organizations, such as the American Health Information Management Association. With the growing role of insurers and third-party payors for health care services, additional requirements for specific data and format may be necessary to expedite the processing of claims. Because of the special requirements of school health, the National Association of School Nurses (NASN) has published *Guidelines for School Nursing Documentation* (Schwab, Panettieri, & Bergren, 1998). These guidelines list the primary objectives of documentation in school nursing practice:

- promotion of high-quality student health services;

- advancement of efficient and effective school health services programs; and

- creation of a legal record of nursing services provided to students.

The NASN guidelines also provide a more specific list of purposes for maintaining school health records, as defined by Kozier, Erb, Blais, & Wilkinson (1995):

- communication;

- legal evidence;

- research;

- education;

- quality assurance monitoring;

- statistics;

- accrediting and licensing; and

- reimbursement.

The NASN *Guidelines* recognize that good documentation is fundamental to good nursing care: From a legal perspective in the health care setting, "if it wasn't documented, it wasn't done." NASN's basic principles of documentation are useful in helping other school staff members understand the similarities and differences between nursing and medical documentation versus educational documentation. (See Figure 9-1.) The NASN *Guidelines* also discuss errors in documentation. (See Figure 9-2.)

Refer to the NASN *Guidelines* for in-depth information on standards of documentation in school nursing, related legal issues, principles for electronic record keeping, and models for adaptation to everyday practice (Schwab et al., 1998).

Changes to Medical Records

Another requirement of medical record keeping that nurses incorporate into their documentation is that health records are cumulative, chronological, and must not be changed. If an error is discovered or a diagnosis added or changed, that information is entered on the record on the appropriate date. The old diagnosis, even when in error, remains on the record as evidence of what occurred or was fact at the time. Therefore, corrections do not result in the expunging of the material corrected. Such alteration, if permitted, would undermine the accuracy of medical records by destroying factual records based on information available at the time of the original documentation.

When school health records are subject to FERPA, parents may use the FERPA provision providing for amendment of education records. Although the FERPA provision limits amendments to situations where the record is inaccurate, misleading, or in violation of the

Figure 9-1.

BASIC PRINCIPLES OF DOCUMENTATION

- Nursing documentation should be accurate, objective, concise, thorough, timely, and well organized.
- All entries should be legible and written in ink (for computerized records, see chapter 10).
- The date and exact time should be included with each entry.
- Documentation should include any nursing action taken in response to a student's problem.
- Assessment data should include significant findings, both positive and negative.
- All records, progress notes, individualized health care plans, and flow charts should be kept current.
- Documentation should include only essential information; precise measurements, correct spelling, and standard abbreviations (only those identified in [school] district procedures) should be used.
- School nursing documentation should be based on nursing classification languages and include uniform client data sets (yet to be defined for school health services).
- The frequency of documentation should be consistent over time and based on district policy, nursing protocols, and the acuity of the student's health status.
- Standardized health care plans increase efficiency of documentation and are acceptable to use so long as they are adapted to the individualized needs of each student.
- Student symptoms, concerns, and health maintenance questions (subjective data) should be documented in the student's own words.
- Only facts (objective data) relevant to the student's care and clinical nursing judgments based on such facts should be recorded; personal judgments and opinions of the nurse should be omitted. For example, "the student is breathing normally" is an opinion, whereas the notation "respirations 20/min.; no retractions, rales or wheezing" provides objective data.

Adapted with permission of the National Association of School Nurses (NASN). Schwab, N., Panettieri, MJ, & Bergren, MD. (1998). *Guidelines for School Nursing Documentation: Standards, Issues and Models,* 2nd ed. Scarborough, ME: NASN.

Figure 9-2.

ERRORS IN DOCUMENTATION

- References to district problems, including staffing shortages, should never be included in student records.
- Terms suggestive of an error should not be used, for example, "accidentally" or "by mistake"; state only the facts of what occurred.
- When an error is made, one single line should be drawn through the error; the word "error" and the nurse's signature should be written directly above it. The correct entry should then follow. Words should never be erased or scratched or whited out.
- When an entry is made in the wrong student's record, the entry should be marked "mistake in entry," and a line drawn through the mistaken entry, as above.
- Late entries should be avoided. When necessary, a late entry may be added, but in the correct date and time sequence. (For example, write today's date and time when entering a note related to care provided yesterday afternoon and mark it "late entry.")

Used with permission of the National Association of School Nurses (NASN). Schwab, N., Panettieri, MJ, & Bergren, MD. (1998). *Guidelines for School Nursing Documentation: Standards, Issues and Models,* 2nd ed. Scarborough, ME: NASN.

student's rights of privacy, there is a direct conflict between FERPA procedures and medical records procedures when the documentary record is questioned by a parent. As a rule, the school nurse should discuss parental requests for amendments with a school administrator and nursing supervisor. If the parent's request for amendment is denied by the school after a hearing, parents retain the FERPA right to insert a statement of their position in the record. The 1984 case of *Carter v. Orleans Parish Public Schools*, discussed above, where parents appealed their children's classification as mentally retarded under FERPA, supports the right of school districts to insist that properly developed, accurate information about students be retained in school records. In this case, the Fifth Circuit held that accurate information was not subject to parental amendment under FERPA.

Record-keeping Issues

To some degree, the record-keeping system used and the location of the school health records will dictate the methods available to insure confidentiality. In a school setting, filing cabinets do not automatically come with locks. Thus, the first step for compliance with FERPA is often a budgetary step toward locked files. Security is a critical issue with electronic records, as well as paper records, and is discussed in chapter 10. The immediate dilemma in the school health office is balancing access to records, to insure appropriate treatment in emergencies, with protection against inappropriate access. In order to provide appropriate levels of protection for student records, many school systems use a classification system based on research by the Russell Sage Foundation (1969). In most cases, three categories of records are recognized:

A. Permanent records showing dates of attendance, grades, graduation, and honors.
B. Temporary records or rough drafts which will be discarded relatively soon; and
C. Highly confidential records, such as results of standardized testing, psychological and psychiatric evaluations, and records disclosed from other agencies.

School systems designate internal access to each category, providing greater protection and limits on access to records assigned to category C. As school nurses and other pupil services providers have become custodians of highly sensitive records, in many cases released from health care providers and including information protected under specific state laws, school health offices are responsible for materials that fall within both category A and category C. School nurses have developed systems for discreet cross referencing, alerting school

health office staff to the existence of additional information about a student, while limiting access to those with a recognized need to know.

Most often, information that other school personnel need to know in order to serve students should be included in an emergency care plan written for school personnel, a Section 504 plan, an individualized education program (IEP), and written instructions for care providers. Also, the standard health record (card), containing basic information for school attendance, such as immunizations and dates and results of screenings, may be accessible to the school principal and health assistant. On the other hand, without the written consent of the parent (and student in some cases), direct access to category C health records, which can include nursing and third party medical records obtained for health services reasons, should be limited to the school nurse, the school nurse's clinical supervisor (nurse or physician), substitute nurse, a school medical advisor, parent, student and university student nurse (with faculty supervisor and under contract).

This type of records system, with appropriate safeguards, can be constructed to be similar to the systems employed by the Multnomah Education Service District in Portland, Oregon, and the states of Washington and Massachusetts, as discussed earlier under FERPA, "Internal Access to Education Records," and later in this section. Variations may be necessary, based on staffing, but the same principles of "need to know" limited to what is needed "for the benefit of the student," as well as consideration of the purpose of different records and who has the expertise to interpret them, should form the foundation and rationale for any school health records system.

When parents provide consent for release of health care records to a school district, it is best practice to inform the health care provider that FERPA access will apply to records included within the school files. For example, a cover letter with the parental consent-to-release form could state:

> Records of individual students are protected by FERPA, a federal law. This law provides that parents have access to ALL records concerning their children. Under FERPA, the school district determines which members of the school staff have a legitimate educational interest in access to which records. In this school district, access to health care records released from health care providers is limited to health care professionals on the school staff, the school principal, and the director of special education and pupil personnel services.

Health care providers wishing to shield information from a parent or adult student should be discouraged from sending it to a school; rather, they should delete it from records that are copied, or they should write a letter or memo which summarizes only information necessary for school personnel to provide appropriate educational programming and health support services in school.

Concerning internal access by other school staff members, two approaches should be considered to implement restrictions to information and records sent to schools by health care providers. The first is the use of the most protective classification provided by the school district records policy. Using a "C" classification, the policy should limit access to information and records from health care providers to professional school health personnel, as discussed above, and, when indicated, one or two administrators. Such records should be stored in a separate locked file. To insure adequate care, reference to "C" material might be made in the regular school health record, an Individualized Health Care Plan (if there is one), and Individualized Education Plan (IEP) (for students receiving special education services) or a § 504 service plan, for students requiring accommodations because of disabilities.

The second approach, used by Washington and Massachusetts and the Multnomah Education Service District in Oregon and others, maintains that records from health care providers and "nursing records" generated in school remain protected under state law as medical, not education, records. This approach, supported by a comprehensive array of state laws, leads to limiting routine access to ONLY licensed health care providers (and, of course, parents and students). Access to the health records by school education staff requires a specific consent from the parent or adult student. However, the school nurse can share functional health information that is educationally relevant, based on interpretation of the health record (for further information on functional health information, see chapter 8, Hootman, 1996a & 1996b, and Schwab et al., 1998). The advantage of this approach is that it maintains the level of protection provided for health care records under state law at their point of origin, but also supports the sharing of relevant information. Medical records law reform has recently expanded the access rights of adult patients and the parents and guardians of minor patients in many states, making parental access rights to medical and education records more similar. As this is an area of legal change, current state laws should be consulted for accurate information.

Of particular concern in the school health office is the log maintained of all student visits. Traditionally, this documentation was a chronological record of students visiting the office, with notes of their complaints, and any assessment or intervention provided. While this form of record keeping was simple and gave a general picture of activity in the health office, it presented two significant problems. Under FERPA, parents have access to their children's records, but not to those of other students; even finding one student's "record of health room visits" over time was nearly impossible. Perhaps more important, however, is that this type of documentation is entirely incompatible with standards of clinical practice for nurses and standards of nursing documentation that support quality care. Scattered entries about an individual student were difficult to track and to access whenever the student sought care from the school nurse, and did not support the nursing process. Current and evolving practice is the use of individual cards, paper files, or computer files for each student.

When a student has on-going medical problems that require the development and use of an Individualized Health Care Plan in school, such plans and necessary supporting documentation are usually kept in individual loose leaf notebooks or computer files for each student. The computerization of school health records, as in other settings, raises unique issues of confidentiality and record keeping. These issues are addressed in chapter 10.

Staffing and Confidentiality Concerns

As more students require a variety of health services in school, the demands on the school health office are also addressed in numerous ways. A minority of public school districts have full-time professional school nurses available in every school building throughout the school day. Due to budgetary restrictions and times or places where there have been shortages of nurses, schools have used other personnel to extend coverage. (See chapters 4 and 5.) Sometimes a paraprofessional, frequently called a "health aide" or a "health assistant", will assist in staffing the health office. Such paraprofessionals are supervised by a school nurse; whether they have any formal training varies by state and school district.

Classroom teachers have also been given added responsibilities. In Connecticut, a classroom teacher is permitted to give medications to students under certain circumstances. They must have general and student specific training and be under the supervision of a school nurse; furthermore, appropriate documentation from physician and parent and a supply of medication must be provided.

In situations where no school nurse is available, the issue of who has access to school health records becomes significant in terms of safety, privacy, and accurate interpretation of medical content. Paraprofessional staff assigned to the school health office must be instructed in the importance of confidentiality and the laws regarding protection of student records. In the absence of regular staffing of the health office, school staff members assigned to work with children who require health support services may require training and on-going supervision both in health care techniques and in access to and use of confidential information in the health records of those students.

Schools relying on adult or student volunteers for health office coverage must carefully define both the confidentiality requirements and access to student records for volunteers. Given that student health office contacts must be recorded, volunteers must also be trained in the requirements of such documentation. Parent volunteers present special issues because they may know and socialize with the families of other children in the school. Jobs requiring access to the confidential health files of students may not be an appropriate assignment for parent volunteers, even with training.

COLLABORATION WITH OTHER AGENCIES SERVING CHILDREN

The IDEA includes provisions concerning the necessity of collaboration between schools and other agencies providing services to children. Interagency agreements are encouraged as one means of facilitating collaboration. The issue of confidentiality of specific student information must be taken into account in establishing interagency agreements or any collaborative project.

In wide use is consultation utilizing hypothetical cases (see chapter 8). The actual identity of the child is not revealed, but specific information, such as age and medical diagnosis, is used in requesting advice or information about available community services. While this technique may be useful in preliminary inquiries, it is better practice to secure parental consent to release information prior to a search for community services or alternative school placements. The minimal information given in a hypothetical may not provide an accurate picture of the child. For example, inquiries about services for a student with a particular disability may be incomplete without the child's age, as many programs are age-limited. For further discussion of problems in sharing information between agencies, see Joining Forces, American Public Welfare Association, Center for Law and Social Policy, Council of Chief State School Officers, and Education Commission of the States (1992).

REFERENCES

Baker, T. R. (1997). Inaccurate and misleading: student hearing rights under FERPA. *West's Education Law Reporter 114:* 721–742.

Billings, J., Pearson, J., Carthum, H., & Maire, J. (1995). *Guidelines for handling health care information in school records.* Olympia, WA: Superintendent of Public Instruction.

Boomer, L. W., Hartshorne, T. S., & Robertshaw, C. S. (1995). Confidentiality and student records: A hypothetical case. *Preventing School Failure 39:* 15, 21.

Cassidy, S. O., & Sepulveda, M. J. (1995). Health information privacy reform. *Journal of Occupational and Environmental Medicine* (JOEM) *37(5):* 605–614.

Cheung, O., Clements, B., & Pechman, E. (1997). *Protecting the privacy of student records: Guidelines for education agencies.* Washington, DC: Council of Chief State School Officers.

Connecticut State Department of Education (1994). *Guidelines for the Development of School District Policy and Procedures: Reporting of Child Abuse and Neglect, Youth Suicide Prevention and Youth Suicide Attempts.* Middletown, CT: Author.

Council on Scientific Affairs. (1993). Users and uses of patient records. *Archives of Family Medicine 2:* 678–681.

English, A., Matthews, M., Extavour, K., Palamountain, C., & Yang, J. (1995). *State minor consent statutes: A summary.* Cincinnati: Center for Continuing Education in Adolescent Health.

Fischer, L., & Sorenson, G. P. (1996). *School law for counselors, psychologists and social workers* (3rd ed.). White Plains, NY: Longman.

Gelfman, M. H., & Schwab, N. C. (1991). School health services and education records: conflicts in the law. *West's Education Law Reporter 64:* 319–338 (Jan. 31, 1991).

Goodman, I. F., & Sheetz, A. H. (Eds.). (1995). *The comprehensive school health manual.* Boston: Massachusetts State Department of Education.

Hill, Education of the Handicapped Law Report (EHLR) (LRP Publications) *211:* 259 (OSEP 1981).

Hootman, J. (1996a). *Quality nursing interventions in the school setting: Procedures, models and guidelines.* Scarborough, ME: National Association of School Nursing.

Hootman, J. (1996b). *Nursing diagnosis: Application in the school setting.* Scarborough, ME: National Association of School Nursing.

Ingram, 23 Individuals with Disabilities Education Law Report (IDELR) (LRP) 445 (OSEP 1995).

Johnson, T. P., Managing student records: the courts and the Family Educational Rights and Privacy Act of 1974. *West's Education Law Reporter 79*: 1 (Feb. 11, 1993).

Joining Forces, American Public Welfare Association, Center for Law and Social Policy, Council of Chief State School Officers, and Education Commission of the States [a joint publication of]. (1992). *Confidentiality and collaboration: Information sharing in interagency efforts*. Denver: Education Commission of the States Distribution Center.

Kelley, EHLR (LRP) 211:240 (OSEP 1980).

Kincaid, EHLR (LRP) 213:271 (OSEP 1989).

Klein Independent School District, 17 EHLR (LRP) 259 (TX SEA 1990).

Kozier, B., Erb, G., Blais, K., & Wilkinson, J. (1995). *Fundamentals of nursing: Concepts, process and practice*. Redwood City, CA: Addison-Wesley Publishing Co.

Letter, EHLR (LRP) 213:188 (OSEP 1988).

Letter to Thomas, EHLR 211:420 (OSEP 1986).

MacDonald, Letter to, 20 IDELR (LRP) 1159 (OSEP 1993).

Mawdsley, R. D. (1996). Litigation involving FERPA. *West's Education Law Reporter 110*: 897–914.

National Conference of Commissioners on Uniform State Laws. (1985). Uniform Health-Care Information Act. Approved by the American Bar Association 1986. Chicago: National Conference of Commissioners of Uniform State Laws.

Purcell, EHLR (LRP) 211:462 (OSEP 1987).

Rosenfeld, S. J. Must school districts provide test protocols to parents? *EDLAW Briefing Paper*, May 1994.

Rosenfeld, S. J., Gelfman, M. H., & Bluth, L. F. (1997). *Education records: A manual*. Hollywood, FL: EDLAW, Inc.

Russell Sage Foundation. (1969, May). *Guidelines for the collection, maintenance, and dissemination of pupils' records: Report of a conference on the ethical and legal aspects of school record keeping* (conference held at Sterling Forest, New York). New York: Author.

Schwab, N. C. (1989). Child abuse and neglect: Legal and clinical implications for school nursing practice. *School Nurse, 5*(4), 17–28.

Schwab, N. C., & Gelfman, M. H. (1991). School health records: nursing practice and the law. *School Nurse, 7*(2): 11–21.

Schwab, N. C., Panettieri, M. J., & Bergren, M. D. (1998). *Guidelines for school nursing documentation: Standards, issues, and models* (2nd ed.). Scarborough, ME: National Association of School Nurses.

Shapiro, R., & Annas, G. (1994). Who sees your medical records? *21 Human Rights 10*, Summer 1994.

Siegler, G. E. (1996). What should be the scope of privacy protections for student health records? A look at Massachusetts and federal law. *Journal of Law and Education 25*(2): 237–269.

Soler, N. I., Shotten, A. C., & Bell, J. R. (1993). *Glass walls: Confidentiality provisions and interagency collaboration*. San Francisco: Youth Law Center.

Student records policies and procedures for the Alpha School District. (1976). Washington, DC: U.S. Department of Education.

Sullivan, F., & Rooker, L. (1990). *School-based Student Assistance Programs: Reconciling federal regulations under the Family Educational Rights and Privacy Act and the Alcohol and Drug Abuse Confidentiality Statutes*, joint memorandum of the United States Department of Education and the Alcohol, Drug Abuse, and Mental Health Administration of the U.S. Department of Health and Human Services (Washington, DC, Sept. 26).

Woodward, B. (1995). The computer-based patient record and confidentiality. *New England Journal of Medicine (NEJM) 333*: 1419-1422.

Zirkel, P. A. (1997a). Disclosure of student records: A comprehensive overview. *The Special Educator 12*: 1.

Zirkel, P. A. (1997b). Caught in the collision: A disabled child's rights to confidentiality and the news media's right to "sunshine." *West's Education Law Reporter 117*: 429-433.

TABLE OF CASES

Aufox v. Board of Education, 588 N.E.2d 316, 18 IDELR (LRP) 727 (Ill. App. Ct. 1992).

Belanger v. Nashua, New Hampshire, School District, 21 IDELR (LRP) 429 (D. N.H. 1994).

Board of Education of the City of New York v. Regan, 500 N.Y.S.2d 978 (Sup. 1986).

Bowers v. Boyd, 22 IDELR (LRP) 139 (D. S.C. 1995).

Carter v. Orleans Parish Public Schools, 725 F.2d 261, EHLR (LRP) 555:419 (5th Cir. 1984).

Fay v. South Colonie Central School District, 802 F.2d 21 (2nd Cir. 1986).

Gebhardt v. Ambach, EHLR (LRP) Dec. 554:336 (W.D. N.Y. 1982).

In the Matter of a Handicapped Child, 460 N.Y.S.2d 256, EHLR (LRP) Dec. 554:477 (Sup. Ct. N.Y. 1983).

John K. and Mary K. v. Board of Education of School District #65, Cook County, 105 Ill. Dec.512, 504 N.E.2d 797 (Ill. App. I Dist. 1987).

Klipa v. Board of Education of Anne Arundel County, 460 A.2d 601 (Md. Ct. Spec. App. 1983).

Korunda v. Department of Children and Family Services, 197 Ill. Dec. 537, 631 N.E.2d 759 (Ill. App. 4 Dist. 1994).

L. R. v. Department of State, Division of Archives, History and Records Management, inter alia, 488 So.2d 122 (Fla. App. 3 Dist. 1986).

Mattie T. v. Johnson, 74 F.R.D. 498 (N.D. Miss. 1976).

Maynard v. Greater Hoyt School District, 876 F. Supp. 1104, 22 IDELR (LRP) 428 (D. S.D. 1995).

Parents Against Abuse in Schools v. Williamsport Area School District, 594 A.2d 796 (Pa. Cmwlth. 1991).

People of the State of New York v. Martin Manzanillo, 546 N.Y.S. 2d 954 (N.Y. City Crim. Ct. 1989).

S-1 v. Turlington, EHLR (LRP) Dec. 557:386 (S.D. Fla. 1986).

S. M. v. State of Florida Department of Health and Rehabilitative Services, 651 So.2d 208 (Fla. App. 2 Dist. 1995).

State of Connecticut v. Martyn D. Bruno, 673 A.2d 1117 (Conn. 1996).

Tallman v. Cheboygan Area Schools, 16 EHLR (LRP) 1117 (Mich. Ct. App. 1990).

Tenenbaum v. Williams, 862 F. Supp. 962 (E.D. N.Y. 1994); affirmed in part, vacated in part, and remanded to the District Court, 193 F.3d 581 (2nd Cir. 1999).

Zaal v. State, 602 A.2d 1247, 18 IDELR (LRP) 901 (Md. 1992).

OFFICE FOR CIVIL RIGHTS (OCR) DECISIONS

Oklahoma Department of Education, EHLR (LRP) 257:622 (OCR 1984).

Oroville (WA) School District #410, EHLR (LRP Publications) 257:147 (OCR 1980).

St. Charles (IL) Community School District #303, 17 EHLR (LRP) 18 (OCR 1990).

Tri-County (IL) Special Education Cooperative, EHLR (LRP) 257:529 (OCR 1984).

See page 625 for Table of Federal Statutes and Regulations.

Chapter Ten
Electronic Records and Technology

Martha Dewey Bergren

INTRODUCTION

This chapter introduces school nurses, administrators, and attorneys to legal issues related to technology and student health information. Issues related to electronic health records, facsimiles, and e-mail are addressed. It is intended as a companion to chapters 8 (confidentiality) and 9 (records and documentation).

ELECTRONIC STUDENT HEALTH RECORDS

Background

For centuries, legal matters regarding records were specific to handwritten and printed paper documents. With the advent of electronic records, the legal system is adapting to a new medium. Legislators are drafting laws, and cases involving digital documents are shaping the parameters of courtroom evidence. Storing and manipulating health records electronically requires additional attention and revision to existing practices and safeguards. School personnel know the legal ramifications and guidelines regarding education, special education, and administrative documents. However, they are often unaware that health records in any setting, including schools, warrant higher levels of legal protection. Medical and nursing informatics professionals continually study and improve standards and guidelines for ensuring the legal value of electronic health records. For sensitive information stored digitally, the highest standards of protection apply. As software and hardware technology improve, the standards applied to the protection and confidentiality of health information also increase. Health professionals who safeguard data in their work setting must stay abreast of technological advances and the concurrent obligation to update hardware and software.

Nurses who work in schools are in a unique situation. They are frequently the only people in the building, or in several buildings, responsible for safeguarding the health data maintained for student and staff care. As the sole health professionals in educational settings, they alone may understand the special nature of health data and the responsibilities of maintaining and protecting a legal record of the health care administered.

When adopting electronic health records, school nurses, admistrators, and attorneys must be cognizant of the issues that are pertinent to electronic records as opposed to paper records. This chapter provides the information necessary to successfully advocate for safe and legally viable electronic student health records.

Why Electronic Records?

Many nurses, faced with the complexities involving electronic records, question why health information in a school setting should be stored electronically. Ten years ago, using a computer to store and manipulate K–12 student health records was rare. However, as information technology has become a standard component in the K–12 curriculum and administrative practices, the computerization of the school health office is a necessary reality. School nurses ask for the technological tools they need to record and investigate student health problems more efficiently and reliably. Whether the ratio of students per school nurse is high or low, manipulating health information in thousands of paper charts in a district is unmanageable. The ability to meet the standards of school nurse practice (National Association of School Nurses, 1998), conduct school community assessments, or analyze patterns of injury for thousands of students is impossible using paper records. Unless it can be manipulated electronically, documentation becomes an exercise in collecting data without any realistic means of producing information, knowledge, or improving student outcomes.

Software designed to meet the current needs of a school health office is widely available. Nurses realize that data formerly stored in rows of file cabinets can be electronically processed to yield information useful for assessing and improving the health and education of the children they serve. Since computerization is now present in the majority of school health offices (Smith, Young-Cureton, Hooper, & Deamer, 1998), nurses will more likely be held to the level of assessment and investigation possible using student health database software. Nurses serving large student populations may incur risk by not adopting technology that enhances practice.

Electronic Student Health Records

Electronic student health records are produced using customized database software. Databases are software programs designed to store and organize all related data. Databases consist of fields, records, and files. A field represents a single piece of information, such as first name, health problem, time of office visit, or reason for being sent home. A record consists of all related fields. In a school setting, one electronic record would consist of all the fields, all information, for a particular student. A file contains all related records, for instance, the records of all students in a single elementary school.

The intrinsic value of a database is the ability to query, or to ask questions of the data. For instance, a database can be queried to identify students with bee sting allergies, students needing vision rescreenings, or the number of health office visits between 11:00 a.m and 1:00 p.m. The information can be sorted in innumerable configurations: by alphabet, by grade, by symptom, by nursing diagnosis. The material can be organized and reformatted to suit many purposes.

Some school nurses are using databases that they designed or others designed using off-the-shelf database software, such as Microsoft Access or Microsoft Works. The quality and usefulness of "homegrown" databases vary widely depending on the skill and resources of the amateur database architect. The number of commercially developed student health software databases available has increased over the last several years. These school health office programs vary a great deal in their complexity, functions, and cost. Some of the commercial products are simple adjuncts to paper records, providing health problem lists, emergency information, or immunization records. However, other more complex products have evolved through many years of revisions and enhancements with the input of practicing school nurses. These databases provide comprehensive student health records and health office logs that aim to mimic and improve every aspect of the paper record. Most of the commercial school health software programs operate on either IBM-compatible

or Macintosh computers. Very few programs are available for both Macintosh and IBM operating systems.

There is a wide variety of computer hardware found in school health offices. Some nurses have free-standing personal computers (PCs), unconnected to other computers in the health office or building. Other nurses use personal computers linked within a network of computers in a building or a district, sharing software and information. Personal computers used for school health include desktop computers and portable notebook computers. Many school districts, in which nurses are responsible for multiple schools, invest in notebook computers that travel with the nurse from building to building.

Many districts install integrated school information systems that aim to manage all school functions: attendance, discipline, grades, scheduling, extracurricular activities, purchasing, and bussing. In the last several years, school information systems vendors have added health modules as an optional add-on to these systems. A mainframe computer or a network server manages these district-wide or building-wide information systems. Mainframe computers process information at a central, remote site. The user at a school site can access records stored in the mainframe using either a PC or a terminal.

Other schools link computers via a client server network. Each personal computer connects to other personal computers and a server. Information can be added or retrieved from the system by computers connected to the network. In a networked school, the student health module and its data reside on a server that is not physically in the health office. School information systems are accessible from anywhere in the building and often from other buildings or from non-district computers with a modem connection. Integrated systems allow the sharing of unprotected data between departments. The school health modules of these systems are usually not as comprehensive as the PC software designed for school health offices (Hedberg, 1997).

Another trend in electronic health records is the introduction of the multi-institution patient-based record. In addition to connecting to local school district networks, a few schools connect to Community Health Information Networks (CHINs). CHINs hold all the health information for an individual in one health care record accessed electronically by several health agencies (R. J. Nystrom, personal communication, 1996, 20 December). This birth-to-death patient record is part of the future of school nursing. The central storage of health data increases access to important information during a student encounter, decreases replication of services, and holds promise for supporting cost-effectiveness of health services in the school setting. However, the transfer or sharing of school-based information with other institutions brings new privacy dilemmas and legal controversies.

The student information stored in school health files is of great value to many parties in addition to the school nurse and the individual student. The vast amount of information stored in the school health office is a rich, untapped data treasury. It is useful for obtaining reimbursement for nursing care and for supporting informed policy and funding decisions at the local, state, and national level. (See Figure 10-1.) Many states are establishing statewide student health databases. School nurses either mail disks of aggregate student information or transfer the files over the Internet to state agency offices. The data is further aggregated at the state level, yielding much information about the health and needs of school-aged children. The ability to quantify needs accurately will influence policy and justify intervention programs (Emihovich & Herrington, 1997).

The data stored in school health records are also a rich resource for researching the health and lifestyle choices of school-age children. The data can provide important information about who is at risk for, and which interventions are most effective in treating and preventing, health problems. Until student health records were computerized, the retrieval of this information was too laborious to be useful on a large scale. However, the ability to store, aggregate, and manipulate large amounts of well-child data transforms the information in school health records into a highly desirable and valuable asset. Sharing student health information for research is a sensitive issue. With automated records, school nurses and administrators will be fielding many requests for access to student data that have been stripped of identifiers. Individuals and groups with legitimate research interests in the health and education of all children will be eager to tap the promise of school health data.

Legislation and Regulation

With computerized health records, school nurses benefit from analyzing data to identify health needs, evaluate nursing interventions, and measure student health and educational outcomes. However, special provisions must be established to protect electronic health records and the student's privacy. The public and legislators are watching closely how we protect their private health information. Regardless of whether bills or regulations are passed, nurses have a professional responsibility to protect the privacy of their clients and their families. The varied methods of storing student health data each pose different threats to the integrity and safety of the information. Protections must take into consideration whether the data are stored on a notebook computer transported from building to building, in a personal computer in a health office, or in a server shared with all administrative and instructional departments.

The public and legislators believe electronically stored information, without stringent protections, poses a serious risk to individual privacy rights. There is no federal health information privacy legislation, and state laws protecting health privacy are inadequate. A survey released by the California HealthCare Foundation in January, 1999 found that the public does not trust private and government health insurers to keep personal information confidential (Koyanagi, 1999). Only one-third of U.S. adults say they trust health plans and government programs like Medicare to maintain confidentiality all or most of the time. The Foundation's survey revealed that one in six people

FIGURE 10-1.

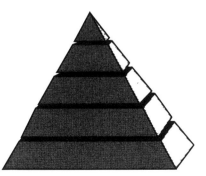

USERS: policymakers, researchers, public health, administrator, care giver

SCOPE: nation, state, district, school, individual student

believes his or her health information has been used or disclosed inappropriately. Personal health data has been used against citizens, relating to insurability, work place, or job discrimination (Braithwaite, 1997), and has been sold to marketers or publicized for profit. The 106th Congress saw 50 bills introduced that concern privacy, primarily health and financial information privacy (Thomas. *The Library of Congress Legislative Information on the Internet*, 2000. URL http://thomas.loc.gov/).

Congress enacted legislation in the electronic health record arena with an amendment to the Health Insurance Portability and Accountability Act of 1996 (HIPAA). HIPAA was designed to enhance the ability to share health information using electronic methods in a standardized format, reducing waste and enhancing the efficiency of reimbursement for health care. However, creating standards that promote transfer and sharing of data heightened public concern for unauthorized and unrestricted access to and dissemination of private health information. In response to these concerns, HIPAA stipulated that Congress must pass a comprehensive health privacy law by August 21, 1999. The goal of legislation is to grant personally identifiable health information, in both paper and electronic form, strong and consistent privacy safeguards. Health privacy bills have been introduced in the Senate and in the House of Representatives. In addition, patients' rights bills introduced in both the House and Senate include provisions related to confidentiality of identifiable health information and the right of individuals to access their personal health information (Legislation. Health Privacy Project, 2000). The August 21, 1999, deadline passed with several pieces of legislation proposed, but none were presented for a vote. In that circumstance, HIPAA required the Secretary of the U.S. Department of Health and Human Services (HHS), Donna Shalala, to issue regulations fulfilling this mandate by February 21, 2000. The Secretary's regulations will be in effect until Congress passes a comprehensive health privacy bill into law.

The HHS-proposed rules were published on November 3, 1999. Public comment was invited until February 17, 2000. Both the proposed rules and the comments can be read or downloaded from the HHS Administrative Simplification web site (http://aspe.os.dhhs.gov/admnsimp/). On August 17, 2000, the final transaction rules were entered into the Federal Register, but the privacy rules were not finalized.

Unlike the privacy bills before Congress, the HHS-proposed rules are limited to the mandate of the HIPAA. Therefore, the proposed rules apply only to electronic health information (or information previously stored in electronic form) and do not protect health privacy for information maintained in a paper system. While both the Senate and House bills aim to provide strong enforcement of individual rights, the HIPAA mandates the HHS rules to enforce minimal necessary disclosure of private health information. Unlike the Congressional bills, the proposed rules do not require specific authorization to release health information for payment or research, but require that policies be in place dictating internal use and external disclosure of health data. Both the HHS-proposed rules and the bills before Congress specify stiff criminal and civil penalties for those who knowingly obtain or disclose individually identifiable information. Health information is the focus, not the setting or type of care provided. The final rules for standards for electronic transactions explicitly state that health information created or received by schools is subject to the provisions.

The proposed bills and the Health and Human Services regulations may directly conflict with the 1974 Family Educational Rights and Privacy Act (FERPA). FERPA allows student health records to be accessed by other school personnel who have a "legitimate educational interest" as defined in school district policy. When all the regulations or Congressional bills are final, FERPA may need to be reconciled with them in relation to student health information and issues of access.

Unrelated to the laws and regulations regarding electronic health data and privacy, the U. S. Food and Drug Administration (FDA) is considering a new policy to regulate software that stores clinical information (FDA plans to revive software regulation effort, 1999). Some within the agency believe that health records software meets the definition of a medical device which falls under the jurisdiction of FDA regulation. Regulating software was first considered in 1986 (Young, 1987), but efforts were set aside when Congress passed the FDA Modernization Act of 1997, restricting what was perceived as regulation overkill. Software connected to medical devices that exert control over diagnosis or therapy (such as heart monitors or chemical analyzers) is subject to strict review. Health record software that does neither, which would include school health software, would be subject to Class One FDA regulation: adopting a standard of manufacturing principles that govern the quality control of the product design ("FDA plans to revive software regulation effort," 1999).

Health care providers who oppose FDA regulation of health records software maintain that FDA oversight would limit the ability of vendors to continue to fine tune health office electronic records. School health software is in its infancy compared to software designed for businesses and acute care settings. Artificial and regulatory barriers to implementing and upgrading such systems would delay needed revisions and improvements to student health software products.

Privacy, Security, and Confidentiality

Frequently, the words privacy, security, and confidentiality are used interchangeably in the literature. Privacy is a right that is protected by the 14th amendment of the U. S. Constitution and is defined by policies and standards within professional groups, local government, and agencies. Included in the definition of privacy is the right to be free from unreasonable intrusions into one's private matters, the right to be left alone, and the right to keep personal information inaccessible to others. Legally, privacy implies some control over information recorded about a person (Steinauer, 1997). An individual is given access to personal information to verify its accuracy and has the ability to challenge it. Privacy is a legal issue, confidentiality an ethical issue. Confidentiality is the expectation that information shared within the relationship will not be shared with others not in the relationship without specific authorization (MacCallum, 1998). Security is the means or methods employed to assure privacy, but it also implies protecting the integrity and reliability of the data (Steinauer, 1997). A privacy law will govern the disclosure of patient-identifiable information. The security provisions within proposed laws and regulations aim to protect all electronic health data in the PC hard drive or data transmitted over a network (Goedert, 1999).

Information Security

Information security is a critical issue in any organization. Health records have fundamental legal requirements whether they are paper or computerized. They must be confidential, accurate, secure, restricted to authorized access (Council on Scientific Affairs, 1993), and protected from destruction or loss of the record (Barber & Douglas, 1994). These standards apply to the security of health data collected and stored in the schools. Information systems are subject to intentional attacks and natural disasters, human error, and external break-ins. Because computer systems store and can copy a large amount of information within moments, a

single breach of security can disclose vast amounts of personal data, resulting in liability for each disclosure (Council on Scientific Affairs, 1993). If a computerized record system lacks reasonable security either in design or operation, the records may not be sufficiently reliable to be introduced as evidence in court (Council on Scientific Affairs, 1993). Viruses and breaches of security can compromise the accuracy of health records. System crashes or lack of skill in using the software can lead to loss of health data. A proactive approach to securing computerized student health information is necessary.

Confidentiality

The protection of confidentiality is the most basic requirement of information technology in the student health office. The use of electronic health records heightens parents' concern over record confidentiality. Measures to ensure confidentiality of electronic records must be as good as or better than those used to protect paper systems. Confidentiality is best ensured by restricting access to health data (Basch, Gold, & Shea, 1988).

When any sensitive or valuable information is stored and manipulated using computers, high technology measures to ensure data security are often considered first. However, technological safeguards do not replace the human factor in confidentiality, the accountability for keeping health information secret. To establish confidentiality standards and protect the integrity of data, districts must develop a security policy.

District Security Policy

A security policy should be established before the installation of any information system (Barber, 1991). Security policies identify those employees who require access to student health records to perform their job. The school nurse should be the one person accountable for granting and approving access to student health records at a particular school. School nurses are the trustees of health information and may be the only employee with formal education and professional standards regarding the legal and ethical aspects of health documentation. The school nurse grants specific staff members health record access and communicates that information to their principal and supervisor. The security policy should cite the criteria to be used for granting access to all or part of the record by a school or health office employee. The policy should also specify the necessary levels of security within the record and explicitly state the responsibilities of health record users to keep student information concealed or secret.

In addition, a security policy should address the school and district's information system administrators' responsibilities. Technical employees have the ability to access student records in order to manage the information systems. They are not likely to be aware of the strict confidentiality requirements for health records and may not be bound by a professional code of ethics regarding the use of such information (Hiller & Beady, 1981). The consequences of inappropriate reading or sharing of student health data by any district employee should be explicitly stated.

To enhance their security policy, some organizations have screen messages that appear when a new user attempts to open a health record and appear intermittently when an established user logs on (Safran et al., 1995). The message advises the user opening the record that each client's confidentiality is protected. Only those persons who have responsibility for that student's health should continue to open the record. Users have to indicate that they read the warning message before reading the record.

In addition to determining who within a school or organization has access to any or all student health data, consensus needs to be reached on who are authorized outside users of the data. For instance, criteria need to be applied to out-of-district health-related, administrative, billing, and research requests for data, who is responsible for processing such requests, and whether or not the student's identifiers are removed.

Employees cannot abide by policies that they do not know (*The Lipman Report*, 1996, February 15). Many schools have already developed and communicated policies and have conducted staff inservice programs regarding confidentiality, including health information issues. Where that is true, a policy must simply be revised to include electronic access to and release of data. If the district does not already have a confidentiality policy, the introduction of information systems is an excellent opportunity to develop one.

Discussion and review of the security policy is integral to the training that precedes the use of a new system, whether it is a PC program or a networked school management information system. Employees should have a copy of the policy or access to a copy in their work area. They should be asked to sign a statement acknowledging that they understand their responsibilities and also understand the consequences of violating the policy. Periodic reviews of the policy should be inte-

grated into regular inservice programs to ensure staff awareness and compliance. Administrators must enforce the policy and, therefore, must participate in determining the consequences of violating the security policy. The message that violating student or family confidentiality will not be tolerated must be validated with administrative action.

Passwords

Both confidentiality and security are enhanced by restricting access to data. The first safeguard to ensuring the protection of data is the use of passwords. As users attempt to open a student data program, they should be prompted to enter a password. Frequently, organizations fail to communicate the importance of passwords to the security of the system. The security policy must explicitly state the need to maintain the secrecy of each password and the consequences of sharing the password with anyone, whether that person has a legal right to access the system or not.

When selecting a password, employees should be advised to select one that can be easily remembered, but not easily guessed. Common safeguards include selecting a password not found in a dictionary, such as nonsense words, words that combine numbers and characters, or special characters. Examples are: *eyescreme, Tea4two, too3four, Ike&Tina.* Long passwords are harder to guess than short passwords. If it cannot be memorized, the password should not be recorded near the computer. A password written on the familiar yellow, 3-inch-square, self-adhesive note adhering to the computer monitor is the most common security threat in institutions (Safran et al., 1995). Employees should be advised never to reveal their password to anyone and to change passwords frequently. Some institutions require employees to change passwords periodically, most commonly, every six months. The deactivation of an employee's password should occur immediately upon termination of employment as part of a standard exit protocol. Passwords enhance security when they allow only the assigned user access to the system.

Partitioning

In addition to requiring a standard password to gain entry to a student health data base, it is also possible to create several levels of access. Software that stores sensitive health or financial information often includes this capability. This feature allows the system administrator to control access to portions of the health records based on a user's responsibilities. The system administrator assigns access to specific users to enter and edit data, and allows others only to read data. The data can be partitioned so that certain passwords give access to only some fields, such as demographics and screening, but not health problems (Safran et al., 1995). In a network, access to the system can be also be limited based on the location of the terminal (Safran et al., 1995). For instance, a school network could be programmed so that access to health records would be blocked from the maintenance and food services offices. If levels of security are designed correctly, electronic records manage limited access to sensitive information more easily than traditional paper ones (Hiller & Bedya, 1981).

If a school installs an integrated school information management system, it should not be assumed that non-health employees are blocked from the health module. The school nurse must verify with the vendor and the district information systems department regarding who may access the school health module. One school nurse discovered in a casual conversation that when the system had been installed, all principals and administrators had been granted full access to the health module without the nurse's knowledge or approval (Anonymous, personal communication, 1999, June 28).

Rejection

Many amateur and professional hackers are middle and senior high school students. If given enough time and an unattended computer, any system's security can be threatened. In at least one documented incident, a student cracked the school health program password, accessed sensitive health information, and disclosed it to several other students (Redes, S., 1999, Apr. 6, personal correspondence). To thwart the student hacker, software can be designed to reject a user when repeated attempts are made to enter an improper password or to access information beyond a password's level of clearance. It is possible to program the computer to sound an alarm when such attempts are made (Council on Scientific Affairs, 1993).

Authentication

To authenticate information is to certify that it was written by the person who signs it. A paper record verifies authentication with the signature. Some older or amateur health office software programs allow access to the database through the use of a common password. Each person logging onto the system uses the same

password. If more than one person accesses and enters information into the health record, a program with a common password should not be used because a common password for all users does not authenticate the author of an entry. Multi-user passwords require personal log-on names and corresponding personal passwords. Each person has his or her own name and access code. If the policy for maintaining the secrecy of passwords is followed, it is likely the person's name following a notation actually represents the person who entered the data.

Digital signatures and smart cards offer even stronger assurance of authentication, but these technologies have yet to reach the school setting. When the Department of Health and Human Services (HHS) issues its final guidelines for electronic health records, electronic signature provisions will be included. Biometric devices to ensure authentication and to restrict access are found in many high level security government and commercial environments. Retinal and fingerprint scanners may be perceived as science fiction, but they are making inroads into electronic health information security systems. Currently, at least one commercial vendor offers a prototype of an updated version of its software program where using a fingerprint scanner logs the user into the database (Redes, S. 2000, July 20, personal correspondence). School nurses can look ahead to increasingly sophisticated biometric and electronic signature devices in school health software.

Audit Capability

Personal passwords also accommodate auditing software. Auditing or tracking software is a standard component of information systems that contain sensitive or valuable information. Designed to discourage unnecessary viewing of a student's or family's sensitive information by persons with authorized access to a system, auditing software provides a detailed access log for each student's record. Each access to the electronic record is recorded with the name of the person who read the information, the type of information retrieved, the location of the terminal (in a network), the date, and the time.

Authorized system users who are not involved in a particular child's care or education are discouraged from reading the record knowing that their voyeurism is being recorded. Demonstrations of this security feature should be included in employee orientations to the system. A security screen message can intermittently remind employees of this capability. Some institutions provide clients with the audit log of their health records on request, listing each time the record was read and altered (Safran et al., 1995). Separate auditing software can be installed to augment the security features in the school health software. Periodic screening of the audit logs for unnecessary access is recommended. The HHS-proposed rules for electronic health information require audit capability in health records software.

Health Office Precautions

One of the simplest strategies to protect confidential information is to arrange the health office with the computer screen facing away from students entering the office or being treated (Bergren, 1999). Another common sense measure is to never leave the computer unattended once the password is entered and a student's records are accessed. However, frequent interruptions and emergencies are the nature of the school health office. School nurses are often called to respond immediately to assess an ill student or report to an accident in the building.

One security program that protects the information on the screen from being read by office visitors and from unauthorized person logging on to the system is the use of a screensaver. A screensaver is commonly a graphics pattern or a blackness that overlays the screen image. Your favorite photo or the school's logo or mascot can be scanned and added to the screensaver choices. Both Microsoft and Macintosh have built password-protected screensavers into their operating systems. On the screensaver set-up, the nurse determines the number of minutes the keyboard can remain untouched before the screensaver is activated. A nurse-selected password is specified. When returning to the unsupervised computer, the nurse enters the password to remove the overlay from the screen. The underlying program, in this case the student database, remains active and no information is lost or altered.

Common school district practices which endanger the confidentiality of health office data are computer upgrades and repairs. Many nurses arrive after weekends or school breaks to find their computer has been upgraded and the previous computer has been removed from the office. Systems professionals often transfer the health office database to the new machine, but may place the outdated computer in storage without erasing the contents. These surplus computers are often used for instruction, tutoring, or student projects. The school nurse must investigate and ensure the removal of all private information from the hard drive.

Another common situation is the need to send a computer out of the district for repair or parts. The easiest way to protect student information is to remove the hard drive before the computer leaves the premises. If the school nurse does not have an information system person available, the hard drive can be removed at the repair shop while the nurse waits. If it is not possible to remove the hard drive, the repair service contract should state that information must be maintained as confidential and private (MacCallum, 1998).

Data Integrity: Overwrite Protection

The integrity of an electronic database system refers to its ability to thwart unauthorized modification or loss of information. Paper documents can be bound and page numbered to prevent additions or alterations. Nurses are well aware that when a paper health record is corrected or altered, the original entry cannot be obliterated, whited out, or blacked out. A single black line is drawn through the entry so that the original notation is legible.

Similarly, software designed to create legal records of health encounters must have overwrite protection. The software must guarantee that information cannot be permanently altered after it has been recorded. A basic tenet of health records is that any additions or deletions to the record must be recorded at the date and time they are entered and must not obliterate the original entry. Within some programs, it is possible to detect that data were altered and when they were altered, but the original notation may be impossible to retrieve. The result is a health record without legal value. Overwrite protection may not be apparent to the user. A demonstration of this feature can be requested from the software vendor.

Data Integrity: Data Loss and Retention

Like paper records, electronic records are vulnerable to loss as a result of all types of natural disasters such as fire, floods, and lightening. Temporary or permanent loss of data can also result from power outages, power surges, magnetic interference, failures of hardware or software, and human error. In addition to acts of nature or equipment failure, loss of data can result from criminal acts such as viruses, sabotage, and theft. Disgruntled employees pose a high risk for sabotaging electronic data (Council on Scientific Affairs, 1993). The potential loss of information must be planned for when electronic records are established.

Viruses are in the news for destroying and corrupting data on home and corporate computers. The key to keeping the student health database free from viruses is to limit the contamination of the system from outside data. Any time a disk that has been in another computer is used on the system, the possibility of introducing a virus occurs.

Downloading documents and programs from email or web sites is another common source of viruses. Virus protection software can be installed to detect and remove a virus in a system. Updates of virus software must be installed promptly upon their release to prevent the intrusion of newly invented viruses. It is recommended that virus protection software be updated every thirty days.

In addition to installing current virus protection software, there are some precautions one can take when receiving attached files via email:

1. Never open files from an unknown person.
2. Do not open any file from friends, coworkers, or relatives without verifying that they emailed it and what the file contains.
3. Avoid opening any attached file with file extensions *.exe* or *.zip*. Exe files are program files that can contain viruses. Zip files are compressed files that may also contain programs.

Another preventable cause of data loss is human error. While the level of computer literacy among school nurses and health office employees increases significantly each year (Smith et al., 1998), some are not even minimally computer literate. Before investing in school health software, the school nurse and all health office employees, should demonstrate a minimum level of computer knowledge and skills. Most school districts, community education programs, and community colleges offer a plethora of classes for the novice. A basic Microsoft Windows or Macintosh introductory class and a beginner's word processing class can convey enough computer sense and confidence to prevent technology disasters. Training specific to newly purchased student health software is necessary to prevent data loss and maximize the benefits of investing in technology, even when all users are computer literate. Unfortunately, many districts and school nurses attempt to reduce the costs associated with high quality software by forgoing training.

Even when a program is used properly, persons adept at keyboarding make data entry errors. When large amounts of data are entered in a short period of time, data samples should be taken to verify the accuracy of the information entered. Randomly selected individual records should be reviewed for errors. Following a mass vision and hearing screening, the data can be sorted to show only screening results and scanned for obvious entry errors. Viewing sample entries on the screen will highlight data entry errors.

Another common reason for the loss of data is poor software design. This can occur in both poorly designed commercial products, or in-house programs designed by the nurse, district employee, or volunteer. Unstable or fragile programs can crash, resulting in data loss. In the health arena, it is necessary to get away from amateur approaches to software development and purchasing (Barber & Bakker, 1994). Efforts to save money result in programs that cannot withstand legal scrutiny and risk losing valuable student data. The lack of familiarity with confidentiality and security requirements of health data can lead system administrators and district supervisors to promote inadequate solutions to health office computing needs.

Another common situation in school health offices is the use of outdated and inadequate hardware. If the capabilities of the computer are stretched to meet the minimal requirements of the software, crashes and freezing during computer processing are a constant risk. All entries made after the last automatic back-up of data will be lost. Using a computer that is not capable of performing its intended function is the equivalent of using a pen that skips for documentation. It is a threat to the coherence and the integrity of the health record and threatens its value as a legal document.

Theft is a real threat to loss of data and valuable hardware and software. Schools are often targeted by thieves as a location for large numbers of computers and peripherals at one time. Alarms or theft resistant locks must be installed on health office doors to prevent access after school hours. Many schools bolt the computers to desks and tables. Identifying information can be etched onto the metal casings of the computer. Notebook computers should never be left unattended in vehicles or in any school offices. Cables with alarms can be purchased to temporarily attach a notebook computer to a desk or other furniture.

The main protection against data loss from any catastrophe is the conscientious maintenance of backup records. Depending on the number of students in a database, the nurse can maintain backups for personal computers with floppy disks, zip disks, recordable CDs, or digital tape storage. For very large student populations, the number of floppy disks needed and the time it would take to load them would be a barrier to consistent daily backups. In large schools investing in a tape or CD backup system as part of the initial hardware purchase would be worthwhile. For health data that is stored in a central server or mainframe, school nurses should verify that the system administrator exercises back-up procedures on a daily basis.

Each state has different requirements for the long time storage of student health data. While the storage of digital records takes up far less space than paper files, the records must be readable long after the computers have lost their value. The district must ensure working hardware is available to read old health records as long as they are required to store them. Outdated computer equipment cannot be scrapped unless other options are available for reading the records. In some cities, universities, government agencies, and research foundations arrange to have electronic equipment available for this purpose.

Until just recently digital storage devices (discs, CDs, hard drives) were considered virtually permanent methods of storing data. It is now known that the integrity of digital data can deteriorate over time. It is too early to say how many years digital data can be reliably stored. School nurses responsible for long-term storage of health records should be alert for new developments and solutions to this problem.

Telecommunication

One of the advantages of electronic records over paper records is that they offer access to a record from another site. Unfortunately, dial-up access allows outsiders to attempt to access a system repeatedly without being visible. Many of the provisions mentioned earlier—passwords, access logs, locking out a user after multiple unsuccessful log-on attempts—can prevent outside intrusion. Alerts can advise a legitimate user how many times their personal user name was used in unsuccessful attempts to get into the system since they last logged on. Some systems require an additional password before users can logon from an outside location.

The transfer of digital electronic student information across the Internet and telephone lines introduces another opportunity for a breach of confidentiality. Many districts and state departments of health are planning to aggregate student health information into a large central database for analysis, planning, and policy purposes. Researchers are also interested in the large data banks for their potential to predict health outcomes. The potential for the capture of sensitive data during its transport over the Internet exists now with hackers' use of sophisticated equipment. One strategy for avoiding interference is to encrypt or encode data prior to transferring it over telephone lines or shared data lines. Additionally, information released for planning, policy, or research purposes should not contain

student identifiers. School nurses who are electronically transferring student information should release only those parts of the record that are requested and necessary. The HHS-proposed privacy rules require the use of encryption if individually identifiable health information is transmitted via the Internet.

Best Evidence Rule

Legal systems have a long history of determining if paper records have been altered or forged and there are extensive legal precedents for lawyers to rely on (Barber & Douglas, 1994). Paper record information is entered at the site of the document with the person in physical contact with the paper (Barber & Douglas, 1994). There is only one main physical original file. In contrast, there is little legal precedent for dealing with electronic records. The records are transient, written on vulnerable equipment, and can be written over (Barber & Douglas, 1994).

Acceptance of computer information as legal evidence in a court of law is subject to the best evidence rule. Within the law, the best evidence rule refers to evidence that in one case might be considered essential but which may be disregarded in another because better evidence is available. Most best evidence case law is based on paper records. In the Federal Rules of Evidence (Fed. R. Evid.) 1002, the best evidence rule provides that in order to prove the contents of a document, the original is required (Fed. R. Evid. or Legal Information Institute, 2000). However, Fed. R. Evid. 1001 makes clear that when it comes to electronic documents, the term "original" has a broad meaning (U.S. Department of Justice, 1994). Fed. R. Evid. 1001 explicitly includes electronic methods of recording letters, words, numbers, or their equivalents. If accurate, paper printouts from electronic storage devices qualify as "original" under the best evidence rule (U.S. Department of Justice, 1994).

Therefore, the ability to document the accuracy of the electronic record affects its weight as evidence. The value of the record as evidence is determined by the ability of those presenting it to verify how and when the record was created, to ensure the inviolability of the record, and to authenticate the author of the information (U.S. Department of Justice, 1994). The biggest risk of using off-the-shelf or poorly designed database products to maintain student health records lies in their capacity to allow changes in health records and logs after the fact. If the information has been altered, the original note may have been overwritten. Even if the alteration is a benign correction, the legal value of the record is in jeopardy.

Another common threat to the legal value of the record is the sharing or public display of passwords. If an employee shares his or her password with a co-worker just once, any entry recorded by that employee after that date cannot be reliably authenticated. If passwords are shared indiscriminately throughout a district or school, the legal value of all records will be weakened.

Software Evaluation

School nurses who manage health offices need to understand the fundamental legal issues and accept responsibility for purchasing and using systems that are appropriate and safe (Barber, 1991). Overwrite protection and multi-user passwords are essential features in health record software if more than one health office employee will be entering data. Multi-level access, auditability, and rejection features limit access and unauthorized alteration of data, enhancing the legal responsibility of the nurse to protect student and family privacy and integrity of the data. These criteria should be applied to systems presently in use and when evaluating new systems.

Some school health databases do not prevent the alteration of data after the fact. Most databases that are created by school nurses or volunteers using off-the-shelf programs do not include overwrite protection. Despite its importance to creating a legal record of a health care encounter, commercially available PC health office software and networked school information system health modules offer overwrite protection inconsistently. It is frequently not specifically mentioned in marketing materials and the nurse should verify this capability before a purchase.

Summary

Risks to the security and confidentiality of electronic student health records cannot be reduced to zero, just as they cannot with paper records (Basch et al., 1988; Rienhoff, 1994; Kluge, 1994). However, computer records can be made as reliable as paper records and, in some respects, even more reliable (Barber & Douglas, 1994). The protection of student information must be addressed even before an information system is implemented, and security and confidentiality require ongoing monitoring and attention. Security policies, compliance policies, and the investigation of possible breaches of information must be addressed on a regular basis (Barber, 1991). School nurses must be knowledgeable and vigilant about maintaining the security of electronic student health information.

School nurses have always needed in-depth knowledge of the legal issues surrounding health records whether the records are paper or digital. As information technology and federal protections of health data evolve, school nurses will need to stay abreast of current standards for maintaining and protecting electronic student health information. Knowledge of these issues is enhanced by reading school nurse, nursing, education, and computer periodicals. The *Journal of School Nursing* publishes a regular column on issues surrounding the use of computers in the school health office. *Computers in Nursing* is a journal dedicated to information technology issues in nursing. Many districts have technology councils composed of employees who have an interest and a stake in electronic record systems. It is imperative that a school nurse be represented on this committee as an advocate for district decisions that protect the privacy of students and their families. The nurse may be the only representative who is cognizant of the security requirements and the legal implications of electronic student health records. Exceptional learning opportunities, networking, and technology coaching are usually benefits of serving on committees for and with district information systems professionals.

There are professional organizations whose primary interest is the use of computers in health care. The American Medical Informatics Association in Bethesda, Maryland, is an organization of physicians, nurses, dentists, pharmacists and other specialists in the use of information technology and telecommunications in health care. AMIA conducts regular workshops on all issues pertaining to electronic health records. There are also many local professional nursing informatics groups that can be used as resources (Newbold, 2000). The National Association of School Nurses in Scarborough, Maine, sponsors a Computer User Special Interest Group composed of nurses presently using information technology in the health office. They meet annually at the national conference.

The World Wide Web and the Internet offer sites that focus on computer issues and the law. The Center for Technology and Democracy maintains a comprehensive web site with frequent updates on Federal legislation regarding electronic health data. An electronic newsletter, The Computer Law Observer, is available through the Internet via email (lawobserver-request@charm.net). Back issues can be read on the World Wide Web (http://www.lawcircle.com/observer). The Library of Congress maintains the Thomas *Legislative Information on the Internet* web site at http://thomas.loc.gov/. The federal and state laws regarding education, health and electronic records can be read in their original form through links at this site.

School nurses have a professional and legal responsibility to safeguard the health information of their students. As computerized health records are becoming a reality, nurses must be able to evaluate the measures that protect this information from disclosure, theft, corruption, and loss. Concerned parents expect nurses to be able to describe the security measures taken to protect student's confidentiality. With a thorough understanding of these issues, nurses can discuss their security and confidentiality needs with software vendors, school administrators, and systems administrators.

FACSIMILES

Broadly defined, the transfer of health data over facsimile is included in the definition of telemedicine (Cohen & Strawn, 1996). The transmission of a fax is electronic, resulting in a paper copy of a health record. School nurses have embraced the technology of facsimiles or faxes. Faxes are used in schools for transfer of health records, doctors orders, pharmacy orders, and student and family communication. The immediacy of acquiring relevant information for decision making and exchanging necessary documentation for treatments and medication administration is highly valued. However, school nurses must address issues regarding the legal status of facsimile documents and ethical issues regarding student and family confidentiality.

Legal Issues Regarding Facsimiles

A facsimile is, legally, a photocopy of a document (Capen, 1995). The Federal Rules of Evidence, Rule 803 of the Uniform Rules of Evidence, recognize that records created in the normal course of business (defined as "a calling of any kind") possess a probability of trustworthiness and are admissible as evidence (Fed. R. Evid., 2000). A duplicate is admissible to the same extent as the original unless the authenticity is questioned. Many states have adopted forms of this act allowing the admissibility of reproductions. State statutes dealing with evidence can be researched through the Cornell Law School Legal Information Institute Web site (http://www.law.cornell.edu/topics/evidence.html).

Regardless of Rule 803, the legal issues regarding the use of faxes for transmission of legal documentation necessary for care is murky. In fact, if a nurse requires a facsimile as evidence in a court of law, a fax

may not be sufficient due to its questioned authenticity or legibility. There are no federal laws that specifically address the issue of the facsimile transmission of physician orders (Hyman, 1998). In a position statement issued by the American Health Information Management Association (AHIMA) (1996), Health Care Financing Administration (HCFA) statements were used to give some direction to health care providers regarding facsimiles. HCFA does not specifically allow or prohibit the use of facsimile for the transmission of health information in its Medicare Conditions of Participation for Hospitals. However, in a Letter No. 90-25, the Bureau of Policy Development of the Health Care Financing Administration stated that it is permissible to accept physician orders via facsimile and that it is not necessary for the physician to countersign at a later date. HCFA noted that facsimile was less prone to error and therefore preferable to verbal orders (AHIMA, 1996).

School nurses must investigate the existence of overriding state laws addressing the acceptability of faxed orders and whether a written original with the physician's signature is necessary. State laws may specifically restrict the facsimile transmission of certain types of information such as AIDS, HIV, or psychiatric care (AHIMA, 1996). State boards of nursing may have issued guidelines for faxed records and physician orders. State school nurse associations, state nurses associations, or a state school nurse consultant may be helpful in locating applicable laws or rulings concerning fax transmissions in a particular state.

In the study of faxed transmission of emergency room data to and from general practitioner offices, Taylor, Chappell-Lawrence, & Graham, (1997) unexpectedly found that 4.3% of the patients refused to allow the transmission of sensitive health data via fax, even when the precautions and safeguards were highlighted. This was a remarkable and unanticipated result of the study. Most forms used to authorized the release of health information do not inquire about the acceptability of fax transmission of data. If information is released in this manner without consent, and if the fax was misdirected containing non-urgent sensitive information, it could cause distress and result in legal action (Taylor, Chappell-Lawrence, & Graham, 1997). Policies addressing informed consent regarding the method of health information transmission must be examined further. The AHIMA (1996) has stated that obtaining authorization to release health records via facsimile is acceptable.

Confidentiality

The use of the fax technology opens new avenues for inappropriate or unintentional disclosure of confidential health information. Fundamental safeguards that protect privacy in paper document transfer, such as direct or certified mail, to a specific individual, at a specific address, in a sealed envelope, are not possible with fax transmission of documents. The sender loses control of the safety of the fax once it is transmitted (Taylor, Chappell-Lawrence, & Graham, 1997). The American Health Information Management Association (AHIMA) recommends sending sensitive health information via mail rather than fax. Facsimile transmission of health information should not used routinely, but only when urgently needed for health care delivery. AHIMA recommends that when health information is transmitted via fax, policies and procedures must be developed to protect confidentiality (1996). AHIMA recommendations for accepting faxed health information include the following:

- Locate the fax machine in a secure area with limited access.

- Assign accountability to one individual to

  - monitor incoming documents.

  - remove documents immediately.

  - verify that all information was received.

- verify that information received is legible.

- Outline procedures for relaying the fax to the appropriate individual in a timely manner.

- If a physician order, verify that it came from an authorized prescriber.

- Thermal paper deteriorates over time. If the fax is on thermal paper, place a photocopy of the document in the record. AHIMA recommends destroying the thermal copy of the document.

When sending faxes with health information, AHIMA recommends the following:

- Verifying that an authorization to release health data is signed, allowing the transfer of the requested information to the recipient.

- Calling first to alert the recipient of the transmission and verify the fax number.

- Including a confidentiality statement on the cover sheet emphasizing the nature of the information and alerting the recipient to contact the sender if the fax is received in error. (See Figure 10-2 for AHIMA's confidentiality sample statement.)

- To eliminate dialing errors, programming fax numbers into the machine.

FIGURE 10-2.

** Confidentiality Notice **

The documents accompanying this telecopy transmission contain confidential information, belonging to the sender, that is legally privileged. This information is intended only for the use of the individual named above. The authorized recipient of this information is prohibited from disclosing this information to any other party and is required to destroy the information after its stated need is fulfilled.

If you are not the intended recipient, you are hereby notified that any disclosure, copying, distribution, or action taken in reliance on the contents of these documents is strictly prohibited. If you have received this telecopy in error, please notify the sender immediately to arrange for the return of these documents.

Sample confidentiality statement for facsimiles, American Health Information Management Association (1996).

The Canadian Health Record Association (CHRA) has additional recommendations regarding best practices for fax transmission (Capen, 1995):

- Transmit only the information requested or needed to provide care.

- Include in the cover page the name, address, phone number and fax number of the intended recipient, the number of pages being transmitted, and a request for a receipt.

These guidelines are directly applicable to the handling of faxes in schools. Many school nurse offices do not have fax machines. It would be prudent to locate machines in health offices for the transmission of student health information. However, even in schools with fax machines in the health office, information is frequently faxed to a general school fax number. Faxed health information may be arriving in a high traffic, central administration office and may sit in the open for protracted periods of time. Often faxes arrive neither labeled as health information nor addressed to the nurse. Well-meaning, but uninformed administrative secretaries, clerks, or parent volunteers have filed sensitive data in student education files, placed it on administrators' desks, or relegated it to dead letter boxes. Other school areas that commonly receive faxed health information are the student activities and sports offices.

Parents and physicians fax physical exam results and health histories directly to expedite student eligibility. On other occasions, health information is inappropriately sent directly to instructional areas for teachers or coaches planning international or domestic student travel. Procedures for handling faxed information should address all areas of the school with fax capability, even when the health office is equipped with a fax machine. The policies and procedures should be communicated to all staff and posted at the fax machine.

The effectiveness of following policy and procedures addressing faxed documents was examined in a study of emergency rooms and general practitioner offices (Taylor, Chappell-Lawrence, & Graham, 1997). The research supported that when safeguards were established for both the sender and receiver, the standard of privacy and protection when using facsimiles was at least as high as that provided by conventional mail.

The use of fax technology is routine in school administration and school health office practice. Although facsimiles can improve care through the efficient, timely, accurate transmission of vital information, nurses must be aware of the legal and professional issues that surround the use of this technology. School nurses need to assist in the establishment of district policies and procedures for the use and handling of facsimile transmissions. They must also verify the legal value of the faxed document and ensure that the student and family privacy is maintained.

EMAIL

Email is an extremely popular method for communicating and sharing resources. Many school nurses are placing their email addresses on their business cards and school health office web sites and in their correspondence to facilitate communication with colleagues, students, and their parents. Similar to adopting the new electronic technology for record keeping, guidelines must be developed and communicated to ensure that email communications meet the legal and ethical standards of care.

Legal Considerations

One preliminary precaution is to be aware of issues that occur when email is exchanged by health providers with out-of-state recipients. Although it is uncommon, some school nurses serve student populations that cross state lines. When a school district straddles state lines, the school nurse maintains a license in the state where the school building is located. Students may be residents of another state, but the nurse may practice in only one state. If the student lives in another state or the parents work in another state, by giving instructions for care, exchanging advice, or providing health teaching via email, the nurse risks practicing without a license in that state. This is equivalent to providing advice or health education over the phone and school nurses should investigate the need for additional state licensure when districts cross state lines.

Preserving the legal value of the email message as evidence is less of an issue than electronic notations in the student health record. Once an email message is sent, it is write protected. Any changes after an email message is sent and received invalidates its authenticity as evidence. Ascertaining that an email message has not been altered verifies its authenticity. Email messages can be printed and placed into a student's paper file or cut and pasted into the student electronic record. Downloading the message into a file preserves the original. It is predicted that future electronic health records will allow direct downloading of email into the health record (Stevens, 1999).

Email's advantage over telephone communication is self documentation (Stevens, 1999). Email documentation is superior to the recording of phone conversations in the record. While a telephone discussion must be recollected, summarized, and written in the student record, email creates its own precise documentation of the exchange, time, and date. Students and families should be informed that email messages are considered documentation and are part of the student health record. Even though phone messages are routinely recorded, parents and students should be made aware that their email correspondence will be placed in the record, much the same as a written letter.

A potential threat to the legal value of email messages is the authentication of the sender. Authentication for a sender of email is identical to that principle applied to health records. That is, a message is authenticated when it is possible to confirm the name signed to the message is indeed the sender. To establish assurances of authentication, each school nurse must have an individual email account with password protected send capability. A school nurse may not share an email account with another employee, nor reveal the password. Some school health offices do not assign email accounts to each nurse or health assistant. That is, the health office has one email account which all employees share. This is done for convenience and to facilitate communication when school nurses job share or health aides staff the office in the nurse's absence. However, legally, it is not possible to attribute an email message to any of the health office staff. Each person in the health office must have their own email account with a personal password. Some mailing software used by school districts requires an employee to enter a password to download new mail, but not to send mail. Any person with access to the computer could send a message masquerading as the school nurse. Software lacking the basic security of password protection for sending mail should not be used for business or communication in any setting, and especially should not be used for student-family communication.

The principle of authentication applies to the student and parents also. Many families subscribe to Internet service providers whose mailers also are not password protected for sending messages. Many families automate the password feature of their email, allowing any family member or visitor with access to the computer to send a message in someone else's name. Students, especially, are not careful about protecting their passwords. There have been circumstances where teachers received email messages from a student's account that were not sent by the student (Educate, K. Personal communication, 1999, May 20). School nurses should be aware that the ability to authenticate the messages received is only as good as the security and password secrecy of the student or family's account.

Confidentiality

Unauthorized access to both the school health office and the home, school, and work computers of the families is also a confidentiality issue. Advise parents not to use employer-owned email accounts (Stevens, 1999), and students not to use school-owned accounts. Email privacy is not guaranteed when the system is owned by a corporation or institution. In some work places, email messages are screened routinely. Although sending email is far superior to leaving messages on an answering machine (Stevens, 1999), the sharing of email accounts and the ability to read old email messages without using a password seriously threatens students' and parents' confidentiality. Students and families should be encouraged not to use email for issues that might be embarrassing or sensitive, and that if they do so, they are taking a risk (Spielberg, 1998). Although the possibility of correctly-addressed mail messages being misdirected or intercepted by a third party is remote, families should be warned that it is technologically possible (Spielberg, 1998). Some telehealth and telemedicine experts advise requiring a signed consent from parents for permission to use email (Appleby, 1999; Stevens, 1999).

Precautions can be taken that will prevent misdirection of email. Many students and parents in a school system have the same name. Communication from school occasionally gets mailed through the post office to the incorrect student or parent, and the same risk exists with email. Request that students include their full names and addresses in their electronic correspondence, and that parents include their names, addresses, and their child's name and grade.

Many people are unsure of their email addresses, yet fill out paper demographic forms with what they think is their email address. Mail containing health information could be inappropriately sent to the wrong address. Rather than writing a 10–25 character email address on a form, parents and students should email the nurse if they wish to communicate in this mode. If email addresses are collected on demographic forms, test the addresses and request a response verifying that they are the correct parent or student.

Protecting student and family confidentiality also requires precautions in the school health office. When communicating with other agencies, each message should contain only information regarding one student (Spielberg, 1998). The confidentiality of other students or families would be violated if the records are examined by a parent. The steps recommended to ensure authentication of the nurse's email messages also protect confidentiality. Each staff member should have their own private email account with a personal password and only the nurse to whom mail was directed should have access to new mail, sent mail or read mail. The password protected screensaver recommended for protecting health records from being read or altered by unauthorized persons protects email left open if the nurse is distracted or called away (Kane & Sands, 1998).

Confidentiality should also be respected when forwarding messages received in the health office. When receiving an email message from an individual, it is unethical to forward it under any circumstance without the permission of the sender. It is especially important to ask parents of students for permission to forward their messages to anyone other than to whom the message was sent. This includes forwarding email to other health professionals for consultation (Appleby, 1999; Kane & Sands, 1998).

Also, when addressing group email to, for example, students identified as asthmatics or diabetics or with anaphylactic allergies, care should be taken not to reveal email addresses, and thus students' identities, in the header. By placing the email addresses of students or parents in the blind copy field (Bcc:) of the email header, the identities of the students are not compromised (Appleby, 1999; Kane & Sands, 1998). To facilitate sending the message, the nurse's own email can be placed in the address field (To:).

Just as you direct families not to use email for sensitive issues, email should never be used by the school nurse or other health office staff for certain types of information. References to AIDS, HIV status, mental health issues (Appleby, 1999), pregnancy results, or birth control are too sensitive to place in an email message, no matter how secure the messages are on either the sender or receiver's end.

Other Issues

Some guidelines should be developed to prevent misuse of email. The nurse should notify students and families that email should never be used for urgent or emergency situations (Kane & Sands, 1998). Even if the nurse believes a response within 24 hours is possible, guaranteeing only a 72-hour turnaround is suggested (Appleby, 1999). This will allow for off campus meetings, substitutes, and illness. Some people expect instantaneous feedback. If an issue is so important that a parent desires a response in less than 3 days, a telephone call is required. It is advised to send a student or family an acknowledgment that you received their message, even if a reply is not warranted (Kane & Sands, 1998).

Some parents are so wired it may be easier and quicker to contact them via email than by phone. In the event that a parent cannot be located by phone for a student illness or injury, a message can be sent to their email addresses notifying them that the school nurse is attempting to contact them, what phone numbers and pager numbers were called, and to respond via phone as soon as possible.

Email tends to promote more complete and accurate instructions or information (Stevens, 1999). For frequently given information, for instance, when a child can return to school following an illness, the school nurse can create a set of standard informational paragraphs which can be attached to a note (Stevens, 1999). This avoids spontaneous responses that omit information or mislead. Imbedded web addresses for the state health department guidelines and lay and professional web sites reinforce or provide additional information.

One disadvantage of using email for nursing care or health information is that there are few ways to ensure it is received and read (Stevens, 1999). If the nurse and the student are using the same Internet Service Provider, an *acknowledge* feature may be available. A receipt mailed to the sender is automatically generated when the message is opened. However, this would apply to only a small proportion of the student population. Just as the nurse sends a courtesy acknowledgment that an email message was received, request that students and parents autoreply an acknowledgment to the nurse.

Email use between clinicians and their clients will continue to grow in all settings. The use of this tool can facilitate communication with school nurses, students, and families. School nurses who wish to use email in their practice must develop guidelines to assure that legal and confidentiality standards are met. For a copy of *Guidelines for the Clinical Use of Electronic Mail* from the American Medical Informatics Association, call 301-657-1291 and request Document No. 406.

REFERENCES

American Health Information Management Association (AHIMA). (1996). Practice brief. Issue: Facsimile transmission of health information. *Journal of the American Health Information Management Association, 67*(7), 2-pp. supplement following p. 40.

American Medical Informatics Association. (1998). Guidelines for clinical use of electronic mail (document no. 406). Bethesda, MD: Author

Appleby, C. (1999). E-mail: New access to care? *Medicine on the Net, 4*(9), 17.

Barber, B. (1991). Disasters, security, and patient confidentiality: Guardians or gizmos. *Health Service Journal, 101*(5262), 33–34.

Barber, B., & Bakker, A. R. (1994). Introduction: A working conference "Caring for health information." *International Journal of Biomedical Computing, 35,* Supplement 1, 3–9.

Barber, B., & Douglas, S. (1994). An initial approach to the security techniques required by the electronic patient record. *International Journal of Biomedical Computing 35,* Supplement 1, 33–38.

Basch, C. E., Gold, R. S., & Shea, S. (1988). The potential contribution of computerized school-based record systems to the monitoring of disease prevention and health promotion objectives for the nation. *Health Education Quarterly, 15*(1), 35–51.

Bergren, M. D. (1999). Legal issues: Office management practices. *Journal of School Nursing 15*(3), 40–41.

Braithwaite, W. (1997). *Security standards. Department of Health and Human Services Administrative Simplification Public Forum: Security standards* [On-line]. Available: http://aspe.os.dhhs.gov/admnsimp/jul9t9.htm

Capen, K. (1995). Facts about the fax: MDs advised to be cautious. *Canadian Medical Association Journal, 153,* 1152–1153.

Center for Democracy and Technology. (2000, June 18). *The Medical Records Confidentiality Act of 1995* [On-line]. Available: http://www.cdt.org/ policy/health-priv/mrca_summary.html (1996, November 20).

Cohen, J. L., & Strawn, E. L. (1996). Telemedicine in the '90s. *Journal of the Florida Medical Association, 83,* 631–633.

Cornell Law School. (2000, June 18). *LII Legal Information Institute Supreme Court collection* [On-line]. Available: http://supct.Cornell.edu/supct/

Council on Scientific Affairs (1993). Feasibility of ensuring confidentiality and security of computer based patient records. *Archives of Family Medicine, 2,* 556–560.

Emihovich, C., & Herington, C. D. (1997). *Sex, kids & politics: Health services in schools.* New York: Teachers College Press.

Family Educational Rights and Privacy Act. *Computer professionals for social responsibility* [On-line]. Available: http://www.cpsr.org/cpsr/privacy/ssn/ferpa.buckley.html

FDA plans to revive software regulation effort. (1999). *Health Data Management, 7*(2), 16, 24.

Federal Rules of Evidence (Fed. R. Evid.) 803 [On-line]. Available: http://www.law.cornell.edu/rules/fre/overview.html (Cornell Law School Legal Information Institute 2000).

Fed. R. Evid. 1001 [On-line]. Available: http://www.law.cornell.edu/rules/

fre/overview.html#article x. (Legal Information Institute 2000).

Fed. R. Evid. 1002. [On-line]. Available: http://www.law.cornell.edu/rules/fre/overview.html#article x. (Legal Information Institute 2000).

Goedert, J. (1999). Data Security: The time to begin is now. *Health Data Management, 7*(2), 108–118.

Hedberg, S. M. (1997). Administrative student information management software (AS/IMS) for school nurse record keeping and reporting. *Journal of School Nursing, 13*(2), 40–48.

Hiller, M. D., & Bedya, V. (1981). Computers, medical records, and rights to privacy. *Journal of Health Politics, Policy, and Law, 6,* 463–487.

Hyman, P. E. (1998, Feb. 9). Memorandum: Nurses' acceptance of electronically transmitted physicians' orders. State of Connecticut, Office of the Attorney General.

Kane, B., & Sands, D. Z. (1998). Guidelines to the clinical use of electronic mail with patients. *Journal of the American Medical Informatics Association, 5,* 104–111.

Kluge, E.-H. W. (1994). Health information, privacy, and ethics. *International Journal of Biomedical Computing, 35,* Supplement 1, 23–27.

Koyanagi, C. Testimony , U.S. Senate Committee on Health, Education, Labor, and Pensions, The Confidentiality Of Medical Information [On-line]. Available: http://www.healthprivacy.org/latest/testimony.4.27.99.html

Legislation. *Health Privacy Project, Georgetown University* [On-line]. Available: http://www.health-privacy.org/legislation/index.shtml

The Lipman report. (1996, February 15). *Cyberspace: The new security frontier.* Memphis: Guardmark, Inc.

The Lipman report. (1996, July 15). *Internet access opens doors to company secrets.* Memphis: Guardmark, Inc.

MacCallum, R. (Late Fall 1998). Nursing informatics and the law. *MANI: Midwest Alliance for Nursing Informatics,* 2–3.

National Association of School Nurses. (1998). *Standards of school nursing practice.* Scarborough, ME: Author.

Newbold, S. (2000). *Nursing informatics special interest groups* [On-line]. Available: http://www.nursing.ab.umd.edu/students/~snewbol/skngroup.htm

Rienhoff, O. (1994). Digital archives and communication highways in health care require a second look at the legal framework of the seventies. *International Journal of Biomedical Computing, 35, Supplement 1,* 13–19

Safran, C., Rind, D., Citroen, M., Bakker, A., Slack, W. V., & Bleich, H. L. (1995). Protection of confidentiality in the computer-based patient record. *Clinical Computing, 12*(3), 187–192.

Smith, C. E., Young-Cureton, V., Hooper, C., & Deamer, P. (1998). A survey of computer technology utilization in school nursing. *Journal of School Nursing, 14*(2), 29–34.

Spielberg, A. (1998). On call and online: Sociohistorical, legal and ethical implications for the patient-physician relationship. *The Journal of the American Medical Association, 280,* 1353–1359.

Steinauer, D. (1997). *Security standards. Department of Health and Human Services Administrative simplification. Public forum: Security standards* [On-line]. Available: http://aspe.os.dhhs.gov/admnsimp/jul9t9.htm

Stevens, L. (1999). Communicating with your patients: The problems and pitfalls of email. *Medicine on the Net, 5*(4), 6–11.

Taylor, D. McD., Chappell-Lawrence, J., & Graham, I. S. (1997). Facsimile communication between emergency departments and GPs, and patient data confidentiality. *Medical Journal of Australia, 167,* 575–578.

Thomas. *The Library of Congress: Legislative information on the Internet* [On-line]. Available: http://thomas.loc.gov/

U.S. Department of Justice (1994). *Federal guidelines for searching and seizing computers* [On-line]. Available: http://cpsr.org/cpsr/privacy/epic/fed_computer_seizure_guidelines.txt. A printed version appears in the Bureau of National Affairs publication, *Criminal Law Reporter,* Vol. 56, No. 12 (December 21, 1994).

Young, F. E. (1987). Position paper: Validation of medical software: Present policy of the Food and Drug Administration. *Annals of Internal Medicine, 106*(4), 628–629.

See page 625 for Table of Federal Statutes and Regulations.

Chapter Eleven

Discrimination in School: § 504, ADA, and Title IX

Mary H.B. Gelfman
with Nadine Schwab

INTRODUCTION

The purpose of this chapter is to discuss the rights of students to be free from discrimination in public school, as provided under federal and state law. Section 504 of the 1973 Rehabilitation Act, the Americans with Disabilities Act of 1990 (ADA), and Title IX of the 1972 Education Amendments are the topics of this chapter. While racial and religious discrimination are not discussed in detail, these and other types of discrimination are illegal under federal, and in many cases, state law. It is the responsibility of all school staff members to be aware of situations in school that are discriminatory, whether by intent or by impact, and to follow school procedures to investigate and eliminate discrimination from the school environment. Discrimination on the basis of disability, which is forbidden by § 504 and the ADA, and on the basis of sex, which is forbidden by Title IX, are problems that students may bring to the attention of school nurses. School nurses should also inform themselves about procedures taken by their school districts to investigate complaints of any type of discrimination, and should counsel students accordingly.

Since children come to school with the same health conditions and health care needs as they have at home, common sense suggest that schools bear some responsibility for knowing what these conditions are and addressing any related learning, health or safety issues. A substantial number of children with chronic health problems have been found eligible for special education, and receive their school health support services as related services provided for in their Individual Education Programs (IEPs). (See chapter 12.) Children with health problems who are not eligible for special education may be eligible for support services under Section 504. This chapter includes selected rulings from the Office for Civil Rights (OCR) of the U.S. Department of Education that address complaints filed on behalf of children with disabilities. OCR handles complaints from students with disabilities who are eli-

gible for special education and also from those who are not eligible, complaints from parents and school employees who have disabilities, and complaints against school districts concerning discrimination on the basis of race, color, national origin, and sex, protected classifications under federal civil rights laws.

Until Congress passed the Rehabilitation Act in 1973, public schools addressed students' individual health needs in ways that varied widely by school district and state; many students who attend school today with significant health-related disabilities would not have attended school at all 30 years ago. Although significant variations still exist, fundamental change has occurred because of these civil rights laws. Section 504 bans discrimination on the basis of disability and requires access to federally funded programs, including public schools, for people with disabilities. Passage of the Americans with Disabilities Act (ADA) in 1990 essentially extended the access rights granted under § 504 to the private sector and to governmental agencies that do not receive federal funding.

There are many parallels and overlaps among § 504, the ADA, and IDEA (the Individuals with Disabilities Education Act; see chapter 12). There are similar cases brought as complaints under § 504 to OCR, or as special education hearings under IDEA. Many cases claim relief under § 504, ADA, and IDEA, and rulings on complaints to OCR and decisions of special education hearing officers may be appealed to court. Therefore, in researching a specific issue, such as a public school's obligation to provide appropriate support services for students who have been diagnosed with attention deficit hyperactivity disorder (ADHD), relevant material can be found in both this chapter and chapter 12. In addition, chapter 13 discusses recent litigation in this area.

Section 504 and IDEA are closely related in that students who are eligible for special education services under IDEA are a smaller subset of all students who are eligible for services or accommodations under § 504.

FIGURE 11-1. RELATIONSHIP OF STUDENTS ELIGIBLE UNDER § 504 AND IDEA

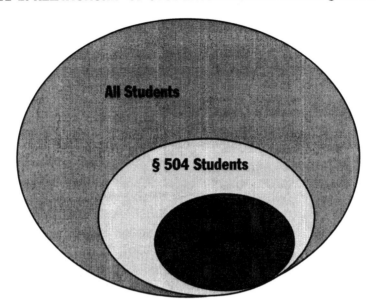

Those who are eligible under § 504 must have a physical or mental impairment that interferes with a major life function. When that major life function is learning or another function that, in turn, interferes with learning, the student should be eligible for special education as well.

The most significant overlap between § 504 and IDEA is that they both require school districts to make an affirmative effort to identify children with disabilities and to evaluate them, and to determine whether they are eligible for individualized support services in school. Many cases in which OCR has found violations of § 504 were brought forward because the school did not seek out or follow up on information about a child's disability. For instance, when parents requested a support service, the school failed to evaluate or failed to discuss the request with the parents and appropriate professional school staff members.

Title IX of the 1972 Education Amendments provides that school districts that permit discrimination on the basis of gender may lose their federal funding. Initially, the impact of Title IX was felt in athletic programs long dominated by boys and men. Requiring equal access to athletics for girls and women resulted in significant changes in physical education classes, intramural athletics programs, and interscholastic team sports. Another reform following the enactment of Title IX was the integration of sewing, cooking, and shop classes at the middle school level, which had traditionally been segregated by gender.

Based on legal precedents from the workplace, sexual harassment is also barred under Title IX. OCR recognizes two types of sexual harassment. In quid pro quo harassment, a sexual favor is requested in exchange for something: "If you have sex with me, you'll get a better grade in English." Hostile environment harassment may make it difficult or impossible for the victim(s) to attend class and learn. This chapter includes discussion of examples of sexual harassment and related current litigation.

REQUIREMENTS OF § 504 OF THE 1973 REHABILITATION ACT

General Protections

Section 504 protects the civil rights of persons with disabilities in their relationships with public programs and activities that receive federal funding. The language of this provision is simple:

No otherwise qualified individual with a disability in the United States shall, solely by reason of her or

his disability, be excluded from the participation in, be denied the benefits of, or be subjected to discrimination under any program or activity receiving Federal financial assistance (29 U.S.C. § 794 (1973)).

The essence of the Act is that no person who would be eligible to participate in a program or activity if he or she didn't have a disability can be excluded from that program or activity on the basis of a disability.

Notice and Coordinator Requirements

Section 504 requires public school districts to provide annual notice to students and their families about the rights of individuals who may qualify under this Act, and how to seek information about, or assistance in determining, eligibility. In addition, each district must appoint a § 504 coordinator who is responsible for overseeing the district's general compliance with the law's requirements. The school nurse may seek out the coordinator to ask how notice is given in the school district, and how families can access additional information, including district procedures for § 504 eligibility determination. Each school health office should have information sheets or fliers on § 504, and school nurses should be advocates for students, not only by informing them, and their families, of their rights under this law, but also assisting them in obtaining factual information and negotiating the district's process for implementing the law.

As an ethical matter, school nurses must be advocates for students regarding their rights under § 504, even when that advocacy may place them in conflict with district administrators. However, many potential conflicts can be avoided by timely and articulate communication, understanding of district concerns and constraints, and a balanced, collaborative approach to problem solving.

Eligibility Requirements—Qualifying Conditions

The Rehabilitation Act of 1973 defines an individual with disabilities as "any person who"

1. has a physical or mental impairment which substantially limits one or more of such person's major life activities,

2. has a record of such an impairment, or

3. is regarded as having such an impairment.

According to the Act, "physical or mental impairment" means

1. any physiological disorder or condition, cosmetic disfigurement, or anatomical loss affecting one or more of the following body systems: neurological; musculo-skeletal; special sense organs; respiratory, including speech organs; cardiovascular; reproductive, digestive, genito-urinary; hemic and lymphatic; skin; and endocrine; or

2. any mental or psychological disorder, such as mental retardation, organic brain syndrome, emotional or mental illness, and specific learning disabilities.

These definitions are more general and far broader than the defined disability categories in the IDEA (see chapter 12). All students eligible for IDEA are also protected by § 504, since "learning" is a major life activity, and disabilities under IDEA are ones which interfere with learning or educational progress. However, some students eligible for services under § 504 may not be also eligible for services under IDEA because their disabilities do not significantly interfere with learning or academic progress. Section § 504 addresses access to educational opportunity, while IDEA addresses free appropriate public education in the least restrictive environment.

Additional definitions are important in interpreting § 504; several follow.

Major life activities means functions such as caring for one's self, performing manual tasks, walking, seeing, hearing, speaking, breathing, learning, and working.

This definition requires a functional analysis of the impact of the disability. A nurse or other medical professional is an appropriate school staff member to make this analysis and to communicate the results to professional educators. For example, a child with an allergy that produces a slight reaction might not be considered "disabled" because the mild allergy does not significantly interfere with a major life function, while another child with moderate to severe asthma, which significantly interferes with breathing, would be considered "disabled" under § 504. It is important for the health professional to articulate the following:

1. how the disability interferes with one or more life functions;

2. how the disability affects the student's functioning (e.g., energy level, exercise needs, medication effects, etc.); and

3. what individualized supports or accommodations in school the student requires in order to access an appropriate education.

Has a record of such an impairment means has a history of, or has been misclassified as having a mental or physical impairment that substantially limits one or more major life activities.

A person who has been cured of cancer has a record of an impairment, yet is not impaired at present. The records of a diagnosis that was later changed would be a "misclassification."

Is regarded as having an impairment means

1. has a physical or mental impairment that does not substantially limit major life activities but that is treated by a recipient [of federal funds] as constituting such a limitation;

2. has a physical or mental impairment that substantially limits major life activities only as a result of the attitudes of others toward such an impairment; or

3. has none of the impairments [listed above] but is treated by a recipient as having such an impairment.

These last two provisions of § 504 ("has a record of" and "is regarded as having") generally pertain to job applicants and employees, but might also be applicable to students. Recent publicized cases of discrimination against individuals who have tested positive for HIV, although currently healthy, and members of the family of someone with AIDS, are examples of students (and staff members) protected under these sections.

Qualified handicapped person means

1. with respect to employment, a handicapped person who, with reasonable accommodation, can perform the essential functions of the job in question;

2. with respect to public preschool, elementary, secondary, or adult educational services, a handicapped person

   a) of an age during which non-handicapped persons are provided such services,

   b) of any age during which it is mandatory under state law to provide such services to handicapped persons, or

   c) to whom a state is required to provide a free appropriate public education under IDEA;

3. with respect to post-secondary and vocational education services, a handicapped person who meets the academic and technical standards requisite to admission or participation in the recipient's education program or activity;

4. with respect to other services, a handicapped person who meets the essential eligibility requirements for the receipt of such services.

All school-aged children who have disabilities that interfere with one or more major life functions are "qualified" under § 504, as are those children with disabilities who are younger or older than the usual school ages, but are eligible under state law for special education, or who qualify under Part C (formerly Part H) of IDEA for early intervention services (aged birth to three).

Section 504 includes exceptions. In the absence of other disabilities, it excludes from protection current users of illegal drugs and alcoholics disabled by current alcohol abuse; people with a current infectious disease who "would constitute a direct threat to the health or safety" of others; and people who "by reason of the currently contagious disease or infection are unable to perform the duties of the job." The Act protects people who have "successfully completed a supervised drug rehabilitation program" and are not using illegal drugs; those who are currently in treatment and are not using illegal drugs; and those who are "erroneously regarded as engaging" in the illegal use of drugs. A "reasonable policy" of drug testing of former users of illegal drugs is not in violation of the Act. Discrimination against current users of illegal drugs is banned in the provision of health care and substance abuse treatment programs. These provisions are probably of greater importance for employees than for students. However, local school districts are specifically permitted to

...take disciplinary action pertaining to the use or possession of illegal drugs or alcohol against any student who is an individual with a disability and who currently is engaging in the illegal use of drugs or in the use of alcohol, to the same extent that such disciplinary action is taken against students who are not individuals with disabilities. Furthermore, the § 504 due process procedures shall not apply to such disciplinary actions.

By definition, in the absence of other disabilities, the Act also excludes from protection individuals who are

• homosexuals and bisexuals;

• transvestites, transsexuals, pedophiles, exhibitionists, voyeurs, those with gender identity disorders not resulting from physical impairments, and those with other sexual behavior disorders;

- compulsive gamblers, kleptomaniacs, and pyromaniacs; and

- current users of illegal drugs who have psychoactive substance use disorders.

In short, the conditions listed above do not, alone, qualify someone as "disabled" under § 504. However, sexual orientation is protected under state constitution or law in many states, and by some municipal ordinances (see chapter 7), and school nurses should familiarize themselves with the laws of their locality.

Who Must Comply with § 504

The requirements that follow apply to programs and activities that receive funding from the federal government. Additional definitions are included in the federal regulations that provide detailed enlightenment on the scope of federal funding.

Recipient means any state or its political subdivision, any instrumentality of a state or its political subdivision, any public or private agency, institution, organization, or other entity, or any person to which federal financial assistance is extended directly or through another recipient, including any successor, assignee, or transferee of a recipient, but excluding the ultimate beneficiary of the assistance.

Most public school districts receive federal financial assistance for school lunch and special education programs, whether the money is paid directly to the district or comes through the state education agency or any other source. This definition distinguishes the "beneficiary" of the program or activity (for example, students in public elementary and secondary schools) from "recipients" of funding, the school districts that provide the services.

Federal financial assistance means any grant, loan, contract (other than a procurement contract or a contract of insurance or guaranty), or any other arrangement by which the U.S. Department of Education provides or otherwise makes available assistance in the form of:

1. Funds;

2. Services of federal personnel;

3. Real and personal property or any interest in or use of such property, including

    a) Transfers or leases of such property for less than fair market value or for reduced consideration; and

    b) Proceeds from a subsequent transfer or lease of such property if the federal share of its market value is not returned to the federal government.

For example, the federal assistance for school lunch programs includes both food and money.

Facility means all or any portion of buildings, structures, equipment, roads, walks, parking lots, or other real or personal property or interest in such property.

Public schools are considered public facilities, whether they are operated in buildings owned or rented by the school district. Programs such as adult education, which are operated by school districts, are included in § 504, as are programs operated in school buildings by other groups or agencies, such as girl and boy scouts, day care, and after school programs. It should be noted that a "reasonable accommodation" standard for § 504 compliance in employment of persons with disabilities does not apply as a limitation of school districts' responsibilities to provide for students with disabilities (Zirkel, 1993). For example:

In a class action on behalf of North Carolina prisoners who were eligible for public education on the basis of their ages and had disabilities, the court ruled that § 504 does apply to prisons (*Anthony D. v. Freeman*, 1996).

Access versus Outcome

An important distinction between an individual's right to equal access and the issue of equal outcome is recognized in regulation under the Act:

For the purposes of this part, aids, benefits, and services, to be equally effective, are not required to produce the identical result or level of achievement for handicapped and non-handicapped persons, but must afford handicapped persons equal opportunity to obtain the same result, to gain the same benefit, or to reach the same level of achievement, in the most integrated setting appropriate to the person's needs.

Least Restrictive Environment

The regulations also support and complement the requirement of IDEA that students who require special education must be placed in the least restrictive environment. In addressing this issue, the regulations for § 504 discuss separate school programs and access to the "regular" school program:

Despite the existence of separate or different programs or activities provided in accordance with this part, a recipient may not deny a qualified handicapped person the opportunity to participate in such programs or activities that are not separate or different.

Physical Access: Program Access or Access to All Buildings

Guarantees of physical access are probably the most well known aspect of § 504 and the ADA, as illustrated by construction of curb cuts, ramps, wider public toilet stalls, elevators and accessible public transportation. In requiring *program accessibility*, § 504 does *not* require that school districts make all their existing buildings accessible.

Case examples:

In a Minnesota case, the parents of a child with spina bifida who used a wheel chair asked that the neighborhood elementary school be made accessible for her. The school district offered placement in another elementary school in the district which was accessible, arguing that it was required to provide program accessibility, not to modify all buildings. The Eighth Circuit Court of Appeals upheld the school district's position (*Schuldt v. Mankato Independent School District*, 1991).

A similar case from Colorado was decided the same way in 1996 by the Tenth Circuit Court of Appeals (*Urban by Urban v. Jefferson County School District R-1*, 1996).

OCR, the division of the U.S. Department of Education that is responsible for enforcement of § 504 in schools, will consider whether alternate facilities are comparable as it did where

> …portable classrooms for children with disabilities in a Michigan school district were found in violation of § 504, on the basis that non-disabled children were not assigned to portable classrooms (Saginaw, 1990).

Independent use of elevator keys has been an issue in at least two cases, where Minnesota and Florida school districts had refused to provide elevator keys directly to individual students. Keys were provided to school staff members who assisted the students, and in each case it had been individually determined that independent use of an elevator

key was not appropriate for the student in question. OCR found no discrimination (*Hoekstra v. Independent School District No. 283*, 1996; Dade County, 1995).

Additionally, in *Hoekstra*, the Eighth Circuit Court of Appeals commented that the ADA provides the same remedies as § 504, and that lawsuits involving access issues cannot recover more money or other benefits by being filed under both the ADA and § 504. In addition to responding to questions about accessibility of school buildings, OCR has reviewed the accessibility of school playgrounds, chorus rooms, auditoriums, football stadiums, parking lots, school buses, school vans, and swimming pools.

Section 504 also requires that private facilities used by public school districts be accessible, as the following cases illustrate:

> High school graduation ceremonies held in inaccessible facilities in Rhode Island (rented or donated theaters, etc.) have been found to violate § 504 (West Warwick, 1993; Coventry, 1993).

> Private schools in Pennsylvania and Massachusetts where public school districts place students with disabilities, and private schools which receive the benefits of federally funded support services, must also be accessible (Radnor, 1993; Uxbridge, 1993).

Procedural Safeguards

Section 504 requires school districts to provide procedural safeguards to insure that students with disabilities and their parents are notified of their rights, are provided with access to relevant records, and know they can have an impartial hearing and a review of the hearing decision when they disagree with a decision of the school district regarding rights or services under the Act. However, § 504 does not include specific procedural requirements: special education procedures and programs are one acceptable method for compliance. School districts are sometimes confused because the lack of specific procedures for students who are eligible for services under § 504 contrasts sharply with the highly prescriptive requirements of IDEA. This is sometimes the cause of noncompliance, such as the case where

> …lack of appropriate notice to parents of § 504 procedures and unreasonable delays in the evaluation process were among the violations found by

OCR when it investigated a complaint about a Pennsylvania school district where "pre-referral strategies" delayed timely consideration of eligibility under § 504 (Curwensville, 1989).

When a referral for program accommodations or related services under § 504 is received, the school is responsible for evaluating the student. The evaluation results and consideration of accommodations or services for eligible students must be discussed by "a group of persons, including persons knowledgeable about the child, the meaning of the evaluation data, and the placement options." For example, when a parent refers a child with juvenile arthritis, the evaluation should include a review of current school performance and standardized testing results. If this record shows weaknesses, individualized testing should be used to obtain a clearer picture of the child's needs.

A statement from a physician, describing the nature of the disability and related problems, including effects of medication, is essential. If the school needs additional medical information in order to plan for the student, the cost of additional medical evaluations is the responsibility of the school. In some cases of juvenile arthritis, physical and occupational therapy evaluations are indicated. The group of knowledgeable persons might include a physician, as well as the school principal, the child's teacher(s), the school nurse and the student's parent.

"Placement" under § 504 may be limited to documentation of the school program modifications and school health services to be provided. In the alternative, "placement" might be a change of classroom or even school to better accommodate the student's needs. As also required by IDEA, placements under § 504 must be in the least restrictive environment for the student, with students who are not disabled as much as possible, and as near to the student's home as possible.

The public school's responsibilities under § 504 were described in a 1987 memorandum from the Pennsylvania Department of Education, informing school districts of the settlement of a class action law suit (*Elizabeth S. v. Gilhool*, 1987) concerning support services for children with chronic health problems. In this case, named plaintiffs included a 6-year-old with insulin-dependent diabetes, who had been denied monitoring of her blood sugar level and administration of insulin shots and snacks in school as needed, and a 6-year-old with spina bifida with various needs, including clean intermittent catheterization (CIC) and flexible homebound instruction to address frequent absences from school. In the memorandum, which introduced state policy modifications concerning children with chronic health needs in school, was this comment:

Thus, what the policy set forth here requires is simply that parents and teachers, principals and others, whose advice and participation are valued because of their knowledge of the child, or the school, or the disability or health condition, should sit down together, together inform themselves and think out loud together about the child's circumstances…and about the arrangements and undertakings which will support and assist the child to participate effectively in school…. In a phrase, a "thoughtful consideration" of the child and his or her circumstances, and action upon it, as with a child remaining in school with a broken leg or arm, a considerate and attentive watchfulness, perhaps a schedule adjustment, adaptive physical education and a thoughtful contingency plan for any acute circumstances which may arise is all that is required (Pennsylvania Department of Education, 1987).

(See also Utah Office of Education, 1992.)

Given OCR's complaint investigation responsibilities, a complainant is usually required to "exhaust administrative remedies" by using this procedure prior to filing suit in court. (See also chapter 2.)

Case examples:

Because the relief sought by parents with siblings who had asthma, allergies, migraine syndrome and sinusitis was available under IDEA, the Eleventh Circuit Court of Appeals upheld a decision dismissing their lawsuit for failure to exhaust administrative remedies within their Florida School District prior to filing a § 504 claim in court (*Babicz by Babicz v. School Board of Broward County*, 1998).

When parents sued for enforcement of a Pennsylvania IDEA hearing officer's order under § 504, the Third Circuit Court of Appeals agreed that to require exhaustion would be futile (*Jeremy H. by W. E. Hunter v. Mount Lebanon School District*, 1996).

REQUIREMENTS OF THE AMERICANS WITH DISABILITIES ACT (ADA)

General Protections and Requirements

The primary thrust of the Americans with Disabilities Act of 1990 is to extend § 504-access rights of people with disabilities to public accommodations in the private sector, as well as to state and local public agencies that do not receive federal funding. Public accommodations are places that are open to the general public, such as stores, theaters, and parks. The ADA uses the § 504 definition of "disability," and includes a similar statement banning discrimination on the basis of disability. Excluded as disabilities under the ADA are current drug and alcohol abuse, and the same additional conditions that are excluded under § 504.

Who Must Comply with the ADA

Generally, the ADA applies to employers of more than 50 employees, and it extends § 504 requirements to employment, public accommodations and services operated by private entities, including private schools from nursery to post-graduate programs, day care centers, adoption agencies and other social service entities.

> *Case example:*
> A Tennessee student with an auto-immune disorder affecting her blood system was expelled from a private school, and alleged discrimination under the ADA. The court issued an injunction, ordering the private school to re-admit her, finding that she was disabled under both § 504 and the ADA; that she was "otherwise qualified" to attend school; that the private school was subject to the requirements of both § 504 and the ADA; and that the private school had not made reasonable accommodations for her disability (*Thomas v. Davidson Academy*, 1994).

There is an exclusion for religious organizations: religious entities are not prohibited from "giving preference in employment to individuals of a particular religion," and schools operated by religious entities are not considered places of public accommodation. Therefore, parochial schools and other educational programs operated by religious organizations are not required to comply with the provisions of the ADA unless they receive federal funding.

ADA Compliance Requirements

The requirements of notice and establishing a grievance procedure parallel the procedural requirements of § 504. Also, self-evaluation and transition plans for compliance with specific deadlines were required. For a summary of ADA compliance requirements for school districts, see the November, 1995, EDLAW Briefing Paper (Rosenfeld, 1995). Checklists for ADA compliance activities appear in this article, and also in a 1994 article in *West's Education Law Reporter* (Kaesberg & Murray, 1994).

Provisions Specific to Public Schools

The ADA includes few provisions with impact on public schools. In general, the ADA applies to employment and to access by members of the public. However, the section prohibiting discrimination in public services requires school districts to provide accessible school buses. (For detailed discussion, see Osborne, 1995.)

Procedural Safeguards

The procedural requirements of the ADA parallel those of § 504. Notice must be provided, including the name of the ADA coordinator and a complaint procedure.

Private Nursery Schools and Day Care Facilities

Section 504 prohibits all programs and services taking place in public school facilities in school districts which receive federal funding of any kind from discriminating against people with disabilities. Thus, children attending nursery schools and day care programs operated in school buildings (often on a contracted or rental basis) fall within the protection of § 504. The enactment of the ADA extended similar protections to children attending private nursery schools and day care centers, and also spelled out requirements for determining whether accommodations requested are "unduly burdensome." OCR and the courts are now struggling with determination of "unduly burdensome" accommodations.

> *Case examples:*
> Responding to a complaint about denial of an aide for one-to-one support services for a California child with disabilities in a parent-funded after school program, OCR found that the child could participate if the aide was not needed, confirming that the child was "otherwise qualified." OCR also determined that providing the aide would not be unreasonably burdensome. This school district voluntarily modified its § 504 notice provisions and procedures for determining whether individual children with disabilities can be accommodated (Conejo Valley, 1995).

A multiply-disabled Kansas 2-year-old in a day care center was threatened with "dis-enrollment" because of his disabilities. The parents obtained an injunction forcing the center to continue to provide services until the completion of a trial (*Ireland v. Kansas District of the Wesleyan Church*, 1994).

A federal district court in Minnesota found that a day care center could not be required to provide a full time personal attendant for a 4-year-old with multiple disabilities. The center had informed the child's parents that admission depended on the parents providing an attendant. The court noted that requiring the center to hire someone to assist with one child only was "an undue financial burden" and therefore not a "reasonable accommodation" under the ADA. After the parents appealed this decision, the Eighth Circuit Court of Appeals upheld the District Court decision, also citing an undue burden on the daycare center (*Roberts v. Kindercare Learning Centers*, 1995).

Parents of a California 9-year-old with multiple, severe disabilities secured an injunction against Kindercare, a chain of day care centers, requiring support services in an after school program pending a full trial (*Orr v. Kindercare Learning Centers*, 1995).

After an injunction has been obtained, a case is sometimes settled without any published final decision.

TITLE IX: DISCRIMINATION ON THE BASIS OF GENDER

The initial, visible effect of the passage of Title IX in 1972 was investment of considerable amounts of thought and money into making school athletic programs equally accessible to boys and girls. Examples of discrimination addressed included more physical education classes per week for boys than for girls; better equipment for boys than for girls; priority on use of facilities (gyms and fields); pay for team coaches; number of interscholastic teams for girls and for boys; and length of interscholastic seasons for boys' and girls' teams. In addition to equalizing funding, Title IX resulted in significant cultural changes, including the encouragement of girls' participation in athletics and the recognition of women team coaches.

Title IX requires school districts to appoint a Title IX coordinator, to publish notice of policies which ban discrimination by gender and sexual harassment, and to establish a Title IX grievance procedure.

Title IX also addresses sexual harassment in schools. Sexual harassment means unwelcome sexual advances, requests for sexual favors, and other verbal or physical conduct of a sexual nature when

1. submission to such conduct is made either explicitly or implicitly a term or condition of a person's employment or advancement, or of a student's participation in school programs or activities;
2. submission to or rejection of such conduct by an employee or student is used as the basis for decisions affecting the employee or student; or
3. such conduct has the purpose or effect of unreasonably interfering with an employee's performance or creating an intimidating, hostile, or offensive work or learning environment (Department of Education, 1997; Bryant, 1993).

A 1993 survey of 1,632 public school students in grades 8–11, in 79 schools in all parts of the United States, reported that 85% of the girls and 76% of the boys had been sexually harassed.

This survey was commissioned by the American Association of University Women and was conducted by Louis Harris and Associates. The students were asked the following questions (*Hostile Hallways*, 1993; Bryant, 1993):

Has another student (or students):
1. made sexual comments, jokes, gestures, or looks;
2. showed, given, or left you sexual pictures, photographs, illustrations, messages, or notes;
3. written sexual messages/graffiti about you on bathroom walls, in locker rooms, etc.;
4. spread sexual rumors about you;
5. said you were gay or lesbian;
6. spied on you as you dressed or showered at school;
7. flashed or "mooned" you;
8. touched, grabbed, or pinched you in a sexual way;
9. pulled at your clothing in a sexual way;
10. intentionally brushed against you in a sexual way;
11. pulled your clothing off or down;
12. blocked your way or cornered you in a sexual way;
13. forced you to kiss him or her;
14. Forced you to do something sexual, other than kissing?

The U.S. Supreme Court has held that school districts can be liable for damages under Title IX of the 1972 Education Amendments, which prohibits discrimination on the basis of sex in programs and activities receiving federal financial assistance (*Franklin v. Gwinnett County Public Schools*, 1992). This case involved sexual advances on a student by a teacher. The school had not responded to the student's complaints. The student's suit focused on the school district's responsibility to comply with Title IX, which requires school districts to designate a Title IX Coordinator and to publish a sex discrimination and sexual harassment complaint procedure. In this case, the court found for the student because her complaints put the district on notice of sexual harassment, and the district had failed to investigate the complaint and stop the problem.

A 1998 Supreme Court decision, *Gebser v. Lago Vista Independent School District*, rejected the plaintiff-ninth grader's claims against the school district for damages based on a sexual relationship with a teacher who had later been fired for that reason. In this case, the court found that lack of notice to school officials, even though the district was in violation of Title IX by having no coordinator or grievance procedure, barred recovery by the student.

Since *Franklin*, the courts, commentators, and school districts have struggled with several related issues:

1. What constitutes appropriate notice to the school district. If a school employee receives a complaint but does nothing, is the district liable? Can school officials who fail to investigate complaints of sexual harassment be found individually liable for damages? These issues are complicated by laws in some states that provide immunity to school districts.

2. Is student-to-student sexual harassment included within Title IX on a "hostile learning environment" legal theory? OCR accepts complaints and investigates instances of student-to-student sexual harassment, on a legal theory that the school district is discriminating if it isn't following the requirements of Title IX.

3. How should the legal principles that have developed around sexual harassment in the workplace be applied to schools? Various courts and commentators have mentioned the mandatory attendance laws, which force children to attend school; the age of students, who are mostly minors; and the possible long-term effects of sexual harassment, especially on younger students, as factors which distinguish sexual harassment of students from that of employees, who can, if all else fails, leave a job.

In 1997, the U.S. Department of Education published guidelines titled *Sexual Harassment Guidance: Harassment of Students by School Employees, Other Students, or Third Parties*. These guidelines were developed from Title IX, which bans discrimination on the basis of sex in any program or activity receiving federal financial assistance, and from the analysis OCR uses in responding to complaints about sexual harassment. Among other matters, these guidelines advise that

1. Sexual harassment includes behavior male on female, female on male, male on male, and female on female, if it is sexual in nature.

2. "Quid pro quo" harassment, when a school staff member conditions a student's grades or participation in a school activity or team on the student's acceptance of sexual advances or other sexual behavior, is unlawful whether the student accepts the behavior or not.

3. A finding of "hostile environment" is based on the severity, persistence or pervasiveness of the sexual conduct.

4. School districts must have grievance procedures and must respond immediately to complaints of sexual harassment from students.

Attorneys defending school districts are arguing about notice; about how difficult it is to draw the line between "normal teenage behavior" and sexual harassment; about "welcome" and "unwelcome" sexual advances; and about the difficulty of preventing actions and words which may be offensive to some students and not to others. An effective defense is a written sexual harassment policy, as well as compliance with the Title IX required appointment of a coordinator and publication of a grievance procedure. Institutional statements of behavior standards, and training for staff members and students about identifying unacceptable behavior are the most effective ways to discourage sexual harassment (Duncan & Rapport, 1998; Doty & Strauss, 1996; Sorenson, 1994; Hassenpflug, 1998; "New Guidelines," 1997; Rossow & Parkinson, 1996a, 1996b, 1997; Thompson & Truelock, 1998; Gorney, 1999).

Allegations of student-to-student sexual harassment have caused considerable debate in the courts. Verbal sexual harassment starting in seventh grade resulted in the plaintiff in *Doe v. Petaluma City School District* (1995) consulting with her guidance counselor during her eighth grade year. The counselor later told the plaintiff's father that he didn't think the complaint important enough to be reported to the assistant principal. The Federal District Court found no "intentional discrimination against the student based on sex." On appeal to the Ninth Circuit Court of Appeals, the counselor's claim of qualified immunity based on ignorance of his duty to report the complaint was upheld, on the theory that at the time in question, it had not been "clearly established" that Title IX applied. However, the court's comments suggested that awareness of school district responsibilities under Title IX would be expected now.

In the case of *Davis v. Monroe County Board of Education* (1996), a fifth grader was sexually harassed by a classmate for six months. The plaintiff and her mother complained frequently, but no action was taken. Eventually the classmate was charged with sexual battery and pleaded guilty. Plaintiff's case, which cited interference with her education, dropping grades, and emotional effects, was dismissed by the Federal District Court, with a finding that the school did not have a responsibility to protect one student from harassment by another student. The Eleventh Circuit Court of Appeals reversed the decision, based on finding that school officials had received notice and failed to stop sexual harassment which resulted in a hostile environment. In May, 1999, the U.S. Supreme Court ruled 5-4 in favor of Davis, holding that in cases like this one, where the school district had notice of the problem and was "deliberately indifferent," and the harassing behavior was "severe, pervasive, and objectively offensive," interfering with the educational opportunity of a student, courts could assess damages against the school district. While the minority of the court found the majority's position an excessive intrusion into local school district operation, the majority stressed that this holding would apply only in extreme cases. For a discussion of *Davis* and of ways that school districts address problems of sexual harassment, see Gorney, 1999.

Case example:
When a Missouri student complained to OCR of sexual harassment by another student, investigation showed that no complaint had been made to the school district. OCR found that without notice, the school district could not be expected to act (Ferguson-Florissant R-II School District, 1997).

In *Seamons v. Snow*, 1996, the plaintiff sued his football coach, high school principal, high school, and school district when his complaint about a sexual prank in the locker room resulted in no investigation and his removal from the team. After the superintendent was informed of the prank, he canceled the last football game of the season, and students blamed and harassed the plaintiff to the point where he moved to another school district. The Tenth Circuit Court of Appeals upheld the District Court's finding of no hostile environment sexual harassment and characterized the harassment as "hazing." The 1997 Guidelines suggest that OCR would have found violation of Title IX in this case.

Since students often consult with the school nurse about troubling issues, awareness of current law regarding sexual harassment is important. A key issue identified by the courts is that if a student has consulted with a school staff member concerning a sexual harassment problem and if the matter is not investigated and appropriate action taken, the school may be liable for damages. From related court decisions, it appears that school districts with clear, published sexual harassment policies, providing notice to students of their rights and procedures for complaints, may limit their liability.

Since the school nurse is likely to be consulted by students about sexual harassment, the health office should have a copy of the school district's policy posted and students should be encouraged to complain to school administrators.

ENFORCEMENT BY THE OFFICE FOR CIVIL RIGHTS (OCR), U.S. DEPARTMENT OF EDUCATION

OCR Jurisdiction

Congress has charged the Office for Civil Rights (OCR), U.S. Department of Education, with enforcement of § 504, ADA and Title IX complaints against public schools. OCR's jurisdiction to investigate parental complaints has been tested and upheld in court (*Rogers v. Bennett*, 1989).

When OCR's authority to investigate has been challenged, states have used claims of immunity—either sovereign immunity, or eleventh amendment immunity. (See chapter 2.)

Case example:
In response to a claim of Eleventh Amendment immunity by state officials, a California federal district court observed that IDEA, § 504 and the ADA each include specific language that waives an eleventh amendment defense. The court then allowed a class action law suit by students with disabilities to proceed against state officials in their official capacities (*Emma C. v. Eastin*, 1997).

Complaints should be submitted in writing to the appropriate regional office. See Figure 11-2.

Figure 11-2. OCR Regional Offices

Eastern Division
- OCR Boston: Maine, New Hampshire, Vermont, Rhode Island, Massachusetts, Connecticut
- OCR New York: New York, New Jersey, Puerto Rico, Virgin Islands
- OCR Philadelphia: Pennsylvania, Maryland, Delaware, West Virginia, Kentucky

Midwestern Division
- OCR Chicago: Illinois, Indiana, Wisconsin, Minnesota
- OCR Cleveland: Michigan, Ohio
- OCR Kansas City: Missouri, Kansas, Iowa, Nebraska, North Dakota, South Dakota

Southern Division
- OCR Atlanta: South Carolina, Georgia, Florida, Alabama, Tennessee
- OCR Dallas: Mississippi, Louisiana, Texas, Arkansas, Oklahoma
- OCR Washington D.C./Metro: North Carolina, Virginia, Washington, D.C.

Western Division
- OCR Denver: Colorado, Utah, Wyoming, Montana, Arizona, New Mexico
- OCR San Francisco: California
- OCR Seattle: Nevada, Hawaii, Idaho, Oregon, Washington, Alaska, Pacific Region

OCR investigations focus on the questions of whether there has been discrimination on the basis of disability or sex, and on whether § 504, ADA, and Title IX procedural requirements have been met. OCR has stated repeatedly that it will not investigate the quality of programs or services, beyond determining whether discrimination has occurred.

In responding to complaints, OCR is currently offering a form of mediation called early complaint resolution (OCR Complaint Resolution Manual, Rev. 1998). If the complainant (usually a parent of a child with a disability) and the school district agree, an OCR representative will meet with the parties and attempt to facilitate a compromise.

Investigations by OCR Regional Offices

According to OCR, the top five reasons for filing of disability complaints in fiscal year 1997 were as follows:

1. Individualized Education Plan Services   436
2. Related aids and services/Auxiliary Aids 372
3. Placement/referral   301
4. Evaluation/classification   269
5. Educational setting   156

(as reported at the 20th National Institute on Legal Issues of Educating Individuals with Disabilities, May 1999).

An investigation by OCR may include file reviews of other students to assist in determining whether the complainant received disparate treatment. Comparisons may be made with other students who have disabilities and with non-disabled students. During the investigation, relevant school district policies and procedures will be reviewed to ensure that they conform to § 504.

After OCR investigates a complaint, it will provide a written letter of findings to the complainant and the school district. The *Individuals with Disabilities Education Law Reporter (IDELR)* (formerly *Education of the Handicapped Law Reporter [EHLR]*), which may be found in university law libraries and the professional libraries of some large school districts, publishes and indexes selected OCR letters of findings. All OCR rulings are accessible from OCR under the federal Freedom of Information Act.

When OCR finds violations of § 504, the school district may choose to implement the recommended remedial actions. In doing so, the school district will avoid possible action by the U.S. Department of Education. (See the section on "Enforcement," p. 347.)

Since investigations by OCR are essentially focused on discrimination, school policies and procedures that apply to all students, both with and without disabilities, usually pass muster with OCR, as illustrated by the following case:

At the Oregon School for the Blind, parents were required to provide current medical information for all children wishing to participate in a camping trip. When a parent withheld information and a medically fragile child was barred from the camping trip, OCR supported the requirement and found no violation of § 504, since the requirement applied to all students (Oregon State School for the Blind, 1990).

OCR has also been designated to investigate complaints of non-compliance with the ADA against public schools. In a 1992 Memorandum to senior staff members (OCR Senior Staff Memorandum, Nov. 19, 1992), OCR pointed out that § 504 civil rights protections had been extended by the ADA to include all public agencies, whether or not they receive federal funding. This memorandum also described investigative procedures to be used for complaints under the ADA. Another policy memorandum advised that ADA complaints against private schools and day care centers that receive no federal funding will be investigated by the U.S. Department of Justice (OCR Senior Staff memorandum, May 4, 1992).

Enforcement: Withholding of Federal Funds

If within a reasonable period of time, the school district does not come into compliance with the recommendations in an OCR letter of findings of violation, the U.S. Department of Education may provide notice and a hearing concerning withholding of federal funds. For example, when the Department terminated federal funding to a Georgia school district because the district had refused to cooperate in an OCR investigation, the school district appealed to court. On appeal of the refusal of the federal district court to issue an injunction, the Eleventh Circuit Court of Appeals refused an emergency petition and upheld the termination of funds (*Freeman v. Cavazos*, 1990, 1991).

If a violation of § 504 is found by a court, the Act provides that a prevailing party, usually the parent who initiated the complaint, may be awarded attorney's fees by the court. Sometimes, OCR rulings are appealed to court by the school district. Occasionally, a law suit citing violations of § 504 will be filed before the plaintiff has exhausted the administrative remedy of a complaint to OCR. A federal court may accept jurisdiction if the plaintiff can establish that exhaustion would be futile, or isn't relevant to the particular case.

Using § 504 to Enforce IDEA Requirements

Perhaps because the filing of a complaint concerning the education of a child with disabilities with an OCR regional office is considerably easier and less expensive than requesting a due process hearing under IDEA, an increasing number of IDEA issues are filed as complaints with OCR. One advantage of complaints to OCR is that OCR does the investigation. On the basis that students who are eligible for special education under IDEA are also eligible for protection under § 504, OCR has found violations where a school district did not conform to the requirements of IDEA. (See chapter 12 for specific requirements). The regulations for § 504 also specifically cite compliance with IDEA requirements as a way of complying with § 504. Examples are:

- OCR found violations of § 504 when a Washington student with traumatic brain injury was denied an appropriate education because the school did not provide adequate training for the staff before placing him in a regular classroom, and he was punished for disability-related behavior (Mansfield, 1995).

- Rejecting the school's argument that a South Dakota student with orthopedic impairments had an excellent academic record and was therefore eligible for support under § 504 only, the Eighth Circuit Court of Appeals ordered specially designed instruction, related services, and transition services (*Yankton School District v. Schramm*, 1996).

- In the case of a California child with a seizure disorder and learning disabilities, OCR found a violation of § 504 because the IEP team did not discuss and plan for health care services he might need in school for the seizure disorder and did not follow correct procedures concerning homebound instruction (Compton, 1995).

- Violations of IDEA procedural requirements concerning notice, consent for evaluation, and special education placement were found to be violations of § 504 as well in a New York case (Sachem, 1987).

IDEA incorporates requirements for parental access to their student's education records, and there is another extensive law, the Family Educational Rights and Privacy Act (FERPA), concerning confidentiality of students' education records. OCR has found violations of confidentiality and records requirements, which are discussed in chapters 8 and 9.

Retaliation under § 504 and the ADA

Section 504 addresses retaliation by referring to anti-retaliation provisions under the Civil Rights Act of 1964. The ADA also bars retaliation against complainants. Retaliation for the filing of a complaint is prohibited, and OCR has applied this provision in a broad context. Retaliation claims must show evidence of an action taken against the complainant, or against the student with disabilities, in relation to the filing of a complaint or asserting of other rights under § 504 or the ADA. Such activities are defined as "protected activities."

Related OCR dicisions and cases are useful—

- OCR has found filing a report of suspected child abuse was required by Kansas state law, and therefore not retaliation (Mill Creek Valley, 1993).

- The actions of a special education administrator in a Rhode Island school district, "taken together, …created a climate of intimidation, threat and coercion" in violation of § 504 (Narragansett, 1993).

- OCR found no retaliation in the assignment of an administrator to attend a Georgia parent-teacher conference: the action was a reasonable response to previous problems with this parent (Rockdale, 1995).

- OCR found no retaliation when a Pennsylvania parent complained that she was required to carry a large, brightly colored visitor's pass when she visited her son's school, and that she had been arrested when she refused to leave another school. In both cases, she claimed she was engaged in advocacy activities. OCR's investigation revealed that all visitors were required to carry visitors' passes, which were sometimes brightly colored, and that she had been arrested as an unauthorized visitor under a general board of education policy (Philadelphia, 1996).

- Maryland parents claimed that a school principal had tried to change the placement of a 7-year-old with Down Syndrome to another school, and had released confidential information about the student without parental consent. A federal court in Maryland denied the school's motion to dismiss the case, citing evidence that the board had knowledge of these claims and of the possibility of retaliation against the parents' raising of § 504/ADA claims (*Gupta v. Montgomery County Public Schools*, 1996).

On occasion, teachers have claimed retaliation for advocacy activities in appeals of adverse employment decisions by local boards of education. Few of these complaints have been found to have merit by OCR. When OCR finds facts supporting an adverse employment decision such as a reprimand in a teacher's personnel file or an involuntary transfer, the investigation seeks to determine whether the reasons for the decision were sound, or whether they were an excuse for discriminatory retaliation.

In a Michigan case, a teacher claimed retaliation for advocacy activities on behalf of students with disabilities. An OCR investigation showed that: 1) notes from the principal questioning classroom decisions were used by that principal with all the staff, and were not made a part of the teacher's personnel file; 2) the principal was not responsible for a mistake in reporting the teacher as absent from a required faculty meeting, and no sanction had been imposed on the teacher; 3) a formal reprimand about "the appearance of impropriety" in having one of the teacher's students work for her as a babysitter and spend the night at her house had been pursued through the grievance procedure, and an arbitrator had upheld the reprimand with modified language; 4) a notice of involuntary transfer was found valid and not pre-textual, and in fact the teacher avoided the transfer; 5) the teacher's conduct at a graduation party for students had been questioned by the superintendent of schools, but no record had been entered into the teacher's personnel file; and 6) denial of the teacher's application to participate in a summer program occurred before her advocacy activities (Anchor Bay, 1996).

DETERMINATION OF ELIGIBILITY UNDER § 504 AND THE ADA
Evaluation Requirements

When a parent requests help for a child with disabilities in school, the distinction between IDEA eligibility and § 504 eligibility may not be known to the parent. When a referral goes the IDEA route and the child is found not eligible for IDEA services, the school team should immediately consider the alternative of § 504 eligibility. If the referral comes in initially under § 504, regulations require an evaluation to be followed by a decision "by a group of knowledgeable people" concerning eligibility for such services. The easiest determinations are made when a parent produces medical documentation of a disability, requesting special education services or some other accommodation.

Related decisions of note include:

- If the IEP team determines, after an evaluation, that the student's disability has no or minimal educational impact and that the child is not eligible for special education, OCR ruled that the school must proceed one more step and determine whether the child is eligible for services under § 504 (Veir, 1994).

- An Arizona school district's limitation of support services to students in particular disability categories (i.e., counseling only for students identified as seriously emotionally disturbed, or occupational or physical therapy only for students with specified physical disabilities), was found to be discriminatory and in violation of § 504 by OCR (Prescott, 1987).

- A Vermont special education hearing officer, with § 504 jurisdiction under state law, found violation of § 504 when a school failed to include someone knowledgeable about ADHD on the school team considering eligibility for a student with ADHD (Lunenberg, 1994).

The evaluation required for determination of eligibility for services under § 504 is not described in detail in law or regulations, although it must meet the same standards as required under IDEA: proper use of validated tests administered by trained staff members; tests "tailored to assess specific areas of educational need, and not merely…to provide a single general intelligence quotient;" and evaluation instruments selected to measure aptitude or achievement levels, not disability. In the case of requests for school health services or program accommodations based on medical conditions, the school team needs appropriate medical documentation. If the parent does not provide the information, the school may need to secure consent for an appropriate evaluation (examination, consultation, test) and provide funding for the evaluation (Veir, 1994).

Case examples:
When a California school district requested an evaluation concerning vision therapy and the parent did not provide it, OCR held that the school must provide the evaluation at no cost to the parent, because it was necessary to determine whether the child required support services in school (San Francisco, 1981).

A complaint against a South Carolina school district listed failure to evaluate for occupational therapy (OT) needs; requirement of a physician's prescription for OT; and denial of payment for such prescriptions unless payment was requested by the parent. OCR found these actions in violation of § 504 (Chester, 1992).

When an Alabama school district delayed an evaluation, imposed conditions on the evaluation and upon services to be provided, and finally suspended a student and insisted that his family institute private therapy for him prior to allowing him to return to school, OCR found the district in violation of § 504 because it had not followed the evaluation requirements and timelines required by IDEA for students in need of special education (Auburn, 1989).

In disputes between parents and school districts over whether a child has a disability, OCR advised in 1992 that it would investigate whether an evaluation has been performed and whether a determination of disability status has been made, as required by § 504 (OCR Senior Staff Memorandum, May 13, 1992). A school district has discretion in determining what an evaluation should include. In some cases, a statement from a physician is enough; in others, more information about the student's educational, psychological, and physical status may be helpful or necessary.

Meeting and Developing a Plan: The Role of the School Nurse

The school nurse is frequently the gatherer of information needed to address § 504 issues, and may also play the role of interpreter and coordinator for the school team. In many cases, school staff members with no health care training will need assistance in understanding the nature of a disability and the validity of a request for school health services or other forms of program accommodation. While school nurses may not be designated to provide direct services in every case, they should be responsible for completing a health assessment, participating in decisions about the student's health and safety needs in school, recommending appropriate accommodations to the school team, developing plans, providing consultation to other team members, and, when appropriate, training and supervising other personnel according to state law and local policy. (See chapter 4 on delegation and supervision.)

At times, it is appropriate for a school nurse to advise the school district to add another health specialist, for example a pediatrician or psychiatrist, to the team discussing support services in school. It is good practice (although not required by law) for the school to consider "matching specialists" when a parent brings a specialist to a school meeting. For example, if a parent brings a psychiatrist, the school should consider bringing its own equivalent consultant.

Another important role for the school nurse is notification of school authorities that a student or category of students may require services under § 504. The school nurse will learn from students' health records, health histories, health room visits, or consultations with parents of the need for an evaluation. The nurse can initiate a meeting of school staff members and parent(s) to discuss the student's needs and appropriate health support services to address those needs in school.

SCHOOL HEALTH SERVICES AS RELATED SERVICES UNDER § 504

An OCR decision, involving a California school district, includes the kind of analysis that a school team should apply when addressing a request for support services under § 504. In this 1993 case, a 6-year-old with mental retardation was scheduled to attend a local pre-kindergarten class for children with disabilities (Conejo Valley, 1993). Over the summer, he was diagnosed as an insulin-dependent diabetic, and his parent requested assistance in monitoring his blood sugar level at school, providing glucose or insulin injections when needed, providing snacks, and development of emergency plans for school and during transportation on the school bus. The district responded with their generic emergency plan: call the school nurse, call paramedics or other emergency services, and call the parent. Because none of these people were on-site at the school at all times, the student's parent objected to the plan, explaining that an immediate response might be needed. The district then offered several alternatives:

1. Homebound instruction for five hours a week;
2. Placement in a school near a hospital which could provide emergency services, in a class for children with communication problems (this child did not have a communication problem);
3. Placement in a school in another school district, where there was a full-time school nurse on-site, which would require an increase in the student's travel time; or
4. Assignment of a paraprofessional to monitor the child, but not to provide emergency assistance.

In its investigation, OCR interviewed the participants in the school team meeting and reported that they had been guided by the district's emergency policy and an interpretation of state law concerning injections for students in school. Pointing out that § 504 requires an evaluation before a significant change in placement, OCR noted the absence of such an evaluation prior to

the district's recommendations for alternative placements. However, OCR's major finding against the school district was failure to provide an individualized emergency plan; application of the school's general emergency plan was found to be insufficient for this student. OCR representatives consulted several nearby school districts, and discovered emergency plans providing for injections for students stung by bees and for diabetic students by school nurses or other trained school staff members. OCR also documented nearby resources for training of school staff members. Finally, OCR noted that the arbitrary limit of five hours per week for homebound instruction failed to allow for individual needs of children with disabilities and was an additional violation of § 504.

This case illustrates both § 504 requirements and the interaction of IDEA and § 504. This child had already been identified as in need of special education and had an IEP and special education placement. When his parent notified the school of additional health needs, the same procedures should have been followed: evaluation followed by planning. This case also raises an interesting contrast between IDEA and § 504 complaints. Here OCR considered services provided in nearby school districts as establishing a "standard of practice." In due process hearings under IDEA, evidence that a health service has been provided in another school district is not always enough to establish that it is required for another student in another district under IDEA. (See chapters 12 and 13.)

SCHOOL DISTRICT RESPONSIBILITIES UNDER § 504 AND ADA

Homebound and Hospital-Based Instruction

When children cannot attend school, the school district's responsibility to provide an education does not cease. Many states limit tutoring or homebound instruction to students who will be out of school for a prolonged period of time due to illness, while students whose chronic health problems result in frequent, short absences from school are often denied support. On an individual basis, students with disabilities may require a mix of homebound and school-based services. In other cases, a homebound program limited to a state minimum, such as five to ten hours a week, may not provide an appropriate full school program. The following cases are instructive—

- When a Washington student with a medical condition that created problems of pain management challenged the homebound tutoring provided by the school district, OCR found that the amount of tutoring provided had not been based on the student's individual needs, and was in violation of both § 504 and the ADA. This school district had provided two hours a week of tutoring without consideration of the student's actual needs (Tacoma, 1996).

- In the case of a North Dakota child with severe asthma, many allergies, migraine headaches, and a record of absences from school, the parent requested a tutor. At first the school district provided the tutor without any evaluation; subsequently, the district performed a variety of evaluations to determine whether the student was learning disabled, or whether the absences were psychological in nature. When the child's physician wrote a description of her medical problems and the various medications she was receiving, the school district refused to provide a tutor and requested a second opinion. In the meetings held by the school principal to discuss services for this student, the school nurse was listed as present, but OCR does not report any specific comments or recommendations from the nurse. The school focused its attention on a psychological evaluation, secured a psychiatric evaluation, and recommended psychotherapy. OCR found a variety of procedural violations prior to the district's realization that it needed a medical opinion concerning the need for a tutor. A proper evaluation, in this case, should have included consultation with the student's physician, and if necessary a school physician, prior to determining what services were needed (Grafton, 1993).

- A Massachusetts school district limited homebound and hospital-based instruction services to four hours per week, scheduled on two days a week in the afternoon. OCR found this policy in violation of § 504 and the ADA, because students' needs had not been individually considered. The district agreed to remedial actions, including removing the limit on the amount of tutoring to be offered and implementing a minimum of six hours of services per week; offering tutoring services during the regular school day; improving coordination of services to provide necessary books and materials; and commencing services promptly (Boston, 1994).

- After investigating a complaint that homebound services were inadequate for an Alabama high school student with a rare blood disease, OCR found that the services provided by the school district were not in violation of § 504 or the ADA. The school had provided instruction in two required courses, and later added four electives as independent study, thereby providing a full course load. The student was provided with tutoring over the summer to make up the course credit he lacked (Mobile, 1995).

- A Missouri family with two children who used wheelchairs required services at home and at school. OCR found that the school district had failed to provide a computer and other assistive devices for use during homebound instruction as required in the children's IEPs; that weekly visits to the school for socialization had not been implemented as planned in the IEP; and that participation in extra curricular activities was limited because of lack of appropriate and timely notice of opportunities, although one of the children had been initiated into the Honor Society (Eldon, 1986).

For students whose chronic health conditions can be anticipated to cause frequent or periodic absenteeism due to illness or for medical treatments such as surgeries or chemotherapy, a plan for homebound tutoring that can be implemented as soon as the student is medically ready is appropriate and should be incorporated into the § 504 accommodation plan.

Program Modifications for Students with Disabilities

Often a student's medical condition requires school program accommodation or modification. The school nurse, as interpreter of medical information, should play an active role in advising school staff regarding specific health conditions, related student needs, and appropriate modifications or accommodations.

For example, an Indiana student with juvenile arthritis was required to participate in volleyball, although the school and her classroom teacher knew of her condition. OCR found a violation of § 504, because her program had not been appropriately modified (Grangeville, 1994).

Students who Require Specialized Transportation

Transportation may be a service available to all students living beyond a specified distance from the school, or it may be a support service for students whose disabilities interfere with their walking to school. Transportation services may be designed to accommodate individual student's needs, such as by using a bus or van with a wheelchair lift, or by providing a bus attendant to assist a student.

Case example:
When a New York school district provided special transportation arrangements only for children who used wheelchairs and denied such transportation to a student with asthma, OCR found that a request from a physician for special transportation for a child with asthma must be honored (York-town, 1989).

In response to such requests, the school should do an evaluation and hold a meeting to plan the service: is the request for year-round service? Should this child be transported on a regular bus route or in a van, and is an attendant needed? When there are questions about the student's medical condition, the physician should be asked for additional information or invited to participate in the meeting at school district expense. Participation by a school medical advisor may also be helpful.

School Attendance Policies

When school districts have attendance policies that impose penalties such as lowering of grades or denial of academic credit for "excessive" absence from class, there may be discrimination against students with disabilities that cause frequent absences. An attendance policy should include provisions for medical excuses and/or review by a school team (IEP team, § 504 team, or attendance review team).

Case examples:
An attendance policy which denied academic credit to a Michigan student who was absent because of injuries in an accident was found to violate § 504 by OCR (Lowell, 1987).

OCR found that a Florida school district had not waived attendance requirements because it had not been notified of a student's depression (Broward, 1994).

An Arizona school district required medical certification for exemption from the district's attendance requirements, and denied course credit if a student exceeded a specified number of absences. OCR upheld exemption for a child who provided a medical certificate, and upheld denial of exemption for another child who had failed to provide a medical certificate (Yuma, 1990).

Monitoring of absences and referral for discussion of program modifications may be appropriate interventions for a student with a chronic health condition.

Students Who Have Shortened School Days

While a student's disabilities may require the accommodation of a shortened school day, this must be done by following proper procedures including an evaluation and a meeting, and the shortened school day must be justified in writing.

Case example:
OCR has ruled in Louisiana, Utah, Maryland, and Indiana that shortening a school day without consideration of the student's individual needs is a violation of § 504. School days have been shortened in violation of § 504 for students with a particular disability (frequently emotional disturbance) or for students in a particular program (frequently because of transportation scheduling) (South Central, 1990; Hartford, 1992; Granite, 1993; East Baton Rouge, 1989; Tippecanoe, 1988).

Access to Field Trips and Extra-Curricular Activities

Section 504 requires that students with disabilities have access to non-academic services.

Case examples:
After investigation of a complaint that an Arkansas student with disabilities had been denied participation in a field trip, OCR found that students with and without disabilities were selected for the field trip, based on the same criteria. No violation of § 504 was found (Conway Public Schools, 1998).

When a California teacher barred a child who used a wheelchair from the school bus for a class field trip, OCR found violations of both § 504 and the ADA. This child's parent had suggested that she ride the bus in a regular seat, with her wheelchair stored on the bus during the trip. The bus driver agreed, but the teacher did not. OCR noted that the school had received adequate notice of the child's deteriorating physical condition and required the district to take remedial action, including notice to staff members concerning accommodation procedures and counseling for the teacher (Elk Grove, 1994).

A Pennsylvania school district used "safety concerns" to bar a student with disabilities from swimming and field trips. OCR found that although the student had fallen frequently in school because of a progressive neurological disorder, she could participate in field trips and swimming if someone accompanied her (Quaker Valley, 1986).

After investigation in another case, OCR ordered a school district to provide notice that children with disabilities had equal access to field trips (Mt. Gilead, 1993).

It may be necessary for the school district to investigate to insure that field trip destinations are accessible, and to consider assigning additional school staff to accompany field trip groups, such as paraprofessionals to assist individual students, and nurses to monitor children with chronic health problems. A serious issue is arrangements for medication administration for those students on a field trip who receive medication during the school day, as well as accommodation on overnight or extended day trips for those who may require medication.

Case example:
The parent of a Washington student with multiple and severe disabilities complained to OCR that the student had been excluded from the school district's after-school recreation program. Investigation revealed that the student had participated in the program with modifications on a trial basis, and the district had determined that although the program provided accommodations for children with disabilities, this student could not participate due to physical limitations. OCR ruled that this student was "not otherwise qualified," and found no discrimination (Shoreline, 1996).

When a field trip involves overnight stays, issues concerning medication and other medical procedures normally provided by the family and not at school should be considered in advance and on a case-by-case basis.

When OCR investigated access to a sixth grade camping program, it discovered that although eligibility requirements for the program were non-discriminatory, children with disabilities were more likely to be found ineligible because of behavior requirements. The California school district agreed to modify eligibility requirements, and to include discussion of the program in IEP meetings for students who were eligible to participate (Ontario-Montclair, 1996).

Access to Interscholastic Sports: Participation Rules

Rules concerning eligibility for interscholastic athletic teams are made by school districts, athletic associations or conferences, and by state law. The intent of such rules varies: to protect students from inappropriate physical competition; to insure that individual students are physically fit to compete; and to require student-athletes to meet academic requirements, to name a few. For HIV issues, see below.

Virtually all public schools that offer interscholastic sports teams require participants to provide evidence that they meet reasonable physical requirements. While this general rule is not discriminatory on its face, it has been used to exclude students with disabilities from school teams.

Case example:
A New Jersey public school district refused to allow a student who had only one kidney to be on the high school wrestling team. The court found this student to be "otherwise qualified" for the team, and held that his exclusion was a violation of § 504 (*Poole v. South Plainfield Board of Education*, 1980).

When students with disabilities are being considered for athletic teams, a case-by-case medical analysis is required to determine whether the impact of individual disabilities results in the student being "otherwise qualified" or not.

When there is a requirement that student athletes meet academic requirements, such as maintaining good grades or earning specified numbers of academic credits, there may be a disparate impact on students with disabilities.

Case examples:
When a Michigan student with ADHD lacked sufficient credits to be eligible for a team, his parents claimed violations of § 504 and the ADA. The court found § 504 violations, and denied summary judgment for the athletic association, since there was a factual dispute concerning the denial of eligibility, which should be addressed at trial (*Hoot v. Milan Area School*, 1994).

After investigating the exclusion of a South Carolina student from the baseball team, OCR found that the student, who had learning disabilities, asthma and hay fever, did not meet team eligibility requirements because of excessive absences, poor school grades, and behavior problems. No evidence of discrimination was found (Beaufort County School District, 1997).

Students with disabilities may have repeated grades in school and/or may continue their education in secondary school until the age of 21. As a result, they may be denied eligibility for interscholastic teams subject to athletic association rules limiting participation by age, or by number of semesters of high school enrollment. Historically, courts have upheld this type of rule on the basis of reasonableness (age limits apply to all students, disabled or not); and on the basis that the athletic association, usually a regional or state association of coaches, is a private organization that does not receive public funding.

Case example:
In a New York case, the federal district court found that age requirements applied to all students seeking participation in interscholastic sports did not violate the ADA (*Reaves v. Mills*, 1995).

Recently, courts are beginning to look more closely at claims of discrimination under the ADA. Injunctions to allow team participation for 19-year-old high school athletes with disabilities have been issued in:
1) Missouri (*Pottgen v. Missouri State High School Activities Association*, 1994); 2) Michigan (*Sandison v. Michigan High School Athletic Association*, 1994; *Frye v. Michigan High School Athletic Association*, 1997; and *McPherson v. Michigan High School Athletic Association*, 1997); and 3) Connecticut (*Dennin v. Connecticut Interscholastic Athletic Association*, 1996)—only to be dissolved on appeal on various grounds.

The Connecticut case is notable because the student involved had Down Syndrome, and the local board of education joined in the lawsuit with the student's parents. The Second Circuit Court of Appeals observed that the case was not a class action, suggesting that a class action might be more successful. This issue is capable of repetition, yet evading judicial review, because individual athletes are usually arguing about one season of team participation, and the judicial process often requires more than one year. In most of the cases where a federal district court issued an injunction permitting the student to play while the case was being litigated, the season was over by the time the case was reviewed at the circuit court of appeals level.

Most cases were dismissed as moot by the circuit courts of appeal, because the season in contention was over. In a class action, the plaintiffs could be named students who wanted to play one more season and had been found ineligible on the basis of age and other unnamed students similarly situated, who might be found ineligible on the basis of age in the future. Commenting that individual consideration of older students with disabilities may find some of them "otherwise qualified" under the ADA, Wolohan (1996) argues that the ADA will prove to be a reasonable vehicle for individual exceptions to age limit rules.

In an attempt to secure placement on a team, parents may request that the IEP team, or a § 504 team, include an athletic team placement in a student's IEP or § 504 plan. While students with disabilities may have rights under § 504 and the ADA to try out for interscholastic teams, no student has an absolute right to play. In other words, each candidate for a team, whether disabled or not, must demonstrate that he or she is "otherwise qualified" in try-outs. Additional perspectives on these topics can be found in Reiser & Cohn's chapter in Goldberg (1995).

Discipline of Students with Disabilities

Through a number of court cases brought under IDEA, it is now well-established that a student with disabilities may not be expelled for misconduct which is found to be a manifestation of, or related to, his or her disability. (See chapters 12 and 13.) Under § 504, discipline for disability-related misconduct is often found discriminatory. OCR has noted that suspension or expulsion of students with disabilities for more than 10 days constitutes a "significant change in placement" and requires an evaluation (OCR Senior Staff Memorandum, Oct. 28, 1988). This memorandum discusses the procedures to be followed in determining whether the misconduct is disability-related, and also mentions that students disabled only by drug and/or alcohol abuse are not eligible for protection under § 504. Short-term suspensions of less than ten days are permissible under § 504.

Case examples:
After investigating a complaint that a California student with ADD had been punished for disability-related misconduct in first and second grade, OCR found that the school district's delay in evaluating the child, despite many requests from the parent, and disciplinary referrals for ADD-related behavior were in violation of § 504 (Rialto, 1989).

While finding no evidence to support allegations that students with disabilities were being suspended for more than ten days without an evaluation, OCR required a California school district to revise its discipline policy to include notice of rights of students with disabilities who are not eligible for special education (Santa Ana, 1992).

The parent of a California student with diabetes complained that her child had been disciplined for carrying a beeper, which he needed for management of his medical condition. OCR determined that when confronted, the student had refused to give his beeper to a school security officer. On investigation, it was learned that the medical documentation for the beeper was dated after the incident, and that the beeper was used to enable family members to keep in touch. Given these circumstances OCR found no violation (Moreno Valley, 1995).

After review, OCR found insufficient evidence to support an Alabama parent's allegations of racial and disability discrimination in the expulsion of a student with learning disabilities. OCR confirmed that a team meeting had determined that the misconduct was not related to disability, proper expulsion procedures were followed, and the student was treated the same as similarly-situated white students (Tuscaloosa City, 1997).

Schools sometimes use "time out" for students with serious behavior control problems. Time out should be identified in school district discipline policy and may be part of an individualized behavior plan under IDEA or § 504. The need for a time out place that is safe and easily supervised has led to development of "time out rooms."
Case examples:
In response to a complaint about the use of specially designed time out rooms in a Florida school district, OCR found no discrimination because the rooms met all state and local safety code requirements and time spent in time out by individual students did not exceed state or local policies (Marion County School District, 1993).

Since use of time out was based on behavior and not on disability, and a Missouri student was allowed to return to his regular classroom seat when his behavior was under control, OCR found no violation of § 504 (Northwest R-I School District, 1996).

OCR found use of "time out" and "composure" rooms in a North Carolina school district to be appropriate (Asheville City School System, 1996).

Behavior plans for severely disabled students may also include other forms of physical restraint or the use of aversives to discourage violent behavior. Zirkel (1998) discusses legal issues that must be considered, including some state statutes forbidding corporal punishment and the need for full discussion with parents in the IEP process prior to implementing such plans. OCR has upheld behavior plans using physical restraint that have been developed through the IEP process and have been applied reasonably in well-documented circumstances. As Zirkel points out, some inappropriate uses of restraint are addressed with teacher discipline by the school district.
Case example:
When OCR investigated a complaint from South Carolina which included allegations of inappropriate behavioral sanctions (taping the student's mouth and sending him to the school walkway), it was found that the school had already investigated and the teacher in question had apologized to the student and had been reassigned. Since the school had taken timely action to remedy the problem, OCR found no violation of § 504 (Aiken County School District, 1995).

While the ADA applies to some aspects of the operation of private schools, it does not replace reasonable contract provisions between parents and private schools.
Case example:
After the Federal District Court in Puerto Rico ordered reinstatement of a student expelled from a private school, the First Circuit Court of Appeals reversed, finding that the contract between the parents and the school required arbitration of any dispute. Arbitration is permissible under both the ADA and § 504 (*Bercovitch v. Baldwin School*, 1998).

Since the enactment of the Gun-Free Schools Act in 1994, which imposes a mandatory 180-day expulsion for students found on school grounds with guns, there have been several communications from the U.S. Department of Education to local school districts concerning application of this law to students with disabilities. This federal law provides for individual consideration of each case, which should provide for the disability relationship determination required by § 504. For discussion of these departmental communications and subsequent related issues, see Hartog (1995) and Rosenfeld (1996a; 1996b).

The 1997 IDEA amendments and related 1999 regulations include extremely specific procedures for determining whether specific misbehavior is a manifestation of a student's disability, and procedures for interim placements in alternative educational settings for students whose behavior poses an immediate danger in their current school setting. (See chapter 12.) A school nurse can be a vital member of a school team reviewing a student's misconduct to determine whether it is disability-related. A nurse's analysis of the disability and medication or other treatment that may impact on behavior will help teachers and other educational personnel understand possible relationships. Regular contacts between the school nurse and the administrator responsible for discipline is good practice.

The nurse may also help the school team devise program modifications and behavior management programs that address the characteristics of individual student's disabilities, medication and treatments. A key to success in these roles is regular communication with the student's parent and health care providers, collaboration with the school team, and constant updating of nursing knowledge and skills.

Participation in School-Wide Assessment

The implications of participation by students with disabilities in school-wide assessment testing have become more complex as states mandate increasing amounts of testing, and as the discussion of possible federal requirements emerges. From the schools' point of view, some students with disabilities may perform so poorly on standardized measures of academic achievement that a class or a school average score may be significantly lowered. One result of this perception is that schools and school districts that routinely exclude many students with disabilities from testing may have artificially enhanced their test results. With publication of scores for each school or school district, school administrators and parents may focus on average scores which are lowered or enhanced by participation or exclusion of significant numbers of students with disabilities.

From the students' point of view, this type of testing may by inappropriate for two small groups of students with disabilities. Those with severe disabilities may be unable to produce meaningful test results, and those with severe attentional or emotional disabilities may find the group testing experience extremely difficult. The appropriateness of participation by students with

severe disabilities in such assessments is a proper topic for discussion by the IEP team, with decisions to be made on an individual basis. The 1999 IDEA regulations require a written statement with the reason why a particular school-wide or grade-wide assessment is not appropriate for a specific student, and how the student will be assessed.

A third concern is the issue of modifications in testing procedures for selected students with disabilities. For example, a student's § 504 plan might include having tests dictated to her, with her spoken answers to be transcribed by a school staff member. Procedures for consistent test administration may, or may not, allow for such modifications. The IDEA regulations require a written statement of modifications necessary for an individual student to be included in the student's IEP.

Case examples:

Texas instituted a minimum skills test as part of eligibility for a state high school diploma. Students with disabilities could be exempted from part or all of the test on an individual basis by the school district's IEP team. Students with disabilities who took the test were permitted the same testing modifications that they were provided in their educational programs, again on an individual basis. Finally, if a student with disabilities failed the test, he could continue in school and retake the test. Given these options for students with disabilities, OCR found no discrimination against learning disabled students (Texas Education Agency, 1990).

OCR found no violation of § 504 or the ADA when a Florida student was denied the modification of having parts of a state high school competency test read and explained to her. While the test administration guidelines provided for accommodations usually given in the classroom, reading and explaining test questions was specifically barred, to protect the validity of the test (Florida State Department of Education, 1998).

The 1997 IDEA amendments and related 1999 regulations require that *all* students participate in system-wide testing, with written justification by the IEP team required for use of alternative testing.

High School Graduation, Diplomas, Grading Systems

Requirements for high school diplomas vary from state to state, and in some states there is a practice of offering several different levels of diploma. For example, one diploma may show that the student has completed courses required for graduation and passed a state competency test; another diploma may show that a student attended and met the graduation requirements of a particular program, such as a vocational program. Recent efforts to raise standards for high school graduation and concern about special education programs provided for students with severe disabilities has led to development of "special education diplomas" and "certificates of attendance" in some school districts.

Case examples:

A Colorado parent complained to OCR that students with disabilities were receiving a different diploma. The school district agreed to offer a "Guaranteed" diploma to all students who earned the required number of credits and passed the state proficiency test, and to provide a different diploma for students who earned the required credits but did not pass the proficiency test. As part of the agreement between the district and OCR, diplomas based on these standards were awarded to all students in the most recent graduating class (Moffat County School District, 1996).

In response to several general questions concerning graduation from the Montana State Director of Special Education, OCR advised:
- "Modified grading schemes" may be used if available to both students with and without disabilities;
- Eligibility requirements for class rank and for honors cannot "arbitrarily discount or exclude" grades from special education classes;
- Students with disabilities may not be excluded from participation in graduation ceremonies; and
- Eligibility standards for diplomas must be the same for students with, and without, disabilities: however, requirements may be modified or waived through the IEP process (Runkel, 1996).

The parent of an Arkansas student complained to OCR that students with disabilities were not eligible for the Honor Roll. Investigation revealed that any "ability/effort" grade disqualified students with disabilities from the Honor Roll, and that one school barred students assigned to resource rooms from the Honor Roll. OCR conducted an investigation and reported that "ability/effort" grades were only given to some students with disabilities, and were considered "noncompetitive" grades. The school district voluntarily modified procedures for Honor Roll eligibility (Fort Smith Public Schools, 1993).

The holding of separate graduation ceremonies for students with disabilities or barring students with disabilities from participation in graduation ceremonies has been found in violation of § 504.

Case examples:

When a Texas school district could not show an educational necessity for a separate graduation ceremony for students with severe disabilities, OCR found violation of § 504 (Aldine Independent School District, 1990).

In 1989, a special school district in Missouri requested advice from OCR concerning special diplomas for students with disabilities who completed their IEP requirements but failed to meet all graduation requirements. OCR found no discrimination if the parents had been advised that completion of the IEP alone would not qualify a student for a regular diploma (Special School District of St. Louis County, 1989).

OCR investigated a complaint that a Pennsylvania student with ADD was required to serve all detentions he owed prior to being permitted to participate in graduation. Since the rule about outstanding detentions applied to all students, those with disabilities and those without, there was no discrimination. The student had made up the detentions and attended graduation (Burrell School District, 1995).

When an Alabama parent complained to OCR that her student was denied participation in graduation, investigation showed that the student and parent had received warnings during the school year that the student lacked the required number of credits, and that all students, those with disabilities and those without, lacking the required number of credits were barred from graduation. OCR found no discrimination (Lauderdale County School District, 1996).

In response to a complaint that a North Carolina student was barred from participation in graduation, OCR found that the student's behavior at graduation practices had led to a limit on participation, and there was no discrimination (Forsyth County School District, 1997).

After an Illinois student was excluded from graduation ceremonies, OCR found that this student was excluded for misconduct (Glen Ellyn Public Schools, 1997).

RELATED § 504 AND ADA ISSUES

School District Employment Issues

Although most of the cases alleging violations of § 504 by school districts involve children with disabilities, § 504 protections are not limited to students. Adults with disabilities are also protected. The first case under § 504 to reach the U.S. Supreme Court (*Nassau County School Board v. Arline*, 1987) concerned a Florida teacher with recurring tuberculosis. The court found that she was eligible for protection under the Act, and that the school district should have conducted an evaluation to determine whether her condition made her "unqualified" for employment as a teacher, rather than terminating her without specific consideration of her disability.

There have been cases brought in Michigan, Pennsylvania, and Nebraska under § 504 or parallel state anti-discrimination statutes, concerning eligibility of people with insulin-dependent diabetes or seizure disorders for employment as school bus drivers (*Wilks v. Taylor School District*, 1988; *Commonwealth of Pennsylvania Department of Transportation, Bureau of Driver Licensing v. Tinsley*, 1989; *Wood v. Omaha School District*, 1993; *Commonwealth of Pennsylvania Department of Transportation, Bureau of Driver Licensing v. Boros, Brown, Clayton and Clayton*, 1993). At this time, it appears that the courts are recognizing the need for individualized fact-finding prior to determination of whether a person with a specific disability is "otherwise qualified" for a particular job.

Access for Parents and Members of the Public

The protection of § 504 extends to parents with disabilities, and public schools must accommodate their needs.
Case examples:
The deaf parents of two non-disabled children appealed the denial of interpreting services for some school events. These New York parents had been asked to attend meetings concerning their children's school problems and group meetings such as "Back to School Night." The district court

found the parents to be "otherwise qualified" and ordered the district to provide interpreters for "school initiated meetings" but not for "extra curricular activities" (*Rothschild v. Grottenthaler*, 1990).

When adults with disabilities made claims under § 504, access to Board of Education meetings in Michigan and Pennsylvania was required by OCR in two cases. These rulings involved one member of the public who was mobility-impaired, requiring that the Board of Education meeting be held in an accessible place, and another parent who required a sign language interpreter (Westwood, 1987; Lake Lehman, 1993).

Do Not Resuscitate Orders in School

Do Not Resuscitate (DNR) orders for terminally ill students or students who are severely disabled with life-threatening conditions are discussed in chapter 6: in addition, chapter 4 addresses nursing practice and licensure issues related to implementing and refusing to implement such orders, chapter 3 includes a care-based ethics perspective on this issue, and chapter 14 discusses the legal issues to be considered in developing school district policies regarding DNR orders. DNR orders are most often written in hospital settings, with the consent of the patient or a minor patient's parent, in consultation with appropriate medical specialists and with review by the hospital's ethics committee. In some cases, a court order is required, with independent legal representation for the patient.

There have been a few rulings that may be helpful to school districts considering policies regarding DNR, or individual requests from parents concerning DNR.
Case examples:
A Maine parent asked the school to accept a DNR order for her child. After characterizing the order as an "individual medical resuscitation plan," OCR upheld the district's general emergency policy because the policy applied to all students—those with and those without disabilities. The general emergency policy was to activate emergency medical services (call 911) and to institute CPR in the event of cardio-pulmonary arrest. OCR ruled that in some cases an individualized emergency plan may be required, which can be acceptable under § 504. In this particular case, the individualized plan had been developed by an appropriately selected team of professionals, and was well documented. In addition, OCR noted that the plan was for a specified time

period and would then be reviewed. OCR found no discrimination (Lewiston, 1994).

After reviewing concerns of pre-school programs for children with severe disabilities, the Maryland Attorney General advised that school districts should not interfere with parents' rights to make medical decisions for their children (Opinions of the Maryland Attorney General, 1994).

When the parents of a severely physically and mentally disabled 4-year-old asked a special education program to honor a DNR order which barred specific invasive procedures, the school asked the court to make a declaratory ruling and issue an injunction prohibiting implementation of the DNR order. The court denied the injunction and ruled that the parents had a right to obtain such an order, and that the school must implement it (*ABC School and DEF School v. Mr. and Mrs. M.*, 1997).

Since state laws vary and this area of the law is changing rapidly, schools receiving DNR orders from parents should immediately consult with legal counsel. A school nurse alone should not decide whether to implement such an order (Beekman, 1994; Brown & Valluzzi, 1995, Herlan, 1994; Kloppenburg & Dykes, 1995; Sapp, 1996).

Use of Restraint and Other Techniques in Behavior Management Programs

In cases of behavior that may be dangerous to the student or others, the school team may consider the use of aversives, including restraint, to assist in helping the student to control behavior. Reasonable use of such techniques should be based on: 1) urgent circumstances, such as avoidance of a clear danger to the child or others; 2) specification in the child's IEP or via some other recognized consultative process; and 3) its use as a last resort after less restrictive alternatives have not proven effective (Zirkel, 1998).

Although corporal punishment is still legal in some states, and the U.S. Supreme Court has ruled that corporal punishment does not violate the U.S. Constitution (*Ingraham v. Wright*, 1977), many states have outlawed it and most educators consider it barbaric and ineffective (Dayton, 1994). The use of physical restraints should only occur after careful analysis of the individual student's behavior, team discussion of alternatives, and development of a written plan.

Staff members who work with the student and may have occasion to use the planned restraints should be trained and supervised carefully to insure that restraint is used only as a last resort and the risk of injury is minimized.

Many schools use time-out facilities. After review of several rulings from the Office for Civil Rights, U.S. Department of Education, Zirkel (1998) lists safeguards for time-out:

- Time-out must be implemented in accordance with state and local school district policies.
- Time-out should be expressly incorporated into the child's IEP.
- Time-out should be used only when less intrusive procedures have proven ineffective.
- Time-out should be limited to short periods of time, typically 2–10 minutes.
- Time-out rooms should be unlocked, monitored, and otherwise in physically safe condition.

Perhaps because of parental concerns, Pennsylvania and Maine have both recently enacted rules that specifically address time-out conditions. Most parental complaints concerning the use of aversives have been resolved either by special education hearing officers or by the Office for Civil Rights. In most cases, the standards have called for planning through the IEP process with notice to and often consent from a parent, reasonable use, and review of use. When these standards have not been met, the school district's claims of immunity are usually met with findings of unreasonable use of force, lack of documentation of planning, and questions concerning the safety of specific techniques (Zirkel, 1998).

Case examples:
When a parent challenged a "blanket-wrapping" technique used for a 9-year-old with multiple mental and physical disabilities, the court found that the technique was reasonable and that school staff members were immune from suit (*Heidemann v. Rother*, 1996).

In responding to a parental complaint alleging use of aversives with an autistic child, OCR found that the school district had a policy barring the use of aversives and that the principal's investigation of several parental complaints had revealed no such use (Los Angeles Unified School District, 1998).

After a settlement of IDEA claims, the parents of a West Virginia student with autism filed suit. After the trial court dismissed the case, citing the agreement, the appeals court found that the agreement was limited to educational claims, and did not address the use of a restraint device which the parents claimed caused physical and psychological damage. The case was remanded for trial, to make factual determinations concerning the restraint device (*Ronnie Lee S. v. Mingo County Board of Education*, 1997).

(For additional discussion of the use of restraints, see chapter 6.)

STUDENTS WITH SPECIFIC HEALTH CONDITIONS

Students who Require Medication During School Hours

Perhaps the most noticeable result of the combination of § 504 and modern medical practice is the increasing numbers of students who have medication administered in school. In almost all cases, the medication is provided by the student's parent, but the responsibility for administration of medication falls on school staff members and is a matter of serious concern for school nurses and all other school staff members who may have been delegated medication duties.

After determining that a particular student is eligible for services and needs medication to be administered during school hours, the school must develop a plan, in keeping with state laws and regulations relevant to medication administration in schools. (See discussion in chapter 5 for further discussion of these laws; understanding their relevance to medication administration under § 504 and IDEA is essential.) The plan should be developed by appropriate members of the school team, usually the school nurse, parent, classroom teacher, and administrator to ensure safe and timely administration of medication and monitoring of the student's underlying health condition. If the school nurse delegates the task of medication administration to personnel other than licensed nurses or physicians, training and supervision of these unlicensed personnel must also be planned, implemented and documented. In states where education administrators make decisions regarding who can administer medication, consultation with the school nurse and, when indicated, a consulting physician or school medical advisor regarding legally permissible and clinically safe practices for medication administration, as well as student-specific concerns in each instance, would be wise from a liability perspec-

tive. (For additional discussion of delegation, see chapter 4.)

When it is agreed that a student may self-medicate and school policy allows such self-medication, that decision should be documented, a plan should be developed, including provisions for monitoring and on-going communication with the student and family, as indicated, and appropriate school staff members should be informed. (See also chapter 8 on confidentiality.)

Case examples:

A Mississippi school district which refused to administer Ritalin during the school day, as prescribed for students with ADD/ADHD, was found in violation of § 504 by OCR (Pearl, 1991).

OCR found no discrimination when an Illinois school sent a student with a mild asthma attack home to get his inhaler, rather than making a call to 911 for paramedics (Burbank, 1991).

When a California parent requested that a child with asthma be allowed to use his inhaler in school, OCR ruled that an evaluation (including appropriate medical documentation), a meeting, and development of a written plan were required (Culver, 1990).

A Colorado school district's refusal to administer eye drops without a physician's prescription was found to be discriminatory by OCR because the policy requiring prescriptions had not been enforced for anyone else in the past 2 years (Pueblo, 1993).

Parental waiver of liability required by a Pennsylvania school district as a condition of administration of medication in school was a violation of § 504. OCR ruled that administration of medication in school is a support service that must be provided (Berlin Brothers Valley, 1988).

Parents questioned the proper maintenance of their child's medication log by the school, and OCR determined that question to be a FERPA issue (see chapter 9) for the Family Policy Compliance Office of the U.S. Department of Education. Upon inspection, the medication log was found to conform to the California school district's policy requirements, and the student was recorded as receiving his medication on all days he was present in school (San Bernardino, 1990).

The Eighth Circuit Court of Appeals found no discrimination in two Missouri school districts' policies which prohibited administration of medication in amounts greater than the *Physicians' Desk Reference* recommended daily dosage (*DeBord v. Board of Education of the Ferguson Florissant School District*, 1997; *Davis v. Francis Howell School District*, 1997).

Some states have laws that permit, but do not require, Boards of Education to develop policies and procedures for the administration of medication. Under § 504, schools no longer have a choice of whether to agree to administer medication when the student has a condition that interferes with a major life function and administration of medication during school hours is necessary.

Nursing Procedures/Medical Treatments During School Hours

School health services have come to include a variety of supportive interventions and treatments, including nursing procedures. Although most of the legal activity concerning access to services such as clean intermittent catheterization has been under IDEA (see chapters 12 and 13), OCR has ruled on some complaints in this area.

Case example:
When a Kansas school district adopted a policy that shortened the school day for children who required tracheostomy care when the school nurse in an early childhood development center was absent and no substitute could be found, OCR found a violation of § 504. It is discriminatory to shorten the school day on the basis of disability, without individual consideration of the needs of each child (Hays, 1991).

(See also the discussion of *Cedar Rapids Community School District v. Garret F.*, 1999, in chapter 13.)

Students with ADD or ADHD

The *Diagnostic and Statistical Manual of Mental Disorders*, 4th ed. (American Psychiatric Association, 1994) provides the following diagnostic criteria:

Diagnostic Criteria for Attention-Deficit/Hyperactivity Disorder (ADD/ADHD):

A. Either (1) or (2):
  1) Six (or more) of the following symptoms of **inattention** have persisted for at least 6

months to a degree that is maladaptive and inconsistent with development level:
Inattention
(a) often fails to give close attention to details or makes careless mistakes in schoolwork, work, or other activities
(b) often has difficulty sustaining attention in tasks or play activities
(c) often does not seem to listen when spoken to directly
(d) often does not follow through on instructions and fails to finish schoolwork, chores, or duties in the workplace (not due to oppositional behavior or failure to understand instructions)
(e) often has difficulty organizing tasks and activities
(f) often avoids, dislikes, or is reluctant to engage in tasks that require sustained mental effort (such as schoolwork or homework)
(g) often loses things necessary for tasks or activities (e.g., toys, school assignments, pencils, books, or tools)
(h) is often easily distracted by extraneous stimuli
(i) is often forgetful in daily activities
(2) Six (or more) of the following symptoms of **hyperactivity-impulsivity** have persisted for at least 6 months to a degree that is maladaptive and inconsistent with developmental level:
Hyperactivity
(a) often fidgets with hands or feet or squirms in seat
(b) often leaves seat in classroom or in other situations in which remaining seated is expected
(c) often runs about or climbs excessively in situations in which it is inappropriate (in adolescents or adults, may be limited to subjective feelings of restlessness)
(d) often has difficulty playing or engaging in leisure activities quietly
(e) is often "on the go" or often acts as if "driven by a motor"
(f) often talks excessively
Impulsivity
(g) often blurts out answers before questions have been completed
(h) often has difficulty awaiting turn

(I) often interrupts or intrudes on others (e.g., butts into conversations or games)
B. Some hyperactive-impulsive or inattentive symptoms that caused impairment were present before age 7 years.
C. Some impairment from the symptoms is present in two or more settings (e.g., at school [or work] and at home)
D. There must be clear evidence of clinically significant impairment in social, academic, or occupational functioning.
E. The symptoms do not occur exclusively during the course of a Pervasive Developmental Disorder, Schizophrenia, or other Psychotic Disorder and are not better accounted for by another mental disorder (e.g., Mood Disorder, Anxiety Disorder, Dissociative Disorder, or a Personality Disorder).

The above Diagnostic Criteria list is reprinted with permission: American Psychiatric Association. (1994). *Diagnostic and Statistical Manual of Mental Disorders* (4th ed.). Washington, DC: Author.

In a U.S. Department of Education joint policy memorandum dated Sept. 16, 1991 (Joint Policy Memorandum, 1991), the Office of Special Education and Rehabilitative Services and the Office for Civil Rights discussed the needs of children with attention deficit disorder (ADD) and attention deficit hyperactivity disorder (ADHD). This memorandum suggested that children with ADD/ADHD be considered as candidates for special education as "other health impaired," "specific learning disability," or "seriously emotionally disturbed": the memorandum also recommended consideration of services under § 504 for those found ineligible for special education. After determining § 504 eligibility, the school district might consider classroom modifications. The 1999 IDEA regulations have added "attention deficit disorder and attention deficit hyperactivity disorder" to the list of examples of health problems which, when resulting in learning problems, may establish eligibility for special education as other health impaired. The school nurse has a vital role in planning for support for students with ADD/ADHD who are on medication: supervision of arrangements for medication in school; observation of a student receiving medication to assist in establishing appropriate dosage and medication schedule; and documentation of possible medication side effects.

Case examples:
A California parent complained to OCR that although the school district had been provided with records of her child's ADD from a prior school district and she had requested meetings to discuss the child's needs, his needs were not being addressed. OCR found that the district did not conduct an evaluation, as required, and failed to notify the parent of her rights, in violation of § 504 (Petaluma, 1995).

OCR found a California school district had punished a student for behaviors that were related to his ADHD, in violation of § 504 (Rialto, 1989).

In a follow-up to earlier communications addressing eligibility of students with ADD, OCR issued a statement that limited the requirement to evaluate (OCR Memorandum, Apr. 29, 1993). When the school district believes that a child does not require special education and denies further evaluation on that basis, the district must inform the parents of their right to challenge the decision.

The IDELR cites dozens of cases of complaints to OCR concerning services for students with ADD/ADHD. In general, OCR investigates the procedures followed by the school district prior to the decision to provide or to deny services. If the procedures conform to the requirements of § 504, the school district is usually found in compliance. Most of the cases in which OCR ruled against the school district showed failure of the school to do a reasonable evaluation or failure to hold a meeting to consider the request.

Students with HIV and Other Infectious Diseases

OCR addressed the issue of § 504 eligibility of students with Acquired Immune Deficiency Syndrome (AIDS), and those students who have tested positive for HIV but who may appear to be completely healthy (OCR Staff Memorandum, April 5, 1990). A summary of court cases involving the exclusion of children with AIDS from school showed universal agreement that children with AIDS were considered disabled under the § 504 definition.

After noting that any child who tested positive for HIV and was within the ages at which a state provides public education should be considered "qualified" to attend public school under § 504, OCR discussed the appropriate issues to consider in determining a school placement for a child with AIDS. OCR used the history of the case of *Martinez v. School Board of Hillsboro County* (1987, 1988, 1989) to illustrate the role of then-current public health information in school policy-making. In this case, a Florida 6-year-old with mental retardation and AIDS had been placed on homebound instruction, and her parent sought an injunction against the school district to require admission to school. The child was described as incontinent and drooling and sucking her fingers continually. The federal district court denied a preliminary injunction, and after a trial that included substantial expert testimony citing the position of the U.S. Centers for Disease Control and the American Academy of Pediatrics, the court ordered placement in a separate, glassed-in area, with visual and auditory contact with the pre-school class for mentally retarded children. The student would be assisted by a paraprofessional at all times. The Eleventh Circuit Court of Appeals vacated the decision and provided guidelines for a correct assessment of the risks of placing the child in the classroom with other children.

On remand, the federal district court considered additional medical opinions and also noted that the child's behavior had improved in the interim, reducing the risk of exposure of others to her body fluids. This court ordered the child admitted to the classroom, with the assistance of a paraprofessional and consultation with a school nurse. Commenting that all subsequent court cases have found classroom placement with individualized support appropriate for children with AIDS, OCR recommended that a school team review the individual child's medical status and "the latest reliable public health information" in making placement decisions. In conclusion, OCR found that children with AIDS were entitled to the procedural protections of § 504, and to confidentiality.

Case examples:
When the New York City Board of Education introduced a policy requiring classroom placement of students with AIDS unless their medical condition required otherwise, and complete confidentiality, a local board of education challenged the policy. In ruling for the city board, the court recognized that children with AIDS were protected by § 504 (*District 27 Community School Board v. Board of Education of the City of New York*, 1986).

When parents challenged a school superintendent's decision that a child with hepatitis B could be assigned to a regular classroom with support, the court upheld the placement citing testimony concerning the student's personal care habits and precautions to be taken in the classroom

(*Community High School District 155 v. Denz*, 1984).

An injunction ordering immediate readmission to school was issued by the court when a Georgia student had been suspended based on a rumor that he was a carrier of hepatitis B (*Jeffrey S. v. State Board of Education*, 1989).

A Virginia boy who is HIV-positive was rejected by a private martial arts school, and he then sued under the ADA, claiming discrimination. The federal district court decision found that there is a significant risk to the health and safety of other martial arts students, and that no reasonable modification could sufficiently reduce this risk without fundamentally altering the nature of the school's martial arts program, and the Fourth Circuit Court of Appeals affirmed (*Montalvo v. Radcliffe*, 1999).

A review of issues involving HIV and school athletics (Bogden, Fraser, Vega-Matos, & Ascroft, 1996) strongly supports inclusion of students who are HIV-positive in athletic programs, on the basis of the extremely remote possibility of transmission of HIV. The ADA standard of "reasonable accommodation" requires less from a private enterprise than Section 504 requires from a public school.

Diabetic Students

Diabetes is a chronic condition that results from failure of the pancreas gland to regulate blood sugar levels. Students with diabetes are eligible for protection under § 504 because diabetes significantly interferes with normal functioning of the endocrine system. The response to an inquiry to the Office of Special Education Programs, U.S. Department of Education, concerning IDEA-eligibility of diabetic students stressed that diabetes is listed as one of the examples of a chronic disease or condition included within the IDEA category of "other health impaired" (Inquiry, 1996). If a child's diabetes significantly affects his or her performance in school, the child should be referred for special education. (See chapter 12.)

Students with juvenile diabetes who are insulin-dependent may require specialized school health services during the school day. Services which have been requested and provided include: monitoring of blood sugar levels; administration of insulin injections (insulin and hypodermic needles provided by parents); monitoring for hypoglycemia, or low blood sugar, and provision of snacks and/or medication when needed; scheduling of classes and lunch periods to accommodate the child's medication schedule; and emergency plans. Current medical practice recommends that for many insulin-dependent diabetics, blood sugar tests and insulin injections be given prior to each meal. People with diabetes also have dietary limitations and must factor their exercise programs into their insulin dosage and schedule. Illness, stressful situations (like final exams), schedule changes (shortened school days, rotating schedules, special schedules to accommodate assemblies, and emotional upsets (all too frequent in adolescence) can also impact the blood sugar level of diabetics. Children with unstable blood sugar levels may require more frequent monitoring in school and consultation with the child's physician.

The case of *Elizabeth S. v. Gilhool* (1987), cited above, was a challenge to school refusals to provide monitoring of blood sugar levels and assistance in administration of supplementary insulin, as well as other support services for children with chronic medical conditions in school. This case was settled by an agreement between the plaintiff students and the Pennsylvania Department of Education in 1987. In a 1995 article, Vennum provides a comprehensive list of services that may be needed for students with diabetes and suggestions for training school staff members. This article cites denial of appropriate services for students with diabetes, based on surveys by the Western Pennsylvania Chapter of the Juvenile Diabetes Association, Pennsylvania Affiliate.

Case examples:
After investigating a complaint concerning support services for a Washington student with diabetes, OCR found that the school district had provided appropriate training for the school staff and had hired an aide to assist with the student's snack schedule and monitoring of various aspects of the student's status, although violations of § 504 were found in other areas (Renton, 1994).

OCR investigations of two California school districts showed that discipline procedures had been appropriately modified and schedule accommodations provided for students with diabetes (Eureka, 1995; Moreno, 1995).

OCR found that a California school district had failed to secure an adequate medical evaluation of a student with diabetes prior to both homebound and in-school placements. School staff members' lack of understanding of the student's disabilities

had led to failure to address his attendance problems appropriately (Yuba, 1995).

A California school-sponsored child development program did not include the supports needed by a child with diabetes. This child required monitoring of his blood sugar, and various treatments when indicated by his blood sugar level, in order to attend the program. OCR found violations of § 504 (Long Beach, 1993).

For § 504 purposes, a suitable team, including the parent, school nurse, school administrator, and other school personnel or health experts from the community, as needed, must develop a plan to ensure that the student receives appropriate services in school. Such services will vary depending on the acuity and stability of the student's condition, the student's age and developmental stage, and the student's knowledge, competencies, and compliance in managing his or her own disease and treatment regimen. It may be appropriate with a young, newly diagnosed and unstable diabetic who needs close supervision, extensive teaching, and support, and glucose monitoring and insulin injections in school to recommend that a nurse be available in the building. For another diabetic student whose condition is relatively stable, and who self-manages the blood glucose monitoring and insulin injections with demonstrated competence, a nurse may not need to be in the building on a full time basis. Assisting and observing the student, as necessary, and implementing an emergency plan can be delegated to other school personnel with appropriate training.

Students who are Substance Abusers

Section 504 does *not* provide protection to current substance abusers, except that it prohibits discrimination in hospital services or treatment programs; the ADA included amendments to § 504 to clarify this exception. The use of "drug screens" to identify possible student substance abusers has recently come under scrutiny.

Case example:
When an Ohio school district included a behavior assessment concerning possible use of drugs or alcohol in evaluating a student for specific learning disabilities, and did not inform the parent of either this aspect of the evaluation or the results, OCR found that such an assessment did not violate § 504, but stated that the parent should have been informed (Marietta, 1989).

A local school district asked OCR to comment on proposed inclusion of a drug and alcohol abuse screen in all evaluations of students with "severe behavior handicaps." OCR questioned whether there was a factual basis to support such screening, and recommended that drug and alcohol screens be used only when an individual student's status suggests such a need (Garner, 1989).

OCR found a violation of § 504 when a Washington school district had a policy of not evaluating students for special education if they were substance abusers. Determining that addiction is a handicapping condition, OCR saw discrimination on the basis of handicap, and noted that addiction could easily mask other disabilities such as emotional disturbance (Lake Washington, 1985).

OCR upheld the right of a Florida school district to expel a student after his second alcohol-related offense; although this student was disabled by his alcohol abuse, the penalty was applied equally to non-disabled students and disabled students (Pinellas, 1993).

Students with Asthma

Asthma is a chronic respiratory disease that is increasing in incidence (The Pew Environmental Health Commissions, 2000) and presents with a variety of symptoms and a wide range of severity. Deaths from asthma are increasing, and can occur quite suddenly. Asthmatic children range from those who need little to no assistance in school to those who require daily medications, respiratory treatments, and professional assessment of respiratory function, and who are frequently absent from school due to exacerbations and fatigue (Rosenfeld, 1999).

Case example:
When the parents of a Connecticut child with asthma complained to OCR about a broken school air cooling system, no violation of § 504 was found when it was determined that air quality was acceptable and there had been no increase in absences of other children with asthma or allergies (Windsor, 1991).

However, it would be wise for the school nurse to consult a child's physician to determine the child's health status and the nature of symptoms alleged to be related to air quality problems.

Case example:
A Connecticut state special education hearing officer found violations of § 504 when a school district failed to properly evaluate an asthmatic student who complained of air quality problems in the building where she was scheduled to attend school (Connecticut Special Hearing Decision, #95-116).

In considering whether students with asthma qualify for services under § 504, it is important to keep in mind the wide variation in severity of the disease. Some students, whose asthmatic symptoms are so mild or occur so rarely that they do not *significantly* interfere with a major life function (breathing) may not be eligible for § 504 services and may not need program modification or classroom accommodations in school. However, the large majority of students with asthma will be eligible for services under § 504, from students who have mild to moderate exertional asthma to those who have severe, debilitating disease.

The latter group of students may also be eligible for special education if their conditions significantly interfere with learning as a result of frequent absences due to exacerbations of the asthma, time spent in the health office for daily treatments, fatigue, decreased self-esteem, and the side effects of medications on learning. Like students with diabetes, the stability of the student's health status, the acuity of the disease, the age and development of the student, and the student's knowledge and self-management skills are important considerations in determining an appropriate plan of services and accommodations. From both a legal and a clinical perspective, assessment of the student's respiratory status before and after medication and treatments may be as important as the treatment itself. Therefore, availability of a school nurse for assessment and decision-making purposes is a critical component of a § 504 plan, especially for asthmatic students whose conditions are at the more severe end of the spectrum. A useful form for school use can be obtained from the Asthma and Allergy Foundation of America. This form is reproduced in Rosenfeld, 1999.

Emergency Services for Students

As in the California case cited above, some students require individualized emergency plans due to their particular health care needs. Most school districts have emergency procedures that are followed for all students who are sick or injured at school, unless there is an individualized plan.

Case example:
OCR investigated a New York parent's complaint about treatment provided to a student with mental retardation whose chin was cut in gym class. The school nurse had stopped the bleeding and bandaged the cut. Unable to contact the parent by telephone, the nurse completed an accident report that noted that stitches might be needed and sent the student home on the bus. The parent argued that the school should have sent the student to the hospital. OCR found that the school had followed its usual procedure and that this student had been treated the same as students without disabilities; therefore, there was no violation of § 504 (New York, 1989).

However, a school nurse in this situation must also consider professional standards of practice and the possibility of a liability action. An attempt to contact an alternate designated by the parent, and documentation of a note sent home with the student and follow-up telephone calls concerning the possible needs for further treatment would have been appropriate in this case, although not within the scope of an OCR investigation.

Case example:
The parent of a non-ambulatory, non-verbal, severely brain-damaged Missouri student complained concerning treatment provided when the student's leg was broken. The school summoned an ambulance after the parent could not be reached by telephone. OCR found no violation of § 504 because: 1) the school followed its usual emergency procedures; and 2) the parent had agreed to an Individualized Education Program for her child which included no special emergency plan (St. Louis, 1989).

It should be noted that a parent might not necessarily be aware that a special emergency plan should have been developed for a child with disabilities; that determination is a school responsibility.

Case example:
After a Ohio student with a seizure disorder and heart problems collapsed on the school bus and died three days later, the parent sued the school district and various school district personnel. The bus driver, thinking that the student was having a seizure, had tried to use her radio to get help, and had then continued on her route to the child's home. The court determined that the school district had no affirmative duty to provide care, the child's rights were not violated, and the school staff

were immune from state law claims unless there was evidence of gross negligence (*Sargi v. Kent City Board of Education*, 1995).

The general standard a court applies in this type of case is whether the school bus driver acted in a reasonable way, given the circumstances. A secondary issue might be whether the school had made sufficient transportation and emergency plans for this child, and whether school staff members and bus personnel had followed the plans. (See also discussion of liability in chapter 4.)

Students with Temporary Disabilities

Section 504 also protects the rights of people who are temporarily disabled.

Case examples:
In the case of a California student with a broken leg who was denied support services, OCR found that an evaluation was required, and that appropriate support services must be provided (Central, 1987).

OCR found a violation of § 504 when a Missouri student who had been injured in an accident was not provided with adequate homebound instruction (Lee's Summit, 1984).

Planning Time

Sometimes a school district will need some time to assemble documentation, locate the appropriate specialists for an IEP meeting, and hire and train people to provide services. OCR has recognized the problem in Seattle (1999) which allows up to 10 school days when a child may be at home, awaiting the development of a program. In this particular case, the school district was seeking updated medical information and developing a health care plan, as well as assigning the student with diabetes to a school with a school nurse available every school day.

REFERENCES

American Psychiatric Association. (1994). *Diagnostic and statistical manual of mental disorders* (4th ed.). Washington, DC: Author.

Beekman, L. E. (1994). DNR orders — what should a school district do? *EDLAW Briefing Paper*, 4(6).

Bogden, J. F., Fraser, K., Vega-Matos, C., & Ascroft, J. (1996). *Someone at school has AIDS*. Alexandria, VA: National Association of State Boards of Education.

Brown, S. E., and Valluzzi, J. L. (1995). Do not resuscitate orders in early intervention settings: Who should make the decision? *Infants and Young Children.*

Bryant, A. L. (1993). Hostile Hallways: The AAUW survey on sexual harassment in America's schools. *Journal of School Health*, 63(8).

Connecticut Special Education Hearing Decision #95-116. (1995). (Unpublished; available from the Due Process Unit, Connecticut State Department of Education, Middletown, CT).

Dayton, J. (1994). Corporal punishment in public schools: The legal and political battle continues. *West's Education Law Reporter 89*: 729.

Doty, D. S., and Strauss, S. (1996). "Prompt and Equitable": The importance of student sexual harassment policies in the public schools, *West's Education Law Reporter 113*: 1.

Duncan, T. K., & Rapport, M. J. (1998). Understanding and implementing OCR's sexual harassment guidance. *West's Education Law Reporter 124*: 21.

Gorney, C. (1999, June 13). Teaching Johnny the appropriate way to flirt. *The New York Times*, Sunday Magazine section, p.43.

Hartog, F. (1995). The new disciplinary rules for students with guns. *EDLAW Briefing Paper, 4*(9).

Hassenpflug, A. (1998). Boys will be boys. *West's Education Law Reporter 126*: 555.

Herlan, E. R. (1994). The legal framework for responding to DNR orders on school grounds, Individual with Disabilities Education Law Reporter (IDELR) Special Report #11. Horsham, PA: LRP Publications.

Inquiry, 24 IDELR (LRP) 853 (OSEP 1996).

Joint Policy Memorandum, 18 IDELR (LRP) 116 (U.S. Department of Education, 1991).

Kaesberg, M. A., & Murray, K. T. (1994). Americans with Disabilities Act. *West's Education Law Reporter 90:* 11.

Kloppenburg, D., and Dykes, M. K. (1995). Do Not Resuscitate! The schools' response to DNR orders. *CEC Today*, May 1995.

Lunenberg School District, 22 IDELR (LRP) 290 (SEA VT 1994).

New guidelines spell out sexual harassment in schools. (1997). *School Health Professional, 4*(6).

Opinions of the Maryland Attorney General, *79*, No. 94-028. (May 13, 1994).

Osborne, A. G. (1995). Court interpretations of the Americans with Disabilities Act and their effect on school districts, *West's Education Law Reporter 95*: 489.

Pennsylvania Department of Education. (1987). Basic Education Circular: *Physically handicapped and other health impaired students.* Harrisburg, PA: Author.

Physicians' desk reference (PDR). (1999). Montvale, NJ: Medical Economics Data Production Company.

Reiser, L., & Cohn, S. (1995). Legal issues regarding children with special health care needs. In Goldberg, B. (Ed.), *Sports and exercise for children with chronic health conditions.* Champaign, IL: Human Kinetics Publishers, Inc.

Rosenfeld, S. J. (1995). Planning for ADA compliance. *EDLAW Briefing Paper, 5*(6).

Rosenfeld, S. J. (1996a). "Kick 'em out!" movement continues. *EDLAW Briefing Paper, 5*(9).

Rosenfeld, S. J. (1996b). "Kick 'em out": An update. *EDLAW Briefing Paper 5*(10).

Rosenfeld, S. J. (1999). Why you should be concerned about asthma. *EDLAW Briefing Paper, 9*(2).

Rossow, L. F., & Parkinson, J. R. (1996a). Another circuit rules on student peer harassment. *School Law Rep. 38*(5).

Rossow, L. F., & Parkinson, J. R. (1996b). New developments in the area of peer sexual harassment, *School Law Rep. 38*(12).

Rossow, L. F., & Parkinson, J. R. (1997). The Fifth Circuit considers standards for school district liability in teacher-student sexual harassment cases. *School Law Rep. 39*(4).

Sapp, S. K. (1996). Compliance with "Do Not Resuscitate" orders in school. *NOLPE Notes 31*(8).

Sorenson, G. (1994). Peer sexual harassment: Remedies and guidelines under federal law. *West's Education Law Reporter 92*: 1.

The Pew Environmental Health Commission. (2000). *Attack asthma.* Baltimore: John Hopkins School of Public Health.

Thompson, D. P., & Truelock, A. (1998). Student-to-student sexual harassment: Sifting through the wreckage. *West's Education Law Reporter 125*: 1037.

U.S. Department of Education. (1997). *Sexual harassment guidance: Harassment of students by school employees, other students, or third parties*, 62 Fed.Reg. 12034.

Utah Office of Education (1992). *Section 504: Guidelines for educators.* Salt Lake City: Author.

Vennum, M. K. (1995 Winter). Students with diabetes: Is there legal protection? *Journal of Law & Education, 24* (33).

Wolohan, J. T. (1996). The Americans with Disabilities Act and its effect on high school athletic associations' age restrictions. *West's Education Law Reporter 106*: 971.

Zirkel, P. (1998). Aversives: A legal look at physical restraint, corporal punishment, time-out. *The Special Educator Bonus Report.*

TABLE OF CASES

Rothschild v. Grottenthaler, 716 F.Supp. 796, EHLR
(LRP) 441:539 (S.D. N.Y. 1989); 725 F.Supp. 776, 16
EHLR (LRP) 78 (S.D. N.Y. 1989); 907 F.2d 286, 16
EHLR (LRP) 1020 (2nd Cir. 1990).

Sandison v. Michigan High School Athletic Association,
863 F.Supp. 483, 21 IDELR (LRP) 658 (E.D. Mich.
1994); 64 F.3d 1026, 23 IDELR (LRP) 222 (6th Cir.
1995).

Sargi v. Kent City Board of Education, 70 F.3d 907, 23
IDELR (LRP) 431 (6th Cir. 1995).

Schuldt v. Mankato Independent School District, 16
EHLR (LRP) 1111 (D. Minn. 1990); 937 F.2d 1357,
18 IDELR (LRP) 16 (8th Cir. 1991).

Seamons v. Snow, 84 F.3d 1226 (10th Cir. 1996).

Thomas v. Davidson Academy, 846 F. Supp. 611, 20
IDELR (LRP) 1375 (M.D. Tenn. 1994).

Urban by Urban v. Jefferson County School District R-1,
870 F.Supp. 1558, 21 IDELR (LRP) 985 (D.Colo.
1994); 89 F.3d 720, 24 IDELR (LRP) 465 (10th Cir.
1996).

Wilks v. Taylor School District, 435 N.W.2d 436 (Mich.
App. 1988).

Wood v. Omaha School District, 784 F.Supp. 1441, 18
IDELR (LRP) 673 (D.Neb. 1992); 985 F.2d 437, 19
IDELR (LRP) 686 (8th Cir. 1993).

Yankton School District v. Schramm, 900 F.Supp. 1182,
23 IDELR (LRP) 42 (D. S.D. 1995); 93 F.3d 1369, 24
IDELR (LRP) 704 (8th Cir. 1996).

OFFICE FOR CIVIL RIGHTS (OCR) DECISIONS

Aiken (SC) County School District, 23 IDELR (LRP)
113 (OCR 1995).

Aldine (TX) Independent School District, 16 EHLR
1411 (OCR 1990).

Anchor Bay (MI) School District, 25 IDELR (LRP) 71
(OCR 1996).

Asheville City (NC) School System, 25 IDELR (LRP)
155 (OCR 1996).

Auburn City (AL) School District, 16 EHLR (LRP) 177
(OCR 1989).

Beaufort County (SC) School District, 26 IDELR (LRP)
1154 (OCR 1997).

Berlin Brothers Valley (PA) School District, EHLR
(LRP) 353:124 (OCR 1988).

Boston (MA) Public Schools, 21 IDELR (LRP) 170
(OCR 1994).

Broward County (FL) School District, 22 IDELR (LRP)
374 (OCR 1994).

Burbank (IL) School District #111, 18 IDELR (LRP)
284 (OCR 1991).

Burrell (PA) District, 22 IDELR (OCR 1995).

Central (CA) Elementary School District, EHLR (LRP)
352:544 (OCR 1987).

Chester County (SC) School District, 19 IDELR (LRP)
545 (OCR 1992).

Compton (CA) Unified School District, 23 IDELR
(LRP) 249 (OCR 1995).

Conejo Valley (CA) Unified School District, 23 IDELR
(LRP) 448 (OCR 1995).

Conejo Valley (CA) Unified School District, 20 IDELR
(LRP) 1276 (OCR 1993).

Conway (AR) Public Schools, 28 IDELR (LRP) 995
(OCR 1998).

Coventry (RI) Public Schools, 20 IDELR (LRP) 1081
(OCR 1993).

Culver City (CA) Unified School District, 16 EHLR
(LRP) 673 (OCR 1990).

Curwensville Area (PA) School District, EHLR (LRP)
353:292 (OCR 1989).

Dade County (FL) School District, 23 IDELR (LRP)
838 (OCR 1995).

East Baton Rouge (LA) Parish School System, EHLR
(LRP) 353:252 (OCR 1989).

Eldon (MO) R-1 School District, EHLR (LRP) 352:144
(OCR 1986).

Elk Grove (CA) Unified School District, 21 IDELR
(LRP) 941 (OCR 1994).

Eureka (CA) City School District, 23 IDELR (LRP) 238
(OCR 1995).

Ferguson Florissant (MO) R-II School District, 28
IDELR (LRP) 885 (OCR 1997).

Florida State Department of Education, 28 IDELR
(LRP) 1002 (OCR 1998).

Forsyth County (NC) School District, 26 IDELR (LRP)
757 (OCR 1997).

Fort Smith (AR) Public Schools, 20 IDELR (LRP) 97
(OCR 1993).

Garner, letter to, EHLR (LRP) 305:53 (OCR 1989).

Glen Ellyn (IL) Public Schools, District #41, 28 IDELR
(LRP) 882 (OCR 1997).

Grafton (ND) Public Schools, 20 IDELR (LRP) 82
(OCR 1993).

Grangeville (ID) Joint District #241, 21 IDELR (LRP)
1139 (OCR 1994).

Granite (UT) School District, 19 IDELR (LRP) 984
(OCR 1993).

Hartford County (MD) Public Schools, 18 IDELR
(LRP) 1114 (OCR 1992).

Hays (KS) Unified School District #489, 18 IDELR
(LRP) 866 (OCR 1991).

Lake Lehman (PA) School District, 20 IDELR (LRP)
546 (OCR 1993).

Lake Washington (WA) School District #414, EHLR

(LRP) 257:611 (OCR 1985).

Lauderdale County (AL) School District, 25 IDELR (LRP) 161 (OCR 1996).

Lee's Summit (MO) Area School District, EHLR (LRP) 257:629 (OCR 1984).

Lewiston (ME) Public Schools, 21 IDELR (LRP) 83 (OCR 1994).

Long Beach (CA) Unified School District, 1 ECLPR (LRP) 335 (OCR 1993).

Los Angeles (CA) Unified School District, 30 IDELR (LRP) 150 (OCR 1998).

Lowell (MI) Area School District, EHLR (LRP) 352:574 (OCR 1987).

Mansfield (WA) School District #207, 22 IDELR (LRP) 1050 (OCR 1995).

Marietta (OH) City Schools, EHLR (LRP) 353:369 (OCR 1989).

Marion County (FL) School District, 20 IDELR (LRP) 634 (OCR 1993).

Mill Creek Valley (KS) Unified School District No. 329, 20 IDELR (LRP) 821 (OCR 1993).

Mobile (AL) County School District, 23 IDELR (LRP) 353 (OCR 1995).

Moffat County (CO) School District RE-1, 26 IDELR (LRP) 28 (OCR 1996).

Moreno Valley (CA) Unified School District, 22 IDELR (LRP) 902 (OCR 1995).

Mt. Gilead (OH) Exempted Village School District, 20 IDELR (LRP) 765 (OCR 1993).

Narragansett (RI) Public Schools, 20 IDELR (LRP) 997 (OCR 1993).

New York, Board of Education of the City of (NY), 16 EHLR (LRP) 457 (OCR 1989).

Northwest (MO) R-I School District, 24 IDELR (LRP) 1193 (OCR 1996).

OCR Memorandum, Apr. 29, 1993, 19 IDELR (LRP) 876 (OCR 1993).

OCR Senior Staff Memorandum, Oct. 28, 1988, EHLR (LRP) SA-52 (OCR 1988).

OCR Senior Staff Memorandum, May 4, 1992, 19 IDELR (LRP) 889 (OCR 1992).

OCR Senior Staff Memorandum, May 13, 1992, 19 IDELR (LRP) 891 (OCR 1992).

OCR Senior Staff Memorandum, Nov. 19, 1992, 19 IDELR (LRP) 859 (OCR 1992).

OCR Staff Memorandum, Apr. 5, 1990, 16 EHLR (LRP) 712 (OCR 1990).

Office for Civil Rights Complaint Resolution Manual (1993), 20 IDELR (LRP) XIV-142 (OCR 1993); rev. 1998.

Ontario-Montclair (CA) Unified School District, 24 IDELR (LRP) 780 (OCR 1996).

Oregon State School for the Blind, 16 EHLR (LRP) 1376 (OCR 1990).

Pearl (MS) Public School District, 17 EHLR (LRP) 1004 (OCR 1991).

Petaluma City (CA) Elementary School District, 23 IDELR (LRP) 245 (OCR 1995).

Philadelphia (PA), School District of, 24 IDELR (LRP) 1188 (OCR 1996).

Pinellas County (FL) School District, 20 IDELR (LRP) 561 (OCR 1993).

Prescott (AZ) Unified School District, EHLR (LRP) 352:541 (OCR 1987).

Pueblo (CO) School District #60, 20 IDELR (LRP) 1066 (OCR 1993).

Quaker Valley (PA) School District, EHLR (LRP) 352:235 (OCR 1986).

Radnor Township (PA) School District, 20 IDELR (LRP) 636 (OCR 1993).

Renton (WA) School District, 21 IDELR (LRP) 859 (OCR 1994).

Rialto (CA) Unified School District, EHLR (LRP) 353:201 (OCR 1989).

Rockdale County (GA) School District, 22 IDELR (LRP) 1047 (OCR 1995).

Runkel, response to letter from, 25 IDELR (LRP) 387 (OCR 1996).

Sachem (NY) Central School District, EHLR (LRP) 352:462 (OCR 1987).

Saginaw (MI), School District of the City of, 16 EHLR (LRP) 801 (OCR 1990).

St. Louis, Special School District of (MO), 16 EHLR (LRP) 117 (OCR 1989).

San Bernardino (CA) City Unified School District, 16 EHLR (LRP) 645 (OCR 1990).

San Francisco (CA) Unified School District, EHLR (LRP) 257:257 (OCR 1981).

Santa Ana (CA) Unified School District, 19 IDELR (LRP) 501 (OCR 1992).

Shoreline (WA) School District #412, 24 IDELR (LRP) 774 (OCR 1996).

South Central (IN) Area Special Education Cooperative, 17 EHLR (LRP) 248 (OCR 1990).

Special School District of St. Louis County (MO), 16 EHLR (LRP) 307 (OCR 1989).

Tacoma (WA) School District #10, 24 IDELR (LRP) 781 (OCR 1996).

Texas Education Agency, 16 EHLR (LRP) 750 (OCR 1990).

Tippecanoe (IN) School Corporation, EHLR (LRP) 353:217 (OCR 1988).

Tuscaloosa City (AL) School District, 27 IDELR (LRP) 53 (OCR 1997).

Uxbridge (MA) Public Schools, 20 IDELR (LRP) 827 (OCR 1993).

Veir, letter to, from Peelan, Director of Elementary and Secondary Education Policy Division, 20 IDELR (LRP) 864 (OCR, no date provided, published in 1994).

West Warwick (RI) Public Schools, 20 IDELR (LRP) 684 (OCR 1993).

Westwood (MI) Community School District, EHLR (LRP) 352:470 (OCR 1987).

Windsor (CT) Public Schools, 17 EHLR (LRP) 692 (OCR 1991).

Yorktown (NY) Central School District, 16 EHLR (LRP) 108 (OCR 1989).

Yuba City (CA) Unified School District, 22 IDELR (LRP) 1148 (OCR 1995).

Yuma (AZ) Union High School District #070, 17 EHLR (LRP) 7 (OCR 1990).

Zirkel, letter to, 20 IDELR (LRP) 134 (OCR 1993).

See page 625 for Table of Federal Statutes and Regulations.

Chapter Twelve
Special Education Law

Mary H. B. Gelfman

INTRODUCTION

This chapter is intended to give the reader specific information about the rights of students with health-related learning problems under the Individuals with Disabilities Education Act (IDEA), (20 U.S.C. 1400 et seq., Regulations at 34 C.F.R. 300) including a few pertinent court decisions. A general overview and history of special education legislation is contained in chapter 2 and should be read as an introduction to this chapter by those less familiar with special education law. Discussion of major areas of litigation under IDEA is found in chapter 13.

The Education of All Handicapped Children Act (EHA) (Pub.L. 94-142) was passed in 1975. This law established national standards for public education of children with disability-related learning problems and offered some financial assistance to states and local school districts providing special education services under the Act. The EHA was renamed the Individuals with Disabilities Education Act in 1990 (Public Law 101-476, 1990) and is now usually referred to as IDEA. Congress made additional amendments to IDEA in 1997 in response to many concerns in the education community. Significant areas addressed in 1997 include: disciplinary procedures for students with disabilities that may, or may not, affect behavior; the contents of the Individualized Education Program (IEP) for each child eligible for special education; addition of mediation to procedures for resolving disputes between parents and school districts concerning special education services to individual children; and membership of the IEP team. Administrative changes affecting the state and federal departments of education were also adopted in 1997. Proposed regulations published in October 1997 evoked varied strong responses, and the U.S. Department of Education released final regulations in March 1999, effective May 11, 1999. Compliance was required on the date that each state received fiscal year 1999 funding from the federal government, estimated to be July 1, 1999, or October 1, 1999, whichever was

sooner. The 1999 regulations include Appendix A, a Notice of Interpretation, which provides additional guidance in question and answer format.

The 1999 IDEA regulations define a child requiring special education as a child

…with mental retardation, a hearing impairment including deafness, a speech or language impairment, a visual impairment including blindness, serious emotional disturbance (hereafter referred to as emotional disturbance), an orthopedic impairment, autism, traumatic brain injury, an other health impairment, a specific learning disability, deaf-blindness or multiple disabilities; *and who, by reason thereof, needs special education and related services* [emphasis added].

Special education is defined as

…specially designed instruction, at no cost to the parents, to meet the unique needs of a child with a disability, including instruction conducted in the classroom, in the home, in hospitals and institutions, and in other settings and instruction in physical education. Speech-language pathology (or any related service) may be considered special education, rather than a related service, under state law.

This distinction is important in states that do not provide related services unless the student is receiving special education. Travel training and vocational education for students with disabilities can also be considered special education.

Specially designed instruction means adapting, as appropriate to the needs of an eligible child under this part, the content, methodology, or delivery of instruction to address the unique needs of the child that result from the child's disability and to ensure access of the child to the general curriculum, so that he or she can meet the educational standards within the jurisdiction of the public agency that apply to all children.

At no cost means that all specially-designed instruction is provided without charge, but does not preclude incidental fees that are normally charged to non-disabled students or their parents as a part of the regular education program.

Physical education means the development of physical and motor fitness; fundamental motor skills and patterns; and skills in aquatics, dance, individual and group games and sports (including intramural and lifetime sports) and includes special physical education, adapted physical education, movement education and motor development.

Travel training means providing instruction, as appropriate, to children with significant cognitive disabilities and any other children with disabilities who require this instruction, to enable them to develop an awareness of the environment in which they live; and learn the skills necessary to move effectively and safely from place to place within that environment (e.g., in school, in the home, at work, and in the community).

Vocational education means organized educational programs that are directly related to the preparation of individuals for paid or unpaid employment, or for additional preparation for a career requiring other than a baccalaureate or advanced degree.

In addition to identifying and providing appropriate services for children with disabilities within the school age population, IDEA requires that pre-school children (ages 3 to 5 years) be identified and provided services if they have a disability that is likely to interfere with learning. Special education services for children of school age (5 to 21) and pre-school children (3 to 5) fall within Part B of the 1975 EHA, and are often referred to as "Part B programs" or "Part B funding." Under another section of IDEA, Part C (formerly Part H), evaluations and services for children with disabilities from birth to age 3 are also available.

During the 1993–1994 school year 5,361,801 students in the 50 states, the District of Columbia, and Puerto Rico, from birth through age 21, were classified as having disabilities and needing early intervention or special education services (U.S. Department of Education, 1995). The U.S. Department of Education estimated the total resident population of children, birth through age 21, at 81,962,968, and gives the special education enrollment as approximately 7.66% of the total.

The 1993–1994 population of school-age children (6–21) served under Part B of IDEA was described as percentages of the total school population, including both those with and those without disabilities:

Students with Specific Learning Disabilities	4.19%
Students with Speech Impairments	1.74%
Students with Mental Retardation	0.93%
Students with Serious Emotional Disturbance	0.71%
Students with Multiple Disabilities	0.19%
Students with Other Health Impairments	0.14%
Students with Hearing Impairments	0.11%
Students with Orthopedic Impairments	0.10%
Students with Visual Impairments	0.04%
Students with Autism	0.03%
Students with Traumatic Brain Injury	0.01%
Students with Deaf-Blindness	[less than 0.00%]
Total receiving special education services	8.19%
Total not eligible for special education	91.81%

These percentages do not include pre-schoolers with disabilities and those in birth-to-three programs. Since autism and traumatic brain injury were added as separate categories by Congressional action in 1991, it is possible that some students with these two disabilities, previously identified as learning disabled, seriously emotionally disturbed, or other health impaired, have not been reclassified.

The determination of "label" or primary disability for each student in need of special education is made by the school team that determines eligibility. When there is a choice, parents sometimes prefer a disability that they perceive carries less stigma, such as learning disabilities. The student's Individualized Education Program (IEP) must address all identified areas of disability: a student with learning disabilities and emotional disturbance must be offered services for both disabilities. The only way the choice of disability category can be challenged for an individual student is through the IEP team and a hearing. Federal and state education department monitors may observe that a state or school district appears to have more students identified in one category than is usual, but they are without authority to change the classification of a specific student.

FEDERAL SPECIAL EDUCATION REQUIREMENTS

In order for a state to qualify for funding under IDEA, special education services must be provided to those students who are found eligible under the provisions of the Act. Such services may include individually designed instruction, as well as related services and program modifications that are necessary in order for the student to make reasonable educational progress. In special education discussions, those public school services that are routinely provided for children without disabilities are usually referred to as "regular education." For example, the fourth grade program is called "regular education." The individual services provided for a fourth grader who has learning disabilities, whether provided in a regular classroom or in a resource room for children with disabilities, are called "special education."

Many states have additional requirements for special education. A few examples are included to illustrate how states incorporated existing law when EHA was enacted and have filled perceived gaps in the federal scheme. These illustrations may not all be current, for two reasons. First, federal compliance monitoring teams have sometimes allowed state-by-state variations and have sometimes found conflict between such variations and federal requirements. States have revised their laws, regulations, and policies in response to federal compliance findings, in order to maintain receipt of federal funding. A second reason for change at the state level is a recent movement to eliminate state requirements that may appear to exceed federal requirements. While legally acceptable, such requirements are perceived as "voluntary" and thus may appear to be areas for possible cost savings in state budgets. The reader is cautioned that examples of state variation used here may not apply in other states and may no longer be in force by the time of publication.

Summary of Legal Requirements Under IDEA

The fundamental requirements for the special education process found in IDEA include the following:

1. Each school district must make an affirmative effort to identify children with disabilities who live in the district and might be in need of special education. This activity is usually called "Child Find."
2. Parents must be notified of and given an opportunity to participate in meetings concerning their child's special education.
3. Parental consent is required prior to the initial evaluation for special education, prior to initial special education placement, and prior to subsequent triennial re-evaluations.
4. The evaluation for special education eligibility must be provided by a multidisciplinary team (professionals with knowledge in areas relevant to the student's disability or suspected disability) and may include school health assessments and medical diagnostic workups as needed to identify a student's unique needs.
5. After an eligibility determination, an Individualized Education Program (IEP) is developed that addresses the student's specialized needs as identified in the evaluation at a multidisciplinary team meeting to which the child's parents have been invited.
6. Parents have the right to appeal disagreements with the school concerning their child's special education identification, evaluation, educational placement, or the provision of a free appropriate public education to their child.
7. Each child enrolled in special education must have an annual review IEP meeting, and must be re-evaluated at least every three years.
8. Under IDEA (as well as FERPA; see chapter 9), parents are guaranteed access to their student's school records.
9. Parents may request an independent evaluation at school district expense if they disagree with the one provided by the school district.
10. Parents must be notified of these and other rights.

Court Interpretations of IDEA: The *Rowley* Standard

The decision of the U.S. Supreme Court in the case of *Board of Education of the Hendrick Hudson Central School District v. Rowley* in 1982 set forth judicial standards for evaluating the appropriateness of a special education program for an individual student with a disability. The Court applied two tests: 1) did the school district follow the procedural requirements of the Act (see chapter 2 and below); and 2) did the individualized special education program (IEP) enable the child to make educational progress. Since this case concerned a deaf and very bright student, the Court called her educational progress of passing from grade level to grade level with As and Bs "appropriate progress." "Educational benefit" is another term used by courts to describe the desired results of an appropriate special education program for a child with a disability.

Procedural Rights of Parents of Children with Disabilities

Notice. IDEA requires public school districts to inform parents of children with disabilities whenever the school proposes or refuses

…to initiate or change the identification, evaluation, or educational placement of the child or the provision of a free appropriate public education to the child.

The specific content of this notice is also delineated in the federal regulations, including a requirement that the notice be written in "language understandable to the general public" and "provided in the native language or other mode of communication of the parent."

Consent. After receiving a referral or identifying a child with a possible disability, the public school district must obtain written parental consent prior to going forward with an evaluation, before an initial special education placement and prior to each triennial re-evaluation. States may have additional consent requirements: Connecticut requires consent prior to placement of a child in a private school for special education services. Many local school districts ask that parents sign consent each year for the Individualized Education Program (IEP) developed for the student. While additional consents are not a violation of IDEA, the federal regulations bar requiring additional consents as a condition for services. When a parent denies consent, or withdraws consent previously given, the school district may use state procedures or a due process hearing under IDEA to challenge, on behalf of the student, the parent's refusal to consent to evaluation and/or placement. (See below.)

Timelines. A meeting to develop an IEP must be held within 30 days of the determination that a student is eligible for special education, and every student in need of special education must have an IEP in effect at the beginning of each school year. While the federal regulations provide that "an IEP must be implemented as soon as possible following [the meeting that developed it]", state requirements may be more specific, including timelines for separate parts of the process. Connecticut requires that there be no more than 45 school days between referral of a child with disabilities and special education placement (if the child is eligible).

Case Example:
Prolonged delays in services for children with disabilities in the New York City schools, due to waiting lists for evaluations and delays in placements, were found in violation of EHA by the federal district court in 1979, and specific timetables for evaluating and placing students in need of special education were ordered (*Jose P. v. Ambach,* 1979).

Confidentiality and Access to Student Records. Included within IDEA are requirements concerning parental access to their student's education records. In brief, parents may request an opportunity to inspect records, and may request copies of most materials in student's school files. All personally identifiable student information must be kept confidential by the school and may not be released outside the school without parental consent. A requirement concerning a student's special education records that appears in IDEA, but not in FERPA, is that when a school district notifies a parent that particular special education records are no longer needed "to provide educational services", the parent may request destruction of the identified records. This provision is problematic, because records of education programs that receive federal funds must be retained after the conclusion of the service provided for auditing purposes (Breecher, 1990, and Cossey, 1984).

State record retention and destruction requirements may also apply. (Record retention issues are covered in greater detail in chapter 9.)

Notice of Parental Rights. IDEA also requires that parents be informed of their rights. Procedural violations, including failure to provide parents adequate notice of their rights, can cause the school district to fail the first Rowley test. However, failure to comply with procedural rights does not automatically invalidate a special education program.

Case example:
In a Louisiana case, the Fifth Circuit held that even though the school district had a record of many procedural errors, including failure to notify parents of their rights, when a child makes reasonable progress in school a minimal penalty for procedural violations can be upheld by the appellate court (*Salley v. St. Tammany Parish School Board,* 1995).

Due Process Appeal Rights

Complaints. When an educational program receives federal financial assistance, there must be a system available in the state education agency to address complaints concerning compliance with federal law. State complaint procedures are varied. In most states, a state complaint officer receives complaints in writing or by telephone, investigates (by telephone, by request for copies of documentation from the school district, or on site), makes a determination of probable cause, and may order corrective action. Many complaints are resolved informally. In most states the complaint procedure focuses primarily on allegations of violations of federal law or regulations, often called "procedural violations."

Mediation. The 1997 IDEA amendments include a requirement that states provide voluntary mediation prior to a hearing. Many states have used mediation successfully. The Due Process Unit of the Connecticut State Department of Education reports that in over 20 years of experience with voluntary mediation, approximately 80% of special education contested cases have been resolved at that level.

Due Process Hearings. Under IDEA, school districts are required to inform parents of their rights, which include the right to request a hearing to challenge almost any aspect of a student's special education, including eligibility, program, or placement, when there is a disagreement. School districts may also initiate special education hearings. These appeals are heard by hearing officers or administrative law judges, depending on state law.

Some states, including Connecticut, Massachusetts, and Utah, have a "one tier" system of hearings: an appeal from a hearing decision goes directly to federal or state court. In other states, including Pennsylvania, Michigan, and New York, there is a "two tier" hearing system. Under this scheme, a hearing decision may be appealed to a state level hearing officer or panel for review prior to a court appeal.

The hearing provided when a parent challenges his or her child's special education program must meet administrative law standards, including the right to be represented by an attorney, to submit documentary evidence, to present and cross examine witnesses, and the right to a timely written decision. An aggrieved party to a special education hearing may appeal the decision in state or federal court. While a hearing or court appeal is pending, the child's school placement may not be changed unless there is an agreement for another placement between the parents and either the school district or the state education agency. However, since 1997 IDEA permits 45-day alternative placements initiated by the school district when a student is considered dangerous after bringing a weapon or drugs to school. Alternative placements for other types of dangerous behavior may be ordered by a hearing officer after hearing from both the school and the parent. When there is a dispute over current placement, a hearing officer may determine placement pending the completion of the hearing.

Attorneys' Fees for Parents. While IDEA requires school districts to inform parents of free and low-cost legal representation, such services are not widely available for special education hearings. In recent years, Congress and the states have reduced public funding for legal services agencies for the poor and for people with disabilities. A 1986 amendment to IDEA making attorneys' fees available to parents who win on one or more issues in a hearing, was seen as an attempt to secure access to legal representation for parents.

Parents who prevail in a hearing may seek reimbursement in court for their attorney's fees from the school district. The IDEA places some restrictions on the attorney's fees provision:

- there is no recovery if the parent gains no more than was offered by the school in a written offer of settlement made by the school at least ten days prior to the hearing;
- attorneys' hourly rates must reflect rates usual in the community for the kind and quality of legal services provided, with no bonuses or multipliers;
- the court may reduce reimbursement if it finds that the parent "unreasonably protracted the final resolution of the controversy, the amount of fees unreasonably exceeds comparable community rates, or the amount of time claimed is excessive", or the parent's attorney did not provide detailed information about the claim in the original due process complaint; and
- since 1997, fees may not be awarded for legal representation in most IEP team meetings or mediation held prior to a request for a hearing.

If the school unreasonably protracted the proceedings, none of the limitations on parental recovery apply.

Case example:
An example of a court award of attorney's fees is a case where a student required medication during the school day. When the school district refused to administer the prescribed drug, the parents requested a special education hearing. Prior to convening the hearing, the matter was settled. A court awarded attorney's fees to the parents, since the request for a hearing was a catalyst in achieving the settlement (*Ian E. v. Board of Education, Unified School District No. 501*, 1994).

In some cases, a school district will settle the claim for attorney's fees, rather than incur the added expense of defending a claim in federal court. If available under state law or practice, special education hearing officers may award attorney's fees. However, hearing officers' findings relevant to the specific issues cited above—such as unreasonable delay—will be considered by a judge addressing a claim for attorney's fees.

IDENTIFICATION OF CHILDREN ELIGIBLE FOR SPECIAL EDUCATION

Child Find and Referrals

The IDEA requires state education agencies to periodically submit state plans for special education to the U.S. Department of Education. State plans must include the procedures that will be followed by each school district in the state in providing special education programs. Under IDEA, children with disabilities who are between the ages of 3 and 21 years may be eligible for special education. Each state must include within its state plan for special education a description of activities designed to locate and identify children with disabilities who may be eligible for special education. Children with disabilities aged birth to 3 are served by a variety of agencies on a state-by-state basis; federal requirements are similar, but states may select the agency or create a new agency to provide and coordinate services. Child Find activities are also required for the birth to three population of children with disabilities.

The school nurse and other school staff members with health-related responsibilities are involved with special education in several ways, including the identification of children with disabilities who may be eligible for special education. Of primary importance is the processing of referrals for special education eligibility evaluation from health care providers in the community, including those from school-based health center professionals. The Child Find mandate requires school districts to seek out children with disabilities who live in the school district and may require special education services. Educating the public, and in particular, collaborating with health care providers and early intervention program staff members in the community are essential components of Child Find.

Other sources of referrals are parents, teachers, and pupil personnel specialists (school counselors, nurses, psychologists, and social workers) who notice that a child is having learning problems in school. Parents should be encouraged to refer their child for evaluation when they suspect a disability is interfering with the child's school performance. Classroom teachers are fre-

quently the first observers of school problems that may be the result of disabilities related to learning. They, in turn, refer these students to the school multidisciplinary team for further evaluation and eligibility determination. The school nurse may also initiate referrals, either from review of the student's health history or because the student comes to the health office frequently and the nurse's assessment suggests a disability that is impacting on the student's learning.

While some school districts will accept a telephone referral from a known source, parents and school staff members may be required to complete a referral form. Parents may also write a letter to the school district requesting evaluation for special education.

Pre-Referral Strategies

Some school districts will implement a "pre-referral" screening process prior to formal referral for evaluation. The intent of such activities is usually both to determine whether less formal interventions might be sufficient, and to gather additional information that may assist in deciding whether and what type of evaluation is indicated. Pre-referral activities that prevent or unduly delay special education evaluation procedures have been found to violate § 504. (See chapter 11.)

One example of a pre-referral procedure is the meeting of a committee of school staff members (sometimes called a Child Study Team) to discuss a reported problem and suggest strategies for the classroom teacher. The Child Study Team may decide to make a referral for evaluation. Since this kind of committee usually doesn't follow the special education procedural safeguards, including notice to the parent, it should *never* be used for special education decisions. Under ideal circumstances, parents would be invited to participate in pre-referral meetings, and might provide information that significantly influences the decision of whether to refer the child for a full evaluation.

EVALUATION FOR SPECIAL EDUCATION

Multidisciplinary Evaluations of Individual Children with Disabilities

A multidisciplinary team meeting determines what an appropriate evaluation should include, based on the child's individual characteristics. Parents can contribute by providing their child's developmental and health histories. Federal regulations require that tests and assessment tools are non-discriminatory, presented in the child's native language, and statistically valid. The evaluation must be provided by knowledgeable professionals selected for expertise in areas related to the student's suspected disability or school difficulty. Evaluation personnel must meet IDEA standards for professional personnel, as defined by the State Education Agency. (See "Staffing for Special Education and Related Services" later in this chapter.)

Children must be evaluated in all suspected areas of disability. Classroom observation of the student, focusing both on learning style and on behavior, may be helpful and is required when a student is being considered for classification as learning disabled. Classroom observation may also yield suggestions for immediate "diagnostic" interventions, such as changing a student's seat. When disruptive behavior is a problem, an observer may be asked to document specific behaviors and frequency of disruptions. In addition to identifying disabilities (if present), a special education evaluation should focus on obtaining information that will assist in the development of an appropriate IEP for the student.

In addition to psycho-educational testing that may be determined appropriate, the evaluation of a student with an actual or potential health-related disability should include a school nursing assessment of the child's health status and health-related education needs. A health history may include health information obtained from the student's school health record; the student's teacher(s) and other school personnel; the student's family; the student's pediatrician or pediatric nurse practitioner; and other health care providers, as indicated. Additionally, a medical evaluation must be provided if the multidisciplinary team determines that one is necessary for education planning. (See below for funding of evaluations.)

In some states, the multidisciplinary team invites parents to participate in the meeting to plan an evaluation. Parents may wish to have evaluation procedures and specific tests explained to them prior to giving their consent for evaluation, and should be given an opportunity to discuss evaluation results with individual evaluators, in addition to the discussion at an IEP team meeting.

Funding Evaluations for Special Education

In most cases, the evaluation for eligibility determination for special education is provided by school staff members or specialists under contract with the school district. When a student's particular needs require an evaluation in a specialized area, the school is responsible for locating an appropriately qualified professional (as required by state certification or licensing agencies) and for funding the evaluation.

Since in some cases parents making a referral for evaluation will base the referral on health information

from the student's primary health care provider or a medical specialist, school staff members may suggest that additional medical information be obtained by the parent. When a child has a chronic health problem requiring frequent visits to health care providers, information requested by the school may not require additional medical evaluation, and therefore no additional fees. Rather, the medical information may be provided in the form of copies of medical records or sections of records, or letters and reports written by the health care providers. Evaluations by physicians must be funded by the school district when the multidisciplinary team determines that the evaluation is necessary either to determine eligibility for special education services or to develop an appropriate IEP for the child.

Records secured from health care providers and other outside agencies become "education records" when they are placed in a student's public school file. Under FERPA (see chapter 9), parents have access to all education records of their child. In some states, medical records are not automatically accessible to the patient, or to the minor patient's parent. Therefore, when a school staff member requests records from a health care provider to be used in educational planning for a child, in addition to the required parental consent, the issue of parental access should be discussed. School nurses must also be aware that medical records are protected under state law (see chapter 8) and may not be accessible to other school staff members unless parents have specifically consented in writing.

Case examples:
A Tennessee case concerned responsibility for a psychiatric evaluation for educational planning, requested by parents of a student who was depressed and had attempted suicide. The court required the school district to fund the evaluation, because it was needed for planning educational services (*Doe v. Nashville*, 1988).

In a New Hampshire case, the parents of a student with a seizure disorder had refused to allow a medical evaluation for school planning. The school district prevailed before a state hearing officer, who found that this evaluation was needed to address the school's medical and safety concerns. This hearing officer also ordered special transportation arrangements to reduce the risk of injury to the student in case of a seizure on the school bus (New Hampshire #95-71, 1995).

A frequent source of disagreement over financial responsibility for medical evaluations is the diagnosis of attention deficit disorder (ADD) and attention deficit hyperactivity disorder (ADHD). Experienced school staff members observing a child's behavior may suggest to a parent that a pediatrician be consulted. Teachers who have observed that some children with ADD or ADHD have benefited from medication may mention "medication," although the recommendation of medication is a medical responsibility and may not be appropriate in all cases. School staff members may make an analogy to referral of a child who may need glasses, or treatment for conditions such as a broken arm: traditionally, such medical treatment has been a parental responsibility. School districts are not responsible under IDEA for providing or paying for medical treatment such as medications. However, the diagnosis of ADD or ADHD also indicates possible eligibility for special education, or support services under § 504. (See chapter 11.)

School staff members should be prepared to make a distinction between referrals for medical care, a family responsibility, and requests for medical information to be used for eligibility determination or educational planning, which is a school district responsibility. When the school IEP team recommends a medical evaluation, the team should clearly state that the school will fund the work and may participate in selecting the physician just as the team selects psychologists and other specialists to do evaluations.

Parents may offer to use insurance or Medicaid to contribute toward the cost of medical evaluations for school planning, (and for health related services in school) and this funding source is recognized by IDEA (Newby, 1990). Under current law, however, schools may not *require* that the family disclose insurance information or use these sources of funding. The IDEA requires that special education services must be at no cost to the parent: utilization of family insurance may result in increases in premiums or in depletion of annual or "lifetime" policy caps on coverage.

Case example:
In a case where parents had provided insurance funding to assist with residential school placement for a student with multiple disabilities, the Fourth Circuit found grounds for a suit for reimbursement under IDEA because depletion of insurance coverage available to the student violated the requirement that special education be provided at no cost to the parent and the student (*Shook v. Gaston County Board of Education*, 1989).

Triennial Re-evaluation for Special Education

Federal requirements include re-evaluation of students in special education every 3 years, although more frequent evaluation may be indicated in specific cases. Since 1997, parental consent is required prior to each triennial re-evaluation. When planning this triennial re-evaluation, the school team should consider the student's current status. It may not be appropriate to repeat all prior evaluations. In some cases, possible new areas will need assessment; in others, where student progress suggests the child may no longer require special education, testing will focus on whether the student is still eligible for services.

It should be noted that § 504 of the 1973 Rehabilitation Act requires an evaluation prior to any "significant change in placement" for a child with a disability. (For more details, see chapter 11.)

Case examples:
A dispute arose between parents of two Michigan hearing-impaired siblings, who preferred continued placement at a residential school for the deaf, and the local school district, which had proposed placement in a day program within the school district. After two special education hearing decisions which supported placement within the local school district, the case was appealed to court. The court noted that failure to provide an evaluation prior to the proposal of a significant change in placement—from the residential facility to day placement in the local school—violated IDEA. Citing the requirement that special education students be re-evaluated every 3 years, "or more frequently if conditions warrant," the court held that the § 504 requirement of re-evaluation prior to a significant change in placement was such a "condition." Because of this need and a variety of other problems in the IEP team representation and decision-making process, this case was sent back to the IEP team with directions concerning the need for evaluations and other factors to be considered in reformulating the IEPs and reconsidering placement (*Brimmer v. Traverse City Area Public Schools*, 1994).

In another case, an Ohio school district that described the triennial re-evaluation as necessary to maintain eligibility for special education prevailed against a parent who had refused to allow re-evaluation (*Andress v. Cleveland Independent School District*, 1995).

Independent Evaluations for Special Education

When a parent disagrees with the results of the school's evaluation, the parent may request an independent evaluation at the expense of the school district. If the school district believes that its own evaluation is suffi-cient, the district may request a hearing to present its case for refusing to provide an independent evaluation. While the regulation does not require parents to notify the school district when seeking an independent evalu-ation (Field, 1989), in most cases parents seek assistance from school personnel in locating independent evalua-tors with appropriate credentials and experience. In some cases a school district will propose an inde-pendent evaluation, usually in cases of unusual disabili-ties or in hopes of addressing parental concerns. In response to an inquiry, the U.S. Department of Educa-tion Office of Special Education Programs (OSEP) advised that there is no legal limit on the number of independent evaluations a school district may arrange for a child with disabilities (Tinsley, 1989). OSEP also noted that an independent psychological evaluation might not fulfill the triennial re-evaluation requirement by itself. When school districts provide parents with suggestions for outside evaluators, it is best to give more than one name.

Case example:

In a 1993 Iowa special education hearing, the parents of a hearing-impaired student attacked the appropriateness of their daughter's special educa-tion program, also complaining of failure to eval-uate and failure to reimburse independent evaluations provided by the parents. Although the hearing officer found the special education program appropriate, he noted the requirement that another evaluation should be provided when requested by the child's parents or teacher. The school district had performed no evaluations between 1986 and 1992, and had used data from independent evaluations secured and paid for by the child's parents in IEP decisions. The hearing officer rejected the school's contention that parents had not "notified the school of a disagreement" with school evaluations: there had been no school evaluations with which to disagree. In ordering reimbursement for the independent evaluations, the hearing officer chastised the school for not meeting its responsibility to provide triennial re-evaluations, as well as evaluations in response to requests from parents (Sioux City Community School District, 1993).

Although the cost of a hearing often exceeds the cost of an independent evaluation, many hearings are requested to dispute independent evaluations. The OSEP has confirmed that fee schedules or "caps" on reimbursement for independent evaluations are allow-able under IDEA, provided that the fees are reasonable and the school is willing to consider the range of pro-fessional opinions that might be needed in an individ-ual case (Anonymous, 1995).

DETERMINATION OF ELIGIBILITY FOR SPECIAL EDUCATION

Perhaps in reaction to widespread exclusion of children with severe disabilities from public education in the early 1970's, IDEA requires that a free appropriate public education be offered to ALL children with disabilities, regardless of the nature or severity of their disabilities. Based on the outcome of the evaluation, the multidisciplinary team is responsible for determining whether or not a student is eligible for special educa-tion. The decision must be made on the basis of the existence of a disability (or disabilities) with demon-strable impact on the child's ability to learn.

Federal Eligibility Requirements for Special Education

Students Aged 5 to 21

The IDEA regulations provide definitions for each disability category that provide some guidance con-cerning eligibility. In 1997, Congress consolidated some categories that had been listed separately in the 1975 law. For example, "deafness" and "hearing impairment" were originally listed as separate categories while the 1997 amendments list "hearing impairments (including deafness)" as one category.

IDEA definitions—

Autism means a developmental disability signifi-cantly affecting verbal and nonverbal communica-tion and social interaction, generally evident before age 3, that adversely affects a child's educational performance. Other characteristics often associated with autism are engagement in repetitive activities and stereotyped movements, resistance to environ-mental change or change in daily routines, and unusual responses to sensory experiences. The term does not apply if a child's educational performance is adversely affected primarily because the child has an emotional disturbance. A child who manifests characteristics of autism after age 3, could be diagnosed as having autism if the above criteria are satisfied.

Deaf-blindness means concomitant hearing and visual impairments, the combination of which causes such severe communication and other developmental and educational problems that they cannot be accommodated in special education programs solely for children with deafness or children with blindness.

Deafness means a hearing impairment that is so severe that the child is impaired in processing linguistic information through hearing, with or without amplification, and that affects a child's educational performance.

Emotional disturbance means a condition exhibiting one or more of the following characteristics over a long period of time and to a marked degree that adversely affects a child's educational performance:
- an inability to learn that cannot be explained by intellectual, sensory, or health factors;
- an inability to build or maintain satisfactory interpersonal relationships with peers and teachers;
- inappropriate types of behavior or feelings under normal circumstances;
- a general pervasive mood of unhappiness or depression; or
- a tendency to develop physical symptoms or fears associated with personal or school problems.

The term *emotional disturbance* includes schizophrenia. The term does not apply to children who are socially maladjusted, unless it is determined that they have a serious emotional disturbance.

Hearing impairment means an impairment in hearing, whether permanent or fluctuating, that adversely affects a child's educational performance but that is not included under the definition of deafness in this section.

Mental retardation means significantly subaverage general intellectual functioning existing concurrently with deficits in adaptive behavior and manifested during the developmental period that adversely affects a child's educational performance.

Multiple disabilities means concomitant impairments (such as mental retardation-blindness, mental retardation-orthopedic impairment, etc.) the combination of which causes such severe

educational needs that they cannot be accommodated in special education programs solely for one of the impairments. The term does not include deaf-blindness.

Orthopedic impairment means a severe orthopedic impairment that adversely affects the child's educational performance. The term includes impairments caused by congenital anomaly (e.g., clubfoot, absence of some member, etc.), impairments caused by disease (e.g., poliomyelitis, bone tuberculosis, etc.), and impairments from other causes (e.g., cerebral palsy, amputations, and fractures or burns that cause contractures).

Other health impairment means having limited strength, vitality or alertness, including a heightened alertness to environmental stimuli, that results in limited alertness with respect to the educational environment, due to chronic or acute health problems such as asthma, attention deficit disorder or attention deficit hyperactivity disorder, diabetes, epilepsy, a heart condition, hemophilia, lead poisoning, leukemia, nephritis, rheumatic fever, and sickle cell anemia, that adversely affects a child's educational performance.

Specific learning disability means a disorder in one or more of the basic psychological processes involved in understanding or using language, spoken or written, that may manifest itself in an imperfect ability to listen, think, speak, read, write, spell, or to do mathematical calculations, including conditions such as perceptual disabilities, brain injury, minimal brain dysfunction, dyslexia, and developmental aphasia. The term does not include learning problems that are primarily the result of visual, hearing, or motor disabilities, of mental retardation, of emotional disturbance, or of environmental, cultural, or economic disadvantage.

Speech or language impairment means a communication disorder such as stuttering, impaired articulation, a language impairment, or a voice impairment that adversely affects a child's educational performance.

Traumatic brain injury means an acquired injury to the brain caused by an external physical force, resulting in total or partial functional disability or psychosocial impairment, or both, that adversely affects a child's educational performance. The term applies to open or closed head injuries resulting in impairments in one or more areas, such as cognition; language; memory; attention; reasoning; abstract thinking; judgment; problem-solving; sensory perception and motor abilities; psychosocial behavior; physical functions; information processing; and speech. The term does not apply to brain injuries that are congenital or degenerative, or brain injuries induced by birth trauma.

Visual impairment including blindness means an impairment in vision that, even with correction, adversely affects a child's educational performance. The term includes both partial sight and blindness.

Pre-School Children Aged 3 to 5

The IDEA regulations give states an option of providing special education services to children aged 3 to 5 years who are "experiencing developmental delays." To be eligible for services, the pre-schooler must demonstrate developmental delays as defined by the state, "as measured by appropriate instruments and procedures", and who, for that reason, needs special education and related services. The developmental delays must be in one or more of the following areas: physical development, cognitive development, communication development, social or emotional development, or adaptive development. However, these preschool special education services are discretionary, and therefore may vary significantly from one state to another.

Examples of children usually receiving such pre-school services are children with mental retardation, hearing or language impairments, and autism. Pre-school children with chronic illness or complex medical problems may be eligible for such services if their condition is likely to interfere with normal development and educational progress.

The school district has a choice of establishing pre-school classes or funding placement in Head Start or private pre-school programs. If a school district program for 3- to 5-year-olds with disabilities is established, it should include normal peers in addition to those eligible for special education.

Federal Requirements—State Requirements

The federal regulations provide detailed requirements concerning identification, referral, and evaluation of children with disabilities who may be in need of special education; most state regulations parallel these requirements. While states may add to or provide more than the federal requirements, they may not provide less than IDEA specifies. For example, Connecticut has an additional disability category, neurological impairment.

Most states have published detailed eligibility criteria for each disability category, providing more detail than the federal definitions. For example, eligibility for the category "other health impaired" is elaborated by two states, Louisiana and Utah, as described below.

Louisiana requires that a student meet one of these criteria:
A. Disabilities which result in reduced efficiency in school work because of temporary or chronic lack of strength, vitality, or alertness, including such conditions as those specified in the [federal] definition, or
B. A severe disability which substantially limits one or more of the student's major life activities (that is, caring for one's self, performing manual tasks, walking, seeing, hearing, speaking, breathing, learning and working) and
C. Impaired environment functioning which significantly interferes with educational performance.
NOTE: These disabilities [categorized as other health impaired] must be other than those defined as handicapping conditions [elsewhere] in the law and regulations (Louisiana Department of Education, 1983).

Louisiana includes minimum standards for evaluation of a child for classification as "other health impaired":
A. A report of a medical examination within the previous 12 months from a physician qualified by training or experience to assess the student's health problem(s), giving a description of the impairment and any medical implications for instruction and physical education.
B. An educational evaluation that identifies educational and environmental adjustments needed.
C. An evaluation of the student's need for adaptive physical education.

Louisiana also requires re-evaluation for students identified as other health impaired. The requirements specify that when requested by the special education supervisor, an annual medical assessment shall be conducted in order to determine any changes in the physical condition of the student.

Utah's procedures for identifying students as *other health impaired* include the following:

The student's medical history must be obtained from the private physician to provide relevant information regarding specific syndromes, health problems, medication, and any information deemed necessary for planning the student's educational program. Eligibility is determined by a multidisciplinary team. Multiple standardized measures should be used to assess suspected educational, adaptive, and behavioral deficits. The student is not identified as manifesting a primary disabling condition [under the special education regulations] other than other health impaired (Utah State Board of Education, 1993).

Special Education Classification

Given the broad nature of the IDEA disability categories, there is sometimes confusion between a medical diagnosis and an educational disability category. Eligibility for special education and related services requires a learning problem or educational impact in addition to a disability. There may be differing opinions about an appropriate "label," and the desires of both parents and school professionals to maintain some flexibility about classification, especially with very young children. Another source of misunderstanding comes from parental (and sometimes school) reluctance to label a child with a category perceived as stigmatizing. The most frequent examples of this problem are mental retardation and emotional disturbance. In some states, the informal practice has been to identify children with mild mental retardation as learning disabled, although this is specifically discouraged by the language of the definition of learning disabilities in the federal regulations.

Pre-schoolers who are identified as eligible for services under IDEA do not have to be specifically labeled under one of the disability categories. These children may be identified as "experiencing developmental delays", and may be classified as "uncategorized." The 1997 IDEA amendments extended flexibility in classification of children with disabilities to age 9.

Since autism and traumatic brain injury were added as separate categories by Congressional action in 1991, it is possible that some students with either of these two disabilities, previously identified as learning disabled, emotionally disturbed, or other health impaired, have not been re-classified.

The definition for the disability category "other health impaired" lists some examples of chronic disease: this classification may be used when a child's learning problem is related to a medical diagnosis. Attention Deficit Disorder (ADD) and Attention Deficit Hyperactivity Disorder (ADHD) are medical diagnoses that are included in the 1999 regulatory list of examples. In responding to demands from parents to Congress that ADD/ADHD be considered as a separate disability category under IDEA, two U.S. Department of Education divisions, the Office of Special Education Programs (OSEP) and the Office for Civil Rights (OCR), issued a joint policy memorandum on September 19, 1991. This policy memorandum advised that school districts could use one of three existing IDEA categories for students who have ADD/ADHD and were eligible for special education because it adversely affected their educational performance. Since "other health impaired" includes "limited alertness," that is, limited alertness for learning, this category would be appropriate for many children with ADD. In some cases, "specific learning disability" or "serious emotional disturbance" would be appropriate categories for children with ADD. In cases where a child with medically diagnosed ADD/ADHD has no significant learning problem in school or where a child's ADD/ADHD is controlled by medication such that there is no significant learning problem in school, the student may not be eligible for special education. However, there may be eligibility for support services under §504, such as monitoring of medication and classroom modifications (Joint Policy Memorandum, 1991). This is still timely advice.

In cases where a child is referred because of suspected ADD or ADHD and there has been no medical diagnosis, the school district is responsible for an appropriate evaluation under IDEA and §504. If the multidisciplinary team determines that a medical diagnosis is necessary, and a child's parents have not provided one, the school district is responsible for providing one. In 1995, OSEP advised that a state policy of requiring a medical diagnosis for classification as other health impaired does not conflict with IDEA, although IDEA does not require it (Hudgins, 1995). OSEP also cautioned that if a medical diagnosis is required, it must be at no cost to the parents. However, it may not always be necessary to have a medical diagnosis to establish that a student is eligible for special education as other health impaired, learning disabled or seriously emotionally disturbed. Decisions by the school's multidisciplinary team regarding whether to evaluate and what an evaluation will include are subject to appeal by parents.

Severity of Disabilities

IDEA mandates educational opportunity for *all* children with disabilities. This mandate extends to children with severe medical problems who were not previously considered eligible for public education.

Case examples:

In a New Hampshire case, the First Circuit Court of Appeals held that a comatose child had rights under IDEA. Physical therapy had been requested by the parents as an educational service, and was denied by the school on the basis of the child's condition. The court determined that no child with disabilities that affect educational performance could be excluded under IDEA, and that an appropriate program, such as physical therapy, must be provided (*Timothy W. v. Rochester, New Hampshire, School District*, 1989).

In the case of a New York child who was hospitalized in a persistent vegetative state after sustaining a head injury, a state hearing review officer affirmed most of an independent hearing officer's decision, providing for 2 hours of instruction per day whenever the child's physical condition was "appropriate for education" (Canastoga Central School District, 1995).

If a physician has determined that a child is "unavailable for education" on a short term basis (due, for example, to brain surgery), the school must maintain contact and continue to offer an appropriate education. When the student is ready, an appropriate program can be provided in a hospital and later at home, while the student is recuperating from the surgery. The concept that *all* children with disabilities are eligible for educational services is often referred to as "zero reject" by educators.

Children with Chronic Health Conditions: IDEA or §504

When an evaluation shows that a child's disability does *not* have an impact on educational performance, the child is usually found not eligible for special education. For example, a child with severe asthma who requires a range of regular and PRN (as necessary) medications resulting in interruptions in classroom participation, careful monitoring and assessment for respiratory distress, periodic emergency interventions and modifications of school program, and who is frequently absent from school due to upper respiratory infections and exacerbations of the asthma, would probably be found eligible for special education as "other health impaired" under IDEA, because the chronic asthmatic condition is interfering with the child's attendance and progress in school.

Another child, who sometimes experiences mild to moderate exertional asthma that is well controlled with medication, is progressing well in school and has no other disabilities, would probably *not* be eligible for special education under IDEA because the child's health impairment is not interfering with the child's educational performance. The second child, however, might be protected and eligible for support services under §504 of the Rehabilitation Act. (For details of services under §504, see chapter 11.)

INDIVIDUALIZED EDUCATION PROGRAM (IEP) DEVELOPMENT

The Individualized Education Program (IEP) and IEP Team

After determining that a child with one or more disabilities that cause a learning problem is eligible for special education, a school staff team must be assembled to develop an appropriate educational program, and the child's parents must be invited to participate in the meeting. In some states, when the eligibility determination is completed, the team moves directly into program development; in other states, the eligibility determination is made in a separate meeting, or by a separate staff team. Although they must be invited to meetings concerning their child's educational program, nothing in the Federal regulations requires that parents be included in the eligibility meeting, although they do have access to copies of all reports considered and any documentation of the meeting and the decision.

The school staff members who compose the IEP team are selected to provide the best knowledge of the child's individual needs and the best understanding of service options. The 1997 IDEA amendments include IEP team membership requirements: the parents, a regular education teacher of the child; a special education teacher; a "representative" of the school district (usually an administrator); someone who can address "the instructional implications of evaluation results"; the student when appropriate; and "other individuals who have knowledge or special education expertise regarding the child." The latter group includes related services professionals. It is useful to note the Congressional Record, in the preface to IDEA 97, in this respect:

Related services personnel should be included on the team when a particular related service will be discussed at the request of a child's parents or the school. Furthermore, the committee recognizes that there are situations that merit the presence of a licensed registered school nurse on the IEP team. The committee also recognizes that schools sometimes are assumed to be responsible for all health-care costs connected to a child's participation in school. The committee wishes to encourage, to the greatest extent practicable and when appropriate, the participation of a licensed registered school nurse on the IEP team to help define and make decisions about how to safely address a child's educationally related health needs (Committee on Labor and Human Resources, U.S. Senate, 1997, p. 23).

It is good practice to allow parents to bring a friend or relative as a support person. Arguably, such a person would have knowledge of the child. Individual states may have more specific requirements for team participation.

When health information has been obtained or a health assessment is completed as part of the evaluation for the IEP team, a qualified school nurse, school physician, consulting physician, nurse practitioner or clinical nurse specialist (or more than one) should attend the IEP meeting to present health assessment findings and to assist with interpretation and educational planning. Occupational and physical therapists and speech/language pathologists may also assist with evaluation of a student's needs and with planning specific aspects of the education program that will address these needs.

When time is needed to obtain additional information for development of an IEP or to hire or train specialized service providers, a student may be excluded from school briefly—for no more than 10 school days (Seattle, 1999). However, it is good practice to offer some homebound instruction while gathering information or preparing staff. Particularly for students with serious health problems, it is safer to delay actual school placement until all necessary medical information is in hand and appropriate individualized health care and emergency plans have been developed.

Among other requirements, the IEP document must include the following:

- individual, measurable student goals and benchmarks or short-term objectives;
- special education and related services planned to address the objectives;

- school staff members (by title) who will provide services;
- a plan for evaluating student progress;
- an explanation of any part of the program in which the student will not be placed in a regular education setting;
- any modifications necessary for the student to participate in district-wide assessments of student achievement;
- the date services will start;
- transition needs for students over the age of 14 and transition plans for students over the age of 16;
- how parents will be informed of student progress; and
- a record of the student's current levels of educational performance.

Each IEP outlines the individual student's education program that may include special education services, regular education services with or without modifications, and related services. While the IEP should be a plan for services reasonably expected to enable the child to make educational progress, schools and school staff members cannot be held liable for a student's failure to achieve a particular annual goal. The federal standard for services is the provision of a free appropriate public education (FAPE) (34 C.F.R. § 300.8, 1993). This standard has been interpreted by the U.S. Supreme Court (*Rowley*, 1982) to mean (1) compliance with the procedural requirements of IDEA, and (2) the offering of an educational program (IEP) that can reasonably be expected to enable the student to make educational progress.

Case example:
The importance of including and identifying staff by discipline in the IEP is demonstrated in the report of an Office for Civil Rights investigation of a complaint at a Missouri school for students with severe disabilities. The complaint concerned staffing: Parents had complained that there was no full-time nurse. OCR determined that none of the IEPs of the students in the school listed availability of a full-time nurse as a related service. Therefore, OCR found no violation of Section 504 (Missouri Department of Elementary and Secondary Education, 1991).

If even one IEP had listed availability of a full-time nurse, the outcome might have been different.

IDEA requires an individualized program based on the student's needs. Under the current notion of educational equity, which is based on the federal constitutional concept of equal protection as well as selected state constitutional provisions defining educational opportunity, many disputed cases include the question of the relationship between an appropriate standard in special education, and the standard for public educational programs in general.

Special education services must address each student's individual needs. Therefore, services may not be linked to disability categories. For example, counseling may not be limited to those classified as "emotionally disturbed," as many students with disabilities may require counseling in school.

For a sample IEP, including a health goal with student objectives, as well as a list of potential health-related student learning objectives by nursing diagnosis, see Appendix K.

Regular Education

Almost all students in need of special education will spend significant portions of their school day in regular education classes. The IEP will show whether regular education placement is to be with or without supplementary aids and services. When a student with disabilities can function without support in any aspect of the regular education program, the IEP will document that class placement without additional support is appropriate.

In many cases, a student with disabilities can be educated in a regular classroom setting if the program is modified to address the student's individual needs. Examples of modifications frequently noted on IEPs include:

- seat the student in the front;
- allow extra time for tests;
- provide tests and classroom notes on paper—do not ask this student to copy from the blackboard; or
- allow the student to use a tape recorder to record lectures and class discussion.

In some situations, a child with disabilities will require significant assistance in a regular classroom. School districts often provide this support by assigning a school staff member called an aide or a paraprofessional to work with the student under the direction of a teacher. The 1997 IDEA amendments provide that states may use paraprofessionals who are properly trained and supervised. (See the section on "Staffing for Special Education and Related Services" later in the chapter.)

Special Education

Special education, again, is defined as

…specially designed instruction, at no cost to the parents, to meet the unique needs of a child with a disability, including instruction conducted in the classroom, in the home, in hospitals and institutions, and in other settings; and instruction in physical education. Speech language pathology (or any related service) may be considered special education, rather than a related service, under state law.

The term *specially designed instruction* is defined at the beginning of this chapter. The IEP team will often refer to services provided by special education staff outside the regular classroom setting as special education placement, but under the language of the federal regulation that distinction is not recognized. Specially designed instruction in a regular classroom setting is also special education.

Related Services

The IDEA requires the provision of related services that may be necessary in order for the student to benefit from his or her special education program. The definition of *related services* under the federal regulations is:

…transportation and such developmental, corrective, and other supportive services as are required to assist a child with a disability to benefit from special education and includes speech pathology and audiology services, psychological services, physical and occupational therapy, recreation, including therapeutic recreation, early identification and assessment of disabilities in children, counseling services, including rehabilitation counseling, orientation and mobility services, and medical services for diagnostic or evaluation purposes. The term also includes school health services, social work services in schools, and parent counseling and training.

The federal regulations provide additional definitions for specific related services. These definitions should be considered "educational definitions." In health care settings, these services might be defined somewhat differently.

Audiology includes the following:
- identification of children with hearing loss;
- determination of the range, nature, and degree of hearing loss, including referral for medical or other professional attention for the habilitation of hearing;
- provision of habilitative activities, such as language habilitation, auditory training, speech reading (lip-reading), hearing evaluation, and speech conservation;
- creation and administration of programs for the prevention of hearing loss;
- counseling and guidance of pupils, parents and teachers regarding hearing loss; and
- determination of the child's need for group and individual amplification, selecting and fitting an appropriate aid, and evaluating the effectiveness of amplification.

Counseling services means services provided by qualified social workers, psychologists, guidance counselors, or other qualified personnel.

Early identification and assessment of disabilities in children means the implementation of a formal plan for identifying a disability as early as possible in a child's life.

Medical services means services provided by a licensed physician to determine a child's medically-related disability that results in the child's need for special education and related services.

Occupational therapy means services provided by a qualified occupational therapist and includes
- improving, developing or restoring functions impaired or lost through illness, injury, or deprivation;
- improving ability to perform tasks for independent functioning when functions are impaired or lost; and
- preventing, through early intervention, initial or further impairment or loss of function.

Orientation and mobility services means services provided to blind or visually impaired students by qualified personnel to enable those students to attain systematic orientation to and safe movement within their environments in school, home, and community; and includes teaching students, as appropriate,

- spatial and environmental concepts and use of information received by the senses (such as sound, temperature and vibrations) to establish, maintain, or regain orientation and line of travel (e.g., using sound at a traffic light to cross the street;
- how to use the long cane to supplement visual travel skills or as a tool for safely negotiating the environment for students with no available travel vision;
- how to understand and use remaining vision and distance low-vision aids; and
- other concepts, techniques, and tools.

Parent Counseling and training means assisting parents in understanding the special needs of their child; providing parents with information about child development; and helping parents to acquire the necessary skills that will allow them to support the implementation of their child's IEP or IFSP.

Physical therapy means services provided by a qualified physical therapist.

Psychological services includes:
- administering psychological and educational tests, and other assessment procedures;
- interpreting assessment results;
- obtaining, integrating, and interpreting information about child behavior and conditions related to learning;
- consulting with other staff members in planning school programs to meet the special needs of children as indicated by psychological tests, interviews, and behavioral observations;
- planning and managing a program of psychological services, including psychological counseling for children and parents; and
- assisting in developing positive behavioral intervention strategies.

Recreation includes:
- assessment of leisure function;
- therapeutic recreation services;
- recreation programs in schools and community agencies; and
- leisure education.

Rehabilitation counseling services means services provided by qualified personnel in individual and group sessions that focus specifically on career development, employment preparation, achieving independence and integration in the workplace and community of a student with a disability. The term also includes vocational rehabilitation services provided to a student with disabilities by vocational rehabilitation programs funded under the Rehabilitation Act of 1973, as amended.

School health services means services provided by a qualified school nurse or other qualified person.

Social work services in schools includes:
- preparing a social or developmental history on a child with a disability;
- group and individual counseling with the child and family;
- working in partnership with parents and others on those problems in a child's living situation (home, school, and community) that affect the child's adjustment in school;
- mobilizing school and community resources to enable the child to learn as effectively as possible in his or her educational program; and
- assisting in developing positive behavioral intervention strategies.

Speech-language pathology includes:
- identification of children with speech or language impairments;
- diagnosis and appraisal of specific speech or language impairments;
- referral for medical or other professional attention necessary for the habilitation of speech or language impairments;
- provision of speech and language services for the habilitation or prevention of communicative impairments; and
- counseling and guidance of parents, children, and teachers regarding speech and language impairments.

Transportation includes travel to and from school and between schools; travel in and around school buildings; and specialized equipment (such as special or adapted buses, lifts, and ramps), if required to provide special transportation for a child with a disability.

Transportation is provided for *all* children who do not live within walking distance of school in most states, although the definition of *walking distance* may vary, and safety factors may also be considered. There

is a technical distinction between transportation provided for a student in need of special education because of distance, which is not regarded as a related service, and transportation provided for a student in need of special education because of the student's disability, which is regarded as a related service. Transportation as a related service is provided because the student's IEP requires it, usually for one of two general reasons. A student with a disability may not be able to walk even a short distance to school, or may require specialized transportation equipment or a different schedule or destination from other students in his or her neighborhood. In some cases, a special van will go directly to the student's home; in others, the student will be accommodated on a regular school bus route. Transportation for students with disabilities may include the services of a paraprofessional on the van or bus, to assist and supervise students. See chapter 11 for school transportation requirements under the Americans with Disabilities Act.

In a few cases, the student's school health needs continue during the trip to and from school. An initial response from some school districts is to offer homebound instruction, arguing that support services are not available on the school bus.

Case example:
In one case, the school district had agreed to provide tracheostomy care and positioning for a student in school, but denied such support service during transportation to and from school. The court required the school district to hire and train someone to provide the service during transportation (*Macomb County Intermediate School District v. Joshua S.*, 1989).

In some cases, school districts are using ambulances with trained emergency services personnel to transport medically fragile children to and from school; in others, RNs, LPNs or paraprofessionals (aides) are used, depending on the needs of the students. In general, if a particular level of health services is determined to be appropriate in school, the same level of service is likely required during transportation to school, and should be provided.

Individualized Transition Plans (ITPs)

IDEA requires the development of Individualized Transition Plans (ITPs) for toddlers who will be moving to pre-school special education programs, at least six months prior to the move, and for adolescents with disabilities who require early and substantial planning in order to optimize students' transitions to adult services before or at the age of 21. The latter ITPs are intended to assist adolescent students with disabilities to move smoothly to one or more of the following: higher education, career preparation, trade skills acquisition, optimal independence in activities of daily living, including management skills for the community, and adult disability services. ITPs are required for special education students aged 16, or in some cases, younger. These plans usually focus on vocational needs and the identification of agencies that will be of assistance to the student after he or she completes public school. Ideally through interagency agreements, representatives of public agencies such as mental retardation or rehabilitation services can participate at IEP meetings to assist in the development of realistic ITPs.

Individualized Health Care Plan

When a special education student requires specialized health care in school, many districts require the student to have an individualized healthcare plan (IHP), alternately referred to as an individualized health care plan (IHCP) or school health management plan (SHMP). The IHP, or relevant aspects of it, are incorporated into the student's IEP or, in some districts, may be attached as an addendum. If a child requires clean intermittent catheterization (CIC), for example, a health goal and specific objectives related to student learning should be included in the child's IEP (see Appendix K), as well as the frequency of services, the amount of time required, the location(s) for the services, and the professional title of the person responsible for the service.

An IHP for that child might include the following:

- student-specific goals of CIC;
- level of student independence or participation in learning to perform the care independently;
- equipment needed;
- specific direct and indirect nursing services to be provided;
- type and frequency of supervision by the professional school nurse when care is delegated (see chapters 4 and 5);
- problems that may arise;
- persons to contact in emergencies; and
- timelines and methods of evaluation to determine student progress toward the goal and objective(s).

The general goal of school health services for students with health-related disabilities should be for the student to achieve maximum independence in self-care and to maintain or improve his or her health status in school in order to be fully available for learning.

Therefore, student objectives related to learning the content and practicing the skills necessary for safe self-care are essential. In addition to providing direct services to a student (e.g., teaching the student self-care, performing tracheal suctioning, or counseling the student regarding necessary lifestyle adaptations), the school nurse may also provide indirect services related to a student's health-related IEP goals, including consultation with classroom teachers and supervision of a health aide or paraprofessional.

Annual Review of IEP

The IDEA requires that each student in need of special education have his or her program reviewed by the IEP team at least once a year. At this annual meeting, the IEP team reviews progress and develops an IEP for the next year. Although IDEA requires an IEP to be in place at the beginning of the school year, many school districts stagger IEP team meetings through the school year. If a student's annual review is scheduled for October, and the plan is for a move to a different school for the next school year, a follow-up IEP team meeting may be needed in the spring.

PLACEMENT DECISIONS AND LEAST RESTRICTIVE ENVIRONMENT (LRE)

The IDEA regulations require a continuum of placement choices, from the regular classroom with additional supports and aids, to special classes, special schools, and hospitals and institutions. Typical supports and aids in a regular classroom setting include modifications of lessons and assignments, use of special materials, technological support such as tape recorders or computers, special seating in the classroom, tutorial support, and individual assistance from a paraprofessional.

Specialized classrooms within regular public schools are usually described as either "learning centers" or "self-contained classes." The learning centers typically provide individualized support services for varying parts of the school day, with students coming from regular classrooms: this is sometimes called "pull-out programming." The self-contained classes usually remain together for most of the school day, and may be provided for students with the same or similar disabilities, or at similar intellectual levels.

Some public schools have adopted policies of providing all support services within regular classroom settings, and do not offer the options of learning centers or self-contained classes. In support of the assumption that most students with disabilities can be accommodated successfully in regular classrooms, IDEA regulations require written justification for placements outside the regular classroom.

The IEP and Placement

The first assumption in devising an educational placement for a child with disabilities is that the child's IEP should be provided in the school that he or she would be attending if not disabled. IDEA establishes that placement must be in the least restrictive environment (LRE) *for the student.* In other words, the placement decision must focus on the student and his or her needs, rather than on the existing array of services or staff configurations. In following the principles of least restrictive environment, the IEP team may consider a placement that will require the re-assignment of staff members or the hiring of additional personnel. School districts have to balance the legislative preference for keeping children with disabilities in their neighborhood schools against staffing efficiency and appropriate peer groupings.

There is no absolute IDEA requirement that *all* children with disabilities be placed in their neighborhood schools, and there is no § 504 requirement that *all* existing schools be made accessible to children with disabilities (see chapter 11). The evaluation for special education eligibility and the IEP must be used in determining placement: the IEP drives the placement. Thus, the starting point for the IEP team is the IEP and the neighborhood school. Only when it can be established that a local placement is not appropriate for the child may the team move further afield.

Placement in a hospital setting or an institution may be the least restrictive environment for an individual student at a particular time. Since the drafting of IDEA in the early 1970s, lawsuits based on least restrictive environment arguments have led to the closing of many institutions for children. Long-term hospitalization of children is now rare, and most hospitals cooperate with nearby school systems to routinely provide educational services.

Private School Placement

Some special schools for children with disabilities are private. A public school district may fund placement in a private school for a child with disabilities if that is the least restrictive environment for that student. As a rule, the public school must consider all possible public school placements (within the district, nearby districts, public regional or state program) prior to considering a private school placement. A private school must have been approved by the state education agency as meeting state standards for special education before a school district may place a student there at public expense.

Case examples:
In a New York case the court found that placement of a student requiring special education, by a local school district, in a non-state approved program does not meet the requirements for state supervision and monitoring of special education programs (*Ankowiak v. Ambach*, 1988).

Subsequently, the U.S. Supreme Court held in a South Carolina case that when the parent of a student needing special education makes a unilateral placement in a private school because the public school program does not meet the student's needs, the parent cannot be held to the requirement of state approval. In this case, the public school program was inappropriate, and the private school program was found to be appropriate. The only significant issue was whether lack of state approval would bar public funding for the placement (*Florence County School District Four v. Carter*, 1993).

There are a group of court decisions, usually involving private day or residential schools, where 1) the public school failed to offer an appropriate program and 2) the parents found an appropriate program. A hearing officer or court will have to find *both* elements before ordering a school district to fund the placement found by the parent.

Case example:
This standard was established by the U.S. Supreme Court, which also held that a parent's removal of his child from a public school followed by a unilateral placement in a private school does not violate the "stay put" provision of IDEA (*Burlington School Committee v. Massachusetts Department of Education*, 1985).

Under "stay put," a school system may not change either the educational program or placement of a student while a due process appeal, or subsequent court appeal, is pending, unless there is an agreement to make the change between the parent and the school district or state department of education. Since 1997, school districts may make 45-day alternative interim educational placements if the student poses a significant safety risk because of bringing a weapon or drugs to school. A hearing officer may order an alternative placement for other types of dangerous behavior, after hearing from the school and the parent. When there is a dispute about what the current placement is, a hearing officer may determine the stay-put placement pending the outcome of the hearing.

Residential Placement for Special Education Services

In some rural areas where population is sparse, schools are small and specialized services are difficult to secure. As a result, students may be assigned to remote schools that require a "boarding placement." This is true for regular education, as well as special education students.

Rural issues aside, residential placement for special education may be required in rare cases. In attempting to avoid responsibility for residential costs, school districts frequently claim that residential placement is either "for non-educational reasons" or that a day program will be sufficient. When the "non-educational reason" is eligibility for residential placement by another public agency, such as a child care agency or department of health, interagency cooperation is required to insure appropriate educational programs. An extended day (and school week or school year), incorporating behavioral programs, life skills, and other services available in a residential setting, may address the needs of a child with complex disabilities.

Case example:
In a California case, the court found residential placement necessary because the school district failed to provide an appropriate placement, and no other option was proposed. This student, who was 20 years old, was seriously emotionally disturbed. In this case, the district's claim that placement was for medical reasons was not determinative, because the district had failed to meet its burden of providing an appropriate program (*Pamela B. v. Longview School District,* 1992).

There are other cases where the child's needs include a residential setting, usually described as "totally structured 24 hours a day" or "professionally supervised around the clock."

Case example:
In an Illinois case, the court ordered residential placement for a child with mental retardation, speech and language impairments, and possible autism (*Board of Education of Murphysboro Community Unit School District No.186 v. Illinois State Board of Education,* 1994).

In general, the few students with disabilities who are found eligible for residential placement by school districts (or by hearing officers) are severely or multiply disabled, or have severe behavioral problems.

It must be mentioned here that in the early 1970s, when the original legislation leading to IDEA was being developed, placement of children with disabilities in residential facilities was more frequent than it is today. It often took place under the auspices of other public agencies, such as those responsible for people with mental retardation or mental illness. With advances in medicine and changes in community attitudes, most children with severe disabilities are now living with their families or in foster family placement. Related to these changes is increasing awareness that many children with severe disabilities may be accommodated in regular classroom settings.

Interagency Placements

Because the state department of education in each state is responsible for the provision of public education to all eligible children within the state, wherever they may be, it is sometimes necessary for a school district (or the state department) to collaborate with another state agency that also has some responsibility for a child. IDEA encourages the use of interagency agreements to expedite cooperative services for children with disabilities who fall within the jurisdiction of two or more state agencies. Examples of other agencies with which cooperation is needed are state child care agencies and state departments of mental retardation, health, and corrections. Depending upon the facts of a case, and the nature of the services provided by the other agency, the school district (or state department) may not be able to exercise complete discretion over the educational placement. (See chapter 13 for a discussion of litigation in this area.)

STAFFING FOR SPECIAL EDUCATION AND RELATED SERVICES

Regulatory Requirements

IDEA 97 specifies general criteria for personnel standards and requires the state education agency to establish specific standards accordingly. These criteria include the following requirements:

- The State educational agency has established and maintained standards to ensure that personnel necessary to carry out [professional special education services] are appropriately and adequately prepared and trained.

- These standards must be consistent with any state-approved or state-recognized certification, licensing, registration, or other comparable requirements that apply to the professional discipline in which those personnel are providing special education or related services.
- To the extent the standards described in [the first bullet above] are not based on the **highest entry-level academic degree needed in the** state for any state-approved or -recognized certification, licensing, registration, or other comparable requirements that apply to that profession or discipline, the state is taking steps to require retraining or hiring of personnel that meet appropriate professional requirements in the state.
- Paraprofessionals and assistants **who are appropriately trained and supervised**, in accordance with state law, regulations, or written policy, in meeting the requirements of this subchapter may be used to assist in the provision of special education and related services to children with disabilities under this subchapter.
- States may adopt a policy requiring local educational agencies to make an ongoing good-faith effort to recruit and hire appropriately and adequately trained personnel to provide special education and related services to children with disabilities, including, in a geographic area of the state where there is a shortage of such personnel, the most qualified individuals available who are making satisfactory progress toward completing applicable course work necessary to meet the standards described above.

These personnel standards are significant for school nursing for two reasons. First, the "highest entry level" degree required for registered nurse (RN) licensure is arguably the baccalaureate degree. Therefore, the baccalaureate degree in nursing might be considered a *minimum* qualification required by IDEA for professional nursing personnel working with special education students, especially in the assessment, planning and evaluation phases of special education-related health services. The second important requirement is that, if paraprofessionals are used to implement health services, as determined by the IEP team, they must be properly trained and supervised, and the supervision should be provided by a baccalaureate or masters-prepared nurse. These requirements must be incorporated into the state education agency's standards for personnel under IDEA, and should be compatible with the state's nursing standards for highest entry level into

practice and for nursing delegation. For nursing standards for entry into practice and into school nursing practice, see chapters 4 and 17; for nursing delegation, see chapters 4 and 5.

The professional titles of service providers must be specified in the IEP, and the school must provide the staffing to implement the IEP. The requirements for appropriate state licensure or certification must be enforced by the state. In other words, IDEA tells school districts to use the IEP team to decide what should be included in the school program for an individual student with disabilities, and then requires the school district to provide the staffing necessary to provide the services. If a school district cannot fill a vacant staff position, interim arrangements must be made. For example, if a speech/language therapist resigns and the district is unable to secure a replacement, the school may contract with a clinic to provide interim services. There cannot be a change in the services specified in an IEP without another meeting of the IEP team, with parents invited to participate. Staffing must be provided for indirect health support services listed in the IEP, and for legally-required professional supervision of paraprofessionals.

Definition of "Qualified School Nurse"

The IDEA regulatory definition of school health services refers to those services "provided by a qualified school nurse or other qualified person," but the "other qualified person" is not defined in any way. Such ambiguity may be responsible, at least in part, for differing interpretations of who else (besides the "qualified school nurse") is qualified to provide school health services. Another major cause of confusion stems from the multiple levels of education and clinical preparation of nurses, such that the public at large, school district personnel and even the courts rarely understand the differences in nursing qualifications and legal scope of practice at each educational level. Thus, a licensed practical (vocational) nurse, allowed in some states to function as a "school nurse" may not, in fact, be qualified to provide many school health services, whereas the professional level registered nurse may be qualified.

State licensing laws for health care professionals, which identify and define professions slightly differently from state to state, and state education certification regulations or other mandates regarding qualifications of school nurses, may also add to differences in interpretation of "qualified school nurse or other qualified person." (See chapter 4 for a review of licensure, scope of practice and education differences among nurses, and their relevance to the qualifications of school nurses, and chapters 1, 17, and 19 for school nurse leaders' perspectives on qualifications of school nurses.)

Staffing for Individualized School Health Services

When a child requires school health support services as part of his or her IEP, the needs should be sufficiently documented to show what professional skills are required, how much service is needed, and how and where it will be provided. For example, in the case of occupational therapy, a child might have two half-hour sessions a week with a licensed occupational therapist. This would be considered "direct services." The therapist might also provide consultation to the child's teachers, helping them to incorporate elements of therapy into the student's total educational program; such consultation services are usually referred to as "indirect services." Such indirect services might include observation of activities in the classroom and instruction of other staff members in appropriate intervention techniques.

As an administrative matter, when the professional nurse delegates to a paraprofessional or other non-nurse an activity such as CIC or oral suctioning, the school must also arrange specialized training for the paraprofessional or ensure that the paraprofessional has received training. Standardized training related to the health care activity and related techniques, such as infection control, should be provided by appropriately qualified health care professionals and the delegating school nurse must provide or ensure the provision of student-specific training. Supervision of the paraprofessional who is providing care, monitoring of the student's health status, and evaluation of student outcomes remains the responsibility of the school nurse. (For further information, see chapters 4 and 5.) It is important to include the child's parents in training sessions for school staff because they know the preferences and idiosyncrasies of their child and because coordinating services provided both at home and at school is critical to the child's health and family's peace of mind.

Where paraprofessionals will augment services provided by professionals, delegation by the professional and training and supervision must be provided to insure continuity and quality of service. Given the dearth of professional nurses in some locations of the country and other school districts' reluctance to hire additional licensed nurses, individualized school health support services are sometimes delegated to paraprofessionals who are individually (and often informally) trained to provide the service. Each state's nurse prac-

tice act and the state board of nursing charged with enforcement may identify health care services that may *only* be provided by a nurse and sometimes only by a registered professional nurse.

When considering a service not previously provided in the school district, the district is responsible for determining the appropriate professional qualifications of potential service providers. A health professional, usually the school nurse, should determine if a specific procedure can safely be delegated to a paraprofessional for the individual student in question. State laws regarding licensure or certification of health professionals and professional standards of practice are the basis for such determinations, in addition to the individual student's health status.

Case example:

In a court case brought by a school health aide who was assigned by the principal to perform CIC for a student, the State Board of Nursing Examiners reported to the court that, indeed, the principal was practicing nursing without a license. The issue was not so much that he had assigned the simple task of CIC, but more that he had presumed to know the health needs of the student, that is, assumed the functions of health assessment, diagnosis and planning, for which he was neither qualified nor licensed (*Mitts, Carol v. Hillsboro Union High School District No.3-8Jt, et al.*, 1990).

As a practical matter school health services are frequently delegated to a paraprofessional working in a school building without a nurse on site. When a supervising nurse is not required on site, there must be a workable plan for nursing consultation and supervision, and for emergencies. Some districts describe these services as "direct" or "indirect," with consulting and supervising considered "indirect" services to the student. These services must be included in the student's IEP. (See chapters 4, 5, and 17 for further discussion of qualifications of health care providers, licensure, and delegation, including related cases and potential liability for school districts, school administrators, and health professionals.)

When Teachers Provide School Health Services

Depending on the particular state, region, and school district, classroom teachers are sometimes asked to provide health support services to students in their classrooms. As a result, many issues related to licensure and union contracts have been and continue to be raised.

Case examples:
In 1991, a Michigan school principal, in consultation with a school nurse, proposed delegation of clean intermittent catheterization, oral and nasal suctioning, deep suctioning, and tracheostomy care to teachers and paraprofessionals. The union representing teachers and paraprofessionals in the school district sued the school district, claiming that the delegation of nursing procedures failed to meet the standards of the state public health code. The Court issued a permanent injunction against the school district's plan, based on the legal requirements for delegation: the decision to delegate, and the decision to whom to delegate, must be made by the professional nurse; and the delegator must meet a supervisory standard, "available for direct communication." The school district's motions to reconsider, to amend judgment, and for a new trial were all rejected (*Macomb Intermediate Federation of Teachers v. Macomb Intermediate School District*, 1991).

Some teachers who had been assigned health support services in their classrooms felt that they were being required to practice nursing without licenses, and that they were not qualified to provide the services assigned to them. The teachers sought a declaratory judgment from a court concerning their status in providing "medical services" at a center for students with varied severe disabilities. The case was dismissed because the State Board of Nursing, which had jurisdiction in these matters, was not a party to the case, and therefore there was no "nursing controversy." The state supreme court upheld the dismissal (*Stamps v. Jefferson County Board of Education*, 1994).

Many special education issues are emerging in teacher union contract negotiations. A few of the issues raised are:

- class size and paraprofessional staffing accommodations when a teacher must provide extensive individualized services for students with disabilities in a regular classroom setting;
- the "right" of a teacher to refuse to accommodate a student whose special needs are challenging;
- the "right" of a teacher to refuse training to prepare the teacher to perform related health services;
- additional stipends for regular classroom teachers who provide specialized support services and supervise paraprofessionals in a regular classroom setting.

While some collective bargaining agreements address these issues, there have not yet been legislative or judicial responses. The National Education Association, the Council for Exceptional Children, the National Association of School Nurses, and the American Federation of Teachers published a joint document with guidelines for providing health services to medically complex students (Joint Task Force for the Management of Children with Special Health Care Needs, 1990). Although an important attempt for all parties to collaborate in resolving these difficult issues, the document's usefulness within specific localities is limited by individual state laws, regulations, rules, interpretations, and practices related to health, nursing, and education services. Updated standards related to delegation of nursing activities in general, and in schools in particular, have been published more recently (*e.g., The School Nurse's Role in Delegation of Care: Guidelines and Compendium* [Luckenbill, 1996]). (For additional information on delegation, see chapters 4 and 5.)

SERVICES FOR INFANTS AND TODDLERS WITH DISABILITIES

Under Part C of 1997 IDEA (formerly Part H), states are also offered the option of coordinating early intervention services for infants and toddlers with disabilities. The definition of those to be served resembles the definition for pre-school children with disabilities. To be eligible for services in states that provide Part C services, infants and toddlers must

- be experiencing developmental delays, as measured by appropriate diagnostic instruments and procedures in one or more of the following areas: cognitive development, physical development, language and speech development, psychosocial development, or self-help skills, or
- have a diagnosed physical or mental condition that has a high probability of resulting in developmental delay.

Participating states may assign this program to the state agency of their choice. Many, including Minnesota and Washington, have chosen the state health department. In a few states, a new agency has been created. State definitions vary for eligibility for birth to three services. In some states eligibility requires demonstrated developmental delays in one or more areas or the medical diagnosis of a condition that leads to developmental delay. In fewer states, infants and toddlers "at risk" for developmental delay may also be served, such as those at risk due to prenatal drug exposure, abuse, or parental neglect.

Part C procedures parallel special education procedures for older children. Evaluation and collection of data concerning the infant or toddler must be followed by a multidisciplinary team meeting with parental participation. An Individualized Family Service Plan (IFSP) is developed (rather than an IEP) and must be reviewed every six months. Each IFSP must designate a case coordinator and provide for transition of the child into special education services, if needed. The IFSP differs from an IEP in that it must also consider family needs and preferences related to the child's disability and the services offered and provided. Parents must consent prior to receiving services and are free to choose whether to participate and to what degree to participate. Services for infants and toddlers with disabilities, "to the maximum extent appropriate, are provided in natural environments, including the home, and community settings in which children without disabilities participate."

Given that participation in Part C is "voluntary," there have been questions about rights of infants and toddlers with disabilities.

Case example:

A Federal District Court in Illinois has certified a class of infants and toddlers with disabilities who claim that services were not provided to meet the needs of members of the class. The District Court ordered the state to provide services, and the state appealed. The Seventh Circuit Court of Appeals upheld the decision, rejecting the state's claim of sovereign immunity and finding the provisions of Part H [now Part C] an enforceable claim under Section 1983 (*Marie O., Gabriel C., Kyle G., and Joanna B. v. Edgar*, 1996).

(See the section earlier in the chapter on "Individualized Transition Plans" for IDEA requirements regarding transition services from infant and toddler to preschool special education services.)

DISCIPLINE

Federal law has recently expanded its reach to include the disciplinary status of students with disabilities. (There is a discussion of the history of court cases concerning school discipline in chapter 13.) Recent amendments to IDEA have included attempts by Congress to address the public perception that students with disabilities are subject to separate, or perhaps less stringent, disciplinary rules and procedures than are nondisabled students. This perception is founded on two legal requirements: 1) students must not be discriminated against on the basis of disability, and

2) students with disabilities may not be denied a free appropriate public education without an opportunity to exhaust their rights under IDEA.

Because of these requirements, cases of students with disabilities whose misbehavior in school reaches the level of a suspendable or expellable offense under state law or local school district policy must be reviewed by an IEP team to determine whether the misbehavior was a manifestation of the student's disability. The school nurse plays a critical role in assisting the IEP team to determine whether a student's chronic health condition or medical treatment, such as medication, may be a contributing factor in misbehavior.

When the special education team and the school discipline team work together, these students should not escape appropriate punishment. However, the specific requirements of the 1999 IDEA regulations can be perceived as burdensome in that procedural requirements and appeals can delay disciplinary action against students with disabilities. A further concern is the confusing legal position of a student with disabilities who has committed a crime at school. In the case of a student who is caught with illegal drugs at school, juvenile court proceedings may run parallel to a school expulsion hearing. If the student has a disability, a third forum may consider whether the misbehavior was related to the student's disability.

REFERENCES

Anonymous, letter to, 22 Individuals with Disabilities Education Law Report (IDELR) (LRP) 637 (OSEP, 1995).

Breecher, letter to, 17 Education of the Handicapped Law Report (EHLR) (LRP) 56 (OSEP 1990).

Canastoga Central School District, # 95-10, 23 IDELR (LRP) 145 (SEA NY 1995).

Committee on Labor and Human Resources, U.S. Senate. (1977, May 9). Senate Report 105-17: Individuals with Disabilities Education Act Amendments of 1997. Washington, DC: U.S. Government Printing Office. Available on-line: http:// www.access.gpo.gov/congress/cong005.html and conduct a search for "sr017.105" in the database for 105th Congress).

Cossey, letter to, EHLR (LRP) 211:351 (OSEP 1984).

Field, letter to, EHLR (LRP) 213:259 (OSEP 1989).

Hudgins, letter to, 23 IDELR (LRP) 347 (OSEP 1995).

Joint Policy Memorandum, U.S. Department of Education, 18 IDELR (LRP) 116 (1991).

Joint Task Force for the Management of Children with Special Health Needs. (1990). *Guidelines for the delineation of roles and responsibilities for the safe delivery of specialized health care in the educational setting.* Reston, VA: The Council for Exceptional Children.

Louisiana Department of Education. *Pupil appraisal handbook* (Rev. 1983). pp. 83–84. Baton Rouge, LA: State Department of Education.

Luckenbill, D. (1996). *The school nurse's role in delegation of care: Guidelines and compendium.* Scarborough, ME: National Association of School Nurses.

Newby, letter to, 16 EHLR (LRP) 549 (OSEP 1990).

New Hampshire #95-71, 23 IDELR (LRP) 588 (NH State Hearing Officer Decision [SEA] 1995).

Sioux City Community School District, 20 IDELR (LRP) 107 (Iowa SEA 1993).

Tinsley, letter to, 16 EHLR (LRP) 1076 (OSEP 1989).

U.S. Department of Education. (1995). *To assure the free appropriate public education of all children with disabilities, 17th annual report to Congress on the implementation of the Individuals with Disabilities Education Act,* Tables AA1, AA14, AF1, AF2. Washington, DC: U.S. Department of Education.

Utah State Board of Education. (1993). *Special Education Rules.* p. 60. Salt Lake City: State Department of Education.

TABLE OF CASES

Andress v. Cleveland Independent School District, 22 IDELR (LRP) 1134 (5th Cir. 1995).

Ankowiak v. Ambach, 838 F.2d 635, EHLR (LRP) Dec. 559:275 (2d Cir. 1988).

Board of Education of Murphysboro Community Unit School District No. 186 v. Illinois State Board of Education, 21 IDELR (LRP) 1046 (7th Cir. 1994).

Board of Education of the Hendrick Hudson Central School District v. Rowley, 458 U.S. 176, EHLR (LRP) 553:656 (U.S. 1982).

Brimmer v. Traverse City Area Public Schools, 872 F.Supp. 447, 22 IDELR (LRP) 5 (W.D. Mich. 1994).

Burlington School Committee v. Massachusetts Department of Education, 105 S.Ct. 1996, EHLR (LRP) 556:389 (U.S. 1985).

Doe v. Nashville, EHLR (LRP) Dec. 441:106 (M.D. Tenn. 1988).

Florence County School District Four v. Carter, 114 S. Ct. 361, 20 IDELR (LRP) 532 (U.S. 1993).

Ian E. v. Board of Education, Unified School District No. 501, Shawnee County, Kansas, 21 IDELR (LRP) 980 (D.Kan. 1994).

Jose P. v. Ambach, EHLR (LRP) 551:412 (E.D.N.Y. 1979).

Macomb County Intermediate School District v. Joshua S., 715 F.Supp. 824, EHLR (LRP) Dec. 441:600 (E.D. Mich. 1989).

Macomb Intermediate Federation of Teachers v. Macomb Intermediate School District, Case No. 88-2474-CZ (Permanent Injunction, Circuit Court for the County of Macomb, August 9, 1991); (Denial of motions for reconsideration, to amend judgment, and for a new trial, December 9, 1991).

Marie O., Gabriel C., Kyle G., & Joanna B v. Edgar, 23 IDELR (LRP) 709 (N.D. Ill 1996); 27 IDELR (LRP) 40 (7th Cir. 1997).

Mitts, Carol v. Hillsboro Union High School District No.3-8Jt, et al., Washington County Circuit Court, case No. 87-1142C (1990).

Pamela B. v. Longview School District, 18 IDELR (LRP) 514 (W.D. Wash. 1992).

Salley v. St. Tammany Parish School Board, 57 F.3d 458, 22 IDELR (LRP) 878 (5th Cir. 1995).

Shook v. Gaston County Board of Education, 882 F.2d 119, EHLR (LRP) Dec. 441:561 (4th Cir. 1989).

Stamps v. Jefferson County Board of Education, 642 So.2d 941, 21 IDELR (LRP) 905 (Ala. 1994).

Timothy W. v. Rochester, New Hampshire, School District, EHLR (LRP) Dec. 559:480 (D N.H. 1988); 875 F.2d 954, EHLR (LRP) Dec. 441:393 (1st Cir. 1989).

OFFICE FOR CIVIL RIGHTS (OCR) DECISIONS

Missouri Department of Elementary and Secondary Education, 19 IDELR (LRP) 463 (OCR 1991).

Seattle (WA) Public Schools, 31 IDELR 193 (OCR).

See page 625 for Table of Federal Statutes and Regulations.

Chapter Thirteen
IDEA: Current Issues in Dispute

Mary H.B. Gelfman,
with Nadine C. Schwab

INTRODUCTION

As discussed in chapters 2 and 12, federal special education legislation was in large part the result of lawsuits brought by parents of children with disabilities. The due process appeal procedures included in IDEA since 1975 continue to generate a significant amount of litigation concerning interpretation of IDEA and the educational rights of individual students with disabilities. This chapter discusses some of the most active areas of current litigation, particularly those that have a relationship to school health and mental health services. The reader is cautioned that these areas continue to be in dispute, and that most court decisions in special education cases are limited to individual facts concerning a single child. In other words, a court decision about special education services for one child may not be applicable to another child with the same disability as the facts of each case may be different.

As also mentioned in chapter 2 and 12, most special education litigation begins as a due process hearing in which school staff members may be called as witnesses. The administrative hearing procedure provided under IDEA for a parent challenging his or her child's special education program must meet administrative law standards, including the right to be represented by an attorney, to submit documentary evidence, to present and cross examine witnesses, and to receive a timely written decision. Some states have an appeal level for review of hearing officers' decisions before an appeal to court, others have a "one tier" system, with appeal directly to court from the hearing officer's decision. Some states refer to the official presiding over a special education hearing as a hearing officer; others have designated administrative law judges for this responsibility. If aggrieved, either party to a special education hearing may appeal the decision in state or federal court. While a hearing or court appeal is pending, the child's school placement may not be changed unless there is an agreement for another placement between the parents and either the school district or the state education agency. In some cases, the issue of "placement pending appeal" has led to a court proceeding and the issuance of an injunction. The 1999 IDEA regulations include provision for school district-initiated placement in an "interim alternative educational setting" for students with disabilities whose misbehavior in school involves drugs or weapons. Interim placements may also be requested from a special education hearing officer on the basis that the student poses a danger to self or others for other reasons. Such interim placements are limited to 45 days.

The decision of the hearing officer and the "record" of the hearing, which includes both the student's documentary records (e.g., school academic, counseling, and health records) that have been entered as exhibits, and the transcript of the hearing, will be the basis for appeal to court. Thus, although school nurses are rarely called to testify in a hearing, a child's school health records may have a significant impact in a contested case.

The topics selected for discussion in this chapter are those that the authors believe have 1) generated the largest amounts of litigation and 2) caused related administrative problems in many public school systems. The primary focus of discussion will be cases that include school health and mental health issues. (For an explanation of the federal and state court systems and of administrative law, see chapter 2.)

COURT INTERPRETATIONS OF IDEA

The *Rowley* Standard

As stated in chapter 12, the U.S. Supreme Court case of *Board of Education of the Hendrick Hudson Central School District v. Rowley* (1982) set forth judicial standards for evaluating the appropriateness of a special education program for an individual student. The Court applied two tests:

1. Did the school district follow the procedural requirements of the Act?
2. Was the individualized special education program (IEP) "reasonably calculated" to enable the child to make educational progress?

"Educational benefit" is another term used by courts to describe the desired results of an appropriate special education program for a child with disabilities. IDEA does not require that students with disabilities be offered the best possible special education program. The IDEA standards of "adequate" and "appropriate" have led to the courts' standard of "educational benefit."

Special Education Hearing Decisions

Special education hearing officers' decisions have little value as legal precedent, because they tend to be specific to the student and a particular state's administrative scheme, but they can be useful as examples of contested cases, and they usually include great detail. In states with two-tier appeal systems, the decision of the state reviewing officer or panel should be consulted (if there was one) as well as the local level hearing decision. These decisions can be obtained from the state education agency in each state, and selected hearing officer decisions are published in the *Individuals with Disabilities Education Law Report (IDELR)*. Some state departments of education are now making hearing decisions available on-line.

Court Appeals of Special Education Hearing Decisions

Most of the court decisions cited in this chapter are the result of cases that started as special education hearings in which the hearing officers' decisions were appealed to court. When the case involves a specific child's rights under IDEA, courts generally require that parents exhaust administrative remedies by requesting a hearing prior to coming into court. For example, when parents sued to obtain implementation of a § 504 plan for their two asthmatic children, the Eleventh Circuit Court of Appeals upheld a district court decision that the court lacked jurisdiction until the parents had exhausted their administrative remedies under IDEA (*Babicz v. School Board of Broward County*, 1998). The court held that the relief sought was available under IDEA. If a parent can demonstrate an emergency or some other reason why exhaustion would be futile, a court may make an exception to the requirement that a hearing be completed prior to filing suit.

Class Action Lawsuits

In some situations, groups of hearing decisions concerning similar situations may be joined into a "class action" in court. In other situations, a class of students suffering from similar or related violations of IDEA may go directly to court, often using a federal civil rights law usually referred to as § 1983. (See chapter 2.) Class actions are permitted in federal courts when it can be shown that the named plaintiffs represent a larger group in the same or similar situation. The federal court will first consider whether the proposed "class" actually has common representative claims. If the court approves, thus certifying the plaintiffs as a class, the case can move forward on behalf of the named plaintiffs plus others who may be similarly situated. In class action lawsuits, the recovery by an individual plaintiff might be relatively small, and attorney's fees per plaintiff are reduced since plaintiffs all share in paying the attorney(s). In most successful civil rights actions, attorneys' fees may be awarded to the prevailing plaintiff by the court.

The 1979 case of *Jose P. v. Ambach* was a class action suit on behalf of children with disabilities in the New York City school system, whose evaluations or special education placements were unreasonably delayed. This case resulted in judicial orders that enforced evaluation and placement timelines, directed hiring of necessary school special education staff, and mandated other actions needed to fully implement the requirements of IDEA, § 504, and related state laws.

A more recent class action, *Marie O., Gabriel C., Kyle G.,* and *Joanna B. v. Edgar* (1996), certified a class of approximately 26,000 Illinois infants and toddlers who alleged eligibility for services under Part H (now Part C) of IDEA that they were not receiving. (See chapter 12.) The federal district court articulated the responsibilities of the state under Part H and set up a compliance schedule, retaining jurisdiction. The Seventh Circuit Court of Appeals rejected the State's appeal in 1997, upholding the District Court's orders.

Applicability of Court Decisions in Special Education

Caution should be used in interpreting court decisions in special education. First, when a case addresses an individual child's rights under IDEA, minimal legal precedent will result. Second, state court decisions do not apply in other states, and federal court decisions do not apply in other federal court districts. However, U.S. Circuit Court of Appeals decisions may establish precedent for all the states in the particular Circuit. (See chapter 2.)

The few special education cases decided by the U.S. Supreme Court do have nationwide impact, and most of them will be discussed in this chapter. For example, the *Rowley* case cited above is quoted in many court decisions as establishing the standard for court review of special education cases. Another case, *Honig v. Doe* (1988), which is discussed below, is frequently cited for providing standards for discipline of students with disabilities whose misconduct may be related to their disability.

As a rule, however, each special education student is evaluated as an individual and offered a free appropriate public education based on individual strengths and needs. This makes most court decisions concerning special education fact-driven and specific to one child.

LEAST RESTRICTIVE ENVIRONMENT (LRE) AND INCLUSION

IDEA Placement Requirements

The provisions of IDEA concerning educational placement, which were originally drafted in the early 1970s, introduced two educational concepts:

- placement must be in the least restrictive environment for the child; and
- a "continuum of alternative placements" must be available for consideration.

IDEA also provides guidance concerning decisions to place a child in an alternative to the regular classroom:

> To the maximum extent appropriate, children with disabilities, including children in public or private institutions or other care facilities, are educated with children who are not disabled, and special classes, separate schooling, or other removal of children with disabilities from the regular educational environment occurs only when the nature or severity of the disability of a child is such that education in regular classes with the use of supplementary aids and services cannot be achieved satisfactorily (Individuals with Disabilities Education Act (20 U.S.C. 1412(a)(5)(A)).

The "continuum of alternative placements" is described as instruction conducted in the classroom, in the home, in hospitals and institutions, and in other settings. Many people refer to placements in regular classrooms as "mainstream," "inclusive," or "integrated" placements, although none of these terms are used in IDEA.

Development of Placement Standards

In the case of *Lachman v. Illinois State Board of Education* (1988), the parents of a profoundly deaf 7-year-old opposed the school district's placement of the child in a program for hearing impaired children, rather than in their neighborhood school. The federal district court and, on appeal, the Seventh Circuit Court of Appeals, upheld the school's placement decision, saying that the mainstreaming preference of IDEA does not override the importance of an appropriate program. Calling the parents' preference for a cued speech program a difference in methodology from the use of total communication including sign language, as proposed by the Board, the court held that the school district has the authority to select educational methodology.

Several court cases have tested the concept of "full inclusion," or placement of all children, regardless of the nature or severity of their disabilities, in regular classes, with whatever support may be needed. In the case of *Daniel R. v. El Paso Independent School District* (1989), the school district tried a regular class placement for a Texas 6-year-old with Down Syndrome, but without needed support services. The school district subsequently proposed placement in a separate class for children with disabilities. The parents challenged the school district's plan. The Fifth Circuit Court of Appeals provided standards for IEP team consideration:

- Can the IEP services be provided in a regular classroom? If so, that is where the placement should be.
- What are the possible benefits the child with disabilities may receive from the regular class placement?
- What is the potential benefit of "mainstreaming," in and of itself?
- What support services (more than "mere token" support) must be in place for an appropriate program in the regular classroom?
- What will be the effect on other children in the classroom?

In *Daniel R.*, the court ultimately upheld placement in a separate pre-kindergarten class because the school district demonstrated that the child received minimal educational benefit in the regular class, and also because the teacher had to spend a disproportionate amount of time dealing with Daniel's behavior, to the detriment of other students. By the time the case had been through a due process hearing, a federal district court decision, and finally a decision by the Fifth Circuit Court of Appeals, the child was attending a private school.

In the Ninth Circuit case of *Sacramento City Unified School District v. Holland* (1994), the school district denied a regular classroom placement to a California 5-year-old with Down Syndrome. Her parents then placed her in a private school for a year, where she was in a regular class with minimal support services. The next year, her parents returned her to the school district and requested a regular class placement, which was again denied. Basing its decision on the child's documented success in the prior year, the federal district court ordered regular class placement. The court questioned the school district's estimate of the cost for support services in the regular class placement and dismissed the school's argument that the state funding formula provided a significantly larger grant for placement in a separate class. This case also provided standards for consideration by the IEP team:

- Will there be educational benefit to the child with disabilities in regular classroom placement?
- Will there be non-academic benefits to the child with disabilities in regular classroom placement?
- Will there be a detrimental effect on the teacher and the other students, either because of disruption or distraction, or because the teacher's time will be taken from other students to provide for the child with disabilities?
- Are there valid cost factors to consider?

This decision was upheld by the Ninth Circuit Court of Appeals. For a detailed discussion of "tests" for LRE cases, see Julnes (1994). Using the *Holland* standards, the Ninth Circuit held in *Clyde K. ex rel. Ryan K. v. Puyallup School District* (1994) that a Washington 15-year-old with ADHD and Tourette's Syndrome and a record of violent behavior in a regular classroom setting should be placed in a self-contained program.

In 1993, *Oberti v. Board of Education of the Borough of Clementon School District* from the Third Circuit presented the case of a New Jersey 8-year-old with Down Syndrome and a record of disruptive behavior. The court found that

- the school district's trial placement in a regular classroom failed because there was no plan to address disruptive behavior; and
- the district should have tried a behavior modification plan before recommending a change in placement.

The standard articulated by this court:

- Did the school make a reasonable effort to accommodate the child in a regular classroom?
- Will there be benefit to the child with disabilities in a regular classroom placement with appropriate supplementary aids and services?
- Will there be negative effects on other children in the class?

Several courts have commented that, while separate programs might offer more rapid academic progress for a child with disabilities, such progress does not outweigh the possible benefits of regular class placement. Several courts have cited the importance for children with disabilities of socialization with non-disabled peers. A few later cases raise the question of who the child's actual peers will be: in the case of a deaf child, other deaf children may be peers. The issue of peers may also include discussion of potential peers in adult life: a child with severe mental retardation may be expected to live as an adult in a supervised setting with other people who are severely disabled, with supervised vocational and community experience.

In many cases, the issue of disruption of a regular classroom will be decided based on documentation of the nature and frequency of the disruptions, and the classroom modifications made in attempting to manage disruptive behavior. In the case of *Light v. Parkway C-2 School District* (1994), the Eighth Circuit upheld a school district placement in a special class for a multiply-disabled Missouri 13-year-old who had mental retardation and autism. After reviewing documentation of the child's disruptive behavior and of school district efforts to modify that behavior in a regular classroom setting, the court noted that removal from the regular class was necessary to provide a safe learning environment, both for this student and for other students. This court discussed standards for placement decisions concerning disruptive and potentially dangerous students:

- Is the student "substantially likely" to injure himself or others?

- Has the school district taken reasonable steps to minimize this risk?

In the Ninth Circuit Court of Appeals case of *Poolaw v. Bishop* (1995), an Arizona school district proposed residential placement in a school for the deaf for a 13-year-old profoundly deaf student. The district argued that a series of mainstream placements in several different school districts had been unsuccessful, and that "total immersion" in sign language was now essential for this student to develop communication skills. The courts held for the school district, and commented that the educational professionals were entitled to deference in the selection of educational methodology.

In a Ninth Circuit case, *Seattle School District No. 1 v. B.S.* (1996), an Administrative Law Judge, the federal district court, and the Ninth Circuit all held that the school district's proposed day program for a Washington 11-year-old with a serious emotional disability would not adequately address her serious needs. The student's behavior had deteriorated to a point where she required hospitalization, and the school district had expelled her. Finding that a residential placement was the least restrictive environment for this student, the court ordered the school district to fund all non-medical costs of such a placement.

A Minnesota state hearing review officer upheld a school district's recommendation, and a special education hearing officer's decision, that "routine" suctioning and tracheostomy care for a severely, multiply-disabled student should not be performed in the classroom. While the school's recommendation that it be done by the school nurse outside the classroom was found to be reasonable, the district was directed to explore locations for suctioning closer than the health office to minimize the student's absence from the classroom (Special School District No. 6, 1994). The parents had requested that this care be provided by a teacher or paraprofessional in the classroom — that is, by regular classroom personnel (personal communication with Carmen Teskey, July, 1999). The school district had argued its position based on standards of nursing care and infection control, as well as the issue of classroom disruption for the other students. See further discussion of this case below.

In 1994, the Sixth Circuit Court of Appeals found that a proposed placement in a comprehensive development class for a Tennessee fourth grader was appropriate. This child was diabetic, with neurological-based problems and limited verbal skills and ambulation. In the prior school district, she had attended a resource room program with some regular classes each day. After the family moved, the new district made a placement in the neighborhood school with services similar to those in the prior school district. Because this student could not perform on the fourth grade level in any subject and was having a variety of other difficulties, placement in a special program in another school was recommended. The Sixth Circuit commented:

> A school district must examine the educational benefits, both academic and nonacademic, available to a child with a disability in a regular classroom. The record shows that [the school district] did so with regard to [this student], and there is no reason to dispute [the school's] conclusion that Crockett School was not able to provide appropriate services. [This student's] IEP requires mainstreaming for classes in art, music, and science or social studies, and that [this student] will eat lunch and [have] recess with nondisabled children. This has been determined by the [school] to be the "maximum extent appropriate" and that determination is supported by the record (*McWhirt v. Williamson County Schools*, 1994, p.511).

When a Minnesota fourth grader's parents unilaterally placed her in a private school for students with learning disabilities and requested reimbursement, the hearing officer ruled that the public school program was appropriate. This student had severe dyslexia, affecting both her reading and math progress, and attention deficit disorder. The state review officer reversed, finding that the public school program was not appropriate and that the private school placement was appropriate. The federal district court and the Eighth Circuit Court of Appeals found with the initial hearing officer that the public school program was appropriate (*Independent School District No. 283 v. S.D.*, 1996). Among many other findings, the Eighth Circuit mentions that the private school placement, with only learning disabled classmates, is not LRE for this student.

The parents of a deaf Texas third grader asked that she be educated in the local school, rather than in a regional program located in a neighboring school district (*Flour Bluff Independent School District v. Katherine M.*, 1996). The child had been doing extremely well, attending mainstream classes assisted by a sign language interpreter and receiving speech therapy. In 1994, the student's parent requested that she be placed in the local school district, and the local district IEP team continued to recommend placement in the regional program. The Fifth Circuit Court of Appeals, in reviewing hearing officer and district court decisions finding that the school closer to home was preferred under IDEA, pointed out the difficulties of securing specialized staff (sign language interpreters and speech pathologists) for deaf children in every district, and the advantages of the staffing at the regional program. The court reversed the earlier decisions, finding the regional program appropriate. Noting an upcoming IEP team meeting and the student's transfer to the local district during the pendency of the case, the court commented that the team should consider that factor in making a placement. The court's discussion of centralizing resources in a regional program is thoughtful and thorough, considering both financial and educational concerns.

In the case of an 11-year-old Virginia student with autism, placement in a regular classroom had become very difficult because of the student's disruptive behavior (*Hartmann v. Loudoun County Board of Education*, 1997). The school recommended placement in a special class for children with autism, with art, music, physical education, library and recess in a regular class. The parents objected, preferring more mainstreaming. The Board requested a hearing, and their program prevailed. The decision was upheld by a state review officer, and the parents appealed in federal court. The district court reversed, rejecting the testimony provided by school staff and finding that the school had not provided sufficient support in the regular class placement. When the school appealed, the Fourth Circuit reversed, citing the *Rowley* standard and the importance of deference to educational experts in matters of program and placement. The Fourth Circuit also noted the record of support services from the hearing, and the record of disruption affecting other students.

A Missouri student with learning disabilities was removed from the public school system and placed in a private school by his parents, who then requested a hearing (*Fort Zumwalt School District v. Clynes*, 1997). The hearing officer held that the public school program had resulted in progress and that the student's disability did not require complete segregation from nondisabled students. A state review officer reversed, and the Board appealed. After another hearing in federal district court, the review officer's decision was upheld. The court found that the student had not received an appropriate program, making extensive findings and ordering reimbursement for the private school program. The Eighth Circuit, however, found for the school district, based on the *Rowley* standard. Acknowledging that the private

school might have been better, the appellate court wrote that the school district had provided an appropriate program and had demonstrated that the student had made progress in that program.

After participating in an "inclusion" program in Minnesota, a student with severe disabilities who functioned at the level of a 2-year-old, moved with her family to Tennessee (*Kari H. v. Franklin Special School District*, 1997). After a year in an "inclusion" program in the new school district, the school recommended placement in a special class for most of the day, with mainstreaming with children who were chronologically younger. The parents objected to the proposed placement. After a hearing, the administrative law judge found that the student received only "marginal benefits" from the regular classroom placement, while learning more in the special education classroom. The record showed significant disruption of the regular classroom. The school's recommended placement was upheld. The Sixth Circuit upheld the district court, noting the greater progress in special education and the disruption of other students' education.

Several decisions at the Circuit Court of Appeals level have ordered greater inclusion and several have ruled for removal from regular education classes. In some cases, the parents sought an "inclusive" placement; in others, the Board argued for LRE. The important thing to remember about these cases is that each one is about a specific child with a specific list of IEP services and a specific prior school history. To a large extent, the outcomes have been driven by those individual facts.

Perhaps because of philosophical differences, the issues of "full inclusion" continue to be raised frequently in special education hearings. According to Maloney and Pitasky (1995, p. 2):

Although some consistency in the factors used by the courts to analyze inclusion cases is readily visible, it is clear that the individual outcomes in these cases are fact-sensitive determinations which escape generalization.

It must also be noted that the positions of the parents and the schools involved are frequently based on strongly-held views of the student's ultimate role in adult society. For further discussion of LRE and inclusion legal issues, see Osborne (1994), McCarthy (1995), Zirkel (1998) and questions and answers on LRE from the U.S. Department of Education (Heumann and Hehir, 1995).

SCHOOL HEALTH SERVICES AS RELATED SERVICES UNDER IDEA

Nursing Services as "Related Services"

The landmark case of *Irving Independent School District v. Tatro* (1984) presented the U.S. Supreme Court with the issue of whether clean intermittent catheterization (CIC) could be considered a related service under IDEA. The school district, claiming that this procedure was a medical service, had offered either homebound instruction or a shortened school day, so that the Texas child's family could continue to provide all CIC for the child. In requiring the school district to provide this service during a normal-length school day, the Court observed that the service itself did not require much time or skill; indeed, the student would eventually be able to perform it for herself. The court also noted that training someone to perform it would require "less than an hour." Finding that CIC was not "burdensome" on the school district, the Court ordered the school to provide it as a related school health service under IDEA. This decision does not reflect any consideration of state nurse practice acts and state boards of nursing, which in some states have defined CIC as a "nursing service" that may only be performed by a nurse.

Intermittent versus Continuous Nursing Services

As more children who are medically complex and technology dependent, and thus in need of more extensive and challenging health services, come to public school, school districts and courts have grappled with making a division between school health services as "related services" under IDEA, and "medical services" that are *not* provided under IDEA. The regulatory definitions categorize "medical services" as services that are provided for diagnostic or evaluation purposes. "School health services" are services provided by a qualified school nurse or other qualified person. The results of these distinctions have not always been consistent.

In a New York case, *Detsel v. Auburn Enlarged City School District Board of Education* (1986), parents requested a full-time nurse to monitor their 7-year-old child's vital signs, respirator operation and oxygen supply, administer medication through a tube to the jejunum, suction the child's trachea, and perform cardiopulmonary resuscitation (CPR) when needed. The federal district court found that these services exceeded "school health services" for several reasons: constant monitoring was required to protect the life of the child; the records in this case showed that the services required were beyond the competence of a school

nurse, and would require a "specially trained health care professional" (i.e., a private duty or one-on-one nurse rather than a paraprofessional); the services would be too costly and burdensome on the school district; and the child's education could be provided at home or in a hospital setting. "Beyond the competence of the school nurse" referred to the extent and nature of the multiple services required, such that the care for this one student was beyond the scope of school nurse responsibilities. In other words,

> …the health care procedures that individually might have been included in [the student's] IEP as school health-related services were, in the aggregate, considered to be so extensive and complex as to consider them excludable medical services beyond the educational obligation of the school district (Rapport, 1996). (See also Dieterich, 1995.)

The Second Circuit Court of Appeals upheld the district court decision, setting a precedent for New York, Connecticut, and Vermont, that the IDEA does not require schools to provide continuous, one-on-one, or private duty nursing care.

In another New York case, *Ellison v. Board of Education of Three Villages Central School District* (1993), a request for full time nursing care to monitor a paraplegic child who required a respirator at an estimated annual cost of between $25,000 and $40,000 was found to be too costly for a local school district. Similarly, when parents in a Utah case requested continuous nursing care for a 6-year-old with a tracheostomy tube and a naso-gastric feeding tube, a court found this care excessively costly, and a burden on the school system and on other children in the school (*Granite School District v. Shannon M.*, 1992). In a Pennsylvania case, a school nurse was requested to serve as monitor for a child with a variety of life-threatening conditions: severe bronchia-pulmonary dysplasia, profound mental disability, spastic quadriplegia, seizure disorder, visual impairment, and hydrocephalus. This child's condition might require life-saving intervention at any time, and thus required continuous one-on-one care. The court held that such care by a school nurse was too expensive, and not a related school health service (*Bevin H. v. Wright*, 1987).

However, similar cases had different results. A 1983 Hawaii case, *Hawaii Department of Education v. Katharine D.*, found "intermittent" nursing services, including care of a child's tracheostomy tube, to be related services and not too burdensome. In *Neely v. Rutherford County Schools*, a 1994 Tennessee case, the federal district court reversed a hearing officer's decision and ordered constant monitoring of the student's tracheostomy by a nurse or a respiratory therapist, as related school health services. Services included suctioning when needed, and ventilation with an AMBU bag when the 7-year-old student's breathing stopped. This court discussed the cost of various options. In conclusion, the court cited the statutory preference for the least restrictive environment, and commented:

> The gains to the child, relative to the burden imposed on the school district, are weightier.

Discussing the apparent conflict between this outcome and that in *Detsel v. Auburn* and other cases, Rosenfeld (1994) cites the following factors in the court's analysis:

- The services required did not require a physician.
- Is the care required a "supportive service" necessary to assist the student to benefit from special education?
- If the answer is "yes," does the care required fall within the "medical services" exclusion?

This court balanced the student's needs and the IDEA emphasis on least restrictive environment, and found for the parents.

However, the Sixth Circuit Court of Appeals reversed the district court's decision, finding the services required by this student to be "medical" and too burdensome (*Neely v. Rutherford County Schools*, 1995). In reversing the decision, Sixth Circuit commented:

> The undue burden in this case derives from the nature of the care involved rather than the salary of the person performing it.

In the *Neely* decision, the Sixth Circuit distinguished its ruling from *Katharine D.*, cited above, in which "a trained lay person or a school nurse" could care for the student's tracheostomy, and the court in Neely drew the line between "constant" and "intermittent" care. In Tennessee, the State Board of Nursing had ruled that tracheostomy care and suctioning must be provided by a properly licensed health professional. Commenting on this decision, Rosenfeld (1996a) notes that the lower court had identified the services in dispute as "medical," and then balanced the interests of the student and the school. The Sixth Circuit points out that *any* medical services, other than those for diagnosis or evaluation, are excluded under the IDEA. Rosenfeld (1996a)

includes in his article two memoranda from the Tennessee State Department of Education to school superintendents and directors of special education, discussing the importance of the state professional practice acts in determining who will be assigned by the school district to perform health support services.

Another example of a court's concern as to whether "continuous" or "intermittent" nursing care was required is *Tanya by Mrs. X v. Cincinnati Board of Education* (1995). This case involved an Ohio child who required tracheostomy care. Based on testimony that a paraprofessional could monitor the child, and that care by a school nurse was needed only "intermittently", the court upheld placement in school over homebound instruction.

Parents of an 11-year-old Rhode Island student with several medical conditions who had a tracheal tube for breathing appealed his placement in the only school in the district with a full-time nurse, preferring that the student be educated in his neighborhood school (*Kevin G. v. Cranston School Committee*, 1997). The hearing officer, state review officer, and federal district court upheld the school's recommended placement, and the First Circuit Court of Appeals affirmed.

A full-time nurse was requested for a 14-year-old Illinois student with a tracheostomy breathing tube, who also intermittently used a ventilator and required a variety of other services as well as continuous monitoring (*Morton Community Unit School District No. 709 v. J.M.*, 1998). These services had been provided in school with funding from the student's parent's employee health plan, which has a lifetime limit on benefits. The parents prevailed through two levels of hearings and in federal district court. The Seventh Circuit Court of Appeals affirmed, finding that the school district had made no argument concerning the financial burden of providing the services and that, since the services were to be provided by a nurse, were not excludable as a medical service.

Although the argument of burdensome costs and responsibilities appeared to be spreading across the country to exclude from school responsibility care for children requiring full-time nursing care, an Iowa case eventually took the issue to the U.S. Supreme Court. An Iowa special education hearing officer analyzed the student's health care needs (catheterization, tracheostomy care, use of an AMBU bag when necessary, monitoring of a mechanical ventilator, and others) in relation to the requirements of the state's nurse practice act and the actual cost of providing the services (Cedar Rapids Community School District, 1994). The Iowa State Board of Nursing had ruled that the services required for this child must be provided by a licensed nurse. The hearing officer ruled that the requested services were related school health services under IDEA. This hearing officer cited several factors that distinguish this case from the cases that follow the standards set forth in *Detsel v. Auburn*:

- the child's general good health;
- his ability to communicate his needs;
- his intelligence.

It was the hearing officer's opinion that, because a "conscientious lay person" had cared for him in the past, a paraprofessional could still do so with appropriate training and the student's continuing stable health status. Even with the cost of a licensed nurse, the hearing officer did not find the provision of such services overly burdensome for the school district in comparison to costs of other special education placements. This decision supports the notion that, contrary to *Detsel v. Auburn* and other decisions cited above, services provided by a nurse are related services under IDEA. Medical services defined in IDEA as services "provided by a physician" are specifically excluded from IDEA. Discussing the Board of Nursing's contention that a registered nurse must be in the school building to either provide the care or supervise care provided by a licensed practical nurse, the hearing officer noted that the same services were provided at home by family members and by a licensed practical nurse with remote supervision by a registered nurse.

It must be noted that "medical" services provided in the home by family members are usually protected from legal action by "family immunity," which is not applicable to school staff members. (See chapter 4 for further information on state nurse practice acts.) On appeal to federal district court, the decision of the hearing officer was upheld (*Cedar Rapids Community School District v. Garret F.*, 1996). The Eighth Circuit Court of Appeals affirmed (*Cedar Rapids Community School District v. Garret F.*, 1997), citing the *Tatro* standard, and the U.S. Supreme Court granted certiorari in 1998. For detailed discussion, see Osborne (1998), Rosenfeld (1998), and Barkoff (1998). Barkoff includes briefs submitted to the Supreme Court.

The U.S. Supreme Court decided in March, 1999, that the services required by Garret were related services under the IDEA, not excludable "medical services." Using the logic of *Tatro*, the court found that the services are required for Garret to attend school, and that they do not require a physician. The court further

rejected the balancing of costs and intensity of services used in *Detsel, Ellison, Granite* and *Neely*, above, commenting that there is no support for this approach in the statute.

It is difficult to estimate the impact of this decision, which applies to the whole country, because under IDEA each individual placement decision is still the responsibility of the IEP team. Students requiring full-time nursing services in school were found in at least four types of placements prior to this decision:

- in school, voluntarily funded by local school districts;
- in school, with nursing services funded by another source (e.g., Medicaid, private insurance);
- at home, receiving homebound instruction; and
- receiving hospital-based instruction.

Some severely-disabled, medically-fragile children have been found by their physicians to be "not medically available for education" from time to time. The immediate effect of the *Cedar Rapids* decision will be more requests from parents for school nursing services; which requests will be granted and how the services will be staffed remain to be seen.

Another confusion about what is required by law occurs because some school districts have voluntarily provided health support services to children with complex, life-threatening conditions, including one-on-one nursing services, while others have not (Osborne, 1998). When families move from district to district, they may discover that services provided in one district are denied in another.

A 1996 article in *The Special Educator* includes a 1991 letter from the Office of Special Education Programs (OSEP) offering a useful test:

- Does the child have a disability as defined by IDEA?
- Is the service necessary to assist the child to benefit from his or her special education program? If the service can be given during non-school hours, then the school district is not required to provide it, even if the burden would be minimal.
- Can the service by provided by a nurse or other qualified professional? If it requires a physician, the school district is not required to provide it.

This article also quotes suggestions to school IEP teams from Mae Taylor, Assistant Director of Special

Education, Utah State Office of Education, and Gary Ruesch, a school attorney:

- Don't have a blanket policy on any particular service or procedure. Consider each request on a case-by-case basis.
- Consult with your school attorney and review your state laws and case law in your region.
- Review your state's medical practice act and nurse practice act. They can offer guidance on what procedures require a nurse or other trained health care professional.
- Think about potential liability. If the service should be performed by or supervised by a registered nurse, but is performed by someone else, both the school district and the individuals involved could be held liable if something goes wrong.
- Establish good, open communication with the family and the child's physician about the requirements for performing the service or procedure.

While the Supreme Court in *Cedar Rapids* has rejected the cost-balancing tests of many earlier court decisions, the IEP team faces many decisions regarding health care in schools. The IDEA mandate, to consider what is appropriate for each child, will continue to shape program and placement decisions.

Professional Status of the Service Provider

Initially, school administrators were uncertain about which services were "medical" and, thus, not a school district responsibility. Some assumed that if a physician performed the service, it was "medical." The problem with this analysis is that in a medical setting, many services directed by a physician are actually performed by other persons. Examples include the prescription of physical therapy by a physician, with delivery of services by licensed physical therapists, and the direction of a program of psychotherapy by a psychiatrist, with delivery of services by psychologists, psychiatric nurses, social workers, and counselors.

Following several rulings by the Office for Civil Rights of the U.S. Department of Education and a similar court decision in response to complaints concerning a Connecticut State Department of Education policy that discouraged school districts from offering "psychotherapy" as a related service under IDEA on the argument that it was a "medical service," the State Department of Education revised its policy in 1983 (Connecticut State Department of Education, 1979;

Simsbury Public Schools, 1980; *Papacoda v. Connecticut*, 1981). In addressing the issue, the Connecticut Attorney General discussed related services:

> In order to give effect to the definition of "related services" in 20 U.S.C. §1401(17), that statute must be read such that a school system will be required to provide "psychological services" or "counseling services" to a student in need of those services whether or not those services might also be considered "psychotherapy…." The inclusion of the definitions of "psychological services" and "counseling services" [in IDEA definitions of related services] would be rendered next to meaningless if the medical services exception were read so as to exclude the same services simply because they might also be referred to as "psychotherapy." In other words, if a child needs psychological or counseling services in order to afford the child the opportunity to benefit from his or her educational program, these services must be provided as related services at no cost to the parents whether or not these services might also be called "psychotherapy…." If the [IEP Team determines that a student needs a related service] it will then go on to determine the type, frequency, and duration of the service as well as the appropriate provider. It is up to the planning team, for instance, to decide whether the child's needs can be addressed by group counseling or individual counseling, by a guidance counselor, a social worker, a psychologist or a psychiatrist, or by daily or weekly sessions. Again, the determination will be based on the individual needs of the student as those needs affect the child's opportunity to receive educational benefit (Opinion of the Connecticut Attorney General, 1983).

Provision of School Health Services

Since school health services as related services under IDEA are distinct from routine health services provided to all students in a school building, school districts may not deny such related services solely on the basis that routine staffing of the school health office provides school nursing services only twice a week. If a student with a health-related disability requires daily nursing services, e.g., for a half hour twice a day, or requires the full-time presence of a nurse in the building for intermittent monitoring and "as necessary" assessments and interventions, the school district will be required to provide the additional nursing services— and staffing, including a full-time nurse in the school building—if the IEP team determines that these services are what the student requires in order to benefit from his or her special education program or to be placed in the least restrictive environment.

Individualized school health services frequently include more than nursing procedures. School nurses may have IEP responsibilities to provide instruction in self-care, on-going assessment of a student's health status, and counseling concerning health issues. In addition, the school nurse can provide informal instruction to other students and to staff members, easing the integration of students with chronic health problems into the life of the school.

In the Minnesota due process hearing decision discussed above (Special School District No. 6, 1994), the hearing officer ruled against parents who did not want their child with multiple disabilities to be removed from the regular classroom, in which he was fully included, for tracheostomy care and suctioning. The parents had wanted their child's tracheostomy to be suctioned, as needed, by the teacher or paraprofessional within the classroom. In the parents' view, this would be the least restrictive environment for their child. The IEP team had recommended that the student's tracheostomy care and suctioning would be provided by the school nurse (for reasons of quality of care and professional practice standards) and outside the classroom (for reasons of noise distraction and infection control). The parents refused this plan, feeling that suctioning outside the classroom infringed on least restrictive environment. In upholding the district's position, the hearing officer cited the state's nurse practice act and declined to interfere in the decision-making process of the professional school nurse (specifically declining to require the nurse to delegate the care to unlicensed persons). While the hearing officer's order permitted suctioning in the health office, it also required the district to "consider establishing alternative procedures and locations for the provision of suctioning when the student is engaged in activities located far from the health office." On appeal in federal district court (*Moye by Moye v. Special School District No. 6, South St. Paul, Minn.*, 1995), the hearing officer's decision was upheld in that it recognized the professional responsibility of the school nurse to make the decision about when and where suctioning should take place, depending on the circumstances. Another way to view this decision is that the court gave deference to school professionals (i.e., the school nurse) in selection of methodology. Since then, the student has been suctioned by the school nurse both in and outside the classroom based

on an assessment of the needs of the student and of other students at the moment (Personal communication with Carmen Teskey, September 9, 1999).

DISCIPLINE OF STUDENTS WITH DISABILITIES

Possible Relationship between Misconduct and Disability

When a special education student is being considered for school disciplinary sanctions, the possible relationship between the child's disability and the misconduct causing concern must be discussed. In effect, it is discriminatory to punish a student with a disability for behavior that is related to his or her disability. The Office for Civil Rights (OCR) of the U.S. Department of Education has investigated many complaints alleging discriminatory school disciplinary practices. When the school district applied a disciplinary policy consistently to all students, those with and those without disabilities, OCR found no discrimination (Warren County (PA), 1997; Abbeville (SC), 1998; Gardner-Edgerton-Antioch (KS), 1998; Castro Valley (CA), 1998).

Some Florida students with mental retardation were expelled from school for relatively minor offenses, including spitting and swearing (*S-1 v. Turlington*, 1981). The court found that students in need of special education could not be expelled without being provided an opportunity to exhaust their appeals under IDEA. In *Honig v. Doe*, a 1988 U.S. Supreme Court case, a seriously emotionally-disturbed California student had been hospitalized. Upon return to public school, he was suspended indefinitely for violent behavior in school. The lower court found that suspension from school should not exceed 10 days, consistent with *Goss v. Lopez*, a 1975 U.S. Supreme Court decision that established due process rights for all public school students being suspended from school. The federal district court ruling in *Honig* was upheld on appeal to the Ninth Circuit Court of Appeals, and again upheld on appeal to the U.S. Supreme Court. The Ninth Circuit commented that if alternate placement arrangements cannot be secured within the ten day suspension period, an injunction to extend the suspension is an option for students who pose a serious threat to school safety (*Doe v. Maher*, 1986).

Special education appeal procedures have been used to slow down or prevent school disciplinary procedures. A 13-year-old Illinois student, not identified as in need of special education, was notified that the school planned to expel him for possession of a master key to school classrooms and theft of money from those classrooms (*Rodiriecus L. v. Waukegan School*

District No. 60, 1996). The student moved for an evaluation for special education and secured a temporary restraining order (TRO) to enable him to remain in school until his eligibility for special education was determined. The school district moved for an injunction to dissolve the TRO, permitting his exclusion from school. The Seventh Circuit Court of Appeals held that he was entitled to remain in school until the IDEA procedures for determining eligibility were completed. Eventually, this student was found not eligible for special education.

The 1999 IDEA regulations include a section that limits the rights of students not identified as in need of special education to claim eligibility after a disciplinary incident (34 C.F.R. 300.527). Such a claim may be made only if the school had knowledge that the child had a disability prior to the disciplinary incident. That knowledge could have come from concerns expressed by the child's parents or teachers, or from prior behavior of the child. The regulations also provide for an expedited evaluation.

In response to increasing concerns about the appearance of a double standard for discipline of students with a disability and those without, Congress included specific procedural details addressing discipline in the 1997 IDEA amendments, and the 1999 regulations reflect these changes. The school must hold a manifestation determination review whenever

- the school recommends an exclusion in excess of 10 school days (usually considered an expulsion) or a change of placement in response to a disciplinary issue;
- the school initiates an interim alternative educational placement based on violations involving weapons or drugs; or
- the school requests that a hearing officer order an interim alternative educational placement based on dangerous behavior.

IDEA now includes specific language concerning the reporting of crimes committed in school by students. Eligibility for special education now includes eligibility for continuing special education services after disciplinary sanctions, an issue that had been litigated prior to the amendments. IDEA now requires that schools perform a functional behavior analysis to assist with planning for services to be provided after placement in an interim alternative educational setting or expulsion. The 1999 regulations also emphasize the importance of individualized behavioral intervention plans, to be included in the student's IEP.

The Gun Free Schools Act of 1994

Acting in response to increasing reports of violence in public schools, the U.S. Congress passed the Gun Free Schools Act of 1994. This law requires that any student who brings a gun to school must be expelled for at least one calendar year. An amendment provides that a school superintendent may modify the penalty on an individual basis. This amendment, intended to address the rights of special education students whose disability is found to be related to their misconduct, is not clearly limited to that group. States that do not modify their state school discipline laws to conform with this federal law risk loss of all federal financial assistance.

State School Discipline Statutes

The *Honig* decision required California to revise its state law regarding discipline of students in public elementary and secondary schools. Other states have made similar modifications in state disciplinary statutes, providing for a limit of 10 consecutive days of suspension and a determination of whether misconduct is related to a disability, prior to expulsion. Under state discipline statutes, school districts must enact and publish detailed discipline codes. The Gun Free Schools Act of 1994 (see above) also required modification of state discipline statutes.

In a discussion of several state proposals to expand school district disciplinary authority over students, Rosenfeld (1996b) concluded that after efforts to promote school safety appeared to have collided with procedural protections for students with disabilities, the real issue is the importance of appropriate educational programs for all students—both those with disabilities and those without disabilities.

The IEP Team and the Manifestation Determination

A school nurse, social worker, or psychologist may be aware of aspects of a child's disability that contribute to behaviors that are in violation of school standards, or that make it impossible for the student to understand the rules or maintain control of his or her behavior. Therefore, the nurse and other pupil personnel services staff play a critical role in explaining the connection between disability and behavior to the IEP team, and in assisting in the development of plans to address and control behavior.

For example, a school nurse may be needed to explain "misconduct" by a diabetic child experiencing insulin shock, a student suffering from Tourette's Syndrome, or a student who falls asleep in class due to side effects of medication. Similarly, the school social worker or school psychologist may be needed to interpret the behavior of a student with a conduct disorder. At other times, school personnel may need to consult with experts outside the school in determining the relationship— or lack of relationship— between a student's disability and misbehavior. Given the current pressure to remove disruptive students from the public schools, the responsibility of the IEP team in making a relationship determination is often subject to considerable pressure.

The manifestation decision may be appealed to a special education hearing. The hearing officer may limit the review to whether the IEP team considered the appropriate information, including the parent's position, and reached a decision supportable by the evidence.

STUDENTS WITH DISABILITIES ENROLLED IN PRIVATE SCHOOLS

Private School Placement by Parents: IDEA Requirements

It is well established that American parents have the right to send their children to private school, or even to instruct them at home. State school attendance requirements vary, but in most cases relatively minimal procedures are required when parents select one of these options for their children's education.

When children with disabilities have been enrolled in private schools, including parochial schools, by their parents, the school district is not responsible for funding the placement. However, the district must locate these children and make an effort to offer special education services to them. (See chapter 12, Childfind, p.378.) The specific requirements are found in the 1999 IDEA regulations at 34 C.F.R. 300.450 through 300.462. Under these provisions, a comparable amount of federal special education funding must be made available for services to private school children. The public school district must "consult" with local private schools to determine numbers of students with disabilities and their needs. The district is not required to provide services comparable to those offered in the public schools to any child enrolled in private school by his or her parents. School districts are responsible for identifying private school students who are eligible for special education, and for offering them a free, appropriate public education. School districts may then offer special education services to these students, supported with pro rata shares of federal funding. Special education services provided to students in private schools may be comparable, the same, or different from those provided to students in public schools, and there is no requirement that all students with disabilities, enrolled in private schools by their parents, receive services.

The per-child allocation of federal grants to the states under Part B of IDEA for 1994 was estimated at $413 (U.S. Department of Education, 1995). This gives the local school district a rather small amount of federal funding to be used to assist children with disabilities placed by their families in private schools. State constitutional requirements and education funding statutes prevent supplementing this federal allocation with state or local revenues in many states. Services for private school children may be offered at the local public school, which may raise the issue of transportation; at a "neutral site"; or on-site at the private school by itinerant teachers and therapists.

The analysis of *Lemon v. Kurtzman,* a 1971 U.S. Supreme Court decision used to determine whether publicly funded assistance to students in private religious schools passes Constitutional muster, could be applied to itinerant special education and related services provided at private schools. The Lemon analysis requires that

- public funding for services in religious private schools must be neutral in intent;
- the use of public funding must not advance the cause of religion; and
- the services provided with public monies must not be "entangled" in the religious mission of the school (Osborne & Russo, 1997).

For these reasons, most public assistance to children in private religious schools has taken a form that can be described as "direct aid to the child." For example, some school districts provide an itinerant teacher to provide individual support to private school students with learning disabilities.

In the 1993 Arizona case of *Zobrest v. Catalina Foothills School District,* the U.S. Supreme Court found that a sign language interpreter for a deaf student enrolled in a parochial high school was a "mere conduit," and that public funding for the interpreter was not prohibited by the then-current version of IDEA. In a similar 1995 Virginia case, *Goodall v. Stafford County School Board,* involving a deaf student in a parochial school, a decision immediately prior to the *Zobrest* ruling had been that the school district was not required, by IDEA or by the Education Department General Administrative Regulations (EDGAR), to provide an interpreter in the religious school setting. In reconsideration requested after the *Zobrest* decision, the Fourth Circuit Court of Appeals affirmed its original *Goodall* decision that services were not required under IDEA. In both *Zobrest* and *Goodall*, the questions asked the courts were very limited: in *Zobrest*, does IDEA prohibit the provision of services by a sign language interpreter in a religious school; and in *Goodall*, does the denial of public funding for an interpreter in a parochial school unreasonably burden the parents' right to the free exercise of religion (Mehfoud, 1994).

In the 1993 Connecticut case of *Crespo ex rel. Rojas v. New Haven Board of Education*, the court upheld the current state interpretation of EDGAR requirements concerning services for students with disabilities enrolled by their parents in private schools. That interpretation requires that the school district

- offer an appropriate program in the public schools;
- consult with the private schools to determine the numbers of students with disabilities and their needs; and
- offer support services with available federal funds (*Crespo ex rel. Rojas v. New Haven Board of Education*, 1993).

This case confirms that EDGAR does not require publicly funded special education services for *all* children with disabilities enrolled in private schools by their parents, nor does it require equal or comparable special education services to those offered in the public school setting. This scheme is essentially adopted by the 1999 IDEA regulations.

The 1996 Indiana case of *K.R. by M.R. v. Anderson Community School Corporation* concerned a 7-year-old with multiple disabilities, who used a wheel chair and required full time paraprofessional support in the classroom. The public school district agreed that it would provide that support if the child enrolled in public school, but refused to provide a full time paraprofessional to assist the child in a parochial school placement. The Seventh Circuit Court of Appeals upheld the hearing officer's ruling and the decision of the federal district court that the school district was not required by IDEA or by EDGAR to provide the same level of support in a private school where the parents had enrolled the child as would be provided in a public school.

Another 1996 case, from the Second Circuit Court of Appeals, *Russman v. Sobel*, held that support services of a consulting teacher and a teaching aide requested for mainstream placement of a student with mental retardation in a parochial school be funded by the school district. The parents had requested an "inclusion" IEP for an 11-year-old, previously placed in a self-contained classroom program for children with disabilities only. The school district developed the IEP, specifying support services necessary, and the parents requested that the support services be provided in a parochial school placement they were initiating. These services were requested for "core academic subjects" only, and not for religious instruction. Citing *Zobrest*, the Second Circuit found that the services would be neutral as to religion; services were to be provided because of parents' placement decision; and services would go to the student, and not benefit the religious school. The 1999 IDEA regulations also provide that only limited appeal rights are available to parents challenging the school district over special education services to children in private schools.

An Alabama 7-year-old required speech therapy. The school district offered the therapy at a school that was three blocks from the private, religious school that the child attended (*Donald B. v. Board of School Commissioners of Mobile Couty, Alabama*, 1997). The parent appealed, requesting either transportation between the two schools or speech services on-site at the private school. The hearing officer, federal district court, and Eleventh Circuit Court of Appeals upheld the school district, finding no requirement to provide transportation for a three-block distance and no requirement for on-site services.

Two Minnesota students who required paraprofessional support in school because of their disabilities requested that those special education services be funded by their school districts in private, religious schools (*Peter and Westendorp v. Wedl*, 1998). The districts denied funding, citing a state law that forbade on-site publicly funded services in religious schools. The parents sued and the federal district court issued a summary judgment against the parents' equal protection claims of discrimination. Between that decision and the decision on appeal to the Eighth Circuit Court of Appeals, legal developments changed the status of on-site services in religious schools, demonstrating that it can make a difference when a case is brought. The U.S. Supreme Court held that the Religious Freedom Restoration Act, passed by Congress in an attempt to clarify issues involving religious use of schools and religious rights of students at school, was unconstitutional. The Court also held that publicly-funded educational services could be provided on-site in religious schools. One of the school districts settled by offering the requested services. The other family prevailed when the

Circuit Court found that the state law that barred publicly funded educational services for students in religious private schools was discriminatory, since services were provided to students in non-religious private schools and home-school students.

Under the pre-1997 IDEA and related court decisions, the Circuit Court found the school district responsible for "comparable" services, while acknowledging that the 1997 IDEA amendments do not require comparable services to private school students. The 1999 IDEA regulations clearly limit both services and appeal rights for children enrolled in private schools by their parents. It is too early to know whether these limits will decrease or increase litigation in this area.

Private School Placement at Public Expense

When a public school system cannot provide a free appropriate public education for a child requiring special education, the school district must consider placing the child in another public school district, in a regional public school program, or in a private school approved for placement of special education students. Each state has its own private school approval standards. In the 1985 U.S. Supreme Court case of *Burlington School Committee v. Massachusetts Department of Education*, the court found that if a parent could show that the special education program offered by the public school was not appropriate and adequate for the child with disabilities, and if the parent could also show that a private school placement, even made unilaterally by the parent, was appropriate and adequate, the cost of that private school placement must be reimbursed by the school district. This case provides the standard of review for unilateral placements by parents.

In a New York case (*Ankowiak v. Ambach*, 1988) the Second Circuit Court of Appeals found that placement (by a local school district) of a student requiring special education in a non-state approved program does not meet the IDEA requirements for state supervision and monitoring of publicly funded special education programs. Subsequently, the U.S. Supreme Court held, in *Florence County School District v. Carter*, a 1993 South Carolina case, that when the parent of a student requiring special education makes a unilateral placement in a private school because the public school program does not meet the student's needs, the parent cannot be held to the same requirement of state approval for the private school that the school district must meet. In this case, the public school program was found to be inappropriate, and the unapproved private school program

was found to be appropriate. The only significant issue was whether lack of state approval would bar public funding for this placement.

INTERAGENCY COOPERATION AND FUNDING

Regulatory Requirements: Examples of Cooperation

The IDEA regulations require that state departments of education assume responsibility for the education of all children with disabilities, including those who are within the custody of other state agencies, or receiving services from other state agencies. In some cases, major questions arise concerning the roles and responsibilities of various state agencies. Such questions include the following:

- Which is the "lead" agency for a child, with final decision making authority?
- Where two or more agencies are involved, how will funding be divided?
- If one agency may charge parents a fee under state law, is that permitted under IDEA?
- May confidential records concerning the child be shared between agencies without parental consent?

IDEA regulations require interagency agreements to address these problems.

Under the IDEA mandate of interagency cooperation, some state interagency agreements have been negotiated. Following are a few examples of agreements that address specific issues. The number and content of such agreements vary from state to state.

In an effort to resolve many issues that arise when a child is "placed out" into a residential treatment facility by the state's child care agency, the Connecticut State Department of Education and Department Children and Youth Services have written an agreement (*Educational services for children who receive services through DCYS within residential facilities*, 1993). This agreement sets forth the principle of least restrictive environment for education and treatment, and establishes planning priorities to be applied on a case-by-case basis by the two agencies.

Addressing the problems of confidentiality requirements within each state agency dealing with children, the Delaware State Departments of Services for Children, Youth and Their Families, Health and Social Services, and Public Instruction developed a policy concerning sharing of confidential data and an interagency consent procedure and form (State of Delaware, 1993).

In a Pennsylvania case, *Cordero v. Pennsylvania Department of Education*, 1993) waiting lists for placement in state residential facilities for children with disabilities were challenged under IDEA. While acknowledging that placement decisions are the responsibility of local school districts, the court also noted that IDEA assigns overall responsibility for special education to the state department of education, including responsibility to enforce IDEA placement timelines.

After the Second Circuit ruled that one-on-one nursing services were not related services under IDEA in *Detsel v. Auburn*, discussed above, the family appealed Medicaid's rejection of their request that the child's Medicaid-funded nurse, who was assigned to give home care for the child, travel with the child and provide necessary health services at school. In *Detsel v. Sullivan*, 1990, the court held that a Medicaid nurse could accompany a medically fragile child with severe disabilities to school, to provide the necessary one-on-one nursing care services.

In a settlement of litigation on behalf of two other New York children with disabilities whose requests for Medicaid-funded nurses who provided home care to also care for them at school, the U.S. Health Care Financing Administration policy regarding nursing services for children with disabilities was revised to provide for Medicaid-funded nursing care to be provided at school (*Pullen by Pullen v. Cuomo*, 1991). This settlement included a commitment to revise the state Medicaid Manuals accordingly. A Connecticut case (*Skubel v. Sullivan*, 1996) also extended Medicaid home health services to eligible children while attending school.

Residential and Day Treatment Programs

Where residential placement is required to provide custodial care and supervision or medical or psychiatric treatment, there is a line of cases that uphold the practice of dividing responsibilities between the agency that initiates placement or that provides medical or mental health care, and the education agency that remains responsible for the child's school program. This division of responsibility varies from state to state. In *Babb v. Knox County School System* (1992), a school district was found responsible for provision of special education services to a student who was hospitalized in a psychiatric facility. In *Clovis Unified School District v. California Office of Administrative Hearings* (1990), the court found that psychotherapeutic services provided in an acute care facility were not related services under IDEA, even though the services were not provided by a physician. The psychotherapeutic care was analyzed as

"medical treatment" rather than as a service "related to education." Hospitalization itself was found not a related service in the cases of *Los Gatos Joint Union School District v. Doe* (1984) and *Tice v. Botetourt County School Board* (1989), since hospitalization is "medical treatment."

While school districts are required to provide educational services to students in substance abuse treatment programs, in the case of *Field v. Haddonfield Board of Education* (1991) a court ruled that drug treatment itself was not a related service. Thus, school districts generally must provide for educational services, but not the "treatment" aspects of a residential or day substance abuse treatment placement. In residential placements initiated by other agencies or by the student or his or her parents, room and board are usually not considered educational costs.

Most states have provisions to insure that educational services are provided when a student is hospitalized. A broader Connecticut law (Section 10-76d[d], Connecticut General Statutes) provides that when a child has been placed by parents or another agency for "services other than educational services[,] such as medical, psychiatric or institutional care or services[,]…the school district meets its obligation by providing special education services in that placement." Services may be provided by sending a tutor, or by contract with a facility-based school program or with the school district where the facility is located.

Because residential placement is an option under IDEA regulations, families dealing with this issue frequently assert that residential placement is necessary to address the needs of a child with disabilities. (See chapter 12 for a discussion of residential placement standards.) Although there has been a considerable amount of litigation in this area, outcomes generally reflect either very individual student programmatic needs or procedural failures by the school district to address identified needs.

Since the original IDEA provisions grant due process rights to parents and require that special education services continue until students reach age 21 if necessary, there has been some dispute concerning the rights of special education students who have attained adult status under state law. In *Mrs. C. v. Wheaton* (1990), the Second Circuit Court of Appeals reversed the hearing officer and federal district court, holding that consent to terminate services was reserved to the parent, even when the student was an adult. The 1997 IDEA amendments provide that due process rights transfer to the student at the state age of majority, except for those determined to be incompetent under state law. IDEA also provides for state procedures to assure representation for adult students who may need assistance with educational decisions. Parents continue to receive notice under IDEA.

Juvenile Corrections Agency Responsibilities

Arguably, the most difficult interagency population to provide with educational services is comprised of those youngsters who are held in secure facilities pending trial, and those who are incarcerated after sentencing. There have been several class action lawsuits against state agency defendants brought into court on behalf of incarcerated youngsters with disabilities. Courts have insured the educational rights of juvenile pre-trial detainees in Illinois (*Donnell C. v. Illinois State Board of Education*, 1993) and Connecticut (*State of Connecticut-Unified School District #1 v. Department of Education*, 1996). Educational rights of juvenile prisoners in South Carolina (*Alexander v. Boyd*, 1995), North Carolina (*Anthony v. Freeman*, 1996), and Massachusetts (*Green v. Johnson*, 1981), and of youngsters placed by juvenile courts in New Hampshire (*Ashland School District v. New Hampshire Division for Children, Youth, and Families*, 1996), Illinois (*David B. v. Patla*, 1996), and Minnesota (*A. A. by B. A. v. Independent School District No. 283*, 1996) have now also been recognized by courts.

The 1997 IDEA amendments include provisions concerning special education services for children with disabilities who have been convicted as adults under state law, and the transfer of rights under IDEA from parents to children who are incarcerated.

ATTORNEYS' FEES

The 1986 Handicapped Children's Protection Act amended the precursor of IDEA to provide that under some circumstances, parents who prevail in special education proceedings may be awarded attorneys' fees in court. Given the increasing shortage of free and low-cost legal representation, there has been a significant amount of litigation concerning this provision. Most of these cases fall within one of the following categories:

1. Did the parents' actions, in initiating a request for a hearing, result in a change of circumstances for the child?
2. Are fees available for parents who prevail in a special education hearing?
3. Are fees available for administrative proceedings such as IEP meetings or mediation, which usually precede filing of a request for a hearing?

4. Whose fees may be reimbursed?
5. Are the fees claimed reasonable?

Some courts have found the parents' actions in requesting a hearing to be a catalyst in securing an improvement in services to the child, although the matter did not result in a full hearing and a decision. Many of these cases had been settled by the parties, with the issue of attorneys' fees unresolved, resulting in a court appeal for attorneys' fees only (*Barlow-Gresham Union High School District No. 2 v. Mitchell*, 1991; *Terefenko ex rel. Terefenko v. Stafford Township Board of Education*, 1991; *Angela L. v. Pasadena Independent School District*, 1990; *Moore v. District of Columbia*, 1990; *Rynes by Rynes v. Knox County Board of Education*, 1993; *Grinsted by Grinsted v. Houston County School District*, 1993).

The issue of attorneys' fees for parents who prevailed in special education hearings has been resolved by several federal circuit court cases holding that fees be awarded (*McSomebodies v. Burlingame Elementary School District*, 1989; *Counsel v. Dow*, 1988; *Mitten v. Muscogee County School District*, 1989).

Fees for legal services in pre-hearing proceedings such as IEP meetings and mediation have been denied on the basis that they were not "actions or proceedings" under IDEA (*Fenneman v. Town of Gorham*, 1992; *Rappaport v. Vance*, 1993; *Kletzelman v. Capistrano Unified School District*, 1995). It has been argued, however, that because such proceedings are required to exhaust administrative remedies under IDEA, attorneys' fee awards are reasonable. This issue was addressed in the 1997 amendments to IDEA, which include specific language that attorneys' fees will not be awarded for participation in IEP team meetings unless the meeting is "a result of an administrative proceeding or judicial action." The 1997 amendments also provide that states may authorize award of attorneys' fees for mediation that takes place prior to the filing of a request for a hearing.

Cases involving the issue of to whom reimbursement may be paid have been less consistent, perhaps reflecting varying local practices regarding attorneys' fees. Expert witness fees have been awarded in some jurisdictions (*McKirryher v. Rochester School District*, 1993; *Aranow v. District of Columbia*, 1992). A pro se parent who was an attorney was denied fees (*Rappaport v. Vance*, 1993), while another pro se parent who was an attorney was denied fees in state court, then won an award on appeal, which was overturned by the Indiana Supreme Court citing *Rappaport* (*Miller v. West Lafayette Community School Corporation*, 1996).

Pursuant to IDEA, a fee award may be reduced when

- a parent has "unreasonably protracted" the process;
- the amount sought unreasonably exceeds the hourly rate prevailing in the community for similar services by attorneys of reasonably comparable skill, experience, and reputation; or
- the time spent and legal services furnished were excessive considering the nature of the action or proceeding.

Thus, requested fees have been reduced (*Barbara B. v. Board of Education of Hardin County*, 1994; *Beard v. Teska*, 1994; *Patrick G. v. City of Chicago School District No. 299, Cook County, Illinois*, 1995; but see *Phelan v. Bell*, 1993). The large volume of disputed claims suggests that attorneys' fee awards have become a way to fulfill the promise of "free and low-cost legal services" for parents mentioned in IDEA. Parents' attorneys' fee awards are paid by school districts or their insurers.

REFERENCES

Barkoff, A. N. (1998). *Serving medically fragile students: The Supreme Court prepares for review.* Horsham, PA: LRP Publications.

Cedar Rapids Community School District, 22 Individuals with Disabilities Education Law Report (IDELR) (LRP) 278 (IOWA State Hearing Officer Decision [SEA] 1994).

Deciding if a related service is medical or educational. (1996). *The Special Educator, 12*(3): 1, 4 & 5.

Dieterich, C. A. (1995). Health-related services under IDEA that are medical in nature. *West's Education Law Reporter 100:* 831.

Heumann, J. E., and Hehir, T. Letter to the Chief State School Officers, dated November 23, 1994, Office of Special Education Programs (OSEP) 95-9, cited by Rosenfeld, S. J. (1995), *EDLAW Briefing Paper IV* (8).

Julnes, R. E. (1994). *The New Holland and other tests for resolving LRE disputes, West's Education Law Reporter 91:* 789.

Maloney, M. H., & Pitasky, V. M. (1995). *Review of special education cases* 1994 (p.2). Horsham, PA: LRP Publications.

McCarthy, M. M. (1995). Inclusion of children with disabilities: Is it required? *West's Education Law Reporter 95:* 823.

Mehfoud, K. S. (1994). *Special education services for private school students.* Horsham, PA: LRP Publications.

Opinion of the Connecticut Attorney General,

addressed to the Acting Commissioner of Education, June 22, 1983 [unpublished].

Osborne, A. G. (1994). The IDEA's least restrictive environment mandate: A new era. *West's Education Law Reporter 88:* 541.

Osborne, A. G. (1998). Where will the Supreme Court draw the line between medical and school health services under the IDEA? *West's Education Law Reporter 128:* 559.

Osborne, A. G., & Russo, C. J. (1997). The ghoul is dead, long live the ghoul: *Agostini v. Felton* and the delivery of Title I services in nonpublic schools. *West's Education Law Reporter 119:* 781.

Rapport, M. J. K. (1996). Legal guidelines for the delivery of special health care services in school, *Exceptional Children, 62*(6): 537-549.

Rosenfeld, S. J. (1994). "Medical services" as limitation for related services. *EDLAW Briefing Paper 4*(4).

Rosenfeld, S. J. (1996a). Who can provide "health related services"? *EDLAW Briefing Paper 5*(7).

Rosenfeld, S. J. (1998). Does U.S. Supreme Court action signal change of course? *EDLAW Briefing Paper 8*(1).

Special School District No. 6, South St. Paul, 23 IDELR (LRP) 119 (SEA Minn. 1994).

State of Connecticut Commissioner of Education and Commissioner of Children and Youth Services. (1993, March 15). *Educational services for children who receive services through DCYS within residential facilities* [Joint Memorandum]. Hartford, CT: Connecticut State Department of Education, Bureau of Special Education and Pupil Services.

State of Delaware. (1993). Interagency consent to release information form, guidelines on confidentiality and use of "Consent to Release Information Form." New Castle, DE: New Castle County Vocational Technical School District.

U.S. Department of Education. (1995). *To appropriate public education of all children with disabilities, seventeenth annual report to Congress on the implementation of the Individuals assure the free with Disabilities Education Act*, p. 3. Washington, DC: U.S. Department of Education.

Zirkel, P. A. (1998), The "inclusion" case law: A factor analysis. 127 *Ed. Law Rep.* (533). (Sept. 17, 1998).

TABLE OF CASES

A. A. by B. A. v. Independent School District No. 283, 24 IDELR (LRP) 553 (D. Minn. 1996).

Alexander v. Boyd, 876 F.Supp. 773, 22 IDELR (LRP) 139 (D. S.C. 1995).

Angela L. v. Pasadena Independent School District, 918 F.2d 1188, 17 EHLR (LRP) 341 (5th Cir. 1990).

Ankowiak v. Ambach, 838 F.2d 635, EHLR (LRP) Dec. 559:275 (2d Cir. 1988).

Anthony v. Freeman, 24 IDELR (LRP) 929 (E.D. N.C. 1996).

Aranow v. District of Columbia, 791 F.Supp. 318, 18 IDELR (LRP) 962 (D. D.C. 1992).

Ashland School District v. New Hampshire Division for Children, Youth and Families, 681 A.2d 71, 24 IDELR (LRP) 165 (N.H. 1996).

Babb v. Knox County School System, 965 F.2d 104, 18 IDELR (LRP) 1030 (6th Cir. 1992).

Babicz v. School Board of Broward County, 135 F.3d 1420, 27 IDELR (LRP) 724 (11th Cir. 1998).

Barbara B. v. Board of Education of Hardin County, 20 IDELR (LRP) 1183 (W.D. Ky. 1993) and 20 IDELR (LRP) 1203 (W.D. Ky. 1994).

Barlow-Gresham Union High School District No. 2 v. Mitchell, 940 F.2d 1280, 17 EHLR (LRP) 1100 (9th Cir. 1991).

Beard v. Teska, 31 F.3d 942, 21 IDELR (LRP) 440 (10th Cir. 1994).

Bevin H. v. Wright, 666 F.Supp. 71, EHLR (LRP) Dec. 559:122 (W.D. Penn. 1987).

Board of Education of the Hendrick Hudson Central School District v. Rowley, 458 U.S. 176, EHLR (LRP) 553:656 (U.S. 1982).

Burlington School Committee v. Massachusetts Department of Education, 105 S.Ct. 1996, EHLR (LRP) Dec. 556:389 (U.S. 1985).

Cedar Rapids Community School District v. Garret F. by Charlene F., 24 IDELR (LRP) 648 (N.D. Iowa 1996); aff'd 106 F.3d 822, 25 IDELR (LRO) 439 (8th Cir. 1997); aff'd 29 IDELR (LRP) 966 (U.S. 1999).

Clovis Unified School District v. California Office of Administrative Hearings, 903 F.2d 635, 16 EHLR (LRP) 944 (9th Cir. 1990).

Clyde K. ex rel. Ryan K. v. Puyallup School District, 35 F.3d 1396, 21 IDELR (LRP) 664 (9th Cir. 1994).

Cordero v. Pennsylvania Department of Education, 19 IDELR (LRP) 623 (M.D. Penn. 1993).

Counsel v. Dow, EHLR (LRP) 441:164 (2d Cir. 1988).

Crespo ex rel. Rojas v. New Haven Board of Education, 20 IDELR (LRP) 1371 (D. Conn 1993).

Daniel R. v. El Paso Independent School District, 874 F.2d 1036, EHLR (LRP) Dec. 441:433 (5th Cir. 1989).

David B. v. Patla, 24 IDELR (LRP) 952 (N.D. Ill. 1996).

Detsel v. Auburn Enlarged City School District Board of Education, 637 F.Supp. 1022, EHLR (LRP) Dec. 557:335 (N.D. NY 1986); aff'd 820 F.2d 587, EHLR (LRP) Dec. 558:395 (2d Cir. 1987).

Detsel v. Sullivan, 895 F.2d 58, 16 EHLR (LRP) 427 (2d Cir. 1990).

Doe v. Maher, 793 F.2d 1470, EHLR (LRP) Dec. 557:353 (9th Cir. 1986).

Donald B. v. Board of School Commissioners of Mobile County, Alabama, 117 F.3d 1371, 26 IDELR (LRP) 414 (11th Cir. 1997).

Donnell C. v. Illinois State Board of Education, 829 F.Supp. 1016, 20 IDELR (LRP) 514 (N.D. Ill. 1993).

Ellison v. Board of Education of Three Villages Central School District, 597 N.Y.S.2d 483, 19 IDELR (LRP) 1027 (N.Y.App.Div. 3rd Dept. 1993).

Fenneman v. Town of Gorham, 802 F.Supp. 542, 19 IDELR (LRP) 155 (D. Me. 1992).

Field v. Haddonfield Board of Education, 769 F.Supp. 1313, 18 IDELR (LRP) 253 (D. N.J. 1991).

Florence County School District v. Carter, 114 S.Ct. 361, 20 IDELR (LRP) 532 (U.S. 1993).

Flour Bluff Independent School District v. Katherine M., 91 F.3d 689, 24 IDELR (LRP) 673 (5th Cir. 1996).

Fort Zumwalt School District v. Clynes, 119 F.3d 607, 26 IDELR (LRP) 172 (8th Cir. 1997).

Goodall v. Stafford County School Board, 60 F.3d 168, 22 IDELR (LRP) 972 (4th Cir. 1995).

Goss v. Lopez, 95 S.Ct.729 (U.S. 1975).

Granite School District v. Shannon M., 787 F.Supp. 1020, 18 IDELR (LRP) 772 (D. Utah 1992).

Green v. Johnson, 513 F.Supp. 965, EHLR (LRP) 552:449 (D. Mass. 1981).

Grinsted by Grinsted v. Houston County School District, 826 F.Supp. 482, 20 IDELR (LRP) 339 (M.D. Ga.1993).

Hartmann v. Loudoun County Board of Education, 118 F.3d 996, 26 IDELR (LRP) 167 (4th Cir. 1997).

Hawaii Department of Education v. Katharine D., 727 F.2d 809, EHLR (LRP) Dec. 555:276 (9th Cir. 1983).

Honig v. Doe, 484 U.S. 305, 108 S.Ct. 592, EHLR (LRP) Dec. 559:231 (U.S. 1988).

Independent School District No. 283 v. S.D. et al., 88 F.3d 556, 24 IDELR (LRP) 375 (8th Cir. 1996).

Irving Independent School District v. Tatro, 104 S.Ct. 3371, EHLR (LRP) Dec. 555:511 (U.S. 1984).

Jose P. v. Ambach, EHLR (LRP) 551:245, 551:412 (E.D. N.Y. 1979).

K. R. by M. R. v. Anderson Community School Corporation, 23 IDELR (LRP) 1137 (7th Cir. 1996).

Kari H. v. Franklin Special School District, 125 F.3d 855, 26 IDELR (LRP) 569 (6th Cir. 1997).

Kevin G. v. Cranston School Committee, 130 F.3d 481, 27 IDELR (LRP) 32 (1st Cir. 1997).

Kletzelman v. Capistrano Unified School District, 20 IDELR (LRP) 1064 (C.D. Cal. 1994); 23 IDELR (LRP) 425 (9th Cir. 1995).

Lachman v. Illinois State Board of Education, 852 F.2d 290, EHLR (LRP) Dec. 441:156 (7th Cir. 1988).

Lemon v. Kurtzman, 403 U.S. 602 (U.S. 1971).

Light v. Parkway C-2 School District, 41 F.3d 1223, 21 IDELR (LRP) 933 (8th Cir. 1994).

Los Gatos Joint Union School District v. Doe, EHLR (LRP) Dec. 556:281 (N.D. Cal. 1984).

Marie O., Gabriel C., Kyle G., and Joanna B. v. Edgar, 24 IDELR (LRP) 846 (N.D. Ill. 1996); 131 F.3d 610, 27 IDELR (LRP) 40 (7th Cir. 1997).

McKirryher v. Rochester School District, 19 IDELR (LRP) 945 (D. Vt. 1993).

McSomebodies v. Burlingame Elementary School District, EHLR (LRP) 441:595 (9th Cir. 1989).

McWhirt v. Williamson County Schools, 23 IDELR (LRP) 509 (6th Cir. 1994).

Miller v. West Lafayette Community School Corporation, 665 N.E.2d 905, 24 IDELR (LRP) 174 (Ind. 1996).

Mitten v. Muscogee County School District, EHLR (LRP) 441:513 (11th Cir. 1989).

Moore v. District of Columbia, 907 F.2d 165, 16 EHLR (LRP) 951 (D.C. Cir. 1990).

Morton Community Unit School District No. 709 v. J.M., 28 IDELR (LRP) 614 (7th Cir. 1998).

Moye by Moye v. Special School District No. 6, South St. Paul, Minn., 23 IDELR (LRP) 229 (D. Minn. 1995).

Mrs. C. v. Wheaton, 916 F.2d 69, 16 EHLR (LRP) 1394 (2nd Cir. 1990).

Neely v. Rutherford County Schools, 851 F.Supp. 888, 21 IDELR (LRP) 373 (M.D. Tenn. 1994); r'ved 68 F.3d 965, 23 IDELR (LRP) 334 (6th Cir. 1995).

Oberti v. Board of Education of the Borough of Clementon School District, 19 IDELR (LRP) 908 (3rd Cir. 1993).

Papacoda v. Connecticut, EHLR (LRP) 552:495 (D. Conn. 1981).

Patrick G. v. City of Chicago School District No. 299, Cook County, Illinois, 23 IDELR (LRP) 327 (7th Cir. 1995).

Peter and Westendorp v. Wedl and Independent School District No. 273, 28 IDELR (LRP) 1071 (8th Cir. 1998).

Phelan v. Bell, 8 F.3d 369, 20 IDELR (LRP) 528 (6th Cir. 1993).

Poolaw v. Bishop, 67 F.3d 830, 23 IDELR (LRP) 406 (9th Cir. 1995).

Pullen by Pullen v. Cuomo, 18 IDELR (LRP) 132 (N.D. N.Y. 1991).

Rappaport v. Vance, 812 F.Supp. 609, 19 IDELR (LRP) 770 (D. Md. 1993); 14 F.3d 596, 21 IDELR (LRP) 709 (D. Md. 1993).

Rodiriecus L. v. Waukegan School District No. 60, 90 F.3d 249. 24 IDELR (LRP) 563 (7th Cir. 1996).

Russman by Russman v. Sobel, 85 F.3d 1050, 24 IDELR (LRP) 274 (2d Cir. 1996).

Rynes by Rynes v. Knox County Board of Education, 907 F.Supp. 1169, 23 IDELR (LRP) 507 (E.D.Tenn. 1993).

S-1 v. Turlington, 635 F.2d 342, EHLR (LRP) Dec. 552:267 (5th Cir. 1981).

Sacramento City Unified School District v. Holland, 4 F.3d 1398, 20 IDELR (LRP) 812 (9th Cir. 1994).

Seattle School District No. 1 v. B.S., 82 F.3d 1493, 24 IDELR (LRP) 68 (9th Cir. 1996).

Section 10-76d(d), Connecticut General Statutes.

Skubel v. Sullivan, 925 F.Supp. 930, 24 IDELR (LRP) 408 (D. Conn. 1996).

State of Connecticut-Unified School District #1 v. Department of Education, 24 IDELR (LRP) 685 (Conn. Super. Ct. 1996).

Tanya by Mrs. X v. Cincinnati Board of Education, 651 N.E.2d 1373, 21 IDELR (LRP) 1120 (Ohio Ct. App. 1995).

Terefenko ex rel. Terefenko v. Stafford Township Board of Education, 17 EHLR (LRP) 573 (D. N.J. 1991).

Tice v. Botetourt County School Board, EHLR (LRP) Dec. 441:485 (W.D. Va. 1989).

Zobrest v. Catalina Foothills School District, 113 S.Ct. 2462, 19 IDELR (LRP) 921 (U.S. 1993).

OFFICE FOR CIVIL RIGHTS (OCR) DECISIONS

Abbeville (SC) School District, 28 IDELR (LRP) 1208, (OCR 1998).

Castro Valley (CA) Unified School District, 29 IDELR (LRP) 615 (OCR 1998).

Connecticut State Department of Education, EHLR (LRP) 257:57 (OCR 1979).

Gardner-Edgerton-Antioch (KS) USD #231, 28 IDELR (LRP) 748 (OCR 1998).

Simsbury (CT) Public Schools, EHLR (LRP) 257:176 (OCR 1980).

Warren County (PA) School District, 28 IDELR (LRP) 485 (OCR 1997).

See page 625 for Table of Federal Statutes and Regulations.

Chapter Fourteen

DNR in the School Setting: Determining Policy and Procedures

Carol C. Costante

INTRODUCTION

Do Not Resuscitate (DNR) orders for students with serious medical conditions are an increasingly prevalent phenomenon for school systems. In the future, this trend will assuredly expand as the numbers of students with health impairments increase, medical technologies that maintain terminally ill children are refined, and diseases such as AIDS continue to steal the lives of our youngest members of society. The legal and ethical considerations surrounding DNR will markedly affect the policies and procedures that school systems develop in response to one of the most complex and challenging issues that they face. A growing number of states and school districts have successfully dealt with this difficult subject, so that there are a number of models to reference.

DEFINING THE ISSUE

Schools are increasingly faced with decisions stemming from end-of-life issues. Federal legislation like the Individuals with Disabilities Education Act (IDEA), Section 504, and the Americans with Disabilities Act (ADA) that guarantee students' rights to an education in the least restrictive environment (LRE), and the increasing number of children with complex medical needs who are able to attend school, are the major reasons that schools must deal with yet another non-traditional educational issue. Given the heightened presence of medically fragile students in public schools, it was inevitable that schools would be presented with requests to comply with physician-issued DNR orders (Herlan, 1995). The challenge of dealing with this issue in schools is that, from both ethical and legal perspectives, the rights of individual students conflict with school responsibilities and other students' rights and interests (Rushton, Will, & Murray, 1994). Ethical and legal decision-making in schools sometimes differ from that in health care institutions because schools deal with populations rather than just individuals (Proctor, 1998).

Havens and Greenberg (1992) define "Advance Directive" (AD) as a document that states what individuals want done if they become unable to make decisions about their own medical care. As this includes decisions about life support measures, DNR requests may be a part of the AD. At present, ADs, except those limited to DNR orders, have apparently not surfaced as an issue in schools and no school jurisdiction is known to have recognized or implemented broader ADs. This is probably because legal uncertainty surrounds the status of "living wills" or durable power-of-attorney documents executed by minors, even those recognized as emancipated or mature. Thus, in most instances, children will not have formal advance directive documents even under the federal patient self-determination act (American Academy of Pediatrics Committee on Bioethics, 1993). It should be noted however, that ADs will undoubtedly become an issue for schools in the future as the schools' delivery of health care services increases.

"DNR" stands for "do not resuscitate" and is the usual acronym for a physician's directive that cardiopulmonary resuscitation (CPR) not be used in the event of a cardiac or respiratory arrest (Beekman, 1995). This includes breathing and ventilation by any assistive or mechanical means including, but not limited to, mouth-to-mouth, mouth-to-mask, bag-valve mask, endotracheal tube, ventilator, chest compressions, and defibrillation (Connecticut Committee on DNR Orders, 1994). CPR is but one of the recognized life-sustaining medical treatments. Other interventions include equally dramatic measures of contemporary health care practice such as organ transplantation, kidney dialysis and vasoactive drugs, as well as less technically demanding measures such as antibiotics, insulin chemotherapy, and nutrition and hydration provided intravenously or by tube (AAP Committee on Bioethics, 1993).

DNR is an explicit directive ordered by a physician and based upon a decision made by an authorized person that *extraordinary* procedures shall not be used to continue a human life (Rosenfeld, 1995). States may define DNR orders differently or use other terms. Until relatively recently, DNR orders were honored only in hospitals and nursing homes. However, a growing number of states are now defining the issue as pertinent to community settings, such as homes and schools.

SCOPE OF THE DNR ISSUE

DNR orders in schools were relatively unknown until the landmark case in Lewiston, Maine, in 1994 where a DNR order for a severely disabled student was not accepted by the school district (Herlan, 1995). Since that time, DNR orders have been the topic of much debate in the education, nursing, medical, legal, disabilities, and ethics literature. As a result, state and local school-based policies have gradually appeared.

Concerned professional organizations have established positions on the subject, as well. The National Education Association (NEA) supports the inclusion of students with DNR orders in the school setting on an individual basis (NEA, 1994). The view of the National Association of School Nurses (NASN) is that DNR orders for medically fragile students must be evaluated on an individual basis in accordance with state and local laws (NASN, 1995). The American Academy of Pediatrics (AAP) issued guidelines that support the withholding of non-beneficial, life-sustaining medical treatment for children in accordance with current medical, ethical and legal standards (AAP Committee on Bioethics, 1993). The AAP has recently taken an organizational stance on DNR orders in schools and supports continuing a child's education and participation in

school for as long as it is reasonable. This may include a DNR plan in school (AAP Committee on School Health and Committee on Bioethics, 2000).

Of the 40 states that responded to a 1994 survey of state representatives to the NASN, only 3 states (7.5%) indicated that they had statewide school DNR policies. Eight states (20%) indicated that there were local school district DNR policies in their states, and 2 states (5%) said that local policies were in the development stage (Ristocelli, Wessel, & Costante, 1994).

In 1995, a poll of 47 school districts, presented at the Annual Convention of the Council for Exceptional Children, indicated that only 2 of the districts (4.3%) had DNR policies (Rosenfeld, 1995). A larger sampling of 1,677 school districts nationwide, with responses by 482 schools (28.8%), revealed a similar 4.7% rate of school districts (University of Colorado, 1995).

Parental requests that schools honor DNR orders for their children appear to be on the rise. A repeat survey of the 47-state NASN representatives in 1998 yielded a response from 42 states. In contrast to the 1994 survey, the 1998 NASN survey resulted in 11 states (26.2%) reporting that they had state policies for addressing DNR orders in schools, and 12 additional states (27.8%) that reported the existence of local school district policies in the absence of state policy. (See Figure 14-1 for a comparison of the 1994 and 1998 NASN surveys.) The states that indicated the presence of statewide DNR policies were Colorado, Connecticut, Idaho, Kansas, Maryland, New Mexico, Rhode Island, Tennessee, Texas, Washington, and Wyoming (Costante, 1998a).

FIGURE 14-1.

DNR POLICIES NATIONWIDE

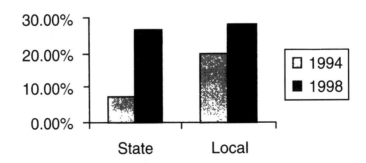

Used with permission. Managing DNR requests in the school setting. Costante, C.C., 1998, *Journal of School Nursing*, 14(4), p. 50.

FIGURE 14-2.
NATURE OF DNR POLICIES NATIONWIDE

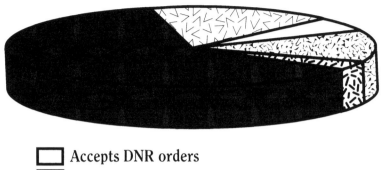

☐ Accepts DNR orders
▨ Denies DNR orders
▨ Vague interpretation
■ No policy
▨ Existence of policy unknown

Used with permission. Managing DNR requests in the school setting. Costante, C.C., 1998, *Journal of School Nursing*, 14 (4), p. 50.

States and school districts are divided in their positions regarding compliance with DNR orders. In one of the 1995 surveys discussed above, the two local school districts that had DNR policies reported opposing stances (Rosenfeld, 1995). In 1998, of the 11 states that reported a statewide DNR policy, 3 supported the acceptance of appropriate DNR orders: Connecticut, Maryland, and Wyoming (Costante, 1998a). The 6 states that held positions against the acceptance of DNR orders included Idaho, Kansas, New Mexico, Rhode Island, Tennessee, and Washington (Costante, 1998a). Texas state law mandates that out-of-hospital facilities follow physician's DNR orders, but whether this requirement includes schools remains uncertain (Costante, 1998b). In Colorado, DNR orders are filed with the local ambulance company, and there is a different implementation standard for school nurses than for education personnel (Costante, 1998a). (See Figure 14-2 for a graphic depiction of these 1998 survey results.)

Many states and school districts that have established DNR policies have done so in reaction to cases that emerged in their jurisdictions, or in response to legal opinions or statutes that are directly related to the issue. Examples of these include the following:

- The landmark case in Lewiston, Maine, occurred during the 1993-94 school year when the mother of a 12-year-old multiply-disabled child requested that the school not institute chest compressions if she went into cardiac arrest. An advocacy group for persons with disabilities became involved in the case and after several reversals, the school board issued a policy that teachers were not to follow a DNR order, but must develop an individually designed resuscitation plan (IRP) to be followed in case of emergency. The Office of Civil Rights stated that the IRP was not discriminatory. Factors considered were that (1) the IRP had been designed by a multidisciplinary team; (2) the IRP was based on expert medical and other relevant information and was appropriately documented; (3) a second medical opinion was required; and (4) the IRP was of limited duration, ensuring that it would be re-evaluated periodically (Brown & Valluzzi, 1995; Herlan, 1995; Rosenfeld, 1995).

- Maryland issued a different policy interpretation in 1994. The Maryland Attorney General advised that if the attending physician of a terminally ill child has issued a DNR order with the authorization of the child's parents, school officials must act in accordance with the order and refrain from medical interventions that are not consistent with it (Maryland Attorney General, 1994). The opinion specifically disclaims any intent that school officials should do nothing if the child suffers a cardiopulmonary arrest at school and clarifies that school personnel must give comfort and reassurance. Furthermore, schools that accept a DNR order are not required to refrain from calling 911 since the act of calling is not a medical treatment. Although it does not have the same force as statute, the Maryland Attorney General's opinion had not been challenged as of December, 2000.

- In contrast, Iowa's Attorney General declared that a school does not have a duty to comply with a decision to withhold life-sustaining procedures because a school is not a licensed health care provider under state law. The opinion also notes that school personnel are not specifically trained, as are medical personnel, to make the medical decisions required. It concludes that a court order or court decision would be needed before a school should agree to refrain from summoning medical personnel or administering first aid to a terminally ill child (Iowa Attorney General, 1988). This position also stands unchallenged at press.

- The legality of mandating DNR orders in public schools has been addressed in Massachusetts. When the parents of a severely physically and mentally disabled 4-year-old asked a special education program to honor a DNR order which barred specific invasive procedures, the school asked the court to make a declaratory ruling and issue an injunction prohibiting implementation of the DNR order. The court denied the injunction and ruled that the parents had a constitutional right to refuse medical treatment for their minor child. The court further ruled that the parents had a right to obtain such an order, and that the school must implement it (*ABC School and DEF School v. Mr. and Mrs. M.*, 1997).

- Washington State's "Natural Death Act" unequivocally states that a teacher, educational staff member, or early intervention practitioner is not authorized to honor a DNR order (Brown & Valluzzi, 1995).

- Colorado state law requires all emergency care responders to honor DNR orders. However, school nurses are not considered "emergency care responders" and other school personnel are to "provide the same care as for any other child" and cannot be asked to withhold life-sustaining measures from a child (Costante, 1998a).

- Direction rendered by legal counsel for the Bucks County, Pennsylvania Intermediate Unit states that schools are not mandated to follow and accede to parental requests (1) to refrain from initiating or to discontinue nutrition or hydration intravenously or through a gastric tube, and (2) to refrain from intervening or to discontinue any life-sustaining treatment in the event that their child arrests. This position was based on the opinion that a minor cannot, even if competent, execute a Living Will; that a parent cannot do so on behalf of the minor child under the auspices of the Living Will statute; and that current Pennsylvania law holds that a parent cannot refuse medical treatment nor authorize removal of life-sustaining measures where the life of a child is endangered (Williams, 1994).

It appears that many state and local educational systems do not comply with DNR orders directly, but summon EMS who are authorized to honor such orders (Costante, 1998a). In a sense, they "pass the buck" in managing DNR requests rather than developing active policies that directly deal with the issue. If, in the meantime, CPR is administered to a terminally ill child, against the wishes of the parents and medical direction of a physician, additional ethical and legal issues surface.

ETHICAL CONSIDERATIONS

What is unusual about a DNR order is that it is a direct contravention of the societal assumption that most people would rather remain alive than die. The societal presumption is that CPR should be initiated on anyone who suffers a cardiac or pulmonary arrest, unless a specific order not to attempt resuscitation has been entered for the individual. This assumption is especially emphatic for children. When CPR is indicated, the usual principle that consent is required prior to a medical intervention is waived due to the emergency nature of the presenting problem and the hypothesis that most persons want efforts made to save their lives. A number of recent studies suggest, however, that automatically providing CPR may not make good sense for everyone. A procedure that was originally developed for otherwise healthy trauma victims can have exceedingly low success rates for persons who have very serious health problems (Maryland Attorney General, 1994).

The surrender-to-death premise of DNR, while increasingly understood in relation to the elderly, may be particularly difficult for many to accept when it pertains to children whom society is charged to protect. It violates many of our individual and societal beliefs, expectations, and fears about death (Scofield, 1992). In addition, it may be viewed as contradictory to the obligation of schools to defend and advocate for children.

However, DNR orders for children should be considered rare and extraordinary measures intended strictly to benefit the child. Such unusual directives should only be used when death is inevitable in the light of a terminal medical condition. The defining principle is that the child will ultimately suffer more harm than good if resuscitated (Costante, 1998b). In addition, a DNR order allows a dying child to maintain some measure of control until the end and to experience death with dignity. The American Academy of Pediatrics Committee on Bioethics (1993) believes that life-sustaining medical care should be provided in conformity with current medical, ethical and legal norms. Allowing non-beneficial treatment can harm a child and may constitute a legal, as well as, moral wrong.

DNR must never mean abandoning the child (Younger, 1992). The needs of the child must remain primary, and measures necessary to assure comfort must be maintained at all times (AAP Committee on Bioethics, 1993). Brown and Valluzzi (1995) clarify that an individual's DNR status does not mean that life will be shortened by direct interventions to hasten death. It means that a natural event will occur with dignity and supportive human comfort measures (Brown & Valluzzi, 1995). CPR is actually an aggressive, intrusive, physical act that can cause pain and injury. As such, CPR is rarely compatible with the concept of a peaceful and dignified death.

Parental decisions regarding advanced directives on their child's behalf are seldom made independently. For the parents, it is a soul wrenching decision to make. After the parents have made this most difficult of decisions with support and guidance from medical profes-

sionals, those same medical professionals and facilities have procedural guidelines to comply with in order to file a DNR order. Ethics committees and ethical consultants are available to review alternatives and to ensure that appropriate medical care is being provided (Brown & Valluzzi, 1995; Rushton et al., 1995). An independent review procedure is an additional protective measure that schools also might consider when they develop policy and procedures or are presented with a DNR order. Having a review process in place ensures that competing interests are considered in the decision-making process (Rushton et al., 1995).

Rejecting aggressive life-sustaining interventions can be ethically justified based on: (1) an assessment that interventions such as CPR will not cure the child's underlying disease; (2) the burdens following such interventions may further diminish the quality of life if the child does survive, and (3) such interventions are only prolonging dying and are, therefore, inhumane. In these situations, DNR falls within a morally defensible range of treatment options (Rushton et al., 1994).

DNR should not be considered as a right-to-die issue, such as suicide or euthanasia. It is a more narrowly defined issue about the right to refuse particular emergency interventions. This point is helpful, contends Herlan (1995), since for individual students there may, indeed, be certain interventions that should not be followed, but others that could be helpful. Thus, he concludes, a general policy prohibiting or encouraging compliance with DNR orders would fail to recognize this distinction, and individual plans are the best approach.

LEGAL PERSPECTIVES

Legal viewpoints regarding DNR orders in schools are varied. Frequently it depends on whether individual rights or the needs of other students are seen as the priority. A compromise viewpoint is that DNR orders should be considered individually and that guidelines should be included in individual student plans (Schultz-Grant, Young-Cureton, & Kataoka-Yahiro, 1998; Herlan, 1995).

State law provides the primary basis for decisions on DNR orders for minors, and states have interpreted relevant federal statutes in different ways. States have also yielded contrasting opinions on the subject due to individual interpretations on various other relevant issues (for example, the scope of responsibility of schools, health care laws, and regulations governing EMS). There are numerous statutes prohibiting societal segregation because of conditions of birth, such as race, color, and sex, or because of religion, but there is nothing to support the public integration of death, the universal condition of birth (Scofield, 1992). Because we have evaded definitive civil involvement with this universal condition, the legal reactions are varied. The law has clearly not kept pace with medical advances, human needs, and ethical issues.

In addition to state-specific statutes, the following federal and state legislative rulings and principles provide the legal basis for states and school districts facing a DNR policy decision:

- Public schools are subject to federal constitutional guarantees concerning equal protection of the law. They are also subject to § 504 of the Rehabilitation Act of 1973 and the Individuals with Disabilities Education Act of 1975, which when combined with the Patient Self-Determination Act of 1991 and the Americans with Disabilities Act of 1990, afford appreciable protection for all students, especially those with special needs. By and large, these statutes have been invoked in order to gain access to public schools or to secure supportive services that enable students with disabilities to attend (Scofield, 1992).

- Most state courts uphold the school's relationship to a student as one of *in loco parentis*. The assumption is that the school protects the child from harm and that it would do what the parent would do in a similar situation. The *in loco parentis* doctrine combined with the doctrine of informed consent enables a school to render emergency medical treatment to a student when the parent has provided no direction. Ordinarily, consent to CPR is implied under the emergency exception to the informed consent doctrine (Scofield, 1992). CPR should not be administered, though, if certain conditions exist, among which is the existence of a DNR order that has been consented to by the individual or, if the person lacks decision-making capacity, the person's lawful surrogate. Consequently, acting contrary to the parent's expressed wishes in the face of a DNR order could put school personnel at risk of liability for battery and a variety of other torts (Beekman, 1995), and also subject the child to an intrusive, aggressive intervention and potential injury.

- Competent adults have the right to decide what medical treatment they will receive and to decline treatment, even if needed, to sustain life.

State statutes determine if this right can be overridden by the interest of the state or a third party (Beekman, 1995). As a general rule, minors do not have the legal authority to consent to or refuse medical care. Nevertheless, as adolescents approach the age of legal majority, they may be considered "mature minors" with the legal capacity to consent to or refuse medical care if they are able to appreciate the consequences of the decision and demonstrate the ability of an average person to understand and weigh the risks and benefits of a given course of action. The mature minor rule varies by state, but is generally considered operational by the age of 15 years, and many state legislatures have codified this exception to parental consent when a child is between the ages of 13 and 18 and is seeking treatment for drug or alcohol addiction, sexually transmitted diseases, and family planning (Brown & Valluzzi, 1995). (See also chapter 7.)

- Although, strictly speaking, the Patient Self-Determination Act does not apply to minors, the spirit of the law implies that minors should be engaged in health care decisions in a meaningful way. The right of minors to be involved in health care decision making is implicit in the moral value of respecting an individual's dignity and autonomy (Rushton et al., 1994). The American Academy of Pediatrics (1993) believes that the gravity of decisions involving life-sustaining medical care requires careful, explicit attention to the wishes and feelings of children, regardless of their legal status (AAP Committee on Bioethics, 1993). At least two courts (Illinois, 1989 and Maine, 1990) have held that the mature minor doctrine extends to decisions to forgo life-sustaining treatment (Scofield, 1992). Thus, the child who is able to participate in decisions about resuscitation and end-of-life care should be permitted to do so (AAP Committee on Bioethics, 1993; Rushton et al., 1994). Additionally, children who meet statutory criteria for emancipation are legally allowed to make health care decisions. Although the definition varies by state, generally legislation defines emancipated minors as those who have graduated from high school, are members of the armed forces, are married, or live apart from and are financially independent of their parents (AAP Committee on Bioethics, 1993).

- As a matter of constitutional law, the "custody, care and nurture of the child resides first in the parents, whose primary function and freedom include preparation for obligations that the state can neither supply or hinder" (Rushton et al., 1994). Under common law, parents have the right to make both educational and medical decisions for their minor children, unless their decisions endanger the health and well being of their children. Generally, courts uphold parents' right to refuse medical treatment as long as such a denial is within the zone of rational medical choices, as normally determined by the child's physician. State law defines who is the ultimate decision maker and is of particular importance when incompetent students have reached the age of majority or "eligibility" to make health care decisions (Beekman, 1995).

- Any state statute that authorizes other persons to make judgments regarding the continuance of life-sustaining care for another individual has application in determining parents' ability to make these decisions for their minor child. For example, Maine has a statute that empowers the guardian of a minor to make decisions in regard to medical treatment and specifically states that the guardian can order discontinuance of life-sustaining care for a minor ward who is in a terminal condition or a persistent vegetative state. Statutes such as these provide helpful guidance on this asserted right. The absence of such statutes may indicate the state's unwillingness to permit others to make decisions for an incompetent person regarding life-sustaining care (Herlan, 1995).

- According to Herlan (1995), another indication of whether schools should comply with requests to withhold life-sustaining care may be found in the process set forth in a state's living will law detailing how health care providers should make decisions to discontinue life-sustaining care in individual situations. That some state laws mandate a specific decision-making process highlights the fact that individuals can encounter life threatening situations in a variety of ways, and that health care providers may consider withholding care only in certain of those situations. The criteria established in a state's living will statute may also provide guidance on the difficult questions concerning what

medically can and cannot be done for those with DNR orders.

- Normally, parents can accept or reject medical treatment that they feel is not in their child's best interest. DNR orders are simply an extension of the right of families to make decisions about medical treatment or nontreatment (Rushton et al., 1994). The legal standard of "best interest" requires that the decision maker (usually the parents in collaboration with the physician) base the decision on what they believe is in the best interest of the child, and this standard is generally used in situations involving minor children.

- According to the American Academy of Pediatrics (Committee on Bioethics, 1993), using the "best interest" standard calls for weighing the benefits and burdens of life-sustaining measures. The benefits may include prolongation of life (understanding that the continuation of biological existence without consciousness may not be a benefit); improved quality of life (including reduction of pain or disability); and increased physical pleasure, emotional enjoyment, and intellectual satisfaction. The burdens may include intractable pain; emotional suffering; invasive or inhumane interventions designed to sustain life; or other activities that severely detract from the child's quality of life. Families and their physicians should work together to make life-sustaining judgments for minors who lack decision-making capacity. Recourse to the courts should be reserved for occasions when adjudication is clearly required by law or when concerned parties have disagreements that they cannot resolve concerning matters of substantial importance (AAP Committee on Bioethics, 1993).

- The doctrine of "substituted judgment," which requires a court to base its judgment on what it determines the patient, if competent, would have done, is generally inapplicable in the case of minors, because it is the parents and their medical advisors who must make these decisions. Also the probable desire of a child cannot be ascertained because he or she most often has never expressed such an intent (Beekman, 1995; Maryland Attorney General, 1994). Nonetheless, children should have the opportunity to participate in decisions about forgoing medical care to whatever extent their abilities allow. Children, even those in the early school years, often appreciate their medical situations far better than their family members, guardians, and health care providers believe. Additionally, physicians and parents should accord considerable weight to the feelings minor children may have expressed at some time regarding life-sustaining medical care (AAP Committee on Bioethics, 1993).

- Nonetheless, family autonomy is not absolute. Under the *parentis patriae* doctrine, countervailing state's interests may supersede the parents' right to make life and death decisions on their child's behalf. State's interests may outweigh a person's rights, whether competent or incompetent, to self determination, as the state has a duty to protect children and other disenfranchised individuals (Brown & Valluzzi, 1995). Those state's interests typically are (1) the preservation of life; (2) the protection of the interests of third parties, e.g., children of the person; (3) the prevention of suicide or wrongful taking of human life; and 4) the maintenance of the ethical integrity of the medical profession (Beekman, 1995; Scofield, 1992). A third party may be able to claim state's interest by contending that the DNR order should not be honored because to do so would not be in the child's best interest (Beekman, 1995). The interests of third parties include family members who may be affected by the decision, just as the ethical integrity of the medical profession concerns the attending physician and other professionals involved in a person's care (Scofield, 1992).

- A potential concern pertaining to the state's interests is the question of whether DNR orders for students constitute medical neglect of a minor. What constitutes neglect of a minor is largely a matter of state law, but it is generally held that the exercise of a constitutional right may not form the basis for criminal prosecution. Neglect is not an issue when a decision to forgo life-sustaining treatment is supported by a reasonably prudent physician who is knowledgeable about the case and the treatment possibilities, and where the treatment would merely prolong the dying process (Scofield, 1992).

In summary, before any school or district establishes a policy or procedure on DNR orders, or responds to any specific DNR order, it is imperative that it closely review state statutes to determine how the state relates to and interprets constitutional rights and protections. (See summary of above points in Table 14-1.)

BARRIERS TO RATIONAL DECISION MAKING

It is one thing to say that students do not shed their rights at the schoolhouse door, and something else to determine how the right to refuse treatment fits into the educational setting (Scofield, 1992). There are several pragmatic issues related to honoring DNR orders in educational settings that hamper school districts from making sensible, objective, student-specific decisions.

Doubting Public Framework

Where there is an established public framework that supports DNR requests, schools may still not understand how or whether this framework applies to them either legally or morally. According to Strike (1992), it is unreasonable to think that it would be easier to die in medical institutions than in schools or that school staff have a more compelling duty to preserve life than do physicians. If state law specifically requires that directives on life-sustaining care be followed outside a health care facility, there is a somewhat greater likelihood that a court would rule that schools are not exempt from this requirement (Herlan, 1995). Certainly, the request is easier to manage in those states that allow EMS to honor DNR orders outside hospitals.

Because educational settings increasingly offer health care services to students, they may be considered health care facilities with respect to provision of services, adherence to guidelines for provision of care under professional licensure or practice acts, delegation of heath care procedures, and confidentiality of health care record keeping (Brown & Valluzzi, 1995). Many school districts are currently billing Medicaid for health care procedures provided by school nurses and other school health professionals. They may, therefore, be considered health care providers under the federal Medicaid law (Schultz-Grant et al., 1998). As health care providers, school-based providers would be obliged to develop appropriate mechanisms for soliciting advanced directives, maintaining confidentiality, and communicating such information to school staff and emergency personnel. The argument by some states and school districts that schools are not

TABLE 14-1.

STATUTE AND LEGAL PRINCIPLES AFFECTING SCHOOL-BASED DNR DECISIONS

- Federal Law: Individuals with Disabilities Education Act (IDEA), Section 504 of the Rehabilitation Act, Americans with Disabilities Act, and the Patient Self-Determination Act

- Doctrines of *in loco parentis* and *parentis patriae*;

- Legal standards of "informed consent"and "best interest"

- Parental sovereignty regarding decisions for minors

- Third party and state's interests

- The principle of emancipation

- Living will and health care decisions statutes

- Minor consent statutes, the standard of "mature minor," and the doctrine of "substituted judgment"

- State licensure laws and professional practice acts

---

health care facilities and, therefore, are not affected by life-limiting legislation may no longer be a valid response.

The liability of schools regarding life-sustaining and life-limiting issues is a matter of state law and subject to varying interpretations of the exceptions to civil immunity that states enjoy. Schools require state specific legal clarification of their responsibility and potential liabilities in this area. However, schools would not be liable for the failure to provide appropriate emergency care if timely treatment would have proven futile (Rosenfeld, 1995). Otherwise, the school's liability for failure to provide emergency medical care depends on the situation in light of state law, which varies considerably.

Whatever duty the school owes its students generally, it is difficult to see how the school would abrogate that duty by not providing CPR to someone with a valid DNR order. If any exception to the duty to provide CPR exists, the presence of a valid DNR order is the most obvious. If a school is concerned about its responsibility to a student, it ought to weigh the prospects for a claim against it for compensatory and punitive damages if it attempts to revive a student against the family's wishes. It is also unlikely that its duty to render care or any protection offered by a good Samaritan law would prevail over a valid DNR order (Scofield, 1992). This issue is clearly a reflection of the societal dilemmas that occur as the right to refuse medical treatment extends beyond health care institutions.

Relinquishing Authority

Perhaps the most prevalent problem faced by local school jurisdictions is that of permitting various interests to supplant the law (Beekman, 1995). This includes using the moral concerns of staff or political viewpoints as primary determiners of school policy. Remarkably, the decision making powers of the family in the matters of life-limiting issues are frequently being negated even in states where family autonomy is clearly supported and court intervention is not required.

Such a response may disregard the child's best interests as well as undermine the parent's presumptive authority, thereby making the school district vulnerable to litigation under IDEA or § 504 (Rosenfeld, 1995). Respecting a child as a unique human being also means honoring the choices made on his or her behalf by the parents (Rushton et al., 1994). Providing a forum in which to develop a public moral consensus is desirable (Strike, 1992), but the community's attitude toward death cannot be allowed to override state law.

Strike (1992) postulates that it is virtually a defining characteristic of modern liberal societies that they distinguish between public and private matters, including matters of ethics. However, no liberal society has found the perfect solution for sequestering public and private obligations. Thus, those who administer public institutions are vulnerable to dilemmas of conscience where they are expected to oversee policies with which they do not agree. Generally, Strike says, it should be recognized that the tension between private conscience and public responsibility is resolved by disentangling the dissenting staff member from the public duty, not by castigating the person nor by nullifying the duty.

Determining Best Interest

Educators, whose professional work is devoted to the betterment of children, sometimes mistakenly believe that they know what is best for children, even when their beliefs conflict with families' desires. Certainly, school staff are under legal obligation to report child abuse and they are ethically obligated to help students distance themselves from self-destructive behaviors. However, the rules that define when they may and when they may not intervene in the decisions made by students and families are far from clear.

Parents can generally accept or reject medical treatment that they believe is not in their child's best interest (Rushton et al., 1994). It must be remembered, too, that a physician, who is held to an even higher standard than an educator to protect and preserve life, is the one who has issued the directive to not resuscitate. Unless there is a valid suspicion of wrongdoing in an individual case, school staff may not substitute their judgment for that of the parent. If there is a reasonable concern regarding abuse or neglect, it should be dealt with through the normal legal channels.

Jeopardizing School Personnel

Simply refusing to honor a DNR order may place a school district and its staff in a high-risk, litigious position. If staff members (at least nurses who are specifically licensed to carry out the orders of physicians and the authorization of a consenting parent or child) refuse to honor a DNR order and initiate CPR in the case of cardiac arrest, per the district's direction, they may be subject to criminal and tort liability, i.e., charged with assault and battery. On the other hand, staff members may countermand their district's refusal to implement a DNR order, because of a personal belief or desire to support the family. In such situations, staff members may be minimally in jeopardy of acting outside of district policy, and potentially in jeopardy of allegations of contributing to the death of a student.

Circumstances that arise in a crisis should never be allowed to dictate an individual response. To help guard against either type of refusal of DNR orders, the district must ensure that employees understand the decision in individual cases and that the decision is based on formal policy that is rooted in the law.

State law defines who can legally decide that extraordinary measures should not be used to continue a human life, as well as who can implement such orders. Only a licensed physician can issue such orders, and medical orders that necessitate situational medical professional judgments making cannot legally be delegated to lay persons. However, there may be a valid state's interest on the part of third parties, such as school administrators or teachers, who lack the competence to assess or respond to the child's medical needs (Rushton et al., 1994).

Even though the decision of whether or not to institute CPR has already been made, managing the child's medical condition on a daily basis in school is a complex issue, not to mention discriminating between such conditions as choking versus pulmonary arrest. Consequently, the presence of a health care professional qualified to make these discriminating judgments should be considered basic to the process of honoring a DNR order in schools. School nursing services, considered "related school health services," are legally supported by the requirements of IDEA and § 504.

One example of such a safeguarding policy is that made in 1998 by the Wayne-Westmoreland School District in Michigan. The local board of education established that DNR orders are to be honored by health care professionals in the schools, but not by other school personnel. The rationale is that in the school setting only a registered professional nurse has the knowledge base to make an assessment as to when and how to render care to a child, and to implement a DNR order. This duty may not be delegated even to other health care personnel such as health assistants or licensed practical nurses (Costante, 1998a).

Misinterpreting Case Law

Due to the paucity of legal decisions regarding children or incompetent adults who are terminally ill or in a vegetative state, some school districts contend that the right to refuse medical treatment does not apply to students with disabilities. Others are of the opinion that such decisions can only be operative in health care settings and do not pertain to schools. Given that the right to refuse medical treatment is based on the U.S. Constitution and not dependent upon whether a student is incompetent, ill, or located in a particular setting, attempts to draw such fine legal distinctions would appear to avoid the real issue (Beekman, 1995; Rosenfeld, 1995). See chapter 7, "Consent to Treatment," p. 231.

Misunderstanding the Necessary Standard

Rosenfeld (1992) points out that a DNR order does not require school personnel to decide whether CPR should be administered. Assuming, as in the majority of states, that the decision is for the family and physician to make (absent third party interest), the decision has already been made. The responsibility of school staff is to refrain from instituting medical interventions inconsistent with the directive (Beekman, 1995).

Inferring that Denying CPR Violates FAPE

Districts may contend that refusing a service such as CPR to a student with disabilities denies the student a free, appropriate public education (FAPE) or that it discriminates against the student under § 504, the IDEA, or both. This reasoning is based on the fact that districts would not honor a DNR order if the student had no disabilities. Appeals to justice and fairness nevertheless require that children with disabilities be treated fairly and in a nondiscriminatory manner (Rushton et al., 1994).

According to Rosenfeld (1995) and Beekman (1995), though, the contention that complying with a DNR request would breach any of these laws would seem to fail for two reasons. First, the right to refuse medical treatment stems from the U.S. Constitution. Therefore, if a DNR order is implemented correctly in accordance with state law, no other law—state or federal, including IDEA, § 504, or the ADA—would likely be permitted to limit or prohibit this fundamental constitutional right. Second, when districts typically refuse parental requests for a particular service, they have to face the possibility of due process proceedings. They encounter the same consequences when they want to provide a service to a child, e.g., CPR, but the parents, on behalf of the child, refuse it.

Caring about the Other Students

One of the most prevalent objections to complying with a DNR order in schools is projecting the impact of that course of action on other students. To some degree, this is deceptive reasoning. Reacting to medical emergencies is part of commonly accepted school procedures. Handling a medical emergency involving a student subject to a DNR order is merely handling another medical emergency (Rosenfeld, 1995). However, the manner in which the DNR order is implemented, both during the planning stage and during the actual episode, is critical to its acceptance by the school community.

Among other things, the reasoning here is that other students will suffer potential harm if the student is not resuscitated in their presence (Rosenfeld, 1995). According to Scofield (1992) the fear about liability to other students stems from concern about the emotional harm they will suffer if the child dies at school or, as Strike (1992) asserts, the students might worry that the school could also decline to assist them if they are in danger.

Scofield (1992) goes on to say that such a claim for the intentional infliction of emotional distress must be based on conduct that is outrageous and that inflicts severe emotional distress. Here the claim would be that the exercise of a lawful right by one person provides the basis for a cause of action by another. If this were the case, anyone upset by the legitimate exercise of constitutional right could litigate based on the distress caused by the very fears and prejudices the law seeks to eliminate. The law's purpose is not to secure universal peace of mind, and certainly cannot do so where death is concerned. From an ethical point of view, one must wonder whether students who observe a peer receiving CPR against his or her wishes would not suffer extreme emotional harm resulting from witnessing such a physically aggressive and defiant act, one that may still result in death, or at least harm to the student.

The death of a student, with or without intervention, should be used as an opportunity for education, exploration of fears, and mutual support (Younger, 1992). Strike (1992) believes that the goal might be to help students understand what has happened and to deal with it suitably so as to help students past an emotional crisis and to restore a positive climate in which the school can get on with its work. Depending on the age and developmental stages of the students, preparation for the death of a classmate and assistance and support in the grieving process are critical. For young children, the issue of CPR versus no CPR is not likely to be understood; loss of a friend and death itself will be the overriding concerns.

Evading the Issue

Some groups take the position that a district should simply refuse to honor any DNR request and instead offer the child educational services in the home. The reasoning is that for this child, given the parent's desires, the home setting constitutes the least restrictive environment (Beekman, 1995).

Given the previous interpretation of the law regarding LRE, Rosenfeld (1992) contends that justifying a home placement on that basis would have no legal support. In addition, refusing to honor a DNR

TABLE 14-2.
BARRIERS TO SOUND DECISION MAKING

- Doubting public framework
- Relinquishing authority
- Determining best interest
- Jeopardizing school personnel
- Misinterpreting case law
- Misunderstanding the necessary standard
- Inferring the violation of FAPE
- Caring about other students
- Evading the issue
- Prioritizing other duties

---

order might cause a claim of discrimination on the basis that CPR for a specific student, given the particular situation, may, in fact, cause more harm than an alternative medical intervention or no intervention at all.

Prioritizing Other Duties

A school district may believe that honoring a DNR order might prove so controversial in the community that it would erode public support for the school's broader educational endeavors. It may, according to Strike (1992), regard its standing with the community as an asset important for the educational welfare of the students and, thus, something that must be protected. Certainly, it may be groundbreaking and brave of a school district to honor a DNR order, just as it was for the first schools that publicly accepted HIV positive students into their classrooms. But it is the law that they must, and fear should not be allowed to prevent schools from doing what is legally or ethically right.

(See summary of above points in Table 14-2.)

ESTABLISHING DNR POLICY

Like many policy decisions, whether to honor DNR orders in schools should be based on an evaluation of the benefits to the individuals affected and society at large of allowing such a policy versus the resulting risks of not doing so (Brown & Valluzzi, 1995). This issue is fraught with enigmatic and often conflicting ethical, moral, and religious views. In addition to legal bases, these less defined areas within the context of the community's personality must be considered when a school system begins to assume the task of developing

policy. This is especially true where state law does not dictate a response. Proactively addressing this subject rather than waiting until forced to deal with it, will result in the development of a sounder and more community-accepted position. See Table 14-3 for a summary of the main considerations when developing DNR policy.

Using a multidisciplinary task force to determine school district or state policy is essential. This will help ensure that the widest range of viewpoints and experiences are examined. Parents, educators, support personnel, and health care team members must be committed to a process that is flexible and responsive to the individual needs of children (Rushton et al., 1994). Among those who should be considered for this important decision-making body are the following: a school nurse, school health services supervisor, school district administrator, both a school board and a health care attorney, classroom teacher, transportation specialist, parent of a medically fragile student, PTA representative (preferably the parent of a student unaffected by the issue), emergency medical services representative, state education department representative, and pediatric or emergency medicine physician. As they draft a policy, the group should consider philosophical, societal, and practical issues of the school-based and community's health care delivery systems, as well as state and federal statutes and regulations. After the Board of Education approves the policy, it should then be explained to school personnel, parents, and appropriate community groups in order to engender the necessary widespread support.

A policy that does not honor physician-directed DNR orders when requested by parents denies families the right to have their decision on behalf of their child honored in the school setting. However, like other services that parents may want for their children, not all family priorities or choices will be compatible with the services that schools can legally or practically offer (Brown & Valluzzi, 1995). Table 14-4 provides a procedural checklist for denying DNR orders.

There are things that school districts have planned or done to help families feel support from schools when their decision is to not comply with DNR orders (Brown & Valluzzi, 1995). One option is to summon emergency medical services without initiating CPR. Knowing that the parents have filed DNR requests with the physician, the hospital, and the school, the ambulance driver may decide to drive slowly to the hospital. Another approach is to page parents by electronic beeper at the same time that 9-1-1 is activated. If the

TABLE 14-3.

DEVELOPING DNR POLICY/PROCEDURES: ISSUES TO DETERMINE

State policy and legislation
- Statute: withholding life support procedures for minors
- Ability to honor DNR options outside medical facilities
- The school's obligation and authority to accept DNR orders
- The school's responsibility *in loco parentis*
- Regulations governing EMS management of DNR orders

Student and Parent Issues
- Parental rights, choices, and purpose
- The student's prognosis and knowledge of medical condition
- The student's cognitive ability and personal preferences
- Acceptable alternatives to a DNR option

Health Care System Resources
- Capabilities of community health and emergency services
- Partnership between the medical community and EMS
- Logistical operations of the EMS system
- Proximity of emergency medical services to the schools
- The existence and functioning of hospice programs

School Considerations
- The perceived mission and responsibilities of schools
- The community's philosophy toward death
- General emergency first aid and resuscitation policies
- Impact on the school community of honoring DNR orders
- Ordinary health care responsibilities assumed by the schools
- Availability of professional school health nurses
- School staff's responsibility regarding the DNR protocol
- Mechanism for maintaining and implementing DNR orders

Adapted from: Costante, C. C. (1998). Managing DNR requests in the school setting. *Journal of School Nursing*, 14(4), p. 43. Used with permission.

parent has filed the necessary DNR requests with the health care community and arrives at school prior to EMS, the parent may take charge and elect not to initiate CPR. A third alternative is for parents to file for "limited" DNR authorization, in which basic school-required CPR is initiated but more invasive procedures such as intubation or tracheotomy may not be used by EMS personnel.

There are many more considerations for those school districts deciding to honor DNR orders in the schools. Refer to Table 14-5 for these primary areas of consideration.

The possibility of a DNR episode in the school demands that the entire school and transportation staff have an opportunity to adequately voice their concerns and feelings. School staff need to learn how to do something other than CPR and feel comfortable doing that (Scofield, 1992). Most importantly, it is essential to help school staff understand that complying with a DNR order does not mean that they stand by and do nothing when an emergent situation occurs for a student with a DNR order. For example, implementing DNR orders does not mean, or even imply, the abandonment of other supportive care such as: administration of oxygen, suctioning, use of the Heimlich maneuver for choking, control of bleeding and pain, and positioning for comfort. Holding and comforting a dying child is not only acceptable, but desirable, regardless of the setting. Such care also preserves the integrity of the dying child (Costante, 1998b). Ironically, these are things that we used to do before CPR appeared (Scofield, 1992).

DEVELOPING PROCEDURAL GUIDELINES

Those deciding to honor DNR orders within a school district face many complex considerations. As a basic requisite, any school having a student with a DNR order should have a full time professional nurse to manage the student's care and implement the medical directives. The legal basis for this requirement has been discussed previously in the sections on "Legal Perspectives" and "Jeopardizing School Personnel." The following issues should be specifically addressed when developing state or local procedures (Baltimore County Public Schools, 1994 [rev. 1997]; Maryland State Department of Education, 1997; and Connecticut Committee on DNR Orders, 1994):

The DNR Order

1. An original, written physician's order and parental authorization should be provided to the school on the appropriate state or local form. Periodically reviewing and updating the directive will assure its currency as related to the student's condition.

TABLE 14-4.

DENYING DNR ORDERS: PROCEDURAL CHECKLIST

- Do not physically accept DNR orders

- Investigate relevant statutes and regulations

- Follow state education agency policies and procedures

- Inform parent in writing of school district's policy

- Get written emergency plan from parent and physician

- Include emergency plan in the IEP, IFSP, or 504 Plan

- Interpret EMS protocols and encourage partnership

Adapted from: Brown, S. E., & Valluzzi, J. L. (1995). Do not resuscitate orders in early intervention settings: Who should make the decision? *Infants and Young Children,* 7(3), p. 25. Used with permission.

2. When the student is "eligible" by state statutes to make medical decisions, the authorization must be signed by the student. A competent adolescent below the legal age of eligibility should be appropriately included in the decision-making. However, if the adult student is also incompetent by state definition, the parent, guardian or state-assigned surrogate must sign the DNR order.

3. The order needs to be accessible to EMS personnel or legal authorities, and the student needs to be distinguished in a manner that is recognized by school and emergency health care personnel who are designated to respond, e.g., by wearing a medical alert bracelet.

4. DNR orders may be legally revoked, so the parameters under which such a revocation may occur should be clearly defined. Families and students may alter their position at any time that there is a medical or personal change of opinion, including at-the-moment verbal wishes to be resuscitated.

Implementing the DNR Order

1. Upon receipt of a DNR order, the school nurse should review it promptly, seek guidance from the school's medical advisor, as indicated, and inform the principal.

2. A meeting should be scheduled to outline expectations and procedures to follow. The meeting should include the parent(s), the student if indicated, and appropriate school and health care providers. Younger (1992) believes that the important goals and fears of each party should be identified and explored in the context of each potential clinical scenario. Such explorations could reveal false assumptions and misguided fears.

3. The written student DNR plan that is subsequently developed should be signed by the parent, principal, physician, and school nurse. If appropriate, the signature of a competent adolescent is desirable.

4. An Individual Healthcare Plan should be developed as part of the overall DNR plan. The plan should be reviewed by the school nurse and parent(s) as needed, and at least quarterly. Areas to be considered in the plan include, but are not limited to, the following:

- parent and school interaction with EMS to develop appropriate protocols;

- regular and periodic assessment of the student's health status;

TABLE 14-5.
HONORING DNR ORDERS: PROCEDURAL CHECKLIST

- Investigate relevant statutes and regulations
- Consider DNR request at multidisciplinary team
- Determine the parameters of the DNR order
- Establish responsibilities of all the stakeholders
- Develop an Individual Student Plan and IHP
- Train the necessary school staff
- Update training and documentation PRN

Adapted from: Brown, S. E., & Valluzzi, J. L. (1995). Do not resuscitate orders in early intervention settings: Who should make the decision? *Infants and Young Children*, 7(3), p. 25. Used with permission.

- guidelines for removal of the student from class activities or school;
- suitable palliative care of the student;
- the medical interventions that are and are not indicated for the student and under what conditions they should be provided;
- the procedures to be followed in the case of impending or actual death;
- who should be contacted in the case of an emergency situation or expiration of the student;
- protocol in the case of an emergency episode on the school bus;
- communication and partnership with the family;
- emotional support of the student and the family;
- training and support of the school and transportation staffs and other students in the school hospice protocol, if indicated;
- removal of the child's body from school; and
- pronouncement of death, signing of the death certificate, and funeral director arrangements if the body cannot be removed immediately from the school.

5. It is critical that student confidentiality be maintained to the extent preferred by the student and family. For minor students, the parent has the ultimate authority in determining who should be informed. Generally, it is recommended that the following persons be informed of the DNR order: all school nursing personnel and other health services personnel assigned to the student's school, the student's teacher(s), school bus staff on the student's bus, all school-based administrators, any CPR-trained school personnel, local EMS personnel and appropriate school district central administration. Those who are advised of the student's DNR status should be listed in the written DNR plan. See Figure 14-3 for a sample DNR-plan form.

Activating the DNR Order

1. Only licensed health care personnel can be expected to assess the health status of a student with a DNR order. The school nurse should determine when activating the DNR order is indicated but should also ensure that all staff members who are informed of the DNR order are trained to respond appropriately when the child shows signs of distress.

2. It should be a priority to transport the student from school at the first signs of deteriorating condition, following the student's established plan.

3. If the student suffers distress that is unrelieved by the predetermined palliative care, summon EMS and/or follow the plan previously established with the physician and parent. This may also include hospice instructions.

4. If the student expires prior to being transported from school, seclude the student in a private area, while maintaining a normal environment in the rest of the building. Activate the EMS, requesting no sirens, and transport the student to the nearest hospital emergency department. If this is not possible in your community, follow the pre-arranged plan for pronouncement of death by the physician who wrote the DNR order, the involvement of the identified funeral director, and transport of the child's body from the school. If the EMS does not transport the student, it is preferable for the transport to take place after normal school hours.

5. If state required, report a death that occurs in school or on the school bus to legal authorities. Appropriate school district personnel should also be notified.

6. If available, secure the assistance of a crisis intervention team to support the school community.

FIGURE 14-3.
INDIVIDUAL STUDENT PLAN: DO NOT RESUSCITATE

BALTIMORE COUNTY PUBLIC SCHOOLS   BALTIMORE COUNTY DEPARTMENT OF HEALTH
Towson, Maryland 21204   Towson, Maryland 21204

INDIVIDUAL STUDENT PLAN
DO NOT RESUSCITATE

STUDENT _____ DOB _____

Original Maryland state physician order/parent authorization form(s) is completed and maintained:

Student ( ) will or ( ) will not wear a DNR identification bracelet.

School staff to be informed of the DNR status:

Staff training and support plans:

School transportation plan:

Allowable medical interventions/palliative care:

Disallowed medical interventions:

FIGURE 14-3. (CONTINUED)
INDIVIDUAL STUDENT PLAN: DO NOT RESUSCITATE

Contact the following persons in the order listed for emergencies:

<u>Name</u>   <u>Title</u>   <u>Telephone(s)</u>

1.

2.

3.

4.

Hospice protocol, if applicable:

Plan for transporting the student from school and referring to appropriate care, when physical condition begins to deteriorate:

_____   _____
        Parent/Guardian   Date

_____   _____
        School Administrator   Date

_____   _____
        School Nurse(s)   Date

_____   _____
        Attending Physician   Date

SUMMARY

School personnel face an array of complex issues when students have serious medical conditions. Increasingly, schools are being asked to make difficult decisions regarding DNR requests in a societal climate of legal, policy, moral, and ethical uncertainty as health care services move more aggressively into community settings. There are no clear answers about whether schools must, or even should, honor DNR orders. This question does not have a definitive policy answer, the issue has yet to be litigated, and there is no ethical consensus (Costante, 1998).

However, DNR orders are not going to disappear, because children with challenging medical problems will remain a part of our educational systems. The ethical and practical issues raised by DNR requests will continue to challenge schools in the foreseeable future. These requests are merely a reflection of the complexity of issues faced by both schools and families today. Successful outcomes of these issues require that all parties collaborate with each other in new and unique ways. Whatever position a school district or state takes, it should be based on what is best for students, within the confines of state law and with consideration for community resources.

REFERENCES

American Academy of Pediatrics, Committee on Bioethics. (1993). Guidelines on forgoing life-sustaining medical treatment. *Pediatric Nursing, 20*(5), 517–5521.

American Academy of Pediatrics, Committee on School Health and Committee on Bioethics. (2000). Do not resuscitate orders in schools [policy statement RE9842]. *Pediatrics, 105*(4).

Baltimore County Public Schools. (1994; rev. 1997). Management of do not resuscitate orders. In *Manual of school health nursing practice* (pp. 43–47). Towson, MD: Author.

Beekman, L. E. (1995, May). *DNR orders: What should a school district do?* Paper presented at the 16th National Institute on Legal Issues of Educating Individuals with Disabilities, Washington, DC.

Brown, S. E., & Valluzzi, J. L. (1995). Do not resuscitate orders in early intervention settings: Who should make the decision? *Infants and Young Children, 7*(3), 13–27.

Connecticut Committee on DNR Orders. (1994). Medical do not resuscitate (DNR) orders in schools: Considerations and recommendations. In *Specialized health care procedure manual for school nurses* (1997)

(Appendix K). Middletown, CT: Connecticut State Department of Education.

Costante, C. C. (1998a). [Do not resuscitate orders in schools, Survey]. Unpublished raw data.

Costante, C. C. (1998b). Managing DNR orders in the school setting. *Journal of School Nursing, 14*(4), 49–55.

Havens, D. H., & Greenberg, P. (1992). Talk about death and dying: It's the law. *Journal of Pediatric Health Care, 2*(3), 158–160.

Herlan, E. R. (1995, May). *Is there a right to die on school grounds? How to respond to "Do Not Resuscitate" orders in school.* Paper presented at the 15th National Institute on Legal Issues of Educating Individuals with Disabilities, San Francisco, CA.

Iowa Attorney General. (Opinion of the Attorney General, no. 88-3-3[L]) (1988, March 10).

Maryland Attorney General. (79 Opinions of the Attorney General, no. 94-028.) (1994, May 13).

Maryland State Department of Education. (1997). Model policy—*Management of do not resuscitate orders in Maryland schools.* Baltimore: Author.

National Association of School Nurses. (1995). *Do Not Resuscitate position statement.* Scarborough, ME: NASN.

National Education Association. (1994). *Policy on Do Not Resuscitate orders.* West Haven, CT: NEA.

Proctor, S. (1998). School nurses and ethical dilemmas. *Journal of School Nursing, 14*(2), 3.

Ristocelli, E., Wessel, G., & Costante, C. (1994, September). [Do not resuscitate policies, Survey] Unpublished raw data.

Rosenfeld, S. J. (1995, August). An overview of DNR orders: Considerations for school districts. *SAARC reports: Emerging issues and trends in education.* Plantation, FL: South Atlantic Regional Resource Center.

Rushton, C. H., Will, J. C., & Murray, M. G. (1994). To honor and obey: DNR orders and the school. *Pediatric Nursing, 20*(6), 581–585.

Schultz-Grant, L., Young-Cureton, V., & Kataoka-Yahiro, M. (1998). Advance directives and do not resuscitate orders: Nurses' knowledge and the level of practice in school settings. *Journal of School Nursing, 14*(2), 4–13.

Scofield, G. R. (1992). A lawyer responds: A student's right to forgo CPR. Kennedy Institute of Ethics Journal, 2(1), 4–11.

Strike, K. A. (1992). An educator responds: School's interest in denying the request. *Kennedy Institute of Ethics Journal, 2*(1), 19–23.

University of Colorado, Health Sciences Center, School of Nursing, Office of School Health. (1995). *A closer look: A preliminary report of some of the findings from the national survey of school nurses and school nurse supervisors.* Denver: Author.

Williams, J. M. (Opinion of legal counsel for Bucks County, PA Intermediate Unit, file no. 0158-19575.) (1994, February 10).

Younger, S. J. (1992) A physician/ethicist responds: A student's rights are not so simple. *Kennedy Institute of Ethics Journal, 2*(1), 13–18.

TABLE OF CASES

ABC School and D.E.F. School v. Mr. and Mrs. M., 26 IDELR 1103 (Super. Ct. Mass. 1997)
Lewiston (Me.) Public Schools, 21 IDELR 83 (OCR 1994)

See page 625 for Table of Federal Statutes and Regulations.

Chapter Fifteen
School-based Health Centers

Ann B. Mech

INTRODUCTION

School-based health centers have caught the attention of health planners and providers during the last decade as a way to provide cost-effective, convenient, and comprehensive primary health care services to children. Despite the expansion of Medicaid and other health insurance programs, there are still children who lack access to basic primary care services. School-based health centers offer one solution by bringing health care to children in their schools where prevention, treatment, and follow-up care can be coordinated at a single location.

OVERVIEW OF SERVICES

School-based health centers expand the concept of school health services into a broader range of primary care services. Such services include diagnosis and treatment of acute and chronic conditions, preventive health and dental services, and mental health counseling (Bureau of Primary Health Care, 1997). While there is physician oversight of the health center program, actual care is often provided by nurse practitioners, with the assistance of school nurses and health assistants (Hacker, Lovick, & Kirby, 1994; Wenzel, 1996).

While there are core primary care services in school-based health centers, additional services are often tailored to the age and needs of the student body. For example, reproductive health services are usually reserved for middle and high schools, while elementary schools may emphasize immunizations and Early Periodic Screening, Diagnosis, and Treatment (EPSDT) services (Wenzel, 1996; Zeanah et al., 1996). Another important function of school-based health centers is referral to other health care and social service providers in the community. Coordinating a student's care among multiple providers presents unique challenges and opportunities for the school's health center.

HISTORY OF EXPANSION OF CENTERS

The first school-based health centers were established almost twenty-five years ago (Lear, Montgomery, Schlitt, & Rickett, 1996). Since that time, and particularly during the last decade, the growth of these centers has been exponential. In the 1988-1989 academic year, there were approximately 150 school-based health centers in U.S. schools. By the end of 1995, the number had grown to 700, and by the end of 1998 to 1,157. Only Idaho, Nevada, North Dakota, South Dakota, and Wyoming reported no school-based health centers (Hurley, 1994; Lear et al., 1996; National Survey SBHC, 1998).

The growth of school-based health centers has stemmed from the need to provide accessible primary care services to students who could not afford them or who might otherwise not be inclined to use them in a traditional health care setting (Lear et al., 1996). The adolescent population has been viewed as a group that could be well served by school-based health centers, especially in light of disturbing rates of teen pregnancy, sexually transmitted diseases, violence, and drug abuse. Therefore, high schools were the sites initially chosen for school-based health centers. Increasingly, though, state and local governments have recognized the value of placing such centers in middle and elementary schools. The 1998 Making the Grade Survey found that 38% of school-based health centers were located in high schools, 33% were housed in elementary schools, 16% were in middle schools, 6% were in K–12 schools, and 7% were located in a mix of other schools (National Survey, SBHC, 1998).

Community support and often community funding have been necessary ingredients in the development of school-based health centers. Until recently, public and private grants have been used to pay both capital and operating expenses of the centers. Unlike other primary care delivery sites, school-based health centers have not relied on patient care reimbursement through private or governmental health insurance programs to sustain their operations. However, schools have found that grant funding cannot guarantee the ongoing revenue stream needed to maintain a full range of primary health care services and are beginning to seek third-party reimbursement for care provided to students covered by health insurance plans (Lear et al., 1996). This comes at a time when states are moving their Medicaid-insured populations into managed care, following the lead of the private sector's switch from fee-for-service to capitated reimbursement ("Enrollments Are Up, Earnings Are Down," 1998). Continued expansion of school-based health centers may depend on how successful schools are in obtaining reimbursement in a managed care environment, a challenge health care providers in other settings have not easily mastered.

DEVELOPMENT OF A SCHOOL-BASED CENTER

The ultimate success or failure of efforts to institute a school-based health center depends on careful planning at the outset. As with almost any new concept or program, resistance to change will be encountered, and unexpected issues may arise. Strategic planning will help to minimize unanticipated problems and increase the likelihood of the center's success.

Community Need for the Center

Goodman and Steckler (1989) state that certain "critical precursor conditions" must be present in order to implement health promotion programs. There must be recognition of and concern about a problem, coupled with receptivity to a particular programmatic solution. There must also be resources available to support the programmatic solution.

Support for school-based health centers to address the health needs of children has come from leaders in health care and education from the Federal government on down (Schlitt, 1991). Elders (1991) outlines the multiple benefits of school-based health centers, and sees them as "the hub for integration of social, health, mental health, and support services for children and families." She also notes the importance of community support and involvement in planning and developing the centers, in order to assure their success.

Identification of the need for a school-based health center at the local level is likely to originate from school officials and health care professionals. Teen pregnancy, drug abuse, poor immunization rates, and lack of access to primary care services are some of the problems to be addressed by school-based health centers

(Hurley, 1994). Rienzo and Button (1993) also cite parents and community groups as others who identify a need for a school-based health center, and who lend their support to efforts to develop one. Since local support for school-based health centers may come from a variety of stakeholders, they can have differing ideas about what services should be offered and differing expectations about what such health centers can accomplish. In order to avoid later disappointment, it is important to discuss community expectations early in the planning process to gain a sense of why different groups value a school-based health center (Dryfoos & Santelli, 1992).

Community Willingness to Use the Center

The allocation of resources to a school-based health center represents a significant financial commitment for most schools. Opportunity to fund other programs, even academic ones, can be lost because of a decision to pay for a health center. Therefore, planners of a school-based health center will want to assure its full use by the student population to be served.

Several policy makers (Center for the Future of Children, 1992; Dryfoos & Santelli, 1992; Hadely, Lovick, & Kirby, 1986) have urged the involvement of parents in the planning phase. It is the parents who best know the needs of their children and who decide which health care services their children will have. Student input is also important for health care services that the student, usually an adolescent, can obtain without parental consent.

In a survey conducted by Weathersby, Lobo, and Williamson (1995), parents and students in a high school in South Carolina were polled to determine their levels of interest in having a school-based health center. Parent interest was rated in the moderate to very interested range. This relatively high rating of interest came from a group of parents who reported that, although private physicians were available in the community, not all health care needs were being met by local practitioners. Parent concerns about a school-based health center related to consent and financial issues, selection of health care providers and services for sexually transmitted diseases and contraception. Students were somewhat-to-moderately interested in having on-site health care services, a level of interest that the researchers believed reflected their stage of adolescent development. As one student stated, "I'm in perfect health, so I don't really care." The services students did identify as needed were counseling, treatment of sexually transmitted diseases, and birth control information.

In a study of rural adolescents' willingness to use a school-based health center, Rickert, Davis, Riley, and Ryan (1997) found more than half of the teens surveyed (55.5%) were unwilling to change their source of health care to a center in the school. Students who did report a willingness to use a school-based health center were three times more likely to be eligible for free or reduced lunches and five times more likely to lack a source of health care when ill.

Other studies indicate adolescents seek health care from a variety of health care settings (Craft, 1987) or use school-based health centers if they have problems related to mental health or weight control, or if they are sexually active (Riggs & Cheng, 1988). Therefore, it is essential that schools explore with students and their parents the services likely to be used in a school-based health center before monies are expended for its implementation. Since ability to afford health care from private providers in the community is a factor in willingness to use a school-based clinic, it should also be worthwhile for local governments to locate health centers in schools with large populations of students receiving free or reduced-priced lunches.

Community Politics

Support for a school-based health center may not be unanimous in the community. Opposition to these centers comes from local citizen groups who may have ties to larger, well-established organizations. Sometimes this opposition is powerful enough to block attempts to start a school-based health care program. Rienzo and Button (1993) studied opposition to school-based health centers at five locations around the country. Their findings indicated resistance to the centers came from socially conservative organizations at the national, regional, or state level working in conjunction with members of the local community. Controversy centered on issues of adolescent sexuality and parental authority. The school-based health centers, the opponents argued, would be nothing more than birth control clinics, encouraging sexual promiscuity and abortion. Similar community reactions to reproductive health care at three school-based clinics in Louisiana were reported in a study conducted by Zeanah et al. (1996).

According to Rienzo and Button (1993), opposition campaigns were well-orchestrated. Opponents presented their arguments at contentious public meetings, lobbied for funding cuts for school-based centers, and elected their own candidates to local school boards. Supporters of school-based health centers countered by enlisting local health authorities to present data through the media identifying health problems in the community that could be addressed by the school-based health center. Sometimes support was secured from local churches as a counterweight to opposition from outside religious groups. Equally important for parents, supporters provided assurances that clinic policy regarding parental permission would be followed.

Thus, in planning a school-based health center, community leaders should develop a strategy to garner community support for the program to meet expected opposition, especially if the center will serve the adolescent population. Increasing public awareness about health care needs of school children makes the community more favorably disposed to the center. Addressing opponent propaganda in a rational and truthful manner helps to create the parental allegiance that is essential to the success of a school-based health center.

CHOOSING A PARTNER TO MANAGE A CENTER

Once the decision has been made to launch a school-based health center, the school must decide how and by whom primary health care services will be provided to the student population. The school could solely own and control the school-based health center, hiring health care providers and purchasing medical equipment through the school's procurement system. But it may be beyond the capability of the school to expand its school health program to include all primary health care services a school-based health center should provide. Schools traditionally have a primary focus on academics; they lack expertise in managing a health care operation. For this reason, a school may look outside the school system for a partner to run its school-based health center.

Health Departments

One logical partner for a school-based health center is the local health department. Health departments often share responsibility for school health services with the school system under state law mandates. Furthermore, an interest in health promotion and disease prevention among children is a key component of a health department's community health focus. The local health department is, at the very least, a provider of some primary health care services and has experience managing health centers and clinics. The health department may already have nursing staff involved in the care of children in the school system who know well the needs of the population to be served by the school-based health center. The health department also has on staff physicians, social workers, counselors, and other health care practitioners who can be accessed to provide a broad range of services in a school-based health center. As Elders (1993) points out, the health department should be involved with the schools in planning school-based health centers, and the health department seems a natural choice of partner in coordinating services in the center.

The local health department, though, may lack the financial resources to extend its operations into school-based health centers. Even if there are funds to establish a center initially, shifts in governmental funding may result in reductions in services and changing priorities that could affect the continuation of school-based health centers run by local health departments. Unless some other revenue or funding source is identified, a school and a health department may not have sufficient funds budgeted by their state or local governments to sustain a school-based health center operation in the long term.

Also, while interagency collaboration can be useful in establishing a school-based health center, there can be problems related to the working relationship. In a 1992 nationwide survey of school health service delivery in urban schools (Hacker, Fried, Bablouzian, & Roeber, 1994), a significant number of respondents cited conflict between organizational structures and institutional culture and other territorial issues as obstacles to interagency collaboration. Conflicts arose over funding control, sharing of employees, and perceived lack of organization for joint support efforts.

Universities

Colleges and universities that educate health professionals are other possible partner choices for managing school-based health centers. As acute care hospitals have downsized over the last decade, clinical education for students in the health care disciplines has moved to the community. Schools of nursing and medicine realize the value of school health practice in the education of future health professionals. These schools may also view school-based health centers as faculty practice sites with the potential to generate revenue for the college or university. Certainly, school-based health centers offer multiple research opportunities on a variety of children's and community health issues.

While colleges and universities may be eager to develop and manage school-based health centers, they may lack experience in running a total clinic operation. A university's involvement in health care service delivery may have been limited to the provision of professional services in facilities managed by a separate corporate entity. Involvement in a school-based health center could entail overall responsibility for the center

itself, including the physical plant, medical equipment and supplies, as well as any third-party billing and collection activities. It is important for a school to consider the prior experience a college or university has in health center management when negotiating a collaborative arrangement to start a school-based health center.

Private Providers

Hospitals, health systems, and health professionals in independent practice are other possible partner choices to run school-based health centers. All have dealt with health center operations, although not necessarily in community settings. These providers may be drawn to school health services because of the potential for patient recruitment into a practice or additional revenue for an integrated health care delivery system, and they may already have an established reputation in the community.

Wenzel (1996) described a partnering model that included a school district, a community hospital, and a private pediatrician to provide health care services to elementary students in Arizona. The school nurse referred children with health care needs to a nurse practitioner who visited one school per day. The nurse practitioner was provided by the hospital, which also furnished pharmacy, laboratory, radiology and emergency department services. The school nurse and health office space were supplied by the school. The private pediatrician served as medical director of the program, as well as collaborating physician for the nurse practitioner.

Political and Regulatory Considerations for Government Contracting

Whenever a school chooses a partner to establish a school-based health center, there may be other interested competitors who were not selected. The school must recognize that the health care provider chosen will have a unique access to a group of children and their families, and a unique opportunity to recruit them as patients. If these families are insured through Medicaid or other health insurers, the school-based provider may stand to make financial gains through third-party reimbursement. Indeed, one reason why private primary care providers in the community have not objected to school-based health centers in the past may be that the centers, in treating the uninsured and underinsured, have not yet cut into private practitioners' patient revenue (Igoe, 1980. But as school-based health centers gain skill in capturing third-party reimbursement, private provider attitudes towards these health centers will likely change. Therefore, schools must consider the financial and political consequences of the selection of a collaborator for a school-based health center.

Schools, under the jurisdiction of local governments, are subject to whatever rules of procurement and contracting the local government has legislated. Often this involves public bidding on government contracts, which would include those to develop, implement, or evaluate school-based health centers. While the open bidding process insures fairness among competitors, it could mean a change in health center partner each time the contract cycle was due for renewal. Frequent provider changes would thwart efforts to develop relationships that foster continuity of care with the student population and the community to be served. Multi-year contracts would decrease the frequency of provider changes in the school setting, allowing sufficient time to establish relationships between practitioner and student, and to evaluate the overall effectiveness of the health center.

If there is to be competitive bidding on school-based health center contracts, the school should have a role in the drafting of the request-for-proposal. The scope of services to be offered should be tailored to the wants and needs of the community. The proposal request should also consider the requirements of any outside reimbursement sources. For example, health insurers (including the public sector insurer, Medicaid) contract directly with health care providers to reimburse them for rendering care to the carriers' enrollees. In addition to specifying treatments and procedures that are covered services, insurance contracts will mandate conditions of participation the health care providers must meet in order to receive reimbursement. Typical conditions of participation include provider qualifications and availability, requirements for a primary care office with point-of-care laboratory capabilities, malpractice insurance, utilization management, credentialing and quality assurance procedures, maintenance of medical and financial records, term and termination of the agreement, and resolution of disputes under the agreement ("Maryland Medicaid Managed Care Program," 1996; Younger, Conner, Cartwright, & Kole, 1995). These conditions of participation can include physician availability (both on-site and by telephone) and coverage or referral for hours when the school-based center is closed, which can impact the school's choice of provider partner as well as overall cost of operating the center. The school would not want to arrange a partnership or collaboration with a health care provider that could not meet the conditions of partic-

ipation necessary for third-party reimbursement.

Any arrangement between school system and outside health care provider to develop and run a school-based health center should be formalized in a written contract. The contract should be drafted after extensive dialogue between the parties to assure conformity in the parties' expectations. The document should be specific and detailed about what services will be provided, by whom, and for how many hours per week. If responsibilities for operating the center are to be shared by the health care provider and the school, contract language must reflect which party has a particular duty (Elders, 1993).

Responsibilities to be addressed in the agreement should include, but are not necessarily limited to, the following:

1. furnishing and equipping the center, specifying:
   a. quantity and quality of medical equipment and other furnishings, including computers
   b. ownership of equipment
   c. disposition of equipment upon termination of the agreement
2. ongoing purchasing of drugs and other medical supplies
3. development of policies and procedures
4. hiring, credentialing, orienting, and supervising personnel
5. billing and collection activities
6. ownership and maintenance of medical records
7. compliance with OSHA bloodborne pathogen regulations
   a. Hepatitis B vaccination for staff
   b. purchase of gloves and other protective equipment
   c. annual training of health care personnel in the prevention of the spread of bloodborne pathogens
   d. arranging and paying for proper disposal of medical wastes, including syringes and needles
8. compliance with federal and state regulations for point-of-care laboratories
9. compliance with fire and safety codes
10. compliance with criminal background checks of personnel who work with children
11. purchase of casualty loss, general, and professional liability insurance
12. maintenance of the physical plant and its equipment, including housekeeping, regular trash and, if necessary, snow removal services
13. coverage of the cost of utilities and phone service
14. costs of marketing the center to the students and the community

15. access to health care data from the center for purposes of research and publication
16. restrictions on contract assignment or subcontracting to other health care providers

There may be a lease covering the matters related to the premises that is separate from the agreement to provide health care services in a school-based center. Since it is advantageous from the school's point of view to facilitate implementation of the school-based health center, the lease payment may be a nominal fee, such as one dollar per year. Attorneys drafting the agreements will also supply standard clauses concerning amendments and termination.

FUNDING A SCHOOL-BASED CENTER

Perhaps the most challenging facet of developing a school-based health center program is securing a funding stream that will pay for both the initial start-up of the center and for ongoing operating costs. With the transformation in this nation's health care system from a fee-for-service reimbursement structure to a managed care environment with built-in incentives to restrict health care resource utilization, school-based health centers face even greater difficulties in covering their costs while providing the level of service needed by the student population. And since schools and some of their health care provider partners may not be as accustomed to dealing with managed care reimbursement as hospitals and established medical practices, they face a learning curve that can have many pitfalls along the way.

Start-up Costs

Finding the resources to expand school health services into a primary care school-based health center has always been difficult (Lear et al., 1996; Yates, 1994). While local governments may view school-based health centers as desirable, they may lack the ability to allocate funds to develop such centers among competing demands for governmental services. Garnering the financial support for school-based health centers presents an ongoing problem.

Initially, the providers of school-based health services must seek monies to develop a center. Sometimes renovation of existing space is needed to turn the school health room into a primary care office. Medical equipment and supplies must be purchased. There are also routine equipment, supply, and personnel costs of running a medical clinic. School staff may require training for new roles. The cost of publicizing and mar-

keting the school-based health center also should not be overlooked.

Grants from public or private agencies have been successfully used to establish school-based health centers. A 1998 survey (National Survey, SBHC, 1998) of funding for school-based health centers showed the following breakdown of funding sources from federal and state programs, as well as third-party insurance:

- State support—$36.8 million
- Maternal Child Health block grants—$8.3 million
- Federal Healthy Schools/Healthy Communities—$8 million (fiscal year 1998 funding)
- Medicaid—$8 million
- Private payors—$0.5 million

One source of federal dollars is the Bureau of Primary Health Care (BPHC), which administers the Healthy Schools, Healthy Communities Program, mandated by Congress in 1994. The mission of the Healthy Schools, Healthy Communities Program is to "promote and establish school-based health centers as an effective way to improve the health of vulnerable children and adolescents" (Bureau of Primary Health Care, 1997). The Program has funded nine rural and seventeen urban sites in twenty states. These school-based health centers serve students from kindergarten through grade twelve who are at high risk for poor health, school failure and other consequences of poverty.

States have undertaken programs aimed at fostering the development of school-based health centers, as well. Colorado's school-based health center initiative is administered through its Department of Public Health and Environment. The goal of this state and local governmental partnership is to "remove financial and organizational barriers that inhibit establishing and sustaining school-based health services" (Colorado Department of Public Health and Environment, 1996). Financing is obtained from diverse sources and includes Medicaid and private health insurance. An objective is to integrate school-based health services into any Colorado health care reform.

Local government monies are also important in funding school-based health centers. While a national figure is not available, local dollars made up almost half of the budgets of 11 cities' school-based health center programs in 1995 (Access to Services, 1998).

Private foundations have been a source of monies to develop school-based health centers. The Robert Wood Johnson Foundation was instrumental in establishing school-based clinics as early as 1978 (DeAngelis, 1981). In the Foundation's National School Health Program, school-based primary care centers served children who otherwise could not afford or would not likely access off-site health care. Since then, a variety of other institutions and charitable foundations have provided funding to begin school-based health centers. For example, in November, 1997, the McKesson Foundation announced a 3-year, $125,000 grant to the Massachusetts Coalition for School-Based Health Centers. This Coalition was established in 1994 to serve as a forum for 43 school-based clinics in 16 Massachusetts cities and towns, with support from the New England Medical Center and Medical Foundation (McKesson Foundation, 1997).

Ownership of Center Equipment

One important consideration in the school-based health center start-up process is reaching an understanding about who owns the center's equipment. It is especially important to determine ownership if the school partners with a private provider. Medical equipment is not inexpensive, and it may be difficult to garner the funds to refurnish a center if the private provider removes the equipment it owns when the partnership is terminated.

It is highly desirable to have the written agreement the parties negotiate address this issue. The parties may not have much flexibility in deciding ownership: grant monies flowing to one party or government procurement rules may dictate that the party purchasing the equipment hold title to it. However, it is possible to include a provision in the partners' agreement that title to equipment will revert to the school if the agreement is terminated.

Ongoing Funding

It is becoming evident that a stable funding source must be found if school-based health centers are to be sustained in the long term. Public and private grants have been used to provide funds to initiate school-based health centers, but increasingly organizations providing school-based health center services are turning to patient care revenues as a source of support. If grant funds are to be used to fund operating costs, those monies are better spent to furnish health care services to the 30% uninsured students seen in school-based centers (McKinney & Peak, 1995; Perino & Brindis, 1994).

Medicaid represents a probable source of reimbursement for school-based health centers. As previously mentioned, students most willing to use these centers are those from low-income families, as demonstrated by their eligibility for free or reduced lunches. Therefore, such students probably meet eligibility criteria for Medicaid coverage. As reported by Perino and Brindis (1994), twenty-four school-based health centers surveyed indicated most of their patient-care revenues for the 1992-1993 school year came from Medicaid. However, patient-care revenues represented only 13% of their operating budgets. In 1998, the amount of revenue from third-party payment services, both public and private, was $9.4 million nationally (National Survey, SBHC, 1998).

A number of factors may be responsible for this relatively low rate of patient care reimbursement (Lear et al., 1996). Medicaid reimbursement for services rendered in schools is relatively recent, beginning with the OBRA 89 expansion of the Medicaid ESPDT program and, at about the same time, coverage for health-related services required to educate disabled children. Also, state Medicaid officials may not understand the nature of health care services provided in school-based health centers, or they may believe other state grants are already funding the full cost of the service. Schools may not know the specific diagnostic and treatment services covered under Medicaid or other insurance benefits, or they may not know the procedures required to process health insurance claims. Furthermore, children covered by private insurance either do not attend schools with school-based health centers or, if they do, their insurance may have large out-of-pocket payments or may not cover the preventive services provided in the centers.

Opportunities exist to increase funding of school-based health centers through Medicaid patient care reimbursement (Lear et al., 1996). Some states, such as New Jersey, New York, and North Carolina, consider school-based health centers managed by private health care organizations to be satellites of the provider and reimburse as they would if care were rendered at the provider's non-school sites. Other states (Massachusetts, Rhode Island, Oregon, Connecticut, California, and Maryland) are taking steps to link school-based health centers and managed care organizations, as part of their Medicaid managed care initiatives. As more states develop programs to move their Medicaid populations into managed care, it will be imperative for schools and health care providers to lobby for state regulations specifically addressing timely reimbursement by managed care organizations for self-referred, school-based health care services (see, for example, "Maryland Medicaid Managed Care Program," 1996).

Billing and Collection

In order to receive reimbursement for patient care services through public or private health plans insurance, a school-based health center provider must furnish services listed as benefits under the applicable health insurance plan, meet the provider qualifications, comply with the conditions of participation required by the insurance plan, and establish a mechanism to bill and collect payment through the health insurance program (Younger et al., 1995).

Considerable administrative time and expense now goes into billing and collecting reimbursement for health care services. Claims are submitted to the insurance carrier; some may be denied reimbursement or sent back for additional supporting documentation (Hilzenrath, 1998). In order to minimize costly delays or denials in reimbursement, providers in the school-based health center must be familiar with the following:

1. Preventative, diagnostic, and treatment services covered under the health insurance plan
2. Which providers are authorized to provide these services
3. What services require pre-authorization of the health insurance plan
4. Limitations on frequency of providing covered services
5. Limitations on furnishing specific services at certain sites, such as at a school-based health center
6. Limitations on referrals to outside providers or facilities

Procedures for processing claims are mandated by each applicable health insurance plan. Errors in processing claims may result in delayed reimbursement, which can create cash-flow problems for the school-based health center. There may be prompt payment incentives for electronic processing of claims, which requires the health center to invest in information technology and personnel trained in its use. The school-based health center must also decide how far it will go in attempts to collect payments for uncovered services from the students' parents, and how much free care it can afford to provide.

MANAGING A SCHOOL-BASED HEALTH CENTER

The day-to-day operations of a school-based health center can run more smoothly if thoughtful strategic planning preceded the center's opening. Managing a school-based health center is similar to managing a large medical office or community health clinic. Each begins with a vision of who will be served, what services will be offered, and what outcomes will be achieved. Once the vision has been articulated, an organizational structure with its accompanying policies and procedures will be readily defined (Elders, 1993).

Scope of Services

When the decision has been made to have a school-based health center, the providers of services must outline which health care services will be supplied to the student population in the school setting. In part, the decision to select specific services to be supplied should be determined by the assessment of wants and needs in the local community, as well as the students' commitment to use the health care services in the school setting. But community wants and needs may exceed the level of services that can be both safely and effectively provided in the school setting.

As more acute care has moved from the hospital into ambulatory facilities in urgi-centers, surgi-centers, and large medical offices, providers and consumers of health care experience a wider range of health care in the outpatient arena. The question arises that if a treatment or procedure can be performed in a large medical office, then why not in the health center of the school? Sometimes the dilemma in school-based health care is whether to provide less health care, rather than more.

Since the decision to implement school-based health care often results from a desire to serve the chronically medically underserved, there may be many health care needs in the student population identified. Preventive health care, treatment for acute episodic illnesses, and mental health services may be some of the health care needs cited for and by the local community. Also, it can be difficult to address the needs of the students without addressing the health care and social needs of their families as well.

A core of health care services most commonly offered in school-based health centers (Elders, 1993; Hacker et al., 1994) includes the following:

Medical Services
1. Comprehensive medical and psychosocial histories
2. Immunizations
3. Comprehensive physical examinations
4. Developmental assessment
5. Assessment of educational, achievement, and attendance problems

6. Vision and hearing screening
7. Referral for dental care
8. Diagnosis and treatment of acute and chronic medical problems
9. Prescription of medications
10. Sports physicals
11. Laboratory testing and interpretation of results
12. Referral for specialty services and well child care
13. Dispensing of medications, per authority of state law
14. Case management based on individual needs
15. Mental health services, including assessment, treatment, referral, and follow-up

Health Education and Disease Prevention

1. One-on-one patient education
2. Group/targeted education at the health center
3. Supplemental classroom presentations and resource support for comprehensive health education, as well as for special topics such as these:
   a. HIV/AIDS
   b. drug use prevention
   c. intentional and unintentional injury prevention
   d. asthma

Social Services

1. Social service assessment
2. Referrals to and follow-up with social service and other public and private agencies

Other services may be offered, depending on the age of the students and the desires of the community. Screening and treatment for sexually transmitted diseases, prescribing and dispensing birth control, and providing addiction treatment services on-site are usually reserved for health centers in middle and high schools (Rickert et al., 1997, Rienzo & Button, 1993). As previously discussed, these services tend to be the most controversial to the community.

Providers of services in school-based health centers should define early in the planning process what medical conditions or injuries will be treated on-site and what will be referred to community practitioners or emergency facilities. Severe asthma or allergic reactions, deep lacerations, and suspected fractures or head trauma are a few of the urgent conditions for which additional medical treatment should be sought. Not only does the typical school-based health center lack the equipment to treat these conditions (i.e. beyond immediate interventions to stabilize a student for transporta-

tion), but there would likely be insufficient numbers of personnel trained in Advanced Cardiac Life Support to furnish assistance if needed. The school already has mechanisms in place to contact local emergency services and parents, and valuable time may be lost if attempts are made to handle severe illness or injury in the health center.

The extent of laboratory services to be offered on-site is another matter for consideration. Laboratory services are now regulated at the federal level under the Clinical Laboratory Improvement Amendments of 1988 (CLIA) (42 USC 263a), and they may be regulated under state laws, as well. Point-of-care laboratories performing simple tests are the most feasible for school-based health centers to operate. The tests that can be performed in point-of-care laboratories are listed in CLIA and any applicable state regulations. More complex laboratory services require specially trained and certified laboratory personnel and regular quality control calibrations of equipment. A school-based health center probably does not need, nor can it afford, a full-service medical laboratory on the premises.

Student Enrollment and Parental Consent

Since most students are minors lacking independent capacity to consent to medical treatment, parental consent to treatment by the providers in the school-based health center is required. State law should be consulted to determine if there are any exceptions to this general rule. States may allow minors to consent to treatment of sexually transmitted infections, as well as treatment related to pregnancy, birth control, mental illness, and substance abuse.

Consent for the student to be examined and treated in the school-based health center must be written and signed by the party having the capacity to consent for the minor (parent, legal guardian, or student). If immunizations are to be administered, separate consent should be obtained. Consent for immunization should list the specific vaccine to be administered, along with its potential risks and side effects. Vaccine purchased through the federal government comes with a vaccine information sheet for the child's parent or guardian; school districts may have additional policies concerning vaccine administration.

Enrollment of students into the school-based health center can be accomplished whenever the school schedules activities involving parents. This is also an opportunity to publicize the center and market its services. Holding open houses or health fairs gives the community a chance to view the center and meet the staff responsible for health care. It is also a time to explain to parents that enrollment in the school-based center is a necessary prerequisite to a child's receiving primary care services there. For, unlike routine school health services, separate informed consent is necessary for the type of treatment rendered in a school-based health center.

Policies and Procedures

Policies are generalized rules and regulations for the center; procedures are the specific steps in implementing those rules. Policy and procedure development is a necessary undertaking in the early phases of school-based health center start-up. Policies and procedures further define the scope of services to be provided in a school-based health center and function as a reference guide for health care practitioners. Policies and procedures inform these practitioners, who may come from several employers, of the standardized practices accepted at the center, as well as what to do when rare but urgent situations arise.

Policies and procedures should cover both routine and emergency patient care at the school-based health center. They should also address routine and emergency matters related to the physical plant, equipment, and supplics (e.g. maintenance safety checks of equipment and removing from shelves out-of-date drugs and sterile supplies).

Maintenance of health care records with provisions to assure confidentiality of medical information should be addressed in a policy. It is not always clear whether the school-based health center record is a school record with rights of access governed by the Family Educational Rights and Privacy Act (FERPA) (20 USC 1232g) or a record of treatment kept by a health care provider that is subject to a state's medical records laws. This distinction can be crucial when faced with questions of authorization to release health care information and rights of access by parents to information about treatment for which a minor has a right to consent without parental notification. The length of time medical records must be maintained is also affected by state records retention laws, third-party payor requirements, and statutes of limitations for malpractice claims.

Ownership of the medical record is another matter for consideration. While students and possibly their parents have a right to information about the health care students receive, there is a legal entity (individual or organization) that owns and carries responsibility for ongoing storage of the record itself (a custodian of the record). If a school has partnered with an out-side provider for school-based health services, the agreement governing the parties' relationship should address which party has those responsibilities. The governing agreement should stipulate that the party who does not own the students' health care records is guaranteed rights of access to those records on a continual basis, and these rights should survive termination of the agreement. There may be need to access health care records for purposes of data collection and substantiation of claims billed to third-party payors, as well as for evidence in the event of malpractice litigation.

Chain of Command

Administrative subjects are an important component of the policies and procedures in a school-based health center. Administrative subjects include job descriptions for different categories of personnel, staffing levels, hours of operation, duties of supervision and chain of command. If multiple employers supply personnel to a health center, as is often the case when a school partners with an outside health care provider, procedures must cover hiring and termination of employees and the steps a supervisor is to take when there is a disciplinary problem with someone else's employee. The relationship of the school principal and other school staff to practitioners in the school-based health center should be determined. Will the principal have the right to direct health care providers in the center, even if the providers are not employees of the school system? Will school staff be involved in enrollment and making appointments for students in the school-based health center program? If there are overlapping responsibilities for school personnel (e.g. school nurse, school health aide, and secretarial staff who schedule appointments), provision should be made for collaboration in health care service delivery and in protecting the confidentiality of medical information.

INTEGRATION OF HEALTH CARE DISCIPLINES
Scope of Practice

When selecting health care practitioners to provide services in a school-based health center, there should be a match between the scope of practice of the health care provider and the services needed by the students. State licensing laws govern the scope of practice of health care professionals, defining what the provider can do independently, and in collaboration with or under the supervision of another health care provider from a different discipline.

For example, physicians, nurses, social workers, dietitians, and others can assess a patient's needs. However, a medical diagnosis may only be made by physicians and certain other mid-level health care providers such as nurse practitioners and physicians' assistants, according to state law. The same holds true for prescribing medications and performing surgery, including the suturing of superficial lacerations.

Dispensing of medications is authorized under a state's pharmacy laws. Not every practitioner who has prescriptive authority also has the authority to dispense medications. This is an important point because of the tendency in ambulatory care settings to dispense starter doses of medications to patients, especially to those who lack the financial or transportation resources to have a prescription filled promptly.

The list of practitioners broadens when ability to counsel and educate patients is considered. Health care practitioners from many disciplines have this authority and responsibility. However, counseling and patient education should be coordinated with a primary care provider's plan of care.

An individual's scope of practice is further defined through credentialing. Credentialing is a process internal to the organization and is done in conjunction with hiring and regular performance appraisal. Current licensure, certification, training, experience, and supervisor and peer evaluations can be checked to determine a practitioner's abilities to perform certain procedures and care for particular patient populations, such as adolescents. Ideally, information from the school-based health center's quality improvement process and evaluation of health care outcomes can be factored into the credentialing process for the center's health care practitioners.

Delegation and Supervision

Health care in a school-based health center is carried out by a team of personnel, some of whom are licensed health care providers and others who are not. Unlicensed personnel, as well as some licensed personnel, must practice under the supervision of other licensed health care practitioners. State health occupations laws may indicate the nature of the relationship among health care disciplines. For example, a health care provider's practice act may state that practice is to be carried out "under the supervision of" or "in a team relationship with" a licensed physician, dentist or other authorized practitioner. Requirements for consultation or collaboration with another practitioner may also be established by state licensing laws. The written agreements that advance practice

nurses, physicians' assistants, pharmacists, and other mid-level providers may be required to have with physicians in order to obtain prescriptive authority signal a collaborative relationship. If practitioners in a school-based health center must be supervised or must have collaborative practice agreements, arrangements for required supervision or written agreements must be negotiated before the school-based health center is established. The personnel involved must understand the responsibilities each has to supervise or be supervised, especially if they are employed by different organizations.

One of the decisions that must be made when starting a school-based health center is what mix of professional and non-professional staff will be present on-site and on-call. While it may be desirable to use only licensed health care practitioners in the health center, the cost of an all-professional staff may be prohibitive. Therefore, it is likely the school-based health center team will consist of unlicensed assistants, such as a health aide or clerk, physicians, mid-level providers such as advance practice nurses, and school nurses. Patient care will be assigned to licensed personnel and delegated to unlicensed staff on the health care team. The physicians, mid-level providers, and school nurse will have both direct and oversight responsibility for care in the center.

State licensing regulations may indicate criteria for delegation of tasks to unlicensed personnel (see, for example, "Delegation of Nursing Functions," 1989). If tasks are delegated by a licensed health care professional to unlicensed assistive personnel, the licensed health care professional retains accountability for the services rendered. Ability to delegate goes hand in hand with the requirement to supervise the assistive personnel. Factors that affect the ability of a licensed health care professional to supervise unlicensed assistive personnel include the following:

1. Training of assistive personnel
2. Training of the professional in the art of management and supervision
3. Number of assistive personnel under the supervision of one health care professional
4. Geographic location of the supervisor (e.g., whether or not the supervisor is on the premises and how long it will take the supervisor to get to the site)
5. The acuity of the patient population (e.g. whether or not any students have unstable medical conditions such as poorly controlled asthma or seizure disorder)

6. The ability to access trained back-up personnel to assist in emergency situations (e.g. whether or not there are others on-site with training in first-aid and CPR)
7. Size of the student population

COORDINATION OF SERVICES

Since it is not likely students will receive all of their health care services at the school-based health center, it is necessary to plan how the health care each student receives will be communicated to other providers and coordinated with health care the student may seek from multiple health care providers at multiple sites. The goal is to facilitate as "seamless" a health care delivery system as possible for the student. Therefore, the providers in the school-based health center should inform outside providers of the role of the center and solicit their participation in the treatment and referral process for students enrolled at the center.

Primary Care Provider

The school-based health center provides a full range of primary care services: routine physical examinations, immunizations, treatment for minor illnesses and injuries, and referral to specialists for more serious problems are but a few. There is a difference, however, between supplying primary care services and being a patient's primary care provider.

A patient's primary care provider serves as the entry point, coordinator and, in a managed care environment, the gatekeeper for the patient's utilization of health care services. The primary care provider treats certain medical conditions and decides when referral to other health care practitioners is warranted. The primary care provider may be designated the "medical home" for the patient (Younger, 1995).

Because medical problems can arise at any time of day, day of week, or season of year, it is necessary for the primary care provider or designee to be available or on-call continually. If the school-based health center is closed at times when the school is closed, it may be difficult for health care practitioners working in the school-based health center to be the students' primary care providers. Even if the practitioners remain on-call for evenings and weekends, it is still difficult to establish the school-based health center as the students' "medical home" unless provisions are made to hold clinic sessions during the summer or other school holidays. However, if the school partners with a private provider that operates nearby health care sites (as the case may be if the school's arrangement includes a hospital, med-

ical group, or managed care organization), the partner could provide the availability of services needed to become the students' primary care providers. Otherwise, the school-based health center must deal with other health care practitioners providing care to the student population.

As states move their Medicaid populations into managed care, Medicaid patients are assigned primary care providers who are supposed to coordinate care. Some providers fill this role better than others. Payment for services rendered can also be a problem: the managed care organization may be delighted that the school-based health center provides services to its enrollees, as long as the managed care organization doesn't have to reimburse the school for those services.

Referral to Specialists

As in any health care practice, access to specialists is often a function of availability, affordability, and proximity. There may be a full complement of medical specialists in the region, but these practitioners may be clustered in areas where patients have the most complete health insurance coverage and, thus, can afford a specialist's care. The uninsured or underinsured may not be able to afford the cost of a specialist's care, and specialists may be unwilling to care for too many patients pro bono. Even if health insurance coverage is present, not every specialist is an eligible provider under every plan, and the student may lack the personal transportation needed to get to the widely scattered specialists who are. When children are referred to specialists, provisions must be made for reciprocal communication between the specialist and the school-based health center concerning the child's condition, treatment, and follow-up disposition.

Coverage When The School-based Health Center Is Closed

Even if the school-based health center chooses not to be a "medical home" for the students' enrolled, attention must be paid to problems that might arise after school hours. Arrangements can be made to provide after hours on-call services with a physician or nurse practitioner. Parents can be instructed to call an answering service after hours to obtain the name of the provider on-call. If these practitioners are not employees of the organization managing the center, they can be engaged as contractual providers paid on a retainer basis. It is best if these practitioners also have referral mechanisms in place to allow the student ready access to more acute levels of care, if needed. This information can be obtained as part of the on-call provider's credentialing procedure.

Authorization to Release Health Care Information

The school-based health center must have written authorization to release health information about the student to external agencies or health care providers. Release of health care information is also necessary to obtain insurance reimbursement for treatment given at the school-based center.

The party holding capacity to consent to the student's treatment (parent, guardian, or child) also has the capacity to authorize release of health care information. Authorizations to release information to other health care providers or to health insurance organizations can be signed at the time the student is enrolled in the school-based health center. It should not be assumed that an authorization to release health information within the normal channels of the health care system translates into permission to release information to school staff, or to include the details of medical treatments in the student's education records.

Maintenance of an Integrated Health Care Record

Continuity of care and today's ideal of seamless care delivery are attempts to counteract the fragmentation and lack of coordination of care seen all too frequently in the past. While it may be impossible to eliminate the multiple sites of health care delivery encountered by most patients, better communication among health care practitioners can be the key to avoiding duplication and gaps in patient care.

In order to foster communication among health care providers, sharing information through the patient's health care record offers the best possibility for coordinating care. Fortunately, advancements in electronic communications facilitate the exchange of needed information, and help to assure that the practitioner has the relevant data required to make a diagnosis or provide a treatment.

These communication systems require financial investments in technology and the personnel to use them. For some school districts such investments can be substantial initially, although they will likely save time and money in the long term. Another issue that arises surrounding an integrated patient care record accessed by multiple providers from different organizations is knowing who owns and has rights to control

the record. Determining ownership is not an insurmountable problem, but should be considered while the school-based health center is in its planning phase.

CONCLUSION

School-based health centers show much promise in meeting the need of access to health care services for children who might not otherwise access them. Many have been started with much enthusiasm, but less attention to how these centers can be financially sustained over time. Careful planning is the key determinant of a center's success starting with early community involvement and willingness to use these centers. Evaluation of student health outcomes and their impact on academic performance will be necessary to convince health care policy makers to continue financial support of the school-based health center. If the center is successful, Elders' (1993) prediction that the school will be the hub of integration of social, health and support services for children and their families will prove true.

REFERENCES

Access to Comprehensive School-Based Health Services for Children and Youth, Spring 1998. *Making the Grade.* Washington, DC: The George Washington University [On-line]. Available: http://www.gwu.edu/~FS/fsdollars.html

Bureau of Primary Health Care. (1997). *Healthy schools, healthy communities.* Health Resources and Services Administration [On-line]. Available: http://www.bphc.hrsa.dhhs.gov/hshc/HSHCfact.htm

Center for the Future of Children. (1992). Analysis. *The Future of Children, 2*(1), 6–18.

Center for Population Options. (1991). *School-based and school-linked clinics, update.* Washington, DC: Center for Population Options.

Colorado Department of Public Health and Environment. (1996). *Colorado School-Based Health Center Initiative* [On-line]. Available: http://www.aclin.org/other/health/cinch/profiles/00447.htm

Craft, M. (1987). Health care preferences of rural adolescents: Types of service and companion choices. *Journal of Pediatric Nursing, 2,* 3–12.

DeAngelis, C. (1981). The Robert Wood Johnson Foundation National School Health Program: A presentation and progress report. *Clinical Pediatrics, 20*(5), 344–348.

Delegation of nursing functions. (1989). Code of Maryland Regulations (COMAR) 10.27.11.

Dryfoos, J., & Santelli, J. (1992). Involving parents in their adolescents' health: A role for school clinics. *Journal of Adolescent Health, 13,* 259–260.

Elders, J. (1993). Schools and health: A natural partnership. *Journal of School Health, 63*(7), 312–315.

Enrollments are up, earnings are down. (1998). *On Managed Care, 3*(4), 1.

Goodman, R., & Steckler, A. (1989). A model for the institutionalization of health promotion programs. *Family and Community Health, 11*(4), 63–78.

Hacker, K., Fried, L., Bablouzian, L., & Roeber, J. (1994). A nationwide survey of school health services delivery in urban schools. *Journal of School Health, 64*(7), 279–283.

Hadely, E., Lovick, S., & Kirby, D. (1986). *School-based clinics: A guide to implementing programs.* Washington, DC: Center for Population Options.

Hilzenrath, D. (1998, March 3). Medicine's growing battle: Getting health plans to pay. *The Washington Post,* A1, A14–15.

Hurley, D. (1994). School-based clinics fill gap. *Medical Tribune, 35*(22), 1, 5 [On-line]. Available: http://www.thriveonline.com/health/Library/CAD/abstract21579.html

Igoe, J. (1980). Changing patterns in school health and school nursing. *Nursing Outlook, 28*(8), 486–492.

Lear, J., Montgomery, L., Schlitt, J., & Rickett, K. (1996). Key issues affecting school-based health centers and Medicaid. *Journal of School Health, 66*(3), 83–88.

Maryland Medicaid managed care program: School-based health centers. (1996). COMAR 10.09.68.

McKesson Foundation. (1997). Announcement: Grant for school-based health centers in Massachusetts. Available: http://f2.yahoo.com/bw/971117/mckesson_foundation_l.html

McKinney, D., & Peak, G. (1995) *Update 1994.* Washington, DC: Advocates for Youth.

National Survey of School-Based Health Centers, 1997–1998. *Making the Grade.* Washington, DC: The George Washington University [On-line]. Available: http://www.gwu.edu/~mtg/FS/fsmap.html

Perino, J., & Brindis, C. (1994). *Payment for services rendered: A report of existing and potential funding sources.* San Francisco: Center for Reproductive Health.

Rickert, V., Davis, S., Riley, A., & Ryan, S. (1997). Rural school-based clinics: Are adolescents willing to use them and what services do they want? *Journal of School Health, 67*(4), 144–148.

Rienzo, B., & Button, J. (1993). The politics of school-based clinics: A community-level analysis. *Journal of School Health, 63*(6), 266–272.

Riggs, S., & Cheng, T. (1988). Adolescents' willingness to use a school-based clinician view of expressed health concerns. *Journal of Adolescent Health, 9,* 208–213.

Schlitt, J. (1991). *Bringing health to school: Policy implications for southern states.* Washington, DC: Southern Center on Adolescent Pregnancy Prevention.

Weathersby, A., Lobo, M., & Williamson, D. (1995). Parent and student preferences for services in a school-based clinic. *Journal of School Health, 65*(1), 14–17.

Wenzel, M. (1996). A school-based clinic for elementary schools in Phoenix, Arizona. *Journal of School Health, 66*(4), 125–127.

Yates, S. (1994). The practice of school nursing: Integration with new models of health service delivery. *Journal of School Nursing, 10*(1), 10–14, 16–19.

Younger, P., Conner, C., Cartwright, K., & Kole, S. (1995). *Legal answer book for managed care.* Gaithersburg, MD: Aspen Publishers.

Zeanah, P., Morse, E., Simon, P., Stock, M., Pratt, J., & Sterne, S. (1996). Community reactions to reproductive health care at three school-based clinics in Louisiana. *Journal of School Health, 66*(7), 237–241.

See page 625 for Table of Federal Statutes and Regulations.

Chapter Sixteen

School Health Services and Managed Care: A Unique Partnership for Child Health

Elizabeth "Nancy" Gaffrey
Wanda R. Miller

Part 1: School Health Services and Managed Care
Elizabeth "Nancy" Gaffrey

INTRODUCTION

The challenge of reforming a system of health care that is presently driven by the goals of quality, access, and cost containment has again turned national attention to the area of school health. In Nursing's Agenda for Health Care Reform, released in 1991, we read of a restructured health care system which "enhances consumer access to services by delivering primary health care in community-based settings" (American Nurses Association, 1991, p. 2). Schools were among the identified settings and the services noted ranged from prevention through treatment. One of the goals of the nursing reform plan was to "guarantee universal access to an assured standard care" (ANA, 1991, p. 2).

In validating this concept of schools as places of "access," McGinnis and DeGraw (1991) estimated that one-third of the Healthy People 2000 objectives could be achieved in the school setting. The same belief can be applied to the Healthy People 2010 objectives. The field of school nursing, practiced "where the action is," provides cost- and outcome-effective health care to school-aged children.

Background

The move toward managed care in this country is dramatically reconfiguring the financing and delivery of health care services. Managed care is a system of prepaid health care services whose goal is to improve both the access to and quality of care while containing costs. Promising and challenging opportunities for Managed Care Organizations (MCOs) and profes-

sional school nurses to work together to provide an effective and efficient delivery system of health care for children within the school community are increasingly available.

Historically, school nurses have met the needs of the school community by expanding their role to provide primary health care and case management as well as disease prevention and health promotion. It is school nurses who possess the education and expertise needed to promote the effective, timely, accessible, cost-efficient delivery of health care services. Since schools can provide services conveniently and cost effectively for students, collaborative systems partnering managed care with school districts must emerge. School nurses need to be involved early in the process of developing these partnerships with MCOs.

Basic to the development of these partnerships is the concept of "systems change." Here we will define it as a revision of the ways that people and institutions think, behave, and use their resources to affect fundamentally the types, quality, and degree of service delivery to children and families (Gaffrey & Bergren, 1998).

Creating a more responsive service delivery system is not easy. Strategies to build more rational and responsive service and support systems for children and families are continuing to gather momentum at the local, state, and federal levels. A national trend has developed for both the privately-insured and Medicaid-insured populations to receive health services through MCOs. Concomitantly, an unrelated trend to develop school-linked and school-based health services has emerged to increase access to a medically underserved population (U.S. Department of Health & Human Services [USD-HHS], 1996).

At present a variety of school-affiliated licensed health care professionals (nurse practitioners, nurses, physicians, mental health professionals, occupational therapists, physical therapists, and speech therapists) provide services essential for meeting managed care goals and do so more efficiently than community primary care sites. School health providers and MCOs share common goals of preventive care, early intervention, and promotion of lifelong health habits to improve an individual's health status.

Neither school health providers nor managed care officials have a realistic understanding of their counterpart's worlds. In anticipation of collaborating with managed care providers, school nurses must have an understanding of managed care and the many forms it takes. They must be able to articulate, for managed care, the type of health services presently delivered in schools, the qualifications of the staff to deliver that care, and its cost effectiveness. On the other hand, managed care officials must recognize that the school setting provides unparalleled access to the school-age population. They need a clear understanding of the expanded role and skills of school nurses. Finally, they must be able to identify the opportunities and limitations of the school setting (Gaffrey & Bergren, 1998).

Current Funding of School Health Services

The majority of school health services are funded primarily by local school districts out of education funds, which are frequently subjected to political winds and competing local needs. Other revenue may come from public health departments, Medicaid, state agencies, federal or private grants, and combinations of these sources (Lear, 1996c). Although Medicaid reimbursement for covered services received increasing

attention over the last decade, school health services have, in general, produced significant revenue for only some of the school districts involved. In the past, most school nurses and many school-based health center (SBHC) personnel have had neither the motivation, the resources, nor the skills to set up the complex data collection, record keeping, and billing procedures required to pursue reimbursements (Zimmerman & Reif, 1995). In 1994, 35% of primarily low-income students using SBHCs had Medicaid coverage, but only 1% of funding came from Medicaid revenues (Brellochs, Zimmerman, Zink, & English, 1996).

Under the federal Individuals with Disabilities Education Act (IDEA), school districts must provide services to ensure that children with disabilities receive an appropriate education (see chapter 12). Special education programs receive limited federal assistance. In addition to federal support for special education, Medicaid programs may pay for those related services specified in the federal Medicaid statute and deemed medically necessary by the state Medicaid agency. However, in addition to the reimbursable, but frequently not claimed, and non-reimbursable nursing services, school districts pay for speech therapy, physical and occupation therapy, and child counseling (Brave New Partnerships, 1997).

The most costly health-related service for special education students is transportation. Health services that must be available under the IDEA legislation are school nursing services, speech pathology, audiology, psychological services, physical and occupational therapy, counseling services, early diagnosis and assessment of disabilities, social work, and medical services for diagnosis and evaluation purposes (Lear, 1996b). Some state programs reimburse school-based professionals, especially school nurses (both those who are nurse practitioners as well as those who are not), for Early Prevention Screening, Diagnosis and Treatment (EPSDT) services provided to Medicaid beneficiaries.

MANAGED CARE ORGANIZATIONS

What is managed care? Managed care is defined as a health care system that integrates financing and delivery of health care services to covered individuals, most often with arrangements by selected providers (ANA, 1995). MCOs offer a specific package of health care benefits, a specific list of health care providers, and financial incentives for its enrollees to use providers and services offered within the organization.

Managed care is usually prepaid or paid at a capitated rate. This means a predetermined dollar amount

is paid periodically, usually monthly, to the enrollee's primary care provider. The provider acts as a gatekeeper, coordinating all the health care services required by the individual member under the terms of a contract. Unlike fee-for-service systems where more care equals more income, prepayment of health care provides a financial incentive for the provider to avoid unnecessary or redundant services and to prevent illness. The assumption is that managed care will reduce costs while improving the delivery and outcomes of health care.

Most managed care organizations are a blend of the following four types (Brellochs et al., 1996):

- **Staff model Health Maintenance Organizations (HMOs)** are the oldest and the most tightly structured organizations for managing care. HMOs own and operate clinics and employ salaried providers.

- **Capitated group networks** are made up of primary care or multispecialty clinics or groups of clinics that contract with a managed care organization to provide care to a designated population. Most group networks contract with several managed care organizations simultaneously.

- **Independent Practice Organizations (IPOs),** the fastest growing type of organizations within managed care, are individual practices or privately owned groups that join together to contract with managed care organizations to serve a specified population. The practices offer their services to a managed care organization as a package and share the financial risk. Their payment may be capitated or a discounted fee-for-service. IPOs abide by rules for referring patients to specialists and prescribe drugs specified in the HMO's formulary.

- **Preferred Provider Organizations (PPOs)** are independent group practices which agree to abide by the same rules as an IPO, but do not share any of the risks. They are usually paid on a discounted fee-for-service basis. The enrollee may visit a provider outside of the organization but will incur a significant co-payment. The plan enrollee has a financial incentive to select providers who are within the PPO.

MEDICAID

The Medicaid program was established under Title XIX of the Social Security Act in 1965 and is administered by the Health Care Financing Administration (HCFA) of the U.S. Department of Health and Human Services (USDHHS). The objective of the Medicaid program is to provide insurance coverage for essential medical care and services to preserve health and alleviate sickness for individuals or families on public assistance or whose income is not sufficient to meet their needs. Medicaid is a state and federal partnership under which the federal government establishes basic program rules. Each state then administers the program, but is free to develop state

rules and regulations for program administration as approved by HCFA to be within the parameter of the federal rules. States meeting federal requirements receive funding at various levels in relationship to their Medicaid expenditures. Medicaid beneficiaries receive their benefits either through the fee-for-service delivery system or, in increasing numbers, through managed care plans.

Current Managed Care Arrangements

Since 1992, the number of Medicaid beneficiaries enrolled in managed care plans has grown sharply, increasing by more than 170%, including a 33% increase from 1995 to 1996. (See Table 16-1.) HCFA, which administers Medicaid, is now the largest purchaser of managed care in the country, accounting for over 15 million enrollees, 48% of Medicaid beneficiaries. At least, 48 states now offer some form of Medicaid managed care. By utilizing federal Medicaid waivers, they are able to increase enrollment in managed care and develop innovative programs to provide care to their Medicaid populations. In limiting fee-for-service and freedom to select any provider, states have realized savings from a reduction in high cost services (e.g., emergency room usage) and have increased the likelihood that Medicaid recipients will obtain preventive care. Several states have used the savings resulting from managed care enrollment to expand either the number of citizens covered by Medicaid or the number of services covered under their programs, or both (Health Care Financing Administration, [HCFA], 1997a).

Waivers

The federal government currently grants an exception for Medicaid managed care under Section 1915(b) and another under Section 1115. Section 1115 demonstrations allow states to experiment with comprehensive health care reform alternatives in Medicaid benefits, services, eligibility, payments, and care delivery. These programs are usually aimed at viewing health care financing and delivery through a new lens, providing care in new and innovative ways, rather than revising old programs. The aim is to reduce costs so that Medicaid coverage can be extended to additional low-income and uninsured people. Between January 1, 1993, and 1997, comprehensive health care reform demonstration waivers were approved for 17 states, and 9 were implemented. HCFA (1997) estimated that, when all 17 were implemented, more than 2.6 million previously uninsured people would receive health coverage.

TABLE 16-1.

NATIONAL SUMMARY OF MEDICAID MANAGED CARE PROGRAMS AND ENROLLMENT

	Total Medicaid Population	FFS Population	Managed Care Population	% Managed Care Enrollment
1991	28,280,000	25,583,603	2,696,397	9.53
1992	30,926,390	27,291,874	3,634,516	11.75
1993	33,430,051	28,621,100	4,808,951	14.39
1994	33,634,000	25,839,750	7,794,250	23.17
1995	33,373,000*	23,573,000*	9,800,000*	29.37
1996	33,241,147	19,911,028	13,330,119	40.10
1997	32,092,380	16,746,878	15,345,502	47.82

*Indicates approximate numbers.

Source: Managed Care Trends, by the Health Care Finance Administration, 1998. Available: http://www.hcfa.gov/medicaid/trends97.htm

SCHOOL HEALTH CARE PROVIDERS AND SERVICES

The range of health services provided in the schools is much more comprehensive and complex than most MCOs realize. Schools employ and house a vast array of health care providers. At one end of the continuum is the school-based health center resembling an outpatient clinic with a combination of professional and support staff. At the other end are schools where there are neither health personnel nor health offices. The breadth and depth of school health services and their program offerings are controlled at both the state and the community level. Services provided range from preventive and primary care to skilled nursing services for students with disabilities, to emergency first aid, to simply mandatory screenings, to none. The type of health care providers employed strongly influences the types of services offered (Gaffrey & Bergren, 1998). To increase MCOs' understanding of the scope of practice of nurses working in the schools and to become involved in continuing or expanding care in this setting requires considerable patience and perseverance on the part of school nursing representatives (Making the Grade, 1995).

School Nurses—Educational Preparation

Not only do school health providers have the required educational preparation and licensure to provide comprehensive health services, they also provide many of the services covered by managed care. Fryer, Igoe, and Miyoshi (1997) found that the large numbers of nursing screening services performed in the schools cost significantly less when compared to screenings

provided in other settings (p. 18). It is estimated that 40,000 school nurses serve 50,709,000 school-aged children (Beverly Farquhar, personal communication, June 30, 1998). Educational preparation and certification requirements for employment as a school nurse vary across the country. Approximately 50% of the states require school nurses to have a four-year college degree. In a 1996 random survey of NASN membership, 5.9% were nurse practitioners, 12% had associate degrees, 76% had baccalaureate degrees, 23.9% had master's degrees, and 1% had doctoral degrees (Davies & Murray, 1997). (Author's note: The survey from which these data were generated queried respondents regarding all college degrees. Percentage total exceed 100%.)

What care do these professional school nurses provide? School nurses are educated to provide comprehensive health services: assessment, referral, management of injuries and illnesses, monitoring chronic diseases, health counseling, health promotion, disease prevention, and case management (NASN, 1997).

School Health Models and Medicaid Reimbursement

School nurses and SBHC staff are reimbursed by Medicaid for services provided in the schools under one of three different models. The first model outlined by the National Association of State School Nurse Consultants (NASSNC, 1993) lists the following nursing services and procedures: (a) case finding, (b) nursing care procedures, (c) care coordination, (d) patient/student counseling/instruction, and (e) emergency care. Table 16-2 details comprehensive Medicaid reimbursable services provided by school nurses in our nation's schools on a daily basis. State standards or mandates for school services typically address provider credentials, student immunizations, health screenings, health records, HIV infection, and medication administration (Lear, 1996c).

The second model demonstrates an increase in service provision. A nurse practitioner (NP) provides comprehensive primary and preventive care. The NP, supervised by a consulting physician, diagnoses and treats a broad range of health conditions in accordance with treatment protocols. In many states NPs who provide direct primary care, including prescriptive authority, also serve as primary care gatekeepers. In states where NPs were not designated as primary care providers, the granting of a Medicaid waiver for managed care has been a catalyst for expanding NPs' scope of practice (Cohen & Juszczak, 1997).

In the third model, school-based centers, an interdisciplinary team (doctors, nurses, counselors, laboratory and medical assistants, and other health professionals) provide comprehensive services in a clinical setting located at the school site. (See chapter 15.) Student health problems are viewed from the broad perspective of comprehensive primary care with special attention to the new morbidities of accidents, violence, and substance abuse that so impact the health of adolescents.

Classifying Services for Reimbursement

While school nurses who are not nurse practitioners hold appropriate licensure and credentials, and currently provide a wide array of health services, much of the care school nurses provide to children goes unrecognized under current medical payment structures. Many nurses are unfamiliar with either the International Classification of Diseases (ICD-9) or the Current Procedural Terminology (CPT) codes that are the basis for many of the fees physicians receive (Fryer et al., 1997). As the number of medically fragile children increases, so do the number of procedures represented by the CPT codes. However, even though using CPT codes would make it easier to quantify nursing health care in the schools, CPTs do not account for a large percentage of nursing activity. In the future, the use of standardized nursing languages (e.g., NANDA nursing diagnoses) to document school nursing services will make it easier to validate the process and outcomes of care and to compare the delivery of health services in schools to other settings. Nursing Intervention Classification (NIC) is a standardized language that codes nursing activities and facilitates research on the outcomes of those interventions using Nursing Outcomes Classifications (NOC). Research is underway to assure applicability of NIC and NOC to school nursing activities (Lunney, Cavendish, Luise, & Richardson, 1997; Redes & Lunney, 1997).

COLLABORATION BETWEEN MCOs AND SCHOOL DISTRICTS

One of the forces bringing together the worlds of managed care and school-affiliated health care providers is mandatory enrollment of Medicaid recipients into managed care plans. The Medicaid program supports using schools as sites for providing health care to eligible children (HCFA, 1998). With the reconfiguring of service delivery and financing, school nurses and the staff of school-based health centers have increased efforts to secure third-party revenues, especially from Medicaid (Brellochs et al., 1996; NASSNC, 1993). Some states have designated school-based health centers (SBHC) as a source of health care for children and adolescents. In 14 states—Colorado, Connecticut, Delaware, Maryland, Massachusetts, Michigan, Minnesota, Missouri, New York, North Carolina, Oregon, Rhode Island, Vermont, and West Virginia—managed care plans are either required or encouraged to include SBHC in their networks (Kendell, 1998).

Challenges that will be Encountered in this Collaboration

As collaboration between school nursing, other school health services, and MCOs takes place, many challenges will be identified and strategies will have to be developed to insure mutually beneficial partnerships. The first challenge is often to raise the level of awareness in the MCOs of the scope of services presently offered by school health providers (Making the Grade, 1995). School-affiliated health care is often isolated from other health care delivery sites. Operating within the confines of the educational community, school nurses, in some cases, are prevented by school boards and other local authorities from offering important services. Some of the problem lies in the invisible nature of the complex health care provided in the schools. Other than school staff and faculty, very few people are aware of the volume of nursing services provided to students. Unmet basic social and health needs and growing numbers of medically fragile children require skilled nursing care during the school day. Another barrier is the lack of data collection on services, utilization, costs, and outcomes of health care delivered in the schools.

TABLE 16-2.

CATEGORIES OF SCHOOL NURSING SERVICES

The following list of potentially reimbursable school nursing services is not intended to be all inclusive. Documentation and quality assurance mechanisms, while not included on the list, are essential components of all service delivery.

Case finding
1. Nursing assessment of applicants registering for early child development programs.
2. Preschool health appraisals for kindergarten children and periodic assessment of eligible students who have not had a comprehensive health appraisal in the past year (EPSDT).
3. Health appraisal with middle school entrants who have not had a comprehensive health appraisal in the past two years (EPSDT).
4. Health assessment of students referred for special education eligibility evaluation.
5. Case-finding screening activities including health history review, developmental maturation/milestones, vision acuity status, hearing acuity status, speech development, dental deviations, spinal deviations, blood pressure abnormalities, growth and nutritional disorders.
6. Nursing assessment of new or previously identified medical/health problems based on student initiated or teacher/staff referral to nurse, including but not limited to substance use assessment, child abuse assessment, and pregnancy confirmation.
7. Home visit for comprehensive health, developmental and/or environmental assessment.

Nursing care procedures
1. Administration of immunizations to students not in compliance with state immunization law.
2. Medication assessment, monitoring, and/or administration.
3. Nursing assessment and interventions related to the Individualized Health Care Plan.
4. Nursing procedures required for specialized health care, including but not limited to the following:
   - Feeding:
     - Nutritional assessment
     - Naso-gastric feeding
     - Gastrostomy feeding
     - Jejunostomy tube feeding
     - Parental feeding (IV)
     - Naso-gastric tube insertion or removal
     - Gastrostomy tube reinsertion
   - Catheterization:
     - Clean intermittent catheterization
     - Sterile catheterization
   - Ostomies:
     - Ostomy care
     - Ostomy irrigation
   - Respiratory:
     - Postural drainage
     - Percussion
     - Pharyngeal suctioning
     - Tracheostomy suctioning
     - Tracheostomy tube replacement
     - Tracheostomy care
   - Medical support systems:
     - Ventricular peritoneal shunt monitoring
     - Mechanical ventilator monitoring and emergency care
     - Oxygen administration

TABLE 16-2. (CONTINUED)

- • Hickman/Broviac/IVAC/IMED
- • Peritoneal dialysis
- • Apnea monitor
- • Medications:
  - • Administration of medications: oral, injection, inhalation, rectal, bladder instillation, eye/ear drops, topical, intravenous, spirometer
- • Specimen collecting:
  - • Blood glucose
  - • Urine glucose
  - • Pregnancy testing
- • Other nursing procedures:
  - • Dressing, sterile
  - • Soaks
- • Development of protocols:
  - • Health care procedures
  - • Emergency protocols
  - • Health objectives for Individualized Education Program (IEP)
  - • Health objectives for Individualized Health Care Plan (IHCP)
  - • Health Objectives for Individualized Family Service Plan (IFSP)

Care coordination

1. Outreach to identify children who are eligible for Medicaid.
2. Follow-up on referrals made for further evaluation, diagnosis, and treatment.
3. Home visit for follow-up, coordination, or home environment assessment of students with health impairments.
4. Interim prenatal or family planning monitoring visit.
5. Visit for arranging transportation of Medicaid-eligible students to medical, dental, or other authorized appointments.

Student health counseling and instruction

1. Limited nursing assessment, health counseling, instruction and anticipatory guidance for an identified health problem or developmental concern.
2. Extended nursing assessment and/or health counseling, instruction, and anticipatory guidance for identified health problem(s) or concern(s).
3. In-depth nursing assessment and health counseling, instruction, and anticipatory guidance for complex or multiple health problems.

Emergency care

1. Assessment, planning, and intervention for emergency management of a student with chronic or debilitating health impairment.
2. Provision of urgent emergency care, to include nursing assessment and emergency response treatment, i.e., CPR, oxygen administration, seizure care, administration of emergency medication and triage.
3. Post-emergency assessment and development of preventive action plan.

Used with permission. National Association of School Nurse Consultants. (1993). *Position statement: Medicaid Reimbursement for School Nursing Services.* [www document]. http://server.aea14.k12.ia.us/swp/tadkins/nassnc/medicaid.html#MEDICAID.

This contributes to the perception that school health professionals are unable to adequately provide the services required by MCOs (Lear, Gleicher, St. Germaine, & Porter, 1991).

Advantages of These Partnerships for School Districts

The most obvious advantage for school districts is the sustainable source of revenue that partnering with MCOs provides. Revenues generated through these partnerships are able to cover the costs of some school health services. Several states with well-established school health care delivery programs have negotiated contracts with MCOs on a fee-for-service basis or a capitated rate. Schools serve all students who visit the nurse's office, and many of those students are from families enrolled in managed care plans.

Schools without managed care agreements find themselves in the position of providing free care for which someone else, the managed care designated primary care provider, is being paid. Children with chronic illnesses and disabilities are frequent users of school health services. Their MCOs receive capitation for many health services that these students require during the school day but assume no financial responsibility for providing these services. In fact, services that are mandated by IDEA for students with disabilities are mentioned in most managed care contracts, and when they are, it is to exclude them from coverage (*Brave New Partnerships*, 1997). By making alliances with managed care organizations, schools can negotiate coverage for the vast array of health services provided to all students, including those in managed care plans (Lear, 1996c).

When a school district negotiates a contract with an MCO to supply health care for members, reporting mechanisms need to be initiated or altered. Some school systems have no experience with procedures required to submit health insurance claims and collect payments and may be overwhelmed with the administrative burdens imposed. HCFA (1997c) published a *Technical Assistance Guide on Medicaid and School Health* to assist schools in applying for Medicaid reimbursement and interfacing with Medicaid managed care. In some managed care markets there are single or only a few MCOs, but in others there are hundreds of organizations. The labor devoted to communicating with multiple payors and meeting each of their reporting standards can be exhausting (Making the Grade, 1995).

School systems frequently lack the ability to provide data needed to answer managed care organiza-tions' legitimate questions concerning rates of school health utilization and costs. When MCOs negotiate with physicians' groups and community primary care clinics, these extensive data are what provide the basis of capitated payment arrangements. Lacking these data, school-based staff may be at a disadvantage when negotiating contracts for managed care enrollees. If data cannot be provided regarding the amount and intensity of services provided, MCOs have only their own data to estimate the costs of care. When school systems have provided utilization data, their rates of utilization far exceeded the rates provided for children, especially adolescents, in the community (Kaplan, Calonge, Guernsey, & Hanrahan, 1998; Lear et al., 1991). Therefore, without their own data, when trying to contract with MCOs, school health providers cannot substantiate their higher rates of utilization and may agree to a contract that does not cover the true costs of care (Making the Grade, 1995).

When school providers of health care are able to demonstrate that the services they provide to students can reduce health care costs or improve health outcomes, these services are more likely to be included in a contract between schools and MCOs. The negotiations will center on the differences in cost of services provided in a primary care clinic when compared to a school setting. It is unlikely that managed care contracts will ever cover the total costs of school health care, regardless of how extensively Medicaid coverage is expanded. There will always be students without insurance. Mental health services are a major component of school health services and frequently are excluded from, or limited in, managed care plans.

There always has been a public health focus in school nursing which is not currently the focus or responsibility of MCOs. School nursing leaders express concern that changes reducing the importance of preventive interventions will be made to the community-driven, social model of school health services in order to secure a place within the current reimbursement system (Making the Grade, 1995). If managed care monies play an increasingly dominant role in school health funding, the needs of the managed care community and the needs and priorities of the school and public health community will have to be a mutually beneficial fit. Despite obstacles, if there is no partnership with managed care, schools will lose opportunities for revenue and may also end up duplicating services for managed care enrollees.

Advantages of These Partnerships for MCOs

Just as schools can establish a revenue stream and improve standard data collection procedures through a managed health care partnership, MCOs can benefit from creating alliances with schools. They may increase revenues by marketing school-based services as a benefit for families with school-age children. The ease and convenience of accessing health care at the school site can attract new enrollees to MCOs that have school district partnership agreements. In fact, the location and convenience of health care at schools is identified as the key reason MCOs consider these partnering arrangements (Making the Grade, 1995). Access to physicians, emergent care, immunizations, health teaching, and monitoring of chronic health conditions at school is an attractive marketing tool.

Igoe and Giordano (1992) further propose the school as a site for family-focused health care. The ease of access to the school makes it an ideal place for health care delivery for entire families, not just children.

As for uninsured children, it is estimated that as many as 25% of children eligible for Medicaid are not enrolled (Making the Grade, 1995). Enrolling these eligible children helps MCOs to increase market share and revenues while providing needy, high-risk children access to health care.

School nurses and SBHC staff can assist MCOs to meet their contractual obligations for school-age groups. One of the evaluation criteria most often used in managed care settings is access to care. School nurses may hold an exemplary record that surpasses primary care clinics in the community in accessibility and utilization of services (Kaplan et al., 1998; Lear, 1996b; Lear et al., 1991). In remote, sparsely settled rural regions, long waiting times for appointments and substantial travel distances discourage families from accessing preventive services (Fryer et al., 1997). By placing health services in consolidated schools, MCOs can efficiently meet their contractual obligations to school-age and adolescent Medicaid beneficiaries in rural areas. With this Medicaid managed care-school health services link, rural states are able to provide more comprehensive health care to previously underserved groups.

Another Medicaid contracted service that school nurses and SBHC staff often can provide more effectively for MCOs than other community primary care providers is Early Prevention Screening, Diagnosis and Treatment (EPSDT). Some of the first Section 1115 waivers allowed schools and day care centers to be sites for EPSDT screening (Cohen & Juszczak, 1997). This mandated federal program has two purposes: to facilitate health care for Medicaid children who are under-served, and, to detect and correct health problems before they lead to serious and costly disabling conditions. EPSDT services include a comprehensive assessment of a child's health status through physical examination, health and developmental history, screening tests and assessments for developmental, dental, vision, hearing, nutritional, and other health concerns, and immunizations. Although it is possible to provide these services in a physician's office, it is more cost effective and efficient to perform these screenings for large groups of children in a child-friendly setting with professionals who have specialized expertise in the needs of this age groups. It has been noted that school-based EPSDT programs meet quality standards better than primary care physicians. One SBHC Neighborhood Health Plan in Boston boasts a 95% compliance rate for EPSDT (Making the Grade, 1995).

Nurses in schools are well qualified and experienced in providing case management for the school-age population. The American Nurses Association (ANA, 1988) defines case management as the comprehensive and systematic approach to providing quality community-based health care. It consists of providing this care along a developmental continuum, decreasing fragmentation of services, enhancing quality of care, and containing costs. NASN, in its 1997 position statement, confirms that being a case manager is intrinsic to the school nursing function. Case management is operationalized in a variety of ways, including that of community liaison, interpreter to school personnel, direct care provider, student advocate, and educator to students, families, and school personnel. NASN identifies five specific skills that school nurses bring to case management: knowledge of available services; experience in collaboration of service plans; skills to assure continuity of service; the ability to assist students and families to understand, select, and obtain services; and the expertise to evaluate outcomes (p. 1).

MCOs that offer case management in the child's everyday environment exert more control and coordination than at a community primary care site. The child and the school nurse occupy the same institution up to five days a week, 10 months of the year. School health care providers, as part of the school community, are well versed in community social and health-supporting agencies and resources. The ability to collect lifestyle information, assess health habits, and monitor compliance with care regimens is optimal. A community health center which sees a child or adolescent as infrequently as three to four times per year cannot compete with the advantages of case management by school-based health personnel.

The advantage of a school-based case manager becomes even more pronounced for students with multiple needs or chronic illness. Parents frequently complain that too many practitioners simultaneously act as their child's case manager. Each sphere of a chronically ill child's world — the medical, the human services, and the educational — manages the care within its own system but often does not coordinate or share information with each other (*Brave New Partnerships*, 1997). The school nurse, within a managed care contract, is ideal to undertake this role of coordinating services among these systems.

With the school nurses a legitimate and fully informed partner in both the managed care and educational system, the coordination with human services agencies would be simplified. Since most physicians manage only a very small number of children with disabilities and chronic illness, they have likely had less opportunity to develop ongoing relationships with community agencies. Schools already have relationships with these agencies and can advocate and communicate efficiently for groups of students with similar needs (Gaffrey & Bergren, 1998).

Some MCOs have little experience with the varied ethnic groups who occupy their service area. Since schools are an integral part of the community they serve, they may be more culturally competent to provide both outreach and health care to minority families. Cultural competence is the ability to provide services and information in appropriate languages and at appropriate education and literacy levels within the context of cultural health beliefs and practices (Jazo-Bajet, 1997). Utilization data supports the ability of school health programs to serve ethnically diverse populations (Lear et al., 1991). Schools can help MCOs navigate the cultural barriers which exacerbate access problems (Taras, 1997).

Research has validated that preventative services for children are cost effective in improving health, but these services are underused (Erkel, 1994). School nurses provide MCOs an opportunity to increase health promotion and prevention efforts among school-aged children and adolescents. Students in both the pre-teen and the teen years are more vulnerable to making poor behavior and health choices that cause morbidity, such as smoking, early and unprotected sexual activity, and substance abuse. Promotion of life-long health habits can improve a client's health status and reduce costs for health systems. Health promotion is the process of enabling a person to increase control over determinants of health, thereby improving health (Nutbeam, 1997). Health promotion is a process, not a single intervention

class or program. On a daily basis, nurses in schools coordinate activities to promote health through wellness and health prevention strategies. The school setting affords MCOs an opportunity to work with school nurses to deliver health education and prevention programs that will greatly impact health behaviors and long-term outcomes.

Although more empirical evidence of the cost advantages of providing care in school settings is needed, schools are able to demonstrate that they can provide savings for MCOs. Transportation costs for needed services during the school day are avoided by on-site services. When school health providers assume the role of case managers, they directly refer students for needed follow up, avoiding duplication of the school's services at a primary physician's or specialist's office.

The more complicated the student's needs, the more case management can help avoid duplications of services as well as gaps in the services provided. A study conducted at a child health clinic serving children from low-income families showed that when a nurse provided both case management and direct services, the adequacy of care was significantly better and 20% less expensive (Erkel, 1994). This cost represents only screenings, just a small portion of the benefits provided within school health programs. Studies that estimate the cost of school health services in the public sector suggest that school clinic services are a good investment (Dryfoos, Brindis, & Kaplan, 1996). More data are needed to isolate differences between costs of providing school-based child health care and providing such care in other health care settings.

Disadvantages of These Partnerships for MCOs

The provision of care in schools has many benefits for MCOs; however, there are some disadvantages. Foremost is concern about losses. Since much of the care that is provided in the schools is not reimbursable, MCOs are concerned with losing some control over the care that they finance. Managed care has been successful in keeping costs controlled, assuring quality and, by assigning one primary care provider, limiting member choices. Most school health programs, including SBHCs, are unable to supply complete primary care services that are required of MCOs when they negotiate with physician groups. Schools usually lack laboratory and x-ray capabilities. With rare exceptions, schools provide services only 10 months of the year; therefore, enrollees need to be assigned a primary health care provider with the schools designated as a secondary source of care (Making the Grade, 1995). Many managed care organizations do not feel the advantages of providing care in the schools outweigh the negatives of having two providers for this group of enrollees.

MCOs are also concerned that, although they are not presently meeting the needs of adolescents for health care, they are hesitant to increase the expenditures and utilization without the promise of concurrent decreases in illness or improvements in behavior and health. The "Woodwork Phenomenon" was seen in long-term care. When you make services convenient and accessible, costs are driven up by people "coming out of the woodwork" to take advantage of them (Making the Grade, 1995).

Partnerships and Contracts

Before schools and managed care organizations can partner, they must learn to negotiate mutually beneficial contracts. Most school districts are uncomfortable negotiating these contracts due to their inexperience in the managed care arena. Many districts hire consultants to assist with all aspects of preparation, service costs, and contract scope and language. Part II of this chapter provides specific information relative to structuring partnerships and contracts.

QUALITY ASSURANCE—QUALITY IMPROVEMENT (QAI) IN SCHOOL HEALTH

In marketing their product, MCOs assure employers and enrollees of a high standard of quality care through accreditation by the National Committee on Quality Assurance (NCQA). The NCQA is an independent, nonprofit accrediting organization composed of health care quality experts, labor union officials, and consumer representatives. NCQA accreditation is designed specifically for managed care models and is mandated by law in some states. The standards that must be met for accreditation address quality improvement, provider credentialing, members' rights and responsibilities, utilization management, preventive health services, and medical records (Gaffrey, 1997).

Accountability

An additional advantage of partnerships between schools and MCOs is the ability to have school nursing and SBHC services measured and evaluated using standards acceptable in the larger health care community. Providers who contract with managed care are accountable for maintaining quality services and documenting quality improvement activities. School nurses and SBHC staff have, with few exceptions, focused intently on providing care, health education, and counseling without measuring the short- and long-term health,

education, and behavior outcomes for clients. In many circumstances, school health professionals neither document the amount of care they provide nor the results of that care. When statistics are kept, they may be limited to immunization rates required by the states and billable services. In a managed care climate, nursing services that prevent illness, promote healthy life styles, and address social behavior problems that lead to disease have value that did not exist in a fee-for-service environment. This focus gives school nurses a chance to showcase the very services that are ideally provided in school settings. The accountability required in the managed care environment will reward school health advocates with the empirical data needed for the expansion of school-affiliated health programs and services.

Assuring Quality

How, then, can school nurses and SBHC staff provide a school health program with an "assured standard of care"? Quality of care has been defined as "health care that effectively betters the health status and satisfaction of the population, within the resources that society and individuals have chosen to spend for that care" (Institute of Medicine, 1974, p. 1). A quality assurance program should evaluate the organization's overall performance in relation to this definition. The program should also quantify the determinants of quality care in a manner that will allow changes to be made to effect improvements in care (Joint Commission on Accreditation of Health Care Organizations [JCAHCO], 1988). The ultimate objective of quality assurance is to improve the health status of the client.

Structured Monitoring System

Control of quality requires clear, reliable measures and an information system that measures quality over time and identifies factors that account for variations in quality (Berwich, 1987). Thus, the ultimate mission of quality assurance is to enable the management of quality. But we will not be able to manage quality until we are able to measure it. To do this, a systematic approach to monitoring is needed. A rational, structured monitoring system is the foundation for an effective quality assurance program (Benson, 1990).

In creating a quality assurance program for school health services, it is necessary to look beyond the school walls to the larger health care community. It is there that we see the components of a valid quality assurance program, which are the elements of structure, process, and outcome for the patient (client), the provider, and the system (Kellett, 1996). A QAI program cannot be a narrow data-gathering activity. It must incorporate the philosophy of quality care and provide a meaningful approach to thinking and acting that can be built into the everyday work style of school nurses and SBHC staff.

With the QAI data produced, it is possible to monitor, evaluate, and ascertain the level of quality of a school health program; to identify deficiencies in medical and nursing procedures and services; and to provide a method to address improvements through changes in policy and procedures, along with planned specific in-service programs.

The role of the school nurse and components of the school health program are continuing to expand to accommodate the multiple needs of a more diverse client population, yet fewer than half of the states require specialized education for the practice of nursing in the schools. A combination of national and state standards of practice and education would provide part of the basis for measuring the effectiveness of a comprehensive school nursing program (Commission on Teacher Credentialing [CTC], 1994; Proctor, 1993; ANA, 1998, NASN, 1998).

We can see, then, how critically important it is to any school health program, especially as partnerships are developed with MCOs, to establish standards and protocols for nursing practice and to clearly define and consistently apply them at all practice locations. There is a need for a tool that can consistently gather data and monitor and improve the program. Such a tool should do the following:

1. Focus on issues that impact client health;

2. Require that clinically valid standards and goals be identified prior to beginning quality assurance activity;

3. Be a structured and comprehensive system;

4. Be based on a system, such as the Health Plan Employer Data Information Set (HEDIS) that standardizes and reports national outcomes data; and

5. Be accepted by national accrediting bodies: Joint Commission on Accreditation on Healthcare Organizations (JCAHO) and the National Committee on Quality Assurance (NCQA).

Our goal remains to provide health care that improves the health of our clients within limits set by the resources available to us. Standards of practice will be consistently applied, nursing care will be monitored, and corrective actions will be designed and implemented.

SUMMARY

The inevitable merging of the world of managed care with school nursing and other school health services will allow both entities to benefit from the resulting collaboration. The inclusion of school nurses in the continuum of health care delivery promotes effective, timely, accessible, cost-efficient services for children. Children's health status will benefit when school nursing services are the focus of cooperative agreements between school districts and MCOs. In preparation for this partnership, school health staff must begin the credentialing, data gathering, and quality improvement activities required prior to entering negotiations with MCOs. Managed care offers an outstanding opportunity to bring to prominence the role of the school nurse and to increase school-based health services. School nurses and allied health professionals provide many of the primary and preventive care services MCOs are obligated to supply, and they do so in a very cost-effective manner. Schools must market their services to MCOs and verify that they can provide the outcomes valued by that system. The success of a partnership between school health and managed care can result in improved access to health care for millions of underserved school-age children, greater attention to preventative services, and the optimal setting for health promotion activities that can lead to improved health for all our nation's children.

Part 2: Partnerships and Contracts
Wanda R. Miller

The material in this part is adapted with permission of the National Association of School Nurses from: Miller, W.R. (1997, September). *Structuring Partnerships Fostering Positive Relationships.* School Health and Managed Care Symposium, Washington, D.C.

INTRODUCTION

Before schools and managed care organizations can partner, they must learn to negotiate mutually beneficial contracts. Given an interest in allocating health resources as effectively and ethically as possible, managed care organizations and school district providers have far more to gain through collaboration than separation. There is simply no rational argument that justifies not using nurses as primary care providers in a retooled and revised health care system (Fagin, 1990; Porter-O'Grady, 1994). The retooled system must be a partnership among managed care organizations, school districts, health care professionals, and school nurses.

An informal agreement, a memorandum of understanding, or a contract is the framework that allows two parties to know the goals and objectives of the other party and to develop common objectives to achieve mutually beneficial goals. A well-written contract can foster a positive relationship between a managed care organization and a school district. The process of negotiation allows potential partners to articulate the rights and responsibilities of the parties.

The purpose of negotiation is not to "win," but to establish a viable framework for future relationships. All partners must be able to operate within the terms agreed upon by the parties. They cannot feel taken advantage of because of inexperience, misrepresentation, or intimidation. An important success factor in negotiating an agreement is understanding the positions and motivations of the other party. Any lack of clarity in the document increases substantially the risk of misunderstanding and the likelihood of disagreements.

Before beginning negotiations, each party must establish within its own organization the issues to be negotiated, the party's desired position on each issue, the minimum position at which the party will enter into a contract, and the extent to which the party will compromise on an issue. In determining a position on the issue, the organization should identify the components of the contract that are essential or highly desirable.

ORGANIZATIONAL STRUCTURE OF THE CONTRACT

Once the priority of the components is established, the parties' organization must strive for clear language to ensure that the essential issues are addressed. A major factor contributing to the clarity of an agreement is the organizational structure of the contract.

This organizational structure of the contract and examples of contract language are presented as initial information to consider internally in developing the organization's position on key components before the school district's or managed care organization's attorney develops a contract. Mark S. Joffe, in *The Managed Health Care Handbook*, recommends the following contract categories: Common Clauses, Provisions, and Key Factors; Provider Obligations; Nondiscriminatory Requirements; Compliance with Utilization Review Standards and Protocols and the Quality Assurance Program; Enrollee Complaints; Maintenance and Retention of Records and Confidentiality; Payment; Use of Name; Relationship of the Parties; Notification; Hold-Harmless and No Balance Billing Clause; Insurance and Indemnification; Term, Suspension, and Termination; Declarations; Closing; and Acceptance of Enrollee Patients (Joffe, 1996). These categories, except for the last one, are relevant to school districts and are discussed below.

Common Clauses, Provisions, and Key Factors

In the Common Clauses section of the contract, the initial paragraph of an agreement identifies the legal name of the managed care organization and school district as the parties entering into the agreement. A shorter name to be used throughout the agreement to designate each party, is then assigned. The legal authority for school districts is usually vested in the Board of Education. Occasionally the Board may designate authority to approve contracts to the Superintendent of Schools.

Following the initial paragraph is a series of statements, frequently entitled Recitals, describing the parties and what they are trying to accomplish. This section declares the agreed upon statements, commonly begun as "Whereas" statements and what is hoped to be accomplished commonly as a "Therefore" statement.

These statements will help to clarify commonalties and goals of the parties. For example in the case of a partnership between a school and a managed care organization the whereas statements might include the following: "We all want children to have access to health care, the quality of their care to be excellent, and the health care programs to be efficient." Schools can provide quality health care in the most cost-effective manner.

The definition section of the contract usually follows and plays an important role in simplifying the contract and in assisting the reader in understanding the contract. Terms that may appear in this section of the contract are words and phrases that have exclusive meaning to the nursing and managed care professions, including the following: advanced practice nurse practitioner, capitation, cost containment, covered services, emergency care, health maintenance organization (HMO), member or enrollee, medical director, primary care provider, quality assurance, and quality of care (HCFA, 1997b; Kelly, Bacon, & Mitchell, 1994). (See Glossary on page 605.)

Provider Obligations

The main purpose of the Provider Obligations section of the contact is to establish the scope of services to be provided. The National Association of State School Nurse Consultants defined the services that are reimbursable by Medicaid in a position statement on *Medicaid Reimbursement for School Nursing Services*. The services include case finding, nursing care procedures, care coordination, student health counseling and instruction, and emergency care (NASSNC, 1993).

- **Case Finding** includes comprehensive health assessments based on the Early and Periodic Screening, Diagnosis, and Treatment(EPSDT) guidelines, nursing assessment of new or previously identified health problems, and comprehensive health, developmental, and environmental assessment of the home environment.

- **Nursing Care Procedures** include administration of immunization and tuberculin testing; assessment, monitoring, and administration of medication; assessment, development, and interventions related to the development of Individual Health Care Plans; and a broad spectrum of skilled nursing procedures provided to students with special needs, such as, feedings through naso-gastric and ostomy tubes; respiratory care, such as, tracheal suctioning, catheterization, medical support systems, medications, specimen collecting, and development of protocols.

- **Care Coordination** includes case management, outreach, follow-up, reevaluation, and referral services.

- **Health Counseling and Instruction** includes nursing assessment, health counseling, instruction, and anticipatory guidance for identified health problem(s) or concerns(s).

- **Emergency Care** includes the assessment and management of children with chronic or debilitating health impairments, provision of urgent emergency care, and development of preventive action plan.

The scope of services may be placed in an attachment or in the body of the contract. Placing services in an attachment enhances the ease of revising specific parts of the service component at a later time without revising the whole contract.

The contract also specifies to whom the school provider is obligated to provide services by defining what is meant by a member or covered enrollee. This should include how the school provider will learn who the member is and should identify who is responsible for the cost of care received by those who are not covered by the plan.

Other services covered include the school provider's responsibilities to refer or to accept referrals of enrollees, the days and times of day the provider agrees to be available to provide services, and the provision of qualified substitute midlevel care providers.

Nondiscriminatory Requirements

The main purpose of the Nondiscriminatory Requirements section is to ensure equitable treatment of members. Provider agreements frequently contain clauses obligating the provider to furnish services to the health care enrollees in the same manner as the provider furnishes services to non-managed health care recipients. Public school districts that receive federal funding require the use of specific contract language to reflect the equal employment opportunities ensured by the Civil Rights Act of 1964, the nondiscriminatory requirements of the Americans with Disabilities Act, 42 U.S.C. Section 12101-12213, and Section 504 of the Rehabilitation Act of 1973, 29 U.S.C., Section 749.

Compliance with Utilization Review Standards and Protocols and the Quality Assurance Program

The main purpose of the Compliance with Utilization Review Standards section is to ensure support for the managed health organization's utilization review. The contract needs to set out the provider's responsibilities in carrying out the managed health care plan's utilization review program. In addition, it is important to ensure that the contract allows amendment of the utilization review standards in the future to comply with federal requirements without the consent of the provider.

The current Health Care Financing Administration (HCFA) guideline for provider contracts requires that the provider cooperate with and participate in the managed health care plan's quality assurance program, member grievance system, and utilization review program (Joffe, 1996).

Enrollee Complaints

The purpose of the Enrollee Complaints section of the contract is to provide a system for addressing member complaints. The contract should require the provider to cooperate in resolving enrollee complaints and to notify the managed health care plan within a specified period of time when any complaints are conveyed to the provider.

Maintenance and Retention of Records and Confidentiality

The purpose of the Maintenance and Retention of Records and Confidentiality section of the contract is to provide a data management system for health and business records. The contract should require the school provider to maintain both medical and business records for specified periods of time. The managed care organization also needs a legal right to have access to books and records. The school provider needs the availability of this information to be limited to services rendered to enrollees, after reasonable notice, and during normal business hours. The cost for performing these services should be identified. Finally, the school provider should be obligated to provide information that is necessary for compliance with state or federal law.

This section also addresses the confidentiality of the members' health records. Some state laws give insurers and managed health care plans a limited right of access to medical records. Managed health care plans should review their state law provisions on this issue and their procedures for obtaining the appropriate consent of their members to allow for sharing of this information. School district providers should review the federal law, the Family Educational Rights and Privacy Act (FERPA), to determine the procedures necessary to

authorize release of information. Release of information is crucial to the sharing of pertinent medical information among the partners. Consent for release of information may be obtained as part of the initial enrollment materials or at the time health services are rendered. Consult state and federal laws regarding privacy of school health records before including provisions in the contract allowing the managed care organization (MCO) a right of access to enrollee records. Many state laws restrict the release of health information more stringently than federal laws. (See chapters 8, 9, and 10.)

Payment

The purpose of the Payment section of the contract is to establish a reimbursement structure for the services provided. The concepts of price, risk, and utilization must be considered in determining this structure.

Price and utilization are intertwined in the economic structure of managed care organizations. To develop an effective contract, school districts must begin to understand the importance of this relationship. The two basic service compensation rate plans approach this concept very differently.

Capitation is a prepaid plan for services provided to members at a fixed rate per member per month. The cash flow in the capitation plan is consistent and allows for a predictable rate of income. However, capitation may place the school provider at risk for assuming a broader expanse of medical expenses based on the complexity, extent, and variety of services needed by students. In open-paneled managed care organizations approximately 60 percent of the plans use a capitation rate for payment (Gold, 1995).

Fee-for-service (FFS) is a reimbursement plan for a specific service provided to members based on a predetermined rate-per-service or rate-per-unit of service provided. The cash flow in fee-for-service is inconsistent and dependent on the volume of service provided. Recovery of costs is also dependent on the efficiency of the school provider's accounting system. Immunizations and EPSDT examinations are good examples of services that may be targeted for fee-for-service reimbursements. Both of these services follow a universally-adhered-to standard of practice and periodicity for utilization. Without a specific periodicity for service, the risk of over-utilization of services exists in a FFS compensation plan. It is the over-utilization of services that MCOs believe drive up the cost of health care.

Carve-outs are funds reserved by the state funding agency to pay for services to special groups of individuals. They are common in states where managed care agencies are responsible for the health care of Medicaid-eligible individuals. They are usually used for populations that are hard to serve or to groups with special needs. These services may previously have been paid as a bundled fee by state human service agencies. Related health services for students who are eligible for special education are services that states are increasingly reimbursing through carved-out funds.

Risk sharing and the cost of risk sharing can be the most difficult to understand in a contract. A broad range of risk sharing responsibilities is possible for providers who include specialty medical and hospital services. MCOs may want to establish risk pools with school district providers by collecting a percent of the capitation or fee-for-service rate to pay for high-cost conditions. School district providers will need to limit their risks by providing only those services that they directly manage or control (Spencer, 1996). Given the limited type of primary health care services provided in a community based, school based, or school district based health service, retention of a percent of payment for a risk pool is probably not necessary. If a risk pool is established in the contract, an incentive clause that provides for reimbursement to the school district for non-use of these funds may be appropriate.

Putting the issue of risk aside, and turning to pricing, there is a growing trend for provider payments to be established at a percentage of the usual and customary service rate. Careful analysis of the cost to the school provider for performing the service must take place prior to the negotiation process to establish reimbursement rates at the actual cost for health care. School districts can not afford to channel educational dollars into health care needs at this time.

Consider fees based on a case mix index in a capitation rate contract and fees based on a percentage of the medical assistance rate in a fee-for-service contract. Most districts will need to contract with more than one managed care organization to provide coverage for all students who need care. Determining that the capitation rate or a FFS rate is the best choice is one of the priorities of the district and establishing one system in the contracts will save the accountants hours of administrative time.

Pricing methodologies may assist school providers to analyze their costs. A common methodology for determining usual, customary, or reasonable service costs is to collect data for charges by current procedural terminology, such as the Current Procedural Terminology (CPT) codes and determine your actual cost for each specific procedure (Kongstvedt, 1996). Another

methodology is an extension of the first and uses a relative value scale where each procedure, defined in CPT has a relative value attributed to it. A resource-based relative value scale (RBRVS) has been produced by the Health Care Financing Administration(HCFA) for Medicaid. Once the procedural cost or the unit cost has been determined, the following steps may be of assistance in establishing a rate (Schroeder, Atkinson, & Armstrong, 1992):

- identify the service unit,
- project cost data on the unit,
- identify total financial requirements,
- project total volume,
- set charges,
- project total gross student revenue and revenue by plan,
- develop data management tracking systems for service,
- determine total return,
- evaluate the results in light of the districts goals, and revise pricing mechanism, price, or service utilization periodically.

Once the rates have been established, the payment schedule should also address who will collect and receive co-payments, and the timeline for submission and reimbursement of claims. If the school district is going to be reimbursed on a fee-for-service basis, a provision needs to delineate who has the responsibility to pay for unauthorized services. The managed care agency needs to have a clear understanding of what is necessary for a service to be authorized. The agreement should establish a reasonable timeline for the provider to submit claims and for the managed care agency to pay claims.

The payment schedule is usually placed in the addendum and referred to in the body of the contract. This allows for the revision of a payment schedule on a periodic basis without requiring a complete review of the contract.

Use of Name

The purpose of the Use of Name section is to restrict the use of the managed care organization and the school district's name and logo from use by another party.

Relationship of the Parties

The purpose of the Relationship of the Parties section is to separate the provider from the management organization to prevent an interpretation of the provider as an employee. The contract should state clearly that the managed care organization and the provider have an independent contractual agreement.

Notification

The purpose of the Notification section is to allow the providers to inform the managed care organization of changes in their ability to fulfill the contract.

Hold-Harmless and No Balance Billing Clauses

The purpose of the Hold-Harmless Clause section of the contract is to establish the protection of each of the parties from an assertion of claims, demands or expenses for any act or cause provided for or alleged against the other party.

Insurance and Indemnification

The purpose of the Insurance and Indemnification section of the contract is to ensure that both parties maintain professional and general liability coverage. The contract should require each party to maintain liability insurance.

Term, Suspension, and Termination

The purpose of the Term, Suspension, and Termination section of the contract is to ensure a term of the contract and the process for termination of the contract. The term of the contract and the term of renewal of the contract should be defined. Some contracts have automatic renew clauses unless one of the parties seeks to terminate. Termination may be defined as termination with or without cause. Termination without cause usually has a 90-day period of notification. School providers that employ staff on a school year contract may wish to restrict termination periods to the end of the school year with a 90-day notification. Termination with cause may need to occur more quickly. Commonly a 30-day notification is provided. The contract language should provide for the orderly exchange of the enrollee's care in the event of termination.

Declarations

The Declarations section allows for unusual occurrences. There should be a clause to relieve a party of responsibility in the event of an occurrence beyond the party's control.

An amendment clause is needed also to clarify how the contract will be amended.

Closing

Finally, the Closing section of the contract identifies the parties in the Common Clause section confirmed as the parties signing the contract.

Strategy Tips

The school nurse in today's health care environment needs to remember that political and social vigilance is necessary (Porter-O'Grady, 1994):

1. Evaluate the attitude of the managed care organization and cultivate a relationship with its officials. In reviewing the contract, keep in mind the objectives of the managed care organization and the school district in determining what are the negotiable and non-negotiable areas of the contract.

2. Work diligently at clarifying ambiguous language. Any lack of clarity in the document increases substantially the risk of misunderstanding and the likelihood of disagreements.

3. Do not expect the MCO to change the principles of the contract after the school district has signed the contract.

REFERENCES

American Nurses Association. (1988). *Nursing case management.* Kansas City, MO: Author.

American Nurses Association (1991). *Nursing's agenda for health care reform.* Washington, DC: Author.

American Nurses Association. (1995). *Nursing facts from the American Nurses Association: Managed care: Challenges and opportunities for nursing.* Washington, DC: Author.

American Nurses Association. (1998). *Standards of clinical nursing practice.* Washington, DC: American Nurses Publishing.

Annie E. Casey Foundation. (1997). *Kids count.* Baltimore: Author.

Benson, D. (1990, March/April). System measures ambulatory care quality. *Physician Executive,* 15–20.

Berwich, D. M. (1987). Monitoring quality in HMOs. *Business Health,* 5(1), 9–12.

Brave new partnerships: Children with disabilities, families, and managed care. (1997). Minneapolis: Center for Children with Chronic Illness and Disability, University of Minnesota.

Brellochs, C., Zimmerman, D., et al. (1996). School-based primary care in a managed care environment:

Options and Issues. *Adolescent Medicine: State of the Art Reviews, 7*, 197–206.

Cohen, S. S., & Juszczak, L. (1997). Promoting the nurse practitioner role in managed care. *Journal of Pediatric Health Care, 11*, 3–11.

Commission on Teacher Credentialing (CTC). (1994). *Standards for professional school nurse preparation in California.* Sacramento: Author.

Davies, L. A., & Murray, M. B. (1997). *Results of the 1996 survey of the National Association of School Nurses.* Rahway, NJ: Merck.

Dryfoos, J. G., Brindis, C., & Kaplan, D. W. (1996). Research and evaluation in school-based health care. *Adolescent Medicine: State of the Art Reviews, 7,* 207–220.

Erkel, E. A. (1994). Case management and preventive services among infants from low income families. *Public Health Nursing, 11,* 352–360.

Fagin, C. (1990). Nursing's value proves itself. *American Journal of Nursing, 90*(10), 17–30.

Fryer, G. E., Igoe, J. B., & Miyoshi, T. J. (1997). Considering school health screening programs as a cost offset: A comparison of existing reimbursements in one state. *Journal of School Nursing, 13*(2), 18–21.

Gaffrey, E. A. (1997, September). *Quality assurance/quality improvement in school health.* Paper presented at Symposium: School health and managed care: A unique partnership for child health, Alexandria, VA.

Gaffrey, E. A., & Bergren, M. D. (1998). School health services and managed care: A unique partnership for child health. *Journal of School Nursing, 14*(4), 5–22.

Gold, M. et al. (1995). *Arrangements between managed care plans and physicians: Results from a 1994 survey of managed care plans.* Washington, DC: Physician Payment Review Commission.

Health Care Financing Administration. (1997a). *Managed care in Medicare and Medicaid* [On-line]. Available: http://www.hcfa.gov/facts/f960900.htm

Health Care Financing Administration. (1997b). *Medicaid managed care enrollment report glossary* [On-line]. Available: http://www.hcfa.gov/medicaid/trends/97.htm

Health Care Financing Administration. (1997c). *Medicaid and school health: Technical assistance guide on Medicaid and school health* [On-line]. Available: http://www.hcfa.gov/medicaid/scbintro.htm

Health Care Financing Administration. (1998). *Managed care trends* [On-line]. Available: http://www.hcfa.gov/medicaid/trends/97.htm

Igoe, J. B., & Giordano, B. P. (1992). *Expanding school health services to serve families in the 21st century.* Washington, DC: American Nurses Publishing.

Institute of Medicine. (1974). *Advancing the quality of health care: Key issues and fundamental principles. Policy statement.* Washington, DC: Committee of the Institute of Medicine, National Academy of Science.

Jazo-Bajet, M. (1997). *Cultural and linguistic competency.* San Diego, CA: Community Health Group.

Joint Commission on Accreditation of Health Care Organizations. (1988). *Ambulatory health care standards manual.* Chicago: Author.

Joffe, M. S. (1996). Legal issues in provider contracting. In P. R. Kongsvedt (Ed.), *The managed health care handbook* (3rd ed.) (pp. 849–887). Gaithersberg, MD: Aspen Publishers, Inc.

Kaplan, D. W., Calonge, N., Guernsey, B. P., & Hanrahan, M. B. (1998). Managed care and school based health centers. Use of health services. *Archives of Pediatric and Adolescent Medicine, 152,* 25–33.

Kellett, A. (1996). *Reports of the task force on standards and regulation of managed care.* Kansas City, MO: American Nurses Association, Congress of Nursing Practice.

Kelly, M. P., Bacon, G. T., & Mitchell, J. A. (1994). Glossary of managed care terms. *Journal of Ambulatory Care Management, 17*(1), 70–76.

Kendell, N. (1998, February). *Managed care legislation.* National School-Based Health Center Forum [On-line]. (Web site address unavailable).

Kongsvedt, P. R. (1996). Compensation of primary care physicians in open panel plans. In P. R. Kongsvedt (Ed.), *The managed health care handbook* (3rd ed.) (pp. 120–146). Gaithersberg, MD: Aspen Publishers, Inc.

Lear, J. G. (1996a). Key issues affecting school-based health centers and Medicaid. *JOSH, 66*(3), 83–88.

Lear, J. G. (1996b). Health care goes to school: An untidy strategy to improve the well-being of school-age children. In I. G. Garfinckel, J. L. Hochchild, & S. S. McLanahan (Eds.), *Social policies for children.* Washington, DC: Brookings Institute.

Lear, J. G. (1996c). School based services and adolescent health: Past, present, and future. *Adolescent Medicine: State of the Art Reviews, 7,* 163–180.

Lear, J. G., Gleicher, H. B., St. Germaine, A., & Porter, P. J. (1991). Reorganizing health care for adolescents: The experience of the school based adolescent health care program. *Journal of Adolescent Health, 12,* 450–458.

Lunney, M., Cavendish, R., Luise, B. K., & Richardson, K. (1997). Relevance of NANDA and health promotion diagnoses to school nursing. *Journal of School Nursing, 13*(5), 16–22.

Making the Grade. (1995). *Medicaid, managed care and school-based health centers: Proceedings from a meeting of policymakers and providers.* Washington, DC: Author.

McGinnis, J. M., & DeGraw, C. (1991). Healthy schools 2000: Creating partnerships for the decade. *Journal of School Health, 61*(7), 292–297.

National Association of School Nurses. (1997). *NASN BOD summary: 1997.* Scarborough, ME: Author.

National Association of School Nurses. (1998). *Standards of professional school nursing practice.* Scarborough, ME: Author.

National Association of State School Nurse Consultants. *Position statement: Medicaid reimbursement for school nursing services.* [www document]. Available: http://ipserv2.aea14.k12.ia.us/swp/tadkins/nassnc/NASSNC.Medicaid.htmlMEDICAID[1993]

Nutbeam, D. (1997). Promoting and preventing disease: An international perspective on youth health promotion. *Journal of Adolescent Health Care, 20,* 396–403.

Porter-O'Grady, T. (1994). Building partnerships. *Nursing and Health Care, 15*(1), 34–38.

Proctor, S. T., (with Lordi, S. L., & Zaiger, D. S.). (1993). *School nursing practice: Roles and standards.* Scarborough, ME: National Association of School Nurses.

Redes, S., & Lunney, M. (1997). Validation by school nurses of the nursing intervention classification for computer software. *Computers in Nursing, 15,* 333–338.

Schroeder, R. E., Atkinson, A. M., & Armstrong, R. N. (1992). Pricing medical services in the managed care environment. *Top Health Care Finance, 19*(2), 58–64.

Spencer, C. D. (1996). Managed care and community health centers. In P. R. Kongsvedt (Ed.), *The managed health care handbook* (3rd ed.) (pp. 234–244). Gaithersberg, MD: Aspen Publishers, Inc.

Taras, H. L. (1997). School health and managed care. *Annals of the American Academy of Pediatrics, 26,* 733–736.

U.S. Department of Health and Human Services. (1996). *Linking local health centers with schools serving low income children.* Washington, DC: U.S. Department of Health and Human Services, Bureau of Primary Health Care, Health Resources and Services Administration.

Zimmerman, D. J., & Reif, C. J. (1995). School based health centers and managed care health plans. *Journal of Public Health Management and Practice, 1,* 33–39.

See page 625 for Table of Federal Statutes and Regulations.

Chapter Seventeen

The Educational Preparation of School Nurses: Implications for Hiring and Liability Protection

Susan E. Proctor

INTRODUCTION

Anyone looking to become a school nurse, hire a school nurse, or arbitrate potential legal conflicts surrounding the practice of nursing in schools would be wise to consider what educational preparation a nurse has and whether the individual's background reflects state nurse practice acts as well as the needs of children, families, and school staff. This chapter will consider the importance of the school nurse's educational background and preparation to nurses, school administrators, and school attorneys, and will highlight laws, professional nursing expectations, and practical perspectives as a framework for designing a role, hiring or evaluating a nurse, and ascertaining the appropriateness and extent of nursing practice.

RELEVANCE OF NURSE EDUCATIONAL PREPARATION TO NURSES, ADMINISTRATORS, AND ATTORNEYS

An understanding of the educational preparation of school nurses is important for school administrators and attorneys, as well as potential school nurses. A parallel may be seen in teacher education models. The preparation of teaching professionals to serve the educational needs of the diverse group of contemporary American children must include the law and its expectations for student outcomes, state legal statutes delineating the educational preparation of classroom teachers, professional standards governing the teaching profession, and the needs of children and families as influenced by current social, political, and economic phenomena. The situation is no less true for nurses in schools. The education of nurses should examine laws governing the practice of nursing in a given state, what a state minimally requires for the delivery of nursing or other health services in schools, professional standards governing school nursing practice, and the educational preparation necessary to meet the complex health needs of today's children.

Relevance to School Nurses

School nurses need and must be concerned about education for practice as it relates to meeting the needs of children, families, and school staff. Several papers have pointed to the overall increase in quality of nursing care with greater levels of educational preparation (Davis-Martin, 1990; del Bueno, 1990; del Bueno, 1993; Howenstein, Bilodeau, Brogna, & Good, 1996; Olson, Kochevar, & McGovern, 1997; Thobaben & Bohannan, 1990). At least one study also correlates higher levels of ethical decision-making to higher levels of education (Dierckx de Casterlé, Janssen, & Grypdonck, 1996). As a general rule, the broader the education, the more the nurse can do to serve the needs of children and families. For example, a registered nurse with a baccalaureate degree in nursing will be prepared as a public health nurse. This background equips the individual to do family and community as well as child assessments and, importantly, make home visits to families in need, many of whom are best and only served by this kind of "outreach." In fact, an assessment of the needs of a school's population and its health issues is essential to ascertain the intensity or complexity of care needed.

School nursing is a specialty within nursing necessitating specialty preparation. A nurse with specific or specialized educational preparation brings a unique perspective to the school population that is often vital to meeting the needs of children and families in a particular school setting or district. Specialty preparation may be attained through a degree program or through enrollment in a self-standing curriculum of study. Mandatory state school nurse certification requirements may be found within both non-degree and degree (undergraduate and graduate) models. There are now many universities and colleges in the United States that have programs to meet the educational needs of the school nurse.

Several institutions offer continuing education certification programs without degrees. Often these are available as summer institutes. Other universities and colleges run ongoing certification programs for school nurses in need of specialty preparation within their states. These non-degree programs may be pre baccalaureate, post-baccalaureate, or post-master's courses of study.

Universities and colleges which have designed curricula incorporating school nurse-specific content into the baccalaureate degree in nursing have only done so in recent years. However, their numbers are increasing. Examples of some of these curricular structures may be found in the literature (Poster & Marcontel, 1999; Spanier & Slater, 1997).

The American Nurses Association has put forth a position paper which espouses the preparation of specialists at the graduate level (ANA, 1980). Practically speaking, specialty preparation, when included in a degree program, either undergraduate or graduate, better serves the nurse educationally and as a consumer of higher education (Proctor, 1997). In the case of master's study, the return to school both awards the individual a graduate degree and increases the individual's employability.

Combining specialization study and the master's degree almost always results in less expenditure than the two would cost separately and requires fewer academic units. Financial aid, federal traineeships, and scholarships are also more available for students pursuing the master's degree.

Additionally, a school nurse with the master's degree gains credibility for nursing judgments in the eyes of school personnel. Schools are an environment where higher education is valued. Many school professionals hold master's degrees, especially "special services" personnel (such as counselors, social workers, psychologists, and speech therapists). For the nurse to be less well prepared than other school colleagues reduces his or her effectiveness and diminishes professional credibility.

The school nurse who seeks specialty education for practice will be of the foremost value to the school community. This individual will be equipped to antici-

pate and meet both the ongoing health needs of students and families as well as changes in the needs of children or the practice environment as they arise.

Relevance to School Administrators and Attorneys

School administrators and school attorneys unfamiliar with nursing and the preparation of nurses may be well served by a understanding of levels of nursing preparation and how they may fit with the needs of a school district. An understanding of nursing background facilitates optimal utilization of the nurse, promotes development of appropriate position descriptions, and most importantly, matches the health needs of the school community with the abilities of the provider. Schools look for the best teachers. Why should they not also look for the best nurses?

As a general rule, nurses are either registered nurses (RN) or licensed practical/vocational nurses (LPN/LVN).

Registered Nurses

Traditionally, registered nurses were prepared in diploma schools of nursing which were housed within hospitals. Coursework was clinically focused with little or no "general education" content and the expense of educating nurses was largely borne by the hospital. Diploma programs were typically three calendar years including summers. Graduates emerged eligible to sit for state board licensing examinations. Today, only a handful of diploma programs remain in the United States.

Due to the cost to the hospital and a need for a broader-based, liberal education foundation for nurses, nursing education moved to the collegiate setting. Today, registered nurses are prepared in either community college or university programs of study. The community college curriculum leads to eligibility for licensure as a registered nurse and an associate of arts or associate of science degree (AA or AS). Originally conceptualized as a two-year program in response to an explosion of technology and a shortage of nurses following World War II, the associate degree nursing program (ADN) was designed to produce graduates who would practice under the supervision of a baccalaureate or master's-prepared nurse (Futch, 1997). Although the course of study is still referred to as "two-year nursing programs," few nurses complete the course of study in two years due to the combined requirements of general education for the associate degree and strict state curricular requirements for nursing content.

Community college programs have proliferated across the country in large part because of the low cost of preparing students in a community college versus a university environment. Educating nurses is expensive, more costly than preparing graduates for other disciplines. This is a result of the many on-site clinical hours required in hospitals, clinics, and health departments as well as the necessity for close faculty supervision characterized by low and costly faculty-student ratios in these clinical settings (Forni & Burns, 1997). Hence, there is a tendency to place curricula within community colleges where state aid to the institutions is more generous and overheads are lower when contrasted with four-year institutions.

Associate degree nursing graduates are well prepared to function in a structured environment such as a hospital. They have little or no preparation for functioning in solo practice, an environment typical of school nursing practice settings. Further, they are not prepared to function in the community nursing role, which is outside the hospital and quite different from an acute care setting.

The remaining registered nurses in the United States are prepared within university programs that, although designed to be four years, are usually closer to five. The curricula are intensive and demanding and there is typically no room for electives as the course of study is composed of required and sequential courses. Students graduate with a bachelor of science degree in nursing, often referred to as a BSN. They are eligible to sit for the same state licensure examination as community college graduates and may refer to themselves as public health nurses.

Although licensure is the same, university curricula differ from community college curricula in several ways that are important to school nursing. First, university graduates have greater preparation in leadership and management and are better equipped to train and supervise paraprofessional health personnel such as classroom health aides. Second, university graduates have had instruction and a clinical practicum in public health nursing. This content provides them with additional knowledge about the identification and management of common communicable diseases, knowledge of the functioning of the health care delivery system, experience in working and collaborating with community agencies, including other health and social service providers, skill in visiting and assessing families within their homes, and the ability to address the health needs of groups as well as individuals. Third, university graduates have been prepared to function autonomously and are comfortable

working without the on-site supervision of another nurse or a physician. None of these knowledge areas are part of the licensing examination.

Despite its intensity and broad curricular preparation, the BS degree in nursing still prepares a "generalist" in nursing. Therefore, many registered nurses go on and obtain the master's degree. The MS in nursing builds upon the BSN and offers specialty preparation. At latest count, there are some fifty plus specialties within the discipline of nursing, one of which is school nursing (ANA, 1998). The areas of specialization often sought by school nurses are community health/school nursing, pediatric nursing, or preparation as a nurse practitioner, most commonly, a pediatric nurse practitioner (PNP). School nurses also seek graduate degrees outside nursing. The two most frequent are the master of education (MEd) and the master of public health (MPH).

Licensed Vocational/Practical Nurses

LVNs and LPNs are the same. They are simply titled differently in different states. The LVN/LPN attends a program of study that may be housed in either a community college or a vocational/technical institute. The LVN/LPN curriculum is approximately one year in length but may differ by state. No degree is awarded upon completion but a state board examination must be passed which is specific to the technical level of practice and differs from that of the professional registered nurse. Upon successful completion of the examination, the candidate is eligible for licensure as either a LVN or LPN depending upon the state.

Generally, LVNs/LPNs practice under the supervision and direction of the registered nurse although contingent upon the nature of the nursing or health care being delivered, states vary on both the scope of practice of the LVN/LPN and the degree of supervision needed.

In summary, making an employment or legal decision regarding the nature, extent, and appropriateness of nursing or health care to be provided in a given school-based and school-related situation may well depend upon the educational preparation of the health care provider involved. Or conversely, the educational preparation of a health care provider may determine the extent of services that may be provided.

FACTORS TO CONSIDER

Laws and Regulatory Statutes

Nurse Practice Acts

Each of the 50 states has a nurse practice act or its equivalent, which specifies the scope of practice of registered nursing in that state. There is frequently a similar statute for licensed vocational or licensed practical nursing. A state's nurse practice act may direct or determine Schools of Nursing curricula and serve as a guide for interpreting scope of practice issues. Some states have broad nurse practice acts, while others are more restrictive. A registered nurse must be *minimally* prepared to meet the nursing functions as delineated within a nurse practice act. Nursing licensure is fundamental to nursing practice in the nation's schools. That is to say, *state certification as a school nurse is predicated upon the active, valid status of an individual's license as a nurse.* It is useful for all parties to understand a state's nurse practice act when hiring a nurse or considering nursing function. A copy of the nurse practice act should be available from the state Board of Nursing.

State Certification Requirements

There are state certification requirements for teachers in virtually all states. Many states also require certification for other school professionals, nurses among them. School nurse certification or licensure is in addition to licensure as a registered nurse. Certification requirements may be similar or identical to those for teachers a few states require school nurses to be certified as teachers. Some states have a two-step certification process affording provisional authorization for practice followed by permanent certification awarded upon completion of certification requirements, usually an educational program of study within an institution of higher education.

The courses of study or required coursework also vary in length, intensity, focus, and level. Some are brief, continuing education venues, while others are required courses taken as part of a baccalaureate degree. Others necessitate completion of a post-baccalaureate or "fifth-year" program, and still others, a master's degree. Some states have no certification requirements for school nurses.

While there are national standards of practice, there are no national standards of education for nurses who practice in schools. Hence, the educational backgrounds of school nurses across the country vary widely. Some school districts employ registered nurses with baccalaureate or master's degrees while others hire registered nurses without a degree. Others hire licensed practical or vocational nurses (LPN or LVN) who work under the supervision of a registered nurse. Some hire health aides to perform simple health services where nursing licensure is not a requisite.

Mandated Services

Nearly every state has law that mandates some health services in schools. Schools have long been recognized as optimal places to deliver health care to children (Igoe & Speer, 1996). Many students are gathered under one roof and "aggregate" or group level public health functions, such as immunizations or health screenings, may be conducted. This approach has proven so successful that it has continued since 1902 (Wold, 1981). For example, most states require periodic screening of student vision and hearing status. This is, unarguably, good public health practice, and study after study confirms the efficacy and cost effectiveness of such services (Brosnan, 1991; Cross, 1985a, 1985b; Lukes & Johnson, 1999; Mannina, 1997; Yawn, Lydick, Epstein, & Jacobsen, 1996). Hearing and/or visual deficiencies that can affect learning are identified, early intervention facilitated, and the public health goal of disease and disability prevention achieved.

Despite the cooperation of school districts in promoting and protecting the health of children, many state laws have not kept pace with the evolving health needs of contemporary youth. Regrettably, in many states, the scope of mandated health services in schools has not been reviewed and updated for decades. Existing statutes, while sufficient at one time, may not address the prevailing needs of children and families. Contemporary health problems, which cost millions of health care dollars in delayed or absent treatment and educational dollars in missed school days, are not systematically looked for because, in many states, the focus remains only on such areas as vision and hearing screening. Such a focus is too narrow for the times. In the early years of the 21st century, there is as great a need to screen children at risk for child abuse, tuberculosis, or depression as for sensory (e.g., ear and eye) deficits.

Mandated services are frequently provided by nurses, although in many cases, state law does not specify a nurse provider or is silent on the person of the provider. Schools, however, have traditionally hired registered nurses to provide these mandated health services as well as to meet non-mandated health needs because their legal scope of practice is broader than that of a LVN/LPN, health assistant, or health aide. Schools can thus use a registered nurse employee to address a greater spectrum of child, family, or staff health concerns much as they use classroom teachers who are authorized to teach in more than one content area.

Advanced Practice Nursing

Some states have separate laws defining and delineating the roles and responsibilities of the advanced practice nurse (APN). In others, APN functions are covered under the existing nurse practice act. The term Advanced Practice Nurse is both a legal and professional definition. It generally refers to nurses who hold master's degrees or are state or nationally certified as nurse practitioners, nurse midwives, nurse anesthetists, or clinical nurse specialists. It may however, refer to other specialties within nursing as well. If a state has defined APN and has passed legislation governing the practice of advanced practice nurses, then the term is a legal one and may further extend the practice of nursing in that state. Many school nurses are now nurse practitioners, although not all are functioning in the physician-extender role in which they diagnose illness, injury, or medical conditions and prescribe medical treatment including medication, if needed. Those who are functioning in this role are frequently associated with school-based clinics or treatment centers providing a wide range of primary care services to children, families, and school district staff. As they can bill for their services, they may be considered as a source of revenue for the school.

Professional Expectations

Standards of Practice

National standards of practice have been written for school nursing as a specialty. The most recent edition (National Association of School Nurses, 1998) was modeled upon standards of practice for the nursing profession as a whole (ANA, 1998). The task force that produced the school nursing standards represented several organizations involved with school nursing and school health: the National Association of School Nurses, the American School Health Association, the American Nurses Association Division on Community Health Nursing, the American Public Health Association, Public Health Nursing Section, and the National Association of State School Nurse Consultants.

The standards constitute a framework within which nursing practice may be assessed and evaluated. Indeed, standards are "authoritative statements describing responsibilities for which its practitioners are accountable" (NASN, 1998, p. 1). They reflect the "values and priorities" of the specialty of school nursing (p. 1). As standards, they are deliberately broad and conceptually written. They therefore tend to avoid language that delineates specific clinical areas of practice. For example, they do not mention the need to assess children for suspected communicable disease, nor do they mention the importance of making home visits to families in need or participating on IEP teams. They do, however,

make it clear that collaboration, management, competent practice, skill maintenance, and effective communication are essential hallmarks of practice.

The scope of practice described in the standards (and in the implementation guides described in the following section) is both expansive and comprehensive. As such, it demands adequate educational preparation to assure the public and a school system that a practitioner of school nursing is meeting the standards. Review of the standards of practice for school nursing would be important for anyone involved in hiring, evaluating, or supervising a nurse in the school setting.

Standards Implementation Guides

Two implementation guides are available to assist the school nurse and others to understand, interpret, and implement the national standards of practice and hence, the school nursing role. Both are based on an early version of the standards (ANA, 1983). As the differences between the early and the most recent versions of the standards are not great, the guides remain instructive to anyone interested in understanding the scope of practice of school nursing as articulated in the late twentieth century.

The two documents, one published by the National Association of School Nurses (Proctor, 1993) and the other by the American School Health Association (Snyder, 1991b) "flesh out" the 1983 standards of practice and provide a detailed guide to implement in a school nursing and school health program. An implementation guide for the 1998 version of the standards is in development by the National Association of School Nurses and will replace the existing NASN guide.

Position Statements, Professional Writings

Two official position statements delineate organizational positions on educational preparation for school nursing, both of which may inform decision makers concerned with nursing practice in schools. One, a statement by the National Association of School Nurses (NASN, 1996), reaffirms an earlier position of the organization which advocated a bachelor's degree in nursing as minimal entry-level preparation for practice. It simultaneously recognizes the growing need for master level preparation as well. As previously noted, the BSN degree carries with it assurance to the employer that the nurse has been grounded in public health nursing concepts, deemed by many as essential for practice. The NASN position statement also makes recommendations for specific curriculum content reflective of an increasingly complex role.

The second position paper is that of the National Consortium of School Nurse Educators, a group of nursing faculty from university settings and others who are involved or interested in the academic preparation of school nurses (National Consortium of School Nurse Educators, 1998). This document advocates a master's degree as necessary for practice and goes on to identify content areas deemed central to any educational program for school nurses. The statement further deems school nursing to be an advanced practice specialty.

Several authors have spoken to the issue of the educational preparation of school nurses within the literature. Four will be mentioned here. Alicia Snyder, in a brief but provocative paper, indirectly makes a strong case for comprehensive preservice education through her description of the contemporary role as viewed from her years of experience as a health services supervisor in a large urban school district (Snyder, 1991a). Carole Passarelli, a nursing faculty member at Yale University and the first Executive Editor of the Journal of School Nursing, addressed a conference of school nursing and school health leaders in which she advocated a baccalaureate degree as minimal practice entry education and also remarked on the need for master's prepared nurses in the school setting (Passarelli, 1993). Master's preparation was advocated by the authors of the NASN implementation guide developed in response to the first national standards (Proctor, 1993). This document noted the comprehensive scope of practice and the need for specialty preparation. Finally, an editorial in the Journal of School Nursing reaffirmed the need for specialty education at the master's level and suggested some critical components of any educational program (Proctor, 1998).

Practical Considerations

Matching the Needs of Students to the Appropriately Prepared Health Care Professional

Perhaps one of the most vital issues for schools and school administrators is finding ways to meet the needs of diverse student bodies with complex educational, social, emotional, and physical needs. Acquiring nursing personnel who are the best prepared educationally to handle the challenges of contemporary American public schools and their children is one way to address some of the student needs. Nurses who have skills in public health nursing and are facile in collaborating with agencies, other professionals, and service providers to meet child health needs can be a true asset for a school district. Two public health perspectives would

seem to be of particular use to schools: family-focused practice and a renewed emphasis on prevention and health promotion.

Family-focused practice. School nursing is, in fact, school-centered public health nursing (Hawkins, Hayes, & Corliss, 1995; Proctor, 1993; Wold & Dagg, 1981). One of the hallmarks of public health nursing is its ability to assess and intervene with at-risk families. These families traditionally have been underserved by schools. However, the need to recognize their individual needs and develop strategies to effectively serve them will assume a greater prominence in the future.

It is becoming increasingly clear that neither school nursing nor schools can continue to focus solely on the child and ignore the family as context. Nursing, especially community nursing, has traditionally had a family orientation. The obvious and expected mission of schools to serve the child and there exists an expectation that all employees do the same. Little time and energy is available to facilitate services for families. An area where family focus is prominent is adherence to the federal law which prescribes the creation of the IFSP (the Individualized Family Service Plan) for children birth through age three who are served by special education programs (IDEA 97, 1998). This plan, very family-focused in its conception, stands in contrast to the IEP (the Individualized Education Program), developed for the older child, which has little or no family emphasis despite parent participation in plan development. Perhaps lessons can be learned from the IFSP model that might apply elsewhere in the school.

Many programs and schools do work diligently to involve parents and families in their child's education. However, for some families, this is not enough. Mission statements do not often include serving at-risk families. Ethically and practically speaking, this posture should be reconsidered because there are families whose social, political, economic, cultural, or emotional estrangement from the mainstream is so severe that the education of their children is seriously and negatively affected. Most unhappily, there is also evidence that American society is becoming more polarized into a nation of "haves" and "have nots" (Children's Defense Fund, 1997; Corcoran & Chaudry, 1997). Some of the "have nots" are only temporarily in this circumstance, e.g., many new immigrants (U.S. Census Bureau, 1993). Others, however, experience poverty that lasts a lifetime and extends to their children and grandchildren. Poor children are severely disadvantaged in the context of modern U.S. society. Despite the best parenting efforts, their success in life is an uphill struggle. Their neighborhoods and physical and social environments consistently threaten their physical and emotional health. Opportunities for healthy group socialization and emotional development are minimized in sections of cities, towns, and countrysides where the daily meeting of the most basic of human needs is the paramount focus of the family (Acquaviva & Lancaster, 1996). It is clear that schools of the future must be the particular champions of the poor and near poor.

In addition to the poor, there are those families who are *both* impoverished and chronically dysfunctional in their communication, family development, and family role patterns (Miller & Winstead-Fry, 1982). Skill in assisting and empowering these families is critical to the school success of the vulnerable, at-risk children who are members of these families. Schools as well as other agencies *must* take a much more active role in reaching out to multi-problem families in attempt to reduce their social isolation. Unless forces external to the dynamics of the family dysfunction can mediate, these children will quickly become part of the generation of children known as "throw-away kids" (Lacayo, 1995).

A broader focus by schools on at least *some* families (those most in need) would mutually benefit all concerned. It is important that all school staff, including nurses, be professionally prepared to serve these challenging families and youngsters. Utilizing the best-prepared nurse would seem likely to make a difference here.

Prevention and the promotion of health. Nurses with public health backgrounds are well briefed in the areas of prevention: primary—acting before a problem begins; secondary—intervention early in the progression of a malady or phenomenon; and tertiary—acting once the problem has developed with the goal of preventing further deterioration or disability. Prevention in health care is a public health term that no longer means prevention of physical illness alone. In the parlance of epidemiology, prevention refers to preventing social and emotional disease, disability, and dysfunction as much as it refers to the traditional areas of communicable disease control, accident prevention, and smoking and sexually transmitted disease avoidance.

A considerable body of literature exists testifying to the ill health of America's children, the inadequacy of the health care delivery system to satisfactorily meet the need of these youngsters, the number of children uninsured or underinsured, and the need for schools to become primary players in this equation (Bourne, 1997; Costante, 1996; Kann et. al, (1997); Lieu, Newacheck, & McManus, (1993); National Commission, 1990); National School Boards Association, 1991). Schools have been quite involved in

public health preventive efforts, most notably in the area of pregnancy prevention, tobacco, alcohol, and other drug use avoidance programs, and violence and dropout prevention. However, further laws are urgently needed which specify the role of the school relative to intervention and early intervention with children and youth at considerable risk for physical, social, and emotional maladies.

Nurses, as healthcare and public health professionals, can be of considerable assistance to schools in spearheading and managing these programmatic efforts. Indeed, Wallinder notes that "In any setting, the role of the public health *[school]* [substitution added] nurse focuses on the prevention of illness, injury, or disability, the promotion of health, and maintenance of the health of populations" (APHA as cited in Wallinder, 1997, p. 79).

Providing the School with a Measure of Liability Protection

Having an appropriately prepared health professional available to the school would go a long way toward protecting a school system from litigation. Many healthcare issues of today's students are of sufficient complexity that facilitating their management by classroom personnel or secretaries risks errors and subsequent lawsuits. Adequately prepared healthcare personnel who can confer with community professionals, make home visits, administer medications, including those that are controlled substances, and participate fully in special education assessments and planning seems intuitively sound and in the best interest of the school. Indeed, having persons who are not licensed perform actions for which they are inadequately prepared puts a school at greater risk for litigation than having a licensed, certified person on staff do so.

Dollars and Sense

School administrators, of course, must be concerned with dollars and their scarcity. Managing school funds to best to serve the needs of today's complex school communities is a growing challenge necessitating not only courage but considerable creativity. Those hiring might be advised, however, that although a well-prepared nurse will cost the school entity more, the outcomes for children, families, and school staff are likely to pay for themselves in reduced absenteeism, better prevention efforts, and higher quality health services.

Fryer and Igoe (1995) looked at the relationship between child well being and the availability of nurses in schools and found there was a strong and direct association between nurse-student ratios and an "index of well being." The index incorporated factors such as teen pregnancy rates, graduation rates, and arrests for violent crimes. Data from 47 states, excluding Hawaii, North Dakota, and South Carolina were examined.

The lower the nurse-student ratio (as determined by state averages) the greater the index of child well being. The correlation was striking: r = .486, p< .001. Nurse-student ratios ranged from one nurse to just over 500 students in Connecticut to one nurse for almost 11,000 students in Tennessee. (Note: special education settings where nurse-student ratios are traditionally lower than in regular education were not treated separately). While other factors could have conceivably been operating to influence the associations i.e., better overall services in those states as well as their schools, the findings are nonetheless instructive in their message that better staffing likely results in healthier children who are *in* school rather than ill, truant, incarcerated, or drop outs.

Kimel (1996) looked at absenteeism among kindergartners following a nurse-delivered handwashing education program. Significant decreases in absenteeism were seen among children receiving the program when contrasted with those who had received no instruction as measured by a chi-square analysis (χ^2 = 22.225; p = .001). Kimel notes that her findings are not unlike those of prior studies where soap and water were available and teachers took the time to have students wash hands.

Health services in schools are a largely unmeasured portion of the total volume of health services delivered in the United States. Since the advent of Medicaid reimbursement for nursing and other health services in schools, schools have begun to take their share of the enormous healthcare dollar. A study in Colorado found that health services for students, if delivered in schools, cost the state millions of dollars less than had the same services been delivered within the traditional health care delivery system i.e., in physicians' offices or clinics (Fryer, Igoe, & Miyoshi, 1997).

Clearly, the contribution of school nurses and others to the total health of the pediatric population is substantial. The potential for generating healthcare dollars as revenue for schools is also an important consideration, as is the use of qualified healthcare personnel who can effectively bring about reductions in absenteeism, target problems early in their development, better assess children who are ill or in distress, and work to improve the overall health of children in order to optimize their education.

CONCLUSION

Legally, professionally, practically and, perhaps, ethically, employing the best-prepared, best-educated nurses in schools will work to the benefit of schools. In the long run, these individuals will be able to affect a broader spectrum of issues and impact a greater range of concerns because of their knowledge, licensure, and expertise.

With many children and families at risk for unremediated, untreated, or undetected problems, disabilities, or dysfunctions, employing such individuals in schools seems not only logical but wise. Students, families, and school staff without health concerns can also benefit greatly from programs that promote health and wellness. Schools are logical places to teach children about wellness. Indeed, staff wellness programs are now components of many schools in the country. The ability of nurses, as healthcare professionals, to promote and maintain wellness among those considered healthy and functional is an added advantage that school boards and administrators should consider when planning and staffing nursing services in school settings.

REFERENCES

American Nurses Association. (1980). *Nursing: A social policy statement.* Kansas City, MO: Author.

American Nurses Association. (1983). *Standards of school nursing practice.* Kansas City, MO: Author.

American Nurses Association. (1998). *Standards of clinical nursing practice* (2nd ed.). Washington, DC: American Nurses Publishing.

Acquaviva, T., & Lancaster, J. (1996). Poverty and homelessness. In M. Stanhope & J. Lancaster (Eds.), *Community health nursing: Promoting health of aggregates, families, and individuals* (pp. 647–654). St. Louis: Mosby.

Bourne, L. C. (1997). Welfare reform: Are our children well cared for? *Journal of School Nursing, 13*(5), 4–14.

Brosnan, H. (1991). Nursing management of the adolescent with idiopathic scoliosis. *Nursing Clinics of North America, 26*(10), 17–31.

Children's Defense Fund (CDF). (1997). *The state of America's children: Yearbook, 1997.* Washington, DC: Author.

Corcoran, M. E., & Chaudry, A. J. (1997). Dynamics of childhood poverty. *The Future of Children, 7*(2), 42–54.

Costante, C. (1996). Supporting student success. School nurses make a difference. *Journal of School Nursing, 12*(3), 4–6.

Cross, A. W. (1985a). Health screening in the schools: Part I. *The Journal of Pediatrics, 107*(4), 487–493.

Cross, A. W. (1985b). Health screening in the schools: Part II. *The Journal of Pediatrics, 107*(5), 653–661.

Davis-Martin, S. (1990). Research on the differences between baccalaureate and associate degree nurses. In G. M. Clayton & P. A. Bay (Eds.), *Review of research in nursing education* (pp. 109–145). New York: National League for Nursing.

del Bueno, D. J. (1990). Experience, education, and nurse's ability to make clinical judgments. *Nursing and Health Care, 11*(6), 290–294.

del Bueno, D. J. (1993). Competence, criteria, and credentialing. *Journal of Nursing Administration, 23*(5), 7–8.

Dierckx de Casterlé, B., Janssen, P. J., & Grypdonck, M. (1996). The relationship between education and ethical behavior of nursing students. *Western Journal of Nursing Research, 18*(3), 330–350.

Forni, P. R., & Burns, P. (1997). Decreasing nursing education costs: Where is the bottom line? In J. C. McCloskey & H. K. Grace (Eds.), *Currents issues in nursing* (5th ed.) (pp. 189–196). St. Louis: Mosby.

Fryer, G. E., & Igoe, J. B. (1995). A relationship between availability of school nurses and child well-being. *Journal of School Nursing, 11*(3), 12–17.

Fryer, G. E., Igoe, J. B., & Miyoshi, T. J. (1997). Considering school health screening services as a cost offset: A comparison of existing reimbursements in one state. *Journal of School Nursing, 13*(2), 18–21.

Futch, C. J. (1997). History of nursing. In K. K. Chitty (Ed.), *Professional nursing: Concepts and challenges* (2nd ed.) (pp. 1–32). Philadelphia: W. B. Saunders Co.

Hawkins, J. W., Hayes, E. R., & Corliss, C. P. (1995). School nursing in America—1902–1994: A return to public health nursing. *Public Health Nursing, 11*(6), 416–425.

Howenstein, M. A., Bilodeau, K., Brogna, M. J., & Good, G. (1996). Factors associated with critical thinking among nurses. *The Journal of Continuing Education in Nursing, 27*(3), 100–103.

IDEA 97: 1997 Amendments to the Individuals with Disabilities Education Act. (1998). *The Special Edge, 11*(2), 8–9.

Igoe, J. B., & Speer, S. (1996). Community health nurse in the schools. In M. Stanhope & J. Lancaster (Eds.), *Community health nursing: Promoting the health of aggregates, families, and individuals* (4th ed.) (pp. 879–906). St. Louis: Mosby.

Kann, L., Kinchen, S. A., Williams, B. I., Ross, J. G., Lowry, R., Hill, C. V., Grunbaum, J. A., Blumson, P. S., Collins, J. L., Kolbe, L. J., & State and Local YRBSS Coordinators (1998). Youth risk behavior surveillance: United States, 1997. *Journal of School Health, 68*(9), 355–369.

Kimel, L. S. (1996). Handwashing education can decrease illness absenteeism. *Journal of School Nursing, 12*(2), 14–18.

Lacayo, R. (1995). When kids go bad. In R. E. Long (Ed.), *Criminal sentencing* (pages unknown). New York: H. W. Wilson Co.

Lieu, T. A., Newacheck, P. W., & McManus, M. A. (1993). Race, ethnicity and access to ambulatory care among U.S. adolescents. *American Journal of Public Health, 83*(7), 960–965.

Lukes, E. & Johnson, M. (1999). Hearing conservation: An industry-school partnership. *Journal of School Nursing, 15*(2), 22–25.

Mannina, J. (1997). Finding an effective hearing testing protocol to identify hearing loss and middle ear disease in school aged children. *Journal of School Nursing, 13*(5), 23–28.

Miller, S. R., & Winstead-Fry, P. L. (1982). *Family systems theory in nursing practice.* Sacramento, CA: Reprinted with permission of Reston Publishing Co., Reston, VA, by Hornet Bookstore, California State University, Sacramento.

National Association of School Nurses. (1996 [draft]). *Education for school nursing: A position statement from the National Association of School Nurses.* Unpublished manuscript in committee.

National Association of School Nurses. (1998). *Standards of professional school nursing practice.* Scarborough, ME: National Association of School Nurses, Inc.

National Commission on the Role of the School and the Community in Improving Adolescent Health. (1990). *Code blue: Uniting for a healthier youth.* Alexandria, VA: National Association of State Boards of Education.

National Consortium of School Nurse Educators (NCOSNE). (1998). *Position statement: Educational preparation of school nurses.* Dayton, OH: Available from the current committee chair, Susan Praeger, RN, PhD, College of Nursing and Health, Wright State University.

National School Boards Association. (1991). *School health: Helping children learn.* Alexandria, VA: National Association of State Boards of Education.

Olson, D. K., Kochevar, L., & McGovern, P. (1997). Form follows function: Occupational health nursing as a member of the management team. *AAOHN Journal, 45*(4), 161–169.

Passarelli, C. (1993). *School nursing: Trends for the future* (Occasional paper #9). Washington, DC: National Health/Education Council.

Poster, E. C., & Marcontel, M. (1999). School nursing role and competence. *Journal of School Nursing, 15*(2), 34–42.

Proctor, S. T. (with Lordi, S. L., & Zaiger, D. S.). (1993). *School nursing practice: Roles and standards.* Scarborough, ME: National Association of School Nurses, Inc.

Proctor, S. E. (1997). On going back to school. [Editorial]. *Journal of School Nursing, 13*(5), 2.

Proctor, S. E. (1998). Education for practice: Identifying a "critical mass" of specialty content for school nursing. [Editorial]. *The Journal of School Nursing, 14*(3), 2; 4.

Snyder, A. A. (1991a). The future of school nursing. In A. A. Snyder (Ed.), Implementation guide for the standards of school nursing practice. Kent, OH: American School Health Association.

Snyder, A. A. (Ed.). (1991b). *Implementation guide for the standards of school nursing practice.* Kent, OH: American School Health Association.

Spanier, A. L., & Slater, P. (1997). Development of a school nurse education model. *Journal of School Nursing, 13*(1), 18–21.

Thobaben, M., & Bohannan, J. (1990). Home health nursing: The relationship between education and practice. *Home Healthcare Nurse, 8*(2), 49–52.

U. S. Bureau of the Census. (1993). *Income, poverty, and valuation of non-cash benefits.* Washington, DC: U.S. Department of Commerce.

Wallinder, J. (1997). Supporting one another: The definition of PHN, awards, and the impromptu. *Public Health Nursing, 14*(2), 77–80.

Wold, S. J. (1981). School nursing: A passing experiment? In S. J. Wold (Ed.), *School nursing: A framework for practice* (pp. 1–19). North Branch, MN: Sunrise River Press.

Wold, S. J., & Dagg, N. V. (1981). A framework for practice. In S. J. Wold (Ed.), *School nursing: A framework for practice* (pp. 30–35). North Branch, MN: Sunrise River Press.

Yawn, B. P., Lydick, E. G., Epstein, R., & Jacobsen, S. J. (1996). Is school vision screening effective? *Journal of School Health 66*(5), 171–175.

See page 625 for Table of Federal Statutes and Regulations.

Chapter Eighteen
Future Directions in School Health Care: The Genetic Revolution

Wendy J. Fibison

INTRODUCTION

In the words of Yogi Berra, "There is nothing so difficult to predict as the future." Predicting how genetics will affect our daily lives, both professional and personal, in the next century is a daunting task. What is certain is that genetic research and biotechnology will radically change how health care and medical care are practiced. Genetic information for an ever-increasing range of conditions will begin to accumulate at birth and, in many cases, before birth. And this information, in turn, will influence how children are viewed, educated, and cared for in our school systems. School nurses have a unique opportunity to lay groundwork in educational settings that will insure that genetic information will be used appropriately to promote educational goals.

BACKGROUND

Many scientific accomplishments and new technologies have contributed to what has been called a Genetic Revolution. Molecular genetics has revealed indisputable scientific evidence for the inheritance of thousands of genetic conditions affecting a person's health. In fact, all human disease has a genetic as well as an environmental component, including cancer and AIDS. It could be argued that even injury has a genetic component when one considers the body's response to the physical insult and to the treatment. We need to broaden our thinking about genetics.

Launching of the Human Genome Project in 1990 gave enormous impetus to the effort to construct a genetic map, identify all human genes, and sequence the human genome. The genetic maps are complete, the physical maps nearly so, and both are in wide use by the scientific community. Current genetic maps are dense enough to locate a gene for a single-gene disorder within a matter of weeks instead of years. An electronic version of the gene map organizes the details into a readily accessible Internet site (www.ncbi.nlm.gov/genemap) with extensive links to supporting data about the DNA structure of the genes and the proteins they encode. To date, over 30,000 human genes have been mapped, about one-half of the estimated 80,000 total (Deloukas, 1998). Sequencing the entire human genome of 3 billion base pairs is targeted for completion by the end of the year 2003, two years ahead of previous projections (Collins, 1997) Researchers in the public and private sectors are developing approaches to accomplishing these goals more efficiently and economically with robotics, miniaturization, chip technology, and informatics. Having the complete set of human genes—the periodic table for biology—will make it possible to unravel how genes function and interact.

In the field of medical genetics, the initial molecular discoveries identified DNA sequence changes associated with congenital disorders, and much work will continue in this domain. The next phase of research will be to discern the function of the genes in isolation and in concert with other genes and environment. Intense efforts are also being directed at understanding the genetic origins of common, adult-onset diseases, such as diabetes, arthritis, cancer, and a host of neuro-psychiatric disorders. These seem to result from the activities of several genes and the interplay between a human body and its environment.

A newly created research center, the Center for Inherited Disease Research (CIDR), focuses on the analysis of common disorders caused by the actions of multiple genes. It is a government-university partnership between National Institutes of Health (NIH) and the Johns Hopkins University School of Medicine. CIDR specializes in a technique known as genotyping—sorting through the entire genome of disease-prone family members to search for not one, but many gene regions associated with that disease. Researchers at

CIDR expect to analyze the genetics of six to nine complex disorders per year. This initiative signals a significant transition in our approach to understanding disease and opens the door to exciting new strategies for treatments and prevention.

The applications of genetic research to health and medical care will continue to broaden in scope. Genetic testing and screening will continue to expand. Disease diagnosis will become more precise, based on a refined understanding of molecular events leading to the pathology. The role of genes in susceptibility to infectious diseases, such as malaria and parasitic, bacterial, and viral infections, will become clearer (Weatherall, Clegg, & Kwiatkowski, 1997). Specifically targeted pharmacologics will be developed based on genomic dissection. Determining the most effective medication for a patient may be based, in part, on genotype. For example, prior to treating an infection, genetic studies may be done to identify any genetic factors that result in antibiotic resistance. As another example, preliminary studies suggest that response to therapeutic doses of albuterol in children with asthma may be associated with a genetic polymorphism in the beta2-adrenergic receptor (Martinez, Graves, Baldini, Solomon, & Erickson, 1997). Behavioral genetics will yield more insights into the genetic contribution to complex human behaviors. And gene therapy, although still in its infancy, holds the promise of providing another treatment modality for certain inherited and acquired disorders and cancers.

In the coming years, school nurses will be confronted with a plethora of new challenges stemming from the availability of genetic information. Children and their families, teachers, and administrators need to be able to rely on school nurses for interpretation of research findings and knowledge of genetic applications as they relate to the mission of education. By looking at trends in genetic testing and research in behavioral genetics, one can begin to project how the practice of the school nurse will be influenced by the genetic revolution.

GENETIC TESTING

Genetic testing has been a part of medical care for many years. The majority of testing is by referral and is performed within the context of a specialty service, a research protocol in a university-based laboratory, or in a private laboratory. The test is generally limited to a specific disorder for which an identifiable risk factor (or factors) exists. For example, the offering of prenatal genetic diagnosis has become the standard of care for women in high risk categories. Carrier testing, for Tay-

Sachs and sickle cell anemia, as examples, and newborn screening for genetic disease are also familiar programs.

Many forces are changing the nature of genetic testing. To begin with, the molecular analysis of disease-causing genes is turning out to be more complex than had been anticipated in the early years of molecular genetics. Looking back, sickle cell anemia was the first genetic disease to be examined at the molecular level. Ingram (1956) discovered that the abnormality in the hemoglobin present in sickle cell disease constituted a replacement of only one of the 287 amino acids present in the hemoglobin molecule. This was the first demonstration in any organism that a single mutation in a structural gene could cause an amino acid substitution in the corresponding protein. The development of DNA tests for prenatal diagnosis of sickle cell disease followed (Orkin, 1984; Embury et al., 1987).

This model, a single base pair change causing disease, appears to be the exception rather than the rule, given what we have been learning about disease-causing genes since then. The majority of inherited disorders are caused by mutations scattered along the length of their respective genes. Cystic fibrosis is one example. Mutations in the cystic fibrosis transmembrane conductance regulator (CFTR) give rise to cystic fibrosis. Over 600 different mutations have been characterized in the gene CFTR gene (NIH Consensus Statement, 1997). Similarly, over 100 mutations are known in the BRCA1 gene (Wagner et al., 1996; Collins, 1996), the best studied of the breast cancer susceptibility genes. In both of these examples, instead of one single mutation responsible for the disease, many different mutations must be checked for. Consequently, DNA testing becomes more complex. Those developing DNA tests must first determine how many of the mutations to test for and which mutations should be included in that number. The proportion of detectable mutations is an important indicator of the utility of a population-screening program. Interpretation of DNA tests is also challenging. What effect the different mutations have on the development and progression of the disorder is not yet known for any genetic condition. Eventually, when more is learned about the genotype-phenotype relationships, genotyping will be helpful in determining prognosis, surveillance, preventive measures, and treatment plans.

In spite of these complexities, more and more genetic tests will be based on the molecular analysis of DNA. In fact, today, the identification of a disease-causing gene mutation is almost immediately translated into a clinical test able to detect the mutation in an individual's DNA. Over 550 genetic tests are being used in the diagnosis of disease. Some are also being used to identify individuals at risk for problems such as colon cancer, glaucoma, and inherited kidney cancer before they become ill, thereby allowing potential life-saving interventions. Since all of a person's genes are present in all nucleated cells from the moment of conception, DNA testing can be performed at all stages of the life cycle, prenatal through senescence, and even after death. DNA testing eliminates the need to obtain a specific tissue or obtain a specific gene product to make a diagnosis, and can be done on a small blood sample.

One of the most significant shifts in DNA testing is the movement from diagnostic to predictive tests. Predictive tests, now available or soon to be available, include: cystic fibrosis, Tay-Sachs disease, Lou Gehrig's disease (ALS), Huntington disease, catastrophically high cholesterol, some rare cancers, and inherited susceptibility to cancer (breast, ovarian, colon, thyroid). Learning presymptomatically that one carries a gene that causes a late-onset disorder is information that may be very hard for an individual to assimilate. This is especially true because our ability to test for a disorder outstrips our understanding of progression of the disorder and what measures should be taken to prolong health. There is usually a gap of time before the clinical research identifies the most effective interventions.

DNA chips, the result of a marriage between molecular biology and precision engineering technologies, are expected to have a formidable impact on both clinical and research genetics. Each DNA chip is the size of a postage stamp and represents a new way of analyzing genetic material. It is estimated that it will be possible to analyze upwards of 150,000 genetic sequences simultaneously with one small tissue (blood) sample from an individual. The implications for genetic testing are astronomic. It will move us from an era of testing for one specific disorder to an era where many different genes are tested at the same time. From a single test, results may inform the client about a diagnosis, carrier status, presymptomatic disease, and a predisposition to disease. Imagine trying to understand the results from such comprehensive testing. Eng and Vijg (1997) predict that although several technical hurdles remain, effective and reliable genetic tests for multigene diseases should be available within the next five years. Typically, these are adult onset conditions. Here again, the client may obtain information about a predisposition to a disorder long before any signs or symptoms are present.

Another trend in genetics relates to location of services. Genetic testing is quickly moving out of the medical genetics specialty clinics into the primary care setting for all age groups. Additionally, commercial laboratories are launching vigorous marketing campaigns to promote consumer interest in genetic testing. Wertz's (1997) survey of the Helix Lab Network in the United States demonstrated that not only can DNA testing be done without a physician or health care provider referral, but many of the laboratories test children at the parents' request. These tests include carrier and presymptomatic testing. For example, approximately 22% of the laboratories had tested children less than 12 years of age for Huntington disease, an adult onset disorder for which there is no treatment. In England, as another example, it is possible to purchase cystic fibrosis test kits with a buccal swab by mail, and to receive results by mail, without going to your general practitioner (The Gene Letter, 1997). Yet, few primary care physicians and nurses have the requisite genetic education to address the many issues surrounding genetic testing. The combination of primary health care professionals who are inadequately prepared regarding genetic testing and interpretation and increased commercial pressures to be tested may result in many individuals having genetic testing information that is misunderstood or troubling, with few supports to assist them in understanding it and using it constructively in their decision-making.

As genetic testing becomes more widespread, schools will inevitably become more involved in issues related to genetic information. These issues are explored in detail elsewhere (Scanlon & Fibison, 1995). Specific issues for schools that will need resolution include the following:

- How can schools protect the privacy of the family with respect to genetic information, since a child's genetic information has implications for other siblings and family members?
- Who in a school system should have access to genetic information on students and for what purposes?
- Is there an advocacy role for the school nurse in protecting the child's right to not know in situations where parents want presymptomatic and/or carrier testing done? (See ASHG/ACMG Report, "Points to Consider: Ethical, Legal, and Psychosocial Implications of Genetic Testing in Children and Adolescents," 1995.)
- What role should school health services play in the future when genes are identified for adult onset disorders and effective interventions have been determined through research that prolong health?
- Should genetic testing be discussed in health classes?
- Should screening programs be set up in schools?

Inevitably, genetic discoveries will require a reevaluation of school policies and educational approaches to curriculum, health services, and record-keeping. *Preparing Schools for the Genetic Revolution* (PSftGR): A National Education Program, is one project that is addressing the ethical and legal questions related to the Human Genome Project and school policy. The PSftGR Registry (http://www.gene.com/ae/tolfa) has been developed in order to document anecdotes, stories, and case studies related to school policy, curriculum decisions, school insurance, and genetics.

GENETICS AND HUMAN BEHAVIOR

Scientists have long been fascinated by the nature-versus-nurture debate, which seeks to identify the elements that contribute to human behavior. The traditional research methodology has been family studies, including identical twins reared together and reared apart, and studies of adopted and foster children. Yet methodologically, family studies are problematic because of small sample sizes and self-selection of research subjects. It has been debated for many years whether it is possible, using this approach, to tease out the complex interactions between genes and human behavior with the same rigor that has characterized the study of genes and human disorders and cancers.

The development of molecular genetics and genetic linkage maps in the past decade offers new possibilities for the study of behavioral genetics. These genetic maps have already made it possible for the mapping of single-locus Mendelian disorders to proceed at an extraordinarily swift pace. As a result, we have evidence for hundreds of genes that cause conditions affecting a person's physical health. Much attention is being focused on using these maps to identify susceptibility genes for behavioral traits. Molecular genetic strategies hold the promise of complementing and extending the traditional methodologies (Sherman et al., 1997). The potential to uncover both genetic and environmental influences on normal and deviant behavior is staggering.

According to Beckwith and Alper (1997), molecular research is focusing on genetic influences of human behavioral traits and can be grouped into three categories: mental illnesses such as bipolar manic depression and schizophrenia; behaviors and aptitudes that have social ramifications associated with them, such as intelligence, alcoholism, homosexuality, and criminal behavior; and behaviors that do not necessarily engender social conflict, such as shyness, the tendency to be happy, and novelty seeking. With some certainty, we can assume that the genetic components of behavior will become clearer in the future. This information will lead to earlier and more accurate diagnosis of behavioral disorders, and better interventions.

A clearer understanding of behavioral genetics will also raise new questions for schools in the area of school policy and classroom management. The study of the attention deficit hyperactivity disorder (ADHD) illustrates the potential complexities of applying research in behavioral genetics. ADHD is the most common childhood-onset behavioral disorder, affecting about 5%-10% of children and adolescents (Wolraich, Hannah, Pinnock, Baumgaertel, & Brown, 1996). School nurses are well-acquainted with the symptoms of ADHD: inability to sit still, difficulty organizing tasks, distractibility, forgetfulness, fidgeting, not listening, and risk-taking behavior. This is a familial disorder with the frequency approximately five to six times greater among first-degree relatives than in the general population (Biederman et al., 1992). According to Smalley (1997), results from twin studies are consistent with the hypothesis that genes account for the observed familiality of ADHD.

Additional evidence for a genetic component is provided by animal models. For example, a knockout mouse for the dopamine transporter gene (DAT1) shows altered dopamine transport and exhibits extreme hyperactivity (Giros, Jaber, Jones, Wightman, & Caron, 1996). Researchers are examining numerous candidate-gene associations in ADHD (Smalley, 1997). It is within the realm of possibility that the identification of susceptibility genes in ADHD will be accomplished using the new molecular approaches.

If such a gene (or genes) is identified by researchers, recent history tells us that it is very likely that a genetic test will quickly be commercially developed. If a test for genetic susceptibility to ADHD were readily available, many issues would be raised for educational systems. Imagine the potential benefits—and harms—of having genetic test information which identifies children at risk for ADHD, keeping in mind that all behavior is a complex interaction of genetic and environmental influences. A partial list of questions that would need to be addressed follows:

- What does the concept of "susceptibility" mean with respect to behavior?
- How will this influence school policy?
- At what point are research findings applicable to a general student population?
- When are research findings generalizable?
- Should genetic testing be recommended or required for all school-age children to assist with placement decisions?

- Regardless of whether testing becomes part of the school entrance requirement or remains a parental decision, what would be the best age for testing: in the preschool years, upon entering kindergarten, or later?
- Besides placement decisions and classroom interventions related to academic work, should other aspects of a child's school life, such as sports or extracurricular activities, be planned based on this information?
- How should planning for a child with the "gene", who shows no behavioral symptoms, be handled?
- Who within a school system, if anyone, should have access to this genetic test information?
- What systems, including records systems, need to be in place to prevent stigma or social stereotyping?
- And most importantly, what role will the parents play in these decisions, beginning with the most fundamental decision, whether to have their child tested at all?

Although at this time, there is no identified gene for ADHD, postulating its existence lets us begin to see what challenges schools will confront when the genetic contribution to behavior is better understood. ADHD was offered as the example because it has clear implications for the classroom. Other areas of genetic inquiry which also have relevance to academic mandates include intelligence and cognitive ability, vocational interests, and communicative disorders. A breakthrough in any one of these behavioral areas will compel those in the education field to examine how genetic information will or will not be used to meet the goals of optimal learning for their students.

Likewise, schools will need to decide which socially important behavioral traits will also be important in the school setting, traits such as shyness, homosexuality, aggression, depression, and alcoholism. Genetic research in these areas may be of considerable interest to older school children as well, and they may come to school with many questions regarding how the new information relates to them. Since it is not uncommon for preliminary behavioral research data to be reported sensationally in the public domain, this may contribute to misinterpretation or misinformation in the minds of children.

It can take a long time to overcome information obtained through an over-eager media, unless there is an easily accessible resource for young people to provide a more balanced perspective. Even rigorously conducted research may create confusion and anxiety when it results in the blurring of traditional boundaries between what is considered normal and abnormal behavior. Schools will need to consider what role they will take in supporting adolescents and young adults as they try to assimilate new information about genetic origins of socially important behavior.

Research in the field of behavioral genetics will continue to evolve. There is growing concern about how the emerging body of information from molecular and behavioral genetics may effect the categorization of children in schools. Genetic explanations of complex behavior—learning disabilities and behavioral problems—may be very appealing to school systems pressured by demands for efficiency and accountability (Nelkin & Tancredi, 1991).

School nurses can play a pivotal role in fostering the wise and careful use of genetic information relevant to behavior. They will have a professional obligation to respond to questions from faculty, administrators, and students or to direct them to the appropriate resources; to protect the confidentiality of students, families, and staff; to prevent abuse of the information; and to prevent or minimize stigmatization. With creative and innovative approaches, school nurses may be able to contribute to solutions that minimize potential harm to those whose behavior differs from the majority, especially if that behavior is shown to have a genetic component.

REFERENCES

ASHG/ACMG Report (1995) "Points to consider: Ethical, legal, and psychosocial implications of genetic testing in children and adolescents." *American Journal of Human Genetics 57*(5), 1233–1241.

Beckwith, J., & Alper, J. S. (1997). Human behavioral genetics. *The Genetic Resource, 11*(1), 5–9.

Biederman, J., Faraone, S. V., Keenan, K., Benjamin, J., Krifcher, B., Moore, C., Sprich-Buckminster, S., Vgaglia, K., Jellinek, M. S., Steingard, R., Spencer, T., Norman, D., Kolodny, R., Kraus, I., Perrin, J., Keller, M. B., Tsuang, M. T. (1992). Further evidence for family-genetic risk factors in attention deficit hyperactivity disorder. *Archives of General Psychiatry, 49*(9), 728–738.

Collins, F. C. (1996). BRCA1—Lots of mutations, lots of dilemmas (editorial). *New England Journal of Medicine, 334*(3), 186–188.

Collins, F. C. (1997). *Statement of the Director, National Human Genome Research Institute, National Institutes of Health.* The 1998 House Appropriations Subcommittee Hearings, U.S. Congress. 27 February 1997, Washington, DC.

Collins, F. C., Patrinos, A., Jordan, E., Chakravarti, A., Gesteland, R., Walters, L., & the members of the DOE and NIH planning groups (1998). New goals for the U.S. Human Genome Project: 1998–2003. *Science, 282,* 682–689.

Deloukas, P., Schuler, G. D., Gyapay, G., Beasley, E. M., Soderlund, C., Rodriquez-Tome, P., Hui, L., Matise, T. C., McKusick, K. B., Beckman, J. S., Bentolila, S., Bihoreau, M., Birren, B. B., Browne, J., Butler, A., Castle, A. B., Chiannilkulchai, N., Clee, C., Day, P. J., Dehejia, A., Dibling, T., Drouot, N., Duprat, S., Fizames, C., Bentley, D. R. (1998). A physical map of 30,000 human genes. *Science, 282,* 744–746.

Embury, S. H., Scharf, S. J., Saiki, R. K., Gholson, M. A., Golbus, M., Arnheim, N., Erlich, H. A. (1987). Rapid prenatal diagnosis of sickle cell anemia by a new method of DNA analysis. *New England Journal of Medicine, 316*(11), 656–661.

Eng, C., & Vijg, J. (1997). Genetic testing: the problems and the promise. *Nature Biotechnology, 15*(5), 422–426.

The gene letter. (1997, January). [On-line]. Available: http://www.geneletter.org.

Giros, B., Jaber, M., Jones, S. R., Wightman R. M., & Caron, M. G. (1996). Hyperlocomotion and indifference to cocaine and amphetamine in mice lacking the dopamine transporter. *Nature, 379,* 606–612.

Ingram, V. M. (1956). A specific chemical difference between the globins of normal human and sickle cell anaemia haemoglobin. *Nature, 178,* 792–794.

Martinez, F. D., Graves, P. E., Baldini, M., Solomon, S., & Erickson, R. (1997). Association between genetic polymorphisms of the beta2-adrenoceptor and response to albuterol in children with and without a history of wheezing. *Journal of Clinical Investigation, 100*(12), 3184–3188.

Nelkin, D., & Tancredi, L. (1991). Classify and control: Genetic information in the schools. *American Journal of Law and Medicine, 17*(1 & 2), 51–73.

NIH Consensus Development Conference Statement. (1997). Genetic testing for cystic fibrosis. Bethesda, MD: National Institutes of Health.

Orkin, S. H. (1984). Prenatal diagnosis of hemoglobin disorders by DNA analysis. *Blood, 63*(2), 249–253.

Scanlon, C., & Fibison, W. J. (1995). *Managing genetic information: Implications for nursing practice.* Washington, DC: American Nurses Association.

Sherman, S. L., DeFries, J. C., Gottesman, I. I., Loehlin, J. C., Meyer, J. M., Pelias, M. Z., Rice, J., & Waldman, I. (1997). ASHG statement Recent developments in human behavioral genetics: past accomplishments

and future directions. *American Journal of Human Genetics,* 60(6), 1265–1275.

Smalley, S. L. (1997). Genetic influences in childhood-onset psychiatric disorders: autism and attention-deficit/hyperactivity disorder. *American Journal of Human Genetics,* 60(6), 1276–1282.

Wagner, T. M. U., M'slinger, T., Zielinski, C., Scheiner, O., & Brelteneder, H. (1996). New Austrian mutation in BRCA1 gene detected in three unrelated HBOC families. *Lancet, 347,* 1263–1264.

Weatherall, D., Clegg, J., & Kwiatkowski, D. (1997). The role of genomics in studying genetic susceptibility to infectious disease. *Genome Research, 7,* 967–973.

Wertz, D. C., & Reilly, P. R. (1997). Laboratory policies and practices for the genetic testing of children: a survey of the helix network. *American Journal of Human Genetics, 61,* 1163–1168.

Wolraich, M. L., Hannah, J. N., Pinnock, T. Y., Baumgaertel, A., & Brown, J. (1996). Comparison of diagnostic criteria for attention-deficit hyperactivity disorder in a county-wide sample. *Journal of the American Academy of Child and Adolescent Psychiatry, 35*(3), 319–324.

INTERNET RESOURCES

Ethical, legal, social implications of the human genome project [On-line]. Available: http://www.nhgri.nih.gov/ELSI/

Genetic education resources, networking and more [On-line]. Available: http://www.kumc.edu/instruction/medicine/genetics/homepage.html

Genetic information for health professionals; policy statements [On-line]. Available: http://cancernet.nci.nih.gov/h genetics.html

Genetic privacy legislation [On-line]. Available: http://www.ornl.gov/hgmis/archive/laws.html

Genetics glossary combining text, audio and visuals [On-line]. Available: http://www.nhgri.nih.gov/DIR/VIP/glossary/

National Cancer Institute [On-line]. Available: http://www.nci.nih.gov/

National human genome research institute [On-line]. Available: http://www.nhgri.nih.gov/

NCI booklet "Understanding genetic testing" [On-line]. Available: http://www.gene.com/ae/AE/AEPC/NIH/index.html

Task force on genetic testing information [On-line]. Available: http://www.med.jhu.edu/tfgtelsi/promoting/

See page 625 for Table of Federal Statutes and Regulations.

Chapter Nineteen

Future Challenges for School Health Services and the Law: A Manager's Perspective

Carol C. Costante

Editor's Foreword

This chapter provides readers with a general summary of current and future challenges for school health services from the perspective of one school nurse manager. Based on her extensive experience as a national leader and manager of school health services, the author offers a road map for addressing several contributory causes of legal confusion and ethico-legal dilemmas in school nursing practice. While these challenges relate to legal issues that are well documented elsewhere in the book, the chapter addresses them in summary form and a call-to-action style.

INTRODUCTION

School nursing is, in many ways, a profession ahead of its time. Created in the early part of the 20th century in response to societal needs related to poverty, communicable disease, and lack of child access to medical care, school-based nursing services have focused on improving the learning and health of our nation's school-aged children. School nurses identify or provide through direct service, or referral to other experts, those health-related services that children and youth require in order to be available for and to maximize learning opportunities. Because the need to bridge health and education has escalated faster than society has made provisions for, the actual practice of school nursing today far exceeds the legal basis for its practice, as well as its public image.

Once part of the public health arena, school nursing services were diminished mid-century by political pressures to eliminate treatment functions in schools. (See chapter 1.) Services have since suffered from a lack of solid investment and ownership by either public health agencies or education systems. Nonetheless, the late 1970s saw gradual growth in the field, again in response to societal needs, but this time the needs were related to the provision of education services to students with disabilities. At the end of the 20th century, amidst mounting child and family needs and adequate resources, school nurses continued to be faced with a multitude of challenges.

The positive aspect of this situation is that society has finally discovered school health services. For decades, school nurses have provided many of the same services that are currently valued by society. That is, they have delivered primary and preventive health care in community settings, where their clients are, in a cost effective manner and in a way that supports the full inclusion into the education environment of a diverse population of children. Because of this emerging societal presence, perhaps school nursing professionals will now have the necessary support to

- address many of the ethical and legal questions that have previously eluded them and
- establish a solid base upon which to build their practice in the 21st century.

School nursing is at the crossroads of its future. As a profession, though, it remains challenged by the following conditions:

- role ambiguity;
- an extremely variable and poorly organized system of services;
- a maturing knowledge base not sufficiently based in research;

- a confused or orphan perspective because it is claimed by both health and education systems, or by neither;
- wide disparity of professional preparation, requirements, and privileges; and
- wavering, multi-source funding streams that are dependent on economic prosperity and politics.

Despite these challenges, external environmental influences have placed school nursing today at its most promising position ever to become full partners in the health care delivery and education systems. School nursing, as a profession, must seize this opportunity to resolve its substantive practice issues.

If school nurses do not take full advantage of the opportunities afforded them now, it is the opinion of this writer that they risk diminishment of their profession or even extinction. In that event, school health services will never take its place as the most appropriate entry point for school-aged children into the health care delivery system. Furthermore, if school nurses and school health services do not survive to effectively and efficiently meet the health care needs of this population, society will pay a much higher price for entry-level prevention, early identification and intervention, and referral and coordination services for children.

Professional school nurses (registered nurses) are the major providers of what schools generally refer to as "school health services." School health services programs are usually school-nurse managed and school-nurse delivered. Physician advisors play an important role on the school health services team, but their role is primarily advisory, rather than direct service or administrative. Many health services programs use assistive personnel, such as clerical staff, health aides, and practical nurses, who work under the direction the school

nurse. Other school health professionals include mental health providers such as counselors, psychologists and social workers, as well as occupational therapists and physical therapists. Comprehensive or coordinated school health programs are usually thought to include a wide array of services:

- school health services;
- health education;
- a healthful school environment;
- food and nutrition services;
- psychological, counseling, and social work services;
- physical education;
- faculty and staff health promotion; and
- integrated school, family and community efforts.

This chapter discusses the future of school health services and professional school nurses as the primary providers and administrators of school health services programs. It is written from the viewpoint of an experienced manager of school nurses and school health services programs in a school system with a diverse student population of over 100,000, and one who has had the advantage of years of national leadership in the field. From this perspective, the foremost legal questions and future needs related to school health services and school nursing practice can be grouped into the following categories: program support; research; health care delivery systems; technology; connection with education; professional nursing issues; program management; and, nursing practice issues. Rather than separate and distinct, these categories often overlap and are inextricably intertwined with the needs of school nursing practice and the need of American children and youth for quality school health services.

PROGRAM SUPPORT

Funding

Basic to the advancement of all public service programs is solid funding. Without a dependable funding stream, the provision of school health services is subject to the priorities of leadership and the existence of substantial budgets. At present, school health services are funded in a variety of ways that are community sensitive, and usually through a combination of funding sources. Refer to Table 19-1 for the major funding sources of school health services.

School health services programs seem to be most successful, prosperous, and able to achieve their poten-

tial in those communities where the programs appear as line items in both the local and state education and health budgets. Communities that have legally cemented a collaborative relationship between health and education agencies, and where they are equally committed to the mission of school health, provide school health services of the highest caliber. However, there is no equity from one school district or community to another, and children are the victims of severe discrepancies in school health and mental health programs. Only by eliminating the bureaucratic, legal and cultural barriers between the health and education systems, and universally applying the fundamental principle that individual health is essential to learning, will school

TABLE 19-1.

Financing School Health Services

General Funds	Categorical Funds	Federal Participation Programs	Other Income
State school district funds	Title One	EPSDT	Private insurance
Local tax revenues	Special Education Safe and Drug-free Schools	Medicaid Child Health Insurance Program	Managed care Public/private partnerships
	Early Periodic Screening, Identification, and Treatment (EPSDT)		Grants
	Title XI for service coordination		

health services programs reach their full potential. As these programs flourish with stable funding streams, they will help communities maximize the full potential of their children. Aren't all children entitled to equal levels of services?

No longer can education budgets continue to bear the whole financial burden of school health services programs. As society has increasingly placed health care responsibilities onto schools, for example, through civil rights and special education federal legislation and related court decisions, it has neglected to transfer to schools sufficient funds to meet those responsibilities. General child health funds should be made available to school districts for the provision of primary and preventive health care services, as well as health maintenance and coordination services for children with chronic health and mental health conditions.

By pooling resources dedicated to child health, communities can access those funds in cost-effective ways that meet their individual, local needs. For example, society is desperately searching for alternatives to our traditional health care delivery model. Why not take advantage of current wellness initiatives and health promotion knowledge by instituting wellness research and programs that are financed through federal health dollars and available to *all* students? A variety of school health professionals, representing all the components of coordinated or comprehensive school health programs, can lead these initiatives and provide school-based, child-wellness services.

In addition to federal funding, contracts developed between school districts and private insurers of health care can make available previously untapped funds to improve, stabilize, and help equalize school health programs. Identifying the unique health care services that schools can (and do) provide in a cost effective, accessible manner and billing third party insurers for those services will allocate increased dollars for school health services. State regulations may need to be promulgated in order to optimize such contracting. Contracting should not be limited to the school-based health center primary care model, but can and should be extended to other effective health promotion and outcome-based school health services programs, including traditional school health services and nursing program models, depending on the extent of established school-based health services available in the district and the district's willingness to go into the "business of health services."

Research

Although predominantly a professional issue, research in the field of school health is directly connected to adequate funding. If school nurses and other school health professionals cannot prove that what they do makes a difference, or what program components are essential to positive outcomes, why should their services be funded? A strong research base that documents the outcomes of school health services will support a convincing impetus for dedicated school health funding. See Table 19-2 for examples of the types of research sorely needed.

TABLE 19-2.

Sample Research Questions To Be Answered

- Which school health services impact child well-being?
- What is the cost benefit of school nursing services?
- What school nursing services contribute to education goals?
- What outcomes valued by the reforming health care delivery system are achieved through the provision of school nursing services?
- What minimum competencies should a school nurse possess?
- What personnel are needed in a comprehensive school health program?
- What increases support for school health services?
- What factors determine school nurse-to-student ratios?

Not only does research support funding decisions, it also provides the necessary data to establish the "why," when legislators question the role of school health services in such things as health promotion and implementation of the Individuals with Disabilities Education Act (IDEA). Only by validating the effectiveness of school nursing services in relation to student outcomes will school nurses be viewed as vital and necessary forces in the delivery of both education and health care services to school-age children and youth. Perhaps, then, political support will exist to establish a legal basis for the stable funding and support of quality school nursing and school health services programs.

HEALTH CARE DELIVERY SYSTEMS

Managed Care

As the managed health care delivery model struggles to contain health care costs, a prime opportunity exists for school health services programs to emerge as major players. It is possible for school health services programs, staffed by qualified, professional school nurses and allied health and other professional school health personnel, to serve as the primary portal into the health care delivery system for school-aged children. School health services programs must no longer be viewed as luxuries that are disposable whenever education budgets are tight, nor should they be considered separate entities from the health care delivery system. Schools serve children and adolescents with developmental delays and other disabilities related to learning from either birth or three years of age to twenty-one years of age, and all children, including a significant population with chronic health and mental health conditions, from five to sixteen or eighteen years of age. The potential for school health services programs to

meet the vast majority of our children's needs for prevention, screening, early intervention, health coordination, health maintenance and referral services is an idea that has come of age.

Although initially perceived by many school health professionals to be a threat to their existence, the managed care environment actually provides school-based health programs an opportunity for prominence in the emerging health care delivery system. Because school health professionals and paraprofessionals provide a myriad of preventive and primary health care services in a very cost effective manner, many managed care organizations (MCOs) are and will be interested in partnering with them to provide population-based health promotion, prevention, and early intervention services to all children attending school. See Table 19-3 for an overview of the advantages of such partnerships.

Several things need to happen before mutually beneficial relationships can evolve. First, both groups must come to the table with open minds and a willingness to learn about the other, sharing information about their structure, mission, goals, values, language, personnel, services, funding, and quality assurance mechanisms. School health services professionals must market their unique and effective services to the managed care system and verify the child health outcomes that are valued by that system. At the same time, MCOs must be willing to work within existing school health services structures instead of attempting to overtake the school-based market with external and seemingly lucrative proposals. Agreement on goals and strategies can result in contracted agreements that advantageously serve both groups, and provide improved health care services to children. Together, MCOs and school districts can collaborate to enact the necessary state and local statutes and regulations to support such mergers.

TABLE 19-3.

Advantages of Partnerships Between Managed Care Organizations and School Health Services

Advantages to Schools	Advantages to Managed Care Organizations	Advantages to the Health System and Consumers
Improved documentation	Cost effective, timely delivery of services	Improved communication among providers
Focus on outcome measures	Accessible site for preventive and primary care	Shared protocols and standard of care
Enhanced value of individual student plans	Case management by closely linked persons	Continuity of care
Determination of cost of school health services	Risk assessments of vulnerable populations	Elimination of duplicative services
Spotlighting of schools for prevention	Identification of potential members	Reduced health care costs
Revenue for school-delivered health services	Management of cultural barriers	Community schools as sites of service
	Efficient care to the Medicaid population	Accessibility to care for school-aged clients
		Removal of transportation as a barrier
		Schools becoming part of the health care system

Further details related to managed care and school health services can be found in chapter 16.

School-Based Health Centers

These primary health care programs expand the role of traditional school health services. School-based health centers (SBHCs) provide diagnostic and treatment services for students on-site and are generally better staffed than traditional school nurse programs. Professional personnel often include masters-prepared nurse practitioners with expertise in pediatric and adolescent primary care, pediatricians, social workers, child psychiatry and psychology consultants, and administrative and assistive personnel.

SBHCs were originally intended to provide services to uninsured children and those without access to health care. In theory, school-based health centers

might cease to be needed because of the federally initiated Child Health Insurance Program (CHIP), whose goal is to guarantee health insurance for all children. CHIP should identify and serve children without current health care access and insurance, assuring them full health care services in a traditional medical setting. Nonetheless, the SBHC model of primary health care delivery continues to expand. Its accessibility for students, cost-effectiveness, and consumer-friendly arrangement are still desired by many communities.

In order for the SBHC model to remain viable, however, states must provide the legal structure for them to access third-party health care financing and establish a stable role in the managed care arena. In addition, their relationship with existing school health services programs and the schools themselves needs to be more clearly articulated. When individual communities negotiate roles and procedures, issues such as programs' rights and responsibilities, confidentiality, revenue sharing, and access to records can be defined. Contracts that carefully stipulate the parameters of these unique partnerships will help prevent misunderstandings that can undermine the programs.

Several issues remain to be resolved. These include:

- role delineation of all school-based health providers;
- the question of 24-hour coverage for members;
- a sustained revenue source;
- quality assurance mechanisms; and
- objective research studies on student outcomes and program cost-effectiveness of different models.

See also chapter 15.

Privatization

Private health care providers, including hospitals and managed care organizations, have taken advantage of the previously described funding chaos of school health services to expand their community-based services. Two scenarios are typical: 1) a private provider proposes to provide basic school health services or primary health care services to a district that has either inadequate health services or none; or 2) a private provider promises to provide services more economically than the district provides them, or to rescue the district in times of challenging budgets.

Certainly, privately-funded services can be beneficial if children receive services that they have been previously denied, or if school health services programs facing extinction can be kept intact. There can be, however,

substantial pitfalls to contracting with private entities for school health programs. First, outside groups may bid for the contract at an unrealistically low rate for the first year or two and, once in control, precipitously raise their fees. Second, personnel working for private, non-board-of-education entities, are rarely viewed by school personnel as integral members of school teams or critical partners in the education system. Opportunities for collaborating with educators and positively influencing day-to-day experiences of children and faculty diminish as services and providers are more remote and less integrated. Third, there can be less administrative overhead with Board of Education models, even though competent school nursing supervision is required. The advantages of Board of Education models need to be researched and then considered as alternatives to privatization. Many of the concerns surrounding privatization of school health services can be avoided if the primary issue of budget allocation for school-based programs is corrected. (See the section "Funding" [above] for additional information.)

TECHNOLOGY

Computerized Information

As for society in general, the development and use of computers have been advantageous to the delivery of school health services. See Table 19-4 for a synopsis of these advantages.

Computerization of the health office enhances the care of students by allowing school nurses to rapidly access a student's full record. Secondly, standardized and computerized record keeping will greatly enhance the ability of clinicians and educators to conduct meaningful research. For example, school personnel can

---

TABLE 19-4.
Use of Computerization in School Health Services

- Documentation of health care
- Standardizing health records
- Identification, tracking, and evaluation of student and community health needs and trends
- Evaluating outcomes of interventions
- Tracking students at risk of lower performance
- Conducting health assessments following individual growth and development
- Correlating student problems and subsequent interventions with education outcomes
- Evaluating school health services programs
- Delivering motivational health education
- Accessing current health information
- Learning via the internet and CD ROM

study the correlation of student problems and subsequent interventions with educational outcomes like school performance, suspensions, and dropout rates. Additionally, school health programs can be evaluated in terms of their effects on both health and education outcomes.

However, "what" needs to be collected and "how" are questions that must be addressed immediately, as the national school nursing community acknowledges. Without standard data collection, comparisons and generalizations cannot be made, yet that is what is necessary to make legal and ethical decisions about health care delivery. This issue will be discussed further in this chapter under "Professional Issues."

An example of the need for computerized record keeping is child immunization data. This has been discussed for years, but without consistent results. While states are now using federal incentive grants to establish standard computerized immunization registries for preschoolers, the use and financial support of these registries for school-age children is unclear or unlikely at this time. Yet, they might go a long way in ensuring appropriate immunization levels and eliminating over-immunization due to poor and inaccessible record keeping.

Telehealth

Telehealth, the application of telecommunications to health care delivery, is just emerging and has entered the thinking of only a few school health leaders. It holds tremendous opportunities for the expansion and improved delivery of school health services. These opportunities are especially important in rural areas and in those communities where human resources are not sufficiently abundant to meet the health care needs of their children and youth.

Where there is a lack of sufficient school nursing personnel on-site, the tele-connection of one nurse to a cluster of schools would enable the professional nurse to delegate a variety of health services and provide immediate, well-informed direction to assistive personnel (e.g. health technicians or on-site education personnel). Another approach is to connect school nurses in their respective buildings with a regional medical center where a physician or nurse practitioner is available for consultation and, if indicated, immediate medical diagnosis and treatment.

Grant funding of pilot sites that model public-private partnerships could spark a new wave of school health services in under-served communities. Of course, there are numerous professional practice and legal issues involved in such models that need to be

dealt with on both the federal and state levels before this type of service delivery can proliferate.

CONNECTION WITH EDUCATION

Health Services and Educational Outcomes

School nurses and health services belong in schools only if they are positively impacting the ability of students to learn and achieve. In order to ensure that they do just that, health services must be consistently linked and delivered in response to the goals of education.

Although there is considerable evidence that good health is a prerequisite to learning, there is a dearth of outcome data to prove that school nursing services positively influence the health and learning of children. Only when there is sufficient, convincing data to prove a positive correlation between school nursing services and health and education outcomes for children will school health services be mandated. In addition, the effects of a wide variety of health services need to be studied, so that funding decisions are based on what really makes a difference. For example, do the results of vision and hearing screenings affect students' availability for learning? We know that vision and hearing are critical to learning, but the next question is whether school-based screening programs are sufficiently low-cost and high-yield to make a difference in the student population for schools to take on this health services responsibility. Another concern is whether a professional nurse needs to provide this service. Can equally valid results be gained by technicians trained and supervised by school nurses to do this type of repetitious work? Using personnel appropriately must be considered when providing services so that resources are expended in a cost-effective manner.

Functional Language

When health and education personnel, each viewing children from their individual professional perspectives, are able to understand children's strengths and needs, and the implications of those needs for successful learning, they are probably using "functional" language. This means terminology that focuses on the functional abilities and limitations of students in the classroom, regardless of medical diagnosis or educational or disability label. For example, instead of labeling a child as "ADHD," identifying the student's functional problems, for example, an inability to attend to tasks and impulsiveness, are far more meaningful to defining strategies that will enable the student to be successful in school. After all, isn't that why both educators and school nurses work in schools? Unfortunately, functional language related to health and educational disabilities is seldom used in schools. Interestingly, nurses today identify the functional health needs of clients through the use of standardized classification languages (e.g. Nursing Interventions Classification and Nursing Outcomes Classification) within their own profession, but have generally not used those languages, which are based on the functional health status of clients, for communications with other professionals.

Used in schools, functional language should not belong exclusively to either health or education and should be readily understood by both. It should be collaboratively developed as a universal language that transcends professional goals, missions, rhetoric and vocabulary. Such a language could result in outcomes that are not dissimilar to the universal understanding and appreciation that is experienced through music. Focusing on the functional abilities and needs of students will increase the likelihood of positive educational and health-related outcomes and better protect student privacy in educational planning and delivery by

- removing the need to use medical, psychiatric, and disability diagnoses;
- shifting the focus of planning appropriate programs to the individual learning strengths and needs of students;
- preventing students from being labeled and compartmentalized; and
- improving communication and collaboration among staff.

An additional advantage of functional terminology is that its use will enable comparisons among and within professions by providing the comparative basis that research demands. Through research on the effects of health and educational interventions for specific functional deficits, data-based determinations for future applications can be made. This will help avoid strategies that merely "seem" right or are presently in vogue.

Comparable terminology will promote trust between health and education providers. It will enhance mutual respect for each other's expertise in the educational process and provide the basis for a comprehensive approach to the needs of students. The current onus is primarily on school health personnel to discontinue the use of medical terminology and diagnoses and to begin communicating health needs by using function-based language. (See discussion in chapter 8.) Educators must also be willing to discontinue the use of generic labels

used for students' disabilities and learning problems and focus instead on their individual learning styles and behaviors. In order for functional language to be institutionalized, there needs to be major collaboration between, and operational shifts by, both professions. These changes must begin at the national level, through professional organizations and at the university level, through pre-service preparation programs. While the operational shift will need to be major, the winners will be children, a worthy incentive, indeed.

Parity with Education Personnel

Even if school nurses are required, or expected, to provide the health care services needed by students on a day-to-day basis, nurses may not be willing to work in schools if they are not regarded as equal members of the professional school team. In the vast majority of school districts nationwide, nurses are compensated on a non-professional scale with custodians and secretaries. Until there is pay equity with other health institutions where nurses work, attracting well-qualified professionals will remain difficult for schools.

Although seemingly a mere personnel problem, parity goes beyond monetary issues to one of professional esteem and expectations. When nurses are on an equal playing field with their education peers, there is a prevailing attitude of teamwork and collegiality that benefits children and families. It is partly related to a philosophy that considers health vital to the education process, i.e. that health goes hand in hand with education. When health is valued, compensation for the services of competent health professionals should follow. When health is valued, and competent school nurses are employed, children benefit from an array of services and professional expertise. However, just being a "nurse" does not and should not translate to parity. School nurses need to be minimally prepared at the baccalaureate level and equipped with special skills and knowledge to be an equal team member with their education peers. This concept is detailed further in the section below on "Professional Issues: Preparation and Continuing Education."

School nurses should be compensated at the same level as their education peers with comparable professional preparation and experience. They should similarly have the same expectations of increased professional preparation and continuing education. Generally, this is a local issue to regulate. Nonetheless, state regulations that are also tied to mandated school health services provided by professional nurses will help ensure standardization across a state. For related information, see the sections on "Preparation and

Continuing Education" and "Certification" under "Professional Issues" below.

PROFESSIONAL ISSUES
Role Definition

One of the most problematic issues in school nursing is the lack of consensus among its practitioners in defining and standardizing a unique set of services. This deficit relates to the fact that school nurses have historically attempted to provide any and all health-related services that children need in the school setting. This desire to help has even expanded to include families and school staff. School health services as a program has, perhaps, suffered from trying to be all things to all people.

School nursing personnel absolutely must determine what they can and should provide, i.e., those services that are most important to removing the health-related barriers to students' achievement and future success. As the school nursing profession makes this determination, educators and communities must also decide the role that health services programs should play in their schools. These determinations require communication and collaboration among school health professionals, educators, families, and other community providers.

Role definition is a critical first step to advancing service delivery and producing quantifiable outcomes of those services. Basic to proving what makes a difference is first standardizing the "what." Unless the profession knows what services it can provide, and those that it can provide better than anyone else, it cannot market those services, for example, to funding sources like MCOs.

TABLE 19-5.
Reasons for Development of Competencies

- Establishes legal performance standards
- Forms the basis for accountability
- Creates a framework for quality assurance
- Standardizes pre- and post-professional preparation
- Institutes universal expectations
- Assists accurate performance assessment
- Formulates a foundation for services

Once the services are defined and a professional framework is institutionalized, school nurses will have the continued challenge of concentrating on the identified core set of services, and not reverting to earlier modes of operation, i.e., doing and giving whatever is needed. When a profession is scattered in its objectives, the lack of clarity and focus in direction makes it appear that the program is "soft" or unnecessary and, therefore, perhaps more expendable when tight budget conditions prevail.

Once the role and services of school nurses are defined, the job descriptions of providers will become clearer. This clarity will help establish the legal framework required to accurately and universally define such things as the necessary preparation and scope of practice of school nurses and, the standards against which negligence claims are measured. In terms of legislation, it will help guide the process of deciding what are appropriate expectations for school health services, such as in the provision of related services under IDEA.

Competencies

The next step after role definition is to establish practice-based competencies for school health nurses. Competencies need to be grounded in research and will be best identified by professional nursing organizations in collaboration with academic institutions. There are a number of compelling reasons for determining what a practitioner must know and be prepared to do to in order to achieve desired outcomes in student populations. See Table 19-5 for a summary of reasons for developing competencies for school health nurses.

Preparation and Continuing Education

The various entry levels into nursing and the wide range of competencies between these levels cause enormous confusion in the public's mind. Not only is there confusion related to registered nurses (RNs) with diplomas and associate, baccalaureate, master's, and doctoral degrees, but the disparate educational content and performance outcomes between each make it legally and practically impossible to expect the same standards and accountability from different levels of RN preparation. Even more problematic, the public does not understand the purely adjunctive role of organized nursing's licensed assistants who receive technical training in ten-to-twelve-month post high school programs. These licensed assistants are usually called licensed practical nurses (LPNs) or licensed vocational nurses (LVNs).

This confusion can be addressed by state legislation requiring one entry level for school health nursing practice. Because of the autonomous nature of the practice, the reasoning required in a multitude of unstructured and demanding situations, and necessary pre-service educational content, such as working with families and within communities, a bachelors degree in nursing should be the minimum entry-level requirement. This would be either equal to or less than qualifications required of other professionals working in schools. It would also help to address related problematic areas, such as parity and the perceived value of health services.

Although advanced professional assessment and problem-solving skills are needed in school nursing, it is the opinion of this author that master's level nurse practitioner preparation is not necessary, or even desirable, for all school nurses. The clinical skills and knowledge of pediatric and adolescent nurse practitioners may be most cost-effective when used in primary health care centers, including school-based health centers, rather than in schools.

Master's degree level preparation, theoretically advantageous but impractical as the universal entry level for all school nurses, must minimally be mandated for those in school nurse management, supervisory, consultant, and other leadership positions. Master's preparation is also critical for school health services models where the school nurse is the sole health professional and must delegate the delivery of certain health services to paraprofessionals. In this situation, the school nurse is more of a consultant than a direct service provider, and has significant responsibilities in leadership, overseeing non-professionals, and ensuring a basic level of student safety. Health and education budgets, in this manager's opinion, cannot support master's-prepared, entry-level school nurses in every school in the United States, nor is there an adequate supply of these nurses, even if money were not an issue. Equity of school nurse qualifications across school districts and states—at a minimum of the bachelor degree for entry into practice—should, perhaps, be the first priority, along with making such qualified school nurses available to every school-age child in the country.

Continuing education should not only be expected, but required of school nurses, just as it is of teachers. Just as teachers in some states are expected to obtain a master's degree within a certain number of years of employment, so should school nurses be required to pursue and complete graduate education in their spe-

cialty practice. Post entry-level education helps ensure a work force that keeps up-to-date and also provides sufficient leadership and mentoring for new school nurses. Moreover, regular, quality, continuing education should be the norm for all professionals and paraprofessionals practicing in health care and education fields.

Advanced knowledge beyond the bachelor-of-science degree in nursing (BSN) is necessary for optimum functioning of school health services professionals, and for their ability to be fully integrated into the school faculty. If the BSN is the required entry-level pre-service preparation, BSN-prepared school nurses will need to pursue certain additional health and education courses in order to be successful in the unique position of school nurse. School nurses must be "bilingual," that is well-versed in the fields of health and education, including, school readiness, basic principles of teaching and learning, and special education law and practice. School nurses must become particularly expert and articulate regarding the effects of good health and health conditions (and their treatments) on student learning.

The school nurse must speak the language of education in order to ensure that the health services provided are meaningful to the education process. These additional requisites for competency in school health nursing speak to Wold's view (see chapter 1) that school nurses require specialty preparation at the Master's level. Practically speaking, achieving this level of school nurse preparation is likely to require the type of two-step process discussed above. The first step is requiring the BSN as the entry-level degree, along with introductory education courses (e.g., a regular and a special education course), for all school nurses. The second step is requiring the Master's degree or equivalency after a standard period of employment.

In addition to professional school nurses, paraprofessionals who assist nurses should have a standard minimal level of preparation. In many jurisdictions, it is a paraprofessional who has the day-to-day responsibility for carrying out routine, basic health services under a professional nurse's direction. States should mandate minimum requirements that include CPR and first aid certification, as well as other standardized content specific to the role and limitations of school health assistants (e.g., Standard Precautions, infection control, body mechanics, confidentiality, screening techniques). Putting instructional assistants or school secretaries with no training in charge of health care constitutes unsafe care for children. Even if they have some basic health care knowledge, these staff members have other responsibilities and cannot be expected to concentrate on the details that comprise safe health care delivery in schools.

Requirements of paraprofessionals who provide health services in school should be regulated by state law. When states require training and certification of nursing assistants and health care technicians, this requirement or a similar requirement should be considered for such assistive personnel in schools. If states do not have standard requirements for nursing assistants, instituting such universal prerequisites should be considered by both state health and education agencies. It must be remembered that paraprofessionals, including LPNs, can legally only operate under the supervision of a registered nurse. This issue will be discussed further in the section on "Assistive Personnel and Delegation."

Certification

Certification of school nurses is the best way to ensure that entry-level school health services providers possess the core knowledge and judgment for competent practice. It also establishes a level of safe, quality services for students beyond those required by state RN licensure.

There are two types of school nurse certification. One is based on clinical nursing practice and is generated by national professional nursing groups, namely the National Board for Certification of School Nurses and the American Nurses Credentialing Center. This type of certification helps to ensure a minimum clinical practice level within the specialty of school nursing, with standards agreed to by school nursing nationwide. One state, North Carolina, uses this type of national certification as a requirement for school nurse employment.

The second type is teacher certification for school nurses, like other student services specialists, as determined by state departments of education. State teaching certification laws mandate minimum requirements for employment, which for school nurses usually include one or more education courses in addition to the BSN. Teacher certification mandates may also spell out requirements for continuing education and graduate preparation for ongoing certification. In some states, such as California, the entry requirements for school nurses are significantly higher than in other states but mirror the expectations for all school professionals in that state. Currently, there are twenty-seven states that maintain some form or level of state certification for school nurses, and others are in the process of standardizing their requirements for school nurses.

Certification is a commitment of value, and the burden is on states to define and demand a minimum but appropriate level of preparation for their school health practitioners. This is essential if states are to succeed in minimizing the disparity of services across districts in their states and to ensure that all students have access to services from equally well-prepared providers. Additionally, where state certification is mandated, required preparation is usually higher and salaries are more substantial.

Sub-specialization

Although school nursing is a specialty practice area of nursing, in many ways it is still a generalist practice. This is true because school nurses are usually responsible for health care delivery to all students served by the school district (sometimes from birth to 21 years of age) and, in some areas, families and school staff. Schools are a microcosm of society, and because the school nurse's role is expanding at a rapid pace in response to health-related societal needs, sub-specialty practices within school nursing should be considered. Examples might include early intervention, adolescent and elementary health nursing, and substance abuse identification and prevention. As school districts commit to and expand their health service delivery programs and as they attain a certain level of sophistication, consideration should be given to establishing sub-specialty practice areas within the program. Of course, graduate preparation programs, job requirements, certification, position descriptions, and professional development will have to reflect these more narrowly defined roles.

Children would likely benefit from increased specialization in school nursing. It is impossible for nurses to keep abreast of all the advances in health to the extent that one's practice is current for all age levels and specific health issues. This is the same challenge that family practice physicians face. If children were served by nurses with specialized expertise in addressing the particular needs of different groups, the services delivered would likely be safer, more current and appropriate, more pertinent to their individual needs, and more effective in terms of student outcomes.

Sub-specialization is currently happening informally with self-selection but, because as it is not yet supported by national certification, state continuing education requirements, or higher education programs, there is no formal designation of sub-specialty expertise in school nursing. Additional consideration must be given to the increased number of health providers that would be required with sub-specialization, and to the funding required to support these additional providers. Although potential benefits are obvious, the corresponding costs cannot, and should not be expected to, be supported by education budgets alone. This sophisticated model of service delivery will depend, in a large part, on major restructuring of health care delivery systems and stable funding to support schools as sites for a wide range of health promotion and intervention services.

PROGRAM MANAGEMENT

Hazardous Practices in Schools

Society increasingly expects schools to ensure the welfare of children including ensuring their good health. Examples of health care procedures that some students need in order to be in school or to fully participate in school activities include: medication administration, blood glucose monitoring, nebulizer treatments, catheterization, tracheal suctioning, and gastrostomy tube feeding.

When health professionals are not available in schools, the health care responsibility for monitoring and interventions needed by students during the school day have fallen to ill-prepared school personnel. Requiring education staff to perform these medical procedures is analogous to expecting nurses to implement the mathematics curriculum. More importantly, though, it is unsafe and potentially very harmful for children. In addition, the delivery of health care by unlicensed individuals may constitute the practice of nursing without a license, which carries legal sanction for those individuals. Even if there is a lack of health professionals to assess student needs, to develop appropriate individualized healthcare plans, and to evaluate the outcomes of the care provided, these critical functions can never be delegated to unlicensed staff. Without these functions, the performance of which require professional expertise, students' health care needs often go unrecognized, unmet, or poorly met, resulting in diminished health and diminished learning.

To prohibit inappropriate and hazardous practices in schools, both education and school health professional organizations must oppose this manner of operating. The support of parent-teacher organizations may be effective in preventing these unsafe practices. Institutionalizing adequate funding for school health programs will serve to significantly reduce or even eliminate these inadequate staffing patterns and unsafe child-health practices. Ultimately, state statute and regulations are required to mandate the use of appropriately credentialed school health professionals to deliver and supervise these specialized health care services in schools.

Staffing Levels and Ratios

Program management issues related to staffing primarily pertain to safety, accountability, and quality assurance. Staffing school health services is most often a local function, although a few states mandate ratios of nurses to students, just as they do for teachers to students. Nonetheless, until school health services are mandated by states, establishing ratios is not very useful.

The National Association of School Nurses and the American Nurses Association recommend certain ratios based on the type of educational programming students require. However, those arbitrary numerical designations do not consider the various models of service delivery, the use and supervision of paraprofessionals, the expanded role of school health nurses, or the increasing needs of students and families that are met today through school programs. Furthermore, these ratios were developed approximately two decades ago and are not relevant to current education settings, i.e., where students with special health care and education needs are expected to be fully included in every school. The complexities related to appropriate staffing today raise critical concerns that the professional organizations and, ultimately, local and state school systems need to address.

More equitable and safer ways to determine staffing requirements need to be established. Assessing the functional health needs of students in every school building and then using this data when budgeting and allocating appropriate resources for the district would provide a comparable, data-based foundation for staffing decisions. The use of functional indicators to create realistic staffing patterns fits well with the concept of school health and education professionals using a common language to address the functional abilities and needs of students, as discussed previously. The already established nursing diagnosis language could provide the functional comparability and standardization needed.

Supervision and Management

In far too many school districts, the only supervision and coordination provided for professional and assistive school health nursing personnel are those furnished by school-based principals or central office education personnel. Despite the fact that many state nurse practice acts require that nurses have supervision by nurses competent to determine another nurse's clinical knowledge and judgment, this practice of supervision by non-nurse administrators continues. A related practice, supervision by non-nurses of unlicensed personnel who are carrying out nursing activities is both dangerous and, in most cases, illegal.

This issue is actually a matter of common sense. Lay persons are not in a position to dictate or supervise clinical health practices. Nor would it be acceptable to have nurses supervising and evaluating the competence of classroom teachers. Certainly, principals have valuable input into the evaluation of school nurses and health assistants, but their scope of concern and expertise must be relegated to non-clinical issues, such as cooperation, productivity, communication skills, and team participation. Performance appraisals of school nurses should be joint initiatives between principals and nursing supervisors.

School districts that provide the most solid, stable, and progressive school health programs are those that have nursing managers to provide the clinical judgment and the infrastructure required for effective service delivery. Even where there are school nurse supervisors and managers, they are frequently faced with unrealistic and unsafe supervisory ratios, e.g., 50 nurses:1 nurse supervisor. Poor ratios take on added significance since school nurses are seldom all in the same building, but spread out across a school district. This is currently a local policy issue, but it needs to be addressed through state regulation.

Substitute School Nursing Personnel

As the health needs of students increase in number and complexity in our schools, thought needs to be given to maintaining safe levels of care when the regular school nursing personnel are not present. Performance-related liability for substitute school nurses and assistive personnel is generally incurred by schools, just as it is for substitute teachers, yet, there are many unanswered legal questions related to substitute school health personnel. Some of these are summarized in Table 19-6.

Although not a strictly legal concern, the monetary reimbursement for substitute school nursing services impacts the supply of substitute nurses which, in turn, can become a legal issue. Generally, the pay is so poor that attracting substitute nurses is virtually impossible or, perhaps worse, only poorly qualified nurses apply. Until schools become competitive with other institutions employing licensed health personnel, this will remain a critical management issue. Certainly increasing the rate of pay for substitutes nurses would be less of a financial burden than having to contract with nursing agencies to supply substitute nurses, or settling a civil case in which damages are sought from the district for negligently employing incompetent staff.

Private Duty Nurses

Even if there is a full-time registered nurse in the school, some children's heath needs may not be safely provided by a nurse who is also responsible for hundreds of other students. There have been multiple federal district court decisions that have drawn the line of schools' responsibilities for providing school health services to disabled students at the point where a private duty (one-on-one) licensed professional or technical nurse is required for a student throughout the school day. However, in March 1999, the United States Supreme Court reversed several previous lower courts' decisions based on the details of case number 96-1793, *Cedar Rapids Community School District v. Garret F.* Central to this case was the question of whether "private duty" nursing is a related school health service under the Individuals with Disabilities Education Act. (See chapter 13 for a fuller discussion of this case and its implications.)

Because the Supreme Court has determined that schools are obligated to fund school nursing services that a student requires to access special education services (and this includes one-on-one nursing services), the implications for school districts are tremendous. There are numerous details yet to decide, not the least of which include:

TABLE 19-6.

Legal Questions Related to Substitute Health Services Personnel

- What type of health services provider is required?
- Should substitute type be decided individually by school?
- What is the minimum qualifications requisite?
- To what extent is the school system required to orient, train, and/or supervise substitutes?
- What are the legal ramifications if the school is unwilling or unable to secure a suitable substitute?

- What criteria will be used to determine when private duty nurses are necessary?
- Can existing, applicable health dollars still be tapped for all or part of the bill?
- Should a new pot of money be established from either health funds or a combination of health and education funds?
- Can Medicaid waivers be expanded to fund private duty nurses that are needed by all such medically-complex students?
- Can schools bill Medicaid and other third party payers for appropriate private duty nursing services, just as they now bill for other school nursing services?

This Supreme Court ruling has interpreted IDEA in an unequivocally distinct and powerful manner that speaks to eliminating any health-related barriers to the education of disabled students. Nonetheless, the financial implications could be overwhelming for many school districts. Of utmost concern, from a manager's viewpoint, is that the finances for complying with the ruling be determined locally in equitable, community-sensitive, and appropriate ways. What must be avoided, at all costs, is the tendency to siphon-off the existing school nurse personnel to meet the now-mandated, in-depth, and continuous health needs of medically complex students to the extent that school health services to other students are diminished.

Services Beyond the Schoolhouse

What is the school's responsibility to students requiring health care services in order to access appropriate education services when the education programs occur off school property? Examples include full-day or overnight field trips, cooperative learning experiences, and outdoor-learning (camp) experiences. If the need for a nursing service is included in a student's 504 plan or individual education program (IEP), then the school is obligated to provide those services. Yet, there remain many unanswered legal questions and difficulties in implementing safe services during overnight field trips and other school-sponsored events off school property.

Despite many decisions by the Office of Civil Rights and the courts to the contrary (see chapters 11 and 12), many schools continue to require parents to accompany students on such trips, or to demand that students remain in the school building if no appropriate person is available to provide the service. These practices, clearly discriminatory under federal and state mandates, continue in large measure because of

inadequate funding of school health services programs. Either revisions to federal legislation are required or new funding streams must be provided to support the existing mandates. Hopefully, the latter will occur, as the outcomes for students with disabilities are extraordinarily improved with their inclusion in regular school programs to the fullest extent reasonable.

Partnerships

Collaboration between both state and local health and education departments in providing school health services is mandated in several states. Where that is not the case, and because public funding is inadequate for school health services, new and creative partnerships are being forged with other community public and private entities. Examples include public health and social services agencies, hospitals, managed care organizations, and private health care agencies. Certainly, partnerships may expand the delivery of health services to school-aged children where it has been non-existent or inadequate but, in the opinion of this author, administrative control should remain with the education agency. If this trend continues, to meet student and programmatic needs certain legal issues must be clarified, such as:

- confidentiality of and access to records;
- employment and personnel issues;
- maintenance of programmatic control; and
- liability issues.

Some of these issues are discussed in this chapter in the section on "Privatization" and in chapters 15 ("School-based Health Centers") and 16 ("Part I: School Health Services and Managed Care").

PRACTICE ISSUES
Medication Administration

Although the administration of medications should be limited to those essential for student participation in schools, the number of students requiring the administration of prescribed medications continues to increase. The types of medications have also changed significantly to include potent psychotropic drugs, and inhaled, intravenous, and intramuscular or subcutaneous medications.

The role of school nurses must be understood to not only include the administration of medications, but also, and sometimes more importantly, to include monitoring for their therapeutic effects and side effects.

Professional judgments about these expanding numbers and types of medications need to be made on a continual basis; safety is an increasing and legitimate concern. While non-health professionals can be trained to safely administer oral medications, monitoring the effects of oral medications and administering medications by routes other than oral or topical must come under the purview of a licensed nurse or physician. In schools where lay persons routinely administer oral medications, nurses need the time and opportunity to supervise and provide consultation for those whom they have trained to administer medications. A few states mandate that all medications in schools be administered by nurses. In order to ensure children's safety, the remaining states should review and, perhaps, eliminate their state laws that permit medication administration by unlicensed individuals in schools or, minimally, require an adequate number of professional nurses to coordinate and supervise this important school activity.

In addition to prescribed medications, there is the issue of over-the-counter (OTC) medications, e.g., mild analgesics and cough suppressants. Since the goal of school health services is to assist students to maintain their health in order to learn, consideration should be given by school districts to providing simple OTCs designed to relieve minor discomfort, so that students can remain in school and focus on learning. When offering this service, schools need to ensure that OTCs will not be dispensed on demand but will be one of several options in a treatment protocol that is based on a health assessment by a professional nurse. In considering an OTC program, schools must abide by state regulations of their boards of medicine, nursing, and pharmacy. Clarification will be needed to determine if the state's licensure provisions that limit dispensing of medications to pharmacists and physicians apply to OTCs. Usually state regulations concerning OTCs require standing physician orders or embedding the OTCs within physician-approved treatment protocols that identify a variety of health care options. This is an example of the kind of collaboration needed between the nursing and medical communities in the delivery of comprehensive school health services.

Confidentiality Issues

Education staff members sometimes believe that they have a right and responsibility to know about a student's personal health issues. This causes both consternation and ethical dilemmas for school health personnel who are required to protect the privacy of

student (client) health concerns. The quandary is that educators do have—and need—some of this information, but not necessarily all.

Pending federal legislation and proposed legislation in many states about these very issues may specifically designate school health records as medical records. This would certainly help protect medical confidentiality in schools, but would necessitate a drastic change of attitude, as well as the practice regulations that govern school health records.

The use of functional language would alleviate many of the problems surrounding confidentiality in schools. See the section on "Functional Language" in this chapter for further details, as well as chapter 8.

Despite many initiatives at the state and national level related to the privacy of health care information, there remains an acute need for health and education professionals, both in pre-service and school settings, and for state leaders and legislators to work together to develop guidelines that will help school professionals to seek appropriate consultation and make well-reasoned decisions when faced with practice dilemmas. Chapter 8 provides an in-depth discussion of confidentiality issues and dilemmas in schools; chapter 9 addresses school health records; and chapter 10 covers electronic records and related technology.

Assistive Personnel and Delegation

In addition to professional nurses, the number of assistive personnel will likely increase in response to the expanding health needs of students. Assistive personnel may include volunteers, school staff, health aides, licensed practical nurses, and RNs who do not meet their state's requirements for qualification as a school nurse. The use of augmentative personnel can extend the delivery of health services, but when used to replace professional healthcare providers, leads to poorer quality of care. Assistive personnel are needed to supplement, not supplant school nurses, nor should they be permitted to practice nursing without a license. For the safe delivery of care to students, the appropriate use of assistive personnel in schools, including their training and supervision, should be state regulated. In the meantime, safe practices should at least by enforced by local policy.

The issue of assistive personnel is closely connected to the issue of nursing delegation of licensed health care activities. (See chapters 4 and 5 for detailed information.) To help ensure safe standards and practices in the provision of health care to minor children in schools, all states need to regulate and restrict nursing delegation to unlicensed assistive personnel in schools and related community settings. In addition, the requirements of licensure and health standards need to be enforced because, even where it is clearly stipulated in the law, compliance is frequently neither monitored nor enforced.

Medically Complex Students

Due to the advances in science and medicine, there are always new health care requirements in the care of children with complex health needs. Schools must keep pace with the services that this special population of children requires so that their care in school keeps pace with technology and knowledge, and further enables their full access to learning. The legal issues previously discussed under funding, private duty nurses, and delegation all pertain to providing safe school-based nursing services for medically complex students.

Communicable Disease Control

Initially the impetus behind the establishment of school health services, controlling communicable disease remains a prime school nursing responsibility. With the advent of AIDS, and with the proliferating strains of hepatitis, sexually transmitted diseases, and antibiotic-resistant bacteria, the role of school health services in the arena of communicable disease control has become even more complex. The main issues in controlling communicable diseases in schools revolve around the following:

- the right of all students to attend school and for school staff to work;
- the right of students and school staff to work in a safe environment
- confidentiality of medical histories and records; and
- practices to prevent the spread of disease to students and staff.

While the right of students to attend school and of employees to work despite having a long-term infectious disease has been well established, confidentiality of medical diagnoses and health care records remain a major issue, as discussed above under "Confidentiality Issues," and in depth in chapter 8. Implementing the OSHA blood-borne pathogen standard is a management strategy for protecting employees from blood-borne disease that usually falls under the purview of school health services. In many states, schools are obliged to comply with the requirements of the Occupational Safety and Health Act (OSHA).

Yet to be explicitly defined in many states is the question of whether and under what circumstances school health professionals should (and should not) notify a child's family or staff member who has been exposed to blood or body fluids that are known to be infected with the AIDS or hepatitis viruses. Children are not covered under the OSHA blood-borne pathogen standard, so their protection and the issues surrounding blood and body-fluid exposures are not as clearly defined as those of employees. Confidentiality demands that the diagnosis be kept private, but the human desire of health professionals to alert the victim can be compelling. Clearly, this issue needs to be addressed by states in a manner that protects societal health and welfare. See the discussion in chapter 8 regarding ethical and legal considerations.

Notification rules are determined by state law and are usually a function only of public health officials and physicians. School health professionals should work collaboratively with public health officials in identifying the rare situations that pose such ethical and clinical dilemmas. Mechanisms for regular consultation and collaboration are greatly needed. For example, school nurses need assistance in explaining to other school officials why the right to privacy is critical and that the "need to know" does not really apply to the medical diagnosis, but usually only to knowing how to implement universal precautions. Again, better pre-service education across disciplines and improved mechanisms for collaboration and consultation between health and education professionals are critical to improving school management of these issues.

Immunizing children against infectious diseases is one of the practices aimed at controlling the spread of these conditions. Even here, though, there remain unanswered legal questions due to variation in state mandates. For example, only some states require immunization compliance prior to school entry. More stringent requirements would greatly enhance communicable disease control in our highly mobile, contemporary society.

CONCLUSION

With increasing demands for school nursing services and more complicated scenarios in schools, old paradigms and established laws and regulations may need to be challenged and revised so that the provision of services to children keeps current with the need. Refer to Table 19-7 for a summary of the future challenges in school health services and school nursing.

TABLE 19-7.

Future Challenges in School Health Services and School Nursing

Program Support	Program Management	Professional Issues	Practice Issues	Health Care Delivery Systems	Connection with Education	Technology
Provide stable budgetary sources	Mandate qualified nurses for school health services	Define and standardize a unique set of services	Require nurses to manage medication administration	Secure schools' position as portal for children and youth	Affirm health as vital to the education process	Support increased computerized recordkeeping
Commit health and education agencies' support	Eliminate educators' responsibility for nursing activities	Clarify job descriptions	Consider over-the-counter medication programs	Render health promotion, prevention, early intervention	Link goals of school health services to education goals	Standardize data collection
Access existing child health funds	Establish safe, realistic staffing levels	Define the role of school health services/nursing in schools	Protect confidentiality of medical information in schools	Partner with managed care organizations	Show positive education outcomes from school nursing	Use computerized data to conduct research
Attach monies to state and federal mandates	Set appropriate, needs-based nurse-to-student ratios	Establish practice-based competencies for school nurses	Give appropriate health information to school staff	Allow SBHCs' access to health care funds	Research and fund effective health services programs	Expand the use of technology to access information
Create new funding streams with partnerships	Strengthen infrastructure with nurse managers	Mandate baccalaureate entry level for school nurses	Disallow replacement of nurses by assistive personnel	Establish role for SBHCs in managed care arena	Use functional language for students' strengths & needs	Promote computerized immunization records
Contract with third-party insurers	Increase requirements and pay for substitute nurses	Establish teacher certification for school nurses	Enforce nurses-only delegation of nursing activities	Solidify operations between schools and SBHCs	Make school nurses equal education team members	Pilot telehealth in underserved school communities
Prove that school health services make a difference	Define legal parameters for substitute health providers	Require advanced education and continuing education	Ensure health services for medically complex students	Demonstrate advantage of Board of Education model	Provide school nurses pay parity with education staff	
Identify programs essential for positive outcomes	Guarantee school nursing services despite location	Require Masters preparation for nurse administrators	Protect students and staff from bloodborne diseases	Avoid need for privatization through secure funding	Equate job requisites for school nurses with educators'	
Connect school nursing with health and education outcomes	Ensure nursing as a related service for eligible students	Enact standards for paraprofessionals	Strengthen immunization requirements			
Document cost effectiveness of school nursing services	Resolve issues related to private duty nurses	Consider subspecialties within school nursing				
	Provide funding for required private duty nurses					
	Mandate health and education agencies' collaboration					
	Forge new public and private partnerships					

SUGGESTED READING LIST

American Nurses Association. (1997). Telehealth: a tool for nursing practice. *Nursing Trends and Issues. ANA Policy Series. 2*(4). Washington D.C.: Author.

Americans with Disabilities Act of 1990 (ADA), 42 U.S.C. §12101 - §12213; Regulations at 28 C.F.R. §35 and §36.

Bradley, B. (1998). Establishing a research agenda for school nursing. *Journal of School Nursing, 14*(1), 4-13.

Brainerd, E. (1998). School health nursing services progress review: A report of 1996 national meeting. *Journal of School Health, 68* (1), 12-21.

Cedar Rapids Community School District v. Garret F., 119 S.Ct. 992, 29 IDELR 966 (U.S. 1999).

Costante, C.C. (1996) Supporting student success: School nurses make a difference. *Journal of School Nursing, 12*(3), 4-6.

Denehy, J. (2000). Measuring the outcomes of school nursing practice. *Journal of School Nursing, 16*(1), 2-4.

Deutsch, C. (2000). Common cause: School health and school reform. *Educational Leadership. 57*(6), 8-12.

Devaney, B., Schochet, P., Thornton, C., Fasciano, N., and Gavin, A. (1997). Evaluating the effects of school health intervention on school performance, *Mathematica Policy Research*, Febuary 27, 1997.

Fryer, G.E.; Igoe, J.B.; and Miyoshi, T.J. (1997). Considering school health program screening services as a cost offset: A comparison of existing reimbursements in one state. *Journal of School Nursing, 13*(2), 18-21.

Gaffrey, N. & Bergren, M.D. (1998). School health services and managed care: A unique partnership for child health. *Journal of School Nursing, 14*(4), 5-22.

Hinshaw, A.S. (2000). Nursing knowledge for the 21st century: Opportunities and challenges. *Journal of Nursing Scholarship, 32*(2), 117-123.

Igoe, J.B. (1998). An overview of school health services. *National Association of Secondary School Principals' Bulletin*, November 1998, 14-26.

Individuals with Disabilities Education Act (IDEA), 20 U.S.C. §1400 et seq.; Regulations at 34 C.F.R. §300.

Institute of Medicine, Committee on Comprehensive School Health Programs in Grades K-12. (Allensworth, D., Lawson, E., Nicholson, L., and Wyche, J., Eds.) (1997). *School health: Our nation's investment*. Washington, DC: National Academy Press.

Klahn, J.K., Hays, B.J., & Iverson, C.J., (1998). The school health intensity rating scale. *Journal of School Nursing, 14*(4), 23-28.

Lessard, J.A., & Knox, R. (2000). Telehealth in a rural school-based health center. *Journal of School Nursing, 16*(2), 38-41.

Marx, E. & Wooley, S. F. with Northrop, D. (Eds). *Health is academic: A guide to coordinated school health programs.* (142-68). New York, NY: Teachers College Press.

National Association of School Nurses. (1995) *Caseload Assignments. Position Statement.* Scarborough, ME: Author.

National Association of School Nurses. (1995) *Delegation.* Position Statement. Scarborough, ME: Author.

National Association of School Nurses. (1995) *Delegation of Care.* Issue Brief. Scarborough, ME: Author.

National Association of School Nurses. (1997) *Managed Care.* Issue Brief. Scarborough, ME: Author.

National Association of School Nurses. (1997) *Managed Care.* Position Statement. Scarborough, ME: Author.

National Association of School Nurses. (1997) *Medication Administration in the School Setting.* Position Statement. Scarborough, ME: Author.

National Association of School Nurses. (1997) *Professional School Nurse Roles and Responsibilities: Education, Certification, and Licensure.* Position Statement. Scarborough, ME: Author.

National Association of School Nurses. (1996) *Regulations on Bloodborne Pathogens in the School Setting.* Position Statement. Scarborough, ME: Author.

National Association of School Nurses. (1996) *School-Based/School-Linked Health Centers.* Position Statement. Scarborough, ME: Author.

National Association of School Nurses. (1994) *School-Based/School-Linked Health Centers.* Issue Brief. Scarborough, ME: Author.

National Association of School Nurses. (1996) *School Health Records.* Position Statement. Scarborough, ME: Author.

National Association of School Nurses. (1995) *School Nurse Supervision/Evaluation.* Position Statement. Scarborough, ME: Author.

National Association of School Nurses. (1996) *School Nurses and the Individuals with Disabilities Act (IDEA).* Issue Brief. Scarborough, ME: Author.

National Association of State School Nurse Consultants (1995). *Delegation of School Health Services to Unlicensed Assistive Personnel.* Position Paper. Kent, Ohio: Author

National Center for School Health Nursing, Brainerd, E., Ed. (2000). *Health of America's children at school:*

Developing a nursing research agenda. Proceedings of the invitational summit meeting, Elkridge, Maryland, March, 1999. Washington D.C.: American Nurses Foundation.

National Nursing Coalition for School Health (1995). School health nursing services: Exploring national issues and priorities. *Journal of School Health, 65* (9), 369-389.

National Task Force on Confidential Student Health Information. (2000). *Guidelines for protecting confidential student health information.* Kent, OH: American School Health Association.

Poster, E. C. & Marcontel, M. (1999). School nursing role and competence. *Journal of School Nursing, 15*(2), 34-42.

Schwab, N.C., Panetierri, M.J. & Bergren, M.D. (1998). *Guidelines for school nursing documentation: Standards, issues and models.* Scarborough, ME: National Association of School Nurses.

Section 504 of the Rehabilitation Act of 1973, 29 U.S.C. §794; Regulations at 34 C.F.R. §104.

Southern Regional Education Board. (April 2000). *Expected competencies for entry-level positions as school nurses.* Atlanta, GA: Author.

Tyson, H. (1999). A load off the teachers' backs. *Kappan Special Report.* (January 1999) Newton, MA: Education Development Center.

U.S. Department of Health and Human Services. (2000). *Healthy people 2010: National health promotion and disease prevention objectives.* Washington, DC: U.S. Department of Health and Human Services, Public Health Service.

Whitten, P.S. & Cook, D.J. (1999). School-based telemedicine: Using technology to bring health care to inner-city children. *Journal of Telemedicine and Telecare, 5*(S1), S23-25.

Wooley, S.F., Eberst, R. M., & Bradley, B.J. (2000). Creative collaborations with health providers. *Educational Leadership, 57*(6), 25-28.

See page 625 for Table of Federal Statutes and Regulations.

Appendix A
Standards of Professional School Nursing Practice

AFFIRMATION

The standards within this document have been accepted and were approved as The National Association of School Nurses *Standards of Professional School Nursing Practice* at a meeting of the Board of Directors, NASN, June 1998.

ACKNOWLEDGEMENTS

The National Association of School Nurses gratefully acknowledges the careful and useful critique of draft manuscripts by the following reviewers:

Standards of Practice Task Force:

Charla Dunham RN, BSN, MEd, Chair; Standards/Practice Issues Committee
National Association of School Nurses, Inc.

Nancy Birchmeier RN, BSN, C.S.N.; Standards/Practice Issues Committee
National Association of School Nurses, Inc.

Linda Edwards RN, DrPH; Organizational Representative
American Public Health Association, Public Health Nursing Section

Beverly Farquhar RN, BS, C.S.N.; Executive Director
National Association of School Nurses, Inc.

Tona Leiker RN, MN; Organizational Representative
American Nurses Association

Doris Luckenbill RN, MS, CRNP; President
National Association of School Nurses, Inc.

Judith A. Maire RN, MN; Organizational Representative
National Association of State School Nurse Consultants

Susan Proctor RN, DNS; Author, *School Nursing Practice: Roles and Standards*
National Association of School Nurses, Inc.

Genie Wessel RN, MS, FASHA; Organizational Representative
American School Health Association

Linda Wolfe RN, BSN, MEd, C.S.N.; Past Chair, Standards/Practice Issues Committee
National Association of School Nurses, Inc.

Other Reviewers:

Donna Zaiger, RN, BSN, C.S.N.; Past President
National Association of School Nurses, Inc.

Elaine Brainerd, RN, MA, C.S.N., Director, National Center for School Health Nursing
American Nurses Association/Foundation

These Standards have been reviewed and approved by the American School Health Association, the National Association of State School Nurse Consultants, and the National Nursing Coalition for School Health.

PREFACE

The contents of this document are the result of an effort by a group of nurses comprised of representatives of several organizations concerned with the practice of nursing in schools. The group, the National Association of School Nurses Standards Task Force, was charged with the development of new national standards of practice for school nursing. In particular, the new standards were to reflect the format and language of the *Standards of Clinical Nursing Practice*, a publication whose intent is to specify areas of responsibility and accountability common to the practice of all professional nurses regardless of nursing specialty (ANA, 1998). Formulated by the Committee on Nursing Practice Standards and Guidelines of the American Nurses Association, the *Standards of Clinical Nursing Practice* are intended to establish criteria for all of nursing practice and serve as a template for the development of specialty standards.

School nursing has had standards of practice since 1983 when a similar task force, chaired by Georgia MacDonough of Arizona, produced the first set of standards specific to the specialty (ANA, 1983). Similarly, these were modeled on early generic (non-specialty) standards also authored by the American Nurses Association. The 1983 standards served school nursing well and were the basis for the development of three implementation manuals: one by the American School Health Association (Snyder, 1991), and two by the National Association of School Nurses (Proctor, 1990; 1993).

The standards within this document are to serve as a definitive guide for role implementation, interpretation, and evaluation. They may be used separately or together with state nurse practice acts, scope of practice statements, and other relevant laws or statutes in determining the adequacy and competency of school nursing practice. They are intended to serve as a framework for the professional expectations of nurses who serve the students in our nation's schools and to further define and clarify the role of nursing in and with schools and the school community.

INTRODUCTION

The language and format of this section is adapted directly from the Standards of Clinical Nursing Practice (ANA, 1998).

Definition and Role of Standards

Standards are authoritative statements by which the nursing profession describes responsibilities for which its practitioners are accountable. Consequently, standards reflect the values and priorities of the profession. Standards provide direction for professional nursing practice and a framework for the evaluation of practice. Written in measurable terms, standards also define the nursing profession's accountability to the public and the client outcomes for which nurses are responsible. (ANA, 1998, p. 1).

Guidelines, as distinguished from standards, "describe a process of patient [client] care management which has the potential for improving the quality of clinical and consumer decision making. Guidelines are systematically developed statements based on available scientific evidence and expert opinion. Guidelines address the care of specific patient [client] populations or phenomena, whereas standards provide a broad framework for practice" (ANA, 1998, p. 4).

Within school nursing, considerable professional literature is available which may be considered guidelines. Position statements and other publications of the National Association of School

Nurses, the American School Health Association, the American Public Health Association's Public Health Nursing Section, the National Association of State School Nurse Consultants, the American Nurses' Association, and others, when specific to aspects of school nursing practice, may be regarded as guidelines.

Development of Standards

"A professional nursing organization has a responsibility to its membership and the public it serves to develop standards of practice" (ANA, 1998, p. 1). This document sets forth standards of clinical practice for the specialty of school nursing and describes a competent level of professional performance common to all nurses engaged in the practice of school nursing.

Assumptions

1. The link between the work environment and the nurse's ability to deliver care and services is recognized, and employers must provide an environment supportive of nursing practice.
2. Nursing care is individualized to meet client needs and situations including family goals and preferences. Given that one of the nurse's primary responsibilities is client health education, the school nurse provides clients with appropriate information to make informed decisions regarding their health care, including information which promotes health, prevents disease, and enhances school performance.
3. The school nurse works collaboratively to coordinate health and other services as needed in order to maximize the educational potential of the client. Collaboration involves partnerships with the family, other school professionals, and with community health and social service providers and agencies.

ORGANIZING PRINCIPLES OF THE STANDARDS OF PROFESSIONAL SCHOOL NURSING PRACTICE

The Standards of Professional School Nursing Practice are modeled on the parent document, the *Standards of Clinical Nursing Practice* (ANA, 1998). The parent document has two sections, "Standards of Care" and "Standards of Professional Performance." The Standards of Care are familiar to all nurses and constitute the nursing process. The Standards of Professional Performance constitute a framework for professional behavior. Consonant with the American Nurses Association's Social Policy Statement (ANA, 1995), "the recipients of nursing care are individuals, groups, families, or communities…the individual recipient of nursing care can be referred to as patient, client, or person" (ANA, 1998, p. 2). Throughout this document, client, when used, may refer to an individual, family, group, or community.

STANDARDS OF CARE

The Standards of Care, comprised of the six steps of the nursing process, describe a competent level of nursing care for all nurses, regardless of practice setting. "The nursing process encompasses all significant actions taken by nurses in providing care to all clients, and forms the foundation for clinical decision making" (ANA, 1998, p. 3).

Standards of Care

- Standard 1: Assessment
- Standard 2: Diagnosis
- Standard 3: Outcome Identification
- Standard 4: Planning
- Standard 5: Implementation
- Standard 6: Evaluation

The original nursing process consisted of four steps: "Assessment," "Planning," "Implementation," and "Evaluation" (Yura & Walsh, 1973). Due in large part to the work of Marjory Gordon, (1976), Lynda Carpenito (1983) and others, "Diagnosis" was separated from "Assessment" and added as a logical outcome of "Assessment." In turn, "Outcome Identification" was identified as a product of "Diagnosis" because of the need to consider goals prior to any planning, as well as the emphasis upon promoting and measuring outcomes of care (ANA, 1991).

In addition to the nursing process and its prescriptive mandate for competent care, "several themes cut across all areas of nursing practice and reflect nursing responsibilities for all patients [clients]." These themes include:

- providing age-appropriate, culturally, and ethnically sensitive care;
- maintaining a safe environment;
- educating patients [clients] about healthy practices and treatment modalities;
- assuring continuity of care;
- coordinating care across settings and among care givers;
- managing information; and
- communicating effectively.

(ANA, 1998, p. 3).

The themes are reflected throughout this document within criteria associated with the standards although the language may differ somewhat. The themes are noted here because they: (1) are fundamental to many of the standards; and (2) consistently and significantly influence contemporary school nursing practice.

STANDARDS OF PROFESSIONAL PERFORMANCE

The Standards of Professional Performance describe a competent level of behavior in the professional role. "All nurses are expected to engage in professional role activities appropriate to their education and position. Ultimately, nurses are accountable to themselves, their patients [clients], and their peers for their professional activities" (ANA, 1998, p.3).

The Standards Task Force added three standards to the grouping, appearing below as the last three standards in the list. Two of the three additional standards (10 & 11) were taken from the *Standards of School Nursing Practice* (ANA, 1983) while the third (9) was gleaned from NASN's standards implementation document (Proctor, 1993).

Standards of Professional Performance

- Standard 1: Quality of Care
- Standard 2: Performance Appraisal
- Standard 3: Education
- Standard 4: Collegiality
- Standard 5: Ethics
- Standard 6: Collaboration
- Standard 7: Research
- Standard 8: Resource Utilization
- Standard 9: Communication
- Standard 10: Program Management
- Standard 11: Health Education

CRITERIA

The criteria immediately following each standard statement are indicators or benchmarks of competent practice. The *Standards of Professional School Nursing Practice* include criteria that allow the standards to be measured. Standards generally remain stable over time reflecting the philosophical values of the specialty. Criteria, however, must be revised to incorporate changes in practice and research and maintain consistency with current advances in scientific knowledge and clinical practice.

Because a document such as this cannot account for all possible developments in practice, modifiers such as "pertinent," "appropriate," and "realistic" may be used which recognize differences in practice arenas, educational preparation, and scope of practice. Guidelines, documents, and local protocols and procedures, as well as state nurse practice acts, may provide additional direction if further interpretation is needed.

SUMMARY

The *Standards of Professional School Nursing Practice* delineates the professional responsibilities of all school nurses engaged in clinical practice. The use of this and other documents could serve as a basis for:

- quality improvement systems;
- data bases;
- regulatory systems;
- health care reimbursement and financing methodologies;
- development and evaluation of nursing service delivery systems and organizational structures;
- certification activities;
- position descriptions and performance appraisals;
- agency policies, procedures, and protocols; and
- educational offerings.

Standards, as well as practice guidelines, must be evaluated on a regular basis. School nurses are invited to provide feedback to the Standards Task Force regarding the utility, effectiveness, and comprehensiveness of these standards.

STANDARDS OF CARE

Standard I. Assessment

THE SCHOOL NURSE COLLECTS CLIENT DATA.
Measurement Criteria
1. Data collection involves the student, family, school staff, community, and other providers, as necessary.
2. The priority of data collection is determined by the nursing diagnosis and the client's immediate condition and/or needs.
3. Pertinent individual and aggregate data are collected, using appropriate assessment techniques, and reviewed in light of relevant supporting information.

4. Relevant data are documented in a retrievable form.
5. The data collection process is systematic, organized, and ongoing.

Standard II. Diagnosis

THE SCHOOL NURSE ANALYZES THE ASSESSMENT DATA IN
DETERMINING NURSING DIAGNOSES.

Measurement Criteria

1. Nursing diagnoses, individual and aggregate, are derived from
   the evaluation of assessment data.
2. Nursing diagnoses, individual and aggregate, are validated with
   the student, family, school staff, community, and other
   providers, when appropriate.
3. Nursing diagnoses, individual and aggregate, are documented in
   a manner that facilitates the determination of expected
   outcomes and the plan of care/action.

Standard III. Outcome Identification

THE SCHOOL NURSE IDENTIFIES EXPECTED OUTCOMES
INDIVIDUALIZED TO THE CLIENT.

Measurement Criteria

1. Outcomes are derived from the nursing diagnoses.
2. Outcomes are mutually formulated with the student, family,
   school staff, community, and other providers, as appropriate.
3. Outcomes are culturally appropriate and realistic in relation to
   the client's present and potential capabilities.
4. Outcomes are obtained in relation to resources necessary and
   attainable.
5. Outcomes include a reasonable time line.
6. Outcomes provide direction for continuity of care and the plan
   of care/action.
7. Outcomes are documented as measurable goals.

Standard IV. Planning

THE SCHOOL NURSE DEVELOPS A PLAN OF CARE/ACTION
THAT SPECIFIES INTERVENTIONS TO ATTAIN EXPECTED
OUTCOMES.

Measurement Criteria

1. The plan is individualized to the student's diagnosis/nursing
   diagnosis.
2. A plan is a component of the individual program for students
   with special health care needs.
3. The plan is developed in compliance with local, state, and federal
   regulations, as needed.
4. The plan is collaboratively developed with the student, family,
   school staff, community, and other providers, as appropriate.
5. The plan reflects current standards of school nursing practice.
6. The plan provides for continuity of care and plan of action to be
   taken.
7. Priorities for care/action and time line for interventions are
   established.
8. The plan is documented in a retrievable form.

Standard V. Implementation

THE SCHOOL NURSE IMPLEMENTS THE INTERVENTIONS
IDENTIFIED IN THE PLAN OF CARE/ACTION.

Measurement Criteria

1. Interventions are consistent with the established plan of
   care/action.
2. Interventions are implemented in a safe, timely, and appropriate
   manner.
3. Interventions are documented in a retrievable form.
4. Interventions reflect current standards of school nursing practice.

Standard VI. Evaluation

THE SCHOOL NURSE EVALUATES THE CLIENT'S PROGRESS
TOWARD ATTAINMENT OF OUTCOMES.

Measurement Criteria

1. Evaluation is systematic, continuous, and criterion-based.
2. The student, family, school staff, community, and other
   providers are involved in the evaluation process, as appropriate.
3. Ongoing assessment data, including incremental goal attainment in achieving the expected outcomes, are used to revise
   diagnoses and outcomes and the plan of care/action, as needed.
4. Revisions in nursing diagnoses, outcomes, and the plan of
   care/action are documented in a retrievable form.
5. The client's responses to interventions are documented in a
   retrievable form.
6. The effectiveness of interventions is evaluated in relation to
   outcomes.

STANDARDS OF PROFESSIONAL PERFORMANCE

Standard I. Quality of Care

THE SCHOOL NURSE SYSTEMATICALLY EVALUATES THE
QUALITY AND EFFECTIVENESS OF SCHOOL NURSING
PRACTICE.

Measurement Criteria

1. The school nurse participates in quality assurance activities as
   appropriate to that individual's position and practice environment. Such activities may include:
   - identification of aspects of care necessary for quality moni-
     toring;
   - development of policies, procedures, and adoption of prac-
     tice guidelines to improve quality of care;
   - collection of data to monitor quality and effectiveness of
     nursing care;
   - formulation of recommendations to improve school nursing
     practice or client outcomes;
   - implementation of activities to enhance the quality of
     nursing practice; and
   - evaluation/research to test quality and effectiveness.
2. The school nurse uses the results of quality of care activities to
   initiate changes in school nursing practice, as appropriate.
3. The school nurse continuously strives to improve the quality
   and effectiveness of school health services.

Standard II. Performance Appraisal

THE SCHOOL NURSE EVALUATES ONE'S OWN NURSING
PRACTICE IN RELATION TO PROFESSIONAL PRACTICE
STANDARDS AND RELEVANT STATUTES, REGULATIONS,
AND POLICIES.

Measurement Criteria

1. The school nurse participates in performance appraisal on a regular basis, identifying areas of strength and weakness, as well as ways to refine professional development.
2. The school nurse seeks and acts on constructive feedback regarding one's own practice.
3. The school nurse takes action to achieve goals identified during performance appraisal.
4. The school nurse initiates and participates in peer review, as appropriate.
5. The school nurse's practice reflects knowledge of current professional practice standards, education and health care laws and regulations, and school policies.

Standard III. Education

THE SCHOOL NURSE ACQUIRES AND MAINTAINS CURRENT KNOWLEDGE AND COMPETENCY IN SCHOOL NURSING PRACTICE.
Measurement Criteria

1. The school nurse acquires knowledge and skills appropriate to the specialty practice of school nursing on a regular and ongoing basis.
2. The school nurse consistently participates in continuing education activities related to current clinical knowledge and professional issues.
3. The school nurse seeks experience to maintain current clinical skills and competence.

Standard IV. Collegiality

THE SCHOOL NURSE INTERACTS WITH AND CONTRIBUTES TO THE PROFESSIONAL DEVELOPMENT OF PEERS AND SCHOOL PERSONNEL AS COLLEAGUES.
Measurement Criteria

1. The school nurse shares knowledge and skills with nursing and interdisciplinary colleagues.
2. The school nurse provides peers with constructive feedback regarding their practice.
3. The school nurse interacts with nursing and interdisciplinary colleagues to enhance professional practice and health care of students.
4. The school nurse contributes to an environment that is conducive to clinical education of nursing students, other health care students, and other employees.
5. The school nurse contributes to a supportive and healthy work environment.
6. The school nurse participates in appropriate professional organizations in a membership and/or leadership capacity.

Standard V. Ethics

THE SCHOOL NURSE'S DECISIONS AND ACTIONS ON BEHALF OF CLIENTS ARE DETERMINED IN AN ETHICAL MANNER.
Measurement Criteria

1. The school nurse's practice is guided by the Code for Nurses (ANA) and Code of Ethics with Interpretative Statement for School Nurses (NASN), and appropriate state nurse practice acts.
2. The school nurse maintains client confidentiality within legal,

regulatory, and ethical parameters of health and education.
3. The school nurse delivers care in a nonjudgmental and nondiscriminatory manner that is sensitive to student diversity in the school community.
4. The school nurse delivers care in a manner that promotes and preserves student and family autonomy, dignity, and rights.
5. The school nurse seeks available resources to formulate ethical decisions.
6. The school nurse acts as a client advocate.

Standard VI. Collaboration

THE SCHOOL NURSE COLLABORATES WITH THE STUDENT, FAMILY, SCHOOL STAFF, COMMUNITY, AND OTHER PROVIDERS IN PROVIDING STUDENT CARE.
Measurement Criteria

1. The school nurse communicates verbally and in writing with the student, family, school staff, community, and other providers regarding client care and nursing's role in the provision of care.
2. The school nurse collaborates with the student, family, school staff, community, and other providers in the formulation of overall goals, time lines, the plan of care, and decisions related to care and the delivery of services.
3. The school nurse assists individual students in developing appropriate skills to advocate for themselves based on age and developmental level.
4. The school nurse consults with and utilizes the expertise of other providers for client care, as needed.
5. The school nurse makes referrals, including provisions for continuity of care, as needed.

Standard VII. Research

THE SCHOOL NURSE PROMOTES USE OF RESEARCH FINDINGS IN SCHOOL NURSING PRACTICE.
Measurement Criteria

1. The school nurse utilizes available research in developing the health programs and individual client plans of care and interventions.
2. The school nurse participates in research activities as appropriate to the nurse's education, position, and practice environment. Such activities may include:
   - identifying of clinical problems suitable for nursing research;
   - participating in data collection;
   - participating in a unit, organization, or community research committee or program;
   - interpreting research findings with others;
   - conducting research;
   - critiquing research for application to practice; and
   - using research findings in the development of policies and procedures for client care and program development.
3. The school nurse contributes to the nursing literature when and if possible.

Standard VIII. Resource Utilization

THE SCHOOL NURSE CONSIDERS FACTORS RELATED TO SAFETY, EFFECTIVENESS, AND COST WHEN PLANNING AND DELIVERING CARE.

Measurement Criteria

1. The school nurse evaluates factors related to safety, effectiveness, availability, and cost when choosing between two or more practice options that would result in the same expected client or program outcomes.
2. The school nurse assists the student, family, school staff, and community in identifying and securing appropriate and available services and resources to address health-related needs.
3. The school nurse assigns or delegates tasks as defined by the state nurse practice acts and according to the knowledge and skills of the designated caregiver.
4. If the school nurse assigns or delegates tasks, it is based on the needs and condition of the client and potential for harm, the stability of the client's condition, the complexity of the task, and the predictability of the outcome.
5. The school nurse assists the student, family, school staff, and community in becoming informed consumers about the cost, risks, and benefits of health promotions, health education, school health services, and individualized health interventions for students.

Standard IX. Communication

THE SCHOOL NURSE USES EFFECTIVE WRITTEN, VERBAL, AND NONVERBAL COMMUNICATION SKILLS.

Measurement Criteria

1. The school nurse communicates effectively with the student, family, school staff, community, and other providers regarding student care and the role of the school nurse in the provision of care.
2. The school nurse employs counseling techniques and crisis-intervention strategies for individuals and groups.
3. The school nurse utilizes communication as a positive strategy to achieve nursing goals.
4. The school nurse demonstrates knowledge of the philosophy and mission of the school district, the kind and nature of its curricular and extracurricular activities, and its programs and special services.
5. The school nurse demonstrates knowledge of the roles of other school professionals and adjunct personnel, and coordinates roles and responsibilities of the adjunct school health personnel within the school team.

NOTE: The language of the Standard Statement and all measurement criteria 2-5 are taken or adapted from *School Nursing Practice: Roles and Standards.* (Proctor, Lordi, & Zaiger 1993).

Standard X. Program Management

THE SCHOOL NURSE MANAGES SCHOOL HEALTH SERVICES.

Measurement Criteria

1. The school nurse manages school health services as appropriate to the nurse's education, position, and practice environment.
2. The school nurse conducts school health needs assessments to identify current health problems and identify the need for new programs.
3. The school nurse develops and implements needed health programs using a program planning process.
4. The school nurse demonstrates knowledge of existing school health programs and current health trends that may impact client care, the sources of funds for each, school policy related to

each, and local, state, and federal law governing each.

5. The school nurse develops and implements health policies and procedures in collaboration with school administration, board of health, and the board of education.
6. The school nurse evaluates ongoing health programs for outcomes and quality of care and communicates findings to administrators and the board of education.
7. The school nurse orients, provides training, documents competency, supervises, and evaluates health assistants, aides, and UAPs (Unlicensed Assistive Personnel), as appropriate to the school setting.
8. The school nurse uses the results of school health/environmental needs, assessment analysis of evaluation data, and quality of care activities to initiate changes throughout the health care delivery system, as appropriate.
9. The school nurse participates in environmental safety and health activities, e.g. indoor air quality, injury surveillance, and prevention.
10. The school nurse adopts and utilizes available technology, as appropriate to the work setting.

NOTE: The language of the Standard Statement and all measurement criteria 2-7 are taken or adapted from *School Nursing Practice: Roles and Standards.* (Proctor, Lordi & Zaiger 1993).

Standard XI. Health Education

THE SCHOOL NURSE ASSISTS STUDENTS, FAMILIES, THE SCHOOL STAFF, AND COMMUNITY TO ACHIEVE OPTIMAL LEVELS OF WELLNESS THROUGH APPROPRIATELY DESIGNED AND DELIVERED HEALTH EDUCATION.

Measurement Criteria

1. The school nurse participates in the assessment of needs for health education and health instruction needs for the school community.
2. The school nurse provides formal health instruction within the classroom based on sound learning theory, as appropriate to student developmental levels.
3. The school nurse provides individual and group health teaching and counseling for and with clients.
4. The school nurse participates in the design and development of health curricula.
5. The school nurse participates in the evaluation of health curricula, health instructional materials, and other health education activities.
6. The school nurse acts as a resource person to school staff regarding health education and health education materials.
7. The school nurse furthers the application of health promotion principles within all areas of school life, e.g. food service, custodial, etc.
8. The school nurse promotes self care and safety through the education of staff regarding their own health and that of their students.

NOTE: The language of the Standard Statement and all measurement criteria are taken or adapted from *School Nursing Practice: Roles and Standards.* (Proctor, Lordi & Zaiger 1993).

GLOSSARY

ASSESSMENT: The first step of the nursing process, assessment is the collection and documentation of data/information about or from individuals, students, families, health care providers, organizations, or communities in a systematic, continuous manner, using appropriate techniques. *

CLIENT: A collective term which may refer to individuals, families, groups, or communities who are the recipients of nursing care. **

DIAGNOSIS: The second step of the nursing process, diagnosis is the analysis of the assessment data to arrive at a conclusion(s) which can be validated by others, is documented, and facilitates the development of outcomes and a plan of care. *

EVALUATION: The sixth and final step of the nursing process, evaluation is a systematic and ongoing appraisal of client responses to interventions and to the effectiveness of interventions in relation to outcomes. Evaluative data are documented and used to revise assessments, diagnoses, outcomes, plans, and interventions. *

IMPLEMENTATION: The fifth step of the nursing process, implementation is the execution of the interventions prescribed in a safe, appropriate manner. Interventions are always documented. *

OUTCOME IDENTIFICATION: The third and newest step of the nursing process, outcome identification is the specification of measurable, appropriate, mutually formulated, attainable, and timely goals which are derived from the diagnosis(es), are documented, and provide for continuity of care. *

PLAN OF CARE: A comprehensive outline of care to be delivered to attain expected outcomes.* Examples may include Individualized Health Plan, Individualized Education Plan, 504 plans, and others.

PLANNING: The fourth step of the nursing process, planning is a prescription of interventions designed to attain outcomes unique to the client which provide for continuity of care, are documented, and are conjointly created, when appropriate. *

SCHOOL NURSING: School nursing is a specialty branch of professional nursing in which nursing care is delivered to children and their families primarily in a school setting. School nursing seeks to prevent or identify client health or health-related problems and intervenes to modify or remediate those problems. ***

STANDARDS: Standards are authoritative statements enunciated and promulgated by the profession by which the quality of practice, service, or education can be judged. *

* From Standards of Clinical Nursing Practice (ANA, 1991).
** From Nursing's Social Policy Statement (ANA, 1995).
*** From Philosophy of School Health Services and School Nursing (NASN, 1988).

REFERENCES

American Nurses Association (1983). *Standards of School Nursing Practice.* Kansas City, MO: Author.

American Nurses Association (1985). *Code for Nurses With Interpretive Statements.* Kerneysville, WV: American Nurses Publishing.

American Nurses Association (1991). *Standards of Clinical Nursing Practice.* Kerneysville, WV: American Nurses Publishing

American Nurses Association (1995). *Nursing's Social Policy Statement.* Kerneysville, WV: American Nurses Publishing.

American Nurses Association (1998). *Standards of Clinical Nursing Practice* (2nd. ed.). Kerneysville, WV: American Nurses Publishing.

Carpenito, L.J. (1983). *Nursing Diagnosis: Application to Clinical Practice.* Philadelphia, PA: J.B. Lippincott Co.

Gordon, M. (1976). Nursing Diagnosis and the Diagnostic Process. *Journal of the New York State Nurses' Association, 76,* 1276-1300.

National Association of School Nurses (1988). *Philosophy of School Health Services and School Nursing.* Scarborough, ME: Author.

National Association of School Nurses (1990). *Code of Ethics With Interpretive Statements for School Nurses.* Scarborough, ME: Author.

Proctor, S.T. (1990). *Guidelines for a Model School Nurse Services Program.* Scarborough, ME: National Association of School Nurses.

Proctor, S.T., with Lordi, S.L., & Zaiger, D.S. (1993). *School Nursing Practice: Roles and Standards.* Scarborough, ME: National Association of School Nurses.

Snyder, A.A., ed. (1991). *Implementation Guide for the Standards of School Nursing Practice.* Kent, OH: American School Health Association.

Yura, H. & Walsh, M.B. (1973). *The Nursing Process: Assessing, Planning, Implementing, Evaluating* (2nd. ed.). New York, NY: Appleton-Century-Crofts.

Appendix B
Codes for Nurses with Interpretive Statements

Committee on Ethics, 1983–1985

Catherine P. Murphy, Ed.D., R.N., chairperson
Mila A. Aroskar, Ed.D., R.N., F.A.A.N.
Sister Karin Dufault, Ph.D., R.N.
Carol A. Jenkins, M.S.N., R.N.
Marilyn Whipple, M.S., R.N., C.S.

Committee on Ethics, 1981–1982

Anne J. Davis, Ph.D., R.N., F.A.A.N., chairperson
Carol A. Jenkins, M.S.N., R.N.
Catherine P. Murphy, Ed.D., R.N.
Rita J. Payton, D.A., R.N.
Joyce Thompson, Dr.P.H., R.N., F.A.A.N.

PREAMBLE

A code of ethics make explicit the primary goals and values of the profession. When individuals become nurses, they make a moral commitment to uphold the values and special moral obligations expressed in their code. The *Code for Nurses* is based on a belief about the nature of individuals, nursing, health, and society. Nursing encompasses the protection, promotion, and restoration of health; the prevention of illness; and the alleviation of suffering in the care of clients, including individuals, families, groups, and communities. In the context of these functions, nursing is defined as the diagnosis and treatment of human responses to actual or potential health problems.

Since clients themselves are the primary decision makers in matters concerning their own health, treatment, and well-being, the goal of nursing actions is to support and enhance the client's responsibility and self-determination to the greatest extent possible. In this context, health is not necessarily an end in itself, but rather a means to a life that is meaningful from the client's perspective.

When making clinical judgments, nurses base their decisions no consideration of consequences and of universal moral principles, both of which prescribe and justify nursing actions. The most fundamental of these principles is respect for persons. Other principles stemming from this basic principle are autonomy (self-determination), beneficence (doing good), nonmaleficence (avoiding harm), veracity (truth-telling), confidentiality (respecting privileged information), fidelity (keeping promises), and justice (treating people fairly).

In brief, then, the statements of the code and their interpretation provide guidance for conduct and relationships in carrying out nursing responsibilities consistent with the ethical obligations of the profession and with high quality in nursing care.

INTRODUCTION

A code of ethics indicates a profession's acceptance of the responsibility and trust with which it has been invested by society. Under the terms of the implicit contract between society and the nursing profession, society grants the profession considerable autonomy and authority to function in the conduct of its affairs. The development of a code of ethics is an essential activity of a profession and provides one means for the exercise of professional self-regulation.

Upon entering the profession, each nurse inherits a measure of both the responsibility and the trust that have accrued to nursing over the years, as well as the corresponding obligation to adhere to the profession's code of conduct and relationships for ethical practice. The *Code for Nurses with Interpretive Statements* is thus more a collective expression of nursing conscience and philosophy than a set of external rules imposed upon an individual practitioner of nursing. Personal and professional integrity can be assured only if an individual is committed to the profession's code of conduct.

A code of ethical conduct offers general principles to guide and evaluate nursing actions. It does not assure the virtues required for professional practice within the character of each nurse. In particular situations, the justification of behavior as ethical must satisfy not only the individual nurse acting as a moral agent but also the standards for professional peer review.

The *Code for Nurses* was adopted by the American Nurses Association in 1950 and has been revised periodically. It serves to inform both the nurse and society of the profession's expectations and requirements in ethical matters. The code and the interpretive statements together provide a framework within which nurses can make ethical decisions and discharge their responsibilities to the public, to other members of the health team, and to the profession.

Although a particular situation by its nature may determine the use of specific moral principles, the basic philosophical values, directives, and suggestions provided here are widely applicable to situations encountered in clinical practice. The *Code for Nurses* is not open to negotiation in employment settings, not it is permissible for individuals or groups of nurses to adapt or change the language of this code.

The requirements of the code may often exceed those of the law. Violations of the law may subject the nurse to civil or criminal liability. The state nurses' associations, in fulfilling the profession's duty to society, may discipline their members for violations of the code. Loss of the respect and confidence of society and of one's colleagues is a serious sanction resulting from violation of the code. In addition, every nurse has a personal obligation to uphold and adhere to the code and to ensure that nursing colleagues do likewise.

Guidance and assistance in applying the code to local situations may be obtained from the American Nurses Association and the constituent state nurses' associations.

CODE FOR NURSES

1   The nurse provides services with respect for human dignity and the uniqueness of the client, unrestricted by considerations of social or economic status, personal attributes, or the nature of health problems.

2   The nurse safeguards the client's right to privacy by judiciously protecting information of a confidential nature.

3   The nurse acts to safeguard the client and the public when health care and safety are affected by the incompetent, unethical, or illegal practice of any person.

4   The nurse assumes responsibility and accountability for individual nursing judgments and actions.

5   The nurse maintains competence in nursing.

6   The nurse exercises informed judgment and uses individual competence and qualifications as criteria in seeking consultation, accepting responsibilities, and delegating nursing activities to others.

7   The nurse participates in activities that contribute to the ongoing development of the profession's body of knowledge.

8   The nurse participates in the profession's efforts to implement and improve standards of nursing.

9   The nurse participates in the profession's efforts to establish and maintain conditions of employment conducive to high quality nursing care.

10 The nurse participates in the profession's effort to protect the public from misinformation and misrepresentation and to maintain the integrity of nursing.

11 The nurse collaborates with members of the health professions and other citizens in promoting community and national efforts to meet the health needs of the public.

CODE FOR NURSES WITH INTERPRETIVE STATEMENTS

1   The nurse provides services with respect for human dignity and the uniqueness of the client, unrestricted by considerations of social or economic status, personal attributes, or the nature of health problems.

1.1   Respect for Human Dignity

The fundamental principle of nursing practice is respect for the inherent dignity and worth of every client. Nurses are morally obligated to respect human existence and the individuality of all persons who are the recipients of nursing actions. Nurses therefore must take all reasonable means to protect and preserve human life when there is hope of recovery or reasonable hope of benefit from life-prolonging treatment.

Truth telling and the process of reaching informed choice underlie the exercise of self-determination, which is basic to respect for persons. Clients should be as fully involved as possible in the planning and implementation of their own health care. Clients have the moral right to determine what will be done with their own person; to be given accurate information, and all the information necessary for making informed judgments; to be assisted with weighing the benefits and burdens of options in their treatment; to accept, refuse, or terminate treatment without coercion; and to be given necessary emotional support. Each nurse has an obligation to be knowledgeable about the moral and legal rights of all clients and to protect and support those rights. In situations in which the client lacks the capacity to make a decision, a surrogate decision maker should be designated.

Individuals are interdependent members of the community. Taking into account both individual rights and the interdependence of persons in decision making, the nurse recognizes those situations in which individuals rights to autonomy in health care may temporarily be overridden to preserve the life of the human community; for example, when a disaster demands triage or when an individual present a direct danger to others. The many variables involved make it imperative that each case be considered with full awareness of the need to preserve the rights and responsibilities of clients and the demands of justice. The suspension of individual rights must always be considered a deviation to be tolerated as briefly as possible.

1.2   Status and Attributes of Clients

The need for health care is universal, transcending all national, ethnic, racial, religious, cultural, political, educational, economic, developmental, personality, role, and sexual differences. Nursing care is delivered without prejudicial behavior. Individual value systems and life-styles should be considered in the planning of health care with and for each client. Attributes of clients influence nursing practice to the extent that they represent factors the nurse must understand, consider, and respect in tailoring care to personal needs and in maintaining the individual's self-respect and dignity.

1.3   The Nature of Health Problems

The nurse's respect for the worth and dignity of the individual human being applies, irrespective of the nature of the health problem. It is reflected in care given the person who is disabled as well as one without disability, the persons with long-term illness as well as one with acute illness, the recovering patient as well as one in the last phase of life. This respect extends to all who require the services of the nurse for the promotion of health, the prevention of illness, the restoration of health, the alleviation of suffering, and the provision of supportive care of the dying. The nurse does not act deliberately to terminate the life of any person.

The nurse's concern for human dignity and for the provision of high quality nursing care is not limited by personal attitudes or beliefs. If ethically opposed to interventions in a particular case because of the procedures to be used, the nurse is justified in refusing to participate. Such refusal should be made known in advance and in time for other appropriate arrangements to be made for the client's nursing care. If the nurse becomes involved in such a case and the client's life is in jeopardy, the nurse is obliged to provide for the client's safety, to avoid abandonment, and to withdraw only when assured that alternative sources of nursing care are available to the client.

The measures nurses take to care for the dying client and the client's family emphasize human contact. They enable the client to live with as much physical, emotional, and spiritual comfort as possible, and they maximize the values the client has treasured in life. Nursing care is directed toward the prevention and relief of the suffering commonly associated with the dying process. The nurse may provide interventions to relieve symptoms in the dying client even when the interventions entail substantial risks of hastening death.

1.4   The Setting for Health Care

The nurse adheres to the principle of non-discriminatory, nonprejudicial care in every situation and endeavors to promote its acceptance by others. The setting shall not determine the nurse's readiness to respect clients and to render or obtain needed services.

2   The nurse safeguards the client's right to privacy by judiciously protecting information of a confidential nature.

2.1   The Client's Right to Privacy

The right to privacy is an unalienable human right. The client trusts the nurse to hold all information in confidence. This trust could be destroyed and the client's welfare jeopardized by injudicious disclosure of information provided in confidence. The duty of confidentiality, however, is not absolute when innocent parties are in direct jeopardy.

2.2   Protection of Information

The rights, well-being, and safety of the individual client should be the determining factors in arriving at any professional judgment concerning the disposition of confidential information received from the client relevant to his or her treatment. The standards of nursing practice and the nursing responsibility to provide high quality health services require that relevant data be shared with members of the health team. Only information pertinent to a client's treatment and welfare is disclosed, and it is disclosed only to those directly concerned with the client's care.

Information documenting the appropriateness, necessity, and quality of care required for the purposes of peer review, third-party payment, and other quality assurance mechanisms must be disclosed only under defined policies, mandates, or protocols. These written guidelines must assure that the rights, well-being, and safety of the client are maintained.

2.3   Access to Records

If in the course of providing care there is a need for the nurse to have access to the records of persons not under the nurse's care, the persons affected should be notified and, whenever possible, permission should be obtained first. Although records belong to the agency where the data are collected, the individual maintains the right of control over the information in the record. Similarly, professionals may exercise the right of control over information they have generated in the course of health care.

If the nurse wishes to use a client's treatment record for research or nonclinical purposes in which anonymity cannot be guaranteed, the client's consent must be obtained first. Ethically, this ensures the client's right to privacy; legally, it protects the client against unlawful invasion of privacy.

3   The nurse acts to safeguard the client and the public when health care and safety are affected by incompetent, unethical, or illegal practice by any person.

3.1   Safeguarding the Health and Safety of the Client

The nurse's primary commitment is to the health, welfare, and safety of the client. As an advocate for the client, the nurse must be alert to and take appropriate action regarding any instances of incompetence, unethical, or illegal practice by any member of the health care team or the health care system, or any action on the part of others that places the rights or best interests of the client in jeopardy. To function effectively in this role, nurses must be aware of the employing institution's policies and procedures, nursing standards of practice, the *Code for Nurses*, and laws governing nursing and health care practice with regard to incompetent, unethical, or illegal practice.

3.2   Acting on Questionable Practice

When the nurse is aware of inappropriate or questionable practice in the provision of health care, concern should be expressed to the person carrying out the questionable practice and attention called to the possible detrimental effect upon the client's welfare. When factors in the health care delivery system threaten the welfare of the client, similar action should be directed to the responsible administrative person. If indicate, the practice should then be reported to the appropriate authority within the institution, agency, or larger system.

There should be an established process for the reporting and handling of incompetent, unethical, or illegal practice within the employment setting so that such reporting can go through official channels without causing fear of reprisal. The nurse should be knowledgeable about the process and be prepared to use it if necessary. When questions are raised about the practices of individual practitioners or of health care systems, written documentation of the observed practices or behaviors must be available to the appropriate authorities. State nurses associations should be prepared to provide assistance and support in the development and evaluation of such processes and in reporting procedures.

When incompetent, unethical, or illegal practice on the part of anyone concerned with the client's care is not corrected within the employment setting and continues to jeopardize the client's welfare and safety, the problems should be reported to other appropriate authorities such as practice committees of the pertinent professional organizations or the legally constituted bodies concerned with licensing of specific categories of health workers or professional practitioners. Some situations may warrant the concern and involvement of all such groups. Accurate reporting and documentation undergird all actions.

3.3   Review Mechanisms

The nurse should participate in the planning, establishment, implementation, and evaluation of review mechanisms that serve to safeguard clients, such as duly constituted peer review processes or committees and ethics committees. Such ongoing review mechanisms are based on established criteria, have stated purposes, include a process for making recommendations, and facilitate improved delivery of nursing and other health services to clients wherever nursing services are provided.

4   The nurse assumes responsibility and accountability for individual nursing judgments and actions.

4.1   Acceptance of Responsibility and Accountability

The recipients of professional nursing services are entitled to high quality nursing care. Individual professional licensure is the protective mechanism legislated by the public to ensure the basic and minimum competencies of the professional nurse. Beyond that, society has accorded to the nursing profession the right to regulate its own practice. The regulation and control of nursing practice by nurses demand that individual practitioners of professional nursing must bear primary responsibility for the nursing care clients receive and must be individually accountable for their own practice.

4.2   Responsibility for Nursing Judgment and Action

Responsibility refers to the carrying out of duties associated with a particular role assumed by the nurse. Nursing obligations are reflected in the ANA publications *Nursing: A Social Policy Statement* and *Standards of Clinical Nursing Practice*. In recognizing the rights of clients, the standards describe a collaborative relationship between the nurse and the client through the use of the nursing process. Nursing responsibilities include data collection and assessment of the health status of the client; formation of nursing diagnoses derived from client assessment; development of a nursing care plan that is directed toward designated goals, assists the client in maximizing his or her health capabilities, and provides for the client's participation in promoting, maintaining, and restoring his or her health; evaluation of the effectiveness of nursing care in achieving goals as determined by the client and the nurse; and subsequent reassessment and revision of the nursing care plan as warranted. In the process of assuming these responsibilities, the nurse is held accountable for them.

4.3   Accountability for Nursing Judgment and Action

Accountability refers to being answerable to someone for something one has done. It means providing an explanation or rationale to oneself, to clients, to peers, to the nursing profession, and to society. In order to be accountable, nurses act under a code of ethical conduct that is grounded in the moral principles of fidelity and respect for the dignity, worth, and self-determination of clients.

The nursing profession continues to develop ways to clarify nursing's accountability to society. The contract between the profession and society is made explicit through such mechanisms as (a) the *Code for Nurses*, (b) the standards of nursing practice, (c) the development of nursing theory derived from nursing research in order to guide nursing actions, (d) educational requirements for practice, (e) certification, and (f) mechanisms for evaluating the effectiveness of the nurse's performance of nursing responsibilities.

Nurses are accountable for judgments made and actions taken in the course of nursing practice. Neither physicians' orders nor the employing agency's policies relieve the nurse of accountability for actions taken and judgments made.

5   The nurse maintains competence in nursing.

5.1   Personal Responsibility for Competence

The profession of nursing is obligated to provide adequate and competent nursing care. Therefore it is the personal responsibility of each nurse to maintain competency in practice. For the client's optimum well-being and for the nurse's own professional development, the care of the client reflects and incorporates new techniques and knowledge in health care as these develop, especially as they relate to the nurse's particular field of practice. The nurse must be award of the need for continued professional learning and must assume personal responsibility for currency of knowledge and skills.

5.2   Measurement of Competence in Nursing Practice

Evaluation of one's performance by peers is a hallmark of professionalism and a method by which the profession is held accountable to society. Nurses must be willing to have their practice reviewed and evaluated by their peers. Guidelines for evaluating the scope of practice and the appropriateness, effectiveness, and efficiency of nursing practice are found in nursing practice acts, ANA standards of practice, and other quality assurance mechanisms. Each nurse is responsible for participating in the development of objective criteria for evaluation. In addition, the nurse engages in ongoing self-evaluation of clinical competency, decision-making abilities, and professional judgments.

5.3   Intraprofessional Responsibility for Competence in Nursing Care

Nurses share responsibility for high quality nursing care. Nurses are required to have knowledge relevant to the current scope of nursing practice, changing issues and concerns, and ethical concepts and principles. Since individual competencies vary, nurses refer clients to and consult with other nurses with expertise and recognized competencies in various fields of practice.

6   The nurse exercises informed judgment and uses individual competence and qualifications as criteria in seeking consultation, accepting responsibilities, and delegating nursing activities.

6.1   Changing Functions

Nurses are faced with decisions in the context of the increased complexity of health care, changing patterns in the delivery of health services, and the development of evolving nursing practice in response to the health needs of clients. As the scope of nursing practice changes, the nurse must exercise judgment in accepting responsibilities, seeking consultation, and assigning responsibilities to others who carry out nursing care.

6.2   Accepting Responsibilities

The nurse must not engage in practices prohibited by law or delegate to others activities prohibited by practice acts of other health care personnel or by other laws. Nurses determine the scope of their practice in light of their education, knowledge, competency, and extent of experience. If the nurse concludes that he or she lacks competence or is inadequately prepared to carry out a specific function, the nurse has the responsibility to refuse that work and to seek alternative sources of care based on concern for the client's welfare. In that refusal, both the client and the nurse are protected. Inasmuch as the nurse is responsible for the continuous care of patients in health care settings, the nurse is frequently called upon to carry out components of care delegated by other health professionals as part of the client's treatment regimen. The nurse should not accept these interdependent functions if they are so extensive as to prevent the nurse from fulfilling the responsibility to provide appropriate nursing care to clients.

6.3   Consultation and Collaboration

The provision of health and illness care to clients is a complex process that requires a wide range of knowledge, skills, and collaborative efforts. Nurses must be aware of their own individual competencies. When the needs of the client are beyond the qualifications and competencies of the nurse, consultation and collaboration must be sought from qualified nurses, other health professionals, or other appropriate sources. Participation on intradisciplinary or interdisciplinary teams is often an effective approach to the provision of high quality total health services.

6.4   Delegation of Nursing Activities

Inasmuch as the nurse is accountable for the quality of nursing care rendered to clients, nurses are accountable for the delegation of nursing care activities to other health workers. Therefore, the nurse must assess individual competence in assigning selected components of nursing care to other nursing service personnel. The nurse should not delegate to any member of the nursing team a function for which that person is not prepared or qualified. Employer poli-

cies or directives do not relieve the nurse of accountability for making judgments about the delegation of nursing care activities.

7   The nurse participates in activities that contribute to the ongoing development of the profession's body of knowledge.

7.1   The Nurse and Development of Knowledge

Every profession must engage in scholarly inquiry to identify, verify, and continually enlarge the body of knowledge that forms the foundation for its practice. A unique body of verified knowledge provides both framework and direction for the profession in all of its activities and for the practitioner in the provision of nursing care. The accrual of scientific and humanistic knowledge promotes the advancement of practice and the well-being of the profession's clients. Ongoing scholarly activity such as research and the development of theory is indispensable to the full discharge of a profession's obligations to society. Each nurse has a role in this area of professional activity, whether as an investigator in furthering knowledge, as a participant in research, or as a user of theoretical and empirical knowledge.

7.2   Protection of Rights of Human Participants in Research

Individual rights valued by society and by the nursing profession that have particular application in research include the right of adequately informed consent, the right to freedom from risk of injury, and the right of privacy and preservation of dignity. Inherent in these rights is respect for each individual's rights to exercise self-determination, to choose to participate or not, to have full information, and to terminate participation in research without penalty.

It is the duty of the nurse functioning in any research role to maintain vigilance in protecting the life, health, and privacy of human subjects from both anticipated and unanticipated risks and in assuring informed consent. Subjects' integrity, privacy, and rights must be especially safeguarded if the subjects are unable to protect themselves because of incapacity or because they are in a dependent relationship to the investigator. The investigation should be discontinued if its continuance might be harmful to the subject.

7.3   General Guidelines for Participating in Research

Before participating in research conducted by others, the nurse has an obligation to (a) obtain information about the intent and the nature of the research and (b) ascertain that the study proposal is approved by the appropriate bodies, such as institutional review boards.

Research should be conducted and directed by qualified persons. The nurse who participates in research in any capacity should be fully informed about both the nurse's and the client's rights and obligations.

8   The nurse participates in the profession's efforts to implement and improve standards of nursing.

8.1   Responsibility to the Public for Standards

Nursing is responsible and accountable for admitting to the profession only those individuals who have demonstrated the knowledge, skills, and commitment considered essential to professional practice. Nurse educators have a major responsibility for ensuring that these competencies and a demonstrated commitment to professional practice have been achieved before the entry of an individual into the practice of professional nursing.

Established standards and guidelines for nursing practice provide guidance for the delivery of professional nursing care and are a means for evaluating care received by the public. The nurse has a personal responsibility and commitment to clients for implementation and maintenance of optimal standards of nursing practice.

8.2   Responsibility to the Profession for Standards

Established standards reflect the practice of nursing grounded in ethical commitments and a body of knowledge. Professional standards or guidelines exist in nursing practice, nursing service, nursing education, and nursing research. The nurse has the responsibility to monitor these standards in daily practice and to participate actively in the profession's ongoing efforts to foster optimal standards of practice at the local, regional, state, and national levels of the health care system.

Nurse educators have the additional responsibility to maintain optimal standards of nursing practice and education in nursing education programs and in any other settings where planned learning activities for nursing students take place.

9   The nurse participates in the profession's efforts to establish and maintain conditions of employment conducive to high quality nursing care.

9.1   Responsibility for Conditions of Employment

The nurse must be concerned with conditions of employment that (a) enable the nurse to practice in accordance with the standards of nursing practice and (b) provide a care environment that meets the standards of nursing services. The provision of high quality nursing care is the responsibility of both the individual nurse and the nursing profession. Professional autonomy and self-regulation in the control of conditions of practice are necessary for implementing nursing standards.

9.2   Maintaining Conditions for High Quality Nursing Care

Articulation and control of nursing practice can be accomplished through individual agreement and collective action. A nurse may enter into an agreement with individuals or organizations to provide health care. Nurses may participate in collective action such as collective bargaining through their state nurses' association to determine the terms and conditions of employment conducive to high quality nursing care. Such agreements should be consistent with the profession's standards of practice, the state law regulating nursing practice, and the *Code for Nurses*.

10   The nurse participates in the profession's effort to protect the public from misinformation and misrepresentation and to maintain the integrity of nursing.

10.1 Protection from Misinformation and Misrepresentation

Nurses are responsible for advising clients against the use of products that endanger the client's safety and welfare. The nurse shall not use any form of public or professional communication to make claims that are false, fraudulent, misleading, deceptive, or unfair.

The nurse does not give or imply endorsement to advertising, promotion, or sale of commercial products or services in a manner that may be interpreted as reflecting the opinion or judgment of the profession as a whole. The nurse may use knowledge of specific services or products in advising an individual client, since this may contribute to the client's health and well-being. In the course of providing information or education to clients or other practitioners about commercial products or services, however, a variety of similar products or services should be offered to described so the client or practitioner can make an informed choice.

10.2 Maintaining the Integrity of Nursing

The use of the title *registered nurse* is granted by state governments for the protection of the public. Use of that title carries with it the responsibility to act in the public interest. The nurse may use the title R.N. and symbols of academic degrees or other earned or honorary professional symbols of recognition in all ways that are legal and appropriate. The title and other symbols of the profession should not be used, however, for benefits unrelated to nursing practice or the profession, or used by those who may seek to exploit them for other purposes.

Nurses should refrain from casting a vote in any deliberations involving health care services or facilities where the nurse has business or other interests that could be construed as a conflict of interest.

11   The nurse collaborates with members of the health professions and other citizens in promoting community and national efforts to meet the health needs of the public.

11.1 Collaboration with Others to Meet Health Needs

The availability and accessibility of high quality health services to all people require collaborative planning at the local, state, national, and international levels that respects the interdependence of health professionals and clients in health care systems. Nursing care is an integral part of high quality health care, and nurses have an obligation to promote equitable access to nursing and health care for all people.

11.2 Responsibility to the Public

The nursing profession is committed to promoting the welfare and safety of all people. The goals and values of nursing are essential to effective delivery of health services. For the benefit of the individual client and the public at large, nursing's goals and commitments need adequate representation. Nurses should ensure this representation by active participation in decision making in institutional and political arenas to assure a just distribution of health care and nursing resources.

11.3 Relationships with Other Disciplines

The complexity of health care delivery systems requires a multidisciplinary approach to delivery of services that has the strong support and active participation of all the health professions. Nurses should actively promote the collaborative planning required to ensure the availability and accessibility of high quality health services to all persons whose health needs are unmet.

Appendix C
United States Federal Circuit Courts of Appeal

FIRST
Boston

Maine	New Hampshire
Massachusetts	Rhode Island
Puerto Rico	

SECOND
New York City

New York	Connecticut
Vermont	

THIRD
Philadelphia

Pennsylvania	New Jersey
Delaware	Virgin Islands

FOURTH
Richmond

Maryland	Virginia
West Virginia	North Carolina
South Carolina	

FIFTH
New Orleans

Texas	Louisiana
Mississippi	

SIXTH
Cincinnati

Michigan	Ohio
Kentucky	Tennessee

SEVENTH
Chicago

Illinois	Indiana
Wisconsin	

EIGHTH
St. Louis

Minnesota	Iowa
Missouri	Arkansas
North Dakota	South Dakota
Nebraska	

NINTH
San Francisco

California	Arizona
Nevada	Washington
Oregon	Guam,
Idaho	Montana
Alaska	Hawaii
Northern Mariana Islands	

TENTH
Denver

Wyoming	Utah
Colorado	New Mexico
Kansas	Oklahoma

ELEVENTH
Atlanta

Alabama	Georgia
Florida	

DISTRICT OF COLUMBIA
Washington, DC

FEDERAL
Washington, DC

The Thirteen Federal Judicial Circuits

See 28 U.S.C.A. § 41

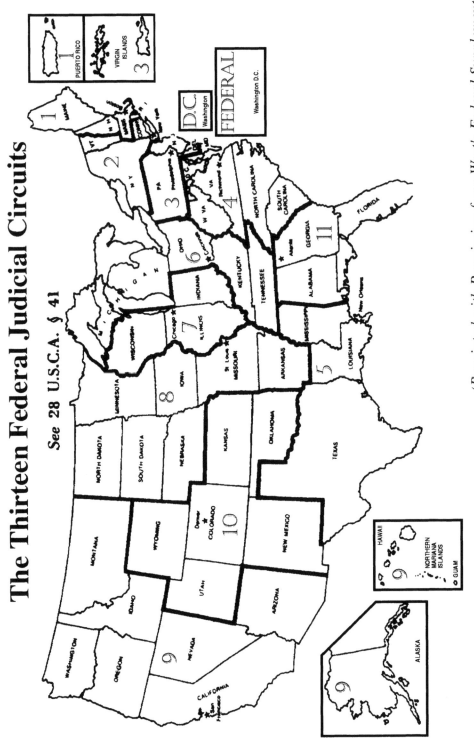

(Reprinted with Permission from West's Federal Supplement)

Appendix D
Office of Civil Rights (OCR) Regional Offices

OFFICE LOCATION	STATES COVERED
EASTERN DIVISION	
Boston	Maine, New Hampshire, Vermont, Rhode Island, Massachusetts, Connecticut
New York	New York, New Jersey, Puerto Rico, Virgin Islands
Philadelphia	Pennsylvania, Maryland, Delaware, West Virginia, Kentucky
MIDWESTERN DIVISION	
Chicago	Illinois, Indiana, Wisconsin, Minnesota
Cleveland	Michigan, Ohio
Kansas City	Missouri, Kansas, Iowa, Nebraska, North Dakota, South Dakota
SOUTHERN DIVISION	
Atlanta	South Carolina, Georgia, Florida, Alabama, Tennessee
Dallas	Mississippi, Louisiana, Texas, Arkansas, Oklahoma
Washington D.C./Metro	North Carolina, Virginia, Washington, D.C.
Western Division	
Denver	Colorado, Utah, Wyoming, Montana, Arizona, New Mexico
San Francisco	California
Seattle	Nevada, Hawaii, Idaho, Oregon, Washington, Alaska, Pacific Region

Appendix E
Selected Resources

ORGANIZATIONS

American Academy of Nurse Practitioners
Capitol Station, LBJ Building
P.O. Box 12846
Austin, TX 78711

American Academy of Pediatrics (& related state associations)
141 Northwest Point Boulevard
Elk Grove Village, IL 60007-1098
(847) 228-5005
http://www.aap.org/

American Association of Colleges of Nursing
American Association for Health Education
1900 Association Dr.
Reston, VA 22091
(703) 476-3437
http://www.aacn.nche.edu/

American Association of Legal Nurse Consultants (AALNC)
4700 W. Lake Avenue
Glenview, IL 60025
(877) 402-2562
http://www.aalnc.org/

American Association of Nurse Attorneys
Belinda E. Peutz, exec. dir.
7794 Grow Drive
Pensacola, FL 32514
toll free 1-877-538-2262 or 1-850-474-3646
http://www.taana.org

American Association of School Administrators
1801 N. Moore St.
Arlington, VA 22209
(703) 875-0755

American Bar Association
Commission on Mental and Physical Disability Law
740 15th St., 9th floor
Washington, DC 20005
http://www.abanet.org/

American College of Nurse Practitioners
503 Capitol Ct. NE, #300
Washington, DC 20002
(202) 546-4825
Email: acnp@nurse.org

American Dental Association
211 E. Chicago Ave.
Chicago, IL 60611
(312) 440-2800
http://www.ada.org

American Federation of Teachers
AFL-CIO
555 New Jersey Ave, NW
Washington, DC 20001
http://www.aft.org/

American Medical Association
515 N. State St.
Chicago, IL 60610
(312) 464-4065

American Medical Informatics Association
4915 St. Elmo Avenue, Suite 401
Bethesda, MD 20814
(301) 657-1291
http://www.amia.org/

American Nurses Association (& related state associations)
600 Maryland Avenue, SW
Suite 100 West
Washington, DC 20024
(202) 651-7000 or 800-274-4ANA (4262)
http://www.ana.org/

American Psychological Association
750 First St., NE
Washington, DC 20002
(202) 336-6126
http://www.apa.org/

American Public Health Association (& related state associations)
800 I St., N.W.
Washington, DC 20001-3710
202-777-2742
http://www.apha.org/

American School Counselor Association
801 N. Fairfax St., Suite 310
Alexandria, VA 22314
(703) 683-2722
http://www.ashaweb.org/

American School Health Association (& related state associations)
PO Box 708
Kent, OH 44240
(330) 678-1601

Association of State & Territorial Directors of Health Promotion
   and Public Health Education
1015 15th St., NW, Suite 410
Washington, DC 20005
(202) 289-6639

Centers for Disease Control and Prevention (CDC) and CDC –
   Division of Adolescent and School Health
U.S. Department of Health and Human Services
1600 Clifton Rd.
Atlanta, GA 30333
(404) 639-3311
Public Inquiries: (404) 639-3534 or 1-800-311-3435
http://www.cdc.gov/
http://www.cdc.gov/nccdphp/dash

Center for School Mental Health Assistance
600 W. Lexington St., 10th Floor
Baltimore, MD 21201
(410) 706-0980

The Children's Defense Fund
25 E. Street NW
Washington, DC 20001
(202) 628-8787
http://www.childrensdefense.org/

Council of Administrators of Special Education (CASE)
See Council for Exceptional Children (CEC) below

Council of Chief State School Officers
One Massachusetts Avenue, NW, Suite 700
Washington, DC 20001-1421
(202)408-5505
http://www.ccsso.org/

Council for Exceptional Children (CEC)
1920 Association Drive
Reston, VA 22091
(703) 620-3660
http://www.cec.sped.org/

Council of Parents' Attorneys and Advocates
PO Box 817327
Hollywood, FL 33081
(954) 966-4489
http://www.copaa.net

Council of School Attorneys
See National School Boards Association below

Education Law Association
Mail Drop 0528, 300 College Park
Dayton, OH 45469
(937) 229-3589
http://www.educationlaw.org/

Employee Assistance Professionals Association
2102 Wilson Blvd., Suite 500
Arlington, VA 22201
(703) 522-6272

National Alliance of Pupil Services Organizations
7700 Willowbrook Rd.
Fairfax Station, VA 22039
(703) 250-3414

National Assembly on School-Based Health Care
1522 K St., NW, Suite 600
Washington, DC 20005
(202) 289-5400
http://www.nasbhc.org/

National Association of Community Health Center
   (Adolescent/School Health Initiative)
1330 New Hampshire Avenue, NW, Suite 122
Washington, DC 20036
(202) 659-8008
http://www.nachc.com/

National Association of County & City Health Officials
1100 17th St., NW, Second Fl.
Washington, DC 20036
(202) 783-5550

National Association of Elementary School Principals
1615 Duke St.
Alexandria, VA 22314
(703) 684-3345

National Association of Pediatric Nurse Associates & Practitioners
   (NAPNAP)
1101 Kings Highway, N., Suite 206
Cherry Hill, NJ 08034-1912
1-856-667-1773 or 1-877-662-7627
http://www.napnap.org/

National Association of School Nurses (NASN) (& related state
   associations)
PO Box 1300
Scarborough, ME 04074-1300
207-883-2117
http://www.nasn@nasn.org

National Association of School Psychologists
4340 East West Hwy., Suite 402
Bethesda, MD 20814
(301) 657-0270

National Association of Secondary School Principals
1904 Association Dr.
Reston, VA 20191
(703) 860-0200

National Association of Social Workers
750 First St., NE, Suite 700
Washington, DC 20002-4241

National Association for Sport and Physical Education
1900 Association Dr.
Reston, VA 20191-1599
(703) 476-3410

National Association of State Boards of Education
1012 Cameron St.
Alexandria, VA 22314
(703) 684-4000
http://www.nasbe.org/

National Association of State Directors of Special Education
1800 Diagonal Road, Suite 320
Alexandria, VA 2314

National Association of State School Nurse Consultants (NASSNC)
c/o ASHA
PO Box 708
Kent, OH 44240
Or contact a consultant through the state department of
    education or health
http://lserver.aea14.k12.ia.us/swp/tadkins/nassnc/NASSNC.html

National Coalition for Parent Involvement in Education
c/o IEL
1001 Connecticut Ave., NW, Suite 310
Washington, DC 20036
(202) 822-8405

National Conference of State Legislatures
1560 Broadway, Suite 700
Denver, CO 80202
(303) 830-2200

National Council of State Boards of Nursing, Inc.
Links to many sites are provided here.
http://www.ncsbn.org/

National Education Association
1201 16th Street NW
Washington, DC 20036
(202) 833-4000
http://www.nea.org/

National Environmental Health Association
720 South Colorado Blvd., Suite 970
Denver, CO 80222
(303) 756-9090

National Institutes of Health (NIH)—Maternal & Child
    Health Bureau
Department of Health and Human Services
Bethesda, Maryland 20892
http://www.nih.gov/

National Institute for Urban School Improvement
http://www.edc.org/urban

National League For Nursing
61 Broadway
New York, NY 10006
1-800-669-9656 or (212) 363-5555
http://www.nln.org/

National Network for Youth
1319 F St., NW, Suite 401
Washington, DC 20004
(202) 783-7949

National Parent Network
http://www.npnd.org/

National PTA
330 N. Wabash Ave., Suite 2100
Chicago, IL 60611-3690
(800) 307-4782
http://www.pta.org/

National Safety Council
1121 Spring Lake Dr.
Itasca, IL 60143-3201
(630) 285-1121

National School Boards Association
1680 Duke St.
Alexandria, VA 22314
(703) 838-6722
http://www.nsba.org/cosa

Office of Elementary and Secondary Education
U.S. Department of Education
600 Independence Avenue, S.W.
Washington, DC 20202

Office of Special Education and Rehabilitation Services
U.S. Department of Education
Mary E. Switzer Building, 330 C Street, S.W.
Washington, DC 20202

Public Risk Management Association
1815 N. Fort Meyer Dr., Suite 102
Arlington, VA 22209
(703) 528-7701

School Health Resource Services
Office of School Health — School of Nursing
University of Colorado Health Sciences Center
1-800-669-9954
http://www.uchsc.edu/sn/shrs/

Society for Adolescent Medicine
1916 Copper Oaks Circle
Blue Springs, MO 64015
(816) 224-8010
U.S. Department of Education
http://www.ed.gov/

U.S. Environmental Protection Agency
http://www.epa.gov/

World Health Organization (WHO)
http://www.who.org

FEDERAL SCHOOL HEALTH-RELATED CLEARINGHOUSES AND RELATED RESOURCES

CDC National AIDS Clearinghouse
1-800-458-5231
1-800-342-AIDS (English hotline)
1-800-344-SIDA (Spanish hotline)
1-800-243-7012 (TTY/TDD)
http://www.cdcnac.org

CDC, National Center for Chronic Disease Prevention and
    Health Promotion
(404) 488-5080
http://www.cdc.gov

Clearinghouse for Occupational Safety and Health Information
1-800-35-NIOSH
(513) 533-8326
(513) 533-8573 (Fax)
http://www.cdc.gov/niosh/homepage.html

Combined Health Information Database (CHID)
1-800-955-0906
http://www.ovid.com/dochome/fldguide/chiddb.htm

CSAP's National Clearinghouse for Alcohol and Drug Information
1-800-729-6686
(301) 468-2600
http://www.health.org

ERIC Clearinghouse on Teaching and Teaching Education
(202) 293-2450
http://www.aacte.org

Food and Drug Administration, Office of Consumer Affairs
(301) 443-3170
http://www.fda.gov

Food and Nutrition Information Center, U.S. Department
    of Agriculture
(301) 504-5719
http://www.nal.usda.gov/fnic

Hotlist of K–12 Internet School Sites (includes links to State
    Department of Education pages)
http://www.gsn.org/hotlist/index.html

Indoor Air Quality Information Clearinghouse
1-800-438-4318
(202) 484-1307
http://www.epa.gov/iaq

National Center for Education in Maternal and Child Health
(703) 524-7802
http://www.ncemch.org

National Clearinghouse on Child Abuse and Neglect Information
1-800-FYI-3366
(703) 385-7565
http://www.calib.com/nccanch

National Clearinghouse on Family Support and Children's Mental
    Health, Portland State University
1-800-628-1696
(503) 725-4040
http://www.rtc.pdx.edu

National Health Information Center
1-800-336-4797
(301) 565-4167
http://nhic-nt.health.org

National Information Center for Children and Youth
    with Disabilities
1-800-695-0285 (Voice/ITT)
(202) 884-8200 (Voice/ITT)
http://www.nichcy.org

National Injury Information Clearinghouse
(301) 504-0424
http://www.cpsc.gov

National Maternal and Child Health Clearinghouse
(703) 821-8955, ext. 254 or 265
http://www.circsol.com/mch

National Oral Health Information Clearinghouse
1-800-402-7364
http://www.nidr.nih.gov

Office of Minority Health Resource Center
1-800-444-6472
http://www.omhrc.gov

U.S. Consumer Product Safety Commission Hotline
1-800-638-2772
http://www.cpsc.gov

Appendix F

Sample State Guidelines for School Nursing Services

Excerpted from: State of Connecticut Department of Education (1999). *Developing Quality Programs for Pupil Services: A Self-Evaluative Guide*. Hartford, CT: Author. Reprinted with permission: pp. i-v and School Nursing-1 through School Nursing-18.

FOREWORD

This compilation of standards has been developed to guide school districts in their efforts to ensure that the programs and services provided by their pupil services staff are of the highest caliber and provide optimal benefit to the school community. The document should help school districts achieve a clear, thoughtful, programmatic focus, plan and implement effective programs and services, enhance the organization and management of pupil services, and provide services in a manner consistent with best professional practice. It should also help inform school administrators and other school personnel about the diverse roles and functions that pupil services specialists can perform, thus promoting understanding and enhanced use of the expertise of these school professionals.

Given the challenges that beset many of today's families and interfere with the healthy development and educational progress of children, schools must become more proactive than ever in helping students connect with school and in engaging parents in the education of their children. Programs and services offered by pupil services specialists can significantly offset the impact of risk factors and stressors. Pupil services programs emphasizing prevention and early intervention and founded upon collaboration with teachers and families serve as models for pursuing these goals. Pupil services specialists can play a key role in initiating and supporting a wide range of collaborative programs and services that promote the physical, mental, and social well-being of all students. These programs and services may include mentoring, peer mediation, violence prevention, character education, development of social and communication skills, health and developmental screening and preventive services, health education, and life planning. Additionally, pupil services specialists can offer targeted parent education programs, consultation with school staff, and, when appropriate, referral to health and mental health services.

Since collaboration with parents, teachers, administrators, and community service providers is a key element in realizing the full potential of pupil services, it is recommended that this guide be made available to the entire school community. I hope you will find them useful in helping to optimize the impact of pupil services on student learning and wellness.

Theodore S. Sergi
Commissioner of Education

INTRODUCTION TO DEVELOPING QUALITY PROGRAMS FOR PUPIL SERVICES

Developing Quality Programs for Pupil Services: A Self –Evaluative Guide is designed to assist school districts to evaluate and enhance their pupil services programs. The concept and structure for this document were derived from previous versions that consultants in the Bureau of Special Education and Pupil Services used for on-site pupil services program review in the mid-1980s. The current version incorporates standards of ethics and professional practice of national pupil services organizations, and position papers, reports and guidelines generated by the State Department of Education. As such, these standards are written for professional staff members. Pupil services professionals are responsible for ensuring that assistive personnel (e.g., assistants, clerical staff, interns, LPNs) are properly credentialed, trained and supervised in order to support the pupil services professionals in meeting these standards. This guide should be regarded as a companion piece to Evaluating Pupil Services Specialists (Connecticut State Department of Education, October 1993), a document modeled on the State's 1987 Guidelines for Teachers Evaluation Programs.

Principles

Developing Quality Programs for Pupil Services: A Self-Evaluative Guide is founded upon the following principles, which are consistent with, or derived from, the *Connecticut Agenda for Improving Education Services to All Students and Report on Special Education and Related Services* (Connecticut State Department of Education, February 1998).

- Pupil services are an integral component of quality education programs for all students.
- Pupil services promote optimal development, health and learning for all students.
- Pupil services are organized and delivered so as to help teachers, parents and other members of the school community provide optimum teaching and learning experiences for students.
- Pupil services are comprehensive in scope, with emphasis on prevention and early intervention.
- Collaboration with students, parents, school personnel and community providers is key to the success of pupil services programs.
- Decision-making and service provision by pupil service professionals are guided by ethical principles.

PURPOSE

Use of this guide by school districts is voluntary. The standards herein are intended for formative, rather than summative, evaluation—that is, to analyze program strengths and weaknesses and promote improvement, rather than to "grade" current programs, services and policies. The standards may also help school personnel and members of the community who are not familiar with pupil services to better understand the nature, scope and value of the programs and services provided by pupil services specialists.

In undertaking a self-evaluation, it is not expected that a school district can or should immediately address all issues that might warrant attention. Districts should use these standards to identify and prioritize areas that most need improvement. This self-evaluation tool will be most effective when pupil services staff, teachers, administrators, parents, students and community providers are involved in the process.

DESIGN

The document begins with a set of "generic" standards for the overall pupil services program. Standards for Pupil Services are followed by a corresponding set for each of five disciplines:

- School Guidance and Counseling,
- School Language, Speech and Hearing,
- School Nursing,
- School Psychology,
- School Social Work.

This enables each of these disciplines to be evaluated separately.

Each of the six sets of standards follows the same basic outline, as shown on page iv. Standards, labeled by capital letters, are divided into three sections: Foundation, Student Services and Systems Operations. Each standard is further defined by selected indicators that are regarded as important for meeting that standard. These indicators have been sequenced so as to keep the numbering as consistent as possible across the six sets.

Depending on the size of the school district and the scope of the self-evaluation, certain indicators in the discipline-specific sets may be addressed in the generic standards (e.g., vision and mission statements), and need not be duplicated. Depending on the size of the school district and the scope of the self-evaluation, certain indicators in the discipline-specific sets may be addressed in the generic standards (e.g., vision and mission statements), and need not be duplicated.

The loose-leaf notebook format of this document allows sections to be easily photocopied. Local education agency administrators are advised to make copies of the generic Pupil Services Section and the relevant discipline-specific sections for each pupil services specialist. Readers are encouraged to provide feedback by completing and returning the reader response form provided.

ACKNOWLEDGEMENTS

The following associations are gratefully acknowledged for reviewing this document during various stages of its development:

Association of School Nurses of Connecticut
Connecticut Association of Counselor Education and Supervision
Connecticut Association of School Psychologists
Connecticut Association of School Social Workers
Connecticut Speech-Language-Hearing Association
Connecticut Council of Administrators of Special Education
Connecticut School Counselor Association

CONTENTS (BY SECTION)*

Standards for Pupil Services
Standards for School Guidance and Counseling
Standards for School Language, Speech and Hearing
Standards for School Nursing
Standards for School Psychology
Standards for School Social Work

OUTLINE THAT EACH SECTION FOLLOWS:

I. Foundation

A. Purpose
B. Program Development
C. Policies and Procedures

II. Student Services

A. Prevention
B. Curriculum
C. Screening and Assessment
D. Intervention
E. Promoting Student Independence/Self Advocacy
F. Referral and Liaison Activities
G. Collaboration and Consultation
H. Evaluation of Student Outcomes

III. Systems Operations

A. Organization and Management
B. Staff Supervision and Evaluation
C. Professional Roles and Responsibilities
D. Students Records
E. Confidentiality
F. Program Accountability
G. Program Support

* Only one section, Standards for School Nursing Services, are included in this index.

STANDARDS FOR SCHOOL NURSING SERVICES

KEY TO RATINGS:

M　= Met
P　= Partially Met
U　= Unmet
NA　= Not Applicable

I. FOUNDATION

A. Purpose

Standard: The school nursing program has clearly written vision and mission statements and related goals and objectives.

INDICATORS	RATING				COMMENTS
1. Vision and mission statements clearly address the needs of *all* students.	M	P	U	N/A	
2. Vision and mission statements complement the vision and mission statements of the district and pupil services program.	M	P	U	N/A	
3. Vision and mission statements reflect collaborative input from other pupil services disciplines and stakeholders.	M	P	U	N/A	
4. Goals and measurable objectives are derived from the vision and mission statements.	M	P	U	N/A	
5. Vision and mission statements, goals and objectives are consistent with the American Nurses Association's (ANA) Code of Ethics for Nursing (1985) ANA's *Standards of Clinical Practice* (1998), National Association of School Nurses' (NASN) *Standards of Professional School Nursing Practice* (1998) and *Nursing's Social Policy Statement* (ANA, 1995).	M	P	U	N/A	
6. Vision and mission statements, goals and objectives are based on periodic needs assessments of students, Families and staff.	M	P	U	N/A	
7. Vision and mission statements, goals and objectives are published and disseminated periodically to families, school personnel and members of the board of education, and made available to students, community agencies and the public.	M	P	U	N/A	
8. Vision and mission statements, goals and objectives are reviewed at least annually and revised as necessary, in collaboration with program stakeholders, preferably through a school health or pupil services advisory council.	M	P	U	N/A	
9. Vision and mission statements support a full range of services that include prevention, assessment, intervention, consultation, and evaluation of student outcomes.	M	P	U	N/A	
10. Vision and mission statements communicate clear expectations for collaboration among pupil services disciplines and with other professionals.	M	P	U	N/A	

B. Program Development

Standard: School nurses collaborate to develop programs that meet the identified needs of students, families and school personnel.

INDICATORS	RATING				COMMENTS
1. School nurses identify program and service needs in collaboration with stakeholders.	M	P	U	N/A	
2. School nursing programs are developed in accordance with current professional standards of practice in nursing and medicine, and legal mandates.	M	P	U	N/A	
3. School nurses plan, develop and evaluate health and pupil services programs in collaboration with stakeholders.	M	P	U	N/A	
4. School nurses participate in the development, implementation and evaluation of other districtwide initiatives and programs.	M	P	U	N/A	

C. Policies and Procedures

Standard: The school nursing program maintains written policies and procedures to ensure quality of services and districtwide uniformity.

INDICATORS	RATING				COMMENTS
1. Policies and procedures are consistent with the program's vision and mission statement, goals, and objectives.	M	P	U	N/A	
2. Policies and procedures are consistent with the ANA's and NASN's professional codes of ethics.	M	P	U	N/A	
3. Policies and procedures are consistent with ANA and NASN professional standards of practice, other applicable professional standards (e.g., guidelines of the American Academy of Pediatrics) and legal mandates.	M	P	U	N/A	
4. School nurses collaborate (e.g., with the school medical advisor, administrators) to develop, review and revise program policies and procedures.	M	P	U	N/A	
5. Policies and procedures allow school nurses to exercise appropriate professional judgment and autonomy in delivering services.	M	P	U	N/A	
6. Policies and procedures promote collaboration among pupil services disciplines and with other school personnel, families and community agencies.	M	P	U	N/A	
7. Policies and procedures ensure effective response to individual and schoolwide crisis situations.	M	P	U	N/A	
8. Policies and procedures require staff compliance with universal precautions and other applicable health and safety standards.	M	P	U	N/A	
9. Policies and procedures are available in writing to all school nursing and health services staff (e.g., school medical advisor, assistants).	M	P	U	N/A	
10. School nurses receive orientation and regular updating on program policies and procedures.	M	P	U	N/A	
11. Policies and procedures are published and disseminated periodically to families, school personnel and members of the board of education, and made available to students, community agencies, and the public.	M	P	U	N/A	
12. Policies and procedures are reviewed and updated annually by the school medical advisor, school nurse supervisor and, as applicable, the school health (or pupil services) advisory council.	M	P	U	N/A	
13. Standing orders for medications and emergency protocols are updated and signed by the school medical advisor at least annually and as needed.	M	P	U	N/A	

II. STUDENT SERVICES
A. Prevention
Standard: School nurses deliver effective prevention programs and services.

INDICATORS	RATING				COMMENTS
1. School nurses collaborate with others to develop, promote and implement prevention programs and services.	M	P	U	N/A	
2. School nurses support and, when appropriate, provide leadership for community and school health programs that promote wellness, reduce risky behaviors and improve school climates (e.g., substance abuse, child abuse, suicide, choosing healthy lifestyles).	M	P	U	N/A	
3. School nurses serve as prevention role models.	M	P	U	N/A	
4. School nurses disseminate information about health practices and behaviors that promote educational success, and risk factors that adversely affect educational success.	M	P	U	N/A	
5. School nurses collaborate with other school personnel, families and community agencies to monitor the development and educational progress of students exposed to risk factors.	M	P	U	N/A	

B. Curriculum
Standard: School nurses coordinate health services for students.

INDICATORS	RATING				COMMENTS
1. School nurses keep abreast of relevant curriculum issues and initiatives.	M	P	U	N/A	
2. School nurses are knowledgeable of school district curriculum, especially health-related goals and content.	M	P	U	N/A	
3. School nurses ensure that nursing services are coordinated and, where appropriate, integrated with curriculum content.	M	P	U	N/A	
4. School nurses participate in the selection, development, delivery, and evaluation of health-related curriculum.	M	P	U	N/A	

C. Screening and Assessment
Standard: School nurses deliver effective screening and assessment services.

INDICATORS	RATING				COMMENTS
1. Health screening programs are designed to ensure coordination of program components (i.e., planning, training, timing and scheduling, implementation, referrals for further assessment, follow through and record keeping).	M	P	U	N/A	
2. Health screening activities are conducted according to current professional standards of practice, school district policies and procedures, and legal mandates.	M	P	U	N/A	
3. School nurses collaborate in the development, implementation and evaluation of screening programs.	M	P	U	N/A	
4. School nurses communicate with families to provide advance notice of screening activities, to provide notice of findings requiring further action, and to ascertain the status of referrals.	M	P	U	N/A	
5. School nurses conduct screenings in a timely manner.	M	P	U	N/A	

II. STUDENT SERVICES (continued)

C. Screening and Assessment (continued)

INDICATORS	RATING				COMMENTS
6. Assessment activities are conducted according to current professional standards of practice, school district policies and procedures, and legal mandates.	M	P	U	N/A	
7. Assessments are conducted for a variety of reasons (i.e., health complaints, program eligibility, determining service needs, monitoring student progress, program evaluation and research).	M	P	U	N/A	
8. School nurses collaborate, as appropriate, with school personnel, students, families and community providers in planning and conducting student assessments.	M	P	U	N/A	
9. School nurses obtain informed written parental consent to conduct individual student evaluations (e.g. comprehensive health assessment).	M	P	U	N/A	
10. School nurses select areas of health assessment, and health and developmental assessment instruments and procedures, on the basis of individual children's needs and presenting problems, as well as appropriate theories in nursing and the biopsychosocial sciences.	M	P	U	N/A	
11. School nurses conduct focussed and comprehensive, multifactored assessments, to diagnose student responses to actual and potential health problems (physical and psychosocial). These assessments may include both informal procedures (e.g., interviews, observations, and behavioral rating scales) and standardized procedures that are valid and reliable for the populations and purposes intended.	M	P	U	N/A	
12. In conducting assessments and interpreting results, school nurses consider factors such as cultural and language background, educational experience, family priorities, health and developmental history, and current student and family concerns. School nurses do not make decisions or recommendations based solely on quantitative formulas.	M	P	U	N/A	
13. School nurses report assessment results, both orally and in writing, in a manner that promotes appropriate understanding and use, and is consistent with confidentiality requirements.	M	P	U	N/A	
14. School nurses write formal assessment reports, either individually or as part of a team, that specify sources of information, results, interpretations and recommendations.	M	P	U	N/A	
15. School nurses conduct evaluations in a timely manner.	M	P	U	N/A	

II. STUDENT SERVICES (continued)

D. Intervention

Standard: School nurses deliver a continuum of effective nursing intervention services from early intervention through crisis response.

INDICATORS	RATING				COMMENTS
1. Intervention activities are conducted according to current professional standards of practice, school district policies and procedures, and legal mandates.	M	P	U	N/A	
2. School nurses provide comprehensive service delivery by using a variety of intervention approaches, including both indirect services (e.g., parent counseling and education, staff training and consultation, monitoring of student status, environmental assessment) and direct services (e.g., the development and implementation of individualized health care plans, health counseling and teaching, casefinding and referral, health maintenance and self-care support and specialized health care treatments).	M	P	U	N/A	
3. School nurses collaborate, as appropriate, with school personnel, students, families and community providers to develop measurable goals and objectives for students receiving health services, as documented in individualized health care plans, Section 504 plans and individualized education programs.	M	P	U	N/A	
4. Goals and objectives are based on assessment and reassessment findings.	M	P	U	N/A	
5. Goals and objectives are educationally relevant, developmentally appropriate and sensitive to the child's and family's social, cultural and linguistic background.	M	P	U	N/A	
6. Strategies, techniques and materials are selected to support goals and objectives.	M	P	U	N/A	

E. Promoting Student Independence and Self-Advocacy

Standard: School nurses assist students in monitoring and directing their personal development and capabilities.

INDICATORS	RATING				COMMENTS
1. School nurses extend services to students in ways that buildon their individual strengths, offer them maximum opportunity to make healthy choices, and allow them to participate in the planning and direction of their own health care and learning.	M	P	U	N/A	
2. School nurses use developmentally appropriate practices to assist students in formulating personal health goals and future plans.	M	P	U	N/A	

F. Referral and Liaison Activies

Standard: School nurses deliver effective referral and liaison services.

INDICATORS	RATING				COMMENTS
1. School nurses keep abreast of current community services and other resources.	M	P	U	N/A	
2. School nurses keep families of school children informed of the community's resources and help families access them independently.	M	P	U	N/A	
3. School nurses make appropriate referrals to other professionals/agencies for evaluation and services, and ensure follow-up.	M	P	U	N/A	
4. School nurses act as liaisons between the school, family and medical community, and as liaisons with other community service providers, as appropriate.	M	P	U	N/A	

II. STUDENT SERVICES (continued)

G. Collaboration and Consultation

Standard: School nurses collaborate and consult with others to provide effective and efficient services.

INDICATORS	RATING				COMMENTS
1. School nurses respect the contributions of all members of school teams (e.g., IEP Team, student assistance team) and integrate the input and recommendations of all team members in making decisions.	M	P	U	N/A	
2. School nurses provide consultative services to parents, students, school personnel and other professionals.	M	P	U	N/A	
3. School nurses seek appropriate consultation to better meet student and family needs.	M	P	U	N/A	

H. Evaluation of Student Outcomes

Standard: School nurses evaluate student outcomes to ensure high-quality services.

INDICATORS	RATING				COMMENTS
1. School nurses collect and maintain relevant data to evaluate student outcomes.	M	P	U	N/A	
2. School nurses monitor student progress to determine the efficacy of direct and indirect interventions.	M	P	U	N/A	
3. School nurses revise interventions on the basis of evaluations of student outcomes.	M	P	U	N/A	

III. SYSTEMS OPERATIONS

A. Organization and Management

Standard: The school nursing program is organized and managed in a manner conducive to effective delivery of services and continuous improvement.

INDICATORS	RATING				COMMENTS
1. The district's organizational chart delineates the relationship between the school nursing program, pupil services department and other departments.	M	P	U	N/A	
2. A designated school nurse supervisor or other appropriate central administrator assumes responsibility for administration of the school district's nursing program. This individual is allotted sufficient time and opportunity to carry out this responsibility.	M	P	U	N/A	
3. A health (or pupil) services advisory council, including representatives of community service providers and parents, advises the district on its delivery of nursing services.	M	P	U	N/A	
4. Organization and funding of the school nursing program assure that all students, both in regular and special education, have access to appropriate health services.	M	P	U	N/A	
5. The school nursing administrator clearly communicates program priorities and provides sufficient resources and direction to help staff organize their work and address priorities in a timely fashion.	M	P	U	N/A	
6. Work assignments are consistent with the qualifications and skills of nursing personnel and are based on current student and program needs identified through a systematic, annual needs assessment.	M	P	U	N/A	

III. SYSTEMS OPERATIONS (continued)

A. Organization and Management (continued)

INDICATORS	RATING				COMMENTS
7. The school nursing program maintains systematic records to ensure that staff members complete assignments in a timely manner.	M	P	U	N/A	
8. Work assignments of school nurses is based on consideration of the full range of responsibilities and logistics. These considerations include: case load; routine and emergency health needs of the student population; number of students requiring individualized health care plans, medication administration and other nursing interventions; consultations with staff, families and community providers; attendance at team meetings; documentation requirements; and if applicable, the numbers of sites to be served, supervision of assistive personnel and travel requirements.	M	P	U	N/A	
9. If contracted nursing services are used, the contractual agreement requires compliance with district policies and procedures, and the district monitors these services to ensure such compliance.	M	P	U	N/A	
10. Contracted nursing services encompass the same continuum of services as those provided by regularly employed school nursing staff and are not used to decrease the amount and quality of nursing services provided by the district.	M	P	U	N/A	
11. School nurses attend regularly scheduled building, school nursing program and interdisciplinary meetings. These meetings afford staff the opportunity to discuss professional issues.	M	P	U	N/A	
12. The school nursing program has mechanisms (e.g., input from outside experts, joint school-community ethics committee) for addressing and resolving staff members' professional, legal and ethical concerns about school district policies, procedures and practices in a constructive and non-threatening environment.	M	P	U	N/A	
13. There are current, written job descriptions for school nurses and other school health personnel including titles, qualifications, professional activities and special responsibilities.	M	P	U	N/A	
14. Sufficient qualified school nurses and assistive personnel are employed to address district priorities and department goals and objectives. Only nurses or nurse practitioners qualified under C.G.S. Section 10-212, and regulations 10-212-1 through 10-212-7, have the title, role and responsibilities of a "School Nurse."	M	P	U	N/A	
15. Delegation by school nurses to assistive personnel (e.g., LPNs, health aides) meets legal mandates and current standards of professional practice for training, supervision, professional-to-assistant ratios, and accountability.	M	P	U	N/A	
16. A school nurse's decision to delegate nursing and school health services responsibilities is based on a multifaceted assessment by the school nurse, including: availability of qualified assistive personnel; availability of the delegating school nurse to provide appropriate training and supervision, and to monitor student outcomes; learning environment(s); the student's health and educational status; and relevant data from other school personnel and the family.	M	P	U	N/A	

III. SYSTEMS OPERATIONS (continued)

B. Staff Supervision and Evaluation

Standard: School nurses are supervised and evaluated in a manner that ensures the provision of high quality programs and services and their own professional growth.

INDICATORS	RATING				COMMENTS
1. School nursing personnel are provided with sufficient administrative and clinical supervision.	M	P	U	N/A	
2. Administrative supervision and coordination are provided by a master's prepared school nurse supervisor (Connecticut Advisory School Health Council, 1988-1997) or, in lieu of such supervision, by appropriately credentialed individuals who are knowledgeable about school health.	M	P	U	N/A	
3. Clinical supervision and consultation, provided by credentialed professionals with discipline-specific training and expertise, are available to all school nurses. See *Roles and Qualifications of School Health Personnel* (Connecticut Advisory School Health Council, 1997).	M	P	U	N/A	
4. Evaluation of school nurses is systematic, appropriate to meet the individual needs of evaluated staff members, and consistent with school nursing standards of practice. See CSDE document, *Evaluating Pupil Services Specialists* (1993); the *Standards of Clinical Nursing Practice* (ANA, 1998); *School Nursing Practice: Roles and Standards* (Proctor, Lordi and Zaiger, 1993); *Roles and Qualifications for School Health Personnel* (Connecticut Advisory School Health Council, 1997); and Standards of Professional School Nursing Practice (NASN, 1998).	M	P	U	N/A	
5. The personnel evaluation process uses data from multiple sources (e.g., work products, self-report, student records, outcome data, observation) and focuses on quality as well as quantity.	M	P	U	N/A	
6. Evaluation of individual school nurses on discipline-specific clinical competencies is conducted only by a supervisor with credentials and expertise in school nursing. (See CSDE document, *Evaluating Pupil Services Specialists*.)	M	P	U	N/A	
7. Evaluation procedures are documented and communicated to all school nurses and their evaluators.	M	P	U	N/A	

C. Professional Roles and Responsibilities

Standard: School nurses assume roles and responsibilities that optimize their contributions to the education of students.

INDICATORS	RATING				COMMENTS
1. School nurses interpret their roles to school personnel so that their professional knowledge and competencies are understood, respected, and effectively used.	M	P	U	N/A	
2. School nurses only provide services within the limits of their individual license, preparation and expertise. In order to provide services in other areas, they must acquire the requisite competencies through additional education (e.g., coursework, in-service training, supervised practice).	M	P	U	N/A	

III. SYSTEMS OPERATIONS (continued)

C. Professional Roles and Responsibilities (continued)

INDICATORS	RATING				COMMENTS
3. School nurses facilitate student achievement by sharing their perspectives and expertise with others (e.g., through consultation, staff in-service, parent education).	M	P	U	N/A	
4. School nurses help families to understand and participate in the communication process between home and school and to access school system resources.	M	P	U	N/A	
5. School nurses serve both as members and as leaders of interdisciplinary teams.	M	P	U	N/A	
6. School nurses assume responsibility for their own continued learning.	M	P	U	N/A	
7. School nurses implement, and model the implementation of, universal precautions and other applicable health and safety standards for staff and students.	M	P	U	N/A	
8. School nurses maintain RN licensure, CPR certification, and continuing education as required by Connecticut Regulations Section 10-212-5.	M	P	U	N/A	

D. Student Records

Standard: School nurses maintain student information and document student services in a manner that meets the needs and protects the rights of students and families.

INDICATORS	RATING				COMMENTS
1. The school nursing program has clearly written policies and procedures about the types of individual student health records maintained by school nurses, where they should be kept, and how they shall be securely protected.	M	P	U	N/A	
2. The school district's records policy and procedures meet federal and state requirements governing education records and, as applicable, medical records, in order to protect student and family privacy.	M	P	U	N/A	
3. School nurses maintain individual student health records that meet current legal mandates and professional standards of practice.	M	P	U	N/A	
4. Access to student health records is limited to school nurses, school medical advisors, assistive school health services personnel (as directed by school nurses), parents, students and, in an emergency, the school principal. School personnel who require student health information for legitimate education purposes should access such information in consultation with the school nurse.	M	P	U	N/A	
5. Student education records maintained by school nurses have an access sheet that meets the requirements of the Family Educational Rights and Privacy Act (FERPA), that is, a record of parties requesting information and their legitimate interest in requesting it (for example, school medical advisors).	M	P	U	N/A	
6. The nature and extent of documentation in student health records is guided by what is necessary and sufficient to inform and support professional decision-making.	M	P	U	N/A	

III. SYSTEMS OPERATIONS (continued)

D. Student Records (continued)

INDICATORS	RATING				COMMENTS
7. The school district provides parents and eligible students annual notice of their rights to inspect and review the student's education records, seek amendment of records and consent to disclosures of personally identifiable information as mandated by FERPA. School nurses are cognizant of these rights.	M	P	U	N/A	
8. School nurses assist parents in inspecting and reviewing student health records that school personnel collect, maintain or use in the course of providing health services to students. In so doing, school nurses protect test security and observe copyright restrictions.	M	P	U	N/A	
9. Procedures for the retention and destruction of student education records meet federal and state mandates.	M	P	U	N/A	
10. The school district procures prior approval from the Office of the Public Records Administrator before destroying any records, whether or not they appear on the *Records Retention/Disposition Schedules.*	M	P	U	N/A	

E. Confidentiality

Standard: School nursing services are delivered in a manner that respects client confidentiality.

INDICATORS	RATING				COMMENTS
1. The school district and school nursing program have explicit written policies and procedures, applicable to all personnel, addressing rules and exceptions for maintaining the confidentiality of student information.	M	P	U	N/A	
2. Confidentiality policies and procedures are consistent with professional nursing standards of practice and code of ethics, as well as applicable federal and state laws.	M	P	U	N/A	
3. Confidentiality policies and procedures include consequences for school health services personnel who fail to act according to policy and procedure. (See draft: *Guidelines for Policy and Practice: Confidentiality of Student Information.*)	M	P	U	N/A	
4. All school health services personnel receive annual training regarding confidentiality, and school nurses contribute to staff education programs and general school awareness.	M	P	U	N/A	
5. Practices of school nursing staff are monitored to ensure that they are consistent with, and serve the intended purposes of, school district confidentiality policies and procedures.	M	P	U	N/A	
6. Practices for obtaining informed consent to share student and family information with outside parties are consistent with legal and professional standards.	M	P	U	N/A	
7. Student and family information is shared among school personnel only as needed for the benefit of the student; informed written consent of the student or parent is obtained before sharing specific medical diagnoses and related information (e.g., HIV status of a student.)	M	P	U	N/A	
8. Resources to assist with confidentiality issues (e.g., supervisors, outside experts, written guidelines) are available to, and appropriately accessed by, school nurses and assistive personnel.	M	P	U	N/A	

III. SYSTEMS OPERATIONS (continued)

F. PROGRAM ACCOUNTABILITY

Standard: Accountability procedures ensure the maintenance of high-quality programs and services.

INDICATORS	RATING				COMMENTS
1. The school nursing program has written procedures for evaluating the effectiveness of its programs and services.	M	P	U	N/A	
2. School nurses collect and maintain relevant data to evaluate program and service outcomes.	M	P	U	N/A	
3. The results of program evaluations are documented and disseminated to appropriate parties.	M	P	U	N/A	
4. Nursing programs and services are modified in response to program evaluations.	M	P	U	N/A	

G. PROGRAM SUPPORT

Standard: The school district provides the necessary supports to enable the school nursing program to realize its vision and mission.

INDICATORS	RATING				COMMENTS
1. Facilities provided for school nurses meet legal requirements (e.g., fire and health codes, Americans with Disabilities Act, Occupational Safety and Health Administration (OSHA) regulations), and ensure adequate office space, privacy, and access to adequate telecommunication equipment for routine and emergency use.	M	P	U	N/A	
2. Facilities accommodate a diverse range of professional activities, including physical assessment, medical treatments, health counseling, screenings, medication administration, emergency interventions and consultation with pupils, parents, and school personnel.	M	P	U	N/A	
3. Clerical support, equipment, materials, and supplies are provided, as needed, to efficiently accomplish program objectives.	M	P	U	N/A	
4. A range of relevant and timely professional development activities is supported in a planned manner consistent with district priorities. The staff development plan includes opportunities for school nurses, as appropriate, to update both *clinical* and other educational knowledge and skills.	M	P	U	N/A	
5. When job responsibilities are changed, school nursing personnel are provided with opportunities for relevant professional development.	M	P	U	N/A	
6. School nurses have sufficient release time for professional development activities in order to support program and department goals and objectives.	M	P	U	N/A	
7. The school nursing program's annual budget is sufficient to support program and school district priorities.	M	P	U	N/A	
8. The annual budget process provides opportunities for cross-disciplinary planning to promote cost effective administration and delivery of services.	M	P	U	N/A	

Appendix G

Delegation of School Health Services to Unlicensed Assistive Personnel: A Position Paper of the National Association of State School Nurse Consultants

Use with permission: National Association of State School Nurse Consultants, Kent, Ohio.

The National Association of State School Nurse Consultants' position on delegation of health services in schools includes the following beliefs:

1. *In order to benefit from educational programs and to maximize energy for learning, students with chronic health conditions must maintain their health at an optimal level in school. This requires access to safe environments and to health care services provided by professional registered nurses (RNs) and, when appropriate, by qualified unlicensed assistive personnel (UAPs) to whom RNs safely delegate aspects of student care.*

2. *Safe delegation of nursing activities in schools requires that:*
   - *the primary goal is to maximize the independence, learning, and health of students;*
   - *individualized student health care plans are developed by the RN in collaboration with the student, family, health care providers, and school team;*
   - *school nurses receive standardized education related to delegation to and supervision of unlicensed assistive personnel (UAPs);*
   - *unlicensed assistive personnel (UAPs) successfully complete standardized training and child-specific training prior to participating in delegated care; and*
   - *the RN has sufficient decision-making authority, administrative support, supervisory responsibility and necessary resources to ensure safe care for students.*

3. *The RN uses professional judgment to decide which [student] care activities may be delegated, to whom and under what circumstances. "This professional judgment is formed by the state nursing practice act and national standards of nursing. Institutional policies cannot contradict state law" (American Nurses' Association, 1994, p. 11).*

DEFINITIONS

Delegation is "the transfer of responsibility for the performance of an activity from one individual to another, with the former retaining accountability for the outcome" (American Nurses' Association (ANA), 1994, p. 11).

While some state rules, regulations or guidelines may use different terms for delegation of nursing care activities, the critical concept is that when the RN determines that someone who is not licensed to practice nursing can safely provide a selected nursing activity or task for an individual student and delegates that activity to the individual, the RN remains responsible and accountable for the care provided.

Unlicensed assistive personnel (UAPs) "are individuals who are trained to function in an assistive role to the registered professional nurse in the provision of [student] care activities as delegated by and under the supervision of the registered professional nurse" (ANA, 1994, p.10).

RATIONALE

Across the nation today, students with special health care needs are attending school and placing new demands on school districts. Local school boards must provide sufficient staff and resources to ensure a level of school health services previously not required. The reasons include:

1. Changes in the health care system resulting in the medical treatment of children, even those with complex medical problems, in out-patient community settings rather than in-patient, acute care settings;

2. Advances in medical technology resulting in far greater mobility of those who are technology dependent, allowing them to live at home and attend school;

3. Federal mandates ensuring students with health-related disabilities access to appropriate educational programs and related services in the least restrictive environment; and

4. Parents' expectations regarding their children's rights to care in school.

These trends raise issues regarding educational placement and maintenance of student health and student safety, as well as school and professional accountability. In making decisions about the educational placement of students with health care needs and the provision of nursing services, the primary concern must be the health and safety of the students. A secondary concern is the liability of all involved parties (e.g., the school board, school administrators, school staff and the school RN). School administrators are legally responsible for the safety of all students, including the provision of required health services by qualified staff. Using non-qualified staff risks harm to students. In addition, non-licensed school staff are liable for their actions if they practice nursing or medicine without a license.

NURSES' RESPONSIBILITY FOR QUALITY CARE

By professional and legal mandate, school RNs are ultimately responsible to the student for the quality of nursing care rendered. If a nurse errs in making decisions regarding care or who can safely perform it, the student suffers. In addition, the RN can be personally and professionally liable for errors in nursing judgment. If the RN's actions violate the requirements of the nursing practice act, the state board of nursing can take disciplinary action against the RN, including revocation of his/her license to practice nursing.

While school district administrators have certain responsibilities regarding the educational placement of students, they cannot legally be responsible for deciding the level of care required by an individual student with special health care needs. The RN, based on the state's nurse practice act and related state rules and regulations, determines whether care should be provided by a licensed nurse or delegated to trained and supervised unlicensed assistive personnel.

The registered professional school nurse is responsible to determine whether delegation of nursing care is appropriate in each individual situation even if a physician or other health professional states or "orders" that such care should be provided by a UAP (unless a physician or other professional takes full responsibility for the training and supervision of the UAP). Furthermore, it must be both legally and professionally appropriate for that professional to engage in delegating the specific health care activity to unlicensed individuals.

While parents sometimes believe that they should determine the level of care required for their child, it is critical for parents to distinguish between themselves as care takers at home and employed school personnel as care providers at school. Among other variables, the school setting is an environment entirely different from the home: school personnel have different responsibilities in their positions and different obligations under the law, school personnel change, and the parent does not have the authority in the school to make administrative decisions or to supervise school staff. In addition, while nursing practice acts make exceptions for parents or family members who provide nursing care to a family member in their homes, this exception to the licensure provisions does not empower families to extend that right to other individuals in other settings. It is essential that the family, school RN, school team and health care providers work in collaboration to plan and provide the student with high-quality care in an environment that is not only least restrictive, but also safe for all students and staff.

QUESTIONS ABOUT DELEGATING CARE

There are two critical questions involved in delegating and supervising a nursing care activity:
1. *Is the activity a nursing task under the state's definition of nursing?* Nursing activities are defined by state statute and interpreted by the state board of nursing. A state's attorney general's opinion, court decision or other mandate may modify the state's definition of nursing or interpretation of its scope or practice. Based on these definitions and interpretations, the nurse decides whether or not the activity or procedure is one that can only be performed by a registered nurse.
2. *Can the activity be performed by unlicensed assistive personnel under the supervision of a registered nurse?*

The delegation of nursing activities to UAPs may be appropriate if:
- it is not otherwise prohibited by state statute or regulations, legal interpretations, or agency policies;
- the activity does not require the exercising of nursing judgment; and
- it is delegated and supervised by a registered nurse.

DETERMINATIONS REQUIRED IN EACH CASE

The delegating and supervising registered nurse makes the following determinations, on a case-by-case basis, for each student with health care needs and each required nursing care activity:
1. The RN validates the necessary physician orders (including emergency orders), parent/guardian authorization, and any other legal documentation necessary for implementing the nursing care.
2. The RN conducts an initial nursing assessment.
3. Consistent with the state's nursing practice act and the RN's assessment of the student, the RN determines what level of care is required: registered professional nursing, licensed practical or vocational nursing, other professional services, or care by unlicensed assistive personnel (UAP).
4. Consistent with the state board of nursing regulations, the RN determines the amount of training required for the UAP. If the individual to whom the nurse will delegate care has not completed standardized training, the RN must ensure that the UAP obtains such training in addition to receiving child-specific training.
5. Prior to delegation, the nurse evaluates the competence of the individual to safely perform the task.
6. The RN provides a written care plan to be followed by the unlicensed staff member.
7. The RN indicates, within the written care plan, when RN notification, reassessment, and intervention are warranted, due to change in the student's condition, the performance of the procedure, or other circumstance.
8. The RN determines the amount and type of RN supervision necessary.
9. The RN determines the frequency and type of student health reassessment necessary for ongoing safety and efficacy.
10. The RN trains the UAP to document the delegated care according to the standards and requirements of the state's board of nursing and agency procedures.
11. The RN documents activities appropriate to each of the nursing actions listed above.

IF CARE CANNOT BE SAFELY PROVIDED IN SCHOOL

After consultation with the family, student's physicians, other health care providers, other members of the school team, and appropriate consultants, the RN may determine that the level of care required by the student cannot be safely provided under current circumstances in the school. In that event, the school nurse should refer the student back to the initial assessment team and assist the team to reassess the student's total needs and explore alternative options for a safe and appropriate program. If such a program is not designed and the student continues in an unsafe situation, the RN should:

1. Write a memorandum to his/her immediate supervisor explaining the situation in specific detail, including:
   a. Recommendations for safe provisions of care in the school; or,
   b. The reason the care or procedure should not be performed in school and a rationale to support this.
2. Maintain a copy of the memo for the RN's personal file.
3. Allow the supervisor a reasonable period of time to initiate action to safeguard the student.
4. If such action does not occur, forward a copy of the memo to the following, as indicated: the state board of nursing, the district superintendent, the state school nurse consultant, and the division of special education, department of education.
5. Regularly notify his/her supervisor and others, as appropriate, that the unsafe situation continues to exist until such time as the issue is resolved.

Revised July, 1995

Note: A revision of this position statement (2000) is available online: http://lserver.aea14.k12.ia.us/swp/tadkins/nassnc/NASSNC.html

Appendix H
Sample Nursing Protocols

PART 1
Reactive Airway Disease/Asthma

Used with permission: Hootman, Janis. (1996). *Quality Nursing Interventions in the School Setting: Procedures, Models, and Guidelines*, pp. 111-REA-1 through 111-REA-4. Scarborough, ME: National Association of School Nurses.

DEFINITION: A Chronic Respiratory Disorder Involving Bronchi and Bronchioles; Characterized by Acute Episodes of Paroxysmal Dyspnea, Expiratory Wheezing, Coughing, and Thick Mucoid Bronchial Secretions That May be Precipitated by Inhalation of Allergens/Pollutants, Infection, Exercise, or Emotional Stress.

GATHER SUBJECTIVE DATA (INCLUDING STUDENT'S PERSPECTIVE) REGARDING:

For Acute Attack:

DO NOT DELAY implementing immediate direct care with students in marked respiratory distress by in-depth history taking.

- Time of attack onset
- Dyspnea
- Cough
- Nausea/vomiting/anorexia
- Intervention tried and effect of such
- Medication taken in past 24 hours and usual/ prescribed medication regimen
- Pain
- Shortness of breath
- Complaints of chest tightness

For Establishing/Maintaining Database:

(Required for all students assessed to be at high risk for reaction at school.)
- Diagnosis confirmed by health care provider
- Age of initial onset of asthma, date of last medication, asthmatic reaction
- Student's understanding of what disease is and impact to him
- Frequency of asthmatic attacks
- Usual precipitators of asthmatic attack
- Usual treatment plan
- Usual preventive measures
- Usual activity tolerance
- Student's feelings about diagnosis and impact on him

INSPECT, PALPATE, AUSCULTATE FOR DEFINING CHARACTERISTICS:

For Acute Symptoms:

- Abnormal breath sounds:
  - Decreased
  - Wheezing
  - Rales (crackles)
  - Rhonchi
- Paroxysmal coughing
- Asymmetric expansion of chest
- Substernal intercostal retraction
- Decreased peak flow rate (peak flow always to be plotted on peak flow graph)
- Tachypnea (respirations greater than 25-30 at rest)
- Cyanotic skin/nailbeds; flushed skin
- Diaphoresis
- Nasal flaring
- Elevated heart rate and pulse
- Fatigue
- Decreased activity tolerance
- Restlessness/posturing

For Establishing Maintaining Database:

(Required for all students assessed to be at high risk for reaction at school.)
- Breath sounds
- Peak flow rate (peak flow always to be
- plotted on peak flow graph)
- Pulse and respiratory rates
- Skin color
- Usual activity level and tolerance

FORMULATE NURSING DIAGNOSIS:

Activity Intolerance, related to:

1. Exercise/stress-induced asthma
2. Other

Anxiety, related to:

1. Dyspnea/shortness of breath

2. Perceived powerlessness
3. Other

Airway Clearance, Ineffective, related to:

1. Airway constriction of smooth muscle or bronchospasm
2. Thick bronchial secretions
3. Wheezing
4. Other

Coping, Ineffective Individual, related to:

1. Denial of illness
2. Crisis—specify type
3. Problem-solving skills deficit
4. Other

Health Maintenance Management, Impaired, related to:

1. Denial of illness
2. Non-compliance with therapeutic recommendation
3. Refusal to practice precautionary/adaptive measures
4. Other

Knowledge Deficit concerning:

1. Medication administration technique/adverse reaction
2. Physiological reaction
3. Preventive measures
4. Other

. . . and related to:

1. Inability to use materials or information resources
2. Lack of interest/motivation to learn
3. Unfamiliarity with information/resources
4. Other

Non-compliance with Therapeutic Recommendation, related to:

1. Cost
2. Denial of illness
3. Dependency on others
4. Knowledge deficit (specify type)
5. Perceived non-susceptibility/invulnerability
6. Perceived therapeutic ineffectiveness

NURSING INTERVENTION PROTOCOL FOR ASTHMA/REACTIVE AIRWAY DISEASE:

FOR ACUTE ATTACK:

1. Assist student in administration of prescribed medication. (Parent's authorization and physician's directions to be on file.)
2. Observe and record student's response to medication.
3. Monitor student's pulse, respiration, and emotional response every 15 minutes until reaction subsides.
4. Call emergency medical system (EMS/9-1-1) for deteriorating respiratory status/level of consciousness.
5. Refer student with cyanosis, 50% reduced peak flow reading, absent/minimal breath sounds, pulse greater than 120, respirations greater than 30, retractions, nasal flaring, severe anxiety/restlessness for immediate medical assessment.
   a. Students presenting with ineffectively controlled or frequent asthma reactions at school will be referred for medical consultation.
6. Assist student to assume comfortable position. If warm, clear fluids (especially tea) accessible, may encourage student to sip such unless student nauseated.
7. Assist student using calm, empathetic approach.
8. Assist student with relaxation techniques as possible:
   a. Deep rhythmical breathing.
   b. Concentrated muscle relaxation.
   c. Imagery.
9. Inform parent promptly whenever student:
   a. Is having respiratory symptoms deviant from usual respiratory pattern.
   b. Has needed and used prn medication at school.
   c. Is unable/unwilling to independently facilitate medical assessment.
   d. Share available community resources if not linked with health care provider.

FOR HEALTH MANAGEMENT OF ASTHMATIC STUDENT:

1. For students assessed to be at potential high risk for altered breathing pattern, review directions at least yearly with parent and physician as necessary on procedures to follow for asthmatic reaction at school.
2. Develop written procedures for school personnel to follow for assisting with asthmatic reaction at school and for planning alternative educational activities.
   - Review procedures with pertinent school personnel. Leave procedures in immediately accessible place.
   - Delegate nursing tasks as necessary following Board of Nursing regulations.
3. Encourage student's verbalization of feelings about diagnosis and impact on his lifestyle using empathetic communications. Document student's concerns.
   - Explore options to facilitate student coping.
   - Share with student available literary and community group support resources.
4. When teaching health management of asthma:
   - Provide information at student's level of understanding.
   - Involve parent, as appropriate, to elicit support.
   - Review may include:
     (1) Etiology:
        - Infection
        - Exercise
        - Allergies to dust, pollens, foods
        - Smoke and pollution
        - Weather changes
        - Stress, anxiety
     (2) Prophylaxis:
        - Predisposition can't be eradicated.
     (3) Benefit of maintenance of good health. Approach includes:
        - Regular, sufficient rest

- Nutritious diet
- Regular exercise
- Avoidance of illness exposure and known irritants (i.e. molds, smoke, animal dander)

(4) Control measures:
- Avoidance of known allergens and respiratory infections
- Dust control at home--no rugs, damp dusting, encased mattress, foam or encased pillow
- Adequate humidification for dry heat and air conditioning in pollen season
- Cleanliness of humidifier to control exposure to molds
- Awareness of initial signs/symptoms and triggers of asthma attack

(5) Appropriate use of medication and inhaler equipment:
- Tilt head back to allow for straighter inhalation. (Encourage, as pertinent, student to discuss use of spacer with physician.)
- Hold inhaler away from mouth. (Spacer can be made by rolling up notebook-size paper with diameter size of quarter; spacer reduces local side effects of thrush, dysphonia, hoarseness, and coughing during inhalation.)
- Blow out as much air as possible; take slow, deep breath while pushing inhaler; hold breath to count of 10; then exhale through pursed lips.
- Wait 5 minutes before using inhaler for prescribed second puff of medication (except in emergency).

(6) Carry inhaler as prescribed to assure immediate access to medication. (Student shall have prescription/physician request to carry medication on person.)

(7) Store inhaler safely to assure potency of medication and prevention of poisoning "curious" classmate.

(8) Sip warm fluids such as tea with teaspoon of lemon juice.

(9) Caution against excessive use of pharmacologic agents.

(10) Diaphragmatic breathing.

(11) Relaxation techniques as breathing in through nose deeply with mouth closed and out slowly through pursed lips.

(12) Breathing exercises as blowing musical instruments, candles, ping pong balls.

(13) Avoid, as necessary and possible, breathing frigid air.

(14) Routine medical evaluation.

(15) Awareness of signs indicating need for prompt medical consultation:
- Decreasing level of consciousness
- Temperature of 101°F or greater
- Intensifying dyspnea
- Ineffective relief of dyspnea from prescribed medication
- Side effects of prescribed medications: vomiting, jitteriness, insomnia

POSSIBLE INTERVENTION CODES

3140	Airway Management
5820	Anxiety Reduction
5604	Teaching: Group
5606	Teaching: Individual
5616	Teaching: Prescribed Medication

PART 2
Diabetes Mellitus Type I

Used with permission: Ridgefield Public Schools, Ridgefield, Connecticut. (1999). Developed by Committee.

CHARACTERISTICS OF CONDITION

Diabetes mellitus is a chronic disease involving primarily carbohydrate metabolism characterized by a deficiency of insulin (relative or absolute), that causes metabolic adjustments or physiologic changes in almost all areas of the body. Type I diabetes mellitus most commonly affects children and young adults and always requires an intake of insulin.

STUDENT HEALTH GOALS

- The student will maximize his/her potential for learning by achieving and maintaining his/her optimal level of wellness.
- The student will become as independent as possible in diabetes self-management.

STUDENT INTERIM HEALTH OBJECTIVES*

Student will be able to:
- List his/her signs of hypoglycemia or hyperglycemia.
- Discuss appropriate personal management of diabetes in school.
- Identify personal blood glucose level goals during day and ways to achieve and maintain such levels.
- Demonstrate correct methods to monitor blood glucose levels with glucometer and correct methods to maintain and secure glucometer.
- Participate in chosen school activities and maintain expected diabetes management.
- Verbalize questions, concerns and feelings regarding diabetes, health issues concerning diabetes including management at school.

*These goals represent a range of possible objectives. Objectives should be tailored to student's specific functional needs.

DEVELOPMENT OF IHCP AND/OR 504 PLAN

The school nurse will collaborate with the student, family, educational team and student's personal health care team to develop an individualized health care plan (IHCP). The IHCP will address the student's individual developmental and health needs in school as well as provide the basis for, or substitute as, a Section 504 accommodation plan. The school nurse will plan and arrange a meeting with the student (as appropriate), family, educational team and other individuals as deemed appropriate to determine 504 eligibility and to complete development of the student's IHCP.

CONSIDERATIONS IN THE DEVELOPMENT OF THE IHCP

Student Specific Considerations:
- Period of time since diagnosis
- Student's current health status
- Student's general developmental abilities (e.g. cognitive skills, fine and gross motor skills, social and emotional considerations)
- Student's level of knowledge related to diabetes self-care skills

- Student's actual performance of self-management skills at home and in school
- Student's personal equipment used to monitor blood glucose levels
- Student's specific medical orders pertinent to management of his/her diabetes at home and at school (e.g. blood glucose monitoring, medication administration, urine testing, dietary and activity modifications).
- Student and family's preference for management of student's diabetes at school.
- Members of the student's personal health care team that work with the student and family

School Specific Considerations:
- Educational team knowledge of student (e.g. how long has student attended the school, familiarity of student to staff).
- School nurse assessment of student's health status and needs at school which will determine level of nursing services required.
- Teacher's assessment of student's functional abilities in the classroom.
- School nurse's assessment of teacher's knowledge and ability to accept delegation of aspects related to the student's management of diabetes.
- Physical design of the student's classroom as well as pertinent characteristics of student's classroom and school building.
- School administration issues.

Other IHCP considerations:
- Classroom accommodations
- Transportation
- Access to methods to communicate with school nurse on school premises
- Field trips
- Family and health care provider communication
- Other

SCHOOL NURSE RESPONSIBILITIES: DEVELOPMENT OF IHCP

Upon notification of the student's medical condition and annually, prior to or during the beginning of each school year, the school nurse will:
- Obtain pertinent student health and school information. The nurse may use the Student With Diabetes Information Sheet (Form H-7) as a guide. The school nurse should incorporate the considerations outlined above in the development of the student IHCP.
- Obtain current relevant medical orders from the authorized prescriber (e.g. blood glucose monitoring, urine testing, and medication administration, dietary and activity interventions, as appropriate). Refer to Form H-2 and Form D-2.
- Review the assessment data to finalize IHCP as needed. The health care plan should include nursing (functional) diagnosis,

student health goals and objectives, health interventions, and individuals responsible for providing, monitoring and evaluating care. The IHCP must also include an Emergency Care Plan for potential crisis episodes. The Emergency Care Plan For The Student With Diabetes (Form H-8) can be used as a guide. The nurse may consult **The School Nurse Source Book of Individualized Healthcare Plans** for assistance in development of the IHCP.

SCHOOL NURSE RESPONSIBILITY IN IMPLEMENTING IHCP

(tasks outlined below are not all inclusive)

- Education of school personnel (as appropriate) regarding functional issues related to diabetes, the student's specific care plan, signs and symptoms of hypoglycemia and hyperglycemia and student's specific emergency care plan.
- Obtain necessary medical supplies from the parent/guardian.
- Assist student, as necessary or appropriate, with blood glucose monitoring, decisions regarding any dietary or activity modifications, or medication administration per medical orders from the authorized prescriber. Form H-9 may be sued for the student or school nurse to record blood glucose monitoring results at school.
- Assist student in attainment of self-care skills and self-care knowledge, as developmentally appropriate.
- Provide counseling to student and family with decisions regarding informing student's peers of the student's medical condition, as developmentally appropriate for student and his/her peers.
- Maintain communication with family regarding student's health status at school and notify family and/or health care provider, as appropriate, of any changes in the student's health status. Determine any changes in the student's health status from the parents.
- Document any change in the baseline health status of the student. Document nursing interventions and student's responses to the nursing interventions.

- The IHCP/504 team will evaluate the effect of the plan on the student's school performance. Adjustments in the IHCP shall be made accordingly through collaboration with the student, family, educational and health care team.

BLOOD GLUCOSE MONITORING

The nurse will refer to the following information:

Specialized Health Care Procedure Manual for School Nurses (State of Connecticut Dept. of Education, 1997)

- Introduction (pp. 1 to 12)
- Specialized Health Care Activity #51 (pp.51-1 to 51-3)
- Appendix B (pp. B 1-5) for management of handling body fluids in school
- Appendix C: In Re: Declaratory Ruling – Delegation By Licensed Nurses to Unlicensed Assistive Personnel – April 5, 1995.

Upon receipt of medical orders for blood glucose monitoring (can be prescribed using From H-2) in school and after obtaining the necessary equipment from the student's parents, blood glucose monitoring will take place according to the specifications of the student's IHCP.

The table above outlines potential symptoms of DKA and hypoglycemia by body systems. The nurse must include in the student's Emergency Care Plan the student's particular symptoms and specific interventions for management of DKA or hypoglycemia. Following are general guidelines for management of DKA and hypoglycemia.

These guidelines DO NOT substitute for the student's individual Emergency Care Plan.

DKA

- Will tend to develop slowly.
- Contact parent to advise.
- Assess student for signs/symptoms of DKA.

GUIDELINES FOR MANAGEMENT OF HYPERGLYCEMIA (DIABETIC KETOACIDOSIS OR DKA) AND HYPOGLYCEMIA
Comparison of Findings for DKA vs. Hypoglycemia*

SYSTEM	DKA	HYPOGLYCEMIA
Blood	50-1500 *could actually be in normal range	50 or under
Eyes	Blurred vision	Dazed, dilated pupils, blurred vision
Gastrointestinal	Thirst, nausea, cramps	Hunger, numb: mouth, tongue
Musculoskeletal	Weak, fatigue	Normal or may be weak
Neurological	Confused, headache, irritable/lethargy	Tremors, headache, confusion, anxiety & delirium
Respiratory	Deep, rapid breathing, fruity breath	Normal to increase, shallow in coma
Skin	Face flushed, skin dry, warm	Pale, diaphoretic, cold, clammy
Urinary	Polyuria, positive glucose, ketones	Negative glucose, ketones by second voiding

*Adapted from the School Nurse Emergency Medical Services for Children Manual: March, 1997, University of Connecticut Department of Pediatrics and J. Ahern, APRN,MSN,CDE Yale University, 1998.

- Discuss with student recent food intake of change in personal health status (e.g recent illness, etc.).
- May monitor student in health room for symptoms of increasing DKA (depending on severity of presenting symptoms and according to medical orders and student's IHCP).
- Types of interventions for students experiencing DKA may include:
- Encouraging student to increase consumption of non-glucose types of fluids such as water and/or diet soft drinks.
- Assisting student with making choices regarding modifications of food intake during rest of school day or ability to increase exercise.

  If have orders for insulin, administer or have student self-administer according to medical orders.

HYPOGLYCEMIA (INSULIN REACTION)

- Develops suddenly.

If student conscious and responsive:

- Depending on severity of symptoms, monitor blood glucose.
- Follow student's Emergency Plan. If students own snacks are not available,

  immediately give any **one** of the following:
  - 4 oz of fruit juice
  - 4 oz of soft drink (non-diet)
  - 1 Tablespoon of honey
  - 1/2 package of sugar mints, chewed and quickly swallowed

- If student is not scheduled to have a meal within   hour of episode, follow with   meat sandwich or peanut butter crackers or cheese crackers and 8 oz glass of milk.
- Contact parents to advise.

Student unconscious, unresponsive and/or disoriented:

- Administer emergency treatment according to student's individual **Emergency Care Plan and call EMS (911).**

  Such emergency treatment may involve placing cake icing or Instaglucose between cheek and gum and massage icing into gum.

  If student becomes unconscious and/or having seizures, glucagon may be administered 1.0 mg. subcutaneously. Place in a side-lying resting position in anticipation of vomiting after glucagon administration. **GLUCAGON IS ONLY TO BE ADMINISTERED ACCORDING TO STUDENT'S SPECIFIC MEDICAL ORDERS AND WITH PRIOR PARENTAL PERMISSION.**

- Contact parents.
- Consult with parents and student's personal medical team regarding any change in student's health plan at school for next few days.

STUDENT WITH DIABETES INFORMATION SHEET

Date: _____

Student Name _____ Grade_____ D.O.B._____

Parent Daytime phone#- Mother _____ Father _____

Primary health care provider _____ Phone #_____

Diabetes Specialist _____ Phone# _____

INSULIN: A.M. _____ Lunch _____
                    Time-Type-Amount   Time-Type-Amount

Dinner _____ Bedtime _____
            Time-Type-Amount   Time-Type-Amount

Will require insulin at school? _____ (Obtain health care prescriber orders)

Does student need assistance with insulin administration?_____

DIET:

        A.M. Snack   _____

        Lunch   _____

        P.M. Snack   _____

    Modifications for parties?   _____

MONITORING:

    Will require routine glucose monitoring at school?   _____ Yes _____ No
        (Obtain health care prescriber orders)

    Will require assistance with monitoring?   _____ Yes _____ No

    Should routinely check blood glucose at _____ (time) each day and record results.

    Type of glucometer _____

    Does student check urine for glucose?   _____ Yes _____ No
        (Obtain health care prescriber orders)

    Will student needs assisting with urine testing?   _____ Yes _____ No

    Routine time for urine testing is _____

Physical Education:

    Scheduled at_____

        Snack required before physical education?   _____ Yes _____ No

    Snack given before physical education if: _____

Management of:

HYPOGLYCEMIA-Insulin Reaction

Student's symptoms are _____

Treatment _____

_____

_____

HYPERGLYCEMIA(DKA)-High Blood Glucose

Student's symptoms are _____

Treatment _____

_____

_____

Ridgefield Public Schools   Diabetes
School Health Procedures Guide   Insulin Dependent—Type I

Date:_____

EMERGENCY CARE PLAN FOR THE STUDENT WITH DIABETES

Student Name _____ Birthdate _____
Parent/Guardian _____
Emergency phone #(home) _____
Emergency phone#(work) _____
Primary health care provider _____
                    Address _____
                    Phone# _____
Hospital _____   Student ID
Diabetes Specialists _____   Photo
Address/Phone# _____

Specifics of Management

1. Insulin Dosage: _____
   Times: _____
2. Glucose monitoring _____
   Location of monitor _____
   Type of monitor _____
   Times to monitor _____
3. Diet _____
   Snack time(s) _____
4. ID bracelet: Yes _____   No_____
5. Time and day of physical education _____
   _____
   School Lunch/Recess _____

Protocol for Hypoglycemic Episode

1. General symptoms: hunger, dizziness, sweaty palms or forehead, and change in behavior.
2. Signs/symptoms particular to this student _____
   _____
3. Action to take: _____
   _____
   _____
   *attach additional information if needed.
4. Contact Parent/guardian if:_____
5. Cake gel or other substance to be given:_____
6. Glucagon ordered: Yes_____   No_____
   *yes (current medical authorization and prior written parent permission forms in health file)

DO NOT LET STUDENT GO TO HEALTH OFFICE ALONE.
CALL 911 IF STUDENT UNCONSCIOUS OR CONVULSING and GIVE NOTHING BY MOUTH.

7. Individual considerations for this particular student _____
   _____
8. Contact parents/guardians if student vomits or has a fever and refer to IHCP.
9. Signatures/photocopies to (where applicable):
        Parent/guardian _____   Principal _____
        Student _____   Teacher _____
        School Nurse _____   Lunch Aide _____
        Physician _____   Bus Driver _____
        Diabetes Educator _____   P.E. Teacher _____
        Other Education specialists : Guidance Dept. _____Music_____
        Art_____Library_____Other_____

Attachment II   Adapted from *J. School Health Nursing*, April 1997

Used with permission. Developed by Committee, Ridgefield Public Schools, Ridgefield, CT. (1999).

Appendix I
Mitts Declaratory Ruling

BEFORE THE OREGON STATE BOARD OF NURSING
Declaratory Ruling

In the Matter of the Petitions For Declaratory Ruling by Hillsboro Union High School District No. 3, Assistant Superintendent of Personnel Gerry C. Elstun for Hillsboro Union High School District No. 3, Linda Potts, and Mary M. Elskamp, R.N., and By Carol Mitts

This matter comes before the Board on a Petition for Declaratory Ruling filed on August 3, 1988 by Hillsboro Union High School District No. 3, Assistant Superintendent of Personnel Gerry C. Elstun, for Hillsboro Union High School District No. 3, Linda Potts, Mary M. Elskamp, R.N. and on a Petition for Declaratory Ruling filed on August 5, 1988 by Carol Mitts.

The petitions for declaratory ruling were filed as a result of an action filed in Washington County Circuit Court in Case No. 87-11420 by Carol Mitts, plaintiff, against Hillsboro Union High School District No. 3; the Assistant Superintendent, Gerry C. Elstun; Laura Potts' physician, Theodore Lehman; Mary M. Elskamp, a registered nurse providing services to the district; and Linda Potts, mother of Laura Potts. In the action, plaintiff sought money damages, a declaratory judgment and injunctive relief on the theory that plaintiff, while employed as a "health assistant" by the school district, was being compelled to practice medicine and/or nursing unlawfully without a license because she was required by the district to provide junior high school Laura Potts with clean intermittent catheterization.

Thereafter, an Amended Complaint was filed naming the State Board of Nursing and the State Board of Medical Examiners as indispensable parties. Subsequently, the parties stipulated to and the court ordered, a stay in the proceedings pending a declaratory ruling from this Board and any appeal taken therefrom.

The Board heard oral argument from petitioners at the November 17, 1988 Board meeting. The petitioners were represented at that meeting as follows: Carrell Bradley for the school district, the Assistant Superintendent and Linda Potts; Vernellia Randall for petitioner Mary M. Elskamp, R.N.; and Paul Meadowbrook for petitioner Carol Mitts.

Following the Board meeting, the petitioners were given until the close of business on Thursday, December 1, 1988 to file written briefs. In addition, all parties were given until the close of business on Friday, December 16, 1988 to file responses to briefs.

STATEMENT OF FACTS

Laura Potts is an 18-year old student at Brown Junior High School, a part of the Hillsboro Union High School District. She is a paraplegic and is wheelchair bound. She is afflicted with spina bifida, a condition which results from failure of formation of the bony arch surrounding the spinal cord. As a result of this condition, Laura has a neurogenic bladder due to lack of sensation at the spinal cord location of the spina bifida. An effect of the neurogenic bladder is that Laura requires clean intermittent catheterization (CIC) to remove urine from the bladder since she is not able to sense when she has a full bladder and cannot control the excretion of urine from her bladder. Clean intermittent catheterization is done several times each day in order to keep her dry, comfortable and prevent bladder infections or other health complications from the buildup of urine in the bladder or incomplete emptying of the bladder.

In August 1987, Carol Mitts, who is employed as a health assistant by the district, was directed by the school's principal, Kenneth Wollman, to perform CIC on Laura. Ms. Mitts was taught the technique of CIC by Laura Potts' mother, Linda Potts. The training was facilitated by use of an anatomically correct mannequin. Other district employees attended the training session, including Mary M. Elskamp, a registered nurse, who is an employee of the Education Service District and under contract to the school district. However, the teaching of CIC was done primarily by Linda Potts. The session lasted approximately two (2) hours. Notes were made during the session by Irene McConaghy, a learning specialist, and distributed to all who attended the session. During the training session, nurse Elskamp occasionally answered questions regarding CIC. Following the initial training session in August 1987, Linda Potts provided additional "hands on" training for Ms. Mitts.

In November 1987, the school district asked nurse Elskamp to periodically observe Mitts' technique in performing CIC, answer questions and regularly supervise her. Regular observation and contact between nurse Elskamp and Ms. Mitts has occurred on a monthly basis from that time forward. Carol Mitts maintains that she is not qualified or competent to perform CIC and that CIC is the practice of nursing. Petitioner district and Mary M. Elskamp maintain that CIC is not exclusively the practice of nursing and can lawfully be delegated to unlicensed persons who have had training.

DISCUSSION AND OPINION
The Practice of Nursing

ORS 678.010(6) defines the practice of nursing as follows:

> "Practice of nursing" means diagnosing and treating human responses to actual or potential health problems through such services as identification thereof, health teaching, health counseling and providing care supportive to or restorative of life and well-being and including the performance of such additional services requiring education and training which are recognized by the nursing profession as proper to be performed by nurses licensed under ORS 678.010 to 678.410 and which are recognized by rules of the Board. "Practice of nursing" includes executing medical orders as prescribed by a physician or dentist, but does not include such execution by a member of the immediate family for another member where the person executing the care is not licensed under ORS 678.010 to 678.410. The practice of nursing includes providing supervision of nursing assistants. (Emphasis added)

This definition has two parts. The first part is a broad description of those activities which nurses perform independent of direction from other health professionals i.e., diagnosing, treating, problem identification, teaching, providing care. The second part is the portion of nursing practice based on direction from other health care professionals through the execution of medical orders.

Nursing is both an art and a science and is based on the nursing process which is a systematic problem-solving method used by nurses in providing nursing care. The nursing process is a five step process that includes:

1. Assessing the client's condition or status.
2. Making nursing diagnoses based on assessment.
3. Planning care.
4. Intervening (treating).
5. Evaluating the effectiveness of the care provided.

The nursing process is ongoing and cyclical in the nurse's contact with the client and involves not only the nurse's goals for the client, but also the client's goals. The focus of nursing practice is to provide support in an appropriate form e.g., direct care, teaching and provision of outside resources in order to improve the client's well-being and to maximize client function related to physical, emotional, and social health. The focus of nursing practice is on the entire person, not only on the client's physical health needs.

The public most clearly sees the intervention or treatment step of the nursing process during which the nurse is either giving direct care to the client or providing health teaching to the client. The public therefore, often mistakenly assumes that the performance of specific tasks is the essence of the practice of nursing. Intervention is only one step in the five step process used in the practice of nursing.

It is often difficult for members of the public to observe each step of the nursing process because the steps are interactive and overlapping. When a client enters a health care setting (acute care, long-term care, community based care), the nurse uses observational skills and problem solving to identify the client's functional status through client interview, physical examination, observation, review of previously generated client health records and diagnostic reports, and discussion with family members and other health care providers. The information or data collected during the assessment phase can be translated into a nursing diagnosis or a statement of the client's wellness state, illness state and responses to actual or potential health problems. The nurse may make an actual nursing diagnosis, e.g., a problem is currently present; a potential nursing problem may occur; or a possible nursing diagnosis, e.g., a problem may be present.

For an actual nursing diagnosis (a present problem), the nurse prescribes interventions or treatments to reduce or eliminate the problem, or to promote healthy activities. For a potential nursing diagnosis, the nurse prescribed interventions to prevent or reduce any risk factors. For a possible nursing diagnosis, the nurse collects additional information to confirm an actual problem or rule out suspected problems.2

Once the nursing diagnosis is established, the nurse plans how to meet client needs based on assessment and diagnosis. The purpose of this planning phase is to decide how to monitor identified problems, and prevent, reduce, or eliminate problems. Priorities for the provision of care are established, outcome goals are established with the client and family, and interventions or treatment strategies are established, including a decision regarding who will provide the direct care.

During the intervention or treatment stage, the nurse may personally give direct care to the client, may assist the client in performing self-care, may provide health teaching and counseling, or may direct and supervise others in their provision of direct care. During this stage, the nurse will continue making nursing assessments to determine the status of already identified problems as well as to identify new problems. The nurse will also provide health teaching to assist clients in the management of their illness or to improve health. This stage of the nursing process involves applying nursing technical skills, as well as additional problem solving activities.

During the evaluation stage, the nurse observes the client and family responses to interventions and determines how effectively the outcome goals have been met. As stated earlier, the nursing process is cyclical in nature and it is during this evaluation stage that the nursing process will begin again if client goals have not been adequately met.

There are two levels of licenses for nurses, the practical nurse and the registered nurse. Their level of functioning in the practice of nursing is based on their education and the scope of practice associated with each type of license.

Practical nursing (LPN) is defined by ORS 678.010(7) as follows:

"Practice of practical nursing" means the application of knowledge drawn from basic education in the social and physical sciences in planning and giving nursing care and in assisting persons towards achieving health and well being.

Registered nursing (RN) is defined by ORS 678.010(8) as follows:

"Practice of registered nursing" means the application of knowledge drawn from broad in-depth education in the social and physical sciences in assessing, planning, ordering, giving, delegating, teaching, and supervising care which promotes the person's optimum health and independence.

Based on these two definitions, it is clear the RN's are given more authority to assess, plan, delegate, and supervise care while the practical nurse performs an assistive role. The Board has further defined the scope of practice for LPN's and RN's in Division 45 of the Board's Administrative Rules. OAR 851-45-005 and 010 compare and contrast the LPN's and RN's responsibilities as members of the health care team. When using the nursing process, although both use all five steps of the process, the LPN contributes to, participates in, and assists with each step of the process under CAR 851-45-005(1); whereas, the RN uses each step of the process fully and independently. The language of 851-45-010(1) directs the RN to perform and to be accountable for the entire nursing process.

The other major differences between LPN's and RN's are in the areas of teaching, delegation, supervision, and independent function. RN's are authorized by CAR 851-45-010(h1) (d) (A) (v) and (2) (n) to teach clients and family members and also to teach health care practices to other health care providers. LPN's are authorized by CAR 851-45-005(1) (d) (E) to provide health care teaching only under the direction of a RN, using established protocols.

TEACHING AND DELEGATING TASKS OF NURSING CARE

Both LPN's and RN's may delegate nursing tasks to others and provide supervision for those to whom nursing care is delegated. However, RN's have a broader, more encompassing role in delegating, supervising, and retaining accountability for the nursing care of clients. LPNs may not function independently; that is, they must always function under the supervision of a RN, licensed physician, or dentist. The level of supervision required is dependent on the condition of the client as described in CAR 851-45-005(1) (d) (B) and (C).

The Board has also adopted administrative rules regulating the delegation of nursing tasks to unlicensed persons. CAR 851-45-011 allows the RN to delegate any task to unlicensed persons. However, in making the decision to delegate, the Board requires the RN to carefully make several decisions.

First, the registered nurse must assess the condition of the client in order to determine whether the task may be safely delegated to an unlicensed person. This decision is based on an assessment of the nature, complexity and severity of the client's health problems. Second, the nurse must assess the nature of the task, its complexity and the skill level necessary for it's safe and proper performance. Third, the registered nurse, in selecting an unlicensed person to whom the task is to be delegated, must assess that person's skills and abilities to perform the task properly.

In order to prevent unsafe delegation practices, the Board requires that the delegation of a task be limited in application to a single client. Consequently, an unlicensed person may not perform a task properly delegated for one client on a third party without receiving express delegated authority from the registered nurse to perform that task on the third party. For example, it may be safe to delegate to an unlicensed person the subcutaneous administration of a daily dose of insulin for an otherwise healthy, active diabetic client. On the other hand, it would probably not be safe to delegate to an unlicensed person the subcutaneous administration of multiple doses of various types of insulin dosage adjustments, since the client's condition requires the constant application of the nursing process in its entirety. Thus, while the task of administering subcutaneous injections is the same for both clients, delegation is proper in the first case and not in the second. Additionally, as the example makes clear, it is both improper and unsafe for the unlicensed person to generalize from the first case and to provide subcutaneous injection to the client in the second case.

Once the decision has been made to delegate a task to an unlicensed person, the registered nurse must teach that person how to perform the task or otherwise assure that the person can perform the task properly and safely. Having taught the selected task and having delegated it to an unlicensed person, the registered nurse must document the process in writing. This includes the process for deciding that this task could be safely delegated to this unlicensed person for this client, how the task was taught, the teaching outcome (how well the unlicensed person learned the task), and how the unlicensed person will deal with any consequences that arise from doing the task. The registered nurse must also leave specific written instruction for the unlicensed person to use as a reference in performing the task, and the registered nurse must arrange for periodic, ongoing supervision of the unlicensed person.

The registered nurse must also, both verbally and in writing, instruct the unlicensed person that the task is not transferable to other clients or to other situations. As noted above, should the same task appear to be required on another client, the RN must assess that client and, when appropriate, teach and delegate the task specific for that client.

The Board intends that RN's take seriously the responsibility of delegating nursing care tasks to unlicensed persons and that they implement as many safeguards as possible to assure that the client's health will not be compromised. The Board intends that delegation be done only in situations where the provision of care by licensed persons is either not possible or is impractical. The Board does not intend that RN's delegate for personal convenience or at the direction of others. Delegation of task of nursing care is the sole responsibility of the registered nurse.

NURSING PRACTICE IN THE SCHOOLS

The primary responsibility of the public school system is to provide students with an education. Students in the school system often have needs to be met, in addition to their normal learning needs. The student enters the school system as a whole being, not just as a mind to be educated.

Under federal law, the school now finds itself in the position of having to meet these other needs through the provision of related services that enhance and facilitate the learning process. This responsibility is mandated by Public Law 94-142, which gives every school age child the right to a free, appropriate public education in the least restrictive environment. The school system must make services available to meet student's special learning needs, e.g., speech and language needs, psychological needs, and health needs.

One of the services that must be provided by the schools under federal law is clean intermittent catheterization. *Irving Independent School District v. Tatro.* 468.US 883 (1984). It is state law, however, that controls the answer to the question of who may perform CIC in the school on students. The Board concludes that when a student enters the school system with a health problem, the nurse, rather than the school authorities, must perform an assessment, develop and implement a plan for meeting the student's health needs. The process of health assessment, planning and implementing care constitutes the practice of nursing.

In the case of Laura Potts, this did not happen. When Laura Potts entered the school system, her mother informed school authorities that Laura required clean intermittent catheterization. Thereafter, the principal directed an unlicensed school employee to meet the need of the student by performing CIC.[3] Presumably, he made this decision based on his assessment of Laura Potts' condition and his assessment that the health assistant's skills were sufficient to perform the task.[4] The principal also directed nurse Elskamp to attend a teaching session for Carol Mitts, but this occurred after the session had already been arranged.

In the Board's view, under the law, the school principal had no authority to assess the health status of Laura Potts and no authority to direct the provision of a task of nursing to an unlicensed person. Furthermore, in the Board's view, the principal and other school authorities, in making the assessment, in directing a health assistant to perform CIC, and in deciding how teaching of that task was to be accomplished, were practicing nursing. As a result of Carol Mitts' implementation of this directive, she was also practicing nursing.

Upon being apprised of Laura Potts' condition, the principal should have referred Laura Potts to the school nurse for an assessment. Following the results of this assessment, if the nurse had decided that delegation or CIC was safe for an unlicensed person to perform, the school nurse should have arranged for teaching of that task to Carol Mitts. Certainly Mrs. Potts should be actively involved in the teaching because Mrs. Potts has first hand knowledge of any idiosyncrasy regarding CIC for Laura. However, it is the nurse, not the parent nor the school principal, who may lawfully assess health conditions and delegate and teach nursing care tasks.

The circumstances in this case, that is, the performance of CIC on Laura Potts by Carol Mitts, with regular supervision by the nurse, apparently has not resulted in a bad outcome. By all accounts, no harm has come to the student. However, the entire process occurred out of sequence and was unlawful. The nurse was involved at the end of the process, rather that the beginning and therefore, the entire health care needs of the student were not appropriately considered.[5]

Thus the central conclusion is that unlicensed persons in the school setting may be required to perform tasks of nursing care when those tasks are properly delegated to them by a registered nurse. Unlicensed persons may not perform those tasks on their own volition nor be required to perform those tasks when directed to do so by school authorities or parents.

The issue here is not merely the performance of clean intermittent catheterization in a school setting and who may perform. Rather, the issue is the identification of health care needs of students and how best to meet those needs. The purpose of hiring individuals with various areas of expertise and credentials in the school setting, is to utilize their knowledge and skills to provide students with an environment for learning and the provision of related services. A nurse employed by, or under contract to, a school system must be allowed to use her skills and expertise in the nursing process to meet identified health care needs of students. The law requires no less.

Questions Presented by Petitioner Mitts and Board of Nursing Answers

The following questions were presented by petitioner Carol Mitts:

1. "Is clean intermittent catheterization a form of cure or treatment of an illness, infirmity, deformity, defect, or abnormal physical or mental condition of Laura Potts?"
   Answer: Yes. Clean intermittent catheterization is a technique or treatment used to keep Laura Potts dry, comfortable and prevent bladder infections because she has a neurogenic bladder and cannot exercise control over excretion of urine from her bladder.
2. "Is Lehman's prescription pad note a medical order within the meaning of ORS 678.010, authorizing Elskamp to catheterize Laura Potts?"
   Answer: No. Dr. Lehman's note is simply a statement addressed to "to whom it may concern" that Laura Potts has a neurogenic bladder and requires clean intermittent catheterization to keep her dry.
3. May a (1) person not licensed by the Board of Medical Examiners or by this Board, or not certified as a nursing assistant, (2) employed by the school district, (3) perform clean intermittent catheterization, (4) on a student who is not a family member, (5) as an assigned employment duty, (6) for which the employee is compensated?"

Answer: Yes, qualified. A school employee who is not licensed as a nurse by the Board of Nursing may perform clean intermittent catheterization on an individual who is not a member of the immediate family only if taught to do so by a registered nurse and only if delegated that responsibility by a registered nurse. Compensation for doing that task is irrelevant to whether or not the unlicensed person may perform the task.

4. "Assuming licensed nurses may delegate clean intermittent catheterization duties to certified nursing assistants, has this Board adopted an approved curriculum and/or appropriate training program for insertion and removal of bladder catheters in a public school setting? Is such an approved curriculum and/or appropriate training program a prerequisite to use of nursing assistants to perform Mitts' duties described above?
   Answer: Registered nurses may delegate clean intermittent catheterization duties to unlicensed persons whether or not they have been certified as nursing assistants.[6] The Board's approved curriculum for basic nursing assistants does not contain content related to CIC because the Board did not intend for unlicensed persons to routinely perform the task of CIC. Instead, the Board intended that tasks, including CIC, may be delegated under specific circumstances to unlicensed persons. The Board has not adopted an approved training program for insertion and removal of bladder catheters in a public school setting or any other setting. It is not a prerequisite that the Board approve a training program for a registered nurse to use in order to teach one specific task to an unlicensed person.
5. "Under Oregon Statutes and this Board's Administrative Rules governing nurses and nursing assistants, may Mitts lawfully conduct clean intermittent catheterization of Laura Potts?"
   Answer: Yes, qualified. The administrative rules related to nursing assistants do not authorize Mitts or anyone else to perform CIC. However, under specific training and delegation by a registered nurse, Mitts, or any other unlicensed person, may perform clean intermittent catheterization under specific circumstances, procedural guidelines, and supervision provided by the registered nurse as set forth in the Board's rules.

Questions Presented by Petitioners Hillsboro Union High School District, Assistant Superintendent Elstun, Mary M. Elskamp, R.N., and Linda Potts

The following questions were presented by petitioners Hillsboro Union High School District, Assistant Superintendent Elstun, Linda Potts, and Mary M. Elskamp, R.N.:

1. "Is clean intermittent catheterization (CIC) performed on a student in a school environment by a health assistant an exclusive nursing task?"
   Answer: No. The performance of CIC is not a nursing task to the exclusion of other licensed health care professionals. It is a task that is performed by licensed nurses and other licensed health care providers. In the school environment a health assistant may only perform CIC upon the delegation of that task from a registered nurse, unless the health assistant is a licensed physician, certified physician's assistant, or a licensed nurse.[7]
2. If this is an exclusive nursing task that may be performed by a parent, may the knowledgeable parent delegate the performance

of CIC on the parent's own child to a health assistant?
Answer: No. When a parent directs others within the immediate
family to perform CIC on that parent's own child that act is
lawful under ORS 678.010(6). However, the parent may not
delegate the task to another person in the school setting or any
other institutional setting. In 42 Op Atty Gen 307 (1982), the
Attorney General concluded that while ORS 126.030 empowers
parents to delegate the power to provide care including the
administration of medication, such delegation probably does
not carry with it the authority to exercise that power irrespective
of the statutes governing the health care professions. The
Attorney General went on to note that an institutional guardian
would not qualify as a "member of the immediate family" under
CRS 678.010(6) and does not, therefore, fall within the statutory
exception of the Nurse Practice Act. The Board concludes,
consistent with the analysis of the Attorney General, that school
employees even when they have been delegated the duty to
provide care under CRS 126.010, are prohibited from
performing CIC on students unless they are legally qualified to
do so under the statutes governing the health care professions.
We also note in regard to CRS 126.010 that there is no evidence
in the present case that Linda Potts ever executed a power of
attorney purporting to delegate to the school administrator the
power.

FOOTNOTES

1   Catheterization of the urinary tract is a common procedure used
for a number of reasons. It may be used on a relatively short
term basis for an individual who has an illness or disease
affecting the kidneys and bladders, or post surgically. It may be
used for longer periods of time for a person who, due to
advanced age or paralysis, is unable to exercise normal control
over bladder functions and, therefore, either retains urine or is
incontinent of urine. The purpose of any urinary tract catheterization is to regularly empty the bladder of the urine, thereby
keeping the person comfortable and reducing risks of skin
breakdown due to retention of urine in the bladder. For urinary
catheterization in health care facilities, a catheter is inserted into
the urinary tract by sterile technique using sterile gloves and
sterile equipment to prevent bacteria outside of the body from
entering the bladder and causing a bladder infection. On a short
term basis, a catheter is usually left indwelling in the bladder and
kept secure by means of a small inflated balloon inside the
bladder. The use of sterile technique and equipment requires the
knowledge and skill of an individual licensed in the health care
field (e.g. a licensed nurse or physician) to ensure that the technique will indeed be done in a sterile manner, to recognize the
signs and symptoms of problems developing with the indwelling
catheter (e.g. inflammation or infection) and to decide what
action is needed to correct the developing problem.

For individuals who require catheterization outside a health
care facility over a long period of time, or even for a lifetime in
the case of an individual who is paraplegic, sterile catheterization is unnecessary. Instead, the technique of clean intermittent
catheterization can be used because the technique differs from
using a sterile catheter in that one does not need to don gloves,
use sterile equipment, or use sterile technique. Instead, clean
hands are used to insert a clean catheter into the bladder for a
short period of time merely to drain off any urine which has
accumulated in the bladder. The procedure is done on a regular
basis, approximately every four (4) hours.

Clean, intermittent catheterization is a simple technique
which can be properly taught in a short period of time (under
one hour) and is sometimes performed by the individual who is
in need of catheterization.

2   Lynda Carpenito, Ed. *Nursing Diagnosis: Application to Clinical
Practice*. (Philadelphia: J. B. Lippincott Company, 1987),
pp. 21-85.

3   It is conceded by all parties that Carol Mitts is not licensed as a
health care professional and is not a certified nursing assistant.
The title of Carol Mitts' position with the school district is
Health Assistant. Mitts' position description was submitted as
Exhibit 3 to petitioner Elskamp's Rebuttal Brief. It appears that
health assistants for the school district are being required to
engage in systematic problem solving which includes the steps of
assessing, making nursing diagnosis, planning, intervening and
evaluating. This constitutes the practice of nursing which health
assistants may not lawfully do unless they are properly licensed.
In this regard, this case is strikingly similar to the case in which
the Attorney General concluded that hospital technicians whose
duties fell within the practice of medicine, pharmacy, nursing
and radiology technology could not perform those functions if
they were not licensed to practice those professions. 45 Op Atty
Gen 188 (1987).

4   Based on the July 10, 1987 letter from Principal Wellman in
which he directed Carol Mitts to receive training and to provide
CIC for Laura Potts, it can be inferred that the assessment and
planning of care were done by him together with Assistant
Superintendent Gerry Elstun and the Director of Special Education for the Hillsboro High School District, "Bud" Moore, Ph.D.
In the letter Mr. Wellman noted that he had requested Mr.
Elstun to have a nurse "available" on a scheduled basis for the
purpose of consultation.

5   Although the focus of the petitioners concerns is whether or not
CIC is the practice of nursing and not on nurse Elskamp, the
Board is concerned regarding the passive role nurse Elskamp
took in this case. The Board expects that licensed nurses take an
active role in applying the nursing process. Nurse Elskamp's role
was passive in that she accepted the assessment by school
authorities regarding Laura Potts' health care needs and acted
upon that assessment by supervising Carol Mitts. Nurse
Elskamp's actions were below the expected standards of nursing
practice.

6   Nursing assistants are defined under CRS 678.440 (4) as follows:
As used in this section, "nursing assistant" means a person who
assists licensed nursing personnel in the provision of nursing
care.

The term "nursing assistant" is most commonly used for
those individuals who are employed in health care facilities to
provide routine simple nursing care. They generally work in
institutions where primary purpose is the provision of health
care, e.g., hospitals, long term care facilities, and infirmaries

contained within correctional or other state-operated facilities.

The Legislature intended that nursing assistants be adequately trained and, therefore, mandated the Board of Nursing under CRS 678.440 (2), to prepare curricula and standards for training programs for nursing assistants to work in health care facilities. Board approved training programs provide standardization of content for nursing assistant training and provide prospective employers with some assurance that those who complete the training program, and are certified as nursing assistants, have basic skills for the provision of nursing care tasks within health care facilities.

The skills and the curriculum content for nursing assistant training programs are described in OAR 851-20-113 and include such things as providing for patient's common daily needs for safety; food and fluids; personal hygiene; rest and comfort; understanding the process of aging; communication skills; taking vital signs such as blood pressure, temperature and pulse, and understanding basic medical terminology.

In health care facilities, nursing assistants are assigned their patient care responsibilities by a licensed nurse and are supervised by a licensed nurse, either directly or indirectly. However, it is not necessary for the licensed nurse to specifically assess their skills in the provision of nursing care tasks for each assignment in that their skills have been verified by certification from the nursing assistant training program.

Certified nursing assistants who provide general basic care to clients under the nurse's direction in a health care facility, are quite different from other unlicensed persons who have had no general training for the provision of nursing care tasks. The latter are under a registered nurse's specific teaching and direction to provide a very specific task of care to only one specific client. In the latter case, the unlicensed person need not be trained under an approved nursing assistant training program because that individual will not be providing general basic nursing care to several clients, but will only be providing one specific task to one client.

7   Petitioner Elskamp in her Rebuttal Brief contends that CIC is a simple, safe and effective procedure to aid toileting which is itself an activity of daily living. She concludes that it is, therefore, to be distinguished from nursing practice. This contention is erroneous. The essence of the practice of nursing is the nursing process as described above and not the specific tasks of nursing care whether simple or complex in nature. Thus, in this case the central analytical focus is on the application of the nursing process to a client who suffers from a dysfunction in the area of one activity of daily living. The focus is not on the skill level required to perform CIC.

8   This does not mean, however, that the nurse is prohibited from relying upon or using the written materials prepared by others. A nurse may use written materials prepared by others if the nurse concludes that those materials adequately convey information and instructions appropriate to the task being delegated.

Appendix J
Private Duty Nurse Contract

Used with permission: Office of Health Services, Baltimore County Public Schools, Maryland.

BALTIMORE COUNTY PUBLIC SCHOOLS
TOWSON, MARYLAND 21204
Agreement

WHEREAS, _____ is a student who
_____ and requires supervision by a skilled
caretaker, parent, or designated direct care giver, and

WHEREAS, all parties to this Agreement are desirous of having the above named student enrolled in the
_____ School, and

WHEREAS, all parties to this Agreement wish to specify procedures and delineate responsibilities among the various
parties, it is therefore,

AGREED, as follows:

THIS STUDENT'S REQUIREMENTS

1. This student will need to be in the presence of a skilled caretaker, parent, or designated direct care giver at all times during the school day. If the skilled caretaker is unable to accompany the student, the student may not attend school.

2. This student will need the following items and supplies in the school: (Attachment A)

THE BALTIMORE COUNTY PUBLIC SCHOOLS (BCPS)

1. Shall enable this student's parent/legal guardian, designee or skilled caretaker to remain in attendance at all times during the school day in order to assist the student's required supportive and medical care.

2. Shall assume no responsibility for the provision and/or maintenance of medical equipment for this student. (See Attachment B—"Understanding Concerning Private Property in School Buildings")

3. Shall assume no liability for this student beyond that which is already assumed for other students in the event of an adverse consequence during a medical emergency.

4. Will provide appropriate home instruction, if necessary, in accordance with the established procedures for referral to its Home and Hospital School.

The Principal or Designee

1. Shall follow agreed upon action and/or call 911 when it is felt that this student requires special or emergency intervention. (See Attachment C — "Physician Notification and Medical Emergency Protocol")

2. Shall advise the parent/legal guardian of any academic or medical concerns.

3. Shall require the parent/legal guardian or the skilled caretaker to remove the student from school, if on any given day this student's medical condition warrants inordinate concern.

4. Shall have complete discretion with regard to any action deemed necessary in order to provide for this student's safety or the safety of other students, faculty, or school staff.

5. Shall assume responsibility for the compliance of school personnel to the guidelines "Private Duty Nurses with Special Needs Students." (See Attachment D)

6. Shall send the student home if the skilled caretaker is unable to accompany the student.

Teacher, Teacher's Assistant, Therapists

1. Shall report medical or academic concerns to the principal or designee, the school health nurse, and/or Pupil Services Team.

2. Shall become familiar with this student's routine medical and crisis procedures.

Private Duty Nurse/Skilled Caretaker (Retained by the Parent/Legal Guardian)

1. Shall be a registered nurse or practical nurse licensed in Maryland and shall, with the parent/legal guardian, be exclusively responsible for this student's daily supportive and medical care. Specific nursing functions will be determined by those individuals directly involved in the student's medical treatment.

2. Shall, at the discretion of the principal, report to the principal or designee each morning prior to accompanying the student to the classroom.

3. Shall accompany the student at all times.

4. Shall become thoroughly familiar with the implementation of this student's transportation procedures and be prepared to carry out these procedures.

5. Shall become thoroughly familiar with the implementation of this student's emergency medical procedures and be prepared to carry out these procedures.

6. Shall become thoroughly familiar with the implementation of this student's fire drill (and other natural disaster) procedures and be prepared to carry out these procedures.

7. Shall continually apprise the principal, teacher, and the school health nurse of the student's health status and any medical and treatment related procedures that might impact on the student's school attendance or performance.

8. Shall participate in the implementation of this student's academic program and other school activities at the discretion of the principal or designee and the classroom teacher.

9. Shall report concerns regarding equipment and supplies to the parent/legal guardian and shall apprise the principal or designee of the same.

10. Shall report to the principal or designee if becoming ill during the course of the day and shall, if at all possible, continue to supervise this student until the parent(s)/legal guardian arrives at the school.

11. Shall adhere to the American Nurse Association 1976 Code for Nurses, particularly Principle #2 (the Nurse safeguards the client's right to privacy by judiciously protecting information of a confidential nature).

12. Shall adhere to all the responsibilities of the private duty nurse in the school setting as delineated by the Baltimore County Public Schools (See Attachment D) and by the Maryland State Board of Nursing.

13. Shall participate as necessary in routine conferences regarding the student.

Private Duty Nurse/Skilled Caretaker

1. Shall adhere to all applicable responsibilities as outlined in the preceding section entitled "Private Duty Nurse/Skilled Caretaker".

Parents/Legal Guardians

1. Shall ensure that persons assigned to accompany this student to school are appropriately trained and qualified for this position.

2. Shall ensure that the skilled caretaker/direct care giver has been apprised about and is in agreement with this student's school procedures and the functions of the skilled caretaker.

3. Shall assume supervisory responsibility for the skilled caretaker/direct care giver and shall recognize the independence of the caretaker from other school-based health professionals.

4. Shall be receptive to judgments by the school principal or designee concerning the competency of the caretaker in the school setting and the overall professionalism displayed by the caretaker in interactions with the school staff.

5. Shall provide all medical orders and other health records, emergency protocol and necessary equipment for school use prior to this student's attendance.

6. Shall be in agreement with "Medical Emergency Protocol", "Fire Drill Procedures", and other appropriate rules, regulations, and procedures of the Baltimore County Public Schools.

7. Shall make arrangements for emergency medical transportation through the Emergency Medical Division of the Baltimore County Fire Department. A copy of this agreement will be in the possession of the principal prior to this student's first day of school attendance.

8. Shall ensure that school-related information obtained in the course of the school day while attending to the student in the classroom remains confidential.

9. Shall take this student home, or make arrangements for same, in the event that the caretaker becomes ill during the school day, if the caretaker is unable to accompany the student, if the principal or designee decides that the student should be sent home, or if for some reason it becomes necessary to close the school.

This Student's Medical Emergency Protocol

1. The skilled caretaker will supervise this student's medical needs at school. This direct care giver will act in conformity with procedures agreed upon by the parent/legal guardian and Baltimore County Public Schools.

2. The skilled caretaker/direct care giver will act in accordance with the responsibility for emergency situations as outlined by Baltimore County Public Schools in Attachment C.

3. Should the classroom teacher have concerns regarding the caretaker's intervention during a medial episode, the principal or designee and the school health nurse should be contacted.

4. The principal or designee has the right to call in other personnel and services if judged necessary for this student's well being. These services may include, but are not limited to, paramedics/ambulances.

5. See Attachment C for specified Medical Emergency Protocol.

This Student's Fire Drill (or other natural disaster) Procedures

1. In the event of fire drill, the caretaker, with the assistance of appropriate school personnel as designated by the principal, will be responsible for ensuring this student's immediate evacuation from the school building.

2. The following equipment will be taken out of the building during a fire drill or actual emergency: _____

   _____

   _____

3. The principal or designee will inform appropriate emergency personnel about a building emergency and, if deemed prudent, this student may be removed from the school grounds.

This Student's Transportation Procedures

1. This student will be transported to and from the school by _____.
    The parent or caretaker will accompany the student in the cases where life support procedures may be needed during transit.

2. If it is determined by the principal or designee that the student's school day must be shortened due to his/her medical condition, the parent or designee will assume responsibility for transporting the student from school to home.

3. If the caretaker becomes ill during the course of the day, the parent will transport the student from school to home or will arrange for same.

4. If this student is transported to school by the Transportation Department of the Baltimore County Public Schools, it has the complete discretion to establish reasonable rules and requirements beyond those contained herein in order to provide for the safe transportation of this student and others.

5. When school bus transportation is provided, the parent shall ensure that the child will be ready to board the bus when it arrives in the morning and will have someone ready to receive the student upon return from school.

In no event shall this agreement be construed to impose any obligation on the Baltimore County Public Schools, or its employees, other than those required by law, and the undersigned do hereby release and discharge the Baltimore County Public Schools from any such obligation.

If any part of this agreement is not complied with, this student's attendance at this Baltimore County Public School may be suspended.

These responsibilities and procedures are agreed to by:

Parent/Legal Guardian _____   Date _____

Parent/Legal Guardian _____   Date _____

Private Duty Nurse/Skilled Caretaker _____   Date _____

Baltimore County Public Schools by:

Principal _____   Date _____

School Nurse _____   Date _____

ADDENDUM TO AGREEMENT

The undersigned parent/legal guardian of _____, a student enrolled in the Baltimore County Public Schools, have heretofore entered into an Agreement dated _____ to which this Addendum is attached. That Agreement provides in part for the execution thereof by a "private duty nurse/skilled caretaker" to be retained or employed by the undersigned. In obtaining the services of such a person, it is the intention of the undersigned to obtain the services of such a person through the

_____

(Name and Address of Agency)

In doing so the undersigned recognizes, agrees, and understands that the aforesaid agency may, from time to time, supply to the undersigned as a private duty nurse/skilled care giver under the terms of the Agreement a person other than the specific skilled care giver who has signed the Agreement to which this Addendum is attached. The undersigned hereby covenant and agree that the Baltimore County Public School System may accept from time to time any person who may be assigned as a private duty nurse/skilled care giver to the above named student by the aforesaid agency, without the necessity of a new Agreement being executed by the parties, and the undersigned do hereby expressly authorize and direct the Baltimore County Public School System to accept as the private duty nurse/skilled care giver under the attached contract any person who shall be so assigned by the aforesaid as a person qualified to fulfill the duties and responsibilities of a private duty nurse/skilled care giver under the attached contract, and the undersigned does hereby further covenant and agree to indemnify and to save and hold the Baltimore County Public School System harmless from any and all claims, demands, obligations, liabilities, debts, damages, and responsibilities generally incurred, or to be incurred, by the Baltimore County Public School System as a result of its compliance with the content of this Addendum.

_____

Parent/Legal Guardian

_____

Parent/Legal Guardian

_____

Witness

_____

Date

EQUIPMENT LIST

ATTACHMENT B

UNDERSTANDING CONCERNING PRIVATE
PROPERTY IN SCHOOL BUILDINGS

The Undersigned owner of certain property or equipment described in Attachment A hereto and intended to be kept or stored in _____ School understands that the Board of Education of Baltimore County and its officers, agents, and employees do not guarantee the safety or security of such property or equipment while it is in the school building, but will take such reasonable precautions as they deem necessary to protect and secure all property in the building.

_____

Parent/Legal Guardian

_____

Witness

_____

Date

ATTACHMENT C

BALTIMORE COUNTY PUBLIC SCHOOLS
Towson, Maryland 21204

BALTIMORE COUNTY DEPARTMENT OF HEALTH
Towson, Maryland 21204

MEDICAL EMERGENCY PROTOCOL

STUDENT: _____ DOB: _____

PRIMARY PHYSICIAN: _____ DATE: _____

NOTIFICATION PROTOCOL

In the event of: Greater Than   Less Than

- Heart Rate   _____   _____

- Respiratory Rate   _____   _____

- Temperature   _____   _____

- Blood Pressure   _____   _____

- Other _____   _____   _____

Notify: _____ at _____
                (Physician)   (Phone)

If unavailable, contact: _____ at _____
                (Physician)   (Phone)

EMERGENCY PROTOCOL

- What constitutes an emergency for this child?

- Who is to be notified? (include name and phone)

- What interventions are to be performed at school?

- When should transport to emergency facility occur?

TRANSPORT PLAN

- Transport to local hospital nearest school? Yes No

- If "No" indicate hospital of choice:

SPECIAL CONSIDERATIONS :

_____
Physician's Signature   Date

BEBCO 82-284-95

PRIVATE DUTY NURSES/SKILLED CARETAKERS IN THE SCHOOLS

As growing numbers of medically fragile children attend regular classes in public schools, private duty nurses/skilled caretakers assigned to those children are increasingly present in the schools. The following guidelines apply when those caregivers are hired by the parents, and the need for the care giver is not part of the Individualized Educational Plan (IEP).

GENERAL CONSIDERATIONS

- School officials are not responsible for the supervision of the private duty nurse/skilled caretaker. School officials are responsible for the safety of the student and therefore have the duty to warn parents if they observe or become aware of inappropriate or deficient care by the private duty nurse/skilled caretaker. This warning should be documented (put in writing), sent to the student's parent/guardian with a copy filed in the principal's office. If a school nurse observes that the private duty nurse/skilled caretaker's services are deficient, the school nurse must first inform the principal and then the parent/guardian. A letter signed by the principal and the school nurse should be sent to the parent/guardian delineating the deficiencies. Copies of the letter should remain with the school principal and school nurse. If a threat to the child's safety continues after the warning, the principal should exercise his/her discretion and exclude the child and the private duty nurse/skilled caretaker from school premises until alternate safe arrangements can be made by the parent/guardian.

- School nurses are not responsible for supervising the private duty nurse/skilled caretaker. School nurses have the same responsibility as school administrators to monitor and warn school administrators and parents of any observed incompetent or deficient actions by the care giver. Under the Nurse Practice Act, school nurses need to decide whether the deficiencies or incompetence warrant notification of the Board of Nursing. This decision should be made in collaboration with the Office of Health Services.

Responsibilities of the Private Duty Nurse/Skilled Caretaker

- The private duty nurse/skilled caretaker performs all tasks agreed upon by the parents and school nurse. These tasks should be put in writing and signed by the private duty/skilled caretaker, the parent/guardian, and the school nurse. This may include but is not limited to: medication administration; toileting; transporting student to classes; performing certain treatments such as, catheterization, suctioning, and tube feeding; and positioning.

- The private duty nurse/skilled caretaker maintains all equipment used by the student.

- The private duty nurse/skilled caretaker apprises school personnel of any changes in the student's health status.

- The private duty nurse/skilled caretaker performs all emergency procedures for the student.

Responsibilities of the School Nurse

- The school nurse informs parents and private duty nurse/skilled caretakers of Baltimore County's policies and procedures relevant to the care of the student.

- The school nurse maintains a safe environment for the student which includes reporting any deficiencies to the principal and the parent/guardian.

- The school nurse maintains health records, including medication and treatment orders, for the student and ensures that the student meets all state and local requirements for school entry.

- The school nurse keeps current regarding the child's health status and conveys concerns to the parents/guardians.

- The school nurse initiates and develops the nursing care plan in collaboration with the private duty caretaker and the parents/guardian.

Responsibilities of the Principal

- The principal requires the parent/guardian to sign the Baltimore County Public Schools agreement delineating responsibilities of all involved parties.

- The principal informs parents that the private duty nurse/skilled caretaker is not supervised by any Baltimore County employee except that deficiencies will be reported and documented. The caretaker and child will be excluded from the school until an acceptable and safe alternative arrangement can be made. The child may be placed on home teaching until this occurs.

- The principal informs the parent/guardian in writing that their child may not attend school without the private duty nurse/skilled caretaker when such care has been deemed necessary.

Appendix K
Sample Student Learning Objectives and IHP

PART 1
Sample Student Learning Objectives by Nursing Diagnosis

Used with permission, Patricia Piatek, RN, MS, August 1999

NURSING DIAGNOSIS	STUDENT OBJECTIVE
At Risk for Alteration in Self-Concept	Student will choose community or afterschool activity and participate in 90% of time while healthy.
Alteration in Nutrition—less than body requirements	Student will follow his prescribed diet 100% of time. Student will demonstrate appropriate lunch program, or in prepared lunches from home, to reflect his high caloric/high protein needs 90-95% of time. Student will tolerate his G-tube feeding by remaining quiet and relaxed during procedure 100% of time.
Altered Growth and Development related to self-care skills	Student will self-direct care during identified activities that require assistance from others 95% of time. Student will use wheelchair independently 95% of time.
Knowledge Deficit and Self-Care Deficit related to age appropriate hygiene	Student will follow daily routine of selfcare to include routine hygiene and, grooming expectations from a prepared list 95% of school days. Student will follow appropriate personal hygiene 4 of 5 days of week. Student will maintain a daily personal hygiene log 80% of time (shower/ bath, handwashing with nail care, toothbrushing, change of clothing).
At Risk for Infection and Ineffective Airway Clearance	Student will cough effectively to clear airway of mucous obstruction 95% of time without adult prompts.
Alteration in Pattern of Elimination-encopresis	Student will verbally indicate to an identified adult the need to access the facilities and supplies kept for him 90% of times he has encopretic problem.
At Risk for Ineffective Breathing Pattern	Student will correctly follow steps for inhaler use 100% of time and selfmonitor time interval steps during that, process.
Knowledge Deficit related to airway management	Student will demonstrate full lung expansion when utilizing her inhaler and peak flow meter 3 of 5 times procedures are followed. Student will increase stamina in physical activities by participating 80% of time in gym.

NURSING DIAGNOSIS	STUDENT OBJECTIVE
Knowledge Deficit related to self-care management	Student will recognize s/s of injury and take proper interventions to treat 3 of 5 reportable occurrences. Student will identify treatments for the following when asked 90% of time: muscle strain, sprain, URI, sore throat.
Knowledge Deficit related to hypertension/renal disease	Student will describe the effects of high BP in relation to renal dysfunction by listing 4-5 resulting effects of nonmanagement of disease 95-100% of times asked. Student will decrease smoking on a sliding scale and consider a StopSmoking program within 6 mos. Student will report to the health room, weekly for BP checks 100% of time.
At Risk for Ineffective Coping	Student will take medication as prescribed 100% of time. Student will list desired effects of the medication 95% of time asked to indicate his understanding of the need to comply with the schedule of administration.
Fear related to medical issues	Student will verbalize his feelings and fears in an appropriate manner 90% of time.
At Risk for Ineffective Airway Clearance	Student will report all signs of airway distress to an adult 100% of occurrences. Student will self-administer inhaler (under adult supervision) correctly 100% of time. Student will tolerate frequent position changes and nursing assessments to facilitate his handling of respiratory secretions 95% of time by allowing such linterventions.
Altered Nutrition—more than body requirements	Student will choose lower caloric foods when offered choices 85% of time. Student will choose food lower in cholesterol when given choice 85% of time. Student will list dietary interventions and will demonstrate a maintenance of or decrease in weight curve over the school year.
At Risk for Infection related to skin integrity	Student will cooperate with daily skin assessments and frequent changes of position by relaxing when asked in order to facilitate staff interventions 95% of time. Student will appropriately use toweling to control oral secretions 80% of time without adult prompts.
At Risk for Infection	Student will tolerate daily nebulizer treatment 100% of time by allowing frequent repositioning of face mask, and coughing to clear airway when asked.
Knowledge Deficit related to puberty changes	Student will demonstrate an understanding of puberty by describing body changes 100% of time subject is reviewed with her. Student will identify the steps appropriate to self-care and management of monthly menstruation by listing 5 of 6 steps in process.

NURSING DIAGNOSIS	STUDENT OBJECTIVE
Knowledge Deficit related to medication	Student will indicate to the classroom staff the appropriate time to access the health room for medication daily, 100% of time. Student will take appropriate dose of medication, per daily schedule, home and school, 100% of time. Student will name 4-5 desired effects of medication, 100% of time requested. Student will name 4-5 possible side effects of medication, 100% of time requested.

SAMPLE INDIVIDUALIZED HEALTH CARE PLAN
Page 1 of 2

NAME: Jane Doe   DOB   2/4/90   SEX   F   ALLERGIES   NKA   PHYSICIAN   Smith

RELEVANT DIAGNOSIS(ES):   Diabetes Type I

DIET   Diabetic   MOBILITY: WNL   EQUIPMENT: Glucometer

MEDICAL HISTORY: Diagnosed as 8 year old: seen at Joselin Clinic

MEDICATION/TREATMENT: NPH Insulin AM,PM, Noon by scale   Reg. NPH AM,PM, Range of Blood sugar levels 90-200 Glucometer test 11:30
AM

SIGNATURE: SIGNATURE: SIGNATURE:

    (Parent)   (Student)   (School Nurse)

HEALTH CARE GOAL: J. will maintain a stable diabetic regime in order attend to classroom activities 95% of educational schedule.

DATE	HEALTH PROBLEM/ NURSING DIAGNOSIS	STUDENT OBJECTIVES	INTERVENTION AND RESPONSIBLE PERSON	EVALUATION AND TIMELINE
——	At Risk for Knowledge Deficit	J. will describe 6 of 8 listed s/s of hyperglycemia 100% of time reviewed.	School nurse to meet monthly with student or on some scheduled basis to discuss diabetic issues. School nurse to collaborate with family, diabetic specialist, MD, family, school team to determine student level of knowledge and understanding of diabetic management.	Monthly with team Orders: (date) Quarterly re. Obj.
		J. will describe 6 of 8 listed s/s of hypoglycemia 100% of time reviewed.		
		J. will remain free of episodes of hyper/ hypoglycemia 90% of time by eating appropriate food choices to keep blood sugar levels between 90-200.	School nurse to complete IHCP, Emergency Care Plan.	(dates completed)
			School nurse to prepare with student lists of symptoms of hyper and hypoglycemia. Knowledge will be revised as necessary.	Monthly

Health-Related Goal and Objectives: Student with Diabetes.
Used with permission, Patricia Piatek, RN, MS, August 1999

SAMPLE INDIVIDUALIZED HEALTH CARE PLAN
Page 2 of 2

NAME: Jane Doe

DATE	HEALTH PROBLEM/ NURSING DIAGNOSIS	STUDENT OBJECTIVES	INTERVENTION AND RESPONSIBLE PERSON	EVALUATION AND TIMELINE
—	Knowledge Deficit related to glucometer testing	J. will identify the 5 steps of glucometer testing, including the safe handling of blood 100% of time procedure is done.	School nurse/staff will assist student to identify steps of glucometer test from prepared 5 step procedure: 1. Select finger. 2. Clean with alcohol. 3. Use lancet. 4. Place blood drop on strip or meter. 5. Apply bandaid to finger. Nurse/trained staff will assist/instruct J. in handling of blood materials. (Nurse to train any designated staff assist)	Monthly
	1. Steps of test			
	2. Interpretation of results	J. will identify blood sugar level on a chart with corresponding interpretations 100% of time following glucometer test.	Nurse will create chart with blood sugar values 40–220, each labeled high, normal, low or very low. Nurse/ designated staff will assist J. in identifying current level.	(date)
	3. Appropriate Interventions	J. will identify and follow appropriate intervention steps for low blood sugar as indicated on chart 100% of time following glucometer test.	Nurse will provide a list of appropriate interventions for each blood sugar value including nutritional intake ranging from no intervention to 3 snacks. 90-above--- none below 90--- 1 snack below 70--- 2 snacks below 50--- 3 snacks	Monthly

Health-Related Goal and Objectives: Student with Diabetes.
Used with permission, Patricia Piatek, RN, MS, August 1999

Appendix L

State Medication Administration Regulations and School District Medication Policy

PART 1
Massachusetts Regulations for the Administration of Prescription Medications

105 CMR: Massachusetts Department of Public Health Regulatory Authority: 105 CMR 210.000: M.G.L. c. 94c, § 7(g); c. 71, §54B.

210.001: PURPOSE

The purpose of 105 CMR 210.000 is to provide minimum standards for the safe and proper administration of prescription medications to students in the Commonwealth's public and private primary and secondary schools. 105 CMR 210.000 permit school nurses to delegate responsibility for administration of prescription medications to trained, nursing-supervised school personnel, provided the school district or private school registers with the Department of Public Health. The aim of 105 CMR 210.000 is to ensure that students requiring prescription medication administration during the school day will be able to attend school and to ensure that prescription medications are safely administered in schools. 105 CMR 210.000 encourages collaboration between parents or guardians and the school in this effort.

210.002: DEFINITIONS

As used in 105 CMR 210.000, the following words, unless the context clearly requires otherwise, shall have the following meanings:

Administration of Medication means the direct application of a prescription medication by inhalation, ingestion, or by any other means to the body of a person.

Prescription Medication means any medication, which by federal law may be obtained only by prescription.

Cumulative Health Record means the cumulative health record of a pupil as specified under M.G.L. c. 71.

Department means the Massachusetts Department of Public Health.

Investigational New Drug means any medication with an approved investigational new drug (IND) application on file with the Food and Drug Administration (FDA) which is being scientifically tested and clinically evaluated to determine its efficacy, safety and side effects and which has not yet received FDA approval.

Licensed Practical Nurse means an individual who is a graduate of an approved practical nursing program and who is currently licensed as a practical nurse pursuant to M.G.L. c. 112.

Licensed Prescriber means a health care provider who is legally authorized to prescribe medication pursuant to M.G.L. c. 94c and applicable federal laws and regulations.

Parenteral Medication means any medication administered in a manner other than by the digestive tract or topical application, as by intravenous, intramuscular, subcutaneous, or intradermal injection.

Physician means a doctor of medicine or osteopathy licensed to practice medicine in Massachusetts or in another state.

School Nurse means a nurse practicing in a school setting, who is:
(1) a graduate of an approved school for professional nursing;
(2) currently licensed as a Registered Nurse pursuant to M.G.L. c. 112; and
(3) appointed by a School Committee or a Board of Health in accordance with M.G.L. c. 71, §§ 53, 53A, and 53B or, in the case of a private school, by the Board of Trustees.

School Physician means a physician appointed by a School Committee or Board of Health in accordance with M.G.L. c. 71,

§§ 53, 53A, and 53B or, in the case of a private school, by the Board of Trustees.

Supervision means guidance by a qualified school nurse to accomplish a task, with initial direction and instruction concerning the task and periodic inspection and oversight of activities related to the task.

Teacher for the purpose of 105 CMR 210.000, means a professional school employee who:

(1) instructs students or serves in the role of administrator below the rank of superintendent; and

(2) is employed by a School Committee or Board of Trustees.

210.003:

POLICIES GOVERNING THE ADMINISTRATION OF PRESCRIPTION MEDICATIONS IN SCHOOLS

(A) The School Committee or Board of Trustees, consulting with the Board of Health where appropriate, shall adopt policies and procedures governing the administration of prescription medications and self-administration of prescription medications within the school system, following development of a proposal by the school nurse, in consultation with the school physician. Review and revision of such policies and procedures shall occur as needed, but at least every two years. At a minimum, these policies shall include:

(1) designation of a school nurse as supervisor of the prescription medication administration program in a school;

(2) documentation of the administration of prescription medications;

(3) response to a medication emergency;

(4) storage of prescription medications;

(5) reporting and documentation of medication errors;

(6) dissemination of information to parents or guardians. Such information shall include an outline of a school's medication policies and shall be available to parents and guardians upon request;

(7) procedures for resolving questions between the school and a parent or guardian regarding administration of medications. Such procedures shall provide for and encourage the participation of the parent or guardian. Existing procedures for resolution of differences may be used whenever appropriate.

(B) The School Committee or Board of Trustees shall submit these policies and procedures to the Department of Public Health upon request.

210.004:

POLICIES REGARDING DELEGATION OF PRESCRIPTION MEDICATION ADMINISTRATION

(A) The School Committee or Board of Trustees, consulting with the Board of Health where appropriate, may approve a proposal, developed by the school nurse and school physician, to permit the administration of prescription medications to be delegated by the school nurse to unlicensed school personnel. Such delegation may occur only if the school district registers with the Department of Public Health pursuant to the applicable provisions of 105 CMR 700.000 and complies with the requirements of 105 CMR 210.000.

(B) In accordance with the proposal of the school nurse and school physician, the School Committee or Board of Trustees may approve categories of unlicensed school personnel to whom the school nurse may delegate responsibility for prescription medication administration.

(1) Said categories of personnel may include administrative and teaching staff, licensed health personnel, health aides and secretaries.

(a) For the purposes of 105 CMR 210.000, health aide shall mean an unlicensed employee of the school district who is generally supervised by the school nurse and performs those health-related duties defined by the school nurse, the School Committee, Board of Health or Board of Trustees.

(b) For the purpose of administering emergency prescription medication to an individual child, including parenteral administration of medication pursuant to 105 CMR 210.004(B)(4), the school nurse may identify individual school personnel or additional categories. Said school personnel shall be listed on the medication administration plan developed in accordance with 105 CMR 210.005(E) and receive training in the administration of emergency medication to a specific child.

(2) An individual in an approved category may be authorized to administer prescription medication if he/she meets the following criteria:

(a) is a high school graduate or its equivalent;

(b) demonstrates sound judgment;

(c) is able to read and write English;

(d) is able to communicate with the student receiving the prescription medication or has ready access to an interpreter when needed;

(e) is able to meet the requirements of 105 CMR 210.000 and follow nursing supervision;

(f) is able to respect and protect the student's confidentiality; and

(g) has completed an approved training program pursuant to 105 CMR 210.007.

(3) A school nurse shall be on duty in the school system while prescription medications are being administered by designated unlicensed school personnel, and available by telephone should consultation be required.

(4) The administration of parenteral medications may not be delegated, with the exception of epinephrine or other medication to be administered in a life-threatening situation where the child has a known allergy or pre-existing medical condition and there is an order for administration of the medication from a licensed prescriber and written consent of the parent or guardian.

(5) Prescription medications to be administered pursuant to p.r.n. ("as needed") orders may be administered by authorized school personnel after an assessment by or consultation with the school nurse for each dose.

(6) For each school, an updated list of unlicensed school personnel who have been trained in the administration of prescription medications shall be maintained. Upon request, a parent shall be provided with a list of school personnel authorized to administer prescription medications.

210.005:

RESPONSIBILITIES OF THE SCHOOL NURSE REGARDING PRESCRIPTION MEDICATION ADMINISTRATION

(A) The school nurse, in consultation with the school physician and the school health advisory committee, if established, shall develop policies and procedures consistent with 105 CMR 210.000 for approval by the School Committee or Board of Trustees, in consultation with the Board of Health where appropriate.

(B) The school nurse shall have responsibility for the development and management of the prescription medication administration program. Such responsibility shall be delineated in policies and procedures adopted by the School Committee or Board of Trustees, in consultation with the Board of Health where appropriate.

(C) The school nurse, in consultation with the school physician shall have final decision-making authority with respect to delegating administration of prescription medications to unlicensed personnel in school systems registered with the Department of Public Health.

(D) Medication Orders

  (1) The school nurse shall ensure that there is a proper medication order from a licensed prescriber which is renewed as necessary including the beginning of each academic year. A telephone order or an order for any change in prescription medication shall be received only by the school nurse. Any verbal order must be followed by a written order within three school days. Whenever possible, the medication order shall be obtained, and the medication administration plan specified in 105 CMR 210.0005(E) shall be developed before the student enters or re-enters school.

   (a) In accordance with standard medical practice, a medication order from a licensed prescriber shall contain:
      1. the student's name;
      2. the name and signature of the licensed prescriber and business and emergency phone numbers;
      3. the name, route and dosage of medication;
      4. the frequency and time of medication administration;
      5. the date of the order;
      6. a diagnosis and any other medical condition(s) requiring medication, if not a violation of confidentiality or if not contrary to the request of a parent, guardian or student to keep confidential;
      7. specific directions for administration.

   (b) Every effort shall be made to obtain from the licensed prescriber the following additional information, as appropriate:
      1. any special side effects, contraindications and adverse reactions to be observed;
      2. any other medications being taken by the student;
      3. the date of return visit, if applicable.

  (2) Special Medication Situations
   (a) For short-term prescription medications, i.e., those requiring administration for ten school days or fewer, the pharmacy-labeled container may be used in lieu of a licensed prescriber's order. If the nurse has a question, she may request a licensed prescriber's order.

   (b) For "over-the-counter" medications, i.e., non-prescription medications, the school nurse shall follow the Board of Registration in Nursing's protocols regarding administration of over-the-counter medications in schools.

   (c) Investigational new drugs may be administered in the schools with (1) a written order by a licensed prescriber, (2) written consent of the parent or guardian, and (3) a pharmacy-labeled container for dispensing. If there is a question, the school nurse may seek consultation and/or approval from the school physician to administer the medication in a school setting.

  (3) The school nurse shall ensure that there is a written authorization by the parent or guardian which contains:
   (a) the parent or guardian's printed name and signature and a home and emergency phone number;
   (b) a list of all medications the student is currently receiving, if not a violation of confidentiality or contrary to the request of the parent, guardian or student that such medication not be documented;
   (c) approval to have the school nurse or school personnel designated by the school nurse administer the prescription medication;
   (d) persons to be notified in case of a medication emergency in addition to the parent or guardian and licensed prescriber.

(E) Medication Administration Plan: The school nurse, in collaboration with the parent or guardian whenever possible, shall establish a medication administration plan for each student receiving a prescription medication. Whenever possible, a student who understands the issues of medication administration shall be involved in the decision-making process and his/her preferences respected to the maximum extent possible. If appropriate, the medication administration plan shall be referenced in any other health or educational plan developed pursuant to St. 1972, c. 766 the Massachusetts Special Education Law (Individual Education Plan under Chapter 766) or federal laws, such as the Individuals with Disabilities Education Act (IDEA) or Section 504 of the Rehabilitation Act of 1973.

  (1) Prior to the initial administration of the prescription medication, the school nurse shall assess the child's health status and develop a medication administration plan which includes:
   (a) the name of the student;
   (b) a medication order from a licensed prescriber, which meets the requirements of 105 CMR 210.005(D)(1);
   (c) the signed authorization of the parent or guardian, which meets the requirements of 105 CMR 210.005(D)(3);
   (d) any known allergies to food or medications CMR 210.005(D)(3);
   (e) the diagnosis, unless a violation of confidentiality or the parent, guardian or student requests that it not be documented;
   (f) any possible side effects, adverse reactions or contraindications;

(g) the quantity of prescription medication to be received by the school from the parent or guardian;

(h) the required storage conditions;

(i) the duration of the prescription;

(j) the designation of unlicensed school personnel, if any, who will administer the prescription medication to the student in the absence of the nurse, and plans for back-up if the designated personnel are unavailable;

(k) plans, if any, for teaching self-administration of the prescription medication;

(l) with parental permission, other persons, including teachers, to be notified of medication administration and possible adverse effects of the medication;

(m) when appropriate, the location where the administration of the prescription medication will take place;

(n) a plan for monitoring the effects of the medication;

(o) provision for prescription medication administration in the case of field trips and other short-term special school events. Every effort shall be made to obtain a nurse or school staff member trained in prescription medication administration to accompany students at special school events. When this is not possible, the school nurse may delegate prescription medication administration to another responsible adult. Written consent from the parent or guardian for the named responsible adult to administer the prescription medication shall be obtained. The school nurse shall instruct the responsible adult on how to administer the prescription medication to the child.

(F) Developing Procedures for Administration of Prescription Medications.

(1) The school nurse shall develop procedures for the administration of prescription medications which shall include the following:

(a) A procedure to ensure the positive identification of the student who receives the medication;

(b) A system for documentation and record-keeping which meets the requirements of 105 CMR 210.009.

(2) The school nurse shall develop a system of documenting observations by the nurse or school personnel and communicating significant observations relating to prescription medication effectiveness and adverse reactions or other harmful effects to the child's parent or guardian and/or licensed prescriber;

(3) The school nurse shall develop and implement procedures regarding receipt and safe storage of prescription medications;

(4) The school nurse shall develop procedures for responding to medication emergencies, i.e., any reaction or condition related to administration of medication which poses an immediate threat to the health or well-being of the student. This includes maintaining a list of persons, with their phone numbers, to be contacted as appropriate, in addition to the parent/guardian, school nurse, licensed prescriber and other persons designated in the medication administration plan. Such persons may include other school personnel, the school physician, clinic or emergency room staff, ambulance services and the local poison control center;

(5) The school nurse shall develop procedures and forms for documenting and reporting prescription medication errors. The procedures shall specify persons to be notified in addition to the parent or guardian and nurse, including the licensed prescriber or school physician if there is a question of potential harm to the student. A medication error includes any failure to administer prescription medication as prescribed for a particular student, including failure to administer the prescription medication:

(a) within appropriate time frames;

(b) in the correct dosage;

(c) in accordance with accepted practice;

(d) to the correct student.

(6) The school nurse shall develop procedures to review reports of medication errors and take necessary steps to ensure appropriate prescription medication administration in the future.

(G) Delegation/Supervision. When a School Committee or Board of Trustees, in consultation with the Board of Health where appropriate, has registered with the Department of Public Health and authorized categories of unlicensed school personnel to administer prescription medications, such personnel shall be under the supervision of the school nurse for the purposes of 105 CMR 210.000. The School Committee or Board of Trustees, in consultation with the Board of Health where appropriate, shall provide assurance that sufficient school nurse(s) are available to provide proper supervision of unlicensed school personnel. Responsibilities for supervision, at a minimum, shall include the following:

(1) After consultation with the principal or administrator responsible for a given school, the school nurse shall select, train and supervise the specific individuals, in those categories of school personnel approved by the School Committee or Board of Trustees, in consultation with the Board of Health where appropriate, who may administer prescription medications. When necessary to protect student health and safety, the school nurse may rescind such selection.

(2) The number of unlicensed school personnel to whom responsibility for prescription medication administration may be delegated is to be determined by:

(a) the number of unlicensed school personnel the school nurse can adequately supervise on a weekly basis, as determined by the school nurse;

(b) the number of unlicensed school personnel necessary, in the nurse's judgment, to ensure that the prescription medications are properly administered to each student.

(3) The school nurse shall support and assist persons who have completed the training specified in 105 CMR 210.007 to prepare for and implement their responsibilities related to the administration of prescription medication.

(4) The first time that an unlicensed school personnel administers medication, the delegating nurse shall provide supervision at the work site.

(5) The degree of supervision required for each student shall be determined by the school nurse after an evaluation of the appropriate factors involved in protecting the student's health, including but not limited to the following:

(a)   health condition and ability of the student;

(b)   the extent of training and capability of the unlicensed school personnel to whom the prescription medication administration is delegated;

(c)   the type of prescription medication; and

(d)   the proximity and availability of the school nurse to the unlicensed person who is performing the prescription medication administration.

(6)   For the individual child, the school nurse shall:

(a)   determine whether or not it is medically safe and appropriate to delegate prescription medication administration;

(b)   administer the first dose of the prescription medication, if:

1.   there is reason to believe there is a risk to the child as indicated by the health assessment; or

2.   the student has not previously received this prescription medication in any setting;

(c)   review the initial orders, possible side effects, adverse reactions and other pertinent information with the person to whom prescription medication administration has been delegated;

(d)   provide supervision and consultation as needed to ensure that the student is receiving the prescription medication appropriately. Supervision and consultation may include record review, on-site observation and/or assessment;

(e)   review all documentation pertaining to prescription medication administration on a biweekly basis or more often if necessary.

(H) In accordance with standard nursing practice, the school nurse may refuse to administer or allow to be administered any prescription medication which, based on her/his individual assessment and professional judgment, has the potential to be harmful, dangerous or inappropriate. In these cases, the parent/guardian and licensed prescriber shall be notified immediately by the school nurse.

(I) For the purposes of 105 CMR 210.000, a Licensed Practical Nurse functions under the general supervision of the school nurse who has delegating authority.

(J) The school nurse shall have a current pharmaceutical reference available for her/his use, such as the Physician's Desk Reference (P.D.R.) or U.S.P.DI (Dispensing Information), Facts and Comparisons.

210.006:

SELF-ADMINISTRATION OF PRESCRIPTION MEDICATIONS

(A) Consistent with school policy, students may self-administer prescription medication provided that certain conditions are met. For the purposes of 105 CMR 210.000, "self- administration" shall mean that the student is able to consume or apply prescription medication in the manner directed by the licensed prescriber, without additional assistance or direction.

(B) The school nurse may permit self-medication of prescription medication by a student provided that the following requirements are met:

(1)   the student, school nurse and parent/guardian, where appropriate, enter into an agreement which specifies the conditions under which prescription medication may be self- administered;

(2)   the school nurse, if appropriate, develops a medication administration plan (105 CMR 210.005(B)) which contains only those elements necessary to ensure safe self-administration of prescription medication;

(3)   the school nurse evaluates the student's health status and abilities and deems self-administration safe and appropriate. As necessary, the school nurse shall observe initial self-administration of the prescription medication;

(4)   the school nurse is reasonably assured that the student is able to identify the appropriate prescription medication, knows the frequency and time of day for which the prescription medication is ordered, and follows the school's self-administration protocols;

(5)   there is written authorization from the student's parent or guardian that the student may self-medicate, unless the student has consented to treatment under M.G.L. c. 112 § 12F or other authority permitting the student to consent to medical treatment without parental permission;

(6)   if requested by the school nurse, the licensed prescriber provides a written order for self-administration;

(7)   the student follows a procedure for documentation of self-administration of prescription medication;

(8)   the school nurse establishes a policy for the safe storage of self-administered prescription medication and, as necessary, consults with teachers, the student and parent/guardian, if appropriate, to determine a safe place for storing the prescription medication for the individual student, while providing for accessibility if the student's health needs require it. This information shall be included in the medication administration plan. In the case of an inhaler or other preventive or emergency medication, whenever possible, a back-up supply of the prescription medication shall be kept in the health room or a second readily available location;

(9)   the school nurse develops and implements a plan to monitor the student's self-administration, based on the student's abilities and health status. Monitoring may include teaching the student the correct way of taking the prescription medication, reminding the student to take the prescription medication, visual observation to ensure compliance, recording that the prescription medication was taken, and notifying the parent, guardian, or licensed prescriber of any side effects, variation from the plan, or the student's refusal or failure to take the prescription medication;

(10) with parental/guardian and student permission, as appropriate, the school nurse may inform appropriate teachers and administrators that the student is self-administering a prescription medication.

210.007:

TRAINING OF SCHOOL PERSONNEL RESPONSIBLE FOR ADMINISTERING PRESCRIPTION MEDICATIONS

(A) All prescription medications shall be administered by properly trained and supervised school personnel under the direction of the school nurse.

(B) Training shall be provided under the direction of the school nurse.

(C) At a minimum, the training program shall include content standards and a test of competency developed and approved by the Department of Public Health in consultation with the Board of Registration in Nursing and practicing school nurses.

(D) Personnel designated to administer prescription medications shall be provided with the names and locations of school personnel who have documented certification in cardiopulmonary resuscitation. Schools should make every effort to have a minimum of two school staff members with documented certification in cardiopulmonary resuscitation present in each school building throughout the day.

(E) The school nurse shall document the training and evidence of competency of unlicensed personnel designated to assume the responsibility for prescription medication administration.

(F) The school nurse shall provide a training review and informational update at least annually for those school staff authorized to administer prescription medications.

210.008:

HANDLING, STORAGE AND DISPOSAL OF PRESCRIPTION MEDICATIONS

(A) A parent, guardian or parent/guardian-designated responsible adult shall deliver all prescription medications to be administered by school personnel or to be taken by self-medicating students, if required by the self-administration agreement (105 CMR 210.006(B)), to the school nurse or other responsible person designated by the school nurse.

(1) The prescription medication must be in a pharmacy or manufacturer-labeled container.

(2) The school nurse or other responsible person receiving the prescription medication shall document the quantity of the prescription medication delivered.

(3) In extenuating circumstances, as determined by the school nurse, the prescription medication may be delivered by other persons; provided, however, that the nurse is notified in advance by the parent or guardian of the arrangement and the quantity of prescription medication being delivered to the school.

(B) All prescription medications shall be stored in their original pharmacy or manufacturer-labeled containers and in such manner as to render them safe and effective.

(C) All prescription medications to be administered by school personnel shall be kept in a securely locked cabinet used exclusively for medications, which is kept locked except when opened to obtain medications. The cabinet shall be substantially constructed and anchored securely to a solid surface. Prescription medications requiring refrigeration shall be stored in either a locked box in a refrigerator or in a locked refrigerator maintained at temperatures of 38°F to 42°F.

(D) Access to stored prescription medications shall be limited to persons authorized to administer prescription medications and to self-medicating students, to the extent permitted by school policy developed pursuant to 105 CMR 210.006(B)(8). Access to keys and knowledge of the location of keys shall be restricted to the maximum extent possible. Students who are self-medicating

shall not have access to other students' medications.

(E) Parents or guardians may retrieve the prescription medications from the school at any time.

(F) No more than a 30 school day supply of the prescription medication for a student shall be stored at the school.

(G) Where possible, all unused, discontinued or outdated prescription medications shall be returned to the parent or guardian and the return appropriately documented. In extenuating circumstances, with parental consent when possible, such prescription medications may be destroyed by the school nurse in accordance with any applicable policies of the Massachusetts Department of Public Health, Division of Food and Drugs.

210.009:

DOCUMENTATION AND RECORD-KEEPING

(A) Each school, where prescription medications are administered by school personnel, shall maintain a medication administration record for each student who receives prescription medication during school hours.

(1) Such record, at a minimum, shall include a daily log and a medication administration plan, including the medication order and parent/guardian authorization.

(2) The medication administration plan shall include the information as described in 105 CMR 210.005(E).

(3) The daily log shall contain:

   (a) the dose or amount of prescription medication administered;

   (b) the date and time of administration or omission of administration, including the reason for omission;

   (c) the full signature of the nurse or designated unlicensed school personnel administering the prescription medication. If the prescription medication is given more than once by the same person, he/she may initial the record, subsequent to signing a full signature.

(4) The school nurse shall document in the medication administration record significant observations of the prescription medication's effectiveness, as appropriate, and any adverse reactions or other harmful effects, as well as any action taken.

(5) All documentation shall be recorded in ink and shall not be altered.

(6) With the consent of the parent, guardian, or student where appropriate, the completed prescription medication administration record and records pertinent to self-administration shall be filed in the student's cumulative health record. When the parent, guardian or student, where appropriate, objects, these records shall be regarded as confidential medical notes and shall be kept confidential, except as provided in 105 CMR 210.000.

(B) Medication errors, as defined in 105 CMR 210.005(F)(5), shall be documented by the school nurse on an accident/incident report form. These reports shall be retained in a location as determined by school policy and made available to the Department of Public Health upon request. All suspected diversion or tampering of drugs shall be reported to the Department of Public Health, Division of Food and Drugs. All medication errors resulting in serious illness requiring medical care shall be reported to the Department of Public Health, Bureau of Family and Community Health.

(C) The school district shall comply with the Department of Public Health's reporting requirements for prescription medication administration in the schools.

(D) The Department of Public Health may inspect any individual student medication record or record relating to the administration or storage of prescription medications without prior notice to ensure compliance with 105 CMR 210.000.

210.100:

ADMINISTRATION OF EPINEPHRINE

A school or school district may register with the Department for the limited purpose of permitting properly trained school personnel to administer epinephrine by auto injector in a life threatening situation, when a school nurse is not immediately available, provided that the following conditions are met:

(A) the school committee or, in the case of a private school, the chief administrative officer, approves policies developed by the school nurse governing administration of epinephrine by auto injector, and renews approval every two years;

(B) the school committee or chief administrative officer provides an assurance to the Department that sufficient school nurses are available to provide oversight of the program, and provides such back-up documentation as required by the Department;

(C) in consultation with the school physician, the school nurse manages and has final decision making authority about the program and selects the persons authorized to administer epinephrine by auto injector;

(D) the school personnel authorized to administer epinephrine by auto injector are trained by a physician or school nurse, and tested for competency, in accordance with standards and a curriculum established by the Department;

    (1)   the school nurse shall document the training and testing of competency;

    (2)   the school nurse shall provide a training review and informational update at least twice a year;

    (3)   the training, at a minimum, shall include:

        (a)   proper use of the device;

        (b)   the importance of consulting and following the medication administration plan;

        (c)   recognition of the symptoms of a severe allergic reaction; and

        (d)   requirements for proper storage and security, notification of appropriate persons following administration, and record keeping;

    (4)   the school shall maintain and make available by parents or staff a list of those school personnel authorized and trained to administer epinephrine by auto injector in an emergency, when the school nurse is not immediately available;

(E) epinephrine shall be administered only in accordance with a medication administration plan satisfying the applicable requirements of 105 CMR 210.005(E) and 210.009(A)(6), updated every year, which includes the following:

    (1)   a diagnosis by a physician that the child is at high risk of a life threatening allergic reaction, and a medication order containing indications for administration of epinephrine;

    (2)   written authorization by a parent or guardian;

    (3)   a home and emergency number for the parents, as well as the name(s) and phone number(s) of any other person(s) to be notified if the parents are unavailable;

    (4)   identification of places where the epinephrine is to be stored, following consideration of the need for storage at places where the student may be most at risk. The epinephrine may be stored at more than one location or carried by the student when appropriate;

    (5)   consideration of the ways and places epinephrine can be stored so as to limit access to appropriate persons, which shall not require the epinephrine to be kept under lock and key;

    (6)   a list of the school personnel who would administer the epinephrine to the student in a life threatening situation;

    (7)   a plan for risk reduction for the student, including a plan for teaching self-management, where appropriate;

(F) when epinephrine is administered, there shall be immediate notification of the local emergency medical services system (generally 911), followed by notification of the school nurse, student's parents or, if the parents are not available, any other designated person(s), and the student's physician;

(G) there shall be procedures, in accordance with any standards established by the Department, for:

    (1)   developing the medication administration plan;

    (2)   properly storing medication, including limiting access to persons authorized to administer the medication and returning unused or outdated medication to a parent or guardian whenever possible;

    (3)   recording receipt and return of medication by the school nurse;

    (4)   documenting the date and time of administration;

    (5)   notifying appropriate parties of administration;

    (6)   reporting medication errors in accordance with 105 CMR 210.005(F)(5);

    (7)   reviewing any incident involving administration of epinephrine to determine the adequacy of the response and to consider ways of reducing risks for the particular student and the student body in general;

    (8)   planning and working with the emergency medical system to ensure the fastest possible response;

(H) the Department of Public Health is permitted to inspect any record related to the administration of epinephrine without prior notice, to ensure compliance with 105 CMR 210.100.

PART 2
Sample Medication Administration Policy—California

Used with permission: Ann F. Holler, 9/98.

The Governing Board recognizes that students may need to take prescribed medication during the school day in order to be able to attend school without jeopardizing their health or potential for learning. Federal and state laws support administration of medications to students while at school.

Section 504 of the Vocational Rehabilitation Act of 1973 (Public Law 93-112); Title II of the Americans with Disabilities Act of 1990 (Public Law 101-336); The Individuals with Disabilities Education Act (as amended by Public Law 105-17); Business & Professional Code 4051; Administration of Medication Letter, California Department of Education, September 1997; Administration of Medication at School, California School Nurses Organization.

All medications administered at school must be prescribed by a physician, licensed in California, even if they are purchased over the counter. The student's health care requirements shall be documented in an Individualized Health and Support Plan (for special education students) or in a Student Accommodation Plan under Section 504 (for other students). The family, credentialed school nurse and other support personnel will develop, evaluate and update an appropriate plan at least annually, or when changes to the prescription are made. The plan will become part of the student's health record.

NOTIFICATIONS

The Superintendent or designee shall inform parents/guardians of the following requirements related to medication administration and monitoring of health conditions at school:

> *Education Code*
> *49422 Medication at School*
> *49423 Authority for Assistance with Medication by the School Nurse*
> *49480 Continuing Medications*

Parent permission and physician authorization forms shall be completed for all medications, including those purchased over-the-counter. The student's physician must provide a written statement indicating the name of the medication, detailing the dose, method and time schedules by which the medication is to be taken. An individualized plan for the student will be developed using the District's Medication Authorization form with a copy kept in the student's health record.

> *Business & Professional Code*
> *2725 Verbal Orders*
> *4033 Definition of a Physician*
> *4036 Definition of a Lawful Prescription*

In addition, the parent/guardian shall provide the medication in a container labeled by a California pharmacist or, in the case of an over-the-counter medication, in the original container. The parent/guardian will deliver the medication to the school personally or send it with a designated adult. There may be an exception for students in special education programs for whom arrangements have been made with the bus driver or other adult transportation provider. Students with consent to self-administer medication may transport their own medication to school.

> *Business & Professional Code 4051 Restrictions on Furnishing Medications without Prescription*

The credentialed school nurse or designated school employee shall maintain a current, confidential list of students needing medication during regular school hours, including students with life-threatening conditions who carry injectable medication. This list shall be available on a need-to-know basis to appropriate school staff, along with emergency measures for allergic and anaphylactic reactions.

> *Cf. 3530 Risk Management/Insurance*
> *Cf. 5141.24 Specialized Health Care Services*
> *FERPA Confidentiality of School Records*

ADMINISTERING MEDICATIONS

All students shall receive necessary services and support from personnel who have been appropriately trained by a credentialed school nurse, public health nurse or physician. A Plan shall be mutually developed by the school nurse or designee and the family, based on the health care provider's order, as stated on the Medication Authorization and Plan. Parents or a designated staff member shall administer medications according to the physician's indicated dosage schedule and follow the Medication Authorization and Plan. A parent may come to school to administer medication on a pre-arranged schedule. The same Medication Authorization and Plan applies to medications administered during field trips and sanctioned off-campus events. The medication(s) shall be in the safe-keeping of the designated school employee or the student with a self-administration order, and shall be dispensed according to the Medication Authorization and Plan.

SELF-ADMINISTRATION OF MEDICATIONS

Under certain circumstances students may self-administer medications. Injectable epinephrine for anaphylactic reactions shall be supplied in the form of an Epi-Pen to facilitate safe, consistent administration. Students who need medication while at school may carry medication (such as asthma inhalers, insulin, severe allergic reaction injections—Epi-Pen and anti-convulsives) and self-administer such medication under the supervision of school personnel, provided the following conditions are met: (1) the student is physically, mentally, and behaviorally capable, in the written opinion of the parent, physician, and the credentialed school nurse, to assume that responsibility and has been adequately instructed at home; (2) the medication is necessary to the student's health and must be taken during school hours; (3) the student has successfully demonstrated self-administration of the medication to the school nurse; and (4) supervision is provided by the credentialed school nurse, when available, or by designated school personnel.

DOCUMENTING MEDICATIONS ADMINISTERED

The student's Medication Authorization and Plan shall be maintained with an individual medication log used to record medication dispensed at school. This log documents all medications administered to the student and serves as protection for both the district and the student. A copy of the Medication Authorization and Plan shall be kept in the student's Health Record.

TRAINING PERSONNEL ADMINISTERING MEDICATIONS

All students shall receive necessary services and support from personnel who are authorized, trained, and supervised in administering medications to students in school. A credentialed school nurse shall conduct an annual in-service instruction for any staff member who will be administering medication. The in-service shall include the following topics:

1. Name of medication and dose
2. Method of administration and universal precautions
3. Time and circumstances medication should be given
4. Contraindications, possible signs and symptoms of adverse effects, omission or overdose
5. Proper handling, storage, circumstances for administration and record keeping
6. Emergency procedures

Education Resource: Medication Administration in Schools–Training Manual and Video, California School Nurses Organization

DISPOSING OF UNUSED MEDICATIONS

If the medication changes during the school year, the remaining medication shall be given to the parent or guardian at the time of the delivery of the new medication. Medication remaining at the end of the school year shall be taken home by the parent or guardian. Any medication not claimed shall be discarded as recommended by the local health officer and appropriate OSHA guidelines. The medication log and Authorization and Plan form shall be placed in the student's health record.

Appendix M
FERPA Regulations and Model Notice

PART 1
Family Educational Rights and Privacy Act—Regulations

[GENERAL OUTLINE:]

34 CFR Part 99

Subpart A—General

Section

Subpart B—What Are the Rights of Inspection and Review of Education Records?

Section

Subpart C—What Are the Procedures for Amending Education Records?

Section

Subpart D—May an Educational Agency or Institution Disclose Personally Identifiable Information From Education Records?

Section

Subpart E—What Are the Enforcement Procedures?

Section

[SPECIFIC POINTS:]

Subpart A—General

§ 99.1 To which educational agencies or institutions do these regulations apply?

(a) Except as otherwise noted in § 99.10, this part applies to an educational agency or institution to which funds have been made available under any program administered by the Secretary, if —

    (1)   The educational institution provides educational services or instruction, or both, to students; or

    (2)   The educational agency provides administrative control of

or direction of, or performs service functions for, public elementary or secondary schools or postsecondary institutions.

(b) This part does not apply to an educational agency or institution solely because students attending that agency or institution receive non-monetary benefits under a program referenced in paragraph (a) of this section, if no funds under that program are made available to the agency or institution.

(c) The Secretary considers funds to be made available to an educational agency or institution if funds under one or more of the programs referenced in paragraph (a) of this section—

  (1) Are provided to the agency or institution by grant, cooperative agreement, contract, subgrant, or subcontract; or

  (2) Are provided to students attending the agency or institution and the funds may be paid to the agency or institution by those students for educational purposes, such as under the Pell Grant Program and the Guaranteed Student Loan Program (Title IV-A-1 and IV-B, respectively, of the Higher Education Act of 1965, as amended).

(d) If an educational agency or institution receives funds under one or more of the programs covered by this section, the regulations in this part apply to the recipient as a whole, including each of its components (such as a department within a university).
(Authority: 20 U.S.C. 1232g)

§ 99.2 What is the purpose of these regulations?

The purpose of this part is to set our requirements for the protection of privacy of parents and students under section 444 of the General Education Provisions Act, as amended.
(Authority: 20 U.S.C. 1232g)

NOTE: 34 CFR 300.560.576 contain requirements regarding confidentiality of information relating to handicapped children who receive benefits under the Education of the Handicapped Act.

§ 99.3 What definitions apply to these regulations?

The following definitions apply to this part:

"Act" means the Family Educational Rights and Privacy Act of 1974, as amended, enacted as section 444 of the General Education Provisions Act.
(Authority: 20 U.S. C. 1232g)

"Attendance" includes, but is not limited to:
(a)   Attendance in person or by correspondence; and
(b)   The period during which a person is working under a work-study program.
(Authority: 20 U.S.C. 1232g)

"Directory information" means information contained in an education record of a student which would not generally be considered harmful or an invasion of privacy if disclosed. It includes, but is not limited to the student's name, address, telephone listing, date and place of birth, major field of study, participation in officially recognized activities and sports, weight and height of members of athletic teams, dates of

attendance, degrees and awards received, and the most recent previous educational agency or institution attended.
(Authority: 20 U.S.C. 1232g(a) (5) (A))

"Disciplinary action or proceeding" means the investigation, adjudication, or imposition of sanctions by an educational agency or institution with respect to an infraction or violation of the internal rules of conduct applicable to students of the agency or institution.

"Disclosure" means to permit access to or the release, transfer, or other communication of personally identifiable information contained in education records to any party, by any means, including oral, written, or electronic means.
(Authority: 20 U.S.C. 1232g(b) (1))

"Educational agency or institution" means any public or private agency or institution to which this part applies under § 99.1(a).
(Authority: 20 U.S.C. 1232g (a) (3))

"Education records"
(a)   The term means those records that are:
  (1)   Directly related to a student; and
  (2)   Maintained by an educational agency or institution or by a party acting for the agency or institution.
(b)   The term does not include:
  (1)   Records of instructional, supervisory, and administrative personnel and educational personnel ancillary to those persons that are kept in the sole possession of the maker of the record, and are not accessible or revealed to any other person except a temporary substitute for the maker of the record;
  (2)   Records of the law enforcement unit of an educational agency or institution, subject to the provisions of § 99.8.
  (3)(i) Records relating to an individual who is employed by an educational agency or institution, that:
    (A) Are made and maintained in the normal course of business;
    (B) Relate exclusively to the individual in that individual's capacity as an employee, and
    (C) Are not available for use for any other purpose.
  (ii) Records relating to an individual in attendance at the agency or institution who is employed as a result of his or her status as a student are education records and not excepted under paragraph (b) (3) (i) of this definition.
  (4)   Records on a student who is 18 years of age or older, or is attending an institution of postsecondary education, that are:
  (i)   Made or maintained by a physician, psychiatrist, psychologist, or other recognized professional or paraprofessional acting in his or her professional capacity or assisting in a paraprofessional capacity.
  (ii) Made, maintained, or used only in connection with treatment of the student; and

(iii) Disclosed only to individuals providing the treatment. For the purpose of this definition, "treatment" does not include remedial educational activities or activities that are part of the program of instruction at the agency or institution; and

(5) Records that only contain information about an individual after he or she is no longer a student at that agency or institution.

(Authority: 20 U.S.C. 1232g(a) (4))

"Eligible student" means a student who has reached 18 years of age or is attending an institution of postsecondary education.
(Authority: 20 U.S.C. 1232g (d))

"Institution of postsecondary education" means an institution that provides education to students beyond the secondary school level; "secondary school level" means the educational level (not beyond grade 12) at which secondary education is provided as determined under State law.
(Authority: 20 U.S.C. 1232g (d))

"Parent" means a parent of a student and includes a natural parent, a guardian, or an individual acting as a parent in the absence of a parent or a guardian.
(Authority: 20 U.S.C. 1232g)

"Party" means an individual, agency, institution, or organization.
(Authority: 20 U.S.C. 1232g (b) (4) (A))

"Personally identifiable information" includes, but is not limited to:
(a) The student's name;
(b) The name of the student's parent or other family member;
(c) The address of the student or student's family;
(d) A personal identifier, such as the student's social security number or student number;
(e) A list of personal characteristics that would make the student's identity easily traceable; or
(f) Other information that would make the student's identity easily traceable.
(Authority: 20 U.S.C. 1232g)

"Record" means any information recorded in any way, including, but not limited to, handwriting, print, computer media, video or audio tape, film, microfilm, and microfiche.
(Authority: 20 U.S.C. 1232g)

"Secretary" means the Secretary of the U.S. Department of Education or an official or employee of the Department of Education acting for the Secretary under a delegation of authority.
(Authority: 20 U.S.C. 1232g)

"Student," except as otherwise specifically provided in this part, means any individual who is or has been in attendance at an educational agency or institution and regarding whom the agency or institution maintains education records.
(Authority: 20 U.S.C. 1232g (a) (6))

§ 99.4 What are the rights of parents?

An educational agency or institution shall give full rights under the Act to either parent, unless the agency or institution has been provided with evidence that there is a court order, State statute, or legally binding document relating to such matters as divorce, separation, or custody that specifically revokes these rights.
(Authority: 20 U.S.C. 1232g)

§ 99.5 What are the rights of students?

(a) When a student becomes an eligible student, the rights accorded to, and consent required of, parents under this part transfer from the parents to the student.
(b) The Act and this part do not prevent educational agencies or institutions from giving students rights in addition to those given to parents.
(c) If an individual is or has been in attendance at one component of an educational agency or institution, that attendance does not give the individual rights as a student in other components of the agency or institution to which the individual has applied for admission, but has never been in attendance.
(Authority: 20 U.S.C. 1232g (d))

§ 99.7 What must an educational agency or institution include in its annual notification?

(a) (1)   Each educational agency or institution shall annually notify parents of students currently in attendance, or eligible students currently in attendance, of their rights under the Act and this part.

(2)   The notice must inform parents or eligible students that they have the right to—

(i)   Inspect and review the student's education records;

(ii) Seek amendment of the student's education records that the parent or eligible student believes to be inaccurate, misleading, or otherwise in violation of the student's privacy rights;

(iii) Consent to disclosures of personally identifiable information contained in the student's education records, except to the extent that the Act and § 99.31 authorize disclosure without consent; and

(iv) File with the Department a complaint under § 99. 63 and 99.64 concerning alleged failures by the educational agency or institution to comply with the requirements of the act and this part.

(3)   The notice must include all of the following:

(i)   The procedure for exercising the right to inspect and review education records.

(ii) The procedure for requesting amendment of records under § 99.20.

(iii) If the educational agency or institution has a policy of disclosing education records under § 99.31 (a) (1), a specification of criteria for determining who constitutes a school official and what constitutes a legitimate educational interest.

(b) An educational agency or institution may provide this notice by any means that are reasonably likely to inform the parents or eligible students of their rights.

(1)   An educational agency or institution shall effectively notify parents or eligible students who are disabled.

(2)   An agency or institution of elementary or secondary education shall effectively notify parents who have a primary or home language other than English.
(Approved by the Office of Management and Budget under control number 1880-0508).
(Authority: 20 U.S.C. 1232g (e) and (f)).

§ 99.8 What provisions apply to records of a law enforcement unit?

(a) (1)   "Law enforcement unit" means any individual, office, department, division, or other component of an educational agency or institution, such as a unit of commissioned police officers or non-commissioned security guards, that is officially authorized or designated by that agency or institution to—
   (i)   Enforce any local, State, or Federal law, or refer to appropriate authorities a matter for enforcement of any local, State, or Federal law against any individual or organization other than the agency or institution itself; or
   (ii)   Maintain the physical security and safety of the agency or institution.
   (3)   A component of an educational agency or institution does not lose its status as a "law enforcement unit" if it also performs other, non-law enforcement functions for the agency or institution, including investigation of incidents or conduct that constitutes or leads to a disciplinary action or proceeding against the student.
(b) (1)   Records of law enforcement unit means those records, files, documents, and other materials that are—
   (i)   Created by a law enforcement unit;
   (ii)   Created for a law enforcement purpose; and
   (iii) Maintained by the law enforcement unit.
   (3)   Records of law enforcement unit does not mean—
   (i)   Records created by a law enforcement unit for a law enforcement purpose that are maintained by a component of the educational agency or institution other than the law enforcement unit; or
   (ii)   Records created and maintained by a law enforcement unit exclusively for a non-law enforcement purpose, such as a disciplinary action or proceeding conducted by the educational agency or institution.
(c) (1)   Nothing in the Act prohibits an educational agency or institution from contacting its law enforcement unit, orally or in writing, for the purpose of asking that unit to investigate a possible violation of, or to enforce, any local, State, or Federal law.
   (2)   Education records, and personally identifiable information contained in education records, do not lose their status as education records and remain subject to the Act, including the disclosure provisions of § 99.30, while in possession of the law enforcement unit.
(c) The Act neither requires nor prohibits the disclosure by any educational agency or institution of its law enforcement unit records.
(Authority: 20 U.S.C. 1232g (a) (4) (B) (ii))

SUBPART B—WHAT ARE THE RIGHTS OF INSPECTION AND REVIEW OF EDUCATION RECORDS?

§ 99.10 What rights exist for a parent or eligible student to inspect and review education records?

(a) Except as limited under § 99.12, a parent or eligible student must be given the opportunity to inspect and review the student's education records.
This provision applies to—
   (1)   Any educational agency or institution; and
   (2)   Any State educational agency (SEA) and its components.
      (i)   For the purposes of subpart B of this part, an SEA and its components constitute an educational agency or institution.
      (ii)   An SEA and its components are subject to subpart B of this part if the SEA maintains education records on students who are, or have been, in attendance at any school of an educational agency or institution subject to the Act and this part.
(b) The educational agency or institution, or SEA or its component, shall comply with a request for access to records within a reasonable period of time, but not more than 45 days after it has received the request.
(c) The educational agency or institution, or SEA or its component, shall respond to reasonable requests for explanations and interpretations of the records.
(d) If circumstances effectively prevent the parent or eligible student from exercising the right to inspect and review the student's education records, the educational agency or institution, or SEA or its component, shall—
   (1)   Provide the parent or eligible student with a copy of the records requested; or
   (2)   Make other arrangements for the parent or eligible student to inspect and review the requested records.
(e) The educational agency or institution, or SEA or its component, shall not destroy any education records if there is an outstanding request to inspect and review the records under this section.
(f) While an education agency or institution is not required to give an eligible student access to treatment records under paragraph (b) (4) of the definition of "Education records" in § 99.3, the student may have those records reviewed by a physician or other appropriate professional of the student's choice.
(Authority: 20 U.S.C. 1232g (a) (1) (A) and (B))

§ 99.11 May an educational agency or institution charge a fee for copies of education records?

(a) Unless the imposition of a fee effectively prevents a parent or eligible student from exercising the right to inspect and review the student's education records, an educational agency or institution may charge a fee for a copy of an education record which is made for the parent or eligible student.
(b) An educational agency or institution may not charge a fee to search for or to retrieve the education records of a student.
(Authority: 20 U.S.C. 1232g (a) (1))

§ 99.12   What limitations exist on the right to inspect and review records?

(a) If the education records of a student contain information on more than one student, the parent or eligible student may inspect and review or be informed of only the specific information about that student.

(b) A postsecondary institution does not have to permit a student to inspect and review education records that are:

    (1)   Financial records, including any information those records contain, of his or her parents;

    (2)   Confidential letters and confidential statements of recommendation placed in the education records of the student before January 1, 1975, as long as the statements are used only for the purposes for which they were specifically intended; and

    (3)   Confidential letters and confidential statements of recommendation placed in the students education records after January 1, 1975, if:

        (i)   The student has waived his or her right to inspect and review those letters and statements; and

        (ii)   Those letters and statements are related to the student's:

            (A)   Admission to an educational institution;

            (B)   Application for employment; or

            (C)   Receipt of an honor or honorary recognition.

(c) (1)   A waiver under paragraph (b) (3) (i) of this section is valid only if:

        (i)   The educational agency or institution does not require the waiver as a condition for admission to or receipt of a service or benefit from the agency or institution; and

        (ii)   The waiver is made in writing and signed by the student, regardless of age.

    (2)   If a student has waived his or her rights under paragraph (b) (3) (i) of this section, the educational institution shall:

        (i)   Give the student, on request, the names of the individuals who provided the letters and statements of recommendation; and

        (ii)   Use the letters and statements of recommendation only for the purpose for which they were intended.

    (3) (i) A waiver under paragraph (b) (3) (i) of this section may be revoked with respect to any actions occurring after the revocation.

        (ii)   A revocation under paragraph (c) (3) (i) of this section must be in writing.

(Authority: 20 U.S.C. 1232g (a) (1) (A), (B), (C), and (D))

SUBPART C—WHAT ARE THE PROCEDURES FOR AMENDING EDUCATION RECORDS?

§ 99.20   How can a parent or eligible student request amendment of the student's education records?

(a) If a parent or eligible student believes the education records relating to the student contain information that is inaccurate, misleading, or in violation of the student's rights of privacy, he or she may ask the educational agency or institution to amend the record.

(b) The educational agency or institution shall decide whether to amend the record as requested within a reasonable time after the agency or institution receives the request.

(c) If the educational agency or institution decides not to amend the record as requested, it shall inform the parent or eligible student of its decision and of his or her right to a hearing under § 99.21.

(Authority: 20 U.S.C. 1232g (a) (2))

§ 99.21   Under what conditions does a parent or eligible student have the right to a hearing?

(a) An educational agency or institution shall give a parent or eligible student, on request, an opportunity for a hearing to challenge the content of the student's education records on the grounds that the information contained in the education records is inaccurate, misleading, or in violation of the privacy rights of the student.

(b) (1)   If, as a result of the hearing, the educational agency or institution decides that the information is inaccurate, misleading, or otherwise in violation of the privacy rights of the student, it shall:

        (i)   Amend the record accordingly; and

        (ii)   Inform the parent or eligible student of the amendment in writing.

    (2)   If, as a result of the hearing, the educational agency or institution decides that the information in the education record is not inaccurate, misleading, or otherwise in violation of the privacy rights of the student, it shall inform the parent or eligible student of the right to place a statement in the record commenting on the contested information in the record or stating why he or she disagrees with the decision of the agency or institution, or both.

(c) If an educational agency or institution places a statement in the education records of a student under paragraph (b) (2) of this section, the agency or institution shall:

    (1)   Maintain the statement with the contested part of the record for as long as the record is maintained; and

    (2)   Disclose the statement whenever it discloses the portion of the record to which the statement relates.

(Authority: 20 U.S.C. 1232g (a) (2))

§ 99.22   What minimum requirements exist for the conduct of a hearing?

The hearing required by § 99.21 must meet, at a minimum, the following requirements:

(a) The educational agency or institution shall hold the hearing within a reasonable time after it has received the request for the hearing from the parent or eligible student.

(b) The educational agency or institution shall give the parent or eligible student notice of the date, time, and place, reasonably in advance of the hearing.

(c) The hearing may be conducted by any individual, including an official of the educational agency or institution, who does not have a direct interest in the outcome of the hearing.

(d) The educational agency or institution shall give the parent or eligible student a full and fair opportunity to present evidence relevant to the issues raised under § 99.21. The parent or eligible student may, at their own expense, be assisted or represented by one or more individuals of his or her own choice, including an attorney.

(e) The educational agency or institution shall make its decision in writing within a reasonable period of time after the hearing.

(f) The decision must be based solely on the evidence presented at the hearing, and must include a summary of the evidence and the reasons for the decision.

(Authority: 20 U.S.C. 1232g (a) (2))

SUBPART D—MAY AN EDUCATIONAL AGENCY OR INSTITUTION DISCLOSE PERSONALLY IDENTIFIABLE INFORMATION FROM EDUCATION RECORDS?

§ 99.30 Under what conditions is prior consent required to disclose information?

(a) The parent or eligible student shall provide a signed and dated written consent before an educational agency or institution discloses personally identifiable information from the student's education records, except as provided in § 99.31.

(b) The written consent must:

(1)   Specify the records that may be disclosed;

(2)   State the purpose of the disclosure; and

(3)   Identify the party or class of parties to whom the disclosure may be made.

(c) When a disclosure is made under paragraph (a) of this section:

(1)   If a parent or eligible student so requests, the educational agency or institution shall provide him or her with a copy of the records disclosed; and

(2)   If the parent of a student who is not an eligible student so requests, the agency or institution shall provide the student with a copy of the records disclosed.

(Authority: 20 U.S.C. 1232g (b) (1) and (b) (2) (A))

§ 99.31 Under what conditions is prior consent not required to disclose information?

(a) An educational agency or institution may disclose personally identifiable information from an education record of a student without the consent required by § 99.30 if the disclosure meets one or more of the following conditions:

(1)   The disclosure is to other school officials, including teachers, within the agency or institution whom the agency or institution has determined to have legitimate educational interests.

(2)   The disclosure is, subject to the requirements of § 99.35, to authorized representatives of:

(i)   The Comptroller General of the United States;

(ii)   The Secretary; or

(iii)   State and local educational authorities.

(4) (i)   The disclosure is in connection with financial aid for which the student has applied or which the student has received, if the information is necessary for such purposes as to:

(A)   Determine eligibility for the aid;

(B)   Determine the amount of the aid;

(C)   Determine the conditions for the aid; or

(D)   Enforce the terms and conditions of the aid.

(ii)   As used in paragraph (a) (4) (i) of this section, "financial aid" means a payment of funds provided to an individual (or a payment in kind of tangible or intangible property to the individual) that is conditioned on the individual's attendance at an educational agency or institution.

(Authority: 20 U.S.C. 1232g (b) (1) (D))

(5) (i)   The disclosure is to State and local officials or authorities to whom this information is specifically—

(A)   Allowed to be reported or disclosed pursuant to a State statute adopted before November 19, 1974, if the allowed reporting or disclosure concerns the juvenile justice system and the system's ability to effectively serve the student whose records are released; or

(B)   Allowed to be reported or disclosed pursuant to a State statute adopted after November 19, 1974, subject to the requirements of § 99.38.

(ii)   Paragraph (a) (5) (1) of this section does not prevent a State from further limiting the number or type of State or local officials to whom disclosures may be made under that paragraph.

(6) (i)   The disclosure is to organizations conducting studies for, or on behalf of, educational agencies or institutions to:

(A)   Develop, validate, or administer predictive tests;

(B)   Administer student aid programs; or

(C)   Improve instruction.

(ii)   The agency or institution may disclose information under paragraph (a) (6) (i) of this section only if:

(A)   The study is conducted in a manner that does not permit personal identification of parents and students by individuals other than representatives of the organization; and

(B)   The information is destroyed when no longer needed for the purposes for which the study was conducted.

(iii)   If this Office determines that a third party outside the educational agency or institution to whom information is disclosed under this paragraph (a) (6) violated paragraph (a) (6) (ii) (B) of this section, the educational agency or institution may not allow that third party access to personally identifiable information from education records for at least five years.

(iv)   For the purposes of paragraph (a) (6) of this section, the term "organization" includes, but is not limited to, Federal, State, and local agencies, and independent organizations.

(7)   The disclosure is to accrediting organizations to carry out their accrediting functions.

(8)   The disclosure is to parents of a dependent student, as defined in section 152 of the Internal Revenue Code of 1954.

[Note: The above section should read "the Internal Revenue Code of 1986."]

(9) (i) The disclosure is to comply with a judicial order or lawfully issued subpoena.

    (ii) The educational agency or institution may disclose information under paragraph (a) (9) (i) of this section only if the agency or institution makes a reasonable effort to notify the parent or eligible student of the order or subpoena in advance of compliance, so that the parent or eligible student may seek protective action, unless the disclosure is in compliance with—

      (A) A Federal grand jury subpoena and the court has ordered that the existence or the contents of the subpoena or the information furnished in response to the subpoena not be disclosed; or

      (B) Any other subpoena issued for a law enforcement purpose and the court or other issuing agency has ordered that the existence or the contents of the subpoena or the information furnished in response to the subpoena not be disclosed.

    (iii) If the educational agency or institution initiates legal action against a parent or student and has complied with paragraph (a) (9) (ii) of this section, it may disclose the student's education records that are relevant to the action to the court without a court order or subpoena.

(10) The disclosure is in connection with a health or safety emergency, under the conditions described in § 99.36.

(11) The disclosure is information the educational agency or institution has designated as "directory information," under the conditions described in § 99.37.

(12) The disclosure is to the parent of a student who is not an eligible student or to the student.

(13) The disclosure is to an alleged victim of any crime of violence, as that term is defined in Section 16 of title 18, United States Code, of the results of any disciplinary proceeding conducted by an institution of postsecondary education against the alleged perpetrator of that crime with respect to that crime.

(b) This section does not forbid an educational agency or institution to disclose, nor does it require an educational agency or institution to disclose, personally identifiable information from the education records of a student to any parties under paragraphs (a) (1) through (11) and (13) of this section.

(Authority: 20 U.S.C. 1232g (a) (5) (A), (b) (1), (b) (2) (B), and (b) (6))

§ 99.32 What recordkeeping requirements exist concerning requests and disclosures?

(a) (1) An educational agency or institution shall maintain a record of each request for access to and each disclosure of personally identifiable information from the education records of each student.

(2) The agency or institution shall maintain the record with the education records of the student as long as the records are maintained.

(3) For each request or disclosure the record must include:

    (i) The parties who have requested or received person-

ally identifiable information from the education records; and

    (ii) The legitimate interests the parties had in requesting or obtaining the information.

(b) If an educational agency or institution discloses personally identifiable information from an education record with the understanding authorized under § 99.33(b), the record of the disclosure required under this section must include:

(1) The names of the additional parties to which the receiving party may disclose the information on behalf of the educational agency or institution; and

(2) The legitimate interests under § 99.31 which each of the additional parties has in requesting or obtaining this information.

(b) The following parties may inspect the record relating to each student:

(1) The parent or eligible student.

(2) The school official or his or her assistants who are responsible for the custody of the records.

(3) Those parties authorized in § 99.31 (a) (1) and (3) for the purposes of auditing the recordkeeping procedures of the educational agency or institution.

(d) Paragraph (a) of this section does not apply if the request was from, or the disclosure was to:

(1) The parent or eligible student;

(2) A school official under § 99.31 (a) (1);

(3) A party with written consent from the parent or eligible student;

(4) A party seeking directory information; or

(5) A party seeking or receiving the records as directed by a Federal grand jury or other law enforcement subpoena and the issuing court or other issuing agency has ordered that the existence or the contents of the subpoena or the information furnished in response to the subpoena not be disclosed.

(Approved by the Office of Management and Budget under control number 1880-0508)
(Authority: 20 U.S.C. 1232g (b) (1) and (b) (4) (A))

§ 99.33 What limitations apply to the redisclosure of information?

(a) (1) An educational agency or institution may disclose personally identifiable information from an education record only on the condition that the party to whom the information is disclosed will not disclose the information to any other party without the prior consent of the parent or eligible student.

(2) The officers, employees, and agents of a party that receives information under paragraph (a) (1) of this section may use the information, but only for the purposes for which the disclosure was made.

(b) Paragraph (a) of this section does not prevent an educational agency or institution from disclosing personally identifiable information with the understanding that the party receiving the information may make further disclosures of the information on behalf of the educational agency or institution if:

(1) The disclosures meet the requirements of § 99.31; and

(2) The educational agency or institution has complied with the requirements of § 99.32 (b).

(c) Paragraph (a) of this section does not apply to disclosures made pursuant to court orders or to lawfully issued subpoenas under § 99.31 (a) (9), to disclosures of directory information under § 99.31 (a) (11), or to disclosures to a parent or student under § 99.31 (a) (12).

(d) Except for disclosures under § 99.31 (a) (9), (11) and (12), an educational agency or institution shall inform a party to whom disclosure is made of the requirements of this section.

(e) If this Office determines that a third party improperly rediscloses personally identifiable information from education records in violation of § 99.33 (a) of this section, the educational agency or institution may not allow that third party access to personally identifiable information from education records for at least five years.

(Authority: 20 U.S.C. 1232g (b) (4) (B))

§ 99.34 What conditions apply to disclosure of information to other agencies or institutions?

(a) An educational agency or institution that discloses an education record under § 99.33 (a) (2) shall:
(1) Make a reasonable attempt to notify the parent or eligible student at the last known address of the parent or eligible student; or
  (i) The disclosure is initiated by the parent or eligible student; or
  (ii) The annual notification of the agency or institution under § 99.7 includes a notice that the agency or institution forwards education records to other agencies or institutions that have requested the records and in which the student seeks or intends to enroll:
(2) Give the parent or eligible student, upon request, a copy of the record that was disclosed; and
(3) Give the parent or eligible student, upon request, an opportunity for a hearing under subpart C.

(b) An educational agency or institution may disclose an education record of a student in attendance to another educational agency or institution if:
(1) The student is enrolled in or receives services from the other agency or institution; and
(2) The disclosure meets the requirements of paragraph (a) of this section.

(Authority: 20 U.S.C. 1232g (b) (1) (B))

§ 99.35 What conditions apply to disclosure of information for Federal or State program purposes?

(a) The officials listed in § 99.35(a) (3) may have access to education records in connection with an audit or evaluation of Federal or State supported education programs, or for the enforcement of or compliance with Federal legal requirements which relate to those programs.

(b) Information that is collected under paragraph (a) of this section must:
(1) Be protected in a manner that does not permit personal identification of individuals by anyone except the officials referred to in paragraph (a) of this section; and
(2) Be destroyed when no longer needed for the purposes listed in paragraph (a) of this section.

(c) Paragraph (b) of this section does not apply if:
(1) The parent or eligible student has given written consent for the disclosure under §99.30; or
(2) The collection or personally identifiable information is specifically authorized by Federal law.

(Authority: 20 U.S.C. 1232g (b) (3))

§ 99.36 What conditions apply to disclosure of information in health and safety emergencies?

(a) An educational agency or institution may disclose personally identifiable information from an education record to appropriate parties in connection with an emergency if knowledge of the information is necessary to protect the health or safety of the student or other individuals.

(b) Nothing in the Act or this part shall prevent an educational agency or institution from—
(1) Including in the education records of a student appropriate information concerning disciplinary action taken against the student for conduct that posed a significant risk to the safety or well-being of that student, other students, or other members of the school community;
(2) Disclosing appropriate information maintained under paragraph (b) (1) of this section to teachers and school officials within the agency or institution who the agency or institution has determined have legitimate educational interests in the behavior of the student; or
(3) Disclosing appropriate information maintained under paragraph (b) (1) of this section to teachers and school officials in other schools who have been determined to have legitimate educational interests in the behavior of the student.

(c) Paragraphs (a) and (b) of this section will be strictly construed.

(Authority: 20 U.S.C. 1232g (b) (1)(I) and (h))

§ 99.37 What conditions apply to disclosing directory information?

(a) An educational agency or institution may disclose directory information if it has given public notice to parents of students in attendance and eligible students in attendance at the agency or institution of:
(1) The types of personally identifiable information that the agency or institution has designated as directory information;
(2) A parent's or eligible student's right to refuse to let the agency or institution designate any or all of those types of information about the student as directory information; and
(3) The period of time within which a parent or eligible student has to notify the agency or institution in writing that he or she does not want any or all of those types of information about the student designated as directory information.

(b) An educational agency or institution may disclose directory information about former students without meeting the conditions in paragraph (a) of this section.

(Authority: 20 U.S.C. 1232g (a) (A) and (B))

§ 99.38 What conditions apply to disclosure of information as permitted by State statute adopted after November 19, 1974 concerning the juvenile justice system?

(a) If reporting or disclosure allowed by State statute concerns the juvenile justice system and the system's ability to effectively serve, prior to adjudication, the student whose records are released, an educational agency or institution may disclose education records under §99.31 (a) (5) (i) (B).

(b) The officials and authorities to whom the records are disclosed shall certify in writing to the educational agency or institution that the information will not be disclosed to any party, except as provided under State law, without the prior written consent of the parent of the student.

(Authority: 20 U.S.C. 1232g (b) (1) (J))

SUBPART E—WHAT ARE THE ENFORCEMENT PROCEDURES?

§ 99.60 What functions has the Secretary delegated to the Office and to the Office of Administrative Law Judges?

(a) For the purposes of this subpart, "Office" means the Family Policy Compliance Office, U.S. Department of Education.

(b) The Secretary designates the Office to:
  (1) Investigate, process, and review complaints and violations under the Act and this part; and
  (2) Provide technical assistance to ensure compliance with the Act and this part; and

(c) The Secretary designates the Office of Administrative Law Judges to act as the Review Board required under the Act to enforce the Act with respect to all applicable programs. The term "applicable program" is defined in section 400 of the General Education Provisions Act.

(Authority: 20 U.S.C. 1232g (f) and (g), 1234)

§ 99.61 What responsibility does an educational agency or institution have concerning conflict with State or local laws?

If an educational agency or institution determines that it cannot comply with the Act or this part due to a conflict with State or local law, it shall notify the Office within 45 days, giving the text and citation of the conflicting law.

(Authority: 20 U.S.C. 1232g (f))

§ 99.62 Where are complaints filed?

A parent or eligible student may file a written complaint with the Office regarding an alleged violation under the Act and this part. The Office's address is: Family Policy Compliance Office, U.S. Department of Education, Washington, D.C. 20202-4605.

(Authority: 20 U.S.C. 1232g (g))

§ 99.64 What is the complaint procedure?

(a) A complaint filed under § 99.63 must contain specific allegations of fact giving reasonable cause to believe that a violation of the Act or this part has occurred.

(b) The Office investigates each timely complaint to determine whether the educational agency or institution has failed to comply with the provisions of the Act or this part.

(c) A timely complaint is defined as an allegation of a violation of the Act that is submitted to the Office within 180 days of the date of the alleged violation or of the date that the complainant knew or reasonably should have known of the alleged violation.

(d) The Office extends the time limit in this section if the complainant shows that he or she was prevented by circumstances beyond the complainant's control from submitting the matter within the time limit, or for other reasons considered sufficient by the Office.

(Authority: 20 U.S.C. 1232g (f))

§ 99.65 What is the content of the notice of complaint issued by the Office?

(a) The Office notifies the complainant and the educational agency or institution in writing if it initiates an investigation of a complaint under § 99.64 (b).

(1) Includes the substance of the alleged violation; and

(2) Asks the agency or institution to submit a written response to the complaint.

(b) The Office notifies the complainant if it does not initiate an investigation of a complaint because the complaint fails to meet the requirements of § 99.64.

(Authority: 20 U.S.C. 1232g (g))

PART 2
Model Notification of Rights under FERPA for Elementary and Secondary Institutions

The Family Educational Rights and Privacy Act (FERPA) affords parents and students over 18 years of age ("eligible students") certain rights with respect to the student's education records. They are:

(1) The right to inspect and review the student's education records within 45 days of the day the District receives a request for access.

Parents or eligible students should submit to the school principal (or appropriate school official) a written request that identifies the record(s) they wish to inspect. The principal will make arrangements for access and notify the parent or eligible student of the time and place where the records may be inspected.

(2) The right to request the amendment of the student's education records that the parent or eligible student believes are inaccurate or misleading.

Parents or eligible students may ask *Alpha School District* to amend a record that they believe is inaccurate or misleading. They should write the school principal, clearly identify the part of the record they want changed, and specify why it is inaccurate or misleading.

If the District decides not to amend the record as requested by the parent or eligible student, the District will notify the parent or eligible student of the decision and advise them of their right to a hearing regarding the request for amendment. Additional information regarding the hearing procedures will be provided to the parent or eligible student when notified of the right to a hearing.

(3) The right to consent to disclosures of personally identifiable information contained in the student's education records, except to the extent that FERPA authorizes disclosure without consent.

One exception which permits disclosure without consent is disclosure to school officials with legitimate educational inter-ests. A school official is a person employed by the District as an administrator, supervisor, instructor, or support staff member (including health or medical staff and law enforcement unit personnel); a person serving on the School Board; a person or company with whom the District has contracted to perform a special task (such as an attorney, auditor, medical consultant, or therapist); or a parent or student serving on an official committee, such as a disciplinary or grievance committee, or assisting another school official in performing his or her tasks.

A school official has a legitimate educational interest if the official needs to review an education record in order to fulfill his or her professional responsibility.

[Optional] Upon request, the District discloses education records without consent to officials of another school district in which a student seeks or intends to enroll. [NOTE: FERPA requires a school district to make a reasonable attempt to notify the parent or student of the records unless it states in its annual notification that it intends to forward records on request.]

(4) The right to file a complaint with the U.S. Department of Education concerning alleged failures by the District to comply with the requirements of FERPA. The name and address of the Office that administers FERPA are:

> Family Policy Compliance Office
> U.S. Department of Education
> 600 Independence Avenue, SW
> Washington, DC 20202-4605

[NOTE: In addition, a school may want to include its directory information public notice, as required by § 99.37 of the regulations, with its annual notification of rights under FERPA.]

Appendix N

Proposed Guidelines for Policy and Practice: Confidentiality of Student Information

Used with permission: Connecticut Committee on Confidentiality of Student Health Information. (1996). *Proposed Guidelines for Policy and Practice: Confidentiality of Student Information* (Draft Document).

Policy Statement

Student information[1] as defined herein must be protected from unethical, illegal and inappropriate disclosure through universal adherence to the principles of confidentiality and privacy by all employees and volunteers of education agencies in the State of Connecticut. Confidential information, unless otherwise defined, is information the disclosure of which would, or would be likely to, constitute an invasion of personal privacy. Accordingly, confidential information concerning a student[2] or student's family must be protected by all personnel in public school districts, approved private programs for special education and Birth To Three, Regional Education Service Centers (RESCs), Regional Family Service Coordination Centers (RFSCCs) and the Department of Education. Confidential student information must be protected regardless of how or where the information is obtained, that is, whether it is obtained through oral, printed or electronic means, on or beyond school or agency grounds, and regardless of what type of record, record-keeping, or method of record-storage is used. The requirements of confidentiality apply to all student information including, but not limited to, academic, family, social, economic, and health information,[3] and to information which is provided orally or electronically, and not solely information contained in "school records."

General Rules Prohibiting Disclosure

Confidentiality of student information is based on legal and ethical precepts derived from constitutional law, federal and state mandates related to health and education, and the ethical standards for health and education professionals. The general rules prohibiting disclosure of student information include the following:

1. *The right to privacy.* This precept can generally be defined as the right to be left alone, with the corollary that certain personal information belongs to the individual who has the right to decide whether that information should be disclosed to others. It further refers to the individual's expectation that information he or she voluntarily discloses to another will not be further disclosed. The right to privacy is founded on federal and state constitutional law, statutes and common law principles.

   Family and Student Privacy. A federal law based on this precept, the Family Education Rights and Privacy Act[4] (FERPA), protects the privacy of students and parents by restricting access to, and guaranteeing the confidentiality of, education records.[5] FERPA defines specific rights of parents and eligible students (students who have reached the age of 18 years) regarding their access to, and the confidentiality of, education records. Student health information which is recorded by any school personnel, including school nurses, school social workers and school health paraprofessionals, and student health information which has been provided to the school by outside health care providers, are considered "education records" within the protection of FERPA.

2. *Provider-client confidentiality.* Provider[6]-client[7] confidentiality means that information gained in the course of the provider-client relationship should not be revealed without the client's consent, unless compelled by law. The belief that a client is more likely to disclose all of the relevant information necessary for proper diagnosis and treatment if he or she knows that private facts will be held in confidence was derived from practice in the earliest days of the medical profession. That concept forms the basis for the client-confidentiality standards incorporated into:

   - the ethical codes of practice for all health professionals, regardless of their practice setting;
   - standards for health care institutions and agencies;
   - relevant state mandates, including minors' rights to seek treatment for certain conditions, and common law principles; and
   - relevant federal statutes and regulations regarding treatment, counseling or assessment and referral of persons, including students, who are receiving alcohol and drug abuse services.[8]

   Accordingly, the health care professional's obligation to maintain client confidentiality extends to all employees and volunteers of health care provider organizations and private practices.

3. *Provider-client privilege.* Established through specific state statutes, this privilege is the right of the client in a judicial proceeding to exclude from evidence confidential communications made to a provider in the course of diagnosis or treatment. In Connecticut, physicians, other licensed health providers and social workers, among others, are prohibited by statute from disclosing such confidential communications without the explicit consent of the

---

[1] Refer to definitions, page 604.
[2] See footnote 1 above.
[3] See footnote 1 above.
[4] 34 C.F.R Part 99
[5] See footnote 1 above.
[6] See footnote 1 above.
[7] See footnote 1 above.
[8] 42 U.S.C. Sec. 290dd-3; U.S.C. Sec. 290ee-3; 42 CFR Part 2.

client, except in specific circumstances (See Connecticut General Statutes [C.G.S.] Sec. 52-146a to 52-146q, inclusive).

Because in the course of their responsibilities, education, health, and early intervention personnel, including volunteers, have access to confidential student and family information, they have a responsibility to ensure that such information is maintained according to the ethical and legal standards of confidentiality. These ethical and legal principles are explicitly recognized in the codes of ethics of national and state teacher, pupil services specialists, and health professional organizations,' and in the "Code of Professional Responsibilities for Teachers," Connecticut Regulations, Section 10-145d-400a.

Confidentiality Practices for Agencies

The following practices regarding the confidentiality of student information should be implemented by all agencies[9] that provide educational services:

- Each agency should have explicit written policies on the confidentiality of student information which may be coordinated or integrated with its student records policies, and which distinguish between categories of internal and external communications, and confidential and non-confidential information.

- Agency policies should include consequences for personnel who fail to act according to the policies.

- Agency policies should require contract personnel (those who work for another organization but are under contract to the agency) to observe the same policies and procedures regarding the confidentiality of student information as other personnel.

- All personnel should be held to the same standard.

- All personnel should be required to sign a "Confidentiality Statement Regarding Student Information"[10] following orientation as a new staff member.

- All personnel, whether employees, contract personnel or volunteers, should receive annual training that includes the principles of confidentiality, relevant policies and procedures, and a review of the "Confidentiality Statement Regarding Student Information" which they signed when first employed.

- When state or federal law further restricts the sharing of specific information, such as the HIV status of a student,[11] the agency's policies and procedures must clearly delineate additional procedures and safeguards that personnel must adhere to in order to protect that information.

- Agencies should regularly evaluate their policies, procedures and practices related to confidentiality for accuracy, clarity, completeness, compliance and efficacy.

Confidentiality Practices for Personnel

General practices related to internal communications, that is, communications among personnel within the same agency, include, but are not limited to, the following:

- Printed, electronic and oral information about students should

be shared internally (unless otherwise prohibited by law) only with other personnel who have an explicit need to know[12] for the benefit of the student, not for the benefit of the provider.

- Only information necessary to provide appropriate services to a student is to be shared.

- The recipient of student information will protect the information from disclosure (for example, a teacher who knows of a student's psychiatric condition is not permitted to share that information with other teachers or anyone else other than appropriate school personnel, i.e., school health and mental health professionals).

- Information about one student is not to be shared with another student or parent unless an imminent life-threatening situation exists, and there is no reasonable alternative.

- Parents should be informed that information made available by a parent will be shared with other agency personnel who need to know the information in order to provide appropriate services for their child and that all agency personnel are obligated to protect student information from disclosure.

- The parameters of confidentiality and the agency's policies regarding internal and external communications should always be clearly explained to students and parents.

- Discussions concerning confidential information should take place in secure locations, not on elevators or playgrounds, in stairwells, halls, teachers' rooms, public gathering places or parking lots, or elsewhere where others may overhear.

- Confidential written documentation or notes of oral confidential communications should be marked "confidential" and stored in secure locations. When in use, such documentation should be shielded from the view of others, and should not be left out unattended.

- Confidential information should not be left as a message with a secretary, on a voice mail or on an electronic mail system.

- Confidential information that must be mailed or carried should be placed in an envelope marked "CONFIDENTIAL."

- Confidential information to be discarded should be shredded or otherwise disposed of securely.

Confidentiality Practices Between Agencies

Appropriate practices related to confidentiality between personnel in an agency and another institution, such as a school-based health center, or third party include, but are not limited to, the following:

- Written consent of the parent or, where applicable, the student must be obtained before requesting or sharing student or family information with representatives of outside institutions or third parties unless otherwise allowed by law.

- When it is appropriate for professional personnel to consult with an outside expert, it may be acceptable to consult about the situation of a particular student so long as it is done in a manner that protects the identity of the student and the family, that is, by withholding the student's name, address, birthdate or any other identifying data. In other words, relevant information must be

---

[9] Refer to definitions, page 604.
[10] See sample attached.
[11] C.G.S., Sec. 19a-583 and Sec. 19a-585 .
[12] Refer to definitions, page 604, "Personnel Who Have an Explicit Need to Know."

presented in a manner that is reasonably calculated to ensure that the identity of the student cannot be determined. Furthermore, information should be shared only to the extent necessary to fulfill the purpose of the professional consultation.

- Confidential information received by an agency which was not requested or is not needed should not be made part of the student's record and should be returned to the sender or shredded. Parents must be notified if this occurs.

Exceptions to the General Rules Prohibiting Disclosure

- *Internal Communications*: Unless otherwise prohibited by law, it is appropriate to share confidential information obtained from a parent or student with other personnel within the same agency who have a need to know the information in order to benefit the student. In all such situations, only that information that is necessary for providing appropriate services to students should be shared. For example, when a staff member seeks supervisory or consultative advice from a supervisor or colleague, and the identity of the student is not essential to the consultation, the student's identity should not be disclosed. Because it may be extremely difficult to protect the identity of a student in some situations, ethical and legal considerations should be weighed in deciding when and with whom to consult about a particular situation.

- *Written Consent*: Confidential information may always be shared with designated individuals inside an agency or with designated personnel in outside agencies when written consent is first obtained from the parent, legal guardian, or surrogate parent, or when appropriate, from the student. The consent may limit the information to be shared.

- *Health or Safety Emergency*: Confidential student information may be shared without consent when a student is, or others are, in danger of imminent harm. Only that information which is necessary in order to reduce the danger is permissible to share and only with necessary medical and/or administrative or law enforcement personnel. A health or safety emergency generally refers to the high probability of suicide, homicide or risk of a life-threatening injury, condition or illness. [Please note: pursuant to C.G.S., Section 10-233h, if police disclose to a superintendent information about the arrest of a student for a felony, the superintendent may further disclose such information to other school authorities as defined therein.]

- *Non-Identifying Information*: Information which is not personally identifiable may be disclosed. Personally identifiable information is that which is reasonably calculated to be associated with a particular individual. For example, a staff member can share with an administrator that students may be engaging in illegal or risky behaviors in the school stairwells without disclosing that an individual student, when seeking counseling, shared that he and two other eleventh graders regularly smoked marijuana in the stairwells [unless the particular activity or issue

would lead to the discovery of the identity of the student(s)].

- *Court Order*: Confidential information can be disclosed in a judicial proceeding when ordered by the court. Privileged information, on the other hand, may not be disclosed unless the court determines that the requested information is, in fact, not "privileged" under the law and orders the information released to the court. Legal advice should always be sought when a court order for information is presented to agency personnel.

- *Crime At Program/Against Personnel*: If a school employee discovers that a crime has been or is being committed in school , and has not learned about the crime through a protected professional communication, the school employee should report the crime to the appropriate school and, if indicated, law enforcement authorities. [Please note: Under Section 10-154a, professional employees shall not be required to disclose any information acquired through a professional communication with a student or the identity of the student, when such information concerns alcohol or drug abuse or any alcoholic or drug problem of such student, but are required to turn over any physical evidence obtained from the student, if such physical evidence indicates that a crime has been or is being committed by such student, to school administrators or law enforcement officials.[13]]

- *Research/Audit*: Valid research studies and audits requiring access to confidential student information are permissible in schools so long as such studies are conducted in a manner that does not permit personal identification of parents and students by "individuals other than representatives of the organization."[14]

- *Abuse*: In the case of suspected child abuse and neglect or imminent danger of abuse, confidential information may be shared in order to make one or more reports (e.g., to the Department of Children and Families or the Superintendent) as required by law,[15] or to assess and monitor the student's health status[16] in relation to suspected abuse, and to intervene accordingly to protect the student.

- *Qualified Service Organizations*: An agency may disclose information to an organization whose members provide direct services to students pursuant to a written contract in which the organization acknowledges that it is fully bound by federal and state confidentiality laws and regulations, and agency policies, and, if applicable, promises to resist, in judicial proceedings, any efforts to obtain access to information pertaining to students except as otherwise permitted by law. [17]

CONCLUSION

Although these guidelines are intended to assist education agencies in the development of appropriate policies and procedures regarding confidentiality of student information, the legal and ethical distinctions required to determine appropriate responses and actions in individual circumstances are frequently complex. Professional personnel require the flexibility to make decisions based on their own level of expertise and their ethical codes of prac-

---

[13] C.G.S., Sec. 10-154a.
[14] 34 CFR Part 99, Section 99.31.
[15] C.G.S., Section 17a-101 to Section 17a-103 inclusive, and Section 17a-106.
[16] Refer to definitions, page 604.
[17] See footnote 8, page 601.

tice; they also need to know to whom they should direct questions
when they are unsure of how to proceed. In legal questions related
to the confidentiality of student health information, it may be critical to consult with attorneys who have expertise in health matters
as well as those who have expertise in education. In addition, education of staff regarding their legal and ethical responsibilities in
protecting the confidentiality of student information is essential.

PERTINENT DEFINITIONS

Terms	Definitions
Agency/Agencies	Public school systems, regional education service centers (RESCs), regional family service coordination service centers (RFSCCs), private approved special education and early intervention organizations, and the State Department of Education.
Client	In education settings, the student; in health care settings, the patient; also, the parent or guardian when the student is a minor, except when the minor student has the right under statutory or common law to privacy around specific personal health information; in early intervention, the infant, toddler and family.
Confidential Information	Unless otherwise defined, refers to information the disclosure of which would, or would be likely to, constitute an invasion of personal privacy.
Education Records	Refers to those records that are (1) directly related to a student and (2) maintained by, or on behalf of, educational agencies or institutions that receive federal financial assistance.
Health Information	Includes, but is not limited to printed, oral and electronic communications regarding: details of a health and developmental history, current health status, illness or developmental concern, examination or assessment findings, medication requirements, treatment or intervention history, and on-going progress notes; records of HIV testing and treatment, drug and alcohol abuse and psychiatric evaluation and treatment; health care facility and provider office records, including evaluation or testing summaries, discharge instructions, prescriptions, psychological evaluation and testing, and neuropsychiatric testing results; nursing, social work and other pupil personnel specialist histories, evaluations and progress notes relating to student or family health; and health-related planning and placement team records and communications.
Health Status	Refers to the physical, developmental, social and mental health condition of an individual client.
Personnel (education, school, agency)	Employees of school systems, RESCs, RFSCCs, private approved special education and early intervention agencies and the State Department of Education; municipal, state and federal employees who may work in any of those agencies; volunteers, contract personnel and anyone else to whom the school permits access to student records or communications.
Personnel Who Have an Explicit Need to Know	Those employees, contract personnel or volunteers of an agency who provide direct services to the student or school officials with a legitimate educational interest as defined in the school records policy.
Provider or Health Care Provider	A licensed provider of health care services, such as a physician, nurse, nurse practitioner, clinical psychologist, physical or occupational therapist, social worker or speech/language pathologist.
Student	any individual who is or has been in attendance at an educational agency or institution and regarding whom the agency or institution maintains education records and any infant or toddler who is or has been in attendance at an early intervention program that is under the auspices of the State of Connecticut Department of Education.
Student Information	Includes, but is not limited to, printed, electronic and oral communications concerning a student's school performance; health and developmental history and current status; disciplinary history; counseling data; testing and evaluation data; disability status; academic, health and other student records; records of evaluation and/or treatment from health care providers and outside agencies; and family information, including but not limited to biographic, socio-demographic, insurance, financial and health data.

CONFIDENTIALITY STATEMENT REGARDING STUDENT INFORMATION

I understand that printed, electronic and oral communications concerning a student's school performance, academic records, disciplinary history, counseling data, health and developmental history and current status, testing and evaluation data, disability status, records of evaluation and/or treatment from health care providers and outside agencies, and family information, including but not limited to socio-demographic, biographic, insurance, financial and health information, are confidential. In the course of my employment or association with [this agency], access to such information from file folders, records, computer display screens, computer printers, telecopying machines and verbal communications may be required for legitimate education purposes.

Release of this kind of information in printed, verbal, electronic, or any other form, except as required in the performance of work, is a major violation of employee conduct standards. As such, it may be considered reason for disciplinary action which may result in termination of employment.

Any computer password assigned to me and keys to any files containing student information for which I am responsible will be kept confidential and will be shared only with specifically authorized fellow employees.

I have reviewed the agency's policies regarding student records and confidentiality that were provided to me. If I have any questions concerning the confidentiality of student information, I will consult with my immediate supervisor or the school building principal.

I have read, understand and agree with the above statements.

_____   _____

Signature of Employee   Date

Glossary

§. The legal symbol for "Section," referring to a section of federal or state law or regulations.

§§. The legal symbol for "Sections," referring to more than one section of federal or state law.

§ 504. See Section 504.

1115 Waiver. Medicaid section 1115 demonstration waivers. Allows states to test new approaches to benefits, services, eligibility, program payments, and service delivery, often on a statewide basis. These approaches are frequently aimed at saving money to allow states to extend Medicaid coverage to additional low-income and uninsured people.

1915(a) Waivers. Permits states to require Medicaid beneficiaries to enroll in managed care plans.

abandonment. In nursing, the nurse's unilateral withdrawal from a professional-client relationship without adequate notice to the client and while the client still requires nursing services. In general, voluntary relinquishment of all title, possession, or claim.

abuse. Physical, mental, and sexual assault, as well as physical, emotional, and medical neglect; usually related to child abuse or elder abuse.

accommodations. In schools, adjustments or modifications made by teachers and other school staff members to enable students with disabilities to have access to education. Examples range from a seat in the front of the classroom to providing a sign language interpreter.

accountability. The state of being responsible, answerable, or legally liable for an action or failure to take action.

accreditation. A process that involves review of an entity (e.g., school, college, hospital) by an external organization, according to certain recognized standards or criteria.

administration of medication. Assisting or monitoring a student in the ingestion, application, or inhalation of medication according to the directions of a legal prescriber, including handling and storage of medication on behalf of a student who applies, inhales, ingests, or injects the medication. *See also* **self-administration (self-management) of medication**.

administrative law. The branch of public law which has been delegated by statute to government agencies to carry out; generally considered a function of the executive branch of government. The responsible federal or state agency, respectively, may develop regulations to interpret the law within the constraints of the authorizing statute.

administrative relief. A legal remedy provided under statutory authority by a government agency, rather than a court.

advanced practice nurse or advanced practice registered nurse (APN or APRN). A registered nurse with a master's degree in nursing, who has satisfied the additional state licensure requirements for advanced practice in nursing (APN or APRN licensure), which usually include advanced education (e.g., in pharmacology, and medical diagnosis and management) and national certification in a specialty area of practice (e.g., as a pediatric nurse practitioner).

affidavit. In law, a sworn statement in writing.

affirmed. In law, a ruling of an appellate court upholding a lower court decision; also affirmed in part, upholding a part of a lower court decision.

age of majority. The age at which a person is considered to be an adult for legal purposes, including but not limited to executing a contract, making a will, and giving consent for medical treatment. The age of majority is determined by state law; in many states it is 18 years.

alternative education setting. In general, an educational placement designed to meet the special interests and talents of students; for example, alternative high schools for students at risk of dropping out, science high schools, and programs in the arts. Under IDEA, a temporary placement for special education students who have serious discipline problems or whose behavior is considered dangerous.

alternative medicine. Approaches to medical diagnosis and therapy for the prevention and cure of illness that have not been developed by use of generally accepted scientific methods. Forms of alternative medicine include acupressure, aroma therapy, herbal medicine, homeopathy, and naturopathy. Some of these alternative approaches are currently under study through the National Institutes of Health to determine efficacy and application.

Americans with Disabilities Act (ADA). A federal law that prohibits discrimination on the basis of disability in privately owned and operated public accommodations, and in state and local government programs and services which receive no federal funding.

anaphylaxis. Extreme hypersensitivity (allergic) reaction to a foreign protein after a previous exposure to the same substance; a medical emergency requiring immediate medical intervention to prevent progression of the reaction and the potential for death.

appellate court (or appeals court). A state or federal court that only hears appeals of lower court decisions.

APRN (or APN). *See* **advanced practice registered nurse.**

assault. An intentional act by one person that causes another person to fear that he or she will be touched in an offensive or injurious manner—even if no touching or injury actually takes place.

asthma (or reactive airway disease). A chronic disease of the respiratory tract characterized by recurrent attacks of difficult breathing, often associated with wheezing and/or coughing. Acute episodes can be precipitated by allergens, infections, environmental conditions (e.g., cold air, airborne pollutants), exercise, and emotional stress. Under Section §504, asthma may be considered to interfere with the "major life function" of respiration and may necessitate school accommodations. It can be life threatening. Under IDEA, asthma is one of the examples of "other health impaired"; students with severe asthma may qualify as in need of special education.

attorney-client privilege. In the law of evidence, the client's privilege to refuse to disclose, and to prevent anyone else from disclosing, confidential communications made between the client and attorney for the purpose of obtaining legal advice. The client, rather than the attorney, owns the privilege and can elect to waive it.

authorized prescriber. Physician, dentist, nurse, or other health care provider who is legally authorized by a state to prescribe medications, and medical devices, procedures, tests, and other medical interventions within the limits of his or her professional license.

autonomy. Personal freedom to make choices or decisions for oneself.

barrier-free environment. In schools, an environment that contains no obstacles to accessibility and usability by students with disabilities. Barriers may be physical (stairs) and non-physical (a class with no accommodation for a deaf student).

basic needs (basic human needs). Essential requirements for survival, including normal development and health, such as food, water, shelter.

battery. An intentional act resulting in unwanted (unconsented) or unlawful physical contact, touching, violence, or constraint that harms someone. A legal action of battery can be brought in either a criminal court, when the contact is unlawful (e.g., a beating) or in a civil court, for example, when consent is not obtained for medical treatment or surgery (e.g., when a surgeon operates on the wrong limb). In some jurisdictions, a charge of battery might be considered against a school nurse who performs cardiopulmonary resuscitation (CPR) on a student who has presented both a valid DNR order from a physician and the parent's express refusal of CPR. Unintentional harmful contact is not battery, regardless of the carelessness of the behavior or severity of the injury.

BOM (board of medicine or board of examiners for medicine). The governmental body to which a state legislature has delegated responsibility for defining the scope of practice of medical practitioners and ensuring the safety of the public regarding medical practice within the state.

BON (board of nursing or board of examiners for nursing). The governmental body to which a state legislature has delegated responsibility for defining the scope of practice of nurses and ensuring the safety of the public in relation to nursing practice within the state.

BRCA1/BRCA2. In human genetics, the first breast cancer genes to be identified. Mutated forms of these genes are believed to be responsible for about half the cases of inherited breast cancer, especially those that occur in younger women. Both are tumor suppressor genes.

breach. The failure of a person (or entity) to perform some agreed-on act, or a legal duty owed to another.

capitated group networks. One of the four types of managed health care organizations; primary care or multispecialty clinics or groups of clinics that contract with a managed care entity to provide care to a designated population. Most group networks contract with several managed care organizations simultaneously.

capitation. A payment system by the health plan to the provider for covered services for each enrolled member for a specific time, usually expressed in units per member per month (pmpm). In other words, the health care provider receives a fixed amount per enrolled client per month and is obligated to provide all covered services at no additional charge. Payments are made by the health plan to the provider regardless of whether services are furnished.

carved out services. In managed care, health care services that are structured and reimbursed separately with no pre-authorization needed. The money is withheld or "carved out" from the total monies and can be used for fee-for-service by other providers.

case law. Successive pieces of litigation and resultant decisions of federal and state courts, often the primary means of determining the specific intent of federal and state legislation.

case management. In health care, the comprehensive and systematic approach to providing quality community-based health care, usually for clients with multiple and complex service needs. It consists of providing this care along a continuum, decreasing fragmentation of services, enhancing a patient's and a family's quality of care, and containing costs.

certification. A process that involves recognition by an entity (usually a state agency or national professional organization) that an individual has mastered a certain body of knowledge and/or expertise, usually demonstrated by the ability to meet certain criteria and/or perform according to certain standards.

certiorari. The notice, called a writ, by which the U.S. Supreme Court reports acceptance of a case for appellate review.

CFR. *See* **Code of Federal Regulations**.

charting by exception. In nursing, a system of client documentation that requires detailed written entries only of significant or abnormal findings and interventions that vary from the standardized protocol of care for the client complaint or problem at hand. This method of documentation requires extensive preprinted guidelines or protocols, standardized care plans, and terminology.

children at increased risk. Children who exhibit certain biological or environmental characteristics that are associated with a heightened probability of developing a chronic physical, developmental, behavioral, or emotional condition. Biological risks are pathologies and physiological abnormalities that have been shown to increase the likelihood of future-onset of chronic conditions, such as very low birth weight, certain metabolic deficiencies, and genetic disorders.

chronic condition. A physical, physiologic, or developmental impairment; an anatomical, physiological, or mental impairment that interferes with an individual's ability to function in the environment.

chronic health condition. One that is long term (usually more than 3 months duration) and is either not curable or has residual features that result in limitations in daily living requiring adaptation in function or special assistance.

chronic illness. A medical condition that interferes with daily functioning for more than three months in a year, causes hospitalization for more than one month in a year, or (at the time of diagnosis) is likely to do either of these.

civil action. A lawsuit involving a private legal right or duty.

civil law. The branch of law that is concerned with non-criminal matters; the rights and duties of persons in such areas as contracts, torts, and patents.

claims-made liability policy. An insurance policy that covers those injuries that (1) occur during the policy period and (2) are reported to the insurer during the policy or tail period.

Code of Federal Regulations (CFR). Regulations adopted by federal agencies, after notice and an opportunity for comment, arranged by general subject and updated regularly.

competencies. Abilities or skills; in a profession, the knowledge, abilities, attitudes, skills, judgments, and values required for successful functioning as a member of the profession.

complainant. The plaintiff or person instituting a civil action (lawsuit) against another.

conditions of participation. The terms in a contract between a provider of health care services and an organization that pays for the services, such as a managed care or health insurance company. The health care provider agrees to abide by the terms of the agreement in exchange for payment by the payor for care rendered to the payor's insureds.

confidential information. Personal information that, if disclosed to others, would be likely to, or would, constitute an invasion of personal privacy; information about a client that, if disclosed, might result in harm or embarrassment to the client. All personal health care information is considered confidential information.

confidentiality. The quality or state of being confidential, private, or secret.

consent. In health care, the client's voluntary act of agreeing to allow someone else (e.g., physician, nurse, therapist) to do something to him or her that would otherwise be considered battery or unwanted touching; provides a defense to a civil (not criminal) lawsuit for battery. In education, a parent's or guardian's voluntary act of allowing school personnel to, for example, administer to his child testing or evaluation that is not administered to every other student, or to disclose to a third party the student's confidential school records. Consent can be express (written or verbal) or implied, and should always be "informed." *See also* **informed consent** and **implied consent.**

conservator/conservatrix. *See* **guardian**. In some states, a guardian is known as a conservator or conservatrix (if a woman).

continuing education. Specified hours of mandatory or voluntary education to promote the continuing competency of a professional, e.g., nurse, teacher.

co-payment. The portion of a claim or medical expense that the insured or covered individual (or health plan member) is responsible for paying out of his or her own pocket.

contract. An agreement consisting of one or more legally enforceable promises between two or more parties—people, corporations, or partnerships. The three elements of a contract include the offer,

acceptance, and consideration. A breach of contract is when the agreed-to contract is broken.

controlled drug. *See* **drug, controlled**.

cost containment (in health care). Terms used to describe efforts to control the growth of medical care costs.

court order (to disclose information). In a law suit, when one party has been denied access to information about the other party which is considered confidential, the party needing access may request an order from the court hearing the case. The court considering the request will review the nature of the information being requested and the reason(s) why it was withheld. After balancing these considerations and reviewing relevant laws, the court may order release. The release may be conditioned to protect against further release. Sometimes the judge will review the actual material prior to determining whether it should be released, in whole or in part.

covered services. Those health services and benefits to which members of an insurance plan or health maintenance organization are entitled under the terms of the contract which may be amended from time to time.

custody. Refers to the right and responsibility to provide for the physical control of a person. Adults who exercise primary control over the rearing of a child, usually the parents, are generally considered to have custody of that child. Custody may be transferred from parents to relatives, foster parents, or a child welfare agency. When parents are divorced, divorce agreements or court documents will determine the custody of the minor children, and may provide for joint custody by both parents.

decedent. In law, one who has died, as used in, "the decedent left no will."

declaratory ruling. A ruling issued by an administrative agency that interprets the law, regulations, or policies of the agency; such rulings are often issued in response to a question.

deductible. That portion of a loss that the insured must bear before the insurer's obligation to pay commences.

defendant. The party against whom a civil or criminal action is brought; in a civil suit, the person who is sued by the plaintiff.

delegation (nursing). The transfer to a competent individual of the authority to perform a selected nursing activity in a selected situation, with the nurse retaining accountability for the outcome. Nursing delegation is governed by the nurse practice act and rules and regulations of the state's board of nursing.

delegatee. The individual to whom a nurse delegates authority to perform a selected nursing activity in a selected situation.

developmental disability. In education, generally refers to chronic impaired cognitive functioning (but may include impaired physical functioning) that is manifested before age 22 years, is likely to continue indefinitely, results in substantial limitation of function, and requires special services.

diabetes (mellitus). A disorder characterized by faulty carbohydrate metabolism due primarily to inadequate insulin production. In children, the condition generally requires insulin injections (one or more daily), diet and exercise management, and frequent glucose monitoring. Uncontrolled diabetic reactions can be life threatening. Under §504, diabetes may be considered to interfere with the "major life function" of metabolism. Under IDEA, diabetes is an example of "other health impaired;" if the condition or its effects (e.g., absenteeism) significantly interfere with a student's learning, the student may be eligible for special education.

diagnosis. The careful, critical study and analysis of something in order to determine its nature. *See also* **nursing diagnosis.**

directory information. Under FERPA, information contained in an education record of a student which would not generally be considered harmful or an invasion of privacy if disclosed. It may include, but is not limited to, the student's name, address, telephone listing, date and place of birth, major field of study, participation in officially recognized activities and sports, weight and height of members of athletic teams, dates of attendance, degrees and awards received, and the immediate past educational agency or institution attended.

disability. The functional limitations imposed by, and the psychological response resulting from, an impairment; a physical or mental impairment that limits any major life activity.

disclosure. The release of confidential information, whether in writing (e.g., a record), or by oral communication, electronic transmission, or other means.

dismissal. In law, the action of a court when a claim cannot be heard for lack of a real dispute, lack of jurisdiction over the parties, or other basic flaw.

dispensing. In medical and pharmaceutical practice, the actions of preparing and delivering medications; generally a licensed function of physicians and pharmacists, but not nurses, except some advanced practice registered nurses. Placing a dose of a medication in a container or envelope for administration to a student at a later time is generally considered dispensing.

DNA. The chemical inside the nucleus of a cell that carries the genetic instructions for making living organisms.

Do Not Resuscitate (DNR) Order. A DNR order is one that orders health care providers to forego resuscitation in the event that the patient suffers a respiratory or cardiac arrest, or both. Currently, these orders are often broader and cover treatments in addition to resuscitation; they may address the withholding of life-sustaining treatments that are commonly available, such as intubation, defibrillation, dialysis, or blood transfusion.

Down syndrome. A congenital condition characterized by varying degrees of mental retardation and multiple defects. (Also called trisomy 21).

drug. Any substance that, when taken into a living organism, may modify one or more of its functions; any medicine or preparation for internal or external use of humans, intended to be used for the cure, mitigation, or prevention of diseases or abnormalities of humans, which are recognized in any published United States Pharmacopoeia or National Formulary, or otherwise established as a drug; includes prescription and non-prescription medications. See also drug, controlled.

drug, controlled (controlled substance). Centrally-acting medication, such as stimulants and depressants, including narcotics and some sedatives, as designated by the Drug Enforcement Administration of the Department of Justice. Controlled substances are subject to the requirements of the Comprehensive Drug Abuse Prevention and Control Act of 1971 and are divided into 5 categories: I–experimental; II–no refills on a prescription permitted; III & IV–can be refilled up to 5 times in 6 months; V–are restricted to the extent that all non-scheduled prescription drugs are regulated.

due process. Formal court or administrative proceedings that include specific rights and safeguards for parties to a dispute. Such procedural rights vary depending on the forum. Examples are: the right to notice of a legal proceeding, the right to present and cross examine witnesses under oath, the right to be represented by counsel, the right to present argument. Under IDEA, the hearing available to parents and local boards of education concerning the special education rights of a student with a disability is sometimes referred to as "due process", although "due process hearing" is more correct.

education code. State laws and regulations concerning public education, education professionals, education agencies, and education programs.

education record. Under FERPA, those records that are 1) directly related to a student, and 2) maintained by an education agency or institution or by a party acting for the agency or institution.

educational setting. Any setting in which a student receives instruction (e.g., school building, institution, hospital, home).

EHA. The Education of All Handicapped Children Act, passed by Congress in 1975. Now referred to as IDEA. *See also* **Individuals with Disabilities Education Act**.

Eleventh Amendment immunity. A provision of the U.S. Constitution that protects states against some kinds of law suits in federal courts by citizens of other states.

eligible student. Under FERPA, a student who is 18 years or older. An eligible student is accorded the same rights under FERPA as the parent or guardian.

emancipation. A legal term defining a situation in which a minor is accorded the rights and responsibilities of an adult, despite his or her age. When a minor is emancipated, the parent is also relieved of financial support obligations and no longer has custody of the minor.

emergency. A serious situation that arises suddenly and threatens the life, limb, or welfare of one or more persons; a crisis. An emergency creates a type of implied consent when the individual is unable to consent to treatment that is immediately necessary.

emergency care. Services needed to treat a condition that if not immediately treated could cause a person serious physical or mental disability, continuation of severe pain, or death.

emergency plan or protocol. *See* **individualized emergency plan or protocol.**

enrollee or member (managed care). Any person enrolled in a contracted health plan and who is entitled to the provision of health care services under the terms of the plan.

EPSDT. Early Prevention Screening, Diagnosis, and Treatment. This is a mandated federal program with two purposes: to facilitate health care for Medicaid children who are underserved and to detect and correct health problems before they lead to serious and costly disabling conditions.

equitable powers. In law, the power given to a court to go beyond technicalities and make a decision that is just and fair in consideration of the facts and circumstances of the individual case.

et seq. An abbreviation for *et sequentia*, meaning "and the following." Often used, for example, as "p. 1 et seq.", meaning page 1 and the pages that follow.

expert witness. In the courts, a person with specialized knowledge used to assist the judge and jury in interpreting information not usually understood by laymen. For example, expert witnesses may be used in a civil case to give evidence regarding the question of whether the defendant(s)health care provider met the applicable standard of care, as well as the nature of the alleged damages.

Family and Medical Leave Act of 1993. Federal law that allows up to 12 weeks of unpaid leave from work for qualified family and medical needs.

Family Educational Rights and Privacy Act (FERPA). The federal law first passed in 1974 that sets standards of confidentiality for education records; sometimes called the Buckley Amendment because it was sponsored by Senator Buckley.

FAPE. *See* **free appropriate public education.**

federalism. A system of government where power is divided between a central government and local governments with each having specific powers. The central government may have the power to revoke the local government's power without consent.

fee-for-service. In managed care, a payment system by which providers are paid a specific amount for each service performed.

FERPA. *See* **Family Educational Rights and Privacy Act.**

first aid. The immediate care that is given to an injured or ill person before treatment by medically trained personnel is available. In schools, this term is often used erroneously to refer to the assessment and management of ill and injured students by professional nurses who, by virtue of their education, are held to a standard of care beyond that of first aid.

free appropriate public education (FAPE). Special education and related services provided at public expense, which meet the standards of the state education agency and are consistent with a student's individualized education program.

gene. The functional and physical unit of heredity passed from parent to offspring. Genes are pieces of DNA, and most genes contain the information for making a specific protein.

genetic map. (Also known as a linkage map). A chromosome map of a species that shows the position of its known genes and markers relative to each other, rather than as specific physical points on each chromosome.

genome. All the DNA contained in an organism or a cell, which includes both the chromosomes within the nucleus and the DNA in mitochondria.

genotype. The genetic identity of an individual that does not show as outward characteristics.

Good Samaritan. In law, someone who volunteers to assist someone else who is in danger or injured; most states provide civil immunity from negligence for Good Samaritans.

gross negligence. In law, the intentional failure to perform a duty in reckless disregard of the consequences as affecting the life or property of another.

guardian. A person appointed by a court who is responsible for managing the financial or personal affairs, or both, of another individual found incompetent to handle these affairs. A guardian of the person manages personal affairs; a guardian of the estate manages financial affairs. These responsibilities may be split between two persons, but are generally handled by one appointee. In the case of a minor, natural parents are guardians unless removed or replaced by a court order. In some circumstances, a guardian will have powers that are specifically limited by a court; this may occur, for example, when a health care facility or provider seeks a court order for medical treatment over a parent's refusal to consent.

harassment. Teasing or other offensive activities of a sufficient intensity and persistence over time that they interfere with an individual's working or learning.

HCQIA. Health Care Quality Improvement Act of 1986.

health assessment. The systematic collection and analysis of information or data about an individual's health situation to determine the individual's general state of health, patterns of functioning, and need for health services, counseling, and education; a licensed function of physicians and nurses. Health assessment of students by school nurses includes data collection, data analysis, and the identification of relevant nursing diagnoses in order to plan interventions and accommodations, make appropriate referrals and collaborate with others (e.g., with families, educators, and health care providers) to promote students' health and learning.

Health Care Financing Administration (HCFA). The federal agency administering the Medicare, Medicaid, and Child Health Insurance Programs, as well as provisions of the Clinical Laboratory Improvement Act.

health care information. Any information, whether oral or recorded in any form or medium that identifies or can readily be associated with the identity of a client and relates to the client's health care. For state-specific details, see individual state laws.

health care plan. *See* **individualized health care plan.**

health care records. The documentary record of an individual's health history, diagnoses, treatments, and outcomes, made by a licensed health care professional (e.g., physician, nurse) or by the professional staff of a hospital, clinic, or treatment facility (e.g., therapist, social worker). See individual state laws for details.

health code. State laws and regulations concerning public health, health agencies, health professionals, and health services.

health impairment. An acute or chronic illness, condition, or disability, or any developmental disability or terminal illness, whether physical or mental in nature.

health maintenance organization (HMO). An organized system of group health care practice that provides an agreed-upon set of basic and supplemental health services to voluntary enrollees for which the HMO is reimbursed through a predetermined, fixed prepayment made without regard to the number or complexity of actual services provided.

health professional. An individual with specialized educational preparation, knowledge, and skill who is licensed under state statute to provide specific health care services to clients, such as a nurse, physician, occupational and physical therapist, speech language pathologist, clinical psychologist, and social worker.

health services. In schools, generally refers to the services provided by, or under the supervision of, a professional school nurse, but may also refer to services provided by other health and mental health professionals. *See also* **health professional.**

hold harmless agreement. A contract in which one party agrees to assume the liability inherent in a situation, thereby relieving the other party of any liability. If questioned, a court will examine the conditions of the original agreement, and such an agreement may be challenged if injury resulted from willful or wanton behavior by a health care provider or other professional.

holistic medicine or nursing. The comprehensive and total care of a client. In this system, the needs of the client in all areas, such as physical, emotional, social, spiritual, and economic, are considered and cared for.

HMO. Health maintenance organization.

home school. Elementary and secondary education provided in the home by parents or others, as provided under state law.

Human Genome Project. An international research project to map each human gene and to completely sequence human DNA.

human rights committee. A group of appropriately qualified professionals designated by an institution to review matters such as the use of physical restraint, DNR orders, and research on human subjects.

IDEA. *See* **Individuals with Disabilities Education Act.**

IEP. *See* **individualized education program.**

IEP team. A multidisciplinary group comprised of parents, teachers, and others (as specified in IDEA and its regulations), that meets to determine a student's eligibility for, and to plan and evaluate the outcomes of, an individualized education program.

IFSP. *See* **individualized family service plan.**

immunity. An American adaptation of the old English legal principle that subjects could not sue their King, immunity is the freedom granted from the usual burdens, duties, or liabilities that arise out of a legal relationship. Immunity is granted to the states under the eleventh amendment to the U.S. Constitution, and under state law, usually granted to an entity or special category of people, such as local governments and public schools.

immunocompromised. Having an immune system incapable of reacting to pathogenic or tissue damage. This may be due to a genetic disorder, disease process, or drugs.

implied consent. Consent that is assumed, rather than expressed, based on the emergency nature of a client's condition (e.g., one assumes consent when an ambulance is called to transport a student with symptoms of anaphylaxis); or consent based on the client's actions in calling or coming to an agency or health care provider to seek services. For example, parental consent to a health history assessment is implied when parents keep an appointment with the school nurse, or permit a home visit, for the purpose of providing the nurse with relevant information about their child's health history. As a legal standard, informed consent that is expressed and written is required whenever possible (e.g., in non-emergency situations).

incident report (variation, accident, situation, unusual occurrence report or form). A written statement by a witness, provided as near the time of the event as possible, which is part of the overall risk management program of an institution. These reports are generally used to review and evaluate client services, to monitor equipment, grounds and buildings for unsafe conditions, and to document events in anticipation of insurance claims.

inclusion. In education, a popular term for placement of children with disabilities in regular classrooms. *See also* **mainstreaming and least restrictive environment.**

indemnification. Reimbursement for a loss already incurred.

indemnification agreement. A contract that shifts the liability for loss from the party who would usually be held legally responsible to another party.

indemnity. An insurance program in which the insured person is reimbursed for covered expenses.

independent practice organization (IPO). One of the four types of managed care organizations, in which individual practices or privately owned groups agree to serve a specified population, abide by rules for referral to specialty care, and prescribe according to a designated list of pharmaceutical preparations or medications.

individualized education program (IEP). A written plan, developed by the IEP team, specifying services for a student (aged three to twenty-one years) in need of special education for a school year or less, as specified in IDEA and state law . *See also* **IEP team.**

individualized emergency plan or protocol. Written school nursing management plan to direct actions that should be taken when a student displays signs and symptoms suggestive of a life threatening or seriously harmful health situation. The protocol, usually considered a part of the student's individualized health care plan, is generally written for the purpose of directing school persons, and may be incorporated into a student's Section 504 plan or IEP.

individualized family service plan (IFSP). A written plan, developed by a multidisciplinary team, specifying early intervention services for an infant or child with disabilities, aged birth to three years, and the child's family, as specified in IDEA.

individualized health [health care] [health management] plan (IHP, IHCP, IHMP). A plan of action to be used by the school nurse and other members of the school team, as appropriate, to meet the actual and potential health care needs of a student during the school day. The plan is written after completion of the nursing assessment and includes written directions for managing student health needs and adaptations for enhancing the student's independent functioning.

individualized transition plan (ITP). A written plan developed by the IEP team for students in need of special education at age fourteen and older, identifying transition services and public agencies appropriate to the needs of the student for post-secondary school planning, as specified in IDEA. May also be developed for children with disabilities who are moving from early intervention into preschool services at age 3.

Individuals with Disabilities Education Act (IDEA). Federal legislation that provides access to school and a free appropriate education in the least restrictive environment for children with disabling conditions that interfere with learning; 1990 updating and renaming of EHA; amended in 1997. *See also* **EHA.**

informed consent. In health care, the considered agreement to do something or allow something to happen after careful consideration of all the facts, including potential benefits, risks, and alternative courses of action; a process of the patient or client gaining information, making an intelligent decision to accept or reject treatment, and giving consent, based on a full disclosure of the relevant facts; agreement in which the individual's full understanding is the most critical element, since a signature alone does not necessarily prove that consent was *informed*.

In education, the considered approval given by a parent or guardian to a school official, based on full disclosure of relevant facts by the official. For example, full disclosure regarding the release of confidential student information to a third party would include potential outcomes—both beneficial and harmful—that might result from the disclosure, as well as alternatives to the disclosure.

injunction. A court order requiring an immediate action or immediate stop to an action, sometimes called a temporary restraining order (TRO) or a preliminary injunction. Used in special education actions to protect the status of a child or group of children while the merits of a case are fully litigated. The general standards for the granting of an injunction are: 1) the likelihood of prevailing on the merits of the case; 2) the relative damage to the plaintiff if action is deferred until the full case is heard; and 3) the relative damage to the defendant if the injunction is issued.

in loco parentis. In place of, or standing in for, the parent; a traditional legal concept describing the authority of a school official or other individual to act in the place of an absent parent.

invasive procedure. In health care, a procedure in which the body or a body cavity is entered (e.g., by use of a tube, needle, device) or any other invasion that could interfere with bodily function.

involuntary commitment. As set forth by statutory provisions, which vary from state to state, the circumstances and procedures for which a person can be detained against his or her will for reason of mental illness or drug or alcohol abuse or intoxication. Provisions dealing with the commitment of minors may differ from those confining adults with regard to reasons for confinement and the circumstances under which the minor may, for example, request a hearing to challenge the commitment.

job description. Written statement of what the jobholder does or is expected to do, including how and why it is done.

judicial bypass procedure. Judicial bypass is a court proceeding used when a State requires parental consent or notice prior to a minor obtaining an abortion. The bypass is used by a minor who feels she cannot or should not involve her parents in the abortion decision. This is further described in Chapter 7.

jurisdiction. In law, the authority of a particular court or administrative forum to hear a case.

law. A set of rules and regulations that govern social conduct and interpersonal behavior. The law includes our state and federal constitutions, enactments of state legislatures, and the U.S. Congress and court decisions.

least restrictive environment (LRE). Under IDEA, the requirement that a student with a disability be educated with children who are not disabled, and that placement of a child with a disability in a special class, separate school, or other separate learning environment may be made only when education in a regular class setting with supplementary aids and services cannot be achieved.

legal prescriber. *See* **authorized prescriber**.

liability. Responsibility for one's own conduct; a duty to be performed; a finding in civil cases that the preponderance of evidence shows that the defendant was responsible for the plaintiff's injuries.

liability insurance. *See* **professional liability insurance**.

liability limits/limits of liability. The amount in an insurance policy that the insurer agrees to pay on behalf of an insured. The policy limits usually consist of two numbers—an amount to be paid per occurrence and an amount to be paid in a single policy year.

license (health care professional). An agency- or government-granted permission issued to a health care professional to engage in a given occupation, or a finding that the applicant has attained the degree of competency necessary to ensure that public health, safety, and welfare are reasonably well-protected.

licensed practical nurse (LPN) or licensed vocational nurse (LVN). A person trained in basic nursing techniques and direct patient care who assists, and practices under the direction or supervision of, a registered nurse, as specified in state law. LPN training usually requires one year of training beyond high school.

licensure (professional). The process by which a governmental entity grants permission to an individual to practice a particular profession, engage in a certain occupation, or perform a certain activity, usually granted on the basis of education and examination. *See also* **license**.

licensure by reciprocity. The method of obtaining a professional license that is based on meeting certain requirements that usually include payment of a fee

and possession of a similar current license in another jurisdiction rather than successful completion of an examination at the time of application.

living will or health care directive. A document created by an adult which describes, in general or specific terms, the types of medical treatment to be provided when that person is unable to make decisions. A living will is generally only applicable if the individual is permanently comatose or in a terminal condition.

locus. The place on a chromosome where a specific gene is located, a kind of address for the gene. The plural is "loci" not "locuses."

malpractice. Negligence by a professional.

managed care. A health care system that integrates financing and management with the delivery of health care services to covered individuals, most often with arrangements by selected providers; a health care organization or system of organizations that attempts to manage the cost and quality of health care, as well as access to health care. Managed care organizations (MCO) offer a specific list of health care providers and financial incentives for its enrollees to use providers and services offered within the organization.

mandated reporters. *See* **reporting statutes**.

mainstreaming. In education, a popular term for placement of children with disabilities in regular education classes. *See also* **inclusion** and **least restrictive environment.**

major life activities (as defined in §504). These activities include, but are not limited to: caring for one's self, performing manual tasks, walking, seeing, hearing, speaking, breathing, learning, and working.

manifestation determination. In special education, the decision by the IEP team that a particular special education student's misbehavior is, or is not, related to his or her disability.

mapping. The process of deducing schematic representations of DNA. Three types of DNA maps can be constructed: physical maps, genetic maps, and cytogenetic maps, with the key distinguishing feature among these three types being the landmarks on which they are based.

mature minor rule. In health care, a legal principle that allows routine medical care and treatment to be provided, without parental consent, to a minor who is 15 years of age or older. This rule exists by case law in some states, and by statute in others.

MCO. Managed care organization.

medical director (in a managed care organization). A physician designated by an HMO to monitor and review the provision of covered health care services to enrollees.

medication. *See* **drug** and **drug, controlled.**

medication errors. Deviations from the standards of care owed to clients in the area of correct medication delivery, including omitted doses, incorrect doses, incorrect time of administration, incorrect client, improper injection techniques, and incorrect route of administration.

mental impairment. As defined in §504, any mental or psychological disorder, such as mental retardation, organic brain syndrome, emotional or mental illness, and specific learning disabilities.

microarray technology. A new way of studying how large numbers of genes interact with each other and how a cell's regulatory networks control vast batteries of genes simultaneously. The method uses a robot to precisely apply tiny droplets containing functional DNA to glass slides. Researchers then attach fluorescent labels to DNA from the cell they are studying. The labeled probes are allowed to bind to complementary DNA strands on the slides. The slides are put into a scanning microscope that can measure the brightness of each fluorescent dot: brightness reveals how much of a specific DNA fragment is present, an indicator of how active it is.

minor. A person who has not yet reached the age of majority. *See* **age of majority.**

morbidity. Illness, disease.

mortality. Fatal outcome or death.

multidisciplinary evaluation. In education, assessment of an individual child with a variety of test instruments and by professionals from several disciplines including, when necessary, medical or psychological assessment.

multidisciplinary team. In special education, generally refers to individuals representing a student's family, school administration, teachers, pupil services, and others (including experts in the community) who have assessed the student or will provide direct or indirect services to the student in school. *See also* **IEP team.**

mutation. A permanent structural alteration in DNA. In most cases, such DNA changes either have no effect or cause harm, but occasionally a mutation can improve an organism's chance of surviving and passing the beneficial change on to its descendants.

mutual recognition licensure. A type of proposed licensure whereby a nurse would hold a license in her state of residency, but be able to practice in any state that has signed onto an interstate compact, provided the nurse follows the laws and regulations of the state in which she practices.

National Committee on Quality Assurance (NCQA). An independent nonprofit HMO accrediting organization composed of health care quality experts, labor union officials, and consumer representatives. NCQA accreditation is designed for managed care models and is mandated by law in some states. The standards focus on quality improvement, credentialing, members' rights and responsibilities, utilization management, preventive health services, and medical records.

national standards (professional). The average degree of skill, care, and diligence that is reasonably expected to be exercised by members of the same profession, regardless of the local community or state in which the services are delivered, usually defined and published by a national organization representing the profession or specialty area of the profession.

NCSBN. National Council of State Boards of Nursing.

negligence. Failure to act in a way that a reasonable and prudent person would act in the circumstance, including the omission of an action that a reasonable person would have taken in the same or similar circumstances; conduct that falls below a reasonable standard of care for the protection of others against unreasonable risk of harm.

non-prescription medication. Medicines that may be obtained over-the-counter without a prescription from an authorized prescriber. *See* **drug.**

nucleotide. One of the structural components, or building blocks, of DNA and RNA. A nucleotide consists of a base (one of four chemicals: adenine, thymine, guanine, and cytosine) plus a molecule of sugar and one of phosphoric acid.

nucleus. The central cell structure that houses the chromosomes.

nurse administrator. A nurse whose primary function is the management of health care services delivery, and who represents organized nursing services in a given institution or agency at the executive or management level. In schools, nurse administrators are generally responsible for organizing, directing, integrating and evaluating the delivery of health services and programs for students, and managing the health services personnel (nurses and paraprofessionals) who provide those services.

nurse manager. *See* **nurse administrator.**

nurse practice act. A state law that defines and regulates the scope of nursing practice in that state.

nursing. The diagnosis and treatment of human responses to actual or potential health problems.

nursing aide (nursing assistant). A nonprofessional health care worker who functions under the direction of a professional nurse and assists the nurse in performing rudimentary patient care procedures. A certified nursing aide (CNA) is one who: (1) successfully completes a required 1- to 3- month course in basic patient care procedures (e.g., taking temperatures, giving baths, making beds, and helping stable patients to ambulate) and (2) thereby receives a credential from a certifying body, usually a state agency. *See also* **paraprofessional.**

nursing diagnosis. A statement that describes the human response of an individual or group to an actual or potential health problem. Nursing diagnoses are those that the nurse can legally identify and for which the nurse can order definitive interventions to maintain a client's health state or to reduce, eliminate, or prevent alterations in a client's health. In schools, nursing diagnoses describe students' responses to actual and potential health problems and the effects of those responses on the students' functioning in school. Nurses may refer to nursing diagnoses as "functional diagnoses" for communication purposes with educators.

nursing process (in educational settings). A systematic approach to the analysis and management of health issues that impact a student's well-being and ability to learn in school.

nursing students. Students officially admitted to a course of study in the nursing discipline, either at entry or advanced levels of nursing.

occurrence-based liability policy. An insurance policy that covers injuries that occur while the policy is in effect.

Occupational Safety and Health Act (OSHA). Federal law that assures healthful and safe conditions for employees in the workplace; may or may not be applicable to governmental entities.

Office for Civil Rights (OCR), U.S. Department of Education. The agency responsible for investigating complaints under Section (§) 504 and the ADA about discrimination on the basis of race, sex, nationality, disability, et al. in public schools, colleges and universities receiving financial assistance from the federal government.

paraprofessional. In health care, a worker who assists licensed health professionals in providing services to clients, but who is not educated or licensed to practice as a professional, e.g., nurse's aide or home health aide. In education, a worker who assists professional teachers, but who is not educated or certified as a professional educator, e.g., teacher's aide. Standards and requirements for the training of health aides and teacher aides for school district positions are variable by state.

parens patriae **power.** Translated literally to mean "parent of the country." This term refers to the role of a state as sovereign and guardian of individuals with legal disabilities. It is the basis upon which a state protects interests, such as the health, comfort, and welfare of people, interstate water rights, and general economic concerns of the state, etc.

partially capitated. In managed care, a stipulated dollar amount established for certain health care services while other services are reimbursed on a cost or fee-for-service basis.

pedigree. In genetics, a simplified diagram of a family's genealogy that shows family members' relationships to each other and how a particular trait or disease has been inherited.

peer review. The process by which professionals review the quality and competence of services provided by their peers.

personally identifiable information. In FERPA, includes, but is not limited to: student's name; name of the student's parent or other family member; a personal identifier, such as the student's social security number or student number; a list of personal characteristics or other information that would make the student's identity easily traceable.

phenotype. The observable traits or characteristics of an organism, for example hair color, weight, or the presence or absence of a disease. Phenotypic traits are not necessarily genetic.

physical impairment. As defined in §504, any physiological disorder or condition, cosmetic disfigurement, or anatomical loss affecting one or more of the following body systems: neurological; musculoskeletal; special sense organs; respiratory, including speech organs; cardiovascular; reproductive, digestive, genito-urinary; hemic and lymphatic; skin and endocrine.

physical map. Chromosome map of a species that shows the specific physical locations of its genes and/or markers on each chromosome. Physical maps are particularly important when searching for disease genes by positional cloning strategies and for DNA sequencing.

physician's (medical) orders. The written directions issued by a licensed and authorized medical provider (e.g., medical doctor or advanced practice registered nurse), usually to other health care providers, for the medical treatment of a client, including orders for medication and other interventions, such as catheterization, glucose monitoring, physical therapy, laboratory or x-ray tests, and activity or dietary restrictions.

P.L. (public law). The indexing method used by the U.S. Congress for new legislation. For example, in P.L. 94-142, the law was the 142nd enactment of the 94th session of Congress. Congressional sessions run for the two years between elections. P.L. 94-142 is codified, or inserted into the United States Code, at Title 20, Sections 1400ff.

plaintiff. The complaining party in a civil suit; the person who sues; the complainant.

policy. Any governing principle, plan, or course of action; in schools, general rules of procedure adopted by a local board of education.

policy exclusion. In malpractice insurance, an activity or circumstance defined as specifically excluded from the obligation to pay assumed by the insurer in an insurance policy.

polymerase chain reaction. In biomedical research, a fast, inexpensive technique for making an unlimited number of copies of any piece of DNA. Sometimes called "molecular photocopying," PCR has had an immense impact on biology and medicine, especially genetic research.

polymorphism. A gene that exists in more than one version (allele), and where the rare allele can be found in more than 2% of the population.

precedent. A decision in a court case which serves as a legal authority in future cases that address the same or similar legal question. Precedent is established within the jurisdiction of the court. Only the U.S. Supreme Court can set precedence for the whole country.

preferred provider organization (PPO). Generally a discounted fee-for-service indemnity product where participants have financial incentives to obtain care from a panel of preferred providers, but are allowed to go outside the network if they pay additional out-of-pocket expenses, abide by rules for referral to specialty care, and accept prescriptions according to a designated formulary. A PPO abides by the same rules as an IPO but does not share any of the risk.

prescriptive authority. The legal authority to prescribe medications and other medical therapeutics.

prevailing party. The winner of a lawsuit or other legal proceeding; a party may partially prevail if he or she wins on one or more issues in dispute, but not all issues in dispute.

prima facie **case.** In law, a case that includes enough supporting evidence to win unless it can be rebutted.

primary care provider. In managed care, a person responsible for supervising, coordinating, and providing initial and primary care to enrollees, and for initiating referrals and maintenance of care to the health plan's enrollees.

privacy. Isolation, seclusion, or freedom from unauthorized oversight or observation; the right to be left alone.

privileged communication. A communication between parties to a confidential relationship which is recognized in state law; the recipient of the disclosed information cannot be compelled to disclose the information in a court of law without the discloser's consent.

PRN. In medication administration, a dosage to be administered "as necessary" or "as circumstances require," rather than regularly at a given time.

procedural objections. In a legal case or proceeding, the objections of one party to actions by the other party that are not in conformity with the rules of the particular jurisdiction.

procedural laws. Laws that dictate the manner in which legal duties, rights, and responsibilities (substantive laws) may be exercised and enforced.

procedural safeguards. In education, administrative requirements such as notice and consent, and appeal rights in special education and student expulsion proceedings.

procedure. In health care, a specific treatment; in law, the administrative requirements in legal proceedings.

professional liability insurance. Insurance that covers the types of losses incurred during the practice of a particular profession.

professional nurse. One who has graduated from an approved professional school of nursing, is prepared to make independent judgments regarding patient or client care, and has passed a state-required examination to practice as a registered nurse (RN).

program accessibility. Under §504, each school district must provide access to all school programs. §504 does not require that all school buildings be made accessible, although all new school buildings and major renovations of old buildings must include accessibility.

protocols (nursing). Procedural statements written and used by nurses that outline the standard of practice for assessing and managing a specified clinical problem and authorize particular practice activities. Nursing protocols vary according to the level of education and licensure of the nurse(s) who will implement the protocol.

public accommodation. Any facility or program that is open to the general public.

pupil services. Contributions made by pupil services specialists to support and enhance the educational programs and experiences of students. *See also* **pupil services specialists.**

pupil services specialists. Professionals who provide skilled support services for students, whether in regular or special education, including school counselors, nurses, occupational and physical therapists, psychologists, speech-language pathologists, and social workers.

pursuant to. In conformance with, or in keeping with, certain requirements.

quality assurance. Activities and programs, including utilization review, intended to assure the quality of care in a defined health care setting or program.

quality of care. The degree or grade of excellence with respect to health care services received by members and administered by providers or programs, in terms of technical competence, need, appropriateness, acceptability, humanity, accessibility, structure, etc.

reactive airway disease. *See* **asthma.**

registered nurse (RN). An individual licensed to practice registered nursing in a state, who has successfully passed the state's licensure examination for registered nursing after completion of an approved university-based program leading to an associate, baccalaureate, or master's degree in nursing or of a hospital-based program.

regulations. When provided by a law, the rules or orders prescribed by a government agency, after notice and an opportunity for public comment. Regulations usually supply additional details and agency procedures for carrying out a law.

related services. As defined in IDEA, related services are transportation, and developmental, corrective, and other supportive services required to assist a child with a disability to benefit from special education. Other supportive services are defined as speech-language pathology and audiology services, psychological services, physical and occupational therapy, recreation including therapeutic recreation, early identification and assessment of disabilities in children, counseling services including rehabilitation counseling, orientation and mobility services, medical services for diagnostic or evaluation purposes, school health services, social work services in schools, and parent counseling and training.

release. A statement signed by a person relinquishing a right or claim against another.

release [of confidential information]. Communication of confidential information, whether by release of a document, oral communication, or electronic transmission. In schools and health care institutions, external release of confidential student information requires a signed statement of the parent or, in some cases the student, giving permission for the release. Internal release of confidential student health information (i.e., to other school personnel) may also require a written release, depending on state laws and regulations, state agency directives or policy, and the information in question. *See also* **disclosure.**

remand. In law, to return a case from the appellate (appeals) court back to the trial court, usually with direction for further action.

reporting statutes. Laws that mandate health care providers or their employees to give certain information to proper state or federal agencies. For example, physicians and laboratories must report the names of individuals with certain communicable diseases to public health agencies, and professionals and paraprofessionals who care for children must report suspected child abuse or neglect to a state child protection agency.

reservation of rights letter. A letter in which a professional liability insurance company advises an insured that the company reserves its right to deny coverage once it obtains all the facts related to a particular claim. A company usually sends a reservation of rights letter when it suspects that there is some chance the claim may not actually be covered, but it is providing defense costs anyway.

research. Scientific study, investigation, or experimentation to establish facts and analyze their significance, including an orderly approach with accurate record keeping. Scientifically valid research requires conduct and description of the research design and methods sufficient for other scientists to repeat it.

respondent. In law, the person against whom relief is sought. *See also* **defendant.**

restraints. Chemical or physical measures employed to curtail a patient's freedom, usually to control behavior which could cause injury to the patient or to others. In schools, the need for and use of restraints should be specified in a student's IEP.

reverse. In law, to set aside or repeal at the appellate level the decision of a lower court. An appeals court may "reverse in part," meaning it sets aside part of the lower court's decision, but not all of it.

risk. In the managed care arena, a system for paying managed care providers under a flat fee for one or more of the services they furnish under their contracts. Providers are at financial risk in the event that the patient costs exceed the payment. In the event that payments are greater than the cost of care, the provider can keep the difference.

risk management. A system of identifying and addressing sources of possible injury and other hazards to clients (students) and employees.

safe environment. One that will not be injurious to an individual's health or well-being; maintaining a safe environment includes the duty to alert others about potentially dangerous situations.

school-based health center. Comprehensive primary health care services provided by an interdisciplinary team—doctors, nurses, counselors, laboratory and medical assistants, and other health professionals—in a clinic setting located in the school or on school grounds; usually operated by a separate health care agency rather than the school.

school nurse. In this book, a registered professional nurse who meets a state's minimum requirements for qualification as a professional school nurse.

school nursing (school health nursing). A specialized practice of professional nursing that advances the well being, academic success, and life-long achievement of students. To that end, school nurses facilitate positive student responses to normal development; promote health and safety; intervene with actual and potential health problems; provide case management services; and actively collaborate with others to build student and family capacity for adaptation, self management, self advocacy, and learning.

scope of practice. Legally permissive boundaries of practice for a health professional; the parameters of professional services, as defined under state law (e.g. medical and nursing practice acts), that a licensed health care provider may deliver.

screening test. A method used to attempt to determine the presence of a treatable disease or condition, or the potential for developing it. Screening programs are usually targeted to a population of persons who are thought to be at risk for the disease or condition, such as vision and hearing screening for school-age children.

Section 1983 (§1983). A federal civil rights law which provides a right of action for persons injured by public officials who abuse their authority.

Section 504 (§504). The civil rights provision of the Rehabilitation Act of 1973 that bans discrimination on the basis of disability in programs and services receiving federal financial assistance.

self-administration (self-management) of medication. Self-administration of one's own medication by a student in school, once it has been established that the student is competent to do so (not usually applicable to controlled drugs). Self-administration of medication means that the student carries the drug on his or her person (or in a school bag) to and from school and is in control of it during the school day; school personnel do not handle or store the medication.

sequencing. In genetics, determining the exact order of the base pairs in a segment of DNA.

sovereign immunity. A legal doctrine that prevents a person from asserting an otherwise valid claim against a governmental entity unless that entity agrees to be sued. *See* **immunity.**

special education. Under IDEA, specially designed instruction, at no cost to parents or guardians, to meet the unique needs of a child with a disability, including instruction conducted in classrooms, in the home, in hospitals and institutions, and other settings.

special health care needs. Health-related services, supports, or adaptations required by a student in order to maintain his or her health status in school, including: medical devices, nursing care, psychosocial care, medically necessary services, specific services and equipment to sustain and enrich life, and adaptations required to maintain life, provide an environment conducive to growth and development, stimulate learning, and maintain the student in the least restrictive environment. Students with special health care needs either have or are at increased risk for chronic physical, developmental, behavioral, or emotional conditions and require health and related services of a type or amount beyond that required by students generally.

specialty (practice). In nursing, a branch of the profession in which the nurse is specially qualified to practice by having met specific requirements beyond basic preparation, usually by completing advanced programs of study (e.g., master's program in school nursing), obtaining specialty practice experience, and passing an examination given by an organization representing the profession.

staff model health maintenance organization. One of the four types of managed health care organizations, it is the oldest form and the most tightly structured organization for managing care. They own and operate clinics and employ salaried physicians.

standard of care. In the law of negligence, the degree of care that a reasonably prudent person would exercise under the same or similar circumstances. In professional negligence, the degree of care that an ordinary prudent professional of the same discipline would exercise under the same set of circumstances; the professional-legal criteria against which a defendant's actions are measured to determine if the actions were negligent.

standards of practice. Authoritative statements, usually created by a professional organization in a particular discipline or industry or by a governmental entity, that define the acceptable practice for that discipline or industry.

standing orders (for medication). In schools, medical directives from an authorized prescriber (usually a school medical advisor), regarding the administration of a medication under specified circumstances, that are written for general application to a group of students, as opposed to an order for a medication written for one specific student by that student's health care provider.

status epilepticus. A medical emergency characterized by continuous seizures, occurring without interruption. It can be precipitated by sudden withdrawal of anticonvulsant drugs, inadequate body levels of glucose, a brain tumor, head injury, fever, and poisoning.

statute. A state or federal law that has been enacted by the state legislature or the U.S. Congress.

statute of limitations. A law that defines the period of time within which a lawsuit must be filed.

statutorily-limited liability. Liability that is limited by a statute in some fashion, usually to a certain dollar level of recovery.

statutory immunity. Immunity defined in a federal or state law rather than obtained through common law. *See* **immunity.**

statutory rape. Every state has a statute that defines the age below which a person is deemed legally incapable of giving consent to sexual intercourse. Although the person may in fact have given consent, prosecution in criminal court for statutory rape may occur.

student. Any infant, child, or adolescent, age 0 to 21 years, who is planning to enter, or has entered, a school program or other setting where educational services are being provided.

students with special health care needs. *See* **special health care needs.**

subpoena. A court order that requires a person to come to court or appear at a specific place to give testimony. A subpoena may require the person called to bring documents related to the case.

substantive laws. Laws that establish legal duties, rights, and/or responsibilities for individuals and entities, as opposed to procedural laws that address the method of enforcing such duties, rights, and responsibilities.

summary judgment. An immediate decision by a court, before trial, usually when there is no argument concerning the law, or the defendant is immune from suit.

supervision (nursing). With respect to nursing delegation, the provision of guidance or direction, evaluation and follow-up by the licensed professional nurse for accomplishment of a nursing activity delegated to unlicensed assistive personnel or a licensed practical (vocational) nurse. **General supervision** includes availability to provide direction through such means as telecommunications, as well as review, observation, and evaluation of the delegatee's performance by the directing nurse, but does not require the delegating nurse to be present on-site at all times. **Direct supervision** requires the delegating nurse to be on-site, physically present, and immediately available to coordinate, direct, inspect, and evaluate the performance of the delegatee.

support services. *See* **pupil services** and **related services.**

Supremacy Clause. The popular title for Article VI, Section 2 of the United States Constitution, which established the federal government's power over the states.

tail policy. A malpractice insurance policy that provides coverage for periods when the insured is exposed to certain professional liabilities but no longer has a claims-made insurance policy in effect.

testamentary will. A testamentary will is the type of will which is used to transmit possessions to another after death. It becomes applicable only after death and is contrasted with a living will, which is applicable in the period prior to death.

tort. A private or civil wrong, other than a breach of contract, giving rise to a lawsuit (civil action) in which the plaintiff seeks compensation for the wrong; a tort can be intentional or unintentional.

Tort Claims Act. A statute that preserves for a governmental entity certain aspects of immunity from liability or suit and/or limits recovery against the governmental entity based upon certain types of claims.

UAP. *See* **unlicensed assistive personnel.**

United States Code (USC). Laws passed by the U.S. Congress, organized by general subject.

unlicensed assistive personnel (UAP). Individuals who are not authorized by state license to provide health care services, including health assessment and health care interventions, acts, or tasks. In nursing, UAP refers to personnel who are not licensed to practice nursing, but who are trained to assist nurses in implementing health care activities that are within the scope of nursing practice and do not require assessment or judgment.

unlicensed personnel. *See* **unlicensed assistive personnel.**

USC. *See* **United States Code.**

writ. Written legal form used by courts, derived from English law.

Table of Federal Statutes and Regulations

U.S.C. – United States Code (laws); C.F.R. – Code of Federal Regulations

Note: Some citations are for a short, specific provision; others are for a complete, extensive law. Not all federal statutes have regulations; regulations are cited only when pertinent. [Information in brackets summarizes the law.] Some of these laws have been amended many times over a period of many years, and some may have been amended since this book was written.

Americans with Disabilities Act (1990) (ADA), 42 U.S.C. §§ 12101 et seq.; Regulations at 28 C.F.R. § 35 and § 36.

Child Abuse Prevention and Treatment Act of 1974, 42 U.S.C. §§ 5101 et seq.

Civil Rights Act of 1964, 42 U.S.C. § 2000c [desegregation assistance]; § 2000d [bars discrimination on the basis of race, color or national origin]; § 2000e [bars discrimination in employment].

Clinical Laboratory Improvement Amendments of 1988, 42 U.S.C. § 263a; Regulations at 42 C.F.R. § 493.

Education Amendments of 1972, Title IX, 20 U.S.C.A. §§ 1681 et seq. [bars discrimination on the basis of sex].

Elementary and Secondary Education Act of 1974 (ESEA), 20 U.S.C. §§ 6301 et seq.

Family and Medical Leave Act of 1993, 2 U.S.C. §§ 60m, 60n; 5 U.S.C. §§ 2105, 6381–6387; 29 U.S.C. § 2601 et seq.

Family Educational Rights and Privacy Act of 1974 (FERPA), 20 U.S.C. § 1232g; Regulations at 34 C.F.R. § 99.

[Federal requirements for retention of documentation for programs receiving federal financial assistance] (1994), 20 U.S.C. § 1232f(a).

Federal Rules of Evidence, 28 U.S.C. §§ 803, 1001, 1002, 2072.

Federal Tort Claims Act, 28 U.S.C. § 2680.

Federal Uniform Administrative Procedures Act (1946 and many later amendments), 5 U.S.C. §§ 551 et seq.

General Education Provisions Act (1968) (GEPA), 20 U.S.C. §§ 1221-1234i; Regulations (called Education Department General Administrative Regulations, EDGAR) at 34 C.F.R. §§ 76, 77, 81, 86.300 and 86.400.

Gun Free Schools Act of 1994, 20 U.S.C. §§ 8921.

Health Care Quality Improvement Act of 1986, 42 U.S.C. §§ 11101 et seq.

Health Insurance Portability and Accountability Act of 1996 (HIPAA), 26 U.S.C. § 294, 42 U.S.C. §§ 201, 1395b-5.

Improving America's Schools Act (1994), 20 U.S.C. §§ 6301, 7703; 8898-8902; 8921, 8922.

Individuals with Disabilities Education Act (IDEA) (1975), 20 U.S.C. §§ 1400 et seq., as amended and incorporating the Education of All Handicapped Children Act (EHA), 1975, P.L. 94-142, and subsequent amendments; Regulations at 34 C.F.R. §§ 300–303 [special education and related services for students, pre-school children, and infants and toddlers].

Ku Klux Klan Act of 1871, 42 U.S.C. § 1983 [provides a civil action for deprivation of rights by a public official].

Medicaid Confidentiality Requirements, 42 U.S.C. § 1396a(a)(7); Regulations at 42 C.F.R. § 431.300.

Medicare Catastrophic Coverage Act of 1988, 42 U.S.C. §§ 411(k)(13), 300aa-12, 300aa-15, 300aa-21.

[National Vaccine Injury Compensation Program] (1988), 42 U.S.C. § 300aa-11 et seq.

Occupational Safety and Health Act (OSHA) (1970), 29 U.S.C. §§ 655, 657; Regulations at 29 C.F.R. §§ 1910.1200 [hazard communication rule]; 1910.1030 [occupational exposure to bloodborne pathogens].

Patient Self Determination Act (1990), 42 U.S.C. §§ 1395i-3, 1395l, 1395cc, 1395bbb; Regulations at 42 C.F.R. 489.100.

[Section 504] Rehabilitation Act of 1973, 29 U.S.C. § 794; Regulations at 34 C.F.R. § 104.

Religious Freedom Restoration Act of 1993, 42 U.S.C. §§ 2000bb – 2000bb-4.

Safe and Drug-Free Schools and Communities (1994), 20 U.S.C. §§ 7101 et seq.; Regulations at 34 C.F.R. § 86.1 et seq. [Incorporates earlier legislation including the Alcohol and Drug Abuse Prevention, Treatment and Rehabilitation Act of 1987, 21 U.S.C. § 1175.

[Social security and Medicaid benefits for people with disabilities, "Title XIX"] (1980), 42 U.S.C. § 405.

[Student Assistance Programs and confidentiality of student information concerning alcohol and drug abuse treatment], 42 U.S.C. §§ 290ee-3, 290dd-3; Regulations at 42 C.F.R. § 2.1 et seq.

Index